FIG. 1. Landscape with deer. Drawing on the wall of Hsing-tsung's tomb; sketched by Miss Midorii Torii (Torii 36 III, pl. 208).

TRANSACTIONS

OF THE

AMERICAN PHILOSOPHICAL SOCIETY

HELD AT PHILADELPHIA
FOR PROMOTING USEFUL KNOWLEDGE

NEW SERIES—VOLUME 36
1946

HISTORY OF CHINESE SOCIETY

LIAO

(907–1125)

KARL A. WITTFOGEL and FÊNG CHIA-SHÊNG

With the assistance of
JOHN DE FRANCIS, ESTHER S. GOLDFRANK, LEA KISSELGOFF, and KARL H. MENGES

THE AMERICAN PHILOSOPHICAL SOCIETY
INDEPENDENCE SQUARE
PHILADELPHIA 6

MARCH, 1949

Published with the cooperation of the
American Institute of Pacific Relations

LANCASTER PRESS, INC.

Reprinted 1961

This book is divided into sixteen sections, each containing an analytic introduction and annotated translations of Chinese texts or a tabulated digest of relevant data. The reasons for the selection and arrangement of the subject matter are given in the General Introduction. The principles underlying the translation are discussed in the Technical Introduction. In the body of the publication, sources are cited by abbreviations which are listed with the full titles in the bibliography.

The main source is the *Liao Shih*, the *Standard History of the Liao Dynasty*. The reference placed at the end of each translated passage indicates the chapter (*chüan*) and page on which the Chinese text appears in the Po-na edition of this work. All sinologists have access either to this or to another edition of the *Liao Shih*. It has therefore been decided not to publish the Chinese originals of the translated texts at this time.

ERRATA AND ADDENDA

An article by Karl August Wittfogel appeared under the title "Chinese Society and the Dynasties of Conquest" in *China*, edited by H. F. MacNair, 1946. Unfortunately no opportunity was given to see the proof or to check certain changes made by the editor. The Chinese History Project therefore is compelled to disclaim responsibility for the form of the published article and for the altered passages. Where discrepancies in meaning, in technical terms or dating appear, the considered opinion of the Project is that expressed in the present volume.

Page 2, note 22: Goës 16, 236, not Goës 15, 577

Page 23, paragraph 3, line 3: *t'a-lin*, not *ta-lin*

  note 335: Schott, not Shott

  notes 348 and 349: Ramsey, not Ramsay

Page 26, note 371: Wittfogel 39, not 40*a*

Page 29, note 409: Febvre, not Le Febvre

Page 58, note 167: Riasanovsky 37, 198, not 37, 16

Page 60, note 9, paragraph 2, line 12: Rashīd ad-Dīn 14, 127, 132, not Yule, CWT III

Page 85, note 11, paragraph 2, line 14: Shiratori 12 TMK, not Shiratori 12

Page 97, no. 22, line 2: Fo-nu, not Fu-nu

Page 102, no. 16: reference should be 46, 25*b*

Page 104, no. 22: T'ung-chia River, not Tung-chia

Page 119, note 88: Frazer 38, not 40

Page 135, note 3: *lang* 朗, not 郎

Page 136, note 16: This note refers to the Yeh-lü T'ang-ku on page 396.

Page 156, right column, paragraph 1, line 18: TPYL 960, 6a, not TYPL

Page 181, note 1: XIII (19) (21), not XII

Page 193, note 21: X, 1 (29), not X, 1 (28). Footnote No. 21 should be placed after the word "well-stocked."

Page 199, left column, last line: quotation should read ". . . when the master is away hunting, or at war, the wife. . ."

Page 213, note 271: *idem* 37*c*, not *idem* 38

Page 222, right column, line 2: burned, not buried

Page 237, note 2 and p. 369, note 11 *la* 剌, not 刺

Page 253, left column, 4th last line: *ch'uan*, not *chuan*

Page 262, note 83: Yeh-lü, not Yah-lü

Page 263, note 99: Hsiao Han-chia-nu's official career began *ca.* 1025, not in 996

Page 272, first reference should be 53, 12*a*–14*b*

Page 317, note 150: X, 2 (86), not X, 2 (78)

Page 369, note 11: see above, p. 237

Page 373, note 47, paragraph 2: Hsi-ching, not Hsi-ch'ing

Page 401, table: Hsi-yin and Wan should be transposed

Page 419 (37), line 4: supervisor of the army, not inspector of the army

Page 433, note 120: Zakharov 75, not 77

Page 445, right column, paragraph 4, line 2: Pien, not P'ien

Page 446, right column, paragraph 2, line 18: Ministry of Civil Appointments, not Ministry of Nominations

Page 452, note 432: Chu-chê, not Chu-chih

Page 453, right column, 3d last line: Hsieh-li, not Chieh-li

Page 454, note 453: Ch'ên S 39*a*, not 39

Page 465, note 587: Riasanovsky 37, 25, not 37, 35

Page 469, right column, 4th line: Ch'ien-wên, not Chien-wên

  note 656: XIV, 4 (29), not XIV 4 (24) (25)

Page 484, 11th line: record keepers, not recorders

Page 500, 4th line: adultery, not unlawful acts

Page 503 (26), line 4: Ho-lu, not Ho-lü

Page 511, left column (4), 4th line: Yün Prefecture, not Yüan

Page 513, note 99: X, 1 (56), not X, 1 (54)

Page 517, left column, paragraph 4, line 17: Yeh-lü Ch'u-ts'ai, not Ch'u-tsai

Page 528, right column, 13th line: Hsi Hsia, not Hsia Hsia

Page 539, right column, paragraph 4, line 8: T'ien-tsu, not Tien-tsu

Page 554 (42), 4th line: Tang-hsiang, not T'ang-hsiang

Page 559, note 1, paragraph 2: 1160, not 1610

Page 581, note 57: Sun Ch'üan-hsing, not Ch'üan-hsing

Page 584, year 989, 3d month: county registrars, not magistrates

Page 593, year 1093, 10th month: Hsia-ti, not Hsiao-ti

Page 596, year 1115, 12th month: Hu-pu-ta-kang, not Hu-pu-ta-kan

CONTENTS

CONTENTS

ILLUSTRATIONS

GENERAL INTRODUCTION

K. A. WITTFOGEL

I. LIAO — CH'I-TAN — CATHAY

This book is a social history of the Liao empire which for two hundred years controlled the regions of modern Manchuria, Mongolia, and the northeastern part of China Proper. As social history, it deals with the empire's economic, cultural, political, and military institutions, with its subject peoples, in the main Chinese, and with its nomad founders and masters, the Ch'i-tan.

Students of the Far East have, until recently, exhibited little interest in the social and cultural growth of the Liao world, but the name of its tribal rulers fired the imagination of Western travelers and writers long after the Liao state had crumbled. In the days of the Orkhon Turks (before 740), the term, Khitāy, referred only to a powerful pastoral people northeast of China Proper.[1] In the tenth and eleventh centuries it was used in Central and Western Asia[2] for the empire of conquest which the Khitāy (Qitā, Qatā) established after the collapse of the great Chinese dynasty, T'ang (618–906). In the twelfth century Liao refugees carried the old "barbarian" name to the oases and grasslands of Turkestan, maintaining "for almost ninety years"[3] a Western Liao state known as Black (Qarā) Khitāy.[4]

But the time-honored designation was not confined to Central Asia. Moslem historians extended the name Khitāy to the new Chin 金 empire (1115–1234) which the Tungus Jurchen, after the destruction of Liao and the defeat of Sung, set up over the whole of North China. Persian historians of the thirteenth century, describing the conquest of this Chin empire, spoke either of Khitāy[5] or "Djerdja" (Jurchen) Khitāy.[6] The earliest Mongol source extant, the so-called *Secret History of the Yüan Dynasty*, composed in 1240,[7] mentioned both Ch'i-ta 乞苔 and Ho-la-ch'i-ta[8] [Qarā-Khitāy]. The Chinese transcription, Ch'i-tan, probably based on a proto-Mongol form, appears in Chinese records[9] that antedate not only the earliest

---

[1] Thomsen 96, 98 and 102; Radloff 97, 131, 134, and 137.

[2] A Manichean Uighur document, written probably about 1000 (Chavannes-Pelliot 13, 141, note 1) mentions the author's return from χ'tai "bei der Rückkehr aus Chatai" (Le Coq 11 TMC, 29). In 1026 the court of Ghazna (modern Afghanistan) was visited by an envoy from Qatā Khan, the ruler of Qatā. Gardīzī, who wrote his history about 1050 (Barthold 28, 20–21), has Qayā (see Nāzim 31, 56, note 2; Barthold [28, 286] follows this reading, though he calls the spelling doubtful); but al-Bīrūnī, in a book composed around 1030 (Minorsky 37, 320) writes Qatā or Qitā (Nāzim 31, notes 2 and 3; Minorsky, *loc. cit.*), a version found also in a newly discovered Arabic manuscript, which was probably completed shortly after 1120 (*op. cit.*, 317 and 319 ff.). The famous Saljūqid vizier, Nizām-al-Mulk (d. 1092) refers in his *Book on the Administration of the State* to Khita and China, evidently considering them two separate countries (Nizām oul-Moulk 93, 194 and 304).

[3] LS 30, 7b. To be exact, eighty-eight years. See below, appendix V.

[4] Nidhāmī-i-'Arūdī-i-Samarqandī, in the middle of the twelfth century (Browne 28 II, 13), speaks of the Gur Khan of Khita (Nidhāmī-i-'Arūdī 99, 650) without adding the epithet Qarā.

[5] Juwaynī 16, 86 ff. (see appendix V B, 2, 1128 *passim*); *cf.* also Marquart 12, 488 ff. Juwaynī completed his history in 1260 (Barthold 28, 39).

[6] En-Nesawi 95, 11. This important work was probably written in A. H. 667 (*op. cit.*, vi), that is, in 1269.

[7] See Barthold 28, 43.

[8] YCPS 6, 26a *passim*; YCPSHC 1, 1a *passim*. The syllable -t'i, which is not infrequently attached in smaller script to the word Ch'i-ta, obviously is the Chinese transliteration of the Mongol plural ending -t.

[9] The *History of the Wei Dynasty*, completed in A.D. 554, gives a relatively full account of Ch'i-tan activities from the fourth to the sixth century (WS 100, 15a ff.). According to the rules of Chinese official historiography, the individual items mentioned in the *Wei History* were probably recorded soon after the events took place (*cf.* Hirth 85, 1; Gardner 38, 88). The occurrence of the name Ch'i-tan in a dictionary, *Tzŭ Lin* 字林, written under the Western Chin (265–317), seems to place Chinese acquaintance with a people called Ch'i-tan in pre-Wei times. But the evidence of the *Tzŭ Lin* upon which the Ch'ing scholar, Chu K'o-pao 諸可寶 (1845–1903) bases this claim (see TLKI, supplement) is of doubtful value because the *Tzŭ Lin* is a late compilation by Jên Ta-ch'un 任大椿 (1738–1789). Even the Sung dictionary *Kuang Yün* 廣韻, which quotes a *Tzŭ Lin* reference to the Ch'i-tan (KY 5, 16a), is not good evidence because before its appearance the *Tzŭ Lin* had already been rewritten several times (HHK 13, 11a–21a), so much so that Sung scholars no longer considered it the original dictionary (CCSLCT 3, 41a–b). Chu K'o-pao's assertion, therefore, does not alter the belief held by the T'ang and Sung authorities that the name Ch'i-tan occurred first under the Wei dynasty, whose rule began in 386 (see TT 200, 1083; TS 219, 1a; WTS 72, 1b; CTKC 23, 1b). This belief is also expressed in the *Liao History* (LS 63, 2b).

Further investigation, however, makes it possible to date the first occurrence of the name still more precisely and, perhaps, even place it somewhat earlier. According

1

Mongol source but also the earliest known Turkic texts, the Orkhon inscriptions.[10]

With the expansion of Mongol power and influence, the old tribal name in its Altaic, Semitic, and European variants emerged in Persia, Arabia, and Europe. By the middle of the thirteenth century, when Carpini and Rubruck visited the Mongol settlements in Inner Asia, the words Kitaia (Carpini) or Cataya or Cathaia (Rubruck) were commonly used to designate the Chinese world.[11] Such different writers as Rashīd ad-Dīn,[12] Marco Polo,[13] Odoric,[14] Hamd-Allāh,[15] and Ibn Batūta[16] applied the term specifically to Northern China to distinguish it from Southern China: Mangi, Manzi, Chin, or Sin.[17] Christopher Columbus, setting forth on his daring adventures, hoped to reach the country of Catayo. On his last voyage he triumphantly described his landing in the Province of Mago[18] "which is contiguous to that of Cathay."[19] In 1497 John Cabot discovered America; he also had sailed for Cathay.[20]

In the tenth century conquest divided imperial China. In the thirteenth conquest again joined the alien-ruled north with the independent south, but the reunification, which outlasted Mongol dominion, was not recognized in western nomenclature for more than three hundred years. Only in 1603 did Bernard Goës learn "to his astonishment" what Bar Hebraeus had realized as early as 1286:[21] "Cathay" and "China" were one and the same country.[22] From Goës' time on, the confusion was largely resolved; the southern term began to replace its northern counterpart. But the word "Cathay" still appeared occasionally in European writings. Even today, in Russia, Greece, Persia, and Turkestan, "Khitāy" in its different variants has remained the general designation for China.[23]

II. THE HISTORICAL POSITION OF THE LIAO DYNASTY

1. TEMPORARY OBLIVION

Thus the name, Ch'i-tan, made history, more successfully it would seem than the Liao empire which the Ch'i-tan founded and ruled. For some time the nature of this empire was wrapped in obscurity, not by accident, but because of a carefully fostered policy.

---

to LS 63, 1a ff., the Ch'i-tan came from a branch of the Hsien-pei people called the Yü-wên 宇文. Between 318 and 385 the Yü-wên had a number of chieftains whose designations sound rather similar. One of them was called Hsi-tu-kuan 悉獨官 (Chin 108, 3a–b); another Hou-tou-kuei 侯豆歸 (Chou 1, 1b) or I-tou-kuei 逸豆歸 (WS 103, 23b ff.; PS 98, 21a); a third Ch'i-tê-kuei 乞得龜 (WS 103, 23b ff.; PS 98, 20b ff.; Chin 108,4a) or Ch'i-tê-kuei 乞得歸 (TCTC 93, 5b); and a fourth Ch'i-t'ê-kuei 乞特歸 (Chin 123, 4a). This designation seems always to consist of two parts. The final -kuei or -kuan may be an early form of a suffix which the Liao Shih renders as ko 哥. The base Hou-tou, Ch'i-tê, etc. may be the root of the later tribal name, Ch'i-tan. After 344, when the Yü-wên split into three tribes (LS 63, 1b), the name evidently remained attached to the K'u-mo-hsi 庫莫奚 division which, in 388, broke up again into the K'u-mo-hsi and the Ch'i-tan. After the year 388 the transcription Ch'i-tan is established as the standard designation in the Chinese historical records. See Fêng CS 33a, 14 ff.

[10] The inscriptions were written in 732 and 735 (Thomsen 24, 136 and 139).

[11] Carpini [d. 1252] 28, 15 ff.; Rubruck [d. 1293 ?] 00, 155: "There is also great Cathay, whose people were anciently, as I believe, called Seres." For the original Latin forms of Cathay given by the two envoys see Rubruck 00, 155, note 1.

[12] Rashīd ad-Dīn [d. 1318] 1833, 336 ff.; idem 14, 113 ff.

[13] Marco Polo [d. 1324] 03 I, 60 passim. Cf. the Moule-Pelliot edition, Marco Polo 38 I, 207 passim.

[14] Odoric [d. 1331] 91, 366 ff. Mandeville [d. 1371], the literary echo of Odoric and other early travelers, also discusses "the great country" of Cathay (Maundeville 1839, 215 ff.).

[15] Hamd-Allāh Mustawfī [completed his book in 1340] 19, 250 ff.; see also Le Strange's note 7 (loc. cit.).

[16] Ibn Batūta [d. 1377/8] 79, 294 ff.; idem 16, 137. In spite of occasional inconsistencies (cf. note 1 to the second reference), the distinction between the northern country, Cathay, and its southern extension, China, is brought out clearly when the author speaks of the Kan or great Emperor as the person "who rules over China and Cathay" (idem 79, 295; idem 16, 137).

[17] "The Mongols call this land [South China] Manzi, while the Arabs name it Sin" (Hamd-Allāh Mustawfī 19, 250).

[18] Mago was Marco Polo's Mangi or Manzi (Marco Polo 03 II, 144 ff.), the territory of the former Southern Sung dynasty mentioned in note 16. Columbus was influenced by the writings of Marco Polo and Mandeville. Cf. Columbus 70, xlix.

[19] ". . . la provincia de Mago que parte con aquella del Catayo . . ." (Columbus 70, 194). While on his first voyage Columbus thought he was nearing "the land of the great Khan, with which there will be vast commerce and great profit" (op. cit., 11). In another letter written during his third voyage he refers to China under the designation "Seres" (op. cit., 136).

[20] Yule, CWT I, 181.

[21] Bar Hebraeus [d. 1286] 32 I, 352.

[22] ". . . and in this way he learned to his astonishment that China was the Cathay that he was in search for" (Goës [d. 1607] 15, 577). For the origin of the name China see Pelliot 12a, 727–742; Yule, CWT I, 2–7; and Barthold 35, 97 ff.

[23] Yule, CWT I, 146; see also Schott 80, 9; and Barthold 35, 97 and 120.

In the second half of the eighteenth century the Manchu government organized a literary inquisition aimed primarily at obscuring the alien character of its power. At the same time it protected from abuse such other dynasties of conquest as Chin, Yüan, and the Ch'i-tan-controlled Liao empire.[24]

A small group of specialists continued to study the non-Chinese features present in these four dynasties, but in general the ban proved effective. For more than a century "many of the authors and poets of China held themselves in check, so as not to incur the displeasure of the ruling house, or run the risk of accusation by a sycophantic fellow countryman."[25] As late as 1924 the Father of the Chinese Revolution, Dr. Sun Yat-sen, bitterly complained of the lack of national pride exhibited by certain scholars and literati.[26]

2. A PATTERN OF CONQUEST

By terror and intimidation the Manchu inquisition emphasized the bond that linked the four last Chinese dynasties of conquest. Interestingly, its instigators showed "no concern over writings about the Wei and other non-Chinese houses, which in earlier times had ruled over the northern part of China."[27] Their attention was focused on that series of conquests which culminated in the Ch'ing and started with the Liao dynasty. Directly or indirectly, the latter served as a pattern for later conquests in Central Asia as well as in China Proper.

Liao culture was directly perpetuated in the state of Qarā-Khitāy. This short-lived but important dynasty of conquest, established by a scion of the Ch'i-tan ruling house, Yeh-lü Ta-shih, controlled the territory between the Oxus River and the Gobi by virtue of a political organization which impressed contemporary writers with its power and statesmanship.[28] Howorth is, therefore, probably correct in assuming that Qarā-Khitāy "in some measure [acted as] a model, upon which the later Mongol empire was framed, assisting, also, very considerably in its formation, since, when it fell, a large, disciplined and compact territory was added to it."[29]

Within China Proper the Jurchen founders of the Chin empire, while adopting in large part the Chinese political organization, did not hesitate to draw on the administrative and military experience of their Liao predecessors which they carefully studied.[30]

The Mongol invaders of China revealed an even closer affinity to Liao culture, due in part to certain fundamental similarities between Ch'i-tan and Mongol tribal society, in part to Chingis Khan's conquest of Qarā-Khitāy, and in part to the active participation of a direct descendant of the Liao imperial family, Yeh-lü Ch'u-ts'ai, whose complete familiarity with Chinese civilization did not impair his understanding of the "barbarian" point of view. Yeh-lü Ch'u-ts'ai, chief adviser first to Chingis Khan and, after 1227, to his son, Ogotai, has been called one of the greatest political figures in the history of Asia.[31] He probably was. For it was Yeh-lü Ch'u-ts'ai who drew the blueprint for Mongol administrative organization which, with all its limitations and shortcomings, represents the most daring attempt to impose the rule of a pastoral people on great agrarian civilizations of the East.

Liao techniques of power were studied again in the formative days of the Manchu dynasty. On the eve of the invasion of China Proper the Manchus ordered selected passages from the Chinese dynastic histories translated into their native tongue. Significantly, they chose the histories of the three preceding periods of conquest: Liao, Chin, and Yüan.[32] Having accomplished their aim, they never denied the tie that held them to their Altaic cousins, though, from the eighteenth century on, they concealed the disturbing realities of conquest by a political taboo which remained in force until the days of Sun Yat-sen.

Japanese scholarship was not hampered by any such restrictions. On the contrary, Japan's expansionist policy in the northeastern regions of the continent proved a powerful directive for the country's scientific activities. In the course of investigations that touched on many aspects of the geography and history of China's dynasties of conquest, considerable attention was given to the Liao empire. Special monographs investigated the Ch'i-tan language and other features of Liao culture. A year before the outbreak of the Sino-Japanese war the distinguished Japanese scholar, K. Torii, published four monumental volumes on Liao archaeology.[33]

The political developments that influenced Japanese scientific interest also affected scholarly trends in China Proper.[34] One of China's prominent contemporary historians, Ku Chieh-kang, becoming "frontier-conscious" after the Japanese occupation of the three northeastern provinces (Manchuria), devoted increasing attention in his magazine, *Yü Kung*, to China's

---

[24] Goodrich 35, 46 and 142.
[25] *Op. cit.*, 65.
[26] Sun CS 37, 37 ff.; *cf.* Sun YS 27, 56–65.
[27] Goodrich 35, 46.
[28] See appendix V.
[29] Howorth 76, 262.
[30] See HCS, Chin, particularly VII, XIV, and XV (ms).

[31] Rémusat 1829 II, 86.
[32] CHTSL 3, 22b–23b; *cf.* Gabelentz 77, 196.
[33] For details concerning the Japanese studies of Liao culture see appendix IV.
[34] See appendix IV.

northern border regions and the problems of invasion. A recent report of the Academia Sinica lists a number of outstanding achievements in the field of Chinese history for the war period, 1937–1942; included is "a notable paper on the method of administering the various racial groups adopted by the Liao emperors."[35]

In view of these facts, the choice of Liao as one of the first dynasties to be investigated needs little justification. The editor presents its social history as a typological complement to the study of the Ch'in and Han periods which is under way. The latter surveys the structure of Chinese society at the moment of imperial consolidation; the former deals with the Liao empire which in diverse ways influenced all the succeeding dynasties of conquest.

3. THE HISTORY OF LIAO AS PART OF THE HISTORY OF CHINESE SOCIETY

In writing Chinese history as a history of Chinese *society* we include the political aspect without however making it the main topic of investigation. The word "society" as used in this publication goes beyond John Locke's "political or civil society";[36] it also comprehends Adam Smith's economic implications[37] and finally that "system of regulatory norms, which exists in every community . . . its institutions."[38]

The institutional patterns shared by members of one society are not necessarily confined within the limits of a political or national unit although on occasion these may coincide. Toynbee concludes a noteworthy methodological analysis by flatly rejecting political communities as "intelligible fields of history." "Societies, not states, are 'the social atoms' with which students of history have to deal."[39] The English scholar suggests the desirability of investigating certain "societies," among them, Sinic society and its extension, Far Eastern society.[40]

The conceptual differences between Toynbee's Asiatic "societies" and "Oriental society," as we see it,[41] cannot and need not be discussed here. Suffice it to say that his methodological intent is much closer

to our own than that of Franke who conceives Chinese history as a history of the Confucian state.[42] Our approach enables us to examine all aspects of China's institutions, economic as well as political, Confucian as well as unorthodox. By the same token, China's dynasties of conquest fall necessarily within the scope of this study. Whatever their "barbarian" background, their dominion over large masses of the Chinese people makes them an integral part of any history of Chinese society.[43]

4. THE INSTITUTIONAL SIGNIFICANCE OF LIAO HISTORY

a. THE TRADITIONAL THESIS

Thus Liao, like Chin, Yüan, and Ch'ing, is an essential part of Chinese social history. Western scholarly opinion has held that the Ch'i-tan conquerors soon became Chinese, and their rule that of a typically Chinese dynasty. Yule, commenting on the Ch'i-tan, writes, "the same curious process . . . took place which seems always to have followed the intrusion of Tartar conquerors into China. . . . The intruders themselves adopted Chinese manners, ceremonies, literature, and civilization. . . ."[44] The second Liao emperor, says Chavannes, made Liao "a truly Chinese dynasty (*une dynastie vraiment chinoise*)."[45]

Pelliot, like Yule, sees a general process of assimilation at work. ". . . it happened to the Khitan as to all nomads who as victors settled on the soil of China and whom, on the rebound, the Chinese civilization soon conquered. After a number of generations the Khitan were civilized, Sinicized (*policés, chinoisés*)."[46] If indeed the Ch'i-tan conquerors had succumbed so completely to the influence of Chinese civilization,[47] then their old tribal organization must have lost its original functions. Stein implies this when he asserts that the "tribes"[48] mentioned in the *Liao Shih* have become simple administrative divisions.[49]

b. NEW RESULTS

It is easy to discover behind such formulas as "always" and "all nomads" the thesis that the Chi-

[35] Yeh CS 43, 8.

[36] Locke 1727, 180 ff.

[37] See Smith 37, 10 ff., 47, 50 *passim*. To be sure, Adam Smith does not discard the political factor: he speaks of "a well-governed society" (*op. cit.*, 11); not infrequently he identifies society with country (cf. *op. cit.*, 264 and 271).

[38] Parsons (37, 231), whose definition we have cited, continues: "In mode of embodiment, whether in custom, or the law of the state, in the type of enforcement, they may vary enormously from one community to another. They form the backbone of the social structure."

[39] Toynbee, SH I, 45.

[40] *Op. cit.*, 88 ff.

[41] *Cf.* Wittfogel, OS (ms).

[42] Franke, GCR I, 30, xx.

[43] The term "Chinese society," which occurs frequently in recent Chinese writings, is also increasingly used by modern Western students of Chinese history and civilization. See Wittfogel 31, *passim*; Linton 36, 97; Lattimore 40, 27 ff.

[44] Yule, CWT I, 147.

[45] Chavannes, "Khitans," 512.

[46] Pelliot 31, 21–22.

[47] *Cf.* Gibert 34, 457 ff.

[48] Stein's quotation marks.

[49] "On voit par la lecture du Leao-che que les noms de 'tribus' (*pou*) sont devenus de simples divisions administratives" (Stein 39, 30, note 1).

nese have always absorbed their nomadic conquerors. Such an assumption has a substantial basis in fact, for Chinese civilization exerted a most important influence on neighboring tribes and states, and particularly on those peoples who succeeded in invading the Middle Kingdom. Chinese writers considered the acceptance of every Chinese culture element a sign of their own society's strength and attractiveness, which indeed it was. The absorption theory, whose validity for the Ch'i-tan has been asserted by some of the greatest authorities in the field, seemed the given starting point for our own investigation; but the further our analysis went, the less the results bore out the original thesis, and this for the following reasons:

(1) The Ch'i-tan achieved only a partial victory over the Chinese. They therefore continued to maintain the center of their political and military power in their old tribal territory of northern Jehol, even while they controlled the northern regions of China Proper. (2) The Ch'i-tan ruling families and nobles came in frequent contact with their Chinese subjects; they adopted numerous cultural elements from them, but they never abandoned their typically tribal political and military organization nor their former secular traditions or religious beliefs. (3) The mass of the Ch'i-tan people continued to pursue their time-honored pastoral activities. Living apart from the Chinese peasants and townspeople, they were little disposed to replace their tribal way of life by "Chinese manners, ceremonies, literature, and civilization." (4) The continuation of a traditional pastoral existence, far from precluding, imperatively demanded that the tribe remain a basic unit of organization. In spite of the many political and military modifications resulting from the conquest situation, the tribes of the Liao empire continued to be tribes—without quotation marks. They fulfilled many administrative tasks, but they were definitely more than administrative units.

c. A NEW METHODOLOGICAL APPROACH

The insight obtained by our preliminary survey strikingly confirms certain recent ideas regarding the character of acculturation and relative, selective, and graded diffusion. The process of acculturation was re-examined[50] in 1935 by three American anthropolo-

gists, Redfield, Linton, and Herskovits, who in a joint memorandum defined it as comprehending "those phenomena which result when groups of individuals having different cultures come into continuous first-hand contact, with subsequent changes in the original cultural pattern of either or both groups."[51] They further state that "acculturation is to be distinguished from *culture-change*, of which it is but one aspect, and *assimilation*, which is at times a phase of acculturation. It is also to be differentiated from *diffusion* which, while occurring in all instances of acculturation . . ., also constitutes only one aspect of the process of acculturation."[52]

This definition implies that culture contact may occur in a variety of circumstances and may be different in degree and intensity. The complete merging of two cultures, as suggested by the simple absorption theory, is only one among many historical possibilities; its realization depends on "the complete amalgamation of the two societies involved."[53] As long as this complete social fusion is not achieved, cultural differences will continue to exist.[54]

The methodological consequences of these observations are evident. Any satisfactory analysis of culture contact must take into consideration the "resistance to traits as well as the acceptance of them";[55] it must be cognizant of the fact that under certain conditions the process of cultural exchange may result, not in the creation of a new homogeneous culture, but in the co-existence of two mutually adapted cultures which "live together in a symbiotic relationship."[56] At times, fusion may result in a configuration so different from the parent cultures that it seems a veritable "third culture."[57]

Examining recent Chinese cultural relations with the West, the Chinese scholar, Dr. Hu Shih, has reached similar conclusions. He stresses the importance of the recipient people's "ethnic, ethnographic, and historical make-up, that constitutes the ultimate core of cultural change," and he concludes: "The adopted culture never succeeds in completely blotting out this ultimate ethnic and ethnographic core unless the people itself is physically destroyed by war or by

[50] For the history of the term acculturation see Herskovits 38, 3 ff. Herskovits traces the word back to 1880 in the U. S. A., where it was first used to describe culture change in Indian tribes after contact with white civilization (*loc. cit.*). The process of acculturation was naturally recognized much earlier—in fact, wherever culture exchange between two societies, based on continuous first-hand contact, has been observed and described in detail. Lattimore, in his recent descriptive and analytic studies

of Inner Asia, has taken great pains to point out varying degrees of cultural exchange and adjustment [acculturation] in nomadic societies at different levels and in different geographical zones. *Cf.* Lattimore 35, 39 ff.; and, in a later statement *idem* 40, 248 ff.

[51] Redfield, Linton, Herskovits 36, 149.
[52] *Loc. cit.;* italics in the original.
[53] Linton 40, 492.
[54] *Loc. cit.*
[55] Redfield, Linton, Herskovits 36, 151.
[56] Linton 40, 493.
[57] For this formula see Redfield 41, 364.

other cruel forces of nature."[58]   There is no need to press Dr. Hu's statement which, probably owing to historical circumstance, is so strongly phrased. It remains significant, particularly since it has been formulated from a non-Western point of view.

The great Arab historian and philosopher, Ibn Khaldūn, was equally aware of the difficulties of cultural fusion which he studied in the main from the standpoint of nomad conquest. According to him, the Arab victors adjusted themselves badly to their new position, so badly indeed that not even the discipline acquired through the Islamic faith could prevent the rapid decay of their power.[59] Ibn Khaldūn's pessimistic analysis obviously reflects the increasing disintegration of Arab rule: Baghdad had fallen; Egypt was in the hands of the Mamlucks; and in Spain the reconquest had deprived the Moslems of most of their territorial possessions. But even if these conditions induced the historian to over-emphasize his co-nationals' maladjustment to the demands of a complex agrarian society, he still has the merit of having drawn attention to a sorely neglected aspect of Arab civilization.   This accomplished scholar and statesman, whose forefathers had left the tribal homelands of Yemen many centuries before his birth, still extolled the nomadism of the desert and decried in contrast the corrupting effect of a sedentary life.[60] Agriculture, despite its great importance for man's material welfare,[61] was still considered a despised occupation, the miserable lot of a subdued and debased people.[62]

Limited or frustrated assimilation has also been noted for Central Asia. According to the Russian Turkologist, Barthold, the cultures of the agrarian countries conquered by the tribal Turks and Mongols primarily influenced the ruling houses and their more distinguished supporters. However, even their cultural tradition "does not vanish suddenly or without traces. The conquerors try to combine the freedom of pastoral life with the advantages of civilized life; under the influence of such attempts peculiar relations develop between the ruler, his fellow-tribesmen and his new subjects. . . ."[63] In his detailed studies of Turkestan and Persia, Barthold is at great pains to describe the stratified and slow advance of such a cultural adjustment,[64] the resistance which it provokes,[65] and the resulting complex which rarely justifies a one-sided absorption theory.

The Mongol conquest led to the creation of strong political organizations in China, Islamic Asia, and Russia, but not in the homeland of the conquerors, Mongolia Proper.[66] The Saljūqids, the Turkic rulers of Persia, "could not assimilate themselves completely" to their subject peoples "because to the end they remained strangers to all culture." Thoroughly reliable records state that the last of the powerful Saljūqid sultans, Sanjar, could neither read nor write, and there is no indication that his predecessors were any better educated.[67] Barthold, who made no special study of the Liao dynasty, repeats the traditional opinion that perhaps this dynasty accepted more of Chinese civilization than any other of the conquest dynasties.[68] But it is interesting that even here Barthold's statement is phrased in terms of partial culture acceptance rather than as an example of complete absorption.[69]

d. LIAO SOCIETY AND LIAO CULTURE

The obstacles to the complete fusion of two cultures which have been formulated in principle and demonstrated in detail by students of acculturation and retarded diffusion were also present in the Liao empire.   Analysis of the institutional history of this dynasty of conquest abundantly confirms Linton's thesis that the complete merging of two cultures should not be expected as long as each society continues its separate existence.

Liao economy was dual in character, the Chinese and some few other subjugated peoples primarily depending upon agriculture, the Ch'i-tan and other less important tribes relying upon stockbreeding, hunting, and some fishing.[70] Dual, therefore, was the attitude of the two main sectors of the population to handicraft ("industry"),[71] to communication,[72] and to the articles, the manner,[73] and the means of exchange.[74] The economy of the two sectors differed with the locale as our geographic data clearly demonstrate. Few Ch'i-tan officials and warriors were stationed in the southern (Chinese) territories of the

[58] Hu S 41, 3.
[59] Ibn Khaldoun, PH I, 311 ff.
[60] *Op. cit.*, 260.
[61] *Idem* II, 368.
[62] *Op. cit.*, 347.
[63] Barthold 35a, 6.
[64] *Op. cit.*, 12; *idem* 28, 306.
[65] *Idem* 35a, 12; *idem* 28, 308.

[66] *Idem* 35a, 6 ff.
[67] *Idem* 28, 308.   The fact that Sanjar's father "is sometimes represented as possessing more culture" (*loc. cit.*) obviously has not made Barthold change his general concept.
[68] Barthold 35, 121.
[69] Toynbee considers degeneration the usual fate of a nomadic conqueror because he "has passed out of his own element and has become economically superfluous" (Toynbee, SH III, 24).
[70] See II.
[71] See III.
[72] See IV.
[73] See V.
[74] See VI.

country; and, although numerous Chinese and Po-hai families were settled in urban and rural centers throughout the northern part of the empire, the grasslands of these tribal regions remained the domain of the Ch'i-tan and their "barbarian" followers.[75]

The ecological and economic symbiosis—not fusion—has it corollary in the social and cultural symbiosis—not fusion—of the empire's two most important nationalities.[76] Many modifications and adaptations are recorded in the sociological and economic sections, but all of them together did not shake the society's dual structure nor its dual folkways and religious ideas.[77]

The same duality permeated the administrative and military organization and policy. The tribesmen were taxed differently (and more lightly) than the settled Chinese and Po-hai.[78] (It is true they were called upon by the government for labor service,[79] but this service was of a somewhat privileged kind.) In time of distress, they were the first to get relief[80] and the last to rebel[81]—if the actions of the Ch'i-tan in the hour of their empire's dissolution can be termed rebellion at all.

The closest collaboration between the Ch'i-tan rulers and their Chinese subjects was achieved in the sphere of political organization; but the key positions of power were carefully retained by the Ch'i-tan conquerors, as shown by our survey of the empire's administrative[82] and military[83] machines.

During the two hundred years of Liao rule Ch'i-tan society adjusted itself to the Chinese manner of living in many ways. Wherever cultural adaptations occurred, an attempt has been made to indicate them clearly, but the duality that remained basic in the socio-economic and political organization of the country found expression until the end in all aspects of the culture. The Ch'i-tan never relinquished their reliance upon horse wealth;[84] their rulers continued to give much of their time to hunting and fishing until the great Jurchen chieftain A-ku-ta openly challenged Liao authority, an event which significantly took place at a great fishing party.[85] Except for one emergency nomination which occurred in the middle of the dynasty, Ch'i-tan nobles headed the most important political and military office, the Northern

Chancellery of the Northern Region;[86] and so completely was the army a Ch'i-tan monopoly that, until the very last, military secrets were withheld from Chinese officials.[87]

A Ch'i-tan who permitted his son to compete in the Chinese examinations was severely beaten.[88] In 1074, two generations before the empire's collapse, Emperor Tao-tsung refused to replace the "improper" Ch'i-tan kinship system by the more civilized Chinese clan system.[89] This same intransigent ruler still underwent the old tribal recognition ceremony;[90] he proudly declared his country's civilization the equal of the Chinese.[91]

Pastoral attitudes towards food were maintained. It was natural enough for the Ch'i-tan soldiers to depend for their main nourishment upon fermented mare's milk or kumiss.[92] But even at court where Chinese dishes were appreciated the Ch'i-tan predilection for dairy products never weakened. After two hundred years of cultural symbiosis, the last emperor of the dynasty, T'ien-tsu, was still unaware of the fact that his Chinese subjects abhorred the curd so dear to his heart and stomach.[93]

There can be no doubt that the great majority of Ch'i-tan people did not become Chinese. When the empire collapsed, few Ch'i-tan crossed the Sung borders. Most of those who left their homesteads[94] drove their carts either into the western borderlands or (and this obviously was the greater number) eastward into the camps of the tribal, though hostile, Jurchen.[95]

The court and the high nobility had accepted much more of Chinese culture; but even this group sought refuge among friendly tribes rather than with their Chinese neighbors. The last emperor fled to the western border zone where he took a wife from the T'u-lü-pu tribe.[96] And the only member of the imperial family who was still capable of planning a new, bold, and successful campaign, Yeh-lü Ta-shih, led his followers, not into China Proper, but into the far western steppes where a reservoir of tribal manpower could be mobilized for a great attack against the agricultural oases of Central Asia.[97]

---

[75] See I.
[76] See VII, 1.
[77] See VII, 2.
[78] See X, 1.
[79] See XI.
[80] See XII.
[81] See XIII.
[82] See XIV.
[83] See XV.
[84] Cf. II, 1 (20).
[85] XIII (42).

[86] XIV, 1 (9) LS 45, 2a; see also XIV, introduction.
[87] XV, 2 (26).
[88] XIV, 3 (9).
[89] VII, 2 (67).
[90] See VII, 2, note 188; reference to YPL 16a ff.
[91] See VII, 1, note 65; reference to SMCW 9a.
[92] II, 1 (2).
[93] CS 8, 13a; PCKT 2, 22.
[94] FHC 28, 354; LCCWP 8, 157.
[95] XIII (50) (57); cf. also CS 133, 5a and 2, 16a.
[96] XVI, 1124, LS 29, 9a.
[97] LS 30, 4b ff.

III. SIMILAR TENDENCIES IN OTHER CHINESE DYNASTIES OF CONQUEST

1. THE CHIN DYNASTY (1115–1234)

The Jurchen founders of the Chin dynasty gave up many of their tribal ceremonies and customs;[98] but they did not yield their political and military domination. They reserved for themselves the key administrative positions, assigning to the Chinese a definitely limited number of offices.[99] To gain their privileged posts the Jurchen did not have to pass the difficult Chinese examinations; their tests were simpler and partly military in character.[100] The special armies of the Chin dynasty, the *mêng-an* and *mo-k'o* 猛安謀克, were at first composed of Jurchen, Ch'i-tan, Hsi, Po-hai, and Chinese. Later they were purged of alien elements,[101] so that for all practical purposes they became a "national" Jurchen body. Jurchen customs and ceremonies became less evident in the new centers of power, but the Jurchen language and script were kept alive and juxtaposed to the Chinese language and script in the official documents of the Chin government.[102] A number of Chinese officials were honored with Jurchen names.[103] For a time Jurchen clothes and haircut were forced on all Chinese men.[104] A nativist movement was inaugurated by Emperor Shih-tsung; in 1187 he ordered the punishment of all Jurchen who had adopted Chinese surnames or wore Chinese clothes;[105] he also reprimanded a Jurchen official who bowed in Chinese fashion.[106]

Nevertheless, the process of Sinicization continued. In 1191, eight years after the fortification of the northern border against the growing Mongol danger, intermarriage between Jurchen settlers and Chinese was permitted.[107] How far-reaching the effect of this measure was, it is difficult to say. As in the other conquest periods, the emperor had Chinese concubines in his harem, but the empress was always chosen from a small number of consort families who could all claim Jurchen nationality.[108] The seemingly curious indulgence of the Chin court towards shamanism[109] (de Groot's *wu*-ism[110]) and a number of other cultural

"anomalies"[111] serve to emphasize the basic differences implicit in Jurchen and Chinese society. These differences are as striking as the trends towards assimilation which were much more marked than under the preceding Liao dynasty.[112]

2. MARCO POLO, EXPONENT OF THE DUAL ORDER WITHIN THE YÜAN DYNASTY

The Yüan dynasty (1206–1368) shows the same socio-cultural[113] rift in a still more conspicuous form. Marco Polo arrived in the Far East almost forty years after North China, the former Chin empire, had been seized by the Mongols and while the conquest of the Southern Sung empire was being completed. He lived in Mongol China for a number of years, a Westerner who enjoyed unique opportunities for travel and observation in the Middle Kingdom. Since he made good use of his privileged position, his limited knowledge of things Chinese has often puzzled his critical readers. "In no respect is his book so defective as in regard to Chinese manners and peculiarities."[114] Marco Polo evidently knew little, if any, Chinese.[115] He does not describe the Chinese script, nor does he mention the favorite Chinese beverage, tea.[116] Yule finds it "difficult to account for these omissions, especially considering the comparative fulness with which he treats the manners of the Tartars and of the Southern Hindoos. . . ."[117]

The Venetian's shortcomings can be readily explained by the fact that he lived in the Far East as an agent of the Mongol government, actively participating, according to his own claim, in breaking down Chinese military resistance.[118] Though his direct contribution to the conquest of Sung China is questioned,[119] his biography leaves little doubt of where his sympathies lay during the conflict. Even in the northern part of China, which had been in Mongol

---

[98] See HCS, Chin, VII, *passim* (ms).
[99] *Op. cit.*, XIV, *passim; cf.* also CS 55, 1*b*.
[100] CS 51, 11*b*–14*b*.
[101] CS 44, 2*b* ff.
[102] CS 55, 20*b*.
[103] CS 7, 10*a* and TCKC 10, 3*a*.
[104] CHHC 7, 80.
[105] CS 8, 20*b*.
[106] CS 88, 16*a*.
[107] CS 9, 11*a*.
[108] CS 64, 11*a*.
[109] TCKC 18, 2*b*.
[110] De Groot, RSC VI, 2, 1187.

[111] HCS, Chin, VII, introduction (ms).
[112] See below.
[113] For this term see Linton 40, 510.
[114] Yule 03, 110.
[115] Lattimore, reviewing the previous discussion on this point, concludes that Marco Polo "had little or no knowledge of either written or spoken Chinese." In a note, he adds that "very likely during his long residence he picked up a smattering of the spoken language; on the other hand his mention of a few words and names shows that he cannot have known the language well and therefore cannot have been able to read and write it. No foreigner ever learned to read and write Chinese without boasting about it" (Lattimore 40, 82).
[116] Yule 03, 110.
[117] *Op. cit.*, 111. *Cf.* also Lattimore 35, 73 ff.
[118] Marco Polo 03 II, 159.
[119] See Yule's discussion of the claim made by Marco Polo for himself, his father, and his uncle (Marco Polo 03 II, 167).

hands for a number of decades, hostility and distrust continued unabated. The Mongol ruler, "having no confidence in the natives, put all authority into the hands of Tartars, Saracens, or Christians who were attached to his household and devoted to his service, and were foreigners in Cathay." On the other hand, "all the Cathayans detested the Grand Kaan's rule because he set over them governors who were Tartars, or still more frequently Saracens, and these they could not endure, for they were treated by them just like slaves."[120]

In this brutally divided world Marco Polo found his place in a foreign bureaucracy[121] which made it possible for Chingis Khan's successors to rule China without yielding the administrative machine to the Chinese officialdom.[122] He accepted Mongol customs, both civil and military, and he learned the Tatar language and script. Discounting his basic Italian orientation, it may be said that he looked on China through Mongol eyes and described it in the terms of its Inner Asiatic conquerors. To him the emperor of China was "the great Kaan."[123] "Whenever the place he speaks of had a Tartar or Persian name he uses that rather than the Chinese one. Thus Cathay, Cambaluc . . . are all Mongol, Turki, or Persian forms, though all have Chinese equivalents."[124] Polo's meagre and distorted knowledge of things Chinese is comprehensible enough when it is recognized as the attitude of the conquering Mongols to a country which they tried to rule and exploit without too much concern for its cultural peculiarities.

The conquest situation described by Marco Polo involved a dual political and social system which, with certain changes and modifications, prevailed until the collapse of the dynasty in 1368. Although the organization of the government was more complex than his description indicates, it was indeed controlled by Mongols, Uighurs, Arabs, and other non-Chinese nationals.[125] So deep was the Mongols' distrust of their Chinese subjects that in the Chinese territories even the local offices were often held by members of the conquering groups.[126] During the greater part of

the Mongol period access to office via examination was barred. Even after 1313, when the examination system was restored, the successful candidates remained few, and their achievement in no way guaranteed them a position of importance. Non-Chinese officials could attain high office without benefit of testing, or at most by submitting to a superficial examination.[127] That the army, the pillar of conquest, was controlled by the Mongols and their foreign assistants goes without saying.[128]

Within the vast empire the official documents were recorded not only in the language of the overwhelming majority, the Chinese, but also in the language—and script—of their rulers, the Mongols.[129] At times announcements were made in several other Asiatic languages[130] as well, a procedure that served the needs of the foreign officials better than those of the Chinese population. The decay of official written Chinese, which has been noted recently,[131] clearly reveals the influence of the non-Chinese bureaucracy on the form and manner of intellectual communication.

The barbarian masters remained socially aloof from the Chinese with whom they did not intermarry.[132] Like the Ch'i-tan, they gave great consideration to the Buddhist clergy, whose "all powerful influence at court" is documented in numerous official Yüan texts.[133] This contrasts strikingly with the policy of the Chinese government which vigorously reduced Buddhist clerical power from the time of the T'ang dynasty on.[134] Again, the Mongols calmly continued to drink their mare's milk so detested by the Chinese. According to Marco Polo, more than ten thousand white mares provided the delectable beverage for the Mongol emperor, for his family, and for one par-

---

[120] Marco Polo 03 I, 418.

[121] Cf. Haenisch 41, 46.

[122] The percentage of non-Chinese officials under the Mongol dynasty was much higher than under the Manchus (cf. Haenisch 41, 42 and Morse 08, 47). More important, however, than the numerical is the dynamic aspect which can be determined only by a study of the distribution of the dynasties' political and military key positions.

[123] Marco Polo 03, passim.

[124] Yule 03, 111.

[125] YS 82, 19b; 110, 1a ff.

[126] In the provinces there were 5,689 foreign offices as compared with 14,236 Chinese (YTC 7, 38a; cf. also YS

39, 8b ff). The central ("court") officialdom comprised 938 foreign and 1,151 Chinese officials (YTC 7, 38a).

[127] YS 81, 1b ff., 16b ff. For the fate of the examination system under Mongol rule see below, XIV, introduction.

[128] YS 98, 1a–3a. The Chinese were strictly forbidden to carry arms (YTC 35, 7a; 38, 5a; Haenisch 41, 46), and while Mongols followed the hunt even when it led through cultivated fields, severe restrictions were imposed on Chinese hunters (op. cit., 34).

[129] YS 102, 13b.

[130] Op. cit., 14a; Yanai 30, 874.

[131] Chavannes was the first Western scholar to investigate the style of documentary writing during the Mongol period. See Chavannes 04 ICC, 417 ff.; idem 05 ICC, 36 ff.; Haenisch 41, 24; and Lattimore 40, 83 ff. and note 31.

[132] YS 106, 1a ff.

[133] De Groot, RSC I, 81. Cf. also Ratchnevsky 37, lxxvii ff., and particularly lxxix ff., where the "all powerful influence at court" of the Buddhist clergy is documented from the official Yüan texts.

[134] See Wittfogel 35, 50; idem 37, 211; idem 38, 109.

ticularly deserving tribe.[135] The official *History of the Yüan Dynasty* gives added evidence of Mongol appreciation of the famous Inner Asiatic drink.[136]

3. THE MANCHU DYNASTY (1616–1912)

When the Manchus came to power, they identified themselves, not with the Ch'i-tan or Mongols, but with the Jurchen, the masters of the Chin 金 dynasty.[137] Both were people of Tungus provenience and both were agriculturists, but the Jurchen relied on a rather primitive agriculture, while the Manchus, before they seized Peking in 1644, had developed a relatively sophisticated agrarian civilization,[138] centered around walled towns,[139] fortified places,[140] and villages.[141] Stockbreeding, while important,[142] was secondary to the cultivation of the soil.[143]

Ogotai considered converting the tilled fields of the Middle Kingdom into pastures[144] but the Manchus entered China already imbued with quasi-Chinese[145] ideas. They did not wish to destroy the Chinese people;[146] they wanted to cooperate with them.[147]

The subtler techniques of Chinese agriculture presented no difficulties. The Manchus had encouraged the use of irrigation before they seized Peking,[148] and in this same early period they had shown interest in matters of flood control.[149] Horses and oxen were still offered in sacrifice,[150] but the great Chinese agricultural rites had been introduced eleven years before the dynasty took the name "Ch'ing" and nineteen years before the conquest of North China.[151] Owen Lattimore seems well justified when he writes: "It has never been sufficiently emphasized how *Chinese* the Manchus were by the time they entered China."[152] De Harlez, a specialist in Jurchen and Manchu history, goes so far as to say that the formation of the Chin empire and the influence of China had developed among the Amur peoples a civilization almost like that of their southern neighbors.[153]

The Manchu invasion was undoubtedly facilitated by the voluntary adoption of many Chinese culture elements both before and during the actual conquest.[154] Marriages between Manchu girls and Chinese deserters were officially promoted during the early years of the dynasty.[155] The first emperor, Shih-tsu (1638–1661), openly expressed his "preference for Chinese officials as over against Manchus."[156] Singde, a Manchu noble,[157] who became one of the great poets of the Ch'ing dynasty, died in 1685, "only forty years after the conquest."[158] Everything pointed to

---

[135] Marco Polo 03 I, 300.

[136] YS 100, 2a; *cf.* also II, introduction, note 50.

[137] WHTSL 36, 10b–11a. The record referred to belongs to the early section of the *Veritable Records of the Ch'ing Dynasty*. At the end of the eighteenth century part of this material was gathered together in a work on the origins of the dynasty, called *Huang Ch'ing K'ai-kuo Fang-lüeh* (HCKKFL), which was translated into German by E. Hauer (*cf.* Hauer 26, xxi ff). Thus WHTSL 36, 10b–11a can also be found in HCKKFL 24, 6b. For its translation see Hauer 26, 488.

[138] KHTSL 1, 17b–18a; 4, 13a–b; 5, 13a; WHTSL 3, 26a; 7, 5b. *Cf.* HCKKFL 1, 4b; 4, 5a; 5, 5a; 10, 14b; 13, 8b and Hauer 26, 9, 50, 64, 179, 236.

[139] KHTSL 1, 12b and *passim*. *Cf.* HCKKFL 1, 1a; Hauer 26, 4.

[140] KHTSL 1, 19a; 3, 6a. *Cf.* HCKKFL 1, 4b; 3, 3a. Hauer (26, 10, 34) translates *sai* 塞 as "Burg"; the word designates all kinds of "blocking" obstacles, particularly those erected for defence purposes at the frontier.

[141] KHTSL 2, 19b; 3, 6a. *Cf.* HCKKFL 2, 7a; 3, 3a; Hauer 26, 29, 34.

[142] KHTSL 1, 17b–18a. *Cf.* HCKKFL 1, 4b; Hauer 26, 9.

[143] WHTSL 47, 27a. *Cf.* HCKKFL 27, 6a; Hauer 26, 493. Horses and oxen meant to be used for war and in the cultivation of the soil.

[144] YS 146, 4a.

[145] Lattimore speaks of the "quasi-Chinese farming" in which the Manchus engaged prior to the conquest (Lattimore 40, 125).

[146] KHTSL 9, 12a–b. *Cf.* HCKKFL 8, 5b–6a; Hauer 26, 128.

[147] WHTSL 5, 38b–39a; 6, 21b–22a; 11, 26b and 29b. *Cf.* HCKKFL 12, 10b; 13, 5b; 16, 2b and 3b; Hauer 26, 213, 231, 296, 300. T'ai-tsung, who in 1632 defeated the Ming Chinese in the region along the Liao River, boasted

that he would not think of taking other men's beautiful wives. He strictly forbade his victorious soldiers to rape the women and girls of the defeated nation. How different is this attitude from that of Chingis Khan who, according to tradition, exclaimed: "It is delightful and felicitous for a man to subdue rebels and conquer and extirpate his enemies, to take all they possess, to cause their servants to cry out, to make tears run down their faces and noses, to ride their pleasant-paced geldings, to make the bellies and navels of their wives his bed and bedding, to admire their rosy cheeks, to kiss them and suck their red lips." See Riasanovsky 37, 91.

[148] WHTSL 31, 17a–b. *Cf.* HCKKFL 22, 7b; Hauer 26, 415. The edict which recommended careful irrigation was announced in the year 1636.

[149] WHTSL 58, 14a. *Cf.* HCKKFL 30, 2a–b; Hauer 26, 536. The event referred to occurred in 1641.

[150] WHTSL 1, 13a. *Cf.* HCKKFL 9, 5a; Hauer 26, 149.

[151] *Cf.* HCKKFL 8, 13b; Hauer 26, 141.

[152] Lattimore 35, 45. Italics in the original.

[153] De Harlez 94, 9.

[154] For a sociological analysis of the interrelation of Manchu and Chinese institutions in the formative period of Manchu rule see Michael 42, *passim*.

[155] 1632: WHTSL 11, 5b and 7a. *Cf.* HCKKFL 15, 13a; Hauer 26, 294–295.

[156] Fang CY, Fu-lin 福臨, in Hummel, ECCP I, 258.

[157] Fang CY, Singde 性德, in Hummel, ECCP II, 662.

[158] Hu S 43, vi.

a rapid absorption of the Manchu victors by their Chinese subjects.

But notwithstanding the many steps taken in this direction during the early years of Manchu rule, no complete cultural fusion took place while the conquest lasted. Political factors present until the close of the dynasty thwarted complete amalgamation. Once the Chinese were subjugated, the Manchus took many measures to safeguard their power and the economic and social privileges arising from it. They organized their national fighters in eight "banners," which were reinforced by reliable Mongol soldiers and by anti-Ming Chinese who in the critical hour threw in their lot with the Manchu invaders.[159] The descendants of the pioneer bannermen, predominantly Manchus and Mongols, like their forefathers[160] continued to serve in the banners which were "the backbone of the military power of the empire"[161] until the T'ai-p'ing rebellion (1850–1864). Then Chinese scholar-officials rescued "the tottering dynasty"[162] by means of a newly raised Chinese army which, after 1864, supplemented but never replaced the traditional Eight Banners.[163]

The Manchus adopted the Chinese political organization, but so modified it that the complete control of their emperor over his bureaucracy was assured. Shih-tsung, who ruled during the Yung-chêng reign period (1723–1736), appointed all functionaries from the highest ministers of state down to the minor officials. This system, which the *Ch'ing Ch'ao Wên-hsien T'ung K'ao* considers unique in Chinese history,[164] concentrated unusual power in the hands of the Manchu monarch.[165] Succession to the throne conspicuously violated the Chinese tradition of primogeniture. Under the Manchu dynasty "not one of the emperors (except T'ung-chih, an only son) was the eldest son of his predecessor,"[166] and consequently "there was no crown prince during the life of an emperor."[167] The few attempts to designate an heir apparent failed, according to one commentator, because "the Manchus originally did not have this institution."[168] But whatever the reason, the preservation of the tribal custom served to demonstrate again the aloofness of the Manchu rulers to certain Chinese political ideals.

Within the high bureaucracy, Manchu leadership was frequently achieved without formal differentiation between the Manchu office-holders and their Chinese colleagues.[169] However, the all-important Council of State, which was set up to allay internal unrest,[170] usually contained a Manchu majority,[171] and "the ranking member was always a Manchu."[172] In spite of the disintegrating power of the Manchus after the T'ai-p'ing rebellion, this principle was maintained until the end of the dynasty.[173] The Chinese statesmen, "brought into national prominence" by the rebellion, were given the title of prime minister, but "they were not asked to stay in Peking and participate in the work of the central government."[174] Manchu nobles continued to be promoted to key positions of power. The Manchus, says de Harlez, "everywhere maintained preponderance either by their number or by superior jurisdiction."[175]

The political separation was paralleled by a social separation which was conspicuously expressed in the serious objections to marriages between the Manchu masters and their Chinese subjects. After the consolidation of the empire, the initial policy of state-promoted intermarriage[176] was suspended and unions between Manchus and Chinese were forbidden. At the same time intermarriage with the tribal Mongols was officially favored.[177]

Marriages were permitted, it is true, between the families of Manchu and Chinese bannermen, but this constituted no real break in the general policy, for Chinese bannermen were considered Manchu and, particularly when they lived in the north, behaved as such, acquiring "not only the speech, but exactly the manners and even gestures of the old-fashioned Manchus of Manchuria."[178] Non-banner Chinese men could not marry Manchu girls,[179] but Manchu bannermen might marry the daughters of non-banner Chinese. In a patriarchal society this irregularity would again tend to strengthen Manchu dominance. For two hundred and fifty years the general ban on intermarriage remained in effect; it was only lifted a

[159] KHTSL 4, 20*a–b*.　*Cf*. HCKKFL 4, 7*b*; Hauer 26, 54.
[160] TCHT 95, 44*a*; *cf*. also Mayers 78, 51 ff.; Brunnert and Hagelstrom 12, 326; Hsieh 25, 60; Mêng S 36, 343 ff.
[161] Bales 37, 38.
[162] Hu S 34, 20.　See also CSK 411, 1*a* ff.
[163] CSK 120, 1*b*; *cf*. also de Harlez 94, 33 ff. and Bales 37, 39 and 43.
[164] CCWHTK 47, 5299; *cf*. also Hsieh 25, 31.
[165] *Loc. cit.*
[166] Morse 08, 47.
[167] Hsieh 25, 41.
[168] *Loc. cit.*

[169] *Op. cit.*, 31.
[170] *Op. cit.*, 77.
[171] *Op. cit.*, 81 ff.
[172] *Op. cit.*, 80.
[173] See CSK 120, 1*b*; Brunnert and Hagelstrom 12, 4*a*.
[174] Hu S 34, 20.
[175] De Harlez 94, 19.
[176] 1644: WHTSL 11, 5*b* and 7*a*.　*Cf*. HCKKFL 15, 13*a*; Hauer 26, 294–295.
[177] Hsieh 25, 50.
[178] Lattimore 35, 62.
[179] *Op. cit.*, 47.

year after the Boxer Rebellion,[180] ten years before the collapse of the dynasty.

An official proclamation made by the T'ai-p'ing rebels described the Manchus as people who "lacked the [five basic] human relations and the rules of civilized life."[181] They particularly objected to the way in which the Manchus married.[182] The critics voicing their disapproval in the heat of civil war were evidently blind to the numerous formalities of even a tribal Manchu wedding ceremony,[183] but they may well have been shocked by the "improper" independence of the Manchu woman. During the heroic era of Manchu history three Manchu women led an armed attack against a besieged town;[184] another discussed peace terms, appearing for her two adult sons.[185] Manchu girls married to Mongols sometimes so frightened their husbands that the emperor encouraged the suffering males to complain openly instead of sighingly accepting the inflicted insults.[186] When a Chinese official was the victim of his ill-tempered Manchu wife, the court held her parents responsible.[187]

Until the close of the dynasty Manchu women continued to "wear their native costume, entirely different from the Chinese women. They still dress their hair in the picturesque Manchu fashion. They not only never bound their feet, but they have as great a horror of it as Europeans have."[188] Walking through life with "big feet," Manchu women were not bound by the same rigid social conventions which prevailed among the Chinese.[189] A Chinese minister to Washington is reported to have said, "The only unmarried woman in the world whose position is analogous to that of the 'American Girl' in her own family is the Manchu girl."[190] This statement confirms the impressions of an American observer, who concludes, "The Manchu women seem to be to other Oriental women what the modern American woman is to her European sisters."[191]

Differences in food habits were sufficiently significant to cause the Manchu Princess Der Ling to comment, "The Manchu people seldom eat rice, but are very fond of bread. . . ."[192] Contrasting Manchu and Chinese table manners, she remarks, "The Manchus eat quite differently and are served with individual bowls and dishes, the same as in any other country. Her Majesty was very proud of this and said it saved time, not to mention being cleaner."[193]

Everywhere within China Proper, Chinese was the medium of intellectual exchange, and the Manchus who resided there were moved by expedience to substitute it for their mother-tongue. But, nevertheless, they insisted on having all court documents recorded in both languages,[194] thus restating the country's socio-cultural duality. "The survival of Manchu, as a dead language confined to the schoolroom use of a social class," has, not improperly, been compared "with Greek and Latin as taught in the eighteenth century and at the English public schools in the nineteenth century."[195] Both languages emphasized social differences, but the use of Manchu asserted social differences that rested on a clear-cut national base.

At times culture unity was frankly achieved at the expense of the Chinese. The Manchus not only preserved their traditional style of dress and haircut, they even compelled Chinese men during the period of invasion to adopt Manchu dress, shave their heads, and grow the queue.[196] This enforced change was so bitterly resented by the Chinese that "many times they chose rather to die, or lose their heads, than obey the Tartars in these ceremonies."[197] The literary inquisition launched during the Ch'ien-lung period reveals that, in the eighteenth century, a Chinese who yearned for "the old cap and garments" was still considered a dangerous rebel.[198]

---

[180] Giles 12a, 117.

[181] 無人倫風化 (TPTKSW 33b).

[182] Loc. cit.

[183] Shirokogoroff 24, 64 ff.

[184] HCKKFL 8, 6a. Cf. Hauer 26, 129.

[185] KHTSL 6, 29a–b. Cf. HCKKFL 6, 11b; Hauer 26, 91.

[186] KHTSL 8, 23a–b. Cf. HCKKFL 8, 2b; Hauer 26, 123 ff.

[187] WHTSL 11, 6a. Cf. HCKKFL 15, 13a; Hauer 26, 295.

[188] Carl 26, 63.

[189] Loc. cit.

[190] Op. cit., 221.

[191] Op. cit., 63.

---

[192] Der Ling 11, 41.

[193] Der Ling 11, 51; cf. also 197.

[194] In 1903, the Empress Dowager was eager to display her knowledge of both Chinese and Manchu to a visitor (Carl 26, 131). Although at that time Manchu was a completely useless language to any foreigner living in China, she praised its simplicity and pointed out how much easier it would be to learn than Chinese (op. cit., 109).

[195] Lattimore 35, 73.

[196] KHTSL 7, 22a; WHTSL 3, 33a; 10, 20a. Cf. HCKKFL 7, 7a; 11, 4a; 15, 7a; Hauer 26, 108, 186, 284. See also Martinius 1654, 108.

[197] Op. cit., 109, 127, 155 ff.

[198] Goodrich 35, 45. Dr. Goodrich's study of this inquisition strikingly reveals the specific Manchu issues hidden behind the policy of the Ch'ien-lung period. Chinese history contains many examples of small native states that attained imperial leadership. But, interestingly enough, the Manchus did not identify with these indigenous usurpers of the throne. Instead they defended the honor of the other barbarian dynasties of conquest, Liao, Chin, and Yüan. Cf. op. cit., 45 ff., 142, 147.

A hundred years later these customs were attacked again. In one of his first proclamations the Eastern King of the T'ai-p'ing rebels stated: "China has a Chinese style. These Manchus have given orders to cut off the hair and to drag a long tail behind. This transforms the Chinese into animals. China has Chinese clothes. These Manchus again have introduced buttons [on the caps], barbarian clothes, and monkey caps, discarding the former dynasties' dress and head-covering. This makes the Chinese forget their origin."[199] Although detested by the Chinese revolutionaries, the queue remained obligatory until, with the fall of the Manchu dynasty, the pigtail also fell.[200]

In certain spheres of life Chinese influence was indeed great. The Manchus, who had lived in settled communities and who had possessed a script before they invaded China,[201] were well-prepared to understand the urban life of the Chinese and their literary interests. Talented Manchus soon began to write in the language of their new subjects, but lack of any scholarly tradition and the privileged position of the conquerors inevitably affected their manner of expression. Among the prominent Manchus of the dynastic period, few excelled in the Confucian branches of learning. Those with literary ambitions were content, in the main, to be translators or compilers,[202] or else they set themselves to writing poetry or popular novels. The great poet Singde distinguished himself particularly in composing tz'ǔ 詞 poems,[203] "songs of irregular lines written to the music of popular tunes,"[204] which were eventually given literary recognition after having been introduced by "dancing girls and public entertainers."[205] Another brilliant Manchu author, Ts'ao Chan, wrote the *Dream of the Red Chamber*,[206] a novel, widely read soon after its appearance but because of its popular form "not appreciated [by the literary critics] until after 1917, when the vernacular style acquired literary importance."[207]

The Chinese scholar-officials, though not without interest in military affairs, emphasized the values of peace and learning. The Manchus, despite demonstrations of reverence for the Confucian sages, insisted that military values were the foundation of their national and imperial well-being. This philosophy prevailed in the formative years of the empire;[208] it persisted during the Ch'ien-lung period;[209] it was present even in the days of open crisis and decay. Any Manchu who wished to participate in the civil service examinations had first to prove his ability as an archer, on horseback as well as on foot.[210] While Chinese candidates made every effort to pass the literary examinations with distinction, the bannermen, mostly Manchus and Mongols, had little reason to master Confucian learning. "According to an unwritten rule of the dynasty," writes one of its recent students, "no bannerman should receive high honors in the civil service examinations, since he presumably had other opportunities to become an official and at any rate should traditionally devote himself to military affairs."[211] This significant rule was broken in 1865, one year after the T'ai-p'ing Rebellion was finally put down, but even then it was a Mongol who won high literary distinction.[212] According to a statistical digest of the records of all candidates who received the degree of *chin-shih* from 1646 to 1894, top honors were obtained by 321 Chinese and three bannermen—two Chinese, one Mongol— and not by a single Manchu.[213]

These figures contrast spectacularly with another set provided in the same statistical investigation. In 1893 the highest government offices were held by 350 Chinese and 398 bannermen. Among these privileged bannermen, thirty-six were Chinese, forty-three Mongols, and the rest, the overwhelming majority, Manchus.[214] In view of such preferential treatment, it is not surprising that, unlike the Chinese upper class which, during the Ch'ing dynasty, furnished many distinguished scholars, the Manchu nobility remained woefully "ignorant,"[215] and that

---

[199] TPTKSW 32b–33a. *Cf.* also Lin-le 66, 90.

[200] Sun Yat-sen initiated his revolutionary career by cutting off his queue. See Wittfogel 27, 42.

[201] KHTSL 3, 2a–b. *Cf.* HCKKFL 3, 1a–b; Hauer 26, 31–32.

[202] *Cf.* Kennedy, Asitan 阿什坦, in Hummel, ECCP I, 13 ff and *passim*.

[203] Fang CY, Singde, in Hummel, ECCP II, 662.

[204] Hu S 31, 136.

[205] *Loc. cit.*

[206] To be accurate, the first eighty chapters which are considered particularly beautiful (see Fang CY, Ts'ao Chan 曹霑 in Hummel, ECCP II, 737). The last forty chapters were written by a Chinese bannerman, Kao Ê 高鶚 (*cf.* Hu S 35, 824 ff. and 861 ff.).

[207] Fang CY, *loc. cit.*

[208] WHTSL 34, 26b–27a. *Cf.* HCKKFL 24, 3a; Hauer 26, 443. *Cf.* Michael's interesting analysis of the military interpretation of certain Confucian concepts by the Manchus (Michael 42, 105–106).

[209] The emperor "loved the show of force and always tried to keep up the military spirit of his people" (Fang CY, Hung-li 弘曆, in Hummel, ECCP I, 369).

[210] Zi 94, 53.

[211] Fang CY, Ch'ung-ch'i 崇綺, in Hummel, ECCP I, 208.

[212] *Loc. cit.*

[213] Zi 94, 221.

[214] *Loc. cit.*

[215] Hu S 34, 19 and 20.

"the scholarship of a Manchu became . . . a bye-word and a joke."[216]

The Manchus also continued to practise their native religion. Emperor Kao-tsung, known by the reign title Ch'ien-lung (1736–1796), carefully observed the ceremonies described in the imperial Chinese code; yet he simultaneously upheld the creed of his Manchu forefathers. In 1747 he ordered the unification of Manchu ritual. A new code, prefaced by his personal introduction which like the entire work was written in Manchu,[217] prescribed ritualistic procedures that differed little from those of the sixteenth and seventeenth centuries.[218] While it revealed strong Chinese influences,[219] it continued to emphasize many tribal features. The Manchu deities were conceived as indefinite "spirits," not as the gods of mountains, rivers, the soil or hearth, so characteristic in Chinese religion.[220] Contact with Manchu spirits was maintained through shamans,[221] while the emperor, who was the spearhead of Chinese ritual observance, acted merely as a helper in Manchu ceremonies.[222] Again in contrast to Chinese custom, Manchu procedure permitted the presence and active participation of women (the empress,[223] female shamans,[224] "women"[225]). Sacrifices and prayers were not only offered in the hope of a good crop;[226] they also asked the welfare of the horse herds and saddle horses.[227] While pork was sacrificed by the Chinese in combination with beef and mutton,[228] the Manchus, firm in their Tungus tradition[229] (and their interest in pig-breeding), continued to make pork their chief offering,[230] even when asking benefits for their horses.[231]

Manchu ritual in the Ch'ing period passed through various phases. The sacrifice of horses and oxen, recorded for the early seventeenth century, is not mentioned in the Ch'ien-lung code. By the twentieth century the shamans had disappeared, but the old deities were still worshipped by nobles and bannermen.[232] After the revolution of 1911–1912 cultural fusion was accelerated. To the casual observer, assimilation now seems complete; actually it is not. The Manchus, while they may explain their traditions by Chinese analogies and frequently recite their prayers in Chinese, still "assure the continuance of the ancient forms of some of their social institutions."[233]

IV. A NEW WORKING HYPOTHESIS

This rapid survey gives no complete picture of the periods under discussion, but, nevertheless, it demonstrates the inadequacy of the traditional absorption theory. During the Liao, Chin, and Yüan dynasties, and even under the rule of the quasi-Chinese Manchus, the great weight of Chinese civilization, which was expressed in innumerable ways, was offset and, on occasion, frustrated by a counter-trend of unusual persistence and vigor. This counter-trend was rooted in the same situation that made contact permanent and promoted intensive culture exchange: conquest and domination.

Speaking of the last dynasty of conquest, Sun Yat-sen stresses the "many precautious measures" taken

---

[216] Giles 12a, 118; cf. also CCWHTK 48, 5307.

[217] De Harlez 87, 61 ff.

[218] According to the emperor's preface, the new code restored the original meaning, which, in a number of cases, had been distorted and modified by the shamans and certain nobles who lived a great distance from the capital (de Harlez 87, 62). For the date of the preface see MCTL, preface, 1a.

[219] Besides the use of rice and silk, a conspicuous Chinese feature is the participation of eunuchs in certain ceremonies (de Harlez 87, 87 and 104).

[220] Op. cit., 202.

[221] Op. cit., 13; cf. also Zakharov 75, 567. The Chinese transliteration, 司祝之人 (MCTL, preface, 1a) "man in charge of the prayers," expresses well the priest-like character of the shaman, but, interestingly, disregards his tribal background.

[222] De Harlez 87, 203 and 79, passim.

[223] Op. cit., 79, 86, 100, 104, 107, 136 ff.

[224] Op. cit., 71.

[225] Op. cit., 87, 105. Possibly the female helpers mentioned are the female shamans discussed in chapter III of the Code. See preceding note.

[226] Op. cit., 73, 87. Besides millet, rice was also offered (op. cit., 75, 76, 158).

[227] Op. cit., 62, 141 ff., 144, 203.

[228] Cf. for the Ch'ing dynasty, TCTL 1, 2b; 7, 2a; 9, 2a; 10, 4b–5a; cf. de Harlez 94, 77, 267, 315, 343.

[229] See I, introduction.

[230] De Harlez 87, 72 ff., 87 ff., 92, 105, 158.

[231] Op. cit., 72 ff., 87, 88, 92, 105, 132, 158. An exception was made for the funeral service; then beef and mutton might be offered instead (op. cit., 77).

[232] Verbal communication from Mrs. C. Ranong at Harvard, October 29, 1943. Mrs. Ranong is the daughter of a Manchu princess who during the days of the Republic still observed Manchu religious ceremonies. According to Mrs. Ranong, noble families held the ceremonies in a room in the rear of their palaces reserved for this purpose. Manchu commoners with less house space available hung a large piece of white cloth on the wall of their main room and held their services there.

[233] Shirokogoroff 24, 2. To Mrs. Ranong's knowledge, religious service under the Republic was held in Chinese by the commoners, but the nobles insisted on using the old Manchu formulas. The only foreigner permitted to witness the wedding of the Manchu "boy-emperor," P'u-yi, in 1922, reports that "in strict accordance with dynastic precedent" the betrothal presents among other things included "two horses with saddles and bridles" and "eighteen sheep" (Johnston 34, 305–306).

to preserve Manchu rule.[234] He further notes that the Manchu or Tatar government (he refused to call it the Chinese government[235]) was absolutely incapable of reforming itself:[236] "By reformation they would be absorbed by the Chinese people and would lose the special rights and privileges which they are enjoying."[237] The correctness of Dr. Sun's observations is confirmed by sixty years of futile attempts at "patching up irreconcilable prejudices between the Chinese and the Manchu."[238]

The limited assimilation of the most Chinese of all four great dynasties of conquest strikingly reveals the importance of "freedom as a determining factor in cultural transmission."[239] Says Dr. Hu: "Wherever a people is denied this freedom of contact and choice, wherever a government or a class or a religious order has the power to decide for the people what to take and what not to take from a foreign civilization, then cultural diffusion becomes impossible or at least exceedingly difficult. Cultural change can be retarded or stopped by authoritarian prohibition, by artificial protection of a whole culture or parts of it from free contact with 'dangerous' alien cultural influences."[240] More specifically, Linton discusses the difficulties of acculturation in a conquest situation. In the subdued group unreconciled hostility creates conditions "least favorable for culture transfer."[241] Conversely, the dominant group, afraid that "the insidious processes of assimilation . . . might, in the long run, destroy their distinctive powers and privileges,"[242] tend to "initiate perpetuative-rational forms of nativism as soon as they achieve power and to adhere to them with varying intensity as long as they remain in power."[243]

---

[234] Sun, TSCQ, 4.

[235] "We say the *Manchu* government, and not the *Chinese* government, with intention. The Chinese have at present no government of their own, and the term 'Chinese Government,' if applied to the present government of China, is a misnomer" (*op. cit.*, 2–3; italics in the original).

[236] *Op. cit.*, 6.

[237] *Loc. cit.* Such was Dr. Sun's opinion when he was fighting the Manchu dynasty. After the revolution he modified his view, and emphasized the absorption both of the Mongols and the Manchus by the Chinese (Sun CS 37, 14; *cf.* Sun YS 27, 23). He did not qualify the later statement, but evidently he was aware of the slowness of the historical process, for he noted that "many 許多 Manchus now have Chinese family names" (*loc. cit.*). Many, but still not all of them—in 1924.

[238] Hu S 34, 21.

[239] *Idem* 41, 1.

[240] *Op. cit.*, 2.

[241] Linton 40, 499.

[242] *Idem* 43, 237.

[243] *Loc. cit.*

Thus, history and anthropology reveal that the absorption theory may obscure rather than clarify the complex character of acculturation under conditions of conquest. Instead of upholding the thesis that the Chinese have always absorbed their conquerors, it seems advisable to make a Copernican turn and ask: *Did the Chinese ever absorb their conquerors as long as the conditions of conquest and political separation persisted?* To be sure, even under the most adverse circumstances, China, old and wise and rich as it was, remained one of the great culture centers of the world. But, for China as well as for other civilizations, conquest not only stimulated culture transfer, but in certain important areas retarded and frustrated it. During the life of the Chinese empire[244] full cultural amalgamation obviously occurred only when the disappearance of the social divide permitted the cultural divide to disappear also—that is, after the period of conquest had come to an end.[245]

From this point of view, acculturation in China's post-Liao dynasties of conquest, Chin, Yüan, and Ch'ing, must be examined. With due modifications, the new working hypothesis may also aid in understanding certain earlier epochs, such as those of the Northern Wei dynasty (386–556) and the short-lived barbarian states which preceded and followed it. The increasing pressure from the mounted tribesmen of Inner Asia[246] led to an increasing infiltration of northern barbarians into the Chinese world. The new-comers—some, forced settlers on Chinese soil, some, "invited" guests, some, regional aggressors—soon sought and often attained power, establishing what may be called dynasties of infiltration rather than dynasties of conquest.

The borderline between the two types of dynasties is fluid; nevertheless, an important difference exists. Semi-peaceful infiltration may ultimately achieve the goals of conquest, but by no means are the two approaches to power identical. The history of the "sixteen states"[247] offers a striking illustration of both techniques. Both finally resulted in a complex dual society. The two Hunnish Chao 趙 infiltration dy-

---

[244] When the contradictions in a complex "Oriental" society led to cyclical crisis and the collapse of the political order. Whether a similar development occurred under the conditions of Chinese feudalism or in other Oriental societies need not be discussed here.

[245] The form of post-conquest fusion apparently differed again according to the structure of the preceding conquest society and in accordance with the new historical situation.

[246] See XV, introduction.

[247] Franke objects to the figure sixteen and counts eighteen instead. He also rejects the traditional date, 265–420, for the period of the sixteen (or eighteen) states, confining it rather to the fourth century, with 304 as the starting point (Franke, GCR II, 116–117).

nasties (304–352) display an institutional and cultural pattern not very different from that of the later conquest dynasties.[248] A detailed study of the dynamics of power and tradition in the T'o-pa (Wei) dynasty may establish a similar convergence.

Furthermore, comparison of the limited acculturation that occurred under the Liao and Yüan dynasties with the greater cultural fusion during the Chin and Ch'ing periods suggests the advisability of distinguishing between two different types of conquest society created by two different types of conquerors—herders, on the one hand, and, on the other, herd-owning agriculturists. The objection may be raised that the Ch'i-tan accepted no more of Chinese civilization because they maintained their old centers of residence outside of China Proper. This is true, but it is equally true that they built urban "Chinese" centers within their northern grazing regions. It is also true that the semi-agricultural Jurchen, who as the rulers of the Chin dynasty controlled North China only, quickly relinquished a large part of their tribal customs, much more than did the pastoral Mongols even after they had occupied the whole of China Proper. The Manchus who merged most successfully and held power longest were the least nomadic of the tribal conquerors of China.

Evidently, the predominantly agricultural conquerors offered less resistance to the "higher" Chinese civilization which, though more complex, was also agricultural, than did the Ch'i-tan and the Mongols who maintained a basically different way of life.[249] The culture history of the Arab conquest, of Saljūqid Persia, and of Osman Turkey[250] strongly supports this thesis.

V. NEW LIGHT ON THE CIVILIZATION OF INNER ASIA

Thus the process of culture change which operated in the Chinese dynasties of conquest was neither simple nor one-sided, but complex and partly reciprocal. In the Liao, Chin, Yüan, and Ch'ing dynasties the acceptance of Chinese culture elements was always selective. This fact, important enough in itself, has far-reaching historical implications, for, if the last four Chinese dynasties of conquest preserved certain aspects of their former tribal life either modified or unchanged, it should be possible to reconstruct, at least in part, their predynastic culture. In any case, success will depend largely on the degree of resistance offered by the conquering peoples to the Chinese ways of life. The less a dynasty of conquest

succumbed to the lure of Chinese civilization, the more it preserved its former tribal tradition. It is from this point of view that the Liao dynasty is of unusual significance.

The Ch'i-tan sector of this dynasty conspicuously reflects the pastoral life of Inner Asiatic tribes as it existed several hundred years before the anonymous author of the *Secret History of the Mongol Dynasty*, or before Carpini, Rubruck, Marco Polo, or Rashīd ad-Dīn recorded their institutions and folkways. True, a number of authors, mostly Chinese, have described the customs of the Huns, the Turks, and other pastoral peoples before the tenth century. But, written from an outsider's standpoint, these descriptions are naturally more concerned with political and military activities than with social structures and customs. To be sure, these sources contain numerous references to institutional and cultural features. In some respects they supplement and clarify other information on Ch'i-tan society; but on the whole they cannot be compared with the historical records of the Liao empire which were written mostly by the Ch'i-tan themselves or by Chinese officials in the service of Ch'i-tan rulers. These recorders felt little need to set down what to them must have seemed obvious facts relating to tribal economy and administration, but their familiarity with the Ch'i-tan elements in Liao culture made possible detailed descriptions when these were considered worth while. Their writings are substantially in agreement with both earlier and later data on the tribal life of Inner Asia. They throw new light on a number of significant aspects of what may be called pre- (or proto-) Mongol civilization.

1. ECONOMIC FEATURES

Concrete data on the economic life of the pastoral tribes of Inner Asia during the first millennium A.D. are few, and the *Liao Shih* like other sources contains little information on this point. Every statement made is therefore a particularly valuable contribution to our fragmentary knowledge. Records dealing with tribal gifts and tributes reflect the variety and number of animals bred.[251] Other passages indicate the size of the tribal herds[252] and the type of ownership, private or public.[253] The presence of these "public" herds is most significant, but there seems no way of determining whether they were established during the khaghanate or only in dynastic times.

The Ch'i-tan tribes were primarily pastoral, but a few members of the confederation are said to have cultivated the soil as well.[254] This would support the

---

[248] See Chin 101, 1*a* ff. and 102, 1*a* ff.; WS 95, 4*a* ff.; *cf*. Eberhard 42, 31 ff.; also Franke, GCR II, 57 ff., 63 ff.

[249] *Cf*. Lattimore 35, 53–60; *idem* 40, 513 ff.

[250] See above, notes 63 ff.

[251] See X, 1, *passim*.

[252] II, introduction.

[253] *Loc. cit.*

[254] *Loc. cit.*

opinion held by a number of modern scholars that the crude auxiliary agriculture practised by some tribes of Inner Asia today is an early rather than a late development.[255]

Hunting and fishing techniques are indicated and, occasionally, they are described in considerable detail.[256] Exchange by barter seems to have prevailed among the tribes, and textiles, the preferred commodity, were as eagerly sought by the Ch'i-tan as by other nomadic peoples of Inner Asia at a later time.[257]

2. TRIBAL MORPHOLOGY (A COMPLEX TRIBAL SOCIETY)

Such data either confirm or elaborate our general concept of the tribal economy of Inner Asia. The Liao material dealing with the social and political organization of the Ch'i-tan has a more far-reaching effect. It leads at times to a fundamental re-evaluation of important aspects of tribal institutions and traditions.

The *Liao History* probably contains the fullest account of tribal genesis and decay to be found in any of the twenty-six Chinese dynastic histories. The fluidity of pastoral tribes is a commonplace, but only in a few rare cases has it been possible to document it from reliable historical sources. The data presented in section I of this volume leave much to be desired from the standpoint of modern anthropology. They nevertheless reveal the mechanics of origin, growth, reorganization, and decomposition of nomadic tribes in Inner Asia long before the days of the Mongol empire.[258]

The inner political structure of the tribes is not as transparent; yet the *Liao Shih* gives at least some idea of the role of chieftainship and officialdom in the various dominant and dependent, simple and complex tribes of the Liao empire.[259]

The distinction between the simple and complex tribes is of the utmost importance for an understanding of the social history of Inner Asia. At the peak of their power, the Huns, as well as the nomadic Turks, were organized in a stratified tribal order, ruled by a well-defined group of officials and dignitaries. Not dissimilar were the Ch'i-tan who, before the establishment of the Liao empire, had grown into a confederation of socially stratified tribes with a fixed nobility and a relatively stable ruling house from which the office of khaghan was filled.[260] The pattern of succession to this office during the pre-

dynastic period is not known, but the names of the chieftains (*i-li-chin*) of the I-la tribe are recorded. An analysis of the genealogies of these early chieftains, and of the struggle for the succession during the Liao dynasty, makes evident how flexible and numerous were the factors which determined the choice of a tribal leader within the complex Ch'i-tan society.

Equally flexible were the rules governing other offices. Certain families had hereditary claims on certain offices, but these claims made due allowance for superior ability and the needs of a changing situation. If Ch'i-tan tradition is in any way representative of a general Inner Asiatic pattern, then the "hereditary offices" of other complex tribal societies, such as those of the Huns and Turks, were probably far less rigidly determined than the records suggest.[261]

The social stratifications found a limited parallel in the hierarchy of the tribe's religious functionaries. Simple shamans (*wu* 巫) performed many of the acts of Ch'i-tan magic, but the most sacred ceremonies were directed by a head shaman whose position and power were far greater than that exercised by his primitive counterparts in the hunting, fishing, and herding tribes of Siberia and Eastern Asia.

3. WOMEN—KINSHIP—MARRIAGE

Early European travelers noted with astonishment the unusual independence and honored position of women in Mongol society.[262] Numerous passages in the *Liao History* describe the participation of Ch'i-tan women not only in economic, political, and religious matters, but even in the military life of their people.[263] The Liao records reveal the extraordinary degree to which such tendencies could develop within a militant pastoral society.

The records also throw considerable light on the formal structure of the Ch'i-tan kinship system. A memorial presented to the Liao throne in 1074 discloses that, except for the two ruling families which adopted certain features of Chinese clan organization, the Ch'i-tan had no "clan names" and did not marry according to the Chinese code of proper behavior.[264] Additional data on the kinship systems of the Ch'i-tan and other Inner Asiatic tribes show clearly that sections of the larger kin group broke off after a number of generations and were no longer bound by their former exogamic rules.[265]

---

[255] *Op. cit.*, notes 133–136.
[256] II, 1, *passim*.
[257] See VI, *passim*.
[258] I, introduction.
[259] VII, 1; XIII, and XIV
[260] XIV, introduction.

---

[261] *Loc. cit.*
[262] See Carpini 00, 10 and 24 ff.; *idem* 28, 9; Rubruck 00, 56 ff. and *passim;* Marco Polo 03 I, 252 and *passim; cf.* also for the time of Timur, Barthold 35a, 41 ff.
[263] VII, introduction.
[264] VII, 2 (67).
[265] *Cf.* Lowie 37, 570.

The two allegedly Sinicized ruling families ("clans") of the Ch'i-tan, the Yeh-lü and Hsiao, actually adopted little more than a permanent name and, with it, permanent exogamy. Their disregard for generation, while utterly shocking to the Chinese, was entirely consistent with Ch'i-tan tribal tradition. Chinese and Western observers have reported that among the Huns, the Ch'iang, the Turks, and the Mongols a son married his father's widows but not his own mother. Among the Turks and other peoples a man married his mother's sister.[266] An analysis of thirty marriages between the two ruling Ch'i-tan families listed in the *Liao Shih*[267] permits us to carry the investigation considerably beyond the general statements of earlier records.

Many Ch'i-tan marriages, as might be expected, occurred within the same generation; but when exception was made, spouses could be one, two, and even three generations removed. However, it was always the men and women of the imperial house who married "upwards," while members of the consort family necessarily took their mates from a lower generation.

This unusual expression of family liens was not without its inner logic. Since the more powerful clan married upwards, it may be inferred that these marriages assured them additional power, prestige, and wealth. Such an assumption is confirmed by two marriages concluded during the formative years of the Qarā-Khitāy dynasty of Kirmān (1222–1303). The founder of the dynasty, Burāq, an emir of the last gurkhan of Western Liao, forced the mother of the legitimate ruler of Kirmān to become his wife.[268] Eighteen years after Burāq's death, his nephew (and son-in-law) married his uncle's concubine, thereby strengthening his hold on the throne which he had just regained from his brother-in-law.[269]

4. SACRED AND SECULAR CONCEPTS AND CEREMONIES

The Chinese habit of describing the ceremonies of a period in detail has produced a unique record for the Liao dynasty. Since much of the Liao ritual was tribal in character, the Chinese and Chinese-trained scribes were forced by necessity to record numerous Inner Asiatic attitudes, customs, and procedures, sacred as well as secular. The silhouette of a peculiarly Ch'i-tan cosmology and religion emerges.[270] A complex tribal world takes shape with ceremonial hunts, rain magic, and devil arrows, with worship of the sun, of the god of Fire, and of awe-inspiring mountains; a world in which shouting shamans unite in their fight against evil demons, and rulers are magically reborn and recognized before investiture; a world in which the tribal ancestress drives an ox-cart, where the path of the bride is blocked by a saddle, and where the final journey of the dead to the mountain of the spirits is eased by the sacrifice of a humble sheep.[271] Details of this kind fill the *Dynastic History of the Liao Dynasty;* information less formal, but equally significant, is contained in many supplementary travelogues and essays. Descriptions of Liao funerals as well as accounts of the customary "stealing" of objects and young girls are an insistent reminder of the dynasty's deep-rooted cultural dichotomy.

5. MILITARY ORGANIZATION AND TECHNIQUES

Conquest is based on military superiority. It is, therefore, entirely logical that the military affairs of the Liao empire are stressed above all others in the historical records of the period. This is especially fortunate, for the great attention paid by recent studies to Chingis Khan's mobile strategy and tactics makes it desirable to see Mongol warfare in historical perspective.[272] Not until the tribal warrior of the steppes mounted the horse, sometime around the middle of the first millennium B.C., did his mobility threaten his Chinese neighbors. To this mobility, the stirrup, which is documented for China from the fifth century A.D. on, added increased hitting power. But cavalry warfare became frighteningly effective only when mobility and hitting power were combined with disciplined, "clock-like" military organization. Such organization was conspicious in the Ch'i-tan (Liao) armies two centuries before it was perfected by Chingis Khan.

The incorporation of Chinese troops in a barbarian army is a matter of early record, but what was sporadic and temporary in feudal and post-feudal China became a well-integrated pattern of warfare in the hands of the Ch'i-tan. Under their rule, nontribal foot soldiers and technical troops became a permanent and numerically important part of the army; Chinese were even included in the empire's mounted elite corps, the ordo guards. This system of complex armies, developed and elaborated by the Ch'i-tan,

---

[266] VII, introduction, notes 234 ff.

[267] *Op. cit.*, tables 10 and 11.

[268] En-Nesawi 95, 239. Subsequent events, which induced Burāq to kill his recently-wedded wife and her son (*loc. cit.*), show that the marriage failed to achieve its purpose; at the same time they underline its political character.

[269] Hamd-Allāh Mustawfī 13, 132.

---

[270] VII, introduction.

[271] For details of these customs and ceremonies see VII, 2, *passim.*

[272] For a full documentation of the facts mentioned see XV, introduction.

remained basic in the military organization of all later conquest societies.

6. THE ORDO ("HORDE")

Among the many unusual features of Liao military organization, one in particular deserves mention: the ordo. The word itself, as *ordo, ordu,* or *orda,* appears relatively early in accounts of Inner Asia. Later the horde[273] struck terror in the hearts of the peoples of western Asia and Europe. The Liao records, incomplete though they are, describe the organization of the ordo in greater detail than any other known source. The *History* reveals that, during the tenth and eleventh centuries, the Ch'i-tan ordo was the camp of the elite cavalry guard of the emperor. An understanding of the composition and functions of the Liao ordo is essential to an analysis of Liao power; it is equally valuable for a comparative study of the elite armies of the Jurchen (Chin), Mongols, and Manchus.

VI. NEW LIGHT ON THE HISTORY OF CHINESE CULTURE

1. SIDELIGHTS ON CHINESE MILITARY HISTORY

The mighty Liao military machine reached its greatest effectiveness in the extensive campaigns against China Proper, but despite frequent early victories the Ch'i-tan eventually bogged down north of the Yellow River. Sung China's defensive strategy dramatically exposes an aspect of Asiatic military history which has been badly neglected in Western writing: the success of Chinese tactics against nomad aggression. In the course of many centuries of border warfare the Chinese system of defence in depth achieved extraordinary flexibility and staying power. Except during the Mongol and Manchu invasions, which exploited the country's inner disunity, the Chinese armies usually succeeded in halting the barbarian invasion, either within the Yellow River basin or somewhere north of the Yangtze River, at the edge of the Chinese rice lands.[274]

The study of the military history of the Liao period is no substitute for the study of the military history of China Proper even during the tenth and eleventh centuries; but the present investigation clearly indicates the desirability of a thorough re-evaluation of the factual and conceptual history of Far Eastern military organization and warfare.

2. MISCELLANEOUS DATA ON THE HISTORY OF CHINESE INSTITUTIONS

The Southern Region of the Liao empire was predominantly Chinese in population and culture. It is necessary, therefore, to include in any history of Liao society a discussion of Chinese civilization as it was perpetuated in this region during the tenth and eleventh centuries. The *Liao Shih* is very articulate on the administrative and military organization of "Liao China," but it has little to say concerning the private life, technical achievements, or material culture of the people. To some extent we have tried to remedy this deficiency by incorporating in our notes data from other sources. Short surveys of the history of coal and petroleum in China have also been added,[275] and the spread of cotton into China Proper via a southern and northern route has been discussed.[276] In connection with this last, the legend of a Central Asiatic "wool"-bearing plant-animal, which was known in China a thousand years before it reached a puzzled European public, is of particular interest. The tribute cloth received by the Liao court from its western vassal states was probably made of that same cotton which Yeh-lü Ch'u-ts'ai observed in Turkestan and which, under Yüan rule, was officially introduced into northwestern China.[277]

The *Liao History* reviews the country's financial organization. Since its agrarian economy was a primary concern of Liao power, more information is given on the taxation of the sedentary populations than on that of the tribesmen, but even for the Chinese regions the data leave much to be desired. Under these circumstances, it is fortunate that the Sung archives have preserved a list of revenues which were collected through the local offices in the Southern Capital at the close of the Liao period.[278] The meaning of certain details is open to question, but a fairly consistent over-all picture emerges nevertheless. The list and the accompanying records contain valuable information on the structure of government finances (revenues, tax conversion, state monopolies) in the most important Chinese territory of the Liao empire.[279]

The significance of a study of the Liao period for an understanding of the character and strength of China's military organization has already been mentioned. Of equal significance is a realistic evaluation of certain hereditary privileges which limited the operation of

---

[273] The word *orda* was taken over unchanged in Russian and Italian; it became *horda* in Polish, Spanish, and Portuguese. The form *horde* is German, Danish, and English. See XV, introduction, notes 33–36.

[274] The southern border of the Liao empire lay north of the Chinese rice region. The southern borders of the Wei and the Chin territories strikingly correspond to the demarcation line between China's wheat and rice region. *Cf.* Herrmann 35, 30 ff., and 46 ff. and Buck 37*b*, 9, map 8.

[275] See III, note 72, and XV, 2, note 43.

[276] See III, note 74.

[277] *Loc. cit.*

[278] A translation of this important document appears in X, 1, note 48.

[279] See III, V, VI, and, particularly, X, introductions.

the Chinese examination system—privileges which, though assuming unusual proportions under Liao rule, were present long before (and after) the tenth and eleventh centuries.[280]

VII. A THIRD CULTURE

Thus, Ch'i-tan and Chinese culture found simultaneous expression within the empire, but their elements blended differently in response to the varying regional and historical conditions under which they met. In the grazing grounds of the north and in the old Chinese territories of the south[281] the conquest situation effected only a limited cultural change. Tribal economy was modified somewhat by the use of grain, textiles, and even money;[282] new methods of administration were introduced in the pastoral regions.[283] Chinese peasants were trained in "barbarian" ways of war which differed widely from the traditional Chinese pattern.[284] Chinese scholars in the northern empire, unlike their brothers in Sung China, boasted few literary achievements.[285] Liao Chinese were duly examined, but the subjects required reflected the naive and unacademic interest of the Ch'i-tan rulers.[286] Moreover, the successful candidates were not assured of a rewarding official career. From the Sui and T'ang periods on, the *yin* 蔭 privilege (the employment of sons because their fathers held government positions) had limited the effectiveness of the newly created examination system. This privilege was particularly favored by the Liao regime[287] and later by the Mongols,[288] evidently because it resembled in intent, if not in detail, the tribal tradition of a hereditary officialdom.

It has been asserted that the process of acculturation is not mechanically cumulative. When contact is established, both native and new traits are changed, and out of their mutual adjustment a third culture[289]

emerges which retains certain ingredients intact, while others appear in a new guise or disappear altogether. To this rule Liao society was no exception. Its political and military organization, its ceremony of investiture,[290] were neither traditionally Ch'i-tan nor traditionally Chinese; rather they coordinated elements of both civilizations. Perhaps the most striking expression of a "third culture" was the Ch'i-tan script,[291] new to the tribal peoples and strange to the Chinese.

Rarely, however, did the third culture lead to a complete fusion of the component elements. More often the "seam across the fabric"[292] remained visible. In the ceremonies Ch'i-tan and Chinese procedures usually followed one upon the other.[293] Shamanistic practice was clearly differentiated from the newly acquired "higher" religion, Buddhism,[294] just as are Christian and Maya observances in the religious ceremonies of a Yucatan village today.[295]

In Yucatan culture contact between the two groups has continued down to the present although varying in intensity in village and town.[296] Liao culture was severely affected by the collapse of Ch'i-tan power. However, it still displayed considerable vitality during the subsequent period, particularly in the Ch'i-tan sections of the Chin empire and beyond this empire's western border. Yeh-lü Ta-shih, the uncle of the last Liao emperor, preserved the dual pattern familiar to him; as head of a great tribal coalition, he established a new variant of Liao culture in the Central Asiatic empire of Qarā-Khitāy.[297]

VIII. DIVERSITIES IN INNER ASIATIC TRIBAL CULTURE

1. CULTURAL SUBDIVISIONS

The Liao records present a picture of the pastoral life of Inner Asia that sometimes elaborates, sometimes contradicts the institutional and cultural data derived from other sources. With the problems arising from elaboration we need not be concerned here, but an attempt must be made to understand and evaluate the contradictions.

At times the Liao data are obviously more concrete and presumably more reliable. For instance, an older text has asserted that in many Inner Asiatic tribes, young men married women of a higher generation.

---

[280] See XIV, introduction.

[281] In this General Introduction we confine our remarks to the Ch'i-tan and Chinese only, as the most important sections of the population. The actual Liao society comprised, in addition, members of many other peoples and tribes whose position, as far as the texts permit, will be discussed later.

[282] VI, introduction.

[283] XIV, introduction.

[284] XV, introduction.

[285] See XIV, introduction, and XIV, 4, *passim*.

[286] See XIV, 3 (10).

[287] See XIV, introduction.

[288] From 1267 on, the Mongols appointed their Chinese officials according to the *yin* principle (YTC 8, 15*a*). Much later, in the year 1313, they introduced the examination system, which incorporated, but did not replace, the *yin* system (YTC 31, 9*b* ff.; *cf.* Ratchnevsky 37, xxvii).

[289] Linton 40, 512 ff.; Redfield 34, 364.

[290] VII, introduction.

[291] VII, 2 (11) and particularly note 25.

[292] For this formula see Redfield 41, 134.

[293] VII, introduction; see also VII, 2 (83).

[294] VII, 2, and IX, *passim*.

[295] Redfield 41, 135.

[296] *Idem* 34, 363 ff.; *idem* 41, 108 ff.

[297] See appendix V.

However, after analyzing specific marriages recorded in the *Liao Shih*, it seems possible that in the earlier time, as in the Liao dynasty, only the princes of the ruling house married thus, the consort family necessarily choosing their mates according to the opposite principle. Furthermore, the detailed Liao descriptions of the overriding of more than one generation suggest caution in accepting as absolute the rather vague statements on the marriage of individuals separated by one generation only.

It is possible that certain tribal customs are more fully discussed in the records of other Inner Asiatic peoples. Among the Turkic Kao-ch'ê the bride's family first received and then presented horses to the groom's family. Among the Jurchen payments to the bride's relatives were customary at the time of the wedding, but the new son-in-law served them for three years before they reciprocated with a substantial gift of cattle and horses.[298] No presentation of animals is mentioned in the rather detailed accounts of the two Liao court marriages or in the descriptions of Ch'i-tan wife-stealing.[299]

Deficiencies in source material explain many but not all such differences. Not infrequently, the descriptions of the same phenomenon given in records that both antedate and postdate the Liao period, while dissimilar, are as concrete and plausible as those contained in the *Liao Shih*. Should we then discard the Liao data? Such action could be justified only by the assumption that all the tribes of Inner Asia had identical institutions and folkways. This certainly was not the case. Even if different peoples are so conditioned that they develop a basically similar cultural pattern, such a pattern, nevertheless, exhibits considerable inner diversity from tribe to tribe because of the specific historical and ecological factors to which each has been exposed. Anthropological opinion holds this to be true for the nomadic tribes of Inner Asia in recent times. Historical information indicates that it was equally true for the earlier periods of Asiatic tribal history.

Thus, the divergencies revealed in the *Liao Shih* need not be a source of bewilderment; they may be the basis for a broader understanding of diversities in folklore and institutions among various groups of Altaic peoples. The Ch'i-tan did not sacrifice pork to their gods as did their eastern Tungus neighbors; nor was the camel as prominent in their ritual as in the ritual of the tribes of the western steppe;[300] but the Ch'i-tan emphasis upon the horse and the ox[301] reflects the importance of these animals in the pas-

toral economy of eastern Mongolia and western Manchuria.[302]

Barthold notes the relative independence of women at the Mongol court of Timur, but he states categorically that these Mongol ladies exerted no political influence.[303] However, at the Liao court and in the Qarā-Khitāy empire Ch'i-tan women repeatedly controlled affairs of state;[304] they might even lead an army in the field.[305]

In some cases, the reasons for diversity are patent. In others, they may be less evident, but even then, the facts themselves have significance for the historian and the anthropologist. The Manchus disregarded the Chinese principle of primogeniture. So, at first, did the Ch'i-tan; but from T'ai-tsu's time on, the eldest son was designated heir apparent and from Ching-tsung's time on this claim, though still contested, prevailed against all covert and overt opposition.[306]

Did Ch'i-tan tradition facilitate the acceptance of direct succession and primogeniture? Theoretically the possibility cannot be denied, but the available data do not favor such an interpretation. The new policy is more satisfactorily explained as a device to protect the power of the ruling family against the traditional aspirations of rival branches of the lineage —aspirations which they had every reason to believe should be recognized in view of the prevailing Ch'i-tan atmosphere at the court.[307]

At times it is easier to suggest diversity than prove it. Did the political head of the Ch'i-tan perform more priestly functions than the rulers of neighboring peoples?[308] Did Ch'i-tan religion have a more stratified shamanism? Did a Ch'i-tan son ever marry his deceased father's widows? Did the Mongol ordo, which differed from the Ch'i-tan ordo, develop from it; or were both variants of an earlier common form; or did they have independent origins?

2. THE HISTORICAL BACKGROUND OF THE CH'I-TAN PEOPLE

Whatever the answers to these questions, the Liao records reveal that the Ch'i-tan people, within the broad frame of a pastoral and nomadic society, developed many institutional features of their own. Abel Rémusat, Klaproth, and Parker were inclined to believe that the Ch'i-tan were of Tungus origin.[309]

---

[298] PS 98, 23*b*; SMCW 14*a*; TCKC 39, 2*b*.
[299] VII, 2 (89) (90) and note 197.
[300] See I, introduction.
[301] VII, 2, *passim*.

[302] I, introduction.
[303] Barthold 35*a*, 42.
[304] *Idem* 35, 126.
[305] VII, introduction, note 133.
[306] See XIII, note 50.
[307] XIII, introduction.
[308] VII, introduction.
[309] See Rémusat 1820, 147; Klaproth 1826, 159; Parker 95, 297 ff.; *idem* 00, 343. Yule mentions the Tungus theory, but characterizes it as doubtful (Yule 03, 11).

Their Mongol affiliation was postulated by Rashīd ad-Dīn in the fourteenth century;[310] a similar claim has been made in recent years by a number of outstanding linguists and historians.[311] The issue is confused by the fact that the terms Mongol, Tungus, and Turk, which primarily designate the three main branches of Altaic speaking peoples,[312] are sometimes applied to tribes whose linguistic affiliations are obscure.

According to Chinese records, the Ch'i-tan were one of three peoples descended from the Hsien-pei, the Hsi and the Shih-wei being the other two.[313] But who were the Hsien-pei? Rémusat, without offering any convincing linguistic evidence, classifies them as Tung-hu whom he erroneously[314] equates with the Tungus.[315] Pelliot, after analyzing a small T'o-pa Wei (Hsien-pei) vocabulary, considers its words Turkic, not Tungus or Mongol.[316] In later statements he still insists upon their Turkic origin,[317] but adds that the people who used them may have been either Turks or Mongols.[318] More recently the analysis of eighteen Hsien-pei words has suggested that this language is mixed Mongol and Tungus.[319] Both assumptions are rejected by Franke who argues that all the data are thin and not sufficiently characteristic.[320] Boodberg considers the T'o-pa words, so far recognized, "essentially Turkish, with a certain admixture of Mongol elements."[321]

If the Hsien-pei handed down their name to the Shih-wei, and if the Shih-wei, northern cousins of the Ch'i-tan, were ancestors of the Mongols,[322] then the Ch'i-tan belonged to a proto-Mongol tribal complex, at least as far as their historical antecedents are concerned. Added weight is given to this assumption by Shiratori's belief that the Ch'i-tan language was predominantly Mongol, although it contained words of Tungus and Turkic origin.[323] Pelliot, who describes the Ch'i-tan language as "strongly palatalized Mongol,"[324] states that the Ch'i-tan people were Mongol mixed with Tungus ("Mongols métissés de Toungous").[325] In large part, the two scholars confirm the conclusions arrived at centuries before by the early Chinese historians and their Persian colleague, Rashīd ad-Dīn.

Whether or not the term "Mongol" should be applied to peoples who lived long before the emergence of the Mongols proper[326] seems a minor issue compared with the historical problems raised. Do the Tungus elements in the Ch'i-tan language suggest an early Tungus origin for the Ch'i-tan? This would imply a similar provenience for the whole Hsien-pei people of which the Ch'i-tan, according to the historical records, formed an indistinguishable part. Shirokogoroff discusses the possibility of a Tungus origin for the ancestors of the modern Dahurs who consider themselves descendants of the Ch'i-tan tribes.[327] But even if "names of clans and a somewhat confused tradition"[328] suggest an early Tungus ancestry for certain Dahur groups, even then they were "Mongolized by direct crossing and cultural assimilation."[329] The same author believes that this culture change, physical as well as linguistic and ethnographic, was already complete when the Dahurs became part of the political organization of the Ch'i-tan.[330] Shirokogoroff fails to state whether he assumes a Tungus origin for all Ch'i-tan tribes and their ancestors, the Hsien-pei, or only for certain sectors within each group.

Without prejudicing further investigation of the historical problems involved, some preliminary insight may be obtained from a linguistic study of Altaic material contained in various Liao records. The last chapter of the Liao Shih, chüan 116, is a glossary of something less than one hundred Ch'i-tan words, many of which are proper names or titles. This is certainly a meagre vocabulary,[331] yet it is considerably larger than the Hsien-pei and T'o-pa lists men-

[310] Klaproth 1826, 159.

[311] See Gibert 34, 453. The views held by Shiratori and Pelliot are discussed below (see notes 322–323).

[312] Pelliot 31, 11.

[313] XIV, 1 (1); WS 100, 12b.

[314] Parker (95, 117 ff.) tentatively and Torii (14, 16–19) definitely refutes this equation.

[315] Rémusat 1820, 147.

[316] Pelliot 21, 328, note 3.

[317] Pelliot 30a, 195 note 1; idem 31, 11.

[318] Pelliot 30a, 195 note 1.

[319] Cf. Franke, GCR III, 177 ff. The Chinese study discussed by Franke was actually based on the work of Shiratori. See the editorial note on the back of the Yenching Hsüeh-pao, no. 9, June 1931.

[320] Franke speaks of the vocabulary of T'o-pa words contained in the Nan Ch'i Shu as of "a dozen words" (op. cit., 170). According to our count the work has about eighteen T'o-pa expressions (see NCS 57, 3b-4a). Boodberg (36, 168 ff. and 179) offers a list of thirty-two T'o-pa words gathered from various sources and mainly identified by Shiratori and Pelliot.

[321] Boodberg 36, 185.

[322] Pelliot 20, 146; idem 34, 35, note 3.

[323] Shiratori 13 TMK, 885.

[324] Pelliot 20, 146 ff. and 174.

[325] Pelliot 31, 21.

[326] In criticizing various attempts to define the ethnic position of the Hsien-pei, Franke attaches no value to the term "Mongol": "mit dem Ausdruck 'Mongolen' ist nichts anzufangen" (Franke, GCR III, 171).

[327] Shirokogoroff 33, 85; Gibert 34, 825.

[328] Shirokogoroff 33, 85.

[329] Op. cit., 84 ff.

[330] Op. cit., 85.

[331] Pelliot 20, 174.

tioned above. Besides, supplementary sources have yielded approximately another hundred Ch'i-tan words.[332] Barthold deems even such fragments most helpful for an understanding of the historical ethnography of Inner Asia.[333]

A tentative survey undertaken by Dr. K. H. Menges reveals Mongol, Tungus, or Turkic affinity for the great majority of recognizable Ch'i-tan words.[334] Certain of the more simple ones, such as the numerals, one, five, and one hundred,[335] and the designation for an important tribal subdivision, the *mo-li* (or *mei-li*, or *mi-li*), are evidently Mongol derivatives.[336] Others, equally elemental, such as *wa-li* (tribal camp) or *cha-sa* (settlement, village) closely resemble Tungus words with identical meanings.[337] To judge from the limited number of Ch'i-tan words whose etymology can be established, the greater part of the common appellatives, including some military and political terms, were either Mongol or Tungus derivatives. Such conclusions, which confirm Pelliot in his opinion, are not surprising in view of the centuries of contact between the Ch'i-tan and their eastern neighbors.[338]

Among the Ch'i-tan tribal titles, however, many (*i-li-chin, yü-yüeh, t'i-yin, i-li-pi, hsien, a-cha-ko-chih, ta-lin*) have a Turkic-Uighur affinity.[339] During the sixth and seventh centuries the Eastern Turks, and in the eighth and ninth centuries[340] their Uighur cousins, controlled the greater part of what is now Mongolia. During these years, the Ch'i-tan again played a secondary role, paying great respect to the rulers of the new steppe empire whose capitals rose from the banks of the Orkhon.[341] Even after the fall of the empire in 840 Uighur influence continued to be felt. Within the Ch'i-tan confederation only the imperial I-la tribe was more distinguished than the I-shih tribe, which may well have been of Uighur provenience;[342] the ancestors of the powerful Shu-lü family (the later Hsiao) who lived in the old Ch'i-tan grazing grounds for four generations are definitely

described as Uighurs.[343] Uighurs taught the Ch'i-tan to grow melons;[344] they probably encouraged the use of the camel;[345] they inspired the creation of the "smaller" Ch'i-tan script.[346] Of all the non-Liao peoples, only the merchants of the Uighurs had special quarters in the Supreme Capital of the Liao empire.[347]

The Turkic-Uighur control over the Ch'i-tan was never as complete as the rule of the Normans over England, but while it lasted, and for some time thereafter, its combined political and cultural impact seems to have wrought changes not unlike those effected by the Norman conquest. In neither case did the native language or culture disappear;[348] but in both instances far-reaching modifications occurred, particularly in the sphere of political and military organization. In Norman England almost all titles were foreign, that is, French;[349] among the less completely subjugated Ch'i-tan the administrative titles were for the most part taken over from Eastern Turks or Uighurs. No organization comparable to the Ch'i-tan ordo, that center of military might, is documented for the early Tungus or proto-Mongols, but the name by which it was known appears almost two hundred years before the foundation of the Liao empire in the Orkhon inscriptions of the Eastern Turks.[350]

3. THE LATER HISTORY OF THE CH'I-TAN

The year 1125 marks the end of the Liao empire but not that of its Ch'i-tan masters. Continuing to dwell in their northeastern homelands, the bulk of this tribal people was first controlled by the Chin state and, after its fall, by the Yüan empire, assuming a not insignificant political role particularly during the earlier period. However, under the leadership of Yeh-lü Ta-shih, a small group of Ch'i-tan escaped the Chin invaders and set out on an adventurous trek to the oasis world of Turkestan. Here for almost a century, they re-established their former glory by founding the empire of Western (Hsi) Liao; better known under its Altaic name: Qarā (Black)-Khitāy.

The history of this Central Asiatic state falls outside the limits of a history of Chinese society; and, consequently, we have refrained from including in our translated texts those passages of the *Liao Shih*

---

[332] This additional vocabulary collected by the co-author of this work, Mr. Fêng Chia-shêng, is part of the unpublished material of our study.

[333] Barthold 35, 25 and 28.

[334] For details of the analysis see XIV, introduction.

[335] Shiratori 13 TMK, 863–885. Schott's claim that the Ch'i-tan numerals two, four, and six were "purely Tungus" (Shott 80, 6, note 1) seems untenable. *Cf.* Shiratori, *loc. cit.*

[336] See XIV, introduction.

[337] *Loc. cit.*

[338] *Cf.* XIV, 1 (1).

[339] See XIV, introduction.

[340] From 742–840. See I, 2 (6), no. 8.

[341] LS 63, 8a.

[342] I, 2 (4), no. 3.

[343] I, 1 (2), I-kun Prefecture.

[344] II, introduction; reference to WHTK 345, 2705 and CTKC 25, 1b–2a.

[345] II, introduction.

[346] VII, 2 (11).

[347] V (19).

[348] See Ramsay 92, 15; Jespersen 05, 92 ff.; Wyld 29, 82 ff.

[349] Bogholm 39, 165; *cf.* also Ramsay 92, 17: Jespersen 05, 85 ff.

[350] Thomsen 96, 113; Radloff 95, 26.

which deal with it. But the significance of a state created and controlled by the dispossessed sons of the "Great" Liao empire of northeast China cannot be overlooked by any student of Liao history. For this reason, we have placed in appendix V a considerable body of Chinese source material dealing with the rise and fall of Qarā-Khitāy power, supplementing it by Central and West Asiatic data which elaborate or qualify the Chinese records in significant ways. The final picture is none too clear, but the new state, despite a certain predilection for Chinese forms and titles, obviously reproduced the basic quality of Liao society with its proud emphasis on a non-Chinese mode of life.

After the collapse of the Hsi Liao empire, certain of its cultural traditions appeared conspicuously at the court of the south Persian country of Kirmān which, for almost a century after the Mongol conquest, was controlled by a Qarā-Khitāy dynasty. During this period Marco Polo visited the "fine kingdom which is called Kerman,"[351] without, it is true, recognizing the Inner Asiatic background of its rulers. Historical records treating of these scions of Qarā-Khitāy exhibit few specifically Chinese traits, whereas the system of marriage and the extraordinary influence of women in government reveal an extreme development of earlier Ch'i-tan features.[352]

IX. BASIC PATTERNS OF CHINESE SOCIETY

The facts revealed by a systematic survey of the Liao and Hsi Liao empires all serve to strengthen our initial thesis: Liao did not follow that pattern of Chinese imperial society which first emerged in the third century B.C. after the collapse of an earlier feudal (or semi-feudal) order.[353] Instead it followed a pattern of conquest which, according to our tentative analysis, also found expression in the Yüan (Mongol) dynasty and, with important modifications, in the Chin (Jurchen) and Ch'ing (Manchu) dynasties.

This distinction has scientific implications. It suggests that the history of imperial China (from 221 B.C.–A.D. 1912) should be studied in relation to two basic categories. The first, the typically Chinese society, is represented by such pioneer dynasties as Ch'in and Han (221 B.C.–A.D. 220) and, after a period of disruption and on a broader territorial base, by Sui (581–618), T'ang (618–907), Sung (960–1279), and Ming (1368–1644). The second finds expression in the four great periods of conquest, with Liao a key dynasty of one sub-type (conquest by pastoral nomads), and

Chin a key dynasty of another (conquest by agriculturists). In the period of disruption (A.D. 220–581) a number of "typically" Chinese dynasties arose in the Yangtze Valley, while in the north there flourished several "infiltration dynasties," the famous T'o-pa Wei (386–556) among them. Each group seems to have followed, in the main, one of the two basic patterns outlined above.

New problems are posed by the last imperial dynasty, Ch'ing. It might be expected that it, too, would fall into the same category as its ethnic and cultural predecessor, Chin. For the first century and a half it actually did, but the growing influence of the Western powers so affected its development that, from the middle of the nineteenth century on, social and cultural trends of a fundamentally different type made their appearance. The growing inner crisis did not lead, as in former times, to the collapse of a disintegrating dynasty only. It ushered in the collapse of imperial Chinese society itself, a society which in one form or another had existed for more than two thousand years.

The history of these last two thousand years falls naturally into ten major divisions: one-half may be subsumed under the "typically" Chinese pattern, one-half under the pattern of conquest.

HISTORY OF IMPERIAL CHINA
(221 B.C.–A.D. 1912)

I. *Typically Chinese Dynasties*	II. *Dynasties of Conquest (and "Infiltration")*
1. Ch'in and Han[354] (221 B.C.–A.D. 220)	
2. (Chinese dynasties during the Period of Disruption (220–581)	
	3. Wei [T'o-pa] (386–556) and other northern barbarian dynasties directly before and after
4. Sui and T'ang (581–907)	
5. Sung[355] (960–1279)	

---

[351] Marco Polo 03 I, 88.

[352] See appendix V.

[353] For a discussion of the character of Oriental feudalism in general and of Chinese feudalism in particular see Wittfogel, OS (ms).

[354] Reasons for combining Ch'in and Han, and Sui and T'ang, are given in Wittfogel 38, 108 ff.; and in HCS, Ch'in and Han, General Introduction (ms).

[355] The Sung dynasty, which after 1127 ruled only South China (the "Manzi" of the Mongols), was preceded by the so-called Five Dynasties (907–960). Among them, the second, third, and fourth were controlled by barbarian groups and emperors, but apparently no clear-cut conquest situation developed. This intermediate period may be treated either as an extension of the T'ang period or, perhaps more appropriately, as a prelude to the Sung dynasty.

6. Liao [Ch'i-tan]
(907[356]–1125)

7. Chin [Jurchen]
(1115[357]–1234)

8. Yüan [Mongol]
(1206[358]–1368)

9. Ming (1368–1644)

10. Ch'ing [Manchu]
(1616[359]–1912)

Each of these ten divisions has a particular historical setting. Each has its particular problems. But among them, five may be considered as key periods, or key dynasties,[360] because they reveal a specific socio-cultural pattern with particular clarity. The Ch'in-Han and the Sui-T'ang dynasties represent the classic form of the "typically" Chinese imperial society in its earlier and later developments; the Liao and Chin dynasties represent the two main sub-types within the pattern of conquest, the culturally resistant (Liao) and the culturally yielding (Chin). The Ch'ing dynasty is transitional: knowledge of its growth and decay is equally essential for an understanding of the disintegrating old order and the new one that is in the making.

X. HOW AN INSTITUTIONAL HISTORY OF CHINA MAY BE WRITTEN

1. THE GROWTH OF A CONCEPT

The foregoing outline and division of the history of imperial China is the result of fifteen years of preliminary experiment and research. Early attempts to examine methodologically[361] and describe systematically the economic development of China[362] may

have succeeded in indicating the general structure of Chinese society. They were, however, handicapped by the character of previous Chinese studies, which, although productive in the fields of art, ceremonial, religious and secular thought, and in the presentation of political events, paid only limited attention to technology and material culture or to social and economic developments.[363] In view of this, a comprehensive selection of texts from the dynastic histories was made in Peiping. This material and preliminary translations were brought to New York in 1937 and 1938.[364] The original texts comprised more than 55,000 items,[365] but large as the compilation was it still proved inadequate. A realization of the bureaucratic structure of Chinese society had, it is true, led to the selection of numerous data on public finance, labor, military service, and public works,[366] but these data were too fragmentary to give a meaningful picture of the political frame within which Chinese economy functioned.

It may be possible, although not ideal, to write an economic history of feudal Europe without giving much consideration to its political institutions. For the complex bureaucratic societies of China, Egypt, India, and the high civilizations of Ancient America,[367] a purely economic history cannot produce satisfactory results.[368] While annotating the texts, we soon discovered that, whether we were dealing with particular passages or with complex problems, the explanations required more than economic data and an administrative background, however valuable both might be.[369]

We therefore redefined and augmented the basic

---

[356] The year in which Ch'i-tan tribal society was transformed into a hereditary monarchy. The *Liao Shih* takes this year as the starting point for its Imperial Annals. In this as in other cases we date "a dynasty according to its own claims as presented in its official annals" (Kennedy 41, 285). Although this method frequently causes the overlapping of the end of the old dynasty and the commencement of the new, it is, as Kennedy remarks, far more realistic than the alternative approach and has therefore been chosen in spite of certain manifest disadvantages.

[357] Year of the establishment of the monarchy.

[358] The same. Kublai Khan (Shih-tsu), whose reign began in 1260, became emperor of the whole of China in 1280.

[359] In 1616 Nuerhachi set up the new dynasty which he called Later Chin in order to present it as the successor of the Chin [Jurchen] dynasty. The new name, Ch'ing, was adopted in 1636, eight years before the conquest of Peking.

[360] In a personal communication this term was suggested by Owen Lattimore for the Liao dynasty.

[361] See Wittfogel 27, 333 ff.

[362] Wittfogel 31 and 35.

[363] Such an attitude was also taken by the students of native American culture. *Cf.* Kroeber 39, 3.

[364] Wittfogel 38*a*, 15.

[365] *Op. cit.*, 17.

[366] *Op. cit.*, 16; *cf.* also 30 ff.

[367] It seems that the complex agricultural civilizations of Ancient America (Toltec and Aztec Mexico, Maya, Inca, and pre-Inca cultures of South America) had economic and political institutions, not identical with, but similar to those of the great Oriental societies of Asia, Egypt, and Moorish Spain. For a preliminary statement see Wittfogel 32, 587 ff.; *idem* 38, 103; for the corrected and amplified concept see *idem*, OS (ms).

[368] This is one of the reasons why M. P. H. Lee's *Economic History of China* (1921) and other modern economic histories of the various periods of Chinese development, although useful in many details, provide such a fragmentary idea even of their special field of research.

[369] The need of considering non-economic factors even for the analysis of economic history has been stressed by leading authorities in the field. R. H. Tawney speaks of "the infinite complexity of human relationships, with their interplay of law with economics, and of economics with politics" (Tawney 12, 402).

categories of our study[370] to include several new aspects of Chinese socio-cultural development that the original work had barely touched upon. Each main category falls into a number of sub-categories, dictated by the general character of the material and its significance for the period or dynasty under discussion. The chapter headings of the sixteen sections of this publication indicate the range of our categories and the type of material collected and analyzed in the course of the investigation.

Section I is devoted to administrative geography and population figures. Sections II–VI contain data on various aspects of economic life: agriculture and stockbreeding (II), handicraft and industry (III), communications (IV), trade (V), and money (VI). Social structure is discussed in the next three sections: social stratification (VII), powerful families (VIII), temples and monasteries (IX). Included also in section VII are texts on social organization and folkways. Sections X–XV are concerned with the structure and functions of the state: financial system (X), compulsory labor service (XI), calamities and relief (XII), rebellions (XIII), administrative system (XIV), military organization and methods of warfare (XV). The main events of the period are tabulated in the last section (XVI), thus presenting chronologically material treated topically in the preceding sections.

2. BASIC SOURCES AND GUIDED SELECTION

a. THE DYNASTIC HISTORIES

Translated passages taken from the dynastic history (or histories) which deal with the particular period under examination are the basic material of the study. The justification for this rests on the assumption that the Chinese dynastic histories really are a basic source of information, and that this source can be rewarding if a technique of guided selection is used.

The dynastic histories cover the whole epoch of imperial Chinese society from the third century B.C. to the beginning of the twentieth century. The earlier history of China, the period of the country's feudal and pre-feudal development, is documented in a number of literary sources and archaeological finds which are less homogeneous than the histories and more difficult of access. These periods can— and should—also be examined in the light of institutional change and culture history, a method which has already revealed the mighty shadow of a substantial and fascinating world.[371]

Short historical records may well have been kept in relatively early times, but the writing of the more extensive histories was probably not begun until the last centuries of the feudal society. The establishment of a new type of state with a centralized imperial bureaucracy paved the way for a new type of systematic, institutional, and cultural historiography. It was this situation that in the Earlier Han dynasty led to the writing of the first dynastic history.[372] From the beginning of the imperial epoch on, the government filed in its archives such documents as edicts, state papers, memorials of important court discussions,[373] as well as the records of daily and ordinary procedure.[374] To all of these the official historian had access. By the twentieth century the number of dynastic histories had grown to twenty-four or, if the New History of the Mongol Dynasty and the Draft of the History of the Ch'ing Dynasty are added, to twenty-six.

To be sure, there are many other sources of great importance particularly for the later dynasties.[375] But a systematic study of Chinese institutional history must still rely upon the Histories as a starting point—and this for a number of reasons: first, because in large part they are based upon official documents and state papers;[376] second, because for the earlier periods the Histories are the chief source of information available to us; third, because even for the late dynasties the Histories in their uniformity and inclusiveness provide the frame into which new and additional material may conveniently be fitted.[377]

All these considerations recommend the Histories to any scholar who does not seek his data in a nar-

---

[370] For the main topics of the original collection see Wittfogel 38, 16.

[371] Recent discoveries and studies enable the historian to supplement such early records as have been preserved in many archaeological finds by the divination texts of the Shang dynasty (trad. date 1766–1122 B.C.), and by a number of bronze inscriptions engraved mainly during time of the Chou dynasty (trad. date 1122–256 B.C.). The analysis and integration of all these sources have led in China as well as in the West to a number of attempts to reconstruct the prehistoric and the feudal society of China. See Creel 37 and 37a, passim; cf. also Wittfogel 40 and 40a, passim.

[372] The Shih Chi 史記. Cf. Gardner 38, 16 ff.

[373] Gardner 38, 89.

[374] See Hirth 85, 1 ff.; Gardner 38, 88.

[375] Wittfogel 38a, 20.

[376] The material of the Bureau of History and other important contemporary sources were selected and edited according to fixed standards which were supposed to insure the greatest objectivity. Usually a comprehensive preliminary compilation of the data, the Veritable Records (shih lu 實錄), preceded the final work. Only the Veritable Records of the Histories of the last two dynasties and some fragments of earlier records are preserved. Cf. Gardner 38, 91 ff.; Moule and Chung 39, 289 ff.; Goodrich 40, 81 ff.

[377] Wittfogel 38a, 20.

rowly circumscribed field but desires to present an integrated picture of the historical process in its entirety. Even though the *Histories* do not deal in detail with the origin of Chinese civilization, they nevertheless have important methodological implications for the study of feudal and prefeudal China. They have particular significance for any study of the country as a living culture, for it is the China of the *Histories* that gives the socio-cultural setting for the China of today.

b. GUIDED SELECTION

Before the institutional data of the *Histories* can be used, they must first be made accessible. Large sections of the two earliest works[378] and fragments of others[379] have been translated into Western languages. But, helpful and valuable as these translations are, they cover only a small part of the twenty-six works. According to a rough estimate, a complete translation of all the *Histories*, properly annotated and prefaced, would fill more than four hundred volumes of five hundred pages each.[380] Such a work may be possible at some future time; it has not been feasible as yet.

A full translation of the more important *Histories* is very desirable, but it is doubtful whether the translation of all twenty-six is imperative. The *Histories* are in part repetitious, and the detailed reports of political, ceremonial, and military events, if they are not used in highly specialized studies, are an obstacle rather than a help to structural insight. Chinese scholars have long tried to mitigate a situation which they were quick to recognize. By a process that may be called *guided* selection they compiled essential data from the *Histories*, supplementing them from parallel sources. Some of the greatest achievements of Chinese scholarship, such as Tu Yu's[381] *T'ung-tien* 通典, Chêng Ch'iao's[382] *T'ung-chih*, 通志, and Ma Tuan-lin's[383] *Wên-hsien T'ung-k'ao* 文獻通考, followed this procedure.

Recent research in the social sciences has led to the realization that culture history must integrate the various aspects of society. The traditional schools of Chinese historiography, while presenting a wealth of detail, have paid little attention to dynamic relationships. On the other hand, some modern scholars who have striven to present society as an integrated whole have too lightly thrust aside categories that were meaningful to earlier historiographers because they functioned more importantly in their society.[384]

The sixteen sections of this publication represent a like number of categories under which the socio-economic, cultural, administrative, and military history of China has been considered. Naturally, certain institutions overlap in function and at times; therefore, classification will be somewhat arbitrary, especially when secondary aspects of a complex and intricate whole are being dealt with. For instance, every administrative unit has its place in the period's administrative geography; it is, therefore, discussed in our section I. But it is also part of the country's political system; as such, it is treated in section XIV. An irrigation canal or a road, from the standpoint of use, is an element in the system of agriculture or communication (II or IV): but as the end result of forced public labor (corvée) it appears again in section XI. The public and private forms of agriculture, industry, and commerce are described in sections II, III, and V, which deal with the dynasty's economic activities from the point of view of the producer and consumer. However, as sources of government revenue they are treated in section X; similarly the excessive taxes (X), labor services (XI), and calamities (XII) must also be discussed in relation to relief measures (XII) and rebellions (XIII). Legal decrees or decisions are presented along with the situations which they regulate (*cf.* below, section VII, 1). But general statements concerned with law and punishment are included in the sections dealing specifically with government functions, such as astronomy, calendar-making, and the maintenance of the official state ideology, Confucianism.

In all these cases, the multiple classification arises out of the complexity of the institution itself or out of its manifold functions. No doubt, at times other scholars might arrive at different decisions. But more important than the placing of individual passages is the question whether or not the categories, as such, enable the scientist to break through the Great Wall set up by the size and form of the dynastic histories and thus gain access to the mass of institutional and cultural information hidden behind it.

---

[378] See Chavannes' monumental translation (MH) of the first forty-seven *chüan* of the *Shih Chi*, and Dubs' translation of the Imperial Annals of the *Han Shu* of which two volumes have been published, while others are in preparation (Dubs, HFH).

[379] Among others, the first sections of the *Yüan Shih* have been translated into Russian by Iakinth. See Barthold 28, 44, note 2.

[380] Suggested by Dr. Homer H. Dubs. His calculation does not include the *New Yüan History* nor the *Draft of the History of the Ch'ing Dynasty*.

[381] 杜佑 died in A.D. 812.

[382] 鄭樵, 1108–1166.

[383] 馬端臨 lived in the thirteenth century.

---

[384] For instances of harmful neglect of basic Chinese categories by modern Western and Chinese scholars see Wittfogel 38a, 21 ff.

c. SUPPLEMENTARY SOURCES

The selected texts of this publication are translated from the dynastic histories. Apart from the scientific considerations mentioned above, this choice was suggested by the conviction that no pioneer study, however comprehensive, could hope to cover the *Histories* and all supplementary sources at the same time. But while making the *Histories* the textual center of our effort we have tried not to disregard the supplementary sources which China, the country of historiography par excellence, places at the disposal of the student of any period, dynasty, or institution.

Literary records and archaeological finds of all kinds provide a vast reservoir of additional information which has been used wherever possible to clarify our notes and to enrich our introductions. A history of the *Liao Shih* and a survey of the main supplementary sources presented in appendix IV of this publication indicate the problems created by the character of both types of source material.

The earliest records in the *Liao Shih* refer to the first century of the Liao empire, when the system of official recording was adopted together with other techniques of administration. The first known official request for a historical account was made in 941.[385] A *Diary of Activity and Repose* was kept during the Liao dynasty.[386] It must have been in existence for some time prior to 991, for in that year there appeared for the first time[387] a preliminary compilation of government records called *Shih Lu, Veritable Records,* which traditionally were based on the daily entries.[388] Thus, although the composition of the *Liao Shih* was not finished until 1343—largely because many scholars objected to a standard history for the barbarian Ch'i-tan[389]—most of its data were taken from the official Liao records brought together in the *Shih Lu* or from a contemporary Sung source, the *Ch'i-tan Kuo Chih,* and a Chin history of the Liao empire.[390] The fact that the *Liao Shih* was written at a relatively late date is, therefore, no argument against the validity of its material, much of which was set down during the periods which it describes.

Many data contained in the *Liao Shih* do not appear in other early sources whose authors had no access to the court records of the Liao government. In spite of an imperial order to exclude "trifling matters" from the *Daily Records,*[391] numerous reports on "barbarian" attitudes and customs found their way into the columns of the *History.* But much additional information is contained in the supplementary texts, for unofficial observers were interested in many aspects of Liao life which for one reason or another did not receive the attention of the Department of National Historiography.

Particularly interesting are conflicting reports of the same event. The controversy between the Liao and Sung governments over the ominous term "tribute" is so concretely and fully reproduced in the *Liao Shih,* and the Liao point of view is so clearly indicated in a contemporary inscription,[392] that this version seems closer to the historical truth than the rather vague statements made in the *Dynastic History of the Sung Dynasty.*[393] On the other hand, A-pao-chi's acquisition of power is so gently pictured in the *Imperial Annals* of the *Liao Shih*[394] that the sanguinary version of the event in the *Dynastic History of the Five Dynasties* appears incomparably more plausible.[395] The credibility of the southern version is strengthened by the vagueness of the official presentation which hides rather than negates A-pao-chi's murderous struggle for power. Its correctness is partially confirmed by another passage from the *Liao Shih* itself, which, though it does not speak of the murder of the rival chieftains, at least admits the grave conflict that arose when A-pao-chi violated the tribal tradition of political succession.[396]

Completely contradictory are the two versions of the scene that occurred after the first emperor's death. According to the *Liao Shih,* the imperial widow wished to follow her deceased husband into the tomb, but her followers persuaded her to disregard this tribal custom.[397] The southern source shows her much less willing to die and much more eager to free herself from her fatal duty.[398] Here, as well as in other instances, the independent source seems more credible than the official record which depicts its Liao heroes as blameless protagonists.

But the critical student has to weigh the motives of each side. The record-keepers of China Proper were certainly ready to exaggerate any unpleasant story about the hated northern court; the Chin emperors who so severely condemned the abuses of the

---

[385] For this event and for the subsequent statements see XIV, 4 (3) and appendix IV, *passim.*

[386] XIV, 4 (16).

[387] XIV, 4 (7) (8).

[388] *Cf.* Gardner 38, 91.

[389] See appendix IV.

[390] *Loc. cit.*

[391] XIV, 4 (10).

[392] See X, introduction and note 213.

[393] SS 7, 7*a*; 281, 9*a* and 20*b*.

[394] LS 1, 2*b*; *cf.* also XVI, 907, LS 1, 2*b*.

[395] WTS 72, 2*b* ff.; for a translation of this passage see III, introduction.

[396] XIII (1).

[397] VII, 2 (12).

[398] WTS 73, 3*a–b*.

former dynasty[399] also had an axe to grind.[400] But if such considerations warn against the acceptance of a foreign record only because it is contemporary and gloomy—a contemporary rumor may be less truthful than a belatedly published state paper—we have, nevertheless, included different versions because they are confirmed by other records, or because the *Liao Shih* does not really refute them, or simply because of the plausibility of their inner evidence. We have generally tried to weigh the relative truth of the divergent statements, deciding either in favor of one of them or, if this appeared inadvisable, ending our discussion on what the layman finds intolerable, but the scholar imperative, "a note of interrogation."[401]

Archaeological data also have significance for a history of the Liao empire. The discovery of the deserted Liao sites has led to many geographical identifications.[402] Inscriptions provide invaluable documentary evidence for various aspects of the empire's secular[403] and religious life.[404] Our list of the coins of the period is based upon a comparison between historical records and numismatic finds, a comparison which speaks well for the reliability of the economic data given in the *Liao Shih*.[405]

Torii's *Illustrations of Archaeology*[406] is a treasure house of information on Liao architecture. Its plates picture in the main imperial tombs and Buddhist temples. Such buildings were, indeed, an important part of Liao culture, but any attempt at reconstruction must define their specific relation to other factors in the whole society. Neither the agricultural world of the Chinese subjects of Liao nor the pastoral life of the mounted herdsmen on the northern grasslands is made visible by these magnificent ruins which survived, not because they were the typical dwellings of the Liao people, but because they were the most durable ones. Accepted uncritically, such archaeological documents would do more to mislead than to enlighten. But, as part of an integrated analysis which assigns them a proper place, they are extremely valuable, for they express important aspects of Liao handicraft and art, the scale of mass labor, the power of the crown and the temples, the worldly pleasures and the religious dreams of the master minds of the Liao dynasty.

---

[399] CS 96, 4*b*. *Cf.* VIII, introduction. CS 47, 15*a*. *Cf.* XI, introduction.

[400] For the methodological problems involved see Oman 39, 39; Langlois and Seignobos, IEH ,131 ff. and 140 ff.; George 09, 41; Bernheim 14, 538 ff.; Droysen 37, 123 ff.

[401] Oman 39, 40.

[402] See I, 1, *passim*.

[403] *Cf.* MCCSC 2, 29*a* (VIII, introduction).

[404] IX, introduction.

[405] VI, introduction.

[406] Torii 36 I–IV.

d. SELECTION—ANNOTATION—INTEGRATION

A preliminary examination of our material leads to several important methodological conclusions. Single documents or facts obviously do not in themselves constitute history;[407] and single documents or facts do not spring into life through the mere act of compilation.[408] A seeming fact may require comprehensive investigation before its actual validity is established;[409] and even a well-established fact has to be seen within its socio-cultural setting before its real historical significance can be determined.

In this sense it has been said that "a collection of facts has no more scientific value than a collection of stamps or shells,"[410] or, more affirmatively, that a fact becomes historical only by its position.[411] Indeed innumerable notes on the tissues of an elephant's tail —however useful for a special study—are no substitute for a few well-selected data that indicate the anatomy and physiology of the whole animal. Even Aristotle, who expected history to produce only "singular statements" such as what Alcibiades did or had done to him,[412] was very eager to select and integrate the political, economic, and psychological data which formed the basis of his many historical examples and excursuses.[413] Selection, the first step taken by all historians,[414] beginning with the authors of the earliest and crudest annals,[415] presupposes a concept, conscious or unconscious, as to the character of history and society as a whole.

If this is true for the first step, it is even more so for the second—interpretation and synthesis—procedures which distinguish the writing of history proper from the mere compilation of annals.[416] The final test of historiography remains its value to man as the maker of history; but the strength or weakness

---

[407] See Langlois and Seignobos, IEH, 181; Shotwell 39, 15.

[408] *Cf.* Creighton 07, 5; Croce 15, 17; Beard 34, 50 ff.; Teggart 16, 164.

[409] Bernheim 14, 544 ff.; Berr and LeFebvre 37, 363.

[410] Berr 11, 19. Of course, even a collection of stamps or of shells may yield interesting information to the historian, geographer, or biologist, if the collection has representative value, and if it is properly analyzed.

[411] Seignobos 01, 3.

[412] Aristotle 41, 1464 (*Poetics*, ch. 9).

[413] *Op. cit.*, 1128 (*Politics,* bk. I), and *passim*.

[414] "In reality . . . all history is selection" (Berr and LeFebvre 37, 363; *cf.* also Creighton 07, 5; Bernheim 14, 254 and 563; Croce 15, 97; Teggart 16, 176; Weber 22, 254; Rickert 29, 293 ff.; Beard 34, 53; Lynd 39, 137).

[415] *Cf.* Robinson 08, 7 ff.; Ritter 19, 97; Teggart 16, 176 ff.; Beard 34, 53 ff. For subject matter favored by early annalists see Shotwell 39, 61 ff.

[416] *Cf.* Langlois and Seignobos, IEH, 181; Teggart 16, 164; Beard 34, 50 ff.; Oman 39, 33.

of the initial concept, the "pre-conception," becomes apparent as soon as the second step is taken. Then the critical scholar has a unique opportunity to re-examine and reshape his original concept, and to organize, reduce, or augment his initial selection of facts.

The present study has passed through both stages of scientific growth and experiment. This is clearly indicated in the arrangement of our material. In each section the translated texts plus the attached notes are separated from the interpretative introductions which are based upon them and the supplementary sources.

The novelty of the task and the wealth of material necessitated an approach which was monographic in form, though synthetic in aim. Each element had to be visualized as a dynamic part of the whole society within which it functioned. It is hoped that the reader by advancing from section to section will gradually recognize the basic structure of Liao society. The political and institutional changes which occurred within the two centuries of Liao rule are briefly indicated in the introductions to sections XII and XVI, where an attempt has been made to subdivide the entire epoch into five main periods.

e. THE CONTOURS OF TRUTH

The foregoing conclusions, plausible as they may seem, are based on a premise whose validity has not been thoroughly scrutinized. Our study assumes that the historical records available are capable of revealing essential features of Chinese institutional and cultural history. Is this premise justified? What is the actual scientific value of the *Liao Shih* and of the other sources which supplement it? The possibility of historical insight has been the subject of innumerable scientific debates. Naive credulity has been replaced at times by critical optimism, at times by scepticism, limited or complete. Attention has been drawn to the inadequacy of most historical records. Thucydides, who did not trust his own impressions,[417] touched upon one of the many difficulties which may discredit even "the most immediate" observation.[418]

Historical documents are always incomplete.[419] What is more, lack of precision, errors, and even lies are their frequent accompaniment both at the time of origin and during the process of transmission.[420] Archaeological remains, other than inscriptions, are not distorted by the subjective factors that influence the written records. But, whatever their special value in the fields of material culture or chronology, they cannot replace the description of human activity and social change contained in the literary sources.

The fact that historical knowledge is limited and indirect[421] and that historical statement rarely passes beyond probability[422] should not lead to a depreciation of history as a basic source of information for the study of man. Completely reliable and exhaustive knowledge is an ideal that is never fully realized, even in the present. "No single individual," says Linton, "is ever familiar with the total content of the culture in which he participates."[423] The Greeks were not too well-informed concerning their own institutions or immediate history;[424] and even modern man has but limited insight into the complex mechanics of the contemporary world. No military leader can base his actions on reliable information alone; he has to make his decisions in accordance with the law of probability.[425] Powerful statesmen are equally restricted, in spite of the elaborate network of intelligence which modern technique and organization place at their disposal. Distrust in the validity of our actual knowledge is so elementary that we often console ourselves with the idea that the riddles of today will be solved tomorrow—that is, when they have become history.

The history of the present is more fully documented than that of the distant past, but within this past the history of China is at least as well documented as that of the Near East, Greece, Rome, and Mediaeval Europe; for many periods and for many aspects the Chinese documentation is infinitely better. The few "often highly fragmentary, literary histories covering Greek and Roman times" are now augmented by numerous valuable inscriptions and archaeological remains; but they still "leave us in the dark upon many vital matters."[426] The lack of coherent data for the earlier periods of Roman history which Mommsen deplored[427] is also noted for Hellenistic society by Rostovtzeff, who, in the preface to his *Social and Economic History of the Hellenistic World*, calls the existing evidence "scanty and hopelessly scattered,

---

[417] Thucydides 34, 14.

[418] Ranke's confidence in "the reports of eye-witnesses and the most genuine, most immediate documents" (Ranke 24, ix) shows that he was not fully aware of the problem which the great Greek historian boldly faced more than two thousand years earlier.

[419] *Cf.* Robinson 08, 22 ff.; Bernheim 14, 185, 199, and 753; Beard 34, 54; Langlois and Seignobos, IEH, 15.

[420] See Seignobos 01, 23 ff.; Langlois and Seignobos, IEH, 130 ff.; George 09, 31; Bernheim 14, 523 ff.

[421] Seignobos 01, 4 ff.

[422] George 09, 26.

[423] Linton 40, 471 ff.

[424] Thucydides 34, 13 ff.

[425] Clausewitz 57 I, 76.

[426] Robinson 08, 23.

[427] Mommsen 23 I, preface to the second edition.

very difficult to date, to arrange, to understand, and to interpret."[428] The unsatisfactory character of the evidence necessitated a circumstantial and sometimes repetitious treatment of the problems,[429] few of which "can be solved with a fair degree of probability."[430] Rostovtzeff's modest remarks, which hide rather than reveal the important contribution he has made, further testify to the limitations of historical evidence on one of the best-known periods of ancient civilization.

The critical student does well to remember this situation when weighing the scientific value of the Chinese official histories in general and of the *Liao Shih* in particular. Among the dynastic histories, the *Liao Shih* is renowned for its deficiencies. While its data on tribal life and traditions are unique, in other areas it compares poorly with the great standard works. Its population data, for instance, are much less complete than those contained in the outstanding *Histories*. For the tribal world there are no systematic population figures—except for the Ch'i-tan ordo garrisons. For the sedentary population there is one set of data, which appears twice—in a civil and in a military list.[431] Undated as these figures are, they give no information on population trends; yet they make it possible to arrive at some reasonable estimate of the total sedentary population of the empire. Together with certain fragmentary data on the tribes, they provide a basis, although a debatable one, for an estimate of the country's total population.[432]

These population figures are admittedly inadequate. But how do they compare with the data available for other large historical complexes, such as the ancient civilizations of Europe before the industrial revolution? According to Rostovtzeff's carefully weighed judgment, "the calculation of the population of the ancient world is based, in some cases, on the few (very few) figures which give the number of inhabitants of a certain part of it at a certain moment, the figures being ambiguous and open to various interpretations. . . . It is obvious that conclusions drawn from such material are necessarily problematical and therefore controversial. Moreover, they refer to certain moments only and very seldom throw light upon the fluctuations of the population in one part or another of the ancient world."[433]

The student writing on European history prior to the seventeenth century is faced with similar difficulties. All estimates of the population of one of the administratively most advanced European states, France, remained hypothetical "until the end of the seventeenth century."[434] In fact, it was several decades after the French intendants prepared the first census in 1697[435] before these estimates were anything more than intelligent guesses. As late as 1753 the English parliament rejected the proposal for a general census which, it was argued, would expose the country's weakness to its enemies.[436] Tawney, discussing the difficulties in studying English economic history, states that before the eighteenth century "for large departments of life, such as population . . . anything approaching satisfactory quantitative description is out of the question."[437] In Austria[438] as well as in Sweden[439] the first real census was taken in the eighteenth century.

The Chinese administrators were more than willing to count their subjects, for knowledge of their number was most vital for the effective execution of financial and military policies. Chinese population data—whatever their inadequacies—are the most complete records of their kind before the time of modern industrial society. These figures require careful analysis, for they sometimes rise above the biological probability. In the pre-industrial periods of Western history, the problems, in the main, spring from a dearth of population data, while in Chinese history they grow out of the contradictions in the abundant material.

Lack of evidence rarely adds to knowledge; abundance may, even if occasionally it seems involved and bewildering. Sudden fluctuations may reflect rural discontent, migrations, or changes in administrative control and management. Properly analyzed, the source of embarrassment may become a source of enlightenment.

The value of Chinese historiography is still more conspicuous when other aspects of the society are examined. The governments of imperial China early considered the keeping and compiling of records an important task. Its execution was entrusted to officials who, always by training and often by practical experience, were familiar with the problems of administration and policy.[440] Their records therefore

---

[428] Rostovtzeff 41 I, ix.
[429] *Op. cit.*, viii ff.
[430] *Op. cit.*, ix.
[431] I, 1, and X, 1, *passim*.
[432] See I, introduction.
[433] Rostovtzeff 41 III, 1604.

---

[434] Levasseur 89, 248.
[435] For the lack of uniformity in this famous attempt see *op. cit.* 202.
[436] See Kulischer, AWMN II, 5.
[437] Tawney 12, viii.
[438] Meyer 18, 85.
[439] Arosenius 18, 538.
[440] Tu Yu, Ssŭ-ma Kuang, and Ma Tuan-lin all held office; so did their fathers (see CTS 147, 3b–7b; SS 336, 1b–12b; HYS 234, 7046). A systematic investigation of the professional background of the authors of the dynastic histories is beyond the scope of this publication. But it goes without saying that these scholars all received a

were not the "interesting" contributions of political amateurs; they were matter-of-fact data put together for the study of statesmen and administrators, acting or potential. The bureaucratic government affected all, and controlled most, aspects of the country's political and ideological institutions. Chinese historiography therefore unfolds a uniquely comprehensive picture of Far Eastern society and culture.

Unique in scope as the Chinese sources are, they naturally vary in their immediacy. How many original notes or memorials were based upon actual observation and how precise such direct observation may have been is, in most cases, impossible to say. In this respect the Chinese sources do not seem to differ much from the records of other great civilizations of the past. In both cases the degree of accuracy achieved is an open question.

Does this mean that the material should not be used to reconstruct the past? By no means. Many conceptions regarding present situations are based upon incomplete data, and not a few practical—and successful—decisions are made in accordance with the principle of probability. If the dynamics of societies other than our own can be disclosed, at least in their essential trends, then the task is surely worth the attempt. In spite of the many difficulties inherent in even the best source material, recorded history offers a reservoir of facts, perhaps not as mighty and unshakable as some scholars assume,[441] but nevertheless one that enables us "to discern the large contours" of the cultural landscape "without securing a microscopic picture of every detail."[442] If this is true for history in general, it is particularly true for the history of "the great political, economic, and cultural institutions," for "the structures of government and the movement of economic forces."[443] All these institutions and trends have been firmly outlined for mediaeval and post-mediaeval Europe,[444] a world which was well, but not too well, described in historical documents.

Chinese historical records, whatever their shortcomings, ought to enable us to etch in at least the larger contours of China's institutional and cultural development. Additional information will, no doubt, modify this picture, revealing in greater detail and greater complexity the institutions and events first described.[445] The original outline will have fulfilled its task if it has succeeded "in properly drawing the directional trend, around which the curve bends."[446]

XI. COOPERATION AND COOPERATORS

The reconstruction of an entire period of Chinese history from an institutional and cultural point of view is a complex undertaking. Its accomplishment, like the recent effort to reconstruct the ancient Maya civilization, requires "cooperation in all aspects of science and knowledge."[447] The situation in eastern Asia differs fundamentally from that in Yucatan; archaeological material does not predominate in the history of Imperial China, but literary sources abound. Under these conditions a less elaborate technical equipment is needed, but the chance of a meaningful interpretation grows. The success of this study depended upon a comparison of the literary sources and their integration with the archaeological material. It depended upon the coordination of the various branches of Sinology with each other, with different sections of Oriental research, and with the many disciplines concerned with the study of man—social history, economics, political science, and anthropology.

In a sense, the decision to broaden the scope of our task resulted from the recognition of the need of cooperative research. This technique was successfully tested in the investigations of Maya culture. Our experience proved what Dr. Merriam assumed: that it could also be "useful for other fields of historical study."[448] Although the actual methods applied differed considerably, the complexity of the problems made the approach valid in both cases.

The general plan of the Maya study "involved, first, the organization of a small, but highly competent staff representing the active body in prosecution of researches in this field"; it involved, second, the "bringing into cooperation representative investigators from various agencies for researches in which expert judgment is needed for study of problems on which the Institution staff is neither highly trained nor widely experienced."[449] This, too, is the methodological ideal of our study. Its realization may be hindered by many factors, the relative novelty of the cooperative approach to Chinese history being only one, but a most important one.

In describing the functions of our collaborators. we have the pleasant opportunity of acknowledging

comprehensive training in the history of Chinese institutions and culture. In many cases the historiographers came from families of officials and frequently they themselves acquired practical administrative experience.

[441] Bernheim 14, 200.

[442] Beard 34, 63.

[443] *Loc. cit.* For the value of revealing the type of economic structure when "accurate results are not to be expected," see Tawney 31, 52.

[444] Beard 34, 63.

[445] Meyer 24, 70.

[446] *Op. cit.*, 71.

[447] Merriam 38, 12.

[448] *Op. cit.*, 1.

[449] *Op. cit.*, 6 ff.

concretely the specific contributions made by both groups and individuals to our work. The inner circle was a small staff whose different qualifications were coordinated in the common effort. The cooperative nature of the work implied planned integration of the various scientific and technical procedures, as evidenced by the linguistic discussions, the appendices, and the longer notes to the introductions and translated texts; nevertheless the particular task of each member was clearly defined. Mr. Fêng Chia-shêng, the co-author, specialized in Liao studies when, as assistant editor of Professor Ku Chieh-kang's well-known journal, *Yü Kung*, he turned his attention to the burning problems of Chinese frontier history. His unusual knowledge of the textual material eminently fitted him for the scholarly work of selection, translation, and annotation, on which all further progress depended. He checked all material previously collected[450] and added many important data to those contained in the texts. Mr. Fêng's familiarity with the *Liao Shih* and the supplementary sources was of utmost value for the factual accuracy of our work and the understanding of institutional processes. His untiring interest in both aspects of our publication established a model of congenial collaboration. The methodological approach and the principles of the guided selection were determined by the editor-in-chief, who later analyzed, integrated, and interpreted the collected material. The process of checking and Englishing the translation, which was entrusted to Mr. John De Francis, required an understanding not only of the translated version but of the Chinese original as well. Competently performed, it paved the way for repeated critical readings of the texts by the editor, his staff, and other collaborators. Mr. De Francis's standardization of the texts, appendices, and bibliography, when the project was still in the blue-print stage, was another valuable contribution. Mr. Wang Yü-ch'üan rechecked the translations, temporarily interrupting his researches on the Ch'in and Han dynasties. In January 1942 Mrs. Lea Kisselgoff, who had studied for a number of years with two of Europe's greatest Sinologists, P. Pelliot and M. Granet, joined our staff. Her knowledge and resourcefulness were of great assistance in solving many of the Sinological problems encountered in the course of our work. She is also responsible for the analytic index that appears at the end of the present volume.

The secretarial tasks, which demanded considerable editorial and research experience, were expertly fulfilled by Miss Tania Manooiloff and Mrs. Ruth

Ricard. Mr. Paul Sherman, whose services were made available through the National Youth Administration, assisted the project in many technical ways. He charted the genealogical tables and aided Mr. Fêng in preparing the map of the Liao empire, which, like the map of Hsi Liao, was drawn by Mr. Nicholas Krijanovsky of the American Geographical Society.

The editor's wife, Esther S. Goldfrank, whose first interest in Liao culture lay in the real or seeming similarities between the subject of her recent research —the Indians of the North American Plains—and the tribal civilizations of Inner Asia, soon participated in our work for its own sake. Examining every detail of the analytic introductions, she has not only improved the style of presentation, but more important, the line and form of the argument itself. Early in 1940, when the unsatisfactory results of the original plan led to the only serious crisis suffered by the project, she more than anyone else understood the issue at stake and encouraged the editor to carry out the methodological change he knew was necessary.

At various times, the Misses Christina Lam, Hu Hsien-chin, and Grace Chinn worked on problems of research or language; Mr. John Prince, Miss Ruth Curran, and Miss Susan Goldfrank on matters of secretarial detail; and Mr. Bruno Lasker and Mrs. Gerda Stein read the manuscript and made numerous helpful editorial suggestions.

No student of China is familiar with all aspects of Chinese history and civilization, just as no student of Europe is an expert in all fields of European culture. To compensate for this scientific limitation we looked to the aid and advice of many Sinologists. Their response was most generous. Dr. H. H. Dubs, Duke University, carefully examined the manuscript, making many helpful suggestions which were incorporated in the final version of the text. Valuable criticism was also given by Drs. Hu Shih, National University of Peking, L. C. Goodrich, Columbia University, J. R. Ware, Harvard, and G. E. Taylor, University of Washington, all of whom contributed to the clarification of important aspects of our study. Special problems were discussed with other experts on the Far East, Drs. K. Biggerstaff, D. Bodde, P. Boodberg, R. S. Britton, H. G. Creel, J. K. Fairbank, Fei Hsiao-t'ung, C. S. Gardner, A. Hummel, G. Kates, E. Kracke, G. Kennedy, K. Latourette, F. Michael, C. H. Peake, N. Peffer, J. Pope, and F. Schultheiss. Dr. H. Wilhelm, Peiping, painstakingly checked the first part of the manuscript. His detailed work and critical suggestions were of great assistance particularly in the revision of the complicated section I. Dr. Hummel kindly made it possible for the editor to see the proofs of his *Eminent Chinese of the Ch'ing Period*, a monumental study which adds considerably

---

[450] A preliminary collection and translation of Liao data was undertaken in 1937 in China by Messrs. Liang Yü, Yao Tsêng-i, and Chao Shu-ch'un.

to an understanding of the last of China's great dynasties of conquest. Professor P. Pelliot's visit to the United States early in 1945 provided a unique opportunity for clarifying a number of important linguistic and historical questions. The distinguished scholar, who has made a special study of the Qarā-Khitāy dynasty in conjunction with his work on the glossary of the new Marco Polo edition, read the whole of our appendix V which deals with the history and culture of this same empire. His suggestions and corrections have, with his permission, been inserted in this publication. Due acknowledgment is made in our notes, but the editor wishes to express here his deep-felt gratitude for the constructive spirit in which the advice was given—a symbol, it is hoped, of a future *universitas literarum*.

Scholars well-versed in other branches of Oriental studies were consulted whenever questions related to their special fields arose. The staff was competent in reading Japanese texts, but in special cases generous help was given by Dr. H. Borton and Mr. R. Tsunoda of the Japanese Department of Columbia. Problems concerned with Sanskrit terms were referred to Drs. S. Elisséeff and J. R. Ware, Harvard. In the field of Altaic languages the project could appeal to Dr. K. H. Menges, Columbia, who gave unstintingly of his time and acted as a permanent collaborator on all matters relating to Central Asiatic linguistics and geography. The etymological analysis of Ch'i-tan words presented in XIV, introduction, is his work. Valuable data on specific points were contributed by Drs. Bernard Geiger, Gustave von Gruenebaum, Ilse Lichtenstaedter, and Alfred Salmony. More general problems were discussed with interested Orientalists at numerous meetings of the Oriental Club of New York.

History, as social and institutional history, could only be written with the aid of the social sciences. The editor was first a social scientist, later a Sinologist. But in spite of his own experience in various branches of social and economic studies—or perhaps because of it— he was fully aware of the need for a cooperative approach in this field as well.

The project was privileged from the start in having as its friend Dr. R. H. Tawney, of the London School of Economics, whose great experience as a social and economic historian was supplemented by his direct contact with recent developments in China. His methodological advice has proved as scientifically valuable as his personal interest was spiritually encouraging. Significant suggestions concerning historical methodology in general and social and economic history in particular were kindly given by Drs. W. L. Westermann and A. P. Evans, Columbia, and Dr. M. Rostovtzeff, Yale.

Among all the social sciences, anthropology has made the greatest contribution to our study. The editor was first attracted to this discipline because the categories of modern industrial society were obviously inadequate when applied to China, India, Babylonia, and Egypt. Anthropology, if merely considered the study of primitive man, could add little to an understanding of the complex civilization which had existed in China since the first millennium B.C. and even earlier. The Durkheimian Granet in his analysis of Chou China[451] was better equipped to trace the primitive aspects of Chinese society than its more complex developments. The same criticism holds for Granet's talented disciple, Stein, whose analysis of certain pre-dynastic Ch'i-tan traditions is excellent, whereas his understanding of the new ("third") Liao culture is limited.[452] Fortunately, however, anthropologists are becoming increasingly interested in the complex "higher" civilizations of America,[453] Africa,[454] and Asia,[455] and the recent discussions of culture change, acculturation, and diffusion are not confined to so-called primitive peoples.[456] In this area of research contemporary anthropology is evolving new concepts. Coordinated with those already established in social and culture history,[457] they constitute a rich arsenal of powerful tools which this study utilized whenever the situation demanded it.

The Department of Anthropology at Columbia University has shown an unusual interest in our work. Dr. R. Linton critically and constructively examined many problems raised by Liao culture in general and Chinese-Ch'i-tan acculturation in particular. Helpful suggestions on specific sections were made by Drs. R. Benedict, W. D. Strong, G. Herzog, and by G. P. Murdock of Yale, who was temporarily attached to the Naval School at Columbia. In addition, a number of other anthropologists in New York, Philadelphia, and New Haven discussed various aspects of our work with us.

The oldest Western friend of the project, Owen Lattimore, brought to it his unique knowledge of Chinese frontier society and history gained through many years of extensive travel and research. He personally watched and scientifically supported our effort from its inception in 1935 until 1941 when he was appointed personal advisor to Generalissimo Chiang Kai-shek. It was Owen Lattimore who drew

[451] Granet 29.
[452] Stein 39, *passim.*
[453] See the immense literature on the ancient higher civilizations of Middle and South America.
[454] *Cf.* Herskovits 40, 375 ff.
[455] *Cf.* Kroeber 23, 247 ff.; Thurnwald 32, 93 ff.; Linton 36, 246 ff.
[456] *Cf.* Herskovits 38, 122 ff.; Linton 40, 510 ff.; Redfield 41, *passim.*
[457] *Cf.* Strong 36, 367.

our attention to many frontier features in Liao society. It was he who pointed out their relation to traditional Chinese culture and to the tribal world of Inner Asia. Other Western friends who aided our work in China were Miss Ida Pruitt, then head of the Social Service Department of the Peiping Union Medical College (P. U. M. C.), and Mr. Edmund Clubb, Secretary at the American Embassy. Among our Chinese friends were Professors W. Hung, Têng Chih-ch'êng, and Ku Chieh-kang, all of the Department of Chinese History, Yenching University, Peiping.

We were fortunate in obtaining the sympathetic assistance of many scholars in many fields of science. We were fortunate also in having placed at our disposal the library and office facilities essential to productive scientific work. The numerous books required for the study were generously and efficiently provided by the East Asiatic Collections of Columbia University and by the main library. Two other great storehouses of Chinese and Japanese books, the Library of Congress and the Library of the Harvard-Yenching Institute, graciously responded to our requests through the inter-library exchange for publications not otherwise available. At all times the staffs were as cooperative as the directors were understanding: Dr. A. Hummel, Washington, and Dr. K. M. Chiu, Harvard, both took a more than technical interest in our work. We are also greatly indebted to Columbia University for the assignment of a convenient and spacious office in the building which houses its Chinese and Japanese Library.

In general academic and editorial matters the project received able counsel from a small committee consisting of Messrs. Dubs, Goodrich, Tawney, Ware, and since 1941, Linton, Taylor, and Menges. For many years the Institute of Social Research and its directors, Drs. M. Horkheimer and F. Pollock, encouraged and enabled the editor to carry on his studies of Chinese society. The Institute of Pacific Relations, in ways too numerous to mention, promoted our work from the start. We are happy in having an opportunity here to thank its interested personnel, and in particular Messrs. E. C. Carter, F. V. Field, W. Holland, W. Lockwood, G. E. Taylor, and Miss Harriet Moore of its International Secretariat and American Council. The Institute of Pacific Relations and the American Philosophical Society have made possible this publication despite the many difficulties inherent in printing such a technically complicated manuscript.

Special gratitude is due the Rockefeller Foundation. Its understanding support permitted us to engage in a study of this size and to initiate what, we hope, may be a new approach to Oriental history.

TECHNICAL INTRODUCTION

The fundamental concepts underlying our project have been outlined in the preceding General Introduction, but special problems of translation and chronology as well as the reasons for certain decisions require further discussion.

I. THE TRANSLATION

1. GENERAL PRINCIPLES

Languages may differ widely in their basic structure, but this does not preclude translation from one to another. While the specific linguistic form of a statement may not be transferable, its content can, nevertheless, be satisfactorily transmitted[1] if the receiving language possesses sufficient "copiousness and flexibility."[2] Experience has shown that Chinese and English exhibit these traits.

The first aim of a conscientious translation is faithfulness.[3] We have tried to follow the Chinese original as faithfully as the different structures and vocabularies of the two languages permit. Structural peculiarities of one language "can but rarely be reproduced in another."[4] This is obvious in translations from Greek and Latin, and still more so for translations from the monosyllabic literary Chinese whose grammar is not a matter of inflection but of word order or position.[5] The Chinese sequence of the semantic elements (words, ideas) has been our guide throughout, but when insistence upon the original order would have resulted in an awkward translation we have resorted to structural inversions, which, being "purely formal or grammatical," may be considered the prerogative of a reasonable translator who is faithful to the spirit of the text without being a slave to the letter.[6] Interpolations which for reasons of meaning or grammar were unavoidable have been bracketed [ ].

Greater difficulty is created by those many Chinese words for which, in spite of a seeming correspondence, the English language provides only partial equivalents.[7] Titles fall in this category, as do the numerous administrative, economic, or cultural terms, which are part of a different historical nexus and, therefore, have widely different factual and psychological implications. In such circumstances the translation cannot furnish a full semantic equivalent for the original meaning. But the reader who is gradually made aware of the term in its different contexts[8] may come to understand the meaning of the original. An explanatory note when the term first occurs partly anticipates, partly initiates its contextual perception.

Chinese and English being what they are, it is certain that our choice of English equivalents or partial equivalents can be improved upon. It is equally certain that at times we may have over-translated[9] or undertranslated a noun, a verb, or a particle. The many difficulties inherent in the task could not be completely overcome, but they were considerably reduced by the fact that Mr. Fêng Chia-shêng, who made the basic translations, had done extensive research in and was thoroughly familiar with the texts of the *Liao Shih* before our study began.[10] The translations have been checked time and again by our own editorial staff and by interested Sinologists.

"There is," writes Postgate, "no such thing as a 'final' translation."[11] But, whatever the limitations, attempts such as ours are technically possible and scientifically rewarding. The emerging mural of a great and distant world ought to encourage, not discourage, those painters of the future who will continue our work.

2. TITLES

In most instances English translations have been given for the many Chinese titles appearing in our texts.[12] Often a term is no more than an index of an official rank or type of duty. The context must supply what the isolated partial equivalent is incapable of doing. In our records the prime minister is a leading official of an autocratic state, not the head

---

[1] Ogden and Richards 25, 363. *Cf.* also Sapir 21, 237 ff.; Postgate 22, 11.

[2] *Op. cit.,* 51.

[3] *Op. cit.,* 3.

[4] *Op. cit.,* 33.

[5] Julien 69, viii; Gabelentz 81, 113 and 121; *cf.* also Bréal 00, 216.

[6] *Cf.* Postgate 22, 34 and 11. Postgate approvingly refers to the famous translator of Sophocles, Sir George Young, who occasionally turned "a whole clause inside out, exchanging the place of the nominative and accusative and substituting a passive for an active voice or turning adjectives into adverbs and redistributing meaning between noun and verb." Quoted by Postgate, *op. cit.,* 34, from Young's preface to his *Translation of Sophocles,* xxii.

[7] See Postgate 22, 44; *cf.* also Ogden and Richards 25, 364.

[8] *Cf. op. cit.,* 146 ff. and 155 ff.

[9] For this interesting term see Postgate 22, 36.

[10] See Fêng CS 33.

[11] Postgate 22, 57.

[12] *Cf.* Dubs, HFH I, xii.

of a modern democracy; a Ch'i-tan chief scribe fulfilled many political functions not implied in his imperial title. In our search for equivalents or partial equivalents we accepted earlier suggestions wherever feasible. We have examined and, when possible, used the translations of Chinese titles made by Chavannes, Dubs, Werner, Balázs, Des Rotours, Mayers, Morse, Brunnert, Hagelstrom, and others, giving preference, in general, to those which appear in studies dealing with our period or closest to it. In many cases these scholars have suggested different equivalents, thus indicating the terminological difficulties that the individual scholar cannot overcome.

The Chinese titles of the Southern Region of the Liao empire derive, in the main, from titles used by governments of the T'ang empire and the Five Dynasties. The Chinese titles of the Northern (Ch'i-tan) Region, though similar in form, nevertheless imply a great variety of non-Chinese functions. They are indeed part of a hybrid "third" culture.

Altaic (Ch'i-tan, Turkic, etc.) titles appearing in the *Liao Shih* have been preserved in our texts in their Chinese transliterations. They are explained in our notes and analytic introductions whenever possible. Such designations are frequent in the historical records; to "translate" them through partial equivalents would mean to create an impression of cultural homogeneity which the texts themselves do not give. Tribal terms, such as *khaghan* or *i-li-chin*, had special meaning for the Chinese, just as the words *führer* and *gauleiter* have for the non-German world today. In general only titles which are used immediately before the name of a person without the definite article are capitalized (e.g., Chancellor Yeh-lü Shih-lu). The names of offices and institutions, however, are always so treated.

3. ADMINISTRATIVE UNITS

More specific, but still none too clear, are terms designating the various territorial units of the Liao empire. Although set up to meet the administrative needs of a partially un-Chinese state, these units were given traditional Chinese names. The obvious difficulty of applying terms used in one Chinese dynasty to another is increased by this peculiar situation. Can the translation for a Han or Ch'ing district be used for the administrative divisions of Liao? The smallest unit directly controlled by the central government, the *hsien* 縣, had changed but little after the unification of China in 221 B.C. The equivalent "county" would, therefore, seem an acceptable translation for the *hsien* of the Liao government. The Liao *chou* 州 differs considerably from the large territorial units of the early dynasties, while resembling in much greater degree its namesake in the T'ang period for which Des Rotours suggests the western

equivalent "prefecture."[13] We accept this for our epoch, well aware that in other periods the word may require a different translation. The Chinese term *fu* 府 is applied to an administrative office, and, by extension, to the area which it controlled. We, therefore, refer to territories so designated as "administrations," a rendering, new in Western translations, but closest to the sense of the Chinese word. The *tao* 道 of the Five Capitals presents a more perplexing problem. The term was used in T'ang China, but under the Liao dynasty it was applied to the newly established territories of the "Five Capitals."[14] Hence we render *tao* as "circuit," a word which, to some extent, preserves its original meaning "way."

Our primary effort was directed toward making our equivalents for the Liao terms as consistent within themselves as they were within the actual Liao administration,[15] using established translations whenever this seemed justifiable, but not hesitating to substitute equations even though these might have to be modified for other periods. Historical change often occurs without a corresponding change in the original terminology. However in our translations we have tried to reflect a changing situation by more suitable equations.

II. PROPER NAMES

1. NOT TRANSLATED

A number of Chinese proper names cannot be rendered at all. But many are translatable and have been given Western equivalents. In our texts, the appellatives, "river," "mountain," "temple," "palace" are translated, but only in rare instances, the proper names preceding them. When the meaning of an untranslated name seems significant for the text, we explain it in a note. The Five Capitals are always referred to as the Supreme Capital, the Central Capital, etc., for these translated forms conveniently indicate their function and geographical position.

2. ROMANIZATION

With minor modifications,[16] the Wade-Giles system[17] has been employed in transcribing Chinese words. It has also been used to render many modern Chinese names with which the Western reader is unfamiliar; but the simplified transcriptions for certain geographical names which have frequently appeared in Western writings—many journalistic—have been retained.

---

[13] Des Rotours 27, 220.
[14] See I, introduction.
[15] For certain inconsistencies in the terminology of the Liao administration see I, introduction.
[16] For example, *yüeh* for yo, and *i* for yi.
[17] As found in Giles 12.

Rigid adherence to the Wade-Giles system would, in these instances, impede rather than aid the reader's understanding. We therefore give the names of the modern Chinese provinces and those of a few well-known rivers in the Westernized form prevailing in non-Sinological publications. Korean names are romanized according to Giles' *Dictionary;* Japanese names according to the Romaji system of Hepburn.[18] The transcription of words from other Oriental languages follows the practice current in English scientific publications in those fields.[19]

The original spelling of proper names has been retained in all quoted passages, a procedure that protects the author but occasionally creates technical inconsistencies in our presentation.

Romanized Chinese words are hyphenated whenever the complex in question seems to form a single concept in Chinese (*shu-mi-shih*, chancellor). In general the unity is obvious, but varying usage in Chinese itself at times makes decision arbitrary. Conforming to prevailing tradition, personal names are always hyphenated.

In view of the present state of Oriental studies, certain inconsistencies are inevitable. E. Meyer,[20] Rostovtzeff, and many other writers on Oriental civilizations have faced similar difficulties with common sense and reasonable compromise. In his last work Rostovtzeff writes, "In the spelling of Greek and Oriental personal names I have not been entirely consistent." After describing the general rules and the necessary exceptions, he concludes that "complete uniformity and consistency were unattainable."[21] Complete uniformity is equally unattainable in dealing with the history of Inner Asia or the Far East. Divergencies may be reduced, but they can never be wholly eliminated because the transcriptions in the available material are not standardized.

III. CHINESE DYNASTIES, EMPERORS, REIGN PERIODS

Since the establishment of a unified empire in 221 B.C., and even before that time, Chinese history has been presented as the history of its ruling dynasties. Such a division still remains most expedient for designating the country's different historic periods. The chronology in all Chinese records is calculated in terms of dynastic reigns, and our own study had no choice but to follow their example.

In Western usage the names of the Chinese dynasties are generally used in their adjectival function (Han dynasty, T'ang period). At times, but less frequently than in the Chinese texts, they appear as nouns (Han, Liao, Sung, Ch'ing).[22] We have employed both forms. Closer contact with Chinese culture and history will, we trust, do much to discourage the present preference for the less concise adjectival construction.

Changes in dynastic names within a single dynastic period raise further problems. Opinion differs regarding the initial use of the name Liao by the Ch'itan rulers. The years 936,[23] 937,[24] and 938[25] have all been recorded as the time of introduction, but the *Liao Shih* places the first appearance no earlier than 947.[26] In 983 the dynasty was again called Ch'i-tan, conforming to the designation that had been official during the early days of the empire.[27] Only in 1066 did the name Liao come into its own again.[28] From that time on until the fall of the empire it continued to be employed. The authors of the *Liao Shih* do not emphasize these changes, perhaps because they considered them an unnecessary complication. Following their example we have designated the whole period from the establishment of the hereditary monarchy in 907 to its collapse in 1125, Liao. Frequent changes in name would, we believe, do more to confuse than inform.

Besides a surname (*hsing* 姓), a given name (*hui* 諱), and possibly a "style" (*tzŭ* 字), a childhood name (*hsiao tzŭ* 小字), or a fancy name (*hao* 號), Chinese emperors received an official office name or title, namely *huang-ti* 皇帝, an honorific title (*tsun hao* 尊號), a posthumous designation (*shih hao* 諡號), and a temple title (*miao hao* 廟號) also bestowed after death.[29] Except for the founder of the Liao dynasty, whose tribal name, A-pao-chi, is used interchangeably with his temple title, T'ai-tsu, particularly for the earlier part of his career, the *Liao Shih*, like other Chinese histories, calls the various Liao emperors by their temple titles: T'ai-tsung, Tao-tsung, etc. We have followed this precedent. Technically,

---

[18] As found, for example in Kenkyūsha's *New Japanese-English Dictionary*, Tokyo, 1931.

[19] For the aid rendered in this regard by Dr. K. H. Menges see General Introduction.

[20] Meyer 26, xii ff.

[21] Rostovtzeff 41 I, xii.

[22] *Cf.* Legge, CC III, Prolegomena 13 ff.; Duyvendak 28, 2 ff.; Gardner 40, 349; Chavannes, MH I, x ff.; Pelliot 29, 115 ff.; Franke, GCR I, 78 ff.

[23] WTS 72, 13*a*; WHTK 345, 2703.

[24] TCTC 281, 7*a*.

[25] TTSL 123, 2*a*.

[26] LS 4, 15*b*; CWTS 137, 10*b*; WTHY 29, 8*a*; TCTC 286, 5*a*; CTKC 3, 7*a*.

[27] In 916, T'ai-tsu called his new empire Ch'i-tan (CTKC 1, 1*b*).

[28] *Cf.* NESKI 83, 3*b*; for a discussion of the whole problem see Fêng CS 34*a*, 22.

[29] For a comprehensive description and discussion of the various names of a Chinese emperor see Dubs 45.

the procedure is as inaccurate as the frequent application of the words "England," "China," "America," and "Australia" to the early history of these countries and continents; but it is equally expedient. After noting the complex nomenclature, we have employed the traditional Chinese simplifications throughout our publication.[30] In Chinese texts the temple title of an emperor is often preceded by the name of his dynasty (T'ang Kao-tsu, Liao Shih-tsung), but the title "emperor" is usually omitted in these instances.[31] Since such formulas as Tudor Henry VII or Bourbon Louis XIV are not used in English, we have avoided this Chinese construction in our interpretative chapters. We have also eliminated the unusual formula from our translations except in those cases where the necessary interpolations became so unwieldy that it seemed wiser to retain the original. Greater familiarity with Chinese writing may ultimately encourage the West to accept the Chinese pattern, as it has other foreign-learned forms of speech.[32]

From the days of Emperor Wu of the Han dynasty, the imperial reigns have been divided into *nien-hao* 年號, a term which we translate "reign periods," or, if considered designations, "reign titles."[33] These titles were considerably reduced in number during the Ming, and still more during the Ch'ing dynasty. Then most reigns had but a single *nien-hao* which thus became a title. During the T'ang, Liao, and Sung dynasties reign titles were frequently changed. No student of Chinese imperial society in general or of these periods in particular can hope to understand the Chinese chronology without understanding the function of the reign titles.

IV. CHRONOLOGY

The texts of the *Liao Shih*, like those of other Chinese records, are abundantly dated. Whenever the year is explicitly mentioned or has been ascertained through research, we have noted its Western equivalent in the margin of our translations. When a longer period is indicated, such as a reign period or an entire reign, Western equivalents are also given.

In the Chinese system a year is defined according to its position in a reign or year period. There are twelve regular months and occasional intercalary months.[34] The exact day is determined by the use of the sexagenary cycle whose sixty combinations are fixed by an interlocking series of ten and another of twelve characters, the so-called *chia-tzŭ*.[35] In our translations we have preserved the original Chinese formulas but, following Western tradition, we have altered the sequence, placing the day and month before the year.

Any non-Sinologist who is familiar with the Chinese cycle can easily calculate the western equivalents of all Chinese dates by using the handy tables prepared by P. Hoang. For the convenience of the reader, however, we have determined the Western year equivalents for all Chinese dates appearing in our texts and for many events that are undated in the selected passages. These dates are recorded in the margin on a line with their occurrence in the text. Within each section (III, IX, etc.) or subsection (VII, 1; X, 2; XIV, 3) the dated texts are given in their chronological order, the first date determining the position of the whole passage. With few exceptions the undated passages follow those that are dated.

The first month of the Liao year, following the Chinese system, begins near the winter's end, and therefore the end of the Liao year overlaps the beginning of the next Western year. For these reasons, the equivalence that can be established between the two calendars for the early months of the year does not hold for the later ones, and certain days in the eleventh and twelfth Liao months[36] have to be assigned to the Western year following.[37] When the Chinese text mentions no day, but only an "overlapping" month, we have placed the entire month in the Western year in which more than half of its days fell. A complete chronological list of the reigns and reign periods of all Liao emperors and of their Western year equivalents is given in the table included in appendix I. The "overlapping" months and days attached to each year are calculated according to P. Hoang's tables.[38]

---

[30] The temple titles of the first emperors indicate their position in the dynastic line. But since they are given names we do not consider it necessary to introduce them with a definite article. For contrary treatment, *cf.* Dubs 45. More information about the designations of the Liao emperors is given in appendix II.

[31] For occasional exceptions see CTKC 1, 1*a*; LS 10, 2*b*; and *cf.* also Dubs (*loc. cit*), who drew our attention to this phenomenon.

[32] *Cf.* Bloomfield 41, 153 ff.

[33] Dubs 45; *cf.* also Gardner 38, 72 ff.

[34] The intercalary month might be inserted at whatever point the astronomers considered convenient. The oracle inscriptions of the Shang dynasty (tr. date 1766–1122 B.C.) reveal that the roots of this procedure go back into the second millennium B.C. *Cf.* Wittfogel 40, 115.

[35] The cycle begins with the combination of the two first characters of both sets, that is, if the first series is symbolized by Roman and the other by Arabic figures, it will be: I, 1 (number one), II, 2 (two) . . . X, 10 (ten). Then the first set begins anew: I, 11 (eleven), II, 12 (twelve); now the second set begins anew: III, 1 (thirteen) . . . up to X, 12 (sixty). *Cf.* Gardner 38, 73.

[36] Hoang 10, 433 ff.

[37] *Cf.* XII (62).

[38] Hoang 10, *passim; cf.* also ESSSJP.

In general, the Western equivalents have only been given for the years. More detailed information can usually be found in the texts. When an exact dating seems desirable as in records dealing with agriculture and labor service, the complete equivalents are inserted in the interpretative analyses.[39]

V. INNER AND CENTRAL ASIA—NAMES OF ASIATIC PEOPLES

The history of the Liao empire touches many areas within the vast Asiatic arena. Its tribal peoples wandered over all of what is now Manchuria and Mongolia; the records mention, besides China Proper, Persia, Tibet, and various parts of Turkestan. The broader term "Inner Asia" has seemed most appropriate in designating the extended inland reaches of the continent;[40] but the heart of "Inner Asia," modern Turkestan and the regions adjacent to it, will still be referred to as "Central Asia."

Names of Asiatic peoples and tribes for the most part unfamiliar to the Western reader are transcribed as uninflected nouns or adjectives (the Ch'i-tan, Nü-chih or Jurchen, Po-hai).[41] In those few instances in which Western forms of Inner Asiatic names are common they are treated like Western proper names with the plural ending in s (Huns, Turks, Mongols, Manchus).[42]

VI. MEASUREMENTS, ABBREVIATIONS

The measurements given in the *Liao Shih* are Chinese. Those occurring in our translated texts are listed in appendix III. Since neither the weights nor lengths, etc. are specified in any known records, we have substituted accepted Western equivalents of

---

[39] See II and XI, introductions.
[40] In this broader sense, the term "Inner Asia" has been adroitly used by Lattimore (40, xvii and *passim*).
[41] *Cf.* the Hopi, Zuni, Dakota.
[42] *Cf.* the Aztecs, Toltecs.

T'ang measurements. Standardized measurements are a basic prerequisite in an orderly sedentary and urban life such as A-pao-chi's Chinese subjects enjoyed. It has, therefore, seemed legitimate to assume that these measurements became part of Liao culture along with the many other elements taken over from the preceding T'ang dynasty.

A number of abbreviations used in the notes follow patterns found in Western presentations of things Chinese. The letter *T.* after the name of a person designated his "style" (*tzŭ* 字). If the exact duration of an individual's life is known, the years of his birth and death are given. Sometimes we have to content ourselves only with the latter. If our knowledge is confined to duration of office or other special events in a man's life, the symbol fl. (flourished) precedes the date.

VII. LITERARY REFERENCES

The passages of the *Liao Shih* translated in this publication are numbered consecutively under each section or sub-section. Reference to such passages is made by noting the section (and sub-section whenever the section has been divided) and in parenthesis the passage number. For instance, XIV, 4 (3) refers to the third passage appearing in sub-section 4 of section XIV. In the case of several long passages, some which appear under a series of dates are cited by number and date; others which cover a number of different *Liao Shih* references are cited by number with the chapter (*chüan*) and page numbers of the original. The tables in section I, 2 have also been numbered, but in the individual tables the other tables are cited under their title, e.g., I, 2, Various Tribes, no. 5.

The full titles of all books and articles quoted in our publication are listed in a bibliography at the end of this volume, but for textual reference abbreviations are preferred. How these have been established is explained in a note preceding the general bibliography.

SECTION I

ADMINISTRATIVE GEOGRAPHY AND POPULATION

INTRODUCTION

1. GEOGRAPHY AND HISTORY

Economic and political institutions, like all others, develop on definite geographical foundations. They function within a specific territorial framework, however temporary its boundaries may be. They grow and change within a physical environment whose influence is determined by the society's historical level, structure, and trends.

Geographical data are essential more to the analysis than to the presentation of institutional history: it is not always necessary to refer to the root in order to identify the flower. But this is true only when the setting is familiar and it can be assumed that the reader is aware of the geographical background; when the main features are known, description can be brief. For example, in presenting the history of a typically Chinese dynasty, confined, in the main, to the relatively familiar environment of China Proper, geographical data may well be limited to a brief sketch of this environment and a survey of the basic territorial divisions of the period. But when considering a border-region dynasty such as Liao, where the natural conditions differ profoundly from those of the typically Chinese dynasties, and where economic and political institutions arise from a dual ecology, more attention must be given to geography than would otherwise be necessary.

2. THE GEOGRAPHICAL DATA OF THE *LIAO SHIH* REARRANGED

The *History of the Liao Dynasty* devotes five chapters (*chüan* 37–41) to geographical information. These chapters, following the principles of traditional Chinese historiography, deal with the sedentary rather than with the tribal sector of the Liao empire although the latter is particularly significant in this dual border society. Any adequate picture of the political geography of the Liao dynasty must consider not only the sedentary but also the tribal world of the country. It should even include the semi-independent and fully independent tribes and states along and beyond the borders of the empire, for these too were important factors in shaping the structure of Liao society.

The present section, therefore, includes not only the relevant data in the geographical chapters but also descriptive material and lists of tribes and "states" hidden in other parts of the *Liao Shih*. A survey of the Ch'i-tan tribes, which is the only one of its kind in the twenty-four dynastic histories, is given in LS 33, 1*b*–9*b*. In addition, the *Liao Shih* contains lists of other tribes which were under the control of, or at least in contact with, the Liao empire.[1] It also enumerates the so-called "subordinate states"[2] which often were neither subordinate to Liao nor real states. Nevertheless, their mere listing is of inestimable value for an understanding of the political geography of eastern and central Asia during the tenth and eleventh centuries. The names of most of the tribes and states mentioned in the Imperial Annals (*pên chi* 本紀), in the Biographies (*chuan* 傳), and in the Chronological Tables (*piao* 表) of LS 69 and 70 appear in these various records.

3. SOME DATA ON THE PHYSICAL AND ECONOMIC GEOGRAPHY OF THE LIAO EMPIRE

At the time of its greatest territorial expansion the Liao empire covered the major part of modern Manchuria, of Inner and Outer Mongolia, and of the northeastern corner of China Proper. It included the boundless steppes and deserts of Inner Asia, a zone of fertile agricultural land in northern China and along the Liao River, the forest regions of eastern and northern Manchuria, and the high wooded grazing grounds of what is now Jehol. In the northern part of Jehol are found the center of political and economic power. Here was the home of the more important Ch'i-tan tribes, the seat of the empire's Supreme Capital and the birthplace of its military centers, the ordos.

The question naturally arises as to whether there were special factors in the natural and economic geography of northern Jehol which under specific political conditions, such as the disintegration of the Chinese empire and (or) the disunity of steppe tribes, favored the growth and concentration, in this particular area, of economic and political power. An examination of the different forms of tribal economy, of the contrast between the stockbreeding tribes of Jehol and their poorer nomadic neighbors to the west seems to indi-

---

[1] LS 33, 9*b*–10*a* and 46, 29*a*–32*b*.
[2] LS 46, 24*b*–29*a*.

cate that the physical and economic geography of northern Jehol explains, in large measure, the growth as well as the limitations of the Liao empire.

When the Ch'i-tan rose to power, the Turkic tribes were retreating from the eastern steppe regions although they still occupied territory along the western borders. Between them and the Tungus lived the expanding tribes of the Ch'i-tan, the Hsi, and the Shih-wei. The Shih-wei were in all probability the ancestors of the Mongols, whose name was at a later date used indiscriminately to designate the descendants of this whole tribal complex.

The fact that the Tungus, the Mongols, and the Turks were members of the same linguistic stock, the Altaic,[3] is important for the earlier history of these peoples. But, whatever their former cultural relations may have been, at the end of the tenth century A.D. the three groups differed significantly in their subsistence economy as well as in their folkways.

The tribal[4] Tungus, whose dialects were closely related, maintained in large part similar economies, but no such correlation can be established for the Turks and the Mongols. The Tungus of eastern Manchuria, living in a well-watered, well-forested region, at an early time combined their hunting with primitive agriculture and its frequent concomitant, the raising of pigs.[5] The old Chinese term Tung-hu 東胡 (eastern barbarians) was formerly believed to be the origin of the name Tungus. But the word Tung-hu was used in a much broader sense by the Chinese to designate barbarian peoples east of the Huns. It is similar to the Turkic word *toŋuz* (pig), which is given in the earliest Turkic dictionary.[6] Torii, however, holds that the terms Tung-hu and Tungus have nothing in common but a fortuitous similarity in sound, and that the latter may have been chosen by the Turkic people to designate their eastern cousins as pig-breeders.[7] The Tungus were indeed great pig-breeders and equally great pig-eaters. Their tribal descendants, the northern Manchus, have pork as "the principal meat food"; they eat it in all religious ceremonies and consider it "the best food for the spirits."[8] In addition to pigs, the Tungus tribes bred horses and where possible oxen, but they had few sheep and no camels.[9]

The tribes on the steppes of Central Asia had almost no agriculture, and therefore no pigs. Instead they raised sheep, horses, and camels in abundance; in certain regions the camel is still found in a wild state.[10] Oxen, although valued as draft animals, prospered only in limited areas, "on meadow and alpine pasture";[11] in the semi-arid regions they are few in number and poor in quality.[12] It is significant that on the steppe the sheep and horse were considered sacred. This is true even today;[13] in an old[14] and solemn ceremony which is still performed in memory of Chingis Khan, the Mongols offer sheep and a horse in sacrifice,[15] while the ritual cart is drawn by two sacred camels.[16]

The Ch'i-tan lived between the camel-breeders of the steppe and the pig-eaters of the east. They used the camel only in some minor ceremonies which probably were of late origin.[17] A legendary ancestor is said to have worn a pigskin,[18] but pork, which was not eaten in everyday life,[19] played no role in the recorded Ch'i-tan sacrifices. In their most sacred rites, they offered a horse and an ox.[20] These different religious traditions aptly reflect the different forms of tribal economy.

The breeding of horses and oxen was well adapted to the terrain of northern Jehol. The pastures of the upper Western Liao River, the hinterland of the modern Shira Muren, were the grazing grounds of the earliest ancestors of the Ch'i-tan and the scene of A-pao-chi's rise to supreme power. Here is the sacred Mu-yeh Mountain on whose slope, according to the tribal legend, the first ancestor, mounted on a white horse, met the first ancestress, who was driving an ox-cart.[21] Here, in the Lung-hua Prefecture of Liao, were located early tribal pastures.[22] Temporary

---

[3] Pelliot 31, 11 ff.; Shirokogoroff 33, 2; Gibert 34, 894 ff.

[4] This qualification is used to exclude people of supposedly Tungus stock, such as the Po-hai, who had developed beyond a primitive tribal culture.

[5] SCPMHP 20, 9*b*.

[6] Brockelmann 28, 213.

[7] Torii 14, 19.

[8] Shirokogoroff 24, 131.

[9] SCPMHP 20, 9*b*; *cf.* also North Manchuria 24, 23; Leonard 94, 208; and Lattimore 40, 73. The Manchu

rulers of the Ch'ing dynasty continued to use pork as the preferred sacrificial meat. See de Harlez 87, 72 *passim*.

[10] *Cf.* Timkowski 1827 II, 285; Howorth, HM IV, 20 ff.; see also Lattimore 29, 217.

[11] Lattimore 40, 74; *cf.* also Timkowski 1827 II, 289.

[12] Howorth, HM IV, 66.

[13] Prejevalsky 76 I, 54.

[14] Lattimore 41, 49.

[15] *Op. cit.*, 35 and 41.

[16] *Op. cit.*, 49.

[17] See IV, introduction, and IV (14).

[18] CTKC, introduction. The story perhaps reflects a certain (early ?) Tungus influence, which is also suggested by the presence of a number of Tungus words in the Ch'i-tan vocabulary. See below, XIV, introduction.

[19] The Sung envoys to Liao embarrassed the Ch'i-tan officials by their requests for pork, which was provided north of the semi-agricultural Hsi country only with considerable difficulty. See VII, 2, note 40.

[20] See below, VII, 2, *passim*.

[21] VII, 2 (84).

[22] See I, 1 (2).

migrations to the northwest (as far as Ching-pien City[23]), to the central plain of Manchuria (T'ai Prefecture[24]), and to the east (Korea[25]) did not make them forget their old pastures. They drifted back to the Shira Muren, where the Ancestral Mountain (Tsu-shan 祖山) and an Ancestral Prefecture[26] recalled to the Ch'i-tan emperors the glory of their predynastic forefathers.

During the Liao period the climate of the highland territory around the upper course of the Shira Muren was apparently similar to that of today. The temperature is relatively low in the mountains of Jehol, and the winter very cold.[27] Only 106 days are frost-less as compared with 145 in the Manchurian plain.[28] No warmer weather prevailed in the time of the Liao empire. It is reported that in the mountainous region two hundred *li* northwest of the Supreme Capital the ice one foot below the surface never thawed.[29] Fur coats were an important article of Ch'i-tan dress.[30]

Today the rainfall in spring is scanty, but in summer it is plentiful.[31] An annual rainfall of ten to fifteen inches[32] in a moderate climate creates a situation highly favorable for herding and moderately favorable for agriculture.[33] This seems to have been as true in the tenth and eleventh centuries as it is in the twentieth. Drought was fought by rain magic,[34] for manifestly it was a serious problem. But the rains were sufficient to send water coursing down the slopes of the Khinghan Mountains, either to become tributaries of the Western Liao River or feeders of lakes. The *Liao Shih*, describing Shang-ching Circuit, mentions fifteen rivers, four lakes, and two salt ponds.[35]

The sandy or marshy stretches[36] limited the development of certain economic pursuits. But the fertile valleys and plateaus offered rich pastures for the herds[37] and even good soil for agriculture.[38] The

mountains and the forests of pine,[39] willow, and elm[40] in the highland and in the lowland supported many kinds of game such as bears, tigers, deer, hares, and eagles.[41] The somewhat greater rainfall[42] in the region south of the Shira Muren river system had made it advantageous for the Hsi 奚 people to carry on a limited agriculture before the Ch'i-tan rulers settled their prisoners of war in the northern regions and forced them to plant crops on a much larger scale.[43]

These factors give special significance to the geographical position of the Ch'i-tan. Their ancestral territory was marginal to the vast pasture lands of what we now call Mongolia Proper, with a rainfall of ten inches or less per annum. It was marginal also to the cultivable plains of the lower Liao River and their eastern extensions, where an annual rainfall of twenty inches or more could be expected. Under the existing cultural conditions, pastoralism was throughout these regions the most advantageous economy. But Ch'i-tan pastoralism, which was concerned with the horse, the ox, and the sheep, differed not only from the pig-breeding of the eastern Tungus; it differed also from the pastoralism of the Central Asiatic tribes with its strong emphasis on camel-breeding and its lesser emphasis on the breeding of long-horned cattle.

During the Manchu dynasty Jehol was treated as part of Mongolia. This can be justified ethnologically; but it must be kept in mind that the territory of Jehol covers only the eastern, not the western, slopes of the Khinghan Mountains and that its main water-course, the Shira Muren, is part of a river system which drains the central and south Manchurian plain. Located within the outer edge of the western curve of the great Manchurian amphitheater, the Ch'i-tan tribes were in an excellent position to subdue the numerous peoples of Manchuria at a time when no outside force (China or the Turkic peoples of Inner Asia) was able to intervene.

Were the Ch'i-tan warriors as effective on the steppes of the west as they were in the river-valleys of the east? Did the stockbreeders of the Shira Muren (then called the Huang 潢 River) adapt themselves as successfully to the mentality of the western sheep- and camel-breeders as they did to the ways of their semi-nomadic southern neighbors, the Hsi? Once Chingis Khan had overcome his tribal enemies of the steppe, he was able to consolidate and mobilize to the full their aggressive strength because of a common and congenial background. On the other hand, the emperors of the Ch'i-tan, relying upon a

[23] I, 1 (5).

[24] I, 1 (2).

[25] XIV, 1 (1), LS 63, 3*a*.

[26] Tsu Prefecture (I, 1 (2); see Mullie 22, 135 ff.).

[27] Franke 02, 7 and 18.

[28] North Manchuria 24, 3.

[29] LS 37, 5*b*. This report is identical with modern observations. See Franke 02, 7.

[30] See VII, 1 (48). *Cf.* also the important role played by furs of all kinds in the tributes paid to the Liao court (X, 2, *passim*).

[31] North Manchuria 24, 3.

[32] Manchuria 32/33, 10 and map.

[33] Franke 02, 7.

[34] VII, 2 (26).

[35] LS 37, 2*b*.

[36] *Cf.* Mullie 22, 211.

[37] I, 1 (2).

[38] I, 1, *passim*.

[39] LS 37, 1*b* and 9*a*.

[40] *Loc. cit.*

[41] *Cf.* II, 1, *passim*.

[42] Manchuria 32/33, map following page 10.

[43] WHTK 346, 2710. *Cf.* Chavannes 97 VC, 438.

Manchurian pastoralism and used to dealing with sedentary peoples, had to control the alien Central Asiatic nomads by institutionalized terror (fortified border cities).

No doubt the extent of China's disintegration was very important for the success of the Mongol invasion. It may well have been the decisive factor. But the development of an inner crisis is also affected by external conditions, and among these the relative strength of the aggressor is particularly significant. The numerous and well-coordinated Mongols spread themselves far more effectively over the decaying empires of Chin and Sung than did the Ch'i-tan over the collapsing T'ang state and the dynasties immediately succeeding it.

A more complete disintegration of China, providing a greater opportunity for easy plunder, might have brought about a coalition of elements far more antagonistic to each other than these. It would in all probability have effected a union of the dissimilar eastern and western nomads for joint attack and for joint looting, just as the expectation of the conquest of Turkestan—which actually occurred—induced a number of western tribes to follow Yeh-lü Ta-shih in 1124. But, conditions being what they were, the economic and religious divergencies between the rich stockbreeders of the east and the poorer—and purer—nomads[44] of the steppe were strong enough to keep these tribes apart. The economic geography of Jehol was obviously a decisive factor not only in promoting but also in limiting the growth of the Liao empire.

4. THE ADMINISTRATIVE DIVISIONS

a. THE ORDER OF PRESENTATION

The *Liao Shih* describes the administrative divisions of the sedentary population of Liao in considerable detail. Clustering about the five capitals, these divisions constitute a convenient starting-point for any comprehensive outline of the empire's political geography. Our geographical section therefore offers first a survey of the five circuits with a list of the entrusted commandery-prefectures and the walled border cities attached to the Supreme Capital. A catalogue of the inner and outer tribes and of the subordinate states follows. The individual administrative units are accompanied by population figures wherever the *Liao Shih* records them. General data concerning the population of Liao are grouped together at the end of this section; they refer mainly to measures for preparing the numerical basis for taxation, forced labor, and military service: the census.

b. THE FIVE CIRCUITS

The authors of the *Liao Shih* preface their description of the five circuits with a general introduction (LS 37, 2a) which is given first in the translated texts of this section. This passage, little more than a bare statement of the empire's territorial growth, fails to mention what tribes were incorporated, but it does give a fairly detailed picture of the diverse sedentary groups that had been added to the population. Its laconic sentences gain more color and meaning when the events to which they refer appear in fuller context in the sections that follow.

Of particular interest is the report concerning the establishment of five "capitals." This unusual system of five administrative centers, well suited to a semi-nomadic government, did not originate with the Ch'i-tan empire builders. They took it over from the semi-agricultural eastern kingdom of Po-hai,[45] though only as a general principle, for they did not establish the seat of their eastern government in any of the conquered Po-hai capitals.[46]

The reader will do well to keep in mind the location of the five capitals of Liao whose names are bound to recur frequently. The Supreme Capital (Shang-ching 上京) was established within the old Ch'i-tan grazing grounds of northwestern Jehol, between the upper course of the Huang River (the present Shira Muren) and the Khinghan Mountains. The ruins found at the site of the Mongol city of Boro Khoton correspond closely to the historical record in general arrangement and conspicuous details: two "cities" with walls of different heights, the same number of gates similarly located, etc.[47] It therefore seems more reasonable to consider this the original site than to follow earlier identifications which locate the city farther to the northwest.

The Eastern Capital (Tung-ching 東京) in the southern part of the great Manchurian plain is now the site of modern Liao-yang. The Central Capital (Chung-ching 中京) was established at a relatively late date.[48] It was located in the mountainous regions of southern Jehol, near the Shira Muren's southern tributary which was then called the T'u River 土河 and which is now called the Lao-ha River 老哈河.[49] The two southern "capitals" were the centers of historically well-known Chinese territories. They are therefore easily defined. The Southern Capital (Nan-ching 南京, also called Yen-ching 燕京) was practically identical with the later Peking or Peiping where a famous modern university adopted

---

[44] Lattimore 38, 15.

[45] *Cf.* I, 1, note 3 and also LS 38, 1*b*.
[46] *Cf.* Gibert 34, 759 ff.
[47] Mullie 22, 156–162.
[48] *Cf.* XI (15).
[49] Mullie 22, 110; *idem* 33a, 219.   *Cf.* also MRC II, 54.

the old name, Yen-ching. The Western Capital (Hsi-ching 西京) was situated in the northern part of modern Shansi, in the region of Ta-t'ung which was known by that name at the time of the Liao empire. Each of the five capitals controlled a territory or circuit (tao 道) of the same name. In order to distinguish the capital cities from their circuits—which the Chinese text often fails to do—the English equivalent is given for the capital while the romanized Chinese form is retained for the circuit. Thus 上京 is rendered according to the context either as Supreme Capital (meaning the city itself) or as Shang-ching (meaning its circuit).

The five circuits were subdivided into administrations (fu 府), prefectures (chou 州), and counties (hsien 縣). These units are supplemented by commanderies (chün 軍), fortified cities (ch'êng 城), or fortresses (pao 堡). Without entering into the details of the administrative organization, the relation existing between the various territorial districts must be briefly explained, for only thus can the following tables be used advantageously.

The term "administration" (fu) designated the metropolitan areas surrounding the five capitals, as well as the prefecture-like district of Chung-ching and the five prefectures that had been consolidated during Hsing-tsung's reign (Hsing-chung 興中 Administration, LS 39, 5b). It is not clear why this last complex was so distinguished, for others seem to have had equal importance. Six outlying regions of Tung-ching were also called administrations, as they had been under the Po-hai Kingdom.[50]

The five circuits were divided into prefectures of varying rank, and these were again divided into counties. However, there were times when prefectures of low rank were classed with counties, but these prefectures might still control other counties. The seemingly confused arrangement was due in part to historical causes. Shang-ching Circuit with its insignificant administrative past was organized in the expected way, but many of the administrative districts of Tung-ching, which were forcibly abolished and then reconstructed, were set up in a less regular manner. In part, however, the confusion resulted from administrative expediency. The larger counties which were subdivided seem to have been classed as prefectures of inferior rank, thus indicating their complex status.

The commanderies were territorial units similar to the prefectures in size but, as will be shown, differing from them in political and military position. A city was frequently a fortified center, and this was particularly so in the border region. The term fortress is self-explanatory. The system in its entirety is well outlined in LS 48, 9b, which states, "Territories which

could not be classified as chou were called chün; those which could not be classified as hsien were called ch'êng; and those which could not be classified as ch'êng were called pao."

The entrusted commandery-prefectures (t'ou-hsia chün chou 投下軍州) are listed in LS 37, after the regular prefectures and counties of Shang-ching. These territories were fief-like in character, but their lords were limited in independent action as well as in number. All had to pay a wine tax to the Supreme Capital, and most of the larger ones had to accept as their head officer a commanding prefect appointed by the central government. LS 48, 9b states that the entrusted territories reverted to the wang fu (歸王府). Fu is "administration," but wang may mean either "kingly" and "governmental" or "princely." The territories were to a large extent held by persons of princely status, mostly by imperial princesses and their Hsiao husbands. Did the fiefs become more princely and more independent in the course of time? Probably not. Many individual examples indicate a development toward a progressive absorption of entrusted districts by the central government.[51]

Both the topography and the size of the fiefs of Liao are of interest. Some smaller ones were located in the old grazing lands of the Ch'i-tan tribes, but the larger entrusted territories were all established within the southeastern periphery of the tribal centers, in the lowlands of modern Liaoning. They formed a girdle of defence against the unruly Eastern Capital, the former kingdom of Po-hai. Hui Prefecture, the largest territory, was considerably smaller than any of the big government centers, but even so small a district was controlled by an official of the Supreme Capital. Significantly, most of the fief-holders were members of the trustworthy consort family, Hsiao.

The fortified border cities are also listed as part of Shang-ching Circuit. As centers of the border garrisons they certainly were under the direct control of the central government in the Supreme Capital. If Mikami's identification is correct, then at least one of these border fortresses was located northeast of the Supreme Capital rather than northwest where our introductory text[52] places the whole complex. The others, however, seem to have been established along the northwestern (and northern) border of the empire. The exact location of some of these garrison centers is disputed, but archaeological evidence and historical tradition[53] point to the existence of several Ch'i-tan cities in the basins of the Orkhon and the Kerulen

---

[50] LS 38, 14b–15a.

[51] Cf. the data given in I, 1, note 29. See also several similar instances recorded in our lists of the five circuits.
[52] I, 1(5).
[53] See the references given in I, 1 (5) and XV, 1. Cf. also Bretschneider 88 I, 53 ff., text and note 127.

Rivers. This is confirmed in the descriptive data of LS 37, 4a–b which in essence is presented in our table of the fortified border cities.

The fact that the Liao government had to resort to fortified military settlements is politically significant. Evidently the Ch'i-tan did not assimilate the north-western tribes; instead they held them in subjection by armed force, proving that the sending of horsemen to the banks of the Orkhon by the Ch'i-tan rulers was not confined to one single reign as Pelliot assumes.[54] In and around the fortified seat of Chên Prefecture on the Orkhon River the Ch'i-tan held seven hundred civilian families and a garrison of more than twenty thousand horsemen.[55] Manifestly the Ch'i-tan were more than casual visitors to this part of Central Asia. The walled settlements which they built in the basins of the Orkhon and Kerulen Rivers indicate that the northwestern boundaries of Liao lay along this border during many decades of their dynastic rule.[56]

The lists given in section I, 1 present the administrative districts of Liao as a whole, because only thus can the structure of this curious border society be concretely demonstrated. Many geographical details will interest only the specialist, yet the cultural historian and the social scientist will find it convenient to consult these lists whenever he wishes to place a historical event in its geographical setting. The tables include statistical and ethnical data on the sedentary population of the circuits, notes on the ordos to which certain districts were attached, and various ecological and economic facts which sometimes supplement and sometimes correct corresponding data given in subsequent sections.

The two most important national groups recorded by the texts are the Chinese and the Po-hai. They were settled in many districts of the old tribal centers of Liao, in Shang-ching and Chung-ching Circuits. The survey of the southern circuits, Nan-ching and Hsi-ching, reveals only occasionally the regions from which the Chinese settlers had come. More detailed information may be found in the Imperial Annals (*pên chi*) and in LS 37 and 39 where the settlement of Chinese colonists is reported as an accomplished fact.

Severe as was the mass deportation of Chinese families, it could not compare with the ruthless treatment accorded the Po-hai whose fierce and sanguinary resistance to the Ch'i-tan conquest[57] was finally broken by counter-measures of extreme harshness. In spite of the enforced transfer, the old Chinese territories of Nan-ching and Hsi-ching Circuits were

never completely depopulated; figures in LS 40 and 41 show that a large and flourishing population still remained. Compared with this, the list of Tung-ching gives a devastating picture. Some sections of the former eastern kingdom weathered the storm without heavy losses but, if the texts can be trusted, many prefectures and counties were seriously depleted at least temporarily. Sometimes only a few hundred families are recorded for the home district while thousands of deported Po-hai families appeared in Shang-ching and Chung-ching Circuits where as farmers, miners, and artisans they served their Ch'i-tan masters.

The data concerning the transplanted groups of settlers are more or less self-explanatory. Some allusions are made to the various ordos which controlled individual districts. The texts show that the ordos were essentially military in character and played a very important role in the military life of the Liao dynasty. Although their garrisons protected the tomb of their overlord after his death, they continued to be part of the shock troops of the nation. The geographical data do not completely clarify the organizational structure of the ordos. Yet they shed considerable light on the relation between an individual ordo and the sedentary and tribal units attached to it and thus furnish significant material for the more detailed analysis of the ordo which appears in section XV.

5. THE TRIBES

The tribal nucleus of the Liao empire, even in its later years, was formed by the eighteen tribes of T'ai-tsu and the thirty-four tribes of Shêng-tsung described in LS 33. The position assigned to these inner tribes in the records hints at their special importance as the source of military strength. From them the most reliable guards and troops were recruited. They raised horses and mobilized special armies for the campaigns of Liao. But these military functions no more converted them into mere military units than did the elaboration of their bureaucratic leadership transform them into mere administrative organizations.

They were and they remained tribes, that is aggregates of a number of local groups, held together by the need for joint military action,[58] by the authority of a head chief,[59] and, after some time, by the adoption of a common myth and a common tribal an-

[54] Pelliot 31, 21.

[55] I, 1 (5).

[56] Cf. I, 1, note 21.

[57] Cf. XIII, passim.

[58] Cf. XIV, 1 (1). Modern anthropology has disclosed the relatively loose social organization of tribes (Boas 40, 359). Cf. also Thurnwald 35, 22, 252, 250; and Linton 36, 231. For the function of the tribe among Asiatic nomads see especially Peisker 24, 334.

[59] Cf. I, 2, passim; see also XIV, 1.

cestor.[60] With the establishment of the empire the chieftains of the individual Ch'i-tan tribes assumed added fiscal, administrative, and military duties, which made their "government" slightly top-heavy. In spite of this, Ch'i-tan tribes continued to exist as cultural, economic, and military units;[61] they were the pastoral and tribal components of the new imperial order.

a. TRIBES AND LINEAGES

The introductory passage of LS 32, 4a, attempts to explain some of the terms basic to the tribal world of Liao. Statements are made with great decision and seeming precision. But their very definiteness limits their scientific value. The real situation was far too complex to be covered by a permutation of the terms *tsu* 族 (kin) and *pu* 部 (tribe). *Tsu* and *pu* are Chinese terms that are nothing more than approximate equivalents for specific and sometimes unfamiliar aspects of Ch'i-tan society. The term *pu* is used as an equivalent for *pu-lo* 部落, tribe; it may also be used to mean a local group or an administrative unit. In our introductory texts, LS 32, 4a and 32, 4a–b, the term is rendered as "tribe."

Tsu is the Chinese word for clan—kin groups whose members claim descent from a common ancestor, bear the same name, and may not intermarry. Since such groups were not the basic social units of the Ch'i-tan tribes, the usual meaning of the term *tsu* cannot be accepted when considering the Liao texts; rather it must be interpreted in the light of Ch'i-tan society. To be sure, the historical records mention two clans, the Yeh-lü and the Hsiao, but documentary evidence makes it certain that these family lines became permanent clans only after the dynasty had been established. A memorial presented in 1074, fifty years before the collapse of the empire, states that at that time no other kin groups had special names or fixed marriage rules.[62] The Ch'i-tan, then, were a tribal society with extended kin groups, not a clan society in the Chinese sense. Except where the two named clans are being referred to, it seems best to render the word *tsu* as lineages, large families, or "houses."

Societies so organized are not unknown to anthropology,[63] and, since a fluid nomadism favors a fluid kinship system,[64] it is not surprising that the kinship system of the Ch'i-tan was loose and flexible. Our notes to LS 32, 4a are only a preliminary discussion of this interesting passage. A more systematic treatment

of the social structure of the Ch'i-tan tribes will be given together with the basic textual material in section VII.

LS 32, 4b and other passages show that the Ch'i-tan peoples preserved the memory of their tribal history long after the establishment of a semi-Chinese empire. At the head of the catalogue of the tribes the *Liao Shih* offers a list of the leading lineages or "families" of Liao (LS 33, 1a–b). The original caption calls the enumerated units *pu-tsu* 部族, thus hinting at their tribal background. Actually, as LS 32, 4b states, the lineages of Yao-lien, the former ruling family, and of the Three Patriarchal Households were cut off from their tribal base obviously for reasons of power politics. Nevertheless the order in which they appear here emphasizes the honorific position still conceded to them. The Nine Tents precede the new imperial family which in turn is followed by the families of T'ai-tsu's uncles and his younger brothers on the one hand and the most distinguished consort lineages on the other. (For the references quoted above see I, 2(1)–(3).)

b. TRIBAL MORPHOLOGY

Pastoral nomadism favored neither a stable clan order nor a fixed place of residence. LS 32, 4a–b tells a story of continual change within the predynastic Ch'i-tan tribes. Around A.D. 600 eight tribes expanded into ten. Under the chieftainship of the Ta-ho family they contracted again into eight; two were added, and "there were again ten tribes." During the latter part of the T'ang dynasty the Yao-lien khaghans once more reorganized the Ch'i-tan people, this time from eight into twenty tribes. Two of these, the Yao-lien and the Three Patriarchal Households, were later set apart by A-pao-chi. While they were raised in social prestige, their tribal status was abolished.

These historical changes are elaborately described in LS 32, 5b–8a. But still more detailed are the data dealing with the late predynastic and dynastic periods of Ch'i-tan history. The essential points have been tabulated in the survey of the tribal groups. They offer a unique picture of the formation, dissolution, and reorganization of Inner Asiatic tribes several hundred years before Chingis Khan.

The first eight of T'ai-tsu's eighteen tribes seem to be simple and homogeneous. But this seeming homogeneity was the result of a long and eventful history. Comparison with the lists of the earlier Ch'i-tan tribes reveals that practically all their names had been changed,[65] and certain changes occur, so to speak,

---

[60] The *Liao Shih* mentions the ancestors of several Ch'i-tan tribes. *Cf.* LS 32, 2b ff.

[61] *Cf.* XIV, 1 and XV, 1.

[62] VII, 2 (67).

[63] *Cf.* Boas 40, 368; Lowie 37, 570.

[64] *Cf.* Linton 36, 201 ff.

[65] *Cf.* the tribes of the time of the Ta-ho family (LS 32, 6b) and the tribes under the Yao-lien khaghanate (LS 32, 7a ff.).

under the very eyes of the historical observer. Before the time of the great Yao-lien khaghan, Tsu-wu, the I-la[66] and the I-shih[67] were a single tribe; so were the Wu-wei[68] and the Nieh-la,[69] and also the T'u-lü-pu[70] and the T'u-chü.[71] LS 33 says clearly that Tsu-wu divided the second and third tribal complexes; the statement on the first is less lucid, but the *Liao Shih* record concerning the "division of the camps" between the two chieftain brothers[72] makes sense only if this case is similar to the two others. The newly formed units were not necessarily permanent; they frequently served as the starting-point for other alignments. The imperial I-la tribe was divided in two and became the famous Five and Six Divisions.[73] Some members of the "old" tribes joined alien groups which had fallen under Ch'i-tan control.[74] T'ai-tsu's tribes from no. 11 to no. 17 were all composites. The non-Ch'i-tan element, which probably constituted the majority of the commoners, was generally designated by the latter half of the tribal name; the Ch'i-tan component was placed first. Only in the case of the Wu-ku Nieh-la tribe was the "foreign" group mentioned first, possibly because of the unusual number of Wu-ku captives which is given as six thousand households.

Similar changes also took place within the other tribal groups. The "simple" Hsi tribe, Ao-li, resulted from the unification of three separate tribes.[75] The Wei-yen Turks stemmed from two different groups.[76] The five Hsi tribes became six by the establishment of a new To-kuei tribe. Under T'ai-tsu the six tribes were temporarily counted as one. Under Shêng-tsung they assumed their original number although some with changed names.[77]

In all these instances relatively large tribal groups were reorganized, either in whole or in substantial part. A second method gathered together small fragments or even individuals and formed them into new groups. These new groups might function at first merely as military or economic organizations; they might be temporarily consolidated into smaller tribal units, *shih-lieh* 石烈, until they finally achieved the status of real tribes. The data here presented show the variations in growth of such synthetic tribes. Among T'ai-tsu's original eight tribes, the P'in and the Ch'u-t'ê were formerly camps (*ying* 營) which the Yao-lien khaghan, Tsu-wu, transformed into tribes.[78] Each of the old eight Ch'i-tan tribes contributed twenty households to a special garrison which, after expanding considerably, developed into the T'ê-li-t'ê-mien tribe.[79] Similarly, three Hsi "camps" eventually became three tribes.[80] The component *chao* 爪 in the name of the second and third tribes still preserves the idea of a sub-tribal camp-settlement.[81] The names of the two K'o tribes of the Hsi people also indicate their military function, even though this function may have been only temporary.[82] In other cases, bondsmen from several Liao camps (ordos) were banded together to act as hunters or ironworkers for their Ch'i-tan masters. Here again a sub-tribal group, the *shih-lieh*, was a step in the development of a recognized tribe.[83] Occasionally when loose tribal groups, *pu-tsu*, gained a certain unity they were permitted "to set up their banners and drums" and thus assume tribal status.[84]

Individual tribes sometimes merged into larger units and sometimes formed confederations, a trend that is clearly demonstrated by the history of the Ch'i-tan people, the Hsi, and many other tribes or tribe-like states included in our tables. The numbers eight and nine, which occur so often in the history of Inner Asiatic tribes,[85] stand out conspicuously in our texts, but other numbers are also frequently mentioned. LS 33, 9b records Eight Tribes of Ti-lieh;[86] LS 46, 29b, Eight P'o-li Tribes.[87] The name Ti-lieh Tribe of the Eight *Shih-lieh*,[88] like the Nine *Shih-lieh*,[89] may refer to large tribes rather than to confederations; but possibly the borderline was not clearly marked. The Five and Three Nations[90] and the Five[91] and Four Fan[92] also appear to have been

---

[66] I, 2 (4), no. 1.
[67] *Op. cit.*, no. 3.
[68] *Op. cit.*, no. 6.
[69] *Op. cit.*, no. 7.
[70] *Op. cit.*, no. 8.
[71] *Op. cit.*, no. 9.
[72] *Op. cit.*, no. 1.
[73] *Op. cit.*, nos. 1 and 2.
[74] The formation of such a composite tribe, Hsi I-la 奚迭剌, is clearly described in the case of the combination of Ch'i-tan and Hsi tribespeople in LS 1, 2a. The principle of this type of formation has been noticed by several scholars. *Cf.* Hirth 99, 44; also Stein 39, 33, note 1.
[75] I, 2 (5), no. 11.
[76] *Op. cit.*, no. 14.
[77] I, 2 (4), no. 10 and (5), nos. 8–13.

[78] I, 2 (4), nos. 4 and 5.
[79] I, 2 (5), no. 5.
[80] *Op. cit.*, nos. 1–3.
[81] For a discussion of the *chao* and *shih-lieh* see XIV, introduction.
[82] For the military significance of the term *k'o* 剋, see LS 46, 13b.
[83] I, 2 (5), nos. 6 and 7.
[84] I, 2 (8), no. 8.
[85] *Cf.* Hirth 99, 34 and 44.
[86] I, 2 (6), no. 2.
[87] I, 2 (8), no. 7.
[88] I, 2 (9), no. 24.
[89] *Op. cit.*, no. 32.
[90] I, 2 (5), no. 34, and (10), nos. 39–41.
[91] I, 2 (9), no. 59.
[92] *Op. cit.*, no. 40.

federated tribes. Side by side with the coordinated groups (federations) were other tribes and "states" which, whatever their former status, seem to have become more or less independent segments of larger cultural units. The Jurchen, the Turks, the various Uighur countries, and many smaller tribes such as the Chih-pu-ku[93] belonged in this category.

c. TRIBAL TOPOGRAPHY

The ever-changing political organization of the inner and outer tribes of Liao clearly expresses the flexibility of their nomadic life. It also explains why it is more difficult to locate these tribes than the sedentary populations of the empire. Most of them, dependent upon a pastoral economy, moved seasonally from one region to another, even choosing completely new grazing grounds if that was expedient for economic or military reasons.

The geographical setting of the Liao tribes is therefore necessarily vague. Some of them are roughly located, and may be placed in certain modern provinces. In every case the military administration to which they were attached contains a directional element (Northern, Southwestern, etc.), which establishes, at least in a general way, their geographical distribution within the Liao empire.

If too much is not expected from the available data, some idea of the tribal topography of Liao, which is equally interesting from the geographical and cultural points of view, may be attained. Out of T'ai-tsu's eighteen tribes, nine can be located in specific territories, even if only for a limited period. All eighteen are described in terms of definite directions. Two-thirds of the nine located tribes lived in what is now Jehol and Chahar, that is, in or near the old grazing grounds of the Ch'i-tan people. The majority of Shêng-tsung's tribes also lived in this region (nos. 1–13, 16, 19, and 20); two were situated in modern Liaoning (14 and 34); seven east and northeast of the Supreme Capital (6, 7, 14, 15, 22, 33, and 34); five in the northern and northwestern regions (17, 21, 23, 24, and 25); and five in the southwest (26–30). The survey shows that the tribal center remained where it had been originally, but that a thin outer circle of tribes had spread out from the south of the former Po-hai kingdom, along the Jurchen border to the Sungari River, to Outer Mongolia (the Orkhon River region), and south of the Gobi into the corner where the land of the Uighur Turks bordered on the Tangut outposts of Tibet.

d. SUBORDINATE, SEMI–SUBORDINATE, AND INDEPENDENT TRIBES AND STATES

The position of the non-Ch'i-tan tribes is geographically and politically less clear. LS 33, 9b–10a

says that the Outer Tribes were unable to maintain their independence. This was equally true for the Large Tribes, which in the main are identical with the Outer Tribes, and for the sixty-one tribes (tabulated in the list of the Various Tribes) as well as for some of the Subordinate States.

In many cases such dependency indicated at least temporary submission.[94] The request of certain tribal chieftains[95] for official status creates an impression of dependency, but this may have been neither great nor lasting. The payment of a substantial tribute may indicate real subordination, if the payment is made by a tribe or a small state,[96] but a different inference seems justified if payment is made by a large country such as Sung China.[97]

The acceptance of relief from the Liao government[98] is no sure proof of a tribe's subordinate position: the Sung government bought peace from a troublesome neighbor whose aggressiveness it could not otherwise control. Nor is the support given by a number of western tribes to Yeh-lü Ta-shih when the Liao empire was collapsing a reliable indication of their former subordination.[99] In some instances loyalty probably played its part, but the expectation of joint conquest and loot attracted tribes, such as the Tsu-pu, which in the past had fought bitterly against the Liao armies. The degree of military cooperation forced upon a tribe is a true index of dependency. The fact that in one case the hereditary officials of a semi-independent tribe were exempted from military service[100] would imply that in other tribes the nobles as well as the commoners had to serve. The tribes that escaped from Liao rule to China Proper complained, not only about the seizure of their sheep and horses, but also about the military duties which the Ch'i-tan government imposed upon them.[101]

The Subordinate States did not always deserve this designation. There might be submissive elements such as the Jurchen "state" whose ruler bore the significant title of the King Who is Obedient to Our Transforming Influence.[102] But often submission was more apparent than real; sometimes it did not exist

---

[93] *Op. cit.*, no. 2.

[94] *Cf.* I, 2 (9), nos. 7, 26, 35, 43, 57; (10) nos. 1 and 4.
[95] I, 2 (9), nos. 22 and 38.
[96] *Op. cit.*, nos. 2, 4, 47, 56, 60.
[97] See X, introduction.
[98] I, 2 (9), nos. 8 and 51.
[99] *Cf. op. cit.*, nos. 5 and 34; also (10), no. 56.
[100] I, 2 (9), no. 52.
[101] WTS 51, 13b–14a; see XIII, introduction, Dependent and Semi-dependent Tribes.
[102] I, 2 (10), no. 1. Designations indicating the submission, complete or limited, of barbarian rulers to the Chinese evidently served as models for this title. For the translation of a number of such formulas see Chavannes 04, 28, 36, 42, 63, 70, 73, 75, 78, 84.

at all. The term Subordinate State must be understood in the light of the old Chinese tradition. Theoretically speaking the emperor controlled all-under-heaven (*t'ien-hsia* 天下), that is, the whole world, and the countries which did not fall directly under his sway were at least considered dependencies in the wider sense of the word. Several "subordinate" states and tribes, like Hsi Hsia and the Jurchen of the border zone, were controlled by Liao, but others, like Japan, Tibet, and Ta-shih, lay for all practical purposes beyond the reach of the empire. In so far as their envoys were political representatives and not men of religion or affairs they came on diplomatic missions which were often nothing more than courtesy calls or visits for information. Their "tributes" were only polite gifts which the court of Liao repaid by presents of a similar kind. Most countries classified as smaller or larger "dependencies" were not only independent *de facto;* they were also acknowledged as such (see LS 46, 23*b*).

The Five Dynasties and Sung are not enumerated among the dependencies, even though some dynasties were temporarily more dependent and paid heavier tributes than most of the so-called "tributary" countries. China Proper obviously fell into a totally different category.

e. THE GEOGRAPHICAL HORIZON OF THE LIAO WORLD

Whatever the political status of the Subordinate States, their mention gives some indication of the political geography of Asia during this period. The present attempt to locate the various tribes and states is based upon the specialized studies of many Chinese, Japanese, and Western scholars, such as Li Shên-ju, Ting Ch'ien, and Ts'ao T'ing-chieh; Tsuda and Ikeuchi; Bretschneider, Chavannes, Hirth, Marquart, Pelliot, Mullie, Gibert, Vladimirtsov, and Barthold. Additional identifications have been ventured whenever our texts or other sources permitted. The frequent use of such terms as "possible," "perhaps," and "probably" indicates that not a few of these equations may be considered tentative rather than final; together with other researches they provide basic material for a political and cultural geography of Inner Asia during the tenth and eleventh centuries, that is, for the period between the collapse of the Turkic steppe empire and the rise of the Mongol world.

The vast regions of China Proper formed the southern border of the Liao empire. Far to the east loomed the island country of Japan whose emissaries on occasion found their way to the Ch'i-tan court (*cf.* IX and X, 2). Silla on the mainland was still an independent state when A-pao-chi seized power. Korea, which later conquered it, remained the strong

eastern continental neighbor, often attacked but never quite subdued by Liao (*cf.* X, 2, and XVI). Between the Korean border, the shores of the Pacific, and the Sungari River there flourished a variety of larger and smaller tribes and states, the Mo-ho (Mukri), the Wu-jo, the T'ieh-li, and—increasingly significant—the Jurchen, the "obedient" ones as well as their "savage" brothers who were destined to become the rulers of the next North Chinese dynasty, Chin.

The people of the northern border have received less attention than the Koreans and the Jurchen. Their geographic location is even less clearly defined than that of the eastern (Tungus) world. Did some of the Ti-lieh live temporarily in western Heilungkiang? The Shih-wei spread out over a far-flung zone along the Amur River. Similarly far-flung, but extending farther to the west, was the territory of the Tsu-pu: the Tatars if Wang Kuo-wei's identification stands.

This same border zone supported predominantly hunting and fishing peoples such as the Wu-ku or Yü-chüeh-li, the Uriangkhai, and perhaps the majority of the Khirghiz who, after their victory over the Uighurs in 840, were soon expelled from the region of the Orkhon River. The names of such northern groups as the Kerait, the Merkits, and the Naiman presage the dawn of Chingis Khan's time when all of them suddenly assumed historic significance.[103]

The San-ho region, which in our list is but one name among many, was later described by Chingis Khan as the tribal home of his ancestors who laid the foundations of Mongol power.[104] Along this northern edge of the grasslands of Inner Asia the Liao government controlled the local remnants of the Uighur people whose country, Shan-yü Administration, still reflected the glorious traditions of the ancient lords of the steppe, the Huns. The Uighur people, after their expulsion from the Orkhon capital, occupied several important areas along the western and southwestern fringe of the Great Gobi Desert, namely the rich oasis country of Kao-ch'ang (Turfan), the smaller key oasis of Tun-huang, and Kan Prefecture in the northwestern corner of what is now China Proper.

Between and beyond the links of this Uighur girdle were located various Turkic groups, including the Sha-t'o people near the Tangut and the Western Turks, whose territory stretched from western Turkestan to the borders of Europe. Yü-t'ien (Khotan) was originally an independent state, free to send a

---

[103] See below, appendix V, *B*, 3, 1194 *passim; cf.* also Vladimirtsov 30, 4, 9, 24 ff., 30 ff., 57–61.

[104] I, 2 (10), no. 73; YS 1, 12*a*.

mission to the Liao court.[105] At the beginning of the eleventh century it fell into the hands of the Qarā-Khānid ruler, Qadir-khan, who gradually acquired control over the whole of Eastern Turkestan.[106] For reasons given in I, 2 (10), no. 46, it seems all but certain that the Ta-shih mentioned in LS 16, 5a and b was Qadir-khan's domain. The Ta-shih of LS 2, 4b may have been the Arabian Caliphate of Baghdad.[107]

The story of the mission sent to Sultan Mahmūd in 1027 by the Liao emperor, Shêng-tsung, reveals the remoteness of Ghazna which was reached via territories ruled by Qadir-khan and Uighur-khan.[108] The

---

[105] X, 2 (49).
[106] Barthold 28, 281.
[107] See I, 2 (10), no. 46.
[108] Marvazī 42, 19 ff. Minorsky (op. cit., 78) assumes an identity between Qadir-khan and Uighur-khan, the latter, in his opinion, being the ruler of Kan-chou (Kan Prefecture), not Qocho (Kao-ch'ang). The fact that Uighur-khan, in a letter, mentions a Khitāy mission which traveled through his country (op. cit., 21) and that Shêng-tsung, in his, refers to an order to permit this mission to pass through Qadir-khan's domain (op. cit., 20) gives some support to Minorsky's thesis. But the mere mention of a passage through the territory of Uighur-khan and Quadir-khan is not convincing proof that the two rulers were one and the same. On the way to Khurāsān and Ghazna the Liao embassy would naturally travel first through a Uighur country (in all probability, Kao-ch'ang) and then through the Qarā-Khānid regions of southwestern Turkestan.

To strengthen his argument, the distinguished Iranist notes that the name of a certain Kan-chou prince, Chaqïr, resembles the name, Chaghrï, given in Shêng-tsung's letter for a son of Qadir-khan (op. cit., 78), but he fails to offer any evidence of the existence of a Qadir-khan in the Uighur countries of the period. However, during the reign of Sultan Mahmūd a Qarā-Khānid ruler bearing this name was one of the most powerful potentates of Inner Asia. This mighty ruler, who in peace and war dealt on an equal footing with the Ghaznevid sultan (Barthold 28, 280 ff.), had gained control over all of Eastern Turkestan before 1020, the year of the first "Ta-shih" mission to Liao. Shêng-tsung's letter, which mentions the marriage of a Liao lady to Qadir-khan's son, was written in 1024, eight years before the death of the famous sovereign. See Barthold 28, 294–295.

Such a marriage involved important questions of diplomatic expediency and prestige. After 840 the Uighur nation ceased to be a leading power in Central Asia. Its scattered fragments remained culturally noteworthy, but the small Uighur states exercised little political influence. The Liao Shih records two official Uighur requests for brides. Both were rejected (XVI, 944, LS 4, 10b; 996/7, LS 13, 7b).

The only western marriage recorded by the Liao Shih for the years immediately preceding 1024 was the one consummated with "Ta-shih" in 1021—and "Ta-shih" was surely not a Uighur country. As will be more fully discussed

southern Uighur states bordered on regions occupied by the Tangut (Tang-hsiang), a Tibetan people whose political power was temporarily centered in Hsi Hsia. The T'u-yü-hun, remote from their northeastern Hsien-pei cradle and expelled from their second home on the shores of Kuku-Nōr, spread out thinly over the northwestern edge of what is now China Proper. Their Tibetan name Ha-za indicates their regional contact with the peoples of the Central Asiatic plateau who had played such an active role during certain phases of T'ang history. The Liao Shih enumerates the T'u-fan together with three other Fan "states," to which modern conjecture adds still another, the T'ieh-pu-tê. Possibly they were the bearers of a name which later designated the entire T'u-fan complex, Tibet.

The countries beyond the icy mountain ranges of Inner Asia were far from the centers of Liao power. Baghdad may have sent an embassy to T'ai-tsu when his star began to shine brightly,[109] yet the Arabian Caliphate, more distant still than Ghazna, lay for all practical purposes outside the Liao world. India too was far away. It is within the realm of possibility that the Ch'i-tan rulers, being devoted Buddhists, should occasionally have established contact with Ceylon, the Chinese Shih-tzŭ, but it is also possible that the Shih-tzŭ Kuo of the Liao Shih was one of a

---

below, the Persian word "Tāzīk" came, in Central Asia, to designate people of Islamic faith, particularly Iranians (see I, 2 (10), no. 46). Although Qadir-khan was a Turk, his country may have been classed as Tāzīk, for it was inhabited by many Iranians and the khan himself was a Mohammedan. But it is most unlikely that the Uighurs, who were the staunchest enemies of Islam, should have been called by this name.

The "Ta-shih" which Yeh-lü Ta-shih seized after the collapse of the Liao empire was a Moslem country located west of the westernmost Uighur territory, Kao-ch'ang, and according to LS, 69, 24b, between the Uighurs and Samarqand (loc. cit.). It seems most improbable that Shêng-tsung, who in the midst of the Sung war was unwilling to consider a diplomatic marriage with the Uighurs, should have accepted such an arrangement after its successful conclusion and at the height of his dynasty's power. More probably, the emperor's boastful remarks on his alliance with Qadir-khan actually reveal his close relations with the country of "Ta-shih" [the Qarā-Khānid state of East Turkestan]—relations that had been established three years before, in 1021.

No Qarā-Khānid prince, Chagrï-tegin, is known to us. The names given by Barthold (28, 284 and 295) for Qadir-khan's two eldest sons reveal no conspicuous affinity to Chagrï-tegin. More suggestive is the similarity of Chagrï to Ts'ê [Ch'ê or Ch'ai]-ko, the name mentioned in LS 16, 5a for a prince of Ta-shih. (See X, 2 (71).)

[109] X, 2 (11).

number of Central Asiatic countries governed by a *shih-tzŭ* [*arslan:* "lion"] king.[110]

Immediately below we present Shêng-tsung's letter of 1024 to Mahmūd,[111] a unique document revealing Ch'i-tan official mentality at the peak of its dynastic power. In it the Liao emperor states in no uncertain terms his supreme control over the numerous king-doms and tribes within his empire. He points to his alliance with Qadir-khan and also asserts close and regular communication with the "nephews among the amirs of the nearer regions," obviously referring to the many countries and tribes listed as "subordinate" by the *Liao Shih*. Shêng-tsung writes:

Concerning [the] welfare [of the Khan]. To the amīr of Khorasan Mahmūd Qarā-khān.

The Lord of the Heavens has granted to us (many ?) kingdoms upon the face of (this) wide earth and placed us in possession of regions occupied by numerous tribes. In our capital we enjoy security and act according to our will. Anyone in the world who can see and hear cannot help seeking friendship and close relations with us. Our nephews from among the amirs of the nearer regions constantly and without exception send their envoys, and their letters and presents follow upon one another. (Only) he (Mahmūd) until now has sent no envoy or messenger, while we hear of his excellence in strength and courage, of his outstanding position in might and elevation, of his supremacy over the amirs by awe, of his control of the provinces by might and authority and of his peace in his homeland according to his own will. As he enjoys such a glorious position it is a duty for him to write his news to the Supreme Khan than whom there is none higher beneath the heavens, and to treat him with consideration according to his state. So we have taken the initiative, limiting ourselves to the dispatch of this lightly equipped envoy rather than someone who would exceed him in rank and equipage, in view of the greatness of the distance and the length of time (necessary) for covering it.

And as there happened to be an alliance with Qadir-khan through a noble lady from the bosom of my house who became married to his son *Chagrī-tegin, and (thus) both houses became united through her, we have ordered Qadir khan to open the road to our envoy to him (*i.e.* to Mahmūd) and to his envoy to ourselves, chosen from among men of sound judgment, intelligent and serious, so that we may inform him of how things stand with us, and communicate with him on what there is in the world, while establishing the custom of mutual donations, in friendship with him.

---

[110] *Cf.* I, 2 (10), no. 46.

[111] This letter, made accessible through Professor Minor-sky's recent translation, was written in the year of the Mouse (Marvazī 42, 20; *cf.* also 76), that is, in 1024. The embassy visited Ghazna only in 1027 (*op. cit.*, 62, 68, 76); or according to other records, in 1026 (*op. cit.*, 76; Barthold 28, 286). Minorsky thinks that the letter "must have been in Turkish" (Marvazī 42, 78); Uighur would probably be the Turkish language in question.

The object in dispatching this envoy Qalitunkā (*Qul-Tonga?*) is to open the road of union and to fasten the ties of amity.[112]

The Liao envoy did not achieve his purpose. Mahmūd was unwilling to entertain closer relations with the Ch'i-tan until they accepted Islam.[113] But the failure of Qalitunkā's mission does not diminish its historical significance. This mission and the ex-change of letters reveal that the names of places and peoples contained in the Liao records, far from being a casual agglomeration of exotic words, reflect a sub-stantial and complex political reality which dynam-ically integrated a considerable part of Central as well as Eastern Asia.

6. POPULATION

In view of the character and purpose of the *Liao Shih*, it is not surprising that data on population are, in the main, incidental to two other types of informa-tion: the geographical descriptions and the military records. The former have been included in the tables of section I, 1; the latter are given below in section XV. Our estimate of the population of the Liao empire has been based on these two series of figures, supple-mented by certain other fragmentary references.

Most conspicuous is the division of the population of Liao into two main groups, the tribal and the sedentary. Each group is again subdivided, the for-mer into a Ch'i-tan and a non-Ch'i-tan sector, the latter into a number of units, the Chinese and the Po-hai being particularly important. These basic divisons were accentuated by economic and cultural differences: the tribal groups were almost entirely nomadic, the others agricultural. Yet their geo-graphical separation is somewhat obscured by the compulsory transfer of numerous people from one part of the country to another. The forced resettle-ment of large numbers of Chinese and Po-hai is described in the data concerning the five circuits. The motives behind this policy are clearly expressed in Yeh-lü Yü-chih's memorial of 929; in his opinion trouble was to be expected if the unruly Po-hai were permitted to remain in their traditional locale, whereas resettlement might result in their ultimate pacification and lead to economic and military benefits as well.[114]

a. METHODOLOGICAL CONSIDERATIONS

A numerical estimate of the population is not easily made. The *Liao Shih* is one of the most obscure of China's dynastic histories; although it is superior to all others in its information on tribal life and tradition,

---

[112] *Op. cit.*, 19–20.

[113] *Op. cit.*, 21.

[114] I, 3 (2).

it is meagre and inadequate in many other respects. Its population figures are poorer than those contained in the larger dynastic histories and certainly not more illuminating. Only one set of figures is given, and these are neither dated nor clearly defined. Data on the three northern circuits probably do not include the tribal population; there is no dependable record of the numerical strength of the Ch'i-tan or the "barbarian" tribes. Thus an ethnical comparison is difficult, a historical one out of the question.

These special factors are aggravated by the general difficulties inherent in the use of all Chinese population data. Chinese histories contain a wealth of population figures, more than any other historical records of similar antiquity; yet these figures are full of contradictions. Sometimes they are not plausible; often they are obviously impossible. Nevertheless they add considerably to an understanding of the administrative organization during the period to which they refer. At times the official population figures may have been close to the truth, but even when this optimum was not achieved the numerical records are still of some value. They may reflect regional differences and historical changes.

The Chinese population figures were probably taken from the reports of local officials to the central government, which used them as a basis for taxation, compulsory labor, and military services. Thus the census figures often represent the admitted population rather than the actual one;[115] and a growing population figure may express a growing administrative efficiency rather than a biological increase. The local tax-collecting agents naturally tended to minimize in their reports the true number of people taxed, for they throve upon taxing as many but reporting as few as possible. The desire of an ambitious official to show striking financial achievements which would bring him honorific recognition and profitable promotion might mitigate this trend. The not infrequent escape of certain sections of the population who, under the pressure of economic distress or warfare, preferred vagabondage to slave-like servitude, probably accounts for occasional records of population decrease.

In the Liao period all these tendencies were intensified by additional difficulties arising from the semi-barbarian character of the state and its administration. At times a general census was attempted[116] but never with full success.[117] The government registers contain no concrete population figures for one of the five circuits, Chung-ching;[118] they are incomplete for part of Tung-ching Circuit. Even for

the Ch'i-tan, the most important tribal complex[119] the information is limited. Equally incomplete are the data on the proportional representation of barbarians (*fan* 番) and Chinese in the various ordos.[120]

In the sedentary region there was much escaping and "hiding,"[121] sometimes more, sometimes less, depending upon the particular economic and political situation.[122] Did the census figures, which Ma Jên-wang contentedly admitted were short a third,[123] refer to the size of the properties or to the number of propertied households? Whatever the situation, his statement expresses a tendency immanent in the traditional Chinese census policy. The numerical results of this policy did not deviate from the truth senselessly but in traditional ways which accorded with well-established social and political procedures. To reject them completely would be as wrong as to accept them uncritically. If read against their institutional background, the Chinese census figures—even those of the *Liao Shih*—assume considerable socio-historical significance.

b. SEDENTARY POPULATION

THE CHINESE

Relatively full data are available for the sedentary sector of the Liao population, particularly the Chinese. Nan-ching and Hsi-ching Circuits were old T'ang territories with a well-developed administrative system. The militia registers of the two regions listed 566,000 and 322,700 adult males respectively.[124] The census admits 247,000 and 167,200 households respectively.[125] If the prevailing custom of counting two adult males per household is accepted, the two sets of figures practically confirm each other. These 414,200 households must have been almost exclusively Chinese.

The three northern circuits disposed over 226,100 adult males according to the authors of the *Liao Shih*.[126] The figures for Shang-ching Circuit is given as 167,200,[127] and that of Tung-ching Circuit as

[115] *Cf.* Wittfogel, OS (ms).
[116] See I, 3, *passim.*
[117] I, 3 (1).
[118] XV, 1 (43).

[119] XV, 1 (3).
[120] XV, 1 (34).
[121] I, 3 (7).
[122] See XII.
[123] I, 3 (6).
[124] XV, 1 (37) (38). This makes a total of 888,700 men. LS 36, 1a gives a somewhat smaller total, namely 806,700 men. Both figures suggest a total of more than 800,000 and less than 900,000 men. If the data originated from two different sources, then their relative coincidence may be taken as particularly instructive.
[125] Our own calculation, based upon LS 40 and 41 (I, 1 (8) and (9)).
[126] XV, 1 (34).
[127] *Op. cit.* (35).

41,400,[128] thus leaving less than 20,000 men for the entire Chung-ching Circuit. The census for this central region was admittedly incomplete.[129] San-han County, the only district for which population figures are given, is credited with 5,000 households[130] and 10,000 adult males. The other prefectures and counties, including the Central Capital, together must have had a population considerably larger than one district. An estimated total of more than 25,000 households and 50,000 adult males for the central territory is probably a conservative guess, making an estimated round total of 220,000 adult males and 110,000 households for Shang-ching and Chung-ching Circuits together. The two regions were settled in the main with "transplanted" Chinese and Po-hai. The Po-hai deportations seem to have been the more radical, but since the number of Chinese subjects in the nation was very large it is more than possible that a considerable Chinese majority was maintained among the settlers of the Shang-ching and Chung-ching Circuits, particularly in the cities with their special Chinese quarters. Assuming that the deported Po-hai (ordo soldiers excluded) almost equalled in number those remaining in Tung-ching Circuit, it seems reasonable to suggest that approximately 40,000 Po-hai and 70,000 Chinese households were settled in Shang-ching and Chung-ching Circuits.

In the old Po-hai territory the precarious political situation distorted the prevailing proportion of potential militiamen in the civilian population. Tung-ching Circuit registered 41,400 adult males for the militia,[131] but if the census figures in LS 38[132] are added a total of 60,000 households, or considerably more than the expected 20,500, is reached. For many prefectures and counties no figures are given, but this does not necessarily mean that the districts were completely abandoned; even after the mass deportations, economic and administrative activities continued in the various parts of the former Po-hai kingdom.

After 926 the territory was no longer inhabited by Po-hai only. Many Chinese and some Ch'i-tan tribesmen were settled in the eastern region[133] to replace the deported Po-hai and to hold the remaining population in subjection. It may be assumed that out of 60,000 Tung-ching households about 50,000 were Po-hai and 10,000 Chinese (the tribal settlers were probably not included in the lists of the Five Capitals). A third group of Chinese was attached

to the imperial guard camps, the ordos. The ordo Chinese are counted with the "barbarians" and their combined maximum number of households is given as 123,000.[134] The actual figures for the ordo armies are considerably less than the mechanical calculations of LS 31 indicate. Instead of the asserted total of over 400,000 adult males, all the ordos considered together did not comprise more than 150,000 men in the last quarter of the tenth century, and less than 300,000 at the beginning of the twelfth.[135] The true figures may have been even smaller. Thus the composite barbarian-Chinese sector mustered not more than 80,000 households at the close of the dynasty and a considerably lesser number during an earlier period. To simplify the presentation, 80,000 households are used as the basis for the following calculations.

Who were the "barbarians" in this composite group? And what was the proportion of Chinese to "barbarians"? The answer to the second question depends on the answer to the first. The Chinese word *fan* 番 designates national or cultural groups other than one's own; like the Greek term "*barbaroi*," it generally implies inferiority. For this reason the translation "barbarian" is acceptable, even if it does not express all the subtle shades of the original term.

In the *Liao Shih* the term generally applies to tribal peoples, never to the Chinese. Occasionally it refers to all the tribes, including the ruling Ch'i-tan. This is the case when the barbarian court officials are juxtaposed to their Chinese colleagues[136] or when barbarian music is contrasted with Chinese.[137] Whenever such comparisons are made, honorific preference is given to the barbarian element. Hence the word "barbarian" has undergone an interesting modification similar to that of the word "Gothic" which in certain contexts has completely lost its originally barbaric connotation.

More frequent is the application of the term *fan* to the non-Ch'i-tan tribes, but in these instances, its meaning is made more explicit by the use of qualifying clauses, such as the "western" barbarians[138] or the "northwestern" barbarians,[139] or by juxtaposition of tribal and barbarian households.[140] The barbarians in these three illustrations were evidently not identical with the Ch'i-tan tribes. It is possible that they lived beyond the border and were forbidden to intermarry with the Ch'i-tan.[141] On the other hand, some

---

[128] *Op. cit.* (36).
[129] *Op. cit.* (39).
[130] See I, 1 (7).
[131] XV, 1 (36).
[132] I, 1 (6), *passim.*
[133] *Loc. cit.*

[134] XV, 1 (3).
[135] See XV, introduction.
[136] VII, 2 (82).
[137] See VII, introduction, notes 485 and 486.
[138] II, 2 (8).
[139] X, 2 (7).
[140] XV, 1 (19).
[141] VII, 2 (73).

were permitted to graze their herds within the confines of the empire. If these barbarians were not identical with "the tribes," then this latter term obviously must designate the empire's inner tribes only.

In records concerning the ordo armies the "transferred"[142] barbarians and Chinese are always mentioned after the *chêng* 正, the "regular" or "principal" people who presumably were the Ch'i-tan.[143] In T'ai-tsu's ordo the second category ("barbarian") was evidently Po-hai; the others, Ch'i-tan and Chinese.[144] Comparison of data in the geographical and military sections of the *Liao Shih* reveals that the Po-hai were also part of the "attached" populations in other ordos.[145] The Po-hai prisoners of war who served in the early ordos may well have included a number of Po-hai tribesmen, but the Po-hai inhabitants of the attached districts must have been predominantly non-tribal, for in general the tribesmen were under the jurisdiction of the government of the Northern Region, not of the Five Capitals.

If all or most of the ordo "barbarians" were Po-hai, it is difficult to understand why, in LS 31 and 35, the barbarians are always referred to before the Chinese whose political status was definitely higher. Such an arrangement is comprehensible only if it is assumed that the barbarian sector included numerous non-Ch'i-tan tribesmen. Mu-tsung's ordo garrison is known to have included Tsu-pu tribesmen;[146] but far more important may have been the "barbarian" element in the empire's fifty-four tribes.

How many of these fifty-four tribes were Ch'i-tan? The eight old tribes may be so considered with certainty. The rest of T'ai-tsu's inner tribes were either composed of Hsi alone or other more or less closely related alien groups which were combined with fragments of the original Ch'i-tan tribes. Again some among Shêng-tsung's tribes, such as the Hsi and Shih-wei, were close relatives; others, composed of Turks, Tanguts, and Jurchen, must have seemed strangers ("barbarian") even when they became part of the Liao empire. The texts do not clearly distinguish between the old, the new, the not-yet, and the definitely non-Ch'i-tan tribes within the empire, perhaps because the fluid political situation made it difficult to draw any exact line. Nevertheless, certain inner tribes must have remained "barbarian." Their members as well as tribal captives and some tribal Po-hai may well have constituted the main "barbarian" component in the ordos.

No data reveal the relative numerical strength of "barbarians" (Po-hai and non-Ch'i-tan tribesmen) and Chinese in the ordos. If, however, for the sake of argument, we assume that the number of non-Ch'i-tan tribesmen and Chinese approximated each other and that the Po-hai group, the least trusted, was somewhat smaller, then a ratio of 3:3:2 seems reasonable. In other words, on the basis of a total of 80,000 non-*chêng* households in the ordos, the Chinese and the non-Ch'i-tan tribesmen would comprise 30,000 each, the Po-hai 20,000.

But a Chinese population total cannot be obtained by simply adding the Chinese ordo households cited above to the population figures of the Five Capitals, for not all ordo soldiers were stationed at the main camp; some lived in the "attached" districts and are counted as inhabitants of the Five Capitals. In table 1, the figures for the ordo Chinese are therefore given after those for the Five Capitals. The total Chinese population of the Liao empire can only be determined by adding a fraction[147] of the ordo figures to the minimum totals.

TABLE 1

ESTIMATED CHINESE POPULATION

Location	Units		
	Adult Males	Households	Individuals
(1) Two Southern Circuits	800,000	400,000	2,000,000
(2) Three Northern Circuits	160,000	80,000	400,000
Total (Minimum)	960,000	480,000	2,400,000
(3) Ordos (Final figures)	60,000	30,000	150,000

The greatest possibility for error occurs in Group 2: more Chinese settlers may have been in Tung-ching and perhaps fewer in the other two northern circuits. To a certain degree, the two possible errors would balance each other out; their numerical importance seems insignificant when compared with the figures in Group 1 which the *Liao Shih* gives with great definiteness.

The estimated total is a minimum rather than a maximum. This is true for three reasons: (1) an average of five members to a Chinese household is somewhat lower than the 5–6 members suggested by historical records for more than two millennia.[148] If

---

[142] For an explanation of this term see VII and XV, introductions.

[143] See below.

[144] XV, 1 (5); *cf.* also analysis in XV, introduction.

[145] See XV, introduction.

[146] XV, 1 (9).

---

[147] Indicating the fraction of Chinese living at the main ordo camps.

[148] See Wittfogel 36, 505–506; *idem* 38, 38.

therefore the household figures are multiplied by 5.5 instead of 5, the total Chinese population of the Liao empire would comprise 2,640,000 individuals; (2) only a fraction of the ordo population is accounted for by the figures of the three northern circuits; (3) in view of the minimizing tendency of the Chinese census, even a corrected maximum is probably below the actual total. This possibility is mentioned, not to depreciate our figures, but to show in what direction further research may modify them.

THE PO-HAI

The great majority of the Liao Po-hai lived in their old eastern homeland or, if transplanted, in Shang-ching or Chung-ching Circuits, in the main ordo camps or their "attached" districts. Analysis of the Chinese sector of the Liao empire has also made possible a tentative estimate of its various groups of Po-hai subjects.

Again the ordo households are not included in our (minimum) total, for some of the Po-hai like the Chinese of the ordo army were counted with the inhabitants of the Five Capitals. A tentative summary of the main groups of Liao Po-hai yields the figures shown in table 2.

TABLE 2

Estimated Po-hai Population

Location	Units		
	Adult Males	Households	Individuals
(1) Tung-ching	100,000	50,000	250,000
(2) Shang-ching and Chung-ching	80,000	40,000	200,000
Total (Minimum)	180,000	90,000	450,000
(3) Ordos (Final figures)	40,000	20,000	100,000

These figures strikingly reveal the extent of the Po-hai mass deportations. The ordos and mausoleums were situated for the most part in Shang-ching Circuit, and the majority of the Po-hai in the main camps must therefore be counted in category 2. The resulting figure suggests that the "transplanted" Po-hai almost equalled those who were permitted to remain in their homeland.

THE CH'I-TAN

No satisfactory total is reported for this dominant group, but LS 31, 1b–2a places the number of *chêng* households in all ordos at 80,000. For contextual as well as linguistic reasons it seems legitimate to consider the *chêng* as the Ch'i-tan. The term is juxtaposed to the "transferred" barbarians and Chinese, that is, to groups that are defined as to nationality and culture. Since the word *chêng* is translated "regular," "principal," "real," this could only be the Ch'i-tan.

At the close of the dynasty, according to LS 31, 2a, the ordos had 80,000 *chêng* households. Since the full strength of all the ordo garrisons reached only three-fourths of the alleged total,[149] the number of Ch'i-tan ordo households at this time can only have been 60,000 and less than 30,000 for the earlier period.

Not all Ch'i-tan were organized within the ordos. The *Liao Shih* leaves no doubt that many of them continued to live with their tribes[150] whose numerical strength is uncertain. Assignment to the ordos may have been the cause of the temporary weakness exhibited by some inner tribes.[151] However, others subjected to similar military demands continued to grow.[152] In general, the Ch'i-tan tribes were strong enough to suffer the loss of many members without any obvious weakness resulting.

How many Ch'i-tan were there at the beginning and at the end of the dynastic era? No direct answer can be made to this question, but some insight may be gained from a record about the Hsi peoples who, during the T'ang period, were as powerful as their northern neighbors, the Ch'i-tan. Midway in the ninth century the T'ang armies defeated the Hsi and destroyed more than 200,000 tent units (*chang-lo* 帳落).[153] Unfortunately, this statement is not only less detailed but also less trustworthy than the information on the ordos contained in LS 31 and 35; it appears in a record that glorifies a military victory and for this reason is in all probability considerably exaggerated. But, even after necessary correction is made, the statement is still ambiguous because of the qualifying word "tent."

The Ch'i-tan moved their tents in carts, and five Ch'i-tan tent carts might service three families.[154] Records on the early Mongols indicate that on occasion there were many more tents or tent carts than men. Rubruck notes that a settlement (ordo) of a rich Mongol looked "like a large town, though there will be very few men in it."[155] One girl led twenty or thirty tent carts.[156] The tent carts of a prince seemed

---

[149] See XV, introduction.
[150] XV, 1 (34).
[151] XI (11).
[152] *Cf.* II, 2 (2); XI (20).
[153] TS 219, 6a–b.
[154] CS 133, 5a.
[155] Rubruck 00, 57.
[156] *Loc. cit.*

like a moving city, but again the number of men attached was amazingly small.[157]

Rejecting half the *T'ang Shu's* claim as a political boast, we assume for argument's sake that 100,000 Hsi tents or 60,000 households were destroyed in the campaign of 847. While it is certain that the Hsi had recovered from their earlier defeat by the tenth century, it is equally certain that at that time they were outnumbered by their Ch'i-tan neighbors. If the Hsi alone had 60,000 households, then the *chêng* population of the Liao empire, which included both Ch'i-tan and Hsi, probably had at least twice that number, or 120,000 households, in the tenth century, and considerably more—perhaps 150,000—after a long period of peace and security. Such a figure does not invalidate the calculated total of 60,000 *chêng* ordo households at the close of the dynasty.

TABLE 3

ESTIMATED CH'I-TAN POPULATION

(at close of dynasty)

Location	Units		
	Adult Males	Households	Individuals
In the Tribes	180,000	90,000	450,000
In the Ordos	120,000	60,000	300,000
Total	300,000	150,000	750,000

The results of our calculations throw some light on the size of the individual Ch'i-tan tribe. Mullie assumes that a family in the predominantly sedentary Shang-ching Circuit consisted of four members only;[158] no attempt is made to explain this low estimate. We, however, accept the average given in the *Liao Shih*, five members per average sedentary family. Since, according to LS 31 and 35, a "regular" household, like a "barbarian" and Chinese unit, could produce two adult males, it can be assumed that all these households had approximately the same number of members, namely, five.

The synthetic T'ê-li-t'ê-mien tribe started with a garrison of 160 households, or 800 persons, if the 1:5 ratio is accepted; but only after a considerable increase was tribal status conferred.[159] Other contemporary records mention tribes with 180,[160] 700,[161] and even 6,000[162] households, figures which correspond roughly to a membership of 900, 3,500, and 30,000 respectively. Still another passage describes a Ch'i-

tan tribe that had 4,000 households in the Sui period. Furthermore, this passage states that at this time a Ch'i-tan tribe could muster somewhere between 1,000 and 3,000 soldiers. In the T'ang period the individual tribe produced approximately 5,000 soldiers; eight tribes had a total of 40,000.[163] This suggests an average of 500–2,500 households and 2,500–12,500 individuals. The maximum figures of the era of semi-dependence undoubtedly became averages, if not minima, after the establishment of the Liao empire. If we assume that forty out of the fifty-four tribes of Shêng-tsung can be classified as *chêng* and if we further assume an average of 2,500 households for each *chêng* tribe, then we arrive at a total of 90,000 households and 450,000 individuals at the end of the tenth century. This figure, which includes the total "regular" population, the tribal and the ordo Ch'i-tan, is somewhat smaller than the 120,000 households suggested in our previous estimate for Ch'i-tan during these years.

OTHER TRIBES

Our general estimates of ordo manpower would seem to indicate that the non-Po-hai barbarians may eventually have numbered 30,000 households. Some of them were captives of war or the descendants of former captives, many of whose fellow-tribesmen still lived beyond the Liao borders.

Among the empire's tribes not a few remained unassimilated and "barbarian" even when they were counted in the fifty-four tribes. If forty of these tribes are assumed to be "regular" (Ch'i-tan), then fourteen may be considered "barbarian." These "barbarian" tribes may well have comprised some 35,000 households in Shêng-tsung's time and perhaps 40,000 at the close of the dynasty. The latter figure more or less confirms our estimate of 30,000 non-Po-hai barbarian ordo households, a total which includes not only the ordo soldiers taken from the non-*chêng* Liao tribes but also certain ordo barbarians whose tribes were located beyond the border.

Because of the presence of this group of ordo barbarians, the total number of non-Po-hai barbarians exceeds that of the empire's inner tribes, but to what extent we have no way of knowing. Our estimate of this category of Liao barbarians (see table 4) is therefore particularly unsatisfactory.

Adding the totals for the four main groups, with full understanding of the limitations of this method, we arrive at the grand totals for the Liao population as shown by table 5.

c. CONCLUSION

The tentativeness of these estimates need not be restated; it has been emphasized again and again.

---

[157] *Op. cit.* 86.
[158] Mullie 22, 211.
[159] I, 2 (5), no. 5.
[160] I, 2 (6), no. 10.
[161] I, 2 (4), no. 13.
[162] *Op. cit.*, no. 17.

[163] *Cf.* XIV (1), LS 63, 3*b*–4*a*.

TABLE 4

ESTIMATED POPULATION OF NON-PO-HAI BARBARIANS

(at close of dynasty)

Location	Units		
	Adult Males	Households	Individuals
Total (minimum)	80,000	40,000	200,000
Ordos	60,000	30,000	150,000
Total (maximum)	?	?	?

TABLE 5

LIAO POPULATION

Population Groups	Units		
	Adult Males	Households	Individuals
(1) Ch'i-tan	300,000	150,000	750,000
(2) Non-Po-hai Barbarians (minimum)	80,000	40,000	200,000
(3) Chinese (minimum)	960,000	480,000	2,400,000
(4) Po-hai	180,000	90,000	450,000
Grand Total	1,520,000	760,000	3,800,000

Nevertheless the estimates serve a necessary purpose: the size and composition of a population are primary factors in its social, economic, and political configurations. The scientific value of even a tentative estimate has lately been confirmed by significant attempts to determine the size of pre-Columbian populations in the Americas. Although the results differ widely,[164] they at least define the limits within which the probable population figure may reasonably be sought.

Analysis of Liao population shows an instructive unevenness. The figures are most definite for the Chinese sector of the Liao population. Although they probably underestimate the actual size of the Chinese population, they are useful for regional as well as for chronological comparisons. They tie in interestingly with corresponding figures for the population of the Chin dynasty[165] for which they are the historical starting point.

The statistics of the Po-hai are much more tentative, but comparison with another available figure may serve as a check. During the T'ang dynasty the population of the Po-hai kingdom numbered over 100,000 households.[166] In view of the losses which these unfortunate people suffered at the hands of their Liao conquerors, our estimate of 90,000 house-

holds seems quite plausible. As a group, the non-Po-hai "barbarians" remain indefinite both in number and character. The extreme caution that must be exercised in interpreting the fragmentary data on the Ch'i-tan reflects the great inadequacies of all numerical information on the tribes of Inner Asia during this period.

Our figures finally invite comparison with that tribal group which gained power in Inner Asia after the decay of the Ch'i-tan, the Mongols. Maisky places their total number at the time of their greatest prosperity at approximately 2,500,000,[167] a figure three times as great as that suggested for the Ch'i-tan at the close of the Liao dynasty. Maisky's figure may be somewhat high and the one offered here somewhat low. But, if they are in any way indicative of the actual numerical difference between the two nomadic complexes, they confirm our belief in the different political and military weight of the two groups. They reformulate in numerical terms the divergencies in tribal economy and custom of the stockbreeders of Jehol and the steppe nomads of Mongolia.

---

[164] Kroeber 39, 164 ff. and 179.
[165] CS 24, 7a ff.
[166] TS 219, 8b–9a.

[167] Riasanovsky 37, 16.

TRANSLATION

1. TERRITORIAL DIVISIONS

1. The territorial development of Liao 2. Shang-ching Circuit 3. Entrusted territories 4. The entrusted prefectures 5. Fortified cities on the border 6. Tung-ching Circuit 7. Chung-ching Circuit 8. Nan-ching Circuit 9. Hsi-ching Circuit.

1. THE TERRITORIAL DEVELOPMENT OF LIAO

907–926 T'ai-tsu, [with the support of] the I-la tribe, replaced the Yao-lien family.[1] He built Lin-huang[2] and there established his imperial capital. In the east he annexed Po-hai,[3] securing 103 urban settlements.

[1] The tribal prehistory of Liao reached its climax in 907. Up to the time when Yeh-lü A-pao-chi 耶律阿保機, the later T'ai-tsu 太祖, made himself the permanent ruler of the Liao people, the family, or lineage, of Yao-lien had ruled the tribal confederacy of the Ch'i-tan. The power of this family faded away (LS 63, 8b) when A-pao-chi established himself and his lineage and tribe as the exclusive center of power. His personal name has various transliterations. For instance, in Chao Chih-chung's 趙志忠 *Lu T'ing Tsa Chi* 虜廷雜記 it is rendered as A-pu(布)-chi while in Li Chi's 李琪 *Chin Men Chi* 金門集 it appears as A-pao-chin (謹) in a Liang document sent to the Ch'i-tan; in many works written in the time of the Five Dynasties it is written A-pao-chi (KTL 2, 2a).

Ou-yang Hsiu 歐陽修 claims that the clan name Yeh-lü was derived from the name of the region where A-pao-chi's Horizontal Tent was established. The passage states that A-pao-chi called his family Shih-li 世里 after the name of the region of the Horizontal Tent where he lived. As the Chinese equivalent for Shih-li the translators chose Yeh-lü (WTS 72, 4b). The author of the CTKC points out that the name Shih-li refers to the region two hundred *li* east of the Supreme Capital. In a note to this passage he says, "At present there is Shih-li Mo-li. Rendered into Chinese this is expressed as Yeh-lü" (CKTC 23, 1a).

It is said that at the beginning of the Chin dynasty the Jurchen did not like to use the name Yeh-lü because it resembled the name of one of their rulers. So it was replaced by I-la 移喇 (MAC 8, 7b–8a). During both the Chin and Yüan periods the name I-la 移剌 (or 喇) was used.

The name Liu 劉, adopted for the Ch'i-tan in Sung, Chin, and Yüan writings, is said to have been somehow related to the name I-la. CKL 1, 27 states that "I-la is Liu 移剌曰劉" (*cf.* also WCTL 5, 55 and CS 135, 12b). The choice of this name, like many which were selected under similar circumstances, may be due merely to some vague phonetic resemblance.

The early location of the I-la 迭剌 tribe has already been mentioned. That of the Yao-lien clan or family is not known.

The word 迭, usually pronounced *tieh* (Giles 12, no. 11,116; Couvreur 11, 933), may also be pronounced *i* if used as a substitute for 逸 and 軼. The latter pronunciation, though apparently not proved for the T'ang period (see Karlgren 23, 880; *idem* 40, no. 402 k), is suggested for

our Liao materials by the fact that the name of A-pao-chi's clan, Yeh-lü 耶律, which was a variant of his tribe's name (Stein 39, 29, note 1), is also rendered as I-la 移剌 (LS 116, 1b ff.; CS 135, 12b). Pelliot calls the family name I-la 移 (or 亦) 剌 the well-known double of Yeh-lü (Pelliot 29, 175; *idem* 31b, 118).

[2] Lin-huang 臨潢 was the metropolitan area within which the Supreme Capital was established. It was located north of the Huang River (the modern Shira Muren) at the same place as the later Mongol city of Boro Khoton (MRC II, 81; *cf.* also Mullie 22, 149 ff. and 160 ff., and Gibert 34, 102).

[3] The first conquered state mentioned here is Po-hai 渤海. The kingdom of Po-hai was established in present Kirin in 712; it existed until 926 when it was overthrown by the Ch'i-tan. Po-hai had five capitals, fifteen administrations, and sixty-two prefectures. Its territory covered nearly the whole of present Manchuria, a part of the Ussuri region, and the northern part of Korea.

The name Po-hai goes back to the Han dynasty; it then designated a commandery (*chün* 郡), with its capital southeast of the present Ts'ang 滄 County, Hopei (*cf.* HS 28A, 26b).

The northeastern kingdom of Po-hai was originally inhabited by the Su-mo-mo-ho 粟末靺鞨; fugitives from Korea as well as Chinese formed another part of the population. The country had walled cities. Horses, beans, honey, furs, grain, linen, silk, pottery, iron, and metal wares comprised the tributes offered by its government (LS 72, 1b; *cf.* also TS 219, 7b–8a; PHKC 2, 28a; and PHKCCP *passim*). The people of Po-hai must have been engaged in a mixed economy of agriculture and stock-breeding; pottery, weaving, and metal work seem to have been developed.

The immediate cause for the final war between Liao and Po-hai is indicated in a report in LS 2, 4a, which states that in the summer of the year 924 the people of Po-hai killed the Ch'i-tan prefect of the newly established region of Liao Prefecture (now Liao-pin-t'a 遼濱塔, Liaoning). A military campaign, headed by T'ai-tsu himself, began in the twelfth Chinese month of the following year (January 926), and brought Po-hai to its end within two months. *Cf.* PHKC 3, 15a–b; Saint Denys 76, 347 ff.; Tsuda 15, 106 ff.; Gibert 34, 761 ff.; see also section XVI, 924, LS 2, 4a; 926, LS 2, 5b and 6b.

927–947   T'ai-tsung established Chin[4] and thereby got sixteen prefectures[5]—Yu, Cho, T'an, Chi, Shun, Ying, P'ing, Yü, Shuo, Yün, Ying, Hsin, Wei, Ju, Wu, and Huan.[6]   Thus [the Liao empire] covered the territory of ancient Yu, Ping, and Ying[7] and even surpassed this.   In the east Korea[8] had to pay homage.   In the west [Hsi] Hsia[9] became a subject.   In the south the Shih [family of] Chin[10] was treated as a son and the Chao [family of] Sung[11] as a brother.   Even Wu Yüeh[12] and Nan T'ang[13] sailed over the sea to pay tribute.   Oh! What prosperity!   37, 1a–b

[4] Chin 晉 is the first Chinese state mentioned in our text. After the downfall of the T'ang dynasty in 907 five short-lived "dynasties" succeeded each other within China Proper. The second, the Later T'ang 後唐, was overthrown in 936 by Shih Ching-t'ang 石敬瑭 who founded the Later Chin dynasty in Honan with the military assistance of the Ch'i-tan. This dynasty, which lasted only ten years, was completely dependent for its existence upon the aid rendered by the Ch'i-tan. Because of their military superiority the Ch'i-tan were able to appropriate the above enumerated sixteen Chinese regions.

[5] The sixteen prefectures were offered to T'ai-tsung in 938 by the ruler of Chin. Of the sixteen prefectures of Chin mentioned in our text two, namely Ying 營 and P'ing 平, had already fallen into the hands of the Ch'i-tan before 938. Another record consequently drops these two prefectures and instead gives two others, namely Ying 瀛 and Mo 莫, as belonging to the sixteen prefectures offered by Chin to Liao in 938 (LS 4, 2b).

[6] These prefectures are all located in the area of present Shansi, Chahar, and Hopei (LSTLCK 8097).

1. Yu 幽 is now Peiping 北平, Hopei.
2. Cho 涿 is now Cho 涿 County, Hopei.
3. T'an 檀 is now Mi-yün 密雲 County, Hopei.
4. Chi 薊 is now Chi 薊 County, Hopei.
5. Shun 順 is now Shun-i 順義 County, Hopei.
6. Ying 營 is now Ch'ang-li 昌黎 County, Hopei. *Cf.* preceding note.
7. P'ing 平 is now Lu-lung 盧龍 County, Hopei. *Cf.* preceding note.
8. Yü 蔚 is now Yü 蔚 County, Chahar.
9. Shuo 朔 is now Shuo 朔 County, Shansi.
10. Yün 雲 is now Ta-t'ung 大同 County, Shansi.
11. Ying 應 is now Ying 應 County, Shansi.
12. Hsin 新 is now Cho-lu 涿鹿 County, Chahar.
13. Wei 嬀 is now Huai-lai 懷來 County, Chahar.
14. Ju 儒 is now Yen-ch'ing 延慶 County, Chahar.
15. Wu 武 is now Hsüan-hua 宣化 County, Chahar.
16. Huan 寰 is now Ma-i 馬邑, Shansi.

[7] According to Chinese legendary traditions, Yu 幽, Ping 并, and Ying 營 were the northern and northeastern territories of ancient China. These three territories are supposed to have covered roughly what is now southern Manchuria, Hopei, and Shansi. In this context, Yu, Ping, and Ying are used in a literary manner, not to designate any special region, but to refer to North China in general.

[8] See I, 2 (10), no. 22.

[9] Wang Ching-ju, basing himself on an investigation of the Hsi Hsia language, claims that the term Hsi Hsia, or Western Hsia, was used by foreigners only, while the official designation was Ta Hsia 大夏, or Great Hsia (Wang CJ 32, 77–78), which was established by Li Yüan-hao 李元昊 who ruled from 1032 to 1048 (MHPT 25, 164; SS 485, 16b).

The country existed as a semi-independent state from 882, when its ruler was invested as Duke of Hsia (夏國公) by the T'ang government and honored with the imperial surname Li 李, until 1227, when it was destroyed by Chingis Khan. Its people, the Tanguts, stemmed from the Tang-hsiang 黨項, a tribal complex of Tibetan background. The name Tangut, the Mongol or early Turkic plural of the name Tang, is mentioned by Mahmūd-al-Kāshgharī, who speaks of a Tangut "country and Turkic [sic!] tribe in the neighborhood of China" (Brockelmann 28, 249). The name is also recorded by Rashīd ad-Dīn and Marco Polo (Yule, CWT III, 127 and 132; Marco Polo 03 I, 203). But it was already in existence in the fifth century (PS 96, 22a). Marco Polo found the people of Hsi Hsia engaged in agriculture rather than in trade (Marco Polo 03 I, 203). The tributes paid to the Liao government reveal that during the eleventh century their agriculture still included a large amount of stockbreeding (cf. section X). A Sung map drawn in the middle of the eleventh century described Hsi Hsia as bounded "by the Sung Empire on the south and east, by the Liao (Kitan) on the northeast, the Tartars (Tata) on the north, the Ouigour Turks (Hui-hu) on the west, and the Tibetans on the southwest" (Bushell 95/96, 144; cf. Rubruck 00, 150, Rockhill's note 2; Marco Polo 03 I, 205, note 1; Laufer 16, 2 ff.; and HKCCC 14, 1a ff.).

[10] The terms Shih Chin 石晉 and Chao Sung 趙宋 are both constructed in the same manner. Chin and Sung are the names of the Chinese dynasties with which Liao was in close contact. Shih and Chao are the names of their respective ruling houses. Formulas such as the Tudors of England, the Hohenzollerns of Prussia, and the Romanovs of Russia offer Western parallels to the Chinese usage.

[11] After the last of the Five Dynasties, Later Chou 後周, had been overthrown, the Sung 宋 dynasty controlled South and Central China and a part of North China. The "brotherly" relation of the Liao emperor towards the emperor of Sung—more exactly, the relation of a younger brother to an elder brother—was based upon a series of military victories gained by the northern state (see X, 2, note 44). It expressed itself in the heavy tributes which, after 1005, Sung had to pay to Liao year after year. For details concerning these two sets of facts see sections XVI and X.

[12] The state of Wu Yüeh 吳越 controlled the coastal regions south of the Yangtze River, including the greater part of modern Chekiang and, for a time, the northern part of Fukien. According to CKC 5, 45, Wu Yüeh was an independent country from 875 until it was absorbed by the Sung empire in 978. It recognized the suzerainty

T'ai-tsung made the imperial capital the Supreme Capital,[14] elevated Yu Prefecture to be the Southern Capital, and changed the [old] Southern Capital to be the Eastern Capital. Shêng-tsung walled the Central Capital and Hsing-tsung elevated Yün Prefecture to be the Western Capital. Thus the five capitals were complete. Furthermore, the families captured during military expeditions were used to establish prefectures in important places, which were generally named after the old residences [of the captives]. In addition, private slaves were used to establish entrusted prefectures.[15] There were altogether 5 capitals, 6 administrations, 156 prefectures, commanderies, or cities, 209 counties, 52 tribes, and 60 subordinate states.[16] In the east [their territory] reached the

of the ephemeral Five Dynasties which claimed to be the legitimate inheritors of the imperial throne. *Cf.* WTS 67, 1a–12a; Chavannes 16, 129 ff.

In general, it is assumed that Wu Yüeh used the calendar of the official Chinese dynasties. This, however, is true only in part. In the eleventh century Ou-yang Hsiu was told by the elders that Wu Yüeh had had its own reign titles, but he tried in vain to prove this fully. He did, however, discover one Wu Yüeh document bearing the reign title Pao-chêng 寶正 which he lists as the sole designation of its kind in his Genealogical Tables (WTS 71, 1a ff.). The *Chiu Kuo Chih* 九國志, written by Lu Chên 路振 (fl. 1000), mentions two other Wu Yüeh reign titles: T'ien-pao 天寶 and Pao-ta 寶大 (CKC 5, 45). Hung Mai 洪邁 (1123–1202), who found the same three titles and no others on various inscriptions, concludes that Wu Yüeh had its own calendar only during the Later Liang and T'ang periods, and that thereafter it used the official imperial calendar and, from 938 to 947, the current Liao reign title, Hui-t'ung (JCSP 5, 9b–10b). This last fact is also mentioned in CKC 5, 45. Another independent Wu Yüeh reign title, Kuang-ch'u 廣初, unfortunately cannot be dated (LTCYK 2, 117).

The adoption of a Liao reign title by the Wu Yüeh Kingdom has been established beyond doubt by the Sung scholar, Wang Hsiang-chih 王象之, who found the designation Hui-t'ung 會同 on six stone tablets of Wu Yüeh origin. Of four inscriptions located in Lin-hai 臨海 (in modern Chekiang), two, one from Ch'ing-ên 慶恩 Temple and one from Ting-kuang 定光 Temple, were dated "Hui-t'ung, first year" (938); two others, one from Ming-chih 明智 Temple and one from Ming-ên 明恩 Temple, bore the Hui-t'ung date without the year number (YTCS 12, 27a; YTPCM 1, 15). An inscription of the Chên-ju 眞如 Temple of I-wu 義烏 (modern Chekiang) and one found in Fu-chou 福州 (modern Fukien) were dated "Hui-t'ung, tenth year" (YTCS 128, 19b; YTPCM 1, 18 and 3, 76). In the first four cases, the reign title Hui-t'ung is preceded by the words Shih Chin 石晉, manifestly referring to the Later Chin dynasty.

Wang Hsiang-chih and Ch'ien Ta-hsin who follows him (SCCYHL 16, 8b) both note the fact that Wu Yüeh had the Liao designation after the defeat of Later Chin in 947 but they fail to comment on its earlier use in 938. The political history of the period, however, leaves no doubt as to the fact or the reason for this earlier use. The Later Chin government officially admitted its submission to Liao, thus also setting a pattern for countries that finally accepted the sovereignty of Chin. The Later Chin court had its own calendar, but it is not impossible that on certain solemn occasions it chose to employ a mixed

formula, such as Shih Chin, Hui-t'ung, in order to please the mighty Ch'i-tan ruler. The existence of such a formula within the domain of Later Chin would make its use in Wu Yüeh more easily understandable.

[13] Nan T'ang 南唐 became independent after 935 and claimed imperial status from 937 to 975. It had its capital at present Nanking and controlled Kiangsu, Anhui, Fukien, and Kiangsi. The diplomatic relations between Liao and Nan T'ang were very close. According to the *Liao Shih*, Nan T'ang sent envoys to Liao who paid tribute and informed the northern court about the political and military activities of Later T'ang and Chin. The second emperor of Later T'ang, Ming-tsung, openly accused Nan T'ang for its secret intercourse with the Ch'i-tan. Diplomatically, the Liao and Nan T'ang rulers called each other brother (HTS 69, 596), a designation which raised the status of the southern state above that of the Chin court.

[14] The present location of this and other places is given in the notes accompanying the next paragraph. The names of the five capitals indicate their relative geographic position. The northern capital is not called *pei ching* 北京 but *shang ching* 上京, the Supreme or Imperial Capital. The name indicates the military and political key position held by the territory of the Supreme Capital.

[15] See I, 1 (3) and note.

[16] The figures recorded here for the most part do not agree exactly with those obtained by a check of the more detailed material given in this section. Thus the number of subordinate states listed is actually seventy-eight. For the number of Ch'i-tan tribes see I, 2, note 24. The following is the checked summary of the geographical subdivisions of the five circuits into which Liao was divided:

Region	administrations	prefectures	commanderies	cities	counties
Shang-ching Circuit		32		5	30
Tung-ching Circuit	6	79		2	80
Chung-ching Circuit	1	22	1		42
Nan-ching Circuit		9			32
Hsi-ching Circuit		15	2		35
		157	3	7	
Total	7		167		219

The administrations of the above table are not identical with the metropolitan administrations, of which there were five. They were instead, under Liao, minor administrative units approximating the status of a prefecture. See introduction.

ocean. In the west it reached the Golden Mountains[17] and also the Flowing Sands.[18] In the north, it reached the Lu-chü River.[19] In the south it reached the Pai-kou [River[20]]. The whole territory covered ten thousand *li*.[21]   37, 2a

2. SHANG–CHING CIRCUIT[22]

REGION	NO. OF HOUSE-HOLDS	MODERN GEOGRAPHICAL EQUIVALENT[23]	REMARKS[24]
Supreme Capital 上京 (Lin-huang 臨潢 Administration)[25]	36,500	Boro Khoton, Jehol (*cf.* also Mullie 22, 162)	Height of outer city walls 20 feet; of (inner) Imperial City 30 feet. Area of entire city 27 *li*. For detailed description see XI (5)
Lin-huang[26] 臨潢 County	3,500	Same	Sedentary population: mostly Chinese captured by T'ai-tsu in Yen 燕 and Chi 薊. Good soil for agriculture
Ch'ang-t'ai 長泰 County	4,000	Northwest of Boro Khoton (LS 37, 3a)	Po-hai and Chinese. Matsui locates this place north of the capital (MRC II, 85)
Ting-pa 定霸 County	2,000	West of Boro Khoton (LS 37, 3a)	Po-hai and Chinese peasants. Good soil. Attached to Empress Dowager Ying-t'ien's ordo

[17] The Golden Mountains (Chin Shan 金山) are the Altai Mountains northwest of Outer Mongolia and most probably their southeastern continuation, called also Ek-Tagh, in northwestern Outer Mongolia.

[18] The Flowing Sands (流沙) are the Gobi Desert.

[19] The present Kerulen River in the northeastern part of Outer Mongolia.

[20] Li Shên-ju states that the old Pai-kou 白溝 River is identical with the present Chü-ma 拒馬 River. The source of this river is about two hundred *li* south of modern Peiping. It receives the waters of several other rivers and discharges into the ocean east of Tientsin (*cf.* LSTLCK 8097). A northern tributary of the Chü-ma River still bears the old name Pai-kou River.

[21] The borders of the Liao empire were less stable than this description implies. That they spread at times far to the west and the east is certain. The Sung delegation which in 981 arrived at Kao-ch'ang in Eastern Turkestan by way of Kan Prefecture traveled along the western Liao frontier (SS 490, 9a). The construction and occupation of fortified cities in the region of the Orkhon and Kerulen Rivers (*cf.* I, 1 (5); see also XV, 1 (51) and Fêng CS 37, 51 ff.) indicates the empire's northern border. A Korean request for land held by the Liao government and located east of the Yalu River (XVI, 1078, LS 23, 6b) marks the country's eastern extension during the later part of the eleventh century. The figure "ten thousand" must not be pressed; evidently it is used to indicate a number of thousands. The distance between the extreme north-eastern corner of the Liao empire and the westernmost border stations may have been around five thousand *li* (less than two thousand miles).

[22] Shang-ching Circuit (上京道) touched the Ying-chin 英金 River in the south, extended to the mouth of the Sungari River in the east, included a part of Outer Mongolia in the west, and reached southern Heilungkiang in the north.

The names of the following geographical units in Shang-

ching and the population figures are taken from LS 37, 2a–11b.

In this and the following tables a number of geographical units are mentioned for which, in order to avoid repetition, no characters are given. These are· circuit (*tao* 道), administration (*fu* 府), prefecture (*chou* 州), commandery (*chün* 軍 or 郡), county (*hsien* 縣), city (*ch'êng* 城), and fortress (*pao* 堡).

[23] Information for this column has been derived mainly from MRC II. References are cited only for other sources from which the present geographical equivalents have been worked out. The modern equivalents given in section I, 1, and I, 2, are place names used during the later part of the imperial epoch of China or under the republic. Sometimes the Ming or Ch'ing identifications worked out by our references have undergone changes in recent years, a new designation either replacing the old one or occurring together with it. But the newest official names of many Chinese cities and towns are often unfamiliar even to Chinese. We therefore indicate only the most familiar designations, leaving to the student interested in topographical detail of this kind the task of tracing the most recent terminological developments.

[24] Wherever possible we state first what peoples inhabit the various geographical areas. Unless otherwise noted the information on the population of these regions, as well as other data, is obtained from the *Liao Shih* passage in which the region is discussed.

[25] In the tables for Shang-ching and other circuits the regions directly controlled by the capital of the circuit are given first. The areas over which the capital "had jurisdiction" follow. Indentation indicates the administrative subordination of the various geographical units.

[26] LS 37, 3a says that "the land was fit for cultivation." For a literal translation and detailed discussion of the texts concerning this and a number of other counties in Shang-ching Circuit see Mullie 22, 119 ff., 135 ff., 149, 166 ff., 177 ff., and 207 ff.

Shang-ching Circuit (*continued*)

REGION	No. of HOUSE-HOLDS	MODERN GEOGRAPHICAL EQUIVALENT	REMARKS
Pao-ho 保和 County	4,000	South of Boro Khoton (LS 37, 3a)	Po-hai and other people. Attached to Ching-tsung's ordo
Lu 潞 County	3,000	East of Boro Khoton (LS 37, 3b)	Chinese and Po-hai. Attached to Empress Dowager Ch'êng-t'ien's ordo
I-su 易俗 County	1,000	North of Boro Khoton (LS 37, 3b)	Po-hai (defeated rebels)
Ch'ien-liao 遷遼 County	1,000	Northeast of Boro Khoton (LS 37, 3b)	Po-hai rebels transplanted here after their defeat
Po-hai 渤海 County			Rebellious Po-hai
Hsing-jên 興仁 County		East of Boro Khoton	Established 1013
Hsüan-hua 宣化 County	4,000	South of Boro Khoton (LS 37, 4a)	Possibly Koreans and Po-hai.[27] Attached to Ching-tsung's ordo
Tsu Prefecture 祖		Monchok Ola, 40 li west of Boro Khoton (Torii 41, 193–201; cf. also Mullie 22, 142)	Birthplace of several ancestors of Yeh-lü family. T'ai-tsu's autumn hunting grounds. T'ai-tsu's mausoleum and temple. Attached to T'ai-tsu's ordo. City walls 20 feet high; area 9 li. Silk brocade shop. See III (26)
Ch'ang-pa 長霸 County	2,000	East of Tsu Prefecture	Po-hai
Hsien-ning 咸寧 County	1,000	West of Tsu Prefecture	Po-hai
Yüeh-wang 越王 City	1,000	20 li southeast of Tsu Prefecture (LS 37, 6b)	Tang-hsiang and T'u-hun captured by T'ai-tsu's uncle
Huai 懷 Prefecture		Southeast of Boro Khoton	Partly Po-hai captured by T'ai-tsu, partly Chinese captured by T'ai-tsung. Attached to T'ai-tsung's ordo. T'ai-tsung's and Mu-tsung's mausoleums located here
Fu-yü 扶餘 County	1,500	Same	Po-hai
Hsien-li 顯理 County	1,000	Not clearly defined	Mainly captive Po-hai
Ch'ing 慶 Prefecture	3,000	Tsaghan Khoton, Jehol	Barbarians[28] and Chinese. Attached to Shêng-tsung's ordo. Shêng-tsung's, Hsing-tsung's, and Tao-tsung's mausoleums located here (cf. Mullie 33, 3 ff.; Torii 36 III, Foreword). A very mountainous and inaccessible landscape. Liao treasures stored here (CS 24, 10b). Ruins called Pai-t'a-tzǔ 白塔子 (Gibert 34, 499)
Hsüan-tê 玄德 County	6,000	Same	Mainly freed bondsmen (落帳人戶) from various camps

[27] According to LS 37, 3b, the population was transplanted from Yalu Administration (鴨淥府) of Po-hai by T'ai-tsu. Yalu Administration corresponds to Lin-chiang 臨江 County, Liaoning (MRC I, 416). This was the location of one of the capitals of Kao-chü-li (see I, 2 (10), no. 22) just before Po-hai came into being. Hence the population may have comprised Koreans and Po-hai.

[28] See introduction.

Shang-ching Circuit (*continued*)

REGION	No. of HOUSE-HOLDS	MODERN GEOGRAPHICAL EQUIVALENT	REMARKS
Hsiao-an 孝安 County		Southwest of Tsaghan Kho-ton (Gibert 34, 237; Mullie 22, 214)	Ruins indicate city of large size; Chinese called it *ta ch'êng* 大城, "the big city" (Gibert 34, 238)
Fu-i 富義 County		North of Lin-hsi 林西 County (Gibert 34, 169)	Mainly Po-hai. Attached to T'ai-tsu's ordo. Gibert 34, 169 says ruins are called Ssǔ-fang 四方 City. See also Mullie 22, 215
T'ai 泰 Prefecture		Southwest of modern Nung-an 農安 County, Kirin	Former grazing ground of the 20 Ch'i-tan tribes. Attached to Hsing-tsung's ordo
Lo-k'ang 樂康 County		Same	
Hsing-kuo 興國 County	700	Exact location unknown	Convicts deported from territory south of the Great Wall
Ch'ang-ch'un 長春 Prefecture		Northwest of Po-tu-na 伯都訥, Kirin	Liao emperors used to hunt here during spring. Attached to Hsing-tsung's ordo
Ch'ang-ch'un 長春 County	2,000	Same	Convicts deported from Yen 燕 and Chi 薊
Wu 烏 Prefecture		140 *li* northwest of Aro Khorchin (LSTLCK 8100)	Built by a Ch'i-tan chieftain. Wu-wan River and Mountain refer to former Wu-wan tribe (part of Tung-hu people). Attached to Shêng-tsung's ordo
Ai-min 愛民 County	1,000	Same	Chinese captives
Yung 永 Prefecture		Near Shira Muren and Lao-ha River	Region of Mu-yeh Mountain. Liao emperors camped here during winter. Attached to Ching-tsung's ordo
Ch'ang-ning 長寧 County	4,500	Same	Po-hai captives
I-fêng 義豐 County	1,500	100 *li* west of seat of Yung Prefecture	Mainly Po-hai
Tz'ǔ-jên 慈仁 County	400	Location not clear	First established as a prefecture. In 1032 changed to a county
I-k'un 儀坤 Prefecture		Between Boro Khoton and Shira Muren	Birthplace of Ying-t'ien, T'ai-tsu's wife, whose ancestors lived here for four generations. Attached to her ordo
Kuang-i 廣義 County	2,500	Same	Former Uighur grazing ground (LS 37, 10a–b)
Lung-hua 龍化 Prefecture		Between the Shira Muren and Lao-ha River, Jehol	Chinese and several hundred Jurchen. First legendary Ch'i-tan ancestors dwelt here. Attached to Ching-tsung's ordo
Lung-hua 龍化 County	1,000	Same	Established by T'ai-tsu with Chinese and Jurchen war prisoners
Chiang-shêng 降聖 Prefecture		Probably 50 *li* west of Lung-hua Prefecture	T'ai-tsung's birthplace. No wood could be cut and no cattle grazed within 30 *li* of city. First attached to Mu-tsung's, later to Ching-tsung's ordo
Yung-an 永安 County	800	Same	Po-hai captives

Shang-ching Circuit (*continued*)

Region	No. of House-holds	Modern Geographical Equivalent	Remarks
Jao 饒 Prefecture		On upper reaches of Shira Muren	Built on site of Sung-mo Prefecture 松漠州 of T'ang. Attached to Hsing-tsung's ordo
Ch'ang-lo 長樂 County	4,000	Same	Po-hai. City built by T'ai-tsu. 1,000 house-holds "offered iron"
Lin-ho 臨河 County	1,000	Near Shira Muren (LS 37, 11b)	Po-hai
An-min 安民 County	1,000	Near Lin-hsi 林西 County, Jehol (Mullie 22, 127)	Po-hai captives

3. ENTRUSTED TERRITORIES

The entrusted commandery-prefectures[29] were all prefectures and counties which princes, relatives of the consort family, high officials, and tribes set up in order to settle in groups the captives whom they had captured on military campaigns or the slaves whom they had made. Princes of the Horizontal Tents,[30] Imperial Maternal Uncles, and princesses were permitted to establish prefectural cities. Others were forbidden to build cities. The imperial court gave names to the prefectures and counties. Their commanding prefects were appointed by the imperial court; positions from the prefects[31] down were all filled by the retainers[32] of the respective lords. The taxes paid by officials

[29] *T'ou-hsia* 投下 or 頭下 is evidently the transcription of a Ch'i-tan term related to the Mongol noun *tüši-yä* (support) derived from the verbal stem *tüši-*, meaning "to rely on, to trust." The term is frequently found in the *Liao Shih* as the initial component before such expressions as commandery, prefecture, commandery-prefecture, or prefecture-commandery. These synonymous expressions, which designate areas of military importance, when preceded by *t'ou-hsia* as an initial component refer to "entrusted" territories. It is evident that we are here dealing with a kind of fief.

LS 37, 11b–13b lists sixteen such areas; CTKC 22, 2b lists twenty-three. These might be handed over to the government and thus become ordinary prefectures either because of a break in the ruling line or because of disloyalty to the government. Hence we find in the geographical section of the *Liao Shih* many prefectures which were originally entrusted prefectures. The following are a few examples:

Kuei-tê 貴德 Prefecture, established by Ch'a-ko 察割 (LS 38, 9b),

Sui 遂 Prefecture, established by Yeh-lü P'o-tê 頗德 (LS 38, 11b),

Shuang 雙 Prefecture, established by Ou-li-sêng 漚里僧 (LS 38, 12a).

The system of entrusted territories was followed by the Mongols, the entrusted areas being called simply *t'ou-hsia*. In 1226 ten *t'ou-hsia* were bestowed upon the same number of high dignitaries (YS 119, 9a). The head official of the *t'ou-hsia*, called *darughatchi* 達魯花赤, was replaced every three years. Mongols were eligible for this position; Chinese were absolutely excluded (*cf.* YTC 9, 9a–16b). For a detailed discussion of the *t'ou-hsia* system see Ch'ên S 39, 387 ff.

[30] The term Horizontal Tents (*hêng chang* 橫帳) designates the descendants of T'ai-tsu alone. According to the Ch'i-tan custom, the tents of this group faced the east; they were therefore named "horizontal." The tents of the Yao-lien family faced the south; those of the senior princes of the collateral line of the imperial family looked northward (LS 45, 20a; Inaba 32, 113 ff.). For more details see section VII.

The specific mention of "princes of the Horizontal Tents, Imperial Maternal Uncles, and princesses" apart from the princes and the relatives of the consort family, who are referred to in the first sentence, is rather difficult to explain. Presumably we are to understand that the first sentence lists all the groups which might possibly set up entrusted prefectures, while the second sentence may mean that in the main only the princes of the Horizontal Tents, Imperial Maternal Uncles, and princesses were permitted to do so. Reference to the list of entrusted prefectures (see below) shows that they were set up almost entirely by members of the latter group. In a few cases, toward the end of the list, entrusted prefectures were set up by individuals not belonging to this group. There is even a case of a Chinese, Han K'uang-ssǔ 韓匡嗣, who was given a princely rank and permitted to establish an entrusted prefecture (LS 13, 2b).

[31] The ranks of the prefects in descending order were commanding prefect (節度使), supervisory prefect (觀察使), defense prefect (防禦使), trainband prefect (團練使), and prefect (刺使). These ranks were each subdivided into three classes (上, 中, 下). The rank and class of the official in charge of the prefecture was determined by the political and economic importance of his territory. See XIV, introduction and XIV, 2 (9). *Cf.* also Des Rotours 27.

from the ninth rank down and by the city merchants went to the respective entrusted [commandery]. Only the wine tax was handed over to the Salt and Iron Office of the Supreme Capital.   37, 11b–12a

4. THE ENTRUSTED PREFECTURES[33]

PREFECTURE	No. of HOUSE-HOLDS	MODERN GEOGRAPHICAL EQUIVALENT	REMARKS
Hui 徽	10,000	Near Fou-hsin 阜新 County, Liaoning	City established by Ching-tsung's daughter with her bondsmen. 700 *li* south of Supreme Capital
Ch'êng 成	4,000	North of I 義 County, Liaoning	City built by Shêng-tsung's daughter. Populated by her personal bondsmen. 740 *li* south of Supreme Capital
I 懿	4,000	10 *li* south of Chang-wu 彰武 County, Liaoning (Gibert 34, 353)	City built by another daughter of Shêng-tsung with her bondsmen. 800 *li* southeast of Supreme Capital
Wei 渭	1,000	Southwest of Chang-wu County, Liaoning	Set up by Hsiao Chang-i, the husband of Shêng-tsung's niece, with her personal bondsmen
Hao 壕	6,000	Southwest of Chang-wu County, Liaoning	City built with Chinese captives by a distinguished member of a lineage of the Maternal Uncles. 720 *li* southeast of Supreme Capital
Yüan 原	500	North of Pei-chên 北鎮, Liaoning	City set up with Chinese captives by a member of a lineage of the Maternal Uncles. 800 *li* southeast of Supreme Capital
Fu 福	300	North of Yüan 原 Prefecture	City built with Chinese captives by a member of the lineage of the Maternal Uncles. 780 *li* southeast of Supreme Capital
Hêng 橫	200	90 *li* northwest of Liao-pin-t'a 遼濱塔, Liaoning	City built and settled by herdsmen under Hsiao K'o-chung, another member of a lineage of the Maternal Uncles. 720 *li* southeast of Supreme Capital
Fêng 鳳	4,000	North of Liao-yüan 遼源, Liaoning	Probably Po-hai and Ch'i-tan. Special land of the Five Tents of the Administration of a Southern King. 900 *li* southeast of Supreme Capital
Sui 遂	500	Southwest of K'ang-p'ing 康平 County, Liaoning	The same Five Tents grazed their herds here. 1000 *li* southeast of Supreme Capital
Fêng 豐	500	Near Shira Muren and Tsaghan Muren, Jehol	Grazing grounds of a member of the Yao-lien family. 350 *li* south of Supreme Capital
Shun 順	1,000	120 *li* northeast of Pei-chên County, Liaoning	Established with Chinese captives by the Administration of a Southern King of the Horizontal Tents. 900 *li* southeast of Supreme Capital

[32] According to special studies undertaken by Ho SC (27, 123–162) and Yang CI (35, 97–107), *pu-ch'ü* 部曲 was originally a kind of a military organization and then became a common term for officers and soldiers. Later *pu-ch'ü* came to mean the private attendants or servants of noble families. During the seventh, eighth, and ninth centuries their position became practically that of bonds-men. Under the Liao dynasty they still seem to have been unfree persons, but of a somewhat higher status. They might replace their masters in rendering services at the court (XI (20)).

[33] The information for the entrusted prefectures is taken from LS 37, 11b–13b.

Entrusted Prefectures (*continued*)

PREFECTURE	NO. OF HOUSE-HOLDS	MODERN GEOGRAPHICAL EQUIVALENT	REMARKS
Lü 閭	1,000	North of Hei-shan 黑山 County, Liaoning	Grazing grounds of Prince Lo-ku 羅古王, about whom no details are known. 950 *li* southeast of Supreme Capital
Sung-shan 松山	500	170 *li* south of Supreme Capital (LS 37, 13*b*)	Grazing grounds of a prince of the Horizontal Tents
Yü 豫	500	North of Lin-tung 林東, Jehol (Gibert 34, 991)	Grazing grounds of another prince of the same lineage. 300 *li* north of Supreme Capital
Ning 寧	300	Northwest of Lu-pei 魯北 County, Jehol (Gibert 34, 671)	Grazing grounds of a prince of the Horizontal Tents. 350 *li* northeast of Supreme Capital

5. FORTIFIED CITIES ON THE BORDER

Border defence cities on the northwestern[34] frontier of the Liao empire were established for the military garrisons. Care was taken to utilize strategic positions.[35] They were not subject to the payment of the poll tax.   37, 13*b*

FORTIFIED CITY[36]	LOCATION	REMARKS
Ching 靜 Prefecture	Probably east of T'ao-nan 洮南 County, Liaoning (Mikami 37, map)	
Chên 鎮 Prefecture	Over 3,000 *li* northwest of Supreme Capital. Located on Orkhon River (LSTLCK 8104)	On guard particularly against Shih-wei, Yü-chüeh, and other countries. 700 Po-hai, Jurchen, Chinese, and banished families were settled here as colonists. More than 20,000 tribesmen
Wei 維 Prefecture	Same	Subdistrict of Chên Prefecture or region controlled by the latter
Fang 防 Prefecture	Same	
Ho-tung City 河董城[37]	1,700 *li* northwest of Supreme Capital (LS 37, 14*a*)	Jurchen settlers
Ching-pien 靜邊 City	1,500 *li* northwest of Supreme Capital (LS 37, 14*b*)	Former pastures of the "20 Ch'i-tan tribes" (LS 37, 14*b*). Now used as defence against thieving Yü-chüeh of the North
P'i-pei-ho 皮被河 City[38]	1,500 *li* northwest of Supreme Capital (LS 37, 14*b*)	
Chao 招 Prefecture	Location not clear	Established with Jurchen families
T'a-lan-chu 塔懶主 City	On Kerulen River (LS 37, 14*b*)	Established 1083

[34] This qualification is valid for all fortified cities, which can be topographically defined, except for the first. Ching Prefecture was probably not located on the northern or western border but in the northeastern corner of the empire.

[35] We follow the Palace edition in reading 形 for the 刑 of our text.

[36] The list of fortified cities is given in LS 37, 14*a–b*. Population figures are recorded for Chên Prefecture.

[37] According to the *Liao Shih*, Ho-tung City was the old Uighur K'o-tun 可敦 City, which had fallen into decay but had been restored for military purposes by the Ch'i-tan. A troublesome Jurchen tribe was transplanted and settled there (LS 37, 14*a*). Matsui endeavors to show that this city was also located on the Orkhon River (Matsui 15, 295 ff.). His assumption is contradicted by the text of the *Liao Shih* which locates the place only 1,700 *li* from the Supreme Capital, that is more or less midway between the Supreme Capital and the Orkhon River

[38] It is difficult to give exactly the present locations of Ho-tung City, Ching-pien City, and P'i-pei-ho City Matsui tries to locate them all along the Orkhon River

6. TUNG–CHING CIRCUIT [39]

REGION	No. OF HOUSE-HOLDS	MODERN GEOGRAPHICAL EQUIVALENT	REMARKS
Eastern Capital (Liao-yang 遼陽 Administration)[40]	40,604	Liao-yang County, Liaoning	City wall 30 feet high. Area of city 30 *li*
Liao-yang 遼陽 County	1,500	Same	Po-hai
Hsien-hsiang 仙鄉 County	1,500	60 *li* west of Hai-ch'êng 海城 County, Liaoning (LSTLCK 8107)	
Ho-yeh 鶴野 County	1,200	80 *li* southwest of Liao-yang County (*loc. cit.*)	
Hsi-mu 析木 County	1,000	40 *li* southeast of Hai-ch'êng County, Liaoning (*loc. cit.*)	
Tzǔ-mêng 紫蒙 County	1,000	East of Liao-yang County (*loc. cit.*)	
Hsing-liao 興遼 County	1,000	South of Kai-p'ing 蓋平 County, Liaoning (*loc. cit.*)	
Su-shên 肅慎 County		Near Liao-yang County (*loc. cit.*)	Po-hai
Kuei-jên 歸仁 County			
Shun-hua 順化 County			
K'ai 開 Prefecture	1,000	Near Fêng 鳳 City. In the southeastern corner of Liaoning	Area 20 *li*. Abolished by T'ai-tsu. Later rebuilt
K'ai-yüan 開遠 County	1,000	Same	Same
Yen 鹽 Prefecture	300	140 *li* northwest of K'ai Prefecture (LS 48, 4*b*)	Four former Po-hai counties abolished. Only 300 families left
Mu 穆 Prefecture	300	Southeast of Hsiu-yen 岫巖 County, Liaoning	Also four Po-hai counties abolished
Hui-nung 會農 County			
Ho 賀 Prefecture	300	In Hamkyung Province 咸鏡道, Korea (LSTLCK 8108)	Four former counties abolished.

(Matsui 15, 295 ff.). The distance between the Supreme Capital and these cities is, however, clearly stated as follows:

Ho-tung City	1,700
Ching-pien City	1,500
P'i-pei-ho City	1,500 (LS 37, 14*a* ff.).

Evidently these cities were much nearer to the Supreme Capital. The order in which they are discussed in LS 37 is from the farthest, Chên Prefecture, to the nearest, P'i-pei-ho City, or from west to east. Hence the three cities in question must have been located between present Boro Khoton and the Orkhon River, possibly in the region of the Kerulen River. *Cf.* also LSTLCK 8104.

This assumption is confirmed by a statement made in LS 37, 14*b*, according to which Ho-tung City was on the Lu-chü River, that is the Kerulen River of today.

[39] The area of Tung-ching Circuit (東京道) covered nearly the whole of modern Kirin and Liaoning plus a fraction of Heilungkiang and Korea.

The names of the geographical units in Tung-ching and such population figures as are given are taken from LS 38.

[40] LS 37, 3*a* says that it "had jurisdiction over eighty-seven prefectures, administrations, and cities and controlled nine counties."

Tung-ching Circuit (*continued*)

Region	No. of House-holds	Modern Geographical Equivalent	Remarks
Ting 定 Prefecture		Chongp'yong 定平 of Hamkyung Province (Tsuda 13 II, 98)	Settled with people from west of the Liao River (Liao-ho). Possibly mainly Ch'i-tan, Hsi, and Chinese, obviously because of the exposed situation of this easternmost military outpost
Ting-tung 定東 County	800		
Pao 保 Prefecture		Wiju 義州, Korea	Territory taken from Korea by Liao in 1014. Government controlled market
Lai-yüan 來遠 County	1,000		First settled with people from Liao-hsi; later 700 Chinese and Hsi soldiers settled as garrison
Hsüan 宣 Prefecture		Sönch'ön 宣川 of Northern P'yongan Province 平安北道, Korea (Tsuda 13 II, 37–38)	In 1014 Liao settled Chinese families here
Huai-hua 懷化 Commandery		Near Wiju, Korea	The region's chief official, a third class prefect (下刺史), indicates that this commandery was equal in importance only to a small county or prefecture
Ch'ên 辰 Prefecture	2,000	Kai-p'ing 蓋平 County, Liaoning	Original population deported by Liao to Tsu Prefecture
Chien-an 建安 County			
Lu 盧 Prefecture	300	Hsiung-yüeh City 熊岳城, Liaoning	Five old counties abolished
Hsiung-yüeh 熊岳 County			
Lai-yüan 來遠 City		On Kimchong 黔定 Island in the Yalu River	Old population of Civilized Jurchen. Later Chinese soldiers settled as garrison
T'ieh 鐵 Prefecture	1,000	T'ang-ch'ih Fortress 湯池堡, Liaoning	Four Po-hai counties abolished
T'ang-ch'ih 湯池 County			
Hsing 興 Prefecture	200	I-lu 懿路, Liaoning	Three old counties abolished
T'ang 湯 Prefecture	500	Near Liao-chung 遼中 County, Liaoning	Five old counties abolished
Ch'ung 崇 Prefecture	500	Southeast of Mukden 瀋陽, Liaoning	Three old counties abolished
Ch'ung-hsin 崇信 County			
Hai 海 Prefecture	1,500	Hai-ch'êng 海城 County, Liaoning	Old Southern Capital of Po-hai. Area 9 *li*. Three prefectures with six counties abolished. After the rebellion of 1029 (see XIII) the entire population deported to Shang-ching Circuit. Replaced by colonists from Tsê 澤 County, Chung-ching Circuit
Lin-min 臨溟 County			

Tung-ching Circuit (*continued*)

REGION	No. of HOUSE-HOLDS	MODERN GEOGRAPHICAL EQUIVALENT	REMARKS
Yao 耀 Prefecture	700	Yao-chou Khoton 耀州和屯, 60 *li* southwest of Hai-ch'êng County, Liaoning (LSTLCK 8110)	Five old counties abolished
Yen-yüan 巖淵 County			
Pin 嬪 Prefecture	500	Northwest of Hai-ch'êng County (*loc. cit.*)	Five old counties abolished
Lu 淥 Prefecture	2,000	Lin-chiang 臨江 County, Liaoning	Former Western Capital of Po-hai. City wall 30 feet high. Area 20 *li*. Four old prefectures with three counties abolished. Remainder of population deported to Shang-ching Circuit after rebellion of 1029
Hung-wên 弘聞 County			
Shên-hsiang 神鄉 County			
Huan 桓 Prefecture	700	90 *li* northwest of T'ung-kou 洞溝 in Chi-an 輯安 County, Liaoning	Old Kao-chü-li capital, Hwanto 丸都 (Gibert 34, 304)
Fêng 豐 Prefecture	300	Near the upper course of Sungari River	Four old counties abolished
Chêng 正 Prefecture	500	East of Ying-ê-pien-mên 英額邊門, Liaoning	
Tung-na 東那 County		70 *li* west of Chêng Prefecture	
Mu 慕 Prefecture	200	Near Liu-ho 柳河 County, Liaoning	Two old counties abolished early
Hsien 顯 Prefecture	300	Pei-chên 北鎮 County, Liaoning (LSTLCK 8110)	In 947, 300 households were moved here from the Eastern Capital to serve the mausoleum of Prince Jên-huang, T'ai-tsu's eldest son. Shih-tsung's mausoleum located here. Attached to Ying-t'ien's and Shih-tsung's ordos
Fêng-hsien 奉先 County		3 *li* southwest of Pei-chên County (LSTLCK 8111)	Population transferred from other counties of Liao-tung in 947. Attached to Ying-t'ien's ordo
Shan-tung 山東 County		Pei-chên County	Populated from Yung-fêng 永豐 County in Po-hai. Attached to Shih-tsung's ordo
Kuei-i 歸義 County		Northeast of Pei-chên County	Attached to Ying-t'ien's ordo
Chia 嘉 Prefecture		Location not clear	
Liao-hsi 遼西 Prefecture		40 *li* east of I 義 County, Liaoning (LSTLCK 8111)	Attached to Ying-t'ien's ordo
Ch'ang-ch'ing 長慶 County			Population from various ordos. Established 990

Tung-ching Circuit (*continued*)

REGION	No of HOUSE-HOLDS	MODERN GEOGRAPHICAL EQUIVALENT	REMARKS
K'ang 康 Prefecture		Near Chin 錦 County, Liaoning (*loc. cit.*)	Po-hai settlers. First attached to Ying-t'ien's, then to Shih-tsung's ordo
Shuai-pin 率賓 County		Same	
Tsung 宗 Prefecture		Probably near Pei-chên County, Liaoning	Mainly Chinese. Attached to a Control Base
Hsiung-shan 熊山 County			
Ch'ien 乾 Prefecture		55 *li* southwest of Pei-chên County (*loc. cit.*)	Ching-tsung's mausoleum. Attached to his widow's ordo
Fêng-ling 奉陵 County			Ching-tsung's mausoleum built here by former bondsmen released from various camps
Yen-ch'ang 延昌 County			Population taken from Mu-tsung's ordo
Ling-shan 靈山 County			
Ssǔ-nung 司農 County			
Hai-pei 海北 Prefecture		40 *li* south of I County, Liaoning	Chinese captives
K'ai-i 開義 County		Same	
Kuei-tê 貴德 Prefecture		Southeast of T'ieh-ling 鐵嶺 County, Liaoning	Settled with Chinese captives. First fief-like, later taken over by central government. Attached to Empress Dowager Ch'êng-t'ien's ordo
Kuei-tê 貴德 County			
Fêng-tê 奉德 County			
Shên 瀋 Prefecture		Modern Mukden (Shên-yang)	9 old counties abolished. First attached to T'ai-tsung's, then to Prince Hsiao-wên's ordo
Lo-chiao 樂郊 County			
Ling-yüan 靈源 County			
Yen 巖 Prefecture		57 *li* northeast of Shih-ch'êng Mountain 石城山, northeast of Liao-yang 遼陽 County, Liaoning (LSTLCK 8112)	Originally attached to Empress Dowager Ying-t'ien's, later to Hsiao-wên's ordo
Pai-yen 白巖 County			
Chi 集 Prefecture		Fêng-chi-pao 奉集堡, southeast of Mukden	
Fêng-chi 奉集 County			
Kuang 廣 Prefecture		Chang-i-chan 彰驛站, 60 *li* southwest of Mukden	T'ai-tsu transferred Po-hai to this region. In 1018 an unknown number of Chinese were settled there
Ch'ang-i 昌義 County		Same	

Tung-ching Circuit (*continued*)

REGION	NO. OF HOUSE-HOLDS	MODERN GEOGRAPHICAL EQUIVALENT	REMARKS
Liao 遼 Prefecture		Liao-pin-t'a 遼濱塔, north-east of Hsin-min 新民 County, Liaoning	5 old prefectures with 18 counties abolished by T'ai-tsu. Attached to his wife's ordo
Liao-pin 遼濱 County			
An-ting 安定 County			
Ch'i 棋 Prefecture		Ch'ing-yün-i 慶雲驛, 50 *li* northwest of T'ieh-ling, Liaoning	Chinese captives. Attached to T'ai-tsu's ordo
Ch'ing-yün 慶雲 County			
Sui 遂 Prefecture		Near T'ieh-ling County, Liaoning	A kind of fief controlled by a member of Yeh-lü clan. Later taken over by central government because founder lacked descendants
Shan-ho 山河 County			
T'ung 通 Prefecture		Southwest of Nung-an County in northwestern Kirin	Filled with over 1,000 captured Po-hai rebels
T'ung-yüan 通遠 County			
An-yüan 安遠 County			
Kuei-jên 歸仁 County		Kuei-jên-pao 歸仁堡, Kirin (LSTLCK 8113)	
Yü-ku 漁谷 County			
Han 韓 Prefecture		Pa-mien City 八面城 in Ch'ang-t'u 昌圖 County, Liaoning	Old administrative division abolished; a new one introduced and modified again. Attached to Mu-tsung's ordo
Liu-ho 柳河 County			
Shuang 雙 Prefecture		West of T'ieh-ling County, Central Liaoning	Old administration abolished; new prefecture replenished with Chinese captives. After Po-hai rebellion completely taken over by central government. First attached to Mu-tsung's, later to Empress Dowager Ch'êng-t'ien's ordo
Shuang-ch'êng 雙城 County			
Yin 銀 Prefecture		T'ieh-ling County, Liaoning	Attached to T'ai-tsu's ordo. Silver smeltery
Yen-chin 延津 County			
Hsin-hsing 新興 County		East of T'ieh-ling County (LSTLCK 8113)	Here the Po-hai had a silver smeltery
Yung-p'ing 永平 County		Northeast of T'ieh-ling County	
T'ung 同 Prefecture		Between T'ieh-ling County and K'ai-yüan 開原 County, Liaoning	Attached to Ching-tsung's ordo

Tung-ching Circuit (*continued*)

REGION	No. of Households	Modern Geographical Equivalent	Remarks
Tung-p'ing 東平 County	300		Iron production
Yung-ch'ang 永昌 County			
Hsien 咸 Prefecture		K'ai-yüan County, north-eastern Liaoning	Terrain mountainous; hiding place for bandits
Hsien-p'ing 咸平 County			
Hsin 信 Prefecture		Near Huai-tê 懷德 County, Liaoning	Old Po-hai administration (*fu* 府) abolished. Later restored with Chinese captives
Wu-ch'ang 武昌 County	1,000		
Ting-wu 定武 County			
Pin 賓 Prefecture		Near juncture of Sungari and I-t'ung Rivers	Populated by Wu-jo 兀惹 settlers, belonging to Po-hai people
Lung 龍 Prefecture	1,000	Nung-an 農安 County, western Kirin	Chinese settlers. T'ai-tsu died here
Huang-lung 黃龍 County			
Ch'ien-min 遷民 County			
Yung-p'ing 永平 County			
I 益 Prefecture		Hsi-hsiao-ch'êng-tzŭ 西小城子, 20 *li* east of Wan-chin-t'a 萬金塔, Kirin (TSSTS 9a)	
Ching-yüan 靜遠 County			
An-yüan 安遠 Prefecture			
Wei 威 Prefecture		43 *li* south of Nung-an 農安 County, Kirin	
Ch'ing 清 Prefecture			
Yung 雍 Prefecture			
Hu 湖 Prefecture			
Ch'ang-ch'ing 長慶 County			
Po 渤 Prefecture			
Kung-chên 貢珍 County			
Ying 郢 Prefecture			
Yen-ch'ing 延慶 County			

Tung-ching Circuit (*continued*)

REGION	No. of HOUSE-HOLDS	MODERN GEOGRAPHICAL EQUIVALENT	REMARKS
T'ung 銅 Prefecture		Hsi-mu 析木 County, Liaoning	
Hsi-mu 析木 County			
Shu 涷 Prefecture		On Sungari River in Kirin (LSTLCK 8115)	
Shuai-pin 率賓 Administration		Corresponds to Shuang-ch'êng-tzǔ 雙城子 or Nikolsk (Voroshilov) in Ussuri Province of the Soviet Far-East	
Ting-li 定理 Administration		North of Nikolsk on shore of Ussuri	
T'ieh-li 鐵利 Administration		Near the A-lo-ch'u-k'o River 阿勒楚喀河, Kirin. *Cf.* Ikeuchi, MSK I, map.	
An-ting 安定 Administration			
Ch'ang-ling 長嶺 Administration		Modern Ch'ang-ling-tzǔ 長嶺子, southwest of Yung-chi 永吉, Kirin (LSTLCK 8115)	
Chên-hai 鎮海 Administration			
P'ing-nan 平南 County			
Chi 冀 Prefecture			
Tung 東 Prefecture			Po-hai settlers
Shang 尙 Prefecture			Same
Chi 吉 Prefecture			
Lu 麓 Prefecture			
Ching 荆 Prefecture			
I 懿 Prefecture		10 *li* south of modern Chang-wu 彰武 County, Liaoning	In 1023 a Liao princess set up the city with her bondsmen. Later taken over by the central government
Ning-ch'ang 寧昌 County		20 *li* north of I Prefecture	
Shun-an 順安 County			
Ying 媵 Prefecture			
Shun-hua 順化 City		Between Fu 復 Prefecture and Chin 金 Prefecture, Liaotung Peninsula	Set up with Chinese families in 1014
Ning 寧 Prefecture		In Liaoning. Exact location not clear	Populated by subdued Po-hai families in 1011
Hsin-an 新安 County			

Tung-ching Circuit (*continued*)

REGION	No. OF HOUSE-HOLDS	MODERN GEOGRAPHICAL EQUIVALENT	REMARKS
Yen 衍 Prefecture		Southwest of Liao-yang County	Chinese settlers
I-fêng 宜豐 County			
Lien 連 Prefecture		Liaoning. Exact location not clear	Chinese settlers
An-min 安民 County			
Kuei 歸 Prefecture		Earth fortress 90 *li* southwest of Kai-p'ing 蓋平 County, Liaoning (LSTLCK 8116)	Po-hai captives
Kuei-shêng 歸勝 County			
Su 蘇 Prefecture		Chin 金 Prefecture, Liaotung Peninsula (*loc. cit.*)	
Lai-su 來蘇 County		Same	
Huai-hua 懷化 County		East of above	
Fu 復 Prefecture		Fu 復 Prefecture, Liaotung Peninsula	
Yung-ning 永寧 County			
Tê-shêng 德勝 County			
Su 肅 Prefecture		North of K'ai-yüan 開原 County, Liaoning	Inhabitants escaped to Jurchen, but were caught and settled here again in 1041
Ch'ing-an 清安 County			
An 安 Prefecture		40 *li* north of Ch'ang-t'u 昌圖 County, Liaoning (Gibert 34, 94)	
Jung 榮 Prefecture Shuai 率 Prefecture Ho 荷 Prefecture Yüan 源 Prefecture Po-hai 渤海 Prefecture			No information exists for these five prefectures. Only their names are listed. Their location appears to have been unknown to the Yüan historiographers themselves (LSTLCK 8116)
Ning-chiang 寧江 Prefecture		Shih-t'ou-ch'êng-tzǔ 石頭城子, southeast of Po-tu-na 伯都訥, Kirin	
Hun-t'ung 混同 County			
Ho 河 Prefecture		500 *li* northeast of K'ai-yüan County, Liaoning (LSTLCK 8116)	Military arsenal
Hsiang 祥 Prefecture		North of Nung-an 農安 County, Kirin	T'ieh-li households 鐵驪戶, originally from northeastern border region
Huai-tê 懷德 County			

7. CHUNG–CHING CIRCUIT [41]

REGION	MODERN GEOGRAPHICAL EQUIVALENT	REMARKS
Central Capital (Ta-ting 大定 Administration)[42]	Tsaghan Suburghan, Jehol	Low city walls. Area "only 4 *li*" (LS 39, 5*a*; *cf*. also XI (15))
Ta-ting 大定 County	Same	Mixture of captives from different states
Ch'ang-an 長安 County	North of Tsaghan Suburghan	Mixture of people from different tribes
Fu-shu 富庶 County	Kung-ying-tzŭ 公營子 west of Ch'ao-yang 朝陽 County, Jehol	In 1013 separated from metropolitan area of Chung-ching
Ch'üan-nung 勸農 County	Northwest of P'ing-ch'üan 平泉 County, Jehol	Same
Wên-ting 文定 County	Southeast of Ch'ao-yang County, Jehol	Established 1013 with people from region of Central Capital
Shêng-p'ing 升平 County	North of Wên-ting County	Same
Kuei-hua 歸化 County	East of Ch'ao-yang County	
Shên-shui 神水 County	Southwest of I 義 County, Liaoning	Set up in 1013
Chin-yüan 金源 County	East of P'ing-ch'üan County	Part of population from region of Central Capital. Set up 1013
Ên 恩 Prefecture	60 *li* north of Tsaghan Suburghan, Jehol	Mainly Po-hai. First attached to T'ai-tsung's ordo, then taken over by Chung-ching Circuit
Ên-hua 恩化 County		
Hui 惠 Prefecture	Berke 博羅科, north of Chien-ch'ang 建昌 County, Jehol	Mainly Chinese
Hui-ho 惠和 County		Former inhabitants of Shang-ching Circuit; former bondsmen of various camps
Kao 高 Prefecture	Near juncture of Lao-ha 老哈 River and Ying-chin 英金 River, Jehol	Korean captives
San-han 三韓 County		Same. 5,000 households
Wu-an 武安 Prefecture	West of Fou-hsin 阜新 County, Jehol	Mainly Chinese
Wo-yeh 沃野 County		
Li 利 Prefecture	70 *li* northeast of Chien-ch'ang 建昌 County, Jehol	Established 1008
Fou-su 阜俗 County		First attached to Ching-tsung's ordo, then taken over by Chung-ching Circuit

[41] Chung-ching Circuit (中京道) covered most of the southern half of modern Jehol, the Great Wall constituting the southern landmark between Chung-ching Circuit and Nan-ching Circuit. The Ying-chin 英金 River formed the northern border between this territory and Shang-ching Circuit. The eastern border of Chung-ching Circuit ran parallel to the Liao River and was intersected irregularly by Tung-ching Circuit. In the west the upper Luan 灤 River constituted an irregular demarcation line between Chung-ching Circuit and Hsi-ching Circuit.

The only population figures for this circuit are for San-han County (in Kao Prefecture) which had 5,000 households (LS 39, 2*b*). The names of the geographical units are taken from LS 39.

[42] The Liao city of Ta-ting, on the left bank of the Lao-ha River, is supposed to correspond to the modern city of Ta-ning 大寧, the Mongol name of which is Tsaghan Suburghan, in Jehol (Gibert 34, 836).

Chung-ching Circuit (*continued*)

REGION	MODERN GEOGRAPHICAL EQUIVALENT	REMARKS
Yü 榆 Prefecture	Hsiao-ch'êng-tzǔ 小城子, 25 *li* north-west of Chien-ch'ang County	Hsi people and—later—Chinese prisoners of war. First held by a member of the Horizontal Tents, then taken over by central government
Ho-chung 和衆 County		
Yung-ho 永和 County		
Tsê 澤 Prefecture	North of P'ing-ch'üan 平泉 County, Jehol	Mainly Chinese. Silver mines
Shên-shan 神山 County		
Luan-ho 灤河 County		
Pei-an 北安 Prefecture	Huang-ku-t'un 皇姑屯, under control of Fêng-ning 豐寧 County, Jehol	Hsi people and—later—Chinese settlers
Li-min 利民 County[43]		
T'an 潭 Prefecture	K'o-la 喀喇 City on upper course of Ta-ling 大凌 River, Jehol	
Lung-shan 龍山 County		Established in 1013
Sung-chiang 松江 Prefecture	Southwest of Ch'ih-fêng 赤峯 County, Jehol (Gibert 34, 810)	Error for Sung-shan 松山 Prefecture (LS 48, 16*a*). Established 1013. Center of trade with the Sung-mo 松漠 region
Sung-chiang 松江 County	West of Ulān Khada, Jehol	Error for Sung-shan 松山 County (LS 13, 1*b*; 15, 6*a*; 105, 3*a*; and also CS 24, 7*b*)
Ch'êng 成 Prefecture	North of I 義 County, Liaoning	Settled with personal bondsmen of a Ch'i-tan princess
T'ung-ch'ang 同昌 County		
Hsing-chung 興中 Administration	Ch'ao-yang 朝陽 County, Jehol	Hsi people and Chinese. Originally attached to Shih-tsung's ordo, later to Shêng-tsung's
Hsing-chung 興中 County		Same
Ying-ch'iu 營丘 County		
Hsiang-lei 象雷 County	West of Ch'ao-yang County, Jehol	Established 1013
Lü-shan 閭山 County	North of Ch'ao-yang County, Jehol	Same
An-tê 安德 Prefecture	30 *li* southeast of Ch'ao-yang County	Established in 990 by separation from an adjacent county (LS 39, 6*a*)
An-tê 安德 County		

[43] The great Ch'ing antiquarian, Ch'ien Ta-hsin 錢大昕 (1727–1786), states that Li-min County was established by the Chin people as late as 1200. Therefore it cannot have been a county of Liao. Pei-an Prefecture actually controlled a county called Hsing-hua 興化 (NESKI 83, 7*b*).

Chung-ching Circuit (*continued*)

REGION	MODERN GEOGRAPHICAL EQUIVALENT	REMARKS
Ch'ien 黔 Prefecture	West of Pei-chên 北鎮 County, Liaoning	Po-hai and Chinese. First attached to T'ai-tsung's ordo, then taken over by Chung-ching Circuit
Shêng-chi 盛吉 County		
I 宜 Prefecture	Near I 義 County, Liaoning	Chinese stone embankments. Attached to Shih-tsung's ordo
Hung-chêng 弘政 County		Chinese captives, skilful weavers
Wên-i 聞義 County		
Chin 錦 Prefecture	Chin 錦 County, southwestern Liaoning	Established by T'ai-tsu with Chinese captives. Attached to T'ai-tsu's ordo
Yung-lo 永樂 County		
An-ch'ang 安昌 County		
Yen 嚴 Prefecture	On Chü-hua Island 菊花島 south of Hsing-ch'êng 興城 County, Liaoning	Chinese and Po-hai. Attached to T'ai-tsu's ordo
Hsing-ch'êng 興城 County		
Ch'uan 川 Prefecture	Ssǔ-chiao-pan 四角板, 67 *li* northeast of Ch'ao-yang County, Jehol	Established by T'ai-tsu's brother An-tuan whose son rebelled. Then district taken over by central government. Temporarily attached to the ordo of Empress Dowager Ch'êng-t'ien. Later to the "mansion" of Han Tê-jang (XV, 1 (3))
Hung-li 弘理 County		
Hsien-k'ang 咸康 County		
I-min 宜民 County		
Chien 建 Prefecture	Shifted from Wu-shih-chia-tzǔ 五十家子 south of Ch'ao-yang County, to K'o-la 喀喇 City, northwest of it	Old Chinese settlement. The imperial family of the Chin 晉 dynasty was placed here after its defeat by Liao. Prefecture first attached to Shih-tsung's, later to Hsiao-wên's ordo
Yung-pa 永霸 County		
Yung-k'ang 永康 County		
Lai 來 Prefecture	130 *li* southwest of Hsing-ch'êng 興城 County, Liaoning (LSTLCK 8122)	5 Jurchen tribes. Attached to Shih-tsung's ordo
Lai-pin 來賓 County	Same	
Hsi 隰 Prefecture	Tung-kuan-i 東關驛, Liaoning	Bondsmen from various camps. Attached to Shêng-tsung's ordo
Hai-yang 海陽 County[44]	Hai-yang-chên 海陽鎮 west of Shan-hai-kuan 山海關	See above. Considerable production of salt. This county, not Hai-pin, should be listed under Jun Prefecture

---

[44] The geographical passages of the *Liao Shih* are full of anachronisms. Often a place name used during the time of Liao is ascribed to Chin 金 and vice versa. Hai-yang County should have been listed under Jun 潤 Prefecture. Hai-pin County should have been listed under Hsi 隰 Prefecture (Fêng CS 34, 6 ff.).

Chung-ching Circuit (*continued*)

REGION	MODERN GEOGRAPHICAL EQUIVALENT	REMARKS
Ch'ien 遷 Prefecture Ch'ien-min 遷民 County	Shan-hai-kuan (LSTLCK 8122)	Po-hai captives
Jun 潤 Prefecture Hai-pin 海濱 County	West of Shan-hai-kuan In the region of Ch'ien-t'un-wei 前屯衛 of Sui-chung 綏中 County, Liaoning (Gibert 34, 203)	Po-hai captives Po-hai captives. This county, not Hai-yang, should be listed under Hsi Prefecture

8. NAN–CHING CIRCUIT [45]

REGION	NO. OF HOUSE-HOLDS	MODERN GEOGRAPHICAL EQUIVALENT	REMARKS
Southern Capital (Hsi-chin 析津 Administration)[46]		Location almost identical with that of modern Peiping	City walls 30 feet high, 15 feet wide. Area 36 *li*. Imperial palace in southwestern corner
Hsi-chin 析津 County	20,000	Ta-hsing 大興 County, Hopei	
Wan-p'ing 宛平 County	22,000	Wan-p'ing County, Hopei	
Ch'ang-p'ing 昌平 County	7,000	Ch'ang-p'ing County, Hopei	
Liang-hsiang 良鄉 County	7,000	Liang-hsiang County, Hopei	
Lu 潞 County	6,000	T'ung 通 County, Hopei	
An-tz'ŭ 安次 County	12,000	An-tz'ŭ County, Hopei	
Yung-ch'ing 永清 County	5,000	Yung-ch'ing County, Hopei	
Wu-ch'ing 武清 County	10,000	8 *li* east of Wu-ch'ing County, Hopei	
Hsiang-ho 香河 County	7,000	East of Hsiang-ho County, Hopei	Salt Monopoly Department
Yü-ho 玉河 County	1,000	Near Yü-ch'üan 玉泉 Mountain west of Peiping	

[45] Nan-ching Circuit (南京道) covered the whole of present northern Hopei. In the northwest the Great Wall was the dividing line between Nan-ching Circuit and Hsi-ching Circuit. In the south the Pai-kou 白溝 River constituted the natural borderline between Liao and Sung.

The names of the geographical units in Nan-ching and the population figures are taken from LS 40. The population in the regions of Nan-ching and Hsi-ching was almost completely Chinese. The sources of information for the location of these territories are LSTLCK and TMTTT.

[46] The Southern Capital had been the seat of the Yu Prefecture during the T'ang dynasty. It was located in what is today the southwestern part of Peiping and the suburb adjacent to it (Chu H 36, 55).

According to the findings of field work done in 1927, the southwestern corner of the Liao city wall was located at Fêng-huang-tsui 鳳凰嘴 outside Yu-an-mên 右安門; the northwestern at Huang-t'ing-tzŭ 黃亭子 outside Hsi-pien-mên 西便門; the southeastern at Ma-chia-p'u 馬家舖 outside Yung-ting-mên 永定門; and the northeastern at Hsi Ch'ang-an P'ai-lou 西長安牌樓 (Nawa 31, 514).

Nan-ching Circuit (*continued*)

Region	No. of House-holds	Modern Geographical Equivalent	Remarks
Kuo-yin 潞陰 County	5,000	45 *li* south of T'ung 通 County, Hopei	The Liao emperors used to hunt swans here
Shun 順 Prefecture		Shun-i 順義 County, Hopei	The Liao emperors built a palace here for sojourns during the spring and summer
Huai-jou 懷柔 County	5,000	Huai-jou County, Hopei	
T'an 檀 Prefecture		Mi-yün 密雲 County, Hopei	
Mi-yün 密雲 County	5,000	Same	
Hsing-t'ang 行唐 County	3,000	East of Mi-yün County	Attached to Ching-tsung's ordo
Cho 涿 Prefecture		Cho 涿 County, Hopei	
Fan-yang 范陽 County	10,000	Same	
Ku-an 固安 County	10,000	Ku-an County, Hopei	
Hsin-ch'êng 新城 County	10,000	North of Hsin-ch'êng County, Hopei	
Kuei-i 歸義 County	4,000	35 *li* northwest of Hsiung 雄 County, Hopei	
I 易 Prefecture		I County, Hopei	
I 易 County	25,000	Same	
Lai-shui 淶水 County	27,000	Lai-shui County, Hopei	
Jung-ch'êng 容城 County	5,000	North of Chü-ma 拒馬 River, Hopei	
Chi 薊 Prefecture		Chi 薊 County, Hopei	
Yü-yang 漁陽 County	4,000	Same	
San-ho 三河 County	3,000	San-ho County, Hopei	
Yü-t'ien 玉田 County	3,000	Yü-t'ien County, Hopei	
Ching 景 Prefecture	3,000	Tsun-hua 遵化 County, Hopei	
Tsun-hua 遵化		Same	
P'ing 平 Prefecture		Lu-lung 盧龍 County, Hopei	
Lu-lung 盧龍 County	7,000	Same	
An-hsi 安喜 County	5,000	30 *li* east of Ch'ien-an 遷安 County, Hopei	
Wang-tu 望都 County	3,000	South of Lu-lung County, Hopei	

Nan-ching Circuit (*continued*)

REGION	No. OF HOUSE-HOLDS	MODERN GEOGRAPHICAL EQUIVALENT	REMARKS
Luan 灤 Prefecture		Luan 灤 County, Hopei	
I-fêng 義豐 County	4,000	Modern I-fêng-shê 義豐社. 90 *li* southwest of Luan County	
Ma-ch'êng 馬城 County	3,000	South of Luan County, Hopei	
Shih-ch'êng 石城 County	3,000	Southwest of Luan County	
Ying 營 Prefecture		Ch'ang-li 昌黎 County, Hopei	
Kuang-ning 廣寧 County	3,000	Same	

9. HSI–CHING CIRCUIT [47]

REGION	No. OF HOUSE-HOLDS	MODERN GEOGRAPHICAL EQUIVALENT	REMARKS
Western Capital (Ta-t'ung 大同 Administration)[48]		Ta-t'ung 大同 County, Shansi	Made Western Capital in 1044. Area 20 *li*. Stone and bronze images of imperial ancestors of Liao
Ta-t'ung 大同 County	10,000	Same	
Yün-chung 雲中 County	10,000	Same	
T'ien-ch'êng 天成 County	5,000	20 *li* northwest of Ta-t'ung County	
Ch'ang-ch'ing 長青 County	4,000	East of Ta-t'ung County	
Fêng-i 奉義 County	3,000	North of Ta-t'ung County	
Huai-jên 懷仁 County	3,000	West of Huai-jên County, Shansi	
Huai-an 懷安 County	3,000	20 *li* east of Huai-an County, Chahar	
Hung 弘 Prefecture		Yang-yüan 陽原 County, Chahar	
Yung-ning 永寧 County	10,000	Same	

[47] Hsi-ching Circuit 西京道 included the southern part of modern Chahar, the northern part of Shansi, and nearly the whole of Suiyuan. In the north the Yin Mountains 陰山 marked the borderline. In the west the loop of the Yellow River was the barrier between Liao and Hsi Hsia.

The names of the geographical units in Hsi-ching and the population figures are taken from LS 41.

Unless otherwise noted, the data for the present geographical identifications are derived from LSTLCK and TMTTT.

[48] Ta-t'ung Administration corresponds to the present Ta-t'ung County (north Shansi). The Liao established their Western Capital here. Because of the importance of this place, the highest positions were exclusively occupied by princes or by relatives of the imperial house.

LS 41, 2a says the Western Capital "controlled two prefectures and seven counties."

Hsi-ching Circuit (*continued*)

REGION	No. OF HOUSE-HOLDS	MODERN GEOGRAPHICAL EQUIVALENT	REMARKS
Shun-shêng 順聖 County	3,000	60 *li* east of Yang-yüan County	
Tê 德 Prefecture		Northeast of Yu-yü 右玉 County, Shansi	
Hsüan-tê 宣德 County	3,000	Same	
Fêng 豐 Prefecture		20 *li* south of Kuei-hua 歸化 County, Suiyuan	Sandy soil. Little cultivable land. Large salt lake
Fu-min 富民 County	1,200	Same	
Chên-wu 振武 County		Ho-lin-ko-êrh 何林格爾, Suiyuan	First 300 soldiers as a garrison; later transformed into county
Yün-nei 雲內 Prefecture		Northwest of Urot Banner, Suiyuan	
Jou-fu 柔服 County			
Ning-jên 寧人 County			
T'ien-tê 天德 Commandery		Region of the Urot Banner	Region of the Great Walls of the Ch'in and T'ang dynasty. Commanders had to be members of the imperial family. A town gradually developed
Ning-pien 寧邊 Prefecture		Ning-pien-ho-tun 寧邊河墩 of P'ien-kuan 偏關 Shansi	
Fêng-shêng 奉聖 Prefecture		Cho-lu 涿鹿 County, Chahar	
Yung-hsing 永興 County	8,000[49]	Same	
Fan-shan 礬山 County	3,000	60 *li* southeast of Cho-lu County, Chahar	Production of white and green alum
Lung-mên 龍門 County	4,000	Near Ch'ih-ch'êng 赤城 County, Chahar	Strategical place in mountainous region difficult of access
Wang-yün 望雲 County	1,000	Ch'ih-ch'êng County, Chahar	Attached to Ching-tsung's ordo
Kuei-hua 歸化 Prefecture		Hsüan-hua 宣化 County, Chahar	Ching-tsung and Empress Dowager Ch'êng-t'ien built summer palaces here
Wên-tê 文德 County	10,000	Same	
K'o-han 可汗 Prefecture		Huai-lai 懷來 County, Chahar	The center of the Western Hsi 西奚 who fled from what is now Jehol
Huai-lai 懷來 County	3,000	Same	

[49] Our text erroneously gives the figure after the eight as 十 (ten), which makes no sense. The Palace edition corrects the figure to 千 (thousand).

Hsi-ching Circuit (*continued*)

REGION	No. OF HOUSE-HOLDS	MODERN GEOGRAPHICAL EQUIVALENT	REMARKS
Ju 儒 Prefecture		Yen-ch'ing 延慶 County, Chahar	
Chin-shan 縉山 County	5,000	Same	
Yü 蔚 Prefecture		Yü 蔚 County, Chahar	
Ling-hsien 靈仙 County	20,000	Same	
Ting-an 安定 County	10,000	Southeast of Yü County	
Fei-hu 飛狐 County[50]	5,000	Lai-yüan 淶源 County, Hopei (LTLCT)	A strategic pass
Ling-ch'iu 靈丘 County	3,000	Ling-ch'iu County, Shansi	
Kuang-ling 廣陵 County	3,000	Kuang-ling 廣靈 County, Shansi	
Ying 應 Prefecture		Ying 應 County, Shansi	
Chin-ch'êng 金城 County	8,000	Same	
Hun-yüan 渾源 County	5,000	Hun-yüan County, Shansi	
Ho-yin 河陰 County	3,000	15 *li* southwest of Shan-yin 山陰 County, Shansi	
Shuo 朔 Prefecture		Shuo 朔 County, Shansi	
Shan-yang 鄯陽 County	4,000	Same	
Ning-yüan 寧遠 County	2,000	Wu-chai 五寨 County, Shansi	
Ma-i 馬邑 County	3,000	Ma-i, Shansi	
Wu 武 Prefecture		Northeast of Shên-ch'ih 神池 County, Shansi	
Shên-wu 神武 County	5,000	Same	
Tung-shêng 東勝 Prefecture		Probably T'o-k'o-t'o 托克托, Suiyuan	
Yü-lin 榆林 County		Same	
Ho-pin 河濱 County		Probably south of T'o-k'o-t'o (LTLCT)	
Chin-su 金肅 Prefecture		Probably Sa-la-ch'i 薩拉齊 [Mongol Sarachi], Suiyuan	Established in 1043 with 300 households from Nan-ching and 1,000 soldiers
Ho-ch'ing 河清 Commandery		West of Pao-t'ou-chên 包頭鎮, Suiyuan	Established in 1043 with 500 households and 1,000 soldiers

[50] The identity of this county is not clear. LSTLCK 8134 locates it at Yeh-hu 野狐 City, 30 *li* east of I 易 County, Hopei. However, the Fei-hu Pass 飛狐口, after which Fei-hu County was named, is placed 20 *li* north of Lai-yüan County and to the west of I County. The atlas LTLCT locates Fei-hu County at Lai-yüan County. This is more reasonable.

2. TRIBES

1. Tribes and lineages   2. Tribal history   3. The four inner lineages of Liao   4. T'ai-tsu's tribes   5. Shêng-tsung's tribes   6. Outer tribes   7. Marginal dependency   8. Large tribes   9. Various tribes   10. The subordinate states

1. TRIBES AND LINEAGES

Tribes are called *pu* and lineages *tsu*.[1] According to the old custom of the Ch'i-tan they settled down by dividing the land; they lived together by combining lineages.[2] There were lineages with tribes as in the cases of the Five Divisions and the Six Divisions.[3] There were tribes with lineages as in the cases of the Hsi kings[4] and the Shih-wei.[5] There were tribes without lineages as in the

---

[1] The reader who feels bewildered by the somewhat loose and arbitrary terminology of our texts does well to remember that even modern anthropology varies widely in its definition of basic terms such as gens, clan, sib, etc. (*cf.* Lowie 20, 111; also Thurnwald 32, 22 and Linton 36, 197 ff.). The same Chinese word not infrequently involves quite different meanings according to the different objective situations described or the nomenclature of the various writers describing them. There is nevertheless a certain order in the terminological arsenal, probably due to a certain order within the defined phenomena themselves. Our text contains the terms *pu-lo* 部落, *pu* 部, *shih-tsu* 氏族, and *tsu* 族. Frequently the term *shih* 氏 occurs alone also. We furthermore find the phrases *pieh-pu* 別部, *fang* 房 (LS 67, 1a ff.), and *pu-tsu* 部族 (LS 33, 1a–b). We have disregarded, for the sake of simplicity, the historical metamorphoses of these terms. Within the *Liao Shih* they tended to have the following meanings:

(1) Kinship terms: *Tsu*—a kin group, a lineage, a proto-clan, a clan, a "family" or "house" larger than the small family (see VII, introduction). *Pu-tsu*—a lineage as part of a tribe. *Shih-tsu*—a lineage-like kinship group (emphasis on the kinship nature of the group). *Fang*—a "house," a branch (of a lineage). *Hsing* 姓—a kin group, a clan (emphasis on clan name). *Shih*—a family (emphasis on the social aspect of the phenomenon), a person of a certain family background, descent, or status; if a married woman: "née. . . ." *Chia* 家—a family (emphasis on the biological aspect, although also used as a part of compounds to describe the social status of a family).

(2) Political and territorial terms: *Pu-lo*—a tribe. *Pu*—a tribe, a group, a local group, a "band" (*cf.* Thurnwald 35, 22, 250; Linton 36, 210, 231 ff.), an administrative unit.

(3) Intermediary terms: *Pieh-pu*—a "special" *pu*, a sub-tribe, used also as an equivalent of *tsu* and *fang* (LS 67, 1a–b). *Tsu* may be used as an equivalent of *fang*. (See preceding case.) *Hu* 戶—household, the family conceived as a unit for taxation and labor and military service. *Pu-tsu*—a compound term with a wide range of meanings with the emphasis either on the kinship aspect or on the regional, non-kinship, "tribal" aspect of the phenomenon.

[2] The text is laconic and not clear. Obviously, several lineages (Stein 39, 30 translates as "families") lived together on a definite tract of pasture land assigned to them.

[3] A-pao-chi's accession to power was followed by a series of rebellions staged by leading members of his own family

and tribe (see XIII). He therefore made several important institutional changes. One of these changes was to split his own powerful I-la 迭剌 tribe into two smaller tribal units, the Five and Six Divisions (*wu yüan* 五院 and *liu yüan* 六院). A Division originally contained "one hundred" families (LS 33, 1b; 45, 5a; 116, 21b). Members of the Yeh-lü clan ruled over the two units, first as *i-li-chin* 夷離堇 (chieftains) and later as *ta-wang* 大王 (great kings). *Cf.* also VII and XIII, introductions.

[4] The Hsi 奚 people are first mentioned in the *Wei Shu* as K'u-mo-hsi 庫莫奚 (WS 100, 14a–15a). Like the Ch'i-tan 契丹 and the Shih-wei 室韋, they are supposed to be descendants of the same ancestral people, the Hsien-pei 鮮卑, whose name, according to Pelliot, was preserved in the name of the northernmost members of the group, the Shih-wei. See Pelliot 34, 35, note 3.

The K'u-mo-hsi, since the time of Sui simply called Hsi, raised livestock in great numbers. In 388, when they were defeated by the Wei, they were plundered of more than a hundred thousand horses, sheep, and pigs. The Orkhon inscriptions frequently mention the Tataby together with the Khitāy (Ch'i-tan). The Tataby are supposed to be identical with the Hsi (see Thomsen 96, 141; Radloff 97, 131 and *passim; cf.* also Barthold 97, 20; *idem* 35, 24). The T'ang armies defeated the Hsi in 847 and the Ch'i-tan subdued them in the beginning of the tenth century (TS 219, 4b–6b; WTS 74, 1a–2a; LS 2, 3b). They continued to reside south of the Ch'i-tan (see Mullie 33, 208 ff. and 223), participating in the military campaigns as well as in the frontier defence service. The rulers of the Hsi people were honored with the title of "king" (*wang* 王). It is obviously this situation to which our text refers. The Hsi represented a tribal complex (*pu* 部) headed by a ruling "family" (*tsu* 族).

[5] The Shih-wei 室 (or 失) 韋, like the Hsi, descend from the Hsien-pei whose name they possibly inherited (see preceding note). Like the Hsi they are first mentioned as an independent people in the *Wei Shu* (WS 100, 12b–13a). Their territory spread widely north of the Ch'i-tan, covering a part of modern Heilungkiang and the banks of the Khalkhin Gol in Eastern Mongolia. After an eventful tribal history they were in part subdued by their ethnical relatives, the Ch'i-tan. According to our text, the subordinated Shih-wei tribes were headed by lineages whose status is unknown.

[6] The T'ê-li-t'ê-mien 特里特勉 originated from T'ai-tsu's original eight tribes. The new group acted first as

cases of the T'ê-li-t'ê-mien,[6] Shao-wa,[7] and Ho-chu.[8]   There were lineages without a tribe as in the cases of the Nine Tents of Yao-lien and the Three Patriarchal Households of the imperial family.[9]

32, 4a

2. TRIBAL HISTORY

After the eight tribes of Ch'i-shou[10] were attacked by Korea and the Juan-juan,[11] they submitted with only ten thousand persons to the Yüan [house of Northern] Wei.[12]   They had been increasing in population for only a short time when they invaded[13] Northern Ch'i[14] but lost by capture more than a hundred thousand men and women.   Later, being pressed by the Turks,[15] they temporarily

---

a garrison against the Hsi people. Later, as the group increased, Shêng-tsung raised it to the position of a tribe (LS 33, 6a).

[7] Whereas the T'ê-li-t'ê-mien tribe was composed of free soldiers, the Shao-wa 稍瓦 and the Ho-chu 曷朮 had a more lowly origin. The Shao-wa were bondsmen ("slaves") taken from different camps of the imperial family and noble clans. *Cf.* LS 33, 6b.

[8] See preceding note. In the case of the Shao-wa as well as in that of the Ho-chu a local group set up for a special economic task evolved into a tribe. The members of all the last three tribes probably were commoners rather than nobles and therefore less *tsu*-conscious than the members of distinguished lineages. It is possible that their marriage customs made them appear *tsu*-less, at least for a certain period of time (VII, introduction).

[9] At the end of a complex tribal history the former ruling family of Yao-lien decomposed and grew weak while the unified I-la tribe became more and more powerful (LS 32, 8a). A-pao-chi then broke the hegemony of Yao-lien by splitting off its Nine Tents. He also detached the families of the Three Patriarchal Households who, like himself, belonged to the Yeh-lü kin group (LS 32, 4b). In both cases he separated the ruling lineages from their former tribes and made them noble houses without tribal power. They now were indeed lineages (*tsu*) without a tribe (*pu*).

[10] The chronological position of Ch'i-shou 奇首, the legendary first ancestor of the Ch'i-tan people, is as nebulous as his actual historical position. Some legends claim that he lived during the time of Ch'in (221–207 B.C.) or Han (206 B.C.–A.D. 220), whereas other records place him back in the era of the legendary Yellow Emperor. These fanciful traditions cannot have been very old, however, since they are all tainted with the Chinese classical tradition (*cf.* Fêng CS 32, 113 ff.). The expression "the eight tribes of Ch'i-shou" is a literary designation for the Ch'i-tan tribes. The attack in question occurred during the time of the first Northern Wei emperor, Tao-wu 道武, who ruled from 386 to 409.

[11] The text here and below has Kao-li, which is an anachronism, since up to the sixth century the country was called Kao-chü-li. See below, The Subordinate States, no. 22.

The stockbreeding Juan-juan tribes first appeared in the historical records in the fourth century A.D. They played a dominant role in Central Asia during the fifth and sixth centuries (Pelliot 31, 12; see also Chavannes 03, 230; Marquart 14, 73; Fujita 23, 55 ff.; *idem* 33, 201 ff.; Franke, GCR III, 283 ff.; Fêng CS 37, 77–80; and above all WS 100, *passim;* 103, 10a; and PS 98, 19a–b). The name

of this people is given in numerous variants such as Jou-jan 柔然, Juan-juan 蠕蠕, Jui-jui 芮芮, Ju-ju 茹茹, and Jou-juan 蝚蠕. An inscription in Yün-kang 雲崗 in Ta-t'ung 大同 County, Shansi, which speaks of the great Ju-ju Empire (*ta ju-ju kuo*), perhaps indicates the name by which the Juan-juan called themselves (Fêng CS 37, 79). The identification of the Juan-juan with the Avars of Western history is not in agreement with the opinions of scholars such as Fujita (33, 188 ff.) and Shiratori (12, 1018–1034) who stress their Mongol provenience. Marquart (14, 73 and 88) claims Mongol affinity for them but also maintains the Avar theory. Boodberg (39, 230, note 2), without arriving at a definite conclusion, also considers the identification with the Avars "by no means certain . . . the whole question deserves careful re-study." However, the existence of Mongol loanwords in Old-Russian prior to the Mongol invasion and even in Proto-Slavic suggests a Mongol origin for the Avars, since they are the only people known to have entered the Slavic world from Inner Asia during this early period. The majority of the Avars, the so-called "Pseudo-Avars," were probably already Turkicized, but it seems that some sections, perhaps the ruling tribe(s), still spoke a proto-Mongol language when, in A.D. 558, they established their first contact with a Slavic people.

[12] The Northern Wei 北魏 dynasty existed from A.D. 386 to 534.

[13] See below, note 16.

[14] A dynasty whose main power was in the northeastern part of China Proper from A.D. 550 to 577.

[15] At the time of the Wei emperor, T'ai-wu 太武 (424–452), the T'u-chüeh 突厥 or Turks (see Pelliot 15, 688) first submitted to the Juan-juan (Sui 84, 1a) but later developed into a great empire under Tümen Khaghan 土門可汗. From the middle of the sixth century to the middle of the seventh century the Turks reached the peak of their power in Northern Central Asia. They assisted in founding the T'ang dynasty. Though the Turks were badly defeated and their khaghan captured in 630 by T'ai-tsung of the T'ang dynasty, the remnants still continued to control the regions beyond the Great Wall until the rise of the Uighurs. For the earliest sources see Chou 50; Sui 84; CTS 194A and B; TS 215A and B. For Western studies see Deguignes, HGH I, 224 ff.; Visdelou 1779, 91 ff.; Julien 64; Parker 92–95 TST. *Cf.* also Thomsen 96, 57 ff.; Barthold 97, 1 ff.; Hirth 99; Chavannes 03; Pelliot 15, 688 ff.; Barthold 28, 186 ff.; Pelliot 31, 12 ff.; Barthold 35, 6 ff.; Grousset 39, 124 ff.; see also The Subordinate States, no. 34.

resided in Korea where they numbered no more than ten thousand families. The tribes became scattered and were no longer the eight tribes of old.[16]

Another group, of which some submitted to the Turks and some became subordinate to the Sui [empire], settled along the Ho-ch'ên River.[17] The tribes gradually became more numerous and split into ten tribes occupying a territory of more than five hundred *li* in Liao-hsi.[18]

During the T'ang period the Ta-ho family[19] re-formed them into eight tribes, but, since those in Sung-mo[20] and Hsüan Prefectures had branched off from them, there were actually ten tribes. The Yao-lien family, after the defeat and dispersion caused by [Li] Wan-jung[21] and K'o-t'u-yü,[22] re-established eight tribes. But, when Yao-lien and I-la branched off from them, there were again ten tribes. Tsu-wu Khaghan[23] divided them into twenty tribes, and the Ch'i-tan became great for the first time.

Coming to T'ai-tsu of Liao, he separated the lineages of the Nine Tents and the Three Patriarchal Households and regrouped them into twenty tribes. During the reign of Shêng-tsung sixteen tribes were established by subdivision, and eighteen were set up by accretion. Including the old ones, there were fifty-four tribes.[24] Inside [the empire] were the Imperial Maternal Uncles of the Pa-li and I-shih-ssŭ lineages. Outside were the ten dependent tribes. Such prosperity!   32, 4a–b

3. THE FOUR INNER LINEAGES OF LIAO[25]

The lineage of the Nine Tents of Yao-lien.[26]
The Horizontal Tent and the lineage of the Three Patriarchal Households.[27]
The Pa-li and I-shih-ssŭ lineages of the Imperial Maternal Uncles.[28]
The other lineages of the Imperial Maternal Uncles.   33, 1a–b

---

[16] This paragraph is rather ambiguous. According to LS 32, 6a; 63, 3a; and PS 94, 19a ff., the Ch'i-tan tribes were north of Ho-lung 和龍 (modern Ch'ao-yang 朝陽 County, Chahar) during the time of the Northern Wei dynasty. Owing to the invasion by the Juan-juan and Koreans, a Ch'i-tan chieftain led some three thousand carts, ten thousand people, and many animals to the region around the Pai-lang River 白狼水 (modern Ta-ling 大凌 River in Jehol and Liaoning) and submitted to Wei in 479. This was only a part of the Ch'i-tan. Later, in 553, the Ch'i-tan invaded Northern Ch'i but were defeated with the tremendous loss of more than a hundred thousand people and several hundred thousand animals.

[17] The modern Lao-ha 老哈 River, Jehol.

[18] The eastern part of modern Jehol. The region had already been established as Liao-hsi Commandery 遼西郡 before the unification of the Chinese empire. It became one of the thirty-six original commanderies of Ch'in (221–207 B.C.).

[19] The Ta-ho family 大賀氏 preceded the Yao-lien clan in ruling the tribal confederacy of the Ch'i-tan (TS 219, 1a; LS 63, 1b). The Yao-lien, Ta-ho, and Shih-li (the later I-la) were classed together as the predominant lineages during the overlordship of the Yao-lien family (LS 32, 8a).

[20] Sung-mo 松漠 was located near the modern Shira Muren. T'ang established a center there called the Administration of the Governor General of Sung-mo (松漠督都府) in order to control the Ch'i-tan.

[21] Li Wan-jung 李萬榮 led some of the Ch'i-tan rebels against T'ang and organized a horrible massacre at Yu Prefecture (Peiping). He was eventually defeated and captured in 697 (TS 219, 2a).

[22] K'o-t'u-yü 可突于 continued the rebellion against the T'ang government by killing his fellow-tribesman, Sha-ku 娑固, who had made far-reaching concessions to T'ang. The struggle which followed temporarily caused a severe weakening of the tribal power of the Ch'i-tan (TS 219, 3a).

[23] Of the Yao-lien clan. *Cf*. XIV, 1 (1), LS 63, 7b.

[24] This statement seems to disagree with LS 37, 2a where the number of tribes is given as having been only fifty-two (*cf*. I, 1 (1)). The discrepancy disappears if we remember that the "twenty" tribes of T'ai-tsu were not more than eighteen plus two "promoted" tents of the Imperial Maternal Uncles (LS 33, 1b).

[25] The term "inner" (內), if used politically, generally refers to the living quarters of the ruler. In the above passage it evidently designates the imperial lineages as well as those that were close to them in social status, either as their predecessors or as consort lineages. LS 45, 19b praises the imperial procedure of T'ai-tsu who replaced the Yao-lien family but honored its Nine Tents by placing them above the imperial camp.

[26] According to LS 45, 20a, nine Yao-lien khaghans ruled successively over the Ch'i-tan tribes. The "Nine Tents" are the descendants of these nine khaghans.

[27] The descendants of A-pao-chi's two uncles and of his brothers were set up as the *san fu-fang* 三父房, the Three Patriarchal Households (LS 64, 2b–3a). Granet suggested that the word *fu* might be taken here as meaning head of a family, not as father (Stein 39, 38).

[28] Literally, "the Pa-li and I-shih-ssŭ lineages of the tents of the uncles of the nation." The term was first used in a narrow sense in 935 by T'ai-tsung who applied it to the brothers and half-brothers of his mother, the wife of T'ai-tsu. A more complete discussion of the name and structure of the Hsiao clan is given in section VII.

4. T'AI-TSU'S TRIBES[29]

No.	NAME OF TRIBE	NO. OF *shih-lieh*	REMARKS
1	Five Divisions 五院 33, 1b–2a	4	The title of its great king (LS 46, 3a), an at least temporary sojourn of members of the tribe near the Mu-yeh 木葉 Mountain (61, 6a), and grants of cultivable land near the Hai-lo River 海勒水[30] to a section of the tribe,[31] all point to a northern location. This location does not exclude military command of its ruler in the southern part of the empire which is indicated in LS 33, 1b. Under the early Yao-lien khaghan, Tsu-wu 阻午, the six camps of the I-la tribe were led by two brothers (LS 33, 1b) who, according to LS 33, 2b, "separated the camp," the younger one controlling the I-shih tribe. Did this I-shih tribe originally form part of the I-la tribe, perhaps presenting an early Uighur admixture, or was it an independent tribe when the brothers parted? See below, no. 3. In 922 the I-la tribe was split into the Five and Six Divisions (cf. XIV, 1 and introduction).
2	Six Divisions 六院 33, 2a–b	4	Tribe of the main imperial line. A-pao-chi was born in the Hsia-lai-i *shih-lieh* 霞瀨益石烈 (LS 1, 1a) which is probably identical with the first of its four subdivisions, the Hsia-lan *shih-lieh* 轄懶石烈 (33, 2a). The title of the tribe's great king possibly implies a southern location (46, 3a). His military duties lay in the south (33, 2a). In 939 one of its *shih-lieh* was shifted northward into the region of the Wu-ku 烏古 tribe and was given cultivable land (33, 2b).
3	I-shih 乙室 33, 2b	2	Was this tribe identical with the I-shih-huo 乙室活 or I-shih-huo-ti (邸) tribe which flourished under the rule of the Yao-lien lineage (WTS 72, 2a; LS 32, 7a; *Han Kao-tsu Shih-lu* 漢高祖實錄 by Su Fêng-chi 蘇逢吉 = LSSI 17, 3b)? Was it also connected with the line of the Maternal Uncles I-shih-ssǔ (巳), that is the leading Uighur complex within the country? In the eighth century the I-shih tribe was once ruled by a younger son of the Yeh-lü lineage; it may even have been part of the I-la tribe itself. This, however, does not exclude a predynastic proto-Hsiao (Uighur) admixture. The ancestors of the Hsiao clan are said to have intermarried early with the ancestors of the Yeh-lü clan (VII, 2 (1)), and the leading position of the I-shih tribe during the dynastic period suggestively parallels that of the imperial I-la tribe. The I-shih tribe was singled out from the mass of the other Ch'i-tan tribes and listed as one of the four "great tribes," the three others being the two imperial tribes and the Hsi tribes whose ruler had kingly status (see XIV, 1, note 88). The head of the I-shih tribe also held royal rank (LS 45, 23a and 46, 3a); T'ai-tsu used it to counterbalance the power of the king of the Hsi people (LS 45, 19b). The head of the tribe was charged with the guard of the southern region. His minister over the masses stayed at the Yüan-yang Lake 鴛鴦泊 (modern Ang-ku-li Lake 昂古里湖 or Arghuli-Nōr in southern Chahar) (LS 33, 2b). Later, in 1122, T'ien-tsu, on his flight from the Jurchen, encountered this tribe west of the Western Capital (CS 2, 17a; *Wu Hsi Chi* 武溪集 by Yü Ching 余靖 = LSSI 13, 2a).
4	P'in 品 33, 2b–3a	2	Probably located northwest of modern Boro Khoton, Jehol (LS 33, 2b). In 997 the emperor urged the prosperous people of the P'in tribe to relieve the poor. He gave orders that the uncultivated land be handed over to the people for cultivation (LS 13, 8a). The tribe was created in the early time of Yao-lien rule when Tsu-wu Khaghan coordinated [a number of ?] "camps" into a tribe (LS 33, 2b).
5	Ch'u-t'ê 楮特 33, 3a	2	Tribal ancestor Wa 洼, possibly the ancestor of the Yao-lien family (LS 45, 20a). Attached to the military organization of the Northwestern Route. Therefore perhaps located in what is now northwestern Jehol. To avoid the summer heat Shêng-tsung went twice to the Pai-p'o 栢坡 Mountain where the chief of Ch'u-t'ê lived (LS 10, 8a and 18, 8a). Origin like that of P'in tribe (LS 33, 3a). The name seems to reoccur in that of the Džotă, a tribe of the Mongol Darxat (cf. Sanžejev 30, 12).

[29] In this and the following tables the name of the tribe, the number of the *shih-lieh* (see XV), and the remarks are, unless otherwise noted, taken from the *Liao Shih* reference which is given immediately below the name of the tribe.

[30] Probably the modern Hailar River (Heilungkiang) which flows into the Argun River.

[31] See II, 2 (2), which gives a somewhat different version.

T'ai-tsu's Tribes (*continued*)

No.	NAME OF TRIBE	NO. OF *shih-lieh*	REMARKS
6	Wu-wei 烏隗 33, 3a–b	2	Under first Yao-lien khaghan separated from Nieh-la 涅剌 tribe with which it had formed a unit. Each independent part was then ruled by one of two brothers who previously had shared a joint command of the undivided tribe (LS 33, 3a–b). In dynastic time attached to Northeastern Route. Northern location also indicated by combination with elements of the northern Yü-chüeh 于厥 or Wu-ku-li 烏古里 which possibly were the same people (see Outer and Large Tribes).
7	Nieh-la 涅剌 33, 3b	2	Attached to Southwestern Route. In 985 the taxes of nos. 6 and 7 were reduced because of sparse population (LS 10, 8a). The name is very probably identical with Mongol *nara(n)*, "sun."
8	T'u-lü-pu 突呂不 33, 3b–4a	2	Originally united with T'u-chü tribe, then forming three camps. Divided by Tsu-wu Khaghan who welded two camps into the T'u-lü-pu tribe, and converted the third into the T'u-chü tribe (LS 33, 4a). Under the Liao dynasty attached to Northwestern Route. Its minister over the masses stationed west of Ch'ang-ch'un 長春 Prefecture (northwest of Po-tu-na 伯都訥, Kirin). In 1123, during the dissolution of the empire, T'ien-tsu took refuge with this tribe which had moved to the east of Hsi Hsia, that is to modern Suiyuan (LS 29, 6b).
9	T'u-chü 突舉 33, 4a	2	Under the Southern Administration. On guard against the Wei Wu-ku 隗烏古 whose location, however, is not clear.
10	The Six Tribes of the Administration of the King of Hsi 奚王府六部 33, 4a–b		The Hsi formerly had five tribes to which the To-kuei 墮瑰 tribe was added in 923 (LS 2, 3b). For further information about the Hsi tribes see above, note 4, and below, particularly X and XIII.
11	T'u-lü-pu Shih-wei 突呂不室韋 33, 5a		Attached to the Northeastern Route. Composed of the Big and Small Yellow Shih-wei and, according to the name, members of the T'u-lü-pu tribe. The T'u-lü-pu Shih-wei heads the list of the composite tribes of T'ai-tsu's period.
12	Nieh-la Na-ku 涅剌拏古 33, 5a		Located east of T'ai 泰 Prefecture (southwest of modern Nung-an 農安 County, Kirin). Ch'i-tan component: Nieh-la.
13	Tieh-la Tieh-ta 迭剌迭達 33, 5a		In the middle period of Yao-lien rule 700 Hsi families were captured by Hsien-chih 鮮質 Khaghan. Their descendants were gathered together into a tribe with fourteen *shih-lieh* by Liao T'ai-tsu. It dwelt south of Ch'ing 慶 Prefecture (modern Tsaghan Khoton, Jehol) (LS 33, 5a).
14	I-shih Ao-wei 乙室奧隗 33, 5a		This tribe, like the next, was established by T'ai-tsu with Hsi captives (LS 33, 5a). Some land was tilled by women (LS 59, 2a). Ch'i-tan component: I-shih.
15	Ch'u-t'ê Ao-wei 楮特奧隗 33, 5b		Ch'i-tan component: Ch'u-t'ê.
16	P'in Ta-lu-kuo 品達魯虢 33, 5b		Probably located north of modern Tsaghan Khoton, Jehol. Southwestern Route. Ch'i-tan component: P'in.
17	Wu-ku Nieh-la 烏古涅剌; also called Nieh-li 涅離 33, 5b		The tribe was set up with 6,000 captive Yü-ku-li 于骨里 households in 921. Southwestern Route. Text proves identity of Wu-ku and Yü-ku-li. Ch'i-tan component: Nieh-la.

T'ai-tsu's Tribes (*continued*)

No.	NAME OF TRIBE	REMARKS
18	T'u-lu 圖魯 33, 5b	Split off from the preceding tribe and therefore probably also composite in character. Southwestern Route.

5. SHÊNG–TSUNG'S TRIBES

No.	NAME OF TRIBE	REMARKS
1	Sa-li-ko 撒里葛 33, 6a	The Sa-li-ko tribe like the two following ones was a "camp" of the Hsi people who had surrendered to T'ai-tsu. Its people were first treated as bondsmen, but in the time of Shêng-tsung they were established as independent tribes. Their tribesmen must have been good hunters, for they assisted in the imperial hunts. The tribes dwelt east of Tsê 澤 Prefecture (north of modern P'ing-ch'üan 平泉, Jehol) (LS 33, 6a).
2	Yao-chao 窈爪 33, 6a	Location south of T'an 潭 Prefecture, on the banks of the upper course of the Ta-ling 大凌 River, Jehol (MRC II, 66).
3	Nou-wan-chao 耨盌爪 33, 6a	Probably situated in southeastern Jehol. No *shih-lieh* is mentioned for any of these three tribes, but the second and the third are called *chao* which, according to LS 116, 21b, seems to have designated a tribal unit, similar if not equivalent to *shih-lieh*. *Cf.* XIV, introduction.
4	Ê-p'u-kua 訛僕括 33, 6a	The text places this tribe, together with the three preceding ones, "east of Wang-yün 望雲 County" (modern Ch'ih-ch'êng 赤城 County, Chahar). This statement would place the Ê-p'u-kua tribe much further west than Tsê Prefecture (see above no. 1). Was the fourth tribe actually located somewhere in between? Or did it move further west at the close of the dynasty?
5	T'ê-li-t'ê-mien 特里特勉 33, 6a–b	Originally 160 households, 20 each from the 8 Ch'i-tan tribes, to guard the Hsi. After considerable increase established as a tribe. The Lo-ma 落馬 River near which the tribe resided is located by CS 24, 7b close to the juncture of the Lao-ha 老哈 River and Ying-chin 英金 River in Jehol. Later the tribe seems to have moved further west into the mountainous region on the border of modern Chahar and Jehol (LS 33, 6b).
6	Shao-wa 稍瓦 33, 6b	First set up as a *shih-lieh* with bondsmen taken from the camps (ordos?) and leading lineages. They caught birds east of the Liao River. Eventually made a tribe.
7	Ho-chu 曷朮 33, 6b	Same origin as no. 6; also first made a *shih-lieh*, then a tribe. The Ho-chu tribesmen were employed to smelt iron in the coastal region. The tribe probably lived near what is now Liao-yang 遼陽 County, Liaoning. For a discussion of the name Ho-chu see III, note 12.
8	Yao-li 遙里 33, 6b–7a	One of the Six Tribes of Hsi (LS 37, 4b). Situated between T'an 潭 Prefecture (on the upper course of the Ta-ling 大凌 River) and Li 利 Prefecture (modern Ta-ch'êng-tzǔ 大城子, seventy *li* northwest of Chien-ch'ang 建昌 County, Jehol). This tribe had three *shih-lieh*.
9	Po-tê 伯德 33, 7a	Another Hsi tribe (LS 37, 4b). Located between modern Lu-lung 盧龍 County, Hopei, and Sung-shan 松山 County (in modern Ch'ih-fêng County, Jehol). Six *shih-lieh*.
10	Ch'u-li 楚里 33, 7a	A Hsi tribe. Located north of T'an Prefecture.
11	Ao-li 奧里 33, 7a–b	Established in 994 with two old Hsi tribes, Ao-li and Mei-chih 梅只, and the additional To-kuei 墮瑰 tribe.
12	Southern K'o 南剋 33, 7b	The two K'o Tribes were set up in 994 with military units, *k'o* 剋, of the Hsi people.

Shêng-tsung's Tribes (*continued*)

No.	NAME OF TRIBE	REMARKS
13	Northern K'o 北剋 33, 7b	See above; no. 12.
14	Wei-yen Turks 隗衍突厥 33, 7b	Established with households of the Ssŭ-p'i-sha 四闞沙 and Ssŭ-p'o-mên 四頗灖 people who possibly were both remnants of the dispersed Turks (T'u-chüeh). The tribe probably lived near modern Nung-an 農安 County, Kirin, where its people garrisoned the Jurchen border.
15	Ao-yen Turks 奧衍突厥 33, 7b	The text says, "Like the Wei-yen 隗衍 Turks," which probably means alike in origin and general conditions.
16	Nieh-la Yüeh-wu 涅剌越兀 33, 7b	Established with Nieh-la and Shih-wei households in order to garrison the region north of the Black Mountain.
17	Ao-yen Nü-chih 奧衍女直 33, 7b–8a	Set up with Jurchen families. The tribe probably lived in the district of Chên 鎮 Prefecture, on the Orkhon River, Outer Mongolia.
18	I-tien Nü-chih 乙典女直 33, 8a	Established with Jurchen families. Situated north of the juncture of the Lao-ha 老哈 River and the Ying-chin 英金 River (MRC II, 59).
19	Wo-t'u-wan Wu-ku 斡突盌烏古 33, 8a	The Wu-ku tribe was one of the northern neighbors of the Liao empire (see the next table). The bravery of its tribesmen made them dreaded enemies and desirable auxiliaries. This is the second Liao tribe in which they appear as components (*cf.* above, the Wu-ku Nieh-la). Wo-t'u-wan may be a qualifying term (LS 31, 7b states that the Ch'i-tan word *wo-tu-wan* 斡篤盌 means "to reproduce the species"). It may also refer to a a border people called Wu-t'u-wan 吾禿婉 who are mentioned twice, as an outer tribe (LS 33, 9b) and as a "large" tribe (LS 46, 29a). The warriors of the Wo-t'u-wan Wu-ku tribe guarded the region north of the Black Mountain, that is the northwestern corner of modern Jehol.
20	Tieh-lu Ti-lieh 迭魯敵烈 33, 8a	The *Liao Shih* offers many variations of the name Ti-lieh, such as 敵烈德, 廸烈, 廸烈得, 迭烈得, etc. Tsuda says that the Ti-lieh tribes probably dwelt near the Ursung River and Khulun-Nōr in Heilungkiang (Tsuda 16, 2). Yanai believes the Ti-lieh to be identical with the Tiriet of the Yüan 元 dynasty. He identifies them also with one of the six Tatar groups near the Bōr [Buir]-Nōr which Rashīd ad-Dīn mentions and which D'Ohsson transcribes as "Terate" (Yanai 30, 543). The attitude of the Ti-lieh tribes oscillated between submission to and struggle against the Liao empire. The Tieh-lu Ti-lieh tribe was probably located northwest of Jehol.
21	Shih-wei 室韋 33, 8a	The Shih-wei have been mentioned above (*cf.* above, note 5). In Pelliot's opinion the Chinese word Shih-wei goes back to an original *Särbi, *Širbi, or *Široi, which formerly was transcribed as Hsien-pei (Pelliot 34, 35, note 3). This etymology, if tenable, makes the Shih-wei the heirs of the name of the ancient Hsien-pei people among whose other descendants the Ch'i-tan and Hsi and later the Mongols all surpassed their backward northern cousins in historical conspicuousness. Some Shih-wei groups were included as components into T'ai-tsu's tribes; under Shêng-tsung a tribe purely Shih-wei in character was set up in addition. It was attached to the Punitive Office of the Northwestern Route.
22	Chu-chê Ta-lu-kuo 尤哲達魯號 33, 8a	The Ta-lu-kuo tribe was probably identical with the Ta-lu-ku 達魯古 tribe which the Ch'i-tan defeated in 926 after a campaign against Po-hai (LS 3, 1b). In 1115 the Jurchen army fought victoriously against the Liao troops at Ta-lu-ku City, which is assumed to have been situated in the vicinity of the Hsing-lung Pao 興隆堡, north of the Sungari River (Ikeuchi, MSK I, 214; *cf.* also Gibert 34, 830). The tribe did garrison service within the border but lived outside of it.

Shêng-tsung's Tribes (*continued*)

No.	Name of Tribe	Remarks
23	Mei-ku-hsi 梅古悉 33, 8b	Established with Tangut households. Belonged to the Northern Administration. Pelliot considers the term Mei-ku-hsi one of the early forms of the word Mongol (Pelliot 29, 127). The Tangut character of the new tribe's masses makes an equation of its name with the non-Tangut word Mongol not very probable. But a tribal name may derive from a noble—superimposed—leader rather than from the inconspicuous and perhaps enslaved commoners. Even a Uighur background for the name is not impossible in a country with as strong a vein of noble Uighur blood as the Liao empire had. One of the nine Uighur tribes was called Mo-ko-hsi-ch'i 貊歌息訖 (CTS 195, 3a; Hirth 99, 36; Chavannes 03, 94). If the final *ch'i* could be explained as a variant of a plural *s* (Pelliot 31b, 118; *idem* 29, 127), or if it were the Chinese transcription of the Altaic suffix -*či*, "related to," "dealing with," then the name would suggest interesting historical possibilities.
24	Chieh-ti 頡的 33, 8b	Established with Tangut households. Also under the Northern Administration.
25	Northern Ti-lieh 北敵烈 33, 8b	Ti-lieh (Tereit?) households. Perhaps located in modern eastern Outer Mongolia.
26	Ni-ch'i Tangut 匿訖唐古 33, 8b	Composed of Tangut households. Attached to Punitive Office of Southwestern Route.
27	Northern[32] Tangut 北唐古 33, 8b	Composed of Tangut households. Attached to Huang-lung Administration in Tung-ching Circuit. (In modern Nung-an 農安, Kirin.)
28	Southern Tangut 南唐古 33, 8b	Composed of Tangut households.
29	Ho-la Tangut 鶴剌唐古 33, 8b	Composed of Tangut households. Attached to Punitive Office of Southwestern Route. Ho-la may be related to the Mongol and Turkic word *qara* (black) which since the beginning of the thirteenth century was transcribed with characters which render these sounds. *Cf.* Pelliot 31a, 419–420.
30	Ho-hsi 河西 33, 9a	The region "west of the [Yellow] River" (Ho-hsi) included the Hsi Hsia empire (*cf.* Bretschneider 88 I, 78 and 185), but was not confined to it. Various Tangut tribes of the Ho-hsi territory were subordinates of the Liao empire. The Ho-hsi evidently belonged to them, as did the preceding tribes who are clearly designated as Tangut.
31	Hsieh-t'ê 薛特 33, 9a	Established in 1015 with Uighur households, which probably were seized during the victorious campaign against the Kan-chou Uighurs in 1010 (see LS 15, 1b and 69, 13a). The new tribe was placed north of Tz'ŭ-jên 慈仁 County, near Yung 永 Prefecture in northeastern Jehol.
32	Po-ssŭ Pi-ku-tê 伯斯鼻骨德 33, 9a	Probably Turkic *boz begüt*, "the beige (grayish-brown) lords." The tribe did garrison service within the border but lived outside of it.
33	Ta-ma Pi-ku-tê 達馬鼻骨德 33, 9a	*Ta-ma* 撻馬, a Ch'i-tan term for an escorting official (LS 116, 2a), is already to be found in the Orkhon inscriptions in the form *taman* (Radloff 95, 71 and 125; Thomsen 96, 131). It later came to mean "a vanguard force." The Mongol title *tamači* designates a special corps of horsemen (Pelliot 29a, 220 ff.). The Taman Begüt were perhaps "lords bearing the title of *taman*." The tribe was attached to the Northeastern Route.

[32] We follow other editions in reading 北 for the 比 of our text.

Shêng-tsung's Tribes (*continued*)

No.	NAME OF TRIBE	REMARKS
34	Five Nations 五國 33, 9*a*	The tribal complex called Five Nations (*wu kuo*) consisted of five smaller tribes, namely, P'ou-a-li 剖阿里, P'ên-nu-li 盆奴里, Ao-li-mi 奧里米, Yüeh-li-tu 越里篤, and Yüeh-li-chi 越里吉. Their territory in the northeastern part of present Kirin was famous for its falcons. The leading settlement of the Five Nations, Wu-kuo City, was probably the center of the P'ou-a-li tribe. Its site corresponds to modern I-lan 依蘭, east of Harbin, Kirin. The two captured Sung emperors were placed there by Chin in 1130 (TSSTS 14*a–b*). The Five Nations became subordinate to Liao in the time of Shêng-tsung. They were, however, never fully integrated into the empire's administration but remained in the category of semi-independent tribes which paid tribute rather than taxes to the Liao government. *Cf.* X, introduction.

6. OUTER TRIBES

No.	NAME OF TRIBE	REMARKS
1	Wu-ku 烏古 33, 9*b*	According to LS 33, 5*b*, identical with Yü-ku-li 于骨里; probably identical also with Wu-ku-li 烏古里 (LS 30, 5*a*), Yü-chüeh-lü 嫗厥律 (WTS 73, 8*b*), Yü-chüeh-li 于厥里 (LS 3, 1*b*), and Yü-chüeh 于厥 (LS 1, 1*b*; 15, 9*a*; 34, 1*b*). The Yü-chüeh-lü are described as a very hairy people, the chiefs with long hair, who lived in cold regions northwest of the Ch'i-tan and provided the Liao empire with large river fish and all kinds of furs (CTKC 25, 2*b*). Possibly identical with the Ongira[t] (Yanai 30, 542). Captured Wu-ku tribesmen were incorporated into the Ch'i-tan tribal order. *Cf.* T'ai-tsu's Tribes, no. 17, and Shêng-tsung's Tribes, no. 19.
2	Eight Tribes of Ti-lieh 敵烈八部 33, 9*b*	For the probable location of this northern people see Shêng-tsung's Tribes, no. 20. Eight Tribes of Ti-lieh is a formula similar to the Six Tribes of Hsi. The eight tribes are considered as one unit of the ten Outer Tribes.
3	Wei-ku 隗古 33, 9*b*	Probably an abbreviated form of Wei Wu-ku 隗烏古. When the Ti-lieh Tribe of the Eight *Shih-lieh* rebelled in 1073, the emperor, Tao-tsung, ordered the armies of Wei [Wu]-ku to attack through two routes (LS 69, 18*a–b*). This tribe must therefore have been located near the Ti-lieh, that is north of Jehol. Liao several times gave silk to them, as in 1087 (LS 25, 1*a*), and sold oxen to them, as in 1096 (LS 26, 2*a*).
4	Hui-po 回跋 33, 9*b*	The Hui-po tribe dwelt near the Hui-fa 輝發 River in the northeastern part of modern Liaoning (MRC II, 107). It paid either local products, as in 1048 (LS 20, 2*a–b*), or horses, as in 1050 (LS 20, 4*b*). Also called Hui-pa 回霸 (WHTK 327, 2570).
5	Yen-mu 巖母 33, 9*b*	Probably situated in modern Kirin, for in 1027 a Jurchen tribesman, P'u-ma 蒲馬, was appointed chieftain with the imposing title of grand preceptor when Shêng-tsung was fishing in the Hun-t'ung 混同 River (the modern Sungari River in Kirin) (LS 17, 4*a*).
6	Wu-t'u-wan 吾禿婉 33, 9*b*	Also transcribed as Wu-tu-wan 吾獨婉 (LS 22, 1*a*). The tribe's exact territory is unknown, but a tribute of horses and camels paid in 1062 indicates a western location. A tribute of 20,000 horses offered to Tao-tsung points to a tribe of major resources. Tribal prisoners were organized in the Wo-t'u-wan Wu-ku tribe of Shêng-tsung. *Cf.* Shêng-tsung's Tribes, no. 19.
7	Tieh-la-ko 迭剌葛 33, 9*b*	Perhaps the ancestors of the Mongol Darxat in eastern Tannū-Tuva.
8	Uighur 回鶻 33, 10*a*	The name Uighur appears in various Chinese transcriptions such as Yüan-ho 袁紇, Wu-hu 烏護, Wu-ho 烏紇, Wei-ho 韋紇, Hui-ho 回紇, and Hui-hu 回鶻 (see TS 217*A*, 1*a*; 217*B*, 1*a*). PS 98, 23*a* and WS 103, 26*a–b* mention a Piao-ho 表紇 tribe as subordinate to the Kao-ch'ê 高車. *Piao* 表 apparently was a misprint for *yüan* 袁, the people in question being really the Yüan-ho (Wang CJ 38, 237) or Uighurs. Whether the Uighurs can be traced back to still earlier times is an open question. The Kao-ch'ê were identical with the Ting-ling 丁令 (零 or 靈) who lived north of the Huns, possibly west of Lake Baikal (Wang JW 36, 83; Maenchen-Helfen 39, 78 ff. and 83). De Groot connects the Hu-chieh 呼揭 of SC 110, 14*a* with the Hu-ku 護骨 who, according to WS 103, 26*b* and PS 98, 23*a*, were a tribe of the

No.	Name of Tribe	Remarks
		Kao-ch'ê (de Groot 21, 79). De Groot's suggested identification of Kao-ch'ê and Uighur (*loc. cit.*), which seems doubtful for a number of reasons, is also contradicted by his own tentative equation of the Uighurs with the Hu-chieh (*op. cit.*, 227) whose successors, according to de Groot himself, were only a subdivision of the Kao-ch'ê people. It seems easier to connect the Yüan-ho tribe of the Kao-ch'ê with the Hu-ku who are also listed as a tribe of the comprehensive proto-Turkic nation. Whatever the roots of the proto-Uighur people may have been, at the beginning of the seventh century the Uighurs shook off the yoke of the ruling Turkic people and settled along the Selenga River in Outer Mongolia (Sui 84, 18*b*–19*a*; TS 217*A*, 1*a* ff.; see also Thomsen 96, 147 ff.). The Turkic Orkhon inscriptions, written between 732 and 735, mention the Uighurs (Radloff 95, 65; Thomsen 96, 127) together with other people, all of whom were Turkic in the wider sense of the term even though they may not have called themselves so (see Barthold 35, 34). A decade later they occupied the territory of the defeated Turks which they controlled from 745–840, almost a century. After their expulsion by the Khirghiz in 840 they established several smaller centers of power in eastern Turkestan (Kao-ch'ang 高昌) and northwestern China (Kan 甘 Prefecture). They are listed by the *Liao Shih* among the Subordinate States (see below). The Uighur tribes mentioned in LS 33, 10*a* may have been split off from the former Uighur empire or border tribes of the newly established Uighur countries. The Ch'i-tan before 840 had been the subjects of the Orkhon ruler. They were deeply influenced by the Uighurs who provided the consort family for their imperial house (see TS 217*A* and *B*; WHTK 247, 2718 ff.). For a translation of the Uighur section of the [*Hsin*] *T'ang Shu* see Visdelou 1779, 128–157 and of the *Chiu T'ang Shu* see Chavannes 03, 87–94. For a survey of later Chinese and Western material see Bretschneider 88 I, 236–263; also Klaproth 1826, 121–130; Hyakinth 1832, 273–279; Schott 74, 102 ff. and *idem* 76, 27 ff.; Chavannes 97 VC, 406, note 3; Hirth 99, 36 ff.; Marquart 14, 61 ff.; Laufer 16, 4; Parker 95, 265 ff.; Franke, GCR III, 256 and 352; Pelliot 31, 13 ff.; Barthold 28, 36 ff.; *idem* 35, 5 and *passim*.
9	The Ch'ang-pai Mountains Tribes 長白山部 33, 10*a*	In the time of Sui and T'ang there existed a Pai Mountains 白山 tribe which was one of the seven Mo-ho 靺鞨 tribes. The tribe, whose name was obviously taken from its locale (in the Pai Mountains), was first under the control of Kao-chü-li. After the defeat of this kingdom by the T'ang armies the tribe submitted to the T'ang government. Later it became dependent on Po-hai. *Cf.* Sui 81, 9*a*; TS 219, 7*b*; also Mullie 33, 201. The change of the name of the mountains to Ch'ang-pai Mountains was either accompanied or preceded by a change in the tribe's (or the tribes') name to Ch'ang-pai Mountains tribe. The group later belonged to the Jurchen complex which like them was descended from the Mo-ho. In 1012 the chiefs of the thirty tribes of the Ch'ang-pai Mountains came to pay tribute, asking at the same time that titles be conferred upon them (LS 15, 3*b*).
10	P'u-lu-mao-to 蒲盧毛朵 33, 10*a*	This tribe probably lived in the eastern part of present Kirin. In 1046, 180 households from the region of the Ho-lan 曷懶 River near P'u-lu-mao-to submitted to Liao (LS 19, 7*b*). The Ho-lan River probably corresponds to the modern Hai-lan 海蘭 River, Kirin. The P'u-lu-mao-to tribe sometimes offered horses, sometimes local products, and once, in 1048, shipbuilders as tribute (LS 20, 2*a*). The latter fact causes Pelliot to suggest a relation between *mao-to*, the second half of the tribal name, and the Mongol word *modo* or *modun*, which means "wood" (Stein 39, 150, note 4).

7. MARGINAL DEPENDENCY

The above ten tribes, unable to achieve an existence as independent countries, became dependent upon Liao. At times they rebelled and at times they submitted. Each had an obligation to pay tribute [to Liao] just as the "attached prefectures" which belonged to the T'ang people.   33, 10*a*

8. LARGE TRIBES

No.	NAME OF TRIBE[33]	REMARKS
1	P'u-lu-mao-to 蒲盧毛朶 46, 29a	See Outer Tribes, no. 10.
2	Hui-po 回跋 46, 29a	See Outer Tribes, no. 4.
3	Yen-mu 巖母 46, 29a	See Outer Tribes, no. 5.
4	Nü-chih of Huang-lung Administration 黃龍府女直 46, 29a	A Jurchen tribe under the control of Huang-lung Administration. This tribe was probably situated near modern Nung-an 農安 County, Kirin.
5	Wu-t'u-wan 吾禿婉 46, 29a	See Outer Tribes, no. 6.
6	Wu-wei Yü-chüeh 烏隈于厥 46, 29a	Probably identical with the Wu-wei Wu-ku-li 烏隈烏骨里 of the Various Tribes (LS 46, 30a). It seems strange that elements of the Wu-wei peoples, who were part of T'ai-tsu's original eight tribes, should have mixed with border tribes of far inferior status to form larger or smaller tribal units at the fringe of the Liao empire. This, however, must have happened if the Wu-wei of this list were indeed the Wu-wei people of T'ai-tsu's confederation. Either the name was borne by two completely different tribes, or else some Wu-wei fractions joined the Yü-chüeh-li people, perhaps before 907; if later, they may have been a garrison force which settled down among the garrison people. In 988 the Liao government allowed them to offer horses and oxen as tribute instead of the skins of sable and dark moles which they had presented previously (LS 69, 9b). Obviously, the Wu-wei Yü-chüeh gradually changed their economic pursuits from hunting to at least partial stockbreeding. Did this occur under the influence of their Wu-wei tribesmen?
7	Eight P'o-li Tribes 婆離八部 46, 29b	LS 20, 2b reports that these tribes submitted to Liao in 1048.
8	Yü-chüeh-li 于厥里 46, 29b	This Yü-chüeh-li complex is identical with the Wu-ku tribe(s) of the Outer Tribes. It is not called a pu 部, a tribe, but a pu-tsu 部族, that is something less definite, perhaps a mixture of local and kinship elements. In 940 they were allowed "to set up their banners and drums." They then evidently assumed the political status of a tribe.

9. VARIOUS TRIBES

| 1 | Savage Nü-chih 生女直 46, 29b | The frequent occurrence of the name Nü-chih in the tribal lists of the *Liao Shih* indicates the importance of this eastern people in the history of the Liao empire. The independent Nü-chih are classified either as tribes or as states. The Nü-chih then formed the largest Tungus complex whose territory, roughly speaking, covered the northeastern part of the Sungari River (PFYSL 24a–b; CS 1, 1b). Their economy was a mixture of agriculture, stockbreeding, and hunting. Their political organization was not highly integrated at the beginning of the Liao period; it became much more so during the latter part of the eleventh |

---

[33] The higher status of the Large Tribes in comparison with that of the tribes in the next list is indicated by the fact that in each case the name of the tribe is followed by the three characters ta wang fu 大王府, the Administration of the Great King. For example, the full designation for the first tribe in the list is "the Administration of the Great King of the P'u-lu-mao-to tribe." In our list we have omitted the repetition of the three characters. *Cf.* also introduction.

Various Tribes (*continued*)

No.	Name of Tribe	Remarks
		century when the Liao state gradually lost its strength. The few Nü-chih tribes which surrendered to Liao were called "civilized" (*shou* 熟); the independent ones were designated as "savage" (*shêng* 生).

Formerly the tribes in question were called Hei-shui Mo-ho 黑水靺鞨. From the time of the Five Dynasties they had a new name which in the *History of the Five Dynasties* is written Nü-chên 女眞. In the Liao records the second part of the name is given as *chih* 直 instead of *chên* 眞 because the latter word occurred in Hsing-tsung's given name, Tsung-chên 宗眞 (SMCW 1*b*), and was therefore taboo. The two next "barbarian" dynasties of conquest, Chin and Yüan, though not bound by any formal obligation, adopted the Liao formula, Nü-chih, whereas Sung writers maintain the Five Dynasties' designation, Nü-chên. Other Chinese variants of the name will be noted in the Chin volume of this series.

The Secret History of the Yüan Dynasty (completed in 1240) speaks of the Chu-êrh-ch'ê 主兒扯 (YCPSHC 2, 28*a*); a Persian work, written in 1269, refers to the Djerdja people of the then Khitay [Chin] empire (en-Nesawi 95, 11). In a dictionary of "Nü-chên" words, written in the Ming period, the name is rendered in two characters which are transliterated in Chinese as Chu-hsien 朱先 (NCIY 2, 10*b*). All these forms, like the Chinese variant Chu-li-chên 朱里眞 (PFYSL 24*a*) suggest a form such as Jurche(n) or Juche(n). Following a suggestion made by Professor Pelliot, we use the designation Jurchen in our introductions and notes, but transcribe Nü-chih or Nü-chên wherever the name appears in a translated text.[34]

No.	Name of Tribe	Remarks
2	Chih-pu-ku 直不姑 46, 29*b*	Also transcribed as Chu (or Shu)-pu-ku 尤 (or 述) 不姑 (LS 46, 25*b*) and Chih-pu-ku 直不古 (LS 60, 3*b*). This tribe first appeared in 912 when T'ai-tsu attacked it and took several tens of thousands of prisoners. According to LS 46, 14*b*, the northwestern part of Liao bordered upon the Tsu-pu 阻卜 and Chu-pu-ku. Hence this tribe must have dwelt in the northern frontier region of the empire. In 940 messengers from three Chih-pu-ku tribes came to present tribute (LS 69, 5*a*). Thus the Chih-pu-ku evidently had a decentralized political organization.
3	Hu-shan 狐山 46, 29*b*	
4	Pa-ssŭ-mu 拔思母 46, 29*b*	There seem to have been two divisions of this tribe, one nearer to and the other farther from the Liao empire. In 1050 the Distant Barbarian (遠夷) Pa-ssŭ-mu came to pay tribute (LS 20, 4*b*). In 1099 Tao-tsung ordered Li Ch'ien-shun 李乾順, King of Hsia, to attack the Pa-ssŭ-mu. These "distant barbarians" seem to be identical with the Basmyl of the Orkhon inscriptions, whose name was transcribed by Radloff in 1895 as Basmal (95, 137) and in 1897 alternatively as Basmyl (97, 179). The Basmyl, who are called Pa-hsi-mi 拔悉蜜 in TS 217B, 9*a*, and Basmyl by Mahmūd-al-Kāshgharī (Brockelmann 28, 241), lived in Eastern Turkestan with Beshbalyq as their capital. The Uighurs after the catastrophe of 840 conquered the Basmyl, taking over their traditions in part (Barthold 35, 48 ff. and 96 ff.). LS 25, 5*b* records for the year 1093 the attack of a Pa-ssŭ-mu tribe in the region of Tao-t'a-ling 倒塌嶺 (probably in the northwestern border region of modern Chahar). This may refer to another, less distant, Pa-ssŭ-mu people.
5	Ch'a-cha-la 茶扎剌 46, 29*b*	Also written Ch'a-ch'ih-la 茶赤剌 (LS 69, 24*b*). Transcribed by Bretschneider (88 I, 213, note 549) as Djadjerats; by Pelliot (20, 146, note 2) as J̌aǰirat; by Yanai (30, 546) as Djadjirat. The tribe, which lived in the region of the Upper Onon and Kerulen Rivers (Yanai, *loc. cit.*), supported Yeh-lü Ta-shih after his flight westward from the collapsing Liao empire (LS 30, 4*b*).
6	Nien-pa-ko 粘八葛 46, 29*b*	Pelliot suggests identity of the Nien-pa-ko with the Nien-pa-ên 粘拔恩 of the twelfth century. Marquart's identification of the Nien-pa-ên with the Mongol Naiman (Marquart 14, 167) does not convince Pelliot though he does not reject completely the possibility of this equation which, if valid, would include also the Nien-pa-ko (Pelliot 20, 173–174). That

[34] For earlier discussions of the words Nü-chên, Nü-chih etc. see Chavannes, Kin, 537; *idem* 97 VC, 404; Pelliot 20, 142; *idem* 31, 22; Gibert 34, 74 ff.; Fêng CS 33*b*, 70.

Various Tribes (*continued*)

No.	NAME OF TRIBE	REMARKS
		the Ch'i-tan knew the name Naiman 乃蠻 is witnessed by LS 30, 7*a* and 69, 24*b*; but this does not exclude the simultaneous existence of the designation Nien-pa-ko. Naiman (or Nien-pa-ên) transcribes the Mongol term *najman*, "eight"; *nien-pa-ko* is possibly a Tungus word for the same number; *cf.* Evenki *dźapkun*, Manchu *dźakūn*, Jurchen *čāh-k'ûn*, Evenki *dźapkun* being the more archaic form and closer to *nien-pa-ko*. Chinese initial *ń-* may stand for *j-* (> *dž-*), and Mongol initial *n-* may stand for initial *j-* (> *dž-*) in other Altaic languages.
7	Yeh-tu-kua 耶覩刮 46, 29*b*	Toward the end of the eleventh century many tribes in the northwestern part of Liao rebelled, among them the Yeh-tu-kua who were brought to submission only after they had suffered a series of defeats (LS 69, 21*a*–22*a*). Probably identical with the Ötükän of the Orkhon Inscriptions (*cf.* Thomsen 96, 152). Mahmūd al-Kāshgharī defines Ötükän as a place in the Tatar Steppe near the Uighurs (Brockelmann 28, 246).
8	Yeh-mi-chih 耶迷只 46, 30*a*	Probably identical with Yeh-mi-chih-li (里). Evidently the Turkic Jämäk (Jimäk) tribe of al-Kāshgharī, "which 'with us' is considered Qyfčaq, while they consider themselves a different tribe" (Brockelmann 28, 245; *cf.* also Marquart 14, *passim*). In 1034 the Yeh-mi-chih received relief from the Liao government. See XII (44) and note.
9	Ta Chu-pu-ku 撻朮不姑 46, 30*a*	Detailed information on this tribe is lacking. In 1042 Hsing-tsung ordered the appointment of its chieftain (LS 19, 2*a*), which indicates an at least temporary dependence upon Liao.
10	Po-hai 渤海	These two Po-hai groups were remnants of the former kingdom of Po-hai. After the kingdom's downfall in 926 many of their nationals fled. Some founded the state of Ting-an 定安 in central Kirin. Others went to the west of the modern Yalu River where they preserved their original name. Still others lived in Heilungkiang under the name Northwestern Po-hai. See SS 491, 3*a*–4*b*; MCYLK 6, 24*a*–25*a*; PHKC 3, 17*b*–19*a*.
11	Northwestern Po-hai 西北渤海 46, 30*a*	
12	Ta-li-tê 達里得 46, 30*a*	Also transcribed as Ta-li-ti (底) (LS 25, 5*b*; 70, 23*b*–24*a*). This tribe attacked the region of Tao-t'a-ling 倒蹋嶺 several times. Hence it probably lived in Outer Mongolia.
13	Wu-ku 烏古 46, 30*a*	For a discussion of this tribe see Shêng-tsung's Tribes, no. 19.
14	Wei Wu-ku 隈烏古 46, 30*a*	One of several compounds in which the name Wu-ku occurs as the second element. Either a sub-tribe of this widespread people or a mixed tribe with a Wu-ku element.
15	San-ho Wu-ku 三河烏古 46, 30*a*	In 953 this tribe came to pay tribute to the Liao court together with three western peoples, the T'u-fan, T'u-yü-hun, and Pi-ku-tê (LS 6, 2*b*). Hence it probably dwelt in present Mongolia. *Cf.* also Subordinate States, no. 73.
16	Wu-wei Wu-ku-li 烏隈烏骨里 46, 30*a*	*Cf.* Large Tribes, no. 6.
17	Ti-lieh 敵烈 46, 30*a*	The Tereits? *Cf.* Shêng-tsung's Tribes, no. 20 and Outer Tribes, no. 2.
18	Ti-li-pi 廸離畢 46, 30*b*	Possibly one of the seventy-two Mongol tribes of the Yüan period. The name is reconstructed as Dörben, Dörbet, and Dörbetei (Yanai 30, 272).
19	Nieh-la 涅剌 46, 30*b*	Either split off from one of T'ai-tsu's old tribes (the Nieh-la), or perhaps organized after the model of the old tribe. According to Hirth (99, 44), such formations occurred frequently in the fluid tribal world of Central Asia. LS 69, 5*a* and 8*b* mention the Nieh-la together with the Wu-wei.

Various Tribes (*continued*)

No.	NAME OF TRIBE	REMARKS
20	Wu-wei 烏隗 46, 30b	According to LS 12, 6b and 46, 30b, nos. 18–20 seem to have been tribes under some sort of [military] obligation to the Northeastern Route of the Liao empire.
21	Ch'u-tê 鉏德 46, 30b	Probably identical with Ch'u-tê 楮特. If so, then parallel case to nos. 19 and 20.
22	T'i-chü 諦居 46, 30b	The location of this tribe is not clear. In 986, during the war between Liao and Sung, the commanding prefect of this tribe, Fu-nu 佛奴, received a beating of fifty strokes for failing to carry out his duties (cf. LS 11, 6b). In 987 one of the members of this tribe, Hsieh-li 解里, was appointed an imperial attendant as a reward for his good work on an espionage mission (cf. LS 12, 1a). In 1020 the punitive commissioner of the Southwestern Route reported that the Sung-hsi clan 宋犀族 of the Tang-hsiang tribe was not fully submissive and that the T'i-chü Tieh-lieh-tê tribe(s) 諦居迭烈德部 had made a request to have the commanding prefect retain his position so as to continue his good administration (cf. LS 16, 5a). Does the above name refer to a composite of two tribes or to two separate tribes governed by a single commanding prefect? If the latter was the case, the T'i-chü tribe may have been located somewhere in present Suiyuan, that is in the southwestern part of the Liao empire.
23	Nieh-la Ao-wei 涅剌奧隗 46, 30b	Another compound with one of T'ai-tsu's tribes (Nieh-la) as an element. Since in two other cases such a compound with the Ao-wei as the second element was established with Hsi families (T'ai-tsu's Tribes, nos. 14 and 15), a similar formation is also possible in the present case. A Ch'i-tan official was a prefect of this tribe (LS 92, 3a).
24	Ti-lieh Tribe of the Eight *Shih-lieh* 八石烈敵烈 46, 30b	For the Ti-lieh see above. The name seems to indicate that this particular complex consisted, at least temporarily, of eight sub-tribes.
25	Tieh-la-ko 迭剌葛 46, 30b	
26	Wu-jo 兀惹 46, 30b	The Wu-jo are identical with the Wu-jo 烏惹, Wu-shê 烏舍, and Wu-jo-chê 嗢熱者. After the fall of the Po-hai Kingdom in 926 their independent remnants set up a state called Ting-an 定安 Kingdom or Wu-jo 兀惹 tribe. The capital of this country, Wu-jo City, was located on the site of the former Supreme Capital of Po-hai (modern Tung-ching 東京 City, Kirin). Cf. Ikeuchi, MSK I, 72–113; Wada 38, 54. The Wu-jo "rebelled" against Liao in 975 (LS 8, 4b). In 994 they fought again for their independence (LS 13, 5b). In 995 they invaded the region of the T'ieh-li 鐵驪 tribe, whereupon the Liao troops attacked them but without success (LS 13, 6b). The campaign probably lasted until 999 when the chieftain Wu-chao-tu 烏昭度 (慶) came for an audience to the Liao court (LS 14, 1b). The Wu-jo captives taken by the Liao army and the T'ieh-li tribe were settled in Pin 賓 Prefecture near the juncture of the Sungari and I-t'ung 伊通 Rivers. This subdued group was called Wu-jo-chê. Cf. SMCW 5b–6b; CTKC 26, 2b–3a; IX (14).
27	Tang-hsiang 黨項 46, 30b	The Tibetan people who founded the Hsi Hsia state were called Tang-hsiang by the Chinese, and Tangu (plural Tangut) by the Liao people (LS 69, 24b) and the Mongols (Bushel 95/96, 142). This and the two following tribes are evidently different groups of the same people. According to SS 491, 12a–24b, the Tang-hsiang consisted of several groups which varied in the number of their men and horses. The Tang-hsiang tribes listed in LS 46, 30b ff. differed in political status (and strength) from the state of the same name, listed below, I, 2, The Subordinate States, no. 20. For further information see *loc. cit.* and above, I, 1, note 9.

Various Tribes (*continued*)

No.	NAME OF TRIBE	REMARKS
28	Wei-yen Tang-hsiang 隗衍黨項 46, 31a	The first element of this tribal name occurs also in the name of the Wei-yen Turks. Does it designate another people or a region?
29	Shan-nan Tang-hsiang 山南黨項 46, 31a	The Tang-hsiang "south of the mountains."
30	Northern Great Nung-wu 北大濃兀 46, 31a	
31	Southern Great Nung-wu 南大濃兀 46, 31a	Split off from the preceding tribe in 922 (LS 2, 3a).
32	Nine *Shih-lieh* 九石烈 46, 31a	The composition of this complex resembles that of no. 24. No other details are known about it.
33	Wu-niang-kai 嗢娘改 46, 31a	For the pronunciation of 嗢 as *wu* see IV, note 1. This seems to be an early record of a tribe called Urjängchan by the Mongols (Ssanang Ssetsen 1829, 87 and *passim;* also Rubruck 00, 198, note 1), Oengai by Rubruck (00, 198), Forest Urianghit by Rashīd ad-Dīn (*op. cit.*, 198, note 1; *cf.* also Bretschneider 88 II, 174), Wu-liang-ha 兀良哈 during Ming times (Wada 38, 101, note 1; Gibert 34, 707), and Urianghai [Uryangkhai] today (Yanai 30, 1–30). The tribe which lived far north of Qaraqorum in the middle of the thirteenth century was famous for its snow (or ice ?) shoes made from polished bones, which made it possible for the tribesmen "to catch birds and beasts" (Rubruck 00, 198). They lived in forests as hunters and as reindeer-breeders (*loc. cit.*, note 1). They are still famous today as reindeer-breeders (Czaplicka 18, 60). They fought bravely in the army of Chingis Khan (Ssanang Ssetsen 1829, 87). Their descendants went as far east as the Shira Muren during Ming times (Wada 38, 101, note 1; Gibert 34, 207) and spread over a wide territory under the Manchu dynasty. Their best known modern representatives live south of Central Siberia near the sources of the Yenisei River between the Sayan Mountains and the Tannu Ola ranges (Czaplicka 18, 58). Their ethnic and cultural affinity has been described as Mongol (Bretschneider, *loc. cit.*, and Gibert, *loc. cit.*), Tungus (Quatremère = Rubruck, *loc. cit.*, note 1), and Samoyed-Yeniseian mixed with Turkic (Castrén = Czaplicka 18, 59 and Jochelson 28, 26 ff.). According to Katanov, their language is Siberian Turkic. Dr. K. Menges considers them Turkicized Southern Samojeds. If indeed one thousand Uryangkhai warriors acted as the guard of Chingis Khan's tomb over a considerable period (Ssanang Ssetsen 1829, 408, note 28), then in all probability the tribe closely approximated a Mongol way of life.
34	Pi-ku-tê 鼻骨德 46, 31a	One of the eighteen western tribes which supported Yeh-lü Ta-shih when he moved toward Turkestan (LS 30, 5a). Its name is transcribed in LS 30, 5a as Pi-ku-tê 鼻古德. *Cf.* also Shêng-tsung's Tribes, nos. 32 and 33.
35	T'ui-yü-tê 退欲德 46, 31a	Evidently one of the not infrequent cases in which a tribe was called after its chieftain. T'ui-yü-tê, the head of a T'u-yü-hun 吐谷渾 tribe, led his people to submit (LS 3, 8a). Besides this tribe there existed also a country of the same name. See The Subordinate States, nos. 25 and 26.
36	Nieh-ku 涅古 46, 31a	LS 16, 3b and 46, 13a mention a Nieh-ko (哥) army of Hsi 奚 tribesmen. Vladimirtsov 34, 105 refers to a Mongol tribe called Negüs. This tribe may well be identical with the Nieh-ku and Nieh-ko, for the form Negüs evidently is a Mongol plural in -*s* of Negü[n].

Various Tribes (*continued*)

No.	NAME OF TRIBE	REMARKS
37	Yao-ssŭ-nien 遙思拈 46, 31*a*	
38	Hua-li 劃離 46, 31*b*	In 983 this tribe's petition that the office of *hsiang-wên* 詳穩 be filled by one of its members was refused by Shêng-tsung (LS 10, 6*b*; 46, 31*b*).
39	Four Tribal Groups 四部族 46, 31*b*	Located somewhere west of Ta-t'ung, perhaps in modern Suiyuan, for T'ien-tsu stayed in the family of its *hsiang-wên* in 1123 when the emperor was defeated by Chin soldiers in Shih-lien-i 石輦驛 (northwest of Ta-t'ung 大同, Shansi). *Cf.* LS 29, 5*a*.
40	Four Fan 四蕃 46, 31*b*	Location not clear. In the year 1010 a Ch'i-tan official, Yeh-lü Yao-chih 瑤質, after the campaign in Korea was appointed the *hsiang-wên* of the Four Fan tribes (LS 88, 6*a*).
41	Three Nations 三國 46, 31*b*	
42	Eastern Tribe of Su-k'un-na Mountains 素昆那山東部 46, 31*b*	In 924 the Ch'i-tan soldiers defeated this almost unknown tribe when T'ai-tsu was proceeding to Outer Mongolia (LS 2, 4*b* and 36, 10*b*). It was therefore probably located in Chahar.
43	Hu-mu-ssŭ Mountain 胡母思山 46, 31*b*	Also written 忽母思. One of the eighteen tribes which followed Yeh-lü Ta-shih (LS 30, 5*a*). Located west or southwest of the Orkhon River, for T'ai-tsu subdued this tribe on his way to the Altai Mountains after he had set up a trilingual tablet at the old Uighur capital in 924 (LS 2, 5*a*).
44	Lu-pu-ku 盧不姑 46, 31*b*	LS 3, 8*b* mentions Lu-pu-ku as a personal name. This may be another case of naming a tribe after a person.
45	Chao-ku 照姑 46, 31*b*	
46	Pai-k'o-chiu 白可久 46, 31*b*	Pai-k'o-chiu was the name of a T'u-yü-hun chieftain. The tribe may have been named after him (Fêng CS 33, 129; *cf.* also above, no. 35).
47	Yü-lu-ku 俞魯古 46, 32*a*	Exact information concerning this tribe is lacking. We know only that in 965 it offered horses to Liao. Mu-tsung in turn granted it 2,000 taels of silver (LS 7, 2*b*).
48	Ch'i-huo Shih-wei 七火室韋 46, 32*a*	For location of the Shih-wei people see above, note 5.
49	Huang-p'i Shih-wei 黃皮室韋 46, 32*a*	*Huang p'i* means "yellow skin." Two "yellow" Shih-wei tribes are mentioned in the administrative list of the empire's tribes (LS 46, 5*a*). According to LS 33, 5*a*, they were merged in the T'u-lü-pu Shih-wei tribe.
50	Yao-wên 瑤穩 46, 32*a*	No details available. In 1048 the tribe received relief from the Liao government (LS 69, 16*a*).

Various Tribes (*continued*)

No.	NAME OF TRIBE	REMARKS
51	Ch'ao-wên 嘲穩 46, 32a	Received relief in 1048 (LS 20, 2a).
52	Two Nü-ku 二女古 46, 32a	The nobles of this tribe who held hereditary positions were not obliged to enlist in the Liao army (LS 21, 3a). The commoners obviously were under this obligation. In 1117 they were stationed at Ch'un 春 Prefecture (northwest of Po-tu-na 伯都訥, Kirin) together with Liao troops (LS 28, 4b). From this record it may be deduced that the Nü-ku tribes probably lived in the northeastern border region of the empire.
53	Mieh-ssǔ-nai 蔑思乃 46, 32a	
54	Ma-ta-li Pieh-ku 麻達里別古 46, 32a	This seems to be either a compound tribe made up of Ma-ta-li and Pieh-ku, or the single Pieh-ku with the designation Ma-ta-li. Pieh-ku may be the simplified form of Pi-kuo-tê 鼻國德, Pi-ku-tê 鼻骨 (or 古) 德, or Pi-ku-li 髀古里. A Sung map of 1180 locates the Pi-ku-li tribe between the Yü-chüeh 于厥 and the Tatar tribes northwest of the Supreme Capital of Liao (CTKC, map 2).
55	Mei-li-chi 梅里急 46, 32a	In the twelfth century the Merkits were a nomad tribe whose territory was north of the Keraits, on the Lower Selenga (Vladimirtsov 30, 9; Rubruck 00, 111, note 2). Rubruck calls them Merkit (*loc. cit.*, 111; *cf.* also Bretschneider 88 I, 28; Barthold 28, 361 ff. and 370 ff.; and Yanai 30, 546). Pelliot (20, 146, note 2) renders the name as Märkit.
56	Wo-lu 斡魯 46, 32a	In 1043 the Wo-lu tribe offered tribute on the same day as the P'u-lu-mao-to tribe which was located in the east (see above, Outer Tribes, no. 10). An earlier habitat to the north is suggested by the possibility that the name Wo-lu is derived from the Tungus word *oron*, "reindeer." The final *n* is dropped before certain declension suffixes.
57	Yü-li-ti-nai 榆里底乃 46, 32b	According to LS 88, 7a, the Liao general Ta K'ang-i 大康乂, a man of Po-hai descent, once held the post of commanding prefect of Huang-lung Administration 黃龍府, controlling the tribes east of that region. The chieftains of the Yü-li-ti-nai tribe came to submit to him. They were sent on to see the Liao emperor. This story indicates that the Yü-li-ti-nai tribe was probably located in modern Kirin.
58	Shuai-lei 率類 46, 32b	
59	Tribe of the Five-tribe Fan 五部蕃部 46, 32b	Apparently identical with the Five Fan tribe. According to LS 82, 4b, Hsiao Yang-a 陽阿 after his father's death transported his coffin from the region of the Five Fan tribe to that region of Hsi-wang-ling 奚王嶺 which was probably in present Jehol Province.
60	P'u-nu-li 蒲奴里 46, 32b	Also transcribed as P'ên-nu-li 盆奴里 (LS 33, 9a). LS 95, 3b reports that the P'u-nu-li tribe rebelled in 1048. Yeh-lü Hsien-t'ung 仙童, commanding prefect of the Five Nations tribe, attacked the rebels and captured their chieftain. Thus it is evident that the P'u-nu-li tribe was located in the eastern part of modern Kirin. This tribe and four other groups paid an annual tribute of 300 horses to Liao (LS 60, 4a). In 1018 the government of Liao ordered the five tribes to pay an annual tribute of 65,000 sable skins and 300 horses (LS 69, 12b–13a).
61	Cha-ku-hu-li-p'a 闸古胡里扒 46, 32b	

10. THE SUBORDINATE STATES

No	NAME OF STATE[35]	TITLE OF RULER	REMARKS
1	Nü-chih 女直 46, 24b	Obedient King 順化王	Among the various Jurchen "states," this one seems to have been particularly close to Liao. In 990 the Liao government conferred upon its ruler the title *shun hua wang* 順化王, "the King who is Obedient to Our Transforming Influence." The people were therefore also called *shun [hua]* Nü-chih 順 [化] 女直 (LS 46, 24b; for parallels to this title see Chavannes 04, 28 ff.). Their territory was probably near Hsien 咸 Prefecture (modern K'ai-yüan 開原 County, northeastern Liaoning), for A-ku-ta 阿骨打 in a quarrel with their king in 1113 brought the case before the government of Hsien Prefecture (LS 27, 7b).
2	Northern Nü-chih 北女直 46, 24b	Great King 大王	According to title and position in our list, nos. 2 and 3 are less important than 1. Their relative locations are indicated by the directional element in their names; the absolute location may be guessed from the data given about the surrounding Jurchen groups. The two states were probably situated between the Ch'ang-pai Mountains in the east or northeast, the Liaoning Peninsula in the south, and Hsien Prefecture in the west.
3	Southern Nü-chih 南女直 46, 25a	Great King	
4	Ho-su-kuan Route Nü-chih 曷蘇館路女直 46, 25a	Great King	Also transcribed as Ho-su-kun 合蘇袞, Ho-su 合素, and Su-kuan 蘇館 (LS 46, 25a), words which are equivalent to the Manchu term *xasxan* (LSYC 3, 8b), "fence, palisades," or to *xasxū*, "left, east(ern), obstinate" (see Gabelentz 64, 95; Zakharov 75, 385). The people of this "state" were shifted by the Liao government to the Liaotung Peninsula to separate them from their native regions. In 1027 they were allowed to set up their own "banners and drums."
5	Ch'ang-pai Mountains Nü-chih 長白山女直 46, 25a	Great King	*Cf.* Outer Tribes, no. 9.
6	Yalu River Nü-chih 鴨渌江女直	Great King	The names of nos. 6 and 7 indicate a location in the region of the Yalu River and along the seashore respectively.
7	Seashore Nü-chih 瀕海女直 46, 25a	Great King	
8	Tsu-pu 阻卜 46, 25a	Great King	Generally used in the *Liao Shih* and *Chin Shih* as a substitute for Tatar. The name Tatar first appears in an Orkhon inscription of 731 (Radloff 95, 5, 11, 45, and 64; Thomsen 96, 102, 126, and 140). A Persian geography which mentions the Tatars and the Turks as belonging to the Toghuzghuz was written in 982 (Hudūd al-'Ālam 37, 94 and 11). In Chinese texts the Tatars 達怛 have been mentioned since 842. They are, however, rarely spoken of in the *Liao Shih* and the *Chin Shih*. According to Wang Kuo-wei, this is due to the derogatory way in which the Sung Chinese applied the word Tatar to the Mongols. Thus the word, though used a few times in the *Liao Shih* for the sake of continuity, was generally tabooed. It was replaced by the word Tsu-pu, written in the *Liao Shih* 阻卜 and Tsu-p'u 阻䪁 in the *Chin Shih* (KTCL 14, 5b–12a; *cf.* also Pelliot 29, 125). Wang Ching-ju accepts the suggested identification of Tatar and Tsu-pu but points out that the word Tsu-p'u had already been used during Chin times; Tsu-pu and Tsu-p'u both resemble

[35] Unless otherwise noted the original text has attached to each of the names in this column the character *kuo* 國 (state).

Subordinate States (*continued*)

No.	NAME OF STATE	TITLE OF RULER	REMARKS
			the Tibetan word for Mongols, *sogpo* (Wang CJ 31, 296–301). These facts explain why the word Tsu-pu was chosen as a substitute for Tatar. That the Yüan writers tended toward such a substitute is proved by the twofold recording of a serious war against an unruly people which occurred during the reign of Liao Tao-tsung. A Liao inscription calls the enemies, whose chieftain was finally executed, Ta-ta 韃靼 (LLSKCL 3, 7*a*). The *Liao Shih* mentions no war against the Ta-ta here but reports instead a long struggle between the Ch'i-tan and the Tsu-pu which ended with the public execution of the Tsu-pu chief by the victorious Liao army (LS 25, 4*b*–26, 5*a*). Wang Kuo-wei (KTCL 14, 5*b*–12*a*) claims an ethnic and linguistic uniformity for the Tartars without, however, defining its character. It seems that the collective Chinese term for Tatar was essentially applied to Mongol-speaking peoples except for the White Tatars, the Öngüt, who were probably of Turkic origin (Pelliot 29, 125 ff.; Yanai 30, 562 ff.).
9	Western Tsu-pu 西阻卜	Great King	
10	Northern Tsu-pu 北阻卜	Great King	Fêng Ch'êng-chün, who considers Tsu-pu a collective term for a great number of Inner Asiatic people, believes that the Eastern Tsu-pu, no. 8 of our list, comprised the Jalair (*cha-la-êrh* 扎剌兒) and Tatars. According to him, the latter were not identical with, but a sub-division of the Tsu-pu. He assumes that the Western Tsu-pu were the Naiman and the Northern Tsu-pu the Kerait. No equation is offered for the Northwestern Tsu-pu (Fêng CC 39, 16–22).
11	Northwestern Tsu-pu 西北阻卜 46, 25*b*	Great King	
12	Ch'i-su River 乞粟河 46, 25*b*	Great King	
13	Ch'êng-ch'ü-li 城屈里 46, 25*b*	Great King	
14	Chu-pu-ku 术不姑 46, 25*b*	Great King	Also written as Shu(述)-pu-ku and Chih(直)-pu-ku. *Cf.* Various Tribes, no. 2.
15	A-sa-lan Uighurs 阿薩蘭回鶻 46, 25*b*	Great King	The character *kuo* 國 is not included in the name. Also called Administration of the A-sa-lan King. This and the next four states are all listed as separate political units of the Uighur people, some of whose representatives we have already encountered among the Outer Tribes of Liao (see no. 8). *Arslan* means "lion." The title "Lion King" was assumed by the ruler of the Kao-ch'ang Uighurs in 981 (WHTK 336, 2639). But the same designation was also used by the rulers of other Uighur countries, such as Kan 甘 Prefecture (LS 93, 1*a*) and Chiu-tzŭ 龜茲 (SS 490, 22*a*). The A-sa-lan Uighurs of the *Liao Shih* are often, but not always, identical with the main center of Uighur power of this period, Kao-ch'ang (see below, no. 19).
16	Uighur 回鶻 45, 25*b*	Shan-yü 單于	The term *shan-yü*, the designation of the ruler of the Uighur state, was the title of the Hunnish rulers. After the fifth or sixth century, when the supreme tribal chieftains of Central Asia assumed the title of "khaghan," *shan-yü* was still occasionally used as an honorific designation for important chieftains. Following the destruction of the Turkic empire by the T'ang forces in 630, a "protectorate general of the Shan-yü" (*shan-yü tu-hu fu* 都護府) was set up in 650 to control the Turks of the Orkhon River region of Outer Mongolia. The office was located close to the T'ang territory, some-

Subordinate States (*continued*)

No.	NAME OF STATE	TITLE OF RULER	REMARKS
			where in Suiyuan (*cf.* TS 43*B*, 1*b*; 215*A*, 10*a*; Des Rotours 27, 255 ff.). The Uighurs of our text may have been remnants of groups which succeeded the Turks in the control of the Orkhon River region. In 924, shortly before T'ai-tsu reached the site of the old Uighur capital, he is said to have halted in the region of the old Shan-yü state (*ku shan-yü kuo*) (LS 2, 4*b*). The Uighurs were governed by an "administration of the Shan-yü" (*shan-yü fu*) which was perhaps an echo of the T'ang "protectorate general of the Shan-yü."
17	Sha Prefecture Uighurs 沙州回鶻 46, 26*a*	King of Tun-huang Commandery 燉煌郡王	The character *kuo* 國 is not included in the name. Marco Polo, after having "traveled thirty days through the Desert" to the east, arrived at a city called Sachiu, which was then part of the Tangut country (Marco Polo 03, I 203). Here, during the Early Han Period, Tun-huang Commandery was set up in 111 B.C. (HS 6, 19*b*; see also de Groot 21, 146). In 622 the T'ang emperors called the region Sha 沙 (Sand) Prefecture. The place which possessed "many amenities and running waters" (Hudūd al-'Ālam 37, 85) was a fertile oasis of about two hundred square miles in the westernmost corner of Kansu, close to Eastern Turkestan (see Marco Polo 03 I, 206–207, note 1; *cf.* also Bushell 80, 514 and 543; and Giles 33–35, 545 ff.). From the ninth century on Tun-huang was nominally under Chinese rule. Actually, however, it was controlled by the Uighurs who in the tenth and eleventh centuries were politically dependent first upon the Liao and then upon the Hsi Hsia. The military importance of this section of the route that linked China and Central Asia is manifest (see Chavannes 03*a*, 388, note 3). Here, a thousand years later, at modern Tun-huang County (LWKKC 3*b*–4*a*), Sir Aurel Stein and Paul Pelliot discovered invaluable manuscripts concerning the life of Central Asia, particularly during the Han and T'ang periods (*cf.* Pelliot 10, 655 ff.; Chavannes 13, *passim;* Giles 15, 468 ff.; Pelliot 31, 18 ff.; Giles 33–35, 556 ff.).
18	Kan Prefecture Uighurs 甘州回鶻 46, 26*a*	Great King	The character *kuo* 國 is not included in the name. Located in the region of Chang-yeh 張掖 County in modern Kansu. After the middle of the ninth century this was the center of power of the southern Uighurs (Chavannes 97 VC, 406, note 3). When A-pao-chi established the dynasty, he still considered it worth while negotiating with them (LS 2, 5*a*; 30, 5*a* ff.). Even after Hsi Hsia and Liao had reduced them to a shadowy political existence in the eleventh century, the Kan Prefecture Uighurs preserved very archaic Turkic features such as the mode of counting revealed in the Orkhon inscriptions and certain Uighur texts (Barthold 35, 49–50).
19	Kao-ch'ang 高昌 46, 26*a*	Great King	The name Kao-ch'ang was already in existence during the Han period. The fort (壁) of Kao-ch'ang, which is mentioned in HS 96*B*, 20*b* and HHS 88, 7*b* (*cf.* also WS 101, 22*b* ff.), was probably located on the site of the later city of Kao-ch'ang 70 *li* east of modern Turfan, in Eastern Turkestan (Chavannes 07, 155, note 1; *cf.* also Pelliot 12*b*, 581). In 460 K'an Po-chou 闞伯周 established a kingdom in this region (WS 101, 23*a*; *cf.* also Pelliot 12*b*, 581; Julien 1847, 196). From the sixth century on another house called Ch'ü 麴 ruled the country (Sui 83, 6*a*). When after the middle of the eighth century a new Kao-ch'ang state was set up, it was also called the country of the Uighurs, for by that time the Uighur population had become quite numerous (WHTK 336, 2638). The collapse of the Uighur empire after the seizure of its Orkhon capital in 840 led to the consolidation of some remnants of Uighur power in Eastern Turkestan. The new country of the western Uighurs (Hsi-chou 西州 Uighurs), which was set up in 860, was designated as Kao-ch'ang or Ho-chou 和州 (also written as Huo-chou 火州 and Huo-chê 火者). The latter group of terms represents the Chinese transcription of the name Qočo, which according to Pelliot (12*b*, 590 ff.) is probably nothing but a Turkic version of the old Chinese name Kao-ch'ang. In the Mongol period there appears the compound form Qarā-khodjo, the forerunner of the modern name

Subordinate States (*continued*)

No.	NAME OF STATE	TITLE OF RULER	REMARKS
			Qarā-khodja (*op. cit.*, 582). The population of the Uighur state of Kao-ch'ang or Ho-chou (*cf.* LS 1, 7*b* and 27, 6*b*) comprised indigenous as well as Uighur elements. Its capital was Beshbalyq. The Sung envoy, Wang Yen-tê 王延德, who visited the country between 981 and 984, that is before the great Liao-Sung war, gave a detailed description of the country. His account has been translated into Western languages. Because of scarcity of rain and snow, irrigation was practised. Grain was cultivated and horses were raised in abundance. A good horse cost only a bolt of lustring, and a poor one not more than a cash. Horsemeat served as food for the nobles; beef and geese as food for the common people. The T'ang calendar was used. Buddha was worshipped in more than fifty temples, one of which treasured Buddhist sūtras and Chinese dictionaries. Wang's report mentions also Persian temples of Mo-ni 摩尼 (Mani). The king was called Shih-tzǔ Wang 獅子王, Lion King. His highest official was the *yü-yüeh* 于越 (SS 490, 8*a*–12*b*; HCCL 4, 129–139). For translations of Wang Yen-tê's report see Julien 1847, 52 ff.; Schott 76, 41 ff.; *cf.* also Chavannes 97, 81–82; Pelliot 12*b*, 579 ff.; Müller 12, 211 ff.; *idem* 15, 4 ff.; de Groot 21, 178 and *passim; idem* 26, 165 ff.; Barthold 28, 388.
20	Tang-hsiang 黨項 46, 26*a*	Great King	The Tang-hsiang people listed here were evidently Tibetans like the inhabitants of Hsi Hsia and the Tang-hsiang tribes mentioned above. The Tang-hsiang were divided into a number of groups which were scattered over the northern parts of modern Shansi, Shensi, Kansu, the Ordos region, and Suiyuan. In 986 Shêng-tsung bestowed a high title upon Ch'i-i 乞移 or Chi-i 佶移, the chieftain of a very powerful group, called Wa-ni 瓦泥 or Wu-ni 兀泥 (LS 11, 1*b*). This group numbered 1,500 households. In 1001 the head of another group, called Pei-ning 卑寧, boasted 30,000 horsemen (SS 491, 18*a*–*b*) which probably was an exaggeration. LS 20, 5*b* compares the Hsi Hsia tributes with those of Tang-hsiang (see X, 2 (83)). The tributes from the Tang-hsiang consisted mainly of horses, camels, oxen, sheep, and deer (see X, introduction, and X 2, *passim*).
21	Hsi Hsia 西夏 46, 26*a*	Hsi-p'ing King 西平王	The kingdom of Hsi Hsia had its capital on the site of Halar west of the Ho-lan Mountain. The territory consisted of five prefectures and seven market towns (*chên* 鎮). At the time of Li Yüan-hao 李元昊 (eleventh century) the Hsi Hsia reached the peak of their power. The people produced barley, beans, and other crops (LS 115, 5*b*); but, judging from their tributes and other indices, stockbreeding must have been an important part of their economy as well. Pelliot calls the Hsi Hsia a half-nomadic, half-sedentary kingdom (Pelliot 31, 21).
22	Korea 高麗 46, 26*a*	King 王	In ancient times there existed in the region of the Tung-chia River 佟佳江 in present Liaoning a people called Kao-chü-li 高句驪. In the fifth century they moved their capital to P'ing-jang. The name of the country was simplified to Kao-li 高麗 (Korea). In 668, attacked by the armies of T'ang and Silla (see below no. 23), Korea lost its independence. It remained under the control of Silla for more than two hundred years. In 918 Korea arose again as a sovereign state, subduing Silla in 936. During the time of Liao the name of the ruling family was changed from Ko 高 to Wang 王. According to the *Hsüan-ho Fêng-shih Kao-li T'u-ching* 宣和奉使高麗圖經, composed in forty chapters by a Sung official, Hsü Ching 徐兢 (T. 明叔, 1093–1155), the preface of which is dated in the year 1124, Korea had then reached the level of a high agricultural civilization. The people built cities, palaces, and temples and established an official hierarchy according to the Chinese pattern. They rode on horseback and had carts pulled by oxen (KLTC 15 and 16, *passim*).

Subordinate States (*continued*)

No.	NAME OF STATE	TITLE OF RULER	REMARKS
			The artisans were skilful (*op. cit.*, 19, 2*a*). The people were not allowed to have private land. From the officials down to the commoners all the people held their land from the government. They produced rice, several kinds of millet, hemp, barley, and wheat (*op. cit.* 23, 1*b*). Another important product was ginseng (*jên-shên* 人參). They wove silk fabrics but were not experienced in rearing silkworms. Gold and silver was scarce, but copper was plentiful (*op. cit.* 23, 3*b*–4*a*).
23	Silla 新羅 46, 26*a*	King	The state of Silla is said to have been established as early as 37 B.C. in the southeastern part of Korea. The country, which had controlled the whole peninsula in the latter part of the seventh and during the eighth and ninth centuries, collapsed in 936. The main source dealing with this kingdom is the *Sam-gook Sa Kii* 三國史記, compiled by a Korean scholar, Kim Poo-sik 金富軾, in 1145. *Cf.* also WHTK 326, 2564–2565; Saint Denys 76, 298 ff.
24	Japan 日本 46, 26*a*	King	For the cultural and political relation between Liao and Japan see X, 2 and introduction.
25	T'u-yü-hun 吐谷渾 46, 26*a*	King	The T'u-yü-hun (谷 here pronounced *yü*, not *ku; cf.* Chavannes 03, 372), also called T'u-hun, were a branch of the Hsien-pei (Pelliot 12, 522; *idem* 21, 323 ff.); they were thus ethnically related to the Shih-wei, Liao, and Hsi. They lived east of the Liao River until the middle of the third century A.D. Then, led by their chieftain, T'u-yü-hun 吐谷渾, one branch migrated westward to the region of Kuku-Nōr (Chinghai). The chieftain's younger brother, Mu-jung Wei 慕容廆, proclaimed himself Grand Shan-yü of the Hsien-pei in the region of modern Manchuria. His successors formed in northeastern China two short-lived dynasties, the Early Yen 前燕 (349–370) and the Later Yen 後燕 (384–409) (*cf.* Chin 108, 1*a* ff.; TS 221*A*, 5*b*–8*a*). The T'u-yü-hun of the *Liao Shih* belonged to the western branch. They had their capital near Kuku-Nōr. After being severely defeated by the T'u-fan (Tibetans) in 663, they temporarily regained their strength at the close of the century (Chavannes 03, 181, 280, 290). The T'u-yü-hun and the Juan-juan are supposed to have been the first people to call their chiefs "khaghan" (Pelliot 31, 12). Under pressure from their stronger neighbors, they decreased in strength in the middle of the tenth century, leading only a shadowy political existence thereafter (TS 221*A*, 8*a*; see also WTS 74, 2*a* ff.). Chavannes (03, 260) believes the T'u-yü-hun to have been Tungus, whereas Pelliot, stressing their Hsien-pei background, assumes their language to have been Mongol (Pelliot 21, 325–330). The designation of the T'u-yü-hun as Ha-ža (*ʔA-ža*) is neither of Mongol nor Tibetan origin. It referred originally to the mixed tribes of northern Kansu whom the T'u-yü-hun subdued (Pelliot 12, 522; *idem* 21, 323 ff.).
26	T'u-hun 吐渾 46, 26*b*	King	See no. 25. Toward the end of the T'ang period, the T'u-yü-hun were frequently called T'ui-hun 退渾 or T'u-hun (TS 221*A*, 8*a*; WTS 74, 2*a* ff.; see also Pelliot 21, 323). T'u-(yü)-hun is possibly the Orkhon-Turkic title *tujγun* (Radloff, WB III, 1432—without translation), "one who notices, perceives," from Turkic *tuj-*, "to notice, perceive."
27	Khirghiz 轄戛斯 46, 26*b*	King	First mentioned as a northern people in the form Ko-k'un 鬲昆 (SC 110, 11*b*) and Chien-k'un 堅昆 (HS 94*B*, 5*b*). Later recorded as Chieh-ku 結骨, Ho-ku 紇骨, Ho-ku-ssŭ 紇扢斯, or Hsia-chia-ssŭ 黠戛斯 (TS 217*B*, 10*b*). The variant of our text, Hsia-chia-ssŭ, is another crude transcription of the original word which according to Barthold would best be transcribed as *ki-li-ki-si* (Barthold 35, 35). The Khirghiz preserved their northern habitat until the time of the Orkhon inscriptions, i.e. 732–735. They then lived

Subordinate States (*continued*)

No.	NAME OF STATE	TITLE OF RULER	REMARKS
			along the upper course of the Yenisei River (Radloff 95, 21 and 425; *idem* 99, 14 ff., 57; Thomsen 96, 98, 102, and 140; Hirth 99, 42). Having overthrown the Uighurs in 840, they probably held the Orkhon region for a while but were driven back again at the beginning of the tenth century when the Ch'i-tan became the masters of Central Asia (Barthold 35, 97). A tenth century record states that they were good fighters, hunters, and breeders of sheep, cows, and horses (Hudūd al-ʿĀlam 37, 96). Rubruck found them north of Qaraqorum and describes them as herdsmen without cities (Rubruck 00, 197; *cf.* also Radloff 93, I, 136 ff.). Their language is very closely related to Orkhon-Turkic and Ancient and Modern Uighur.
28	Shih-wei 室韋 46, 26*b*	King	The large northern branch of what had formerly been the Hsien-pei people. See above, note 5.
29	Black-cart Shih-wei 黑車子室韋 46, 26*b*	King	The first part of this name seems to be a Chinese designation of a particular Shih-wei tribe rather than of another tribal element (Pelliot 29, 124). The men of this tribe were renowned cart-makers (WTS 73, 9*a*; *cf.* also Chavannes 97 VC, 407). Wang Kuo-wei thinks that they shifted from the north of the Ch'i-tan territory to the region of the Yin 陰 Mountains (KTCL 14, 1*a*–3*b*), probably somewhere in modern Chahar.
30	T'ieh-li 鐵驪 46, 26*b*	King	The T'ieh-li, also written 鐵利, must not be identified with the Turkic T'ieh-lo 鐵勒 or Tölös who spread over Central and Western Asia during the eighth century (see Hirth 99, 37–43; *cf.* also Radloff 95, 496; Marquart 98, 48; Chavannes 03, 368; and with new arguments Boodberg 34). The T'ieh-li tribe of our text first appeared in the time of T'ang (*cf.* TS 219, 8*a*). It became one of the fifteen administrative units (府) of the Po-hai kingdom (*cf.* TS 219, 10*b*). After the fall of the latter country the T'ieh-li continued to be organized as an administration under the Liao government, but their former importance was lost. The T'ieh-li were located near the A-lo-ch'u-ko 阿勒楚喀 River, Kirin (*cf.* Ikeuchi, MSK I, 21 ff.). In 1012 a T'ieh-li tribesman presented more than a hundred Wu-jo captives to Pin 賓 Prefecture and asked for Buddhist images and Chinese classics in return. This request was granted (IX (14)).
31	Mo-ho 靺鞨 46, 26*b*	King	Called Wu-chi 勿吉 during the time of the Southern and Northern dynasties (fourth to sixth century). The name Wu-chi may have been formed under the influence of another early tribal name, Wo-chü 沃沮, which possibly corresponds to the Manchu term *wedži*, forest. The tribe was called Mo-ho during the Sui and T'ang periods and after (TS 219, 7*b*). Its various groups spread over a wide territory from the Amur and Sungari Rivers to the Pai 白 Mountains and the northern border of Korea. The Mo-ho had a mixed economy of agriculture, pig- and horse-breeding, and extensive hunting. They sought shelter in dugouts against the abundant rains. Although their civilization was much simpler than that of their Korean neighbors, their old name Wu-chi or Mo-ho has been mistaken for that of Korea. The Turkic name for Korea was Mug-lig. The Sanskrit name was Mukri or Mukuri (Pelliot 20, 145; Stein 39, 43; and Boodberg 39, 239, note 46). This parallels the usage of a modified form of the name Ch'i-tan—Kathai and Cathay—to designate China. The question whether the Wu-chi or Mukri were identical with the Avar group, Mukri, of Theophylaktos Simokattes (*cf.* Chavannes 03, 230 and Marquart 14, 88) cannot be treated here. Pelliot, though not excluding this possibility, prefers to identify the Avars in question with the Märkit. As to the Mo-ho, Pelliot rejects an assumed Tatar-Mongol affiliation and suggests instead a Tungus background (Pelliot 20, 145 ff.; for a translation of Ma Tuan-lin's description of the Mo-ho or Wu-chi see Saint-Denys 76, 333–346).

Subordinate States (*continued*)

No.	NAME OF STATE	TITLE OF RULER	REMARKS
32	Sha-t'o 沙陀 46, 26*b*	King	The Sha-t'o, a Western Turkic tribe (Pelliot 29, 126), lived near Lake Barkul in Eastern Turkestan, with their capital at Beshbalyq. Pressed by other Western Turkic groups, they migrated eastward and in the ninth century established themselves north of the Great Wall (Barthold 35, 49). In consideration of their growing strength the T'ang court appointed their chieftain to the position of commanding prefect of northern Shansi. In 923 their ruler, Li Ts'un-hsü 李存勗, even established a short-lived dynasty, the Later T'ang (923–935). The Sha-t'o possibly set up the Later Chin (936–946) and certainly the Later Han (947–951) dynasties, which both more or less depended upon the Liao government. See TS 218, 1*a* ff.; also Bushell 80, 533, note 57; Bretschneider 88 I, 47; Chavannes 03, 272.
33	Wei-mo 濊貊 46, 26*b*	King	The term Wei-mo in its broader sense covers all tribes which spread over modern Kirin, Liaoning, and Korea before and during the Han dynasty. In its narrower sense the term refers to the tribes which lived in eastern Korea (Fêng CS 34*a*, 3).
34	Turks 突厥 46, 26*b*	King	The early history of the Turkic tribes and the name under which they were subsumed may be studied in the special literature devoted to this topic (*cf.* Chavannes 03, 217 ff.; Barthold 35, 33 ff.). The Chinese equivalent, T'u-chüeh 突厥, transcribing Türk-üt, an archaic plural in -(*ü*)*t* of the tribal name Türk, already appears in the history of Northern Wei. The oldest preserved literary documents of the Turkic language, the Orkhon inscriptions, contain the word "Türk" frequently (Radloff 95, *passim;* Thomsen 96, 98 and *passim*). Barthold, however, doubts that it was used there as a proper name (Barthold 35, 33). It certainly was not yet the name for all Turkic speaking tribes. In this wider sense the word seems to have been first employed by the Chinese historians and Arabian authors; their example was followed by many but not all branches of the Turkic people when they turned Mohammedan (Barthold 35, 34). The *Liao Shih* mentions, besides the Turks proper, all kinds of Turkic groups whose names do not reveal their Turkic background. The reader must therefore keep in mind that the Turkic people within and around the Liao empire were much more numerous than is indicated by the nomenclature. For more details, see above I, 2, note 15.
35	Western Turks 西突厥 46, 26*b*	King	The Western Turks lived in the region of the Ili 伊犁 River in present Sinkiang and south of Lake Balkhash. The country was very strong at the beginning of the seventh century. It was to these Turks or their ancestors that the Byzantine emperor sent a delegation in 568 to form an alliance against the Sassanids. The country of the Western Turks was destroyed in 659 (*cf.* Chavannes 03, 268). The people mentioned in our text were perhaps the remnants of the Western Turks.
36	Wo-lang-kai 斡朗改 46, 27*a*	King	Uryangkhai. See Various Tribes, no. 33.
37	Ti-lieh-tê 廸烈得 46, 27*a*	King	*Cf.* Shêng-tsung's Tribes, no. 20.
38	Yü-chüeh 于厥 46, 27*a*	King	Reading *yü* 于 for the *Kan* 干 of our text. Identical with the Wu-ku, Yü-chüeh-li or Yü-chüeh-lü. *Cf.* Outer Tribes, no. 1.
39	Yüeh-li-tu 越離覩 46, 27*a*	King	Probably identical with the Yüeh-li-tu of the Five Nations tribe. See Shêng-tsung's Tribes, no. 34.

Subordinate States (*continued*)

No.	NAME OF STATE	TITLE OF RULER	REMARKS
40	A-li 阿里 46, 27a	King	Possibly identical with the P'ou-a-li 剖阿里 of the Five Nations tribe.
41	Ao-li 襖里 46, 27a	King	Possibly identical with the Ao-li-mi 奥里米 of the Five Nations tribe.
42	Chu-hui 朱灰 46, 27a	King	
43	Wu-sun 烏孫 46, 27a	King	The Wu-sun people lived north of present Kansu until 175 B.C. when they migrated to the Ili River, Sinkiang. No record mentions the state as still existing during the time of Liao (HS 96B, 1a–8b; Fêng CS 36, 1–18; Bretschneider 88 I, 123).
44	Khotan 于闐 46, 27a	King	The Chinese transcription is Yü-t'ien. This country is first mentioned during the Early Han dynasty. It covered modern Khotan in southern Sinkiang. Yü-t'ien paid tribute to the court of Sung several times in the period from the ninth to the twelfth centuries (SS 490, 4a–8a; cf. also Hirth 85, 151; Bretschneider 88 II, 246; Chavannes 03, 9 and passim).
45	Shih-tzǔ 獅子 46, 27a	King	Shih-tzǔ is the Chinese equivalent of the Sanskrit word Simhala in the name for Ceylon (cf. Pelliot 04, 349; Ware 33, 131). But were the Liao people really in contact with this remote island? Shih-tzǔ, like arslan, and simhala, means "lion." Lion Kings are mentioned for a number of Central Asiatic countries in our period (see above, no. 15). The tributes which Liao received in 989 from the "Lion Country" may have been sent by any one of them and not necessarily by the remote island of Ceylon.
46	Ta-shih 大食 46, 27b	King	The Chinese term Ta-shih is a transliteration of the Persian word Tāzīk which in Turkic became Tadžik (Radloff, WB III, 913). Originally applied to the Arabs, Tāzīk later was used in Central Asia to designate people of the Islamic faith, particularly Iranians (Barthold 35, 42). In the Liao Shih the name Ta-shih may well refer to two different countries: the mission of 924 (LS 2, 4b) possibly came from the Arabian Caliphate of Baghdad; the Ta-shih, which in 1020 sent a mission to Liao and in 1021 received a Liao bride for the ruler's son (X, 2 (71)), was the country of Qadir-khan as a letter to Sultan Mahmūd suggests (Marvazī 42, 20; see also I, introduction, note 108). Qadir-khan's dynasty, the Turkic Qarā-Khānids, adopted Islam long before the mass of nomad Turks (cf. IX, note 52). The term Ta-shih, as used in LS 16, must have implied adherence to the Mohammedan faith and may, therefore, have referred both to the large sedentary Iranian population of Eastern Turkestan and their Qarā-Khānid rulers. Yeh-lü Ta-shih marched westward through the Uighur country of Kao-ch'ang in search of Ta-shih (appendix V, B, 2, 1130, LS 30, 5b). According to LS 69, 24b, he seized Hui-hui [Islamic] Ta-shih after having passed through a "Uighur city" and before taking Hsin-ssǔ-kan [Samarqand]. During this period he occupied Eastern Turkestan which was controlled by various branches of the Qarā-Khānid dynasty (see appendix V, B, 2, passim).
47	Hsi-fan 西蕃	King	Here the list enumerates four Fan countries. The fourth is T'u-fan which is the ancient Chinese name for Tibet. The Hsi (Western), the Ta (Great), and the Hsiao (Small) Fan were no longer part of the unified Tibetan country, which, during the middle of the T'ang period, exerted its influence upon China as well as upon part of Central Asia (cf. Franke, GCR II, 371 ff.; Petech 39, 60 ff.). After 842 the Tibetan empire dissolved into a number of small states

Subordinate States (*continued*)

No.	NAME OF STATE	TITLE OF RULER	REMARKS
			ruled by "petty local chieftains" (Petech 39, 83) of which the four countries of our list seem to have been conspicuous representatives. During the T'ang period the Chinese designation of the Tibetan people was T'u-fan (TS 216*A*, 1*a* ff.; *cf.* also Chavannes 03, 46 and *passim*). At the same time the name Tüpüt (or Tüpöt, Töpüt, Töpöt; see Pelliot 15*a*, 20 ff.) appears in the Turkic
48	Ta-fan 大蕃	King	Orkhon inscriptions (see Radloff 95, 5, 74, 336; Thomsen 96, 98, 115 and 140). The name is taken as referring to Tibet by Radloff, Thomsen, and Pelliot (*loc. cit.*). A Chinese manuscript of the tenth century discovered at Tunhuang contains the name T'ê-fan 特番 (reconstructed pronunciation *Dak-p'ʷan) which is similar to T'u-fan (Pelliot 15*a*, 18–20). *Dak-p'ʷan is evidently the Chinese rendering of the word Drok-pa by which the Tibetans designate themselves. In Persia the name Tubbat was known in the tenth century (Hudūd al-'Ālam 37, 92). Mahmūd-al-Kāshgharī's Turkic dictionary
49	Hsiao-fan 小蕃	King	of 1066/7 has Tübüt (Brockelmann 28, 250). Thus both designations existed side by side. Gradually the word Tibet gained ground also in China.
			The Chio-ssǔ-lo 唃廝羅 tribe, a tribe of T'u-fan descendants, occupied part of modern Kansu and Chinghai. During the tenth and eleventh centuries the Chio-ssǔ-lo reached the peak of their strength. The Sung government treated them preferentially, for they served to check the Hsi Hsia whom they defeated several times. Around 1058 Liao offered a bride to a young chieftain, Tung Chan 董氈. Obviously, Liao was suspicious of the policy of the Sung empire which, later on, expanded its territory into this tribal
50	T'u-fan 吐蕃 46, 27*b*	King	region (SS 492, 14*a*; HWKC 19, 256).
			The Chio-ssǔ-lo tribe is not mentioned in the *Liao Shih;* it seems possible that it is hidden behind one of the four Fan of our list.
51	A-sa-li 阿撒里 46, 27*b*	King	A-sa-lan 阿薩蘭. *Arslan?*
52	Po-la 波剌 46, 27*b*	King	The second character *la* 剌 is possibly a mistake for *tz'ǔ* 刺. If so, Po-tz'ǔ may be a variant of Po-ssǔ 波斯, Persia, which is mentioned several times in the *Liao Shih* (2, 3*b*; 36, 10*b*; 70, 2*a*) whereas no records are given about a country called Po-la.
53	T'i-yin 惕隱 46, 27*b*	King	Lo Chi-tsu 羅繼祖 proposes reading T'i-tê 惕德 instead of T'i-yin (LSCKC 5, 38*a*). This is a plausible suggestion, for the T'i-tê people, who are frequently mentioned in the *Liao Shih* (25, 4*b*, 6*b*, 7*b*), would not otherwise appear in the lists of the tribes and states.
54	Hsien-mên 仙門 46, 27*b*	King	LS 20, 1*b* speaks of a certain Hsien-mên as the leader of a T'ieh-li mission to the Liao court. According to the *Ching-shih Ta Tien T'u* 經世大典圖, identical with Hsi-mu-niang 西模娘 City near the Ta-pa-li-ssǔ-tan 達拔里斯單 tribe (HYS 50, 6729). Obviously the city of Semnān, south of Tabaristān, the ancient Hyrcania in northern Persia.
55	T'ieh-pu-tê 鐵不得 46, 27*b*	King	Offered its assistance to Liao Hsing-tsung when the latter prepared a military campaign against Hsi Hsia in 1048; the offer was refused (LS 20, 2*a*). The country evidently was located in the west near Hsi Hsia. Yanai (30, 279) equates its name with Tibet which is not impossible.
56	Pi-kuo-tê 鼻國德 47, 28*a*	King	Also transcribed as Pi-ku-tê 鼻古 (or 骨) 德 (*cf.* LS 30, 5*a*; 69, 22*b*, and Various Tribes, no. 34). When the founder of the state of Qarā-Khitāy, Yeh-lü Ta-shih, was on his way to Central Asia, he summoned the chieftains of eighteen tribes, the Pi-kuo-tê state among them. It therefore seems legitimate to assume that the territory of this people was located somewhere in present Outer Mongolia. Throughout the whole course of the Liao dynasty the Pi-kuo-tê offered tribute to the imperial court.

Subordinate States (*continued*)

No.	NAME OF STATE	TITLE OF RULER	REMARKS
57	Hsia-la-kuo-chih 轄剌國只 47, 28a	King	Probably identical with Hsia-lieh 轄烈, a state which in 989 paid tribute to Liao together with A-ssǔ-lan 阿思蘭 and Yü-t'ien 于闐. The Hsia-la-kuo-chih were possibly identical with the Khirghiz, the greater part of whom dwelt in the northwestern part of modern Sinkiang, in the T'ien Shan Mountains (LS 12, 5a; 70, 8a–b).
58	Lin-lieh 賃烈 46, 28a	King	The country paid tribute to Liao in 940 and 944 (LS 70, 5a).
59	Huo-li 獲里 46, 28a	King	
60	P'a-li 怕里 46, 28a	King	
61	Sao-wên 噪温 46, 28a	King	
62	A-po-p'o-tê 阿鉢頗得 46, 28a	King	
63	A-po-ya 阿鉢押 46, 28a	King	
64	Jên-mo-li 紝沒里 46, 28a	King	Offered tribute to Liao together with the Yao-li 要里 state in 944 (LS 4, 10b).
65	Yao-li 要里 46, 28a	King	Offered tribute in 944 and 945 (LS 70, 5b).
66	T'u-tu-ku 徒覩古 46, 28b	King	LS 4, 8b mentions a people called T'u-lu-ku 徒魯古 who paid taxes to Liao in 942. Whether this name is a distorted form of the T'u-tu-ku, perhaps caused by a clerical error, we do not know.
67	Su-sa 素撒 46, 28b	King	Paid tribute in 942 (LS 4, 8b).
68	I-tu-kun 夷都袞 46, 28b	King	
69	P'o-tu-lu 婆都魯 46, 28b	King	
70	Pa-ssǔ-hei 霸斯黑 46, 28b	King	
71	Ta-li-chien 達離諫 46, 28b	King	During T'ang times there existed a city called To-lo-chien 多勒建 (Tālikān) in Tokharistan and another city of the same name west of Balkh (Chavannes 03, 278, text and note 10). It is impossible to decide whether either city is

Subordinate States (*continued*)

No.	NAME OF STATE	TITLE OF RULER	REMARKS
			related to our state or whether Ta-li-chien of LS 46, 28*b* is merely another transliteration of the subsequent name, Ta-lu-ku.
72	Ta-lu-ku 達盧古 46, 28*b*	King	Also transcribed as Ta-lu-ku (or kuo) 達魯古 (or 虢). Ikeuchi suggests for this tribe's location the region north of the Sungari River (Ikeuchi, MSK I, 216). Whether the Ta-lu-ku are identical with the Ta-la-kuai 達刺乖 we do not know. A people of the latter name is mentioned among the western tribes which attended the great gathering convoked by Yeh-lü Ta-shih before his attack against Turkestan (see LS 30, 5*a*; 69, 24*b*). Whether in this case an eastern tribe migrated far to the west, or whether the slightly different names refer to two tribes who were either totally independent or became partially so through separation, we have no means of ascertaining.
73	San-ho 三河 46, 28*b*	King	According to YS 1, 12*a*, Chingis Khan, criticizing the chieftain of the Kerait tribe, Wang-Khan 汪罕, called San-ho "the region where our ancestors laid the foundation of the country." He warned the Kerait nobles not to lose it. The Kerait tribe lived between the K'ên-t'ê 肯特 [or Kentei] Mountains and the Khinghan Mountains (Vladimirtsov 30, 4). Therefore the San-ho state was probably situated in the same region.
74	Ho-lieh-ko 聶列哿 46, 28*b*	King	The location of the Ho-lieh-ko tribe is not clear. According to LS 11, 5*b*, Liao messengers who were on their way to the Uighur and Ho-lieh-ko states were intercepted by the Chu-pu-ku 尤不姑 people. Since the latter seem to have lived in the northern border region of the Liao empire (see above, no. 14, also Various Tribes, no. 2), the Ho-lieh-Ko state probably was located still further to the west or northwest.
75	Shu-lü-tzŭ 述律子 46, 28*b*	King	The final *tzŭ* 子 may stand for a final *s* with the meaning of a plural suffix as Pelliot (31*b*, 118) points out for similar cases. Shu-lü-tzŭ then could signify the Shu-lü "people." But who were the Shu-lü? Shu-lü 述律 became the name of the imperial consort family of Liao during the time of T'ai-tsu (CWTS 137, 6*b*, *cf.* VII, 2, note 3). Did the name exist earlier with a somewhat different meaning, as a designation for certain branches of this Uighur kin-group? Or did a more or less independent people, perhaps of Uighur background, use the name of the distinguished clan as the name for their own state? The form of the name raises these questions but offers no answer.
76	Shu-pao 殊保 46, 29*a*	King	
77	P'u-ni 蒲昵 46, 29*a*	King	CS 1, 4*b* mentions a P'u-nieh 蒲聶 tribe which lived near modern Ninguta, that is midway between Harbin and Vladivostok. If this tribe is the same as the P'u-ni of the *Liao Shih*, then the location of the latter state as well as that of no. 78 would be defined approximately. The P'u-ni continually quarreled with the neighboring Wu-li state. In 1018 the P'u-ni state sent messengers to the court of Liao asking for mediation. An imperial decree ordered the two countries to stop fighting (LS 16, 2*a*).
78	Wu-li 烏里 46, 29*a*	King	See no. 77.

3. POPULATION

1. Census organized   2. Reason for transfer of conquered people   3. Census studies   4. Transfer of wealthy families disputed   5. Census studies   6. An exhaustive census unnecessary   7. Hidden families

1. CENSUS ORGANIZED

911–916   In regard to the system of taxation, national expenditures were first systematized when T'ai-tsu placed Han Yen-hui[1] in office.   T'ai-tsung had the adults of the five capitals registered in order to determine the taxation.   There is no way of knowing the number of adults.   *59, 3b*

2. REASON FOR TRANSFER OF CONQUERED PEOPLE

929   After the accession of T'ai-tsung, [Yeh-lü Yü-chih[2]] memorialized, "When our Great Divine Heavenly Emperor[3] first acquired the eastern territory, he selected worthy assistants to care for these people.   In spite of my stupidity, he appointed me.   When the national interest is concerned, how would I dare not to express my opinion?

"The Po-hai, who formerly feared the Southern Court,[4] relied upon [natural] obstacles for their protection and settled in Hu-han City.[5]   Now, since they are far remote from the Supreme Capital, they are not put to use nor is the garrison abolished.   What indeed is to be done?   Our former emperor, taking advantage of their dissension, seized the opportunity to put troops in motion. Hence they were subdued without a fight.   It was truly granted by Heaven and given by man. This was the situation at that time.

"The remnants [of the people] have grown by gradual propagation.   They dwell at present in a distant region, and I am afraid that they may cause trouble later on.   The region of the Liang River[6] is after all their original home.   [There] the land is rich and the soil fertile, and there are also benefits from wood, iron, salt, and fish.   To take advantage of their weakness and to move the people back [to the Liao region] would be a permanent scheme for ten thousand generations.

"If they get back to their old homes and also obtain the bounties of wood, iron, salt, and fish, they will certainly live in peace and enjoy their work.   Afterwards we may select some [from them] and move[7] them to guard our left [flank], while the Turks, Tang-hsiang, and Shih-wei aid our right. We can thus sit here and control the Southern Countries,[8] unify the whole world, complete the enterprises that have not been achieved by our divine ancestors, and bequeath boundless happiness to later generations."

When the memorial was presented, the emperor accepted it with approval.   In this year an imperial decree ordered the people of the kingdom of Tung-tan[9] to be moved to the Liang River.   At that time it was praised as excellent.   *75, 1b–2a*

---

[1] Han Yen-hui 韓延徽 (T. 藏明 D. 959) was the first distinguished Chinese official to be taken over by the Ch'i-tan people after the establishment of the Liao empire. He was sent as an envoy to the Ch'i-tan and was detained by T'ai-tsu.   He drafted a scheme for the organization of the Chinese segment of the country's administration (LS 31, 2a–3b; *cf.* LS 74, 2a–3b).

The exact date of his appointment is not known. LS 31, 2a–3b and CTKC 1, 2a record all these activities under the year 916.   But the appointment may have been made between 907 and 916.   Gabelentz, in his translation of the Manchu version of the *Liao History*, places the appointment of Han Yen-hui in the year 911 (Gabelentz 77, 10).

[2] Yeh-lü Yü-chih 羽之 could speak the languages of several tribes which participated in the military expedi-

tions in the time of T'ai-tsu.   In 926 he was appointed left prime minister and assisted T'ai-tsu's eldest son to administer the kingdom of Tung-tan in the eastern part of the empire (*cf.* LS 75, 1b–2a).   According to LS 3, 3a, he presented this memorial in 929.

[3] T'ai-tsu's posthumous title.

[4] That is, the T'ang court.

[5] Modern Tung-ching 東京 City, Kirin.   It was first the capital of Po-hai and later on important in the Tung-tan kingdom.

[6] T'ai-tzǔ 太子 River, Liaoning.

[7] 徙 is probably an error for 徙.

[8] In China Proper.

[9] After the conquest of the Po-hai in 926 T'ai-tsu transformed their country into the kingdom of Tung-tan, the "Eastern Tan," a name perhaps derived from the fact

3. CENSUS STUDIES

929　　　　On the day *kêng-hsü* of the second month [in the fourth year of T'ien-hsien] the register of households of the Yao-lien family was examined.　　*3, 3b*

991　　　　On the day *kuei-mao* of the seventh month [in the autumn of the ninth year of T'ung-ho] a general census was taken.　　*13, 2b*

997　　　　On the day *jên-wu* of the third month [in the fifteenth year of T'ung-ho] a general survey of the households attached to the ordos[10] was carried out.　　*13, 8a*

1031　　　　In this year a general census was taken.　　*59, 2b–3a*

4. TRANSFER OF WEALTHY FAMILIES DISPUTED

Ca. 1036–1055　　An imperial decree ordered that the rich people be moved in order to fill up the two prefectures of Ch'un[11] and T'ai. [Liu] Shên[12] thought it was not right and memorialized that it be stopped.　　*98, 4a*

5. CENSUS STUDIES

1039　　　　On the day *i-ch'ou* of the sixth month [in the eighth year of Ch'ung-hsi] an imperial decree ordered a census to be taken.　　*18, 9a*

1052　　　　On the day *ping-shên* [of the eleventh month in the twenty-first year of Ch'ung-hsi] a general census was taken of the tribesmen of the Southern Division.　　*14, 4b*

1055–1100　　At that time the court sent emissaries to ascertain the number of hidden households in the three [northern] capitals, but they were unsuccessful. [Yeh-lü] Yin-chi[13] was chosen to replace them and discovered several thousand households.　　*97, 3a*

6. AN EXHAUSTIVE CENSUS UNNECESSARY

1065–1075　　It happened that a census [conducted by Ma Jên-wang[14]] was completed in less than twenty days. The assistant acting vicegerent, Hsiao Pao-hsien,[15] was surprised and asked him about it. [Ma] Jên-wang replied, "If the people's property were relentlessly assessed,[16] it would later increase the abuses of heavy taxation. In general, it is enough to get six- or seven-tenths."

---

that Po-hai was situated east of the Ch'i-tan. The territory gradually lost its special character and was abolished in 982, becoming the eastern section of the imperial administration, Tung-ching Circuit (LS 2, 6b; 3, 5a; 5, 2a).

The capital of Tung-tan, T'ien-fu 天福, was first located at the site of the old Po-hai capital, Hu-han 忽汗, in modern Kirin; in 929 it was moved to Liao-yang in modern Liaoning. The first king was Pei, T'ai-tsu's eldest son, who ruled until 930. From 947 to 953 An-tuan, T'ai-tsu's fourth younger brother, was in charge of the government. For the period after 953 information concerning its ruler is lacking (PHKCCP 19, 45b ff.).

[10] We follow the Palace edition in reading 宮 for the 官 of our text.

[11] Ch'un 春 Prefecture is not listed in the geographical section of the *Liao Shih*. The name is probably an abbreviated form of Ch'ang-ch'un Prefecture, northwest of modern Po-tu-na 伯都納, Kirin, which was walled in 1039 (LS 18, 9a).

[12] Liu Shên 劉伸 (T. 濟時). A native of the Southern Capital. He acquired the degree of *chin-shih* in 1036.

He was later appointed assistant vicegerent of the Supreme Capital. He died in 1086 (LS 98, 4a–b).

[13] Yeh-lü Yin-chi 引吉 (T. 阿括) was a man from the P'in tribe. He was appointed vicegerent of the Eastern Capital, then scribe of the herds, and finally grand guardian of the horse herds in the Hua River Region North of the Desert (LS 97, 2b–3a).

[14] Ma Jên-wang 馬人望 (T. 儼叔) was greatly respected for his honesty in financial affairs. He received the *chin-shih* degree in 1070 and later became chancellor of the Southern Region. He died at the end of the Liao dynasty and was given the posthumous title of Wên-hsien 文獻. According to his biography, the event mentioned above must have taken place between 1065 and 1075.

[15] Hsiao Pao-hsien 保先, a brother-in-law of Emperor T'ien-tsu, administered Tung-ching Circuit so badly that a rebellion, in which he was killed, broke out among the Po-hai people in 1116 (XIII [48]).

[16] Literally, "without exemption." The idea of Ma Jên-wang was obviously to simplify the procedure and to spare the people. The fiscal history of China shows,

[Hsiao] Pao-hsien acknowledged this and said, "Your foresight reaches far into the future.   I am unable to keep pace with you."   105, *3b*

7. HIDDEN FAMILIES

1083   On the day *kêng-wu* of the sixth month [in the ninth year of Ta-k'ang[17]] a decree ordered all routes[18] to investigate the households which had evaded [the census]. Those which incurred the death penalty were pardoned.   24, *4b*

---

however, that it was in most cases the officials rather than the taxpayers who benefited from this kind of policy.

[17] The word 太 in the text should be read 大.

[18] Geographically the territory of Liao was organized into five circuits (*tao* 道); economically it was divided into eight routes (*lu* 路), namely Shang-ching, Nan-ching, Hsi-ching, Chung-ching, Tung-ching, Hsing-chung Administration (present Ch'ao-yang County, Jehol), Lung Prefecture (present Nung-an County, Kirin), and P'ing Prefecture (present Lu-lung, Hopei).   Each route had a high official who was responsible for the collection of taxes (CTKC 22, 1*a*).

The term *lu* was also applied to a number of military regions designated by the directions, such as Northwestern Route (西北路), Northeastern Route (東北路), etc.

SECTION II

PASTORALISM AND AGRICULTURE

INTRODUCTION

1. CH'I–TAN PASTORALISM

In all typically Chinese dynasties, from Ch'in and Han to Sui, T'ang, Sung, and Ming, agriculture was basic. Pastoralism, though pursued, was of minor importance and had little influence on the country's political structure.

The Liao dynasty differed in this respect. Although the bulk of the country's population—Chinese and Po-hai—was agricultural, a considerable tribal minority lived a nomadic life with animal husbandry as the economic mainstay and hunting and fishing as subsidiary occupations. From such a mixed tribal economy the Ch'i-tan rose, fought, and flourished. They continued to breed animals even after they succeeded in appropriating the services of neighboring peoples who were engaged in agriculture and in the extraction of salt and iron. Thus the new empire's subsistence economy was in the main agricultural; its power economy in the main pastoral.

The texts of this section not only describe the two basic elements of Liao economy, animal husbandry (II, 1) and agriculture (II, 2), but also throw some light on their interaction. Because Liao society developed from a tribal base, we present the pastoral data before those on agricultural activities. Various records concerning hunting and fishing are attached to the subsection on pastoralism, II, 1.

a. SOURCES OF WEALTH IN ANIMALS

Centuries before A-pao-chi established his rule[1] Ch'i-tan herds are mentioned in the Chinese annals,[2] and tribal tradition and ceremony indicate the early presence of sheep,[3] oxen, and horses.[4] Although reference is made to the camel, everything points to its late introduction from the western steppes, perhaps through the Uighur Turks as intermediaries. A camel was used by the empress dowager who rode in a camel-drawn cart[5] when the sacrificial offering was made to Mu-yeh mountain, and by the imperial princesses[6] in their wedding ceremonies; but both the empress dowager and the husbands of the princesses belonged to the Hsiao clan which was rooted in a Uighur lineage.

On the other hand, the horse had long been of importance, and as the Ch'i-tan rose in power it became their most valued possession. Not only did they reckon their wealth in horses[7] but, when the political situation demanded, this wealth could be directly translated into aggressive military strength. The Liao empire augmented its animal wealth by seizing great herds from defeated tribes and sedentary southern neighbors.[8] In addition it demanded heavy tributes from semi-dependent border states and tribes which were paid chiefly in horses.[9]

Both the growth and stagnation of a pastoral people "depend on the capacity of their winter quarters, which can support far less live stock than the almost unbounded country over which they range in summer." Consequently, "the nomads can keep only as many [animals] as have a chance of living through the winter, when grazing is limited."[10] This general rule, valid enough for the earlier pastoral life of the Ch'i-tan, lost much of its significance after their victorious conquest of a rich agricultural population. Now the non-pastoral foodstuffs eagerly sought by herdsmen[11] became available in large quantities; more milk could be spared for the young animals;[12] winter quarters could be occupied without fear of attack. Though the well-being of the herds depended primarily upon an adequate snowfall,[13] pastoral life as a whole became less arduous since it was better protected against those crises which it had previously faced. The new conditions of security and the large animal tributes could not fail to affect the number of the Liao livestock which is said to have increased "to a total of more than a million."[14]

---

[1] II, 1 (3).

[2] XIV, 1 (1), LS 63, 3a.

[3] Cf. VII, 2 (83). The birth of an imperial prince or princess was supposed to be facilitated if the empress heard the bleating of sheep outside the delivery tent (YPL 17a–b).

[4] In the most sacred tribal sacrifice oxen and horses were offered (see VII, 2, passim). The sacred imperial funeral-cart was drawn by an ox (IV (14)).

[5] Loc. cit.

[6] Loc. cit.

[7] II, 1 (2).

[8] II, 1 (3).

[9] Loc. cit.; cf. also X, 2, passim.

[10] Lattimore 30, 242. See also Radloff 93 I, 415 ff.; Peisker 24, 337; Schakir-zade 31, 113 ff.

[11] Peisker 24, 340.

[12] Personal communication of Mr. Owen Lattimore.

[13] II, 1, note 2, reference to TCCS 5, 33.

[14] II, 1 (3); cf. also II, 1 (20).

b. CHANGING VALUES

The new economic and political symbiosis which the Ch'i-tan established with the subjugated Chinese apparently altered the relative importance of the animals raised. In the four main categories, sheep, oxen, camels, and horses, less attention was now paid to the first two, whereas camels, and particularly horses, became increasingly significant.

SHEEP AND OXEN

The tribesmen derived a considerable part of their food, clothing, and leather goods from these animals, and the ox was an important aid to transportation throughout the dynastic period.[15] Curd was consumed ceremonially;[16] it was also considered a proper food for the masses.[17] Cream and other dairy products were even offered to Chinese visitors.[18] Among the pastoral peoples of Inner Asia, meat has remained a luxury food and, with the possible exception of mutton, was reserved for wealthy and honored guests.[19] The Ta-ta, tribal neighbors of Liao, drank the milk of cows and mares but did not eat the flesh,[20] a practice that may well have been current also among the predynastic Ch'i-tan. The growth of political power, however, increased meat consumption, certainly among the ruling class and probably among the tribal commoners. A Liao spokesman boasted that his country's supply of meat was greater than that of Sung;[21] the last Liao emperor, T'ien-tsu, was criticized by the Chin 金 emperor, Shih-tsung (1161–1189), because he permitted the daily slaughter of three hundred sheep for court consumption.[22]

In spite of the growing interest in horses, sheep remained indispensable. Their skins were converted into clothing,[23] and felt tents, undoubtedly processed

from the wool,[24] were still considered the most appropriate dwelling for a good Ch'i-tan, high or low.[25] Sheep were offered in payment of taxes[26] and salaries;[27] they were also given as presents.[28] On occasion the government sold large numbers of them to its southern neighbors; HTS 69, 594–595 speaks of thirty thousand sheep which, together with two hundred horses, were exchanged for Chinese silk, tea, and medicine in 938. Yet in a critical period the sale of sheep,[29] particularly of ewes,[30] was restricted by administrative order. Both sheep and oxen were accepted as tribute from neighboring tribes[31] and sold at the Liao markets.[32] Oxen were given as a form of governmental relief to poor people of certain tribes.[33]

Whether the newly acquired great stores of grain reduced the use of mutton as a basic food is doubtful. Grain had probably been part of the pastoral diet long before dynastic times.[34] But after the conquest, and with the incorporation of large agricultural areas into the new empire, more of this desired foodstuff became available. If Liao was able to send a shipment of two hundred thousand bushels of grain to its southern neighbor, Eastern Han,[35] it is more than probable that great quantities of grain were also distributed as subsidies to the tribal sector of the empire which after all was its military and political backbone. The relief records describe the transfer of government grain to the tribes.[36] An increasing number of Ch'i-tan, particularly those engaged in the frontier service,[37] received grain from the government, but while this enriched their diet it does not seem to have radically affected their consumption of meat.

Changes in clothing are clearly noted. The customary sheep-skins were in part replaced by valuable tribute furs, in part by the silk, which the states of China Proper sent to the Liao capital.[38] After satisfying its own needs the court distributed furs and fabrics to the imperial attendants[39] and officials[40] and

---

[15] XII (84).

[16] YPL 17a–b.

[17] CS 8, 13a. Dairy products, both liquid and solid, were in all probability kept in leather bags such as the *hun-t'o* 渾脫 which are documented for the tribes of Inner Asia during the Yüan period. The *hun-t'o* were made from calf skins which were left intact except for a hole behind the head through which the flesh and entrails were removed (TMT 4, 21a).

[18] HCLY 77, 4b; PCKT 2, 22; cf. also II, 1, note 6.

[19] For the principle, see Thurnwald 32, 74; for the Inner Asiatic situation, cf. Peisker 24, 340, Rubruck 00, 64 ff.; Timkowski 1827 I, 214 and II, 296; Prejevalsky 76 I, 54 and 56; Radloff 93 I, 428 and 298.

[20] LSSI 24, 5a, quoting a passage in *Tung-chai Chi-shih* 東齋紀事 which we were unable to locate in the present TCCS.

[21] KLTY 2, 10.

[22] CS 6, 22a.

[23] VII, 1 (9) (48).

[24] Lattimore 40, 74; cf. also Rubruck 00, 54; Laufer 30, 1 ff.

[25] III (11) and *passim*, particularly VII, 2.

[26] X, 1 (25).

[27] V (4).

[28] VII, 2 (83).

[29] V (10).

[30] II, 1 (8).

[31] X, 2—Sheep: (83); Oxen: (48) (83).

[32] V (4).

[33] XII (103).

[34] Cf. the use of millet cakes in the sacred New Year Ceremony (VII, 2 (83)).

[35] II, 2 (7).

[36] See XII *passim*.

[37] XV, 1 (45).

[38] See X, 1 and 2 *passim*.

[39] X, 1 (16).

[40] VII, 2 (83).

even to the tribes.   The use of silk increased among the officials;[41] the tribes also received lustring.[42]   The enormous flow of tribute silk into Liao may have led to an occasional and undiscriminating give-away to all tribesmen, but the detailed record in LS 26, 5b indicates that in this instance the silk was given to the poor of the Five Divisions, that is, to the less affluent members of the imperial tribe.   In 1042 the government followed a similar policy when it offered special benevolences to the poor members of the Three Patriarchal Households.[43]   It is possible, therefore, that in the less fully described cases relief silk was not equally distributed either, but went for the most part to privileged tribesmen or to members of privileged tribes.

Sheep and oxen, unlike the horse and camel, are rarely mentioned in the tributes paid to Liao.   To some degree this may be due to the introduction of new foods and textiles.   However, the improved conditions of grazing may have assured so adequate a supply of these animals that the everyday needs of the people were satisfactorily met.

CAMELS

In the western border zone of the Manchurian basin the camel was a stranger.   In the past, as in the present, it was of no particular use in a region of woodland and prairie.   In modern Barga, which stretches from the Kerulen River to the old Shang-ching Circuit of Liao, a few camels are kept by the local Mongols, but because there are no sandy roads or great steppes they "have no special need for keeping many camels."[44]   The Ch'i-tan no doubt valued the animal for its wool[45] and milk.[46]   But apart from this practical aspect—which was limited—the camel symbolized for them the tribal world of the steppes which they tried in vain to assimilate during two hundred years of tribal warfare and border diplomacy. Numerous camels were received from tributary tribes and states.[47]   Camels paraded in ceremonies of a minor order,[48] and in an emergency even an emperor might ride on camelback.[49]   But the prestige value of the camel was not paralleled by its utility.   When

Yeh-lü Ta-shih deserted his clan and home, he seems to have been more interested in the horses than in the camels of the crumbling dynasty.

THE HORSE

The horse provided the Ch'i-tan with milk which in its raw and in its fermented state, as kumiss, was and still is the favorite beverage of the herdsmen of Inner Asia.[50]   The military value of animals that can carry and feed a soldier is obvious, and this fact explains to no small degree the extraordinary strength and terrifying successes of the Mongol cavalry.[51]   Our texts properly emphasize Ch'i-tan dependence on the horse[52] during the era of expansion.   To secure its position the Liao empire had to maintain or, preferably, to extend its horse wealth.   The horse became "the" animal and horse herds "the" herds.[53] Reduced dependence on their former subsistence economy and the increasing importance of their power economy led the Ch'i-tan to prize above all others the animal that had been instrumental in making possible their glorious rise.

c. THE HERDS

Originally government-owned horses were maintained in large and concentrated herds but, since this soon proved unsatisfactory,[54] they were distributed over a number of suitable pastures.[55]   The text speaks of herds of about a thousand head each,[56] a figure confirmed by the report[57] of a Sung writer, Su Sung.[58] In part these were owned by private individuals, and the wealth of a family depended upon their number.[59]

---

[41] VII, 1 (7).

[42] XII (96).

[43] X, 1 (46).

[44] North Manchuria 24, 128.   A statistical survey of the various kinds of animals in present-day Northern Manchuria (op. cit., 127) does not even mention the camel.

[45] III (22).

[46] Cf. Peisker 24, 339.

[47] See X, 2 (18) (25) (57) (70) (72) (75) (80) (81) (83) (86) (88) (91).

[48] IV (14).

[49] IV (3).

[50] Among the Ch'i-tan soldiers, as among the Mongols, mare's milk was the favorite drink.   Except for the game it might be the only item in their diet during a campaign of a month's duration (Marco Polo 03 I, 260).   In such a situation the milk was probably drunk fresh.   Its fermented form, kumiss, is pungent on the tongue like wine. "When a man has finished drinking, it leaves a taste of milk of almonds on the tongue, and it makes the inner man most joyful and also intoxicates weak heads . . ." (Rubruck 00, 67).   Lattimore (30, 254) very appropriately calls the drink "horse-milk wine."   For further details see Marco Polo 03 I, 300; YS 100, 2a; Timkowski 1827 I, 214; Prejevalsky 76 I, 54; Howorth, HM IV, 58 ff.; Vámbéry 85, 209; Radloff 93 I, 450 ff.; Pelliot 20, 169–171; Jochelson 28, 80 ff.; Lattimore 29, 88 ff.

[51] See Marco Polo 03 I, 260.

[52] II, 1 (2).

[53] II, 1 (3).

[54] XV, 1 (45).

[55] Loc. cit.   See also II, 1 (3).

[56] II, 1 (3).

[57] LSSI 13, 4a.

[58] 蘇頌 (T. 子容 1020–1101).   His writings were gathered in a collection called Su Wei-kung Chi 蘇魏公集.

[59] LSSI 13, 4a.

Government horse herds in the main served a military need;[60] the large hunts in which tens of thousands of horses were used[61] gave added opportunity for cavalry maneuvers.

Government-owned oxen were employed as draft animals; government-owned sheep are referred to as "salary sheep."[62] If the Liao administration could sell thirty thousand sheep in a single transaction,[63] its sheep herds must have been large.

Especially designated herdsmen or stock-breeding families[64] were placed in charge of the imperial herds, but the local population was also mobilized for herding service.[65] Su Sung claims that two or three men could handle a herd of a thousand horses.[66] During the Manchu period government-owned animals were pastured in somewhat smaller units, herds of three hundred head with one man in charge,[67] oxen and stallions in herds of a hundred.[68] The Manchu units were smaller than those of the Ch'i-tan, but their care and arrangement were apparently similar.

In both dynasties a high official was responsible for all the imperial herds.[69] In the Liao empire the pastoral hierarchy was headed by a commissioner of the herds of the various routes who was also called the grand guardian.[70] While he seems to have had some clerical assistance, the bulk of the clerical work remained in the hands of the general commissioner of the herds. The commissioner as well as his vice-commissioners were local officers, and no doubt it was their subordinates who personally tended the animals.[71] LS 46 lists the titles of the offices whose special concern was with the horse herds of the Western Route in the region north of the Hun River (north of the Gobi) and in the territory south of the desert. The titles of those in charge of the imperial stables are also reported as well as the office that supervised the ox herds. Government-owned camels and sheep are not expressly mentioned; they were probably included in the general "herds."

Government-owned animals were branded on the left side,[72] but we do not know whether horses marked with a tribal insignia[73] were owned jointly by the tribe or by individual herdsmen. Marco Polo found the Mongol "mares, camels, oxen, cows, or other great cattle" marked with the individual owner's "peculiar brand," and recent observers noted group ("sib") marks.[74] The *Liao Shih* does not mention private animal marks, but many passages indicate the existence of private herds besides those belonging to the government.

Private herds were the basis of the tribes' early economic power; it must have been the owners of such herds who "exchanged [good] government horses"[75] —evidently for privately-owned animals of poor quality—or who purchased government-owned horses when the dynasty was decaying.[76] The conflict between private and government interests, which then assumed disastrous dimensions, must have smoldered throughout the period. Powerful individuals tried to take over imperial grazing grounds for their own herds, and because the available pastures were limited in size such infringements seriously interfered with the natural increase of the herds owned by the government.[77] In 994 rich tribesmen avoided registering their horse herds for the army, and the government had to provide the necessary animals.[78] Indeed irregularities of all kinds resulted from the great increase in the country's equine wealth and aristocratic power.[79] The outcome of the request for the registration of horses shows that in a conflict between a government agency and the pastoral nobility the former could not always hold its own.

How numerous and how large were the privately owned herds? If LS 24, 7a[80] refers only to government-owned horse herds, while LS 60, 4a[81] refers to the total horse wealth of the Ch'i-tan, public as well as private, then the Liao government would have owned about a million head and the private tribesmen several million. Both figures are probably inflated for reasons of political prestige and glory, but there is little doubt that private herds accounted for a large part of the total horse wealth of the country. T'ai-tsu mentions wealthy tribesmen who owned ten thousand horses.[82] This figure need not be taken literally; yet it may refer to herds of at least a few thousand head. The *Liao Shih* also notes that a powerful Ch'i-tan could purchase honorary rank with ten oxen and

[60] II, 1 (3).
[61] *Loc. cit.*
[62] IV (14); V (4); XV, 1 (51).
[63] LSNTS 15, 3a.
[64] II, 1 (18); V (18).
[65] XI, introduction.
[66] LSSI 13, 4a.
[67] Timkowski 1827 I, 201.
[68] *Op. cit.*, 265.
[69] For the Manchu dynasty, *cf.* Timkowski 1827 I, 201.
[70] *Cf.* II, 1 (18).
[71] XIV, 1 (26).
[72] II, 1 (14).
[73] II, 1 (15).
[74] Marco Polo 03 I, 266 ff.; Radloff 93 I, 279 ff. and 455 ff. *Cf.* also Hudson 38, 31 ff.
[75] XIV, 4 (15).
[76] II, 1 (3).
[77] II, 1 (19).
[78] X, 1 (29).
[79] II, 1 (18).
[80] II, 1 (20).
[81] II, 1 (3).
[82] XIII (11).

camels and a hundred horses[83]—a standard that obviously did not threaten the economic status of the applicant.

The poor tribesmen boasted no such animal wealth. According to LS 28, 4a there were tribal commoners who had less than ten animals all told,[84] a few sheep and perhaps one or two horses. Most of the Ch'i-tan herds probably fell below the upper limit and above what may be called the tribal poverty line.

Recent investigations among Central Asiatic nomads suggest several thousand head as the upper limit of a Mongol noble's herds,[85] and ten thousand head of cattle and horses "for those of a rich Khirghiz tribesman."[86] Our estimate of a few thousand head is based only on horse wealth; if sheep and oxen are included, the total would be considerably higher. Since political conditions in Inner Asia were at least as conducive to cattle-raising in the time of the Ch'i-tan as they are today, it is more than probable that the Ch'i-tan herds were as large, and perhaps even larger, than the herds of their tribal successors.

2. HUNTING

From earliest times hunting was an integral part of nomadic life;[87] pastoralists, fearful of killing off their milk-producing animals, looked to the game to augment their meat supply.[88] However, the hunt also provided valuable military training. This was recognized by Chingis Khan who included rules of the communal hunt in his "Laws."[89] In another connection he refers to the duties of soldiers in wars and in hunts in the same sentence.[90] These two aspects of the hunt also characterized the Liao period; even though the economic function shrank in significance, hunting still remained part of the life of the Ch'i-tan horsemen "in order to provide for their daily needs."[91] The statement, which is none too explicit may refer chiefly to conduct during military campaigns, but peace-time needs, too, were served.

Large-scale hunts were organized by the court[92] or under regional direction.[93] The kill might be "given to the army as food supplies";[94] it might feed all the soldiers.[95] At the same time the hunt offered an opportunity for maneuvers which were of value in military training; LS 32, 3a asserts that the imperial winter hunt was definitely related to military practice.

While special officials supervised the activities on the imperial hunting grounds,[96] most of the huntsmen seem to have been drawn from the local population.[97] The thousands of light horsemen chosen to hunt in the mountains in 929[98] may have been regulars in the army or only mounted tribesmen; yet the latter too were potential soldiers. It is quite within the range of possibility that the large winter hunts were, at least in part, undertaken by regular army detachments.

The hunts referred to in LS 46, 6b, whether under the supervision of central government officials or tribal dignitaries, probably preserved tribal hunting practices of long standing. Our geographical notes mention the available game;[99] and a number of passages, especially those dealing with the imperial seasonal hunts, describe the methods used. The deer,[100] tiger,[101] bear,[102] and fox[103] were particularly worthy of an emperor's effort; the hare was hunted during the annual hare-shooting ceremony.[104]

Bird-hunting with the aid of falcons and eagles was a favorite sport of Asiatic nomads in early times, during the Mongol period,[105] and is so even today.[106] The Liao emperors, who had special aviaries,[107] spent much of the spring in hunting swans and wild geese.[108] The tribute deer,[109] hares,[110] magpies,[111] and pheas-

---

[83] VIII (12).

[84] XV, 2 (25).

[85] Riasanovsky 37, 16; Lang 40, 54.

[86] Timkowski 1827 I, 213. Timkowski got his information from a Chinese official; it must not be considered more accurate than T'ai-tsu's figure whose vagueness it shares.

[87] Cf. Peisker 24, 340.

[88] For the principle see Thurnwald 32, 74 and 83. For Africa: Frazer 40, 33, 44, 56, 237, 290, etc. For Asia: Peisker 24, 340; Rubruck 00, 69 ff.; Marco Polo 03 I, 252; Vámbéry 85, 196 ff.; Howorth, HM IV, 40; Radloff 93 I, 298.

[89] Riasanovsky 37, 85.

[90] Op. cit., 87.

[91] II, 1 (2).

[92] II, 1 (3); see also XI (27).

[93] II, 1 (12); II, 2 (18); XV, 2 (6).

[94] II, 1 (5) (text one).

[95] Loc. cit. (text two).

[96] XIV, 1 (26).

[97] See XI (27).

[98] II, 1 (7).

[99] See I, introduction.

[100] II, 1 (26). See also X, 1 (8).

[101] VII, 2 (83). Cf. also II, 1 (26).

[102] XIV, 3 (10).

[103] II, 1 (9).

[104] VII, 2 (83); cf. also LS 51, 1b.

[105] Rubruck 00, 69 ff.; Marco Polo 03 I, 402 ff.

[106] See Vámbéry 85, 196; Lattimore 30, 106 ff.; Radloff 93 I, 467 ff.

[107] XIV, 1 (26).

[108] II, 1 (24).

[109] X, 1 (7) (18) (21) (45) and passim. The deer-callers whom the Jurchen presented in 991 were of course meant as a contribution to the emperor's team of skilled huntsmen.

[110] X, 1 (9).

[111] X, 2 (34).

ants[112] were probably kept in the court's animal quarters.[113] The continued requests for tribute falcons and eagles[114] must be taken as an index of the passion with which the Ch'i-tan rulers clung to their traditional tribal hunts.

The imperial seasonal hunting grounds all lay within the Manchurian basin[115] which includes modern Jehol. But to shoot swans[116] the Liao emperors went southward to the old Chinese territory of Nan-ching Circuit, and during an occasional military campaign[117] they hunted on the wide western steppes of present day Mongolia.

3. FISHING

Still more conspicuous is the eastern orientation of the Ch'i-tan rulers in fishing. Peisker remarks that the "long-wandering tribes" of Inner Asia do not engage in fishing even if the rivers are well stocked, whereas "fishing is an important source of food among short-wandering nomads."[118] The Mongols practised fishing earlier in their history; according to the *Secret History of the Mongol Dynasty*, the young Chingis Khan and his brothers caught fish with hooks and nets.[119] Later the Mongols—or at least some of their tribes—seem to have neglected fishing if they did not forsake it altogether. Rubruck "passed many fine sheets of water full of fish, but the Tartars [Mongols] do not know how to catch them. . . ."[120] Timkowski never found fish on the frugal tables of the Mongols.[121]

The Ch'i-tan followed a very different tradition. Bordered on the north and east by tribes whose economy depended in large part upon fishing,[122] they engaged in this pursuit as one of their "long-standing practices."[123] Each year during the winter months the Liao emperor hooked fish through holes cut in the ice,[124] employing a technique still used by some Tungus tribes along the Sungari[125] and Amur Rivers.[126] The fact that the emperor himself was so ready to fish indicates that it was an old and honored occupation.

The announcement of war by a fish tally[127] is cul-

turally less revealing. The fish tally was known to the Chinese long before the Liao dynasty,[128] and the resemblance of the Ch'i-tan tally[129] to the Chinese form makes it all but certain that the northern people took it over from their southern neighbor. Its acceptance accorded well with an established tribal esteem for fishing, but it may also have been valued as a symbol of imperial prestige.

During the time of the Liao empire the Ch'i-tan even imported large fish from the Yü-chüeh-li (Wu-ku) people who lived in the well-watered regions beyond their northern border.[130] Compared with animal husbandry and agriculture, fishing was economically of little importance; yet the fact that it remained a favorite sport of the Ch'i-tan rulers reveals its traditional significance for the culture as a whole.

4. LIAO AGRICULTURE

a. ITS TWO ROOTS

The greater part of the population of the Liao empire was sedentary and agricultural. The grain surplus produced by its labor supported the country's government and army; it supplemented its tribal economy.

The *Liao Shih* does not describe the agriculture of the epoch in detail, for this was the economy of the subject population, not of the conquerors. LS 59, 4a gives a brief survey of the land system of Liao, and 59, 1b a sketch of the origin of agriculture among the Ch'i-tan themselves. The Chinese sector of Liao agriculture, rooted in thousands of years of Chinese sedentary life, needs little comment, but the presence of even a limited agriculture in the predominantly pastoral Ch'i-tan tribes may seem surprising.

Contrary to popular belief, modern studies have revealed that pastoralism rarely depends upon a single economy.[131] It develops out of other systems of economy and tends to preserve elements of such earlier forms as food-gathering, hunting, fishing, and even agriculture.[132] Lattimore's contention that "there has always been a minimum of rough agriculture among the Qazaqs and Qirghiz"[133] is supported by Vámbéry for the Turks,[134] and by Radloff and Peisker for the Central Asiatic nomads in general.[135] At the beginning of the nineteenth century the Mongols sowed

---

[112] X, 2 (39).

[113] XIV, 1 (26).

[114] X, 2 (17) (38) (51) (52) (54) (55) and *passim*.

[115] See II, 1 (24) (25) (26) (27) and notes 54, 62, and 65.

[116] II, 1 (28).

[117] See II, 1 (5).

[118] Peisker 24, 340.

[119] YCPS 2, 7a–b; *cf.* also Ssanang Ssetsen 1829, 65.

[120] Rubruck 00, 97.

[121] Timkowski 1827 II, 296.

[122] See I, 2 (6), no. 1.

[123] XIV, 1 (26).

[124] II, 1 (24). *Cf.* also II, 1, note 30.

[125] For the modern Gold Tribe see Lattimore 33, 33 ff.

[126] For the Northern Tungus *cf.* Shirokogoroff 33, 26 and 306.

[127] XV, 2 (3).

[128] LTFPTL 1, 21a ff.

[129] For the form of the Ch'i-tan tallies see LTFPTL 1, 28b–29a and LLSKCL 5.

[130] CTKC 22, 4b–5a.

[131] *Cf.* Lattimore 40, 518.

[132] Peisker 24, 329.

[133] Lattimore, 30, 241.

[134] Vámbéry 85, 173 ff.

[135] Radloff 93 II, 134 ff.; *op. cit.* I, 297; Peisker 24, 340.

some millet, barley, and wheat, "but in small quantities, and in a most careless manner."[136] Elements of this careless Mongol agriculture existed even in the thirteenth century; Marco Polo refers to the "crops" of the tribal Mongols,[137] and Rubruck speaks of certain southern villages which provided "millet and flour" to the great Mongol lords.[138] While both travelers allude only vaguely to this aspect of early Mongol life,[139] they leave no doubt that in the years following Chingis Khan's aggressive rule animal husbandry and hunting were still the basic subsistence economies of the tribes of Inner Asia.

The Ch'i-tan rose to dynastic power three hundred years before Chingis Khan. Their ceremonies suggest that they were familiar with millet centuries earlier, for the sacred cakes which were baked on the eve of the New Year contained the marrow of a white sheep and glutinous millet.[140] In general, such ritual integration bespeaks long knowledge of a plant.

Historical records refer to a tribal agriculture in predynastic times. In the eighth century Yün-tê-shih, who placed great emphasis upon animal husbandry, also promoted agriculture.[141] Whether he really introduced it, as one record claims,[142] or whether the recital of his achievements merely imitated the legends of early Chinese culture heroes will probably never be satisfactorily answered. Some new agricultural techniques were introduced only a few decades before the establishment of the empire. Hu Chiao, who traveled through Shang-ching Circuit in the middle of the tenth century, found the Ch'i-tan tribesmen growing melons. They treated the plant carefully, applying cow-dung to it and protecting it with mats; they claimed they had obtained it from the defeated Uighurs.[143] According to the *Liao Shih*, the cultivation of hemp and mulberry trees was initiated by T'ai-tsu's uncle, Shu-lan.[144]

A few tribes of the Ch'i-tan confederation seem to have been especially interested in agriculture. In 940 the two branches of the imperial tribe were given land for cultivation.[145] The record indicates that the I-la tribe, whose rulers exploited their neighbors' iron and salt industry at a relatively early date,[146] may also

have been the leaders of this agricultural progress. The other tribes, though certainly aware of the advantages of sedentary pursuits, apparently hesitated to practise them. In 997 a government decree stipulated as part of a program of governmental relief[147] that the P'in tribe use some of its land for agriculture.

Women of the I-shih Ao-wei tribe tilled the soil.[148] This fact is significant for two reasons: the Ao-wei captives, who constituted the mass of the composite tribe, belonged to the semi-agricultural Hsi people;[149] and the I-shih tribe possibly contained some Uighur elements. If the reported agriculture in the I-shih Ao-wei tribe reflected a similar economic trend in the I-shih tribe, then all four leading Ch'i-tan tribes had engaged in some agriculture. Growing wealth and power seem to have facilitated the cultivation of the soil. According to a recent observer, only rich herdsmen could afford to leave any of their retainers on the land while they themselves followed the herds.[150]

The acquaintance of the Ch'i-tan with the elements of agriculture must have been of utmost importance politically since it enabled them to understand and thus more easily to control groups habituated to gaining their livelihood from the soil; but this limited cultivation did not fundamentally change the pastoral pattern of their life. Herds had been their pride in the "barbarian" past. Herds remained their pride in the dynastic present. Where agriculture was practised in the tribal territories, it was probably carried on by poor tribesmen, by women, and by prisoners of war from the agricultural regions.

b. TECHNICAL ELEMENTS

Under these circumstances, the tribal agriculture of Liao was only the politically significant fringe of a complex and non-tribal agricultural economy, for agriculture completely dominated the two old Chinese circuits of the south and flourished in the old settled region of Tung-ching Circuit. It spread out to many new centers in Shang-ching and Chung-ching Circuits inhabited by peasant settlers of Chinese, Po-hai, or Korean descent. The technical methods and legal forms which governed the pursuit of agriculture in these sectors are described in a general way in our texts.

The *Liao Shih* calls the main crop *su* 粟. Originally this word seems to have referred to millet, but later it designated grain in general.[151] What did the word mean during the time of the Liao dynasty? The

---

[136] Timkowski 1827 II, 289.

[137] Marco Polo 03 I, 257.

[138] Rubruck 00, 68.

[139] It seems possible that Rubruck's "southern villages" were inhabited, not by Mongols, but by a sedentary population—perhaps Chinese.

[140] VII, 2 (83).

[141] II, 2 (1).

[142] III (1).

[143] WHTK 345, 2705; CTKC 25, 1b–2a.

[144] II, 2 (1).

[145] II, 2 (2).

[146] See III, introduction.

[147] See II, 2 (20) and XII (25).

[148] II, 2 (10).

[149] WTS 74, 1b; CTKC 22, 2b and 6b; KSC 28, 334; HCLY 77, 11a. See II, 2, note 9.

[150] Radloff 93 II, 135.

[151] *Cf.* HCS, Ch'in and Han II, introduction (mss.).

northern and western parts of Manchuria were, and are, particularly suited to the cultivation of millet.[152] In A.D. 1000[153] wheat and barley were grown in what is now southern Chahar though to what extent is not clear. According to a modern source, wheat has been introduced only recently into North Manchuria.[154] In 1901 the "tall" millet, kaoliang, was still the staple food of the Manchurian population,[155] and as late as 1924 more millet, if all varieties are included, was planted in Heilungkiang and Kirin than wheat and barley together.[156]

The testimony of western travelers makes it evident that millet was the principal cereal of the early Mongols;[157] it is the standard crop of the steppes of Inner Asia even today.[158] It may therefore be reasonably assumed that the northern and western parts of the Liao empire depended upon millet primarily, or at least so much so that it outweighed all other crops in importance. In passages referring to these regions the term *su* no doubt preserved its original meaning—millet. In doubtful cases in general and in descriptions of the southern territories in particular the more inclusive translation "grain" has been adopted.

Rice was, and still is, grown in certain geographically favorable sections of modern Hopei. Its cultivation was tolerated and even encouraged by the Ch'i-tan when it did not interfere with important military considerations;[159] yet it never became a significant item in mass consumption. This is also true for silk. The government suggested the planting of mulberry trees,[160] but nevertheless hemp maintained a natural advantage in these regions, and most of the highly desired silk continued to come from China Proper either through trade[161] or tribute.[162]

In Manchuria today the frost "begins to relax its grasp of the soil towards the middle of March"[163] and in the northern regions slightly later, at the beginning of April.[164] Wheat and barley are sown first; millet (including kaoliang) follows in April. The first two are harvested in June, the wheat a few days before

the barley.[165] Millet remains standing in the fields much longer; usually it is not harvested until the middle or end of September.[166] The agricultural reports of the *Liao Shih* do not always specify the section of the empire referred to; nevertheless it is evident that the Liao agricultural year is not dissimilar to that of modern Manchuria and the northeastern borderzone of China Proper.

Instruction in sowing and spinning was sometimes given during the early winter months,[167] but in general the important preliminaries of the spring planting were commenced somewhat later. Decrees encouraging the cultivation of crops were issued by the court on February 15, 24, and 26 in the years 995, 997, and 1028 respectively.[168] These orders, like those referring to the planting of fruit trees,[169] were made public in the villages shortly before the spring plantings in March and April.[170] In 997 two measures concerned with the tilling of waste land were announced on April 2 and 13;[171] one decree affecting the planting of rice was issued sometime between February 20 and March 21, another on April 17.[172] From April on the crops stood in the field. A warning against possible damage by careless herders was given on April 9, 989.[173] Prolonged law suits involving peasants engaged in agriculture were prohibited; a decree to that effect is dated May 4, 1014.[174]

A local gazetteer states that in one section of Hsi-ching the tax on barley, wheat, and peas was collected from July 13 to October 1 because of unfavorable weather.[175] In normal years, therefore, collections must have been somewhat earlier, an assumption that accords with the time for harvesting wheat and barley in modern Manchuria, namely June. South of the Great Wall the growing season is longer by several weeks.[176] Significantly, in Nan-ching Circuit taxes were collected twice during the year, in the summer and again in the fall,[177] a schedule rooted in the seasonal order of China Proper.[178]

The information regarding the taxing of wheat and

---

[152] Franke 02, 7.

[153] *Hsüan-fu Chên Chih* 宣府鎮志 (Ming) = LSSI 15, 28b.

[154] North Manchuria 24, 73 and 74. Had wheat never been grown at all in this region or was its cultivation merely intensified because of better marketability?

[155] Hosie 01, 174.

[156] North Manchuria 24, 62.

[157] Rubruck 00, 68 and 132.

[158] Vámbéry 85, 210; Peisker 24, 340; Jochelson 28, 80.

[159] II, 2 (31).

[160] II, 2 (1).

[161] *Cf.* V, introduction.

[162] See X, 1, *passim; cf.* also X, 2 (74).

[163] Hosie 01, 174.

[164] North Manchuria 24, 4.

[165] Hosie 01, 174.

[166] *Op. cit.*, 175 ff.

[167] II, 2 (3).

[168] II, 2 (16) (23).

[169] II, 2 (19). Apparently fruit trees might also be planted during the early summer. *Cf.* Hosie 01, 174.

[170] For the beginning of the planting season in North China see Buck 37a, 55, 69, 73, and 103.

[171] II, 2 (20).

[172] II, 2 (30) (31).

[173] II, 2 (12).

[174] II, 2 (21).

[175] *Hsüan-hua Fu Chên Chih* (Ming) = LSSI 15, 28b.

[176] Buck 37a, 7.

[177] SCPMHP 13, 7a.

[178] TS 52, 5a; *cf.* also Balázs 31 BWT, 85 ff.

barley in one of the old Chinese territories of the empire is certainly of great value, but it is equally significant that this record appears in a local report, not in the official history of the Liao dynasty. It is evident that some wheat and barley were grown, particularly in the two southern circuits, and that both crops were cut some time after June, that is, in the middle of the summer,[179] but the big crop, the one which claimed the special attention of the government, remained in the fields until August and September, the seventh and eighth months of the Liao year. On August 12, 946, an imperial order was issued warning soldiers not to damage the crops.[180] Harvesting might commence around the middle of August; on August 14 and 27 in the years 1046 and 994 the emperor watched the grain fall,[181] perhaps at the first solemn cutting. Weather conditions necessarily affected the time of maturing, but as a rule most of the crop was still standing at the end of August and during September. Ch'i-tan courtiers were told not to trample the people's fields on August 27 in the year 1046;[182] and special officials were dispatched "to inspect the crops" on September 1 and 18 in 992 and 1033 respectively.[183] In 952, on September 22, a remarkable plant with four stalks each bearing two ears was presented to the court.[184] Considered together, such data reveal the agricultural year of Liao. Its progress accords with our agronomical knowledge on the growth and harvesting of the northern staple crop, millet.

The time of harvesting was carefully watched by the government for fiscal reasons. No comparable data describe agricultural techniques. Obviously Chinese peasants continued their traditional agriculture which depended upon intensive cultivation and familial cooperation. Under "Oriental" conditions, intensive cultivation implies the use of irrigation above and beyond other horticultural methods. The existence of irrigated fields is documented in the inscriptions[185] as well as in the historical records.[186] Oxen, wherever available, assisted the farmer in his agricultural efforts.[187]

Cultivation must have been intensive, for it supported a dense population. Even the northern regions, which had formerly relied upon a mixed tribal economy—animal husbandry, hunting, and fishing—

now maintained a surprisingly large number of people.[188] A gift of ten thousand *mou* of irrigated rice fields was accompanied by a gift of a hundred households, presumably to work them.[189] The garrison fields also seem to have been managed by households rather than by the combined efforts of individual soldiers.[190] We may therefore assume that in the main agricultural production in the Liao empire followed the traditional Chinese family pattern.[191]

Intensive Chinese agriculture often needed government support. Its low-lying regions had to be protected against too much water; wherever possible its fields had to be watered by irrigation. Apart from this, the peasants needed a reliable calendar to carry out successfully the seasonal operations.

The Ch'i-tan rulers of Liao were none too well prepared for these Chinese tasks. There was conspicuous need for a proper calendar, but what astronomy the Liao government required was taken over, after the Ch'i-tan invasion, from the successors of the T'ang dynasty in China Proper. Only in 994 did the Liao rulers set up an official calendar of their own; and even this "new" calendar was based on an earlier Chinese system of astronomical calculation.[192]

A change from the economic mentality (the *Wirtschaftsgesinnung*)[193] of pastoralism to that of intensive agriculture is difficult. Although eager to exploit their agricultural subjects, the Ch'i-tan were too deeply rooted in their pastoral mores to understand fully the economic order of the people they had conquered. Traditional Chinese waterworks constructed in an earlier time were still used,[194] irrigation techniques were still employed, and a number of minor governmental measures actually encouraged agriculture.[195] But no large waterwork project was reported during the two hundred years of Liao rule. This cannot be explained solely by the fact that the agricultural regions of Liao were located in the north, for even there the need for waterworks was evident, and long river dikes had been erected in certain parts of the territory.[196] But in case of doubt the government was inclined to decide against work on the

[179] Besides Hosie 01, *cf.* also Buck 37*a*, 55 and 103.
[180] II, 2 (4).
[181] II, 2 (15) (26).
[182] II, 2 (26).
[183] II, 2 (14) (25).
[184] II, 2 (5).
[185] MCPL 2, 49*a*. *Cf.* IX, introduction.
[186] II, 2 (6) (30) (31).
[187] II, 2 (11).

[188] Mullie 22, 210 ff.
[189] MCPL 2, 49*a*. *Cf.* also a gift of three hundred thousand *mou* of land and fifty households (MCCSC 2, 18*b*). In the second case the proportion between land and families is quite different, perhaps because the land was not irrigated or perhaps in part not even cultivated.
[190] See below.
[191] *Cf.* Wittfogel 31, 347 ff.
[192] See XIV, 4 (4) and XIV, introduction.
[193] Sombart 19, I, 13.
[194] See XI (14).
[195] *Cf.* II, 2 and XII, *passim*.
[196] XI (22).

embankment system[197] or against the further expansion of the area under irrigation.[198] Nor did it resist the spread of water-mills, as did the governments of T'ang and other typically Chinese dynasties.[199] In the *Liao Shih* the occurrence of water-mills is mentioned only once: the *History* tells of an estate with a water-mill (or water-mills) which was given as a present.[200] The not irrigation-conscious Ch'i-tan probably failed to recognize the threat of the water-mill to intensive irrigation agriculture.

c. LAND TENURE

A survey of the different categories of land tenure is given in LS 59, 4*a*, and this is instructive as far as it goes. It contains no reference to the tribal form of land-ownership, but fortunately some information on this point is found in other sections. The grazing grounds were occupied by a few lineages which divided up the land between them.[201] In all probability this refers only to the winter quarters which are still limited today in Inner Asia and are usually allotted to individual families while the summer pastures are communally owned.[202] In recent time the attempts of wealthy herd-owners to enlarge their holdings[203] were aimed at increasing their winter pastures. Evidently Ch'i-tan herders were similarly concerned. The "land" in the northern (tribal) part of the empire[204] bestowed upon a skillful huntsman no doubt assured him good winter quarters, and the government pastures coveted by a powerful aristocratic stock-breeder[205] may well have been desired for the same reason.

The survey of LS 59 deals exclusively with those forms of landed property familiar to the sedentary regions of the empire. They are classified according to the degree of government control.

The "public land" described in the survey was used to maintain the border garrisons. It was permanently held by the government. Whether the soldiers tilled it individually or in cooperation is not clear, but the fact that they were exempted from taxation by a special law points to semi-private management; otherwise the problem of taxation could scarcely have arisen. The T'ang dynasty had some of its military land—rice fields in the interior—worked on a large scale,[206] whereas the garrison fields of the frontier regions might be cultivated by individual families. The latter arrangement probably appealed strongly to the Chinese peasant soldiers who were employed in the frontier service.

A second category consisted of wasteland which the government allotted to peasant families. This might never have been cultivated or it might have been abandoned by peasants forced to flee their homes. It was given to new colonists and remained tax-free for about ten years. Later these colonists became regular taxpayers[207] and, it may be assumed, the owners of the allotted lands.

A third category of land was privately held from the beginning. Such lands, which had to be registered,[208] could be mortgaged and sold.[209] The wealthy were permitted to own fields in different districts but were expected to pay taxes,[210] an obligation they sought to avoid by spreading their property beyond the borders of their home country.

Large landed properties were held by the Liao nobility and bureaucracy[211] and by the Buddhist temples, whose wealth continued to increase during the course of the dynasty.[212] The families of the retainers who were controlled by these landlords[213] must have worked as tenant-farmers. What their actual reward was is not known, but the offer of fifty per cent of the crop to men enlisted for agricultural work in 986[214] indicates a rate of land-rent similar to that of the preceding T'ang dynasty.[215]

Tenancy does not exclude the use of hired labor; prosperous peasants as well as the wealthier tenants may have employed some wage labor. A decree of

---

[197] *Loc. cit.*

[198] II, 2 (6).

[199] Wittfogel 27, 319. Water-mills, though not necessarily harmful, might under certain conditions interfere with the unhampered utilization of water for the irrigation of the fields. In view of this possibility, the T'ang government decided, "Wherever a water-course has irrigation, water-mills must not interfere with its benefit" (TLT 7, 9*b*). This means that wherever water was not abundant the mill dams were to be closed for a certain period (*loc. cit.* original note). In case of a conflict the mills were completely destroyed. THY 89, 1622 records the destruction by the government of over seventy and eighty water-mills in 764 and 778 respectively. In both cases the motive was the protection or development of irrigation. *Cf.* also Balázs 31 BWT, 36 ff.

[200] II, 2 (17); *cf.* also LS 48, 5*b*.

[201] I, 2 (1).

[202] Radloff 93, I, 417; *cf.* also Hudson 38, 32 ff.

[203] Radloff 93 I, 415 ff.

[204] X, 1 (8).

[205] II, 1 (19).

[206] See CTS 151, 7*b* and 139, 15*b*–16*a*. Balázs (31 BWT, 73) erroneously assumes the existence only of large scale garrison farms in the T'ang period.

[207] *Cf.* II, 2, *passim* and XII, *passim*.

[208] II, 2 (24).

[209] VI, 2 (3).

[210] II, 2 (9).

[211] *Cf.* VIII.

[212] *Cf.* IX.

[213] *Cf.* VIII (3).

[214] XII (6).

[215] TS 153, 2*b*.

1013 prescribes a wage of ten coppers per day[216] for men and women who because of famine fell into bondage. Was the decreed rate exceptionally low because of the distressing situation, or was it exceptionally high because of the government's desire to offer effective relief? Did the set wage rate refer to all kinds of work, or did it refer chiefly to the most common occupations, agriculture and animal husbandry? The text gives no clue to the answers.

d. AGRICULTURAL POLICY OF THE CH'I–TAN RULERS

The agricultural policy of the Liao government was that of a conquering people who attempted to exploit for their advantage an economic situation which they did not fully understand. The resettlement of large groups of peasants in the old tribal regions of the north was undertaken in order to increase the food supply and provide additional labor power. The reclamation of wasteland was encouraged as were also the planting of mulberry trees and [silk?] spinning,[217] the raising of fruit trees,[218] and the growing of crops in general.[219] Near the close of the dynasty Nan-ching Circuit was ordered to cultivate rice except in those places which were necessary for the movement of the Liao cavalry,[220] an indication that even at that late date the fundamental conflict in the country's economic system was still unresolved. The mounted masters of Liao, clinging to their pastoral ways of life, were bound to clash with and infringe upon the interests of their agricultural subjects. They restricted the development of irrigation agriculture; they turned irrigated fields into pastures;[221] they interfered with seasonal agricultural requirements[222] or ruthlessly destroyed the crops when they herded or hunted.[223]

The imperial government fought against excesses of this kind, for they threatened the much-desired agricultural surplus. But restrictions upon a negative attitude do not always lead to a positive one; no really positive attitude was possible where the basis for a full understanding was absent. A story circulated at the court of the succeeding dynasty, Chin, reveals how little the Ch'i-tan rulers knew of the life and habits of their agricultural Chinese subjects. When the last Liao ruler, T'ien-tsu, heard that starvation was ravaging his sedentary population, he is said to have naively asked, "Why don't they eat curd?"[224] This Ch'i-tan emperor had learned nothing from two hundred years of conquest and domination; he was still unaware of the fact that the Chinese in the course of a long cultural development had acquired a deep-seated aversion to the pastoral diet which seemed natural and attractive to him.[225]

---

[216] XII (34).

[217] II, 2 (1).

[218] II, 2 (19) (28).

[219] II, 2 (14) and *passim*.

[220] II, 2 (31).

---

[221] LWT 5, 21b–22a; see VIII, introduction.

[222] II, 1 (12).

[223] II, 1 (12); II, 2 (27).

[224] CS 8, 13a.

[225] At the end of the eleventh century (about 1096) a Chinese envoy to the Liao empire was offered a milk gruel to which some kind of cream (生油) was added. He was unable to swallow the dish (不可入口). Yet he enjoyed the gruel when it was left "pure," that is without the cream (PCKT 2, 22).

TRANSLATION

1. PASTORALISM

1. Economic base of the northern people 2. The strength of the Ch'i-tan 3. Animal husbandry 4. Fishing 5. Game as army supplies 6. Herds inspected 7. Large-scale hunting 8. Ewes precious 9. Legend of a fox hunt 10. Huge loot of horses 11. Roebucks and deer 12. Seasonal hunting and grazing 13. Fishing 14. Government animals branded 15. Tribal brands for horses 16. Fishing 17. Horses requisitioned 18. Livestock census 19. Pastures limited 20. A million horses 21. Horses requisitioned 22. A levy of horses 23. The emperor's seasonal residences 24. The spring *na-po* 25. The summer *na-po* 26. The autumn *na-po* 27. The winter *na-po* 28. Spring hunting in Nan-ching

1. ECONOMIC BASE OF THE NORTHERN PEOPLE

[The people of] the Northern Desert[1] made animal husbandry and hunting their occupations, just as the Chinese people encouraged agriculture from which they derived the means of subsistence.[2] After Liao became an empire, it established the five capitals and set up the Southern and Northern Divisions and controlled the whole of China.[3] But the customs of hunting still followed the old course.   68, 1a

2. THE STRENGTH OF THE CH'I-TAN

In the ancient Ch'i-tan way of life their wealth consisted of horses and their strength of soldiers. The horses were released in the open country and the soldiers were demobilized among the people. Whenever a military campaign occurred, they were called to arms. The mounted archers and armored soldiers received their orders at the hour *mao*[4] and assembled at the hour *ch'ên*.[5] The horses went after water and grass and the men depended on kumiss.[6] They bent the powerful [bow]

---

[1] The term *shuo mo* 朔漠, "the northern desert," is frequently applied to the regions north of the Great Wall.

[2] The Liao official, Hsiao Ch'ing 慶, speaking with a Sung envoy in 1055, said, "The Ch'i-tan oxen and horses sometimes reach maturity and sometimes do not, just as is the case in the Southern Country [Sung] with the breeding of silkworms." The envoy was surprised and asked for an explanation. Hsiao Ching continued, "If there is snow above which the grass shows an inch or more, then the oxen and horses will come to successful maturity. If there is no snow, or if the snow covers the grass, they will not come to maturity. Generally the Ch'i-tan consider this the reason for prosperity or calamity" (TCCS 5, 33).

Another dialogue in 1007 between a Sung envoy and a Ch'i-tan official also is based upon the differing subsistence economies of the two countries. At a banquet a Ch'i-tan dignitary asked the Sung envoy, T'êng Shih 滕涉, "Why does the Southern Country eat meat without removing the skin?" T'êng replied, "Our country raises silkworms, therefore we do not remove the skin from the meat" (KLTY 2, 10). The Ch'i-tan question implies a not too subtle boast about the abundance of meat in the northern empire. The Sung spokesman points to the high development of Sung sericulture which (he tacitly admits) does not make for an equally satisfactory development of animal husbandry.

[3] The statement, though manifestly exaggerated, contains a grain of truth. During the period of the Five Dynasties, particularly at the time of Later Chin, Liao influence was indeed paramount throughout China. Even after the establishment of the Sung empire the northern state remained a factor of supreme importance. A Sung

scholar, Ch'ên Liang 陳亮, in his memorial to Emperor Hsiao-tsung 孝宗 (1163–1189) of the Southern Sung dynasty explains the situation: Before 1005 Liao stood as a rival side by side with China. If it had not been for the battle of T'an-yüan 澶淵, the Chinese situation would have been much worse and there might not have been an independent China at all. In 1042 Fu Pi 富弼 succeeded in persuading the Liao emperor not to use force, but he did not dare to boast of this great achievement. He clearly noted the superior position of the northern state: "An order for a punitive expedition issued by the Ch'i-tan rests upon the overlord's authority; the tribute paid by the [Sung] Son of Heaven is an act of propriety rendered by a subordinate" (LCWC 1, 5).

[4] Between five and seven o'clock in the morning.

[5] Between seven and nine o'clock, that is immediately after the orders were given.

[6] According to a poem written by the Sung official, Pi Chung-yu 畢仲游, on the occasion of an embassy to Liao in 1055, the Ch'i-tan ate *lo chou* 酪粥:

The region of the Sang-chien is cold	桑乾地寒
Felt is used to make dwellings. . . .	氈作屋
[People] with gifts for the guests come and go	饋客往來
Bearing the *lo chou*. . . .	隨酪粥
Behind the mountains	山後猶存
The old customs still exist	舊風俗
The women of Yu and Yen	幽燕婦女
Are white as suet;	白如脂
They show their faces	露面來覘
Coming to peek at [our] Chinese caps and garments.	漢冠服

(HTC 18, 7a ff.).

and shot living [animals] in order to provide for their daily needs. [They also had] dried food[7] and fodder. Such was their way of living. On account of this, they held the upper hand and encountered no opposition wherever they went. 59, 1a

3. ANIMAL HUSBANDRY

901   Previously, when T'ai-tsu was the *i-li-chin*[8] of the I-lieh Administration,[9] he took warning from the fact that the Yao-lien family had been weakened by isolation and therefore treated all tribes kindly, made the rewards and punishments equitable, and abstained from wanton military campaigns. He benefited his people by pursuing their interests. The herds flourished, and both the government and the people were sufficiently provided for. After he had ascended the throne, he attacked Ho-tung,[10] subdued the commanderies and counties of Tai-pei,[11] and seized more than a hundred thousand oxen, sheep, camels, and horses. Chancellor Yeh-lü Hsieh-chên[12] in subduing the Nü-chih also captured more than two hundred thousand horses. The herds were distributed among pastures where water and grass were plentiful. Within a few years they increased beyond number. Taking over the horses from the rich at this time did not seem to increase the number, and granting more than ten thousand horses to the Greater and Smaller Hawk Armies[13] did not seem to decrease it. Such were the results of [excellent] methods of animal husbandry.[14] . . .

Afterwards, the kingdom of Tung-tan paid an annual tribute of one thousand horses; the Nü-chih ten thousand; the Chih-pu-ku and other countries ten thousand; the Tsu-pu, Wu-tu-wan, and T'i-yin[15] twenty thousand each; Hsi Hsia and Shih-wei three hundred each; and the Yüeh-li-tu, P'ou-a-li, Ao-li-mi, P'u-nu-li, and T'ieh-li tribes three hundred each. Furthermore, the exportation of sheep and horses into Sung by way of Shuo Prefecture[16] was prohibited, as well as the sale of horses from the T'u-hun and Tang-hsiang to [Hsi] Hsia.

As a result of this the herds flourished and grew to a total of more than a million. The stock-breeding officials were promoted according to their rank. During the almost[17] two hundred years from T'ai-tsu down to Hsing-tsung the prosperity of the herds continued undiminished. During the early years of T'ien-tsu there were still several tens of thousands of herds of horses, each herd comprising not less than a thousand animals.

In the old system of the ancestors usually several tens of thousands of horses were selected for southern expeditions. They were grazed in Hsiung,[18] Pa,[19] Ch'ing,[20] and Ts'ang[21] in preparation

---

Lo chou was probably identical with *ju chou* 乳粥, mentioned by another Sung author, Wang Chu 王洙, and was a sort of milk gruel. When offered as food to guests, the *t'ieh chiao* 鐵脚 plant was added. The Ch'i-tan considered this very delicious (WSTL 14b; cf. also PCKT 2, 22).

[7] According to the Sung commentator, Shih Chao 史炤, the term *ch'iu-liang* 糗糧 means dried food broken into small particles (TCTCSW 26, 9a).

[8] The significance of the term *i-li-chin*, which designates a chieftain, and its probable etymology are discussed in XIII, introduction and XIV, introduction.

[9] Identical with I-la, T'ai-tsu's tribe. The lack of institutional stability is well expressed in the unstable nomenclature even of this important tribe.

[10] The regions east of the Yellow River covering approximately the whole of modern Shansi (JCL 31, 29 ff.).

[11] Corresponding to the northeastern part of modern Shansi.

[12] For the title see XIV, 1 (9), LS 45, 2a–3b. Yeh-lü Hsieh-chên 斜軫 was a military strategist. In 969 he was recommended to the emperor, Ching-tsung, who put him in charge of the military affairs of Shan-hsi—during the war against Sung (LS 83, 3b). He died in 999.

[13] A name for armies composed of Shih-wei horsemen (LS 46, 12b).

[14] We follow the Palace edition in reading 畜 for the 蓄 of our text.

[15] See I, 2 (10), no. 53.

[16] Modern Shuo County, Shansi.

[17] The period from T'ai-tsu's accession to the throne in 907 to the death of Hsing-tsung in 1055 covered exactly one hundred and forty-eight years.

[18] Modern Hsiung 雄 County, Hopei. Hsiung and Pa prefectures were established by the emperor of Later Chou after he had reconquered the region of the three passes of I-chin 益津, Wa-ch'iao 瓦橋, and Yü 淤口 from Liao in 959. See WTS 60, 6b; WHTK 316, 2479.

[19] Modern Pa 霸 County, Hopei.

[20] Ch'ing 清 Prefecture was set up in the region of modern Tientsin (Hopei) by the Sung government as late as 1113.

[21] East of the preceding prefectures. Both territories were firmly in the hands of the governments of Later Chou and Sung (WTS 60, 7b; SS 86, 4b).

for emergencies in Yen[22] and Yün.[23]   Besides these, several tens of thousands of horses were selected for the quarterly hunting tours.   The rest were assigned to different places for grazing.   This system worked very well.

During the last years, because of frequent wars with Chin, six or seven out of ten barbarian[24] and Chinese[25] war horses were lost.   Although the price increased many fold, horses could not be purchased anywhere.   Then, in disregard of the law, government horses were purchased for the army and private sales of herds increased daily.   Even the [emperor's] needs for hunting [horses] could not be satisfied.   Consequently [Emperor T'ien-tsu] was defeated by Chin, deserted the people, and fled continuously until the fall [of the dynasty].   All the horses[26] formerly kept north of Sung-mo[27] became the possession of the scribe[28] [Yeh-lü] Ta-shih.[29]   60, 3b–4a

4. FISHING

915   On the day *mou-shên*[30] of the tenth month in the winter [of the ninth year of T'ai-tsu's accession to the throne the emperor] fished[31] in the Yalu River.   1, 8b

5. GAME AS ARMY SUPPLIES

924   On the first day *ping-yin* of the tenth month in the winter [of the third year of T'ien-tsan] a hunt in the Yü-lo Mountains[32] resulted in the capture of several thousand wild animals which were given to the army as food supplies.   2, 5a

---

[22] Modern Peiping, here obviously used for Nan-ching Circuit as a whole.

[23] Modern Ta-t'ung, Shansi, here obviously used for Hsi-ching Circuit as a whole.   The passage seems to refer to the earlier period of the Liao empire, probably to the reign of T'ai-tsung when these regions were temporarily used by the Ch'i-tan armies as starting points for their southward thrusts into the region of the Yellow River.

[24] Here evidently all tribes, including the Ch'i-tan.

[25] The Liao army comprised Ch'i-tan, "barbarian," Chinese, and Po-hai soldiers.   The mounted Ch'i-tan soldiers were the backbone of the army.   The other tribal and Po-hai soldiers included both horsemen and infantry. The Chinese militia were mainly foot soldiers.   The Chinese regular troops were made up of horsemen and foot soldiers.   Their cavalry was probably a crack force belonging to special armies, such as the Shu-shan Army of Empress Ying-t'ien (LS 35, 1a).   Li Hsin 李信, a Chinese employed as a Liao official, reported to the Sung court after his surrender in 1003 that there were several detachments of Chinese cavalry totaling more than eighteen thousand men (SHYK 196, 27a; see also XV, introduction).

[26] CTKC 19, 4b relates that at the end of the dynasty there were several hundred thousand imperial horses in the territory of modern Mongolia, a region which the Chin soldiers could hardly reach.   Yeh-lü Ta-shih took these horses with him when he left Emperor T'ien-tsu.   Of course, the horses trained for military use were but a small percentage of the total number in the combined herds.   CS 3, 5a–b states that Yeh-lü Ta-shih possessed ten thousand war horses when he established himself as king in 1124.

[27] This term originated during the seventh century as the name of a prefecture in modern Jehol.   Later it became a common term denoting the regions of modern Jehol, Chahar, Suiyuan, and Mongolia.

[28] The *lin-ya* 林牙 (scribe) was the Ch'i-tan equivalent of the Chinese *han-lin* 翰林, a position of high scholarly status.   See XIV, 1 (9), LS 45, 8b–9b.

[29] See below, appendix V.

[30] The word 戊, which is now colloquially pronounced *wu*, was originally pronounced *mou*.   In 907 the then emperor of the Liang dynasty decreed that the word *wu* 武 should take the place of *mou* 戊 to avoid the latter sound in the name of the emperor's great-grandfather, Mou-lin 茂琳 (WTS 2, 2b).

Hung Mai 洪邁 (1123–1202) claims that in North China during his time the word 戊 was generally pronounced *wu* 武, but the Sung standard dictionary *Chi Yün* 集韻, completed in the eleventh century, gives the earlier pronunciation, *mou* (JCHP 6, 5a; CY 6, 26a).   We therefore transcribe the word as *mou* rather than *wu*.

[31] Most later editions have the word 釣, "to fish with a rod"; our Yüan text, however, has 鈎, "to hook."   This version coincides with a description of Ch'i-tan fishing given by Ch'êng Ta-ch'ang 程大昌 (1123–1195), who says, "They do not fish with the rod (非釣也), but they hook (鈎也)."   For a detailed discussion see Fêng CS 33, 25–27.   Fishing with nets was also sometimes practised (see II, 1 (24)).

Most of the Liao fishing expeditions were made when the rivers were frozen over in the winter and spring months. The tents of the emperor and his retinue were pitched on the river.   The fish were attracted by kindling fires in hollows cut into the ice and were caught by a hook at the end of a line dropped through a hole in the ice.

The *niu-yü* 牛魚, "sturgeon" (Read 39, no. 139), was the most prized of the river fish.   Success or failure in catching the sturgeon was believed to foretell whether the coming year would be good or bad.   The first sturgeon caught was called 頭魚, "First Fish."   A feast was given by the emperor to his followers and the chieftains of nearby tribes and was called the First Fish Feast (頭魚宴). *Cf*. XIII, (45); YFL 3, 6b–7a; HLWC 3a; *T'ung-ya* 通雅 by Fang I-chih 方以智 = LSSIP 5, 24b.   See also Stein 39, 95.

[32] Probably in present Outer Mongolia.

On the first day *i-wei* of the eleventh month [in the third year of T'ien-tsan . . . T'ai-tsu] shot tigers from the Wu-la-hsieh-li Mountains[33] to the Pa-shih Mountains.[34]   He hunted while advancing over a distance of more than six hundred *li*.   There was fresh food daily and the soldiers were all well supplied.   2, 5a

6. HERDS INSPECTED

928   On the day *hsin-mao* [of the twelfth month in the second year of T'ien-hsien] the herds were inspected [by T'ai-tsung] in the nearby suburban region.[35]   3, 2a

7. LARGE–SCALE HUNTING

929   On the day *chi-wei* [of the sixth month in the fourth year of T'ien-hsien] several thousand light horsemen were recruited to hunt in the nearby[36] mountains.   3, 3b

8. EWES PRECIOUS

939   On the day *i-ssŭ* of the fifth month [in the second year of Hui-t'ung] the export of ewes from the territory of Nan-ching was forbidden.[37]   4, 3b

9. LEGEND OF A FOX HUNT

947   In this year [the first year of Ta-t'ung] more than ten horsemen, hunting in the large mountains fifty *li* west of Tsu Prefecture, saw T'ai-tsung, mounted on a white horse, in solitary pursuit of a white fox.   He shot one arrow and killed it.   Suddenly he disappeared. They found only the fox and the arrow.   On the same day T'ai-tsung died in Luan City.[38]

Later a temple was built at this place.   On the Phoenix Gate of [Huai] Prefecture[39] was painted a picture of T'ai-tsung galloping on a horse and shooting at a fox.   37, 7a

10. HUGE LOOT OF HORSES

986   On the day *ping-tzŭ* [of the first month in the fourth year of T'ung-ho] Chancellor Yeh-lü Hsieh-chên, Scribe [Hsiao] Ch'in-tê,[40] and others offered more than a hundred thousand captives, over two hundred thousand horses, and other objects which they had seized during the punitive campaign against the Nü-chih.   11, 1a

11. ROEBUCKS AND DEER

994   In the twelfth year of T'ung-ho [Hsiao Kuan-yin-nu[41]] became the *hsiang-wên*[42] of a group of the emperor's right attendants and [then] was transferred to the [position of] great king of the Six Tribes of Hsi.   Previously [a great king], in addition to the emoluments of his rank, was provided with more than a hundred roebucks and deer, all of which were exacted from the common people.   On the suggestion of [Hsiao] Kuan-yin-nu, this was stopped.   85, 2a

---

[33] Perhaps in the western part of Kansu.

[34] Probably in the western region of present Outer Mongolia.   During this period T'ai-tsu led his great expedition through this region to eastern Sinkiang.

[35] Of Lin-huang, the later Supreme Capital, the only capital of that period.

[36] Near the emperor's stopping place on a trip west of the Supreme Capital.

[37] In 938 Liao envoys went to Nan T'ang offering sheep and horses as a gift to the king.   At the same time, they sold thirty thousand sheep and two hundred horses, and purchased silk, tea, and drugs (HTS 69, 594–595).   Thus the prohibition of the export of ewes from Nan-ching occurred one year after the great sale of sheep to Nan T'ang.

[38] Luan 欒 City (north of present Luan-ch'êng 欒城 County, Hopei), where T'ai-tsung died, was many hundred miles distant from Tsu Prefecture (southwest of present Boro Khoton, Jehol) where the emperor appeared in a vision to the huntsmen.

[39] The information contained in this passage is presented in the description of Huai Prefecture which was located southeast of present Boro Khoton, Jehol.

[40] Hsiao Ch'in-tê 勤德, whose name is also given as K'ên-tê 肯德 and Hêng-tê 恆德, distinguished himself during the war against Sung (LS 88, 3a–b).

[41] Hsiao Kuan-yin-nu 觀音奴 came from a noble Hsi family (LS 85, 2a).

[42] The title *hsiang-wên*, which was applied to the chief of various governmental organizations, originated in 938 (LS 4, 2b).   It was also applied to the chief of an army, a camp, a small tribe, or a group of imperial followers. See XIV, 1, *passim*.

12. SEASONAL HUNTING AND GRAZING

997   In the fifteenth year of T'ung-ho an imperial decree ordered the remission of the grain long in arrears to the charity granaries in Nan-ching. The military officers were again forbidden to hinder agriculture by engaging in hunts or grazing cattle at improper seasons.
59, 2b

13. FISHING

1002   [In the ninth month of the twentieth year of T'ung-ho] fish were forked from the Liao River.   68, 9b

14. GOVERNMENT ANIMALS BRANDED

1026   On the day hsin-ch'ou of the sixth month [in the sixth year of T'ai-p'ing] an imperial decree ordered that all animals belonging to the government should be branded on the left side so as to identify[43] them.   17, 3a

15. TRIBAL BRANDS FOR HORSES

1038   The emperor, considering that [Yeh-lü] Hsi-sun[44] possessed merit for assisting him to ascend the throne and grieving because his son had died for a crime, wanted to make his official position hereditary but found that Hsi-sun lacked tribal origin. It happened that he saw a pattern branded on a horse with the mark of the P'in tribe; he ordered him to belong to this tribe and appointed him as prime minister of the Southern Administration.   97, 4b

16. FISHING

1039   [In the first month of the eighth year of Ch'ung-hsi[45]] fish were forked from the Chih River.[46]   68, 14a

17. HORSES REQUISITIONED

1046   On the day chi-hai [of the eleventh month in the fifteenth year of Ch'ung-hsi] there was a general requisition of army horses among the [Po-] hai[47] tribes[48] in accordance with the procedure among the Ch'i-tan households.   19, 8a

1048   On the first day i-wei of the eleventh month [in the seventeenth year of Ch'ung-hsi] emissaries were sent out to requisition horses.   20, 2b

---

[43] We follow other editions in reading 識 for the 職 of our text.

[44] Of Yeh-lü Hsi-sun's 喜孫 background we know nothing except that he belonged to T'ai-tsung's ordo (LS 97, 4a) which was established about a hundred years previously. Either Hsi-sun's family may have belonged to no tribe at all (the garrison of T'ai-tsung's ordo included people from the old Po-hai and Chinese regions), or the memory of its tribal provenience may have been wholly lost. Hsi-sun was called a Yeh-lü probably as result of the aid which he rendered to Hsing-tsung before the latter ascended the throne. He became prime minister in 1038 (LS 18, 8b; 27, 8b).

[45] In the time of T'ien-tsu this reign title was changed to Ch'ung-ho 重和 in order to avoid the use of hsi 熙 which had the same sound as hsi 禧 in his personal name. The Sung empire, knowing that Ch'ung-ho was used by Liao (in 1119), changed its reign title, which was also Ch'ung-ho, to Hsüan-ho 宣和. Cf. TWSTT 1, 16a; LHAPC 1, 10.

[46] We follow the Southern Academy, Northern Academy, and Palace editions, and also 8, 4b of this edition in reading 治 for the 冶 of our text. The Chih River is mentioned twice in the Liao Shih: once here and once in 8, 4b. Its location may be traced from the latter source. In the seventh month of the seventh year of Pao-ning (975) a Po-hai descendant, Yen-p'o 燕頗, slew a Liao official and rebelled in Huang-lung Administration. In the ninth month he was defeated at the Chih River. Since Huang-lung Administration corresponds to modern Nung-an County, Kirin, the Chih River must be close to or identical with the modern I-t'ung 伊通 River, a branch of the Sungari River, Kirin.

[47] The word po 渤 is missing in our text. We have followed other editions in adding it.

[48] The population of the former Po-hai kingdom comprised tribal as well as other elements. After the kingdom was destroyed in 926 by T'ai-tsu, some Po-hai tribes became independent and others were taken over into Shang-ching and other circuits. The tribes referred to in the present passage must have been the ones under the control of the Ch'i-tan.

18. LIVESTOCK CENSUS

1069　　　In the beginning of Hsien-yung, [Hsiao T'ao-wei[49]] was appointed grand guardian[50] of the herds of horses.　　Having learned that herds nominally in existence were actually non-existent, he made a minute check of the old registers in order to eliminate the weak and the sick and to record the real number.　The herdsmen were won over by their respect for him.

[Hsiao] T'ao-wei sent up a memorial saying, "The herds when small have been reported to be large, and when non-existent have been reported in existence.　Superiors and inferiors deceive each other; evils accumulate and become habitual.　It would be best to ascertain the real figures and to record the actual number.　The government and private persons would both profit."

The proposal was approved.　The livestock in consequence propagated abundantly year after year.　　90, 2b–3a

19. PASTURES LIMITED

1075　　　In the first year of Ta-k'ang, [Yeh-lü] I-hsin[51] made a request for pasture land. [Yeh-lü] Yin-chi memorialized, "The present pastures are limited and the herds do not propagate abundantly.　How can they be distributed among subordinates?"

The emperor then terminated [this matter].　　97, 3a

20. A MILLION HORSES

1086　　　On the first day *ting-ssŭ* of the fifth month [in the second year of Ta-an], because the herds of horses had propagated so abundantly that they had reached a total of a million, the stockbreeding officials were rewarded and promoted according to their rank.　　24, 7a

21. HORSES REQUISITIONED

1094　　　On the day *chia-yin* of the fifth month [in the tenth year of Ta-an] horses were requisitioned.　　25, 6b

22. A LEVY OF HORSES

1120　　　On the day *chi-yu* of the third month [in the tenth year of T'ien-ch'ing] one tenth of the horses possessed by the common people were taken to supply the armies of the Eastern Route.[52]　　28, 7b

23. THE EMPEROR'S SEASONAL RESIDENCES

The Liao empire included all of the great desert and also covered the region of the Great Wall. They followed expediency in carrying on the government.　During the autumn and winter they shunned the cold; during the spring and summer they avoided the heat.　Following water and grass and engaging in hunting and fishing made up the yearly routine. For each of the four seasons [the emperor] had a temporary place in which to reside.　This was called a *na-po*.[53]　　32, 1a–b

---

[49] Hsiao T'ao-wei 陶隗 was a descendant of a noble family.　According to LS 60, 3b, he was appointed grand guardian in 1069.

[50] The title of grand guardian was used to designate one of the three highest dignitaries of China's imperial hierarchy.　The Ch'i-tan applied it to officials of widely differing rank.　Cf. XIV, 1, *passim*.

[51] Yeh-lü I-hsin 乙辛 was a descendant of the Five Divisions lineage.　He was first honored as Prince of Chao 趙 and later held other princely titles.　When he was prime minister, he plotted to kill the empress and the heir apparent of Tao-tsung (LS 110, 1a–3b).　For the story of his birth, see VII, 2 (72).　In a contemporary inscription the name I-hsin was transcribed 乙信 (MCCSC 2, 27b).

[52] From 1114 down to this time (1120) Liao dispatched several expeditions to the region of the Sungari River, but all were defeated by the Jurchen with great losses in equipment and horses.

[53] WCTL 6, 61 explains *na-po* 捺鉢 as designating a temporary residence of an emperor (行在).　TCKC 11, 6b gives the pronunciation *la-po* 剌鉢 for this expression. According to Shiratori (13 TMK, 19–20), *na* or *la* is equivalent to the Mongol *nutuk*, meaning a camp in the wilderness, and to the Tunkinsk *nutuk* and the Selenginsk *nütük*, meaning a village; *po* is equivalent to the Manchu and Japanese *ba* and Korean *pa*, meaning a place.　*Na-po* or *la-po* is equivalent to *nutuk-ba*, a combination of the word *nutuk* plus the suffix *ba*.

The institution of the *na-po* prevailed also during the Chin and Yüan dynasties.　According to the Yüan poet, Yang Yün-fu 楊允孚, the Yüan temporary residence was called *na-pao* 納寶 or *na-po* 納鉢 (LCTY 1, 1a).

24. THE SPRING *NA–PO*

It was called Duck River Lake.[54] During the first ten days of the first month the emperor moved his tent, arriving there in about sixty days.[55] Before the swans[56] came, tents were erected on the ice in order to catch fish by cutting into the ice. When the ice melted they released eagles and falcons to catch swans and wild geese. Going out in the morning and returning in the evening, they devoted themselves to hunting.

Duck River Lake was twenty *li* from east to west and thirty *li* from south to north. It was situated thirty-five *li* northeast of Ch'ang-ch'un Prefecture. It was surrounded by sandy tracts and by many groves of elm, willow, and apricot trees.

Whenever the emperor arrived, all the imperial attendants donned dark green clothes. Each had ready a multiple hammer, an eagle's food-bowl, and an awl for piercing the swans. They placed themselves around the lake five to seven paces from each other. The emperor, wearing a cap and clothes according to the season and with a belt ornamented with jade tied around his waist, stood with his back to the wind and watched them from a distance. Places with swans were signaled by the raising of banners; messengers[57] on horseback rushed with reports. At the beating of drums around the pond,[58] the swans were frightened and flew up. The surrounding horsemen to the left and right all raised banners and waved them.

[Attendants of] the Five Animal Quarters[59] bowed and handed gray falcons from east of the sea[60] to the emperor who released them. As the falcons caught the swans and fell down exhausted, the attendants, lined up nearby, seized the awls and dug into the swans, taking out the brains to feed the falcons. Those who revived the falcons were generally granted silver and lustring.

When the emperor obtained the First Swan,[61] he offered it as a sacrifice to the ancestral temple. Each official offered refreshments. Music was played and they toasted each other with wine and expressed congratulations. Everyone stuck swan feathers on his head to make merry. [The emperor] granted wine to his followers and distributed the feathers among them.

He caught birds, hunted animals, and fished with nets until the spring was over. Then he returned. 32, 1b–2a

25. THE SUMMER *NA–PO*

There was no fixed place. It was usually in the T'u-êrh Mountains. Every year Tao-tsung first went to the Black Mountain to do homage to the mausoleums of Shêng-tsung and Hsing-tsung[62] and to enjoy the golden lilies. Then he proceeded to the Tzŭ River to avoid the heat.

The T'u-êrh Mountains were three hundred *li* northeast of the Black Mountain near the Man-t'ou Mountains. The Black Mountain was thirteen *li* north of Ch'ing Prefecture.[63] On the mountain

---

[54] A lake formed by the overflow of the Ya-tzŭ 鴨子 River (Duck River), the modern Sungari River. The name was changed by imperial order to Hun-t'ung 混同 River in 1024, but the earlier designation was still used to the end of the Liao period (LS 16, 8b). In 1054 a Sung envoy, Wang Kung-ch'ên 王拱辰, who visited the northern court, reported that every spring the Liao emperor set up his tents on the river to fish and to feast with a limited number of nobles and courtiers. Each time the emperor caught a fish he personally served wine to the Sung envoy; he also played the guitar to entertain his guest (CSCSI, 307).

[55] Sixty days seems a long time but, according to CTKC 23, 4b, the emperor hunted on his way to the Lake.

[56] *T'ien-ê* 天鵝, "swan" (*cf.* Read 32, no. 254). Wherever the word *ê* is used alone, it is assumed that *t'ien-ê* is meant.

[57] We follow other editions in reading 探 for the 深 of our text.

[58] We follow CTKC 23, 4b in reading 泊 for the 洎, and 遶 for the 遠 of our text.

[59] XIV, 1 (26) and note 96.

[60] *Hai-tung ch'ing hu* 海東青鶻. The "sea" was the modern Sungari River. These falcons were sometimes called simply *hai-tung ch'ing*. Laufer (16a, 353, note 3) equates them with gyrfalcons.

[61] According to SCHY 21b, *t'ou-ê* 頭鵝 means *t'ien* (天)-*ê*. However, in another description of the hunt the term *t'ou* has to some extent the meaning "the foremost," that is the largest or best (*Yen-shan Ts'ung-lu* 燕山叢錄 = LSSI 17, 8b–9a).

[62] These mausoleums were located at modern Warmanha (War-in-manha), about twenty *li* northwest of Tsaghan Khoton, Jehol (LLSKCL 6, 3a; Torii 36 III, foreword; Mullie 33, 3). See frontispiece.

[63] According to LS 37, 8a, this mountain was located twenty *li* west of Ch'ing Prefecture (modern Tsaghan Khoton, Jehol). A Sung scholar, Shên K'uo 沈括 (T. 存中

was a pond with golden lilies.   The Tzŭ River was three hundred *li* northeast of the T'u-êrh Mountains.   In the mountains west of Huai Prefecture[64] was the Ch'ing-liang Hall.   This too was a place which the emperor visited to avoid the heat.

During the second ten days of the fourth month [the emperor] moved his tent and sought out by divination an auspicious place as a cool retreat.   During the last ten days of the fifth month or the first ten days of the sixth month he arrived there.   He stayed fifty days discussing national affairs with the officials of the Northern and Southern [Regions] and hunted on days of leisure.   During the second ten days of the seventh month he departed.   *32, 2a–b*

26. THE AUTUMN *NA-PO*

It was called the Forest of Vanquished Tigers.   During the second ten days of the seventh month the emperor moved his camp from the cool retreat into the mountains to shoot deer and tigers.   This forest was situated fifty *li* northwest of Yung Prefecture.[65]   Once tigers infested the forest and killed the inhabitants and the herds, so Ching-tsung directed several horsemen to carry out a hunt there.   The tigers crouched in the grass trembling and dared not raise their heads to look up, so the emperor let them go.   Hence it was called the Forest of Vanquished Tigers.

Every year when the emperor came people from the imperial clan down scattered alongside the pond and waited until about midnight when deer came to drink the salty water. Hunters were ordered to blow horns and imitate the cry of the deer which were shot as they came together.   This was called "salt-licking deer" or "calling the deer."   *32, 2b–3a*

27. THE WINTER *NA-PO*

Called Kuang-p'ing-tien.   It was thirty *li* southeast of Yung Prefecture and was originally named Pai-ma-tien.   It was more than twenty *li* from east to west and more than ten *li* from south to north. The land was very flat and as far as one could see there were sand dunes.   The trees were chiefly elms and willows.   The region had much sand.   As it was somewhat warmer during the winter months, the emperor[66] generally spent the winter here discussing national affairs with the high officials of the Northern and Southern [Regions].   Frequently he went out to engage in hunts and military practice. He also received tributes from Sung in the south[67] and from other countries.

The imperial tent had a strong stockade made of spears which were joined together by hair ropes. Beneath each spear was a black felt umbrella to protect the guards from wind and snow.[68]   Beyond the spears was a row of small felt tents.   Each tent held five men, all of whom carried arms.   This was the Forbidden Enclosure.

To the south was the Shêng-fang Hall, and about two *li* to the north of the hall was Shou-ning Hall.   Both were built with wooden pillars and bamboo rafters and were covered with felt.   The pillars were enveloped with colorful designs.   The walls were clothed with brocade, and above the door there hung a piece of purple embroidery.   The floor was made of yellow cloth embroidered with dragons.   The window curtains were all made of felt covered with lustring [imbued with] Yellow oil. The foundation was more than a foot high.   The side chambers and verandahs were also covered with felt but had no doors or windows.

1030–1094), gives a different location.   He states that it was situated northeast of Ch'ing Prefecture.   As an envoy he had stayed in a camp at the foot of the mountain. The color of the mountain was black and blue like loadstone (MHPT 24, 156).

[64] Southeast of Boro Khoton, Jehol.

[65] Near the juncture of the Shira Muren and the Lao-ha River.

[66] The term *ya-chang* 牙帳 usually designates the imperial tent or camp.   As this meaning does not fit here, the term must be explained as referring to the emperor himself, as in the expression 車駕

[67] *Nan Sung* 南宋 must be taken as expressing the relative geographical location of Sung.   It does not refer to Southern Sung which existed from 1127–1180, that is after the fall of the Liao dynasty.

[68] This terse and rather ambiguous description seems to indicate that the imperial tent was protected by a kind of fence consisting of spears planted in the ground a few yards apart and joined together by ropes.   The felt umbrellas, evidently of considerable size, may have been attached to the spears with the sharp point protruding above the covering.

North of the Shêng-fang Hall was the Deer-skin Tent. Further to the north of the tent was the Pa-fang-kung-yang Hall. North of the Shou-ning Hall was the Ch'ang-ch'un Tent which was protected by a strong stockade.[69]

The imperial tent employed four thousand Ch'i-tan soldiers rotating in groups of a thousand daily for sentry duty. Beyond the Forbidden Enclosure spears were planted in the ground as a stockade.[70] At night they were taken up and placed around the imperial sleeping tent.[71]

Beyond a barrier against [enemy] horses there were set up outposts and warning bells for protection during the night.

Each year during the four seasons [the emperor] made the rounds [of the *na-po*] and then started all over again.[72]   32, 3a–b

28. SPRING HUNTING IN NAN–CHING

Kuo-yin County[73] originally was Huo-ts'un Chên of Ch'üan-shan[74] of Han. Every year in the late spring[75] the Liao [court] engaged in hunting at Yen-fang-tien[76] [where] the residents had established a town. Then the old Kuo-yin Chên was walled and later changed into a county. It was situated ninety *li* southeast of the [Southern] Capital.

Yen-fang-tien covered several hundred square *li*. In the spring it was the gathering place of swans[77] and ducks. In the summer and autumn many water chestnuts and foxnuts grew there. When the ruler engaged in the spring hunt his guards all donned dark green clothes. Each man carried a multiple hammer, eagle's food, and an awl for piercing the swans. They lined up by the water five to seven paces from each other. The drums were beaten with the wind; the swans were frightened and flew up from the water. The ruler[78] personally released the falcons from east of the sea to catch them. As the swans fell down, fearing that the falcons would become exhausted, those who stood in the line pierced the swans with the awls that they carried; quickly taking out the brains, they fed the falcons. Whoever seized the First Swan[79] was as a general practice granted silver and lustring.   40, 3b

---

[69] The word 梗 is probably a misprint for 硬 which is used above in describing the stockade around the imperial tent.

[70] We follow other editions in reading 槍 for the 搶 of our text.

[71] Presumably the additional row of spears was planted in the ground beyond the strong stockade of the imperial tent during the day and was brought closer around the tent at night to afford a maximum of protection.

[72] This description indicates that the imperial winter residence was an elaborate camp which included many large and small tents. The Sung official, Pi Chung-yu, (see above, note 6), appropriately calls it a "felt city":

The wind from the frontier blows the snow,	邊風吹雪
It covers the felt city.	罨氈城
Where the felt city stands,	氈城在處
There is the military camp.	爲屯營
Traveling over the Yellow Sands	黃沙行盡
Hsüeh-tien is reached;	到靴淀
On New Year's Day	新年下馬
The shan-yü's court is visited	單于庭

(HTC 18, 7a–b)

Hsüeh-tien was the place where the Liao emperor spent the winter. In Han times the word *shan-yü* designated the supreme ruler of the Huns. Here it is a poetic reference to the Liao emperor.

[73] Forty-five *li* south of Lu 潞 County, Hopei.

[74] According to LSTLCK 8125, Ch'üan-shan 泉山 should read Ch'üan-chou 泉州 which in the time of Han was administered by Yü-yang 漁陽 Province.

[75] Though the Liao emperors did not hunt in the Southern Capital every spring, it is true that since 938 they usually engaged in hunting whenever they went there. According to the *Kao Mu-wu Wang Shên-tao Pei* 高穆 武王神道碑, in the winter of the year 1022 Shêng-tsung conducted a large-scale hunt in the south between Cho 涿 and I 易 Counties. The Sung government, noticing the maneuver-like display, feared that the Liao army might launch an attack against its southern neighbor (HYC 36, 474).

[76] The location of the lake is still problematic. One authority states that it is a place about forty-five *li* south of modern Lu County (TSFYCY 11, 21a), while another locates it at Nan Yüan 南苑 outside the Yung-ting Mên 永定門 of Peiping. During the eighteenth century it still covered an area of one hundred and twenty square *li*. The imperial guard used to hold hunting maneuvers there (CCITC 7, 27a).

[77] According to another text which describes the same hunt, we read *t'ien-ê* instead of *ê* (*Yen-shan Ts'ung-lu* = LSSI 17, 8b–9a).

[78] According to the context and to CTKC 23, 4b, we read 主 instead of 王.

[79] See above, note 61.

2. AGRICULTURE

1. BEGINNINGS OF AGRICULTURE

8th century   Previously, when the imperial ancestor, Yün-tê-shih, was the *i-li-chin* of the great I-lieh Administration, he had a liking for agriculture and was well versed in animal husbandry. He studied the advantages of the land in order to instruct the people in cultivation.

ca. **900**   When [T'ai-tsu's] uncle, Shu-lan, was the *yü-yüeh*,[1] he ordered the people of the country to plant mulberry trees and hemp and to learn weaving. After T'ai-tsu suppressed the rebellion staged by his brothers, he put an end to military operations, lightened the taxes, and devoted his entire attention to agriculture. Because the population had greatly increased

922   and the administrative control grown remote, the Northern Great Nung-wu[2] were divided into two tribes. [T'ai-tsu] set examples in horticulture for the tribes to emulate.

938–947   At the beginning of [the reign period] Hui-t'ung, when T'ai-tsung was about to start out eastward on a hunt, the three *k'o*[3] requested that he reduce the supplies for the expedition, make a quick trip to the Northern Mountains,[4] and obtain materials to meet the needs of the nation without harming agricultural activities. Later an imperial decree ordered the authorities to encourage agriculture and the planting of mulberry trees, and to teach spinning.

59, 1*b*

2. LAND GRANTS

940   On the day *ping-ch'ên* [of the eighth month in the third year of Hui-t'ung] it was decreed that the land adjacent to the Yü-hsieh-li[5] and Lu-ch'ü Rivers should be granted to the people of the three *shih-lieh* of Ou-chin,[6] T'u-lü, and I-ssŭ-p'o[7] of the Southern Division, and to the people of Wên-na-ho-la[8] of the Northern Division, to be used for cultivated fields.   4, 5*b*

---

[1] Shu-lan 述瀾 is the style of Shih-lu 釋魯, the third uncle of T'ai-tsu. According to LS 112, 1*b*, he held the post of *yü-yüeh* during the time of Hên-tê-chin 痕德堇, khaghan of Yao-lien (901–906). In 903 his nephew A-pao-chi (T'ai-tsu) (LS 1, 2*a*) succeeded to this position. At an earlier time the Ch'i-tan had paid tribute to the Turks; Shu-lan put a stop to this practice (LS 64, 3*a*). For the title of *yü-yüeh* see XIV, introduction and XIV, 1 (9), LS 45, 7*b*.

[2] See I, 2 (9), nos. 30 and 31.

[3] The term *k'o* 剋 (also transcribed as 尅) was a Ch'i-tan expression of predynastic origin (see LS 112, 5*b*). It may designate a group of people, as in LS 33, 4*b* and 7*b*, according to which the two *k'o* of the Administration of the King of Hsi (奚王府) were ordered to become two tribes. Generally, however, the term connotes a military officer. The glossary of LS 116, 6*b*–7*b* defines it thus. LS 46, 13*b* lists the armies of different kinds of *k'o*

(see XV, 1 (30)). For several camps *k'o* are given as military chiefs. The position of the *k'o* was apparently of considerable importance, for we find that the men who assumed this office were sent as envoys to foreign countries. Thus Shih-lu 實魯 was sent to Later T'ang in 933 (LS 3, 6*b*) and Lang 郎 to Wu Yüeh in 940 (LS 4, 6*a*). For a linguistic discussion of the term *k'o* see XIV, introduction, text and notes 123–128.

[4] Probably some mountains in the northeastern part of modern Jehol. Presumably a quick trip to these mountains would entail less of a drain on the national resources than a longer hunting expedition to the east.

[5] According to Tsuda, the Yü-hsieh-li 于諸里 is the same as the Khalkha River in modern Heilungkiang (Tsuda 16, 6).

[6] Also written Ou-k'un 甌昆 (LS 33, 2*a*).

[7] Also written I-hsi-pên 乙習本 (LS 33, 2*a*).

[8] Also written Wo-na-a-la 斡納阿剌 (LS 33, 2*b*).

3. AGRICULTURAL INSTRUCTION

940   On the day *ting-ch'ou* [of the eleventh month in the third year of Hui-t'ung] an imperial decree ordered the officials to instruct the people in sowing and spinning.[9]   4, 6a

4. AUTUMN CROPS

946   On the day *hsin-ch'ou* of the seventh month in the autumn [of the ninth year of Hui-t'ung] it was decreed that the soldiers conscripted from the various circuits who dared to damage the crops were to be punished according to military law.   4, 12b

5. EXCELLENT CORN

952   On the first day *chia-yin* of the ninth month [in the second year of Ying-li], Yün Prefecture presented a remarkable [millet] plant of four stalks with two ears [on each].   6, 2a

6. RICE IN NAN-CHING

969–979   During [the reign period] Pao-ning, since much land on the outskirts[10] of the Southern Capital was vacant, [Kao Hsün[11]] asked permission to divide the land into plots in order to cultivate rice.   The emperor was inclined to consent to it.   The scribe Yeh-lü K'un, however, made a statement before the court, saying, "This request of Kao Hsün must have some other purpose.   If permission is actually given to canalize water and divide the land into plots for the cultivation of rice, in case of a rebellion based on the [Southern] Capital, whence would the government troops effect an entry?"

The emperor became doubtful about it and did not accept [the proposal].   85, 4b

7. SURPLUS OF GRAIN

975   In the seventh year of Pao-ning,[12] [Eastern] Han,[13] facing a military invasion by Sung, sent an envoy [to Liao] to ask for food supplies.   It was decreed that two hundred thousand bushels of millet should be provided to help them.   Unless [Liao] had a surplus beyond its expenditures, how could this have been done?   59, 2a

8. COST OF MILLET

982–1031   At this time[14] most of the western barbarians[15] were in a state of rebellion.   The emperor, desiring to provide for defence and protection, ordered Yeh-lü T'ang-ku[16] to take charge of agricultural activities in order to furnish supplies for the western armies.   [Yeh-lü]

---

[9] The preceding passage speaks of gifts of land to the imperial tribes for the purpose of agriculture.   This decree possibly is part of the same story.   The Ch'i-tan were essentially stockbreeders, after 907 as before.   Their cousins, the Hsi, were far better acquainted with the art of husbandry (CTKC 22, 6b).   Many Sung envoys watched the Hsi till the soil in the valleys (KSC 28, 334; CTKC 24, 2a).   In 1008 a Sung envoy, Lu Chên 路振, noticed that the Hsi guards in charge of the traveling stations beyond Ku-pei Pass 古北口 were all granted land for cultivation (HCLY 77, 11a).

Besides the Hsi, there were also Chinese settlers.   In 1086 an imperial decree ordered the removal of four hundred Chinese to another region.   But the plan was not carried out because of objections by Chia Shih-hsün 賈師訓 (MCCSC 2, 29b).

[10] *Chiao* 郊 means the suburb of a city.   It may also signify border or wasteland.   The territory discussed in the above text must have been situated on the outskirts of the Southern Capital, for the capital itself, it was feared, might be strategically endangered by the establishment of inundated fields.   The passage indicates that under favorable conditions rice could be grown near Peiping during the tenth century as it can be today.

[11] Kao Hsün 高勳 (T. 鼎臣) a Chin official who surrendered to Liao in 946.   In 947 he was appointed chancellor of the Southern Division in charge of Chinese military affairs.   He was executed in 978 for the murder of Hsiao Ssǔ-wên 思温.   Cf. LS 85, 4a ff.

[12] For the exact date see X, 2, note 34.

[13] This small kingdom, located in what is now Shansi, was founded in the year 951 and destroyed by Sung in 979.

[14] LS 59, 3a places this passage after material on the reign of Tao-tsung (1055–1101), but according to LS 91, 2a it refers to conditions in the time of Shêng-tsung (982–1031).

[15] The tribes and people who led a more or less nomadic life north of the Kerulen River such as the Tsu-pu and Wu-Ku.   Cf. LS 91, 2a; 103, 2a; and 104, 2a–3a.

[16] Yeh-lü T'ang-ku 棠 (or 唐) 古 (T. 蒲速宛) was a noble of the Six Divisions.   The people called him "Strong (強) T'ang-ku" (cf. LS 100, 1a ff.).   He was appointed commanding prefect.   He retired in 1035.   See XV, 1 (44).

T'ang-ku led the soldiers to cultivate the land along the Lu-ch'ü River. The harvest flourished exceedingly well. He was moved to garrison Chên Prefecture,[17] where, in the course of fourteen harvests, several hundred thousand bushels of millet were accumulated. [As a consequence] one peck cost no more than a few cash.[18]   59, 3a

9. THE LAND SYSTEM OF LIAO

983–1012   During the T'ung-ho period Yeh-lü Chao[19] stated that among the people of the northwest each year during the agricultural season, for each person engaged in patrol service, another cares for the public land and two render service to the *chiu*[20] officers.

During that time garrison fields were set up along each of the borders. The soldiers on frontier duty cultivated the fields and stored up grain in order to provide food for the army. Therefore, in the seventh year of the T'ai-p'ing period it was decreed to the garrison fields that not a bushel of millet belonging to the government should be loaned out without authority, and that the military settlers engaged in tilling the public land need not pay taxes. This was the public land system.

Other people answered the call to till uncultivated land or to cultivate private fields. They had to pay out grain according to the [number of] *mou* as a tax to the government. In the fifteenth[21] year [the government] called on the people to till the vacant land along the Luan River. Tax payments were to begin after the tenth year. This was the system concerning the uncultivated land under government administration.[22]

It was further decreed that the families before and behind the mountains[23] who had not yet paid taxes might occupy fields and establish property in the two counties of Mi-yün[24] and Yen-lo[25] and should pay taxes. This was the system of private land holding.   59, 4a

---

[17] This walled city, built in 1003, was named by the emperor in 1004. It was situated on the Orkhon River in modern Outer Mongolia (Matsui 15a; LSTLCK 8104).

[18] The coinage of Liao, according to LS 60, 2b, was first established in the time of T'ai-tsu's father. Some coins made during the time of T'ai-tsu are still preserved by Chinese numismatists. *Cf.* VI, 1 (1).

[19] Yeh-lü Chao 昭 (T. 述寧) was an accomplished essayist. He died in the middle of the K'ai-t'ai period, that is about 1016 (LS 104, 1b–2b).

[20] The word *chiu* 紏 occurs in the description of the government organization (LS 45, 21a; 46, 13b) and also in several biographies. According to Ch'ien Ta-hsin, it is identical with the word 糺 in the *Chin Shih*, a word which he was unable to find in any dictionary (CSSI 5, 6b). In the glossary of the LS (116, 4a) *chiu* is explained as the designation of an army, the name connoting "to control." Yanai says that it may have been an original Ch'i-tan word pronounced either "*tu*" or "*tyu.*" According to the *Hei-ta Shih-lüeh* 黑韃事略, written by Hsü T'ing 徐霆 in 1237 (Yanai 30, 71–6), a "*tu*" detachment probably consisted of fifty mounted soldiers. Wang Kuo-wei says that 紏 or 糺 is probably identical with the word *chi* 紀 as used in the *Mêng-ta Pei-lu* 蒙韃備錄, written by Chao Kung 趙珙 in 1221. He assumes that during the end of the Chin dynasty the "*chi*" army referred mainly to the Ch'i-tan soldiers (MTPLCC 8a).

The Ch'ing scholar, Yü Chêng-hsieh 俞正燮 (1775–1840), does not consider 紏 or 糺 a Ch'i-tan word but identifies it with *chiu* 糾, "to assemble." According to him, the Liao, Chin, and Yüan *chiu* were detachments of garrison soldiers stationed at the frontier (KSTK 3, 83).

Yanai manifestly misunderstands the text of the *Liao Shih* which says, "*chiu* is the name of an army" (紏軍名). Overlooking the third word, *ming* 名, he equates *chiu* 紏

with *chün* 軍, thus missing the meaning of the original definition. Wang Kuo-wei's tentative explanation, which is based upon reference to a single passage, does not classify the enigmatic term either.

Probably, Yü Chêng-hsieh's commentary is closest to the truth. *Chiu* 紏 obviously is the name of a detachment of frontier soldiers. The term was used during the Liao, Chin, and Yüan periods. Whether *chiu* is the Chinese transcription of a Ch'i-tan word we do not know. The existing word seems identical with the Chinese *chiu* 糾. During the Chin period the *po-chi-lieh* 孛極烈 (*po-chin* 孛菫 or *bogin*) was a *chiu* official (糾官也) who in Chinese was called *tsung-kuan* 總管, general officer, controlling different groups of households numbering from five to ten thousand (SCPMHP 3, 5b). The term *po-chi-lieh* was a part of various official designations, beginning with the highest, while the term *po-chin* denoted a small tribal chieftain (CS 55, 1a ff.; 135, 9a–b).

[21] This could not have been the fifteenth year of T'ai-p'ing as there were only eleven years in this reign period. LS 13, 8a has a similar passage concerning the vacant land along the Luan River. The passage is dated the fifteenth year of T'ung-ho (997).

The previous reference in our text to the seventh year of T'ai-p'ing (1027) is corroborated by LS 17, 4a which has the same date for the event mentioned in our passage.

[22] We follow the Palace edition in reading 官 for the 宮 of our text.

[23] Since 938 the terms 前 and 後 were generally used to designate the regions south of ("before") and north of ("behind") the mountain ranges in northwestern Hopei.

[24] Modern Mi-yün 密雲 County, Hopei.

[25] Yen-lo 燕樂 was seventy *li* northeast of modern Mi-yün County. It is not listed in the geographical section of the *Liao Shih*.

10. AGRICULTURE UNDERTAKEN BY WOMEN

985   Once the emperor, in passing by Kao-ch'êng,[26] noticed that the glutinous millet of the woman Ti-lien and others of the I-shih Ao-wei tribe was over-ripe but had not yet been harvested.   He sent men to help them cut it.[27]   59, 2a

11. LAND GIVEN TO THE PEOPLE

989   Furthermore,[28] three hundred households among the inhabitants of the outpost of Chi-pi were removed to the three prefectures of T'an,[29] Shun,[30] and Chi.[31] Fertile land was selected, and they were provided with oxen in order to cultivate grain.   59, 2b

12. HERDS DAMAGE SPRING CROPS

989   On the first day *jên-wu* of the third month [in the seventh year of T'ung-ho] . . . it was forbidden to let grazing herds damage the crops.   12, 5a

13. LAND GIVEN TO THE PEOPLE

989   On the day *hsin-yu* [of the sixth month in the seventh year of T'ung-ho] it was decreed that the people be allowed to cultivate the land in the two counties of Yen-lo and Mi-yün, and that they be exempted from taxation and labor service for ten years.   12, 6b

14. CROPS INSPECTED

992   On the day *kuei-hai* of the eighth month [in the tenth year of T'ung-ho the emperor] inspected the crops and sent emissaries in all directions to inspect the crops.

13, 3b

994   On the day *chia-yin* [of the seventh month in the twelfth year of T'ung-ho] emissaries were sent to inspect the crops of all the circuits.   13, 5a

15. HARVESTING TIME

994   On the day *mou-ch'ên* [of the seventh month in the twelfth year of T'ung-ho the emperor] watched the harvesting.   13, 5a

16. AGRICULTURE ENCOURAGED

995   On the day *kêng-shên* [of the first month in the thirteenth year of T'ung-ho] an imperial decree ordered the circuits to encourage agriculture.   13, 6a

On the day *ping-hsü* a decree was issued granting the request for the occupation of wasteland by the people of Ch'ang-p'ing, Huai-jou,[32] and other counties.   13, 6b

17. A FARMSTEAD WITH WATER–MILLS

995   On the day *mou-wu* of the ninth month [in the thirteenth year of T'ung-ho], because the students of the Imperial Academy of the Southern Capital had gradually[33] increased in number, it was given a special grant of a farmstead with water-mills.   13, 6b

---

[26] The location of this place, like that of the I-shih Ao-wei tribe, is not known.

[27] The present passage occurs among a number of items recorded after the year 983. However, as a similar passage in LS 69, 8b is more specifically dated 985, we give this date for our passage.

[28] This paragraph, erroneously listed under 988, belongs here, for in the first month of 989 a Sung general, Kuo Jung 郭榮, who was guarding the outpost of Chi-pi 鷄壁, surrendered with his troops and was ordered to settle in Nan-ching. It was in the second month of that year that the above mentioned families were transferred to the three prefectures (LS 12, 4a–5a).

[29] Modern Mi-yün County, Hopei.

[30] Modern Shun-i 順義 County, Hopei.

[31] Modern Chi 薊 County, Hopei.

[32] Both north of Peiping.

[33] We follow other editions in reading 浸 for the 侵 of our text.

18. HUNTING AND AGRICULTURE

996   On the day *chia-hsü* of the eleventh month [in the fourteenth year of T'ung-ho] an imperial decree ordered that military officers were not to cause damage[34] to agriculture by hunting at improper times.   13, 7*b*

19. ARBORICULTURE

997   On the day *kêng-ch'êng* [of the first month in the fifteenth year of T'ung-ho] a decree was issued to all the circuits to encourage the people to plant trees.   13, 8*a*

20. EXTENSION OF CULTIVATED LAND

997   On the day *ting-ssǔ* [of the second month in the fifteenth year of T'ung-ho] it was decreed that the people should be permitted to till the wasteland of the P'in tribe.[35]

13, 8*a*

On the day *mou-ch'ên* [of the third month in the fifteenth year of T'ung-ho] the people were called upon to till the wasteland of Luan Prefecture.[36]   They were exempted from taxation for ten years.

13, 8*a*

21. BUSY AGRICULTURAL SEASON

1014   On the day *mou-wu* of the fourth month in the summer [of the third year of K'ai-t'ai] an imperial decree ordered that, within the area controlled by Nan-ching, agricultural activities were not to be hindered by prolonging litigation.   15, 7*b*

22. CROPS INSPECTED

1019   On the day *mou-ch'ên* [of the seventh month in the eighth year of K'ai-t'ai] the emperor inspected the crops.   16, 3*b*

23. AGRICULTURE ENCOURAGED

1028   On the day *chia-tzǔ* [of the first month in the eighth year of T'ai-p'ing] an imperial decree ordered the superior officials of the prefectures and counties to encourage agriculture.   17, 4*b*–5*a*

24. THE WEALTHY EVADE TAXATION

1031   When Hsing-tsung[37] took the throne, he sent officials to inspect the crops of all the circuits.   In this year a general census was taken.

An imperial decree said, "From earlier years I learned that in husbandry those who are affluent extend their undertakings in the cultivation of land but rarely pay taxes, while those who have to live off their families are entirely lacking in [opportunities for] sowing and planting and often reach the point where they run off.   Therefore a general census[38] should be taken in order to achieve a general equalization."[39]   59, 2*b*–3*a*

25. CROPS INSPECTED

1033   On the day *i-mao* [of the eighth month in the second year of Ch'ung-hsi] emissaries were sent to inspect the crops of all routes.   18, 4*a*

26. HARVESTING

1046   On the day *mou-tzǔ* [of the seventh month in the fifteenth year of Ch'ung-hsi] the emperor watched the harvesting.   19, 8*a*

---

[34] We follow other editions in reading 妨 for the 放 of our text.

[35] According to LS 33, 2*b*, this region was situated in the northwestern part of Shang-ching. It therefore probably corresponds to the northwestern part of modern Jehol.

[36] Modern Luan 灤 County in northeastern Hopei.

[37] He ascended the throne in 1031, but his mother actually held the reins of government until 1034. *Cf.* VII, introduction.

[38] This is the same census referred to in the first paragraph.

[39] We follow the Palace edition in reading 爲 for the 遂 of our text.

27. FIELDS DAMAGED BY IMPERIAL FOLLOWERS

1046   On the day *hsin-ch'ou* [of the seventh month in the fifteenth year of Ch'ung-hsi] the emperor's followers were forbidden to trample on the people's fields.   19, 8a.

28. HORTICULTURE

1053   On the day *jên-yin* of the fifth month [in the twenty-second year of Ch'ung-hsi] it was decreed that fruit trees be planted in the prefectures and counties of the inner region.[40]   20, 7b

29. LOW PRICE OF GRAIN

1055–1071   In the beginning of the reign of Tao-tsung[41] the northwest had a rain of grain [within an area of] thirty *li*.   One peck of millet cost [only] six cash in Ch'un Prefecture.   59, 3a

30. IRRIGATION MUST NOT ENDANGER THE RIVER DIKES

1064   In the second month [in the tenth year of Ch'ing-ning] the people of Nan-ching were forbidden to open the river [dikes] for the planting of rice.[42]   22, 2b

31. RICE IN NAN–CHING

1068   On the day *i-yu* [of the third month in the fourth year of Hsien-yung] it was decreed to [the authorities of] Nan-ching that all land, except that through which the army traveled, might be used for the planting of rice.   22, 5b

32. COST OF MILLET

1071   In this year [the seventh year of Hsien-yung] in Ch'un Prefecture one peck of millet [cost only] six cash.   22, 8a

---

[40] This term was used to designate the region of Shang-ching.

[41] According to LS 22, 5b, the Northwestern Route had a rain of grain in an area of thirty square *li* in 1068. According to LS 22, 8a, in the year 1071 one peck of grain cost only six cash in Ch'un Prefecture (northwest of modern Po-tu-na, Kirin).   Whether the present text is a combination of the above passages, which were compiled by the Yüan historians, or occurs independently is not clear.   Hence we give the approximate date, 1055–1071.

[42] The text says *ying tao* 粳稻 which means non-glutinous or ordinary rice (*oryza sativa*) as opposed to the glutinous variety (*oryza glutinosa*) which is used to make sweets and glue.

SECTION III

INDUSTRY

INTRODUCTION

1. THE PROBLEM

If the Ch'i-tan rulers hoped to benefit fully from their conquest of the agricultural territories in the south, they had to preserve the industrial level that had been attained there.[1] If they expected the transplanted settlers in the north to approximate their southern brothers in effectiveness, they had to introduce Chinese industry along with Chinese agriculturists and Chinese agriculture. To be sure, while satisfying their new subjects' need for industrial products, the Ch'i-tan rulers never lost sight of their own power, security, and comfort. It was only natural that they used the new industries directly for their own advantage—for the equipment of powerful armies, for the construction of walled cities, fortresses, carts, and boats, and for the production of the many material conveniences attractive both to those in power and to their followers.

2. THE TRIBAL INDUSTRIES

The tribal industries did not disappear with the growing use of products derived from the industrially more advanced Chinese communities. In many ways the primitive crafts were in greater harmony with the tribesmen's principal occupations and modes of life. Though there was little of that division of labor which we associate with the ordinary use of the word "industry," manufacture was sufficiently widespread and important in the economy of these people to justify the term. Despite the importation of many articles of use, the production of felts and tents continued;[2] so did the making of fur garments.[3] The "regular" soldiers were equipped with armor, saddles, and a great variety of weapons and tools, such as bows and arrows, spears, clubs, axes, and knives. All this, according to the Liao Shih, each soldier had to provide for himself.[4]

The record raises an interesting question. Was the individual soldier able to manufacture all his military equipment himself, or did he rely for his armor and heavier weapons upon special artisans, either within the tribe or outside it? A partial answer may be found in Rubruck's comments on the tribal Mongols of Central Asia shortly after Chingis Khan had set up his great Asiatic empire. Even more than the Ch'i-tan, the Mongols at that time dominated large agricultural areas; yet the men in the tribal sectors pursued many industrial activities. They "make bows and arrows, manufacture stirrups and bits, make saddles, do the carpentering on (the framework of) their dwellings and the carts. . . ."[5] The crafts observed in Inner Asia in the thirteenth century are still practised there to the present day.[6]

It seems legitimate therefore to assume that the Ch'i-tan men also were capable of producing the military equipment of their soldiers within the framework of their tribal industry. Whether this industry remained undifferentiated or was delegated, at least in part, to certain artisan groups is not explained by the texts of the Liao Shih. It is probable, however, that certain crafts requiring a high degree of technical skill were entrusted to specialists. The making of iron implements and artifacts in Inner Asia long before the time of the Liao empire[7] must have led to the establishment of professional smiths at a relatively early date. Specialization must have occurred among the Shih-wei and Hsi who were famous for their skill in working metal[8] and in making carts.[9] Specialization of some sort probably existed in most of the Ch'i-tan tribes in such crafts as metal work. But if iron was known and used by the early inhabitants of the Shira Muren region[10] it was not necessarily smelted.

The Liao Shih notes certain industrial innovations that were introduced by A-pao-chi's father and uncle prior to the establishment of the empire. His father, "the first to establish iron smelteries," began the casting of metal implements. His father's younger brother, Shu-lan, was interested in weaving.[11] Such reports indicate a relatively primitive industry for the preceding periods, but we do not know whether the Ch'i-tan lacked all knowledge of metal work in those

---

[1] See Wittfogel 31, 496–501.
[2] III (11); see also VII, *passim*.
[3] VII, *passim*.
[4] XV, 2 (1).

[5] Rubruck 00, 76.
[6] See Vámbéry 85, 195 ff. and 198 ff.; Prejevalsky 76 I, 58; Howorth, HM IV, 41.
[7] Radloff 93 II, 129 ff.; Torii 14, 70; Barthold 35, 20.
[8] III (3).
[9] IV (3).
[10] Torii 14, 71 ff.
[11] III (1).

times or whether they engaged in crude metal work with little specialization.

The establishment of smelteries must have led to some specialization in the hands of particular artisan groups or families. Were these families tribal or were they Chinese artisans imported by the Ch'i-tan chieftains to operate the newly installed iron works? It must be remembered that the economic reorientation of the Ch'i-tan occurred at the end of the ninth century when the T'ang empire was slowly disintegrating. This situation left a large group of Chinese border settlers, who were without an effective government, ready to accept protection anywhere if it was offered under not too unfavorable conditions.

Such an offer came from the I-la tribe of the Ch'i-tan. Their chieftains had married into a lineage (later called Hsiao) of the Uighur Turks. The Turks were iron workers of reputation even before the time of T'ang,[12] and their famous semi-agricultural branch, the Uighurs, acquired a relatively high technical skill before their Orkhon cities were destroyed in 840. The evident superiority of Uighur material culture and its accessibility through long continued contact make it highly probable that the I-la chieftains used iron products even if their own people could not make them. Under A-pao-chi's father the I-la tribe engaged in a more advanced agriculture and industry.[13] Under A-pao-chi the tribe was stimulated anew by the Ch'i-tan conquest of the metal-working Shih-wei people.[14] It was the I-la chieftain, A-pao-chi, who first employed the subdued sedentary peoples of the south to till the soil, to extract salt, and to work iron.

This step marked a great change. From now on the I-la surpassed all other Ch'i-tan tribes in wealth and power. The Sung author of the *Wu Tai Shih* states positively that it was this new economic power which enabled A-pao-chi to challenge and destroy all his political rivals. His account, given in WTS 72, 2b–3a, runs as follows:

---

[12] See Julien 64, 349; confirmed by Turkic folklore (Barthold 35, 20).

[13] III (1).

[14] III (3). This record ascribes the beginning of Ch'i-tan mining and smelting to A-pao-chi's victory over the Shih-wei. If we accept it as correct (or probable), we have to reject the other passages which date the beginning of the new industrial phase one generation earlier. The acceptance of the Shih-wei version would not affect our argument concerning a possible Uighur influence. This influence might have facilitated the taking over of Shih-wei as well as Chinese techniques. We hesitate, nevertheless, to accept the Shih-wei version because the well-documented story about A-pao-chi's relations with Chinese settlers points to a significant contact with Chinese economic life at the end of the predynastic period.

"At this time Liu Shou-kuang[15] was despotic, so that most of the people in Yu and Cho fled to the Ch'i-tan. A-pao-chi, taking advantage of the opportunity, crossed the frontier, attacked and seized the cities, and captured their people. Following the prefectures and counties of T'ang, he built cities to settle them.

"The Chinese told A-pao-chi that there was no case of a Chinese ruler being replaced on the throne Thereupon A-pao-chi made increasing use of his power to control the tribes, and refused to be replaced. After he had been in power for nine years, the tribes reproached him for not being replaced in such a long time. A-pao-chi had no alternative but to pass on his banner and drum. But he said to the tribes, 'The Chinese whom I have obtained during the nine years of my rule are numerous. I should like to organize an independent tribe to govern the Chinese City. Is this permissible?' The tribes consented to it.

"The Chinese City, which was situated southeast of Mount T'an and on the Luan River, enjoyed the advantages of salt and iron. This was the Hua-yen County of Later Wei. Its land was suitable for the cultivation of the five grains. A-pao-chi led the Chinese in cultivating the land and constructed for them a city, houses, and markets after the system of Yu Prefecture. The Chinese were satisfied with this and had no further thought of returning.

"A-pao-chi, realizing that the people could be used, followed the plan of his wife, Shu-lü, and sent emissaries to inform the tribal chieftains, 'I own the salt-lake from which you eat [salt]. But though the tribes know the advantages of eating salt, you do not realize that this salt has an owner. Is this fair? You should compensate me.'

"The tribes, considering that this was right, all assembled at the salt-lake with oxen and wine. A-pao-chi had placed soldiers in ambush nearby. When the wine began to take effect, the hidden soldiers came forth and killed all the tribal chieftains. Then he set himself up and was not replaced again."

3. IMPORTATION OF TECHNIQUES AND TECHNICIANS

Thus the stage was set for a new industrial policy. Complex "Chinese" techniques were preserved in the old agricultural regions. Their introduction was encouraged in the newly settled rural and urban centers. A steady stream of cultural elements drifted northward from the empire's old Chinese territories, Nan-ching and Hsi-ching Circuits. But this spontaneous

---

[15] A war-lord who temporarily controlled part of what is now northern Hopei. See XVI, 907, LS 1, 3a; 909, LS 1, 3b; 911, LS 1, 4a; 912, LS 1, 4b; 913, LS 1, 4b ff.

diffusion did not satisfy the increasing demand for superior manufacture. By governmental action fine Chinese carriages were introduced from China Proper in 937 when the ruler of the Ch'i-tan donned the awe-inspiring attire of a real Son of Heaven.[16] Ten years later, after the conquest of the capital of Chin 晉, a large quantity of Chinese products was seized. Armor and weapons, all kinds of imperial equipment, bronze statues, a water-clock, musical instruments, astronomical charts, etc. were carried off to the Supreme Capital.[17]

Not content with the mere possession of such desirable objects, the Liao emperors endeavored to draw to their territory those men who had been trained to produce them. They imported iron workers from Po-hai[18] and silver workers from China.[19] Shipbuilders came to them as tribute from the P'u-lu-mao-to tribe.[20] Weavers were transferred from what is now Ting County, Hopei.[21] In Tsu Prefecture silk brocade was made in a special workshop by Chinese, Po-hai, and "barbarians."[22]

When T'ai-tsu conquered an extensive territory and took large numbers of prisoners, the skilled artisans were set apart and brought to the northern sections of the country. They were called *shu-shan* 屬珊,[23] "precious as coral."[24] The great loot seized by T'ai-tsung in 947 included not only utensils but also "artisans."[25] Recent archaeological finds show that in structure the tombs and temples of the Ch'i-tan followed the Chinese pattern and that decorative designs on large buildings and on small objects, such as tiles and jars, were also faithfully copied from the Chinese.[26] Thus the Ch'i-tan, while preserving the basic features of their pastoral life, were ready to incorporate many elements of the more advanced civilization of the peoples they had conquered.

4. INDUSTRIAL RAW MATERIALS

The information in the *Liao Shih* on mineral resources and raw materials is rather thin, but what little there is seems to agree with statements made in a number of recent publications.[27] The *Liao Shih* notes the presence of copper, iron, gold, and silver in the north (Shih-wei[28]) and iron in the east (in modern Liaoning[29]) and perhaps in the old grazing-grounds of the Ch'i-tan.[30] The center of the iron mining and smelting activities was "in the east" of Liao, that is in Liaoning, where it still is today.[31] Silver and gold were also worked in Liaoning,[32] Jehol,[33] and Hopei.[34] Salt and salt-like minerals were procured at the salt-lake near the old Chinese City[35] (in modern Chahar), in the mountainous regions of modern Hopei,[36] and along the seashore.[37] The pastoral, agricultural, and wooded regions of the empire and its tribal borderlands[38] provided organic raw materials such as hides, wool, wood, grain, hemp, and silk. These and various minerals found their way to the country's industrial centers where, separately or in combination, they formed the basis of its finished products.

5. PRODUCTION

a. GOVERNMENT AND PRIVATE ENTERPRISE

The economic history of imperial China records innumerable attempts to establish a proper balance between public and private management in industry as well as in agriculture, in commerce as well as in money-lending. All these attempts reflect both the power possessed by a complex Oriental government and its limitations. For, although such a government was strong enough to make itself felt in all economic activities, it was rarely efficient enough to administer them successfully. As long as the economic and political key positions remained in the government's control, there was no danger in permitting private enterprise.

The Liao government which inherited a relatively advanced industry from China Proper adopted also the legal forms which regulated this industry's growth and functioning. Certain key positions were government-managed for economic and military safety or for the benefit of the court; the rest were in private hands, either without regulation or as licensed monopolies.

---

[16] III (10).
[17] VII, 2 (22).
[18] III (9).
[19] III (6).
[20] III (20).
[21] III (12).
[22] III (26).
[23] III (2).
[24] LS 116, 19a.
[25] VII, 2 (22).
[26] *Cf*. Torii 36 I, pl. 37, 71; II, pl. 98 ff., 105, 116, 137–145; III, pl. 173 ff., 205 ff.; IV, pl. 292 ff., 337 ff.
[27] *Cf*. Hosie 01, 151 and 217; North Manchuria 24, 210 ff.; Manchuria 32/33, 156 ff.; Progress in Manchuria 32, 152 ff.; Yano and Shirasaki 36, 468 ff.
[28] III (3).
[29] *Loc. cit*.
[30] III (1).
[31] Yano and Shirasaki 36, 468.
[32] III (5).
[33] III (17).
[34] *Loc. cit*.
[35] III (4).
[36] III (28).
[37] III (4) (13).
[38] For the raw materials and finished goods sold to Liao by various border tribes, see V (4).

Private management may be inferred from the issuance of licenses, from taxation, or from regulations governing standardization. Textiles that were offered as taxes had to be standardized. In this way the government nipped in the bud any ingenious attempts on the part of weavers, whether professional or not, to cheat the tax-collectors; a fight against the manufacture of textiles of inferior quality had been energetically waged by the T'ang government in 846 when the collection and burning of all small weaving shuttles were ordered.[39] In 956 a decree was issued by the government of the last of the Five Dynasties warning the makers of linen and silk not to produce tissues which were too light and thin and of poor quality.[40] The fiscal purpose of the campaign for standardization is clearly indicated for the beginning of the Sung dynasty when a specific size and quality were prescribed for textiles "paid to the government."[41] The decrees of the Liao government dealing with the standardization of textiles are in line with the Chinese administrative tradition of this epoch. The Liao empire had a tax called *tiao* 調[42] which probably was paid in textile products.[43]

GOVERNMENT MANAGEMENT

A number of industries which the Liao rulers deemed important for their political and military safety or for the convenience of the court were administered directly by the government. Minting of money seems to have been one of these. The minting and smelting of gold and silver was supervised by government officials,[44] though perhaps not exclusively.[45] The position of the iron smelteries of Liao is not clear. LS 60, 2a (III (3)) seems to refer to the establishment of government smelteries; an office of the "Five Smelteries (五冶)" is mentioned in LS 46, 7a, but without details. The eight imperial workshops included an arsenal (單器坊[46]) which probably absorbed part of the iron provided by the Five Smelteries. Even if the tribal soldiers furnished their own arms, the Chinese and Po-hai in the sedentary regions were certainly not permitted to manufacture weapons for their militia service. Military equipment (器甲) was kept in special armories (武庫[47]).

[39] CTS 18*B*, 2*b*–3*a*.
[40] CWTS 116, 8*b*.
[41] SS 175, 1*a*–*b*.
[42] X, 1 (23).
[43] See X, introduction.
[44] III (6) (17).
[45] The last record cited in note 44 mentions the production of gold and silver in the Yin Mountains. This was evidently prior to the suggested establishment of a government smeltery.
[46] XIV, 1 (26).
[47] XIII (44).

Part of it was probably transferred there from the imperial workshops and arsenals. Walls and towers, palaces, and even a few temples were constructed by mobilizing the corvée,[48] the most direct means of government control and supervision.

The *Liao Shih* speaks of "government coal,"[49] but whether this means government production or government ownership we do not know. Public management is documented for the Silk Workshop of Tsu Prefecture. The cloth manufactured by this shop expressly served the needs of the court.[50]

MONOPOLIES

Government "monopoly" (*ch'üeh* 権[51]) was not identical with government management, but it is difficult to determine how this monopoly was exercised. Apparently, its organization varied both in time and space and probably even from trade to trade. In the commercial sphere state monopoly merely entailed supervision and taxation on the spot.[52] In industry the methods employed were somewhat different. In 1123 the two government-controlled Yung Salt Departments of Nan-ching Circuit evaporated and sold a considerable quantity of salt. The income from other items marketed by government offices even exceeded the salt revenue.[53] The nature of these other items can be inferred, in part, from a comparison of the tax policies of Tung-ching and Nan-ching Circuits which implies that in the southern territory the liquor and yeast trade suffered restrictions similar to those imposed on salt,[54] and in part from LS 22, 3a which notes that in 1064 private trade in iron was forbidden.[55]

Other records clearly indicate the existence of private enterprise in the same fields. Salt permits (鹽筴) were first issued under T'ai-tsu.[56] In Nan-ching Circuit the Triple Office collected taxes from salt and iron, originally in money, later in silk.[57] What is the economic reality hidden behind such seemingly contradictory accounts?

Any attempt at an explanation must consider the organization of the trades in question and then the changes that may have occurred over time. It is possible that one section of an industry (for instance, salt) was privately run while another was government-

[48] XI, introduction.
[49] III (24).
[50] III (26).
[51] *Cf.* X, 1 (1) and *passim*.
[52] *Loc. cit.*
[53] SCPMHP 14, 11*a*–*b*.
[54] X, 1 (2).
[55] III (23).
[56] III (4).
[57] X, 1 (2).

controlled both as to production and sales. Such a possibility is not excluded by the fact that the *Liao Shih* refers in a general way to government monopolies. But the independent enterprises that may have existed must have been relatively insignificant when compared with these monopolies.

Did the government itself manufacture the two hundred and twenty thousand piculs of salt referred to in the document of 1123, or did the holders of salt permits produce the salt under close government control, following a pattern still operating today?[58] The finished product may then either have been marketed directly by special government bureaus, or the sales may have been merely supervised by these offices. The record of 1064 reveals a shift to government management in the sale of iron. A similar development may have also occurred in the salt and other trades, at least in Nan-ching Circuit—a development that would inevitably have led to the monopolistic situation suggested by the Chin statement of 1123. Whether under these circumstances private enterprise was excluded from production, too, we do not know. But even if, in the Southern Capital, salt was evaporated by government workers, as SCPMHP 14, 11b claims, it does not necessarily follow that all other government-sold goods were government-produced.[59]

PRIVATE MANAGEMENT

Private enterprise certainly prevailed in the manufacture of textiles. Tissues presented by the Liao government to the Sung court frequently bore the inscription, "Paid as tax by Pai-ch'uan Prefecture."[60] An edict forbidding the private production of colored satin[61] implies that the manufacture of other textiles was not so restricted. Regulations governing the standardization of textiles refer to linen as well as to silk cloth.[62] If these regulations were observed, the goods could be sold in the market-places[63] as well as in the emperor's temporary residences.[64] In 1081 the regulations for silk fabrics were suspended.[65] Did the rising economic crisis lead to the disappearance of these fabrics from the market?

Among other commodities that were manufactured privately iron may be mentioned first. The iron tax of Nan-ching Circuit, which is mentioned together with the salt tax,[66] was paid most probably by iron manufacturers; the families who gave iron in payment of taxes[67] were evidently permitted to consider the remainder of their output as their property. For the greater part of the dynasty, if not for its duration, "wine"[68] must have been produced privately, for the government taxed wine and also yeast for fermenting liquor.[69] Restrictions on the distilling of wine by officials[70] may reflect (temporary? or regional?) government production; more probably the prohibitions were directed against the illegal use of public (granary) grain.

b. TECHNICAL FEATURES

Historical records collected by a scholarly bureaucracy stress the administrative side of the country's industry more than its technical aspects. Thus no comprehensive picture of industrial production in the Liao empire can be drawn. Only a few facts may be gleaned from our textual data and the parallel sources which supplement them.

A division of labor according to sex is inevitable in all tribal industry, but this was so much taken for granted that practically nothing is said about it in the *Liao Shih.* Some idea of how the Ch'i-tan divided work between the sexes may be gathered from Rubruck's classic on the Mongols. He states that it was the duty of women "to drive the carts, get the dwellings on and off them, milk the cows, make butter and *gruit* [curd], and to dress and sew skins, which they do with a thread made of tendons. . . . They also sew the boots, the socks, and the clothing. . . . They also make the felt and cover the houses."[71] The men make weapons and saddles; they do the carpentering on the dwellings and carts. They "take care of the horses, milk the mares, churn the *cosmos* [kumiss] or mare's milk, make the skins in which it is put."[72]

In most instances technical specialization did not require the coordination of large capital and much labor. Large-scale organization was necessary or profitable only in a few metallurgical industries and

---

[58] To the present day the salt-lake of An-i in southern Shansi is exploited by private enterprise under government control. A wall surrounds the lake; the wall and the gates are guarded by government soldiers. Personal observation made in 1936 by K. A. Wittfogel.

[59] III (4); XIV, 2 (7).

[60] WCTY 16B, 16a. Pai-ch'uan 白川 Prefecture was the earlier name of Ch'uan 川 Prefecture in Chung-ching (LS 39, 7b).

[61] III (23).

[62] III (25).

[63] V (4).

[64] V (5).

[65] III (25).

[66] X, 1 (2).

[67] III (3).

[68] In accordance with the general usage, we employ the word "wine" to designate the alcoholic drink which the Chinese made from grain, particularly from millet or rice. It differs from grapewine less than kumiss which, nevertheless, is also called wine, "horse wine" (HS 22, 29b).

[69] X, 1 (2).

[70] III (19).

[71] Rubruck 00, 75–76.

[72] *Op. cit.,* 76.

in the manufacture of salt and certain textiles. According to the records, minerals were often mined and smelted at the same place.[73] Our data indicate a considerable concentration of workers at some mining centers; they speak of three hundred families in one case and as many as a thousand in another.[74] An average family was expected to provide two male adults between the ages of fifteen and fifty as soldiers; and young boys could be used for industrial work before they were fit for military service. Therefore the actual number of workers in these settlements may easily have reached six hundred or two thousand respectively.

The organization of the complex industries of Liao no doubt followed the Chinese pattern. In China Proper coins were made from metal extracted from pits (坑). During the T'ang dynasty the copper mines of P'ing-yang County are reported to have had 280 such pits. Ore from these pits was smelted in two furnaces (爐[75]) and yielded when minted twenty strings of cash daily or seven thousand strings annually,[76] a much higher productivity than is recorded for the one mint of the Liao empire on which numerical data are available. Whether this mint and its annual output of approximately five hundred strings of cash[77] can be considered typical for Liao will be discussed in section VI.

The production of salt from two lakes in what is now southern Shansi was carried on by three hundred and eighty families during the Sung period. Since each family provided two workers,[78] a total of seven hundred and sixty were employed. The lakes, still exploited today, yielded great quantities of salt in the past. The production of salt from the lakes of the Liao empire was probably less; unfortunately "the method of evaporating salt and the amount of the annual production" are not clear.[79] It is probable that in all these centers work was carried on by a number of small units rather than by a single large integrated organization, but even within the small units a certain division of labor was suggested by the nature of the task and the technical tradition.[80]

The silk workshop of Tsu Prefecture employed three hundred Chinese, Po-hai, and "barbarians," but no information is given as to the sex of the workers. That female labor was used in certain industrial enterprises may be inferred from the fact that women

prisoners were sentenced to work in the Hard-labor Embroidery Workhouse.[81]

When little is known of the organization of the large industries, it is not surprising that nothing is known of the structure and size of the innumerable small workshops which, under the management of artisans with perhaps a few journeymen and apprentices, must have constituted the major part of all the industrial enterprises of Liao.[82]

c. LABOR

The actual work in these industrial enterprises was carried out by a great variety of persons whom the texts make visible only in dim silhouette. Men and women of the tribes, perhaps assisted by slaves, must have attended to the immediate manufacturing needs of the pastoral regions. Free tribesmen ("barbarians"), possibly including some Ch'i-tan, are the first category of workers mentioned in the silk brocade workshop of Tsu Prefecture. As their social position was higher than that of the Chinese and Po-hai, they must have acted as superintendents in this and similar government establishments.

Prisoners of war constituted the second category of laborers. Either captured in war or transferred from conquered territories, they were classified in accordance with the needs of the moment and their own qualifications. The majority were settled in the rural or industrial regions of Liao, but others were used for military or technical services in the camps. Their social status gradually improved; as militia soldiers in the prefectures and counties they were permitted to carry weapons; they might join the imperial standing armies; or they might even become "free" members of a new tribe such as the Ho-chu. It may therefore be assumed that the captured artisans who worked in the camps were not too badly treated either; their name, *shu-shan*, clearly expresses the esteem in which they were held by their new masters. Less favorable treatment was probably accorded those captives who were settled in the centers of industry, particularly if they were assigned to crude work as certain processes in mining and salt-making certainly were.

Those subject peoples who continued to live in their native land even after they had been conquered by Liao enjoyed a somewhat better position. The three hundred Chinese families of iron-workers in Tung-p'ing County who paid taxes to the government were obviously considered free people, superior in status to the transplanted Po-hai families of Ch'ang-lo County. Together with the native artisans of the urban centers the "captives" formed the nucleus of a more or less free class of industrial laborers and independent

[73] Iron: III (3). Gold and silver: III (3) (5) (6) (17).
[74] III (3) (9).
[75] CTS 48, 11a; see also TS 54, 8a.
[76] CTS 48, 11a.
[77] LTCSL 1, 20b.
[78] SS 181, 13a.
[79] III (4).
[80] See Wittfogel 31, 527–558.

[81] XIII (47).
[82] Cf. Wittfogel 31, 520–524, 569 ff.

artisans. As the captives' status improved, the two groups were bound to merge sooner or later.

Slaves and convicts also worked at industrial tasks; their legal status and their economic functions varied considerably. Their families, if attached to camps, were mainly concerned with domestic duties. In addition they saw to the brewing of medicine.[83] Female convicts were assigned special work in the Hard-labor Embroidery Workhouse.

According to the textual evidence, the range of industrial work performed by full slaves was rather limited, but former slaves or prisoners were permitted to engage in industrial activities to a considerable degree. Although not free in the modern sense of the term, skilled artisans were kept in good humor by an honorary designation ("the precious ones") and by bonuses given for special achievements. The artisans who worked at the tomb of Ching-tsung received "rewards befitting their positions."[84]

If conditions of labor were at all similar to those of the T'ang and Sung dynasties, then the labor regulations in those epochs will give some idea of working conditions in the Liao empire. The T'ang working day was short in the winter, long in the summer, and of medium length in the spring and fall,[85] obviously depending on the amount of daylight. The Sung government granted particularly favorable conditions to artisans who minted coins and made swords. They had to work only half-time during the summer season (during the fifth, sixth, and seventh months). Besides their regular wages they received additional pay for medicine.[86]

The time of apprenticeship varied, being four years for engravers, three years for makers of chariots and musical instruments, two years for manufacturers of arrows, arrowheads, etc., and nine months for hat- and cap-makers.[87]

Work at the salt-lakes of South Shansi was rewarded as follows: a family was expected to provide two laborers, each of whom received two pints of grain daily while the family received forty thousand cash per year.[88]

For the Liao period we have only one wage figure. We know that ten cash per day was the expected pay for the work of a person in bondage.[89] If the year had three hundred and fifty working days, as one calculation for the copper mines and furnaces of P'ing-yang County[90] suggests, then the temporary bondsmen were supposed to receive about three thousand five hundred cash or three and a half strings per year.

d. THE PRODUCTS

This industrial realm of mines, smelteries, and textile manufactures, of small-scale workshops and organized state labor produced raw materials or turned them into the variety of objects mentioned in the archaeological and literary records. Among these were such articles as armor and weapons, agricultural implements, Ch'i-tan fur coats, Chinese silk gowns, cymbals, drums and bells, all sorts of temple offerings made of paper, colored fans, powder-bags and cosmetics; such aids to transportation as carts and boats; such architectural achievements as palaces and temples, and the walls and towers in the urban centers and along the borders. Recent excavations show that the Chinese artisans of the Liao empire kept the country's sedentary and urban sector supplied with goods that in many ways equalled those produced in the great southern world of China Proper.[91] Yet we may ask to what extent did the newly established industries penetrate the cultural orbit of Ch'i-tan society? To what extent did they replace the products of pastorally oriented craftsmen?

In 1005, almost a hundred years after the birth of the empire, Shêng-tsung, the powerful northern ruler, sent some birthday gifts to Chên-tsung, the emperor of Sung China. These gifts, which were displayed before the officials of the Southern court, included, among other things, the following items:

Shirts of silk gauze decorated with flowers
Sable skin coats
Belts ornamented with gold and silver dragons and offered in a silver box
Green rough-grained leather boots and shoes
Light tan leather boots and shoes
Three hundred bolts of silk brocade
Saddles decorated with gold and silver dragons and phoenix, with saddlecloths of red silk and gold thread
Two leather block saddles with felt saddlecloths
Two green leather saddles with saddlecloths of swordfish skin
A whip made of tendons
A set of imperial ornaments embroidered with clouds and dragons

---

[83] VII, 1 (1).
[84] XI (9).
[85] TS 48, 17b.
[86] SS 180, 5a.
[87] TS 48, 15b–16a.
[88] SS 181, 13a.
[89] XII (34).
[90] CTS 48, 11a.

[91] See figure 27; cf. also Torii 36 passim. A number of porcelain and earthenware jars, excavated in the old Liao territory and kept in the Museum of Mukden, bear a certain resemblance to the leather bags of nomadic peoples; they may have been modelled after them. The location of the site and their style suggest that they were made in the Liao era, "but the exact date is impossible to determine owing to lack of details" (Yamashita 36/37).

A leather-covered birch bow
A red silk quiver
Twenty jars of wine
Twenty packages of candied fruit
Four packages of pears and persimmons
Twenty boxes of chestnuts, plums, jujubes, etc.
Ten bowls of white salt
Ten boxes of blue salt
Twenty boxes of salted meat of calf, lamb, wild boar,
    fish, and deer
Six horses from the imperial stable
Two hundred common horses[92]

This list must not be taken as a statistical average of the industrial production of Liao, for on an occasion of this kind an emperor would offer those articles he valued most highly. The exhibit held in 1005 shows that the products of Liao, although "more skilfully made than formerly,"[93] were still largely pastoral. Agriculture contributed a few items such as fruits and wine. Silk was presented by the Liao ruler in limited quantity, perhaps because his country produced little or because the defeated Sung had to supply him with two hundred thousand rolls of silk annually as tribute. The presence of two varieties

of salt is significant as is the absence of wood-work, bronze statues, or other large pieces of metal work. Only a few silver and gold ornaments and a silver box are mentioned.

A hundred years after the establishment of the Chinese City, more than fifty years after the looting of Chin, and after the transference of many artisans and technicians to the northern region, the Liao emperor could not boast of an industrial production in any way comparable to that of the Five Dynasties or Sung. A beautiful leather saddle, skin coats, tanned leather boots, and a good whip were still the most highly prized industrial achievements of the mounted empire-builders of the north.

The second hundred years of the Liao empire saw the sedentary habits of its rulers intensified. Mausoleums, Chinese in style, were erected[94] and numerous Buddhist temples and towers were built. But, although the shift was toward a more settled life, the earlier economic duality was maintained, and many tribal elements persisted. The Ch'i-tan emperors, who still spent much of the year in tent camps and on horseback, could ill afford to neglect or abandon those tribal crafts that added so much to their hours of leisure but, more importantly, helped to clothe and arm the fighting forces of the empire.

[92] SHYK 196, 35b–36a.
[93] Loc. cit.

[94] Cf. Torii 36 III and IV, passim.

TRANSLATION

INDUSTRY

1. Pioneers of economic development 2. Skilled artisans 3. Mining and smelting 4. Salt from lakes and sea water 5. A "silver prefecture" 6. Silver industry 7. Cart-pullers presented 8. Iron smelting 9. A thousand households in the iron industry 10. Chinese carts 11. Tents of blue felt 12. Skilled weavers 13. Salt-pans 14. Silk brocade 15. Palaces and carriages 16. Gold and silver articles 17. Gold and silver 18. Armor 19. Wine made from grain 20. Shipbuilders 21. Articles of jade prohibited 22. Camel wool and otter skins 23. Ban on private manufacture of colored satin 24. Coal 25. Standardization 26. An imperial silk workshop 27. A government-controlled salt office 28. Mineral products.

1. PIONEERS OF ECONOMIC DEVELOPMENT

8th century   I-tsu[1] begot Yün-tê-shih who was the first to teach the people to sow and reap. He was skilled in stockbreeding. The country thereby became rich. He was Hsüan-tsu.[2]

9th century   Hsüan-tsu begot Sa-la-ti who was humane toward people and kind toward living creatures. He was the first to establish iron smelteries. He taught the people to cast [iron implements]. He was Tê-tsu,[3] that is the father of T'ai-tsu.[4] For generations [members of this family] were the *i-li-chin* of the Yao-lien lineage of the Ch'i-tan and held the political power.

Before 903   Tê-tsu's younger brother, Shu-lan,[5] attacked the Yü-chüeh and Shih-wei in the north. In the south he invaded the I and Ting[6] [regions] and the Hsi[7] and Hsi[8] [tribes]. He was the first to practise masonry and to establish walled cities. He taught the people how to plant mulberry trees and hemp and how to weave. Already he had the ambition of making his territory large and his people numerous.   2, 8*a–b*

2. SKILLED ARTISANS

907–926   When T'ai-tsu was expanding [his territory] in the four directions and conquering Po-hai, the empress[9] played the greatest part in this. Most of the captives with technical skill were generally transferred to the camps. They were called *shu-shan*.[10]   37, 10*a*

---

[1] The temple title of T'ai-tsu's great-grandfather. It was conferred upon him in 1103 (LS 27, 3*b*). No dates are given in the *Liao Shih* for the early ancestors of Liao, possibly because the Ch'i-tan did not have an exact calendar before 947 (LS 42, 1*b*). For defining events of T'ai-tsu's time and the decades following 947, the Chinese calendar was used by the later historiographers of Liao. Traditions concerning the period before T'ai-tsu were transmitted mainly by memory. However we may secure at least an approximate date of I-tsu's period by examining a story in the Liao *Veritable Records* as preserved by the Yüan historians. LS 63, 7*b* states that in 745, during the lifetime of Su-tsu 蕭祖, the father of I-tsu, the Ch'i-tan fought a decisive battle against An Lu-shan 安祿山. Judging by this date, I-tsu must have lived during the middle or second half of the eighth century.

[2] The temple title of T'ai-tsu's grandfather. It was conferred upon him in 1052 (LS 20, 6*b*).

[3] This temple title was conferred upon Sa-la-ti in 1052 (LS 20, 6*b*).

[4] T'ai-tsu was born in 872 (LS 1, 1*a*).

[5] See II, 2, note 1.

[6] In 922 and 923 T'ai-tsu invaded the area of present Hopei from Cho 涿 and Wang-tu 望都 Counties down to Ting 定 County but was defeated by the founder of Later T'ang, Li Ts'un-hsü 李存勖 (*cf.* LS 2, 3*a*; WTS 5, 4*b*). Hence I 易 and Ting here apparently refer to modern I and Ting Counties in Hopei.

[7] The two tribes mentioned here are both romanized as Hsi; their Chinese names, however, differ completely, the first being written 奚 and the second 霫. Before T'ai-tsu's time the territory of the Hsi 奚 was equivalent to the southern part of modern Jehol.

[8] The Hsi 霫 tribe first appeared during the time of Sui (589–618). TT 200, 1084 and CTS 199*B*, 13*b* describe them as living north of the Ch'i-tan. The Hsi probably migrated southward to the Shira Muren at the end of the T'ang dynasty.

[9] Empress Ch'un-ch'in 淳欽, T'ai-tsu's wife. Her honorific title was Ying-t'ien 應天. Once, when T'ai-tsu was engaged in a distant expedition, she launched a successful attack on two rebellious tribes. Whenever a military campaign was planned, the empress joined the preliminary discussion. She died in 953 (LS 71, 1*a*–3*b*).

[10] According to LS 116, 19*a*, this group of people was called *shu-shan* 屬珊 because they were as valuable as coral. The Ch'i-tan word for "coral" is given as *shu-shan*. It is obvious that the Ch'i-tan must have become acquainted with coral through the Chinese or Koreans or some other coastal group. A "precious" army of Liao was called the Shu-shan Army (*cf.* XV, 1 (25)).

3. MINING AND SMELTING

907–926   Mining and smelting began when T'ai-tsu first annexed the Shih-wei.   Their territory produced copper, iron, gold, and silver, and their people were skilled in making copper and iron articles.

There was also the Ho-chu tribe[11] where iron was abundant.   *Ho-chu*[12] in the [Ch'i-tan] national language means "iron."   In this region three smelteries were established, namely those of Liu-shih-ho, San-ch'u-ku-ssŭ, and Shou Mountain.[13]

At the beginning of the reign period Shên-ts'ê,[14] when Po-hai was conquered, Kuang Prefecture was taken.   Originally the T'ieh-li Administration of Po-hai, it was renamed T'ieh-li Prefecture.[15] This place also had an abundance of iron.

Tung-p'ing County,[16] originally the old territory of Hsiang-p'ing County[17] of Han, produced iron ore.[18]   Three hundred households were established here to refine [the metal].   Together with their taxes, they paid [iron].[19]

Since the mining and smelting was conducted mostly in the eastern part of the country, an Office of the Ministry of Revenue was therefore established in the Eastern Capital and an Office of Money and Silk[20] was created in Ch'ang-ch'un Prefecture.

Returning after his punitive campaign against Yu[21] and Chi,[22] T'ai-tsu encamped with his army at the foot of a mountain [where] silver and iron ore were found.   He ordered the establishment of

1021–1031   a smelting plant.   During [the reign period] T'ai-p'ing of Shêng-tsung, both at the Yin Mountains[23] north of Huang River and at the source of the Liao River,[24] gold and

---

[11] For the history of this tribe *cf.* I, 2 (5), no. **7**. The tribesmen were given the task of smelting iron. Their territory was probably near what is now Liao-yang 遼陽 County in Liaoning (LS 33, 6*b*).

[12] It is impossible to establish any direct etymology for this word. It may however be related to certain words in the Tungus languages of the lower Amur River which mean "heavy": Olča *xudžösi*, etc. (*cf.* Schmidt 23, 256). On the other hand the word may be related to Jurchen *huô-čōh* (beautiful) and Manchu *xočžo* (beautiful, rare) (Grube 96, 93; Zakharov 75, 432).

Ho-chu is equated by Shiratori with the Khirghiz word transcribed in TS 217*B*, 11*a* as *chia-sha* 迦沙, for which Karlgren (23, nos. 342 and 841) gives *ka* and *sa*. Shiratori (12 TMK, 1266 ff.) equates this with the Samoyed words for iron, *kuose, kuese, kueś*, etc., and with the Dahur word *kasó* (iron), evidently quoted from Ivanovski's *Mandjurica*. Whether or not the equation between *chia-sha* and the Ch'i-tan word *ho-chu* is tenable cannot yet be decided. If the equation is valid, Shiratori has revealed an interesting linguistic relation which might of course be due to borrowing. Only one relationship can be definitely established for this word series: the relation of the proto-Khirghiz word *chia-sha* with the Samoyed words for iron. This presents the first linguistic proof of the hitherto assumed Samoyed origin of proto-Khirghiz.

[13] Also called Shou 首 Mountain or Chu-pi 駐蹕 Mountain. It is situated fifteen *li* southwest of modern Liao-yang County, Liaoning. According to CKTLHC 7, 7, Liao-yang still produces iron today.

[14] Shên-ts'ê (916–922) must be an error for T'ien-hsien 天顯 (926–938), for the friendship between the Ch'i-tan and Po-hai was not broken until 924 (LS 2, 4*a*). Po-hai was not conquered until 926 (LS 2, 6*a*–*b*).

[15] T'ieh-li Administration was renamed T'ieh-li Prefecture in the reign of T'ai-tsu (907–926). It was renamed Kuang 廣 Prefecture in the seventh year of K'ai-t'ai (1018) (LS 38, 10*b*). It is equivalent to modern Chang-i-chan 彰驛站, Liaoning (MRC II, 25). The name T'ieh-li 鐵利 probably indicates the "profit from iron" which this locality offered. *Cf.* III (5).

[16] Probably between modern T'ieh-ling 鐵嶺 County and K'ai-yüan 開原 County, Liaoning. According to the table in CKTLHC 7, 31, the region has continued to produce iron ore up to the present. The passage concerning the iron-smelting families of Tung-p'ing County can also be found with some slight variations in LS 38, 12*b*.

[17] The region was called Hsiang-p'ing 襄平 County from the Han dynasty down to the time of Chin 晉 (265–420).

[18] The character used is an obsolete orthography for 礦 (ore).

[19] For a slightly different version of this passage see LS 38, 12*b*.

[20] There were three of these offices: the first (established in 1053 by Hsing-tsung) in Ch'ang-ch'un 長春 Prefecture (northwest of modern Po-tu-na, Kirin); the second in Hsing-chung Administration 興中府 (modern Ch'ao-yang 朝陽 County, Jehol); and the third in P'ing 平 Prefecture (modern Lu-lung 盧龍 County, Hopei). The function of the office is indicated only vaguely in the *Liao Shih* and the *Ch'i-tan Kuo-chih*. We can merely assume that it belonged to the category of the tax offices, since the *Liao Shih* lists it among them. See XIV, 2 (10); CTKC 22, 1*a*.

[21] Modern Peiping.

[22] Modern Chi 薊 County, Hopei.

[23] Probably part of this big range in northwestern Jehol.

[24] Modern Shira Muren, Jehol.

silver ore was discovered.[25]   Smelteries were established for refining [the ore].   From this time down to T'ien-tsu the state depended throughout on these benefits.   60, 2a–b

4. SALT FROM LAKES AND SEA WATER

907–926   The system of salt permits originated with T'ai-tsu.   Because he had secured many Chinese [subjects], he set apart from the eight tribes the ancient Chinese City[26] and made it into another tribe to govern it.   The city, situated south of Mount T'an, enjoyed the advantages of a salt-lake.   This was the Hua-yen County of Later Wei.[27]   All eight tribes extracted [the salt] and ate it.[28]

Then, after the expedition to Yü and Chi, [T'ai-tsu] returned and halted at Ho-la Lake[29] where he ordered salt to be taken to supply the army.   Afterwards the amount of salt from the lake increased so much that both the government and the people were fully provided.

938–947   In the beginning of the Hui-t'ung period T'ai-tsung was very benevolent toward Chin.   Chin offered sixteen prefectures,[30] among which were Ying[31] and Mo.[32]   Now for the first time they obtained the benefits of evaporating water [for salt] in Ho-chien.[33]   A Salt Monopoly Department was set up in Hsiang-ho County.[34]   As a result the people to the north of Yen and Yün[35] were temporarily provided with the salt of Ts'ang.[36]   At this time the Offices of the Accountants of the five capitals for such salt-producing areas as Po-hai, Chên City, Hai-yang,[37] Fêng Prefecture,[38] Yang-lo City,[39] and Kuang-chi Lake[40] each controlled its own region.   As to the method of evaporating salt and the amount of the annual production, no details are known.[41]   60, 1b–2a

---

[25] Gold and silver are found all over Jehol. See the table in CKTLHC 6, 19. Cf. also Franke 02, 45 ff.; and for the northern regions, North Manchuria 24, 217 ff.

[26] The Chinese City (Han-ch'êng 漢城) corresponds to modern Shih-t'ou Ch'êng-tzŭ 石頭城子, the Mongol name of which is Chilun Balghasun, in Chahar (Yanai 30, 835).

Besides this Han-ch'êng, several other "Chinese cities" are mentioned in the *Liao Shih*: (1) the southern city of Lin-huang Administration 臨潢府 (Boro Khoton, Jehol); (2) a place outside Liao-yang Administration 遼陽府 (Liao-yang County, Liaoning); (3) a city near Chien 建 Prefecture in Chung-ching (south of Ch'ao-yang County, Jehol). The names of these cities were probably derived from the Chinese who were settled there after having been captured in various wars. Walled cities were built by and for these captives partly to preclude their escape and partly because they were accustomed to urban life. Cf. LS 37, 5a; 38, 2a; 39, 7b; cf. also Yao TW 35, 53 ff.

[27] The Wei dynasty (386–534).

[28] A Ch'i-tan official in a conversation in 1008 with the Sung envoy, Lu Chên, mentioned a large salt-lake west of the Supreme and Central Capitals. The lake, whose circumference was given as about three hundred li, produced salt on its shore like ice. The largest pieces were like rocks; the Ch'i-tan cut and used them as pillows. When it was reduced to grains, it was sold to the people (HCLY 77, 10a).

The Liao salt is said to have been cheaper than that produced in the Sung empire in the regions adjacent to the Liao territory. As a result, a lively illicit salt trade developed across the Sung border. In the beginning salt was smuggled into the southern empire by Liao merchants; later Sung merchants also engaged in the dangerous, but profitable, business. In 987, 1046, and 1100 the Sung officials hotly discussed the problem, but the only effective

measure taken was severe persecution of Sung smugglers. A Sung subject who smuggled a catty or more of salt was punished. Persons who smuggled fifty catties or more were either banished or subjected to hard labor; those who smuggled more than a hundred catties were sent to the court for special investigation (SS 181, 13a, 27a ff.; 182, 1a ff.).

[29] Probably in modern Jehol.

[30] See I, 1, note 5.

[31] Modern Ho-chien 河間 County, Hopei.

[32] Modern Jên-ch'iu 任邱 County, Hopei.

[33] Another name for Ying 瀛 Prefecture. See note 31.

[34] Modern Hsiang-ho 香河 County, Hopei.

[35] This refers to the regions north of modern Peiping in Hopei and Ta-t'ung in Shansi.

[36] Near modern Ts'ang 滄 County, Hopei.

[37] The present market town of Hai-yang 海陽鎮, west of Shan-hai-kuan.

[38] There were at least three Fêng Prefectures in the time of Liao; one in Shang-ching (between the rivers Shira Muren and Tsaghan Muren, Jehol); one in Tung-ching (near the Sungari River, Liaoning); and one in Hsi-ching (modern Kuei-sui 歸綏, Suiyuan). The text probably refers to the third, for a great salt lake was located there. See LS 41, 4a.

[39] Corresponds to modern Tung-kuan-i 東關驛 near Sui-chung 綏中 County, Liaoning.

[40] This lake belonged to Shang-ching. It probably corresponds to the present Dalai Nōr in Chahar.

[41] During the negotiations of 1123 between the Sung government and the Chin conquerors of Nan-ching Circuit mention is made of an annual government income from this territory of three hundred and ninety thousand strings of money which was derived from the sale of two hundred and twenty thousand piculs of salt (SCPMHP 14, 11b). According to this figure, a picul sold at this

5. A "SILVER PREFECTURE"

907–926   Yin Prefecture[42] (Fu-kuo Commandery,[43] third class prefect[44]) was originally Fu Prefecture of Po-hai. T'ai-tsu changed its name because of the silver smelting [carried on there].   38, 12a

6. SILVER INDUSTRY

907–926   Tsê Prefecture (Kuang-chi Commandery, third class prefect) was originally the region of T'u-yin County of Han. T'ai-tsu captured the people of Yü Prefecture and set up a fortress in which he settled them. They extracted and refined silver in the smelteries of Hsien-ho.[45]   39, 3b

7. CART–PULLERS PRESENTED

909   On the day chi-ssŭ[46] of the tenth month in the winter [of the third year of T'ai-tsu's accession] . . . the Wu-niang-kai tribe of the northwest presented cart-pullers.[47]

                                                       1, 3b

8. IRON SMELTING

911   On the day mou-wu of the tenth month in the winter [of the fifth year of T'ai-tsu's accession] iron smelteries were established.   1, 4a

9. A THOUSAND HOUSEHOLDS IN THE IRON INDUSTRY

926   Ch'ang-lo County[48] was originally the name of a county in Liao-ch'êng.[49] T'ai-tsu attacked Po-hai and transferred its people. He set up a county in which to settle them. The population consisted of four thousand households, of which a thousand households provided iron.   37, 11b

10. CHINESE CARTS

938   In the first year of Hui-t'ung of Emperor T'ai-tsung[50] [the court of] Chin sent Fêng Tao,[51] Liu Hsü,[52] and others to furnish imperial carriages and ceremonial equipment and to present honorific titles[53] and the document for the investiture ceremony for the emperor

---

time for one and three-fourths strings, a catty for something over fourteen cash. For the inflationary character of these prices see op. cit. 13, 11a; 14, 11a; cf. also VI and X, introductions and X, 1, note 48.

[42] Yin 銀 means "silver." Modern T'ieh-ling 鐵嶺 County, Liaoning. The existence of silver in this region is also reported in CKTLHC 7, 44.

[43] The former subdivision of China into regions called chün 軍 was probably for reasons of military expediency. During the time of Liao the nomenclature was occasionally retained even though much of the military significance had been lost. Many areas were designated both as prefectures (州) and commanderies (郡 or 軍). Yin Prefecture, for example, is explained as being the same as Fu-kuo 富國 Commandery.

[44] In Liao the importance of a prefecture was indicated by the rank of the official in charge of the area (see I, 1, note 31).

[45] Hsien-ho was probably the name of a small area in P'ing-ch'üan County, Jehol (our Tsê 澤 Prefecture). CKTLHC 6, 13 states that silver ore was to be found in P'an-chia-kou 潘家溝, Yen-t'ung 煙筒 Mountain, and Ku Hill 孤山子, all of which were in P'ing-ch'üan.

[46] 紀 is an error for 己.

[47] For the possible development of carts in the realm of Ch'i-tan culture see IV, introduction.

[48] In Shang-ching near the upper course of the modern Shira Muren, Jehol (MRC II, 93).

[49] Presumably a place in Tung-ching, the former territory of Po-hai. No Ch'ang-lo County in Tung-ching is recorded in the geographical section of the Liao Shih, but the name is mentioned in LS 38, 8b. Possibly there formerly existed a Ch'ang-lo County in Tung-ching which was later abolished. The present text points out that some inhabitants were transferred to a new Ch'ang-lo County in Shang-ching. LS 38, 8b states that others were transferred to Fêng-hsien County (southwest of present Pei-chên 北鎮 County, Liaoning).

[50] The year when the Chinese name of the dynasty, Liao, was assumed. This is why the government of the semi-barbarian state of Liao obtained advisers from China Proper to regulate ceremonial matters according to the prevailing Chinese tradition.

[51] Fêng Tao 馮道 (T. 可道, 881–954) served ten emperors during the time of the Five Dynasties. As far as we know, he was the first person to use wooden blocks in printing the classics (CWTS 126, 4a; MHPT 18, 117; AJCTC 1, 5a; SLYY 8, 74; cf. Carter 31, 49 ff.).

[52] Liu Hsü 劉煦 (T. 耀遠, 887–946) was the president of the editorial group which prepared the Chiu T'ang Shu.

[53] The title of a Liao emperor generally had to contain the word "heaven" and to consist of between ten and twenty characters. These long titles were frequently built up by successive additions of laudatory expressions. Cf. appendix II.

and the empress dowager.   From this time the carriages[54] and robes of the Son of Heaven became known in Liao.   55, 2b

11. TENTS OF BLUE FELT

940   [On the day *i-ssŭ* of the eighth month in the third year of Hui-t'ung], Nan T'ang sent envoys to ask for tents made from blue felt.[55]   These were given to them.
4, 5b

12. SKILLED WEAVERS

947–951   Hung-chêng County[56] was established by Shih-tsung with captive households from Ting Prefecture.[57]   The people were adept at weaving and possessed many skills.
39, 6b

13. SALT–PANS

982–1031   Hai-yang County,[58] originally a county of Han, was near the sea.   The soil contained much alkali.   [Therefore] salt-pans were established at this place.   39, 8a

14. SILK BROCADE

984   On the day *ting-hai* [of the twelfth month in the first year of T'ung-ho] the damask and brocade offered annually by Hsien Prefecture[59] were distributed as gifts to the right and left attendants [of the emperor].   10, 6a

15. PALACES AND CARRIAGES

1001–1032   [The empress[60]] once made models of palace halls from stalks of straw.   She secretly gave these to the officials and ordered them to construct three halls, the Ch'ing-fêng Hall, the T'ien-hsiang Hall, and the Pa-fang Hall.   After their construction the emperor's favor increased inordinately.   The chariot in which she rode was embellished with a dragon's head and an owl's tail and was decorated with gold.   She also [had] constructed a nine-dragon carriage and a princely[61] carriage with silver pagodas, each with ingenious designs.   71, 5a

16. GOLD AND SILVER ARTICLES

1025   On the day *ting-ch'ou* [of the twelfth month in the fifth year of T'ai-p'ing] artisans were forbidden to melt down and destroy articles of gold or silver.   17, 2a

17. GOLD AND SILVER

1027   In the fifth month [of the seventh year of T'ai-p'ing], when the emperor took shelter from the heat in Yung-an Mountain,[62] the Punitive Office of the Southwestern

---

[54] The imperial carts of Chinese style followed the T'ang pattern. A comparative study of the Histories of the T'ang and Liao dynasties reveals that the section in the *Liao Shih* concerning the carts of Liao (LS 55) was probably copied from TS 24.

[55] Blue felt seems to have been esteemed early by the Ch'i-tan. When thirty Ch'i-tan tribesmen came to the court of Wei in 517, they were presented by the empress with a gift of this material amounting to two rolls for each tribesman (WS 100, 16a).

[56] Probably in the vicinity of I 義 County, Liaoning.

[57] Modern Ting 定 County, Hopei.

[58] The present market town of Hai-yang, west of Shan-hai-kuan. It was set up during the time of Shêng-tsung (982–1031). According to CKTLHC 5, 54, because of the proximity of the sea, salt was produced here in great quantities.

[59] East of modern Pei-chên 北鎮 County, Liaoning. A number of prefectures, Ling 靈, Chin 錦, Hsien 顯, and Pa 霸 of Chung-ching or Tung-ching respectively, are known to have produced mulberry trees, hemp, and variegated silk. The people of these prefectures who paid the land tax in the form of silk were called "the empress dowager's silkworm families" (太后絲蠶戶) (HCLY 77, 9a). The regions of Nan-ching also produced silk. Their brocade, variegated silk, and embroidery were unsurpassed in fineness in the world (CTKC 22, 7a). This is probably why the Liao gifts to Sung frequently included silk.

The Liao pattern of assigning silk producing territories to imperial relatives was also followed by the Yüan dynasty. Mongol empresses, concubines, princes, princesses, and meritorious officials were all granted "fiefs," which periodically delivered money and silk to government offices. These officials, in turn, distributed the precious revenue in accordance with an established pattern (YS 95, 1a ff.).

[60] Empress Jên-tê, wife of Shêng-tsung. She received the title of Empress Ch'i-tien in 1001. She was killed in 1032 (LS 71, 6a–b).

[61] 諸子 means "the princes." The vehicle probably was a carriage used by the imperial princes.

[62] A mountain about twenty *li* northwest of Tsaghan

Route memorialized that gold and silver were produced in the Yin Mountains and requested that a smeltery be set up. This was approved. Emissaries were also sent to trace[63] the Liao River[64] to its source in search of gold and silver producing areas.   17, 4a

18. ARMOR

1031   On the day *hsin-yu* [of the intercalary tenth month in the first year of Ching-fu] the newly manufactured armor was inspected [by the emperor].   18, 2b

19. WINE MADE FROM GRAIN

1031–1055   Officials were forbidden to waste[65] grain by making wine without authorization. It was allowed for weddings and sacrificial offerings if a written permit was first obtained from the authorities.[66]   59, 3a

20. SHIPBUILDERS

1048   On the day *chia-shên* [of the fourth month in the seventeenth year of Ch'ung-hsi] the great king of the P'u-lu-mao-to tribe,[67] P'u-lien, came [to Liao] and offered shipbuilders.[68]   20, 2a

21. ARTICLES OF JADE PROHIBITED

1059   On the day *ping-hsü* [of the eleventh month in the fifth year of Ch'ing-ning] . . . it was forbidden to make articles of jade.[69]   21, 5b

22. CAMEL WOOL AND OTTER SKINS

1060   On the day *hsin-ch'ou* of the twelfth month [in the fifth year of Ch'ing-ning] the prohibition against the use of camel yarn[70] and otter skins was relaxed.   21, 5b

23. BAN ON PRIVATE MANUFACTURE OF COLORED SATIN

1064   [On the day *kêng-ch'ên* of the eleventh month in the tenth year of Ch'ing-ning] an imperial decree was issued to the Southern Capital forbidding the private manufacture of the colored satin[71] used by the emperor, the private trade in iron, and also the drinking of wine at improper times.   22, 3a

24. COAL

1065–1075   During the reign period Hsien-yung, [Ma Jên-wang] received the *chin-shih* degree and was appointed to the post of magistrate of Sung-shan County. As the task of yearly transporting government coal[72] from Tsê Prefecture devolved upon Sung-shan alone, [Ma]

Khoton, Jehol, where the Liao emperors Shêng-tsung, Ching-tsung, and Tao-tsung were buried (LS 18, 1b; Torii 40, 171).

[63] We follow the Palace edition in reading 循 for the 遁 of our text.

[64] The present Shira Muren, Jehol.

[65] The word 糜 is used as equivalent to 靡.

[66] This order was issued during the time of Hsing-tsung (1031–1055).

[67] This tribe probably occupied the region which is now eastern Kirin (*cf.* I, 2 (6), no. 10). According to LS 19, 7b, one hundred and eighty families of the P'u-lu-mao-to people who had resided on the shore of the Ho-lan River (the modern Hai-lan River, Kirin) came and submitted to Liao.

[68] They were probably used to build ships for military campaigns against Hsia. According to LS 20, 3b, Hsing-tsung led an army across the Yellow River by boat in the eighth month of 1049. LS 93, 2b reports also that a general, Hsiao Hui 惠 (d. 1056), moved a fleet on the

Yellow River from Ho-nan 河南 (the modern Ordos region) into the territory of Hsia. His boats are said to have spread out over several hundred *li.* *Cf.* IV (10) (11) (12).

[69] The prohibition of making jade objects was probably due to the fact that jade was considered as precious as gold; therefore the common people were not to use jade. Several imperial decrees interdicted its use by persons without special privilege (LS 21, 2a).

[70] The word 尼 is identical with 呢 which signifies yarn made from the wool of animals.

[71] The Southern Capital at that time was renowned for its embroidery products and silk brocades (see CTKC 22, 7a). 段 is usually written 緞. The meaning of the two words is the same.

[72] The term 炭 may designate either coal or charcoal. In early Chinese books "coal" is sometimes rendered as *shih mo* 石墨, and sometimes as *shih t'an* 石炭. Coal must have been known to the Chinese before the third century. From the third century down to the fourth

Jên-wang sent a petition to the vicegerent of the Central Capital, Hsiao T'u-hun, requesting an equalization of the service with other counties.[73]   105, 3a–b

25. STANDARDIZATION

1071   On the day *i-hai* [of the fourth month in the seventh year of Hsien-yung] cloth[74] in sizes which did not conform with the standard measurements was forbidden.   22, 7b

---

and fifth centuries they not only used it for writing but also knew about its value as a fuel.

Lu Yün 陸雲 (A.D. 262–303) wrote in a letter to his brother, Lu Chi 陸機 (261–303), "One day, on climbing San-t'ai 三臺 Mountain, I discovered that Mr. Ts'ao 曹公 had stored up several hundred thousand catties of *shih mo*. He claims that after being reduced by fire it can still be used again. I do not know whether you have ever seen this or not. I am now sending you two lumps" (TPYL 605, 5a).

A footnote to the History of the Later Han dynasty (HHC 22, 15b) quotes the *Yü-chang Chi* 豫章記 by Lei Tz'ǔ-tsung 雷次宗 (386–448) as saying, "Ko District 葛鄉 of Chien-ch'êng 建城 County [modern Kao-an 高安 County, Kiangsi] had two hundred *mou* of *shih t'an* which could be burned by cooking."

The *Shui Ching Chu* 水經注 by Li Tao-yüan 酈道元 (d. 527) quotes from the *Hsi-yü Chi* 西域記 the words of the Buddhist monk Tao-an 釋道安 (314–385), "two hundred *li* north of Ch'ü-tz'ǔ 屈茨 [modern Kucha 庫車, Sinkiang], there is a mountain which sheds light at night but simply emits smoke during the daytime. The people take *shih t'an* from this mountain for smelting the iron of the same mountain. It supplied the needs of thirty-six states" (HCSCC 2, 13a).

During the Sui period (581–618) the use of coal evidently spread. According to Wang Shao's 王劭 memorial about fire, coal was used for warming wine and roasting meat (Sui 69, 1b).

From the fifth century to the eleventh and twelfth centuries coal gradually became popular as a fuel among the people, at least in some regions. Thus in 828 the Japanese monk Ennin 圓仁, on his way to Ch'ang-an 長安 (modern Sian 西安, Shensi), passed some rocky mountains called Chin Shan 晉山 (west of T'ai-yüan 太原 in modern Shansi), in which he was surprised to find coal (*shih t'an*) everywhere. He remarks, "All the people from far and near come to take it for fuel. It has a good flame for cooking. It looks as if it had been transformed from rocks. Someone says it is made through the burning of a heavenly fire, but I do not think this is so. As a matter of fact, it is a reward for the people's sincerity" (NGJG 3, 76–77).

The Sung empire, contemporary with Liao, controlled more than twenty coal fields in the region corresponding to modern Honan. The people of Ho-tung 河東 (modern Shansi) used to derive their livelihood from coal. It is interesting to note that most of the coal mines in Hopei, Shantung, and Shensi were first developed under the Sung dynasty. In 1078 a coal mine in Hsü 徐 Prefecture was opened for the first time (*cf.* SS 179, 17b; 186, 14b; ICLTC 1, 11b–12a; TCP 110b). Su Shih 蘇軾 (1036–1101) relates that in 1079 a coal mine was opened at a place north of Pai-t'u Chên 白土鎮 and southwest of P'êng 彭 City.

The mineral obtained there was used to smelt iron which served as raw material for the production of sharp weapons (TPCC 10, 6b). Formerly "several million" people in the capital, Pien, all used coal as fuel, and no wood at all (CLP 2, 62).

A Sung scholar, Lu Yu 陸游 (1125–1210), states that the northern regions of Sung produced much coal, the southern regions much charcoal, and Shu 蜀 (modern Szechuan) much "bamboo coal" (*chu t'an* 竹炭) (LHAPC 1, 9). Chu Pien 朱弁 claims that coal appeared everywhere in the northwestern part of Southern Sung (CYCW 4, 30).

Many territories of Sung were taken over by Chin which thus gained control over a number of coal-producing areas. For example, Mien-ch'ih 澠池 (Mien-ch'ih County, Honan) is reported by a garrison soldier, Chia Ho-ch'un 賈合春, as having an abundance of coal in open mines. He adds that a very strong fire is obtained by heaping coal over a wood fire (HICC 4, 6b).

The region of T'ai-yüan, which lay just to the south of the Liao empire, had a considerable coal mining industry under the T'ang dynasty. It is therefore quite likely that the *t'an* of our text refers to coal mining within the Liao country. This interpretation is strengthened by the impressive development of coal mining in the contemporary Sung empire.

The possible existence of coal mining does not exclude the simultaneous continuation of the time-honored charcoal industry. Chinese travelers noticed a flourishing charcoal industry in the central region of Liao, Chung-ching Circuit (CTKC 24, 2a; Chavannes 97 VC, 428). For a recent discussion of the earliest industrial use of coal in Europe and Asia see Read 39/40, 119–133.

[73] For a fuller version of this passage see XI (21).

[74] The question whether the "cloth" of this and similar passages has to be interpreted as cotton or linen depends on the answer to the question as to whether or not cotton was known in present Manchuria, Mongolia, and North China during the tenth and eleventh centuries. Doubtless, the Chinese knew cotton long before they began to grow it. The earliest source which mentions cotton is probably the *I Wu Chih* 異物志, written by a Han author, Yang Fu 楊孚, either in the second half of the first century A.D. or in the second (PHHIWC 82). According to this "*Record of Curiosities*," there grew in the regions of present Indo-China and Kuangtung a tall *mu-mien* 木棉[絲?] tree whose fruit, shaped like a wine cup, contained a very white silk-like fibre and yielded several catties (IWC 7b). The *Hou Han Shu* (composed between 318 and 445 from Han material) says that the Ai-lao barbarians who lived along the Irrawaddy River produced *pai-tieh* 帛疊. The early Chinese works also use other

1081   On the day *hsin-hai* [of the eleventh month in the seventh year of Ta-k'ang] regulations concerning silk fabrics and lustrings of narrow and short measures were abolished.   24, 3*b*

---

terms for cotton such as *pai-tieh* 白疊 (or 㲲 or 㲲), *ku-pei* 古貝, *chi-pei* 吉貝, *chieh-pei* 刧貝, *chia-po-lo* 迦波羅, *chieh-po-yü* 刧波育, *ku-chung* 古終, *t'u-lu* 土蘆, and *ch'ü-shun* 屈朐.

Hirth and Rockhill (11, 218) consider *pai-tieh* equivalent to Chaghatai *pakhta* ["cotton"—an Iranian loan word], and conclude therefore that cotton must have been introduced into China through Central Asia. Fujita (32, 545) rejects this theory, claiming erroneously that the appearance of the term *pai-tieh* in the *Hou Han Shu* indicates that China knew cotton in pre-Turkic times. He states further that, since the *pai-tieh* producing region of the Ai-lao people was established in A.D. 61 by Emperor Ming of Later Han as Yung-ch'ang Commandery 永昌郡, China may have learned of cotton directly from that place. Laufer (19, 489–490) correctly etymologizes *pai-tieh* from Pahlavi **bak-dib < *pambak-dīp* "cotton brocade" which has no direct connection with *paxta*. Fujita (32, 552) suggests a relation to a Pali word *pataka*.

The other terms for cotton, *chi-pei*, *ku-pei*, *chieh-pei*, *chia-po-lo*, and *chieh-po-yü*, are derived from the Sanskrit *karpāsa* and the Pali *kappāsa*, from which stems the Malayan *kapas* as a loan word (Fujita 32, 575; Dr. K. Menges, personal communication; for a detailed discussion of the Chinese terms for cotton see HCS, Ch'in and Han, I, 2, The Ai-lao Barbarians, HHS 86, 23*a*–26*a*, mss. See also Laufer 19, 488 ff.).

Among the Chinese scholars from Sung down to Ch'ing times there has been a dispute concerning the meaning of the terms *ku-pei* and *chi-pei*. Ch'êng Ta-ch'ang is unable to determine whether these two terms indicate two different plants or whether one is simply an error for the other (YFL 10, 6*b*). Yü Chêng-hsieh considers *chi-pei* the correct form to which the terms *chieh-po-lo* and *chia-po-lo* in the Buddhist sūtras and *chieh-pei* in a T'ang poem by P'i Jih-hsiu 皮日休 are similar (KSLK 7, 21*a*–*b*).

There are different earlier explanations of *ku-pei* and *chi-pei*. The *Sung Shu* 宋書 (completed in 488) is the earliest document so far known to have the term *ku-pei*. Under the year 430 it lists *pai-tieh* 白疊 and *ku-pei* as two different items (Sung 97, 6*a*). In Liang 54, 2*a* and NS 78, 1*b*, *ku-pei* is said to be a tree, while in CTS 197, 1*a* and TS 222B, 2*a* it is called a plant. During and after the Sung period the term *ku-pei* was no longer used; only *chi-pei*, which clearly designates cotton, was employed (CFC 2, 35; LWTT 6, 6*b*). According to Chao I 趙翼 and Ling Yang-tsao 凌揚藻, before the Sung period, *ku-pei* was considered a tree because scholars were unfamiliar with the plant, while in Sung time and later, *chi-pei* is used for cotton because by then the plant was well known (KYTK 30, 26*b* ff.; LSP 40, 648).

Mu-mien 木棉 (or 枛 or 緜 or 緤) (KY 2, 5*a*; CY 3, 6*b*; TPYL 960, 6*a*) first appears in Yang Fu's *Record of Curiosities* (see above) and not long afterwards in the

Wei Chih 魏志 (written by Ch'ên Shou 陳壽 233–297). Here it is stated that Japanese men tied it around their heads (SKC, Wei 30, 27*b*). The *Wu Lu* 吳錄, written by the Chin 晉 author, Chang P'o 張勃, and quoted in the *Ch'i Min Yao Shu* 齊民要術 (composed under the Northern Wei dynasty), says that in Chiao-chih 交趾 [Indo-China] *mu-mien* grew very high, bearing fruits like wine cups with a silk-like fibre. The textile made from this material was called *pai-tieh* 白緤 (CMYS 10, 45*a*). The *Liang Shu* 梁書, compiled by Yao Ssŭ-lien 姚思廉 (d. 637), records that Emperor Wu of the Liang dynasty (464–549) was so frugal that he had his bed-curtains made of *mu-mien* (Liang 3, 38*b*). It is however impossible to determine whether this *mu-mien* is the cotton plant or the silk-cotton tree (*Bombax malabaricum*) since some pre-Sung and Sung works, such as Yang Fu's *I Wu Chih*, the *Wu Lu*, the *Lo-fu Shan Chi* 羅浮山記, the *Kuang-chou Chih* 廣州志 (TYPL 960, 6*a*), and the Sung dictionaries, the *Kuang Yün* 廣韻 (KY 2, 5*a*), and the *Chi Yün* 集韻 (CY 3, 6*b*), all say it is a tree, whereas the *Nan Yüeh Chih* 南越志 describes it as the cotton-plant (NCCS 35, 1*b*). Li Shih-chên 李時珍 and Hsü Kuang-ch'i 徐光啓 (1562–1633) describe both types, pointing out their differences (PTKM 36, 71*b* ff.; NCCS 35, 2*a* ff.).

Yü Chêng-hsieh says that the word *mien* 棉 was created in Sung times in order to distinguish cotton from *mien* 緜 or 綿, "floss silk" (KSLK 7, 21*b*). As shown above, the new word was variously written. Its meaning was uncertain; it sometimes denoted cotton and sometimes the silk-cotton tree. Many authors from Sung to the Yüan period still used the old forms instead of the new one.

The terms *pai-tieh*, *ku-pei*, and *chi-pei* are all foreign in origin, while *mu-mien* is a purely Chinese term. From the Yüan period to the present, *mu-mien* has been used to denote cotton only.

Cotton is indigenous to India. It was introduced into China by two routes: the southern and the northern. The former led across the sea to Kuangtung and then over-land from Burma to Yünnan, while the latter started in India and continued overland through Central Asia.

In the south Kuangtung and Yünnan first produced cotton as shown in certain writings of the fourth or fifth to the sixth century, which note that Kuangtung and Kuangsi produced *mu-mien* or *ku-pei* (TPYL 960, 6*a*; NCCS 35, 1*b*). Its cultivation and use were, however, generally limited to the tribal peoples. Not until about the tenth or eleventh century did the Chinese in these regions use the plant. The *Daily Records* of the Yüan-fêng and Hsi-ning periods (1068–1085), *Hsi-fêng Jih-li* 熙豐日曆, edited by Wang Ming-ch'ing 王明清 (1127–?), state that when Ch'ên I 陳繹 was prefect of Kuang-chou (Canton) in 1078–1079 he was guilty of allowing soldiers to engage in the weaving of *mu-mien* for a living. He was degraded and exiled (HFJL 4*a*). About 1178 Chou Ch'ü-fei 周去非, an official in Kuangsi, stated that Lei-hua

26. AN IMPERIAL SILK WORKSHOP

In the east[75] were the prefectural offices, various [other] government buildings, and the silk brocade shop.[76] The servitors assigned to the shop—three hundred barbarians,[77] Chinese, and Po-hai—supplied the demands of the imperial palace.　　37, 6a

---

雷化 and Lien-chou 廉州 produced *chi-pei* which he clearly describes as cotton (LWTT 6, 6b). About the same time Chao Ju-k'uo 趙汝适 says that regions, such as Ch'iung-chou 瓊州, Ch'ang-hua 昌化, and Wan-an 萬安 Commanderies produced *chi-pei* which he too describes as cotton (CFC 1, 1, 2, and 12; Hirth and Rockhill 11, 46, 48, 96).

When cotton was first planted in Fukien is not known. In 1275 the Sung prime minister, Chia Ssŭ-tao 賈似道, was killed at Mu-mien Monastery 木綿庵, twenty *li* south of the present Lung-hsi 龍溪 Prefecture (CTYY 19, 10a; SS 474, 21a; CCITC 429, 19a). The fact that this monastery was already named Mu-mien certainly suggests familiarity with cotton. A southern Sung scholar, Fan Chêng-min 范正敏, states that in his time (dates of his life-span unknown) the natives of Fukien emulated one another in planting *mu-mien* (TCHL 3a).

Another Sung work, *Po Chai Pien* 泊宅編, written by Fang Shao 方勺, reports that in Kuangtung and Fukien the people planted *mu-mien*, a plant seven or eight feet high with leaves resembling oak leaves and with blue fruit which looked like large water-chestnuts. In the late autumn the fruit opened and the white fibre emerged. The natives picked out the fibre from the bolls and beat it with an iron stick. The lint was then separated from the seeds with a small bow and woven into a fabric which was called *chi-pei*. The various types of the cloth worn by the people were called *pai-tieh* (PCP 3, 3b).

In the north cotton was introduced into China from Central Asia probably in the thirteenth century. The textile came from Kao-ch'ang 高昌 (Liang 54, 40a; NS 79, 14b; TS 221A, 4a; SS 490, 10a–b), Ts'êng-t'an 層檀 (SS 490, 21b), and Tukhara 吐火羅 (TS 221B, 7a). In Kao-ch'ang and other Inner Asiatic regions recently investigated by archaeologists (see Stein 21, 160, 399, 435, 786, 1315; *idem* 28, 70, 247, 664; Bergman 39, 57, 103, 105; *cf.* also Goodrich 43, 409) the cultivation of cotton may date from the fifth or sixth century. According to the *Liang Shu* (54, 40a), the cotton plant (*pai-tieh*) bears fruit like cocoons with fibres inside. The cloth made from these fibres was used as a means of exchange.

In 981 a Sung envoy, Wang Yen-tê 王延德, traveled to Kao-ch'ang. On his trip, which lasted until 984, he observed that Kao-ch'ang produced *pai-tieh* and *hua-jui pu* 花蕊布, tissues made of flower buds (SS 490, 10b).

According to SC 123, 8a, Chang Ch'ien 張騫 saw in Ta Hsia 大夏 *shu* 蜀 cloth which the T'ang commentator, Chang Shou-chieh 張守節, relates to *t'u-lu* 土蘆 cloth. Hung Hao 洪皓, who was sent to the Chin court in 1129 and remained there for fifteen years, reported that the Uighurs possessed *tou-lo mien* 兜羅綿 (SMCW 4b). In 1221 the Taoist, Ch'ang-ch'un 長春眞人, noticed in Almaliq 阿里馬 a textile called *t'u-lu ma* 禿鹿麻 (HYCCC 1, 24b).

Evidently, the terms *t'u-lu, tou-lo, t'u-lu* or *tu-lo* 妬羅

(FIMIC 7, 21a) are identical with the *tu-lo* 都落 which, according to a work of the late tenth century, was produced in Hsin 新 Prefecture (modern Kuangtung) (TPHYC 163, 4b–5a). The terms are also identical with the *tou-lo* of the *Chu Fan Chih* 諸藩志, a cloth woven of *chi-pei* and equated with the Sanskrit word, *tūla*, cotton (CFC 2, 35; Hirth and Rockhill 11, 217–219; Laufer 19, 491).

Yeh-lü Ch'u-ts'ai 楚才 (1190–1244), who in 1218 accompanied Chingis Khan to Central Asia and who stayed there several years, states in his travelogue, *Hsi Yu Lu* 西遊錄, that Samarqand had mulberry trees but no silkworms; and that the people wore clothes made of *ch'ü-shun* (HYLC 12). A Buddhist dictionary of Sanskrit words, written in 1157, explains the term *ch'ü-shun* as a fine cloth woven from the heart of the *mu-mien* 木綿 flower (FIMIC 7, 20b). A Ming compendium of agriculture lists it as an equivalent for cotton (NCCS 35, 2b).

A poem written by Yeh-lü Ch'u-ts'ai (CJCSWC 12, 147) contains the following passage:

The Western Regions have fine climate and soil;　西方好風土
Generally there are no silkworms or mulberry trees.　大率無蠶桑
Each family plants *mu-mien*;　家家植木緜
It is called the mound-planted sheep.　是爲壠種羊

The author's identification of the mound-planted sheep with *mu-mien* provides a realistic variant of the story of a miraculous plant-animal. This story was told in China from the earlier part of the first millennium A.D. on; from the fourteenth century on it bewildered the Western world. The earliest known source, Sung Ying's 宋膺 *I Wu Chih*, which was probably written under the Chin 晉 dynasty (265–420) (PCSIWC 41), relates that in the north of Ta Ch'in 大秦 there grew a lamb that remained attached by its navel to the soil from which it had sprung. The lamb died when the [stem-like] navel was cut (LCIWC 6a and 15a). The story is repeated in a number of versions in many subsequent Chinese writings devoted to the "western lands." For books that were either written under the T'ang dynasty or, after its fall, with T'ang data, see PHL 1, 16; THY 99, 1778; CTS 198, 16b; TS 221B, 11a. Chin 金 and Yüan writers, besides emphasizing the usefulness of the plant-animal's meat and fur, state that it was reproduced by planting the sheep's wool, navel, or bones (HYCCC 1, 24b; *cf.* Waley 31, 86; *Pei Shih Chi* 北使記 and *Hsi Shih Chi* 西使記 in KHCCL 6b and 10a; LCSY 10b–11a; YYC 7, 215–216). Ch'ang-ch'un equates the *t'u-lu-ma* textile plant with the miraculous sheep, thus arriving at a conclusion similar to that reached by his contemporary, Yeh-lü Ch'u-ts'ai, when the latter visited Central Asia: the "mound-planted sheep" was cotton. (Besides Yeh-lü Ch'u-ts'ai's above quoted poem, see CJCSWC 6, 73.) Wang Kuo-wei concludes that the term "mound-planted sheep" was but another designation

27. A GOVERNMENT–CONTROLLED SALT OFFICE

Hsiang-ho County was originally Sun Village of Wu-ch'ing [County].   Liao established in Hsin-ts'ang[78] a Salt Monopoly Department.   Settlers flocked there.   40, 3a

for cotton; in his opinion, the stories of Chinese travelers about the planting of sheep in the ground should be discarded (HYCCC 1, 25a).

The identification of the legendary sheep with the cotton plant is obviously correct.   There is, however, a folkloristic aspect of the fable which deserves attention.   The story of the miraculous lamb, which appears in Chinese records from the earlier part of the first millennium on was also known in the Western world, although it is recorded in its complete Eastern form only at a relatively late date.   The motive of a navel-supported creature can be found in the *Jerusalem Talmud*, a work completed in the fourth century A.D.   In the section *Kilᶜayin* of this famous Hebrew work, chapter 8, 31c [*Talmud Yerushalmi*, Berlin 1929 I, 306], the explanatory *Gemara* interprets the biblical phrase *adne sadeh* as meaning beasts that "live by their navel; if the navel is cut, they can't live." (Translation kindly provided by Dr. Ilse Lichtenstaedter.)   A distinguished commentator, Rabbi Schimschon (fl. second half of twelfth century), ascribes a human shape to the fabulous creature which grew on a navel-stem like a gourd or melon. The monster lived on the grass around it, and could not be approached unless its navel was broken; it then died (see Fink 07, 176; *cf.* also Dr. Hermann Adler's translation of this commentary in Lee 87, 7).   Thus, the *adne sadeh*, in spite of its dependence on vegetable food, is considered a man-like creature, according to L. Ginsberg (25, 50): "undoubtedly a certain species of ape."

In the fourteenth century another part of the Chinese legend made its appearance in the West, namely the idea of a plant-born lamb; this time the navel motive is absent. In 1330 Friar Odoric, depending on hearsay, told of a miraculous Asiatic plant whose melon-shaped fruits yielded little lambs (Odoric 91, 425 ff.; *cf.* also Maundeville 1839, 264).   It was only in the first part of the sixteenth century, in 1526, that the story of a navel-supported lamb was brought to the court of Emperor Maximilian V, significantly from Moscow, where Maximilian's ambassador, Sigismund von Herberstein, had heard it told of the Tatar regions near the Caspian sea (Herberstein 52 II, 74–75). The controversies aired subsequently in Western literature cannot be presented here, but the Western fable of the Vegetable Lamb of Tartary, or the Scythian Lamb, or Borametz, like the earlier Chinese versions, was evidently derived from descriptions and myths concerning the Central and Western Asiatic cotton plant (*cf.* Lee 87, 46).

In 1273, three years before the capture of the Sung Capital and six years before the annihilation of Southern Sung, Kublai Khan ordered the Bureau of Agriculture to compile the *Nung Sang Chi-yao* 農桑輯要 which contains several passages entitled *mu-mien*.   The book states that ramie was produced in the south and *mu-mien* in the west and that ramie had recently been introduced into what is now modern Honan, and *mu-mien* into what is now modern

Shensi.   Since the people of these regions benefited greatly from them, they were advised to cultivate both plants everywhere in spite of certain objections based on differences of climate and soil (NSCY 2, 21b ff.).

Judging from the above, it seems evident that in North China cotton came not from the south, but from the west, the place of entry being modern Shensi.

The exact date of the introduction of cotton into Shensi from Central Asia cannot be given, but it probably occurred between 1234 and 1264.   From 1213 to 1234 the Mongols conquered North China.   Many people were killed and captured, gardens were destroyed, and mulberry trees hewn down.   In 1234, when the whole territory of the Chin empire was occupied by the Mongols, there must have been an acute shortage of textiles. Under these circumstances, the cultivation of the quick growing cotton plant naturally suggested itself to the Mongols who controlled the Central Asiatic cotton centers. According to Wang P'an's 王磐 preface to the *Nung Sang Chi-yao*, the Yüan government between 1230 and 1264 officially promoted agriculture and sericulture.

The introduction of cotton into Northwest China in the thirteenth century implies that the valuable textile was not yet cultivated there during the Liao period.   It would, however, be precipitate to conclude from this that cotton was unknown in the Liao empire.   The Ch'i-tan maintained political, commercial, and religious relations with a number of Central Asiatic states whose governments frequently presented tributes and gifts to the Liao capital (see X, introduction, and X, 2, *passim*).   In CTKC 21, 4a the tribute paid by Kao-ch'ang, Chiu-tzǔ, and Yü-t'ien to the Liao court is called *ho-hei* 揭黑 silk, *mên-tê* 門得 silk, *p'a-li-ho* 怕里呵 and *ho-li* 褐里 silk.   These names are transcriptions of various Central Asiatic terms for textiles which, either in part or in whole, may have been made of cotton.

The records are not sufficient to prove the production of cotton in the earlier centers of the Liao state, but they make it all but certain that the Liao rulers were familiar with the "western" textile which probably came to them from Central Asia and from Sung China.   Even the less civilized eastern neighbors of the Ch'i-tan, the Jurchen, were familiar with cotton at the close of the Liao dynasty. In 1123 a Chin spokesman requested from the Sung government not only silk but also *mu-mien* (SCPMHP 14, 2b).

[75] The above text is part of a description of the seat of Tsu 祖 Prefecture, a region southwest of modern Boro Khoton, Jehol.   *Cf.* Mullie 22, 137.

[76] Liao, Sung, and Chin each had a silk brocade shop. It was obviously a weaving shop run by the government, for its director, an official of the eighth rank, was in charge of matters concerning weaving (SS 175, 1a and CS 57, 17b).

[77] *Cf.* II, introduction.

28. MINERAL PRODUCTS

Fan-shan County[79] was originally Chün-tu County of Han.   It was so named because of the alum and acetate of copper produced in the mountains.   41, 5*b*

---

[78] The town of Hsin-ts'ang 新倉 was located in Hsiang-ho 香河 County in Liao times and is now situated in the modern Pao-ti 寶坻, Hopei.

[79] Seventeen *li* west of modern Ch'ang-p'ing 昌平 County, Hopei. The name means Alum Mountain County.

COMMUNICATIONS

INTRODUCTION

1. MEANS OF COMMUNICATION

a. ROADS AND WATERWAYS

Until recent times the pastoral life of the Inner Asiatic steppes required no elaborate system of roads. There were trails made by the feet of camels and oxen and by the wheels of ox-carts.[1] But these trails were none too well marked and were not roads in the narrow sense of the term.[2] Easily made, they were easily changed and easily abandoned.[3] Such "roads" existed in the pastoral regions of the Liao empire. Cart followed cart over the trails; a single turn would destroy the ruts.[4]

The roads in the Chinese territories of the empire were vastly superior to the trails in the pastoral regions. In the tenth century Chinese observers commented on the postal stations along the wayside where the weary traveler could rest and change horses. At the close of the dynasty five roads led over five passes from the old Chinese regions to the north. Four of them could be used only by men and horses, but the main road was wide enough to permit the passage of large carts and the transport of food.[5] If it followed the Chinese pattern, it must have been adapted not only to wheeled traffic but also to "the orderly supervision of officials and tax collectors."[6] To what extent its Chinese character was preserved beyond the passes, we do not know.

A large levy was raised to build or repair the mountain roads in the northern section, but service was demanded for one day only.[7] The interest in roads was growing; yet the standard of achievement was still none too high. LS 17, 4a mentions the fact that nothing could be planted within thirty paces of the imperial highways; obviously this was a measure of protection. The imperial roads must have led through the agricultural sections of the country, for otherwise the restriction against planting would make little sense.

All these roads were extremely useful to a government which frequently shifted large armies to its borders and beyond. They were equally useful in the development of trade. New roads might be built expressly for commercial purposes.[8] In the tenth century Chinese travelers measured their journey in days spent on the road;[9] in the eleventh century they often counted the distances between places in *li*,[10] a change in emphasis that may have reflected a more precise feeling for topography, induced perhaps by the improved quality of the roads.

Bridges, which were a necessary adjunct to overland traffic in the agricultural regions, were both stationary[11] and of the floating type.[12] Warships plied the rivers,[13] but the use of the ocean for the transportation of relief grain was rejected because of the danger and inconvenience involved.[14] The horsemen of the steppe put even less confidence in the open sea than did the agricultural Chinese. The lack of information concerning canals and freight-boats is no proof of their complete absence in the Liao empire; but for geographic as well as cultural reasons they must have played a minor role in the country's system of communications.

b. ANIMALS AND VEHICLES

Overland traffic prevailed in the Liao empire. In the tribal regions, whenever possible, men and women rode on horseback,[15] but the legend of the eight tribes[16] and similar records[17] reveal that the women of Liao also drove the ox-cart. The same custom was noted by early observers of the Mongols.[18] The art of making *ch'ê-chang* 車帳, "cart tents," or better "tent carts," is said to have been learned from the expert Hei-ch'ê-tzŭ,[19] a tribe belonging to the Shih-wei

---

[1] Gilmour 93, 228.

[2] Lattimore 28, 517; Riasanovsky 37, 15; Karamisheff 25, 62.

[3] Gilmour 93, 229.

[4] VII, 2 (72).

[5] WTS 73, 6b ff. and Fu LH 35, 165 ff.

[6] Lattimore 28, 517.

[7] IV (4).

[8] IV (7).

[9] *Cf.* WTS 73, 6b ff.

[10] *Cf.* LS 37, 5b; SHYK 196, 44b–46a; CTKC 24, 2b; WHTK 346, 2709–2710.

[11] IV (5).

[12] IV (10).

[13] *Loc. cit.* See also IV (11).

[14] IV (9).

[15] IV (14).

[16] VII, 2 (84).

[17] VII, 2 (24).

[18] See Rubruck 00, 57 and *passim*.

[19] CTKC 25, 2b.

nation which was renowned for its metal workers.[20] A few hundred years later the Mongols, descendants of the Shih-wei,[21] are reported to have used very elaborate carts[22] which they may have developed from the earlier and simpler forms.

A light cart drawn either by man[23] or camel[24] is believed to have been taken over from the Hsi, another proto-Mongol people. Such carts were used by the Liao rulers,[25] and, although no identity can be established between them and the small carts favored by the Ch'i-tan nobles,[26] it is possible that they were one and the same. The large freight carts,[27] which in all probability served the needs of the army,[28] were of different construction. Ox-carts also were used by soldiers who transported the grain provisions over the long road to the northwestern border stations.[29]

Simple Chinese carts were brought to the Ch'i-tan by those Chinese peasants, traders, officials, and soldiers who, in the wake of a series of military defeats, were drawn into the orbit of the newly rising northern empire. Fine Chinese carriages appeared at the imperial court in 937.[30] The sedan chair used in the investiture ceremony by the emperor's mother may have come to the Supreme Capital along with other Chinese imperial conveyances.[31]

The ships of the Ch'i-tan varied in style and use. The Chinese had an old tradition of navigation, particularly for river-traffic, and the Po-hai certainly had some naval experience, as is indicated by their use of "pirates" for an attack against China Proper.[32] Whatever Po-hai ships were left after the conquest of 926 must have passed into the hands of their new Ch'i-tan masters. It is significant that an expansion of naval transportation was proposed by a Chinese official when grain had to be carried from the old Po-hai territory to Nan-ching Circuit. It is equally significant that the proposal was turned down by the Ch'i-tan court because the route was "dangerous."[33] This was in 1029. Seventeen years later, in the campaign against Hsia, the Liao government faced an enemy familiar with water-courses and naval warfare. To bring their fight to a successful conclusion the

Ch'i-tan had to use warships. They even built new ones,[34] probably with the help of Chinese artisans, thus proving that they could manufacture ships[35] which though smaller than those of Sung were still of considerable size. In 1111 two Liao vessels, carrying two hundred persons,[36] arrived in Sung waters. These facts are worthy of note but whether they imply any basic change in the Ch'i-tan attitude toward naval affairs is doubtful.

2. COMMUNICATIONS
a. GOVERNMENTAL SERVICE

Oriental absolutism has generally organized the control of the nerve centers of communications with great care.[37] When the Ch'i-tan took over part of the former T'ang empire, they inherited a well-developed governmental system of communications.[38] This the northern conquerors eagerly adapted to their own political needs.

The Liao government freely mobilized its subjects and their draft animals. Grain was transported to the granaries by families who were in charge of government herds.[39] These herds, which must have included horses and oxen, obviously served the needs of government traffic, as did the imperial herds of the Manchu dynasty a thousand years later.[40] Each year a corvée was imposed upon the people in order to move the government coal.[41] The official who criticised certain inequalities in this corvée belonged to the government of the Southern Region; evidently the business of transporting coal was handled by persons attached to the "southern" administration. However, the Ch'i-tan tribes also had to render labor service.[42] Early and late Mongol parallels indicate that these services consisted chiefly in transporting government officials and government freight.[43]

For the quick dispatch of messages and men a special organization, usually referred to as a postal service, was set up. In view of its functions, however, it seems more appropriate to speak of it as a courier and relay system, a system which has a long history in China.[44] The T'ang government maintained more than 1,500 individual relay stations: 1,297 were inland

[20] See III (3).
[21] See I, 2 (5), no. 21.
[22] Rubruck 00, 55.
[23] CTKC 24, 2a–b.
[24] TCTC 284, 9a, note.
[25] IV (3).
[26] IV (14).
[27] Loc. cit.
[28] IV (12).
[29] XV, 1 (51).
[30] III (10).
[31] Loc. cit.
[32] WHTK 326, 2567.
[33] IV (9).

[34] IV (11).
[35] JCSP 9, 4a–b; AJCTC 5, 199–200; see IV, note 19.
[36] SCPMHP 1, 2a; see IV, note 16.
[37] See Wittfogel, OS (ms).
[38] Cf. Balázs 32 BWT, 38–41.
[39] V (18).
[40] Timkowski 1827 I, 202.
[41] XI (21).
[42] XI, introduction.
[43] Cf. Riasanovsky 37, 95; Lattimore 30, 233; idem 41 12 ff. and 34.
[44] Cf. HCS, Ch'in and Han, IV, introduction (ms).

stations, 260 were "water posts," and 86 were mixed in character.[45]

Like that of T'ang, the relay system of the Liao empire was reserved for government use. The decree of 1082 imposed great restrictions upon the transport of goods and made no provision for private travelers.[46] Naturally envoys from foreign countries were expected to travel by courier post. They were provided with lodgings at the stations[47] and had to be fed by the local population.[48] LS 12, 2b records the establishment of new courier stations in the southern sector of the empire.[49] Every county was supposed to have its own relay stations for which the local population had to provide the necessary horses and oxen.[50]

To be safe the courier service had to be exclusive; to be effective it had to be fast. Chinese envoys sent from the Sung court to the old territory of Chin 金 rested at the stations provided for such high dignitaries in China Proper as well as in the northeastern border territory. They covered an average of seventy, eighty, or ninety li a day.[51] But the courier service was much faster; couriers of the Chin 金 dynasty attained a maximum speed of three hundred li a day,[52] while the first Liao emperor, T'ai-tsu, once covered the tremendous distance of six hundred li in a day.[53] This may be considered unusual, for in hurrying to his mother, who was ill, the emperor probably did not consider the number of horses he ruined. Still another record indicates the extraordinary speed of which the Liao courier service was capable. In an emergency an imperial message might be dispatched at a daily speed of seven hundred li; in a less serious situation an average of five hundred li was set as the standard.[54]

If the Ch'i-tan couriers, who seem to have had more endurance than the horsemen of Chin, achieved a maximum speed of five to seven hundred li a day and if the distance between the eastern and western limits of the empire was approximately three thousand li, then an imperial message could be carried by the courier service from the Korean border to the far western garrisons in about six days; from any point near the center it could be carried in three or four. The political significance of these figures is evident.

---

[45] TLT 5, 12a–b.
[46] IV (13).
[47] IV (15).
[48] XI (7).
[49] IV (6).
[50] XIV, 2 (9).
[51] TCKC 40, 1a ff. and *passim*.
[52] CS 55, 15b.
[53] IV (2).
[54] IV (16).

b. PRIVATE COMMUNICATIONS

The official history pays little attention to the movements of private individuals within the Liao empire. Uighur merchants traded with the Supreme Capital. Buddhist monks, Chinese students, and business men visited the centers of worship, learning, and trade, and each no doubt availed himself of those means of communication permitted to his status and suitable to his needs. A high Buddhist dignitary might with propriety be offered a comfortable chariot;[55] merchants probably preferred horses for themselves and carts for their goods.

The tribes in the grasslands and valleys still followed the old nomadic way of life. The records show that they migrated from place to place as did their tribal "cousins" in the vast steppes of western and Central Asia. Rubruck, describing his first meeting with a caravan of Mongol tent-carts, wrote, "a city was coming towards me. I was also astonished at the size of the herds of oxen and horses and flocks of sheep, though I saw but few men to manage them."[56] A recent description of the spring trek of a Turkestan tribe gives some idea of the orderly way in which many animals can be directed by a few young people and a few old ones. Says Lattimore: "First came pony herds, driven ahead to trample down the going, herded by the most hardy and skillful of the young men, armed with long poles with a running noose of rope at the end,—a crude anticipation of the lasso,— the herding pole of the Qazaqs and Mongols. After them came oxen and cows, loaded with tents, babies in their cradles, new-born lambs; or bestridden by women with babies in front of them and puppies or cooking pots tied on behind. Behind them again were the camels, more heavily laden still, sprawling frequently on the slippery footing that camels hate most and having to be rescued with digging, beating, and pulling of the tail. Many of the cow camels carried their January-born calves lashed on top of their own loads, bulging with yurt-felts and the tent-chests in which the nomad carries his more precious things. The calves nodded and bobbed unconcernedly in their high nests; but the mothers could not see them, and, thinking them lost, howled and moaned bubblingly, one of the worst of noises. Last of all came the sheep, in bumping, humping, struggling flocks; slowest and most unhandy of all the stock, but precious, being the basis of wealth in the nomadic life; thousands of sheep and a few hundred goats. They were in the charge of half-grown boys and girls, riding half-grown ponies and bullocks and cows, who leaned frequently from their crude saddles to pick up exhausted lambs until cantle and pommel were all

---

[55] IX (42).
[56] Rubruck 00, 86.

hung about with little bleating bundles of wool and snow. The lambs ranged all the way from the autumn-born, already able to fend for themselves, through the winter-born to the spring-born; nor was the season over, for at least one ewe cast her lamb on the march, as I saw. The great camp dogs ran where they liked, quiet on the march as a good dog should be, but the shivering greyhounds were dragged in leash. Most valuable of all, the hooded berkut, the magnificent hunting eagles, were in the charge of graybeards not fit for active work up and down the line of the caravan, whose burdened wrists were supported on crutches, socketed in the stirrup."[57]

In general the trek of the Ch'i-tan followed the Turkestan pattern, but some differences may be noted. The Ch'i-tan had few camels and as far as we know their women did not ride the ox; they rode on horseback or drove the ox-cart which carried the family tent and other belongings. The *Chin Shih* tells of three thousand Ch'i-tan families who, led by Yü-tu 余睹, surrendered to Chin in 1121. They had with them many thousand cattle and five thousand carts.[58] Loaded with goods and tents, these thousands of carts must indeed have been another city on wheels slowly wending its way over the hilly northeastern grasslands.

---

[57] Lattimore 30, 117–118.

[58] CS 2, 16*a*; 133, 5*a–b*.

COMMUNICATIONS

1. Cart-pullers offered   2. Six hundred *li* covered in one day   3. The emperor rides a Hsi cart and a camel   4. Mountain roads   5. Boats and a bridge   6. The courier service   7. New roads   8. Nothing may be planted near imperial highways   9. Sea transport considered dangerous   10. Boats and bridges   11. Warships   12. An army on the march   13. Regulations for the imperial courier service   14. Chariots and other means of communication   15. Courier stations   16. Conveyance of imperial orders

1. CART–PULLERS OFFERED

909   [In the tenth month of the third year of T'ai-tsu's accession] the Wu-niang-kai[1] tribe of the northwest[2] offered cart-pullers.   69, 2a

2. SIX HUNDRED *LI* COVERED IN ONE DAY

919   In the ninth month [of the fourth year of Shên-ts'ê], while on his way to attack the Wu-ku tribe, [the emperor] heard that his mother was not well.   In one day he galloped back six hundred *li* to attend to her illness.   When she recovered somewhat, he returned to the army.   2, 1a

3. THE EMPEROR RIDES A HSI CART AND A CAMEL

945   Fu Yen-ch'ing[3] attacked the flank of the Liao army with ten thousand mounted soldiers and at the same time led an infantry force forward.   As the Liao army was at a disadvantage, the emperor, riding a Hsi cart,[4] retired more than ten *li*.   The pursuing army of Chin pressed forward.   He obtained a camel, mounted it, and returned.[5]   4, 11b

4. MOUNTAIN ROADS

984   In the autumn [of the second year of T'ung-ho] an imperial decree ordered the building of mountain roads.   [Shih] Fang[6] mobilized two hundred thousand people and finished the work in one day.   79, 1b

---

[1] According to the glossary in LS 116, 3b, 唱 has the sound of *chiu* 九, but probably is an error for *wan* 九. In Mongol and Manchu the final consonant -*n* may in special cases be omitted; thus the phoneme *wan* 唱 may have resembled either *wa*, *wu*, or *wo*.

The location of this tribe, the Uriangkhai, was originally in Outer Mongolia or Siberia (*cf.* I, 2 (9), no. 33).

[2] The Supreme Capital was the political center of the whole empire.   Such terms as southeast, northwest, etc. were generally formulated in relation to the Supreme Capital.

[3] Fu Yen-ch'ing 符彦卿 (T. 冠侯), a general of Chin 晉, served four short-lived dynasties in succession, namely Later T'ang, Later Chin, Later Chou, and finally Sung. He died in 975 (SS 251, 6b–10b).

In 943, after friendly relations between Liao and Chin had been broken off, the emperor of Liao personally led a campaign southward into the territory of Chin.   A battle was fought north of modern Ting 定 County, Hopei, in which the Ch'i-tan soldiers were defeated.

[4] A Sung scholar, Shên K'uo, describes the Hsi cart as narrow in the front and wide in the rear, with large wheels and a long body.   It was made of light material and thus easily broke down.   These carts, drawn by camels, were unsuited for heavy loads but were very useful for traveling through hilly country (TCTC 284, 9a, note).

Su Sung, in a poem on the Hsi, says,

Blue felt curtains with window openings: 青氈通幨
These are the carts of the nobles.   貴人車
He adds in a note, "The enclosures of the carts of the noble families were chiefly made of blue felt" (LSSI 13, 24a).

Liu Ch'ang 劉敞 (T. 原父, 1019–1068) in a poem speaks of

Barbarian horses grazing in the cold;   虜馬寒隨草
Hsi carts nightly covered by the stars.   奚車夕戴星
He remarks in a note, "The Hsi people live in cart-tents (車帳) which move day and night" (KSC 22, 256).

Wang Tsêng 王曾 (T. 孝先, 978–1033), during his journey to Liao in 1017, found that most of the people in Chung-ching, the old center of the Hsi people, were cart-makers (SHYK 196, 46a).   The carts of the Hsi were obviously as famous as the horses of the Ch'i-tan.

[5] According to CTKC 3, 2a and TCTC 284, 9b, the Ch'i-tan were badly defeated by Chin and lost a great number of horses and large quantities of armor, weapons, and other military equipment.   T'ai-tsung escaped (the text merely says "returned") on camel-back to Yu Prefecture (modern Peiping) where the generals responsible for the defeat were punished.

[6] Shih Fang 室昉 (T. 夢奇), a native of the Southern Capital, gained a good reputation because of his honesty and scholarship.   He received the degree of *chin-shih* in the middle of the tenth century and in 991 compiled

5. BOATS AND A BRIDGE

985   On the day *ping-yin* [of the seventh month in the third year of T'ung-ho] the emperor halted at the T'u River. Because the river suddenly rose, the emperor ordered the construction of boats and a bridge.[7]   10, 8*a*

6. THE COURIER SERVICE

988   On the day *kuei-ch'ou* [of the seventh month in the autumn of the sixth year of T'ung-ho, Hsiao] P'ai-ya[8] requested the establishment of an additional courier post in Cho Prefecture.[9]   12, 2*b*

7. NEW ROADS

989   On the day *ping-shên* [of the third month in the seventh year of T'ung-ho] an imperial decree ordered roads developed in Ch'i-fêng[10] in order to establish communications with I Prefecture market.   12, 5*b*

8. NOTHING MAY BE PLANTED NEAR IMPERIAL HIGHWAYS

1027   On the day *i-ssŭ* [of the seventh month in the seventh year of T'ai-p'ing] an imperial decree stated that the land within thirty paces of the imperial highways, which was forbidden to be cultivated, was not within[11] the scope of the [regular] jurisdiction.[12]   17, 4*a*

9. SEA TRANSPORT CONSIDERED DANGEROUS

1029   In the ninth year [of T'ai-p'ing] a famine occurred in the region of Yen.[13] The vice-commissioner of the Ministry of Revenue,[14] Wang Chia, requested that ships be built and that men familiar with sea transportation be recruited in order to transfer the grain of Liao-tung[15] to supply Yen. The persons who discussed [the plan] said that the route was dangerous and inconvenient.[16] Therefore [the plan] was set aside.   59, 2*b*

10. BOATS AND BRIDGES

1046   In the fifteenth year [of Ch'ung-hsi, Hsiao P'u-nu[17]] was appointed punitive commissioner of the Southwestern Region. During the western punitive campaign[18]

---

twenty chapters of the *Veritable Records*. He died in 994. When the above mentioned event took place, he had just become chancellor and prime minister of the Northern Administration (LS 79, 1*a* ff.). The roads were therefore located in the northern part of the empire, a fact which explains well the speed with which they could be built or repaired.

[7] A Liao inscription of 1084 says that the Sang-ch'ien 桑乾 River overflowed during the summer, causing a great loss in people and animals. To build a bridge, Buddhist monks collected donations to the amount of one thousand strings of cash. Rocks were used for the foundation and the arches, and lumber for the roadway. The large logs were fifty-five feet long and a foot and a half in diameter; the small logs thirty-five feet long and a foot and a half in diameter. The rails consisted of a number of sections, each of which was five feet long (TCHC 3, 35*a* ff.).

[8] Hsiao P'ai-ya 排押 (or 亞). A descendant of the empress' clan who married Ching-tsung's second daughter. He reached the position of prime minister and obtained the title of Prince of Tung-p'ing 東平. He died in 1023 (LS 65, 2*b*; 88, 2*b*–3*a*).

[9] Modern Cho 涿 County, Hopei.

[10] The only other mention of this place is in LS 60, 1*b* (see V (4)). Its location, though not exactly known, may have been near I Prefecture (modern I 易 County, Hopei).

I Prefecture had just been captured from Sung in the first month of 989. Hence the roads in question may have been developed between the Southern Capital and I Prefecture for military as well as commercial reasons.

[11] We follow the Southern Academy edition in reading 在 for the 得 of our text.

[12] The land used by the emperor was called "the forbidden land" (禁地). As a rule it was not taxed. Any crime committed in this region was punished with particular severity. The area was not within the jurisdiction of the courts.

[13] Modern Peiping.

[14] This office was located in the Eastern Capital. See VI, 1, note 10 and XIV, 2 (7).

[15] An old term for the modern province of Liaoning.

[16] In 1111 the head of Têng 登 Prefecture of Sung submitted a report to his government about two Liao boats with two hundred persons which had arrived at T'o-chi 駝基 Island. The sailors said that they had intended to go to Korea in order to escape from the war but the wind had altered their course (SCPMHP 1, 2*a*).

[17] Hsiao P'u-nu 蒲奴, a descendant of a noble Hsi family, several times held the position of great king of the Six Tribes of Hsi (LS 87, 4*b*).

[18] From 1049 to 1050.

against the state of Hsia, [Hsiao] P'u-nu, with two thousand soldiers, held a [floating] bridge on the [Yellow] River and assembled several tens of large war-junks.[19]   He also had some large hooks made [for some purpose] which the people did not understand.   On the day of the battle he spread the boats out over the river in a long line of more than thirty *li*.   He dispatched men to watch the upper course of the river and to pick up immediately whatever floated down.

That the main army had already been defeated was not yet known to [Hsiao] P'u-nu.   It happened that large logs floating downstream threatened to destroy the floating bridge[20] and to cut off the line of retreat.   The men who manned the boats struggled to divert them with the hooks, so that the bridge managed to escape destruction.   87, 4*b*–5*a*

11. WARSHIPS

1048   In the seventeenth year [of Ch'ung-hsi], while walled cities were being built along
                   the western frontier, [Yeh-lü] To-chên[21] was ordered to inspect the terrain and to construct warships.[22]   Thereupon he completed one hundred and thirty multiple-decked ships. Soldiers were put on the upper decks; horses were stowed below.   Their construction was sturdy and accorded with the will of the emperor.

At the time of the western campaign [against Hsia] an imperial decree ordered To-chên to lead his troops via a by-path and to come together on the bank of the [Yellow] River.   The enemy soldiers drew up their lines with the river as a barrier.   The emperor led the warships across the river and attacked them.   He gained a great victory and then returned.   93, 6*a*

12. AN ARMY ON THE MARCH

1049   The next year the emperor[23] led another punitive campaign against the state of
                   Hsia.[24]   [Hsiao] Hui[25] advanced south along the [Yellow] River[26] with warships and supply boats which were spread out over several hundred *li*.   When he had penetrated enemy territory, the patrols did not go far, the armor was packed into carts, and the soldiers were not permitted to mount their horses.   All the generals demanded that preparations be made against an emergency. [Hsiao] Hui said, "[Li] Liang-tsu[27] will himself surely go to meet the emperor.   How will he have

---

[19] Before the war against Hsia the Liao government had boats built at T'ien-tê 天德 Commandery (in modern Suiyuan) for navigation on the Yellow River (WKC 36, 438).   Judging from a statement made by a Liao monk to the Sung scholar, Hung Mai, these Liao boats were not so large as those of the Sung empire: "The Southerners do not believe the Northerners have tents that cover a thousand persons, while the Northerners do not believe that the Southerners have boats that carry ten thousand bushels" (JCSP 9, 4*a*–*b*; AJCTC 5, 199–200).

[20] They were probably made of beams, small boats, or hollow floats, somewhat similar to modern pontoon bridges.

[21] A member of the Chi-ch'ing Palace who gained renown during the war between Liao and Sung (LS 93, 6*a*).

[22] The transportation of military provisions both on land and water was sometimes effected by large boats with four wheels which could move like carts on land, and which when the wheels were removed could be used on the Yellow River or elsewhere (PCP 10, 1*b*).

[23] Hsing-tsung.   He failed in this campaign as his father, Shêng-tsung, had failed in Korea.

[24] In 986 Hsia for the first time submitted to Liao: Liao, in turn, honored Hsia by presenting its ruler with a princess to be his wife.   In 1044 Hsia rebelled again and several expeditions were sent against it, but without success.   In the same year an expedition led by Em-

peror Hsing-tsung himself also failed (LS 115, 6*b*–8*b*). After the failure of the campaign Hsing-tsung in a proclamation boasted of his "victory" over Hsia.   The Sung spies, however, inferred the truth from the numerous corpses and wounded soldiers who were taken back from the west.   The Hsia troops used several devices to weaken the Liao assault.   First, they burnt all the provisions and the grass along the road; then they retreated several hundred *li*.   The Liao soldiers and horses found no food and starved before they saw the enemy (MHPT 25, 164; JLKI 2, 27).   In 1049 the emperor again attacked the western country, but his army suffered a second defeat. The latter campaign is the subject of our text (LS 115, 8*b*–9*a*).

[25] Hsiao Hui 惠, a descendant of the consort family and husband of Hsing-tsung's sister, was promoted to the position of northern chancellor in spite of his lack of ability.   He died in 1056 (LS 93, 1*a*–3*a*).   Probably his name was Hsiao Hsiao-hui 孝惠 since the names of his brothers and cousins all included the word *hsiao* as shown in Sung literature (*cf.* TPCCTL 8, 47*b*).

[26] Probably in the vicinity of modern Pao-t'ou 包頭, Suiyuan.

[27] Li Liang-tsu 李諒祚, the king of Hsia who ruled from 1048 to 1068, proved to be as able as his father, Li Yüan-hao 元昊, the former king.

time to make contact with us?   To make preparations without reason means only to wear oneself out to no purpose."   93, 2b

13. REGULATIONS FOR THE IMPERIAL COURIER SERVICE

1082   On the day *hsin-yu* [of the second month in the eighth year of Ta-k'ang] an imperial decree was issued to the officials of the Northern and Southern Divisions ordering that anyone given permission to use the courier service had first to be reported to the throne.   Only for tributes of fresh things[28] and for memorials concerning litigations might the express service be used.   With these exceptions it was forbidden in all cases.   24, 3b

14. CHARIOTS AND OTHER MEANS OF COMMUNICATION

The Ch'i-tan by ancient custom found it convenient to use saddled horses.   For moving in search of water and grass they used felt carts.   For carrying loads they had big carts.   The women rode horses.   There were also small carts which those who were noble and rich decorated with elegant ornaments.   Restrictions [on the use of ornaments] were lax and lenient.   Serviceability alone was considered important.   That the emperor and empress were invested with regal trappings was natural.   We collect what can be known and list it here:

The Great Imperial Chariot.   In the Firewood Investiture Ceremony[29] and in the Rebirth Ceremony[30] it could be seen carrying the ancestral tablets.[31]

The Imperial Chariot.   In the La Ceremony[32] it could be seen when the emperor and empress ascended and descended the Imperial Chariot.

The Imperial Chariot with a Grand Banner.   It was pulled by an imperial camel.   In the Ceremony of the Sacrificial Offering to the Mountain it appeared when the empress dowager ascended the Imperial Chariot with a Grand Banner.[33]

The Chariot.   In the Wedding Ceremony of the Empress it appeared when the empress ascended the Chariot.

The Chariot with a Blue Curtain.   Two dragon heads covered the [upper] section.   Both were decorated with silver.   To draw it a camel was used.   It was bestowed upon a princess who was being married. . . .

The Funeral Chariot.   The body of the chariot was completely decorated with brocade and with silver dragon heads.   Bells were suspended below; a large [piece of] felt hung down in the rear. To draw it an ox was used.   On the chariot was carried a single lamb which was called the "sacrificial lamb."   It was supposed to be used in the funeral.   It too was bestowed upon a princess.

The [Sedan] Chair.   In the Investiture Ceremony for the Empress Dowager the emperor mounted a [sedan] chair[34] which was carried from the Private Hall to Hsi-pien Gate.[35]

Saddled horses.   In the Ceremony of the Sacrifice to the Mountain the emperor rode a horse in attendance on the empress dowager.   In the La Ceremony the emperor descended from the Imperial Chariot, offered his sacrifice to the east, and then rode a horse into the place of the battue.   In the Sê-sê Ceremony[36] both mounted horses and rode toward the east [between] the courtiers on the south and titled ladies on the north.   55, 2a–b

---

[28] Obviously meaning perishable goods such as fruits, fish, etc.

[29] For the full description of this ceremony see VII, 2 (87).

[30] An old Ch'i-tan ceremony originally held in honor of an *i-li-chin*. See VII, 2 (86).

[31] LS 49, 4b enumerates the seven ancestral tablets, namely those of T'ai-tsu, T'ai-tsung, Shih-tsung, Mu-tsung, Ching-tsung, Shêng-tsung, and Hsing-tsung.

[32] Held annually during the twelfth month at a hunting ground. See VII, 2 (93).

[33] In 1005 Ts'ao Li-yung 曹利用 saw the Empress Dowager Ch'êng-t'ien ride in a camel-drawn chariot. She was accompanied by the northern chancellor Han Tê-jang with whom she discussed military problems (LCPC 2b).

[34] This passage speaks only of a "chair" (椅), but the description of the Investiture Ceremony of the Empress Dowager in LS 52, 4b mentions a "shoulder-carried chair" (肩輿), evidently a sedan chair. *Cf.* also SS 150, 2a ff. and 9a ff.

[35] The Private Hall was probably not used for formal audiences but as a residence for the emperor, the empress, and the court ladies. The Hsi-pien Gate was probably west of the palace.

[36] This ceremony was held in order to procure rain when the country suffered from a drought. See VII, 2 (81).

15. COURIER STATIONS[37]

In the southwest[38] was the T'ung-wên courier station. The envoys from foreign countries lodged there. Southwest of the courier station was the Lin-huang courier station. It was used for receiving emissaries from the state of Hsia.[39] West of the courier station was the Fu-hsien Temple.   37, 5a

16. CONVEYANCE OF IMPERIAL ORDERS

Two hundred silver tablets[40] a foot long were engraved with [Ch'i-tan] national characters which read, "Speed!" or "Tablet to gallop a horse by imperial decree." When the state was confronted with a serious affair, the emperor personally gave the tablets to the messengers and noted the number of relay horses to be supplied. In case relay horses were lacking, other horses were taken over as substitutes. According to the law, in a day and night they had to make a run of seven hundred li, the next being five hundred li. The arrival at a place was as if the emperor himself had arrived. No one dared object to any demands or changes [of horses]. When a messenger returned, the emperor personally received the tablet and affixed a seal to it with his own hands. It was taken over and cared for by the court gentleman for tablets and seals.   57, 3a

---

[37] In 1055, when the Sung envoy Liu Ch'ang moved beyond the Ku-pei Pass toward the Central Capital, he was led along a mountainous road more than a thousand li away from his destination. The Liao escorts when interrogated replied that the route could not be changed as the stations were arranged in this way. The envoy suspected a political motive, namely the attempt to impress upon the Sung visitor the size of the Liao territory (PCC 35, 468; KSC 22, 256). In view of the fact that many Chinese visitors had traversed the Liao empire, this explanation is not very plausible. Besides topographical reasons, the detour may have been organized as a means of hiding certain temporary or permanent features of the Liao defence system.

[38] In the southwestern section of the Supreme Capital.

[39] Of course, the Liao courier system was extended also to the eastern border. From 1056 on, the Korean government several times demanded the abolition of the "postal station" (郵亭) outside the gate of Kung Ku 弓口, east of the Yalu River, because it encroached upon Korean sovereignty. The Liao government did not comply with the request (TKTK 17, 439–440).

[40] According to the *Yen-pei Lu*, there were three kinds of tablets: (1) silver tablets (銀牌) with an engraved Ch'i-tan word equivalent to the Chinese word 朕, which were used only for mobilizing troops (see fig. 2 (b)); (2) long tablets (長牌) with three engraved Ch'i-tan words equivalent to the Chinese expression 敕走馬, which were used for delivering tributes (see fig. 2 (a)); (3) wooden tablets (木刻子牌) with an engraved Ch'i-tan word equivalent to the Chinese word 急, which were used for demanding tribute and soldiers from the Jurchen and Tatars (see fig. 2 (c)). Tablets of these kinds were already used under the T'ang dynasty from which they were evidently adopted by the Liao government (KTLYK 12, 106).

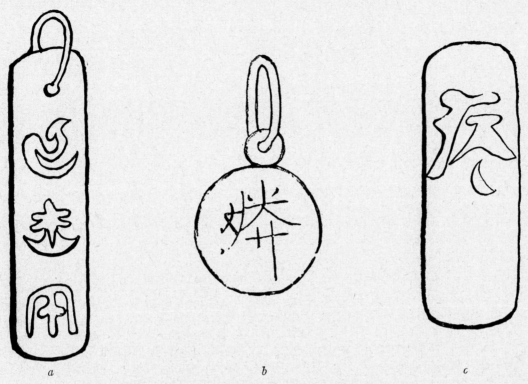

FIG. 2. Three inscribed Ch'i-tan tablets: (*a*) a gilt tablet, (*b*) a silver credential, (*c*) a wooden tablet. Copied from the *Yen-pei Lu* in a Ming edition of *Shuo-fu* 56.

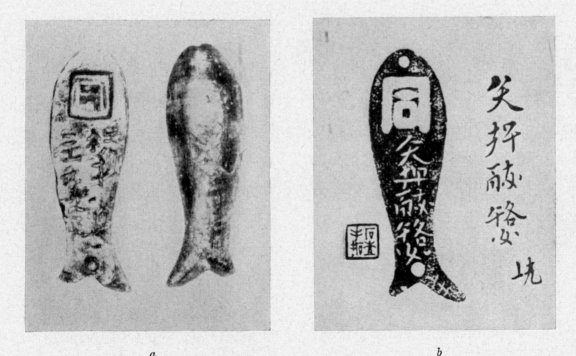

FIG. 3. Fish-tallies with Ch'i-tan characters: (*a*) (HCCSC 1, 39*a*), (*b*) (LLSKCL 5).

SECTION V

COMMERCE

INTRODUCTION

1. MORE PRODUCTS THAN MERCHANDISE

The Liao government, like its typically Chinese predecessors, penetrated all aspects of the country's economic life. Many of the commodities produced, transported, and consumed were handled directly by the government, which left little opportunity to the private entrepreneur to act as middle-man. Quantities of grain, cattle, and textiles passed from producer to consumer through such channels as taxes or tribute and were again paid out as salaries, presents, or relief without ever entering into the country's commerce. Our examination of the commerce of Liao does not concern itself with such areas of public administration.

2. TRADE AND TRADERS

a. TRIBAL TRADE

To the markets of Liao the tribes brought their many products. The survey in LS 60, 1a[1] looks like a catalogue of their pastoral, hunting, fishing, and industrial achievements. There are listed the animals of the herds—oxen, sheep, camels, horses—and the felt made from wool. Hunters brought the skins of moles and sables; fishermen, their catch of fish and pearls. The semi-sedentary Jurchen sold honey, wax, gold, and hempen cloth.

The tribal trade of Inner Asia depended until recently upon barter. This system, which has interested travelers and sociologists[2] and bewildered and inconvenienced economists and business men,[3] was typical for the tribes of Inner Asia; it prevailed in the tribal sectors of China's great dynasties of conquest. Turkic tribes are known to have exchanged their animals, hides, and furs for textiles before and during the time of the Liao dynasty.[4] The Chinese envoy to the new Chin capital saw the Jurchen trade product for product without the use of coined money.[5] Carpini found the Mongols eager for all kinds of cloth.[6] Rubruck saw sheep and skins pass in exchange be-

tween tribal Mongols.[7] The famous traveler "could find nothing to buy with gold and silver, but only with linen or other tissues."[8]

It is therefore not surprising to learn that in the middle of the tenth century the commercial transactions in the Supreme Capital of the Liao empire were carried on not in cash but in a natural money which Hu Chiao calls *pu* 布.[9] Within China Proper the term *pu* was applied to a spade-shaped copper coin which was minted approximately a thousand years before the Liao dynasty, in the Chou period,[10] and under Wang Mang in the middle of the Han period.[11] But no spade-shaped money for the Liao period is mentioned in the historical texts or in the reports of numismatic investigators.

The original meaning of the word *pu* is cloth.[12] Chavannes translates the term *pu* as cloth, and Mullie follows him.[13] Taking into consideration the basic meaning of the word and the trade habits of the Inner Asiatic nomads this translation seems fully justified. Cloth in general may have served as the preferred medium of exchange; it may even have been standardized money. According to Barthold's translation of a statement made by Mahmūd-al-Kāshgharī, the Uighurs used as money a piece of cloth of a definite size, called *qamdu*. *Qamdu*, which was stamped with the seal of the Uighur khan for authenticity, was washed, repaired, and restamped every seven years.[14]

Another interpreter of the same passage assumes that the *qamdu* were standardized pieces of cloth on which trade agreements were recorded. Every seven years the texts were washed off, then restored, and the cloths restamped.[15] Such a procedure would seem to be not only troublesome but precarious.

The idea of a standardized form of cloth money is much more plausible; its temporary diffusion to the northern Ch'i-tan capital through Uighur merchants

---

[1] V (4).

[2] See Timkowski 1827 II, 315; Prejevalsky 76 I, 58; Riasanovsky 37, 15; Lattimore 29, 60; *idem* 30, 13 and 37.

[3] *Cf.* North Manchuria 24, 153; Karamisheff 25, 38.

[4] Barthold 28, 237 ff.; *idem* 35, 71.

[5] SCPMHP 20, 12a; TCKC 40, 8a; *cf.* Chavannes 98 VC, 425.

[6] Carpini 00, 23 ff.; *idem* 28, 49.

[7] Rubruck 00, 68.

[8] *Op. cit.*, 90.

[9] V (3).

[10] Traditionally 1122–255 B.C. For pictures of the Chou coins see Coole 36, 29.

[11] A.D. 9–23. For Wang Mang's *pu* money *cf.* HS 24B, 24a ff.

[12] SWCTC 7B, 107.

[13] Chavannes 97 VC, 399.

[14] See Barthold 35, 118.

[15] Brockelmann 28, 144.

would be natural enough in view of the close Uighur-Ch'i-tan contact and the unusual position of the Uighur merchants in the Supreme Capital. But, whether Barthold's interpretation of Mahmūd-al-Kāshgharī's report is accepted or not, our texts leave little doubt that the Ch'i-tan rulers of Liao valued textiles as highly as did the other pastoral people of contemporary Inner Asia. Even after the spread of coined money, textiles, particularly silk, were still used instead of cash. The designation of the regional treasuries as Offices of Money and Silk,[16] although formally following an old Chinese nomenclature, may also have given concrete expression to the convergence of two different traditions.

These considerations have led us to accept Chavannes' translation. When Hu Chiao visited the northern regions of the Liao empire, the tribal form of exchange still seems to have prevailed.

b. TRADE IN THE AGRICULTURAL CENTERS

Although the government claimed a considerable share of the country's production, what remained was enough to supply the markets of the interior and those along the far-flung borders of Liao with large quantities of varied merchandise. A lively trade is reported in the administrative centers of Shang-ching Circuit,[17] in the seat of the "ancestral" district (Tsu Prefecture[18]), in the Eastern Capital,[19] and in smaller cities of the old Po-hai kingdom.[20] The Southern Capital (Yen-ching) had three markets filled with "all the products of the soil and the sea."[21] Besides these, markets were established at other important trade centers. The region along the Shira Muren with its many agricultural settlements had a special market center in Sung-chiang County.[22] Commercial life flourished in government-controlled markets near the Korean border,[23] near the Hsia border,[24] and far to the west in the Turfan border region.[25] Hsiung Prefecture in modern Hopei was a gateway of commerce with China Proper.[26]

In metropolitan market streets that ran between double rows of houses, in crowded town squares below the watch-towers, in the emperor's splendid traveling camps, and in picturesque border bazaars, the government officials supervised the private sale of salt, metal goods, wine, and pastoral products for coined money, cloth, or other commodities.

c. MEASURES AND PRICES

Chinese artisans and Chinese merchants probably set the technical standards of industry and trade for the agricultural centers of the empire. At first they must have used measurements valid in the T'ang period. Whether they later accepted the somewhat larger measurements of the Sung dynasty we do not know. The T'ang *shêng* 升 (pint) was equal to 0.5944 liter and the *tou* 斗 (peck), to 5.944 liters. During the Sung dynasty a pint was equal to 0.6641 liter and a peck to 6.641 liters.[27] Unfortunately no details can be found regarding the Liao measures which were fixed anew in 1082.

Money equivalents are given for grain. The government tended to keep the price of grain low when it calculated tax money in terms of grain, and five cash were originally equated with one peck of millet. This rate was considered unfair to the taxpayer and the money equivalent was raised to six cash.[28] In the free market, prices must have differed considerably according to regional and historical conditions, but they had one thing in common, namely—they were generally higher than the rate of conversion fixed by the government. Six cash for one peck was considered worthy of note;[29] "a few cash" (the exact figure is not given) was looked upon as extraordinary.[30] If five to six cash for one peck of grain was the average government and a low private price, then the average high price must have been considerably above this level.

During the negotiations in the inflationary year of 1123 over the revenue of Nan-ching Circuit a Sung representative stated that a peck of grain (*su* 粟) formerly costing a hundred cash was selling for a thousand.[31] The last figure is consistent with the picture of economic chaos in this period given in the *Liao Shih:* during the famine of 1118 a peck of grain was traded for several bolts of lustring,[32] each probably worth from two to five strings of money.[33] More difficult to explain is the assertion that in Nan-ching the price of grain, prior to the extreme inflation, was as high as one hundred cash. It is possible that the Sung spokesman was ignorant of price conditions

---

[16] XIV, 2 (10).

[17] V (19).

[18] V (20).

[19] V (21).

[20] V (4).

[21] SCPMHP 20, 3b; TCKC 40, 2a.

[22] V (23).

[23] V (4), LS 60, 1a (Po-hai); op. cit., 1b (Pao Prefecture).

[24] Op. cit., 1b (Chên-wu Prefecture).

[25] Op. cit., 1a (Kao-ch'ang).

[26] Loc. cit.

[27] Cf. Wu CL 37, 71.

[28] X, 1 (2).

[29] II, 2 (32).

[30] II, 2 (8).

[31] SCPMHP 13, 7b.

[32] XII (118).

[33] In the course of the Sung-Chin negotiations of 1123 the money value of a number of categories of silk is given. The conversion rate, according to quality, ranged from two to five strings of money per bolt (SCPMHP 13, 8a–b).

prevailing in the golden days of Liao rule; or perhaps he shrewdly offered this round number which accorded with the one to ten ratio given in the Chin documents, but which may have been well above the real price. If he had admitted a lower "peace-time" price, he would have given a dangerous new argument to his Chin opponent whose demands were based on a ten-fold increase of the old figures.[34]

A comparison with the grain prices of the T'ang dynasty, though not conclusive, is suggestive for, in this case as in that of Liao, prices rose from a strikingly low to an astronomically high level. In 679 a hundred cash in bad money were added to the regular price in exchange for one peck of government grain (*mi* 米 and *su* 粟[35]). In 759 the inflation reached such a point that the price soared to seven thousand cash.[36] Where *mi* and *su* are mentioned separately, *mi*, rice, cannot include *su*, millet, which is expressly excluded by the above formula. In other cases *mi* stands for grain in general, including millet. During the T'ang dynasty the capital was still in the north, and the greater part of the country's population lived in the millet and wheat belt of what is today Hopei, Shantung, Honan, Shansi, Shensi, and Kansu.[37] TS 51, 4a describes the favorable conditions prevailing in the year 746 and puts the price of one peck of grain (*mi*) at thirteen cash for the empire as a whole and at three cash for the territory which is now modern Shantung. The cash referred to here was obviously still good "full" money. The grain in question must have been mainly millet or wheat, certainly as far as Shantung was concerned. Even if the weight of the good copper coins of T'ang in 746

was not identical with that of the cash of Liao, this year's "low" price of three to thirteen cash offers an interesting background for our recorded millet prices of a "few" and of "five to six cash" for the time of Liao.

As to the weight of the cash, it seems that in 746 the T'ang government still used the K'ai-yüan T'ung-pao coin which was put into circulation again after a short inflationary experiment in 766. This coin weighed two *shu* 銖 four *lei*[38] 絫 as did the Liao cash used in the good year 1071. The low grain price of three to thirteen cash in the pre-inflationary period of the T'ang dynasty is similar to the grain price paid in cash in the Liao empire in 1071.

Only a few commercial equations are recorded in addition to the data on grain prices discussed above. None of them can be made the basis for any calculation of averages. The fact that an honorary title could be purchased for ten oxen and camels and a hundred horses[39] seems to imply that camels and oxen were either less numerous than horses or less eagerly desired by the government. But no conclu-

TABLE 6

EQUIVALENCE OF EXCHANGE VALUES

DATE	EQUIVALENT	REMARKS
Tenth century	1 peck of grain = 5 cash	Conversion ratio; average market price probably considerably higher
End of tenth century	1 peck of grain = 6 cash	
1071	1 peck of grain = 6 cash	Extremely low market price
The two hundred years preceding 1123	1 peck of grain = 100 cash	(Exaggerated ?)
1118	1 peck of grain = several bolts of silk	
1123	1 peck of grain = 1,000 cash	Inflation
	2 pecks of grain = more than 1 sheep	
	1 ox = 3 sheep	
	1 horse = 5 sheep	
	1 camel = 8 sheep	
	1 picul of salt = 1¾ strings of money	Government price

[34] SCPMHP 13, 7a.

[35] CTS 48, 7b.

[36] *Op. cit.*, 10a.

[37] According to Balázs' calculation (31 BWT, 20) in the middle of the eighth century the population of China was distributed as follows:

North China
(Kansu, Shensi, Shansi, Hopei,
Shantung, and Honan)   about 30,500,000
Central and Western China
(modern Anhui, Kiangsu, Chekiang,
Fukien, Hupei, Hunan and
Szechuan)   about 19,500,000
South China   about 2,000,000

The central and southern regions are the main centers of rice cultivation, not the north where the crop can be grown only under especially favorable circumstances (*cf.* Wittfogel 31, 64 and 72 ff.). Dr. Buck's agricultural atlas draws the "Rice Line" south of North China, generally in keeping with the provincial divisions given above. "North of this line . . . rice is grown only in scattered patches. South of it is the Rice Region. This marks the main agricultural division line in China" (Buck 37b, 10; *cf.* also *idem* 37a, 174 ff.).

[38] *Cf.* TS 54, 5a; *cf.* also Balázs 32 BWT, 30 and Coole 36, 111–114.

[39] VIII (12).

sion can be drawn as to the relative value of the three animals mentioned.

More representative perhaps is another set of figures recorded for the year 1123. For government grain stolen by certain herding families, the ephemeral emperor, Ya-li, demanded restitution in terms of cattle. The price of one sheep for one cart of grain was obviously much too low; the courtiers asserted with justice that even one sheep for two pecks of grain would have been too low a price. In addition to the rather inconclusive reference to the relative values of grain and sheep at this time, the record gives the ratio of sheep to oxen, horses, and camels as 1:3:5:8.[40] For obvious political reasons the "emperor" named an abnormally low sheep price for the stolen grain. However, no political motives affected the ratio of value established for the four most important categories of animals. The figures, though probably not exact, may well have approximated the actual price relations between them.

Thus some numerical information emerges from the Liao records, much of it based on price relations in 1123 and two statements noting grain prices prevailing in the empire's earlier period. The data are combined in table 6, not because they give a comprehensive picture of Liao commerce, but because they are a unique, if incomplete, index of certain exchange values during the Liao dynasty.

d. THE TRADERS

The official records of Liao say little about persons engaged in commerce. Traders of low status are mentioned among the groups excluded from access to examinations.[41] Certain families, such as the *yün-wei* 云爲 of the Supreme Capital, although classed among the commoners, were powerful enough to avoid public labor service. They owned extensive property, part of which was in money, as LS 59, 3b ff. shows. The glossary, LS 116, 21a, equates the *yün-wei-so* 云爲所 with the *ying-yün* 營運. In the succeeding Chin 金 dynasty the *ying-yün* were rich families who owned houses and land.[42] Since *ying* means "to manage," "to promote business," and *yün* "to move," the term *ying-yün* may have designated persons active in commerce and dealing in movable property.

The Liao government kept its eye on these upper class business people.[43] In 982–983 restrictive measures were taken against what were considered excessive profits.[44] In 1105 members of merchant families

were forbidden to take the examination for the *chin-shih* degree.[45] But, even if they suffered certain discriminations, they were not completely eliminated, for their functioning was indispensable to the economic life of the country.

Officials were known to have engaged in commerce and money-lending, but they were severely attacked when their activities threatened the stability of the Ch'i-tan tribes[46] or when they appropriated government grain for their own purposes.[47]

The Chinese communities within the northern urban settlements naturally harbored many Chinese merchants. The decrees which excluded peddlers and merchants from taking examinations must have been chiefly aimed at the latter, for only they had any chance of satisfying the requirements of Chinese scholarship in the traditional way.

Besides Chinese business men, the texts also mention Uighur merchants who received special residential privileges in the Supreme Capital.[48] In spite of occasional restrictions upon the export of iron to the Uighurs,[49] these traders were obviously treated with greater consideration than were the commercial representatives of any other neighboring people.

3. COMMERCIAL POLICY

a. INTERNAL TRADE

The varying attitudes of the Liao government toward different groups within its merchant class was but one expression of its general economic policy. This policy, following the established Chinese tradition, leaned more to the supervision and regulation of business than to the direct participation of the state in production or trade.

Within the limits set by the political situation the government endeavored to encourage private trade which was a welcome source of additional government income and served the convenience of the tribal and sedentary populations. The government set up markets which it "controlled" (*chüeh* 榷[50]), that is policed and taxed. It standardized the size of the pieces of cloth which were to be sold; it regulated the size of dry measures;[51] it established new markets[52] and laid out new trade routes;[53] and it even ordered the mobili-

---

[40] V (18).

[41] XIV, 3 (13).

[42] CS 46, 13b. For discussion of the philological problem involved in the term *yün-wei* see VI, 2, note 2.

[43] VI, 2 (1).

[44] See VI, introduction.

[45] XIV, 3 (28).

[46] VI, 2 (4).

[47] III (19); *cf.* also II, 2 (9).

[48] V (19). Some of these Uighur merchants traveled in Sung China as well as in the Liao empire (CTC 5, 61–62; see V, note 46).

[49] V (15).

[50] V (4).

[51] V (17).

[52] V (1) and *passim*.

[53] V (4).

zation of carts so that the tribespeople might visit the market centers.[54] The trade tax, though certainly not instituted for the good of the merchants, could be managed in such a way that private enterprise would not be too severely handicapped.

A request mentioned in LS 60, 1b asks a reduction in the toll levied at a pass between Nan-ching and Hsi-ching.[55] The passage indicates some kind of intra-territorial customs stations, similar to the *likin* of recent times. Was this "tax" (*shui* 稅) demanded only at the borders of the five circuits, or was it levied wherever economic and geographic conditions favored the establishment of such stations? No other passage in the *Liao Shih* throws light on this unique record.

b. FOREIGN TRADE

The foreign trade of the Liao empire can be properly understood only when it is considered in relation to the country's internal and foreign policy. The extended frontiers of the vast empire were not clearly defined. A good deal of border trade certainly flowed back and forth without official interference, but the bulk of the commercial transactions between Liao and the neighboring countries was government-managed or at least government-controlled.

The attitude of the Liao government toward foreign trade rested upon a number of elementary considerations:

1) The empire received a large amount of valuable foreign products as tribute, that is without recourse to commercial exchange.

2) Whatever goods were desired in addition to tributes—and there always were such additional demands—had to be paid for with national merchandise. This national merchandise was limited in kind; it consisted chiefly of pastoral products such as animals, skins, and wool, and of metals such as iron, silver, gold, and copper.

3) The merchandise which was available for export might be withheld because of political considerations. Iron and copper were not to be sold abroad[56] if the sale entailed military or monetary disadvantage. Ewes were not to be traded away,[57] for the natural increase of the flocks had to be assured. Horses, the foundation of the frontier defence,[58] were likewise protected from injudicious exportation. LS 60, 3b considers these and other similar restrictions responsible for the country's pastoral strength and prosperity.[59]

Particularly complex were the commercial relations with the various states and dynasties of China Proper. The southern regions produced many precious things which the rulers of Liao intensely desired. As demand grew with the increasing tribute payments of silk and silver, the traditionally frugal tribal life was transformed and softened. Thus the trade policy toward China Proper shifted from one of severe restrictions on the export of such vital commodities as cattle, felt, silver, and gold to an attitude of *laissez faire* and even encouragement.

With sheep, horses, and camels the people of the Liao empire purchased from China Proper medicine, incense, rhinoceros horns, ivory, tea,[60] sapanwood (蘇木), lacquered objects, pearls, sulphur, niter, porcelain ware, and books.[61] The numerous fragments of Sung porcelain recently discovered in Liao sites[62] reflect clearly the appreciation of the masters of the northern empire for the fine handicraft of contemporary China. But the most coveted Chinese product was silk. After 1005 the Sung government paid the Ch'i-tan two hundred thousand pieces annually and even then the domestic demands of the Liao were not satisfied. An official order shortly after that fateful year strikingly illustrates the economic relations between the two countries. The order consents to the exchange of skins, wool, and even live sheep for the south's most precious product, silk.[63]

The economic resources of the Sung empire were sorely strained by the huge tributes paid to the Liao court. The income of the Sung government was furthermore curtailed by the sale of cheap Liao salt which was smuggled across the border in such large quantities that it caused deep concern among the southern officials.[64] The losses suffered through the payment of the tribute and the salt smuggling were somewhat mitigated by the expanding trade relations between the two countries. Some idea of the extent of their commercial transactions can be gleaned from the fact that in 983 the Liao government sold as many as thirty thousand sheep to Nan T'ang.[65] The profits reaped by the Sung empire from their trade with Liao are estimated to have reached a total of four hundred thousand strings of cash annually.[66]

---

[54] *Loc. cit.*

[55] *Loc. cit.*

[56] V (15) (13).

[57] V (2).

[58] V (6) (7) (11).

[59] II, 1 (3).

---

[60] The people of Liao purchased tea with grain even though the export of grain was prohibited by the government (SHYK 140, 4b).

[61] SS 186, 22b–24a.

[62] See Torii 36 I, 24 ff.

[63] V (4).

[64] SS 181, 13a, 27a–b; 182, 1a ff.; see III, note 28.

[65] HTS 69, 595; *cf.* II, 1, note 37.

[66] SS 179, 9b; 186, 22b–23b; see V, note 31.

TRANSLATION

COMMERCE

1. A trade center established   2. Sale of ewes banned   3. The economic center of West Tower   4. General picture of trade   5. Cloth for sale must be standardized   6. No horses to Sung   7. Against smuggling of horses   8. A government-controlled market in Korea   9. Restrictions on sale of gold and iron   10. Restrictions on exports to Sung   11. Sale of horses to Hsia   12. A government market   13. Ban on the sale of copper   14. Restrictions on colored satin and iron   15. No iron trade with the border tribes   16. The emperor visits a market   17. Measures of capacity   18. Values at the close of Liao   19. Markets in the Supreme Capital   20. A market place   21. Markets in the Eastern Capital   22. A great eastern trade center   23. A trade center near the Shira Muren

1. A TRADE CENTER ESTABLISHED

909   On the day *chia-shên* of the fifth month [in the third year of T'ai-tsu's accession] Yang City[1] was established north of Mount T'an[2] in order to open up market exchange.[3]   1, *3b*

2. SALE OF EWES BANNED

939   On the day *i-ssŭ* of the fifth month [in the second year of Hui-t'ung], Nan-ching was forbidden to sell ewes beyond the borders.   4, *3b*

3. THE ECONOMIC CENTER OF WEST TOWER

951–953   During [the reign period] Kuang-shun of the Chou [dynasty] Hu Chiao said in his memoirs,[4] "The Supreme Capital (West Tower[5]) had houses and market places.   In

---

[1] Yanai (30, 628) suggests that the location of this trade center was near modern Pain Tsaghan Nor, Chahar.

[2] Probably a mountain thirty *li* southwest of Ch'a-han Ko-êrh 察汗格爾, [Mongol "Tsaghān-gōl," White River?], Chahar (Yanai 30, 834).

[3] The term *shih-i* 市易, market exchange, assumed a special meaning during the Sung dynasty.   It was then used to designate one point of the economic policy which Wang An-shih 王安石 (1021–1086) adopted in 1072. Because the markets were dominated by powerful families and big merchants, the government established its own trade bureaus (*shih-i wu* 務) in the imperial capital and in five other large cities.

The *shih-i* of Liao was of a simpler nature.   In the *Liao Shih* this term indicates only that the Ch'i-tan carried on an urban market trade in addition to local tribal exchange.

[4] The work is entitled *Hsien Pei [Lu] Chi* 陷北[虜]記. It has been preserved in WTS 73; CTKC 25; and LS 37.

[5] The location of this West Tower (Hsi Lou 西樓) has been disputed.   Hu Chiao identifies it with the Supreme Capital (see, besides our text, the full version of Hu Chiao's story in WTS 73, 6a–10a).   His identification is controverted by LS 37, 6a, according to which West Tower was Tsu Prefecture 祖州, about forty *li* southwest of the Supreme Capital.   Chavannes (97 VC, 398, note 1) accepts LS 37, 6a; Mullie and Pelliot follow him (see Mullie 22, 138, note).   This interpretation is favored by the fact that in the settlement described by Hu Chiao no coined money was used during his visit, but only cloth, which indicates a primitive state of economy more adequate to a local center than to the national capital.   No conclusive evidence can be drawn from the ruins of a

House of Stone found at the site of the former seat of Tsu Prefecture (Mullie 22, 141).   The construction, which is unique in shape, does not present the appearance of a tower.   Mullie himself, though tempted to identify it with the West Tower, hesitates to do so (*op. cit.*, 142).

The correctness of Chavannes' and Mullie's view is however strongly challenged by a series of textual and material arguments.   CTKC 23, 4a enumerates four places which were called "towers" (*lou* 樓).   They are South Tower on Mu-yeh Mountain (between the Shira Muren and the Lao-ha River), East Tower or Lung-hua Prefecture (probably at the juncture of the Shira Muren and Lao-ha River), North Tower or T'ang Prefecture (three hundred *li* north of the Supreme Capital), and West Tower or the Supreme Capital.   This description is repeated in LSSI 13, 5b quoting from *Lu T'ing Tsa Chi* 虜廷雜記 by Chao Chih-chung.   It is confirmed by several passages of the *Liao Shih*.   According to LS 1, 4b, at the West Tower there was a T'ien-hsiung Temple 天雄寺; this temple is mentioned in LS 37, 5a as having been located in the Supreme Capital.   At West Tower a Ming-wang Tower was destroyed at the beginning of the Liao period (LS 1, 5b); on its site was erected the K'ai-huang Hall 開皇殿 (LS 1, 8b) which again is recorded in the geographical section as one of the edifices of the Supreme Capital (LS 37, 4b).

This textual proof is strengthened by several significant material considerations.   The Supreme Capital had a Confucian temple as well as Buddhist and Taoist temples, whereas the old city of Tsu Prefecture was devoted to the memory of the Liao ancestors rather than to the cult of the Three Doctrines.   Hu Chiao's description mentions Confucianists, Buddhists, and Taoists as a conspicuous

commercial transactions they did not have cash but used cloth.[6]   There were all kinds of silk brocade workers, officials, scholars,[7] magicians, musicians, wrestlers, Confucianists,[8] Buddhist monks and nuns, and Taoist priests.   Of the Chinese people, those from Ping,[9] Fên,[10] Yu,[11] and Chi[12] were the most numerous.   *37, 5a*

4. GENERAL PICTURE OF TRADE

In the [capital] city of Tung-p'ing Commandery[13] a watch tower was erected separating the southern and northern markets.   In the forenoon[14] trade was conducted in the northern market.   In the afternoon business was transacted in the southern market.

In Hsiung Prefecture,[15] Kao-ch'ang,[16] and Po-hai[17] markets were also set up in order to open a way for commodities from southern Sung, the northwestern tribes, and Korea.   As a result, with the Nü-chih bringing gold, cloth, honey, wax, and the raw materials for various drugs, and the T'ieh-li,[18] Mo-ho,[19] and Yü-chüeh[20] bringing pearls, skins of gray moles, sables, and glue fish,[21] oxen, sheep, camels, horses, and fine felt, those who came to trade in Liao formed a continuous stream along the road.

983					During [the reign period] Ch'ien-hêng of Shêng-tsung[22] the office of the vicegerent[23] of Yen-ching stated that the people were short of food and requested that the duties at Chü-yung Pass[24] be relaxed so as to open a way for the purchase of grain from Shan-hsi.[25]

---

feature of the city called West Tower.   Silk workshops existed in Tsu Prefecture and in the Supreme Capital, but the presence of officials and men of letters must have been a characteristic feature of the capital which besides numerous government headquarters also contained important centers of learning.   This again harmonizes with Hu Chiao's description.

The use of natural (cloth) money in the northern capital, though surprising at first sight, can be explained by the relatively early date of Hu Chiao's visit (*cf*. VI, introduction).   The length of this visit may be considered another argument.   Hu Chiao lived in the Liao country from 947 to 953, that is for about six years.   Chavannes (97 VC, 391), who seeks Hu Chiao's West Tower in Tsu Prefecture, assumes nevertheless that the Chinese official visited the Supreme Capital.   It seems difficult to believe that someone who was so familiar with the conditions of Liao should have believed that the seat of Tsu Prefecture was the national capital.   We ourselves believe that his description really pertains to the capital.   LS 37, 6a does not speak of the seat of the Tsu Prefecture as West Tower.   It says that T'ai-tsu erected a West Tower at this place where he frequently hunted.   The report continues, "Later he established a city called Tsu Prefecture."   It seems perfectly plausible that the name West Tower was first applied to this region and was then shifted to the growing national capital, Shang-ching.

[6] See introduction.

[7] The *han-lin* 翰林 were members of the highest learned body of China, the Han-lin Academy.   These scholars must have come from China as fugitives or captives or may have obtained their degree from the Liao emperor.

[8] Instead of the term *ju* 儒 a parallel version in CTKC 25, 1b has *hsiu ts'ai* 秀才 which in the T'ang period was used to designate a talented scholar (JCL 16, 33 ff.).   Our version seems preferable because it coordinates the representatives of the Buddhist, the Taoist, and the Confucian creeds.   This way of presentation, which harmonizes well with the conception of the Three Doctrines

(*san chiao* 三教), seems particularly appropriate in the description of a city which had Confucian, Buddhist, and Taoist temples.

[9] Modern T'ai-yüan 太原, Shansi.

[10] Modern Fên-yang 汾陽, Shansi.

[11] Modern Peiping.

[12] Modern Chi 薊 County, Hopei.

[13] Modern Liao-yang 遼陽 County, Liaoning.   Tung-p'ing Commandery was established in 919.   Its name was changed first to Southern Capital in 928 and then to Eastern Capital in 938 (LS 38, 1b–2b).

[14] *Yü* 禺 literally means the time between 9 and 11 A.M.

[15] Modern Hsiung 雄 County, Hopei.

[16] See I, 2 (10), no. 19.

[17] In LS 38, 17a a place called Po-hai 渤海 Prefecture is listed just before Ning-chiang 寧江 Prefecture (modern Shih-t'ou Ch'êng-tzŭ 石頭城子, Kirin), but this does not mean that the two places were closely connected geographically.   From the text we can only assume that its location must have been near the border of Korea, perhaps somewhere in the eastern part of modern Liaoning.

[18] See I, 2 (10), no. 30.

[19] *Op. cit.*, no. 31.   Our passage probably refers to the Hei-shui Mo-ho 黑水靺鞨, a tribe dwelling in the northeastern part of present Kirin (LWKKC 6a–b).

[20] I, 2 (10), no. 38.   Wu-ku or Yü-chüeh people spread out over the eastern part of modern Outer Mongolia.

[21] *Chiao* 膠, "glue," made from the skins of fish was used as a medicine (Read 39, no. 192b).

[22] Ch'ien-hêng was the second reign period of Ching-tsung.   It lasted from 979 to 983.   According to LS 9, 5a, Ching-tsung died in the ninth month of the fourth year of Ch'ien-hêng (982).   His son, Shêng-tsung, who succeeded him, continued to use his father's reign title until the sixth month of 983 when he changed it to that of T'ung-ho which was made retroactive to the first day of the first month of 983 (see appendix I).   However, it seems that these first six months of 983 were considered as the fifth year of Ch'ien-hêng as there are few records

The officials were also ordered to notify all imperial traveling camps that cloth which did not conform to the standards by being too short or too narrow should not be sold in the market.

The next year an imperial decree ordered that, because of the scarcity of people in the markets of the Southern and Northern Administrations, a hundred carts should be sent from [each of] these tribes to the gathering places.

Roads were developed in Ch'i-fêng in order to establish trade relations with I Prefecture.[26]

1005 In the twenty-third year [of T'ung-ho] markets controlled by the government were set up in both Chên-wu Commandery[27] and Pao Prefecture.[28] At this time the great king of the Northern Divisions, Yeh-lü Shih-lu,[29] considering the great deficiency of salary sheep and the poverty of the tribesmen, requested that lean and old sheep as well as skins and wool be exchanged against the lustring from the south,[30] which would be advantageous to both sides.[31]

During the disturbances at the time of T'ien-tsu the collection of taxes became heavy and the system of exchange fell to pieces. The wealth dwindled away daily, and the people became daily more miserable.[32]   60, 1a–b

5. CLOTH FOR SALE MUST BE STANDARDIZED

986 On the day *kuei-ssŭ* [of the eleventh month in the third year of T'ung-ho] it was forbidden to trade in the emperor's temporary residence in cloth which did not conform to the regulations for length.   10, 9a

6. NO HORSES TO SUNG

997 On the day *hsin-wei* [of the seventh month in the fifteenth year of T'ung-ho] the sub-tribes of the T'u-yü-hun were forbidden to sell horses to Sung.   13, 8b

7. AGAINST SMUGGLING OF HORSES

1006–1009 [Yeh-lü T'ang-ku] set up strict regulations forbidding crafty people to sell horses to the territories of Sung and Hsia. Then he sent up a petition on the importance of exterminating smugglers and of tranquillizing the frontiers. The empress dowager[33] accepted it with approval. An imperial decree ordered the frontier regions to carry it out. It was made into law.
91, 1b–2a

8. A GOVERNMENT–CONTROLLED MARKET IN KOREA

1012 At the end of [the reign period] T'ung-ho, Korea surrendered. A market controlled by the government was established there.[34]   38, 5a

---

in the *Liao Shih* using this date (see LS 59, 2a). According to LS 10, 5a, the vicegerent of the Southern Capital made this request in the ninth month of the first year of T'ung-ho (983).

[23] Each of the five capitals of Liao had a vicegerent who exercised full authority over his territory. See XIV, 2 (8).

[24] Northwest of Peiping.

[25] This term probably refers to the area west of the T'ai-hang 太行 Mountains, a mountain range located on the present Hopei-Shansi border. The region would be roughly equivalent to modern northern Shansi.

[26] *Cf.* IV, note 10.

[27] As early as the T'ang period this designated a region corresponding to Xorin-gōl, "Twenty Rivers," in Suiyuan.

[28] Modern Wiju 義州, Korea.

[29] Yeh-lü Shih-lu 室魯, a native of the Six Divisions tribe, lived from 971 to 1014 and at one time achieved the position of chancellor of the Northern Division.

[30] *Nan-chung* 南中, according to LS 81, 1a, refers to Sung which was located to the south of Liao.

[31] LS 81, 1a reads 彼此 (mutually). The implication would be that the measure proved advantageous to Liao

as well as to Sung. During the early years of the Sung dynasty no government offices at the border controlled the trade between Sung and Liao. In 977 Sung set up monopoly offices at I 易, Hsiung 雄, Pa 覇, and Ts'ang 滄, through which incense, drugs, ivory, rhinoceros horn, and tea were sold to Liao. In turn, Sung purchased cloth, sheep, horses, and camels with a total value of four hundred thousand strings of money annually. The sale to Liao of books, with the exception of the Classics, and of sulphur and saltpetre was prohibited. The sheep and camels, which reached the Sung capital worn out by the long march, looked lean and as if about to die. *Cf.* SS 179, 9b; 186, 22b, 23b.

[32] See XII, introduction.

[33] Empress Dowager Ch'êng-t'ien 承天. Her posthumous title was Jui-chih 睿智. A member of the Hsiao family, she was offered by the officials to the Emperor Ching-tsung in 969. Until her death in 1009 she dominated her husband as well as her son, Shêng-tsung. Her greatest achievement was the famous treaty of T'an-yüan concluded between Liao and Sung in 1005.

[34] The record refers to Pao Prefecture (modern Wiju, Korea).

9. RESTRICTIONS ON SALE OF GOLD AND IRON

1034   On the day *chi-yu* [of the twelfth month in the second year of Ch'ung-hsi], Hsia envoys were forbidden to make private purchases of gold and iron along their route of travel.   18, 4*b*

10. RESTRICTIONS ON EXPORTS TO SUNG

1039   On the day *ting-ssŭ* [of the first month in the eighth year of Ch'ung-hsi] the sale of sheep from Shuo Prefecture to Sung was prohibited.   18, 9*a*

1042   [On the day *jên-wu* of the sixth month in the eleventh year of Ch'ung-hsi] the sale of felt and silver to Sung was prohibited.   19, 2*b*

11. SALE OF HORSES TO HSIA

1043   On the day *jên-tzŭ* [of the twelfth month in the eleventh year of Ch'ung-hsi], since the T'u-hun[35] and Tang-hsiang[36] frequently sold horses to the country of Hsia, an imperial decree was issued ordering [increased] attention paid to the frontier defences.   19, 3*b*

12. A GOVERNMENT MARKET

1054   On the day *ping-hsü* of the second month [in the twenty-third year of Ch'ung-hsi] a government-controlled market was reestablished in Chên-wu Commandery.[37]   14, 6*a*

13. BAN ON THE SALE OF COPPER

1063   On the day *hsin-wei* [of the first month in the ninth year of Ch'ing-ning] the people were prohibited from selling copper.   22, 1*b*

In the first month of the ninth year [of Ch'ing-ning] the people were prohibited from selling copper to Hsia.   115, 9*b*

14. RESTRICTIONS ON COLORED SATIN AND IRON

1064   [On the day *kêng-ch'ên* of the eleventh month in the tenth year of Ch'ing-ning] an imperial decree was issued to [the government of] the Southern Capital forbidding the private manufacture of the colored satin[38] used by the emperor, the private trade in iron, and also the drinking of wine at improper times.   22, 3*a*

15. NO IRON TRADE WITH THE BORDER TRIBES

1071   On the day *i-mao* of the eleventh month [in the sixth year of Hsien-yung] the sale of iron, raw or manufactured, to the Uighurs and Tsu-pu[39] was prohibited.   22, 7*a*

16. THE EMPEROR VISITS A MARKET

1080   On the day *mou-ch'ên* of the seventh month in the autumn [of the sixth year of Ta-k'ang] the emperor visited the market.[40]   24, 2*b*

---

[35] This tribe originally dwelt in modern Chinghai. It later migrated to the northern part of modern Shensi and Shansi. See I, 2 (10), no. 26.

[36] Of Tibetan origin, the Tang-hsiang flourished during the fifth century and at first occupied the territory of modern Szechuan and Chinghai. The people were divided into a number of units which differed according to local conditions. The Tang-hsiang tribesmen raised yaks, cows, horses, sheep, and pigs. They had no elaborate calendar, but distinguished the seasons by observing the grass and trees. Every three years a tribal assembly was held at which a sacrifice was offered to Heaven. In the eighth century the oppressive policy of the T'u-fan 吐蕃 induced them to migrate northeastward to Kansu, Shensi, and Inner Mongolia (WHTK 334, 2622; see also I, 2 (10), no. 20).

[37] See above, note 27.

[38] 段 is usually written 緞.

[39] The Tsu-pu 阻卜 are probably identical with the Tatars (see I, 2 (10), no. 8). The exportation of iron to the border tribes might well result in an improvement in their tools and weapons. Hence there was a prohibition on the selling of iron to the powerful neighboring peoples. Li Hsin-ch'uan 李心傳 (T. 微之, 1166–1243) stressed the point that the Ch'i-tan never allowed iron to be sold to them. Later, during the time of Chin, iron was allowed to go out to the Tatars from Ch'in (modern Shensi) and Chin (modern Shansi); in consequence their weapons became better and their military strength grew to a dangerous degree (CYTC *B* 19, 590).

[40] Probably in the Supreme Capital.

17. MEASURES OF CAPACITY

1082   During this month [the third month of the eighth year of Ta-k'ang] an imperial decree was issued enforcing the use of [the dry measures] *shêng* and *tou*,[41] which were fixed according to [a certain amount of] black millet.   24, 4a

18. VALUES AT THE CLOSE OF LIAO

1123   When T'ien-tsu was a fugitive, Yeh-lü Ti-lieh and others forced Ya-li, Prince of Liang,[42] to ascend the throne.   He ordered the stock-breeding families to move the millet in the granaries of Yen-p'o.[43]   When these families embezzled [the millet], a discussion arose concerning the confiscation of their property as a means of compensation.   Ya-li personally fixed the values in this way: a sheep was made equivalent to one cart of millet, an ox to three carts, a horse to five carts, and a camel to eight carts.   His followers protested that since one sheep could not be exchanged for even two pecks of millet, his valuation [of grain] was too low.   Ya-li replied, "If the people have, I have.   If complete compensation were ordered,[44] how could the people bear it?"
59, 3b

19. MARKETS IN THE SUPREME CAPITAL

The southern city[45] was called the Chinese City.   In the southern part were transverse streets with storied buildings facing each other.   Below spread the market-place.   North of the East Gate was Lu County; to the southwest was Hsing-jên County.   East of the South Gate was the settlement of the Uighurs.   The Uighur merchants who remained in the Supreme Capital established a settlement and lived there.[46]   37, 5a

20. A MARKET PLACE

In the southeast[47] was a crossroad on the four corners of which were storied buildings facing each other.   Below were rows of markets.   37, 6a

21. MARKETS IN THE EASTERN CAPITAL

The outlying section of the city,[48] called the Chinese City, was divided into a southern and a northern market.   In between was a watch tower.   In the morning the people gathered in the southern market.   In the evening they gathered in the northern market.   38, 2a

22. A GREAT EASTERN TRADE CENTER

In Ch'ên Prefecture, which obtained its name from Ch'ên Han,[49] were row on row of markets. It was a very important center of communications.[50]   38, 5a–b

---

[41] See appendix III.

[42] Ya-li 雅里, who had the honorary title of Prince of Liang, was the second son of the last Liao emperor, T'ien-tsu.   He was kidnapped by his followers and made emperor (LS 30, 3a–b).   According to LS 29, 6b, the event occurred in 1123.

[43] Yen-p'o 鹽濼 was probably situated in the northern part of modern Suiyuan, for Ya-li was kidnapped north of modern Kuei-sui 歸綏 (Suiyuan), where the emperor lived.   The same name is mentioned in the memorial of the essayist Liu Hui 劉輝 who toward the end of the reign period Ta-an (1085–1095) suggested that Chinese families be sent there to till the land in order to increase the garrison's food supply (LS 104, 3a).

[44] The word 今 is probably a misprint for 令.

[45] The record refers to the Supreme Capital, for a more detailed description of which see XI (5).

[46] In 1093 a Sung visitor of the Liao empire, Ho Wei-li 郝惟立, met a Uighur merchant who had seen him before in Sung China.   A Liao official whom Ho Wei-li interrogated explained the presence of such people by the fact that the empire included a number of Uighur prefectures, and that Uighurs usually went to court to offer tribute but occasionally came to the capital to trade (CTC 5, 62).

[47] The passage refers to Tsu Prefecture, southwest of modern Boro Khoton.

[48] The text is a description of the Eastern Capital (modern Liao-yang County, Liaoning).

[49] During the Han dynasty the southern part of Korea was occupied by a people called Han 韓.   They were divided into three groups, the Ma Han 馬韓 in the west, the Ch'ên Han 辰韓 in the east, and the Pien Han 弁韓 in the south (HHS 85, 14a–16b).

[50] The strategical location of Ch'ên Prefecture (present Kai-p'ing 蓋平 County, Liaotung Peninsula) gave it a position of vital political, military, and economic importance.   During the time of Han and T'ang, whenever a barbarian invasion cut the connection between the region

23. A TRADE CENTER NEAR THE SHIRA MUREN

Sung-chiang County was originally the territory of Wên-chêng County of Han. It bordered Sung-mo and was an important gathering place for merchants.   39, 4a

---

of modern Peiping and the area east of the Liao River, the only line of communication between the Liaotung region and China Proper was that via Ch'ên Prefecture, the Liaotung Peninsula, and across the Gulf of Po-hai to Shantung.

A few casual records throw some additional light upon the commercial relations between Liao and Korea. In 1101 the Korean government established two lodges, Yöng Pin 迎賓 and Hwe Sön 會仙, for Liao merchants. In 1055 Liao merchants came and went, trading valuable merchandise; in 1062, therefore, a special Liao Trade Department (遼國買賣院) was established south of Sön Ïi 宣義 Commandery (CPMHPK 164, 1b).

In 1088 the Liao government intended to set up government-controlled markets (権場) at the Yalu River, but Korean envoys argued against the measure which their court considered unnecessary (op. cit. 122, 12a).

In 1093 a Korean official, Ch'o T'e-po 邵台輔, suggested in a memorial that the Korean envoys should select servants who were able to discover the strategic plans of Liao. These spies enjoyed their task because it gave them an opportunity to engage in a profitable exchange of goods with the Liao people (loc. cit.).

SECTION VI

CURRENCY AND MONEY-LENDING

INTRODUCTION

1. THE CURRENCY OF LIAO

a. ORIGINS

When Hu Chiao visited the bazaars of the Supreme Capital sometime between 947 and 949,[1] he was surprised to find that cloth was used instead of coined money. Do the historical and archaeological data on Liao currency confirm his observation?

Investigations of Chinese numismatists have yielded considerable information on the coins of the Liao dynasty, their inscriptions, and their weight. We offer a chronological list of all Liao coins that have been found so far (see table 7). An asterisk * in front of an inscription means that the coin in question is also mentioned in the survey of Liao currency in LS 60, 2b–3b.

TABLE 7

COINS OF LIAO

EMPEROR[2]	REIGN PERIOD	INSCRIPTION	WEIGHT[3]	REFERENCE
T'ai-tsu 907–926	T'ien-tsan 922–926	T'ien-tsan T'ung-pao (通寶)	3 shu 6 lei	CC 11. 4b LTCSL 1, 8b
Mu-tsung 951–969	Ying-li 951–969	Ying-li Chung-pao (重寶)		CC 11, 4b–5a LTCSL 1, 10a
Ching-tsung 969–982	Ch'ien-hêng 979–983	*Ch'ien-hêng Yüan-pao (元寶)		LTCSL 1, 10a–11a
Shêng-tsung 982–1031	T'ung-ho 983–1012	T'ung-ho Yüan-pao		LTCSL 1, 10b–11a
	K'ai-t'ai 1012–1021	K'ai-t'ai Yüan-pao		LTCSL 1, 11a–b
	T'ai-p'ing 1021–1031	*T'ai-p'ing Yüan-pao		LTCSL 1, 11b–12a
		*T'ai-p'ing Hsing-pao (興寶)		LTCSL 1, 12a
		*Tai-p'ing T'ung-pao		LTCSL 1, 12b
Hsing-tsung 1031–1055	Ch'ung-hsi 1032–1055	Ch'ung-hsi T'ung-pao	3 shu	CC 11, 5a LTCSL 1, 14a–b
Tao-tsung 1055–1101	Ch'ing-ning 1055–1065	*Ch'ing-ning T'ung-pao	3 shu	CC 11, 5a LTCSL 1, 15a–b
		*Ch'ing-ning Yüan-pao		KCCL 13, 3b
	Hsien-yung 1065–1075	Hsien-yung T'ung-pao		LTCSL 1, 15b
	Ta-k'ang 1075–1085	*Ta-k'ang T'ung-pao	2 shu 4 lei	CC 11, 5b LTCSL 1, 16a

[1] Hu Chiao together with his patron Hsiao Han 蕭翰 entered the Supreme Capital as followers of the victorious emperor, Shih-tsung, in 947. Hsiao Han was arrested for high treason in 948 and executed in the spring of 949 (cf. XII (19) (21) (22)). His accomplices fled to the east. Among them was Hu Chiao, who thus must have been in the Supreme Capital in 947 or 948 or at the beginning of 949. Cf. also Chavannes 97 VC, 390 ff.

[2] Emperors for whose reigns coins have been found.

[3] In the T'ang and Sung dynasties there were ten lei 枀 to a shu 銖. A lei was equivalent to 0.155 gram and a shu to 1.55 grams. Cf. Wu CL 37, 237 ff.

Coins of Liao (*continued*)

EMPEROR[2]	REIGN PERIOD	INSCRIPTION	WEIGHT[3]	REFERENCE
		*Ta-k'ang Yüan-pao	2 *shu* 4 *lei*	CC 11, 5*b* LTCSL 1, 16*a*
	Ta-an 1085–1095	*Ta-an Yüan-pao	2 *shu* 8 *lei*	CC 11, 5*b*–6*a* LTSCL 1, 17*a*–*b*
		*Ta-an T'ung-pao		KCCL 13, 4*b*
	Shou-ch'ang[4] 1095–1101	*Shou-ch'ang Yüan-pao	2 *shu* 4 *lei*	CC 11, 6*a* LTSCL 1, 18*a*
T'ien-tsu 1101–1125	Ch'ien-t'ung 1101–1111	*Ch'ien-t'ung Yüan-pao	3 *shu* 2 *lei*	CC 11, 6*a*–*b* LTCSL 1, 19*a*
	T'ien-ch'ing 1111–1121	*T'ien-ch'ing Yüan-pao	2 *shu* 4 *lei*	CC 11, 6*b* LTCSL 1, 20*b*
		*T'ien-ch'ing T'ung-pao		KCCL 13, 6*a*

Most of the coins that have been found are mentioned in literary records from the year 1021 on; before that time the records and the collections do not completely correspond. No coin has been discovered for the reign of T'ai-tsung who, the *Liao Shih* claims, promoted metallurgy and minting. Again according to the *Liao Shih*, Sa-la-ti made the first coins, and his son, T'ai-tsu, used them.[5] The archaeological collections contain one coin from the reign of the son; there are none for the time of his father. The numismatic evidence is incontrovertible as far as it goes; whether or not there were other early coins can be decided only by further archaeological investigation.

It is theoretically possible, though not probable, that there were early experiments with a crude currency in the agricultural fringe of the country, but if such experiments were made they do not seem to have been successful. The sixteen southern prefectures were only acquired in 938, and the Chin capital was looted in 947. Until then the Chinese forms of production and exchange, though used by the Ch'i-tan, probably were confined to the southern zone and to a few scattered northern colonies. The *Liao Shih* does not mention a single inscribed coin before the time of Ching-tsung, and the collections have only one coin, inscribed T'ien-tsan T'ung-pao, for the first two rulers of Liao. This lonely pioneer certainly circulated in the agricultural south and perhaps in the east. When Hu Chiao, immediately after the death of the second emperor in 947, visited the political centers of the north, he found the traditional system of exchange by barter or cloth money still in use. The emperor, Shih-tsung, for whom Hu Chiao's patron fought, minted no new money. Mu-tsung seems to have contributed only a single coin. It was more than a generation after Hu Chiao's sojourn in the Supreme Capital that Liao currency began to spread over the country. Then for the first time the *Liao Shih* records money-lending in the Supreme Capital by the *yün-wei* families.

b. EXPANSION OF MONEY ECONOMY

A number of circumstances contributed to the increased circulation of money at the end of the tenth and during the whole of the eleventh century. The natural resources of copper were more fully exploited; and they were augmented by the discovery of a huge treasure of old coins.[6] Even in Tung-ching money was minted and issued.[7]

How much money was put in circulation annually? As noted in section III,[8] a mint in the time of Ching-

---

[4] Throughout the *Liao Shih* the fifth reign title of Tao-tsung is written as Shou-lung 壽隆 except in 43, 9*b* where the title is rendered as Shou-ch'ang 壽昌. Since Shêng-tsung's Chinese name was Lung-hsü 隆緒, Tao-tsung would not, on account of the taboo, have used the first part of his grandfather's name for his reign title. We find that the reign title in question is rendered as Shou-ch'ang not only in the Liao inscriptions but also on the preserved Liao coins. This proves that Tao-tsung had not adopted Shou-lung but Shou-ch'ang as his reign title. The *Liao Shih* writes Shou-lung instead of Shou-ch'ang because during the time of Chin and Yüan the word *ch'ang* must have appeared in the name of a member of the Chin or Yüan house and was therefore taboo. Hence the original reign title was Shou-ch'ang because of the taboo of the word *lung* during the Liao period, but was changed later to Shou-lung because of the taboo of the word *ch'ang*.

[5] VI, 1 (1).

[6] VI, 1 (2).

[7] VI, 1 (3).

[8] See III, introduction.

tsung turned out five hundred strings of cash annually. If a string contained a thousand cash, then the mint coined about five hundred thousand pieces of money per year. This assumption conforms to the historical picture. Until the time of Ching-tsung's successor, Shêng-tsung, money was still rare. Only then were more and varied coins minted. In addition, Sung copper coins entered the Liao empire, partly in payment of salt[9] and other northern commodities, partly by exchange for a Liao iron coin that circulated for some time along the frontier. This limited iron issue[10] seems to have had little if any effect on Liao economy, but it was otherwise with the influx of Sung copper coins and the increased production of Liao copper money which even influenced the monetary policy of Korea.[11] Su Ch'ê 蘇轍 (T. 子由 1039–1112), who visited Liao territory during the later part of the dynasty, was so astounded by the number of Sung coins in use in the northern empire that he suggested iron coins be made available in the Sung border regions as a protective measure.[12] Recent archaeological discoveries confirm Su Ch'ê's observation. Torii found many more coins of Sung than Liao origin in the excavated Jehol sites;[13] and a vase dug up in Hsing-ching 興京 (Kirin), and apparently buried there during Chin 金 times, contained primarily Sung coins, Liao coins being the next most numerous.[14] The expanding production of copper coins within the northern empire and the influx of Sung currency were probably, in the main, responsible for an increasingly conspicuous money economy during the later years of the dynasty.

Yang Tsun-hsü 楊遵勗 was able to collect four hundred thousand strings of money for taxes in arrears. Liu Shên 劉伸 collected an annual sum of more than three hundred thousand strings. Both did so while holding office in Tung-ching Circuit.[15] The first amount is said to have been only tax money, and taxes surely contributed in large part to the second item. Naturally the amount of money possessed privately must have been considerably in excess of the sums paid out. According to archaeological evidence, Tao-tsung and his wife, I-tê, presented fifty thousand and a hundred and thirty thousand strings respectively to a Buddhist temple.[16] According to our texts, a prime minister was able to accumulate seventy thousand strings,[17] and a temple could turn over ten thousand strings to the government.[18]

It would, of course, be a mistake to assume that an annual income of, let us say, three hundred thousand strings meant the actual presence of this sum in the treasury at the end of the fiscal year. The Ministry of Revenue took in and paid out monies at the same time, and in spite of a considerable revenue the treasury might find itself without any reserve.[19] Similarly it would be erroneous to think only of the production of new coins without considering reductions in the old ones by loss, export, and destruction.[20]

An annual income of three hundred thousand strings of money for Tung-ching Circuit is mentioned as an all-time high;[21] Chung-ching Circuit once accumulated two hundred thousand strings in half a year.[22] Both figures are marginal; the normal income must have been much less. The revenue of Hsi-ching seems to have been small: during the discussions of 1123 neither side stressed the economic significance of this territory.[23] The revenue of Shang-ching Circuit, which included the Supreme Capital, probably was at least equal to that of the Eastern Capital whose older agricultural civilization had been weakened by a harsh anti-Po-hai policy.

The wealthiest region in the empire, however, was Nan-ching Circuit. In 1123 its annual revenue was said to have been the equivalent of 5,492,906 strings of money,[24] while only one-tenth of this amount is claimed to have been the norm for the preceding "two hundred years."[25] The figures for 1123 are calculated on the basis of sharply inflated prices due to the chaotic political situation.[26] But the earlier peace-time figure seems extremely low. Could the explanation lie in the fact that the anti-Chin officials of the Southern Capital, mostly Liao Chinese, purposely understated the totals in the hope of reducing the payments that the Sung government was expected to make for the cession of the territory? Whatever the background of these calculations of 1123, four-fifths of the revenue was "converted,"[27] that is, defined in money but, as a rule, collected in kind. The remaining fifth, 1,208,416 strings (in 1123), the so-called k'o-ch'êng money 課程錢 and a composite of

---

[9] See III, note 41.
[10] Between 1041 and 1048 (SS 180, 7b). The event is not mentioned in the *Liao Shih*.
[11] KRS 79, 607; see VI, 1 (3) and note.
[12] LCC 41, 12a–b.
[13] Torii 37, 239 and 349.
[14] See Wei CH 37, 154.
[15] VI, 1 (1), 1055–1101.
[16] MCPL 2, 49a.

[17] VIII (11).
[18] VI, 1 (1), 1055–1101.
[19] *Loc. cit.* See also X, 1 (66).
[20] VI, 1 (4) (5).
[21] VI, 1 (1), 1055–1101.
[22] X, 1 (66).
[23] SCPMHP 13, 10a ff.
[24] *Op. cit.* 14, 11a.
[25] *Op. cit.* 13, 11a.
[26] *Op. cit.*, 7b.
[27] *Op. cit.*, 14, 11a.

miscellaneous fiscal items (house tax, salt revenue, and income from other government monopolies[28]), may have been gathered at least in considerable part, in cash. In the two hundred years before 1123 the annual k'o-ch'êng (cash ?) income amounted to no more than 120,842 strings if the ten-to-one ratio also applied to this item; more probably it amounted to a figure above this sum and considerably below 1,208,416 strings.

This estimate, based though it is on most limited data, accords well with information on the cash revenue of Tung-ching and Chung-ching Circuits. The data concerning the "eastern" and the "central" territory are maxima figures; the average years certainly yielded much less. No other circuit exceeded Nan-ching in wealth; none, in all probability, equalled its cash revenue. If the Southern Capital collected more than 120,000 strings annually, all five capitals may well have had a combined cash income of half a million strings per year.

Barter and natural money were the classic forms of exchange among the tribes; the spread of coined money must have provoked their distrust and resistance. Only in the middle of the eleventh century, when a considerable amount of cash had accumulated in the Supreme Capital, did money appear conspicuously in the tribal world. The government, which so far had relieved the needy tribes with grants of grain and textiles, now began to distribute both produce and money[29] or even money alone.[30] At the same time the administrative officials were forbidden to lend out money to the tribes or conclude commercial transactions with them.[31]

A new monetary trend appeared among the tribal peoples of Liao, but this trend remained feeble. It was the last weak ripple of a movement which was bound to lose its drive as soon as the dynamic center of power collapsed. When the Liao empire was crumbling, the monetary system temporarily lost its hold even in the agricultural regions. During the famine of 1118 grain was sold in Nan-ching Circuit, not for cash, but for silk.[32] Small wonder that in this crisis the tribes continued to cling to their time-honored national economy. In 1123, when the herdsmen of the southwest were forced to make restitution for stolen grain, the amount was calculated, not in money, but in sheep.

2. A DYNASTY WITHOUT AN INFLATIONARY POLICY

Our table of the currency of the Liao dynasty shows great stability in the weight of the coins until the end of Shêng-tsung's reign. The first coin issued under T'ai-tsu was relatively heavy (three shu six lei). The exact weight of the new coins issued during the reign of Shêng-tsung (982–1031) is not known, but the T'ai-p'ing Yüan-pao and the T'ai-p'ing T'ung-pao are described as heavy, the latter being coarsely stamped. About this time more money was minted. The two coins appearing after the issue of the T'ai-p'ing series weighed only three shu. These lighter coins, which circulated together with the older and heavier pieces, no doubt invited counterfeiting by private producers. It is interesting to note that just "at this time" measures had to be taken against the private production of coins.[33] The simultaneous suppression of the sale of copper and iron to the Uighurs was probably for military rather than financial reasons.

In the reign period Ta-k'ang (1075–1085) a coin was issued which weighed not more than two shu four lei. It is difficult to understand why at the end of this period private smelters began to destroy copper coins and use the metal for tools.[34] Yet this behavior is comprehensible for the period Ta-an (1085–1095) when a heavier coin of two shu eight lei appeared. Obviously there was a tendency to take "good" money out of circulation. In 1086 the government had to fight the flow of Liao coins across the border.[35] During the next reign new coins were made which again weighed two shu four lei. The first coin issued under the last emperor, T'ien-tsu, was decidedly heavier. The political purpose of this change is not clear; but, even if it did not stem the tide of financial decay, it certainly shows that the government did not expect relief from a radical inflationary policy. The excessive rise in prices which occurred in Nan-ching Circuit prior to 1123 was obviously due to a scarcity of goods rather than to a deterioration in Liao currency.

The replacement of "good" coins by "bad" ones, which played so important a role in the internal policy of typically Chinese dynasties such as Han and T'ang, was not a significant factor in the time of Liao. The Ch'i-tan rulers were not threatened by a powerful class of independent business men whose financial strength had to be undermined by an energetic inflationary policy.[36] The wealth of the yün-wei families

---

[28] Op. cit., 14, 11a–b.
[29] XII (70) (86).
[30] XII (82) (101).
[31] VI, 2 (4).
[32] XII (118).

[33] VI, 1 (1), 1055–1065.
[34] VI, 1 (4).
[35] VI, 1 (5).
[36] This was an avowed motive in the inflationary policy of Emperor Wu of the Han dynasty. Cf. HCS, Ch'in and Han VI, 117 B.C., HS 6, 14a ff., ms.

was no major problem in a society whose main centers of power depended little upon industry and commerce. Indeed there are many indications that the greater part of the country's wealth in money and in property was concentrated in the hands of the imperial family, the Ch'i-tan nobility, and the high Chinese officials.[37] An inflation which would have hit hardest those who alone could effectively initiate it naturally had no chance of developing.

3. MONEY AND GRAIN LENDING

Since money-lending is an organic corollary to financial transactions of all kinds, it is not surprising to find it reported for a society such as Liao. But money was not the only commodity that was borrowed and loaned. In any country, which depends almost exclusively upon agriculture, grain is a highly valued commodity and in an emergency is more eagerly borrowed than money which would still have to be converted into grain. The lending of grain therefore played a large role in the economic history of China.

In the Liao empire grain was produced by a great agricultural majority; it was eaten by almost everyone. It may be readily surmised that in this country the lending of grain would equal in importance the lending of money. The recorded data on these points are neither detailed nor clear, but they are sufficient to establish beyond doubt the practice of grain- as well as money-lending.

a. GRAIN–LENDING

Grain-lending seems to have been largely in the hands of the government which kept in its numerous granaries great reserves of millet for military defense and civilian relief. The accumulated stock was issued in case of emergency or when the annual crop fell short.[38] It had to be replaced from time to time to keep the supply fresh.[39] A grain loss might be offset by the interest accruing on loans; a grain debt might be cancelled if it dragged on for a long period.[40] But, while a loan might be converted into government relief, the usual procedure was expressed in the regulations of the Eastern Capital where the people were permitted to borrow grain from the graneries at an interest of twenty per cent.[41]

At first glance, the Liao rate of twenty per cent for a grain loan seems similar to the rate fixed by Wang An-shih for the Sung empire in his famous Green Sprout Measure of 1069. But the Green Sprout

loans, offered in the spring, were made in money; they had to be repaid in the fall.[42] Calculated on an annual basis, these loans yielded forty per cent. It is possible that the Liao terms resembled those of Sung. But since the administration of Tung-ching Circuit was firmly established by the first half of the eleventh century, it is difficult to believe that it was based upon Wang An-shih's reforms which were not instituted until 1069. It seems much more probable that both measures developed independently from the lending of grain in China Proper during the early years of the Sung dynasty and long before. Grain, stored in the charity granaries, was lent out to needy people during the T'ang period[43] and under the Five Dynasties.[44] Early in the Sung dynasty the size of the loans depended on the size of the needy families.[45] In serious cases, either postponement or complete suspension of payment was ordered.[46] An interest rate of twenty per cent for the summer season or forty per cent for the whole year resembles the rates demanded for loans in cash. That grain and money were lent by private persons on the same terms, and occasionally at oppressive rates, is shown by an order of the Sung government issued in 988.[47]

The rates of interest demanded and paid for loans of grain or money in the course of Chinese history startle the present-day observer. Even the historical Chinese records show that the current rates were often considered usurious. But ideas on what might be a normal rate of interest or an oppressive one differ widely from those of our modern industrial world.[48] There is no need to enter into any comparative sociological investigation here, but a few examples chosen at random reveal that a high rate of interest was normal in higher agrarian societies, whether in mediaeval Europe or in the Asiatic Orient.

---

[37] See VIII and IX, introductions.
[38] XI (16).
[39] VI, 2 (6).
[40] XII (28).
[41] VI, 2 (6).

[42] SS 327, 4b. Dr. Williamson (WAS I, 143) speaks of the conversion of granary grain into a capital fund which was made available to the people "at the rate of 2 per cent per mensem, or 24 per cent per annum." The numerical examples used in the ensuing discussion—10,000 cash yield 2,000 cash after half a year and 4,000 after a year (SS 176, 23b)—show that Dr. Williamson's interpretation is untenable. The money in question was not converted from existing granary grain; it was a fund held by the granaries for the purchase of grain (常平糴本), and the rate of "two" (二分) as usual means two parts of ten, not of a hundred.
[43] CTS 49, 7a ff.
[44] CWTS 90, 11b and 81, 9a.
[45] SS 176, 14a ff.
[46] 984 (SS 4, 19b); 1008 (SS 7, 16a); before 1061 (SS 330, 3a). In the last case money was given out and grain was expected in return. This was the core of Wang An-shih's famous Green Sprout Loan.
[47] SS 173, 5a.
[48] Wittfogel 31, 739 ff.

TABLE 8

RATES OF INTEREST IN HIGHER AGRARIAN SOCIETIES

COUNTRY	DATE	GRAIN OR MONEY	RATE OF INTEREST	SHORT OR LONG TERM	REFERENCE
Japan	8th century	Rice	50%	From sowing to harvesting	Nachod, GJ II, 778
Japan	16th century	Rice or money	Actually: 40–50; desired: 20–30%		Takekoshi 30 I, 263
Bengal (India)	Until recently		24% and more	Long term	Saha 30, 136 ff.
			75% and more	Short term	
Egypt	Ptolemaic period		2%	Per mensem	Westermann 29, 32
Babylonia	Latter part of early Babylonia		20%	Per annum	Knight 37, 139
	Neo-Babylonian period		40%	Per annum	
Europe	Mediaeval		Average loans for consumption 43⅓%	Per annum	Schulte 00 I, 317 ff.
			Low average 20–25%	Per annum	Sombart 19 I, 626 ff.; Kulischer, AWMN I, 350 ff.; Lipson 37, 137; Knight 37, 139
			Medium average 40–50%	Per annum	
			Upper margin: 120, 173, 202, 266⅔, and 300%	Per annum	

b. MONEY-LENDING

Additional understanding of the administration of the grain loans of Liao may be gained from a survey of the records that deal with money-lending. Buddhist priests are said to have lent out money at exorbitant interest.[49] The yün-wei families demanded so high a rate that the accumulated interest tended to equal the capital. The Liao government punished the receipt of interest which exceeded the original capital loan. It followed the Chinese tradition which prohibited the capital (pên 本) from bearing interest (li 利) beyond its own amount: i pên i li 一本一利. This policy had been pursued during the T'ang dynasty.[50] Yet certain T'ang regulations were directed to cases where the accrued interest was five or even ten times as great as the capital.[51] Even when the law was upheld, long-term loans at twenty per cent, thirty-three per cent, and fifty per cent per annum

were possible; the rate on short-term loans might be much higher.[52]

In the agricultural sector of Liao, the direct heir of certain T'ang traditions, a similar situation seems to have developed. A passage (LS 103, 2a) that evidently refers to the country's sedentary population speaks of debtors who ceded their fields and sold their children. The interest charges described as 十倍其息 correspond to T'ang precedents in which the interest amounted to ten times the capital. The children and fields mentioned in our text may not always have been part of the original credit arrangement, but valuables were pledged[53] and both male and female members of a destitute family were sold into temporary bondage.[54] In the famine of 1012 the pawning of persons became nation-wide and threatened the very security of the country. The government then felt compelled to interfere, not by immediately freeing

[49] LCC 41, 14a.
[50] T'ao and Chü 36, 114.
[51] THY 93, 1683–1684.

[52] THY 88, 1618; 93, 1675–1692; cf. also T'ao and Chü 36, 114–117.
[53] Cf. op. cit., 114.
[54] XII (34).

those who had been pawned, but by outlining a scheme for paying off the original debt.

When small loans were involved there was little government interference. In one instance, however, the government took action: local officials were strictly forbidden to lend money to the tribes.[55] Whatever

---

[55] VI, 2 (4).

undermined their economic stability also undermined the political foundations of the masters of Liao.

The growing money economy was penetrating even the remote grazing grounds of the Liao empire. Nevertheless, it was limited in extent as well as in effectiveness; it may have hastened, but it certainly did not cause, the downfall of the Liao dynasty.

TRANSLATION

1. CURRENCY

1. Currency of Liao   2. Search for buried treasure   3. Money minted in the Eastern Capital   4. Making implements from coins forbidden   5. Export of money banned

1. CURRENCY OF LIAO

The system of coinage:

End of 9th century   During the preceding period, when Sa-la-ti was *i-li-chin*, because his locality produced much copper, he for the first time made coins.   T'ai-tsu, his son, continued to use them.   He thereby attained wealth and power, and began his imperial career.

927–947   T'ai-tsung set up a grand preceptor[1] of the five smelteries to take charge of the cash and the iron of the whole country.   Shih Ching-t'ang[2] offered the cash which had been accumulated along the border in order to provide supplies for the army.

969–982   Ching-tsung, considering that the old cash did not suffice to meet the need, began to cast the new Ch'ien-hêng cash.   The use of cash became widespread.

982–1031   Shêng-tsung had some digging done at Ta-an Mountain,[3] recovered the cash hoarded by Liu Shou-kuang,[4] and distributed it among the five Offices of the Accountants. He also cast the T'ai-p'ing cash.   The old and new [money] was used jointly.   From this time on the national coins circulated throughout the empire. . . .

Annually in the spring and autumn government funds were used to give feasts to the officers and soldiers.   As cash existed in incalculable amounts, it was not until the Ch'ing-ning period that the cash minted in the Eastern Capital was used for the first time.[5]

1055–1065   At this time an imperial decree prohibited all routes to trade in copper and iron in order to prevent counterfeiting.   The sale of copper and iron to the Uighurs[6] was also forbidden.   The regulations became increasingly strict.

1055–1101   At the time of Tao-tsung there were four kinds of cash,[7] namely Hsien-yung, Ta-k'ang, Ta-an, and Shou-lung.   In each case the change of name was due to a change in the reign title.   There are, however, no means to determine their shape and weight.[8]

Yang Tsun-hsü[9] was ordered to collect the old accounts of families in arrears to the Office of the

---

[1] The title *t'ai-shih* 太師 in the Chinese sense designated a grand preceptor; it was generally granted only to very high officials.   Here it means merely a director or head of a government department.   For the use of Chinese titles in the Northern Administration of the Liao empire see XIV, introduction and XIV, 1 *passim*.

[2] The founder of the Later Chin dynasty (936–946). Being politically dependent on Liao, he was considered a "son" of the Liao emperor, T'ai-tsung.   The Liao emperors called him Êrh Huang-ti 兒皇帝, the "Son" Emperor (CWTS 137, 8*b*).

[3] Northwest of modern Fang-shan 房山 County, Hopei.

[4] All other available sources connect this story with Liu Shou-kuang's father, Liu Jên-kung 劉仁恭, and not with the son.   Liu Jên-kung usurped the throne of Yen 燕 in the beginning of the tenth century.   He built his palaces in the region of Ta-an 大安 Mountain and ordered his subjects to use an inferior kind of money made of glue and clay.   The copper coins were taken away from the people and hoarded in a cave at the top of Ta-an Mountain (CWTS 135, 4*a–b*).   Our text obviously refers to Liu Jên-kung's treasure.

[5] That is to say, the coins were minted previously but owing to the abundance of funds were not needed until this period.

[6] And to the Tsu-pu (Tatars).   See V (15).

[7] *Ch'ien* 錢 (coined money).

[8] The exact years when the Liao coins were struck are mentioned in the *Ch'ien P'u* 錢譜 of Tung Yu 董逌:

1.	982	Ch'ien-hêng T'ung-pao
2.	983	T'ung-ho Yüan-pao
3.	1021	T'ai-p'ing Yüan-pao
4.	1055	Ch'ing-ning T'ung-pao
5.	1065	Hsien-yung T'ung-pao
6.	1074	Ta-k'ang Yüan-pao
7.	1074	Ta-k'ang T'ung-pao
8.	1084	Ta-an Yüan-pao
9.	1102	Ch'ien-t'ung Yüan-pao
10.	1112	T'ien-ch'ing Yüan-pao (CP 9*a–b*)

[9] A native of Cho Prefecture (modern Cho 涿 County, Hopei) who acquired the degree of *chin-shih* in 1050 and was made prime minister of the Northern Administration at the end of the eleventh century.   *Cf.* LS 105, 5*a–b*.

Ministry of Revenue.[10]   He obtained more than four hundred thousand strings of cash and was installed as assistant amanuensis[11] of the Chancellery.   Liu Shên, who as commissioner of the Ministry of Revenue had brought about an additional annual revenue of more than three hundred thousand strings of cash, was promoted to the post of chancellor of the Southern Division.   In case of a calamity this [surplus] money was given out to relieve the poor and distressed together with the families of the different camps who were distributed along the frontier for guard service.

At this time, although there was no such accumulation that the strings [holding the cash] rotted away so that [the cash] could not be counted, yet it could be called rich indeed.

When it came to the last years of his [Tao-tsung's] reign, expenditures were tremendous.   The coining [of money] was carried on as ever, but the national expenses could not be met.   Even a contribution of ten million [cash] offered by the Buddhist Hai-yün Temple[12] was not refused but accepted.   Before long the people were forbidden to take money beyond the borders.

1101–1125   At the time of T'ien-tsu two issues of new coins, called Ch'ien-t'ung and T'ien-ch'ing, were minted in addition.   Nevertheless, both the government and the people were exhausted and in distress, and the treasury had no reserves.   60, 2b–3b

2. SEARCH FOR BURIED TREASURE

996   On the day chi-hai [of the fourth month in the fourteenth year of T'ung-ho] digging was undertaken at Ta-an Mountain in order to recover the cash hidden by Liu Shou-kuang.   13, 7a

3. MONEY MINTED IN THE EASTERN CAPITAL

1056   On the day chi-hai of the intercalary [third] month [in the second year of Ch'ing-ning] cash minted in the Eastern Capital was put in circulation for the first time.[13]   21, 3b

4. MAKING IMPLEMENTS FROM COINS FORBIDDEN

1084   On the day jên-ch'ên of the sixth month [in the tenth year of Ta-k'ang] a prohibition was issued against destroying copper coins to make implements.   24, 6a

5. EXPORT OF MONEY BANNED

1088   On the day chi-ssŭ [of the seventh month in the fourth year of Ta-an] it was forbidden to allow cash to go out from the territory [of Liao].   25, 2b

---

[10] The Office of the Ministry of Revenue (戶部司) was presumably the same as the Office of the Commissioner of the Ministry of Revenue of the Eastern Capital (東京戶部使司).   See XIV, 2 (7).

[11] An official in the Chinese Chancellery.   Cf. XIV, 2 (5), LS 47, 3b.

[12] See IX (40).

[13] According to the Korean official history, Korea up to the beginning of the twelfth century still used plain cloth together with coins as a medium of trade.   In 1112 the Korean king urged the increased use of coins, remarking that "Great Liao also has begun to use coins in recent years" (KRS 79, 607).   The Korean statement probably refers to the circulation of coins in the adjacent Eastern Capital.

Recent finds have reemphasized the importance of Sung coins in the Liao territory.   Torii (37, 239 and 349) discovered many Sung and but few Liao coins in Jehol.   According to a note in the Peiping newspaper *I-shih Pao* 益世報, Henry P'u-i 溥儀 presented the archaeologist Lo Chên-yü with a vase filled with ancient coins which had been buried in what is now the capital of Kirin, Hsing-ching 興京.   The vase is said to have been buried in Chin 金 times, but most of the coins are of Sung origin; Liao coins follow in number (Wei CH 37, 154).

2. MONEY–LENDING

1. Money-lending families   2. "Interest" of an ordo used for relief   3. Money-lending and rate of interest   4. Money-lending in the tribes   5. Grain-lending   6. Grain loans from granaries

1. MONEY–LENDING FAMILIES

982–983   During [the reign period] Ch'ien-hêng of Shêng-tsung,[1] because the *yün-wei*[2] families of Shang-ching were indeed rich in property and were adept at avoiding the labor service, leaving this affliction to the poor people, therefore each of these families, whenever its interest [on a loan] became as great as the principle, was compelled to turn over all [the interest] to the government for equal distribution among the common people.   59, 3b–4a

2. "INTEREST" OF AN ORDO USED FOR RELIEF

1013   On the day *mou-shên* [of the seventh month in the second year of K'ai-t'ai] an imperial decree ordered that the interest of Tun-mu Palace[3] be used to relieve the poor people.   15, 6b

3. MONEY–LENDING AND RATE OF INTEREST

1035–1044   "The families without adults [capable of military service] offer double prices for hired [substitutes], but these men fear the hardships and run off in the middle of the journey, so that provisions for the frontier troops frequently cannot be supplied, and if they seek a loan from a person, tenfold interest has to be paid. Things go so far that repayment is impossible even if children are sold and fields ceded."[4]   103, 2a

4. MONEY–LENDING IN THE TRIBES

1058   On the day *kêng-hsü* of the twelfth month [in the third year of Ch'ing-ning] the administrative officials were forbidden to lend out money or to carry on commercial transactions within the tribes.   21, 5a

1083   On the day *kuei-hai* [of the seventh month in the ninth year of Ta-k'ang] it was forbidden for local officials to lend money at interest within the tribes,[5] and for messengers to take lodgings in the families of the people.   24, 5a

5. GRAIN–LENDING

1088   On the day *kuei-wei* [of the tenth month in the fourth year of Ta-an repayment] of government grain loaned to the people was remitted.   25, 2b

6. GRAIN LOANS FROM GRANARIES

Among the more than fifty cities [in Tung-ching] each of the prefectures situated along the frontier had a Fair Purchase Granary.[6] Following the ancestral system, the stale grain was removed and replaced with a new supply. The people were permitted of their own accord to borrow [the grain] at an interest of twenty per cent.[7]   59, 3a–b

---

[1] See V, note 22.

[2] From a philological point of view it is possible to punctuate differently, to place a comma between *yün* 云 and *wei* 爲; this reading would eliminate the term *yün-wei* and with it the idea of a special social category of *yün-wei* families. But the authors of the *Liao Shih* (116, 21a) list the *yün-wei-so* (所 may be an error for 戶) as a special term which they relate to the *ying-yün* 營運 families of the subsequent Chin dynasty (*cf.* CS 46, 13b). Our interpretation therefore follows that of LS 116, which assumes the existence of a special type of business family, called *yün-wei*. See above, V, introduction.

[3] This ordo was established by Shêng-tsung's brother near the region of modern Pei-chên 北鎮 County, Liaoning (see XV, 1 (16)).

[4] This passage is part of a memorial by Hsiao Han-chia-nu 韓家奴 (see XV, 1 (51)).

[5] This order, announced in 1083, closely resembles the prohibition issued in 1058. The fact that the malpractice had to be attacked again after twenty-six years shows that it was deep rooted and difficult to combat.

[6] For the granary system of the Liao dynasty *cf.* XII, introduction.

[7] For the notes and complete text of this passage see XII (119).

SECTION VII

SOCIAL ORGANIZATION, KINSHIP SYSTEM, CUSTOMS AND TRADITIONS

INTRODUCTION

1. SOCIAL STRATIFICATION

The social stratification of the Liao empire was determined by the same forces that shaped Liao economy. Military conquest superimposed a crudely stratified pastoral society upon a highly differentiated agricultural civilization, creating a new social order which was in part maintained, in part modified, during two hundred years of political domination and culture contact.

A survey of the social strata of Liao society paves the way for an understanding of the customs and traditions in the two main sectors of the Liao empire. Comparative analysis reveals a complicated two-way process of culture borrowing and rejection, a process of culture change, sometimes complete, sometimes restricted, sometimes frustrated. It reveals the forms and limitations of Ch'i-tan and Chinese acculturation in its many secular and religious aspects.

a. THE CH'I–TAN

THE TWO RULING CLANS

At the apex of the Ch'i-tan social pyramid were the Yeh-lü and Hsiao clans which replaced the former ruling family of Yao-lien.[1] Members of these two clans occupied most of the political and military key positions[2] and owned most of the empire's wealth. The extent of their property is in some degree indicated by the huge presents made by some of them to the Buddhist temples.[3]

The Hsiao clan, which was of Uighur origin, was subdivided into a number of higher and lower lineages.[4] The imperial Yeh-lü clan, like the I-la tribe from which it stemmed, was split into two sections, the Five Divisions or the Northern Division and the Six Divisions or the Southern Division. These two tribal sections were controlled by a northern and a southern great king chosen respectively from the remoter Five Divisions and the more distinguished Six Divisions of the Yeh-lü clan.[5] T'ai-tsu's direct descendants, the Horizontal Tents (hêng chang 橫帳), and the descendants of his two uncles and his brothers, the Three

Patriarchal Households (san fu fang 三父房), grew out of the Six Divisions of the Yeh-lü clan. Together they formed its four leading lineages. The outline (fig. 4) may clarify the main sub-divisions of the Yeh-lü clan.

The men of the Yeh-lü clan had a permanent lien on the women of the Hsiao clan, and vice versa. But this claim was restricted. The decree of 1019 which forbade the members of the four leading Yeh-lü lineages to marry members of the "lesser [Hsiao] lineages"[6] provides a starting-point for an analysis of the marriage regulations and for an understanding of the relative positions of the various Yeh-lü and Hsiao lineages. In 1029 the two leading families of the Hsiao clan and the families of the Southern and Northern Divisions were officially proclaimed the noble lineages of the nation.[7] The four leading Yeh-lü lineages are not mentioned, probably because their imperial status placed them above the category of nobility. Of the four "noble lineages of the nation," those of the two great kings were Yeh-lü, and therefore automatically excluded from marriage with the four leading imperial lineages. The latter then must have intermarried exclusively with the two noble Hsiao lineages.

By 1029 Shêng-tsung had fused the two distinguished Hsiao lineages, the Pa-li and the I-shih-ssǔ. To these he added an "other group" (pieh pu 別部[8]) of the Maternal Uncles.

The decrees of 1019 and 1029 reveal the outstanding position of the four imperial lineages, the two leading lineages of the Imperial Maternal Uncles, and the families of the two great kings. The relative status of the eight lineages was stabilized only after a series of conflicts and open rebellions,[9] but their social and political superiority over the lesser lineages remained unshaken until the end of the dynasty.

Clan membership did not signify joint ownership of property. The relief measure of 1100[10] indicates that the Yeh-lü clan included both rich and poor. The family of the poor Yeh-lü clansmen Tieh-la belonged to the more remote branch of the so-called

---

[1] See XIV, 1 (1), LS 63, 8b; cf. also XVI, 907, LS 1, 2b.

[2] See I, and XIV, introductions.

[3] See IX, introduction.

[4] See VII, 2, note 3.

[5] For a more detailed description of the ramifications of the Yeh-lü clan see XIII, introduction.

[6] VII, 1 (24).

[7] VII, 1 (29).

[8] See VII, 2, note 3.

[9] See XIII, passim.

[10] XII (108).

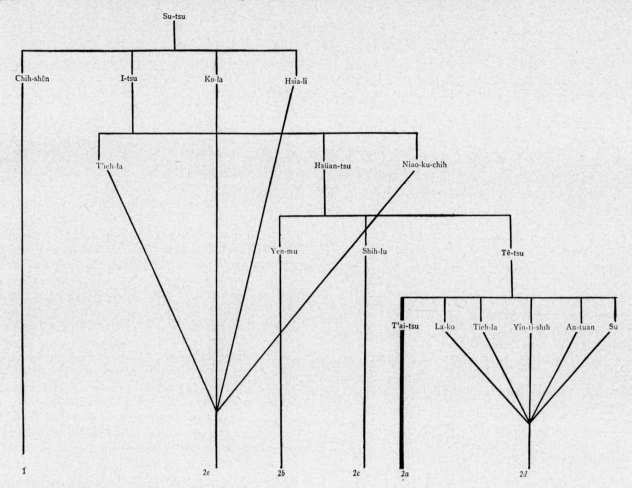

1   Five Divisions or Northern Division
2a Horizontal Tents (the imperial lineage)
2b First Patriarchal Household
2e Six Divisions or Southern Division (all lineages of the Six Divisions except the four leading lineages 2a–d)

2c Second Patriarchal Household
2d Third Patriarchal Household

FIG. 4.   The two divisions and the main lineages of the Yeh-lü Clan.

Five Divisions.[11]   But even a member of a leading lineage might be without means; Yeh-lü Hai-ssǔ came to the court riding an ox and wearing a coat made of sheep-skin.[12]   A Ch'i-tan who had no horse to ride was indeed destitute.

In Tieh-la's case as well as in that of Hai-ssǔ their poverty may have been exaggerated for literary reasons, but the fact remains that among members of the Yeh-lü clan poverty was well within the realm of possibility.   However, an originally low economic status did not necessarily frustrate a successful political career; Tieh-la's son and Hai-ssǔ both attained high governmental positions.

Members of other lineages and tribes might be given the name Yeh-lü or Hsiao.   The Chinese who held posts of exceptional importance and were credited

with exceptional achievements were all called Yeh-lü. As a rule, the tribesmen in question were descended from the former ruling houses of Yao-lien,[13] from one of T'ai-tsu's old tribes,[14] or from the Hsi[15] (nos. 1–10 of our list of T'ai-tsu's tribes).   The Chinese so honored were dignitaries of great importance, such as Han Tê-jang, the man who headed the Liao empire during the critical years of the Sung war.[16]

_____

[13] LS 73, 7a (two cases); 79, 4a; 88, 5b; 91, 3a (all included in the Yeh-lü clan).

[14] LS 76, 1a (provenience T'u-lü-pu); 85, 2b (T'u-chü); 85, 5b (I-shih); 97, 2b (P'in)—all made Yeh-lü. LS 74, 1a (I-la); 81, 3b (T'u-lü-pu); 96, 5a (Ch'u-t'ê); 99, 1a (I-shih); 103, 1a (Nieh-la)—all included in the Hsiao clan. Cf. VII, 2, note 3.

[15] See LS 94, 1b and 85, 2a (included into the Yeh-lü or Hsiao clan respectively).

[16] See VII, 2, note 76.

_____

[11] VII, 2 (72).
[12] VII, 1 (9).

THE FORMER RULING FAMILIES

Special policies determined the status of former ruling families and their descendants. The Hsi princes still succeeded in preserving some of their earlier power; the families of the Ch'i-tan khaghans (the Yao-lien) and the royal house of Po-hai were completely stripped of real authority. Yet all three families were permitted to retain the appearance of royalty and were surrounded by small, if shadowy, courts. Such treatment indicates that the new rulers of Liao had learned how to remove the substance of power without destroying its shell.

THE LESSER NOBILITY

LS 31, 9b speaks of the [imperial] clan, of the relatives of the empress (that is, the Hsiao clan), and of "the hereditary officials." The last category refers in a general way to the privileged strata of the Ch'i-tan conquerors[17]; it includes members of the Yeh-lü and Hsiao clans as well as other important personages, such as "the elders of each tribe."[18] While the *Liao Shih* is not specific on the point, it can be assumed that these families which had a hereditary claim to office constituted what may be called the tribal nobility. However, if a member of this stratum committed a crime he might be reduced to the rank of a commoner, *shu jên* 庶人[19] or *min* 民.[20]

In all probability the Ch'i-tan nobles had considerable wealth, for the empire provided a constant revenue from without and economic security within. While they seem to have been taxed but lightly,[21] they, like the nobles of the subdued tribes, had to keep the government herds well-stocked. However, as imperial guardsmen and attendants or tribal administrators in the pastoral grounds, they were spared the drudgery of frontier service, the lot of the common people.[22] They were certainly free from labor service which was not imposed even upon the Chinese officials.[23] If a member of the aristocracy committed a serious crime, he might merely be fined or sent upon a mission abroad in deference to his noble status.[24] If he was imprisoned, he was treated as a noble camp attendant,[25] a kind of gentleman-convict, and was not called upon to render the menial services required of the inferior tribal prisoners.[26] It

seems probable that a nobility of wealth and power existed during the predynastic period of the Ch'i-tan, but the privileges this class enjoyed were increased by the establishment of an empire of conquest which needed faithful followers to fill the numerous important military and political posts, and which was able and willing to give ample rewards for the loyal service it received.

THE COMMONERS

The text speaks of commoners[27] without defining the character of their status. However, it may be inferred that they ranked below the nobility in social position as well as in wealth. Most of them may have owned livestock below the upper limit of thousands of head and above the tribal poverty line.[28] Those who had only a few sheep and oxen and one or two horses, or perhaps no riding horse at all, probably became dependent upon their wealthier fellow-tribesmen, but whether this led to actual economic subordination or only to a nonchalant gentleman-beggardom,[29] we do not know.

b. THE NON–CH'I–TAN TRIBES

The non-Ch'i-tan tribes included in the Liao empire had either submitted more or less voluntarily to its newly risen power or, after serious resistance, had been defeated and taken captive. Any of these people might be taken to another part of the country;[30] the best fighters were often "transferred" to the camps where they were used as Liao soldiers.[31] LS 8, 3a shows that hundreds of tribal families approached the Liao authorities voluntarily, submitting politically and requesting to be attached to the camps. In this instance the request was granted.[32]

An edict of 921 placed the Ch'i-tan and the pacified barbarians[33] in the same political category, a procedure dictated no doubt by the desire to gain and maintain the allegiance of the tribes. This seeming equality was possible only because of a basic institutional similarity: the subdued tribes were ruled by chieftains, as were the Ch'i-tan; like them, they had rich and poor elements.[34] To be sure, there was less wealth among their rich and more downright destitution among their poor, but a decree mobilizing men who owned ten or more animals referred to all stockbreeding tribes, the lower limit probably marking the

---

[17] See XIV, 3, *passim*, and introduction.
[18] XIV, 3 (12).
[19] *Cf.* LS 23, 1b; 29, 6a.
[20] LS 24, 3b.
[21] See II, 1 (3); and X, 1 (28). *Cf.* also CS 3, 15b.
[22] XI (20).
[23] CS 47, 15a.
[24] VII, 1 (15) (25). *Cf.* VII, 1, note 4.
[25] VII, 1 (1).
[26] *Loc. cit.*

[27] *Cf.* VII, 1 (42) (43).
[28] See IX, introduction.
[29] *Cf.* Radloff 93 I, 295 and 298.
[30] *Cf.* I, 3 (2).
[31] *Cf.* XV, 1, *passim*.
[32] VII, 1 (11).
[33] VII, 1 (3).
[34] XV, 1 (45).

general tribal poverty line. The political and social status of the tribal upper stratum was carefully restricted by the administrative measures of a vigorous and suspicious central government. To be rich did not necessarily mean to be powerful.

c. THE CHINESE

Like the tribal barbarians, the Chinese subjects of Liao were incorporated into the empire either after voluntary surrender or as captives of war. Their manner of entry was one, but not the only, factor which determined the social status of the Chinese newcomers within the developing border society. That status was further modified by the functions which the new subjects were called upon to perform in their new social environment. The prisoners of war, both Chinese and others, were either "transferred" to one of the imperial camps to be used as government soldiers,[35] or they were handed over to individual princes and dignitaries who forced them to cultivate new lands and to build new cities and fortresses.[36] Living in a state of semi-serfdom, they paid rent to their personal overlords, and perhaps taxes to the government as well.[37]

Considerably better was the position of the Chinese inhabitants in those regions which had been taken over entirely. Ruled by a government of conquerors, they enjoyed less freedom than the free subjects of a typically Chinese dynasty, such as T'ang, but they were more independent in their movements than their captive or bonded co-nationals. The Chinese families, resettled in the north, became part of an administrative organization similar to that of the old Chinese territories. Surrounded by their tribal masters, they were probably less free than their brothers in the Nan-ching and Hsi-ching Circuits, even though legally their status was identical. Thus an intricate system of personal and collective bondage, of half and full freedom arose—a system that was extremely complex in the northern tribal regions and relatively simple in the old Chinese provinces of the south.

The peasantry of the Chinese villages was stratified. Naturally the village head came from the upper group[38] whose members could well afford to hire a substitute for frontier service; the middle group could barely do so.[39] The position of the villagers below this stratum may be readily imagined; members of their families lived on the fringe of the subsistence level and even hired themselves out to the two upper groups as substitutes. In case of calamity, they must

have been the first to be sold,[40] to sell themselves into bondage,[41] or to run off and become vagabonds.[42] The three strata of the rural population revealed by the texts are confirmed by archaeological data.[43]

The Chinese artisans in the camps were not free, but they were treated with conspicuous esteem.[44] The families whose members engaged in metallurgical work might be either bonded or free. Those who, like the silver smelters of Hsien-ho,[45] were under government control probably achieved a status equal if not superior to that of the artisan retainers of Po-hai provenience. The Po-hai iron workers of Tung-p'ing County contributed iron[46] either in part or full payment of taxes;[47] the thousand households of Ch'ang-lo County "provided iron,"[48] perhaps to meet similar fiscal obligations. The "government people" (*kuan min* 官民), who are mentioned in the negotiations of 1123 along with "officials, wealthy families, . . . and [free] artisans"[49]—all groups which the victorious Chin government intended to transfer to the north—must have been artisans of this semi-free type. The bulk of the tax revenue collected by the Control Office of Nan-ching Circuit was provided by the territory's "government people."[50]

Free Chinese artisans and business men formed a large part of the population in the old agricultural centers of Nan-ching and Hsi-ching. They also filled large sections of the new northern cities, converting the Chinese quarters into veritable Chinese cities like the one in the Supreme Capital.[51] Their streets and markets were lined with customers. Craftsmen and business men, big and small, carried on a lively trade.[52] Here were the stores of butchers, wine-dealers, cloth-merchants, and other Chinese traders. Here must have been the headquarters of the *yün-wei* families whose business practices, though feared, were deemed indispensable.[53]

The economic power of business men like the *yün-wei* was considerable, but their political career was

---

[35] *Cf.* XV, *passim.*

[36] *Cf.* I, 1.

[37] See X, 1 (38); and CSCSPM 1, 33a.

[38] See XIV, 2, note 29.

[39] XIII (39).

[40] XII (34).

[41] VII, 1 (47).

[42] II, 2 (24).

[43] See LWT 4, 17a.

[44] III (2).

[45] III (6).

[46] III (3)

[47] As did the inhabitants of certain prefectures who paid no tax except textiles. See HCLY 77, 9a.

[48] III (9).

[49] 職官富戶官民工匠 (SCPMHP 14, 1b).

[50] SCPMHP 14, 11b; for the position of the Control Office in the financial organization of the territory see X, introduction.

[51] See XI (5).

[52] See V, *passim.*

[53] VI, 2 (1).

blocked. Together with butchers, doctors, diviners, and slaves, traders were excluded by edict, from the examinations,[54] that is, from access to those government offices open to properly accredited Chinese candidates. The measure failed to mention the artisans who along with the merchants had suffered similar restrictions during the Sui, T'ang, and Sung dynasties.[55] Another edict of 1105 excluded only the merchants. Both orders probably reflect an appreciation of craftsmen and, certainly, a growing concern with the power of trade and traders.

The position maintained by Chinese officials in Liao society clearly expresses the political problem created by the growth of the new Ch'i-tan state. When A-pao-chi took under his protection the Chinese settled in the Chinese City and around the western salt-lake, he was forced to continue some form of Chinese administration and to keep in office some qualified Chinese officials. The acquisition of additional Chinese territory and populations demanded the employment of additional Chinese organizers and administrators. Han Yen-hui directed the new efforts. He was the first of a long series of Chinese officials who served the Liao court, mainly as members of the "southern" government but to a limited extent also as incumbents of certain offices in the government of the Northern Region. The political problems involved in this development are discussed in XIV, introduction; the social implications are obvious.

The power of the Chinese officials was restrained by the overlordship of an alien group of conquerors who, while willing to delegate numerous administrative functions, were equally eager not to delegate the essentials of political and military power. Within these limitations the Chinese officials enjoyed a status far above that of the Chinese commoners and, in a number of cases, even above certain noble Ch'i-tan. Some leading Liao Chinese, as they may be called, were made honorific Ch'i-tan and after this distinction was conferred, their relatives were permitted to marry members of the ruling nationality. Numerous marriages occurred between Han Tê-jang's family and the Hsiao clan after Han was named Yeh-lü.[56]

These upper class Liao Chinese exercised considerable influence on the policies of the central government; for the most part they administered the civil affairs of their co-nationals. They were exempted from the compulsory labor service which Chinese and in a modified form even Ch'i-tan commoners had to render.[57] Their income might not equal that of the highest Ch'i-tan dignitaries; yet as holders of certain offices they could accumulate great fortunes in a short time.[58]

d. THE PO–HAI

The edict of 921[59] formally placed the largest non-Chinese sedentary group, the Po-hai, in the same category as the Chinese. But this equation, like that of the "barbarians" and the Ch'i-tan, expressed a cultural relationship rather than a social status.

The Chinese subjects of Liao were acquired gradually and in part peaceably. Their treatment was no doubt influenced by the presence of the huge unconquered Chinese hinterland beyond the southern frontier. The Po-hai enjoyed no such protection. Conquered after a violent military assault, they were governed with great severity. Repeated attempts to shake off the hated Liao yoke resulted in intensified measures of repression, which culminated in large-scale deportations.[60]

Under these circumstances the number of Po-hai who became Ch'i-tan soldiers was unusually small, particularly in their old eastern homeland.[61] LS 81, 2b shows that one hundred years after their submission the Po-hai were still not permitted to play their national game of polo,[62] no doubt because it offered an opportunity for military training. The workers of the Imperial Silk Workshop in the Supreme Capital were barbarians, Chinese, and Po-hai.[63] The order of enumeration well expresses their respective status: the barbarians headed the social hierarchy; the Po-hai were at the foot.

The records disclose the existence among the Po-hai of civil and military officers,[64] of artisans[65] and peasants,[66] and probably, since there was trade,[67] of merchants. A decree exempting "poor people" from the land tax[68] indicates some kind of economic stratification within the Po-hai villages. Whether this stratification was as elaborate as that within the Chinese villages we do not know.

---

[54] See XIV, 3 (13) (28).

[55] TT 14, 81; TS 45, 1a; SS 155, 3a.

[56] MCCSC 2, 2b ff.; see VII, 1, note 17.

[57] Cf. CS 47, 15a; see also XI, introduction.

[58] See VIII (11).

[59] VII, 1 (3).

[60] Cf. I, 1 and 3 and XIII, passim.

[61] See I, introduction.

[62] VII, 1 (31).

[63] III (26).

[64] Cf. LS 88, 7a; 105, 1a ff.

[65] Cf. III (9). The position of the Po-hai "artisan retainers" has been discussed above with that of their Chinese counterparts.

[66] See VI, 2 (6).

[67] Cf. V (4). Part of the trade in the old territory of Po-hai seems to have been in the hands of Chinese merchants. The two markets of the Eastern Capital were both located in the so-called Chinese city. See V (21).

[68] XII (94).

e. SPECIAL GROUPS: THE MONKS

The great influence attained by Buddhism under the rule of the Ch'i-tan can be inferred from the high position of the Buddhist priesthood. Its prestige was extraordinary; its temple wealth startling. As a special section (IX) is devoted to the discussion of the sociology of Liao Buddhism, it is enough here merely to note its presence.

f. SPECIAL GROUPS: THE SLAVES

Although special aspects of slavery in the time of Liao have already been discussed, its many and complex forms demand a more comprehensive statement.

ORIGIN

Those members of the society who were not free had been, for the most part, brought in from the outside as captives of war. They were either soldiers of a defeated army who as individuals were forced into slavery, or they were inhabitants of a conquered region who were still permitted to live with their families.

But even those subjects of the Liao empire who had enjoyed freedom might be denied it. Families of convicts attached to camps,[69] persons bonded and sold by their families,[70] and poor people who sold themselves into bondage[71] fell within this group. The attitude of the authorities toward the last two categories makes it evident that such situations were considered completely normal. Under special conditions the government might reduce the number of slaves, but it never made any attempt to abolish slavery as an institution.

OWNERSHIP

Slaves might be attached to ordos, tombs, palaces, or administrative offices; they might be bestowed upon temples, or they might be assigned to individuals, to Ch'i-tan dignitaries in particular[72] or to "officials" in general.[73] The Ch'i-tan were forbidden to sell their slaves to Chinese,[74] obviously to make certain that prisoners of war who had been enslaved remained in the hands of the ruling group. This prohibition did not prevent the Chinese from owning slaves. Internal slavery, arising out of economic distress, was particularly frequent in the agricultural sector. There wealthy Chinese (or Po-hai) pressed poor Chinese (or Po-hai) into domestic bondage, just

as they hired substitutes for labor or frontier service. As frontier strife and war persisted, the slaves grew in number and were increasingly concentrated in the hands of the ruling group of Liao and on the land of its dominant religious institutions, the Buddhist temples.

NUMBERS

Ten "households" were given to Yeh-lü Chüeh, and fifteen to Hsiao Tê.[75] An important Chinese official received a grant of thirty households.[76] Women of the ruling clans offered fifty and one hundred families respectively as gifts to two temples.[77] From a Liao emperor the Lung-kung Temple received six hundred persons who at first were permitted to pay taxes but later were treated as slaves.[78] A "frugal" member of the Hsiao clan, Hui 惠, was satisfied with the possession of a thousand slaves.[79] The wife of Ching-tsung gave ten thousand slaves to a particularly beloved princess.[80]

TREATMENT

Slaves given in such numbers were generally prisoners of war, who after a period of initial hardship gradually achieved some sort of semi-freedom. The situation differed fundamentally from that of the classic period of slavery in Rome. There large groups of slaves were kept in barracks and treated as chattel. Under the conditions of Liao economy, family agriculture was preferable to large-scale "chattel" work. Liao slavery drew from different social strata; it involved different forms of labor, and different methods of treatment.

As indicated in our preceding remarks, the status of Liao slaves varied greatly. There might be practically no freedom, even the right of property and family being denied. When a slave-owner was plotting treason, then—and then only—could his slave appear in court against him.[81] At other times the master might exercise extraordinary authority; he might imprison his slave or torture him. Only when he killed him was the master punished, for then he interfered with a prerogative which the government reserved for itself. It is not clear how many cases of this kind actually reached the courts. Perhaps there were not many, but, when they did, the hand of the state was heavy although leniency increased with the rising rank of the killer. Yeh-lü Niao-lü, the husband of a princess, killed a slave and at first was sentenced

---

[69] VII, 1 (1).
[70] Cf. XII (34).
[71] VII, 1 (47).
[72] VII, 1 (6) (30) (44).
[73] VII, 1 (14).
[74] VII, 1 (36).

[75] VII, 1 (44) (30).
[76] VII, 1 (19).
[77] MCCSC 2, 18b and MCPL 2, 49a.
[78] IX, note 48; CS 96, 4b.
[79] VIII (7).
[80] VII, 1 (12); cf. also I, 1 (4).
[81] VII, 1 (20).

to death; but his portrait of Shêng-tsung had been highly praised, and he was therefore only banished to the frontier for life.[82]   Princess Sai-ko, who murdered a slave, was lowered in rank but did not lose her royal status, while her husband was only deprived of his honorary title.[83]

The lot of the slaves differed according to the work assigned them and the conditions under which it had to be done.   If they were permitted to have families and to acquire some property as industrial laborers, they were not full slaves but only half-slaves in the more precise sense of the term.[84]

Most of the enslaved workers in the agricultural or pastoral regions should be so considered.   They are generally referred to as "families," not as "individuals."   The decree of 989 makes explicit the government's preference for family rather than individual status of the captured Chinese.[85]   United in families and having property of their own from which they paid "taxes" to masters or temples and perhaps also to the government,[86] they enjoyed a position which had within it elements of freedom and of slavery. When they were given as presents, they were handed over as "families," not as persons attached to the land.   In the latter case they would have been serfs; actually, however, they must be considered half-slaves.   The term pu ch'ü 部曲 seems to refer to a group of persons whose status was below that of free men,[87] but who nevertheless might act for their masters in rendering certain services at the imperial court.[88]

The "transferred" (chuan 轉) families lived in a state of semi-bondage, from which they might advance into full freedom if they showed unusual military prowess.   They were frequently attached to ordos and thus were part of the standing army of the country.   Or they might continue in civil life as subdued families with a semi-free status.   Evidently, the artisan retainers became a not unimportant factor in the country's economic life.   But, even though this was the case, the "government people" remained bondsmen.   Full freedom was generally open to them only when—or just before—they joined the army. Two passages in the Ch'i-tan Kuo Chih show this clearly.   The first reads, "At this time [1116] the unemployed men of Liao-tung were enrolled and the strong adults from the transferred families were urged to enter the army.   Since the [people of] Liao-tung

used to be at odds with the Nü-chên and Po-hai, if the transferred families were made free they were likely to exert themselves for the country."[89]   The other says, "The so-called transferred families began to be enlisted. Since the [people of] Liao-tung used to be at odds with the Po-hai, if the transferred families were made free they would probably sacrifice their lives with passion."[90]   The "precious" artisans evidently were well treated; only thus could they be encouraged to render their needed services with a maximum of skill and effectiveness.

The status of the personal slaves varied, as did the treatment accorded them.   They were exposed to any outrage short of murder, yet at times great confidence was reposed in them.   That Yeh-lü A-mo-li dared to consider making his slave Yen-kuei the prefect of a newly established region[91] reveals the lengths to which recognition might be carried.   The Ch'i-tan certainly did not resemble the Romans; yet an individual Ch'i-tan might become as dependent upon a favorite Chinese slave as the wealthy Roman upon his educated Greek bondsman.   Chinese slaves might act as brain-trusts even for the government.   The edict of 1048 decreed that slaves should not offer their advice to the court in person.   Obviously this had been done previously.   But the court still found ways of benefiting from their valuable ideas: "The views of slaves might be presented to their masters. . . ."[92]

A slave girl might become a concubine.   She often did.   Her son would then be free because of her newly acquired status, but he could not enjoy the social privileges of his father. He could not claim a hereditary official position,[93] although the heated arguments over the status of concubines' sons[94] seem to indicate that there were many such claims.   The law tried to keep the sons of slave-mothers in a low position, but their real status varied with the father's power and intent.   Recourse could be had to legal appeal, but according to LS 80, 4a it was frequently difficult to arrive at a decision.   In spite of the law, the son of a concubine might frequently obtain a high position and keep it.

g. TRENDS TOWARD SOCIAL CHANGE

Did the consolidation of the Liao empire modify the status of its social strata?   In a pacified country the opportunity for advancement because of civil achievement could be expected to increase.   In 989 prisoners of war were redeemed and reunited with

[82] LS 86, 3b.
[83] VII, 1 (23).   See also LS 93, 5b.
[84] Cf. Wittfogel, OS (ms).
[85] VII, 1 (16).
[86] X, 1 (38).
[87] VIII (3).
[88] XI (20).

[89] CTKC 10, 8a.
[90] CTKC 19, 1b.
[91] VII, 1 (18).
[92] VII, 1 (37).
[93] VII, 1 (28).
[94] VII, 1 (26).

their families,[95] no doubt because the government desired to ameliorate their discontents. A similar attitude may have inspired the redemption edict of 1013[96] which attempted to reunite peasant families threatened by famine. For fiscal reasons the government was interested in again registering those families[97] which, because of the connivings of influential nobles and temples, had disappeared from the public rolls.

According to CS 96, 4b, the Buddhist temples had control over enslaved peasant families even after the collapse of the Liao dynasty. Government effort to consolidate the free peasant families was counterbalanced by the greed of private individuals and institutions. The growth of this greed coincides with the increasing decay of Ch'i-tan power and Liao society.

h. CHANGING RELATIONS BETWEEN CH'I-TAN AND CHINESE

In general the *Liao Shih* texts treat slavery purely as a social manifestation. We therefore have had to treat it in the same way, but it must be kept in mind that the status of the individual was affected not only by his position among his co-nationals, but also by the relation of his ethnic group to the entire imperial order. As has frequently been stated, Liao society consisted of two main divisions, the tribal with the Ch'i-tan people at its core and the sedentary with the Chinese as the major group. The two divisions, which we have examined separately, were actually component elements in a single conquest situation. This situation determined the initial status as well as the changing position of its parts.

Most conspicuous among the subordinate groups were the Chinese. For obvious reasons, their fate is recorded by the authors of the *Liao Shih* in more detail than that of the Po-hai or Koreans. Submission and conquest initially placed the new Chinese subjects in a clearly inferior position, a situation which was in all probability mitigated by the relatively peaceful surrender of some of the Chinese territories. But the sociology of conquest demonstrates that surrender is no guarantee of considerate treatment. It was political expediency and economic necessity rather than any sentimental motive which influenced the status of the Chinese within the social order of the Liao empire. Ch'i-tan statecraft and economy being what they were, Chinese officials had to be employed and Chinese trade and agriculture had to be maintained. Taking advantage of this situation, the various Chinese groups pressed toward

better positions, administrative as well as social. While the Ch'i-tan handed over certain technical posts to the Chinese, they strove hard, and not without success, to preserve as much of their original superiority as possible. The political mechanics of this struggle will be described in section XIV; its social and legal forms may be inferred from a number of passages given in VII, 1.

The edict of 921 announced one legal status for the tribal groups headed by the Ch'i-tan, and another for the Chinese.[98] But the increasing weight of the Chinese sector soon found expression. During the reign period Hui-t'ung (938–947) the examination system (symbol of the indispensability of Chinese officialdom) was reestablished.[99] Chinese clothes were worn by the emperor and by the Ch'i-tan officials of the southern or Chinese section of the empire.[100] In 941 these "southern" officials received formal permission to take Chinese wives.[101] A few decades later (after 983) Chinese clothes were worn on important ceremonial occasions by all high officials[102] without any geographical restriction. The acceptance of the dragon as a sacred emblem which ranked with the sun, the mountains, and—interesting feature —the moon[103] definitely pointed in the same direction.

The decree of 994 proclaiming the validity of Chinese law for the Ch'i-tan[104] was a war measure; it did not create real equality. According to the new code, a Chinese who killed a Ch'i-tan was condemned to death, and his wife and children became government slaves, but a Ch'i-tan who killed a Chinese was not executed. His family might be enslaved; he himself might merely be banished to the frontier,[105] or if he was a member of the nobility he might escape personal punishment altogether.[106] This state of affairs caused influential Chinese circles to ask for additional legal guarantees, and these were granted. Special Chinese officials were appointed to examine cases of this kind, but under pressure from a dissatisfied Ch'i-tan, Chung-yüan 重元 (Hsing-tsung's brother), it was decided in 1044 to appoint five Ch'i-tan police commissioners to handle homicides involving Ch'i-tan.[107]

The legal struggle reflects an underlying economic and social conflict. During the eleventh century the Chinese became richer and more influential. They

---

[95] VII, 1 (16).
[96] XII (34).
[97] VIII (3).

[98] VII, 1 (3).
[99] See LS 79, 1a; cf. also XIV, introduction.
[100] VII, 1 (7).
[101] VII, 1 (8).
[102] See note 100.
[103] VII, 1 (46).
[104] VII, 1 (17).
[105] See SMCW 10a.
[106] See above.
[107] VII, 1 (35); cf. also OYWCCC 118, 10a.

began to buy slaves from the Ch'i-tan. Their cultural prestige rose. Numerous Chinese features modified the ceremonial and religious order of the Ch'i-tan. The wearing of Chinese clothes at the great ceremonies was no longer confined to the three highest ranks within the Ch'i-tan hierarchy; after 1055 it was expected of all Ch'i-tan officials.[108] Even the restrictions concerned with intermarriage between Ch'i-tan, Hsi, Po-hai, and Chinese seem to have been relaxed.[109]

But the tendency to accept elements of Chinese culture provoked a vigorous countermovement. In the middle of the eleventh century the attempt of a Ch'i-tan to participate in the Chinese examinations was drastically punished;[110] the sale of slaves to Chinese was forbidden by law.[111] The next to last emperor, Tao-tsung, saw no reason to be ashamed of his own civilization which he considered as good as that of the Chinese.[112] Small wonder then that in 1070 a new decree again proclaimed the basic difference between the Ch'i-tan and the Chinese.[113] Although a formal revision of the previous laws was not achieved,[114] perhaps because of secret Chinese resistance, the edict of 1070 and the succeeding legislative efforts express clearly the continued tension between the two competing ethnic factions within Liao society.

2. THE POSITION OF WOMEN

Even a cursory survey of the social order must consider the position of women, for an understanding of their status illuminates many other aspects of the society. The pastoral economy of Inner Asia made man the uncontested master of its most important property, the big animal herds. The master of the herds allocated the use of property within the family group, just as he controlled power within the tribe. Ch'i-tan society seems to have followed this general pattern; it was patriarchal in its authority and patrilineal in its succession.

The situation, however, was not one-sided. The necessities of a nomadic life affected both sexes, but during the man's frequent and extended absences for hunting and warfare his tent and certain of his animals were turned over to the care and control of women. Chingis Khan with unconscious humor compares the Mongol man to the sun which cannot shine in two places at once: "when the master is away or

at war, the wife must keep the household in good condition and order. . . ."[115] An early European historian elaborates this point further by saying, "The management of the man's fortune, among the Tartars, belongs to the women. . . . The husbands wholly employ themselves with hunting and war and trouble themselves with nothing else."[116] This description fails to mention those day-by-day herding activities of the men which were of particular importance in a pacified pastoral society where men were increasingly taken up with the herds and women with the yurt.[117] In the early days of independent nomadic life the men often left camp and cattle for a considerable time. Then the economic functions of the women necessarily went beyond the limits of the family home.

To what degree the Ch'i-tan women were actually engaged in caring for the herds is not clear. LS 104, 2a records a frontier situation in which the soldiers' women and children took care of the family animals.[118] In this case the men camped and fought nearby. But, when the soldiers of the ordo families had to go to distant battlefields, they had to leave their wives at home with the herds for weeks and months. Certainly Ch'i-tan women knew how to drive ox-carts,[119] and riding on horseback was their normal mode of travel.[120] It is not too much to assume that the wives of the commoners, besides managing the affairs of the "household," were capable of attending to the tasks of herding when their husbands' absence in wars or hunts required it.

Description of the tribal marriage customs of the northeast indicate that the Ch'i-tan girls enjoyed a freedom of action[121] which was strictly interdicted to their Chinese sisters. Further evidence of this independence is given in numerous passages in the *Liao Shih* which relate in considerable detail the spectacular deeds of various female members of the imperial family, empresses, empress dowagers, and princesses. During the long period of imperial China (221 B.C.–A.D. 1912) few empresses played a conspicuous political role. Yet during the relatively short Liao dynasty, with only nine emperors, an unusual number of powerful female co-rulers emerged.

After the death of their husbands these ladies took full advantage of the immaturity of an heir apparent, not infrequently going so far as to insure their own influence by conspiracies and intrigues against an

---

[108] See VII, 1 (7).

[109] According to a proposal made before the middle of the eleventh century by the Chinese official, Han Shao-fang 韓紹芳 (*Wu Hsi Chi* by Yü Ching = LSSI 15, 15b).

[110] XIV, 3 (9).

[111] VII, 1 (36).

[112] VII, 1 note 65.

[113] VII, 1 (45).

[114] XIV, 4 (30).

[115] Riasanovsky 37, 87 ff.

[116] Petis de la Croix, quoted by Vernadsky 38, 357. See also Barthold 97, 15.

[117] *Cf.* Prejevalsky 76 I, 69.

[118] XV, 1 (45).

[119] *Cf.* IV, introduction.

[120] IV (14).

[121] See VII, 2, note 197.

eldest son.[122] Even during a husband's lifetime Ch'i-tan matrons participated openly in the country's political affairs. A-pao-chi's wife, Ying-t'ien, offered her husband a scheme for murdering the rival chieftains;[123] she told him how to deal with the Uighur mission in 924.[124] She had her own military camp,[125] mobilized the Shu-shan Army,[126] and carried on campaigns of her own against tribal enemies;[127] she promoted industry by bringing artisans to the camps.[128] Opposing her will to tribal tradition,[129] she refused to be buried with her dead husband, and established herself instead as temporary regent over both military and civil affairs.[130]

No Liao empress equalled Ying-t'ien in ruthlessness, vigor, and effectiveness, but on several later occasions the empire was controlled by the young emperor's mother or spouse rather than by the ruler himself. Ching-tsung's wife was influential even during her husband's lifetime; she became all-powerful after his death[131] when as empress dowager she had complete control over her son, the Emperor Shêng-tsung. Her authority was so great that, according to CTKC 7, 6b, she scolded and beat him. She too had a military camp and army of her own;[132] she personally led the Liao troops against Sung and concluded the fateful peace treaty of 1005.[133] Shêng-tsung's grandaunt, Hu-lien 胡輦, also excelled in military achievement and in 994 was made commander in chief of the expeditionary force against border tribes of the west. She is credited with the establishment of the famous northwestern city of K'o-tun. In 1006 her ambitious intrigue to overthrow the empress dowager was uncovered; a year later she was put to death in the prison where she was being held.[134]

After the death of Shêng-tsung's mother, his wife, Ch'in-ai, exerted a considerable political influence which reached its peak immediately after her husband's death in 1031. The second wife of Hsing-tsung, the next emperor, also exercised no small power during her husband's reign, but she too achieved her greatest influence in the early years of her son's rule. In general, Liao empress dowagers held so distin-guished a position that every imperial envoy sent to the Sung court was accompanied by another delegate of the same rank, sent by the emperor's mother.[135]

Among the entrusted prefectures of the empire the three particularly large ones which head our list were set up by imperial princesses with their personal bondsmen.[136] Since the records depict the Ch'i-tan men as anything but effeminate weaklings, the extraordinary power of their women probably reflects strong matriarchal tendencies within the older Ch'i-tan society.

The unusually high political and military status of these women found its natural corollary in their economic independence. An empress could give a princess a large number of slaves.[137] Buddhist temples received huge donations from the Princess of Ch'in and Yüeh, from Tao-tsung's wife, I-tê, and from a noble Hsiao lady.[138] Obviously great fortunes in land, money, and slaves were held by female members of the ruling families who were free to dispose of them at will.

Contrary to Chinese tradition, which gave little opportunity to a wife to divorce her husband, the Mongol tribes of Inner Asia permitted not only the husband but also the wife to initiate a divorce.[139] Were the Ch'i-tan women equally free in these domestic arrangements? For the commoners we can say nothing, but we do know that women of noble rank could divorce an unsatisfactory husband and marry again.[140] Ch'in-ai's daughter, Yen-mu-chin, was divorced several times; she married four times.[141] Matrimonial fidelity was considered meritorious, but again contrary to Chinese tradition it was by no means taken for granted. A princess might divorce an exiled husband; if she refused to do so she was considered extremely loyal.[142]

According to our texts, divorced women were permitted to remarry without interference, but the remarriage of widows was restricted. Until the death of T'ai-tsu the widow of a khaghan was buried with her husband. But T'ai-tsu's widow, the first empress, demurred at this questionable honor,[143] and her power was so great that she was not forced to

---

[122] See XIII, introduction.

[123] CTKC 23, 2a. See III, introduction.

[124] VII, 2 (11).

[125] XV, 1 (8).

[126] XV, 1 (25).

[127] Cf. LS 71, 2a ff.

[128] III (2).

[129] See VII, 2, note 27.

[130] VII, 2 (12).

[131] See XVI, 983, LS 10, 4b.

[132] XV, 1 (11).

[133] LS 71, 4a–b.

[134] XV, 1, note 120.

[135] SHYK 196, 36b ff; Nieh CC 40, tables.

[136] Cf. I, 1 (4).

[137] VII, 1 (12).

[138] See IX, introduction, Donations made to Buddhist Temples.

[139] Riasanovsky 37, 241. Cf. also for the nineteenth century Timkowsky 1827 II, 310 ff.

[140] VII, 2 (35).

[141] VII, 2 (75).

[142] VII, 2 (69).

[143] VII, 2 (12) and note 27.

follow traditional behavior. From then on the practice seems to have been abolished.

T'ai-tsu's mother-in-law was married twice.[144] Was her first husband dead, or was she divorced when she married again? Yen-mu-chin's first husband was executed, but the record concerning her second marriage[145] suggests that she may have remarried after a divorce. A decree of 941 providing mates for the widowers and widows of three Ch'i-tan tribes who found it impossible to live alone[146] would seem to imply that poorer tribesmen were disinclined to marry widows. The same aversion is reported for various branches of the Altaic world before and after the Liao period. The proto-Turkic Kao-ch'ê pitied widows, but disliked marrying them.[147] Among the ethnic cousins of the Ch'i-tan, the Shih-wei, a widow did not remarry because she was considered "the dead man's wife."[148] This coincides with the explanation which the Mongols of the thirteenth century gave to Rubruck. According to the famous Western traveler, "No widow marries, for the following reason: they believe that all who serve them in this life shall serve them in the next, so as regards a widow they believe that she will always return to her first husband after death."[149] That the Ch'i-tan had a similar belief may be inferred from the decree of 941 and the traditional burial of a khaghan's wife with her dead husband.

The Chinese also hesitated to marry widows, but their religious formulation[150] differed considerably from that of the Ch'i-tan. Whatever modifications occurred after the establishment of the dynasty, the Ch'i-tan attitude obviously expressed a general Inner Asiatic rather than a Chinese tradition.

The Ch'i-tan disapproval of the remarriage of widows would seem to conflict with the levirate which is documented for the imperial family of the Liao dynasty[151] and which no doubt functioned also in the wider tribal society. The levirate is recorded for Inner Asia in the time of the Huns;[152] it was still practised by the Mongols[153] who also restricted the remarriage of widows. The histories offer no explanation of this seeming contradiction. However, the contradiction disappears if we assume that the disapproval of remarriage did not extend to the husband's

brothers, but was in fact a means of assuring the claim of the husband's family upon the widow.

Rubruck found the Mongols of the thirteenth century still marrying "at the same time or successively two sisters."[154] That the sororate also functioned among the Ch'i-tan is certain for, in 940, the Liao government decreed that such marriages were no longer compulsory. It is doubtful whether this measure affected to any large degree the marriage customs of the tribal commoners. Within the ruling clans the old practice may have become less prevalent, but by no means was it abandoned. Sisters appear in the harems of both Tao-tsung and T'ien-tsu.[155] At the wedding of a Liao emperor the sisters of the bride participated with her in making ceremonial offerings to the imperial ancestors and in turn receiving presents from them.[156]

Legally the position of Ch'i-tan concubines was not high; practically it was not very different from that of the concubines of the early Mongols whose sons were considered legitimate.[157] But, whatever the status of concubines and widows in Liao society may have been, there can be no doubt of the unusual independence enjoyed by Ch'i-tan women in general. This independence is further reflected in their important position in tribal religion and ritual.

In Ch'i-tan cosmology the [male] heaven had as his complement the female earth. According to popular tradition, the deity of the earth was an old woman who rode a gray ox.[158] At first glance she seems to resemble the Chinese earth goddess, Ti-ch'i 地祇 or Hou-t'u 后土. But the Chinese goddess is definitely part of an agricultural world,[159] whereas the Ch'i-tan deity is typically pastoral in her activities. Even if both deities have a common origin—which is none too probable—their concrete historical setting is completely different.

Like their cosmology, the origin myth of the Ch'i-tan also reflects the strong position of women in their society. On the sacred Mu-yeh Mountain stood not only the temple of the first tribal ancestor but that of the first ancestress as well. Throughout the dynasty the horse and the ox, the companions of the

[144] The mother of Ying-t'ien, the first Liao empress, was married twice (see VII, 2, note 3).
[145] See VII, 2 (75) and notes.
[146] VII, 2 (21).
[147] PS 98, 23b. Cf. Radloff 93, I, 127.
[148] Sui 84, 21a.
[149] Rubruck 00, 78.
[150] See de Groot, RSC II, 1, 757 ff.
[151] LS 65, 5b and 111, 2b.
[152] SC 110, 2a.
[153] See Carpini 28, 8 and Marco Polo 03 I, 253.

[154] Rubruck 00, 77.
[155] See LS 71, 7b and 8b.
[156] VII, 2 (89).
[157] For the attitude assumed under Chingis Khan and shortly afterwards see Riasanovsky 37, 86, Vernadsky 38, 357, and Carpini 28, 9. Later the status of sons of concubines seems to have deteriorated, perhaps under the influence of the Manchus who, according to Hyakinth, tried to introduce monogamy in the middle of the seventeenth century. Cf. Hyakinth 1832, 136 ff.
[158] VII, 2 (24).
[159] See de Groot 86 I, 147 ff.; idem 18, 187.

original ancestors, were offered to these tribal progenitors in the spring and autumn sacrifices and before the start of a military campaign.[160]

Women participated conspicuously in numerous important ceremonies. Weddings were directed by the so-called *ao* woman who impersonated the tribe's ancestral mother. During an imperial wedding a woman invited the bride to attend, another held a magic mirror, and a third personified fertility.[161]

That women should have a significant role in essentially domestic ceremonies is readily understandable, although Ch'i-tan participation goes considerably beyond Chinese custom. But that she should be conspicuous in public ceremonies is most extraordinary from a Chinese point of view.[162] Yet this was the case in Liao society. The empress accompanied the emperor to the ceremonial hare hunt and, as the lines of hunters formed, she and her husband offered their prayers to the great Ch'i-tan deity, the sun.[163] In the annual worship of Mu-yeh Mountain, a rite whose antiquity is attested by the presence of a head shaman and some lesser ones, the emperor and his consort made the great initial sacrifice in the presence of their cortege composed of noble women as well as noble men.[164]

The mystic rebirth of the tribal chieftain and of his historical successor, the Liao emperor, was supervised by an old man and an old woman.[165] But it was not enough for the greatest of the Ch'i-tan matrons that their imperial sons should experience this ancient ceremony; some even insisted upon undergoing the magical rebirth normally reserved for the emperor alone. Among them were the mothers of Hsing-tsung and Tao-tsung.[166] They performed the ceremony at a time when their imperial sons were still young and great power rested with them as empress dowagers. Especially spectacular was the performance of Empress Dowager Ch'êng-t'ien, the mother and tutor of the boy emperor Shêng-tsung, who obtained rebirth in 984 and again in 986, in the latter year twice at short intervals.[167] Her will to power, real as well as magic, could only be satisfied when translated into ritual terms. It probably was no accident that this same empress dowager who was "reborn" with such

intensity led the mounted warriors of Liao in their most glorious triumph against the great Sung empire.

3. THE KINSHIP SYSTEM OF THE CH'I-TAN

The Ch'i-tan who faithfully preserved many of their economic, social, and military traditions were equally conservative regarding their traditional kinship patterns. Ch'i-tan kinship terms are not recorded in any texts known to us. In the Chinese sources Chinese terms are used instead.

The *Liao Shih* speaks of the *tsu* 族, a kinship unit extending beyond the limit of the small family.[168] The term *tsu*, like *tsung* 宗 and *hsing* 姓, has had an interesting semantic history. Within imperial China all three terms, over and above their general meaning, designate specific aspects of the patrilineal exogamous clan: the word *tsung* stresses the origin of all clan members from a common ancestor; *hsing* refers to their common name and implies exogamy; *tsu* emphasizes the unity of "the generations which compose the clan."[169] This last term may also refer to those generations that are united by the mourning rituals, the "nine *tsu*,"[170] but such a special application in no way negates the conception of the clan as an unbroken line of a "hundred generations." Since Inner Asiatic tribal society differs in structure from the Chinese, it is well to inquire what the Chinese word *tsu* connoted when applied to the Ch'i-tan kin organization.

LS 32, 4a states that various tribes within the empire had *tsu* while others did not.[171] As examples of *tsu* with tribes or tribes with *tsu*, the text cites the two branches of the imperial tribe as well as the Hsi and the Shih-wei. The *tsu*-less organizations referred to are two tribes composed of former camp bondsmen[172] and one other consisting of members of the eight Ch'i-tan tribes.[173] The bondsmen were probably tribal prisoners of war. Were they split up into individual families, when as captives they were assigned to various camps and again later united in proto-tribal groups, the *shih-lieh?* This is not beyond possibility, but it is difficult to understand why, if they ever had *tsu*, these *tsu* were so quickly forgotten, even when a restored tribal status would naturally have suggested the restoration of their traditional kinship organization.

Why particularly did the third tribe, the T'ê-li-t'ê-mien, remain *tsu*-less? Its members were free Ch'i-

---

[160] VII, 2 (84).

[161] VII, 2 (88) (89).

[162] When the Chinese empress ceremonially cared for the silkworms, male observers were excluded. Only court ladies and eunuchs were allowed to assist her (de Groot 18, 251 ff.).

[163] VII, 2 (93).

[164] VII, 2 (85).

[165] VII, 2 (86).

[166] VII, 2 (57) (62).

[167] VII, 2 (39).

[168] The term *chia* 家 occasionally may designate a larger complex. See I, 2, note 1.

[169] De Groot, RSC I, 562.

[170] For an early appearance of this formula see SSCS 2, 5a; Legge, CC III, 17; KHTT sub *tsu* 族.

[171] See I, 2 (1).

[172] See I, 2 (5), nos. 6 and 7.

[173] *Op. cit.*, no. 5.

tan men and women. During the long process of their tribal consolidation they had ample time and opportunity to organize *tsu* if they had wanted to. How readily this could be done is shown by the tenacity with which the Chinese subjects of the empire preserved their clan affiliations even when they were shifted to the remote corners of the country.

A partial answer to some of these questions is suggested by a memorial presented to the Liao throne by Yeh-lü Shu-ch'ên in the year 1074. This document stated that the otherwise enlightened dynastic regime had set up only two clan names (*hsing shih* 姓氏), Yeh-lü and Hsiao, and suggested that all tribes should establish special *hsing-shih* "so as to make the marriages between men and women harmonize with the code of proper behavior."[174] Yeh-lü Shu-ch'ên's words are confirmed by the *Ch'i-tan Kuo Chih* which states that originally the Ch'i-tan had no clan names (*hsing-shih*) and that even in dynastic time they set up only two clans (*hsing*), namely those of the two ruling houses.[175]

To be sure, the absence of Chinese clans does not necessarily imply the absence of extended kin groups among the Ch'i-tan. Their two ruling families were complex exogamic units long before they were Sinicized.[176] Numerous Chinese sources besides the *Liao Shih* call the larger kin groups among Inner Asiatic tribes *tsu*. Western scholars have often referred to these aggregations as clans[177]—a term that is entirely permissible if it is adequately defined.[178] But the significant differences in structure between the Inner Asiatic and Chinese type of kin organization would seem to be more strikingly exposed if, in line with certain recent anthropological studies, the extended families of the former were designated as lineages.

A patrilineal lineage may be defined as "an exogamic unit containing a man and his descendants through males."[179] As long as the male descendants continue to share their fathers' residence, while the females move away at marriage, the group is unilocal and patrilocal.[180] When the group expands and some

of its male members take up residence elsewhere, "the new alignment of relatives may be described as an exogamic multilocal patrilineal lineage."[181] Under fluid living conditions there is a strong tendency for the cut-off groups to forget former ties and consider themselves separate units. Stable conditions, on the other hand, aided by such devices as a common name, exogamic marriage regulations, and, at times, common ownership of property or joint ceremonial participation[182] favor the perpetuation of early affiliations. The resulting multilocal, patrilocal organization, "a unilateral group of kindred derived in the male line from the same real or supposed ancestor"[183] is conveniently—and reasonably—called a patrilineal clan.[184]

It is evident that the Chinese extended kin group, which developed in a relatively stable agricultural society, follows the clan pattern.[185] It is equally evident that the pastoralism of Inner Asia required

---

[174] VII, 2 (67).
[175] CTKC 23, 1a.
[176] *Cf.* VII, 2 (1).
[177] *Cf.* Shirokogoroff 24, 15 ff.; *idem* 33, 120 ff.; Riasanovsky 37, 254 and *passim*.
[178] This has been illuminatingly done by G. P. Murdock in a paper delivered at the annual meeting of the American Ethnological Society at Andover, Mass., in December 1941.
[179] Titiev 43, 524.
[180] *Loc. cit.* The unilocal, matrilocal counterpart is the "maternal lineage" (Murdock 43, 302). The importance of residence in the organization of kin (as over against blood) while temporarily slighted has recently received increased attention in anthropological writings. *Cf.* Gold-

enweiser 16, 353; *idem* 22, 235 ff.; Lowie 19, 39; *idem* 40, 263 ff.; Linton 33, 36, 137 and 209 ff.; Kroeber 38, 299 ff.
[181] Titiev 43, 525. For the roots of Titiev's thesis see, among others, Rivers 24, 52; Gifford 26, 389 ff.; Linton 33, 133 ff.; *idem* 36, 192 ff. The term "lineage" has been used recently by a number of anthropologists to denote kin groups more complex than a simple unilocal family and less complex than the clan; the phenomenon itself, however, has been observed for a considerable time, particularly in Inner Asia, but in other parts of the world as well. For instance, the wealthy stratified fishing tribe, the Kwakiutl, on the northwestern coast have "no clear-cut clan organization" (Lowie 37, 570) such as the neighboring Tsimshian boast (Boas 35, 173 ff.). The Kwakiutl were organized in exogamic kinship units, *numayms*, which Boas designates as tribal subdivisions (*op. cit.*, 41) or more frequently as families (*op. cit.*, 117). On page 97 the term "clan" is used, but this isolated occurrence is supported neither by the context nor by the terminology used elsewhere. The detailed *numayn* histories given by Dr. Boas (21, 836–1277) are called "family histories." In a general anthropology recently edited by him these units which extended beyond the small family (Boas 35, 3, 28 and 66) and repeatedly broke off (*op. cit.*, 42) have been called lineages (Bunzel 38, 357). *Cf.* also Lowie 19, 37; Rivers 24, 20.
[182] Linton 36, 198 ff.
[183] Titiev 43, 527.
[184] In the past the term "clan" primarily designated the matrilineal unit, "gens" the patrilineal unit, and "sib" either phenomenon. More recently the term "clan" has also been applied to both types of descent group. *Cf.* Lowie 20, 111 ff.; Kroeber 23, 232; Linton 36, 197; Murdock 43, 235 ff. and 272.
[185] Linton sees the development of a "strong functional clan organization . . . correlated, in a very general way, with stability of culture and fixity of residence." He suggests: "The stability of clans as functional units in China may well have been due to the relative stability of Chinese culture" (Linton 36, 201–202).

a much more flexible economic, political, and kin organization. Here instability was not a vice, but a virtue—so much so, in fact, that according to Radloff it constituted "the chief condition for the wealth of a nomadic people."[186] True, even in this world of tribal movement and frequent aggression, self-preservation demanded strong local or kin solidarity,[187] but the pattern of this solidarity changed with the changing economic, military, and political situation. "The conglomeration of the political nomadic units transforms itself continually and within it there originate always new tribes, kinship groups, and sub-groups."[188]

This general Inner Asiatic picture also mirrors the life of the Ch'i-tan. The data presented in section I show the tribes of Liao in almost continuous political flux. The memorial of 1074 suggests corresponding instability in their organization of kin. Chinese observers were amazed at the attitude of the early Ch'i-tan toward their ancestors: they did not cry at the death of a parent; they did not bury the corpse, but placed it in a tree where it was left for three years, after which time they removed the bones and burned them.[189] Such disposal of the dead fitted the exigencies of nomadic life, but it did not encourage stability of interest in a common ancestral tradition. The Ch'i-tan worshipped their tribal ancestors, the progenitors of the eight original tribes, and, after the establishment of the dynasty, the ancestors of the emperor also; but worship of the ancestors of the individual groups is not recorded in our texts.

In China such rites were important in the annual ceremonial calendar. The people honored their family ancestors in the tenth month[190] and at other times as well.[191] In the tenth month the ceremonial calendar of the Liao empire also records a sacrifice by the emperor to the god of the Black Mountain, who cared for the souls of the people.[192] Even if influenced by Chinese ideas of the continued existence of souls, this Ch'i-tan ceremony remained tribal and contained no hint of the worship of family ancestors.

The absence of clan names as well as the limited development of family ancestor worship was probably the result rather than the cause of Ch'i-tan nomadism. But, whatever their interrelation, all three factors tended to increase family segmentation. The question then arises: at what point would the descendants of a common ancestor disregard the original family nexus?

A survey of the social history of Inner Asia shows that many pastoral tribes counted their kin for a limited number of generations only. In the time of Han, the Ch'iang 羌, nomadic inhabitants of the Kuku-Nōr region, might marry within their own group if both the man and the girl were twelve generations removed from their common ancestor.[193] Until recent times other Central Asiatic groups have counted their kin in a similar way. Among the Khirghiz marriages within the same kin group were forbidden "up to the sixth degree of relationship exclusively."[194] Beyond this limit marriage was permitted. Hudson reports that the Qazaqs, who significantly did not distinguish terminologically between tribe, clan, and generation,[195] forbade their young men to marry girls of their own uru, an exogamic complex which shared a common male ancestor over several generations, usually seven,[196] but sometimes six or ten.[197] Recently the number has been reduced to two or three.[198] The ancient Yakuts "reckoned relationship only to the ninth generation." More remote relatives were considered members of other kinship groups, "with whom it is possible to marry."[199] The breaking-off of the kinship relation in the ninth generation is well documented in an old proverb that reads, "I need not disturb myself over such relatives if they fall in the water. . . ."[200]

A similar arrangement existed among eastern groups of Inner Asiatic tribes. The northern Tungus even today have no special name for their extended kin group[201] which foreign observers have conventionally called "clans."[202] Each unit has its "clan" spirit, but that does not prevent the breaking of the so-called clan "as soon as it does not satisfy the practical needs. . . ."[203] The shamans find a simple solution by dividing the spirits also.[204]

The Manchus of Manchuria organize their kin into hala and mokun. These have no proper names,[205] but nevertheless they restrict marriage for a limited number of generations. Members of two mokun within the same hala may marry if they have "two

[186] Radloff 93 I, 517.
[187] Op. cit., 418.
[188] Hirth 99, 45.
[189] See Sui 84, 19b; WTS 72, 4b; CTKC 23, 1a–b.
[190] CCYL 2a.
[191] De Groot 86 I, 16 ff.
[192] VII, 2 (83).

[193] HHS 87, 1b.
[194] Riasanovsky 37, 256.
[195] Hudson 38, 17 ff.
[196] Op. cit., 43.
[197] Op. cit., 44.
[198] Op. cit., 43.
[199] According to an informant of Seroshevskii, quoted by Hudson 38, 98.
[200] Loc. cit.
[201] Shirokogoroff 33, 122 and 203.
[202] Loc. cit.
[203] Op. cit., 203.
[204] Op. cit., 204.
[205] Shirokogoroff 24, 18, 19, and 50.

different ancestors in the fifth senior class,"[206] five generations being the lower limit and nine the upper for the exogamic unit.[207]

In special circumstances, such as the ceremonial mourning, the Chinese also recognize numerical limitations, but in theory at least all generations in a particular clan are indissolubly linked by their descent from a common ancestor. In the tribal instances cited above the numerical formulas envisage and sanction the breaking-off of a lineage.

The Ch'i-tan, whose kinship organization was admittedly non-Chinese, in all probability also recognized a numerical limitation of generations included in their extended families. The sources do not contain any definite statement on this point, but indirect evidence strongly suggests restrictions of this kind. Among the peoples mentioned in our brief survey the lineages comprised the following number of generations:

Ch'iang	12
Qazaq	6, 7 or 10
Khirghiz	6 or 7
Yakut	9
Manchu	5 or 9

The number "nine," which played a significant role in the kin organization of the last two groups, seems to have been of considerable importance in the tribal life of the Uighur Turks.[208] It is also conspicuous in a number of texts dealing with the social and political organization of the Ch'i-tan.

The Horizontal Tents of the imperial lineage were referred to as "the nine tents of the Emperor T'ai-tsu's descendants."[209] The formula was obviously inaccurate during the dynasty. If used after its collapse, it was still incorrect for only eight descendants of T'ai-tsu ascended the throne. However, a point may have been stretched to include the father of the last emperor who was killed while heir apparent. In either case it is remarkable that these Horizontal Tents, which were set up after the establishment of the dynasty and patterned on Chinese principles of clanship, were still characterized by the tribal formula of broken lineages.

The importance of the number nine is further emphasized by the following facts. According to tradition, nine Yao-lien khaghans ruled the Ch'i-tan people. Although it is more than possible that the earlier khaghans were at times the brothers rather than the

fathers of their successors, they are described as *chiu shih* 九世, "the nine reigns."[210] The descendants of each reign constituted a special "tent" or palace.[211] A-pao-chi was not a member of the Yao-lien family. Why then did he call his *tsu* the tenth tent?[212] Manifestly he expressed the political relationship of his family to the former ruling house, but at the same time he announced the establishment of a new and independent line. In the recognition ceremony before the imperial investiture, the new emperor took his place with nine other men all dressed alike and each occupying his own tent.[213] Evidently, nine was as important for the Ch'i-tan as it was for other peoples of Inner Asia.

But practice does not always follow theory. The fact that a number was traditionally preferred is no reason for believing that reality never deviated from it. The powerful and noble lineages would certainly keep their genealogies in mind, whether they had ancestor worship or not. Such knowledge might justify the branching off of an independent unit,[214] but more particularly it might aid in preserving power and prestige within the group. Poor families and weak ones might remember "the genealogies of their immediate ancestors,"[215] yet their "hope of better things" had to be satisfied by association with the strong and rich.[216]

Seen thus, the actual functioning of the *tsu* within the traditional Ch'i-tan society becomes more comprehensible. They were patrilineal exogamic lineages that broke off after a certain number of generations, probably nine. Strong and noble lineages eager to validate their status would be fully aware of their genealogies as a means of enhancing their prestige through regulated marriage. These noble lineages were the *tsu* that appeared on all important occasions as the emperor's tribal escort.[217]

The common people also had *tsu*. The statement in the *Liao Shih* that the Ch'i-tan associated together in lineages (*tsu*) and settled down[218] can only mean that all members in the tribal society belonged to some lineage or other. But, even if this were so, the extended genealogies remained the concern of the powerful families. The warrior families who had been merged into the new T'ê-li-t'ê-mien tribe were

---

[206] *Op. cit.*, 66.

[207] *Op. cit.*, 50 ff.

[208] *Cf.* the "Toguz (nine) Oguz" and the "nine Tatars" of the Orkhon inscriptions (Radloff 97, 142; *cf.* Hirth 99, 43 ff.).

[209] XIV, 1 (14).

[210] XIV, 1 (20), LS 45, 20a.

[211] *Loc. cit.*

[212] XIII (2).

[213] VII, 2, note 188.

[214] For the branching off of "the richest families" among the Mongols see Hudson 38, 87.

[215] *Op. cit.*, 23.

[216] *Op. cit.*, 87.

[217] See VII, 1 and 2, *passim.*

[218] I, 2 (1).

apparently not *tsu*-conscious, and their marriage customs probably made them appear *tsu*-less to the Chinese.

Thus, in the Liao texts the word *tsu* has several meanings which have to be carefully distinguished. In conformity with Chinese usage it designates such "true" clans as the Yeh-lü and the Hsiao, including their subdivisions (family lines or lineages). But the Chinese term is also applied to the traditional Ch'i-tan kin aggregates which lacked essential features of the full-fledged clan.

Greater insight into the nature of the Ch'i-tan *tsu* provides a suggestive working hypothesis for the study of other Asiatic tribal societies. It may even give meaning to one of the earliest Chinese records of a nomadic steppe civilization, that of the Huns. At the end of the first millennium B.C., the Hunnish tribes aroused the fears as well as the curiosity of their sedentary southern neighbors. Ssŭ-ma Ch'ien notes that as a rule the Huns had no clan names (*hsing* 姓), only personal names (*ming* 名[219]). But the same Han author reports that the great, hereditary officials all belonged to "three *hsing*," which constituted the people's "noble stock" (*kuei chung* 貴種[220]); and the official historiographers of the Early and the Later Han dynasties refer to royal and noble *hsing*.[221] The *History of the Later Han Dynasty* designates the distinguished Hunnish kin groups (which at that time were four in number) as the country's noble *tsu*. A permanent marriage arrangement existed between the ruling house and the noble *tsu*.[222]

These data interestingly parallel certain features of the Ch'i-tan kinship system. It is not impossible that the Hunnish *hsing* or *tsu* resembled the Ch'i-tan lineages. This hypothesis implies, first, that the Hunnish commoners also belonged to larger kin groups of some kind and, second, that the *hsing* or *tsu* of their nobles instead of being "true" clans were nothing more than extended and cut-off lineages similar to those of the tribes of Inner Asia at a later period.

4. THE TWO RULING CLANS

a. TRIBAL ROOTS AND IMPERIAL CHANGES

While emphasizing the "clanless" structure of Ch'i-tan society as a whole we noted two exceptions: the imperial family, Yeh-lü, and the consort family, Hsiao. These two kin groups were veritable clans. After the establishment of the dynasty they received clan names.[223] Their members could then be easily distinguished, and exogamy, no longer limited to a few generations, became a permanent factor in their kinship order. The criticism levelled by the memorial of 1074 against the marriage customs of the un-Sinicized majority of the Ch'i-tan people implies that the marriages of the two ruling clans were "properly" concluded. Indeed our texts do not reveal a single transgression of the exogamic rule by either of them.

The Yeh-lü and the Hsiao families existed long before the dynastic period, though they were somewhat differently designated.[224] It is doubtful whether marriage between the two groups was institutionalized in early times, yet LS 71, 1*b*[225] indicates that intermarriage occurred between the two lineages in predynastic days.

However, early in the dynasty these lineages were set up as exogamous clans with obligatory reciprocal marriage arrangements for reasons of political power and prestige. The Hsiao obviously had been almost as influential as the rapidly rising Yeh-lü. Together they could dominate all other lineages, as indeed they did. An analysis of the political machine of Liao[226] and a survey of the dynasty's court rebellions[227] show how carefully the two clans were weighted in the centers of power.

The Chinese kinship organization proved a convenient model for the establishment of the Ch'i-tan clans. The consolidation of kin must have appealed to the ruling group as an expedient device for increasing power; and it is an interesting political fact that the emperor refused to extend the new kinship technique beyond the consort lineage of Hsiao.

Ancestor worship was also stimulated by Chinese contact, but here political expediency dictated that it should remain the exclusive practice of the Yeh-lü, the imperial clan. Sacrifices were offered to the spirits of deceased emperors[228] and members of the imperial lineages.[229] No sacrifices are recorded for any Hsiao ancestor.

---

[219] SC 110, 2*a*. HS 94*A*, 1*b* has the same statement but omits the word "*hsing*." Obviously the meanings are identical.

[220] SC 110, 9*b*. The term *chung* is also used by the eunuch Chung-hang Yüeh who defends Hun society against Chinese criticism (SC 110, 17*a*). De Groot (21, 82) translates *chung* as "tribes" (*Stämme*); we prefer "stock," which according to the SOED (II, 2024) may mean "a line of descent, the descendants of a common ancestor; a family, kindred."

[221] HS 94*A*, 7*a*; HHS, 89, 7*b* ff.

[222] *Op. cit.*, 7*b*–8*a*.

[223] CTKC 23, 1*a*.

[224] See I, 1, note 1 and VII, 2, note 3.

[225] VII, 2 (1).

[226] See XIV, 1, and introduction.

[227] See XIII, introduction.

[228] VII, 2, *passim*; CTKC 23, 3*b*.

[229] LS 49, 4*b*.

TABLE 9
Marriage Relations: The Emperors

Genera-tion	Temple Title	Empress Posthumous Title	Wife Genealogical Position	Reference*
1	(a) T'ai-tsu	Ch'un-ch'in 淳欽	Daughter of P'o-ku 婆姑. Genealogical position unknown	71, 2a
2	(b) T'ai-tsung	Ching-an 靖安	Mother's brother's daughter	71, 3b; CTKC 17, 1a
3	(c) Shih-tsung	Huai-chieh 懷節	Father's mother's brother's daughter	71, 3b
3	(d) Mu-tsung	unknown	Daughter of Hsiao Chih-fan 知璠, whose genealogical position is unknown	71, 4a
4	(e) Ching-tsung	Jui-chih 睿智	Granddaughter in male line of a man in same generation as e's father's father's mother	71, 4a; 78, 2a; CTKC 13, 3b
5	(f) Shêng-tsung	1 Jên-tê 仁德 2 Ch'in-ai 欽哀(愛)	Mother's brother's daughter / Descendant in fourth generation from f's father's father's father's mother's brother	71, 4b–5b / 73, 4b; 71, 5b–6a; CTKC 13, 4b–6a
6	(g) Hsing-tsung	1 Concubine San-ch'a 三㽪 (personal name) 2 Jên-i 仁懿	Daughter of g's half-sister's husband / Mother's brother's daughter	71, 7a; 65, 3a; / 71, 6b; 87, 1a–2b CTKC 13, 6a
7	(h) Tao-tsung	Hsüan-i 宣懿	Father's mother's brother's daughter	71, 7a; 93, 1a ff
8	Heir apparent killed before reaching throne			
9	(i) T'ien-tsu	To-li-lan 奪里懶 (personal name)	Descendant in fourth generation from i's father's father's father's father's mother's brother	71, 7b; 78, 3a–b

* Unless specified to the contrary the references given in tables 9 and 10 are to the *Liao Shih*.

It is possible that in the predynastic period tombs of some sort may have been erected for chiefs and nobles,[230] but it was only after the establishment of the dynasty when the ruling house became more ancestor-conscious that impressive mausoleums were built for the deceased emperors and their wives.[231]

b. UN–CHINESE MARRIAGE FEATURES

In spite of their interest in the Chinese clan the Ch'i-tan rulers retained important features of their traditional kinship system. Not only did they restrict the privileges of clanship to the imperial and consort lineages, but contrary to the Chinese pattern they continued to marry outside their own generation.[232]

Marriages which override generation have a long history among pastoral and semi-pastoral peoples of Inner and Eastern Asia. Han Fei claims that Shun, an early Chinese culture hero with a stockbreeding background, "married his own mother."[233] Among the Huns of the Han period, a son married his father's widows, but not his own mother.[234] A similar custom is reported for the Ch'iang,[235] the Turks,[236] and the Mongols.[237] The Turks also married the wives of deceased older brothers.[238] To this day the pas-

[230] See Hyakinth 1832, 137 ff.; Lattimore 38, 12; *cf.* also Radloff 93 II, 121 ff.
[231] See XI and XV, 1, *passim.*
[232] See tables 9 and 10 and figure 5.

[233] HFT 20, 2b; *cf.* Erkes 39, 214 ff.
[234] SC 110, 2a.
[235] HHS 87, 1b.
[236] Sui 84, 2a–b.
[237] Rubruck 00, 78; Marco Polo 03 I, 253. *Cf.* also Vernadsky 38, 357; Riasanovsky 37, 159; and Hudson 38, 80.
[238] Sui 84, 2a–b.

TABLE 10

Marriage Relations: Imperial Princesses

Genera-tion	Princess		Husband		Reference
	Name	Genealogical Position	Name	Genealogical Position	
2	(a) Chih-ku 質古	T'ai-tsu's daughter	Hsiao Shih-lu 實魯	a's mother's brother	65, 1b; CTKC 15, 1a
	(a') Ai-yin 藹因	Daughter of T'ai-tsu's brother, An-tuan	Hsiao Hai-li 海璨	A Hsiao man in the generation of a' or of her father	78, 1b
3	(b) Lü-pu-ku 呂不古	T'ai-tsung's 1st daughter	Hsiao Ssŭ-wên 思温	Son of a Hsiao man in the same generation as b's father's mother	65, 1b; 78, 2a
	(c) Ch'ao-kuei 嘲瑰	T'ai-tsung's 2nd daughter	Hsiao Hai-li 海璨	A Hsiao man in c's mother's generation. Married also to a'	65, 2a; 78, 1b
5	(d) Kuan-yin-nü 觀音女	Ching-tsung's 1st daughter	Hsiao Chi-hsien 繼先	d's mother's brother	65, 2a; 78, 3a
6	(e) Yen-ko 燕哥	Shêng-tsung's 1st daughter by a concubine	Hsiao P'i-li 匹里	A Hsiao man in e's father's 1st wife's generation. His daughter was married to Hsing-tsung	65, 3a; 71, 7a
	(f) Yen-mu-chin 巖母堇 (married 4 times. The 1st two husbands unknown)	Shêng-tsung's 2nd daughter by Empress Ch'in-ai	(1) Hsiao Hu-tu 胡覩	f's mother's brother's son	65, 3b; 71, 7a; 87, 4a; 114, 1a
			(2) Hsiao Hui 惠	f's mother's brother	65, 3b; 93, 1a ff.
	(g) Shuo-ku 槊古	Shêng-tsung's daughter by Empress Ch'in-ai	Hsiao Hsiao-chung 孝忠	g's mother's brother	65, 3b; 81, 2b
	(h) Ts'ui-pa 崔八	Shêng-tsung's daughter by a concubine	Hsiao Hsiao-hsien 孝先	h's father's 2nd wife's brother	65, 4a; 87, 3a
	(i) Tien-ni 鈿匿	Shêng-tsung's 6th daughter by a concubine	Hsiao Shuang-ku 雙古	A Hsiao man whose generation is unknown. His grandfather was married to a' and c, and his father to j	65, 4a; 93, 5b
	(j) Sai-ko 賽哥	Shêng-tsung's 13th daughter	Hsiao T'u-yü 圖玉	Hsiao man whose son was married to i and whose father was married to a' and c	65, 4b; 93, 5a–b
7	(k) Pa-ch'in 跋芹 (married 3 times. The last husband is unknown)	Hsing-tsung's 1st daughter by Empress Jên-i	(1) Hsiao Sa-pa 撒八	k's father's mother's brother's son	65, 5a; 87, 2b
			(2) Hsiao A-su 阿速	k's father's mother's brother's son. His father married g (Shêng-tsung's 3rd daughter)	65, 5a; 81, 3a

TABLE 10 (*continued*)

| GENERA-TION | PRINCESS | | HUSBAND | | |
	NAME	GENEALOGICAL POSITION	NAME	GENEALOGICAL POSITION	REFERENCE
	(*l*) Wo-li-t'ai 幹里太	Hsing-tsung's 2nd daughter by Empress Jên-i	Hsiao Yü-li-yeh 余里也	father's mother's brother's son's son	65, 5*a*; 111, 1*a*
8	(*m*) Chiu-li 紃里	Tao-tsung's 2nd daughter by Empress Hsüan-i	(1) Hsiao Ta-pu-yeh 撻不也	father's father's mother's brother's son's son	65, 5*b*; 91, 2*b*; 99, 3*a*
			(2) Hsiao Ê-tu-wo 訛都幹	father's father's mother's brother's son's son	65, 5*b*; 111, 2*b*
	(*n*) T'ê-li 特里 (married twice, then captured by Chin soldiers)	Tao-tsung's 3rd daughter by Empress Hsüan-i	(1) Hsiao Ch'ou-wo 酬幹	father's father's mother's brother's son's son's son	65, 6*a*; 100, 3*a*
			(2) Hsiao T'ê-mo 特末	father's father's mother's brother's son's son's son	65, 6*a*–*b*; CS 82, 14*b*

toral Barguzin and the Nerchinsk Tungus marry their mothers' sisters.[239] Even the Silla might disregard generation, a possible survival of an old pastoral tradition. The direct line of their king was called "the first bone." Individuals in this line were forbidden to marry into the "nine lineages" or "second bone," but instead married "the daughters of their older or younger brothers, paternal or maternal aunts, or parallel cousins."[240]

According to CTKC 23, 1*a*, marriage without consideration for generation was commonly practised by the two ruling houses of the Ch'i-tan. Tables 9 and 10, which list the marriages of the Liao emperors and some imperial princesses as recorded in the *Liao Shih*, confirm this. These marriages have been charted in the diagram (fig. 5), so that the principles underlying them may become more apparent.

The chart reveals important features of the Ch'i-tan marriage system, but it must be remembered that our data are confined to a few distinguished lineages. It does not necessarily follow that the lesser lineages intermarried in exactly the same manner. The reader must also keep in mind that no Liao kinship terms are known to us. The relationships noted in the *Liao Shih* are expressed in Chinese terms which frequently are unable to reveal Ch'i-tan kinship principles contrary to Chinese tradition.

When the head of a lineage gives the women of his family line to men of a different lineage and the arrangement becomes reciprocal, a lien of one lineage upon the other is set up. In such a system the over-

riding of generation need not offer any difficulty, whether the society is clanless or has clans. However, where an alien terminology is superimposed, as was Chinese usage upon Ch'i-tan, the relationships may not always be clearly expressed.

The decree of 1019 prohibited the leading Yeh-lü lineages from marrying into the lesser lineages. By implication this set up a lien of the imperial family upon the lines of the "Maternal Uncles." Our chart reveals the family line of one "maternal uncle," that of a brother of the first empress; a second line, that of her mother's first husband, does not appear as such. The first may be incomplete, and the second cannot be defined because of inadequacy of the genealogical data. The few disconnected Hsiao lineages on the chart may therefore belong to either of them. While these relationships cannot be definitely established, it is clear that only a few lineages intermarried with the imperial family. The exercising of a lien within a small family is evidenced by the marriages of three sisters of the emperor Hsing-tsung (*g*) with their mother's brothers.

But the liens established by the Liao were not entirely reciprocal. True, the two clans set up at the beginning of the dynasty were exogamous, and men or women of either clan could marry in their own generation: a Yeh-lü with mother's classificatory brother's children, and a Hsiao with father's classificatory sister's children. However, marriages were commonly with spouses of ascending or descending generation, and in these the Yeh-lü always married into ascending generations (parents, grandparents, great grandparents) and the Hsiao reciprocally into descending generations (sons, grandsons, great grand-

[239] Shirokogoroff 33, 213.
[240] WHTK 326, 2564.

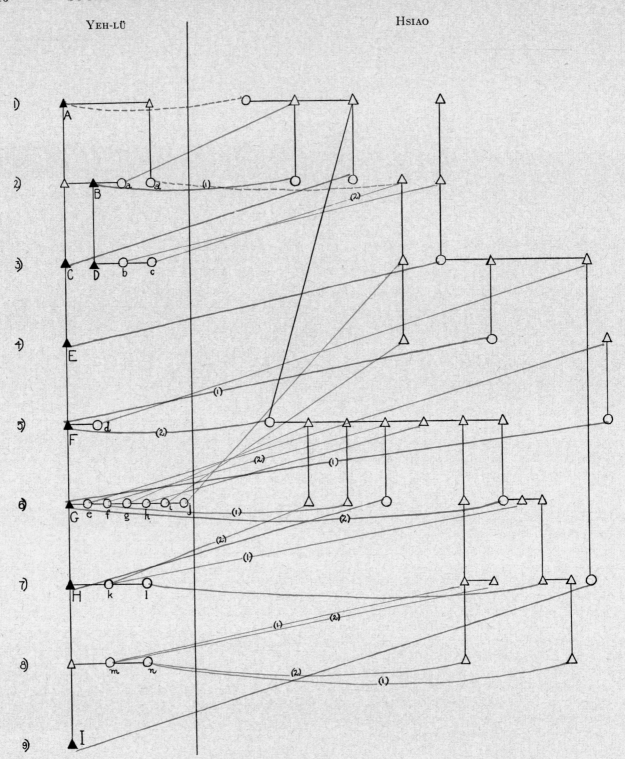

FIG. 5. Marriages between distinguished members of Yeh-lü and Hsiao Clans

△ Male members of both clans.
○ Female members of both clans.
Emperors (▲) designated by capitals.
Imperial princesses designated by small letters.

–––––––– Generation uncertain.

Note: As the society is patrilineal, the position of the fathers in the imperial line has been the determining factor in the position of his descendants.

sons).[241] Evidently, the form in which generation was overridden reflected the rising power of the Yeh-lü, and bulwarked the supremacy of the imperial clan.

The first emperor may well have married within his own generation for his energetic empress survived him by many years. For the second ruler, who was not the eldest son, such a marriage is actually recorded. But the first wives of all the succeeding emperors were all chosen from a higher generation. The last emperor, who was the first to wear the Chinese funeral gown, was also the first to choose a bride two generations senior, perhaps because he felt the need for the added support of age and position in the collapsing dynasty. Second marriages possibly gave greater latitude for romantic expression; the emperors who married again chose their second wives from their own generation.

The order of marriage was less fixed for the junior members of the imperial house. First marriages occurred between cross-cousins, but the trend even here was for marriage with a higher generation—sometimes, according to our way of reckoning, three generations removed.

Unlike the sororate which, from 940 on, was no longer compulsory,[242] the levirate seems to have persisted without any similar restriction. It may even have been encouraged by the laws governing the remarriage of widows. The successive marriages of *m* with two brothers, and of *k* and *n* with two of their cross-cousins, show that the institution still functioned. However, *f*, who first married her cross-cousin, later became the bride of her mother's brother. It is possible that a man of a higher generation took precedence if he so desired.

Indifference to generation—particularly when combined with levirate and sororate—may have been a means of maintaining population strength so frequently strained by a militant nomadic life. In the Early Han period a spokesman of the Huns used this very argument to defend their "improper" marriage practices against Chinese criticism.[243] While such considerations may have influenced the perpetuation of the custom, there can be little doubt that its retention during the Liao dynastic period was not divorced from the power politics of the imperial family.

It is more than probable that the Ch'i-tan, like the early Mongols, had practised polygamy in predynastic times and perhaps during the earlier part

of their dynastic rule. The contradictory statements concerning Shih-tsung's two "empresses" may well reflect a conflict between an early tribal tradition of polygamy and a Chinese system of concubinage. Shih-tsung married a Hsiao woman shortly before he became emperor.[244] At that time he had in his harem a lady named Chên 甄 who had belonged to the household of the last ruler of the Later T'ang dynasty.[245] In 947, when he ascended the throne, he made this Chinese lady, and not his Hsiao wife, the empress.[246] Subsequent events are not entirely clear, but it is evident that the Hsiao clan felt cheated of its most prized prerogative, the right to provide the imperial consort. The rebellion of 948 found Hsiao support,[247] and the conspiracy of 949 was led by a noble of the consort clan, Hsiao Han 翰.[248] In 950 Shih-tsung finally did what according to established tradition he should have done in the beginning—he raised his Hsiao wife to the rank of empress.[249] A belated concession! He and both his wives lost their lives in the rebellion of 951.[250]

A contemporary Sung version, given in the *Ch'i-tan Kuo Chih*, recognizes only the Lady Chên as Shih-tsung's empress, and states categorically that she is the mother of the later emperor Ching-tsung.[251] No doubt the Sung author was biased, and his claim that Lady Chên bore Shih-tsung six children after her forty-first

---

[241] In the present discussions of kinship western anthropological practice has been followed in counting generations, i.e., the count does not start with ego as is the Chinese custom, but with the parent generation if ascending, the children's if descending.

[242] VII, 2 (20); see also above.

[243] SC 110, 17a.

[244] LS 71, 3b states that Shih-tsung married (納) her after receiving the title, Prince Yung-k'ang 永康. According to LS 5, 1a, he was thus honored in the second month of the reign period Ta-t'ung, that is, early in the year 947. He declared himself emperor in the fourth month of that year (cf. XIII (19)). He must, therefore, have married the Hsiao woman sometime between the second and fourth months of 947.

[245] It seems that Shih-tsung met Lady Chên shortly before he took his Hsiao relative (his father's cousin) as wife. LS 71, 4a notes that he "obtained" (得) the Chinese lady when he accompanied T'ai-tsung on his southern campaign. CTKC 13, 2b states more specifically that he "obtained" her after T'ai-tsung entered Ta-liang 大梁. The ancient Wei 魏 capital, Ta-liang, was the site of the Later Chin capital, Pien, and the author of the Ch'i-tan Kuo Chih uses the older name to designate it. The Ch'i-tan army entered Pien in the first month of 947 (see XVI, 947, LS 4, 14a). It thus seems that Lady Chên lived in or near the imperial palace in Pien when Shih-tsung met her a few months before his official marriage with his classificatory aunt.

[246] LS 71, 4a.

[247] XIII (21).

[248] XIII (22); cf. also XIV, introduction.

[249] LS 5, 2b.

[250] LS 71, 3b and 4a.

[251] CTKC 13, 2b–3a.

year[252] does not increase confidence in the trustworthiness of his other statements.

The *Liao Shih* introduces its record by designating Lady Chên as Shih-tsung's concubine (*fei* 妃).[253] While this evidently expresses the later official Liao attitude, it is interesting to note that the text itself does not make any such distinction. After his investiture Ching-tsung, who is referred to as the son of Shih-tsung's Hsiao wife,[254] gave a solemn funeral "to the two empresses."[255] This formulation would be most unusual if Lady Chên had actually been deprived of her rank. However willing Ching-tsung might have been to provide an official burial for his father's murdered concubine, he probably would not have referred to her as empress if she had yielded that title to his mother. But, even if political inhibitions were overcome by considerations of etiquette, either in the mind of Ching-tsung or a Liao record-keeper, there is little reason for the failure of the *Liao Shih* to mention the reduction of Lady Chên to the rank of concubine. The fact that the Yüan authors of the official *History* who call Shih-tsung's Chinese wife a concubine have nothing to say concerning her reduction in rank would seem to indicate that no such procedure was mentioned in the original records. Thus, even if the critical reader questions the prejudiced version of the *Ch'i-tan Kuo Chih*, which presents Shih-tsung's Chinese wife as his only empress, he may equally question the validity of the official Liao version which labels Lady Chên a concubine in one passage and in another refers to the "two empresses."

The story, in spite of, or perhaps because of, its inner contradictions, seems to indicate that the Ch'i-tan had not as yet abandoned their tribal habit of polygamy for a Chinese system of concubinage. The advantages of the latter would, however, be increasingly recognized in a developing hereditary monarchy; it lessened the conflicts over imperial descent and, at the same time, fortified the position of the heir apparent and the ruling house.

For the student of social change the introduction of the Chinese clan and the Chinese system of concubinage into Ch'i-tan life is of unusual interest. Particularly important was the manner in which these transfers were effected.[256]

1. Clans were established, but for the two ruling families only. They grew in stability and strength, while as late as 1074 the emperor considered a similar change for the other lineages inadvisable.

2. Ancestor worship was established—or reinforced—but for the ancestors of the stronger of the two clans only. While permanent exogamic regulations had to be extended to the consort clan, ancestor worship could be monopolized by the imperial clan. It obviously was.

3. The generation taboo so important in the Chinese kinship system was not accepted at all. Few benefits would have derived from such a regulation, whereas the marriage with a mature and established Hsiao man or woman cemented the imperial lineage's power and support.

4. The Chinese system of recognizing only one "legal" wife, while it functioned to the disadvantage of the co-wives, solidified the position of the imperial family and safeguarded the hereditary marital prerogative of the consort clan, Hsiao.

From a formalistic standpoint, the unequal diffusion of the elements of Chinese kinship to the Ch'i-tan may seem queer and inconsistent. Viewed realistically, the apparent contradictions emerge as a consistent program to bolster the power and security of the ruling families of the Liao empire.

5. THE CHINESE FAMILY

The *Liao Shih* has little to say about Chinese family life in our period. Ch'i-tan mores may have exerted some influence on the Chinese, particularly where the ruling peoples had intimate personal contacts with their Chinese subjects as in the Chinese diaspora in the north or in the ordos where Chinese and Ch'i-tan lived side by side for generations. In the south the marriage of Ch'i-tan officials with Chinese girls was legally sanctioned by the decree of 941.[257] From the wording of this decree it may be inferred that in general such marriages had not been encouraged; and it is doubtful whether the formal relaxation of the general restriction which is reported for the eleventh century[258] produced any radical change: the two groups maintained their different ways of life until the end of the dynasty. The imperial clan saw to it that its members took only Ch'i-tan wives, at least as legal mates. Nor did the situation created by Shih-tsung's marriage with Lady Chên encourage imitation.[259] After his death the imperial harem still included Chinese and, for that matter, Po-hai concubines,[260]

---

[252] *Loc. cit.* The biological achievement claimed by the *Ch'i-tan Kuo Chih*, although not altogether impossible, is certainly exceptional. It remains so even if, according to western reckoning, Lady Chên was "only" forty years of age at the time of her marriage.

[253] LS 71, 4a.

[254] *Op. cit.*, 3b.

[255] *Op. cit.*, 4a.

[256] See Linton 40, 472.

[257] VII, 1 (8).

[258] *Wu Hsi Chi* by Yü Ching = LSSI 15, 15b.

[259] See above.

[260] LS 65, 3a and 4a ff.

but the daughters of these non-Ch'i-tan women were often (always ?) married to Chinese dignitaries.[261] Never again was a Chinese girl raised to the rank of a Liao empress.

Thus intermarriage between Ch'i-tan and Chinese was limited and consequently those cultural influences that are its normal accompaniment. Exposed to foreign rule, the great majority of the Chinese probably stuck with increased tenacity to their traditional way of life. The numerous and violent court feuds of the Ch'i-tan express an overt aggressiveness completely at variance with those Chinese family mores formulated by Confucius. Brothers who shot devil arrows at each other,[262] who did not stop at murder,[263] and sons who conspired against their own fathers[264] were moral monsters from a Chinese point of view. Rivalries of this kind remained the privilege of the Ch'i-tan masters of the empire.

The Chinese maintained their family tradition and code of behavior. The decree prohibiting the second marriage of women of distinguished status (because their deceased husbands had possessed honorary titles[265]) reveals that the Liao government accepted this time-honored Chinese custom, though, as it seems, only for the non-Ch'i-tan sector of the country's population.[266] The official encouragement of families of more than two generations must have been directed primarily to the Chinese, for the pastoral peoples frequently permitted their grown sons to set up their own tents and care for their own herds.[267] Our texts report only one family within the tribal sector who approached the Chinese ideal: in 1074 a Hsi family was publicly rewarded because it included three generations.[268] However, it should be added that the Hsi were a semi-agricultural people and therefore less inclined to split their families than were the more purely pastoral tribes.

The law of 983 forbidding separate residence for parents and children[269] was certainly influenced by Chinese custom, but the number of generations coexisting in one Chinese family has been overestimated by many writers. If during the last two millennia an average Chinese family numbered less than six members,[270] then the presence of three generations

under one roof, particularly if the roof covered a poor family,[271] was not realized as often as desired.

Conditions in the Liao empire did not alter this fundamental trend. A family of three generations living together was honored by the government.[272] While some few families of more than three generations are mentioned, instances of four,[273] six,[274] or eight[275] generations in one household are rare. The presence of eight generations[276] under one roof, although startling, is not impossible. If over the years the young men of a family all marry before they are twenty and quickly beget their first son, then the family head may not have reached his one hundred and fortieth year when the first baby of the eighth generation is born. In 994 the court publicly honored an old man who had reached an age of one hundred and thirty-three years.[277] Theoretically speaking, it is not beyond the range of possibility that in a span of two hundred years all marginal biological and economic factors may combine in producing an amazing pyramid of six, seven, or eight generations.

But such phenomena, although statistically intriguing, are sociologically significant only because of the family ideal which they reflect. This ideal of a stable sedentary family which builds up generation after generation like a coral reef is not Ch'i-tan, but definitely Chinese. Why Chinese society which nourished such an ideal was built primarily on families of two or perhaps three generations is a fascinating question which cannot be answered but only posed in the present analysis.

6. CH'I–TAN TRIBAL RELIGION

a. THE FOUR DOCTRINES OF THE LIAO EMPIRE

As late as the reign of Tao-tsung the Ch'i-tan boasted of "a civilization not inferior to that of the Chinese."[278] They saw no reason, therefore, for abandoning their ancient religious traditions and substituting Chinese concepts instead. When they accepted Buddhist ideas eagerly, they did so, not because these ideas were so popular in China Proper (as a matter of fact they were rapidly losing ground in T'ang and Sung China), but because with few exceptions they fitted into the established pattern of Ch'i-tan religious life. In the main Buddhism was concerned with those spheres of man's fate that dealt

[261] VII, 1, note 17.
[262] VII, 2 (8).
[263] XIII, introduction and text, *passim*.
[264] VII, 1, note 1.
[265] See de Groot, RSC II, 1, 767 ff.
[266] VII, 2 (50) and note.
[267] See Hudson 38, 35 and 82.
[268] VII, 2 (66).
[269] VII, 2 (38).
[270] See I, introduction, note 148.

[271] *Cf.* Buck 30, 334; *idem* 38, 371.
[272] VII, 2 (38) (76).
[273] VII, 2 (47) (70).
[274] VII, 2 (47).
[275] VII, 2 (65).
[276] *Loc. cit.*
[277] X, 1 (24).
[278] SMCW 9a.

with the occult possibilities of transmigration, of eventual escape, and ultimate rest, while the day-by-day supernatural needs of the Ch'i-tan remained the care of their tribal religion as they had been since time immemorial.

If we disregard Manicheism and Nestorianism, which seem to have played a rather insignificant role,[279] four doctrines flourished within the borders of the Liao empire—Confucianism, Taoism, Buddhism, and the tribal religion of the Ch'i-tan. Confucianism and Taoism were more or less limited to the Chinese territories, while the tribal population experienced little difficulty in combining their devotion to the Buddhist creed[280] with a pious adherence to the religious concepts and practices of their forefathers.

b. POWERS AND SPIRITS

The Ch'i-tan people believed that their world was inhabited by supernatural powers, both "wonderful"[281] and frightful.[282] In many cases these powers were immanent in the objects themselves, in trees,[283] banners and drums,[284] mountains, sun, heaven, and earth,[285] but not infrequently the object was personified. LS 34, 3a mentions the gods of Heaven, Earth, and Sun[286] and the god of Mu-yeh Mountain. Another passage speaks of the god of the Black Mountain;[287] further records refer to the deities of the deer[288] and white horse.[289] The Earth deity is the only one concretely described in the *Liao Shih;* she appears as an old woman.[290] While both animate and inanimate[291] powers were present in the Ch'i-tan pantheon, they are not always clearly differentiated.

Our texts are filled with references to deities and spirits, both good and bad. Hostile spirits (*mei* 魅) threatened the relation of husband and wife.[292] Evil spirits (*kuei* 鬼) were overcome when salt and moles were roasted in the New Year's ceremony.[293] The god of Fire, perhaps the prototype of the sacred fire of the Mongols,[294] received considerable attention during the winter.[295] The god of War[296] and the god of Metal[297] are mentioned in Chinese descriptions of ancient Ch'i-tan ceremonies. As certain contemporary Chinese observed, the Ch'i-tan had indeed "a predilection for spirits (好鬼[298])." Most frequently natural phenomena were set in motion by specific spirits or deities, but at times they were considered the acts of more impersonal agents. The magic influence of the directions, particularly the east,[299] is a case in point.

Included in the Ch'i-tan pantheon were also the endless legions of the souls of the dead. The spirits of the two tribal ancestors[300] and those of the imperial clan[301] were appealed to at the temple seats. The souls (*hun p'o* 魂魄) of the general populace were protected by the awesome god of the sacred Black Mountain.[302]

The texts do not explicitly describe the hereafter. But if the destruction of clothes and weapons, saddles and riding animals at the funerals of the Ch'i-tan rulers indicates the kind of life they expected to lead after death, then that life manifestly was pastoral and militant. More than a century after the end of the Liao dynasty Carpini found that the tribal "Tartars" believed in a future world where their livestock would multiply, where they would eat, drink, and "do other things which living men perform here upon earth."[303]

The nature of the Ch'i-tan pantheon becomes clearer when the status of the leading deities is examined. Strangely enough, the moon was not included.[304] In this the Ch'i-tan differed from the Mongols who, Carpini reported, call "the moon the Great Emperor and worship it upon their knees."[305] Chinese observers during the Five Dynasties were impressed by the prominent position the Ch'i-tan gave to the sun which they worshipped on the first day of every month.[306] The emperor himself made the special sacrifice to the sun,[307] but he omitted the sacrifice to the moon which followed in the Chinese ceremony. The great reverence paid to the sun seemed so extraordinary to the Chinese that they spoke of their

---

[279] See IX, note 52.
[280] IX, *passim.*
[281] *Cf.* Boas 37, 94; Benedict 38, 639 ff.; Lowie 24, 323.
[282] Radin 37, 9 ff.
[283] VII, 2 (26).
[284] VII, 2 (32).
[285] VII, 2, *passim.*
[286] VII, 2 (82).
[287] VII, 2 (83).
[288] VII, 2 (13).
[289] VII, 2 (45).
[290] VII, 2 (24).
[291] Boas 37, 94.
[292] VII, 2 (68).
[293] VII, 2 (83).
[294] See Carpini 28, 10 ff.

[295] VII, 2 (80).
[296] VII, 2 (31).
[297] YPL 16a ff.   See VII, 2, note 188.
[298] WTS 72, 5a.
[299] VII, 2 (78) and note 130.
[300] VII, 2 (84).
[301] See VII, 2, *passim.*
[302] VII, 2 (83).
[303] Carpini 28, 11.
[304] VII, 2 (82).
[305] Carpini 28, 11; *cf.* also Koeppen 59, 89 and Howorth, HM I, 112.
[306] WTS 72, 5a.
[307] VII, 2 (79).

northern neighbors as the Sun Ch'i-tan (*t'ai-yang Ch'i-tan* 太陽契丹[308]).

The sun was worshipped at the winter solstice[309] and again on such occasions as the ceremonial hunt,[310] mobilization for war,[311] and the ceremonial "recognition" of the ruler. After his discovery the emperor, dressed in Ch'i-tan clothing, emerged from his tent, faced the sun, and bowed four times. Then in turn he bowed to the temples of his imperial ancestors, to the god of Mu-yeh Mountain, to the god of Metal, to his mother, to the tribal ancestress, and finally to his own blood relatives.[312] The Chinese observer may not have been completely accurate in all the ceremonial details, but there is little probability that he could have been mistaken about the conspicuous position of the sun or the extreme awe in which it was held.

Equally conspicuous in Ch'i-tan religion were the two other great cosmic principles, Heaven and Earth. They were usually worshipped together and were appealed to particularly in the grim times of rebellion, war, and death. When A-pao-chi usurped supreme power, he announced it to Heaven;[313] when he pardoned his rebellious brothers, he announced his decision to Heaven and Earth.[314] In the mobilization ceremony a sacrifice was offered to Heaven and Earth and to the Sun, but after the war had actually begun, not the Sun, but only Heaven and Earth were appealed to at each critical turn in the campaign.[315] During the funeral ceremony, which was performed inside the tent and before the fire, the emperor bowed twice to Heaven and Earth.[316]

c. TREATMENT OF THE SUPERNATURAL POWERS

Gods, spirits, and impersonal powers were immanent in the "wonderful" world of the Ch'i-tan. To live among them naturally would mean to be influenced by them—and in turn to influence them. Ch'i-tan religion expressed itself in a continued effort to win the magic support of potentially friendly supernatural powers and to ward off real or possible danger at the hands of supernatural enemies.

The great gods of Heaven, Earth, and Sun were treated as powerful potentates. Solemn announcements were made to them, sometimes by the rising flames,[317] sometimes on a mountain top,[318] sometimes without mention of place or form.[319] To gain their favor the Ch'i-tan sacrificed horses and oxen,[320] sheep,[321] and geese.[322] Wine offerings were generously poured upon the ground[323] as if the gods were capable of enjoying frequent and heavy potations. The prayers which accompanied such sacrifices were more than idle words. They were an integral part of a substantial gift in return for which a substantial favor was expected.

Twice a year the two great tribal ancestors were officially honored by the sacrifice of a horse and an ox;[324] on the fifteenth day of the tenth month the spirits of all dead ancestors were worshipped,[325] but offerings were made to them at other times as well. The imperial ancestors were appealed to on important political occasions, such as the investiture of the new ruler,[326] or the commencement of a war,[327] because their approval was obviously a prerequisite of success.

The life of an ancestral spirit began at the moment of death. At the funeral ceremonies of the Ch'i-tan emperors human beings were sacrificed,[328] and saddle horses, saddles, clothes, and other objects were burned.[329] The living sacrifices no doubt supplied the dead with fit companions in the next world and the destroyed property assured their comfort.

The aid of powers immanent in objects was invoked by sympathetic magic, imitation, and contact.[330] It was hoped that thus the ambivalent potentials of rain and vegetation could be influenced, that the evil spirits could be paralyzed, and the political strength of the ruler could be maintained.

The ceremonies of rebirth[331] and recognition[332] which established the position of the emperor by a magical repetition of his physical and political "birth" recapitulated the original scene so realistically that the presence of a ceremonial midwife and child was necessary in the former, while the "nine tents" (of the previous rulers) and the "tenth tent" of the em-

[308] LTCL 5b.
[309] VII, 2 (23).
[310] VII, 2 (93).
[311] VII, 2 (82).
[312] YPL 16a ff.
[313] VII, 2 (5).
[314] VII, 2 (6).
[315] VII, 2 (82).
[316] VII, 2 (91).

[317] VII, 2 (5).
[318] VII, 2 (6).
[319] VII, 2 (82).
[320] VII, 2, passim.
[321] VII, 2 (83). See also (85).
[322] LS 53, 14a.
[323] VII, 2, passim.
[324] VII, 2 (84).
[325] VII, 2 (83).
[326] VII, 2 (87) and note 188.
[327] VII, 2 (82).
[328] VII, 2 (34).
[329] VII, 2 (91).
[330] See Frazer 40, 11; cf. also Boas 37, 96 and Benedict 38, 638 ff.
[331] VII, 2 (86).
[332] VII, 2 (87) and note 188.

peror were erected in the latter. Rainfall was induced by asperging individuals,[333] by standing in water,[334] or by shooting at willow trees,[335] a ceremony which may have symbolized birth after death.[336] During a marriage ceremony an imperial bride offered a jug of wine to a woman of unusual fertility[337] in the hope of transferring to herself that woman's proven motherhood.

The same magic techniques that moved friendly supernatural agencies to favorable action were also used to counteract hostile forces. Evil spirits were fought by roasting moles,[338] animals living a dark and secretive life. Sleeping tents were protected by the solemn sacrifice of white dogs in an autumn ceremony, and dog images were placed in the emperor's mausoleum.[339] The Ch'i-tan shot magic "devil arrows"[340] into their prisoners, hoping thus to affect their real enemies.

Exorcism was also employed. At the New Year the evil spirits were intimidated by bells and arrows, singing and shouting;[341] at an imperial funeral they were combatted with prayers.[342] The doctor who treated Yeh-lü Hsieh-chên's wife apparently displayed his primitive techniques[343] with as little emotion as a modern physician. To quote Dr. Boas' general formulation, he approached his task "purely as a relation of cause and effect, from his point of view as a practical or scientific process."[344]

No more "scientific" yet no less technical were the divinations to which the Ch'i-tan looked for direction. To determine what were the chances of success in a contemplated military expedition, a shoulder blade of a white sheep was exposed to the heat of a fire kindled with mugwort and horse manure. If the bone cracked, the Ch'i-tan went to war: if not, peace was maintained.[345] Other ways of divining were also favored, as the story of the two fish indicates,[346] but obviously the scorched bones were preferred on important occasions.[347]

Divination by means of animal bones may be expected among peoples whose essential economy is hunting[348] or animal husbandry.[349] However, it has also been recorded for certain societies that combine agriculture with stockbreeding.[350] Shang China (traditional dates 1766–1122 B.C.) is an example, but in this instance archaeological finds indicate that the origin of the practice must be looked for in pre-Shang antiquity.[351]

Bone divination in its more primitive form[352] is well-documented for the tribes of Inner Asia. Rubruck found the tribal Mongols completely dependent upon bone oracles for divination. Khan Mangu "does nothing in the world without first consulting these bones. . . ."[353] Radloff reports that the scorching of shoulder blades of sheep was used for divination not only by the Khirghiz but also by all other Inner Asiatic people who still adhered to their ancient religion.[354] And today the eastern Golds still divine "by burning the shoulder blade of a roedeer, or rather scorching it over hot coals."[355] The Ch'i-tan diviners obviously shared an ancient tribal technique with most of Inner Asia, and they practised it in its most orthodox form.

d. RELIGIOUS FUNCTIONARIES

The relations between man and the supernatural world were maintained by the tribal priests or shamans and by certain individuals who exercised political as well as religious power. Preeminent among these last was the emperor who obviously perpetuated the religious functions of the Ch'i-tan chieftains. In time of war or during a ceremonial hunt it was the emperor who dealt with the gods;[356] he paid reverence to the sun;[357] he (or his delegated official) invoked the rain magic.[358] A survey of the calendar reveals that in almost every ceremony of importance the emperor played a leading role.[359] While those described in

---

[333] VII, 2 (26) and (81).

[334] VII, 2 (26); cf. Frazer 40, 70 and 438.

[335] VII, 2 (26) (81).

[336] See Frazer 40, 296 ff.

[337] VII, 2 (89).

[338] VII, 2 (83).

[339] Loc. cit. and note 166.

[340] VII, 2 (8) and also (82).

[341] See VII, 2 (83).

[342] VII, 2 (91).

[343] VII, 2 (45).

[344] Boas 37, 96; see also Benedict 38, 637.

[345] CTKC 27, 3b.

[346] VII, 2 (30). Cf. also VII, 2 (83) where divination by means of the weather is recorded.

[347] Cf. VII, 2, note 139.

[348] Speck shows that among certain Algonquian and Athapascan hunting tribes along the northern fringe of North America "shoulder blade divination appears to be still as important as among the culture groups of Asia" (Speck 35, 137).

[349] For Asia cf. Laufer 27, 253 ff.

[350] Creel 37, 1 ff.; idem 37a, 21 ff.; Britton 38, 1ff.; see also Wittfogel 40, 110 ff.

[351] Cf. Wu CT 33, 631; Liang SY 35, 558 and 561.

[352] The diviners of Shang, unlike those of more primitive peoples, incised their questions on bone (mainly shoulder blades). Only in a few cases do pre-Shang divination bones show any trace of inscription.

[353] Rubruck 00, 187.

[354] Radloff 93 I, 474 ff.; cf. also Menges 33, 1252 ff.

[355] Lattimore 33, 66.

[356] VII, 2 (82) (93).

[357] VII, 2 (79).

[358] VII, 2 (26) and subsequent texts.

[359] VII, 2 (83) and passim.

the text were observed in dynastic times and may have been embellished or modified, they still preserved much of their early character. Some, like the rain ceremony, seem to have remained practically unchanged.

Certain other religious functionaries of obvious tribal provenience continued to perform the ceremonial duties of a predynastic past. Among them were the *i-li-pi* who directed the ceremonial participants;[360] the *t'i-yin*, who conducted certain sacrificial ceremonies of his own;[361] the *i-la* of the banners and drums who killed the animals for the great sacrifice to Mu-yeh Mountain;[362] and particularly the *ti-lieh-ma-tu*, who was in charge of ritual and etiquette,[363] and made the sacrifices to Mu-yeh Mountain.[364] When the great rain ceremony achieved its purpose, he was rewarded; when it failed, he was doused with water.[365]

Besides the political functionaries, Liao society supported a number of professional seers and soothsayers, exorcists, and physicians, the *wu* 巫.[366] This term, still in use today, originally designated the priests of ancient China.[367] During the Shang dynasty the *wu* were highly esteemed[368] and the Shang king, who danced with them for rain,[369] may in an earlier period have been their religious chief. However, the separation of powers already noticeable in Shang times became increasingly marked. The growing political centralization which gave the key positions for magic control to the ruler and his secular officials inevitably reduced the functions and powers of the *wu*. In the course of a long and dramatic struggle the *wu* priests became merely the guardians of a subsidiary, but not always tolerated, popular religion.[370] Tribal conquerors of China paid greater respect to the primitive priesthood and what it stood for. Until well along in the T'o-pa Wei dynasty female *wu* and male sorcerers beat drums and danced at the sacred sacrifices.[371] During at least some part of the Chin 金 and Mongol dynasties a similar indulgence was shown.[372] Even the highly assimilated Manchus who officially accepted the orthodox Chinese attitude[373] continued to use

shamans in their own religious ceremonies, at least until the Ch'ien-lung period.[374] The Chinese *wu* (native priests) were officially registered and limited in number, but otherwise they were tolerated.[375] In fact, Manchu women sought the magic services of female *wu* with great eagerness.[376] The maintenance or rejection of what de Groot calls *wu*-ism is an interesting chapter in the cultural history of China's dynasties of conquest.

The Ch'i-tan, who so proudly clung to their tribal traditions, had little reason to abandon the services of their former religious functionaries. The government in 957 executed a female *wu*, not because she practised magic, but because her particular magic had been unsuccessful and had caused the death of several persons.[377] The records tell of attempts to regulate the growth of Buddhism,[378] but no measures to restrain the practice of *wu*-ism are reported. In view of the decrees against the *wu* announced in 472 by the Wei dynasty and in 1186 by the Chin dynasty,[379] the unperturbed attitude of the Liao government acquires especial significance.

In our translation we have called the *wu* shamans. This term is generally used to designate the religious functionaries of Inner and Northern Asia whose status does not depend upon an officially institutionalized position but is derived from power received "directly from the spirits as a gift or grant."[380] Shamans are employed to "foretell the future, change the weather, blast the crops or multiply game, avert catastrophes or precipitate them on foes; above all, to inflict and cure disease."[381]

In Asia two types of shamans may be distinguished —the arctic and subarctic.[382] The latter exhibit less ecstacy and only rarely have recourse to frenzy or trance in the performance of their magic and prayers.[383] Among the Ch'i-tan, as among most Altaic peoples, shamanism was definitely "subarctic" and possession was more the exception than the rule.

At the year's end the shamans, led by a "great"

[360] VII, 2 (80).
[361] VII, 2 (85).
[362] *Loc. cit.*
[363] XIV, 1 (9), LS 45, 9a.
[364] VII, 2 (85).
[365] VII, 2 (81).
[366] De Groot, RSC VI, 2, 1212.
[367] *Op. cit.*, 1187.
[368] Ch'ên MC 36, 533–539.
[369] *Op. cit.*, 535.
[370] See de Groot, RSC VI, 2, 1188 ff. and 1198 ff.
[371] WS 7A, 2b; cf. de Groot, *op. cit.*, 1234.
[372] TCKC 18, 2b.
[373] De Groot, *op. cit.*, 1242.

[374] See above, General Introduction, note 221.
[375] De Groot, *op. cit.*, 1243 ff. and 1251 ff.
[376] *Op. cit.*, 1332.
[377] VII, 2 (25).
[378] De Groot, *op. cit.*, 1187 and *passim*.
[379] See notes 371, 372.
[380] Kroeber 23, 363 ff.; cf. also Potapov and Menges 34, 68 ff.
[381] Kroeber 23, 364.
[382] For an illuminating study of the subarctic "Kleinschamanieren" see Ohlmarks 39, 40 ff. and 94 ff.
[383] According to Ohlmarks (39, 84), the subarctic form of shamanism is found among most Altaic peoples, the Turkmens, Mongols, Manchus, the peoples north of the Amur, and the Koreans.

one (大巫), invoked the god of Fire by their prayers.[384] The next day twelve shamans sang, shouted, rang bells, and walked (or danced) around the tents with arrows in their hands, fighting off the evil spirits. They then retreated to special tents for seven days.[385] During the great rain ceremony they magically encouraged the growth of the newly planted willow trees by offering wine, millet, and prayers.[386] At the rebirth ceremony[387] the head shaman covered the emperor's head and offered presents to him. During the sacrifice to Mu-yeh Mountain the head shaman poured wine on the sacrificial animals; and another uttered magical incantations, while the emperor, the empress, and their attendants all bowed.[388] During an imperial funeral both the "great" one and other lesser shamans were required to ward off evil spirits.[389] In 980, while war was being waged against Sung China, shamans were ordered to "worship" (祀) Heaven and Earth and the god of War,[390] a function normally performed by the emperor. Evidently in a military crisis the power of the Ch'i-tan shamans gave added hope of military success.

The Ch'i-tan *wu* are not listed as members of the "northern" government, but whatever their formal status their position in the dynasty was high, their professional task complex. The men who offered ceremonial gifts to the ruler when he was "reborn," who might call upon the highest powers in an important ceremony, and who forced the entire court to bow at the sound of their voices exercised a religious function that differed as strikingly from a primitive tribal shamanism[391] as the stratified society of the predynastic Ch'i-tan people differed from the simple democratic tribes of Siberia, Manchuria, and Mongolia.

7. SECULAR TRADITION

No clear distinction can be made between what a people, such as the Ch'i-tan, considered extraordinary or "wonderful" and what seemed to them ordinary and matter-of-fact.[392] But, even if the border-line was somewhat indefinite, it existed nevertheless. Certain ceremonies, such as the sacrifice to Heaven and Earth and to the Sun, were patently religious no matter what their secular setting may have been. Con-

versely, many customs and ceremonies reported in our texts were primarily secular although religious elements of some kind or another might also be present.

a. POLITICAL TRADITIONS

The great political ceremonies, as well might be expected, included significant secular features. During the investiture ceremony the emperor was accompanied by elders of "the eight tribes."[393] Such a statement, if taken at face value, clearly indicates that A-pao-chi's eight Ch'i-tan tribes still maintained an unusually privileged position; or, if the reference is rhetorical and all the Ch'i-tan tribes were actually represented, then it reveals the extraordinary strength of a formula that had originated many centuries before A-pao-chi came to power.

Chinese elements were also present in this ceremony, but nevertheless the tribal atmosphere was carefully preserved. The ceremonial argument between the emperor, his tribal chieftains, and high officials to determine whether an uncle or a brother should be elected in his stead[394] clearly reflects the ideological recognition of fraternal succession, a principle strikingly at variance with Chinese ideas of direct descent and primogeniture.[395] The ceremony itself was held in no city palace, but far from any fixed settlement. Temporary structures were erected and the ten men who symbolized the possible choices waited in tents during the recognition scene. While the election was being debated, the emperor and his followers appeared on horseback, and as a final gesture tribal chieftains and high officials offered the emperor what their Ch'i-tan forefathers had appropriately offered a newly elected khaghan, a herd of cream-colored sheep.[396] Such a gift was no mere anachronism. Its usefulness was still recognized: at a military spectacle during the year-end ceremonies the emperor bestowed on his followers armor, weapons, "sheep, and horses."[397]

b. TRIBAL TRADITION IN PERSONAL LIFE

The ceremonial data on political events are more fully documented than those on the personal life of the Ch'i-tan, but what is known of birth, marriage, and death shows the strength of the tribal tradition. T'ai-tsung, who was born in 902, first saw the light of day in a delivery tent,[398] a birthplace that con-

---

[384] VII, 2 (80).

[385] VII, 2 (83).

[386] VII, 2 (81).

[387] VII, 2 (86).

[388] VII, 2 (85).

[389] VII, 2 (91).

[390] VII, 2 (31).

[391] For the activities of such shamans *cf.* Radloff 93 II, 17 ff.

[392] See Boas 37, 94; *cf.* also Benedict 38, 630 ff.

[393] VII, 2 (87).

[394] *Loc. cit.*

[395] See XIII, note 50.

[396] VII, 2 (87).

[397] VII, 2 (83).

[398] VII, 2 (2). Delivery tents are still used today by the Northern Tungus (see Shirokogoroff 33, 274 ff.) and by the Finno-Ugric and Palaeo-Asiatic tribes of Siberia.

tinued to find favor in dynastic times. A Sung traveler in the middle of the eleventh century reports as many as forty-eight tents surrounding the large delivery tent where the empress awaited her critical hour, while the shouts of men and the cries of sheep frightened away the evil spirits.[399]

At marriage a Mongol bride hid from her groom who, assisted by his friends, would finally succeed in locating her and carrying her off "with a semblance of violence."[400] Ch'i-tan folkways also reveal the persistence of wife-stealing, though the abducted girl was manifestly in collusion with the "thief." On certain days of the first month young tribesmen were expected to run off with the girls of their choice and, if the experiment was successful, to maintain them as wives. Ceremonial gifts were then offered to the bride's family. Equally un-Chinese were the elopements of the sons of noble and wealthy Ch'i-tan families with "local" girls in the territory of the Wu-jo-chê tribe after hours of dancing and drinking under the light of the moon. Some of the girls may have been of Wu-jo-chê nationality; some possibly were Ch'i-tan, for the region was inhabited by a mixed population. But whatever their provenience, they were evidently considered worthy of marriage to upper class Ch'i-tan. Upon the birth of a child, the young couple customarily presented itself to the wife's parents who then formally recognized the young son-in-law.[401]

Marriage ritual at the Liao court appeared overwhelmingly Chinese; yet a number of significant Ch'i-tan features were prominent in the ceremonies. A lambskin garment was held over an imperial Ch'i-tan bride "as if to cover her" and a saddle was placed in her path.[402] Wrestling bouts and horse-racing entertained the wedding guests.[403]

Tribal custom prescribed the burning of bodily remains three years after death. *The History of the Five Dynasties* notes the old practice.[404] In 1055 a Sung report mentions the burning of Ch'i-tan commoners.[405] Nothing in the text indicates whether this was done in conformity with ancient tribal or Buddhist custom. If the latter, early traditions no doubt facilitated acceptance.

Tribal protocol and tradition are more clearly revealed in the imperial funeral ceremonies, the only ones that are described in any detail in the *Liao Shih*.

In the solemn procession that attended Tao-tsung's burial a *t'i-yin* is mentioned first, evidently representing the imperial family.[406] He is followed by members of the Three Patriarchal Households of the Yeh-lü clan and the prime minister of the Southern Administration who, at least in theory, was a Yeh-lü clansman.[407] Next appear the patriarch of the former ruling family (Yao-lien), certain courtiers, apparently of that same group, and then representatives of the distinguished Hsiao lineages. Lesser tribal nobles conclude the list of those present, a list that makes no mention of a single dignitary of the government of the Southern (Chinese) Region.

The burning of a dead emperor's bows and arrows, saddles, bridles, horses, and camels,[408] and the burial of living persons with the corpse[409] repeated tribal mores of great antiquity. The sheep that was sacrificed at the emperor's funeral,[410] and also at the funeral of a princess,[411] continued an old Ch'i-tan custom.[412] The offering is historically significant, for a world in which a single inconspicuous sheep insured the well-being of a tribal chieftain in the hereafter was far removed from the late predynastic and dynastic periods of Ch'i-tan wealth and power.

8. CULTURAL CONTACTS AND CULTURAL TRANSFER

Tribal customs continued to manifest themselves in innumerable ways, but they were modified by contact with the neighboring "barbarian" peoples on the one hand, and with the great southern civilization of China on the other.

No details of cultural exchange between the Ch'i-tan and the "barbarian" peoples are known. However, it seems safe to assume that the Ch'i-tan, whose position of power and prestige in the tribal world was assured, would play an active rather than a passive role in any culture transfer. Tribal chieftains participated in the Ch'i-tan ceremonies; tribal delegations visited the court to render homage and offer tribute; barbarian warriors served in the Ch'i-tan ordos and in the tribal armies under Ch'i-tan leadership. The subdued Silla of Kuei Prefecture were given schools "to educate them."[413] Whether these schools taught the Chinese or the "national" (Ch'i-tan) script is not recorded, but the students certainly were instructed

[399] YPL 17*a*–*b*. *Cf.* also VII, 2 (72) and note.
[400] Rubruck 00, 78.
[401] See CTKC 26, 2*b* ff.; SMCW 6*a* and 15*a*; LTSS 48*b*. *Cf.* VII, 2, note 197 and Stein 39, 145 ff.
[402] VII, 2 (89).
[403] *Loc. cit.*
[404] WTS 72, 4*b*.
[405] HJC 2*a*; HML 33*b*. See VII, 2, note 215.

[406] See XIV, 1 (9), LS 45, 8*a*; also (13).
[407] See XIV, introduction.
[408] VII, 2 (91); *cf.* also VII, 2 (54). The emperor's favorite belongings might also be burned with him.
[409] VII, 2 (12); CTKC 13, 2*a* ff.; VII, 2 (33).
[410] VII, 2 (91).
[411] VII, 2 (90); see also IV (14).
[412] VII, 2 (91).
[413] VII, 2 (48).

in the religious and secular traditions of the Ch'i-tan which were so prominent in the great political ceremonies of the empire.

The cultural contact established by the conquest affected both Ch'i-tan and Chinese society. Its influence on the Ch'i-tan was complex and obvious; its influence on the Chinese, though less conspicuous, was still evident. In the old Chinese territories of Nan-ching and Hsi-ching Chinese life seems to have continued as of old; but north of the mountain ranges, where the Chinese peasants settled among the Hsi and Ch'i-tan tribes, the new environment created a new situation. The Sung traveler, Su Ch'ê, in a short but instructive poem set down his impressions of the mixed population in the country of the Hsi:

奚君五畝宅	The Hsi ruler has a residence of five *mou*.
封戶一成田	The households bestowed on him cover a *ch'êng*[414] of land;
故壘開都邑	The old stronghold has grown into a capital.
遺民雜漢編	The remnants [of the Hsi] mix with Chinese peasants.
不知臣僕賤	Without knowing the humiliation of servitude
漫喜殺生權	They greatly enjoy the power of killing what is alive.[415]
燕俗嗟猶在	Behold, the customs of Yen are still carried on:
婚姻未許連	Intermarriage is not allowed.[416]

The poetic form may have led the traveler to overemphasize the persistence of Chinese ("Yen") customs. In a more prosaic passage he adds an important item of information: In the land north of the Yen Mountains where the Hsi dwelt in grass huts and the Ch'i-tan drove their carts along the watercourses, where camels, sheep, and horses bore witness to the pastoral pursuits of the tribal inhabitants, here the Chinese, though clinging to their mother tongue, had changed their manner of dress.[417] To what extent so external a transformation affected other aspects of their life Su Ch'ê does not say. It is probable that in the tribal territories of Liao, Chinese settlers merely clothed the "customs of Yen" in the more suitable garments of their pastoral neighbors. The process of Ch'i-tanization probably went much further among the Chinese soldiers of the ordo armies; during the Manchu dynasty Chinese bannermen who lived in the north of Liaoning, tended "to become actually Manchu bannermen."[418]

Ch'i-tan culture and political organization exercised its peculiar influence over still another section of the Liao Chinese, the bureaucracy. Officials in the lower ranks may have been little affected if they held office in the old Chinese territories. But those who lived in the northern circuits and, more particularly, close to the court were extremely susceptible to Ch'i-tan example. Some distinguished Chinese received honorific Ch'i-tan names;[419] some Chinese fathers gave Ch'i-tan personal names to their young sons.[420] A high Chinese official might take a Ch'i-tan wife;[421] he might prefer hunting to calligraphy and learning. The nephew of Han Tê-jang (Yeh-lü Lung-yün), Han Chih-hsin was an expert in taming eagles;[422] two other relatives of the chancellor held the tribal office of *t'i-yin*.[423]

It is not easy to determine to what extent Liao military organization and warfare modified Chinese tradition. But the extreme emphasis on horsemanship even in certain Chinese detachments, the life in the ordos and in the frontier garrisons must have exerted a considerable, if varying, influence.

While difficult to document, the effect of Liao values and ways of living on the spiritual attitudes and literary interests of the Chinese intelligentsia must not be overlooked. Ruled by a people who preferred riding, shooting, fishing, and hunting to reading, writing, and other subtle Confucian pursuits, the Chinese literati of Liao lived in an atmosphere which definitely discouraged higher forms of intellectual activity. During the tenth and eleventh centuries, which saw unique achievements in many fields of Chinese culture in Sung China, the Chinese scholars of the Liao empire did not make a single conspicuous contribution to Chinese literature, history, or philosophy.

The effect of Ch'i-tan culture on the Liao Chinese,

---

[414] Ten square *li*.

[415] Evidently referring to hunting.

[416] LCC 16, 14b.

[417] *Loc. cit.*

[418] Lattimore 35, 61. *Cf.* Lattimore's description of a

Chinese from China Proper who became "in his own lifetime an out-and-out 'Manchu'" (*op. cit.*, 62).

[419] *Cf.* LS 82, 1a; 98, 2b.

[420] Han Tê-wei's 韓德威 son was called P'ang-chin 雱金, and his two grandsons Hsieh-shih 謝十 and Ti-lu 滌魯 (LS 82, 2b–3a). These three names, as well as Ti-lu's style, Tsun-ning 遵寧, all seem to be Ch'i-tan rather than Chinese. Another scion of the same family, Chih-hsin 制心, had the servile childhood name of K'o-han-nu 可汗奴, "the khaghan's slave" (LS 82, 3b). The half-Ch'i-tan, half-Chinese compound expresses well the peculiar status of this group of semi-Ch'i-tanized Chinese dignitaries.

[421] *Cf.* LS 65, 3a and 4b and 82, 2b (see VII, 1, note 17).

[422] LS 82, 3b. In the *pên chi* Chih-hsin 制心 is sometimes written as one character 憇 (LS 16, 2b ff.). But in a Liao inscription it is given as 直心 showing that the name was pronounced Chih-hsin (MCCSC 2, 3a).

[423] LS 82, 3a.

notable though it was, is only one aspect of culture transfer under the Liao dynasty. The reverse process was equally important and perhaps even more complex. To a considerable degree the political and military superiority of the Ch'i-tan was balanced by the enormous prestige which Chinese civilization possessed among its barbarian neighbors. Even if the major part of an aggressive barbarian people consciously and proudly preserved many of its ancient mores, the upper stratum, thrown into closer contact with the Chinese population, was more susceptible to Chinese influence.[424]

In order to impress their subject peoples, the Ch'i-tan rulers were eager to introduce those political symbols with which Chinese tradition surrounded a "real" emperor. In order to control their sedentary population they were prepared to promote Chinese administrative and economic techniques wherever such techniques were required. Temporary or even permanent residence in the empire's cities, both new and old, and regular contact with the cream of Chinese officialdom and scholarship promoted the spread of numerous elements of Chinese life which enriched rather than destroyed Ch'i-tan culture.

a. NEW ELEMENTS ACCEPTED

When A-pao-chi abolished the semi-democratic tribal khaghanate and instituted a hereditary monarchy, he found direct and indirect sanctions for his act in a number of Chinese institutions. He proceeded to introduce the imperial reign title,[425] to set up an heir apparent,[426] and to proclaim Confucius the supreme sage of his new state.[427] For obvious reasons his appointed successor, Pei, was most eager to adopt Chinese manners and customs. T'ai-tsung, though disregarding primogeniture, nevertheless strove to emphasize the Chinese aspects of his court and administration, particularly after having attached new Chinese territory to his empire. In 938 two high officials from China Proper were called in to supervise the construction of the imperial carriages and other paraphernalia and to pass upon the making of proper gifts and the presentation of honorific titles.[428] In 947 the dynastic name Great Liao was introduced,[429] and Chinese court ladies and eunuchs, astronomical maps and classics cut in stone, musical instruments and treatises, armor and weapons[430] were carried from

the Chinese court to the Supreme Capital. The victorious war against Chin 晉 China was evidently "favorable to culture transfer."[431]

The waves of culture transfer in 938 and 947 were primarily political. So were the establishment of the two ruling clans and the typically Chinese ancestor worship practised by members of the imperial clan who even used the traditional Chinese ancestral tablets (shên chu 神主[432]). The retention of Chinese titles for officials in the Southern (Chinese) Region was just a matter of common sense, whereas the application of such titles to numerous offices in the tribal region[433] may at first glance seem strange. But the new nomenclature, though probably influenced by external considerations of prestige, was not without its inner justification; while the political organization of the tribes was maintained, a greater degree of centralization was achieved. China was the classic example of a workable centralized political machine.

The investiture ceremony offers an even more striking expression of Chinese influence on the Liao political structure. The new emperor's offer to cede the throne to one of his more worthy relatives was formulated according to the Chinese tradition of "yielding,"[434] and reference to his alleged lack of virtue (tê 德) was typically Confucian.[435] The Sinicized argument, though retaining certain tribal elements, was made in a political setting that had outgrown its former tribal structure. Both the tribal leaders as well as the new imperial officials participated in the ceremonial discussion; but, as might be expected in a growing bureaucracy, the latter were mentioned first.[436]

The adoption of Chinese political ideas and institutions favored the adoption of many other Chinese features. T'ai-tsu recommended the acceptance of Confucianism rather than Buddhism as the state creed because it was the doctrine of the Chinese.[437] He learned the Chinese language and ordered the introduction of a script.[438] Calligraphy, one of China's most valued arts, was encouraged by his over-powering widow who made her emperor son and his unfortunate brother Pei write "in front of her."[439] During T'ai-tsung's reign both he and the officials of the Southern Region began to wear Chinese clothes.[440]

---

[424] For the motives which lead to culture acceptance see Linton 40, 470 ff.

[425] LS 1, 9a.

[426] Loc. cit.

[427] IX (3).

[428] See III (10).

[429] XVI, 947, LS 4, 15a.

[430] VII, 2 (22).

---

[431] For war as an important means of culture transfer see Linton 40, 498.

[432] See VII, 2, passim.

[433] See XIV, 1, passim.

[434] MTCS 9B, 1a–2b.

[435] Loc. cit.

[436] VII, 2 (87).

[437] IX, 916 (3).

[438] VII, 2 (11).

[439] VII, 2 (15).

[440] VII, 1 (7).

The Chinese sedan chair and fine Chinese carriages appeared at the Liao court.[441]   The use of silk spread,[442] as it did again a few centuries later among the tribal Mongols.[443]   The astronomical cycle of twelve animals that appeared on several Liao structures,[444] and that played so conspicuous a role in the three dreams preserved from the early days of the dynasty,[445] may well have been rooted in a Chinese concept, a possibility that has been suggested also for the earlier Turkic form.[446]   While direct borrowing from Turkic Uighur culture is documented in many instances, and the empress who dreamed of the twelve animals was of Uighur descent, it must not be forgotten that long before the establishment of the dynasty China had contributed many elements to Ch'i-tan and to Uighur culture.   Manicheism itself which may have influenced the incidence of these zodiac-like animals in the recorded dreams is said to have been introduced into the Uighur empire from the second T'ang capital, Lo-yang.[447]

Buddhism may also have been accepted from either or both of these civilizations.   T'ai-tsu seems to have tacitly acknowledged the Uighur root, for in comparing Buddhism with Confucianism he referred to the latter as purely Chinese.   But no matter which influence prevailed in this case, the new cultural developments undoubtedly encouraged the adoption of many Buddhist ideas.   The increasing consideration for animals, the release of captured birds,[448] the temporary suspension of the butchers' activities,[449] and the reduction in animal sacrifice[450] are all definitely Buddhist in formulation, though not necessarily in motivation.

The gradual abolition of the burial of the living with the dead[451] was accomplished in line with Chinese thought and tradition.   Similar influences may be seen in the changing attitudes toward the destruction of property at death.[452]   At Shêng-tsung's funeral in

1031[453] favorite animals and fine presents were still buried with the emperor, but at Tao-tsung's funeral in 1101, near the close of the dynasty, only lists enumerating the valued objects were burned.[454]

The discontinuance of joint fraternal responsibility for a crime[455] may have been inspired by juridical procedures in T'ang China.[456]   The festival of the seven days, which the Liao celebrated in the spring, had been held in China for centuries.[457]   The Chinese Dragon Boat Festival[458] and the Taoist Buddhist Chung-yüan Festival were celebrated not only by the Liao Chinese, but by their Ch'i-tan rulers as well, the latter marking the feast days in accordance with certain of their own national traditions.[459]   Chinese elements such as the silk flag and the dragons,[460] the colored fans and the written welcome to spring[461] appeared in other more particularly Ch'i-tan ceremonies.   Chinese became the *lingua franca* not only of the various subjugated peoples and tribes who could not understand each other,[462] but also of the educated Ch'i-tan themselves.

b. MODIFICATIONS AND LIMITATIONS

But, evident as this process of culture transfer was, it was definitely limited in scope and effect.   The Liao empire remained a border society politically as well as culturally.   China Proper was seriously defeated and temporarily invaded, but only the northeastern region was permanently occupied.   The relative success of the Chinese armies made Chinese civilization politically more impressive but at the same time less accessible.

The great majority of the Ch'i-tan tribesmen were little affected by their Chinese contacts which, confined primarily to military campaigns and the business of the market place, were too short and too superficial to establish the foundation for far-reaching culture exchange.   Except for the use of silk and a few other commodities, only the upper stratum and a limited number of city-dwelling commoners were disposed to accept Chinese cultural elements.

---

[441] IV (14).

[442] See III, V, and X, 1, *passim.*

[443] *Cf.* Rubruck 00, *passim.*

[444] LLSKCL, 2.   See rubbings.

[445] VII, 2 (2).

[446] Hirth 99, 117 ff.

[447] See IX, note 52.

[448] IX (6); *cf.* also LS 6, 6*a*; 13, 3*a*; and VII, 2 (61).

[449] IX (26) (31).

[450] VII, 2 (43) (58).   *Cf.* also Fêng CS 32, 108.

[451] In 926 Empress Ch'un-ch'in survived T'ai-tsu's burial, but hundreds of men were killed and buried with him (CTKC 13, 2*a*; *cf.* VII, 2 (12).   In 983 a few persons were interred with Ching-tsung's corpse (VII, 2 (33)).   The descriptions of the later emperors' burials do not refer to human sacrifices (see VII, 2 (91)).

[452] The Chinese, who in early times placed valuable objects in a ruler's grave, had before the time of Han

begun to substitute crude imitations.   During the Han period this became the prevailing practice, though on occasion objects of value were still buried with the dead.   See de Groot, RSC I, 706 ff.

[453] VII, 2 (54).   See also VII, 2 (91).

[454] VII, 2 (91).

[455] LS 79, 4*a* ff.

[456] Lesser punishment for the brother of a person guilty of high treason (THY 39, 707–709).

[457] CCSSC 4*a*.

[458] VII, 2 (83).

[459] *Op. cit.*

[460] CCSSC 5*a*; SSKC 21, 235.

[461] VII, 2 (83).

[462] SCPMHP 20, 11*a*.

Chinese influence spread from the imperial court and the high Ch'i-tan bureaucracy to the local centers of political and military power, reaching down to the commoners only casually and uncertainly. But, even when Chinese traits were conspicuously accepted, they underwent considerable modification. Often they were completely distorted.

The new Chinese nomenclature did not destroy the traditional tribal political organization; the vital local units continued to function.[463] The Ch'i-tan rulers accepted many of the paraphernalia of Chinese emperorship; their city palaces[464] and their somewhat Chinese education[465] certainly affected their manner of living[466] and social attitudes. But whatever Chinese influences were present they were balanced by a continued recognition of institutions that had been developed by nomads in a tribal setting.[467] The newly assumed imperial responsibilities created no serious conflict with the older way of life; the Supreme Capital and the imperial ordo were located in the northern tribal region.

The investiture ceremony, whose primary design was to install the Ch'i-tan ruler as a "true" (Chinese) emperor, commenced with two manifestly tribal rites, the "rebirth" and the "recognition" ceremonies. Even the final ceremony, apparently so Chinese, retained many tribal elements although these were disguised or modified.[468] The remains of a great pile of

firewood which had been burned to announce the event to Heaven served as the investiture platform. Later the announcement by fire was abandoned, but the pile of wood and the old name were retained.[469]

Equally evident are the tribal implications of two other rituals. While the emperor was being invested, he galloped off[470] and fell from his horse and was covered with a blanket, probably a ceremonial capture to insure his taking office. The following day the carpet rite was performed. High dignitaries grasped the carpet on which the emperor sat and raised it.[471]

The carpet rite seems to have been widely practised in Inner Asia; it is recorded for the T'o-pa Wei as late as 532: seven dignitaries stood under a black carpet, the ruler on it.[472] It was performed by the Turkic contemporaries of the Northern Chou dynasty (557–581): tribal grandees lifted the new khaghan on a carpet and moved in nine sunwise circles.[473] When Chingis Khan was proclaimed supreme Mongol ruler, the rite was repeated again with great solemnity:

---

[463] See XIV, 1, and introduction.

[464] See XI (5).

[465] See XIV, introduction.

[466] Cf. VII, 2 (52).

[467] See II, 1 (23)–(27).

[468] LS 49, 3b says that the rebirth ceremony preceded the investiture. It does not mention the recognition ceremony, but according to YPL 16a–17a (see VII, 2, note 188), the recognition also led up to the investiture. ("Finally the emperor ascended the wooden platform to receive investiture.") Thus it may be asked whether these two descriptions are two versions of the same investiture ceremony or whether they describe an earlier tribal form and a later somewhat Sinicized form that replaced it. The first hypothesis can be discarded at once, for the two descriptions differ not only in details but in their whole content. Theoretically speaking, the tribal recognition rite might well have been replaced by the investiture ceremony with its conspicuous Confucian features. But the introduction of elements of Chinese court ceremonial goes back to the first half of the tenth century (III (10)), whereas the recognition ceremony was still observed in 1058 under the next to the last Liao emperor. This encourages the belief that the recognition was part of the general investiture ceremony. LS 49, 3b states that other buildings (室) were erected besides the investiture platform for the rebirth, for the empress dowager, and for the "seeking" (搜索). Stein is puzzled by the last term and ties it in with the rites of ancestor worship

mentioned for the rebirth ceremony (Stein 39, 68 ff.). "Seeking" is a very unusual term for the establishment of religious contact with one's ancestors, but it is a perfect description of those actions which led to the recognition of the emperor in the recognition ceremony. Since the latter was held before the solemn investiture, it seems much more reasonable to interpret the building (or buildings) for the "seeking" as identical with the tents noted in Yen-pei Lu. This source does not specify the number of the buildings erected. Parallel descriptions such as that of the winter na-po (II, 1 (27)) show that the temporary buildings of the Ch'i-tan were felt tents of various sizes.

Our earlier folkloristic analysis of the recognition ceremony does not depend for its validity upon the role played by this ceremony in the official part of the investiture rites. The erection of the "seeking" building(s) at the ceremonial grounds makes it more than probable that the recognition (or "seeking") rite was performed upon the occasion of the investiture. It may have taken place after the "rebirth" and before the final investiture. At what particular moment it occurred we do not know.

[469] VII, 2 (87).

[470] Stein (39, 70) interprets the passage as possibly describing a race between the Hsiao elders and the emperor. This is indeed suggestive. Unfortunately, Stein's punctuation, on which the interpretation depends, is not valid for any text we have seen. Stein reads ma yeh 馬也. In our texts ma and yeh are two parts of a single character, ch'ih 馳.

[471] VII, 2 (87).

[472] PS 5, 9b. The seven men were covered (蒙) by the carpet. Boodberg (39, 242) translates: "Seven men . . . held up (lit. 'were covered by') a black felt rug. . . ." But a Sung scholar discussing the T'o-pa custom says that the seven men were "covered" (覆) by black felt (TWSTT 2, 13a; see VII, 2, note 190).

[473] Chou 50, 4b.

seven chieftains raised the black felt on which the great khan was seated.[474] The records differ in detail possibly because the ceremony itself was differently performed, but the basic idea is manifestly the same. Like the Turkic throttling test[475] the carpet rite may originally have been a tribal method of determining physical and mental fitness for leadership.

The "yielding" which climaxed the investiture ceremony had a definitely Chinese appearance, and its form may well have been influenced by the ancient Chinese custom. But even this seemingly non-Ch'i-tan procedure was performed à la Tatar, on horseback; and the reverence paid by it to the new emperor's "uncles and elder brothers" was probably a symbolic concession to the tribal principle of fraternal succession, which greatly affected the political history of the Liao dynasty.[476]

The triple investiture ceremony has been discussed in considerable detail to make clear how completely the tribal elements permeated even a procedure whose chief intent was to identify the Liao ruler with his Chinese prototype. Small wonder that many ceremonies less influenced by "imperial" trends clung so tenaciously to Ch'i-tan tradition. Small wonder that the limited number of borrowed elements were often so altered that the final synthesis had little resemblance to the Chinese original.[477] The Ch'i-tan probably accepted the idea of a script as well as certain technical details from the Chinese. But other influences, among which the *Liao Shih* specifically mentions that of the Uighurs,[478] were also present. In spite of a few princely adventures in calligraphy, literary pursuits remained definitely limited. Chinese books were officially collected,[479] and some classic works published and distributed,[480] expounded and copied.[481] A small number of Ch'i-tan nobles delighted in collecting and writing books.[482] But, while literary studies were respected and encouraged in Chinese circles, most of the Ch'i-tan nobility looked upon the reading of books with suspicion until the end of the dynasty.[483]

T'ai-tsu recommended Confucianism, and a handful of Ch'i-tan outsiders sincerely embraced the great Chinese doctrine. A few Confucian temples were erected,[484] but the failure of Confucianism to become a state doctrine is too obvious to need elaboration. The idea of clanship was taken over by a limited group which so "tribalized" the honored system that the result was more a caricature than an adaptation of the original Chinese institution.

Chinese music was played during the gentle Chinese Chung-yüan Festival, but tribal music introduced it and a vigorous display of Ch'i-tan horsemanship climaxed it.[485] Chinese music celebrated the birth of a princess, but Ch'i-tan music announced the birth of a prince.[486] Chinese and even Po-hai food might be appreciated by the Ch'i-tan rulers,[487] but the Ch'i-tan warriors continued to live on kumiss.[488] The last Liao emperor, T'ien-tsu, was so conditioned to the pastoral diet that he did not understand his Chinese subjects' aversion to it.[489] The three Liao stealing days which coincide with the Chinese merry celebrations of Chinese New Year remained typically "barbarian." While the Liao emperor might visit the market place incognito as the Chinese emperor did, his tribal subjects playfully stole their friends' property and abducted unmarried girls. The practice must have persisted throughout the Liao dynasty, for it was still observed after its collapse.[490]

Despite the presence of Chinese specialists in acculturation at the court, the Liao emperor, contrary to Chinese custom in this period, continued solemnly to clasp the hand of an honored vistor.[491] Chinese clothes, while worn by the northern (tribal) officials on important ceremonial occasions,[492] were not generally accepted by the tribal commoners. During the early days of the eleventh century[493] and even after 1055[494] the empress and the Ch'i-tan officials in their routine activities at court wore the traditional northern dress. Portraits preserved in the inner chambers of Hsing-tsung's mausoleum reveal the Ch'i-tan dignitaries clothed in garments that differed strikingly from those of their Chinese colleagues.[495]

---

[474] See the Armenian Hethum's description of Chingis Khan's inauguration (Boodberg 39, 242 ff).

[475] The Turkic dignitaries made the new khaghan mount a horse and throttled him almost to the point of strangulation. Immediately after this test they asked him to announce quickly the number of years he expected to rule (Chou 50, 4b).

[476] See XIII, note 50, and introduction.

[477] For a description of this process of adaptation and synthesis cf. Linton 40, 476 ff., 486 ff., and 492 ff.

[478] See VII, 2 (11).

[479] XIV, 4 (23).

[480] XVI, 1056, LS 21, 3a; XIV, 4 (25).

[481] XIV, 4 (29).

[482] VII, 2 (15) and note; XIV, 4 (2); LS 96, 4a.

[483] VII, 2 (77).

[484] IX (3); XI (5).

[485] VII, 2 (83).

[486] YPL 17b. See VII, 2, note 118.

[487] See VII, 2 (83).

[488] II, 1 (2).

[489] CS 8, 13a.

[490] SMCW 15a; cf. also Stein 39, 145 ff.

[491] VII, 2 (17) (49). See also Creel 38, ix.

[492] VII, 1 (7).

[493] SHYK 196, 48b; see VII, 1, note 16.

[494] VII, 1 (7).

[495] Torii 36 III, pl. 180 ff. [our fig. 6] and 191 ff.; for the Chinese officials see op. cit., pl. 183 ff.

Most significant, however, is the ceremonial attitude of the Ch'i-tan rulers to the basic economy upon which Chinese sedentary life and culture had rested for millennia. The emperor attended many ceremonies on horseback. Without concern for the Confucian warning against such occupations[496] he hunted and fished at his pleasure. But the great agricultural rite in which the Chinese emperor ceremonially ploughed the land and magically promoted his country's prosperity[497]—this great agricultural rite is not even mentioned in the ceremonial calendar of the Liao dynasty.

---

[496] The *Ch'un-ch'iu*, whose authorship is ascribed to Confucius himself, notes Duke Yin's interest in fishing. According to the *Tso Chuan*, his passion for the sport was improper. A good ruler should engage in hunting and fishing only for specific purposes, in the main to provide sacrificial animals (CCTCCS 3, 10a and 11b ff.; *cf.* also Legge, CC V, 18 ff.).

[497] See WHTK 87, 788 ff.

TRANSLATION

1. SOCIAL ORGANIZATION

1. Noble and common camp attendants 2. Dual order of dress 3. Different laws for various ethnic groups 4. Laws codified and ranks defined 5. Ch'i-tan ranks 6. Captured households bestowed 7. Ch'i-tan and Chinese clothes 8. Ch'i-tan officials marry Chinese 9. A poor but daring imperial clansman 10. Ch'i-tan and Chinese clothes 11. Subdued households attached to the ordos 12. "Ten thousand" slaves given 13. Sons of wives and concubines 14. Captives become personal property 15. A noble criminal treated leniently 16. Captives scattered and reunited 17. Formal equalization of the law 18. Can a slave become a prefect? 19. Ordo household presented 20. Master and slaves 21. Nobles and commoners to be punished equally 22. Changing status of a Yeh-lü clansman 23. Killing a slave 24. High and low Ch'i-tan may not intermarry 25. Privileged culprits 26. Sons of wives and concubines 27. The dress of the imperial family 28. Sons of concubines 29. The noble lineages of Liao 30. Ordo households given to an official 31. Po-hai allowed to play polo 32. A remote branch of the Hsiao clan 33. Special mourning customs for privileged groups 34. Property of heirless Chinese 35. Ch'i-tan police commissioners 36. Selling of slaves to Chinese 37. Political advice given by slaves 38. Emperor's paintings are tabooed 39. Weapons and caps 40. *I-li-chin* ranked with lower officials 41. Chinese and barbarians 42. People permitted to tame eagles 43. Restrictions on taming falcons 44. Households as presents 45. Ch'i-tan and Chinese different 46. Dress regulations 47. Selling oneself into slavery 48. Regulations for fur clothes 49. Imperial prerogative

1. NOBLE AND COMMON CAMP ATTENDANTS

Before 907   Previously Hên-tê-chin, khaghan of Yao-lien, because three lineages, P'u-ku-chih's and two others, had murdered the *yü-yüeh*, Shih-lu, seized their families[1] and put them into a *wa-li*.[2] Empress Ch'un-ch'in[3] pardoned them and made them noble camp attendants.[4]

947–951   Shih-tsung released all of them. Thereafter the members of the [imperial] clan, the relatives of the empress, and the hereditary officials[5] who committed crimes were seized and placed [in a camp].

The common camp attendants[6] were originally people who had been taken from the various ordos and criminals who had been seized and placed [in camps]. The tasks of the servitors who took care of the imperial storehouses, eagle aviary, boiled medicines,[7] beverages, ablutions, food, valet service, and tailoring, as well as of the attendants and actors of the imperial princes in the court, were all undertaken by them.   31, 9b–10a

---

[1] P'u-ku-chih 蒲古只, at one time the *i-li-chin* of the I-la tribe, avenged the murder of T'ai-tsu's grandfather by Hên-tê 很德. Later he plotted the murder of T'ai-tsu's uncle, Shih-lu 釋魯, with Hsiao T'ai-shên 臺哂 and Shih-lu's son, Hua-ko 滑哥. The families of Hsiao T'ai-shên and Hua-ko were forced into a *wa-li*, while that of P'u-ku-chih managed to escape punishment (LS 75, 2b; 90, 3b; 112, 5b).

[2] For a discussion of the nature of the *wa-li* 瓦里 see XV, introduction.

[3] T'ai-tsu's wife.

[4] *Chu-chang lang-chün* 著帳郎君 literally means "nobles attached to the camps." They were some sort of gentlemen prisoners. During the tribal period justice was simple and culprits were dealt with quickly and severely, mostly by execution. After the establishment of a more elaborate political system, the noble criminals were sentenced to detention in the [palace] camps and forced to perform various duties such as driving carts, tending lamps, and serving in the imperial tents (LS 61, 1a–2a; 88, 5a–b; cf. also 45, 13b). For minor crimes they were banished to the frontier tribes. A serious offender might be punished by exile beyond the border, or if qualified by status and training he might be sent to distant countries on a difficult mission. If successful in his mission, he was pardoned on his return and even rewarded (LS 61, 1b). For instance, Han Ch'un 韓橁, according to the inscription on his tomb, was beaten in 1005 for an undefined offence, and then the following year was dispatched to the Sha Prefecture Uighurs to invest the king. Upon his return he was granted two hundred taels of gold, one hundred bolts of silk, and eighty pieces of yarn (MCCSC 2, 4a–b).

[5] The term *shih hsüan chih chia* 世選之家 refers to families whose members had a hereditary claim to be selected to certain offices. For details concerning this important Ch'i-tan institution see XIV, introduction, and XIV, 1 and 3, *passim*.

[6] *Chu-chang hu* 著帳戶 literally means "households attached to the camps." These families were evidently much lower than the noble camp attendants, for their original social status was inferior. The term *chu-chang lang-chün* still marks the members of this group as officials. The *chu-chang* households occupied the lowest position. Their members had to perform all kinds of menial work.

[7] We follow LS 45, 16b in reading 藥 for the 樂 of our text.

2. DUAL ORDER OF DRESS

907–947   T'ai-tsu became emperor over the north; T'ai-tsung controlled China. . . . Then the regulations for clothes were defined. The northern section was based on the national system, and the southern section on the Chinese system. Each followed its convenience.
56, 1b

3. DIFFERENT LAWS FOR VARIOUS ETHNIC GROUPS

921   In the sixth year of Shên-ts'ê all barbarian tribes were pacified. . . . Then the high officials were ordered by edict to establish [special] laws for the Ch'i-tan and for all barbarians, while the Chinese were sentenced according to [their own] laws and decrees. . . . Until the time of T'ai-tsung the Po-hai people were all governed according to Chinese law; no changes were made for the rest [of the population].   61, 3a

4. LAWS CODIFIED AND RANKS DEFINED

921   On the first day ping-hsü of the fifth month in the summer [of the sixth year of Shên-ts'ê] an imperial decree ordered the codification of the laws and the definition of ranks and grades.   2, 2a

5. CH'I-TAN RANKS

According to the old system, the imperial house from Su-tsu down was designated as "Divisions." Tê-tsu's house was known as the Three Patriarchal Households and the Horizontal Tents.[8] The children of officials and people who were deprived of their property and enslaved were said to be "attached to the camps."[9]

Yeh-lü Hsieh-ti expressed the opinion that the standing of the Horizontal Tents should not be [simply] equated with that of the Northern and Southern Divisions.[10] When T'ai-tsung ordered it discussed

927–947   in the court, all agreed. Therefore an imperial decree ordered that the standing of the Horizontal Tents be placed higher. [Yeh-lü] P'o-tê[11] memorialized, "In my humble opinion, according to the government system the rank of the great kings of the Northern and Southern Divisions is higher than that of the t'i-yin.[12] While the Horizontal Tents, who desired in the beginning the highest position, were willing to participate in appointment to office along with the Northern and Southern Divisions, they are now however shamefaced about the equal standing. Since the Horizontal Tents and the various [other] lineages are all imperial subjects, why should there be these differences in standing?"

The emperor then reproved the officials, saying, "It is not proper for you to be acquiescent to Our face about what is not known to Us."[13] He ordered that the old system be followed again.   73, 6b

6. CAPTURED HOUSEHOLDS BESTOWED

930   On the day ping-wu [of the second month in the fifth year of T'ien-hsien] the Po-hai households which had previously been captured were bestowed upon Li-hu.[14]
3, 4a

7. CH'I-TAN AND CHINESE CLOTHES

938–947   This was the system of Liao: During the Hui-t'ung period the emperor's mother and the officials of the Northern Region dressed according to the national [Ch'i-tan] style. The emperor and the officials of the Southern Region dressed according to the Chinese style.

---

[8] See introduction.

[9] The term chu-chang 著帳 is here the abbreviated form of chu-chang lang-chün, nobles attached to the camps, and of chu-chang hu, households attached to the camps (see above, notes 4 and 6). Our text obviously juxtaposes the highest and the lowest social stratum of Ch'i-tan society.

[10] These were the two sections of the imperial I-la tribe. See VII, introduction and XIV, 1.

[11] Yeh-lü P'o-tê 頗德 was great king of the Southern Division of the I-la tribe (LTCNP 8047).

[12] The official in control of the administration of the Horizontal Tents (see XIV, 1, (9), LS 45, 8a).

[13] That is, they should not have kept silent and simply agreed with Yeh-lü Hsieh-ti when the issue was first brought up and discussed in the court. For the political problems involved, cf. below, XIV, introduction.

[14] Li-hu 李胡 was the childhood name of Hung-ku 洪古, the third son of T'ai-tsu (LS 64, 8b–10a; 72, 4a–5b).

After 983

After [the reign period] Ch'ien-hêng, at big ceremonies even officials of the third rank[15] and above in the Northern Region also wore Chinese clothes. After the [reign period]

After 1055

Ch'ung-hsi at big ceremonies all [officials] dressed in the Chinese style. During regular court audiences they still complied with the system of Hui-t'ung.[16]   56, 4a

8. CH'I–TAN OFFICIALS MARRY CHINESE

941

On the day *ping-ch'ên* [of the twelfth month in the third year of Hui-t'ung] it was decreed that Ch'i-tan individuals who held Chinese offices were to follow Chinese customs and might intermarry with the Chinese.[17]   4, 6a

9. A POOR BUT DARING IMPERIAL CLANSMAN

942

In the fifth year of Hui-t'ung the emperor asked for straightforward advice. At that time [Yeh-lü] Hai-ssŭ[18] was eighteen years old. Dressed in a sheepskin garment and riding an ox, he came to the court. The officials asked, "Why have you come here?"

He replied, "In answer to the decree on discussion of state affairs. If I am not rejected for being poor and young, I too can be selected to give straightforward advice."

The officials reported this to the throne. It happened that the emperor was about to go out hunting. He sent a messenger to say, "Wait for my return. Then I will see you."

Hai-ssŭ said, "I thought Your Majesty was in a hurry to find worthy men, so I came here, but now it is put off until after the hunt. Please let me go back right now."

On hearing of this the emperor immediately summoned him and, letting him be seated, inquired

---

[15] The Liao records offer no details concerning the ranks and degrees of the officialdom. Under the Chin the officials who held positions of the third rank were governors, governors-general, prefects, or generals (CS 55–57).

[16] In 1008 the Sung envoy to the Liao Court, Lu Chên, observed that the Liao emperor, Shêng-tsung, wore Chinese clothes. Yeh-lü Lung-yün and the emperor's brother, Lung-ch'ing 隆慶, were dressed in the same manner, while officials holding the tribal offices of *t'i-yin* and *ch'ang-wên* 常溫 (or *ch'ang-kun* 常衮) appeared in Ch'i-tan costume (HCLY 77, 7a ff.). Another Sung envoy, Sung Shou 宋綬, who visited Liao in 1020, learned that the emperor and his Chinese officials wore Chinese clothes, while the empress dowager and the Ch'i-tan officials were dressed in the Ch'i-tan style (SHYK 196, 48b).

On diplomatic missions the various national representatives usually wore different styles of clothes. The head envoys of a Liao mission to the Sung court, who always were Ch'i-tan, appeared in national costume; the Chinese vice-envoys wore Chinese dress. Sung emissaries to the Liao capital presented themselves in their traditional raiment. On special occasions both governments asked the foreign delegates to follow the style of the country that they visited (*cf.* WWC 12, 8b ff.; WWCPL 4b; SLYY 9, 89).

The most conspicuous piece of Ch'i-tan dress was the felt hat. From 1102 down such hats were fashionable even in the Sung capital. Between 1111 and 1119 several imperial edicts forbade the wearing of felt hats by civilians (*cf.* SHYK 196, 48b; NKCML 1, 14).

The dichotomy in Liao clothing is also documented by archaeological finds. The murals discovered on the walls of Hsing-tsung's mausoleum show two types: one is Chi-

nese (see fig. 7), the others Ch'i-tan (see figs. 6, 8, and 41). Some Ch'i-tan officials are shown bareheaded with the hair hanging in front of their ears; some wear caps or felt hats, long gowns with a round neck and a belt. They hold staffs with knobs and carry bows and quivers on the left. The wooden idols discovered in the mausoleums also show the dual style of dress (Torii 36 III, pl. 220 ff.).

The Ch'i-tan continued to dislike Chinese official dress during the Chin period. Wên Wei-chien 文惟簡, a Chin scholar who flourished around 1138, reports that after the establishment of the *hsing-t'ai shang-shu shêng* 行臺尚書省 certain Ch'i-tan officials in high positions were to wear formal Chinese dress and hold ivory tablets, according to Chinese rules. The Ch'i-tan considered this a most cumbersome imposition and said to their Chinese colleagues, "All these rules which you Chinese have set up constrict us in a fatal manner!" (LTSS 48b).

[17] The imperial harem included Chinese concubines though the empress had to be Ch'i-tan (see VII, introduction). Princesses born of imperial concubines of Chinese or Po-hai origin were given as wives to Chinese officials, such as Lu Chün 盧俊, Liu San-ku 劉三嘏, and Liu Ssŭ-tuan 劉四端 (*cf.* LS 65, 3a and 4b). Liu San-ku fled to Sung to avoid a marriage of this kind (JLKI 2, 34). Members of the Han 韓 clan frequently intermarried with the Hsiao clan, perhaps because one of its distinguished members, Han Tê-jang, was classed as a member of the Imperial Horizontal Tent (*cf.* MCCSC 2, 2b ff.).

[18] Hai-ssŭ 海思 was a son of Shih-lu, T'ai-tsu's uncle. He was appointed master of court etiquette. He was involved in a conspiracy against the throne and died in prison (LS 113, 3b–4a).

Fig. 6. Ch'i-tan dignitary; above his left shoulder are some Ch'i-tan words. Drawing on the wall of the entrance passage of Hsing-tsung's tomb (Torii 36 III, pl. 180).

Fig. 7. Persons dressed in Chinese style. Drawing on the wall of Hsing-tsung's tomb; sketched by Miss Midorii Torii (Torii 36 III, pl. 186).

Fig. 8. Ch'i-tan dignitary holding a staff. Drawing on the wall of Hsing-tsung's tomb; sketched by Miss Midorii Torii (Torii 36 III, pl. 194).

about the methods of good administration. An-tuan, Prince Ming,[19] and Yeh-lü P'o-tê[20] were ordered to examine him. After a few days An-tuan and the other memorialized, "The ability of Hai-ssǔ is superior to ours."

The emperor summoned Hai-ssǔ and asked, "What are those men who talked with you like?"

He replied, "An-tuan speaks without control like an empty cart rolling along a precipitous slope. P'o-tê is like a man who clumps along on boots through the wilderness to shoot bustards."

The emperor burst into loud laughter.[21]   113, 3b–4a

10. CH'I-TAN AND CHINESE CLOTHES

947   In the Liao empire after T'ai-tsung entered Chin the emperor and the Chinese officials of the Southern Section wore Chinese clothes, while the empress dowager and the Ch'i-tan officials of the Northern Section wore their national clothes. The Chinese clothes followed the traditional style of Chin of the Five Dynasties.[22]   55, 1b

11. SUBDUED HOUSEHOLDS ATTACHED TO THE ORDOS

971   On the day kêng-tzǔ of the eleventh month [in the third year of Pao-ning] the yü-yüeh Yen-ni-li and other [dignitaries] of the Lu-ch'ü River led four hundred and fifty households to submit and asked that they be included in the ordo registers.[23]   A decree decided that the households be permitted to remain, that they be distributed among the three palaces of Tun-mu, Chi-ch'ing, and Yung-hsing, and that [Yen-ni-li and the others] be sent back with generous rewards.

8, 3a

12. "TEN THOUSAND" SLAVES GIVEN

979–983   The empress,[24] who greatly loved [Kuan-yin-nü],[25] granted her ten thousand slaves.[26]   65, 2a

13. SONS OF WIVES AND CONCUBINES

983–1014   Yeh-lü Shih-liang,[27] whose childhood name was Wo, was a member of the Six Divisions lineage. He was gifted and quick-witted and well versed in the dynasty's historical precedents and genealogies. When he sent up a memorial about a debate with his cousin, Ti-lieh, concerning the sons of wives and concubines, the emperor began to take notice of him.

94, 4a

---

[19] An-tuan, Prince Ming, was one of T'ai-tsu's younger brothers. In 947 he helped Shih-tsung become emperor and received the title of King of Tung-tan 東丹 (LS 64, 6a).

[20] Yeh-lü P'o-tê acquired a reputation during the military expedition against Later T'ang in 936. He made up for lack of brilliancy by his great earnestness (cf. LS 73, 6a–b).

[21] And began to use Hai-ssǔ's services.

[22] The Chinese clothes donned by the Liao Chinese in the main followed the T'ang style (MHPT 6, 37). Our text says that the Liao Chinese dressed according to the style of the Chin dynasty. The seeming contradiction disappears if it is remembered that the clothes of the Chin dynasty were those of T'ang.

[23] The term kung chi 宮籍, which is not explained in the Liao Shih or elsewhere, probably means the list of people belonging to the different ordos. These persons may originally have been captives of war. In 986 six special officials were appointed to take charge of the Yü-ku-li, Jurchen, Ti-lieh-yü 迪烈予, and other tribesmen "who belonged (隸) to the kung chi" (LS 11, 6a). They may also have entered the kung chi voluntarily, like Yeh-lü Yü-wên 欲穩 of the T'u-lü-pu tribe, who was the first person to do so (LS 73, 7a). These people were obliged

to render various services to the ordos as well as to the mausoleums. On achieving merit, as on the field of battle, they could "leave (出) the kung chi." Such was the case with Yeh-lü Lung-yün 隆運, who instead of having to render services was granted land, a residence, and a tomb (LS 82, 2a–b).

[24] Empress Jui-chih.

[25] The eldest daughter of Ching-tsung. She was married to Hsiao Chi-hsien 繼先.

[26] In other passages dealing with the presentation of slaves to daughters of the emperor, the term nu pi 奴婢 of our text is replaced by the expression ying-ch'ên hu 媵臣戶 (LS 37, 12a) or ts'ung-chia hu 從嫁戶 (LTHPC 4a). Both expressions refer to households which the emperor and empress gave to their daughters when they married. With persons of this kind Princess Kuan-yin-nü built up Hui 徽 Prefecture (cf. LS 37, 12a), one of the country's "entrusted" territories. The donation was made during the great war against Sung; the slaves given were in all probability Chinese prisoners of war.

[27] This Ch'i-tan noble was promoted to the post of northern chancellor in 1014 (LS 15, 7a). His memorial was sent up some time during the reign of Shêng-tsung (983–1031), most likely well before 1014 when he was already sufficiently important to receive a high position.

14. CAPTIVES BECOME PERSONAL PROPERTY

986   On the day *hsin-ssŭ* [of the seventh month in the fourth year of T'ung-ho] . . . two hundred and forty persons of Sung who had surrendered were presented as gifts to attendant officials.   11, 5*b*

15. A NOBLE CRIMINAL TREATED LENIENTLY

988   On the day *ting-wei* of the second month [in the sixth year of T'ung-ho], Ch'ou-ning,[28] Prince of Hsi, murdered an innocent man, Li Hao.   The officials concerned, considering his noble status, petitioned that he be pardoned for his crime and that he be made to furnish funds for the support of [Li] Hao's family.   The request was granted.   12, 1*b*

16. CAPTIVES SCATTERED AND REUNITED

989   On the day *chia-tzŭ* [of the second month in the seventh year of T'ung-ho], it was decreed that those captives who were taken during the southern expedition and had relatives attached to the various camps should be redeemed with government money so that they might join each other.   12, 5*a*

17. FORMAL EQUALIZATION OF THE LAW

Previously, when a death occurred in a brawl between Ch'i-tan and Chinese, justice was not even-handed.   Now it was applied impartially.[29]

994   In the twelfth year of T'ung-ho it was decreed that Ch'i-tan who had committed one of the ten crimes[30] should also be sentenced according to [Chinese] law.   61, 5*a*

18. CAN A SLAVE BECOME A PREFECT?

995–996   [Yeh-lü] A-mo-li was covetous by nature.[31]   He brought together those whom he had captured whenever he participated in a military expedition and had them build a walled city.   He requested that it be named Fêng Prefecture[32] and that one of his house slaves, Yen-kuei, be appointed its prefect.   Contemporary public opinion held him in contempt.   79, 4*b*

19. ORDO HOUSEHOLD PRESENTED

After 1003   Because the family of [Wang] Chi-chung[33] had no slaves, it was granted thirty ordo households.   81, 2*a*

---

[28] Ch'ou-ning 籌寧 was the style of Ho-shuo-nu 和朔奴. His surname is not known (LS 85, 5*a–b*).

[29] At least theoretically and temporarily.   For the real situation see VII, introduction.

[30] The Chinese traditional code listed ten grave crimes. According to TLT 6, 7*a–b*, the ten crimes were: (1) Plotting rebellion (謀反); plotting to overthrow the state; (2) Plotting treason (謀大逆); plotting to destroy the imperial ancestral temples, mausoleums, and palaces; (3) Plotting revolt (謀叛); joining the enemy in a revolt against the state; (4) Family crimes (惡逆); striking or plotting to kill a parent, uncle, aunt, brother, sister, etc.; (5) Inhumanity (不道); killing, dismembering, or poisoning several persons; (6) Great disrespect (大不敬); making illegal use or appropriation of imperial possessions; (7) Unfilial conduct (不孝); cursing one's parents, or grandparents; living apart from one's parents; giving insufficient support to one's parents, etc.; (8) Discord (不睦); striking or plotting to kill a husband or his parents; (9) Insubordination (不義); plotting to kill an official in one's district; (10) Incest (內亂); having sexual relations with a concubine of a close relative.

[31] Whether he really was as selfish as the text asserts may be questioned.   His appreciation of a slave's achievement shows him as an unconventional and bold character. It was he who suggested to Empress Dowager Ch'êng-t'ien the abolition of the rule that persons be held responsible for crimes committed by their brothers (LS 79, 4*a–b*; *cf.* LS 13, 6*b*–7*a*).

[32] The name means Prosperous Prefecture.   This area corresponds to the region between the Shira Muren and the Tsaghan Muren, Jehol (MRC II, 96).   In another part of the text Fêng Prefecture is described as a "grazing ground" (LS 37, 13*a*), which may refer to the pastoral economy of the tribal population.

[33] Wang Chi-chung 王繼忠 was a Sung official captured by Liao in 1003.   He reached the position of chancellor in the court of Liao.   He made great contributions to the maintenance of peace and friendship between Liao and Sung during his lifetime (LS 81, 1*b*–2*b*).   He was honored by the bestowal of the imperial clan name, Yeh-lü; his personal name was changed first to Hsien-chung 顯忠 and later to Tsung-hsin 宗信.   Whenever a Sung envoy visited the Liao court he always brought Wang Chi-chung presents from the emperor (SS 279, 2*a*).

20. MASTER AND SLAVES

1006   In the twenty-fourth year [of T'ung-ho] it was decreed that except in cases of plotting rebellion or treason or committing crimes punishable by hard labor or death, a slave could not act as first informant against his master.   In case of slaves committing a crime deserving the death penalty, they were to be surrendered to the authorities.   The master was not allowed to slay them on his own initiative.   61, 5*a–b*

21. NOBLES AND COMMONERS TO BE PUNISHED EQUALLY

1011   In the twenty-ninth year [of T'ung-ho], according to the old law, the descendants of the hereditary families[34] of prime ministers and commanding prefects who committed a crime were sentenced to hard labor and beaten like the commoners but were exempted from the tatooing of the face.   It was decreed that henceforth whenever they deserved tatooing for committing a crime they were to be punished equally according to the law.   61, 5*b*

22. CHANGING STATUS OF A YEH–LÜ CLANSMAN

1013–1020   Previously, when [Yeh-lü] Tzŭ-chung[35] was in Korea, his younger brother Chao was a noble camp attendant.   In punishment for a crime[36] the family property had been confiscated.   Now [Tzŭ-chung] was restored to the Horizontal Tents and the old property was returned.   An imperial decree ordered that a daughter from the imperial consort family be married to him.   88, 5*a–b*

23. KILLING A SLAVE

1017   On the day *chia-hsü* of the second month [in the sixth year of K'ai-t'ai], because Princess Sai-ko[37] killed an innocent girl slave and because her husband, Hsiao T'u-yü,[38] could not control his family, the princess was degraded to the rank of *hsien chu*,[39] and T'u-yü was deprived of his position as associate administrator of the affairs for the Political and Court Councils.[40]

15, 11*a*

It happened that the princess was found guilty of murdering a household girl-slave.   She was degraded to the rank of *chün-chu* and T'u-yü was removed from his *shih-hsiang* position.[41]   93, 5*b*

24. HIGH AND LOW CH'I–TAN MAY NOT INTERMARRY

1019   On the day *kuei-ssŭ* [of the tenth month in the eighth year of K'ai-t'ai] it was decreed that the Horizontal Tents and the Three [Patriarchal] Households could not intermarry with the lesser tents and lineages.   All marriages had to be reported to the throne before being concluded.   16, 4*a*

25. PRIVILEGED CULPRITS

1020   [On the day *mou-yin* of the tenth month in the ninth year of K'ai-t'ai] a court noble, Lao, returned from a mission to Sha Prefecture[42] and was ordered to be pardoned for an old crime.   In the past the country, in sending missions to distant states, in most

---

[34] See above, note 5.

[35] Yeh-lü Tzŭ-chung 昚忠 (T. 沃衍) was versed in literature.   He was sent to Korea twice, the first time in 1013 and the second time from 1014 to 1020 (LS 15, 6*a* and 7*b*; 16, 4*b*).

[36] Yeh-lü Kuo-liu 國留, the eldest brother of Tzŭ-chung and Chao, killed his wife's brother's wife and a slave because of adultery.   He was sentenced to death and his relatives were thrown into prison.   Tzŭ-chung was sent to unfriendly Korea and Chao died as a gentleman-prisoner (*cf.* LS 88, 4*b* ff.; 104, 1*b* ff.).

[37] The thirteenth daughter of Shêng-tsung.   She died in exile (LS 65, 4*b*).

[38] Hsiao T'u-yü 圖玉 (T. 兀衍) gained fame for his

military expedition into what is now western Mongolia and Kansu (LS 93, 5*a–b*).

[39] A princess could possess the most honored rank of *kung chu* 公主, the less honored rank of *chün* (郡) *chu*, or the lowest rank of *hsien* (縣) *chu* (LS 65).

[40] When it first originated in 634, this rank was as high as that of a prime minister, but by the time of Liao it had become a mere honorary title.   See XIV, 2 (5), LS 47, 3*b* ff.

[41] *Shih-hsiang* 使相 was a term designating officials who held such military positions as that of commanding prefect or chancellor along with a civil position of the rank of prime minister.

[42] An oasis state then controlled by the Uighurs.   See I, 2 (10), no. 17.

cases used capable men who had been sentenced to hard labor for a crime.   On returning from the mission they were pardoned for their crime.   16, 5a

26. SONS OF WIVES AND CONCUBINES

1024   At this time it had long been peaceful. The emperor devoted his attention to literature. For the first time he drew up genealogical tables in order to differentiate the descendants of wives from those of concubines. Thereupon quarrels and lawsuits arose continuously. [Hsiao] P'o,[43] who had administrative ability and understood the ruler's intentions, had presented memorials which accorded with the emperor's will. The discussions in the court were in the main decided by him.   80, 4a

27. THE DRESS OF THE IMPERIAL FAMILY

1025   On the day *mou-wu* of the second month [in the fifth year of T'ai-p'ing] the empire was forbidden to have garments using variegated silk with bright gold and golden thread. The imperial relatives who had to wear them were to memorialize before using them.
17, 1a

28. SONS OF CONCUBINES

1027   On the first day *ting-mao* of the tenth month [in the winter of the seventh year of T'ai-p'ing] it was decreed to all tents and households that the standing of a concubine's son should be decided according to the social standing of his mother.[44]   17, 4a–b

1029   On the day *ting-ch'ou* [of the twelfth month in the eighth year of T'ai-p'ing] it was decreed that a son of a concubine, even though he was already considered a free man, was not eligible for hereditary selection.   17, 5b–6a

29. THE NOBLE LINEAGES OF LIAO

1029   [On the day *ting-hai* of the twelfth month in the eighth year of T'ai-p'ing] it was decreed that the Two [sections of] Imperial Maternal Uncles and the Administrations of the Southern and Northern Kings were the noble lineages of the nation. Low and common persons were not allowed to hold offices in these groups.   17, 6a

30. ORDO HOUSEHOLDS GIVEN TO AN OFFICIAL

1036   [Hsiao Tê][45] was ordered to revise the code with the scribe Yeh-lü Shu-ch'êng.[46] He was shifted to the position of chief controller of the Ch'i-tan traveling camps and was presented with fifteen ordo households.   96, 5a–b

31. PO-HAI ALLOWED TO PLAY POLO

1038   In the seventh year of Ch'ung-hsi [Hsiao Hsiao-chung[47]] was vicegerent of the Eastern Capital. At this time the Po-hai people were not allowed to play polo.[48] Hsiao-chung said, "The Eastern Capital, a very important military center, has no hunting ground.

---

[43] Hsiao P'o 朴 (T. 延寧) was a very learned man. In 1024 he became prime minister of the Northern Administration and then chancellor of the Northern Division. At the end of his life he was raised to the rank of Chancellor of the Southern Division. He died in 1035 (LS 80, 4a–b).

[44] Concubines might be either slave girls or daughters of a commoner or sometimes of a noble.

[45] Hsiao Tê 德 (T. 特末). In LS 89, 1a, his name is written as Yeh-lü Tê. He held the position of prime minister of the Southern Administration (LS 96, 5a–b).

[46] Yeh-lü Shu-ch'êng 庶成 was skilled in the Chinese and the Ch'i-tan languages. He translated a medical work from Chinese into Ch'i-tan (LS 89, 1a–b). His

younger brother, Yeh-lü Shu-chên 庶箴, suggested the reform of the Ch'i-tan kinship system in the memorial of 1074. See VII, 2 (67) and VII, introduction.

[47] Hsiao Hsiao-chung 孝忠 was a brother of Empress Ch'in-ai, Shêng-tsung's second wife, and was married to her daughter. He was made prime minister of the Northern Administration. In 1043 he became northern chancellor. See XIV, 2 (3).

[48] Literally, "ball," here obviously referring to polo. The suppression of physical training among the Po-hai people was similar to the prohibition of hunting among the Chinese enforced by the Liao government in 1071 (LS 22, 7a).

Except for polo how can [the people] get military training? And, since the Son of Heaven considers All Within the Four Seas as one family, why is there a differentiation between this and that?[49] It would be advisable to relax the ban." The request was granted.   81, 2b

32. A REMOTE BRANCH OF THE HSIAO CLAN

1041   On the day kêng-yin of the twelfth month [in the ninth year of Ch'ung-hsi], because the court noble[50] of the Pu-wei tent of the Administration of the Northern Great King claimed that since his forbears had been connected by marriage with the imperial [house] permission should be given to set up a directing secretary, it was ordered that Hsiao Hu-tu[51] of the same tent should be this official.[52]   18, 9b

33. SPECIAL MOURNING CUSTOMS FOR PRIVILEGED GROUPS

1043   On the day ping-wu of the sixth month [in the twelfth year of Ch'ung-hsi] it was decreed that the lineages whose members had a hereditary claim on the posts of prime minister and commanding prefect,[53] as well as[54] the families of those who personally[55] were commanding prefects, might use silver utensils but were still[56] forbidden to kill animals for sacrifices[57] in the burials.   19, 4a

34. PROPERTY OF HEIRLESS CHINESE

1043   On the day kêng-hsü [of the sixth month in the twelfth year of Ch'ung-hsi] it was decreed that, if the Chinese families assigned to the different camps[58] had no offspring, their permanent property was to be inherited by their near relatives.   19, 4a–b

35. CH'I–TAN POLICE COMMISSIONERS

1044   Previously, when a Ch'i-tan committed a crime, he was generally examined by a Chinese. Many people suffered wrong. Chung-yüan,[59] in a memorial, requested that a Ch'i-tan police commissioner be appointed in each of the five capitals. It was approved by an imperial decree.[60]   112, 5a

---

[49] Meaning, of course, between the Ch'i-tan and the Po-hai people.

[50] In 938 the court noble, an official in the tent of an Imperial Maternal Uncle, was renamed directing secretary (cf. LS 4, 2b). From this time on this title was given to some of the court nobles.

[51] Hsiao Hu-tu 胡覩 was a nephew of the Empress Ch'in-ai and was married to her daughter. He held high official positions during the Ch'ing-ning period (1055–1065). In 1063 he unsuccessfully plotted high treason and was drowned (LS 114, 1a–2a).

[52] The passage shows that the northern great king, who was a Yeh-lü, had members of the Hsiao clan among his officials.

[53] See XIV, introduction.

[54] We follow other editions in reading 及 for the 反 of our text.

[55] As juxtaposed to those whose families held a hereditary prerogative.

[56] This refers to the previous decree on funerals. See VII, 2 (58).

[57] This order shows that in the middle of the eleventh century Buddhism played a great role in changing the Ch'i-tan customs. Statistics of the animal sacrifice, based mainly upon the Imperial Annals (pên chi), show clearly the difference before and after Shêng-tsung (982–1031). Before Shêng-tsung the killing of animals for sacrificial purposes was very frequent; after Shêng-tsung only seven cases are recorded (Fêng CS 32, 108).

[58] Those attached to the kung 宮 (palaces) of T'ang were generally children and wives of criminals, whereas those assigned to the kung 宮 (camps) of Liao were not only the families of criminals but also families captured during war (NESCC 19, 17b–18b).

The households attached to the camps for service were divided into two groups, the kung hu 宮戶 (or chang hu 帳戶) and kung fên hu 宮分戶 (or kung fên jên hu 宮分人戶). Sometimes the kung hu was also called ling hu 陵戶 after an emperor's death. The difference between the kung hu or chang hu and the kung fên hu or kung fên jên hu lies in the fact that the former belonged to the camp of a living emperor, while the latter were variously distributed among the other camps.

These families could be presented as gifts, but they were allowed to possess some property, to be enrolled as soldiers, and occasionally even to rise to the rank of officials. Cf. LS 89, 3a; 94, 4a; 108, 2a; 114, 2b.

[59] Chung-yüan 重元 was the second son of Shêng-tsung and the younger brother of Hsing-tsung. In the Liao Shih, Ch'i-tan Kuo Chih, and other works, the names of Shêng-tsung's sons generally begin with the word tsung 宗. It is possible that Tsung-yüan was renamed Chung-yüan after his rebellion and death in 1063 (cf. LS 16, 1b).

[60] In 1044 the offices of the Ch'i-tan police commissioners were set up (LS 19, 5b).

36. SELLING OF SLAVES TO CHINESE

1046   On the day *i-yu* [of the first month in the spring of the fifteenth year of Ch'ung-hsi] . . . the sale of slaves to the Chinese by Ch'i-tan people was prohibited.   19, 7*b*

37. POLITICAL ADVICE GIVEN BY SLAVES

1048   In this month [the second month of the seventeenth year of Ch'ung-hsi] an imperial decree ordered that officials and commoners who expressed their opinions on the national interest should not mention their own affairs at the same time.

The views of slaves might be presented to their masters but could not be presented [to the government] by themselves.   20, 2*a*

38. EMPEROR'S PAINTINGS ARE TABOOED

1052   On the day *kuei-hai* [of the seventh month in the twenty-first year of Ch'ung-hsi] a personal imperial servitor,[61] Lu Pao, who had copied a painting by the emperor, was spared the death penalty but was punished by hard labor for life.   20, 6*b*

39. WEAPONS AND CAPS

1055   On the day *kêng-shên* [of the ninth month in the first year of Ch'ing-ning] an imperial decree ordered that with the exception of the soldiers of the imperial guard, no one who entered the palace was to carry a sword and that no one except the descendants of meritorious consort family relatives and the *i-li-chin*, subordinate officials, servitors, and attendants on duty was to wear a cap.[62]   21, 1*b*

40. *I-LI-CHIN* RANKED WITH LOWER OFFICIALS

1055   On the day *jên-hsü* [of the ninth month in the first year of Ch'ing-ning] it was decreed that the lineages of the *i-li-chin* and of the subordinate officials and also the people of the lower class were not to wear camel yarn [clothes] and otter furs. For sword-hilts, *t'u-hu*[63] [belts], and saddle and bridle ornaments they were not allowed to use rhinoceros [horn], jade, or *ku-tu-hsi*.[64]   Only grand generals were not restricted.   21, 1*b*–2*a*

---

[61] The term *hsiao-ti* 小底 often appears in the literature from the time of the Five Dynasties to that of Yüan. It was probably a colloquial term for a servant. In the time of Liao the *hsiao-ti* served the emperors, taking care of yet stationery, bedrooms, Buddhist temples, stores, horses, eagles, medicine, beverages, ablutions, food, clothes, etc. (LS 45, 16*a–b*).

[62] The headgear of the Ch'i-tan officials consisted from early times of a felt hat, called *pu yao kuan* 步搖冠, which was decorated with golden flowers, pearls, jade, and kingfisher feathers. Also worn was a black cap, decorated in front with golden flowers and strings of pearls and further embellished with two ear-flaps sticking out horizontally. Another cap, dark purple and green in color, was worn with tight-fitting robes of the same color. From the back hung a tuft of hair like a queue (CTKC 23, 4*a–b*).

[63] *T'u-hu* 兔鶻 (also written 吐鶻 in LS 96, 6*b* and CS 64, 3*b*) was a belt with a buckle, according to Hung Hao 洪皓 (T. 光弼 d. 1155) (SMCWPI 16*a*). It was probably pronounced *t'u-hu* in the Ch'i-tan language. According to Laufer (13, 359) and Pelliot (13, 366–367), the word is a transcription of a Ch'i-tan word and designates a kind of belt or a pendant on a belt.

[64] 骨突犀 (also written 㨉柮犀 in LS 96, 6*b* and 116, 24*a* and 骨睹犀 in CS 64, 3*b*) was the horn of a thousand year old snake (LS 116, 24*a*). According to one eleventh century tradition it was considered poisonous and yet antitoxic (YYKYL 1, 16–17). According to SMCWPI 16*a* it was an ivory-yellow plant from which the Ch'i-tan made belts. Laufer (13, *passim*) identifies it with walrus or narwhal ivory: "It seems to me that the Kirgiz were the mediators in the trade of *ku-tu-si* between the Chinese and the Turks, and possibly the Arabs . . . it seems to me that the foreign word *ku-tu-si* was taken by the Kirgiz or a related Turkish tribe on account of some real or alleged similarity in sound in the sense of a word of their language signifying 'bull.' At all events, while I strictly adhere to the conclusion that Arabic *chutww* and Turkish *ḥutū* like Chinese *ku-tu-si* principally denote walrus and narwhal ivory, it must be admitted that a confusion with mammoth ivory was possible, in view of the fact that it seldom was the complete tusk which was the object of trade, but prepared fragments or wrought articles" (*op. cit.*, 354–356). Pelliot (13, 365) endorses this view. See also Laufer 16*a*.

41. CHINESE AND BARBARIANS

1057   On the day *hsin-hai* of the eighth month [in the third year of Ch'ing-ning] the emperor presented to the empress dowager a poem on the subject, "Sovereign and subjects have the same interests; Chinese and barbarians[65] have the same customs."   21, 4*b*

42. PEOPLE PERMITTED TO TAME EAGLES

1058   On the day *i-ssŭ* [of the twelfth month in the fourth year of Ch'ing-ning] officials and commoners were allowed to tame eagles.[66]   21, 5*b*

43. RESTRICTIONS ON TAMING FALCONS

1061   On the day *hsin-wei* of the fourth month in the summer of the seventh year [of Ch'ing-ning] the lower officials and common people were forbidden to tame the gray falcons from east of the sea.[67]   21, 6*b*

44. HOUSEHOLDS AS PRESENTS

1065–1073   [Yeh-lü] Chüeh[68] did not like to amass wealth. The emperor, knowing the state of his poverty, bestowed upon him ten camp households.   91, 3*b*

45. CH'I-TAN AND CHINESE DIFFERENT

1070   In the sixth year [of Hsien-yung] the emperor, considering that the customs of the Ch'i-tan and the Chinese were not the same and that the national law should not be applied indiscriminately, therefore ordered the *t'i-yin* Su[69] and Chancellor [Yeh-lü] I-hsin to revise the regulations.[70]   62, 3*a*

46. DRESS REGULATIONS

1078   On the day *ting-hai* of the eleventh month [in the fourth year of Ta-k'ang] the common people were forbidden to wear brocade and variegated silk with decorations of the sun, moon, mountains,[71] or dragons.   23, 6*b*

47. SELLING ONESELF INTO SLAVERY

1088   On the day *chia-hsü* [of the first month in the fourth year of Ta-an], because of the famine in Shang-ching and Nan-ching, free persons were permitted to sell themselves.   25, 1*b*–2*a*

---

[65] Once Tao-tsung ordered a Chinese official to expound the *Lun Yü* 論語. When the latter reached the passage, "The rude tribes of the east and north have their princes" (Legge, CC I, 156), he dared not explain it but passed over it quickly. Tao-tsung said, "The ancient Hsün-yü 獯鬻 and Hsien-yün 獫狁, who were without good manners and laws, were because of this called 'barbarians.' As to our country, we have a civilization which is not inferior to that of the Chinese. Why should we feel ashamed of it?" He ordered the official to continue expounding the text (SMCW 9*a*).

According to the Chin scholar, Wên Wei-chien (see above, note 16), the old Liao Central Capital had a Temple of Confucius in which during the middle of the spring and autumn sacrificial ceremonies were performed. Once, when a Ch'i-tan official, Ku-ko 固哥, was occupied in preparing a feast at the temple, several well-dressed barbarian women entered. One of them asked, "What kind of a god is this bearded one?" to which another replied, "This is he who slandered us by saying 'The barbarians who have a ruler.'" All burst into laughter and went away (LTSS 49*a*).

[66] According to the Liao custom, only the prime minister, besides the emperor, was allowed to hunt with falcons (LS 110, 4*b*). The present text shows that the common people were previously not even permitted to have eagles.

[67] See II, 1, note 60.

[68] Yeh-lü Chüeh 玦, a descendant of the Yao-lien family, was known for his straightforwardness (LS 91, 3*a*–*b*).

[69] Su 蘇 was the childhood name of Yeh-lü Liang 良. He edited Tao-tsung's collected works, *Ch'ing-ning Chi* 清寧集. A collection of his own works was given the title *Ch'ing-hui Chi* 慶會集 by Tao-tsung (LS 96, 3*b*–4*a*).

[70] This code of Liao, which consisted of more than a thousand clauses, was never put into practice. It was formally abolished soon afterwards, in 1089 (XIV, 4 (29) (30)).

[71] The moon pattern is here mentioned together with the dragon decoration. The moon was not worshipped by the Ch'i-tan; the dragon was definitely Chinese. Could it be that the moon pattern was also introduced from China Proper?

48. REGULATIONS FOR FUR CLOTHES

The nobles wore sable furs, those of purplish black being most prized, with plain black next. They also had ermine of a very pure white. The lower classes [wore] the furs of the sable, sheep, mole, and corsac.[72]   56, 2b

49. IMPERIAL PREROGATIVE

According to Liao law, stags with antlers could be shot only by the Son of Heaven.   78, 1b

2. CUSTOMS AND TRADITIONS

1. Traditional exogamy 2. The twelve animals 3. A political alliance concluded 4. Rebirth Ceremony of the *i-li-chin* 5. Fire informs Heaven of the emperor's accession 6. Sacrifice on a mountain 7. Chinese culture encouraged—for Chinese subjects 8. Invoking a curse with devil arrows 9. Ceremonies fixed 10. Selective culture transfer 11. The Ch'i-tan script 12. Should the empress be buried with the emperor? 13. The deity of the deer 14. Entertainment 15. Calligraphy 16. The Imperial Maternal Uncles 17. Clasping a high visitor's hand 18. Ceremony of Entering the Side Hall 19. The Dragon Boat Festival 20. Sororate 21. Remarriage of widowers and widows 22. Loot from Chin 23. Worship of the sun 24. The deity of the Earth 25. A female shaman's medicine fails 26. Rain magic 27. The emperor drinks in the market 28. Beating the clay ox 29. Card playing 30. Accurate divination 31. Shamans perform important rites 32. War magic 33. A favorite asks to be buried with the emperor 34. Buried with the emperor 35. Divorce of a Ch'i-tan princess 36. Ceremony of establishing a friendship 37. Banners and drums for victorious generals 38. Honors for three generations living together 39. Rebirth Ceremonies of the empress dowager 40. Sacrifice to Mu-yeh Mountain 41. The game of "double sixes" 42. Rebirth Ceremony of a prince 43. Costly funeral customs abolished 44. Koreans study the Ch'i-tan language 45. The deity of the white horse 46. Primitive psychotherapy 47. Four and six generations living together 48. Schools for uncivilized settlers 49. Clasping a meritorious general's hand 50. Distinguished widows may not remarry 51. An eclipse 52. The emperor in Yen 53. A tribe sets up its own banners and drums 54. Burning the former emperor's favorite possessions 55. Reason for a divorce 56. A high official is beaten 57. Rebirth Ceremony of the empress dowager 58. Reduction of animal sacrifice 59. System of ritual 60. Pardon for a sonless bandit 61. Men and animals freed 62. Rebirth Ceremony of the empress dowager 63. A good miracle 64. Rebirth Ceremony of the heir apparent 65. Eight generations living together 66. Three generations living together 67. Clan names and marriage system 68. Ethical idealism versus shamanism 69. A wife's loyalty to her exiled husband 70. Four generations living together 71. Rain magic 72. Legend of a poor tribesman 73. No intermarriage with barbarians 74. Old age honored 75. A Ch'i-tan princess marries four times 76. Three generations living together 77. Reading of books 78. Directions 79. The sun worshipped 80. The god of Fire 81. The Sê-sê Rain Ceremony 82. War magic 83. Miscellaneous annual ceremonies 84. Legend of tribal origin 85. The sacrifice to Mu-yeh Mountain 86. The Rebirth Ceremony 87. The Investiture Ceremony 88. The *ao* woman 89. Marriage of an emperor 90. Marriage of a princess 91. Funeral ceremonies 92. Honoring the emperor's death place 93. Ceremonial hunt 94. Hunting clothes 95. A successful diviner

1. TRADITIONAL EXOGAMY

Ca. **800**   Su-tsu,[1] on a visit to her[2] family, said, "Those who bear the same family name may become friends. Those who bear different family names may marry." Knowing that she was born a Hsiao,[3] he betrothed I-tsu to her.   71, 1b

---

[72] This paragraph was obviously taken over from the description given in CTKC 23, 4b which is practically identical with it.

[1] T'ai-tsu's great-great-grandfather. His original name was Nou-li-ssŭ 耨里思 (LS 63, 7b; 64, 2a).

[2] The future wife of Su-tsu's son, Sa-la-tê 薩剌德, who was later given the temple name of I-tsu. He was well-known for his skill in archery (LS 2, 8a).

[3] The kin group from which the empress came probably received its Chinese clan name, Hsiao 蕭, in the year 947 after the conquest of the Chin capital of Pien, that is at a moment when Chinese cultural influence grew particularly intense. According to LS 67, 1a and CTKC 17, 1a, T'ai-tsung granted to Hsiao-han 小漢, a meritorious brother-in-law who was then commanding prefect of the conquered city, the homonymic name Hsiao Han 蕭翰.

Thereafter the name Hsiao was applied to the whole clan. WTS 72, 18b asserts that the name was first assigned by a Chinese official, Li Sung 李崧 (d. 948), to this person and was then extended. The two reports, which coincide in substance if not in detail, dispose of other stories which assign an earlier origin to the name. CHWC 27, 4b claims that the Ch'i-tan who followed the empress neé Hsiao of the Sui dynasty (581–618) into T'u-chüeh territory adopted her name. This story is one of several legendary reports of an early origin of the name Hsiao (*cf.* PYC 1, 10; LS 116, 1b ff.; LCYHP 2a; YS 150, 1a).

According to Chou Ch'un 周春 (1729–1815), this story originated during the Yüan dynasty (LCYHP 2b). It is contradicted by the memorial of 1074 which denies the existence of Chinese clan names among the predynastic Ch'i-tan (see VII, introduction). If it has any factual

2. THE TWELVE ANIMALS

902   Empress Ying-t'ien dreamt of a god wearing a golden crown and plain clothes and holding a weapon.[4] His countenance was very handsome. He was followed by twelve strange animals,[5] among them a black hare which jumped into the bosom of the empress. As a result she became pregnant and later bore T'ai-tsung.[6]

foundation at all, it may possibly refer to an early development of the kin group which later was named Hsiao.

The origin of the name was also ascribed to A-pao-chi who out of admiration for Liu Pang 劉邦 and Hsiao Ho 蕭何 of the Han dynasty gave his clan the name Liu and that of his wife the name Hsiao (LS 71, 1b; WCTL 5, 55 ff.). This story can have no validity either, because the name Liu did not appear until the time of Sung, Chin 金, and Yüan (see I, 1, note 1). No Ch'i-tan is referred to in the *Liao Shih* by the name of Liu. The name Hsiao is consistently applied to the clan of the empress only from the time of T'ai-tsung (927–947).

With regard to the Ch'i-tan pronunciation of the name, the Yüan historiographers advanced Shih-mo 石抹 as an equivalent (LS 116, 2a). The name is not applied to any individual in the *Liao Shih*, *Ch'i-tan Kuo Chih*, or other early sources. In the Chin and Yüan periods it was applied to some members of the Hsiao clan. CS 135, 12b and CKL 1, 27a both state that the Chinese name for Shih-mo is Hsiao. In the Liao period the equivalent for Shih-mo seems to have been Shên-mi 審密, a name applied not to individuals but to the Pa-li 拔里 and I-shih-ssŭ 乙室巳 lineages of the clan of the Liao empresses (LS 32, 8a; 67, 1a).

There is also a possibility, though no proof can be adduced, that the name of the first empress, Shu-lü 述律, may have been related to Shên-mi, both having been derived from a common source. There is more evidence to indicate that Shu-lü may have been related to Yeh-lü 耶律, the name of the imperial clan. Shu-lü evidently contains the idea of "imitating" or "following" (*shu* 述) the name of the imperial clan.

On the basis of the foregoing comments the following chart may be drawn up to indicate the derivation of the name of the empress' clan:

The clan name Hsiao referred to several groups, namely:

(1) Pa-li 拔里, the lineage of T'ai-tsu's wife's father. This lineage had two branches, the Senior Patriarchal Tent 大父帳 and the Junior Patriarchal Tent 少父帳, probably descended from T'ai-tsu's wife's blood brothers, Ti-lu 敵魯 and A-ku-chih 阿古只 respectively (XIV, 1 (21); and LS 67, 1b and 2a–b; cf. also Hashiguchi 39, passim. In LS 67 the two branches are called Households 房, not Tents 帳).

(2) I-shih-ssŭ 乙室巳, the lineage of the first husband of T'ai-tsu's wife's mother. This lineage had two branches, the Senior Elder Tent 大翁帳 and the Junior Elder Tent 小翁帳.

The following chart explains the relationship of the above groups:

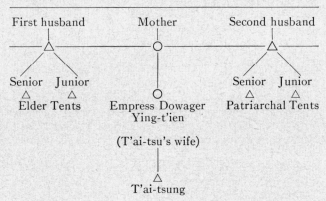

(Set up the lineages of "Imperial Maternal Uncles")

(3) Another lineage of Maternal Uncles was established by Shih-tsung who made an outstanding tribesman (noble ?) of the Six Divisions, the honorific Hsiao T'a-la-ko 塔剌葛, its head (LS 90, 3b).

Together the first three groups constituted the distinguished lineages of the Hsiao clan mentioned in LS 33, 1a–b (cf. I, 2, (3)). They are also called the five tents of the Imperial Maternal Uncles (XIV, 1, (9), LS 45, 4b–5a). The Pa-li and the I-shih-ssŭ were combined by Shêng-tsung, who thus reduced the three lineages to two (LS 67, 1b).

(4) The genealogical affiliations of many clansmen are not given. It is more than probable that some of them belonged to other than the distinguished lineages (LS 67, 5b).

(5) There were also a number of non-Hsiao who for one reason or another (usually outstanding military or political achievement or marriage) were honorifically awarded the clan name, Hsiao.

Examples of this last group are Hsiao Hên-tu 痕篤 of the I-la 迭剌 tribe (LS 74, 1a); Hsiao Ho-cho 合卓 of the T'u-lü-pu 突呂不 tribe (LS 81, 3b); Hsiao Tê 德 of the Chu-t'ê 楮特 tribe (LS 96, 5a); Hsiao Yen-shou 嚴壽 of the I-shih 乙室 tribe (LS 99, 1a); Hsiao Han-chia-nu 韓家奴 of the Nieh-la 涅剌 tribe (LS 103, 1a); and Hsiao Kuan-yin-nu 觀音奴, a descendant of a king of Hsi 奚 (LS 85, 2a).

R. Stein's attempt to construct a Hsi 奚 background for the Hsiao clan, based upon CS 67, 14b (Stein 39, 38, note 1), is not convincing. Even if the remarks of the Yüan historiographer were without contradictions, which

At the time [of his birth] black clouds covered the tent, the light of a fire lit up the dwelling, and there was a noise like thunder.   All the tribes considered it strange.[7]   37, 11a

3. A POLITICAL ALLIANCE CONCLUDED

905   [In the tenth month of the winter T'ai-tsu and Li K'o-yung[8]] exchanged their gowns and horses and agreed to be as brothers.[9]   1, 2a

4. REBIRTH CEREMONY OF THE *I-LI-CHIN*

Before 907   According to ancient practice, those who were *i-li-chin* were permitted to perform the Rebirth Ceremony.

Just when Yen-ku-chih[10] went to a tent to change clothes, Hsia-ti stole the red robe and the sable cicada hat[11] and came out riding a white horse.   He ordered his partisans to shout loudly, "The *i-li-chin* has come out!   All flocked around and knelt before him.   Then he performed the Firewood Investiture Ceremony[12] and made himself *i-li-chin*.   112, 1b

5. FIRE INFORMS HEAVEN OF THE EMPEROR'S ACCESSION

907   On the day *kêng-yin* of the first month in the spring of the first year [of T'ai-tsu's accession] officials were ordered to erect an altar at Ju-yü-wang[13]-chi-hui-kuo.[14]   Firewood was burned to announce to Heaven the accession to the imperial throne.   1, 2b

---

they are not, they would only prove that the royal clan of the Hsi people intermarried with "the Ch'i-tan" and that its name was attached to that of the Shu-lü 述律 family.   It is quite possible that the Hsi formerly intermarried to some extent with a certain family of the Ch'i-tan, perhaps even with the group which later intermarried exclusively with the imperial I-la clan.   But this would neither make the intermarrying group identical with the Hsi people, nor would it make the ruling clan of Hsi the marriage partners of the I-la clan.   Stein himself states, "Je n'ai pas trouvé d'autres textes qui confirmeraient l'affirmation du *Kin-che*" (*loc. cit.*).   Indeed, neither the *Liao Shih* nor the *Chin Shih* seems to contain any record concerning the Hsi background of any of the empresses of Liao.   The *Liao Shih* instead speaks clearly of the Uighur ancestry of the first empress of Liao (LS 71, 2a and 37, 10a).   Stein admits the textual strength of the Uighur argument.   "L'origine Ouigoure de l'impératrice est affirmée par tous les textes" (*loc. cit.*).   The Uighur origin of the powerful consort family helps to clarify several important elements of Ch'i-tan culture which we otherwise have great difficulty in explaining.

[4] We follow other editions in reading 使 for the 伏 of our text.

[5] Obviously inspired by the cycle of twelve animals. It is interesting to note that some steles discovered in the Liao mausoleums in Jehol have carved human figures with the twelve animals depicted above their heads.   *Cf.* LLSKCL 2; see rubbings.

[6] According to the *Lo-chung Chi-i Lu* 洛中紀異錄, quoted in CTKC 2, 6a–b, this dream is ascribed to T'ai-tsung who is said to have dreamt it before he carried out his military expedition against Later T'ang in aid of Chin 晉.   He reported the dream to his mother and summoned a shaman to determine its significance.   (*Cf.* IX, note 52.) This text explains the presence of the black hare by the fact that T'ai-tsung was born in the year *kuei-mao* which is the year of the hare.   Another record, however, men-

tions that he was born in 902 (LS 3, 1a), which was the year of the dog.

[7] The part of the story concerning the birth of T'ai-tsung is also related in CTKC 2, 1a and in the Buddhist book *Fo-tsu T'ung-tsai* 佛祖通載 which was completed by a Yüan monk, Nien Ch'ang 念常, at about the same time as the *Liao Shih* was composed (FTTT 25, 310a).

[8] Li K'o-yung 李克用 was a warlord of Turkic descent whose military and political center was in what is now Shansi.

[9] The purpose of this agreement was to conclude a military alliance.   Another text gives a different description of the ceremony: the two clasped hands and agreed to be as brothers (WTS 72, 3a; for the exact date, *cf.* XVI, 905, LS 1, 2a).   According to Wang Kuo-wei, the conclusion of an agreement of friendship by means of exchanging clothes, horses, or other objects was also a Mongol custom.   For instance, when Chingis Khan was a young man, he made friends with Cha-mu-ho 札木合 by exchanging certain objects.   Later the two friends reasserted their relationship by exchanging belts and horses.   Wang assumes that the Mongol custom must have derived from the Ch'i-tan and that the Mongol word, *anta* 安答, "friend, objects for making friends," derived from the Ch'i-tan language (KTCL 16, 19b).

[10] He was succeeded as *i-li-chin* by his younger half brother, Hsia-ti, who was *i-li-chin* of the I-la tribe about 901–907.   *Cf.* XIII, introduction.

[11] These were the *i-li-chin's* badges of office.

[12] A-pao-chi announced to Heaven his accession to the imperial throne by burning firewood (see below, (5)). This passage shows that the burning of firewood was originally part of the Investiture Ceremony.   See introduction.

[13] The word *wang* 王 is written *chêng* 正 in LS 3, 5a. It is impossible to decide which form is correct since the name appears only twice in the entire *Liao Shih*.

[14] This place was probably located in Shang-ching Circuit.

6. SACRIFICE ON A MOUNTAIN

911   The emperor, who could not bear to execute them, then climbed to the top of a mountain with his brothers, killed animals as a sacrifice, made an oath to Heaven and Earth, and pardoned their crime.[15]   1, 4a

7. CHINESE CULTURE ENCOURAGED—FOR CHINESE SUBJECTS

911–916   Han Yen-hui . . . then asked that cities be established and market places and living quarters be delimited so as to settle the Chinese who had surrendered. He also arranged marriages for them and taught them cultivation in order to provide for their propagation and livelihood. As a result those who fled away became very few.   74, 2a–b

8. INVOKING A CURSE WITH DEVIL ARROWS

913   On the day chi-mao [of the fourth month in the summer of the seventh year of T'ai-tsu's accession, when the emperor] halted at a mi-li,[16] he learned[17] that his brothers had shot "devil arrows"[18] in the direction of Mu-yeh Mountain[19] to bring a curse upon him. So he seized the rebel Hsieh-li[20] and, facing in their direction, invoked a curse upon them in the same way.   1, 5b

9. CEREMONIES FIXED

913   In the eleventh month [of the seventh year of T'ai-tsu's accession] the ceremonies for auspicious and inauspicious events were fixed.   1, 7a

10. SELECTIVE CULTURE TRANSFER

916–926   At this time the ceremonial regulations were loose. [Han] Chih-ku,[21] basing himself on the old regulations and comparing the national customs with the Chinese ceremonies, combined them and created [a new ritual] so that it might be easier for the Ch'i-tan to understand and to practise it.   74, 4a

11. THE CH'I-TAN SCRIPT

920   On the day i-ch'ou of the first month in the spring of the fifth year [of Shên-ts'ê] the larger Ch'i-tan script was formulated for the first time. . . . On the day jên-yin [of the ninth month], the larger script was completed. An imperial decree ordered it to be circulated.
2, 1b

[Tieh-la[22]] was endowed with a quick mind. T'ai-tsu said, "As to Tieh-la's cleverness—his quickness in accomplishing feats is beyond my powers. But for deliberateness in planning affairs I am

---

[15] That is, the crime of the emperor's brothers who had revolted against him. Cf. XIII (4).

[16] According to the glossary (LS 116, 2a), mi-li 彌里 was a term for a small settlement.

[17] Reading 聞 for 問 of our text, which makes no sense.

[18] See VII, 2 (82) and note.

[19] The sacred mountain between the Shira Muren and Lao-ha River (Jehol) where, according to the tribal tradition, the earliest ancestors of the Ch'i-tan met and mated (LS 37, 9a). Here it evidently symbolizes the emperor T'ai-tsu.

[20] Apparently a follower of the emperor's rebellious brothers.

[21] Han Chih-ku 韓知古, a Chinese captured at the age of six by a Ch'i-tan noble. His family was the most powerful Chinese family in the Liao empire. One of his grandsons, Han Tê-jang, whose Ch'i-tan name was Yeh-lü Lung-yün, was the first Chinese to receive a really important position of power in the government.

By the end of the eleventh century the Han clan had furnished seven prime ministers, nine masters of court etiquette, and more than a hundred ministers and generals (MCCSC 2, 3a). Even in the Yüan period, the people of Yenching when talking about the four leading Chinese clans, Han 韓, Liu 劉, Ma 馬, and Chao 趙, placed the Han family above the others (cf. CCWC 73, 7b ff.).

[22] A younger brother of T'ai-tsu.

FIG. 9. An inscription written in Ch'i-tan seal script from the stele of Tao-tsung's tomb (LLSKCL 2, 13).

FIG. 10.   Epitaph from Tao-tsung's tomb—Ch'i-tan characters (LLSKCL 2, 11).

his superior." Uighur messengers[23] came [to court],[24] but there was no one who could understand

925   their language. The empress said to T'ai-tsu, "Tieh-la is clever. He may be sent to welcome them."

By being in their company for twenty days he was able to learn their spoken language and script. Then he created [a script of] smaller Ch'i-tan characters which, though fewer in number, covered everything.[25]   64, 4*b*–5*b*

---

[23] The Uighurs held a geographically intermediary position between China and the West. This position is also reflected in their script. Though they knew the Chinese script, they used a phonetic script which was first shaped after an unknown Syriac pattern from Mesopotamia by the Sogdians in present Western Turkestan; it was adopted with new changes by the Uighurs in Eastern Turkestan. Under Chinese influence the Uighurs abandoned their horizontal writing and substituted the vertical lines still found in modern Mongol, Qalmyq, and Manchu. See Schott 76, 35 ff.; Bretschneider 88 I, 237 and 262; Wang CJ 38, 240 ff.

[24] According to Shiratori (98, 926), this event occurred either in 924 or 925 when Uighur missions visited Liao (see fig. 32). Of the two dates the second seems more probable, for in 924 T'ai-tsu undertook his great expedition into western Mongolia, returning to the capital only in the fourth month of 925. In that same month an envoy of the Uighurs of Kan Prefecture arrived and offered tribute (LS 2, 5*b*).

[25] These records on the creation of the Ch'i-tan scripts during the later part of T'ai-tsu's reign imply that until 920 the Ch'i-tan had no script of their own. In predynastic days it was their custom to make notches on wood (WTHY 29, 4*a*; WTS 72, 4*b*); but a few distinguished tribesmen may have had some knowledge of written Turkic or Chinese. When A-pao-chi in 924 visited the old Uighur capital, he ordered the inscriptions on the stone tablet of the Uighur Bilgä Khaghan erased and replaced with writings in Ch'i-tan, Turkic, and Chinese (XVI, 924, LS 2, 4*b*–5*a*). Marquart's doubts regarding the execution, or even the authenticity, of this particular command (Marquart 12, 499 ff.), whether justified or not, do not dispose of the Ch'i-tan recorders' belief that some variant of the Turkic script was still known in the northwestern border regions of the Liao territory.

If the smaller Ch'i-tan script was only introduced in 925, then T'ai-tsu's scribes must have employed the larger script. This assumption is strengthened by the *Liao Shih* record which notes that the larger script was created in the year 920, thus ruling out both 926 and 927 as possible dates of origin. (The first year is given in CTKC 1, 6*a*; the second is suggested in NESCC 29, 35*a* by Chao I who based himself on a passage of the *Chi-i Lu* 紀異錄.)

The existence of a Ch'i-tan script was known in China Proper from the second reign period of the Later T'ang dynasty on; after 925/926 generals of the southern armies not infrequently seized documents written in a Ch'i-tan script which the Chinese were unable to decipher (WTHY 29, 4*a*).

The first work written in the larger script, which is said to have comprised "several thousand characters" (WTS 72, 4*b*), seems to have been a dictionary of sorts supplemented by a list of Ch'i-tan tribal names (LS 2, 1*b*; *cf.* also VII, 2 (67)). The Ch'i-tan who undertook this task in collaboration with some Chinese were later assigned positions as scribes and appointed supervisors of national historiography (LS 76, 2*a*; WTHY 29, 4*a*; WTS 72, 4*b*).

There has been considerable discussion regarding the nature of the larger and smaller Ch'i-tan scripts. Lo Fu-ch'êng believes both are distant variants of a single system of writing derived from the Chinese, the smaller simpler than the larger. To make his point he emphasizes the differences between the script in the body of the main epitaph on Tao-tsung's tomb and that used in the heading (see figs. 9 and 10). The differences are indeed apparent, but they are differences of arrangement and style rather than of basic structure. The characters in the body usually are the more complex, their elements combined in a single compact form, while those in the heading follow one upon the other in a manner reminiscent of the Chinese seal style. In addition, the Ch'i-tan "seal" symbols are at times composed of simpler elements than the corresponding character in the main inscription. Both devices seem to be essentially aesthetic, creating an impression of simple dignity and strength.

Wang Ching-ju, who has painstakingly studied the Hsi Hsia script, emphasizes its divergences from the Ch'i-tan symbols. He assumes that the compound Ch'i-tan characters express polysyllabic words and, perhaps, also inflected forms (Wang CJ 33, 471–474).

No illumination can be gained from an inscription, *Ching-an Ssŭ Pei* 靜安寺碑, which seems to be composed in Ch'i-tan (MCCSC 2, 19*b* ff.). The symbols used are simpler than those found in the Liao imperial mausoleums (see fig. 17), but the epigraph as a whole is too seriously damaged to admit of any definite conclusions. No more helpful is the alleged reproduction of a Hsi Liao banknote contained in the *Ch'üan-pu T'ung-chih* 泉布統志, a source of doubtful reliability. Theoretically, the two forms that flank the Chinese inscription (CPTC 7*B*, 46*a*) may be characters of the smaller Ch'i-tan script, but thus far no linguist has identified either of them.

In our opinion, all the known Ch'i-tan characters are variants of a single larger script modelled on the Chinese. At first glance, the Ch'i-tan symbols appear very like Chinese words, but closer examination reveals marked differences either because of additional strokes or fewer ones. It has been claimed by some Chinese authors that the larger Ch'i-tan script was patterned after the Chinese "clerkly" (*li* 隸) style of writing (SSHY 8, 1*a*; WTS 72, 4*b*); but like their Chinese models, the Ch'i-tan characters were written in a number of different ways, the *li* style being only one (see fig. 11).

According to LS 64, 5*a*–*b* the smaller Ch'i-tan script was created by Tieh-la immediately after he had studied

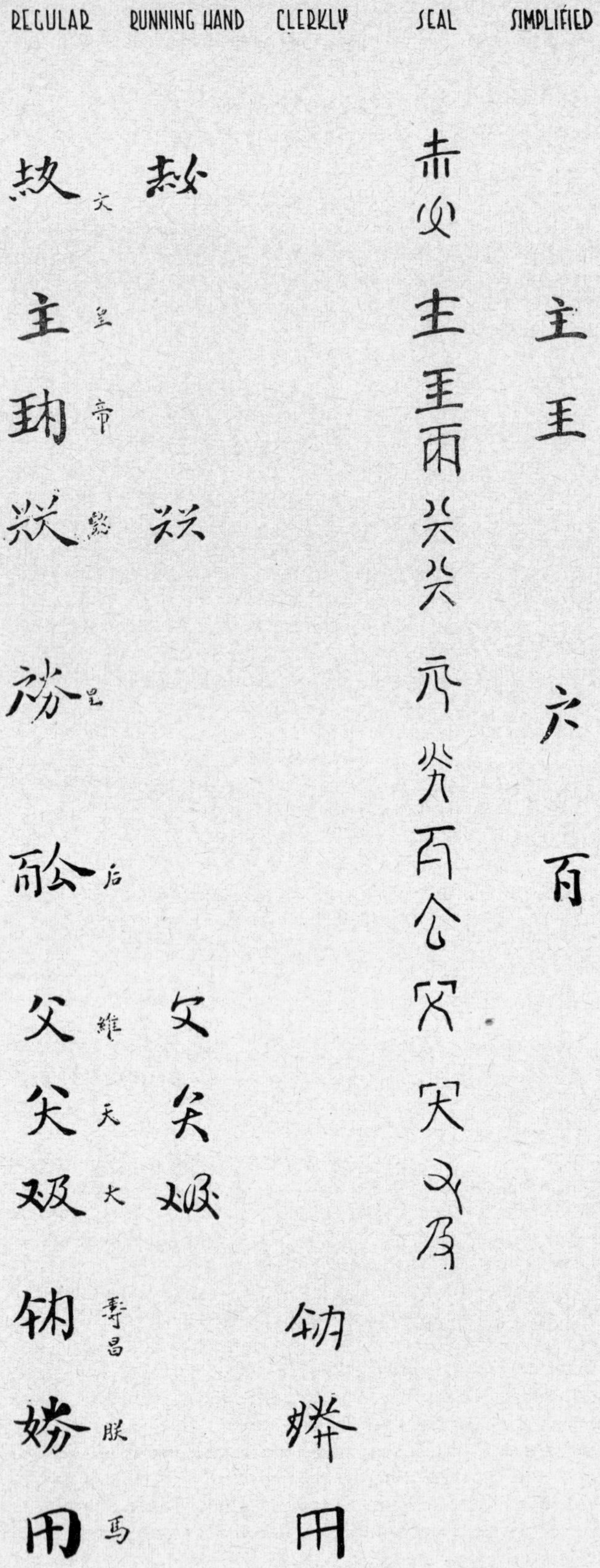

244 SOCIAL ORGANIZATION, KINSHIP SYSTEM, CUSTOMS, TRADITIONS [VII]

REGULAR	RUNNING HAND	CLERKLY	SEAL	SIMPLIFIED

FIG. 11. Five types of Ch'i-tan script.

the Uighur system of writing. Unlike the larger script, this smaller Ch'i-tan script was alphabetic: it had few *tzŭ*, characters or letters, which "covered everything." De Groot translates 該貫 somewhat differently: "alle aneinander gereiht [all lined up together]"; Marquart concludes on the basis of this rendering that the letters were written in rows and connected by ligatures (Marquart 12, 500–501). De Groot's translation varies considerably from the one given in our publication, but our interpretation and Marquart's are in agreement on the decisive point: the manifestly alphabetic character of the smaller script.

Few samples of Ch'i-tan writing have been discovered thus far; all of them are, if our interpretation is correct, composed in the larger script. As the archaeological finds (tablets, murals, tallies, seals, mirrors—see figs. 2, 3, 6, 12, 13, 14, 15, 16, 18, 19) and the casual references to Ch'i-tan writings reveal, the Ch'i-tan script served many political, religious, and literary purposes (see below, XIV, 4, *passim*). None of the writings mentioned in the *Liao Shih* and other sources have come down to us in their original form; but a few fragments give some indication of Ch'i-tan literary achievement, style, and syntax. Yeh-lü Ch'u-ts'ai translated into Chinese a Ch'i-tan poem, entitled in Chinese *Tsui-i Ko* 醉義歌. The famous statesman stressed the profundity of the original which he compared to writings of the great Sung poets, Su Shih 蘇軾 and Huang T'ing-chien 黃庭堅 (CJCSWC 8, 109 ff.).

Another record throws some light on Ch'i-tan syntax. The Sung envoy, Hung Mai, heard from Wang Pu 王補 that a Ch'i-tan child in the process of learning Chinese would first be taught the vernacular rearranged to mirror Ch'i-tan sentence structure. To illustrate his point, Wang Pu cited two lines of a poem by the T'ang writer, Chia Tao 賈島, which literally may be rendered:

鳥	宿	池中	樹
Birds	sleep	pond-in	tree

僧	敲	月 下	門
Monk	knocks	moonlight-under	gate.

These verses would be rephrased in the vernacular; at the same time, the word order would be modified, as follows:

月明裏	和尚	門子	打
Moon-in	monk	door	knocks

水底裏	樹上	老鴉	坐
Water-in	tree-on	crows	sit.	(ICPC 18, 136).

It is impossible to make any comprehensive linguistic analysis from two short sentences. Yet one thing is evident. The "Ch'i-tan version" of the T'ang poem is in complete accord with the rules of Altaic syntax, which require the following sentence structure: attribute or attributes—subject—(attribute)—object—predicate. In the rearranged sentences the attributes precede the subjects and the verb is placed at the end. The first change somewhat alters the meaning, but is not unknown in Chinese usage; the second establishes a position of the verb which syntactically is as un-Chinese as it is typically Altaic.

The Ch'i-tan script was widely used during the Liao dynastic period. The government of the Northern Region had a Department of the Grand Scribe which handled the

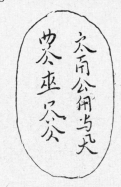

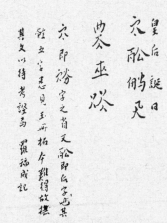

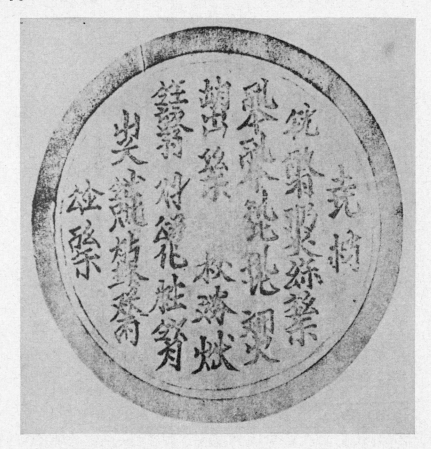

a

b

FIG. 12.   Two bronze mirrors with Ch'i-tan characters (LLSKCL 5).

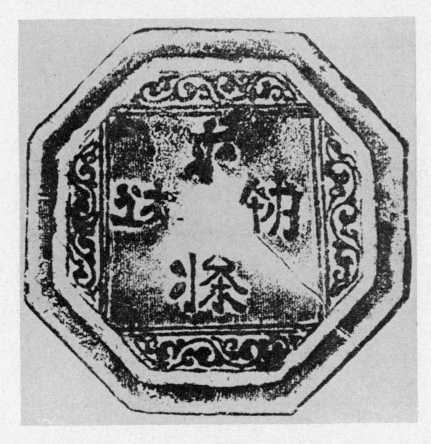

FIG. 13.   (*a*) Ch'i-tan inscription from a jade vessel. At the top, the text is copied by Lo Fu-ch'êng; below Mr. Lo's rearrangement of the symbols and explanatory remarks in Chinese; (*b*) Two seals with Ch'i-tan characters (LLSKCL 5).

FIG. 14. Ch'i-tan epitaph for Hsing-tsung (Mullie 33, photographic reproduction facing p. 24; the author erroneously ascribes the site to Shêng-tsung).

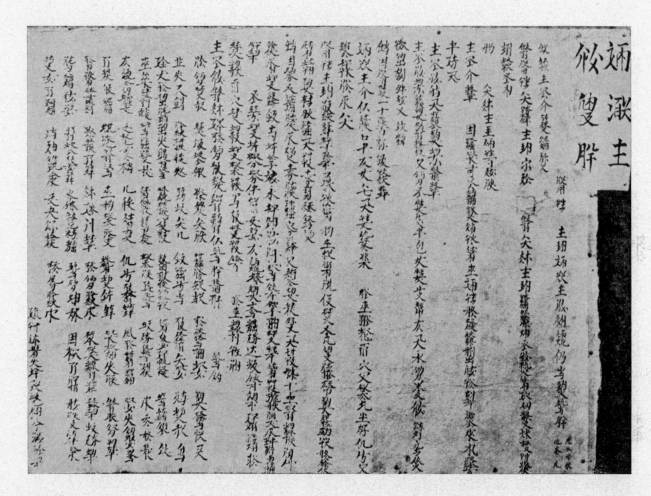

FIG. 15. Ch'i-tan epitaph for Empress Jên-i, wife of Hsing-tsung (Mullie 33, photographic reproduction facing p. 24; the author erroneously ascribes the site to Shêng-tsung).

FIG. 16. A broken brick, showing a large character and a sentence in smaller characters, both in Ch'i-tan (Torii 36 IV, pl. 336). To the left, the Ch'i-tan sentence from the brick rewritten and accompanied by a Chinese translation. The inscription reads: "On the third day of the first month of the first year of Ta-k'ang [1075] of the Great Liao Empire."

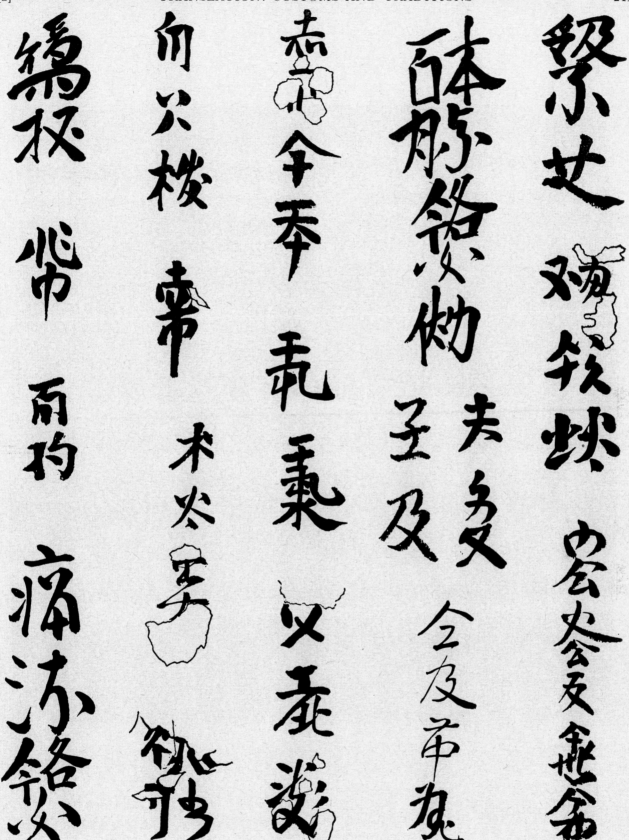

FIG. 17.   Ch'i-tan inscriptions accompanying figures of Ch'i-tan dignitaries drawn on the walls of Hsing-tsung's tomb (Torii 36 III, pls. 213–215).

FIG. 18.   Inscription from the tomb of Empress Hsüan-i written in Ch'i-tan characters (LLSKCL 2, 16).

FIG. 19.   Epitaph on the stele of Empress Hsüan-i written in Ch'i-tan characters (LLSKCL 2, 15).

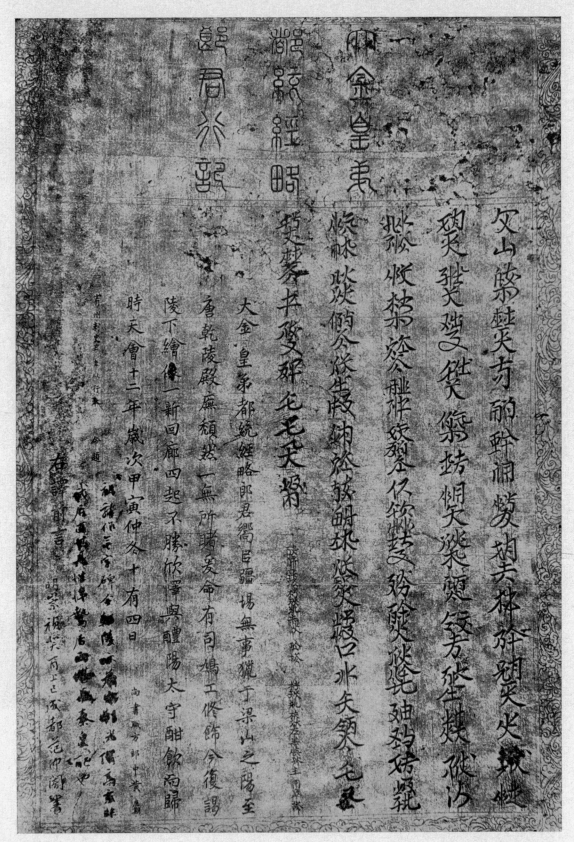

FIG. 20.   Tablet with Ch'i-tan inscription erected in 1134 by a Jurchen general at the mausoleum of the T'ang emperor, Kao-tsung, located in modern Ch'ien County, Shensi.   (The inscription has been reproduced in several Chinese works without the tablet.)   From a photograph in *Shigaku Zasshi* vol. XXI, no. 6, 1910, opposite p. 636.

"literary affairs" of the tribal administration (XIV, 1 (9), LS 45, 8b–9a). It seems reasonable to assume that the business of this department was carried on in Ch'i-tan, whereas the chief scribe of the "southern" Han-lin Academy (XIV, 2 (5), LS 47, 8b–9a) may have used both the Ch'i-tan and Chinese scripts.

The vitality of the Ch'i-tan script is further demonstrated by its role in the cultural life of the succeeding dynasty, Chin. Besides the Ch'i-tan themselves, their new Jurchen masters employed both forms of Ch'i-tan writing (see fig. 20) before and even after the creation of a special Jurchen script. The "large" Jurchen script was officially introduced in 1119, the "small" one in 1138 (CS 2, 14a and 4, 3b). At first, all literary activities were in the hands of the Ch'i-tan and Liao Chinese, but in time the Jurchen princes and nobles learned to read and write (CS 66, 1b; 73, 9b; 84, 5a). An edict, in 1138, ordered that official diplomas be written in the Jurchen, Ch'i-tan, and Chinese scripts for the officials of the three main sections of the population, the Po-hai being classed with the Chinese (CS 4, 4a). But the introduction of the new national script did not cause the Jurchen to abandon the Ch'i-tan way of writing which they had obviously learned to use with ease. More than thirty Jurchen mentioned in the *Chin Shih* were familiar with the Ch'i-tan script, many of them still ignorant of their own (CS 66, 4a and 5a; 73, 2b and 9b; 82, 7a; 120, 5a and 7b). In 1139 the Ho-nan branch of the Presidential Council received an order from the court concerning the affairs in the northern border zone, written entirely in Ch'i-tan (HNYL 125, 2042). In 1150 a distinguished Jurchen statesman is said to have written a confidential political letter to his son in the small Ch'i-tan script; this interesting document, translated into vernacular Chinese, is preserved in the *Chin Shih* (CS 76, 12a ff.; 84, 3a ff.). Jurchen nobles were entitled to the rank of *mêng-an* 猛安 if they mastered one of the three national scripts (CS 73, 4b–5a).

The Chin government assigned a number of posts to officials who were familiar with the Ch'i-tan script and language, some close to the emperor (CS 4, 4a; 86, 6b), others in the Presidential Council (CS 53, 2a; 90, 5b and 9a), still others in the Ministry of Civil Appointments (CS 55, 13b). In 1151 the staff of the Han-lin Academy included seven persons familiar with the Ch'i-tan script (CS 55, 20b). In 1156 it was officially ordered that in the examination for copyist in the Department of National Historiography the Jurchen copyists were to translate Ch'i-tan into Jurchen and the Ch'i-tan copyists Chinese into Ch'i-tan. The topics were written in Ch'i-tan characters (CS 53, 8a). The prestige of the Ch'i-tan script among the Jurchen is reflected in a statement made in 1180 by Emperor Shih-tsung who extolled its age and fitness to express profound and subtle poetry: "The new Jurchen script cannot match it" (CS 51, 13a).

Thus, the Ch'i-tan script continued to be the medium through which Chinese literature was introduced to the educated Jurchen. The Chinese original was first "written" in the Ch'i-tan smaller script and then "*chuan*" 傳 (annotated in or translated into ?) the Jurchen script. This was the procedure followed by Yeh-lü Ch'u-ts'ai's father, Yeh-lü Lü 履, when he translated the (Old or New ?) *History of the T'ang Dynasty* (ISHSC 27, 18a ff.; CS 125, 7a).

At the close of the twelfth century the Chin government tried to break the influence of the Ch'i-tan script. In 1191 Emperor Chang-tsung ordered that Jurchen political and literary writings should be directly translated into Chinese, eliminating an intermediate version in the Ch'i-tan script. The clerks of the Department of National Historiography, who knew only the Ch'i-tan script, were dismissed (CS 9, 11b ff. and 13b). In 1192 the position of Ch'i-tan secretary was abolished in all ministries (CS 52, 12a).

It is difficult to evaluate the effect of Chang-tsung's policy. It probably stopped the use of the Ch'i-tan script in government bureaus, but those familiar with the outlawed system may well have continued to employ it in private. Yeh-lü Ch'u-ts'ai, who "learned" the Ch'i-tan language so proficiently during his stay in Qarā-Khitāy that he was able to translate a Ch'i-tan poem into Chinese, could easily have received some earlier instruction from his father whose knowledge of the (smaller) Ch'i-tan script has already been mentioned. In 1221 when Ch'ang-ch'un's party on its way from Chin China to Central Asia stopped at the ruins of a deserted Liao city in northern Mongolia, it found a tile covered with writing which was identified as Ch'i-tan (HYCCC 1, 15b; cf. Waley 31, 68).

Many Chin records describe the continued use of the Ch'i-tan script during the early and middle years of the Chin dynasty. Unfortunately, they do not make it clear whether this also involved the use of the Ch'i-tan language. There must have been a number of Jurchen who spoke Ch'i-tan, but the question still arises whether such knowledge was necessary to the use of the Ch'i-tan script. In the formative period of their power the Mongols wrote their documents in the Mongol language but in the alphabetic Uighur script (Browne 28 II, 441; cf. Barthold 28, 41). The Manchus until the year 1599 wrote their documents in Mongol and used the Mongol script (KHTSL 3, 2a–b). The Jurchen may have availed themselves of either method exclusively, or of both at different periods of time, first adopting an alien language and script and later using the alien script for transcribing their own language. In the latter case the smaller script would seem particularly appropriate, for as an alphabetic system of writing it could easily be adjusted to the needs of another language, especially if this language belonged to the same Altaic complex.

The larger Ch'i-tan script presents a very different problem. It is possible, of course, for the symbols of an ideographic script to become associated with words of an alien language (witness written Chinese and Japanese), but whether the Jurchen used the larger Ch'i-tan script to such purpose, we do not know. Frequently, if not always, a knowledge of the Ch'i-tan language may have accompanied a knowledge of the Ch'i-tan "characters." The smaller Ch'i-tan script, being alphabetic, was an incomparably more convenient device for transcription than the larger script—and obviously it enjoyed a much greater popularity. It is probably no accident that Yeh-lü Lü, when translating the *T'ang Shu*, used not the larger but the smaller Ch'i-tan script.

12. SHOULD THE EMPRESS BE BURIED WITH THE EMPEROR?

926   When T'ai-tsu died, the empress assumed the reins of government and took over the management of military and civil affairs. When the time to bury T'ai-tsu arrived,[26] she wished to be buried [with him]. The relatives and officials remonstrated vigorously. She therefore [only] cut off her right hand at the wrist and placed it in the coffin.[27]   71, 3a

13. THE DEITY OF THE DEER

928   On the day *chi-mao* [of the fourth month in the third year of T'ien-hsien] sacrifice was offered to the deity of the deer.   3, 2a

14. ENTERTAINMENT

929   On the first day *jên-shên* of the first month in the spring of the fourth year [of T'ien-hsien] a feast was given for the courtiers and for the envoys of various countries. [The emperor] watched theatrical performances and wrestling bouts.[28]   3, 3b

15. CALLIGRAPHY

930   On the day *ping-ch'ên* [of the second month in the fifth year of T'ien-hsien] the emperor and Prince Jên-huang[29] visited the empress dowager. Their mother, knowing that both were skilled in calligraphy, ordered them to write in front of her so that she might look on.   3, 4a

16. THE IMPERIAL MATERNAL UNCLES

935   On the day *ping-hsü* [of the third month in the tenth year of T'ien-hsien] two tents—the lineage of the empress dowager's father and the lineage of her mother's former husband—were made the Imperial Maternal Uncles.[30] Hsiao Mien-ssŭ was appointed the chief patriarch[31] to exercise authority over them.   3, 8a

17. CLASPING A HIGH VISITOR'S HAND

936   [On the day *kêng-tzŭ* of the ninth month in the eleventh year of T'ien-hsien, when Shih] Ching-t'ang[32] led his subordinates for an audience, the emperor[33] clasped his hand[34] and comforted him.   3, 9a

---

[26] T'ai-tsu died in 926 after the conquest of Po-hai, but was buried several months later.

[27] A contemporary Sung source does not describe the empress as being nearly so willing to follow the emperor in death as our text would have us believe. CTKC 13, 1b–2a relates that after the death of T'ai-tsu hundreds of men were killed and buried in his mausoleum. A Chinese official, Chao Ssŭ-wên 趙思溫, was invited by T'ai-tsu's wife, Empress Ying-t'ien, to meet the same fate.

"You were very close in serving the deceased emperor," she said. "Why don't you go?"

Chao Ssŭ-wên replied, "As for intimacy, no one equalled Your Majesty. If Your Majesty goes, I will follow."

The empress dowager said, "I am not unwilling to follow the deceased emperor underground. But my sons are young and the country has no ruler. I cannot go."

Then, according to WTS 73, 3a–b, she offered to cut off an arm to accompany the emperor. The courtiers are said to have remonstrated with her, whereupon she cut off a hand.

[28] Wrestling bouts were called 角觝戲 by the state of Ch'in in the period of the Warring States. For their origin and other details see HCS, Ch'in and Han, XV (mss.). Wrestling has remained a favorite pastime of

Mongol tribes until recent times (*cf.* Timkowski 1827 II, 297).

In 1931 Torii discovered at Liao-yang 遼陽, Liaoning, certain Liao objects, among them the remains of a piece of white pottery on which were painted the black figures of two wrestling boys (see Torii 41, 193–201 and fig. 21). The sport as depicted here is very like a description given by the Sung scholar, Chang Shun-min (HML 4a ff.).

[29] The honorific title of Pei 倍, the eldest son of T'ai-tsu. He was skilled in composing essays in both the Ch'i-tan and Chinese languages. He also showed ability in painting Ch'i-tan hunters and horsemen. He was fond of books and had a library of ten thousand *chüan*. Disliked by his mother, he yielded the throne to his younger brother, the later T'ai-tsung, who persecuted him. Consequently, in 930 he fled to Later T'ang where he was killed in 937 (LS 72, 1a ff.).

[30] See above, note 3.

[31] For the title *shang-fu* 尙父 see Chavannes, MH I, 225, note 3.

[32] Shih Ching-t'ang, the founder of the contemporary state of Chin, ruled from 936 to 943.

[33] T'ai-tsung.

[34] This ceremony probably resembled that of shaking

937   [On the day *jên-shên* of the eleventh month in the eleventh year of T'ien-hsien],
when the emperor of Chin departed, the emperor gave him a banquet.   Merry with
wine, they clasped hands and agreed to be as father and son.   3, 10*b*

18. CEREMONY OF ENTERING THE SIDE HALL

940   On the day *kêng-tzŭ* [of the fourth month in the summer of the third year of Hui-
t'ung the emperor] arrived at Yen[35] and together with the imperial equipage[36] entered
through the Kung-ch'ên Gate.[37]   He gave an audience in the Yüan-ho Hall where the Ceremony of
Entering the Side Hall was performed.[38]   4, 4*b*

19. THE DRAGON BOAT FESTIVAL

940   On the day *kêng-wu* of the fifth month [in the third year of Hui-t'ung], because of
the Fifth Day of the Fifth Moon,[39] [the emperor] gave a banquet[40] for the officials
and envoys of the various countries.   He ordered the two emissaries from the Uighurs and Tun-
huang[41] to perform their native dances so that all the envoys might see them.   4, 4*b*–5*a*

20. SORORATE

940   On the day *ting-ch'ou* [of the eleventh month in the third year of Hui-t'ung] an
imperial decree . . . abolished the law that after the death of an older sister a younger
sister should succeed her.[42]   4, 6*a*

---

hands.   When a general reported a victory over the forces of the enemy, the emperor ordered a personal attendant to perform the ceremony of holding the hand for him (see below, (49)).   The glossary (LS 116, 10*a*) remarks also that the emperor personally took the hand of a victorious general as a token of encouragement and gratitude.   If the generals remained with their army, a messenger was dispatched to represent the emperor.   In 1063 Tao-tsung clasped the hand and comforted the Sung envoy who was sent to announce to Liao the death of Jên-tsung of Sung (SSWCHL 1, 4).

[35] This was the first time that a Liao emperor entered Yen (modern Peiping).

[36] A description of an imperial procession with its courtiers, equipment, horses, etc. is quoted in LS 58, 4*a*–5*a* from the *Liao Ch'ao Tsa Li* 遼朝雜禮.

[37] The Kung-ch'ên Gate 拱辰門 was the northern gate of the city of Yen (LS 40, 1*b*).

[38] This was a T'ang ceremony.   Here the Ch'i-tan were probably imitating the T'ang system.   The ceremony was performed before an audience and was given in the palace (*cf.* SS 117, 1*a* ff.).

[39] The date of the Chinese Dragon Festival.

[40] A Sung envoy who visited the Liao court in 1008 observed that at a Ch'i-tan banquet the food consisted mainly of meat of various kinds.   For the first course the so-called *lo-mi* 駱麋, a sort of cream soup, was usually served, and was eaten with a spoon.   Dishes of lamb, pork, pheasant, rabbit, veal, venison, goose, etc. followed. The meat was cut into small pieces by two servants neatly dressed, who then served the envoy (HCLY 77, 4*b*).

The above list includes pork, a type of food not common in the Ch'i-tan part of the Liao empire.   According to a Sung report, the Ch'i-tan envoys who traveled through Sung territory always demanded unusual food.   These requests greatly embarrassed the prefectures and counties situated along their road.   Later a Sung envoy on his way to the Liao capital requested pork and pork sausage.

This proved bothersome for the Liao hosts.   The officers of the relay stations sent horses far into Ch'i-tan territory in search of pork.   The underlings were often beaten because of their inability to procure the desired food. The envoy explained the curious phenomenon by the scarcity of pigs in the Ch'i-tan territory.   According to him, no pigs were bred north of the Southern Capital (TYCH 5*a*; CCHT 2*a*).

This statement needs qualification.   In 1012, when another Sung envoy, Wang Tsêng, traveled north of the Great Wall, the Hsi people kept numerous yellow pigs in the mountain valleys (CTKC 24, 2*a*).   Probably pigs were rare north of the Hsi region.

[41] The Tun-huang oasis was inhabited by Uighur people (*cf.* I, 2 (10), no. 17).   Hence we would expect the text to read Tun-huang Hui-hu (the Uighurs of Tun-huang) rather than Hui-hu Tun-huang 回鶻燉煌 which does not make good sense whether rendered as "Uighurs and Tun-huang," "Uighur Tun-huang," or "Tun-huang of the Uighurs."

Under the T'ang dynasty the prefectures, Kan 甘 (Chang-yeh 張掖), Liang 涼 (Wu-wei 武威), Kua 瓜 (west of An-hsi 安西), and Sha 沙 (Tun-huang 燉煌), possessed great significance because of their location between China and the "Western Regions."   At that time the territory was inhabited by a million Chinese and occupied by a strong army.   When An Lu-shan rebelled, the troops were withdrawn, and the Chinese civilians fell under the rule of the Uighurs and T'u-fan.   Kan Prefecture was the center of Uighur power; their supreme ruler resided there (WTS 74, 6*b* ff.).   Sha Prefecture was controlled in the ninth century by the Chang 張 family whose national status is not clear.   From the beginning of the tenth century to the eleventh century the region was controlled by the Ts'ao 曹 family whom the *Liao Shih* calls Uighurs (LS 15, 7*b*; 16, 4*b*).

[42] We follow other editions in reading 續 for the 績 of our text.

21. REMARRIAGE OF WIDOWERS AND WIDOWS

941   On the day *jên-hsü* [of the first month in the spring of the fourth year of Hui-t'ung] the widowers and widows of the three tribes of I-shih,[43] P'in-pei,[44] and T'u-kuei[45] who were unable to live alone were granted mates by the government.   4, 6a

22. LOOT FROM CHIN

947   On the day *jên-yin* [of the third month in the first year of Ta-t'ung] the members of the various governmental departments of the Chin [empire]; the court ladies, eunuchs, specialists,[46] and artisans; the maps and books, astronomical charts, classics cut in stone, bronze statues, the water-clock[47] of the Ming T'ang,[48] the music treatises from the department of ceremonies, and all the imperial suspended musical instruments,[49] the imperial equipage and the various impedimenta displayed upon the emperor's official appearance, and armor and weapons—all these were transported to the Supreme Capital.   4, 15a

23. WORSHIP OF THE SUN

952   On the day of the Winter Solstice, *chi-mao* [of the eleventh month in the second year of Ying-li], the ancient practices were used for the first time to make obeisance[50] to the sun.[51]   6, 2a

24. THE DEITY OF THE EARTH

Before 953   [The empress[52]] once went to the place where the Liao[53] and the T'u[54] Rivers meet. There was a woman riding a cart drawn by a gray ox[55] who hurriedly fled from the road and suddenly became invisible.   Before long there was a children's ditty saying,

> The crone who had a gray ox
> Went fleeing from the road.

It is commonly said that the deity of the Earth was the old woman with the gray ox.   71, 2b

25. A FEMALE SHAMAN'S MEDICINE FAILS

957   On the first day *mou-wu* of the fourth month [in the summer of the seventh year of Ying-li the emperor] returned to the Supreme Capital.   Previously, a female shaman, Hsiao-ku, had offered a prescription for lengthening life which had to be mixed up with a man's

---

[43] One of the old eight tribes of the Ch'i-tan (WTS 72, 2b).   Its territory probably corresponds to the region southwest of modern Boro-Khoton, Jehol.

[44] Probably identical with the P'in 品 tribe which lived northwest of modern Boro-Khoton, Jehol (LS 33, 2b).

[45] Probably identical with the T'u-chü 突舉 tribe whose location is not clear (LS 35, 4a).

[46] The term *fang chi* 方技 refers to specialists such as astrologers, diviners, doctors, etc.

[47] The 刻 (or 更) 漏 is a Chinese water-clock.   Giles (12, no. 5990) describes it as "an arrangement by which the regular leakage of water from a large jar is shown upon a bamboo index inside."

[48] The palace where the emperor discussed and announced his governmental measures and received foreign envoys.

[49] The *Chou Li* 周禮 states that the 宮縣 was a special set of musical instruments used exclusively by a king or ruler.   It differed from the 軒縣 of the marquises, the 判縣 of the ministers, and the 持縣 of the lower officials (CLCS 23, 5b).

[50] The word *pai* 拜, according to SWCTC 12A, 46 means "to bow the head to the hands" (首至手也).   Ku

Yen-wu 顧炎武 says that in ancient times the act represented by the word *pai* assumed various forms (JCL 28, 59).   In the *Liao Shih* the term *pai* is used so loosely that it is impossible to tell whether it means to bow or to prostrate or to make obeisance in the Ch'i-tan fashion. The Ch'i-tan salutation for both men and women was to kneel down on one leg while alternately raising the arms up and down.   This was probably similar to the Jurchen style (*cf.* CTKC 27, 4a; CS 35, 10b–11b).   For the sake of simplicity we generally translate the word *pai* as "to bow" or "to make obeisance," even though these renderings do not fully convey the precise meaning of the word.

[51] The Ch'i-tan worshipped the sun, as WTS 72, 5a states, on the first day of every month.   A special ceremony emphasizes the importance of the sun in the life and religion of the Ch'i-tan people (VII, 2 (79)).

[52] T'ai-tsu's wife.

[53] The modern Shira Muren, Jehol.

[54] The modern Lao-ha River, Jehol.

[55] The word *ch'ing* 青 signifies various natural colors, such as green, black, blue, and gray.   It frequently indicates a blue color for cloth and a gray color for animals. The sacred animals of the Ch'i-tan (*ch'ing niu pai ma*

gall.   In only a few years many men were killed.   Now the fraudulence of this was discovered.   On the day *hsin-ssŭ* she was shot to death.[56]   6, 4a

26. RAIN MAGIC

962   On the day *kêng-wu* of the fifth month in the summer [of the twelfth year of Ying-li the emperor], because of a drought, ordered his attendants to pour water on each other.[57]   Presently it actually did rain.   6, 5b

966   On the day *chia-shên* of the fifth month [in the sixteenth year of Ying-li the emperor], because of the year's drought, floated a boat in a pond and prayed for rain. No rain came.   He left the boat, stood in water, and prayed.   A short time later it rained.   7, 3a

967   On the day *ping-tzu* [of the fourth month in the seventeenth year of Ying-li the emperor] shot at willow trees to pray for rain, and water was poured on the courtiers.
7, 3b

27. THE EMPEROR DRINKS IN THE MARKET

968   On the day *chi-hai* [of the first month in the eighteenth year of Ying-li the emperor] looked at the lanterns in the market places.[58]   He bought wine at a cost of a hundred taels of silver and ordered the courtiers also to buy wine.   They drank without restraint for three nights.   7, 4a

28. BEATING THE CLAY OX

969   At the beginning of spring on the day *chi-ch'ou* [of the first month in the nineteenth year of Ying-li the emperor] became intoxicated.   He ordered the chief palace superintendent,[59] [Yeh-lü] I-la-ko,[60] to take his place in performing the ceremony of beating the clay ox.[61]
7, 5a

29. CARD PLAYING

969   On the day *chia-wu* [of the first month in the nineteenth year of Ying-li the emperor] played cards[62] with the courtiers.   7, 5a

30. ACCURATE DIVINATION

Ca. **969**   One day, when the commanding prefect summoned [Wei] Lin,[63] someone happened to offer a brace of carp.[64]   The prefect said jokingly, "Divine, sir, when I shall be able to eat these fish."

青牛白馬) are also described as *hui* 灰 *niu pai ma*, that is an ash-colored ox and a white horse (CTKC introduction, 1a; HCLY 78, 2a–b and TCCS 5, 32).   This seems to justify the translation "a gray ox and a white horse" for the above phrase.

[56] LS 61, 4a describes the punishment meted out to Hsiao-ku 肖古 in more detail: "Whistling arrows were showered upon her; [then] she was trampled to death by horsemen."

[57] According to the Sung scholar, Li Hsin-ch'uan, this ceremony still prevailed under the Chin dynasty, and not only among the Jurchen, but also among the Chinese inhabitants of the Ch'i 齊 territory (approximately modern Honan and Shantung), established by Liu Yü 劉豫.   A Chinese, Sun Chao 孫肇, placed in the hot sun and wet with many pails of water, fell ill and died (HNYL 55, 975).   In modern North China the villagers in praying for rain often pour water into the gutter on the roof so that it will run down onto a man kneeling below.

[58] The day *chi-hai* fell on the fifteenth day of the first month.   The reference is therefore to the Lantern Festival which was held in the market places.

[59] During the Chin 金 period this official belonged to the third rank and had charge of protecting the emperor (CS 56, 1a).

[60] Yeh-lü I-la-ko 夷臘葛 was first a noble camp attendant.   After the accession of Mu-tsung he gradually came to hold positions in the court, eventually becoming a favorite of the emperor.   He was sentenced to death in 969 for dereliction of duty when Mu-tsung was assassinated (LS 78, 1a–b).

[61] Reference to a "clay-ox" (土牛) is also found in early Chinese sources.   In the *Lü-shih Ch'un-ch'iu*, *Li Chi*, *Huai-nan-tzŭ*, and *Hsü Han Chih*, it is said that at the end of winter the clay ox was carried out in a ceremony bidding farewell to cold weather (LSCC 12, 1b; LCCS 17, 12a; HNT 5, 15b, and HHC 4, 2a).

[62] The *yeh ko* 葉格 or *yeh-tzŭ ko* 葉子格 were made of thick dotted paper.   The game, already known during the ninth century, remained very popular during the following centuries.   The *yeh ko* were perhaps the early form of the modern *chih-p'ai* 紙牌, the Chinese gambling cards (KTL 2, 13b ff.; TLCY 2, 26b; *cf.* also Carter 31, 243, note 5).

[63] Wei Lin 魏璘, a well-known diviner, was captured from Chin by T'ai-tsung.   He was banished to the Wu-ku tribe for treason in 969 (*cf.* LS 8, 1b; 108, 1b ff.).

[64] Since the Wu-ku tribe lived in the vicinity of the Kerulen River in eastern Outer Mongolia, the carp were probably taken from that river.

After a long time [Wei] Lin replied, "Your Excellency and I before this day is gone will meet an unknown misfortune. How will there be time to eat fish?"

The prefect immediately ordered that the fish be cooked, but they had not yet begun to eat when bandits came. Both of them met their death.   108, 2a.

31. SHAMANS PERFORM IMPORTANT RITES

980   On the first day *hsin-wei* of the tenth month in the winter [of the second year of Ch'ien-hêng] the shamans were ordered to worship Heaven and Earth and the god of War.   9, 4a

32. WAR MAGIC

980   On the day *hsin-ssŭ* [of the tenth month in the second year of Ch'ien-hêng], just before starting on the southern punitive expedition, a sacrifice was offered to the banners and drums.   9, 4a

33. A FAVORITE ASKS TO BE BURIED WITH THE EMPEROR

983   A Po-hai escorting official, Hsieh-li, because he had received great favors from the former emperor,[65] asked permission to be buried with the deceased emperor. A decree refused approval but bestowed gifts upon him in order to honor him.   10, 2a

34. BURIED WITH THE EMPEROR

983   On the day *chia-wu* [of the second month in the first year of T'ung-ho] Emperor Ching-tsung was buried in Ch'ien Mausoleum.[66] A close favorite, Lang, and the entertainer[67] in charge of wine, Ta-lu, were interred with him.   10, 2b

35. DIVORCE OF A CH'I-TAN PRINCESS

983   On the day *chi-ch'ou* [of the sixth month in the first year of T'ung-ho] the officials memorialized that Lu Chün, who was associate administrator of the affairs for the Political and Court Councils and imperial son-in-law chief commandant, was not getting along with the princess.[68] A decree ordered their divorce. [Lu] Chün was then sent out to become the commanding prefect of Hsing-kuo Commandery.[69]   10, 4b

36. CEREMONY OF ESTABLISHING A FRIENDSHIP

983   On the day *chia-wu* [of the eighth month in the first year of T'ung-ho] the emperor[70] and [Yeh-lü] Hsieh-chên, in front of the empress dowager,[71] exchanged bows, arrows, saddles, and horses, and agreed to be friends.   10, 5a

---

[65] Ching-tsung (969–982).

[66] Southwest of modern Pei-chên 北鎮 County, Liaoning (MRC II, 21).

[67] According to Shih Chao, a *ling-jên* 伶人 is a musician (TCTCSW 28, 6a). The term seems, however, to have designated not only a musician but also an actor. Wên Yen-po 文彥博 (1006–1097) communicated to Ssŭ-ma Kuang 司馬光 (1019–1086) the following story which he had been told: When the Liao ruler feasted his officials, the *ling-jên* donned official hats and garments and seized any objects they cared to (SSWCCL 10, 70).

These musician-actors were also called *yu-jên* 優人 and *yu-ling* 優伶. In 1106 Liao envoys went to Sung to mediate the quarrel between Hsi Hsia and Sung. On this occasion they were entertained by *yu-jên* dressed in Taoist style (LS 27, 4b; 86, 4a). During the Ch'ung-hsi period a Liao envoy to the Sung court was provoked by a Chinese *yu-ling* who jested about the Hsi Hsia victory over Liao. He was impetuous enough to reply with similar jests about Chinese defeats; after his return he was punished with two hundred lashes (see XV, 2 (17)).

[68] The fourth daughter of Ching-tsung; her mother was a Po-hai concubine. The princess was married to Lu Chün 盧俊, a Chinese, in 980 (LS 65, 3a).

[69] Southeast of the juncture of the Shira Muren and the Lao-ho River, Jehol (MRC II, 93).

[70] Shêng-tsung.

[71] Empress Dowager Ch'êng-t'ien.

37. BANNERS AND DRUMS FOR VICTORIOUS GENERALS

983   On the day *ping-wu* [of the tenth month in the first year of T'ung-ho] the master of court etiquette[72] and concurrently inner chamberlain, [Yeh-lü] P'u-ling,[73] the scribe [Hsiao] K'en-tê, and others were ordered to lead troops in the eastern campaign.[74]   They were presented with banners, drums, and silver tallies.   10, 5b

38. HONORS FOR THREE GENERATIONS LIVING TOGETHER

983   In the case of those among the common people whose parents were registered separately and who had separate domiciles, they should be exposed by their neighbors and made to suffer punishment.   In the case of those who were filial toward their parents and had three generations living together, honorific insignia were bestowed upon their households and villages.

10, 6a

39. REBIRTH CEREMONIES OF THE EMPRESS DOWAGER

984   On the day *kuei-ch'ou* of the seventh month in the autumn [of the second year of T'ung-ho] the empress dowager[75] performed the Rebirth Ceremony.   10, 7a

986   On the day *chia-wu* [of the ninth month in the fourth year of T'ung-ho] the empress dowager performed the Rebirth Ceremony.   11, 7a

On the day *ting-yu* [of the tenth month in the fourth year of T'ung-ho] the empress dowager again performed the Rebirth Ceremony.   On behalf of the emperor she worshiped the gods and prayed for good fortune.   11, 7a

40. SACRIFICE TO MU–YEH MOUNTAIN

988   On the day *kuei-hai* [of the eighth month in the sixth year of T'ung-ho], because the campaign against Sung was about to begin, envoys were sent to offer sacrifice to Mu-yeh Mountain.   12, 2b

41. THE GAME OF "DOUBLE SIXES"

988   On the day *ting-yu* [of the eighth month in the sixth year of T'ung-ho], when the empress dowager visited the camp of Han Tê-jang,[76] rewards and gifts were generously bestowed.   She ordered the attendants accompanying her to divide themselves into groups for the game of "Double Sixes"[77] and thus to enjoy themselves to the full.   12, 3a

42. REBIRTH CEREMONY OF A PRINCE

989   On the day *mou-tzŭ* [of the third month in the seventh year of T'ung-ho] the *yü-yüeh*, the Prince of Sung,[78] was granted red pearls and cords made of sinews and was ordered to enter the imperial divine tent to perform the Rebirth Ceremony.   The empress dowager bestowed presents very generously.   12, 5b

---

[72] For this and other titles in the present passage see section XIV, 1 and 2.

[73] P'u-ling (or lin) 蒲領 (or 鄰) was the style of Yeh-lü A-mo-li 阿沒里, a descendant of the Yao-lien clan (LS 79, 4a).

[74] That is, in the expedition against Korea.

[75] Empress Dowager Ch'êng-t'ien. See fig. 23.

[76] Han Tê-jang 韓德讓 was a Chinese official whose Ch'i-tan name was Yeh-lü Lung-yün 隆運. According to a Sung source, Empress Dowager Ch'êng-t'ien 承天 fell in love with him (CTKC 13, 4b). It was said that he was made grand prime minister because of his close personal relations with the empress dowager. Whatever his personal affairs may have been, his nomination to a high honorary position and the posthumous grant of an ordo-like mansion are explained fully by the unusual services which he rendered to the Liao government during its war against Sung China (XV, introduction).   In 1004 Emperor Shêng-

tsung gave him the imperial name Yeh-lü and, in 1010, changed his whole name to Yeh-lü Lung-yün.   He died in 1011 at the age of seventy-one (LS 82, 1a–2b).   He was buried beside the mausoleum of Ching-tsung and Empress Dowager Ch'êng-t'ien (LS 31, 9b).

[77] A chess-like game played by two persons.   A Sung scholar, Hung Tsun 洪遵 (T. 景嚴 1120–1174), in his *P'u Shuang* 譜雙, a book of five chapters, describes several variations of this game.   According to him, the game was popular in Yen-ching among both the Chinese and the Ch'i-tan.   Wealthy gamblers usually made their bets in gold, silver, slaves, sheep, or horses, while the poor gambled for wine (PSHT 5, 22a–23a; see fig. 22).   In the Yüan period the game was almost forgotten (TC 4b; *cf.* also Stein 39, 105 ff. and Culin 98, 841).

[78] Yeh-lü Hsiu-ko 休哥 (T. 遜寧) whose grandfather was T'ai-tsu's uncle.   He won fame for his tactics in the war with Sung from 979 to 989.   He died in 998 (LS 83, 1a–3b).

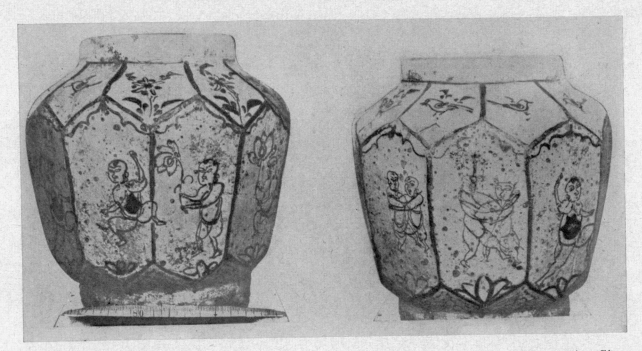

Fig. 21. Vase with pictures of Ch'i-tan wrestlers. The vessel was found at the site of Tung-ching City, Liaoyang (Torii 41).

Fig. 22. The game of Double Sixes (PSHT).

43. COSTLY FUNERAL CUSTOMS ABOLISHED

992   On the day *ting-yu* of the first month in the spring of the tenth year [of T'ung-ho] it was forbidden in funeral rites to kill horses and bury armor or gold and silver jewelry.   **13, 3a**

44. KOREANS STUDY THE CH'I–TAN LANGUAGE

995   On the day *mou-ch'ên* [of the eleventh month in the thirteenth year of T'ung-ho] Korea sent ten boys to study the [Ch'i-tan] national language.[79]   **13, 6b–7a**

996   On the day *kêng-ch'ên* [of the third month in the fourteenth year of T'ung-ho] Korea again sent ten boys to study the [Ch'i-tan] national language.   **13, 7a**

45. THE DEITY OF THE WHITE HORSE

998   On the day *chia-tzŭ* of the fifth month [in the sixteenth year of T'ung-ho] sacrifice was offered to the deity of the white horse.   **14, 1a**

46. PRIMITIVE PSYCHOTHERAPY

10th century   Previously, when the wife of Chancellor Yeh-lü Hsieh-chên contracted a serious ailment, several doctors prescribing in succession had been unable to effect a cure. [Yeh-lü] Ti-lu[80] examined her and said, "Her heart contains accumulated heat. This [heat] cannot be reached by medicine or acupuncture; it must be cured through the mind. If we take advantage of her coma to drive her into a frenzy by dinning her, so as to drain off her poison, then she may be cured."

Therefore he had cymbals and drums beaten loudly in front of her. The next day she actually did fall into a frenzy, raging and cursing until her strength was exhausted, whereupon she stopped. Thereafter she recovered. Many of his remedies were of this sort. People could not understand them.   **108, 2a–b**

47. FOUR AND SIX GENERATIONS LIVING TOGETHER

1012   On the day *kuei-mao* [of the eleventh month in the first year of K'ai-t'ai] the former record-keeper of Liao Prefecture, Chang T'ing-mei, who had six generations living together, and Liu Hsing-yin of I-k'un Prefecture, who had four generations living together, were both granted exemption from labor service for three years.   **15, 5a**

48. SCHOOLS FOR UNCIVILIZED SETTLERS

1013   [On the day *chia-shên* of the twelfth month in the first year of K'ai-t'ai], Kuei Prefecture[81] reported that its inhabitants, who had originally been moved from Silla,[82] were illiterate, and that schools should be set up to educate them. This request was approved by imperial decree.   **15, 5a–b**

---

[79] This record is confirmed by the Korean official history which relates that in 995 the Korean government sent ten boys to Liao to study the Ch'i-tan language (KRS 3, 46). However, this effort seems to have produced very poor results. In 1010, when the Liao vanguard general sent a document written in Ch'i-tan to the Korean court, no one could read it (KRS 94, 86). Although Korea was "subordinate" to Liao, using the Liao calendar and paying tribute regularly, the Korean ruler felt a deeper respect for China Proper. In 943 the founder of the first Korean dynasty in a talk with his descendants called Liao a "country of birds and beasts" with a strange way of life and language. He ordered his people not to imitate their institutions (KRS 2, 26). Indeed, in subsequent generations the Koreans paid little attention to Liao institutions.

[80] Yeh-lü Ti-lu 敵魯, a member of the imperial clan, achieved the position of commanding prefect (LS 108, 2a).

[81] Southwest of Kai-p'ing 蓋平 County, Liaoning. This city was first established in 926. It was later abolished and then reestablished in 1011 (*cf*. LS 38, 16a).

[82] The Silla Kingdom is said to have been founded during the Han period; it ended in A.D. 936 when the Silla king surrendered to the Korean founder of the Korean state (KRS 2, 24). Liao and Sung authors still used the word Silla when referring to Korea. For instance, in CTKC 21, 3a, the tribute is said to have been paid by Silla, but a note to the text states: "Another edition says 'Korea.'"

49. CLASPING A MERITORIOUS GENERAL'S HAND

1015   [On the day *ping-ch'ên* of the fourth month in the fourth year of K'ai-t'ai], Chancellor Kuan-ning[83] submitted a memorial reporting that he had badly defeated the Eight Tribes of Ti-lieh-tê.[84] A decree ordered the imperial attendant, Sa-la, to praise and exhort him and to perform in the emperor's place the ceremony of clasping his hand.   15, 8*b*

50. DISTINGUISHED WIDOWS MAY NOT REMARRY

1017   On the day *jên-ch'ên* [of the fourth month in the sixth year of K'ai-t'ai] titled ladies[85] were forbidden to remarry.   15, 11*a*

51. AN ECLIPSE

1020   On the first day *kêng-hsü* of the seventh month in the autumn [of the ninth year of K'ai-t'ai] there was an eclipse of the sun. An imperial decree ordered an intimate courtier to represent the emperor in praying for the rescue of the sun.[86]   16, 4*b*

52. THE EMPEROR IN YEN

1025   During this year, owing to the abundance of the year's crops and a visit from the emperor, the people of Yen[87] vied with each other in offering up local products. The emperor paid his respects to the aged, showed his kindness to widowers and widows, and gave a banquet. The drinking lasted until nightfall. Six streets were lighted by lanterns as if it were daytime. Officials and commoners strolled about, enjoying themselves. The emperor also looked on incognito.   17, 2*a*

53. A TRIBE SETS UP ITS OWN BANNERS AND DRUMS

1027   On the day *kêng-ch'ên* of the twelfth month [in the sixth year of T'ai-p'ing] the Ho-su-kuan tribe[88] requested permission to set up banners and drums.[89] Approval was granted.[90]   17, 3*b*

54. BURNING THE FORMER EMPEROR'S FAVORITE POSSESSIONS

1031   On the day *ting-mao* [of the seventh month in the first year of Ching-fu the emperor, Hsing-tsung,] paid a visit to the T'ai-p'ing Hall and burned the bows and arrows[91] which the former emperor had used.   18, 2*a*

On the day *mou-wu* [of the ninth month in the first year of Ching-fu the deceased emperor's] bows, arrows, saddles, and bridles[92] were burned in the funeral hall.[93]   18, 2*a*

---

[83] Yah-lü Shih-liang. See VII, 1, note 27, and XII, note 39.

[84] LS 33, 9*b* transcribes the term as *Ti-lieh-pa-pu* 敵烈八部 which is more in keeping with what we would expect grammatically. The Ti-lieh or Ti-lieh-tê lived in the region of Bŏr Nōr in the eastern part of modern Mongolia (MRC II, 545; see also I, 2 (6), no. 2).

[85] The "titled ladies" (*ming fu* 命婦) were women to whom the emperor granted honorific titles. The "titled ladies inside the palace court" were imperial concubines; the "titled ladies outside the palace" were wives of princes, dukes, prime ministers, or other officials (see TS 46, 5*a*; SS 163, 8*a*). Our passage evidently refers to women of the second group, particularly to wives of Chinese officials, for the Ch'i-tan women were not subjected to this typically Chinese restriction.

[86] According to YPL 17*b*, when an eclipse of the moon occurred, the Ch'i-tan people prepared a feast. When an eclipse of the sun occurred, they spat toward the sun and turned their backs to it.

[87] Modern Peiping.

[88] This tribe lived in modern Liaotung.

[89] Banners and drums were granted not only to a supreme khaghan but also to the chieftains of smaller tribes, or to higher officials.

[90] We follow other editions in reading 許 for the 訴 of our text.

[91] This was the first of three reported ceremonial burnings performed because of Shêng-tsung's death. It took place at T'ai-p'ing Hall before the emperor's body was carried in a coffin to the funeral hall.

[92] From our text it is not clear whether these objects actually belonged to the former emperor. It is possible that they were funeral offerings presented by the relatives and the high officials (see below (91)).

[93] The funeral hall (菆塗殿) was the last place in which the emperor's coffin was set up prior to burial. Usually the Liao emperors were interred a few months after death.

1032   On the day *jên-ch'ên* of the eleventh month [in the first year of Ching-fu] the emperor led the officials and made libations in the funeral hall. The deceased emperor's
equipment for chariots and horses, and favorite objects were taken out and burned. The eagles and
falcons of the Five Animal Quarters were set free.   18, 2b–3a

55. REASON FOR A DIVORCE

1032–1055   [Yeh-lü Shu-ch'êng] was convicted of a crime through his wife. When the case
came up for judgment, it was decided that they should be divorced.[94]   89, 1b

56. A HIGH OFFICIAL IS BEATEN

1037   In the sixth year [of Ch'ung-hsi], Hsiao Ti-lieh[95] received an imperial order to go
as an envoy to Sung. He was lame owing to an injury to his foot, but he went to
Sung without reporting it to the throne. The emperor became angry and, when he returned, had
him punished with a large stick.[96]   95, 1b–2a

57. REBIRTH CEREMONY OF THE EMPRESS DOWAGER

1039   On the day *mou-shên* [of the eleventh month in the eighth year of Ch'ung-hsi] the
empress dowager[97] performed the Rebirth Ceremony. An amnesty was announced.
                                                                                        18, 9a

58. REDUCTION OF ANIMAL SACRIFICE

1043   On the day *ting-mao* [of the twelfth month in the eleventh year of Ch'ung-hsi] it
was forbidden in funerals to kill oxen and horses and to bury valuable objects.[98]
                                                                                        19, 3b

59. SYSTEM OF RITUAL

1046   In the fifteenth year [of Ch'ung-hsi] another imperial decree said, "The ancients
who ruled the empire brought to light propriety and righteousness and standardized
laws and regulations. Since the establishment of our dynasty there has been a ruler with enlightened
virtue in every generation. Although the inside and outside incline toward our culture, yet a ritual
has not been worked out and there is none to show to later generations. You should collaborate
with [Yeh-lü] Shu-ch'êng to formulate a code of ritual by consulting the past and conforming to the
present. If there are questions, you should discuss them with the northern and southern chancellors."
After [Hsiao] Han-chia-nu[99] had received the order, he made an extensive study of old works.
The customary practices and traditional usages from the Son of Heaven down to the common people
which might be put into effect without violating the past[100] were written up in three chapters and
presented to the emperor.   103, 5b

60. PARDON FOR A SONLESS BANDIT

1050   On the day *chi-mao* [of the twelfth month in the eighteenth year of Ch'ung-hsi the
emperor] reexamined the criminals. In cases where a younger brother had followed
an elder brother as a bandit, if both elder and younger brothers were without sons, then the younger
was specially pardoned.   20, 3b

---

[94] Yeh-lü Shu-ch'êng was accused of a crime by his wife. He was removed from his official post, sent into exile, and forced to divorce his spouse. Later the accusation was proved to be false, and Shu-ch'êng was restored to his official position. His wife had died in the meantime.

[95] Hsiao Ti-lieh 滴冽 reached the position of the vice-chancellor of the Northern Division and the vicegerent of the Western Capital. He died in 1050 (LS 95, 1b–2a).

[96] The lameness of Hsiao Ti-lieh was obviously a blot on the prestige of Liao and an insult to the honor of Sung.

[97] Empress Dowager Ch'in-ai, the mother of Hsing-tsung.

[98] This order expressly refers to the sacrifice of oxen and horses during the funeral ceremony. It does not affect the great national ceremonies described below.

[99] Hsiao Han-chia-nu 韓家奴 was a scholar who began his political career in 996. He compiled, in cooperation with others, a twenty *chüan* 卷 history of Liao from the time of the rule of the Yao-lien lineage down to his own time. He also translated several Chinese histories into the Ch'i-tan language.

[100] The Ch'i-tan past? This passage obviously refers to one of the many steps taken by the Liao government to coordinate the Chinese ceremonial with the tribal traditions of the Ch'i-tan.

61. MEN AND ANIMALS FREED

1055   On the day *mou-tzŭ* [of the eighth month in the twenty-fourth year of Ch'ung-hsi] a general amnesty was proclaimed. The eagles and falcons of the Five Animal Quarters were set free and the equipment for catching fish was burned.[101]   20, 9*a*

62. REBIRTH CEREMONY OF THE EMPRESS DOWAGER

1063   On the day *mou-tzŭ* [of the twelfth month in the eighth year of Ch'ing-ning], because the empress dowager[102] performed the Rebirth Ceremony, the prisoners of the Western Capital were given a special imperial pardon.   22, 1*b*

63. A GOOD MIRACLE

1068   On the day *jên-tzŭ* of the sixth month [in the fourth year of Hsien-yung] in the northwestern route it rained husked millet in an area of thirty square *li*.[103]   22, 5*b*

64. REBIRTH CEREMONY OF THE HEIR APPARENT

1070   On the day *chia-tzŭ* of the twelfth month [in the fifth year of Hsien-yung] the Rebirth Ceremony for the heir apparent[104] was performed. In each route sentences from hard labor down[105] were reduced by one degree.   22, 6*b*

65. EIGHT GENERATIONS LIVING TOGETHER

1072   On the day *chi-mao* of the seventh month in the autumn [of the eighth year of Hsien-yung], Chin Wên-kao of Ch'ing Prefecture,[106] who had eight generations living together, was granted an official rank by imperial decree.   23, 1*b*

66. THREE GENERATIONS LIVING TOGETHER

1074   On the day *hsin-wei* [of the fourth month in the tenth year of Hsien-yung], because Ta-lu, a Hsi, had three generations living together, he was given an official position to honor him.   23, 2*b*

67. CLAN NAMES AND MARRIAGE SYSTEM

1074   The next year [in the tenth year of Hsien-yung, Yeh-lü Shu-chên[107]] was transferred to the post of chief scribe. He submitted a memorial requesting the extension of the national[108] [Ch'i-tan] clan names. It said, "Since our dynasty was founded, the laws and regulations have been made enlightened, but, as to our clan names, only two have been set up, namely the Yeh-lü and the Hsiao. Previously, when T'ai-tsu formulated the Larger Ch'i-tan Script, he wrote the tribal place-names[109] into the end of the book as a supplementary chapter. I request that they be widely spread and that each tribe may set up clan names so as to make the marriages between men and women harmonize with the code of proper behavior."

The emperor, thinking that the old order should not be changed suddenly, refused consent.

89, 1*b*–2*a*

---

[101] The day after the onset of the emperor's final illness these two acts of charity were performed. The day after the amnesty for men and animals was announced the emperor died.

[102] Empress Dowager Jên-i 仁懿, the mother of Tao-tsung.

[103] The story was obviously made up by the local official or by the emperor himself in order to demonstrate that good fortune favored his reign.

[104] The eldest son of Tao-tsung and the father of T'ien-tsu. He was killed in 1077 while he was still heir apparent.

[105] Excluding the severest sentences such as exile and death.

[106] Ch'ing 慶 Prefecture, modern Tsaghan Khoton, Jehol.

[107] Yeh-lü Shu-chên 庶箴 (T. 陳甫) was an accomplished essayist. He died in 1082 (*cf.* LS 89, 1*b*–2*a*).

[108] 本國, "our" country, meaning the Ch'i-tan as contrasted with the Liao Chinese.

[109] Literally, "names of village communities." The "villages" here were the more or less fixed places where the pastoral tribes used to camp.

68. ETHICAL IDEALISM VERSUS SHAMANISM

Before 1077 Once, at a gathering with her brothers' wives, there was a dispute about the repression of evil spirits as a means of winning a husband's favor. [Hsiao] I-hsin[110] remarked, "The repression of evil spirits is not as good as proper behavior."

When they all inquired the reasons for this, [Hsiao] I-hsin replied, "To cultivate yourself with purity, to honor elders with respect, to serve husbands with tenderness, to direct subordinates with generosity, and not to let gentlemen see one frivolous—this is proper behavior. It naturally gains the respect of one's husband. Are you not ashamed to gain favor by repressing evil spirits?"

The listeners were deeply mortified.   107, 2b

69. A WIFE'S LOYALTY TO HER EXILED HUSBAND

1077 Previously, a rift had occurred between [Yeh-lü] Nu[111] and Chancellor [Yeh-lü] I-hsin. When the imperial heir apparent was deposed,[112] [Yeh-lü Nu] was falsely accused. He was deprived of his rank, taken into the Hsing-shêng Palace,[113] and exiled to the Wu-ku tribe.[114] Because [his wife, Hsiao] I-hsin, was the daughter of a princess, the emperor wished to dissolve the marriage.

I-hsin refused, saying, "Your Majesty, because I am a relative of yours, has let me be spared exile. This is really boundless grace.[115] But the relationship of husband and wife must be followed in life or in death. Since the year of the hairpin[116] I have followed Nu. If in a moment when he has fallen into trouble I suddenly desert him, violating the principles of duty and morality, how would I be different from the birds or the beasts? I pray that I may be favored with Your Majesty's compassion and that I may go with Nu. Then even if death comes I shall feel no regret."

The emperor, moved by her plea, consented to this.   107, 2b

70. FOUR GENERATIONS LIVING TOGETHER

1078 On the day hsin-mao [of the eleventh month in the fourth year of Ta-k'ang], because Chang Pao, a native of Chin Prefecture, had four generations living together, all his sons were ordered to become attendants in the Three Sections Department.[117]   22, 7a

71. RAIN MAGIC

1080 On the day kêng-yin [of the fifth month in the sixth year of Ta-k'ang], because there was a drought, the emperor prayed for rain. The left and right attendants were ordered to pour water on each other. Soon the rains came.   24, 2a

72. LEGEND OF A POOR TRIBESMAN

–1081 Yeh-lü I-hsin, whose style was Hu-tu-kun, was a member of the Five Divisions lineage. His father was called Tieh-la. The family was so poor that it lacked clothing and other necessities. The tribesmen called him Poor Tieh-la.

---

[110] Hsiao I-hsin 意辛, a daughter of the imperial son-in-law Hsiao T'ao-su-wo 陶蘇幹 of the T'u-lü-pu tribe, was married to Yeh-lü Nu 奴. She gained fame by her filial piety and by her loyalty to her husband (see below, (69)). She was killed in the course of a rebellion which broke out in the Supreme Capital at the end of the Liao dynasty.

[111] Yeh-lü Nu was the husband of Hsiao I-hsin (see note 110).

[112] The heir apparent of Tao-tsung was deposed and put to death in 1077 because of a false accusation made by Yeh-lü I-hsin 乙辛 (LS 72, 6a–b).

[113] An imperial ordo established by Shêng-tsung. Its Ch'i-tan name was Nü-ku Ordo 女古幹魯朵 (see XV, 1 (12)).

[114] In Outer Mongolia.

[115] Literally, "grace of Heaven and Earth."

[116] Formerly, when a Chinese girl reached the age of fifteen, she was allowed to wear a hairpin. This pin indicated that she was grown-up. In recent times the hairpin has come to indicate a marriageable girl in general, regardless of age.

[117] According to the glossary of LS 116, 12a, this department was divided into a Left Section (左班), a Right Section (右班), and a Delivery Section (寄班). The Left and Right Sections probably served inside the office; the Delivery Section served outdoors, delivering government documents, etc.

Previously, when the mother of I-hsin was pregnant, she dreamed one night of seizing a ram with her hands and pulling out its horns and tail.[118]   Upon awakening she sought divinatory advice about it.

The diviner said, "This is a good omen.   The character for sheep with the horns and tail removed forms the character for prince.   You will have a son who will be a prince."[119]

When I-hsin was born it happened that they were on the road.   There was no water for the bath. In turning the cart around they demolished the ruts, from which they suddenly saw a spring of water gush up.   As a son had been born to him, Tieh-la wanted wine to celebrate.   They scented the aroma of wine in the brambles and obtained two vessels [of wine].   So they offered a sacrifice to the east.[120]

110, 1a–b

73. NO INTERMARRIAGE WITH BARBARIANS

1094   On the day *chi-hai* [of the fifth month in the tenth year of Ta-an] the frontier people were forbidden to intermarry with the barbarian tribes.   25, 7a

74. OLD AGE HONORED

1095   On the day *kuei-yu* of the twelfth month [in the tenth year of Ta-an], because Sun Pin, a native of San-ho County and his wife were both a hundred years old, his family was exempted from labor service.   25, 7b

75. A CH'I–TAN PRINCESS MARRIES FOUR TIMES

11th century   Empress Ch'in-ai[121] bore two daughters, the second of whom, Yen-mu-chin, . . . [first] married Hsiao Cho-pu.[122]   She was married again, [this time] to Hsiao Hai-li. As they were not compatible, she divorced him and then married Hsiao Hu-tu.[123]   [Again] there was incompatibility.   She divorced him and then married[124] the Prince of Han, Hsiao Hui.[125]   65, 3a–b

76. THREE GENERATIONS LIVING TOGETHER

1100   On the day *jên-shên* of the eleventh month [in the sixth year of Shou-lung], because T'ien Shih-jung, a native of T'ien-tê,[126] had three generations living together, it was decreed that he be granted an official position.   One of his sons was permitted to become an attendant of the Three Sections Department.   26, 5b

---

[118] Another story of childbirth involving rams is told in YPL 17a–b.   The empress, about to give birth to a child, made obeisance to the sun eight times and entered the central tent which was surrounded by forty-eight smaller tents, each of which sheltered a ram with big horns. Immediately before the birth of the child the horns of the rams were twisted to the accompaniment of noises made by other rams and by men.   According to the *Yen-pei Lu*, the Ch'i-tan people believed that such noises would relieve the labor pains of the empress.   If the child was a boy the empress ate half a cup of curd with almond oil; the emperor donned a red suit and Ch'i-tan music was played in the front camp.   If the child was a girl the empress drank some black pulse soup with a little salt; the emperor donned a black suit and Chinese music was played.   The wounded rams were not slaughtered but were left to die in their own time.   The empress returned to the emperor's camp on the ninth day.

[119] This story, whose legendary character is obvious, implies that the sorcerer had some knowledge of the Chinese or Ch'i-tan script.   If from the Chinese character

yang 羊 (sheep) the two upper dots and the lower part of the vertical stroke are removed, the word *wang* 王 (king or prince) remains.   We do not know if the two Ch'i-tan characters for sheep and king were similar to the Chinese forms.

[120] According to WTS 72, 5a, the Ch'i-tan held the eastern direction in greatest esteem.   Windows and doors generally faced east (see VII, 2 (78)).

[121] The wife of Shêng-tsung.   In an inscription discovered in the northern part of Jehol in 1930 *ai* is written 愛 instead of 哀 as in our text (LLSKCL 3, 6a).

[122] Hsiao Cho-pu 啜不, also transcribed as Tsu-pu-li 鉏不里 or Cho-pu 浞卜.   This Ch'i-tan noble was sentenced to death for treason in 1031 (LS 18, 1b).

[123] A nephew of Empress Ch'in-ai.

[124] An analysis of the Table of Princesses in LS 65 shows that six of the recorded Liao princesses remarried.

[125] A descendant of the clan of Empress Ch'un-ch'in 淳欽, T'ai-tsu's wife, and the brother of Empress Ch'in-ai.

[126] This place was located north of the modern Ordos region in the western part of Suiyuan.

77. READING OF BOOKS

At this time,[127] when people were seen reading books in court, they were reproved.   Once Ao-lu-wo[128] entered the imperial sleeping chamber and saw a servant, Ch'a-la, reading a book.   He took it and glanced at it.   When some princes happened to arrive, he hid it in his sleeve and then returned it, saying, "Don't let the others see it."   At this time he got the reputation of an elder.[129]   72, 7a–b

78. DIRECTIONS

It was the Liao custom to face the east[130] and to esteem the left.   The imperial tent faced the east, the nine tents of Yao-lien faced the south, and the Three Patriarchal Tents of the imperial clan faced the north.   The east-west line was the warp; the north-south line was the woof.   Hence the imperial camp was called the Horizontal Tents.[131]   45, 20a

79. THE SUN WORSHIPPED

In the ceremony for the worship of the sun the emperor ascended the open-air terrace[132] where a mat was placed.   He bowed twice towards the sun and offered incense.   49, 4b

80. THE GOD OF FIRE

On the eve of the last day of the year emissaries and the *i-li-pi*[133] were ordered to lead the responsible court nobles[134] to the front of a hall.   Salt and sheep fat were placed in a stove for burning.   The shamans and the head shaman, in accordance with their ranks, recited incantations to invoke the god of Fire.   Then the commissioner of court ceremonies called the emperor to bow twice before the fire.[135]   49, 6a

81. THE SÊ-SÊ RAIN CEREMONY[136]

In case of drought an auspicious day was chosen for performing the Sê-sê Ceremony to pray for rain. Previous to this date an awning was set up with a hundred poles.   When the day arrived, the emperor offered wine to the images of former emperors and then shot at willow trees.   The emperor shot twice; the imperial princes and the ministers, in the order of their rank, each shot once.   Those who hit the willow trees received as pledges the hats and robes of those who had marked the trees.[137] Those who did not make a hit gave up their hats and robes as pledges.   The losers offered wine to the winners.   Afterwards the hats and coats were returned to each person.

Further, on the next day willow trees were planted southeast of the awning.   The shamans making the sacrifices of wine and glutinous and panicled millet and praying, planted the willow trees.   After the emperor and the empress had worshipped the east, the younger men shot at the willow trees. Members of the imperial clan and of the Imperial Maternal Uncles and the various courtiers who participated in the ceremony were granted presents according to their rank.   After three days, if rain fell, four horses and four suits of clothes were granted to the *ti-lieh-ma-tu*[138]; if not, water was spilled upon him.   49, 3a–b

---

[127] During the youth of Ao-lu-wo 敖盧斡.

[128] He was born of an imperial concubine in the first years of the Ch'ien-t'ung period (*ca.* 1101. LS 71, 8a), and was granted the title of Prince of Chin in 1106. He was put to death by the emperor in 1122 for high treason (*cf.* LS 72, 7a–b).

[129] He was actually an adolescent. His reputation was earned by his poise and maturity, as in the present case in which he kindly let the servant go instead of reporting him.

[130] The Sung envoys who visited the Liao empire noticed that the huts and houses, as well as tents and cart tents, all faced the east (*cf.* PFTL 24; CTKC 24, 2b; WTS 72, 5a).

[131] *Hêng* 橫 means "east to west," "horizontal."

[132] A construction used to observe the heavens. Emperor Wên of Han once wanted to build a terrace, but because it would have cost one hundred catties of gold he dropped his plan (SC 10, 17b).

[133] See XIV, 1 (9), LS 45, 8a–b.

[134] The term *lang-chün* 郎君 (court nobles) is used loosely in the *Liao Shih*. Officials of various offices were called *lang-chün*.

[135] *Cf.* VII, 2 (83), where this ceremony is described from a slightly different aspect.

[136] The ceremony had been performed long before this in the tribal period of the Ch'i-tan. According to LS 49, 1b, it was established by Su 蘇 Khaghan, probably during the T'ang period.

[137] The willow trees had been marked by peeling off some of the bark. See Stein 39, 86 ff., where a somewhat different account of this ceremony is translated from the *Liao Shih Shih-i.*

[138] The *ti-lieh-ma-tu* 敵烈麻都. For the position of this tribal official see XIV, 1 (9), LS 45, 8b–9a.

82. WAR MAGIC

Whenever the army was being mobilized, the emperor, at the head of the barbarian and Chinese civil and military officials, sacrificed a gray ox and a white horse and reported to the gods of Heaven, Earth, and Sun. The moon, however, was not worshipped. The intimate courtiers were ordered to report separately to the mausoleums of T'ai-tsu and [of the emperors] after him and to the god of Mu-yeh Mountain.   34, 3a

The ceremony for a military campaign personally directed by the emperor regularly took place during the autumn or winter. To meet the enemy and control an emergency, it sometimes took place without regard to the season. Before the army was sent out it was first necessary to report to the ancestral temples. At this time three divine tablets were set up and sacrificed to. They were called "the deceased emperors," "the highways," and "the armies."[139] A gray ox and a white horse were killed and offered to Heaven and Earth. The sacrificial offering was usually presented near a solitary tree. If there was no lone tree, it was done at the place where the emperor halted. Sometimes the emperor, dressed in armor and helmet, offered sacrifice to the mausoleums and temples of the deceased emperors. Then the soldiers were reviewed.

When the troops were about to move, one female and one male deer were sacrificed to drive away evil spirits.[140] When the troops were about to contact the enemy, the horses' tails were knotted and Heaven and Earth were implored and worshipped. Then they advanced. When a city was captured or the enemy defeated, the sacrifices offered to Heaven and Earth consisted of a white and a black sheep. When the troops were brought back, a captured stallion and a bull were sacrificed to Heaven and Earth. Using a criminal condemned to death when the army set out and a spy when the army returned, they planted a stake in the ground, tied him to it, and, facing the direction in which they were moving, shot at him haphazardly until the arrows collected like [the spikes of] a hedgehog. This was called "shooting devil arrows."[141]   51, 1a–b

83. MISCELLANEOUS ANNUAL CEREMONIES

On New Year's day, in accordance with the national custom, glutinous millet[142] and the marrow of white sheep were made into cakes which were rounded like fists. Each tent was given forty-nine balls. Just before dawn everyone from within his tent threw the balls outside through the windows. If the number was even,[143] they played music, drank, and feasted. If the number was odd, they had twelve shamans ring bells, hold arrows, and circle the tents singing and shouting. Inside the tents they exploded salt in stoves and roasted moles. This was called "frightening the demons."

---

[139] CTKC 27, 3b reports that the Ch'i-tan, while conducting a military operation, did not wait to choose a lucky day. Instead they daily subjected the shoulder blade of a sheep to a fire made of mugwort and the droppings of horses. If the shoulder blade was cracked by the fire, the soldiers would begin the campaign; otherwise they would not march.

This description is taken from the *Yen-pei Tsa-chi* 燕北雜記, (YPTC 9a), written by Wu Kuei 武珪, a singer who in the middle of the eleventh century lived in the Liao country for more than ten years. A Yüan scholar, Li Yeh 李冶, criticizes Wu Kuei's statement as based upon too narrow and too casual observation. Li Yeh enumerates a number of other types of bone divination practised by Inner Asiatic tribes, especially the Mongols. He concludes that very possibly the Ch'i-tan also used bone divination for various purposes not mentioned by Wu Kuei (CCKCT 9, 57–58).

[140] According to the glossary in LS 116, 14a, a male

and a female deer were killed in order to bring a curse upon the enemy.

[141] This magic technique was usually employed before or during the initial period of a campaign (LS 2, 5b; 3, 11a; 12, 4b; 14, 1b, 3a). The arrows were shot either at prisoners of war (LS 9, 4a; 11, 4b, 8b) or at captured spies (LS 14, 5a; 19, 6a; 70, 17b), obviously in the hope of injuring more important if more distant enemies. The sanguinary device was also employed by or against rebellious Ch'i-tan (VII, 2 (8) and LS 1, 6b; 2, 3b). On occasion a criminal official was thus punished (LS 4, 3b). The Hsi Hsia in a similar practice killed captured men and horses (LS 115, 6a).

[142] *No* 糯 may mean either glutinous rice or millet. Since in the border regions millet constitutes the oldest and most common crop, it seems reasonable to translate *no* as millet (*cf.* II, introduction).

[143] That is, if the number of balls recovered was even.

They remained [in the tents] for seven days and then came forth.   In the national language New Year's day was called *nai nieh-i-êrh*.   *Nai*[144] means "first."   *Nieh-i-êrh*[145] means "day."

On the first day of spring women presented the spring writings.   They cut gray silk cloth into banners and carved dragon images to hold them.[146]   Sometimes they made toad [images].[147]   The flags were inscribed with the words, "Propitious Spring."

The day of the Man.   Among the days of the first month the first was that of the Cock; the second, of the Dog; the third, of the Pig; the fourth, of the Sheep; the fifth, of the Horse; the sixth, of the Ox; and the seventh, of the Man.   If, as forecast, the day was clear, this was auspicious; if cloudy, this was inauspicious.   Customarily cakes were fried and eaten in the courtyard.   This was called "smoking the sky."[148]

The first day of the second month[149] was the Festival of Harmony.   The clan of the Imperial Maternal Uncles, the Hsiao family, arranged a feast to which they invited the imperial clan, the Yeh-lü family.   Year after year this was considered regular practice.   In the national language this day was called *hsia-li p'o*.   *Hsia-li*[150] means "to invite."   *P'o*[151] means "time."

The eighth day of the second month[152] was the birthday of Prince Siddhārtha.   The capitals,

---

[144] *Nai* is equivalent to the Mongol word *nige, nigen,* and *nege* and the Dahur word *nége* or *néke,* all of which signify "one" or "first" (Shiratori 13 TMK, 882).

[145] The term is equivalent to the Mongol and Buryat word *nara(n),* to Dahur *nara,* and to Oročon-Solon *nari,* all of which mean "sun" and "day" (*cf.* Shiratori 13 TMK, 23).

[146] In our translation we follow the parallel version in CTKC 27, 1*a,* as it is clearer.

[147] It is possible that 蟾蜍 refers to the three-legged toad in the legend of Hêng-ê 姮娥.   She stole the Drug of Immortality and ran away to the moon where she was transformed into a toad (see HHC 10, 4*b,* note to the text).

[148] The *hsün t'ien* 薰天 of our text is repeated in *Ch'i-tan Kuo Chih* and in the Han-fên Lou 涵芬樓 edition of the *Liao Chih.*   (CTKC 27, 1*b*; LC 6*b*).   The Ku-chin Shuo-hai 古今說海 edition of the *Liao Chih* has *hsün yao* 夭.   CCSSC 5*a* simply has *hsün huo* 火.   The phrase conveys the idea of smoking out the evil spirits in the sky.   *Cf.* Stein 39, 121–122.

[149] The traditional loosening of property regulations in the middle of the first month is not mentioned in the ceremonial calendar, probably because it did not have the distinction of being an official institution.   Yet the custom seems to have enjoyed great popularity; folkloristically it is highly significant.

From the thirteenth to the sixteenth day of the first month playful stealing was permitted.   According to the *Ch'i-tan Kuo Chih,* objects up to the value of ten strings of money might be taken; the *Sung-mo Ch'i-wên* defines no such limit, but says that the "thieves" used to seize jewelry, carts, and horses; it also mentions the carrying off of girls as a regular part of the stealing license.   Objects were taken preferably during visits.   The host and his wife tried to prevent the "theft," but they were seldom completely successful.   A noble lady, who was carefully watched, might let her maid act for her.   Afterwards, either the robbed family discovered its loss or else the malefactor voluntarily revealed the deed.   Sheep and wine were then offered to redeem the appropriated articles.   Abducted girls were eventually married to the "thief" if they desired it (CTKC 27, 3*b*; SMCW 15*a*).

[150] *Hsia-li* 恓里 is equivalent to the Gold word *galign* or *goli,* to Olča *gali,* and to Oročen *kala,* all of which mean "to invite" (*cf.* Shiratori 12 TMK, 1269).

[151] *P'o* 叵, according to Shiratori (12 TMK, 1244), is equivalent to Gold *bao,* Manchu *fon,* "time."   These words are related to old Mongol *hon,* literary Mongol *on,* "time."   The Jurchen equivalent is transcribed as *fu-wan-to* (Grube 96, 92).

[152] The fact that the (Sanskrit) Lalitavistara and the later (Pali) Nidānakathā place Buddha's birth in two different months (Beck 16, 35, note 2) has affected the dating of the sacred event by the Buddhists of the Far East.   According to CTKC 27, 1*b* and SMCW 14*b,* Buddha's birthday was celebrated on the eighth day of the fourth month.   The same date is given by the *Yen-pei Tsa-chi* = SSKC 20, 227, a source which described later Liao and early Chin customs.   Contradicting these records, which Ch'ien Ta-hsin considers valid (NESKI 83, 39*a*), the present text (LS 53) mentions the eighth day of the second month as the Liao date of Buddha's birthday.   The second month was favored also by the Chin and Yüan dynasties.   The Chin emperor, Hai-ling 海陵, on the eighth day of the second month, in 1156, watched the procession and granted silk and silver to the monks of various temples (CS 5, 14*b*).   On January 8, 1157, the same emperor prohibited the celebration of Buddha's birthday on the eighth day of the second month (CS 5, 15*a*) but in 1199 the then Chin emperor, Chang-tsung 章宗, again revived the celebration on the eighth day of the second month (CS 11, 3*a*).

According to the Chao-kung Shên-tao-pei 趙公神道碑, during the Yüan period the Buddha's birthday was celebrated annually on the eighth day of the second month; commoners, nobles, and courtiers all enjoyed the elaborate festival which forced both government and governed to spend huge sums of money.   The Mongols set up numerous tents outside the capital to watch the various performances given on the occasion (TYHKL 42, 10*b*).

CSHC 1, 39*b*–40*a,* after discussing the contradictory Liao dates, suggests that the *Ch'i-tan Kuo Chih* and the *Sung-mo Ch'i-wên* follow the Sung custom in giving the fourth month.   This explanation, however, is inadequate

administrations, and prefectures carved wooden images [of him]. Ceremonial equipment and various kinds of performances were paraded throughout the cities in celebration. Prince Siddhārtha was the son of King Suddhodana of the Western Regions.[153] He had the surname of Gautama and the personal name of Śākyamuni. Because of his enlightened nature[154] he was called Buddha.

The third day of the third month was *shang-ssŭ*. In accordance with the national custom, hares were carved from wood. [The people] divided themselves into [two] groups[155] and rode on horseback to shoot at them. The first to score a hit was the winner. The defeated group dismounted, knelt down in a line, and offered up wine, which was drunk by the winning party on horseback. In the national language this day was called *t'ao-li hua*. *T'ao-li*[156] is "hare." *Hua*[157] means "to shoot."

At noon on the double-fifth day[158] of the fifth month, mugwort leaves were picked and combined with silk for padded garments. Seven [of these garments] were presented to the Son of Heaven. The northern and southern officials were each given three. The emperor and the officials were entertained at a banquet at which a Po-hai cook offered mugwort cakes. Silk threads of five different colors were made into a cord which was tied around the arms. These were called the Knots of Mutual Rejoicing. Coils of colored silk threads were made into a human figure which was pinned on the hair. These were called the Threads of Long Life. In the national language this day was called *t'ao sai-i-êrh*. *T'ao*[159] means "five." *Sai-i-êrh*[160] means "month."

The day of the summer solstice was customarily called the *Ch'ao* Festival. Women presented colored fans and sent bags of powder and cosmetics as gifts to one another.[161]

On the eighteenth day of the sixth month, as a national custom, the Yeh-lü family arranged a feast and invited the Hsiao clan of the Imperial Maternal Uncles. This was also called *hsia-li p'o*.[162]

During the night of the thirteenth day of the seventh month the Son of Heaven set up a tent thirty *li* west of the [traveling] camp and slept there. Wine and viands had been prepared beforehand. The next day the escorting armies and tribes played barbarian music,[163] feasted until evening, and then returned to the traveling camp. This was called "welcoming the festival." On the fifteenth day, which was Chung-yüan,[164] Chinese music was played and there was a great feast. At early dawn of the sixteenth day the emperor went westward once more and the escorting armies and tribes shouted aloud three times. This was called "bidding farewell to the festival." In the national language this was called *sai-i-êrh shê*. *Shê* means "good."

---

since we find the eighth day of the fourth month mentioned as Buddha's birthday also in a Liao inscription (LWT 5, 13a). Could it be that there existed within the Liao empire two traditions based on the two versions of the original Indian story?

In present Peiping the memory of Buddha's birthday is still honored on the eighth day of the fourth month (Bodde 36, 36). The famous pilgrimage to the top of Mount Miao-fêng which is undertaken in the first part of the same month seems also devoted in large part to Buddhist worship (*op. cit.*, 38 ff.).

[153] The term 西域 (Western Regions) is generally applied in Chinese history to all countries west of modern Kansu, such as Persia, India, and Arabia. It denoted more particularly the Central Asiatic regions.

[154] This enlightened nature refers to the concept of Bodhi, or Enlightenment (Soothill and Hodous 37, 480).

[155] CTKC 27, 1b adds the word 兩 (two).

[156] In the Khalkha language and in the Buryat dialects of Tunkinsk, Aral, Selenga, and Khori the word for hare is *tūlaj*. The Mongols near the Great Wall call it *taolai*. The Ölöt term is *tōlai* or *tūlai* (*cf.* Shiratori 13 TMK, 39).

[157] Equivalent to the Gold word *harpé*, "to shoot" (*loc. cit.*).

[158] The fifth day of the fifth month, the date of the Chinese Dragon Festival. Because the date contains two fives, it is called the double-fifth.

[159] Shiratori (12 TMK, 1261) equates this word with literary Mongol *tabun*, "five."

[160] The term is equivalent to literary Mongol *sara(n)*, "moon, month."

[161] The Liao women and girls used yellow powder on their faces; they painted their eyebrows red and their lips black. This type of make-up, which was called *fo-chuang* 佛裝, "Buddhist cosmetic," did not originate among the Ch'i-tan, but had existed in North China from the sixth century on (PCKT 2, 25; NKCML 2, 12a; KSTK 4, 101). The Liao women also used a sort of rose oil which was bright and fragrant (MCML 3, 32). They used isinglass to attach fish-shaped ornaments to their faces (KSTY 1, 9).

[162] *Cf.* notes 150 and 151.

[163] Here the word "barbarian" manifestly designates tribal music in general as contrasted with Chinese music. According to LS 54, 1a ff., Ch'i-tan and other tribal ("barbarian") music as well as Chinese music was played within the Liao empire.

[164] A festival celebrated by Taoists and Buddhists.

On the eighth day of the eighth month, as a national custom, white dogs were killed seven paces in front of the sleeping tents and were buried with their muzzles uncovered. After seven days, on the Mid-Autumn Festival,[165] the sleeping tents were moved over upon them. In the national language, this was called *nieh-ho nai*. *Nieh-ho*[166] means "dog." *Nai*[167] means "head."

On the double-ninth day of the ninth month the Son of Heaven led the courtiers and tribes to shoot tigers. Those who shot the fewest were the losers and had to pay a penalty by preparing a banquet for the double-ninth. After the shooting an elevated locality was selected for the erection of the tents. The barbarian and Chinese courtiers were granted drinks of chrysanthemum wine. The livers of hares were made into pickled meat and the tongues of deer into gravy. Dogwood was pressed into wine and sprinkled in the doorways in order to keep out the evil spirits. In the national language this day was called *pi-li-ch'ih li* which means "the ninth day of the ninth month."[168]

In the tenth month of the year the five capitals offered ten thousand paper sets of short coats, armor, spears, swords, and [other] weapons. On the fifteenth day the Son of Heaven and the courtiers made obeisance to Mu-yeh Mountain from a distance. They used the national script to write the [ceremonial] statements and burned them together [with the paper sets]. In the national language this was called *tai la*. *Tai*[169] means "to burn." *La* signifies "armor."

On the day of the winter solstice, as a national custom, a white sheep, a white horse, and a white goose were slaughtered. The blood of each was taken and mixed with wine. Then the Son of Heaven worshipped the Black Mountain from a distance. The Black Mountain was in the northern part of the country. Tradition says that the souls of the national [Ch'i-tan] people were cared for by its god, as in the case of Mount T'ai in China. Each year on this day the five capitals offered more than ten thousand sets of paper men and horses, which were sacrificed to the mountain and burned. According to the custom [the Black Mountain was considered] very majestic and awe-inspiring. Without offering a sacrifice [the people] dared not approach the mountain.

On a *ch'ên* day of the La [Ceremony][170] the Son of Heaven led the northern and southern officials, all of whom wore military clothes. Just before dawn they took their seats in court, played music,

---

[165] The Chinese Moon Festival. The historian uses the Chinese term, but the recorded ceremony is obviously Ch'i-tan in character.

[166] Equivalent to Mongol *noqaj* and Khalkha, Ölöt, and Buryat *noxaj, noxoj* (*cf.* Shiratori 12 TMK, 1262).

When T'ai-tsung entered the capital of Chin in 947 and occupied the imperial palace, dogs were slaughtered and their skins were hung at each door in order to bring good luck (WTS 72, 16b; *cf.* also TCTC 286, 2a and CTKC 3, 5b which describes the slaughtering of dogs and the hanging of sheepskins in the courtyard).

White dogs are said to have been used for warding off spirits also in the Chin period. A Sung envoy who traveled to the Chin capital (modern Peiping) observed near Han-tan 邯鄲 (in modern Hopei) the impaling of a white dog on a long stake and the sprinkling of wine on its corpse. He was told that the Jurchen used dog sacrifices to worship Heaven and for magic cures (LPL 4b).

In 1105 the Sung envoy, Lin Shu 林攄, aroused the anger of the Liao officials by his refusal to rehearse the Liao ceremonial before going to court. His food supply was cut off, and he was led to a place where tigers were kept. He did not lose his self-control, but remarked contemptuously, "These are dogs of the Southern Country!" His words startled the Liao officials because of a Ch'i-tan taboo which forbade the use of the word "dog" (TWSTT 3, 17a–b). The wooden dogs found in Tao-tsung's mausoleum reflect the Ch'i-tan attitude toward this animal (Torii 36, IV, pl. 262; see fig. 26). Originally

the deceased emperors were probably given live dogs as magic protectors. Under Buddhist influence wooden images were used instead.

[167] *Cf.* above, note 144.

[168] Shiratori equates *pi-li-ch'ih* 必里渥 with Mongol and Turkic *bars*, "tiger," and *li* 離 with *sara*, "month." Thus the whole term, literally translated, would signify "the month of the tiger" (Shiratori 12 TMK, 1252–1253). Linguistically this derivation is untenable.

[169] The word seems to be equivalent to Goldi *tawa, taua*. It closely resembles Evenki Tungus *toγo, toγa, tō*, "fire" and Korean *t'ăi, töi, t'ă*.

[170] The word *la* 臘 connotes both a hunt for sacrificial animals (獵) and a transition from the old to the new (接) (see VII, 2 (93)). From the time of the Sui dynasty (581–618) the La Ceremony usually occurred in the last month in the year (*cf.* SSKC 39, 422).

The Liao dynasty, following the Chinese tradition, selected one of the five elements as its national symbol. According to a Chin document, it chose the "water" element (CWT 56, 6b) which made the La Ceremony fall on the *ch'ên* 辰 day of the twelfth month (*cf.* SSKC 39, 421).

The aforesaid ceremonial day is different from the *la* day, which, according to CCSSC 16a, was the eighth day of the twelfth month. The modern colloquial Chinese designation for this day, *la pa* 八, was already in use in the Sung period. On this day the Buddhist temples provided a gruel which was called *la pa chou* 粥 (MLL 6, 3a).

and drank wine. Armor,[171] weapons, sheep, and horses were bestowed according to rank. In the national language this day was called *ch'ao-wu-êrh p'o*. *Ch'ao-wu-êrh*[172] means "to fight."

53, 14a–12b

84. LEGEND OF TRIBAL ORIGIN

There was Mu-yeh Mountain on which temples for the earliest ancestors of the Ch'i-tan were built. Ch'i-shou Khaghan was [worshipped] in the southern temple and his *k'o-tun*[173] in the northern temple. They modelled and painted likenesses of these two sage rulers and their eight sons.

Tradition has it that a divine man riding a white horse floated along the T'u River[174] from the Ma-yü Mountains[175] to the east. A heavenly maiden riding a cart drawn by a gray ox floated down the Huang River[176] from P'ing-ti Sung-lin.[177] On reaching Mu-yeh Mountain, where the two rivers joined courses, [the two persons] met and mated. They had eight sons. Later on their descendants gradually prospered. They split up into eight tribes.[178] In each military undertaking and in the seasonal sacrifices of spring and autumn they had to use a white horse and a gray ox[179] [as sacrificial animals] to show that their origin was not forgotten.[180]   37, 9a

85. THE SACRIFICE TO MU–YEH MOUNTAIN

In the ceremony of sacrificing to the mountain the tablets of the gods of Heaven and Earth were set up facing the east on Mu-yeh Mountain. A "master" tree was set up in the middle and a group of trees was planted in front like the arrangement of the court. Two trees were also planted side by side as a divine gate.

When the emperor and empress arrived, the *i-li-pi*[181] prepared the ceremonies. The animals used for the sacrifice were a cream-colored horse, a dark ox, and a reddish-white sheep, all male. An imperial servant who was called the *i-la*[182] of the banners and drums slaughtered the sacrificial animals, cut up their bodies, and hung them on the master tree. The head shaman poured wine on the animals. A ritual official called the *ti-lieh-ma-tu*[183] reported on the performance of the ceremonies. . . .

---

[171] We follow other editions in reading 甲 for the 申 of our text.

[172] Shiratori (12 TMK, 1246) tries to relate this word to Mongol and Uighur *čärik*. But in both ancient and modern Mongol and Turkic *čärig*, a loan word from Sanskrit *kšatriya*, means "army" only. Hence its derivation from an original longer Mongol form **čägärik* is impossible. Concerning *p'o*, "time," cf. note 151.

[173] Equivalent to Orkhon Turkic and Uighur *qatun;* an early Turkic loan word from Sogdian *xwatēn*, lady.

[174] Modern Lao-ha River, Jehol.

[175] These mountains extended through Shang-ching and Chung-ching Circuits (LS 37, 2b; 39, 1b). Their location must therefore correspond to a region near Boro Khoton and the Lao-ha River, Jehol.

[176] The modern Shira Muren.

[177] Probably in the western part of Jehol.

[178] This story is also related in the introduction of *Ch'i-tan Kuo Chih*, in HCLY 78, 2a, and in TCCS 5, 32. The Liao historiographer tried to trace it back to the Ch'in and Han periods (221 B.C.–A.D. 220) without, however, arriving at a definite conclusion.

[179] Because this animal pulled the cart of the female ancestor of the Ch'i-tan, Mullie (22, 105) translates *niu* 牛 as "cow." R. Stein (39, 11) draws attention to a passage of the *Liao Shih* which points in another direction. According to LS 49, 2a, Heaven and Earth were worshipped by offering a sacrifice of white horses, gray *niu*, and red and white sheep, all of which were male animals. To this passage may be added LS 51, 1a–b (see above (82)),

according to which a stallion and a bull were sacrificed to Heaven and Earth before the troops were withdrawn from an expedition. These descriptions support Stein's interpretation of the *niu* as a male animal.

[180] Yeh Lung-li, the author of the *Ch'i-tan Kuo Chih* presents another Ch'i-tan origin story in which three phantasmal early "rulers" figure prominently. The first was merely a skull covered with felt which lived hidden in a tent inaccessible to the Ch'i-tan people. When an important tribal event occurred, a white horse and a gray ox were offered as sacrifice, whereupon the skull emerged in human shape to attend to the affair in question. Afterwards it was transformed again into a skull. Eventually this "ruler" vanished completely because in violation of the regulations the people had peeked at it.

The second "ruler" had a boar's head and was dressed in pigskin. He also lived in a tent which he left only to attend to important tribal affairs. Later he also disappeared because his wife had stolen his pigskin.

The third "ruler" kept twenty sheep, of which he ate nineteen each day. The following day the original number was present, and he proceeded in the same way.

These three rulers are said to have been capable administrators (CTKC, introduction, 1a–b; cf. also Stein 39, 11 ff.).

[181] The *i-li-pi* 夷离畢 was a high judicial official (cf. XIV, 1 (9), LS 45, 8a–b).

[182] Officers who took charge of banners and drums (LS 46, 12a).

[183] Cf. XIV, 1 (9), LS 45, 9a. Cf. also LS 45, 1b.

The emperor and empress, riding on saddled horses, were followed by the courtiers in the south and the titled ladies in the north, each dressed according to the color of the banner of his tribe. The emperor and empress dismounted on reaching the master tree and ascended the southern platform where they sat on a couch. The courtiers in one group and the titled ladies in another, all arranged according to their rank, entered and went to their places. They bowed in one group and then resumed their places.

The emperor and empress proceeded to the tablets of Heaven and Earth to offer wine, and after the commissioners of court ceremonies had read prayers they resumed their places. The prime minister of the Northern Administration and the *t'i-yin*, according to their rank, made offerings of wine to the master tree and to the other trees.

With the playing of music the courtiers and the titled ladies retired. The emperor, leading the lineages of the First, Second, and Third Patriarchal [Households], circled the trees of the divine gate three times. The other lineages circled it seven times. The emperor and empress bowed twice, as did the whole company. Incense was offered, and they bowed twice as before.

The emperor and empress ascended the platform and sat on square cushions with dragon designs. At the second signal they went to the east-worshipping place. The courtiers and the titled ladies followed and arranged themselves in groups as before. A shaman put on a white robe. The *t'i-yin*, who had a plain cap, bowed and put it on. The shaman spoke thrice. Each time the emperor and empress bowed once, and the whole company bowed once. The emperor and empress, each of whom held two cups of wine and two dishes of meat, made two offerings of wine. The high courtiers and the titled ladies, each of whom held a cup of wine in the right hand and a dish of meat in the left, made one offering while standing a little to the rear. The *t'i-yin* was ordered to throw offerings towards the east. The emperor and empress bowed six times, and the whole company bowed six times. Then the emperor and empress returned to their seats.   49, 1*b*–2*b*

86. THE REBIRTH CEREMONY

For the Rebirth Ceremony an auspicious day was selected every twelve years in the last month of the winter preceding the year [of the duodenary cycle] of the emperor's birth.[184]

Previously the ground north of the Forbidden Gate was cleared and the rebirth building and the building of the emperor's mother were set up. A chariot with the tablets of the deceased emperor stood southeast of the rebirth building. Three V-shaped timbers were planted upside down in the ground.[185]

On the day selected a young boy and an old midwife were placed in the building. A married woman holding wine and an old man carrying a quiver with arrows stood outside the building. The officials took the tablets down from the chariot and made offerings of wine. After the libations had been made the emperor left his sleeping chamber and went to the rebirth building. The courtiers welcomed him with two bows. The emperor entered the building and took off his clothes and shoes. Followed by the boy, he passed thrice under the V-shaped timbers. At each passage the midwife recited some words and stroked the emperor's body. When the boy went through the V-shaped timbers for the seventh time, the emperor lay down by the timbers [?]. The old man struck the quiver and shouted, "A boy is born." Then the head shaman covered the emperor's head. When [the emperor] stood up, the courtiers offered congratulations and bowed twice. The old midwife took the wine from the woman who was holding it and presented it [to the emperor]. The head shaman took some swaddling clothes, colored ribbons, and other objects and recited incantations. Seven previously selected old men, each of whom suggested a name for the emperor [on a document] tied with colored ribbons, all knelt down and offered them. The emperor chose the most auspicious name and received it. After being granted presents [the old men] bowed twice and retired. The

---

[184] The phrase refers to the cycle of twelve years symbolized by the animals of the Duodenary Cycle: the rat, ox, tiger, hare, etc.

[185] According to the context it seems that these timbers were placed inside the rebirth building. See also below, (87), "The emperor entered the rebirth building and performed the rebirth ceremony."

courtiers all offered swaddling clothes, colored ribbons, and other objects. The emperor made obeisance to the images of the former emperors and then gave a feast to the courtiers.   53, 14b–15a

87. THE INVESTITURE CEREMONY

For the Firewood Investiture Ceremony[186] an auspicious day was selected. Before this date a hall and a platform[187] for the Firewood Investiture were set up. For the construction of the platform firewood was piled up high, logs were made into three layers, and the altar was placed on top of it. This was covered by a carpet a hundred feet long and by square cushions decorated with dragons. The rebirth building, that for the emperor's mother, and those for seeking [the emperor][188] were also built.

The emperor entered the rebirth building and performed the rebirth ceremony. When he had finished, the elders of the eight tribes preceded him in front, followed him behind, protected him on the right and left, and invested him in the northeastern corner of the hall. After worshipping the sun he mounted a horse. The oldest men among the imperial maternal relatives were chosen to be his grooms. The emperor galloped off and fell down. The grooms and followers covered him with a felt rug.[189]

---

[186] Firewood (柴) was burned to announce to Heaven an emperor's accession to the throne (see above (5)). Throughout Chinese history high officials were given a tablet or document (册) to confirm their appointment to office. In our text we may therefore translate the word as "investiture," even though, in the present case, the emperor actually ascended the throne several years before the ceremony was performed.

[187] Also called 柴龍 or 籠 (standing for 壟 or 隴) (YPL 16b–17a).

[188] According to YPL 16a–17a, a recognition ceremony was performed as part of the investiture rites by Tao-tsung in the year 1058. The description reads as follows:

On the twenty-third day of the tenth month in the fourth year mou-hsü of Ch'ing-ning [1058] the barbarian emperor together with his followers left Hsüeh Tien 靴甸 [near Tsaghan Khoton, Jehol] for a place some two hundred odd li to the northwest called Yung-hsing Tien 永興甸 where the Firewood Investiture Ceremony was held.

On the first day of the eleventh month the emperor first entered the Small Forbidden Enclosure to stay overnight. On the second day nine men similar in size to the barbarian emperor were first of all selected from among the Ch'i-tan officials. Each was given a suit of the barbarian emperor's clothes and was ordered to don it. The nine men were thus disguised as the barbarian emperor himself. This was not permitted to be disclosed to others. At midnight of the same day these men and the barbarian emperor, to a total number of ten, left the Small Forbidden Enclosure separately and entered the Large Forbidden Enclosure. Each entered a tent which contained only a wax candle and a chair. On the morning of the third day a Ch'i-tan dignitary stood before each tent and then went inside to identify the real emperor. The one who recognized the barbarian emperor was granted a thousand head each of oxen, sheep, camels, and horses. On this day [in 1058] the Prince of Sung [Tao-tsung's brother] recognized the barbarian emperor in the eighth tent. The latter, according to the barbarian ceremony, had to say, "I am not the emperor!" The Prince

of Sung said, "You are the emperor!" They said this in the barbarian language three times; then the barbarian emperor had to say, "It is so."

Afterwards he came out of the tent and put on barbarian ceremonial garments taken from a chest. Then he performed rites in a certain order. First he bowed four times towards the sun; then to the Hall of the Seven Ancestors and the god of Mu-yeh Mountain; then to the god of Metal; then to the emperor's mother; then to the Red Woman [a female deity from whom the Ch'i-tan are said to have sprung]; and then to the family of the seven ancestors. Finally the emperor ascended the firewood platform to receive the tablet of investiture. He then entered the Black Dragon Hall to accept congratulations. The day's ceremonies over, the emperor together with his mother and his father's younger brother left the Large Forbidden Enclosure, making their way to the Small Forbidden Enclosure, where in the evening and until midnight he feasted with his close Ch'i-tan and Chinese officials. Then he retired.

On the fourth day he rested. On the fifth day he went to Hsüeh Tien to receive the presents of the Southern Court [Sung].

The Small Forbidden Enclosure, which was outside the northeastern corner of the Large Forbidden Enclosure, contained two or three felt tents. The Large Forbidden Enclosure was one hundred and ten paces long on each side; in it were ten felt tents and seven black felt military tents. Outside the Large and Small Forbidden Enclosures were ten thousand armored Ch'i-tan soldiers equipped with lances, swords, banners, drums, bows, and arrows. The banners were decorated with the Ch'i-tan word for "army."

[189] This seems to be a survival of an old Inner Asiatic practice. When a Turkish khaghan was invested, he was first carried on a felt blanket which the bearers turned around nine times. After this he mounted a horse and was choked so severely he almost suffocated. While he was still dizzy, his followers asked how long he expected to be khaghan. His reply determined the length of his rule (Chou 50, 4b).

When the emperor reached an elevated place, the high officials and tribal leaders marshalled the ceremonial equipment and made obeisance to him from a distance. Then the emperor sent a messenger to say, "After the death of the late emperor my uncles and elder brothers remain. One who is virtuous should be selected. I am without virtue; how can I manage the administration?"

The dignitaries replied, "Because of the late emperor's generous grace and Your Majesty's brilliant virtue your subjects all wish to be completely loyal to you. How could we presume to have other desires?"

The emperor decreed, "If I must follow what you wish, I will make rewards and punishments honest and clear. When you are meritorious, you will be promoted and given office. When you are guilty of crimes, you will be demoted and discharged. If you submit to my orders, you should execute them faithfully."

All replied, "We will certainly follow the commands of Your Majesty." In the place which was to be commemorated the emperor assembled earth and stones to mark it. Then he went away. He venerated the images of the former emperors and gave a feast for the courtiers.

The next day the emperor came out from the Investiture Hall and was escorted to the platform by the grand guardian of the imperial bodyguard. The ancestral tablets from the seven temples were placed on the square cushions decorated with dragons. The prime ministers of the Northern and Southern Administrations, at the head of the courtiers, stood in a circle, and each raised the carpet by the edges while pronouncing a eulogy. Then the chancellor carried in the imperial jade seal and jade tablet of investiture. An official read from the tablet, after which the chancellor proclaimed the honorific title [of emperor] and offered it [to the emperor]. The courtiers shouted "Ten thousand years" three times and all made obeisance.[190] The prime ministers, the great kings of the Northern and Southern Divisions, and the tribal leaders each offered a flock of cream-colored sheep. The emperor changed his garments and bowed to the images of the emperors. Then he gave a feast to the courtiers and granted them gifts, each according to his rank.   49, 3b–4b

88. THE *AO* WOMAN

According to the old Ch'i-tan custom, during the ceremony of the wedding banquet a woman deserving of respect was chosen to sit in the position of honor.[191] She was called the *ao* woman.
                                                                                                          65, 1b

89. MARRIAGE OF AN EMPEROR

For the ceremony of the marriage of an emperor to an empress, an auspicious day was selected. When the day arrived, the whole clan of the empress [to be] assembled. In the early morning she left her private dwelling and sat in a hall.

---

[190] The ceremony resembles the investiture rite performed in 532 by the Wei emperor, Hsiao-wu. Outside of the capital seven men were covered by a black felt blanket. The emperor standing on the blanket turned west and worshipped Heaven. The custom is said to be based on ancient T'o-pa tradition (PS 5, 9b).

In the second half of the eleventh century a Sung envoy, Li Shih-mei 李士美, once attended a feast given by the Liao emperor in celebration of his investiture. The emperor sat on a bed. Behind him loomed a large form covered with a black bearskin against which the emperor on occasion leaned. At times a human hand or foot was exposed at the base. His curiosity aroused, the envoy inquired regarding these strange sights and learned that the bearskin concealed a number of Ch'i-tan children. When he related the story to Ts'ai T'ao 蔡絛, the latter explained that in this the Ch'i-tan followed the custom of the T'o-pa who covered seven men with a sheet of black felt during the ruler's investiture (TWSTT 2, 12b ff.).

[191] According to Chinese tradition, the word *ao* 奥 designates the southwestern corner of a room where the spirits of the dwelling resided. This explanation, however, does not fully fit the meaning for Liao as, according to LS 116, 9b and 52, 8b–9a, the term *ao* refers to the person who sits at the *ao* place and directs the wedding ceremony. The full title of the *ao* woman was *lüeh-hu-ao* 掠胡奥 in the Ch'i-tan language, or Red Woman (赤孃子) in the Chinese translation. She impersonated the earliest Ch'i-tan ancestress who as the mother of the whole people was worshipped at Mu-yeh Mountain. Whenever an investiture ceremony or a wedding took place she received special reverence (YPL 16b). The *ao* woman obviously acted as her representative.

The emperor sent messengers and the go-between with sacrificial animals, wine and food[192] to the gate [of the empress]. When they were announced by officials entrusted with the matter, the messengers and the go-between entered, made obeisance twice, got up and stood erect. After a moment they made obeisance and offered wine to the empress and then to her parents, relatives, brothers, and cousins, bowing twice after the wine was served. [Wedding] gifts were presented and speeches were delivered. They bowed twice and then the empress' relatives all sat down.

The wife of the *t'i-yin*, bowing four times, invited [the bride] to get on the cart. The empress took her departure, bowing four times to each of her parents, father's brothers and their wives, and elder brothers, and twice to the clan elders.

As the empress ascended the cart, her parents offered wine and gave advice to the empress. [Wine was served] to all the messengers, the go-between, and the escort. As the cart started, her father's brothers and their wives and her elder brothers also offered wine to the empress. Musicians blocked the road and struck up a laudatory air. The empress ordered them to be given presents. Her clan pursued her bowing and offering wine. Then she went on.

When the cart was about to arrive at the gates of the court, the prime ministers passed down an imperial order granting wine to the empress and to the entire escort. When the cart arrived, the *t'i-yin* led the imperial clan to welcome it with two bows. The cart of the empress stopped at a distance of seventy paces southeast of the private hall. The *t'i-yin*'s wife invited her to descend from the cart. The empress, carrying a silver jar on her back and holding a warp-spacer[193] in her hands, walked along a yellow path. Behind her a man held out a lambskin garment as if to cover her. A married woman holding a mirror walked backward in front of her. A saddle was placed on the path, and the empress walked over it.

Then the empress went to the hall of the ancestral tablets and bowed three times. She bowed once towards the south and once toward the north and offered wine. She made obeisance once to those who came to visit, stood up, and then bowed twice. Next she went to the images of her father-in-law and mother-in-law, made obeisance, and offered wine. Towards a woman selected from the imperial clan for her [abundant] offspring she bowed twice and gave her the jar and the warp-spacer.

She also went to the images of all the emperors, made obeisance, and offered wine. The spirits gave her clothing and pearls, jade, and other jewels. Bowing, she accepted them and put them on. The empress' sisters who had bowed with her were each granted presents. Those of the imperial clan who had welcomed the empress and those of her clan who had escorted her were given wine which was drunk by all in pairs.

Then the empress sat in a side hall. Those who had escorted her retired somewhere to eat. The go-between announced an imperial decree ordering the escort to line up in the northern part of the hall. As soon as the emperor ascended the imperial seat, a person worthy of respect was selected from the imperial lineage to take the seat of honor[194] and to direct the marriage ceremony.

The officials entrusted with the matter were ordered to go back and forth and proffer greetings to the empress' clan. Her clan elders, leading her escort, advanced towards the imperial seat and bowed twice. Then they bowed again and, proceeding a little farther, presented a message [to the emperor] concerning the escorting of the empress. Returning to their original positions, they made obeisance twice.

The elders of the empress' clan and the empress' escort bowed three times towards the *ao* woman, once towards the south, and once towards the north, and once again towards the visitors. Kneeling, the elders of the empress' clan greeted the emperor, "Myriads of good luck to Your Majesty." Bowing twice, they again presented the message concerning the empress.

---

[192] In the expression *shêng chiu yung ch'i* 牲酒饔餼 the term *yung ch'i*, which literally means "living and dead sacrificial animals," must refer to sacrificial food in general, for the sacrificial animals are already covered in this expression by the word *shêng*.

[193] According to KHTT, sub 滕, this character means a contrivance to hold the warp in position on the loom. The Palace edition has 縢.

[194] See VII, 2 (88).

The *ao* woman and the go-between served three rounds of wine. The empress' escort was ordered to make obeisance twice. All sat down until the banquet ended.

The next day the emperor rose in the early morning and went to the image of the former emperor to make his obeisance and to offer wine. Then he returned to preside in the hall where he gave a banquet for the empress' clan and all the courtiers. The members of the imperial clan and those of the empress' clan drank wine in pairs as before. All kinds of entertainments, wrestling bouts and horse-racing contests were performed for their enjoyment.

The third day the emperor, presiding in the hall, granted gifts to the empress' clan and to those who had given the empress parting gifts, each of varying value. The recipients made obeisance twice. When the wine was served, they bowed twice again.

Then the emperor presided in the side hall where the officials presented him with a list of the wardrobe of the empress. After the wine was served five times, the escort of the empress made its farewell. The imperial clan offered gifts to the empress' clan. The empress' clan thanked the *ao* woman with presents.

The ceremony was over.   52, 8a–9a

90. MARRIAGE OF A PRINCESS

In the ceremony for the marriage of a princess one of the princess' uncles was appointed as the master of the wedding. The whole ceremony of acting as *ao* woman[195] and as go-between and of delivering speeches, from the presentation of [wedding] gifts to the end of the ritual, was about the same as the ceremony for the marriage of an empress.

An auspicious day was selected. In the early morning the go-between went to the family of the bridegroom. [The bridegroom] proceeded to the court and, waiting until the emperor and empress came to the private hall, led in his clan for an audience. Wine was offered. Then the members of the imperial clan were commanded to drink in pairs with the members of the bridegroom's clan.

The next day the bridegroom's family, with the princess and bridegroom, led in his clan for an audience. They were given a feast by the emperor and empress. The presents of those who had brought farewell gifts were presented. Then they departed from the court.

The princess was presented with two blue-curtained carriages whose dragon-head ornament and covering were both decorated with silver. They were drawn by camels.[196] [She was also given] a funeral carriage whose superstructure was decorated with simple brocade, silver dragons and hanging bells, with a large piece of felt suspended in the rear. It was drawn by oxen and carried a sheep called the "sacrificial sheep." This was supposed to be a funeral object. Even the ceremonial objects to cover the corpse were all there.

The bridegroom was presented with court clothes, suits for the four seasons, and saddles and horses. Everything needed was provided.

A member of the imperial clan was selected to escort them back to his home.[197]   52, 9a–b

---

[195] See note 191.

[196] We follow other editions in reading 馳 for the 馳 of our text.

[197] This passage and the one preceding describe court marriages of the most formal kind, the first that of the emperor himself, the second that of an imperial princess. In both instances Chinese elements conspicuously overlay Ch'i-tan features. No report of a traditional Ch'i-tan marriage is given in the *Liao Shih*, but a number of Sung nationals, who were familiar with the ordinary life of the Ch'i-tan, claim that the latter resorted to elopement or "wife-stealing," a custom which they shared with other non-Chinese peoples of the northeast.

In Pin 賓 Prefecture where the Wu-jo-ch'ê 嗢執者 were settled, interspersed with other groups, young and wealthy Ch'i-tan and Jurchen nobles were in the habit of going out together to a trysting place, racing their horses there, and gambling and drinking. Women and girls in the locality gathered to watch them, joining the young blades in drinking, dancing, and song. If during the festivities a young girl was seduced she followed the young man, a development that met with no opposition on the part of the girl's parents. When a child was born, the couple visited the girl's parents, bringing food and wine in carts. This was called 拜門, "to pay respect to the family." Thereafter the young man was recognized as a son-in-law.

The report concludes with the following statement: "As to their custom, it is said that a marriage determined upon by a man and woman themselves is superior to one which is fixed by the presentation of gifts" (SMCW 6a). This is a version given by Hung Hao, who visited the Chin

91. FUNERAL CEREMONIES

When Shêng-tsung died,[198] Hsing-tsung lamented at the funeral hall.[199]   On the night preceding the transfer of the coffin [to the mausoleum], when the fourth drum[200] had been struck, the emperor led the courtiers in and offered libations thrice before the coffin.   The coffin was taken out through the northwestern gate of the hall and was placed on a hearse.   It was covered with a plain mat. The shamans purified it [from evil spirits].   At dawn the next morning the funeral cortege went to the sacrificial place.   Libations were offered five times.   The head shaman offered up prayers. The imperial clan, the relatives of the empress, high officials, and all the officials of the capitals made

territory in 1129, shortly after the fall of the Liao dynasty. The story is vague as to the nationality of the girls, but since the young men, Ch'i-tan and Jurchen, were eager to establish themselves as the accepted husbands of their newly chosen mates, it must be concluded that marriage by elopement was not only recognized but proper. CTKC 26, 2b–3a, which deals with this subject, uses almost identical words although only Ch'i-tan males are referred to, probably because the Ch'i-tan were the subject of this work. And similarly SCPMHP 3, 4b, which treats of Jurchen life and manners, gives the story without mentioning the Ch'i-tan.

Hung Hao also notes the custom of wife-stealing in the region of Yen from the days of Liao on. A young man who had been accepted by a girl "stole" her in the middle of the first month. If she wished to stay with him she was permitted to do so (SMCW 15a).

Wên Wei-chien, who lived at the beginning of the Chin dynasty, observed the same custom, but his account differs slightly from those just given. In accordance with a Ch'i-tan tradition and without any successful opposition on the part of the officials, wife-stealing was freely indulged in throughout the sixteenth day of the first month. A girl who had accompanied her family for a stroll or one whose family was staying at a lonely place might well be kidnapped. After at least a month had elapsed, her abductor informed the girl's parents of their daughter's whereabouts and formally married her by offering the ceremonial presents (LTSS 48b; cf. Stein 39, 145 ff.).

Wife-stealing seems to have been a long-established custom among the Ch'i-tan and related tribes. In its description of the Shih-wei, significantly attached to that of the Ch'i-tan, the *Sui Shu* states that after the two families had come to an understanding the young man was supposed to steal and carry off his bride (Sui 84, 21a).

Without reference to wife-stealing, but with specific mention of the Ch'i-tan nationality of the women, a Sung poet, Chiang K'uei 姜夔 (fl. in the twelfth century) gives a description of a spring festival similar to that described above for Pin Prefecture. When the peonies bloomed in Yün-sha 雲沙, Ch'i-tan men, both young and old, danced, played on their guitars, and flirted with Ch'i-tan girls (PSTJSC 1, 12).

[198] Shêng-tsung's funeral is also described in the inscription found in his mausoleum (MCCSC 1, 45a–b).

[199] This is the only systematic description of the imperial funeral ceremonies appearing in the *Liao Shih*. However, numerous other passages, mainly in the first chronological section, supplement and to some degree modify the picture given here.

The chronological section, the *pên chi*, clearly indicates

that a relatively long time elapsed between the death of an emperor and his burial.   During this period the body usually lay in state in a coffin in some hall (Shêng-tsung's rested at T'ai-p'ing Hall) before being finally transferred to the funeral hall near the mausoleum.   In general, the period lasted some five or six months, but after T'ai-tsu's death thirteen months elapsed before burial; after Hsing-tsung's three; no mention is made of the interval after Shih-tsung and Mu-tsung were murdered.   Shêng-tsung died in 1031 in the sixth month of the Liao calendar; his funeral took place in the eleventh month, that is, six months later (the year having an intercalary month which fell between the regular tenth and eleventh months).   The delay made the preservation of the body a necessity; embalming devices were used for this purpose (CWTS 137, 11a–b; WTS 72, 19b; see below, note 215).

The description of Shêng-tsung's funeral contained in LS 50 refers only to the final ceremonies.   The recording, while somewhat stylized, notes certain important details that are not mentioned in the *pên chi*.   According to LS 17, 8b and 18, 1b ff., Shêng-tsung died on the third day of the sixth month in a traveling camp.   On the nineteenth day his body was placed in a coffin in T'ai-p'ing Hall 太平殿.   In the seventh month a mourning procession of the imperial relatives led by the emperor's widow went to T'ai-p'ing Hall.   (Ch'ing 慶 Prefecture had been chosen as the site for Shêng-tsung's mausoleum, and special families were dispatched there to care for and guard it.)

A portrait of the late emperor had been ordered and his son, the new emperor, Hsing-tsung, lamented before it. Ten days later he visited the T'ai-p'ing Hall and burned his father's bow(s) and arrows.   In the eighth month the coffin was taken to the funeral hall.   In the ninth month on the third day Hsing-tsung visited the mausoleum; on the thirteenth day certain objects [funeral presents?] were burned in the funeral hall.   Meanwhile messengers had notified the courts of the neighboring states who sent emissaries to present condolences and funeral gifts.   In the intercalary tenth month the emperor Hsing-tsung visited the funeral hall and examined the funeral paraphernalia.   In the eleventh month on the nineteenth day he led the officials in a libation ceremony in the funeral hall.   Shêng-tsung's favorite clothes were burned, eagles and falcons were released (VII, 2 (54)).   On the twenty-first day Shêng-tsung's body was placed in the mausoleum. The next day a sacrifice was offered to Heaven and Earth. On the third day following the final burial Hsing-tsung visited the mausoleum and distributed the personal effects of his father to all the officials.

[200] Between one and two o'clock in the morning.

offerings according to their rank.   Then clothes, bows, arrows, saddles, bridles, pictures,[201] horses, camels, imperial equipment, and other objects were all burned.

The coffin went to the mausoleum and was entombed.   Then an epitaph was offered up.   The emperor presided in a tent.   Ordering a fire to be made,[202] he faced the fire, made a libation, and bowed thrice.   Then he faced east and bowed twice to Heaven and Earth.   He mounted a horse and led the funeral company through the logs of the divine gate.[203]   Then he dismounted and bowed twice toward the east.

The next day, early in the morning, the emperor led the courtiers and titled ladies to the mausoleum to perform the first libation ceremony.   Ascending the hall of the deceased emperor's image, he received[204] the objects bequeathed [by the latter].

On the third day the second libation ceremony was performed as before.

After the death of Hsing-tsung, Tao-tsung personally selected the place for burial.   When Tao-tsung died, the coffin was placed in Yu-hsien Hall.[205]   The officials presented the funeral clothes. Emperor T'ien-tsu asked the general functionary of the Han-lin Academy, Yeh-lü Ku,[206] about the ritual.   The emperor for the first time donned the [Chinese] unhemmed mourning garments.   The imperial clan, the maternal clan, the military and civil ministers, the officials of the lower platform,[207] and the court nobles were similarly dressed.   Other officials as well as the servitors all wore white linen and caps.   They entered and lamented.

The t'i-yin, the Three Patriarchal Households, the prime minister of the Southern Administration, the ch'ang-kun[208] of the Yao-lien [tents], the court nobles of the nine hsi-shou,[209] the i-li-pi, the hsiang-wên of the Maternal Uncles, the court nobles of the ten cha-sa,[210] the great king of the Southern Division, and the court nobles, each according to his rank, made libations and offered saddled horses, clothing, belts decorated with rhinoceros [horn?] and jade, and other objects.   The items were enumerated in a list.   After being read, the list was burned.   The funeral equipment and clothing contributed by the various states and the various objects presented for the funeral and sacrifices by the imperial princes and vicegerents of all the capitals were treated in the same way.

The day before the deceased emperor's preliminary dressing[211] the emperor, wearing funeral clothes, offered incense and a libation and lamented.   During the night the chancellor of the Northern Division

---

[201] The passage may also be translated as "pictures showing horses and camels . . . ," but our interpretation is suggested by a number of parallel texts (VII, 2 (43) (58); VII, 1 (33)) all of which mention the killing of animals as a funeral custom.   The government tried to suppress the custom in 992, and again in 1043.   Whether the prohibition referred also to the imperial funeral is not said, but it is probable that it did, for after Tao-tsung's death only a list of horses and objects was burned (see our text below).   The burning of animals is reported for Inner Asia as early as the third century A.D.   At that time the Wu-wan 烏丸 are said to have burned horses, clothing, and other objects belonging to a deceased person during the funeral ceremony (SKC, Wei 30, 2b).   In post-Liao time the Mongols are reported to have burned horses on similar occasions (TMT 3, 27b).

[202] 改火 is a literary expression for making a fire by rubbing sticks together.   The kind of wood used was changed according to the season (LYCS 17, 5a).

[203] See VII, 2 (85).

[204] The 受 of the text probably is an error for 授.   LS 18, 3a relates that Hsing-tsung "granted" (賜) the bequeathed objects to his courtiers.   After Tao-tsung's death a similar procedure was followed: T'ien-tsu granted (授) the bequeathed objects to relatives and officials.

[205] The name of this hall appears in Tao-tsung's epitaph as Hsien-yu 僊遊 (LLSKCL 3, 6b; see fig. 10).

[206] Yeh-lü Ku 固 was ordered by Hsi-tsung 熙宗 of Chin 金 to compile a history of Liao, but the assignment was not completed.   His student, Hsiao Yung-ch'i 永祺, finished it (cf. CS 125, 7a).

[207] A description of a picture (Liao P'ai-pan T'u 遼排班圖) notes that officials from prime ministers to a-cha-ko-chih 阿札割只 stood on high, low, or square platforms according to their rank when attending ceremonies.   Such officials were called 墩官, "platform officials" (cf. LS 116, 12a).

[208] See XIV, 1 (20).

[209] According to LS 116, 14a, hsi-shou 奚首 is the name of a cantonment or tent, and therefore the nine hsi-shou may mean the nine tents of the Yao-lien lineage.

[210] A tribal subdivision called cha-sa 閘撒 is mentioned in LS 31, 2a (XV, 1 (3)).   The ordos are said to have had nineteen cha-sa attached to them.   The nature of these units is not clear (see XV, introduction).   Does our passage refer to the cha-sa of the ordos?   If so, it may originally have read "nineteen" instead of "ten."   Errors of this kind are not infrequent in Chinese texts.

[211] The ceremony called hsiao lien 小斂, the preliminary ceremonial dressing of the corpse, was usually followed by the ta lien 大斂 ceremony when the body of the deceased was finally dressed and prepared for the coffin.   See Couvreur 13 I, 151 note.

and the chief controller of the Ch'i-tan traveling camps came in for the ceremony of preliminary dressing.

The next day the vice-chancellor of the Northern Division and the scribe were ordered to put the funeral equipment and clothes in the funeral palace.

The coffin was placed on a cart which the imperial princes pushed to the place where a ram was offered.[212] It was an old custom of the Liao empire to slaughter a ram here as a sacrifice. The imperial clan, the relatives of the empress, and the officials of the capitals and prefectures offered sacrifices according to their rank. After they arrived at the burial place, the coffin was taken down from the cart and placed on a sedan chair. The emperor took off the mourning dress and went ahead of the coffin on foot to Ch'ang-fu Hill.

During this night the emperor entered the mausoleum and granted the objects bequeathed by the deceased emperor to the imperial clan, the relatives of the empress, and high officials. Then they came out.[213] It was ordered that the former emperor's sleeping tent be passed through the logs of the divine gate which was in front of the mausoleum. The emperor did not go personally but sent a close attendant dressed in regular court clothes.

In the first libation the emperor and the empress led the imperial clan, the consort clan, the military and civil ministers, the commanding prefects, and the titled ladies from the rank of fu-jên[214] up in making obeisance and offering sacrifice. They went twice around the mausoleum and then descended. Libations were made again as before. They took their departure from the mausoleum and returned.[215]   50, 1a–2b

---

[212] Literally, "eaten," but the next sentence shows that the ram was a sacrificial offering. According to the glossary (LS 116, 14a), when the emperor's coffin started out for the mausoleum, officials offered a ram as sacrifice on the road.

[213] The Liao mausoleums were probably kept open even after the coffin had been placed in them. Hu Chiao reports that Shih-tsung and some of his dignitaries once carried sacrificial utensils into a mausoleum. The door was then shut and kept shut until the next morning. This was called "the ceremony of throwing away the goblets" (抛盞禮). The Ch'i-tan refused to tell Hu Chiao the significance of this ceremony (WTS 73, 7b–8a). A number of other passages in the Liao Shih confirm the story that the new emperor visited the mausoleum of his predecessors (LS 3, 3b, 5a, 6a; 10, 3b, 5a; 18, 9a; 19, 4b; 20, 6b; 21, 2b, 4b, 5a; 23, 6a; 24, 3a–b).

[214] According to CS 57, 1b, the fu-jên 夫人 equalled the fifth rank of the Chin hierarchy.

[215] According to the Chinese records, Ch'i-tan funeral customs changed greatly from predynastic to dynastic times. The Sui Shu relates that the Ch'i-tan considered a man who cried over his parents' death a weakling. They placed the corpse on a tree in the mountains; after three years they collected the bones and burned them. They then spilled wine and prayed: "During the winter months [you] eat facing the sunlight. When I am hunting, help me to obtain many boars and deer!" (Sui 84, 19b ff.). WTS 72, 4b, with a few modifications, repeats this description which certainly was considered valid for the Ch'i-tan people of the first half of the tenth century, and perhaps even later. (The Wu-tai Shih-chi was composed in the second half of the eleventh century.)

When the old traditions began to change, it is difficult to say. Our text shows the imperial funeral pattern strongly permeated with Chinese culture elements; but,

to judge from other instances of Liao acculturation and from the funeral customs observed during the Mongol period, Chinese influence was probably strongest at the court and among the nobles, whereas the tribal commoners in the main still followed their national customs.

In 927 T'ai-tsu was buried in Tsu Prefecture. In this region a square dolmen was found at the foot of modern Mount Monchok which is said to be his tomb (see fig. 25). After T'ai-tsung's death in 947 his corpse was opened and filled with salt to preserve it. The Chin 晉 people called this procedure 帝羓 (WTS 72, 19b), literally "imperial dried meat." Filling a body with salt had been practised previously in China (NS 80, 25a; cf. de Groot, RSC II, 371); whether the Liao technique was modelled after the Chinese or a national pattern, we do not dare to decide.

In 1055 a Liao envoy who returned from the Sung court died in Hua 滑 Prefecture. His corpse was hung upside down so that the waste ran out through the mouth and nose. In addition, the flesh was drained by stalks of straw which pierced the skin. The corpse was then treated with white alum in order to shrink it. Actually only the bones were carried home. Embalming was confined to persons of noble rank; the corpses of the lowly were simply burned (HJC 2a; HML 33b).

According to the Chin scholar, Wên Wei-chien, the Ch'i-tan continued to embalm upper class persons even after 1125. When a Ch'i-tan of wealth or rank died, his abdomen was cut open, the intestines removed, and the corpse after being cleansed and filled with aromatic herbs, salt, and alum, was sewed up with a five-colored wire thread. The flesh was then drained with stalks of straw. When this was done, the face was covered with a mask made of gold and silver and the hands and feet were tied together with copper wire (LTSS 49a).

Whether the burning of the dead is a continuation of an

FIG. 23. Chinese inscription from an octagonal stone found at Ch'ing-chou, recording the establishment of Shêng-tsung's mother as regent (Torii 36 II, pl. 129).

FIG. 24. Interior of Tao-tsung's tomb (Torii 36 IV, pl. 259).

FIG. 25. Dolmen-like stone chamber found at foot of Mt. Monchok. According to Torii, "closely associated with the tomb of the founder of the Liao dynasty" (Torii 36 II, pl. 88).

FIG. 26.   Three views of a wooden dog found at the entrance to Tao-tsung's tomb (Torii 36 IV, pl. 262).

FIG. 27.   Pottery discovered in the imperial Liao tombs at War-manha (Torii 36 IV, pl. 302).

92. HONORING THE EMPEROR'S DEATH PLACE

After the accession of an emperor, for the people captured from rebellious countries during military campaigns, persons offered by officials, and criminals seized as government families, the emperor personally inspected vacant fields and established prefectures and counties to settle them and set up officials to manage their affairs. And, after the death[216] of an emperor, households [of retainers] were assigned, and a treasury for money as well as a depot for grain was set up. Within the domed tent a small felt hall was built; gold images of the deceased emperor, empress, and concubines[217] were cast and placed in it.[218] On all festivals, anniversaries of imperial deaths, and the first and fifteenth days of each month sacrifices were offered up in front of the domed tent.

---

old tribal custom or whether the old custom was modified or completely altered under Buddhist influence, we do not know. There is evidence that in the Liao empire Chinese officials, and perhaps even commoners, burned their dead; they certainly followed the Buddhist practice which during this period was widely accepted in China Proper. In the city of Mukden a stone coffin has been discovered which, according to the attached inscription, received in 1027 the remains of a certain Sun Yün-chung 孫允中. The coffin is only three feet long, one foot high in the front, and nine and a half inches wide. It contained an earthen vessel, probably for ashes, and two stone idols, but no bones (MCCSC 1, 41b). No details are given regarding a stone coffin of the same date, that of a woman called Ts'ai 蔡 discovered in Jehol (op. cit., 41a), or the one found at the site of the Liao Supreme Capital (Torii 36 I, pl. 17).

In the Chin 金 dynasty it was still the custom to burn the dead (HNYL 149, 2405). A stone coffin discovered in Nung-an 農安 County, Kirin, is said to belong to Chao Ching-hsing 趙京興 who was buried in 1182. The coffin is one foot, four inches in height and one foot, eight inches in width (MCCSC 3, 25a–b).

The mausoleums of the emperors are located in four different regions: (1) that of T'ai-tsu at Tsu Prefecture; (2) of T'ai-tsung and his son Mu-tsung at Huai Prefecture; (3) of Shih-tsung and his son Ching-tsung at Hsien and Ch'ien Prefectures; (4) of Shêng-tsung, Hsing-tsung, and Tao-tsung at Ch'ing Prefecture (see fig. 24). All seem to have been built on the slopes of high mountains.

The mausoleums of Shêng-tsung, Hsing-tsung, and Tao-tsung have been excavated. Each tomb resembles a mound and is built of bricks. The dome has windows which were blocked up with rocks. The walls are decorated with murals depicting clouds, mountains, water, deer, and human figures. Within the chambers idols and dogs, pottery and stone tablets with carved Chinese and Ch'i-tan inscriptions are found (see figs. 1, 6, 7, 8, 26, 27, and Torii 36 III and IV, passim).

The presence of Chinese and Ch'i-tan figures and wooden idols both outside and within the Liao mausoleums reveals the strength of Chinese customs at the Liao court and also the outstanding position of Buddhism at that court. However, the strength of Ch'i-tan tradition is demonstrated by the use of Ch'i-tan words above the portraits of high officials which were painted inside the tombs of deceased rulers (see LS 18, 2a).

According to WTS 73, 3a ff. and CTKC 13, 1b ff., human sacrifice was still practised on a large scale in 926: when T'ai-tsu died over a hundred courtiers were buried in his mausoleum. Owing in part to Buddhist influence the practice seems to have been gradually weakened.

Were the Ch'i-tan emperors and nobles eventually burned or were their mummified bodies left untouched? Neither the written records nor archaeology answers this question. In Tao-tsung's mausoleum four skulls were found (Torii 36 IV, pls. 274–277). Did they belong to the bodies of the emperor and his wives or were they the remains of all or only some of the courtiers who had been buried alive. The original arrangement was evidently destroyed by the robbers who, in the Chin period, opened the tombs (CHC 3, 13a).

Chinese influence though revealed in many features of the imperial funeral ceremony did not cause the abandonment of Ch'i-tan customs. Nor did it lead to a strict observance of the newly adopted traits. Contrary to Chinese custom, a Sung envoy, Lu Tien 陸佃, was welcomed by music on the anniversary of an imperial death. Furthermore, while proceeding homeward, Lu Tien noted that the Liao officials, who accompanied him did not change their dress, but merely blackened the bright parts of their hats for a few days. One high official who failed to remove the black covering was laughed at by other members of the escort (CSCW 2a–b; see also a different version in SS 343, 14b).

[216] Judging from two similar passages in CTKC 23, 3b and WHTK 346, 2711, the word 所 seems to be superfluous.

[217] Metal or stone images of the Liao emperors or empresses were also made in the capitals and prefectures. For instance, in the Supreme Capital there were images of the Ch'i-tan ancestors of the predynastic period and of Liao emperors of various generations (LS 37, 4a). In Tsu Prefecture there was a silver image of T'ai-tsu (op. cit., 6a). In I-k'un Prefecture there were silver images of T'ai-tsu and his wife (op. cit., 10a). In 1062 Hua-yen 華嚴 Temple was built in the Western Capital, in which stone and bronze images of the former emperors were placed (LS 41, 2a). According to SHTC 37, 40a, these images could still be found in the western part of Ta-t'ung 大同 City, Shansi, during the Ch'ing dynasty. There were five stone figures, three male and two female, and six bronze figures, four male and two female. One of them, resembling an emperor with a crown and majestic garments, was seated with legs hanging; the others wearing only caps and ordinary clothes were in a standing position.

[218] This passage can also be translated: "The [new] emperor, empress, and concubines all cast gold images [of the deceased emperor] and placed them in it."

The earth was also built up into a platform more than ten feet high.   On it a large plate was placed for offering sacrifice; wine and food were spread out on it and burned.   According to the national custom, this was called the Burning Festival.[219]   49, 6a

93. CEREMONIAL HUNT

The La [Ceremony][220] was held on the *ch'ên* day of the *la* twelfth month.   On the day before, the officials in charge of the hunt were ordered to choose the hunting ground.   On the day *ch'ên* the emperor and the empress burned incense and bowed to the sun.   After this was finished, the battue was organized, the hunters being ordered to spread out to the left and right wings.   The officials in charge of the hunt reported that the formation was completed.   Then the emperor and the empress ascended a carriage.   The *ti-lieh-ma-tu* offered up two cups of wine and a plate of food, and the officials from the great kings of the Northern and Southern Divisions down presented horses and clothes [to the emperor and empress].

After the emperor had descended from the carriage and offered sacrifice to the east, he mounted a horse and entered the beaten area.   The heir apparent and imperial princes led the courtiers to offer wine to the emperor and then went forth in two wings.

When the emperor first caught a hare, the courtiers offered wine and toasted him.   Each in turn was granted wine.   On arriving somewhere for lunch, the imperial princes and high officials each presented their catch.   [After the emperor and empress] had drunk, the courtiers were granted wine.   Then they returned to the court.   51, 1b

94. HUNTING CLOTHES

The emperor wore a cap and armor as a military costume and had ermine or goose-neck and duck-head [feathers] as a loin-protector.   Leading officials in the various barbarian and Chinese offices all wore military costumes.   Their clothes, all of which fastened on the left side,[221] were dark green in color.   56, 3a

95. A SUCCESSFUL DIVINER

[Yeh-lü I-pu-ko[222]] once selected a burial spot for a man.   He said, "After three days there will pass by an ox riding on a man pursuing another ox.   You may then open up the ground."   When the day came there actually was a man who passed by carrying a new-born calf on his back and pulling a cow.   The man said, "This must be the prediction of an ox riding on a man."   Then he opened up the ground.   After the burial good and bad fortune was entirely as predicted.

He also divined for a man who had lost an eagle, saying, "The eagle is perched on an elm-tree west of a pond thirty *li* northeast of your home."   The man proceeded to search for it there and really did find it.   At that time he made no prophecy which was not fulfilled.   108, 2b

---

[219] The ceremony of Burning Food (*shao-fan* 燒飯) was also held by the Jurchen of the pre-Chin (SCPMHP 3, 5a) and the Chin (CS 85, 2b) periods and by the Mongols (TMT 3, 27b).   This ceremony was performed not only at funerals but on other occasions as well.   A report of 1140 under the Chin dynasty states that if the Liao emperor visited the Southern Capital, Yen, on the first day of the tenth month or during six other festivals, food was to be burned by the metropolitan officials (TCCL 38, 318).   According to Wang Kuo-wei, the term *shao-fan* originated in the Liao-Chin period.   It is his opinion that the ceremony is perpetuated in the modern custom of sending away a deceased person's spirit, *sung-san* 送三 (KTCL 16, 18b–19a).

[220] See note 170.

[221] Unlike Chinese clothes which fasten on the right side.

[222] Yeh-lü I-pu-ko 乙不哥 was a descendant of the Six Divisions.   He was skilled in divination and was fond of books, but disliked being an official (*cf.* LS 108, 2b).

SECTION VIII

POWERFUL FAMILIES AND INDIVIDUALS

INTRODUCTION

1. "POWERFUL FAMILIES" IN BUREAUCRATIC SOCIETIES

Powerful (*hao* 豪) families and individuals are frequently mentioned in Chinese historical records. The early history of the term does not concern us here but, after the beginning of imperial China, the word *hao*, either alone or in combination,[1] always designated persons of economic, political, social, and personal independence. The "powerful ones" were contemplated with awe by the masses, for on occasion they acted independently of and even contrary to official intent. Almost without exception these people were not in office although most of them were members of the scholarly bureaucracy. At times acting officials were also designated as "powerful and distinguished" (*hao chieh* 豪傑); they then became the targets of government policy rather than its agents.[2]

In a simple bureaucratic society all power rests in the state and its officials.[3] Where the society is more complex, conditions may favor the development of independent economic and political nuclei either within the government machine or outside of it.[4] But whether these nuclei remain part of the ruling bureaucracy or not, their centrifugal tendencies threaten the central government which in turn must block, or at least restrain, their independent movements. The ability to control these centrifugal "private" tendencies[5] is an index of the stability and strength of a bureaucratic society.

2. POWERFUL FAMILIES IN A DYNASTY OF CONQUEST

The powerful families, who played an important role in the history of the typically Chinese dynasties, were also a significant factor in the dynasties of conquest, not excluding the none too well assimilated Liao. Here their specific character and status were determined by the conquest situation and the tribal background of the ruling group. The descriptive material at our disposal is very limited; yet it is possible to reconstruct in rough outline the position and function of the various types of powerful families within Liao society.

a. PO–HAI AND CHINESE

Even among those peoples who had been subdued by the Ch'i-tan, the powerful families still maintained some influence. Their former ruling class was, no doubt, looked upon with suspicion by the central government. When the first emperor of the Ch'in dynasty (221–209 B.C.) unified China, he brought the powerful families of the defeated feudal states into his capital.[6] More than a thousand years later the Ch'i-tan conquerors followed his example and resettled the great and important families of the Po-hai kingdom in the Central Capital[7] where the government could more easily control them.

The coordination of the Chinese into the new political system was less abrupt and less violent. The administrative skill of their ruling bureaucracy was frequently utilized by the expanding Liao empire, and new opportunities favored the rise of powerful families in the Chinese tradition; yet the inferior position of the Chinese within the conquest society restricted their growth and influence.

The wealth of the families of retired officials or of potential ones (in reality often two sides of the same coin) is indicated in a number of records.[8] Shih Li-ai's 時立愛 father was "the outstanding man of his community because of his wealth."[9] In a crisis he wrote off old debts and opened his granary to the poor, but, when conditions were normal, he made loans from his accumulated property.[10] The position enjoyed by the two retired officials who aided the government in giving relief[11] must have been more or less similar. Families of such men may have done business with the *yün-wei* families, who constituted a marginal type of economically influential people. But the two groups differed widely in professional interest as well as in social status. The "business families" had to

---

[1] *Cf.* SC 6, 13*b*; HS 92, 1*b*; SC 122, 2*a*; HS 92, 2*a*; SC 30, 3*a*.

[2] See HS 6, 28*a* ff.

[3] See Wittfogel 38, 103.

[4] *Op. cit.*, 110 ff.

[5] *Op. cit.*, 112 ff.

[6] SC 6, 13*b*.

[7] VIII (2).

[8] See VIII (10) (11); and CS 78, 6*b*.

[9] *Loc. cit.*

[10] *Loc. cit.*

[11] XII (85).

render labor service,[12] while the members of the literary bureaucracy were usually exempted from this onerous duty.[13] The former were excluded by law from participating in the official examinations, while the latter were expected and encouraged to take them.[14]

b. CH'I-TAN "POWERFUL FAMILIES"

The "powerful families" of Ch'i-tan provenience differed as widely from the Chinese *hao chia* 豪家 as a complex tribal despotism differed from a complex Chinese bureaucratic society. Tribal wealth and power were fluid. Those who possessed them did not hesitate to strive openly for supreme power, but they soon discovered how firmly that supreme power was held by the emperor.[15] The ruling lineages and the court nobles were more than ready to mulct and plunder the new state, but they continued to use, or abuse, their rank and power in a typically pastoral way. The members of the imperial clan took advantage of their status to "encroach upon the common people,"[16] a formula that may refer to the seizure of land as well as to the acquisition of families.

Influential persons, whose position is not specified, converted registered commoners into personal retainers.[17] Similar action is recorded for the temples[18] as well as for a tribal chieftain who also robbed the people of their movable property.[19] Those activities of the imperial clan that aroused government criticism may well have been, in whole or in part, of this kind.

Land was given to the Buddhist clergy, but their right to ownership might be contested by people of still greater power and influence. An inscription tells of pressure exerted by certain powerful people (*hao min* 豪民) which led to the withdrawal of fertile wheat fields from the temple lands and their transformation into pastures.[20] Although the inscription does not specify the nationality of these powerful individuals, the conversion of the arable land into pastures makes their Ch'i-tan origin highly probable. LS 97, 3a notes that an influential Yeh-lü openly demanded valuable grazing grounds.[21]

The imperial princesses "borrowed" regularly from the important Office of Money and Silk of Ch'ang-ch'un Prefecture;[22] an official who refused them a loan had to defend his action against "many spiteful remarks."[23] The Hsiao clansman who took several hundred bushels of grain from the state granaries without permission[24] is an even more blatant example of undisguised plunder.

The imperial courtiers and the tribal nobles also abused their position, although their derelictions were of lesser degree. Some destroyed cultivated fields while satisfying their passion for hunting.[25] Certain officials lent money to the tribes, a practice that must have been politically undesirable, for the government tried to stop it.[26] A high territorial officer might compel the local population to herd "his family's oxen, sheep, camels, and horses."[27]

In most reported instances the government criticized and endeavored to suppress the "centrifugal" use of position and influence. In the main, the texts and inscriptions emphasize the effectiveness of the restrictive measures, but nevertheless there are many cases when members of the two ruling clans, who had violated the law, were pardoned illegally because of favoritism or bribes.[28] It is, therefore, difficult to say how vigorously the government policy was carried out and how satisfactorily it stabilized the general situation. Its varying success must be viewed in relation to the rise and decay of the dynastic power of Liao as a whole.

3. DIGNITARIES, GOOD AND BAD

Objectively, the society's centripetal tendencies can be inferred from the numerous government decrees and acts. Subjectively, they were expressed in the wariness of the court and its loyal officials on the one hand, and in the cooperative, "virtuous," and "frugal" attitudes of certain powerful families or individuals on the other. The retired Chinese officials who supported the local government in an emergency and the high Yeh-lü and Hsiao dignitaries who practised and promoted "righteousness" and "frugality"[29] exemplify these two aspects.

The model dignitaries were neither ascetics nor impoverished hangers-on. Hsiao Hui enjoyed a satisfactory emolument from the government, and owned more than a thousand slaves.[30] Shih Li-ai's father,

---

[12] VI, 2 (1).
[13] CS 47, 15a.
[14] Cf. VII and XIV, introductions.
[15] See XIII.
[16] VIII (8).
[17] VIII (3).
[18] See CS 96, 4b.
[19] MCCSC 2, 29a.
[20] LWT 5, 22a.
[21] II, 1 (19).

[22] See XIV, 2 (10); cf. also X, introduction.
[23] X, 1 (57).
[24] VIII (6).
[25] II, 2 (27).
[26] VI, 2 (4).
[27] MCCSC 2, 28a.
[28] XIV, 2 (2).
[29] VIII (4) (5) (7).
[30] VIII (7).

who had his own granary, was rich enough to engage in lending activities.[31] But a status such as theirs was obviously considered normal, and the country's economic system seems to have been adapted, either actually or at least theoretically, to their enterprise and income. These men represented the economic and political golden mean[32] as against the unchecked greed of the "powerful families" whose "centrifugal" activities contributed to the weakening and final collapse of the Liao empire.

---

[31] CS 78, 6b.

[32] For a description of this phenomenon in China *cf.* Weber 20, 345.

TRANSLATION

POWERFUL FAMILIES AND INDIVIDUALS

1. Conditions under Ching-tsung 2. Powerful Po-hai families 3. People forced to become retainers 4. A model Yeh-lü dignitary 5. A model Hsiao dignitary 6. Venality of an Imperial Maternal Uncle 7. Slaves held by a frugal dignitary 8. Encroachment by the imperial clan 9. Overbearing courtiers 10. How wealthy should a high official be? 11. Wealth acquired in three months of premiership 12. Rank bought by powerful tribesmen

1. CONDITIONS UNDER CHING–TSUNG

969–978   The grand prime minister, Kao Hsün, and the chief controller of the Ch'i-tan traveling camps, Nü-li,[1] relying on the emperor's favor, knew no restraints, and the influence of the emperor's aunt and nurse-mother was overwhelming for a time. What with persons coming to offer bribes and to ask for interviews, the doorways were like market places.   79, 2b

2. POWERFUL PO–HAI FAMILIES

983–1011   Ta Kung-ting[2] was a Po-hai man whose ancestors were registered as natives of Shuai-pin County[3] in Liao-yang. During the T'ung-ho period the powerful and influential families of Liao-tung were removed to fill up the Central Capital. Hence he made his home at Ta-ting.[4]   105, 1a–b

3. PEOPLE FORCED TO BECOME RETAINERS

995

951–969   On the day ping-hsü [of the fourth month in the thirteenth year of T'ung-ho] it was decreed that the people of the various circuits who had been forced to become retainers since the Ying-li period should again be registered in the prefectures and counties.   13, 6a

4. A MODEL YEH–LÜ DIGNITARY

1032–1052   [Yeh-lü] I-hsien[5] constantly admonished his clansmen, "[The members of] the Three Patriarchal Households of our country, since they are all brothers of the emperor, especially may not behave without filial piety or righteousness." In dealing with inferiors he paid no regard to nobility or baseness, virtue or imperfection, but treated them all in the same manner. His wife, the daughter of the eldest princess of Chin,[6] whenever she encountered her cousins, would not see them unless she wore formal clothes. As a result, the close and distant [relatives] were largely transformed.   90, 2a–b

5. A MODEL HSIAO DIGNITARY

Ca. 1037   [Hsiao] Hsiao-mu,[7] even though he was a relative of the empress, became more apprehensive the higher he rose in position. Whenever the empress extended grants to him, he always refused to accept them. His wife and sons did not have a haughty appearance. His friendship toward a person remained always the same. The persons whom he recommended were all loyal and straightforward officials.   87, 2a

---

[1] Nü-li's 女里 family background is unknown. He assisted Ching-tsung to ascend the throne. He was executed in 978.

[2] Ta Kung-ting 大公鼎 was one of those officials whose assistance enabled the Liao government to crush the Po-hai rebellion of 1116. He died in 1121.

[3] Near Chin 錦 County, Liaoning.

[4] Another name for the Central Capital.

[5] Yeh-lü I-hsien 義先 was a descendant of the Third Patriarchal Household. He died at the age of forty-two.

[6] Yen-mu-chin 嚴母菫, the second daughter of Shêng-tsung.

[7] Hsiao Hsiao-mu 孝穆, a brother of Empress Ch'in-ai, suppressed a Po-hai rebellion and was appointed vicegerent of the Eastern Capital in 1030. In 1037 he became the northern chancellor. He was a strong advocate of peace between Liao and Sung. He wrote a work entitled *Pao-lao Chi* 寶老集. He died in 1042 (LS 87, 1a ff.).

6. VENALITY OF AN IMPERIAL MATERNAL UNCLE

1055–1065   In the beginning of the Ch'ing-ning period [Hsiao Chu-chê[8]], who was *hsiang-wên* of the Imperial Maternal Uncles and punitive commissioner of the Northwestern Route, embezzled three hundred bushels of government grain. When he was replaced he left some livestock behind and had the men in charge sell it to make compensation. Later [Hsiao] Hu-tu, his cousin of the same lineage, went to the government office and revealed his activities. The emperor, becoming angry, punished him with a large stick and deprived him of his official positions.   91, 2*b*

7. SLAVES HELD BY A FRUGAL DIGNITARY

Before 1056   [Hsiao] Hui[9] was generous by nature but frugal and simple in his own expenditures. Once, when Hsing-tsung urged Hui to take whatever treasures he desired, Hui said, "As an imperial relative I hold an important position. My emoluments are sufficient to maintain my integrity.[10] My male and female slaves number more than a thousand. This is not insufficient. If Your Majesty gives me still more grants, how will you treat those who are poorer than I?"   93, 3*a*

8. ENCROACHMENT BY THE IMPERIAL CLAN

1069   On the day *kuei-wei* [of the seventh month in the fifth year of Hsien-yung] an imperial decree forbade the imperial clan to make use of its power to encroach upon the common people.   22, 6*a*

9. OVERBEARING COURTIERS

1079   On the day *jên-wu* [of the ninth month in the fifth year of Ta-k'ang] members of the imperial entourage were forbidden to molest the people.   24, 1*b*

10. HOW WEALTHY SHOULD A HIGH OFFICIAL BE?

11th century   [Chang] Hsiao-chieh,[11] who for a long time held a ministerial position, had an insatiable greed[12] for wealth. At this time, in drinking together with his relatives, he once said, "Without a million taels of gold it is impossible to be classed as a prime minister's family."

    110, 4*b*

11. WEALTH ACQUIRED IN THREE MONTHS OF PREMIERSHIP

1122   The father, [Li] Ch'u-wên,[13] and his son, [Li Shih], fearing disaster,[14] communicated with T'ung Kuan[15] in the south with the aim of forcing the empress dowager née Hsiao[16] to hand over the territory to Sung. In the north they communicated with Chin, planning

---

[8] Hsiao Chu-chê 术哲, a member of the imperial consort family, gained fame during the punitive campaign against Hsia in 1044. He was granted the title of prince (LS 91, 2*b*–3*a*).

[9] Hsiao Hui was Emperor Hsing-tsung's uncle and was also married to the latter's sister.

[10] Besides their regular salaries, officials generally received an extra allowance in the hope that this would discourage their recourse to corrupt practices. The special allowance was called 養廉費 (expenditure for the maintenance of integrity). The first two words of this expression are used in the present passage.

[11] Chang Hsiao-chieh 張孝傑, a native of the Central Capital, acquired the degree of *chin-shih* in 1055. In 1075 he was granted the imperial surname of Yeh-lü and two years later the name of Jen-chieh 仁傑. He cooperated with the northern chancellor, Yeh-lü I-hsin 乙辛, in deposing and killing the heir apparent in 1077. In 1080 he was degraded to the rank of commanding prefect, and in 1082 to that of commoner when the emperor discovered that the accusation against the heir apparent was not true.

He died in his village during the reign period Ta-an (1085–1095) (LS 110, 3*b*–4*b*).

[12] We follow the Palace edition in reading 貪 between 位 and 貨.

[13] The Chinese official Li Ch'u-wên 李處温, a nephew of the Liao historiographer Li Yen 李儼, together with his son, Li Shih 奭, placed Ch'un 淳 on the Liao throne in the Southern Capital and assumed for himself the position of prime minister for the three months (third to sixth in 1122) of this brief reign.

[14] They were involved in an attempt to prevent the empress dowager, the widow of Ch'un, from ascending the throne on his death.

[15] T'ung Kuan 童貫, a powerful eunuch, became chancellor of Sung in 1111. He advocated the alliance of Sung with Chin 金 as a means of regaining the northern territory lost to Liao. He failed in this and was put to death in 1125 (SS 468, 9*a*–14*a*).

[16] After the death of Ch'un in the sixth month of 1122 his widow seized the imperial power and set up a new reign period, Tê-hsing 德興. But her rule was quickly over-

treason from within. Externally they paraded as persons with the great merit of having supported the accession [of Ch'un]. The empress dowager née Hsiao execrated them, saying, "The ones who led astray the Prince of Ch'in and Chin[17] were you yourselves, father and son!"

Enumerating in detail their crimes, which numbered several tens, she permitted [Li Ch'u-wên] to kill himself.[18] His son, [Li] Shih, was sliced and quartered. When their household was confiscated, seventy thousand strings of cash and an equal value of gold, jade, and valuables were seized. This was what had been acquired during a few months of premiership. 29, 4b

12. RANK BOUGHT BY POWERFUL TRIBESMEN

Powerful Ch'i-tan individuals who wanted to wear turbans paid ten head of oxen and camels and one hundred horses. Then they were given the official title of shê-li.[19] Henceforth it became an official title in the ordos. Lang-chün was attached to it.[20] 116, 5a

---

thrown. In 1123, when the Southern Capital was conquered by Chin, she fled to the court of the old emperor, T'ien-tsu, where she was executed.

[17] This honorary title which refers to Ch'un is in the Chinese tradition. Outstanding nobles were made princes of feudal states which had flourished prior to the Ch'in period (221–207 B.C.). Under the Chin 金 dynasty, which may have taken over its system from Liao, the honorary titles were divided into three classes. The first had reference to the largest of the pre-Ch'in states; the second and third, to the smaller ones (CS 55, 10b). Frequently, as in the present case, the nobles were made princes of more than one of these ancient states.

[18] In Liao, as in other dynasties, the highest officials were placed in a special category even if they had committed serious crimes. Instead of being publicly executed

they were allowed to kill themselves by means of poison, rope, or sword.

[19] Giles (12, no. 9789) explains the term shê-li 舍利 as probably related to a Sanskrit word sâria [śārya], "crane." But the reference to a turban suggests another etymology. The Chaghatai, Taranchi, and Özbek Turks designate the ordinary turban as sällä (Radloff, WB IV, 481), a loanword from Persian salla, "a wicker basket" (Steingass 30, 694).

[20] Thus forming the title shê-li lang-chün 舍利郎君. This title is also transcribed 赦例郎君 which, according to Wang Kung's 王鞏 explanation, was an imperial messenger who galloped five hundred li a day with the announcement of an amnesty (CSTC 7b). This explanation seems to be based on the meaning of the Chinese characters, and makes no sense in our passage.

TEMPLES AND MONASTERIES

INTRODUCTION

1. LIAO BUDDHISM

Buddhist temples and monasteries have added to the weight and to the danger of the "private sector" in Chinese society since the middle of the first millennium A.D. The influence of Buddhism decreased in the typically Chinese dynasties such as T'ang, Sung, and Ming.[1] It reached its peak under the pseudo-assimilated dynasties of conquest such as the Liao and Yüan.

Liao Buddhism is barely mentioned in the Western histories of the creed.[2] This is a serious omission, for it was under the Liao dynasty that Buddhism spread to the vast eastern expanses of Inner Asia. By the end of the ninth century Chinese Buddhism had experienced both prosperity and decline. From the Middle Kingdom the doctrine had spread to the northeastern regions, to Korea and Japan, and to the Po-hai.[3] In Tibet it took a peculiar ("lamaistic") form,[4] and, after a period of severe persecution in the later part of the T'ang dynasty,[5] it flourished again, acquiring new strength during the Liao period. In a great part of Turkestan, Buddhism had spread hundreds of years before the T'ang dynasty.[6] In Kao-ch'ang in Eastern Turkestan, Buddhist temples received their names from the T'ang government; the Ying-yün T'ai-ning 應運泰寧 Temple was erected in A.D. 640.[7] Thus a huge semicircle of countries where Buddhist influence was important, Japan, Korea, Po-hai, China, Tibet, and Turkestan, fringed the pastoral regions of what is now northwestern Manchuria and Outer and Inner Mongolia.

There is no detailed information regarding the religious situation in this vast region at the end of the ninth century. In China, Nestorianism[8] was practically eliminated by the persecutions of 845; farther to the north, its continued, if limited, practice is attested to by a number of literary records and archaeological monuments. Manicheism seems to have weathered the storm somewhat more successfully, possibly because it could adjust more easily both in form and substance to the most powerful of the outlawed creeds, Buddhism. This religion, which within China Proper soon regained part of its previous strength, spread rapidly to the northern grasslands when the T'ang government collapsed. In 902 the Ch'i-tan built what seems to have been the first Buddhist temple, "The Commencement of Teaching."[9] In all probability, its erection was preceded by a period of ideological penetration. A-pao-chi's courtiers, who in 916 unanimously declared themselves in favor of Buddha,[10] obviously were already indoctrinated. But, whatever Buddhist elements may have existed along with the old tribal religion during the predynastic period, it seems beyond doubt that the establishment of a powerful empire paved the way for the rapid development of the creed. The new government could mobilize many skilled workmen to build temples and monasteries; it could also appropriate large surpluses of food for the use of the temples' monks and retainers.

A-pao-chi justified his usurpation of the throne in terms of Chinese political customs,[11] and his eldest son, Pei, naturally favored Confucianism with its implied hereditary rule and succession. But even the first Liao emperor built Buddhist temples[12] and encouraged his family to visit them.[13] He himself honored the An-kuo and Hung-fu Temples with his

---

[1] See de Groot, SRP I, 51 ff., 72 ff., 77 ff., 81 ff.

[2] Demiéville's scholarly treatment of the Chinese versions of the Milindapañha, which discusses the Ch'i-tan editions of Buddhist texts (Demiéville 25, 193 ff. and 207–212), is exclusively concerned with the comparison of successive editions of the Canon.

[3] The existence of Buddhism in the old kingdom of Po-hai has been shown by fragments of statues and a stone lamp with a lotus-carved stand which were excavated recently in the ancient Po-hai site of Lung-ch'üan 龍泉 Administration, modern Tung-ching 東京 City (TCC, pls. 107–120; Mikami 34, 73 ff.).

[4] Grünwedel 00, 56; cf. also Koeppen 59, 81 ff.; Waddell 95, 28; Bell 31, xvi, note.

[5] Bu-ston 32, 182–197; Petech 39, 69–81; Waddell 95, 34; Bell 31, 48 ff.

[6] SKC, Wei 30, 32a; Rémusat 1836, 7 ff.; 16 ff. and passim; Rockhill 84, 231; Wassiljew 60, 43 ff.

[7] SS 490, 10b–11b. Cf. also WHTK 336, 2639 and Schott 76, 43–44.

[8] For details concerning the following statements see IX, note 52.

[9] IX (1).

[10] IX (3).

[11] WTS 72, 2b.

[12] IX (2) (4).

[13] IX (5) (6).

presence[14] and offered food to Buddhist monks. His successors, firmly entrenched in their imperial position, continued to pay lip-service to Confucianism, but within the Ch'i-tan world only a limited group[15] favored this doctrine whose anti-barbarian overtones were still resented by the northern nobility in the Chin period.[16] The Liao rulers, despite their partially Chinese education, remained emotionally tied to the ideas of their nomadic tribesmen. They were eager to clothe their new imperial experience in the garments of a new "imperial" religion; and this new religion had to be compatible[17] with their old tribal beliefs which they did not intend to discard. Cherished tribal traditions might be reasserted in new and significant ways,[18] but, since the new ideas had to be congenial emotionally as well as intellectually, they could not embody the sophisticated "learning" of Confucianism. Buddhism, however, which offered its followers metaphysical ideas, complex and difficult in some aspects, yet attractive because of the power and simplicity of its basic vision,[19] could appeal to the mounted Ch'i-tan rulers who were pushing their domain farther and farther along an increasingly glorious if increasingly dangerous road to victory and conquest.

The Ch'i-tan had been in contact with Chinese life and thus with Chinese Buddhism for centuries before 907. By the seizure of Chinese subjects, cities, and finally large territories, they incorporated into their empire numerous Buddhist temples, monks, and believing laymen. All the preserved Buddhist inscriptions are written either in Sanskrit or in Chinese.[20] Demiéville claims that the Liao edition of the Canon, which differs in arrangement from the Sung and the Korean texts, resembles the one used in China Proper between 930 and 940.[21] He concludes that in all probability the Ch'i-tan received the Buddhist Canon either from the Later T'ang or the Later Chin dynasty.[22]

Did the Ch'i-tan acquire the Canon as part of the war loot of this period, as Demiéville suggests? Such an assumption seems to be confirmed by a *Liao Shih* passage which reports that in 947 *shih ching* 石經, classics cut in stone, were brought from the capital of Chin to the Liao empire.[23] The use of the word *ching* offers no insurmountable difficulties, for this term, which usually refers to the Confucian classics, was also applied to the sacred books of Buddhism. A temple south of the Southern Capital of the Liao empire is known to have contained *shih ching*, the Buddhist Canon cut in stone.[24]

But this very fact, which at first seems to simplify the problem, actually complicates it. The engraving of the *shih ching* of the Yün-chü 雲居 Temple was begun long before 947, during the years 605–618, under the Sui dynasty.[25] The work was well under way at the end of the T'ang dynasty, and it was completed during the Liao period.[26] The importation of any other *shih ching* from the south seems highly improbable, for this would only have duplicated work already done and made the continuation of an extremely complex and expensive enterprise superfluous.[27] It is hard to believe that the Liao government would have strained its resources to finance the completion of the Canon, as it did, if a Canon cut in stone had been taken from Pien to the empire.[28] Whatever the classics acquired in 947 may have been,[29]

---

[14] IX (6).

[15] *Cf.* VII, introduction; see also IX (14) (23).

[16] LTSS 49a. See VII, 1, note 65.

[17] *Cf.* Linton 40, 488.

[18] *Loc. cit.*

[19] See the respect which other Chinese dynasties of conquest, such as the T'o-pa Wei, the Chin, and Yüan, rendered to Buddhism. Barthold noted a similar attitude among the nomads of the Near East, "not excluding the Arabs." They regarded Islam in its official legislative form "as a religion unsuited to their requirements." The various forms of Moslem mysticism "had incomparably more influence, and still have to-day the greatest number of adherents in the steppes" (Barthold 28, 255).

[20] See LWT, *passim;* Torii 36 I, pls. 23, 59, 64–66; III, 241–244.

[21] Demiéville 25, 211.

[22] *Loc. cit.*

[23] VII, 2 (22).

[24] Vaudescal 14, 385 ff.

[25] *Op. cit.*, 381 and 456.

[26] *Op. cit.*, 382 ff.; 385–390, see also 456 ff.

[27] *Op. cit.*, 387 ff.

[28] When, under Shêng-tsung, a high Ch'i-tan dignitary visited the temple and surveyed the work done, he commented in great detail upon it (*op. cit.*, 385), but neither he nor his successors ever referred to any other Canon cut in stone extant within the Liao empire.

[29] The Confucian classics were cut in stone during the Han-Wei (魏) epoch, under the T'ang dynasty, and again several decades after the latter's collapse in the state of Shu 蜀 (modern Szechuan) which had acquired temporary independence. The T'ang *shih ching* was used as the basis of the Confucian classics which were printed under the Later T'ang, Chin, Han, and Chou dynasties between 932 and 953. (See CWTS 43, 2a; Carter 31, 50 ff., 212 ff.; *cf.* also WTHY 8, 2b ff.; in the copy of the latter work used by us the date of the completion of the printing blocks is given as the sixth year of the reign period Kuang-shun. This is a manifest error. The period Kuang-shun lasted only three years, from 951–953.) The new printed edition was definitely inspired by the extraordinary growth of printing in Shu (*cf.* Carter 31, 50 and 212), but, contrary to Carter's opinion, the stone-cut classics of Shu cannot have exerted a similar influence, for the work of cutting them began only in 944 (LTSCL 2, 26b ff.).

they obviously were not identical with the Buddhist stone-cut Canon of the Yün-chü Temple whose last sections were engraved with the aid of the Liao court from 1027 to 1094.[30] There is a slight possibility that they were individual sūtras cut in stone; but, although such sūtras, some written in Sanskrit, most written in Chinese, have been found in old Liao sites,[31] they would scarcely have been designated as *shih ching*. In any event, the critical Liao edition which was not engraved, but printed, is much more important in the history of the Canon. Sponsored by Hsing-tsung, this edition was in the main prepared during his reign (1031–1055);[32] supplements were completed in 1062[33] and perhaps in 1068[34] under Tao-tsung, whose reign is characterized by great activity in the printing and reprinting of Buddhist texts.[35] Demiéville asserts that the arrangement of the printed Liao Canon as well as that of the Canon cut in stone corresponds to the Chinese edition used from 930 to 940.[36] Thus no connection can be established between the *shih ching* of the Yün-chü Temple and the mysterious *shih ching* of 947; and any connection between the latter and the printed Liao Canon is equally problematic. But, even if the Buddhist Canon was not part of the imperial loot of 947, it may well have been transferred under similar circumstances. The Ch'i-tan, who in 912 transplanted fifty Buddhist monks from China Proper to the West Tower of their home territory,[37] were probably also eager to acquire the sacred scriptures which would insure a proper growth for the favored religion.

The Chinese root of Liao Buddhism is beyond doubt. It is confirmed by the recent discovery in old Liao sites of many Buddhist structures definitely Chinese in character.[38] However, also beyond doubt is the decay of T'ang and post-T'ang Buddhism. The T'ang government persecuted those who espoused the doctrine so severely[39] that onlookers might easily have gained the impression voiced by A-pao-chi in 916 that "Buddhism is not a Chinese religion."[40] The deterioration of the sacred texts under the Sung dynasty[41] indicates the gradual loss of the creed's prestige and importance.

Was Liao Buddhism influenced by any other impulse? In the Uighur countries of Central Asia the religion flourished side by side with Manicheism and Nestorianism; in 966 two hundred Uighurs appeared in the Liao border region of Shuo-fang, in the company of sixty Chinese monks who were on their way to India;[42] a Chinese delegation visiting Kao-ch'ang in 981 observed that the Uighurs possessed the Buddhist Canon.[43] LS 97, 1b ff. also gives the life story of a high official, Hai-li 孩里, a believing Buddhist[44] of Uighur descent. We do not know whether his forefather, who came to the Ch'i-tan court at the time of T'ai-tsu, was already a Buddhist. But there is clear evidence that a century later religious elements flowed from the Uighurs and, still later, from their neighbors,

---

When, in 947, the Liao army occupied Pien (modern Kaifeng) and carried away "classics cut in stone," these classics cannot have been the *shih ching* of Shu on which work was only just commencing and which remained in Shu until their later destruction by the Mongols (KTCL 20, 9a). They cannot have been the remains of the Han-Wei *shih ching* or the T'ang *shih ching*, because the former were in Lo-yang and the latter in the Western Capital, in modern Shensi (NESKI 85, 19b). Ch'ien Ta-hsin's conclusion that the Liao conquerors cannot have seized any of the existing stone-cut classics (*loc. cit.*) is supported for the T'ang *shih ching* by the fact that after 947 the officials of the Imperial Academy of Later Han and Chou continued to cut the wood-blocks of the new edition, based upon the T'ang classics cut in stone, without indicating in their reports any serious disturbances or loss.

There is a certain possibility that the *shih ching* of our text was a poetic essay, called the *Lan-t'ing Shih-k'o* 蘭亭石刻, written in 353 by one of the great early Chinese calligraphers, Wang Hsi-chih 王羲之 (321–379). The essay was first cut in stone in the T'ang capital, Ch'ang-an, by T'ai-tsung. During the Liang period it was moved to the new capital, Pien. In 947 it was carried north by the Liao emperor, T'ai-tsung, to Chên-ting 眞定 (modern Hopei) where the Ch'i-tan left it after his death. Between 1041 and 1048 the stone was discovered by a certain Mr. Li 李 whose son derived a handsome profit from selling rubbings made from it. Later, Sung Ch'i 宋祁 obtained the precious object and deposited it in a government treasure house, permitting no one but his intimate friends to see it. In 1126 the stone "and the stone drums" were seized by the Jurchen invaders and carried north (PTL 1, 3b–5a; CCCW 5, 4a ff.).

[30] Vaudescal 14, 385, 387, and 390.
[31] See note 19.
[32] Demiéville 25, 209.
[33] *Loc. cit.*
[34] *Op. cit.*, 209 and 210.
[35] See notes 48–51.

[36] Demiéville 25, 211.
[37] IX (2). The name West Tower was originally applied to Tsu Prefecture, then to the Supreme Capital. See V, note 5.
[38] See Torii 36, *passim*.
[39] For the sociological reasons of this persecution *cf.* Wittfogel 35, 50; *idem* 38, 107–109.
[40] IX (3).
[41] Demiéville 25, 212.
[42] SS 492, 3a; see IX, note 38.
[43] SS 490, 10b. *Cf.* also Schott 76, 36–44. Demiéville does not compare the Uighur Canon with the Ch'i-tan edition, nor does he mention the contacts between Liao Buddhism and the western countries of the Uighurs and Hsi Hsia.
[44] LS 97, 2a.

the Hsi Hsia, to the Liao court.   In 1001 "the Uighurs [the country is not specified] presented Fan [Mani-chean?] monks."[45]   In 1067 the kingdom of Hsi Hsia offered a Sanskrit sūtra and golden Buddhas together with "Uighur monks."[46]   Another Buddhist sūtra, this time an original manuscript, arrived from Hsi Hsia in 1095.[47]

In all three cases the Liao rulers were on the receiv-ing end of the culture transfer.   They participated more actively where their eastern neighbor, Korea, was concerned.   A set of the newly printed Liao Canon[48] was presented to the king of Korea in 1063;[49] another set followed in 1074.[50]   In return Korea also offered Buddhist texts, which Tao-tsung ordered re-vised and published in 1083.[51]   The superiority of the Liao texts as compared with the Sung editions was so striking that even Sung scholars had to acknowledge it.   It was the Liao Buddhists who "established the first critical edition of the Canon."[52]   Their work was carried on by Korean and, much later, by Japanese scholars.   In contrast, in China Proper "each new edition was more mediocre than the last; this reached such a point that the edition in the Manchu dynasty was ignored by the scholars."[53]

2. THE INFLUENCE OF BUDDHISM IN THE LIAO EMPIRE

Literary records and contemporary inscriptions both confirm the importance of Buddhism to the masters of Liao.   LS 3, 8a revealingly portrays the devotion to the creed shown by T'ai-tsu's immediate family, including his second son, T'ai-tsung, the next emperor. Shêng-tsung's religious inclinations are reflected in his Buddhist childhood name Wên-shu-nu 文殊奴 (the servant of Mañjuśrī[54]) and also in several inscrip-tions.[55]   Hsing-tsung accepted the five great Budd-hist commandments,[56] an unusual step for a Chinese

emperor; he also organized a discussion of Buddhist doctrines.[57]   Tao-tsung composed and copied Budd-hist texts with his own hand.[58]

Buddhist ceremonies marked military victories[59] and mourning at the death of an empress.[60]   Animals were treated with greater kindness; birds were released;[61] even the slaughter of animals for meat was tem-porarily suspended.[62]   The celebration of Buddha's birthday was included in the list of national festivals,[63] a list which does not mention the birthday of Con-fucius.   Buddhist scriptures were used in educating the heir apparent.[64]   Buddhist altars were set up throughout the country,[65] even in the Inner Hall,[66] where the visits of fortune-telling Buddhist monks and nuns became so frequent that emperor Tao-tsung, himself a firm believer, was compelled to interfere, no doubt because of the excessive emoluments offered them.[67]

In 991 and 997 Buddhist monks and nuns had become so numerous that membership in the organiza-tion was restricted.[68]   Both the increase in adherents and the counter-measures were probably related to the war against the Sung empire, just as the regula-tions of 1015,[69] and perhaps the order of 1020 against self-mutilation,[70] may have been inspired by the exigencies of the conflict with Korea.   Yet when im-perial power was stabilized, the power of Buddhism was stabilized also.   Monks were appointed to high honorary positions;[71] a clerical dignitary was allowed to ride in an imperial carriage.[72]   Even in the hour of decay, when the government needed to mobilize all its manpower, it still admonished the Buddhist monks and nuns not to break their vows.[73]

---

[45] IX (13).   According to Ch'ên Y 23, these Fan monks may have been Manicheans.   The possible existence of traces of Manicheism in the Liao empire is discussed in IX, note 52.

[46] IX (28).

[47] IX (41).

[48] The Canon was printed in 1063 (Demiéville 25, 209).

[49] IX (24); cf. also KRS 8, 118.   See IX, note 34.

[50] IX (34).

[51] IX (39).

[52] Demiéville 25, 212.

[53] Loc. cit.

[54] LS 10, 1a.

[55] Cf. LWT 4, 4a and 6a.

[56] IX (18).   Cf. also LWT 4, 8a and 6, 3a.   These five commandments are taken by believing laymen, who thereby vow (1) not to kill any living thing, (2) not to steal, (3) not to commit adultery, (4) not to lie, (5) not

to take intoxicating liquors.   In addition the monks abstained (6) from perfumes and flowers, (7) from singing and dancing, (8) from using comfortable beds, (9) from taking meals at regular intervals, and (10) from acquiring or possessing valuable things (Reichelt 27, 241 ff.).

[57] IX (19).

[58] IX (29) (33).

[59] IX (9).

[60] IX (20).

[61] IX (6).

[62] IX (26) (31).

[63] VII, 2 (83), and note 152.

[64] IX (35).

[65] IX (37).

[66] IX (38) (43).

[67] IX (25).

[68] IX (10) (12).

[69] IX (15).

[70] IX (16).

[71] IX (21) (27) (30).

[72] IX (42).

[73] IX (44).

3. THE ECONOMIC ASPECT OF LIAO BUDDHISM

Parallel to its rising influence in religious life was the increasing importance of Buddhism in Liao economy. The temple property of Liao derived from the devotion and generosity of its believers who at the same time were the most powerful and wealthy elements in the empire. The reservoir of the temples' economic strength was therefore almost unlimited. In 902, when the Temple of the Commencement of Teaching was set up, the new religion may not have possessed great worldly wealth; but at the close of the dynasty the property of the Buddhist temples could only have been matched by the wealth of the two ruling clans and, perhaps, some few other families. How did this come about? The literary texts throw little light on the economic aspects of Liao Buddhism.

Fortunately contemporary inscriptions are more revealing. The pride of donors and the gratitude of lavishly endowed temples have led to the tabulation of some of these gifts which consisted of money, land, grain, cattle, bondsmen, and other miscellaneous items. In table 11 we give the most important of these, listing also the donor, the recipient temple, and the grant.

Other inscriptions tell of Buddhist possessions without naming their source. An inscription of 1056 records the ownership of ten thousand *mou* of land and more than two thousand fruit trees[74] by the Ch'ao-hua 超化 Temple. An inscription of 1107 refers to the three hundred Buddhist monks of the Kan-hua 感化 Temple as the owners of more than ten thousand *mou* of good land and more than ten

[74] LWT 6, 21b.

TABLE 11

DONATIONS MADE TO BUDDHIST TEMPLES

DATE	DONOR	TEMPLE	LAND	GRAIN	BONDS-MEN	CATTLE	HORSES	MONEY	MISCEL-LANEOUS	REFER-ENCE
949	Shih-tsung	Hsien-lu 仙露						300 strings		LWT 4, 1a
1022	Shêng-tsung	Hsüan-hua 玄化	fields	more than 3,000 bushels				more than 2,000 taels of silver		LWT 4, 4a
1059	Princess of Ch'in and Yüeh 秦越公主	Hao-t'ien 昊天	10,000 *mou* of irrigated rice fields		100 families				fruit trees	MCPL 2, 49a
1059	Tao-tsung	Hao-t'ien						50,000 strings		MCPL 2, 49a
1059	Empress I-tê 懿德	Hao-t'ien						130,000 strings		MCPL 2, 49a
1068	Têng Ts'ung-kuei 鄧從貴 (a Chinese official)	Ch'ing-shui Yüan 清水院						800,000 cash		LWT 4, 9b
1072	Lady Hsiao 蕭夫人	Ching-an 靜安	300,000 *mou*	10,000 bushels	50 families	50	40	2,000 strings		MCCSC 2, 18b
1095	Tao-tsung	Chin-yang 縉陽						10 taels of silver and 700 strings	10 bolts of silk	LWT 4, 11b–12a
1101	T'ien-tsu	Hao-t'ien						more than 80,000 strings		MCPL 2, 51b
1115	Lord Ch'ung 冲公 (details unknown)	Shang-fang 上方						5,000 strings		LWT 4, 20b

thousand chestnut trees; in addition, the Kan-hua Temple owned three thousand *mou* of land, of which a thousand *mou* were sown in wheat.[75]

These data present no complete picture, but they give some indication of the kind and amount of wealth amassed by the temples. Besides owning great tracts of land and large sums of money, they had control over considerable numbers of people. The inscriptions refer to donated families that obviously lived in a state of bondage.[76] Above and beyond the enslaved families were the free monks and nuns. According to the texts, their numbers swelled beyond belief; 50,000 monks and nuns are listed for the year 942,[77] but in 1078, one hundred and thirty-six years later, 360,000 are mentioned.[78] It was usual for tribal believers to select the eldest son for the priesthood.[79] This principle was observed by the later Mongols, most of whose lamas, male as well as female,[80] lived at home and, exempted from military service, continued to attend to domestic affairs.[81] The records do not state whether the monks of Liao were also exempted from military service and from the payment of taxes;[82] it may be assumed that the majority stayed with their families and pursued their regular occupations, while their position remained somewhat privileged.

The priestly status must have been most attractive, for otherwise it would be difficult to explain the collective conversions of thousands of individuals or an order of several hundred thousand members. The nature of the privileges enjoyed by the monks can only be conjectured. Since the temples tried to remove their secular retainers from the public registers[83] which were used in imposing taxes and labor service, they probably sought similar means of exempting their religious followers. They set up granaries[84] for the benefit of the poor; they established charity schools;[85] they lent out grain and money at a nominal rate of interest.[86] The monk who gave alms to more than two million people[87] must have subsidized whole districts, and at that several times over. The story seems barely credible; it was probably exaggerated to emphasize the temple's unusual generosity.

These benefactions were counter-balanced by economic enterprises far from charitable. Kan-hua Temple leased its fertile wheat land to tenants;[88] the Lung-kung 龍宮 Temple enslaved its tenants and treated them cruelly.[89] The story that tells of the five hundred strings lent out annually at only one per cent interest by the Chin-yang Temple[90] can be matched by the report that the pawnshop of the Shang-fang Temple earned more than a thousand strings of money yearly.[91] The latter proceeding seems to have been the more typical. A Chinese traveler, Su Ch'ê, in his report to the Sung court describes the situation in Liao as follows: "Temples are being built everywhere and monks are very numerous. The monks indulge in licentiousness. They lend money at exorbitant interest and plunder the common people, who have become very desperate."[92]

To be sure the possible prejudice and exaggeration in all Chin and Sung sources must not be lost sight of. The monasteries and temples certainly engaged in charitable activities, and the excesses may not have been as flagrant as the report suggests. But in general it confirms our other information too well to be lightly dismissed. Whatever their spiritual influence may have been, from an economic standpoint the temples obviously were the centers of a growing accumulation of wealth, which led to grave social and political consequences.

4. THE GREAT INVESTMENT

The extraordinary growth of Liao Buddhism was approved and consciously fostered by the rulers of the country. They made enormous gifts to the temples. They permitted the monks to become "very numerous"; thousands accepted the commandments in a single region and at one time. They provided meals

---

[75] LWT 5, 21*b*.
[76] See VII, introduction.
[77] IX (7).
[78] IX (36).
[79] MCWP 18*b*.
[80] Women "above a certain age" were accepted as nuns. Prejevalsky's additional statement that nuns were "often met with among aged widows" also indicates the numerical inferiority of this category. On the other hand, according to the same explorer, the institution of lamahood affected "the best part of the male population" (Prejevalsky 76 I, 80).
[81] Timkowsky 1827 II, 353, 356.
[82] As stated for the later Mongols (*cf.* Prejevalsky 76 I, 78).
[83] CS 96, 4*b*.
[84] According to an inscription of the year 1110, the Pao-shêng 寶勝 Temple set up granaries to relieve the people in case of calamity (LWT 4, 19*a*).

[85] An inscription of 1103 relates that the Yen-chiao Temple 演教院 first promoted charity schools (義學) (LWT 4, 13*b*).
[86] The Chin-yang Temple lent more than a thousand bushels of grain and five hundred strings of money to the people at an annual interest of only one per cent. (Inscription of 1095. See LWT 4, 12*a*.)
[87] LWT 6, 20*b*.
[88] LWT 5, 22*a*.
[89] CS 96, 4*b*.
[90] LWT 4, 12*a*.
[91] LWT 4, 20*b*.
[92] LCC 41, 14*a–b*.

in honor of the Buddhist clergy, following an old established custom.   But the outlay surpassed anything that had been previously done in China Proper or Japan.   Vegetarian meals were offered in Southern Sung to an unspecified number of Buddhist monks.[93] The Japanese court entertained numerous Buddhist priests and nuns as shown by the following data:

10,000 priests in 752
1,000 priests in 756

1,500 monks in 756
600 priests in 767
269 nuns and girls in 773
1,049 men of all kinds in 773.[94]

But, impressive as these figures are, they cannot be compared with the 50,000 and 360,000 monks and nuns who are said to have been fed by two of the Liao emperors at the monster entertainments in the years 942 and 1078.

[93] De Visser 35, 51 ff.

[94] *Op. cit.*, 28–41.

TRANSLATION

TEMPLES AND MONASTERIES

1. The "Commencement of Teaching" 2. The Temple of Celestial Heroes 3. Buddha and Confucius 4. Temples for the three doctrines 5. Imperial worship 6. Buddhist monks granted food 7. Fifty thousand monks granted food 8. Buddhist monk honored 9. Victory celebrated by Buddhist ceremonies 10. Ordination limited 11. Periodic religious worship 12. Ordination limited 13. Uighurs 14. Buddhism and Confucianism spread northeast 15. Restrictions during Korean war 16. No self-mutilation 17. Mourning for a Sung emperor 18. Hsing-tsung accepts Buddhist commandments 19. Discussion of Buddhist doctrines 20. Buddhist ceremonies on an empress' death-day 21. Buddhist monk honored 22. Amnesty follows casting of a silver Buddha 23. The three doctrines may not be insulted 24. Buddhist Canon given to Korea 25. Private court visits of monks and nuns 26. Buddhist fast days 27. Buddhist monk honored 28. Hsia offers Uighur monks 29. Tao-tsung writes on Buddhism 30. A Buddhist monk honored 31. Buddhist ceremony halts killing of animals 32. Men and women take the full Buddhist vows 33. Tao-tsung copies scripture 34. Buddhist sūtras as an imperial present 35. Buddhist education for an heir apparent 36. Three hundred sixty thousand monks and nuns granted food 37. No hampering of Buddhist activities 38. A Buddhist altar for an empress 39. Sūtras received from Korea 40. A temple gives relief money 41. Hsia offers a manuscript sūtra 42. Buddhist monk honored 43. A Buddhist altar for an empress 44. Commandments must be kept

1. THE "COMMENCEMENT OF TEACHING"

902 In the ninth month [of the second year of the reign period of T'ien-fu of T'ang], Lung-hua Prefecture,[1] south of the Huang River, was built up as a walled city, and the construction of the Temple of the Commencement of Teaching[2] was begun. 1, 1b

2. THE TEMPLE OF CELESTIAL HEROES

912 This year, armies were dispatched to attack Liang-yeh.[3] The fifty Buddhist monks —Ch'ung-wên and others—who were captured were brought back to West Tower.[4] The Temple of Celestial Heroes was built as their residence to show that the courageous and militant were assisted by Heaven.[5] 1, 4b

3. BUDDHA AND CONFUCIUS

916 In the spring of the first year of Shên-ts'ê, [Pei] was made the heir apparent. At that time T'ai-tsu asked his attending courtiers, "The ruler who receives the mandate should serve Heaven and revere the gods. I want to worship those who have great merit and virtue. Who is the foremost?"

All replied, "Buddha."

T'ai-tsu said, "Buddhism is not a Chinese religion."

Pei said, "Confucius, the Great Sage, who commands the reverence of every age, should be the foremost."

T'ai-tsu was greatly pleased and thereupon founded the Temple of Confucius.[6] A decree ordered the imperial heir apparent to offer sacrifices in the spring and autumn. 72, 1a

---

[1] Probably located at the juncture of the modern Shira Muren and the Lao-ha River, Jehol (MRC II, 92).

[2] See introduction.

[3] Probably in present Hopei.

[4] The Supreme Capital. Cf. V, note 5.

[5] These early constructions initiated a period of great activity in the field of Buddhist architecture. Recent archaeological studies (Torii 36, passim) confirm the impression gained by contemporary Sung travelers concerning the splendor of the Liao Buddhist temples.

One record speaks of a large and beautiful temple inside which was a large statue of Buddha cast in silver and covered with gold. Sung envoys who arrived at this temple had to burn incense (SKTP 2,7b). Unfortunately the temple cannot be identified, for the record does not define its location. See figs. 28 and 30.

[6] It was ordered to be built in 918. See below, (4).

Fig. 29. Liao stele. On the shaft is an inscription concerning the "Stone Buddhist Sūtra." The carving was begun under Shêng-tsung and continued down to the time of Tao-tsung. Reproduced from a photograph in *Toho Gakuho*, Kyoto, March, 1935, pl. 17 in Studies on the Yün-chü-ssǔ, Fang-shan.

Fig. 28. Lower part of an octagonal brick tower found on the elevated ground of the southern [Chinese] part of the Liao Supreme Capital (Torii 36 I, pl. 34).

FIG. 30.   Two Buddhas from a Liao temple (IHC, fasc. 1).

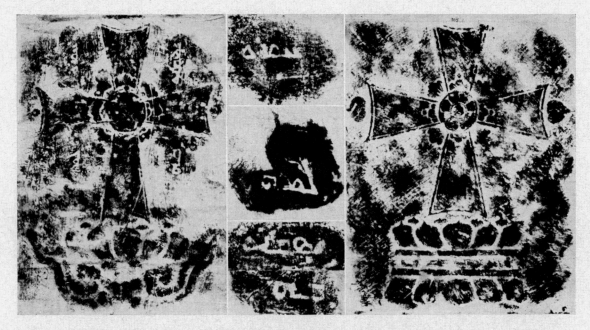

FIG. 31.   Two crosses found in the "Temple of the Cross," Shih-tzŭ Ssŭ, near Peiping.   In the center, on a larger scale, the Syriac inscription.   Reproduced with the author's permission from A. C. Moule's *Christians in China before the year 1550*, plate facing p. 87.

4. TEMPLES FOR THE THREE DOCTRINES

918   On the day *i-hai* in the fifth month [of the third year of Shên-ts'ê] an imperial
decree was issued ordering the construction of Confucian, Buddhist, and Taoist
temples.[7]   1, 10*b*

5. IMPERIAL WORSHIP

919   On the day *ting-yu* of the eighth month in the autumn [of the fourth year of Shên-
ts'ê the emperor] visited the Temple of Confucius and commanded the empress and heir
apparent to visit separately the Buddhist and Taoist temples.[8]   2, 1*a*

6. BUDDHIST MONKS GRANTED FOOD

925   On the day *ting-yu* in the eleventh month [of the fourth year of T'ien-tsan the
emperor] visited the An-kuo Temple and presented food to the monks.[9]   An amnesty
was proclaimed for the prisoners of the capital, and the eagles and falcons of the Five Animal Quarters
were set free.[10]   2, 5*b*

935   On the day *ping-wu* in the eleventh month in the winter [of the tenth year of T'ien-
hsien the emperor] paid a visit to the Hung-fu Temple and presented food to the
monks on behalf of the [deceased] empress.[11]   As he contemplated the portraits of Kuan-yin,[12] which
had been offered by Emperor Ta-shêng, Empress Ying-t'ien, and Prince Jên-huang,[13] he glanced at

---

[7] Our text uses three different terms, *miao* 廟, *ssŭ* 寺, and *kuan* 觀, to designate the sacred buildings ("temples") of the three doctrines. In addition, *miao* refers to the temples of the imperial and tribal ancestors (see VII, 2 (82) (84)). Although in recent times the word *miao* is also applied to Buddhist temples (*cf.* Reichelt 27, 264), it seems safe to say that in general the common designation for Buddhist temples was indeed *ssŭ*, that for Taoist temples *kuan*, and that for the temples associated with the state-cult *miao* (Duyvendak 35,337; for the earliest use of the term *ssŭ* for a Buddhist temple, in the second century A.D., see Maspero 10, 228, note 5). The English language distinguishes between temples and monasteries There exists also a special Chinese term for monastery (*yüan* 院, see LWT 4, 9*b*), but the preferred term for both types of Buddhist buildings is *ssŭ*. According to our records, there were *ssŭ* in the cities (see XI (5)) as well as in the mountains (IX (12)). Of the former several probably were primarily for public worship; most of those in the second group and perhaps some of the city *ssŭ* were monasteries, as is indicated by the number of their monks (*cf.* IX (2)) and the amount of property controlled by them (*cf.* introduction, table 11). Since we often have no means of establishing the exact character of the *ssŭ*, we translate the term as "temple." This word is sufficiently indefinite to include also the idea of a home for monks, whereas the term monastery definitely excludes the idea of a temple which has only a few monks attached to it for the service.

The same considerations as in the case of *ssŭ* make it impossible always to translate *kuan*, a term designating religious buildings of the Taoist faith, as "abbey" or "phalanstery." We therefore translate *kuan*, *ssŭ*, *miao*, and other names for religious buildings as "temple," leaving it to the context or explanatory notes to determine the more specific nature of the building in question.

[8] In these visits to the Confucian and Buddhist temples the imperial family was presumably following the T'ang custom of offering sacrifices there in the spring and autumn.

[9] Acts of charity of this kind were, and still are, performed by persons desiring to support Buddhism. The donor (施主) expressed his reverence toward the creed by offering alms, expecting in return good fortune in his present or future life.

[10] See XIV, 1, note 96.

[11] T'ai-tsung's wife, who had died in the fifth month of the same year.

[12] The Indo-Tibetan Bodhisattva Avalokiteśvara was worshipped in China under the name Kuan-yin as a male deity from the third to the seventh century A.D. (Doré, RSC VI, 139; for the male character of Avalokiteśvara see also Wassiljew 60, 135; Waddell 95, 15, 22, and *passim;* Grünwedel 00, 118, 127 ff.; Reichelt 27, 39, 179 ff.; Petech 39, 32). Chao I 趙翼, quoting many sources, contends that the deity appears as a female as early as the fifth century (KYTK 34, 19*b* ff.). The male giver of children, Sung-tzŭ Kuan-yin 送子觀音 (*cf.* Peri 17, 68), certainly was replaced in some cases by a female in the eighth and ninth centuries (Doré, RSC VI, 142). In the Sung period the female character of Kuan-yin seems definitely established (*op. cit.,* 143 ff.; for details other than the chronology see also Peri 17, 67–76). In what way Liao Buddhism followed or paralleled the change in concept which took place in China Proper during the T'ang and Sung periods is not clear. Several statues of undetermined sex recently discovered on Liao sites are said to represent Avalokiteśvara (Torii 36 I, pls. 10–13; II, pl. 119). Did the Ch'i-tan preserve, along with the Indian designation, the original conception of the deity as a male?

[13] These titles refer respectively to T'ai-tsu, the wife of T'ai-tsu, and the eldest brother of T'ai-tsung.

those attending him and said, "Formerly I visited here together with my father, my mother, and my brothers. Now, only a few years later, I come alone!" He sighed sadly. Then he himself made a composition and wrote it on the wall in order to express to the utmost his feelings for them. Those who read it were filled with pity.   3, 8a

7. FIFTY THOUSAND MONKS GRANTED FOOD

942   On the day *ting-ch'ou* [of the sixth month in the fifth year of Hui-t'ung], on hearing that the empress dowager[14] was ill, the emperor hastened in to wait on her and always tasted her medicinal decoction himself. He also reported to the temple of T'ai-tsu, went to the Hall of the Bodhisattva,[15] and gave food to fifty thousand monks.   4, 8b

8. BUDDHIST MONK HONORED

975   On the day *mou-tzŭ* of the twelfth month [in the sixth year of Pao-ning] the *śramaṇa* Chao-min was made the chief general officer of the monks and nuns of the circuits of the three capitals.[16] He was also granted the concurrent rank of inner chamberlain.[17]   8, 4a–b

9. VICTORY CELEBRATED BY BUDDHIST CEREMONIES

986   Furthermore, because many enemies were slain, [on the day *hsin-ssŭ* of the seventh month in the fourth year of T'ung-ho] an imperial edict was issued to K'ai-lung Temple in the Supreme Capital ordering that Buddhist ceremonies be held for one month and that ten thousand monks be presented with food.   11, 5b

10. ORDINATION LIMITED

991   On the day *ping-tzŭ* [of the first month in the ninth year of T'ung-ho] the private ordination[18] of Buddhist monks and nuns was prohibited.   13, 2a

11. PERIODIC RELIGIOUS WORSHIP

995   On the day *jên-ch'ên* [of the eighth month in the thirteenth year of T'ung-ho] it was ordered to repair the shrines on the mountains and rivers together with the temples of deceased worthies in order to worship there seasonally.   13, 6b

12. ORDINATION LIMITED

997   On the day *ting-yu* [of the tenth month in the fifteenth year of T'ung-ho] the Buddhist temples in the mountains were forbidden to make excessive ordination of monks and nuns.   13, 9a

13. UIGHURS

1001   [In the first month in the nineteenth year of T'ung-ho] the Uighurs presented Fan monks[19] and noted doctors.   70, 10b

---

[14] Empress Dowager Ying-t'ien.

[15] See below, note 52.

[16] The term "three capitals," which often appears in the text, generally includes: (a) the Eastern, Central, and Southern Capitals (LS 48, 1b); or (b) the Eastern, Central, and Supreme Capitals (LS 36, 1a). We find from the text (LS 8, 4a) that Shêng-tsung was in the Supreme Capital at the time he granted Chao-min the title. Hence the term employed here may refer to the Eastern, Central, and Supreme Capitals.

[17] Liao priests were frequently given high titles. Li T'ao 李燾, a historian of Southern Sung, records the granting by the Liao emperor Hsing-tsung of such high titles as Three Teachers, Three Dukes, or chief of the Political Council to Buddhist monks, honoring in all twenty persons, and the admonishment by an official for his loose way of granting such titles to people without merit (HTCCP 180, 16a–b).

Because of the high status of the monks, and probably also because they were exempted from various services and taxes, common families with three sons had the eldest son become a monk (CS 6, 20a; *cf.* also Fêng CS 32, 105 ff.).

[18] That is, ordination without the sanction of the government.

[19] See below, note 52.

14. BUDDHISM AND CONFUCIANISM SPREAD NORTHEAST

1012   On the day *ping-shên* of the eighth month [in the first year of K'ai-t'ai], Na-sha and others of T'ieh-li, who had sent more than a hundred Wu-jo[20] households to Pin Prefecture,[21] were granted silk and lustring.   On this day Na-sha asked that he be granted Buddhist pictures and Confucian books.   An imperial decree ordered that he be granted a Buddhist picture of the Benevolent King Who Guards the Country[22] and a copy each of the *Book of Changes, Book of Odes, Documentary Classic, Spring and Autumn Annals,* and *Book of Rites.*   15, 4*b*

15. RESTRICTIONS DURING KOREAN WAR

1015   On the day *kêng-shên* of the eleventh month [in the fourth year of K'ai-t'ai] an imperial decree ordered the Buddhist monks of the Eastern Capital to be reduced in number.   The Supreme Capital and the Central Capital, and the various ordos, were also ordered to select fifty-five thousand well-trained soldiers in order to prepare for an eastern expedition.[23]

15, 9*b*

16. NO SELF–MUTILATION

1020   On the day *ting-hai* of the twelfth month [in the ninth year of K'ai-t'ai] the Buddhist monks were forbidden to burn their bodies and to sear their fingers.[24]   16, 5*b*

17. MOURNING FOR A SUNG EMPEROR

1022   On the day *mou-tzǔ* [of the third month in the second year of T'ai-ping], in behalf of the [deceased] Sung ruler,[25] the Buddhist monks of the three capitals were fed.[26]

16, 6*b*

18. HSING–TSUNG ACCEPTS BUDDHIST COMMANDMENTS

1039   [In the twelfth month of the seventh year of Ch'ung-hsi, Hsing-tsung] visited a Buddhist temple and accepted the Buddhist commandments.   68, 14*a*

19. DISCUSSION OF BUDDHIST DOCTRINES

1039   On the day *mou-hsü* [of the eleventh month in the eighth year of Ch'ung-hsi the emperor] paid a visit to the empress dowager[27] and summoned the monks to expound the Buddhist doctrines.   18, 9*a*

20. BUDDHIST CEREMONIES ON AN EMPRESS' DEATH–DAY

1043   On the day *chi-yu* [of the twelfth month in the eleventh year of Ch'ung-hsi], because it was the anniversary of the death of Empress Hsüan-hsien,[28] the emperor and the empress dowager donned plain clothes and presented food to the monks of the three temples of Yen-shou, Min-chung,[29] and San-hsüeh.   19, 3*b*

---

[20] The Wu-jo tribe was composed of Po-hai remnants who originally dwelt near the T'ieh-li tribe and in 1012 moved to Pin Prefecture (*cf.* I, 2 (9), no. 26). Most of the people had the family name Li 李. In the time of Chin 金 the family of Li Ching 李靖 enjoyed an outstanding political and scholarly position (*cf.* SMCW 6*a–b*).

[21] A city at the juncture of the Sungari River and the I-t'ung River (MRC II, 31).

[22] A title given by the Liao emperor. It refers to Buddha.

[23] Against Korea. See XV, 2, note 50.

[24] According to the inscription *Ch'ung-hsiu Fan-yang Pai-tai-shan Yün-chü-ssǔ Pei* 重修范陽白帶山雲居寺碑, not only the monks but also the common people who came to worship in the temples sometimes tortured themselves by burning their fingers and heads, or committed suicide by throwing themselves into a gorge (LWT 5, 12*b*–13*a*).

[25] According to CTKC 7, 8*a*, after the Sung emperor, Chên-tsung, died, Shêng-tsung commanded that the former's image be set up in the Min-chung 悯忠 Temple of the Southern Capital and that prayers be said for him for one hundred days. The playing of music in the prefectures along the frontier was stopped and the name of Chên-tsung was tabooed.

[26] If a Sung diplomat died in Liao territory, the Liao government also paid homage to him by providing a coffin and appropriate clothes. When, in 1092, Yü-wên Ch'ang-ling 宇文昌齡 came to Liao as an envoy, and his assistant, Chang Tsao 張璪, died, the Liao government, in accordance with the tradition concerning the treatment of diplomats, spent three hundred taels of silver for his coffin and garments (HML 36*a*).

[27] Empress Dowager Ch'in-ai.

[28] This was the posthumous title of Ching-tsung's wife, the grandmother of Hsing-tsung. In 1052 it was changed to that of Empress Jui-chih. She had died in 1009.

[29] Wang Tsêng who visited Liao in 1013 described this temple in a memorial (SHYK 196, 44*b*).

21. BUDDHIST MONK HONORED

1050   On the day *kêng-yin* of the first month in the nineteenth year [of Ch'ung-hsi] the monk Hui-chien was granted the additional title of superior grand commandant.[30]

20, 3*b*

22. AMNESTY FOLLOWS CASTING OF A SILVER BUDDHA

1054   On the day *kuei-ch'ou* [of the tenth month in the twenty-third year of Ch'ung-hsi], because the silver Buddha of the K'ai-t'ai Temple was cast, the prisoners of the [Supreme] Capital were pardoned by special action of the emperor.   20, 8*b*

23. THE THREE DOCTRINES MAY NOT BE INSULTED

1056   In the second year of Ch'ing-ning the people of T'ung Prefecture[31] wantonly insulted the three doctrines.[32]   [Chao] Hui[33] examined them.   He then submitted a report concerning the case which the emperor considered satisfactory.   97, 3*b*

24. BUDDHIST CANON GIVEN TO KOREA

1063   In the twelfth month of the eighth year [of Ch'ing-ning] a Canon of the Buddhist sūtras was granted to [Wang] Hwi.[34]   115, 4*a*

25. PRIVATE COURT VISITS OF MONKS AND NUNS

1064   On the day *hsin-ssŭ* [of the seventh month in the tenth year of Ch'ing-ning] Buddhist monks and nuns were forbidden to pay private visits[35] to the imperial residences in order to secure rewards by making senseless predictions of good or bad fortune.   22, 2*b*–3*a*

26. BUDDHIST FAST DAYS

1064   On the day *hsin-wei* [of the eleventh month in the tenth year of Ch'ing-ning] the slaughter of animals on the six fast days[36] was prohibited.   22, 3*a*

---

[30] *Chien-chiao t'ai-wei* 檢校太尉. In the T'ang and Sung dynasties the expression *chien-chiao* was prefixed to a number of titles to form new and higher titles (*cf.* CYTC *A*12, 159).

[31] Modern Hsi-mu 析木 City, Liaoning.

[32] Of the "three doctrines," Buddhism, Taoism, and Confucianism, the third was obviously not as highly respected as the first. In 1027 a Sung envoy, K'ung Tao-fu 孔道輔, visited the court of Liao. In his honor a play was performed in which an actor took the role of Confucius. The Chinese envoy became very angry and asked that the performance, which he considered an insult to the Great Sage, be forbidden (SS 297, 2*a*).

[33] Chao Hui 趙徽 achieved the rank of *chin-shih* in 1036.

[34] Wang Hwi 王徽, the king of Korea, reigned from 1047 to 1083. The text here states that 一藏 was granted to him, thus indicating merely a collection of sūtras. See Soothill and Hodous 37, 467 for an interpretation of this, and an explanation of the twofold Canon etc.

The influence of Liao Buddhism on Korea and the importation of Liao Buddhist texts into that country are discussed by Tsukamoto Zenryū, who notes that during the reign of Hsing-tsung (1031–1055) the Tripiṭaka was compiled in 579 cases and in 1068 it was printed with a financial subsidy contributed by Têng Ts'ung-kuei (Tsukamoto 36, 275 ff.; *idem* 36*a*, 89). A copy of the precious work was sent to Korea four years later. The Korean official history, completed in 1451 by Chöng Nin-chi 鄭麟趾, states that in 1063 the Liao court gave a set of the Tripiṭaka to Korea. When the Liao delegation arrived at the Korean capital with the Canon, the Korean king in

a formal equipage welcomed the guests in the western suburb (KRS 8, 118).

The Liao edition was printed with small characters on thin sheets of paper which were attractively bound. In the thirteenth century, between 1236 and 1251, a Korean monk Su-ki 守其, when preparing a new Korean edition of the Canon, compared the existing texts. He found the Sung and Korean versions less accurate and less complete than their Liao counterpart. He therefore inserted in the new edition many chapters and details from the Liao Canon. He adopted from the Liao work seven *chüan* of original textual material not contained in the Sung and Korean editions; he added thirty-five chapters with new contributions made by Liao Buddhists; he replaced seven *chüan* of the Sung edition with the corresponding Liao version. In eleven *chüan*, Sung and Korean versions were corrected by recourse to the Liao text; in fifteen *chüan* the Sung edition was corrected by means of the Liao and the Korean texts. Only two *chüan* of the final Korean edition were lacking in the Liao Canon; distortions of the text were discovered in five *chüan* of this Canon; in eleven *chüan* Sung versions were used to correct the Liao and Korean texts (Kamio 37, 87–150).

[35] We follow other editions in reading 私詣 for the 和諧 of our text.

[36] The Buddhist six fast days 六齋日 are the eighth, fourteenth, fifteenth, twenty-third, twenty-ninth, and thirtieth of each month. Originally no meal was to be eaten in the afternoon of these days, but later the rules were changed and only the eating of meat and the drinking of wine was forbidden.

27. BUDDHIST MONK HONORED

1066   On the day *mou-tzŭ* [of the twelfth month in the second year of Hsien-yung] the monk Shou-chih was granted the additional title of minister over the masses.[37]   22, 4b

28. HSIA OFFERS UIGHUR MONKS

1067   On the day *jên-ch'ên* of the eleventh month in the winter [of the third year of Hsien-yung] the country of Hsia sent an envoy to offer Uighur monks,[38] golden Buddhas, and the *Sūtra of Enlightenment* in Sanskrit.[39]   22, 5a

29. TAO–TSUNG WRITES ON BUDDHISM

1068   On the day *kuei-ch'ou* [of the second month in the fourth year of Hsien-yung] the *Eulogy on the Avataṁsaka Sūtra*, which was compiled by the emperor, was published.
22, 5b

30. A BUDDHIST MONK HONORED

1070   On the day *chi-wei* of the intercalary [eleventh month in the fifth year of Hsien-yung] the monk Chih-fu was granted the additional title of minister over the masses.
22, 6b

31. BUDDHIST CEREMONY HALTS KILLING OF ANIMALS

1071   On the day *hsin-ssŭ* of the eighth month [in the seventh year of Hsien-yung], while a bone of Buddha was being placed in the Chao-hsien Pagoda, hunting was stopped and the slaughter of animals was forbidden.   22, 7b

32. MEN AND WOMEN TAKE THE FULL BUDDHIST VOWS

1072   On the day *kuei-mao* of the third month [in the eighth year of Hsien-yung] the authorities memorialized that in the three prefectures of Ch'un,[40] T'ai,[41] and Ning-chiang[42] more than three thousand[43] persons had expressed the wish to become monks and nuns and to accept the Buddhist commandments in their entirety.   They were permitted to do so.   23, 1a–b

33. TAO–TSUNG COPIES SCRIPTURE

1072   On the day *ting-wei* [of the seventh month in the eighth year of Hsien-yung] the *Five Stanzas of Eulogy on the Avataṁsaka Sūtra*, which had been copied by the emperor, was shown to the courtiers.[44]   23, 1b

---

[37] The minister over the masses was one of the Three Dukes. As mentioned in section XIV, his rank was very high. Many contemporary inscriptions and books written by Sung scholars mention the fact that during the Liao period Buddhist monks were given titles of the highest order. Since this was against Chinese tradition, the emperor Shih-tsung of the Chin dynasty condemned the usage very sternly. *Cf.* Fêng CS 32, 110; see above note 17.

[38] In 966 a prefect of Hsi-liang 西凉 reported to the Sung court that more than two hundred Uighurs and more than sixty Chinese monks coming from the Shuo-fang 朔方 region had been robbed by tribesmen. The monks, who said they were on their way to India to obtain an original Buddhist sūtra, were escorted to Kan 甘 Prefecture (SS 492, 3a). Were the Uighurs believing laymen who accompanied the monks on their pilgrimage?

[39] A Liao inscription says that a Yeh-lü clansman owned 5,048 *chüan* of the Buddhist sūtras (JHC 118, 1b). This indicates that during the Liao period there existed private collections of the sūtras of considerable size.

[40] Northwest of modern Po-tu-na 伯都訥, Kirin.

[41] Southwest of Nung-an 農安 County, Kirin.

[42] Modern Shih-t'ou Ch'êng-tzŭ 石頭城子, Kirin (MRC II, 50).

[43] Our edition has 三千 (three thousand), but the Northern and Southern Academy editions and most of the later editions have 三十 (thirty). In another part of the *Liao Shih* containing a résumé of the important events of Tao-tsung's reign, to which our passage refers, only one record concerns the taking of vows by a number of laymen, and this record gives the figure as three thousand, not thirty (LS 26, 6b). The passage is uncontested; our version of the text supports it. Although the version of the Northern and Southern Academy editions has been widely quoted, it seems an error for three thousand.

[44] Liao rulers and officials reproduced Buddhist scriptures. Work on the stone-cut Canon of the Yün-chü 雲居 Temple, which began under the Sui and T'ang dynasties, was completed in Liao times (see IX, introduction, note 30). According to an inscription dated 1118

34. BUDDHIST SŪTRAS AS AN IMPERIAL PRESENT

1073   On the day *kêng-yin* [of the twelfth month in the eighth year of Hsien-yung, Tao-tsung] granted Korea a Canon of Buddhist sūtras.   23, 2a

35. BUDDHIST EDUCATION FOR AN HEIR APPARENT

1075   On the day *i-ssŭ* in the third month [of the first year of Ta-k'ang the emperor] commanded the heir apparent to write out the Buddhist scriptures.   23, 3a

36. THREE HUNDRED SIXTY THOUSAND MONKS AND NUNS GRANTED FOOD

1078   On the day *chia-hsü* of the seventh month in the autumn [of the fourth year of Ta-k'ang] all routes memorialized that they had presented food to three hundred and sixty thousand Buddhist monks and nuns.[45]   23, 6b

37. NO HAMPERING OF BUDDHIST ACTIVITIES

1079   On the day *chi-mao* of the ninth month [in the fifth year of Ta-k'ang] an imperial decree ordered all routes not to forbid monks to set up altars for religious ceremonies.   24, 1b

38. A BUDDHIST ALTAR FOR AN EMPRESS

1079   On the day *ting-ch'ou* of the eleventh month [in the fifth year of Ta-k'ang] the *śramaṇa* Shou-tao was summoned to install an altar in the Inner Hall.[46]   24, 2a

39. SŪTRAS RECEIVED FROM KOREA

1083   On the day *chia-yin* [of the eleventh month in the ninth year of Ta-k'ang] an imperial decree ordered the Buddhist monk, Shan-chih, to collate the Buddhist sūtras presented by Korea in order to publish them.[47]   24, 5b

40. A TEMPLE GIVES RELIEF MONEY

1087   On the day *kêng-shên* [of the fifth month in the third year of Ta-an] the Hai-yün Temple presented ten million cash as relief for the people.[48]   25, 1b

---

(see fig. 29), the engraving activities of the eleventh century were subsidized by three Liao emperors: Shêng-tsung, Hsing-tsung, and Tao-tsung. One hundred and eighty large and four thousand and eighty small stone tablets were buried in the ground; their location was marked by a pagoda which was built over them (LWT 4, 21a ff.).

Laymen followed the example set by the temples and reprinted Buddhist texts. A Liao inscription mentions a man named Tung 董 who went so far as to sell his property in order to purchase and reprint the Buddhist scriptures (LWT 4, 13a–b). They also recite the Buddhist scriptures. A Liao Chinese, Han Chêng 韓正, who between 1119 and 1125 was appointed to the post of commanding prefect, went each day to an open place, loudly reciting a Buddhist text, *T'ien-t'ung Ching* 天童經, many times. He objected to the word "I" (我家) as improper for communicating with the divine powers (in everyday life a superior used it when speaking to an individual of lower status). In more than twenty passages he replaced it by the phrase 小人, "the small person" (CSSC 9a).

Most of the Liao writings which are preserved today are Buddhist texts. Not less than fourteen are now known (cf. PLSIWC 1a ff.).

[45] A similar record (LS 26, 6b) mentions three hundred and sixty thousand monks as benefiting from the emperor's generosity. The passage adds that during a single day three thousand persons cut off their hair, thus entering the ranks of the Buddhist clergy.

[46] The residence of the empress.

[47] Tao-tsung's attitude toward Buddhist Korea is illustrated by an incident which happened some time before 1099. Wang Ê 王蕚, who was sent as an envoy to Korea, saw a small, but beautiful, bell in the Hing-wang 興王 Temple. He expressed his admiration, whereupon the monk suggested that, inasmuch as the Liao emperor believed in Buddhism, two gold bells should be offered to him. When the bells were sent to Tao-tsung, he refused them and punished Wang Ê for his unreasonable demand from a subordinate state (TKTK 18, 464).

[48] The Hai-yün 海雲 Temple was situated on the mainland across from Chüeh-hua 覺花 Island (modern Chü-hua 菊花 Island near Hsing-ch'êng 興城, Liaoning, in the Gulf of Liaotung). During Hsing-tsung's reign this temple was headed by Hai-shan 海山, a man who in his earlier days had obtained the *chin-shih* degree and had held several regional positions, and who later, as a Buddhist dignitary, was highly respected by the emperor and the imperial princes and princesses (cf. LTHPC 3a).

On Chüeh-hua Island was Lung-kung 龍宮 Temple, which was famous for the splendor of its buildings and notorious for the enslavement of its retainers (CHC 1, 9b–11a; CS 96, 4b).

41. HSIA OFFERS A MANUSCRIPT SŪTRA

1095   On the day *chia-chên* [of the eleventh month in the first year of Shou-lung] the country of Hsia offered a Buddhist sūtra written on palm leaves.[49]   26, 2a

42. BUDDHIST MONK HONORED

1097   On the day *mou-wu* [of the eleventh month in the third year of Shou-lung] the monk Chih-ta from I-wu-lü Mountain[50] was summoned to court in a Comfortable Chariot.[51]   26, 3a–b

43. A BUDDHIST ALTAR FOR AN EMPRESS

1100   On the day *ping-tzǔ* [of the eleventh month in the sixth year of Shou-lung] the monk Chih-ta from I-wu-lü Mountain was summoned to install an altar in the Inner Hall.   26, 5b

44. COMMANDMENTS MUST BE KEPT

1113   On the day *chia-hsü* [of the first month in the third year of T'ien-ch'ing] the monks and nuns were forbidden to break the Buddhist commandments.[52]   27, 7a

---

Li Yen 李晏 (d. 1197), who for a while held the post of censor in the Chin 金 government, reported to Emperor Shih-tsung of Chin, "Formerly the Lung-kung Temple of Chin 錦 Prefecture (modern Chin County, Liaoning) was presented by the Liao emperor with families of common people who were to pay taxes to the temple. But after a while they were considered slaves. Those who tried to appeal [to the government] were killed on the island." Li Yen concluded by asking that this malpractice be stopped. Shih-tsung followed his advice and freed more than six hundred persons who had lived under the bondage of the Lung-kung Temple (CS 96, 4b).

The wealth of Liao Buddhism at the close of the dynasty, which is revealed by the above passage, is also reflected in an inscription of 1093 concerning the Kuan-chi 觀雞 Temple in Ching 景 Prefecture. This temple possessed cash amounting to five thousand strings, three thousand *mou* of farm land, several hundred *ch'ing* of forests, seven thousand fruit trees, one hundred and seventy resident houses and inns, and a pawnshop. The monks numbered more than a hundred (FJHC 4, 13b ff.).

[49] 貝多, the *peito* or palmyra palm, the leaves of which were used to write on (Giles 12, 8793).

[50] In modern Pei-chên 北鎮 County, Liaoning.

[51] The *an ch'ê* 安車, a term which may be translated as Comfortable Chariot, was used from Han or pre-Han times by the emperor and empress and by distinguished officials and their wives. It was also used to summon aged and respected officials to court (*cf.* CLCS 27, 3b–4a; LCCS 1, 9a; TS 24, 1a ff.). During the Chin 金 and Sung dynasties it was used only by the empress (CS 43, 3b ff.; SS 150, 1a). A detailed description of the *an ch'ê* of the Sung period is given in WHL 1a–b. It is described as low-wheeled with a body six feet long so that a person could lie in it comfortably. During the Sung dynasty the *chin-hsien* 進賢 chariot was used instead of the *an ch'ê* to summon aged and respected officials to court (SS 149, 13b).

[52] The *Liao Shih*, which is so articulate on the development of Buddhism in the Liao empire, has little if anything to say on other contemporary religions such as Islam, Christianity, or Manicheism. During the tenth and eleventh centuries Mohammedanism advanced impressively in Central Asia, converting not only large sections of the urban population, but also many nomadic groups, among them the Qarā-Khānids around 960 (Marquart 12, 493; Barthold 28, 254; *idem* 35, 78), the Saljūqids before 1043 (Barthold 01, 50), and other Turkic tribes in 960 and 1043 (Barthold 28, 254; Marquart 12, 493 and 496; Barthold 01, 50–51). The Moslem creed spread primarily because of the growing political power of Islam (Barthold 35, 51). It is therefore understandable that it did not conspicuously affect the mighty and independent Liao world.

Nestorian Christianity, which had been tolerated in China from 635 on (Pelliot 14, 624), was outlawed together with Buddhism and Manicheism by the T'ang government in 845, a few years after the collapse of the Buddhist-Manichean Uighur empire (*cf.* de Groot, SRP I, 59 ff.; Marquart 12, 489, Chavannes-Pelliot 13, 284 ff.). The persecutions that followed interfered much more seriously with Christianity than with the two other proscribed creeds. In 987 a Christian monk, after his return from the Far East, reported in Constantinople that "the Christians of China had disappeared and perished for various reasons and that in the whole country only one was left" (Kitāb al-Fihrist = Ferrand 13, 129; *cf.* also Moule 30, 76 and Pelliot 14, 626). To be sure, some fragments survived north of China, but the second wave of Christian expansion did not get started until the eleventh century (Barthold 35, 58); according to Bar Hebraeus, the Keraits south of Lake Baikal adopted Nestorianism in 1007 (Bar Hebraeus, Chron. Eccles. II, col. 279 = Browne 33, 101–102; *cf.* also Barthold 01, 51 and Pelliot 14, 627).

Buddhism weathered the storm more successfully, and even Manicheism was not completely suppressed, although it had to resort to camouflage in order to carry on (*cf.* Chavannes-Pelliot 13, 318 ff.). No precautions or disguises were necessary in those regions of Inner Asia that lay beyond the reach of Chinese power. The Uighurs, who lost their empire between 840 and 843, did not disappear from the political scene. Having embraced Manicheism in 763 (Chavannes-Pelliot 13, 190 and 199) and Buddhism in 778–779 (Marquart 12, 496–497), they continued to practise both creeds even after 843. A hundred years later, the importance of Manicheism among the Uighurs is still emphasized by Mas'ūdī (Maçoudi, PO I, 288; cf. Barthold 35, 58); it is documented for the Kan Prefecture Uighurs in 951 (CWTS 138, 5b; cf. Chavannes-Pelliot 13, 305 ff.); and for the Kao-ch'ang Uighurs in 983 (SS 490, 10b). Al-Bīrūnī claims that in his time (the earlier part of the eleventh century) "most of the eastern Turks, of the people of China and Thibet and some of the Hindus, adhere still to his [Mani's] law and doctrine" (Bērūnī 79, 191). The statement is obviously exaggerated; the author, like other Islamic writers, probably drew no clear distinction between Manicheism and Buddhism (Barthold 35, 58). But such a lack of clarity does not completely invalidate al-Bīrūnī's testimony. As his *Chronology* reveals, he had a very fair understanding of Manicheism (Bērūnī 79, 189–192), and his remark on the spread of the Persian creed among the "Eastern Turks" appears correct, especially insofar as the Uighurs, then also called Toghuzghuz (Barthold 35, 58; cf. also Flügel 62, 106 and 388 ff.), are concerned.

When the Liao government took over the northeastern territories of the former T'ang empire, it had no interest in implementing the severe edict of 845. Buddhism enjoyed great favor at the "northern court"; and Manicheism and Christianity seem to have been tolerated, though neither attained major importance. West of Fang-shan 房山, some forty miles southwest of Peiping, is the Buddhist "Temple of the Cross" 十字寺 which, sometime around 1896, was included by a Chinese official in a list of antiquities (IFCSWT 13, 1b). From 1919 on, this temple attracted international attention, for it contained two crosses carved on stone (see fig. 31), similar to the cross appearing at the top of the famous Nestorian tablet of 781 in Hsi-an. One of the Fang-shan crosses bears, in Syriac, the words: "Look ye unto it and hope in it" (Psalm 34, 5). Also preserved in the temple are two inscribed tablets, one Liao, the other Yüan. The former, dated 960, ascribes the erection of two stone *ch'uang* 幢 (pillars) to Chin 晉 and T'ang times (BCP 22, 290 ff., 464 ff.; *idem* 23, 218 ff.; cf. also Moule 30, 86 ff.; *idem* 31, 82 ff.). These *ch'uang* are generally identified as the stones on which the crosses appear. While such an identification may be entirely correct, the presence of crosses on the two stones is no sure index that Christianity played a significant role in the Liao empire. It may, however, be argued that the inscription suggests a not antagonistic Liao attitude toward an unmistakably Christian symbol.

Crosses have also been discovered in other parts of the old Liao territory, and these with varying degrees of certainty have been assigned to the Liao period: The seven crosses of Shih-chu-tzǔ-liang 石柱子梁 in Inner Mongolia stand in a cemetery that also yielded Liao coins dated Shêng-tsung (BCP 24, 54 ff.; cf. Moule 30, 74 ff., note 93; *idem* 31, 83). In the ruins of an old northern Liao city on the T'ao-êrh 洮兒 River, a metal cross was found in 1927 (Saeki 35, 984–993). A number of large earthen crosses appeared in some recently investigated Liao tombs in Liao-yang; and at the site of the Liao Supreme Capital Torii collected a number of objects which he claims are Nestorian (Torii 37, 344).

These archaeological finds are supplemented by written records that, directly or by implication, indicate the Nestorian affiliations of certain individuals during the Liao period. The Yüan scholar, Huang Chin 黃溍, traced the genealogy of his famous contemporary, Ma Tsu-ch'ang 馬祖常 to Ho-lu Mi-ssǔ 和祿釆思, a scion of a distinguished Nestorian family who, in the eleventh century, came from the Western Regions to the Liao empire. Ho-lu Mi-ssǔ, whose name may originally have been Horam Michael, refused the official title offered him by Emperor Tao-tsung, but his son served as an officer in the Liao army (CHWC 43, 1a; Ch'ên Y 23a, 594; Chang HL 30 II, 267 ff.). An inscription made in 987 in Chi 薊 County, northeast of modern Peiping, speaks of an abbot who belonged to "the Nestorian sect (*ching p'ai* 景派) which is of foreign origin. Its god is unfathomable. Suffering which follows desire is brought to an end. Happiness is shared with others" (LWT 5, 15a). In 962, under this same abbot's direction, the temple was enlarged by the addition of a new hall which contained a single statue —that of Buddha (*op. cit.*, 15b).

The curious mixture of Nestorian and Buddhist elements revealed by this story is less bewildering if it is remembered that Nestorianism, as well as other religions of refuge including Manicheism, exhibits syncretistic combinations of all kinds. The cross on the Nestorian tablet in Hsi-an, as well as the two crosses found near Fang-shan, rests on a lotus flower (cf. Moule 31, 81, and 82)—that is, they appear in a typically Buddhist setting.

The various elements blended in Empress Ying-t'ien's dream of a god with a golden crown who is followed by twelve animals (VII, 2 (2)) are difficult to identify; but more detailed and therefore more suggestive are the records of two dreams ascribed to the empress' second son. In the first, T'ai-tsung saw a god, handsome in appearance, wearing a chaplet and attended by a ceremonial cortege. Suddenly this god, scepter in hand, descended from heaven, his white clothes held together by a golden belt. Twelve strange animals followed him, and one, a black hare, leaped into the emperor's bosom and disappeared. Addressing T'ai-tsung, the god said: "When Shih Ching-t'ang [the founder of the Later Chin dynasty] dispatches a messenger to call upon you, you must go!"

T'ai-tsung told his mother of his dream, and at first she gave it little attention, but when her son dreamed again of the same god, dressed the same way, and speaking the same words, she advised him to consult a *hu wu* 胡巫 (a *hu* "shaman"). The *hu wu*, after completing his divinations, declared: "T'ai-tsu on his return from the West Tower said, 'China is going to set up a heavenly king who needs your help. You must go.'" T'ai-tsung, thereupon, supported Shih Ching-t'ang in his fight against the tottering Later T'ang dynasty, urged to action not by worldly motives, but—so at least the record claims—by the heavenly lord's command (CTKC 2, 6a–b).

Some time later, on a visit to the seat of Yu 幽 Prefecture, T'ai-tsung identified an image of a Bodhisattva which he saw there with the god of his dreams. While their gowns differed in color, both wore the same head-dress. The emperor therefore erected at Mu-yeh Mountain a Hall of Bodhisattvas, P'u-sa T'ang 菩薩堂 (*loc. cit.*).

The *Liao Shih*, in a somewhat different version, which ascribes the dream to T'ai-tsu, states that the emperor had the Kuan-yin in the White Dress removed from Yu Prefecture to Mu-yeh Mountain, establishing it as his family deity (家神), to whom he announced his military plans and achievements (LS 37, 9a–b; 49, 3a; T'ai-tsu is obviously a mistake for T'ai-tsung).

T'ai-tsung's two dreams end on an unmistakably Buddhist note. They contain, however, a number of features suggestive of other religious creeds. Nestorian Christianity, documented by archaeological and literary evidence, may well have provided some elements in the miracle story: the scepter-bearing god, the non-Buddhist white gown, the twelve strange followers, the idea of a directing father. But it is equally probable, if not more so, that these features derived primarily from other sources. The father motif may be plausibly explained by Ch'i-tan or Chinese tradition. The possibility of Manichean influence is suggested by the Uighur background of Ch'i-tan civilization in general and of the Hsiao clan in particular. The color white, which had an honorific significance in Ch'i-tan tradition (*cf.* VII, 2, *passim* and index, sub: white) was also favored by the Nestorians (Saeki 35, 662), but it assumed particular prominence among the Manicheans who considered light the manifestation of the Supreme Being (Bērūnī 79, 190; *cf.* also Jackson 32, 7 *passim*). White gowns and headdresses are documented for the Manicheans both in Turfan and in China (Chavannes-Pelliot 13, 262, note 1, and 333, note 1; also Le Coq 22 TMC, 46–47). Even in Sung China, where the adherents of the then outlawed creed are said to have changed the color of their garments, they still worshipped a "white Buddha," whom they identified with Mani (Chavannes-Pelliot 13, 333 ff.).

The twelve animals, which also appear in Ying-t'ien's dream, seem to have nothing in common with the twelve apostles except their number. However, the figure twelve is conspicuous in Mani's cosmology (*cf.* Jackson 32, 25 ff., 37 ff.), having been derived from the "twelve hours" (Chavannes-Pelliot 13, 545; Le Coq 22 TMC, 18; *cf.* Schaeder 27, 94)—that is, from the twelve "signs of the zodiac" (Jackson 32, 192 ff.; for reference to the zodiac and the "twelve hours" in Manichean sects see Le Coq 11 TMC, 15 and 19; and 22 TMC, 6, 12, 16 ff. and 18 ff.).

In the records dealing with the history of Manicheism translated by Chavannes and Pelliot the term *hu* has been rendered either as "Iranian" or "Soghdian" (Chavannes-Pelliot 13, 166, 171, 173, and 268–269, note 3). If this rendering is accepted, the *hu wu* of our story would have been a Central Asiatic priest. However, in other contemporary sources the word *hu* has the general connotation "barbarian" or tribal. The diviner consulted by the disturbed emperor was obviously not a Buddhist, but whether he was a Nestorian or a Manichean cannot be determined.

Concrete and incontrovertible evidence of Liao Manicheism is scanty. According to a Uighur document recently discovered in Qarā-Khodja [ancient Kao-ch'ang] a Manichean *auditor* returned to Central Asia with a Manichean text from "Chatai" ٮڡٮٮ (Le Coq 11 TMC, 29). Unfortunately the attached note written by the *auditor* and dated by Chavannes and Pelliot (13, 141), "des environs de l'an 1000," yields no significant data on the Manichean's experiences in "Chatai"; it merely states that he recited the text twice after returning from that country (*loc. cit.*).

In 1001 the Uighurs sent *fan sêng* 梵僧 to Liao (IX (13)). In Buddhist writings the term *fan* usually designates a Brahman; and a *fan sêng* is "a monk from India," or, more generally, "a monk who maintains his purity" (Soothill and Hodous 37, 353). However, in view of the importance of the Manicheans in Uighur society, Ch'ên Yüan assumes that the monks sent in 1001 possibly were Manicheans (Ch'ên Y 23, 225).

An inscription made during the Chin 金 dynasty discusses heretic religious trends that developed under the guise of Buddhism at the close of the T'ang period and during the Liao and Sung dynasties. The heretics prefer *wu hsin* 無心 (no desire) to fasting, *wu yen* 無言 (no words) to the expounding of texts, and *wu wei* 無爲 (no action) to the exalting of pagodas and temples (MCWP 40b). The Three Seals—abstention from evil thoughts, words, and deeds—are fundamental in the Manichean ethical code (Jackson 32, 334 ff.). Manicheism, which grew from a synthesis of ancient Persian ideas with elements of Buddhism, Christianity, and Gnosticism (*cf.* Jackson 32, 7; Schaeder 27, 73 ff.), was particularly well-prepared for further syncretistic adjustment when historical circumstance demanded it. (See Müller 15, 5; Le Coq 19 TMC, 4 and 7 ff.; 22 TMC, 3 and 46 ff.; *cf.* also Chavannes-Pelliot 13, 319 ff. and 377; Schaeder 27, 92; Barthold 28, 389; Jackson 32, 7.) In view of this, it is not impossible that whatever remnants of Manicheism existed within the Liao empire were gradually associated and merged with the country's outstanding religion, Buddhism.

SECTION X

THE FINANCIAL SYSTEM

INTRODUCTION

1. THE POWER ASPECT OF LIAO SOCIETY

For certain periods history may be written—and has been written—from an exclusively social and economic point of view. Such an approach, which is never fully satisfactory, is conspicuously inadequate when a society like that of imperial China is under consideration, for then the political (bureaucratic) organization so permeates all aspects of the civilization that no clear understanding of its dynamics is possible without a presentation and analysis of the political and military framework within which it functions.

Even more important is a political analysis of China's dynasties of conquest. Here the coercive role of the state is particularly conspicuous. A complex (dual) political organization is built up and maintained by a strong army which, in turn, depends upon an effective civil service. Taxes and tributes feed the military as well as the administrative machine. Forced labor provides manpower for the construction of fortifications, palaces, and roads. Relief measures maintain the population's ability to pay taxes and serve in the corvée.

The analyses given in this and subsequent sections, therefore, deal first with the financial organization of the Liao government (X), next with its labor service (XI), its relief policy (XII), its conflicts and crises (XIII), and finally with the structure and activities of its political and military machines (XIV–XV).

2. THE FINANCIAL ORGANIZATION

a. ITS DEVELOPMENT

Every government seeks an income large enough to cover its needs, both present and future; it raises the necessary revenue according to the country's present situation, recent experience, and historical tradition. The financial system of the Liao dynasty was no exception: it clearly reflected the national and international configurations within which it developed.

At the beginning of the dynasty the financial situation, according to the *Liao Shih*, was very simple.[1] Concrete statements dealing with matters of taxation at this time are few and fragmentary, possibly because historiography in the new state was still an undeveloped art, possibly because the financial system was

still rudimentary, possibly because of both factors. A-pao-chi taxed the salt production of his newly acquired Chinese subjects;[2] he "lightened the taxes" after his victory over the rebellious brothers,[3] a measure which, in all probability, affected those Ch'i-tan tribespeople who were temporarily impoverished by the widespread unrest among the camps and lineages.[4]

The first step toward establishing a comprehensive financial organization in the Chinese style was taken by Han Yen-hui.[5] Under T'ai-tsung the population was registered "to determine the taxation."[6] But it was only after the conquest of the capital of Chin in 947 that the empire's settled territories were organized into a Southern Region, complementing the tribal Northern Region. The Southern Region had its own financial administration which differed from and was seemingly independent of the financial organization of the Northern Region.

b. ITS STRUCTURE (THE TRIBAL WORLD)

The fiscal administration of the tribes was centered in the Southern Chancellery of the Northern Region,[7] an office which demanded so much technical skill that it was generally headed by a Chinese.[8] Details of regional organization are practically non-existent: large as well as small tribes had a "minister over the masses"; the latter also had a "minister of works,"[9] but it is an open question whether these officials were the active administrators of fiscal affairs or whether their titles were purely honorific.

c. ITS STRUCTURE (THE FIVE CAPITALS)

The texts are not clear as to the functional interrelation of the various metropolitan and regional financial bureaus. However, we know that the central government of the Southern Region, which had its seat in the Supreme Capital, included a Ministry of Revenue, probably identical with the bureau of similar name under the general control of the Chinese

---

[1] XIV, 2 (10).

[2] III (4).
[3] II, 2 (2).
[4] XIII (11).
[5] I, 3 (1).
[6] *Loc. cit.*
[7] XIV, 1 (9), LS 45, 3*a*–*b*.
[8] XIV, introduction
[9] *Cf.* XIV, 1 (23) (24).

Chancellery.[10] The government and imperial treasuries were administered by the central government of the Southern Region,[11] and to judge from their titles, they must have received the revenues destined for the use of the government and court. Whatever income was brought to the metropolitan storehouses was forwarded either from the tribes or from the territorial administration of the Five Capitals whose growth, responding to regional needs and traditions, was "not uniform."[12] Shang-ching Circuit had an Office of the Salt and Iron Commissioner. Hsi-ching Circuit boasted an Office of the Accountant, and the Southern Capital, a Triple Office.[13] This last bureau, which controlled the empire's wealthiest territory,[14] was no Liao innovation; it was already in existence at the time of the Five Dynasties.[15] It probably had originated in 906 at the end of the T'ang dynasty,[16] and continued to function under the Sung dynasty. Wang An-shih temporarily held office in one of its three departments.[17] In the Sung period the Triple Office managed the salt and iron administration, kept account of the national revenues, and controlled the system of taxation.[18] The Triple Office of Chin, which apparently had the same three main divisions,[19] may have followed Liao as well as Sung tradition.

The creation of Money and Silk Offices in certain regions of the Liao empire satisfied special territorial needs. An Office of the Ministry of Revenue in the Eastern Capital and an Office of Money and Silk had been established farther to the north in Ch'ang-ch'un Prefecture because the mining and smelting operations were carried on primarily in that part of the empire.[20] Offices of the same name west of the Liao River and in the northeast of Nan-ching Circuit[21] may have been created for similar reasons, while salt control offices were established wherever the local extraction of the mineral made its supervision by the government desirable.[22] Whether the trade tax[23] was collected by agents responsible to particular offices, or by officials of the general territorial financial administration is not clear.

The county magistrates were the intermediaries between the territorial government and the villages whose community life in the Chinese regions centered around the village altars. The officials of these altars recorded all compulsory contributions to the local granaries[24] in registers that, in all probability, were either identical with or similar to[25] those upon which the general taxation of the peasant families was based.

The fief-like Entrusted Prefectures retained their local revenues, except for the not inconsiderable wine tax which was handed over to the financial headquarters of Shang-ching Circuit—the Salt and Iron Office of the Supreme Capital.[26]

d. STRATIFIED TAXATION

Taxation was graded in the typically Chinese dynasties as well as in border societies such as the Liao empire. But in the Liao world, with its conspicuous military and political stratification, little effort was made to conceal privileged tax exemptions. An emperor of the succeeding Chin dynasty criticized the Liao administration because it treated the officials (士) and the commoners (庶) differently.[27] The description of the taxation of the Entrusted Prefectures implies that officials above the ninth rank paid no taxes;[28] instead they made annual contributions, saddled horses being the most important.[29] Other gifts were offered on special occasions, for the mausoleum of a deceased emperor[30] or at the time of the heir apparent's marriage.[31]

Different from the government-approved grading of taxes for officials and commoners were the attempts of powerful families and temples to prevent the taxing of their retainers. These attempts were frequently successful.[32] In 994[33] an imperial order demanded an equitable system of taxation, and in 1056[34] another asked for the equalization of taxes. Both decrees may have been issued in the hope of reducing surreptitious tax evasions, but, whatever the intent, they did not succeed in abolishing the established tax privileges. The critical comments of the second emperor of the Chin dynasty on the different fiscal

[10] See XIV, introduction and XV, 2, *passim.*

[11] XIV, 2 (5), LS 47, 14a.

[12] XIV, 2 (6), LS 48, 1a.

[13] XIV, 2 (7).

[14] See below.

[15] *Cf.* CWTS 42, 7a; 149, 7b–8a.

[16] In 906 Chu Ch'üan-chung 朱全忠 refused to accept the Triple Office which the last T'ang emperor conferred upon him (NKCML 2, 3a–b).

[17] Williamson, WAS I, 85 ff.

[18] SS 162, 11b–12a.

[19] CS 55, 19b ff.

[20] III (3).

[21] XIV, 2 (10).

[22] III (4).

[23] See V, *passim.*

[24] XII (21).

[25] Kept or controlled by the village head. For details about his position, see XIV, introduction.

[26] I, 1 (3).

[27] CS 3, 15b.

[28] I, 1 (3).

[29] X, 1 (15).

[30] X, 1 (13).

[31] X, 1 (42).

[32] See VIII and IX, introductions.

[33] X, 1 (26).

[34] X, 1 (52).

policies displayed toward the upper class and the commoners indicate that the system continued even after the fall of the Liao dynasty.[35]

3. TAXES FROM THE SETTLED REGIONS

The income of the Liao empire consisted of taxes from its sedentary and nomadic subjects, revenue from additional internal sources, and, last but not least, tribute from abroad.

a. TERMS

The taxes collected in the agricultural sector of Liao were called *shui* 稅,[36] *tsu* 租,[37] *tsu shui* 租稅,[38] *ch'ien* 錢,[39] *shui ch'ien* 稅錢,[40] *shui fu* 稅賦,[41] *shui wu* 稅物,[42] *fu* 賦,[43] *tiao* 調,[44] or *k'o-ch'êng* 課程.[45] All these terms have a long and complex history which cannot concern us here. Under the Liao dynasty the term *shui* might be used as "tax" in general or in combination with or as a substitute for more specific terms. *Tsu* designated the land tax; *ch'ien*, a tax assigned in cash or the cash value of a tax which was collected in kind. The *shui wu* probably means "tax in kind."[46] In the negotiations of 1123 the summer tax was called *shui*, the autumn tax, *fu*.[47] The compound *shui fu* designated all (converted ?) taxes,[48] as opposed to the *k'o-ch'êng* money[49] which (always ? or preferably ?) was collected in cash. *Tsu shui* or *shui tsu*[50] seems to have referred to the land tax and other taxes. *Fu* was used for miscellaneous taxes such as the trade tax and the wine tax.[51] The fee levied at the passes might be designated simply as *shui*.[52]

During the early years of the T'ang dynasty—before 780—the *tiao* tax was levied in textile products.[53] The Double Tax of the year 780 included the *tiao* as well as other former taxes.[54] Within its framework, however, the *tsu*, the *yung* 庸, the labor

service levy, and the *tiao* continued to be counted as separate items.[55] In the course of the disintegration of the Double Tax System,[56] its original components emerged in various new forms. It is, therefore, not surprising to find the *tiao* tax levied in the Liao empire whose agricultural population produced considerable quantities of textiles.[57]

b. THE LAND TAX

The collection of the land tax was based on a census[58] whose details were fixed rather generously[59] and, as various records indicate, none too fairly.[60] In the succeeding Chin dynasty the summer tax was collected between the sixth and the eighth months, and the autumn tax between the tenth and the twelfth months,[61] that is in the fall and winter. During the negotiations of 1123 a spokesman for the Chin government referred to these two taxes in relation to Nan-ching Circuit, without, however, specifying their due date.[62] Apparently, some sort of double tax was also imposed in the more northerly regions of the Liao empire, but in these parts, crops were harvested and taxes collected somewhat later than in China Proper and, for that matter, in the territory of the Southern Capital. A local gazetteer of Hsüan-hua (in modern Chahar) relates that in the year 1000, because of a late harvest, the taxes on barley, wheat, and peas should be collected from the tenth day of the sixth month to the tenth day of the ninth month, whereas the trade and liquor taxes should be collected from the twentieth day of the sixth month to the twentieth day of the tenth month.[63] The regular dates were evidently somewhat earlier.

The land tax was fixed in terms of money but collected in grain in accordance with an officially determined rate. This system had operated during the T'ang dynasty when, as in earlier periods, it had given rise to much corruption.[64] The Liao government inherited the abuses as well as the principle of conversion. In 986 the conversion rate of the salt and iron tax was increased because it "did not accord with the value."[65] At about the same time it was charged that the government rate of exchange for grain "did

---

[35] CS 3, 15*b*.

[36] X, 1 (2).

[37] XII (6) and *passim*.

[38] X, 1 (35).

[39] X, 1 (27).

[40] X, 1 (20).

[41] SCPMHP 13, 7*a* ff.

[42] *Op. cit.* 14, 11*a*.

[43] X, 1 (2).

[44] X, 1 (23).

[45] SCPMHP 13, 7*a*.

[46] *Op. cit.* 14, 11*a*.

[47] *Op. cit.* 13, 7*a*.

[48] *Op. cit.* 6*b*; *cf.* also 14, 11*a*.

[49] *Op. cit.* 11*a*–*b*.

[50] *Op. cit.* 11*b*.

[51] X, 1 (2).

[52] X, 1 (35).

[53] CTS 48, 3*a*.

[54] T'ao and Chü 36, 153 ff.

[55] TS 52, 5*a*.

[56] WHTK 3, 50 ff.; *cf.* also T'ao and Chü 36, 160.

[57] *Cf. op. cit.*, 138.

[58] *Cf.* I, 3 (1); II, 2 (24) and *passim*.

[59] I, 3 (6).

[60] *Cf.* X, 1 (43).

[61] CS 47, 13*b*.

[62] SCPMHP 13, 7*a*.

[63] *Hsüan-fu Chên Chih* = LSSI 15, 28*b*.

[64] LHKTI 6, 8*b* ff.; *cf.* also CTS 48, 1 ff.; and T'ao and Chü 36, 145 ff.

[65] X, 1 (17).

not conform to the real value."[66] The report probably refers to a suggestion of Yeh-lü Mo-chih to increase the conversion price of a peck of grain from five to six cash.[67] But despite the government's willingness during the Sung war to adjust the official rates, conversion continued to be used as a means of exploitation. At the close of the dynasty, when the growing political disintegration bared many weaknesses in the Liao administrative system, thoughtful officials again turned their attention to the problem of conversion. In 1114 Ma Jên-wang sought to combat "the abuses in paying and receiving cash and grain," which were particularly serious in Nan-ching Circuit.[68] Ma lost his fight against the corrupt fiscal functionaries, in all probability not because of lack of ability but because the disease was too deeply rooted in the administrative pattern to be remedied by the good intentions of any one individual.

Quantitatively speaking, the land tax seems to have yielded a larger return than any other fiscal device. The figures for Nan-ching Circuit given in the list of 1123 are inflated, but nevertheless the relation between the separate items is worthy of note. The regular taxes, among which the land tax is specifically mentioned, amounted to around 4,285,000 strings as compared with 1,208,000 from salt and other government monopolies, house tax and other dues.[69]

c. OTHER TAXES AND REVENUES

The revenue of Nan-ching Circuit, as given for 1123, comprised, besides regular taxes, the income from the sale of salt and other goods. Salt is said to have been evaporated and sold by the two government-controlled Salt Departments; the "other" commodities were marketed by "various departments and bureaus."[70] The true nature of the government monopolies (榷) is not clear. Certain records point to the existence of partial, others to that of full monopolies. The texts do not say whether the purchaser of a salt permit[71] could produce and sell at his discretion after paying a fee. The record referring to the prohibition of private iron trade in 1064[72] and the statement concerned with the government sale of salt and other items in 1123 both point to direct state management, at least during the later part of the dynasty.[73]

But, whatever the technical arrangements and legal forms may have been, one thing appears certain: the administration derived a considerable income from its licensed or monopolized industries which, besides salt and iron, seem to have included liquor and the yeast to ferment it.[74] The "government people" (官民) paid taxes which, in Nan-ching Circuit in 1123, were levied by a special bureau, the Control Office, and listed separately.[75] The return from this tax, though small in comparison with land and other imposts, was not insignificant; the tax money from the "government people"[76] of the Southern Capital exceeded not only the revenue from the salt monopoly but also from that accruing from other government "sales."

In Nan-ching Circuit the revenue from salt and iron was converted from money into silk,[77] a type of exchange current in other parts of the empire as well. Special Offices of Money and Silk functioned not only in the old Chinese territory but also to the north and east of it, in the region west of the Sungari River and in what is now eastern Jehol.[78] Silk and money were exchanged in accordance with rates standardized in 1123 and probably earlier. A bolt of one kind of silk was valued at five strings of money (1123) if of superior quality, or at two and a half if of medium grade. A bolt of another variety brought four and two strings respectively.[79] In the oft-quoted statement of Nan-ching taxes the income from salt and other government sales is given in money. Whether the payments were actually made entirely in cash or in part in silk, we do not know. The house tax (房錢), listed together with the revenues from salt, etc., was collected in money,[80] but again it is not impossible that, in this case also, silk was an ultimate substitute.

Besides silk, gold and silver were greatly desired and were accepted without conversion.[81] Less valuable goods were also collected in kind, if and when the government needed them: iron[82] (for the state workshops and arsenals[83]), possibly coal,[84] and perhaps salt for the armed forces.[85]

The taxes on salt and wine were among the important sources of government income during the time of T'ang, the Five Dynasties, and Sung. The wine

---

[66] X, 1 (20).
[67] X, 1 (2).
[68] X, 1 (66).
[69] SCPMHP 14, 11a–b.
[70] Op. cit. 11b.
[71] X, 1 (3).
[72] V (14).
[73] See III, introduction.

[74] X, 1 (2).
[75] SCPMHP 14, 11b.
[76] See VII, introduction.
[77] X, 1 (2).
[78] XIV, 2 (10).
[79] SCPMHP 13, 8a–b.
[80] Op. cit. 14, 11a.
[81] X, 1 (58).
[82] III (3).
[83] See XIV, 1 (83).
[84] III (24).
[85] X, 1 (3). This rests on the assumption that the actual production of salt was undertaken privately, either at certain places or in general.

tax, also a significant item in the Liao budget, was administered by Chinese officials enjoying the *yin* 蔭 privilege, the "sponsored sons."[86] It was the only revenue which the central government collected from the Entrusted Prefectures.[87] Various branches of industry had government monopolies imposed upon them.

The taxes on trade were collected either at the markets[88] or passes,[89] as in the T'ang period.[90] In the later part of that period most commodities paid a transit fee of twenty coins per string of value, or something more than two per cent, since the string contained less than one thousand coins. On bamboo, timber, tea, and lacquer a fee of ten per cent was levied; foreign goods were taxed thirty per cent.[91] No details are given regarding the trade tax of Liao, but since the fiscal policy of its southern regions followed the T'ang tradition we may assume that this form of Liao taxation, like others, was either a continuation or a modification of T'ang practice. The Sung government modified the old rates to a certain extent; it imposed a transit tax of two per cent and a market tax of three per cent.[92]

The tax on agricultural implements, which was levied in China Proper in 932 during the early part of the Five Dynasties at a rate of one and a half cash per *mou*,[93] was also collected in the Liao empire at the end of the tenth century,[94] but the rate is not stated.

The regular taxes were supplemented by temporary levies for special purposes, particularly for military campaigns. In 1020 an order requisitioned horses from "Chinese in all circuits" for the war against Korea.[95] More a matter of curiosity than of revenue was the payment of black hares and a crow with three feet;[96] in the same category were such tribal tributes as a white wolf[97] and a boy who had hair on his nose.[98]

d. THE ASSIMILATION OF THE FORMER PO-HAI KINGDOM

The political submission of Nan-ching Circuit to the Liao government apparently implied no important

financial changes, for it was relatively peaceful. Besides, the Ch'i-tan rulers had every reason to avoid unnecessary interference with the fiscal system of a territory which, as indicated by the number of its tax collectors,[99] was the empire's richest domain.

The conquest of the Po-hai kingdom was a much more violent affair; its incorporation into the sedentary sector met with more political—and even military—resistance. For a considerable period, therefore, this rebellious land was treated as a tributary border state and, as such, not subject to the empire's internal administration of finance. After its conquest in 926 Tung-tan 東丹, the former Po-hai kingdom, had to pay an annual tribute (*kung* 貢) of one thousand horses and one hundred and fifty thousand *tuan* of linen cloth (布).[100] This differed conspicuously from payments received from those settled regions of the empire where Han Yen-hui had installed the traditional Chinese system of taxation more than twelve years earlier.

The Liao government did not dare to impose immediately on its new Po-hai subjects the taxes on liquor, salt, and yeast which its Chinese population had to pay.[101] Several generations later, when these taxes were demanded from the eastern territory, the unruly Po-hai objected violently; the *Liao Shih* attributes Ta Yen-lin's rebellion in 1029 directly to the new financial system.[102] Certain high officials were imprisoned, but not before the rebels had killed the commissioner and vice-commissioners of revenue.[103] The revolt which had led to the establishment of the independent but short-lived state of Hsing-liao 興遼 was finally broken; yet years passed before the pacified population was required to pay the land tax.[104]

As the dynastic period progressed, an increasing number of temporary tax exemptions were reported for Tung-ching Circuit. These records as well as the extensive description of the region's granaries[105] may be considered a symptom of the gradual integration of the conquered Po-hai territory in the new administrative and financial order.

4. INCOME FROM THE EMPIRE'S TRIBES

a. TERMS

The payments made by the empire's tribes to the Liao government were usually called taxes, not tribute. The *Liao Shih* speaks of tribal *ting fu* 丁賦,[106] obviously

[86] ISHSC 27, 12*a*; CS 7, 17*a*. See also XIV, introduction.

[87] X, 1 (2).

[88] See V, introduction.

[89] X, 1 (25) (34).

[90] T'ao and Chü 36, 170 ff.

[91] *Op. cit.*, 171.

[92] SS 186, 1*a*.

[93] *Cf.* WHTK 3, 51; see also CWTS 42, 9*b*–10*a*.

[94] X, 1 (27).

[95] X, 1 (39).

[96] X, 1 (9); X, 2 (50).

[97] X, 2 (13).

[98] X, 2 (43).

[99] XIV, 2 (6), LS 48, 1*a*.

[100] X, 1 (4).

[101] X, 1 (2).

[102] *Loc. cit.*

[103] XIII (38).

[104] XIII, *passim*.

[105] XII (119).

[106] XIV, 1 (9), LS 45, 3*a*.

referring to taxes (*fu*) paid by adults (*ting*). At another point the taxes offered by the tribes are called *tsu shui* 租稅[107] which here seems to designate taxes in general rather than land tax and other taxes. The word tribute (*kung* 貢) covers the many and varied offerings to the court,[108] but is rarely applied to the regular payments made to the fiscal offices. When used in relation to certain inner tribes, such as the Hsi people and the Five Nations, the term refers to a "tributary" status which will be more particularly discussed below.

b. ANIMAL TAXES

From Chingis Khan's measures regulating exemption from taxation[109] it may be inferred that most of his own tribesmen had to pay taxes. The two passages quoted from the *Liao Shih* show that the tribal population of the Liao empire was under similar obligation.

The primary wealth of the tribes was in animals and the primary wealth of the Chinese and Po-hai people was in grain. Apart from products of the hunt, the tribes offered their taxes mainly in domesticated animals; the agricultural population rendered them in grain. But the burden of taxation varied according to the political status of the taxpayer. The Chinese peasants paid a considerable tax in peace times and a lesser one in time of war, when tax remission was often a form of relief[110] and a veiled plea for loyalty. The tribal taxes, although paid annually, seem to have been lighter in peace time than during or before a military campaign. The *Liao Shih* mentions annual taxes of sheep only.[111]

Could the tribal herds have remained untaxed in times of peace because the government considered them an important adjunct to their military reserves? Large herds were owned by the state,[112] and these were augmented by heavy horse tributes demanded—and received—from neighboring tribes and countries. LS 13, 6a reveals the antagonistic interests of the government and the owners of private herds. During the great war against Sung, high officials suggested a tax upon the horse wealth of the rich people in order to supply the army; the government rejected the idea and used horses from the government herds instead.[113] But appealing as this course was to the native Ch'i-tan, it could not always be followed, perhaps because the demand was too great or because cautious officials

were afraid to make serious reductions in the government herds. Horses were requisitioned whenever military requirements made it necessary;[114] it goes without saying that those owned by Chinese, although limited in number, were also demanded when the army needed them.[115]

c. THE HSI TRIBES AND THE FIVE NATIONS

If the measures for levying horses affected all inner ("Ch'i-tan") tribes as LS 19, 3b and 45, 3a suggest, then naturally they also affected the Hsi listed among the empire's fifty-two tribes. But the Hsi were a strong complex and did not submit as readily as certain others to the new dynasty. Although culturally closer to the Ch'i-tan people than the Po-hai, they fought against their powerful cousins with bitter and repeated violence. After having "pacified" them in 911,[116] T'ai-tsu a few years before his death had to crush them again.[117] The list of Shêng-tsung's tribes shows that until the end of the tenth century these obstinate people were frequently reorganized and resettled.[118] After that time they seem to have definitely accepted a political situation which, while preventing them from living independently outside the empire, offered them a kind of junior partnership within it.[119]

The change in the political status of the Hsi people is clearly reflected in the changing form of their payments to the Liao government. The Hsi were great hunters.[120] Appropriately they presented a tribute of deer to the Liao court in 943,[121] and they continued to render such tribute until 997. From that year on the deer payments as well as other regular tribute were discontinued,[122] perhaps because of the Sung war, but perhaps also because of the changing status of the Hsi within the empire. The coming of a new administrative order was heralded by the memorial of 994 which suggested the abolition of the customary deer tribute to the great king of Hsi because this "king," now an appointed official, received sufficient emolument.[123]

When the war against the Sung empire came to an end, the victorious Liao ruler could concentrate all his energies upon the final consolidation of the central government in the Hsi territory. Shêng-tsung him-

[107] X, 1 (47).
[108] X, 1 (15).
[109] *Cf.* Riasanovsky 37, 83 and 85.
[110] See XII, *passim*.
[111] X, 1 (25).
[112] See II, 1, *passim* and introduction.
[113] X, 1 (29).

[114] II, 1 (17) (21) (22).
[115] X, 1 (39).
[116] XIII (4).
[117] XIII (14) and XVI, *passim*.
[118] *Cf.* I, 2 (5), nos. 1–3, 8–13.
[119] See XIII, introduction.
[120] TS 219, 4b ff.
[121] X, 1 (7) (evidently two records of the same events).
[122] X, 1 (31).
[123] II, 1 (11).

self visited the region (whether before or after the conclusion of the peace treaty is not quite clear); and, following his vision, work on a new city close to the former Hsi capital was started. In 1006, a year after the Sung court began paying its heavy tribute, the Hsi tribes handed over their former royal site to the imperial government of Liao,[124] thus signalling the end of the tribes' semi-independent status. In 1007 the new city, filled with Chinese settlers, was walled and officially established as the Central Capital.[125] From that time on the Hsi no longer appear among the tribute-paying tribes.[126] If they were as completely integrated as they seem to have been during the eleventh century,[127] it was only natural that they, like the other inner tribes of the empire, should have become taxpayers.

One exception, however, must be noted. The Five Nations, listed among Shêng-tsung's tribes,[128] paid tribute until the beginning of the twelfth century.[129] Again the political status explains the financial relation. Located in the northeastern corner of the empire, the Five Nations were not as completely subdued as their inclusion in the inner tribes suggests.[130] During Shêng-tsung's reign they did not pay taxes, nor were they ruled directly by officials of the central government. Under Hsing-tsung, the next emperor, the chieftains came again to pay tribute,[131] but in 1037 the Liao government tightened its control by replacing the native ruler with a prefect.[132] In the years that followed, the authority of the central government must have again weakened, for in 1049 it was the chieftains of each of the Five Nations who came to submit.[133] Once more we hear of a prefect of the Nations,[134] but neither the extent nor the duration of his jurisdiction is clear. Shortly thereafter the tribes

were again represented by their chieftains who offered local products as tribute.[135] Another rebellion and another submission followed.[136] In 1070 the chieftains (not the prefect) appeared at the court and had an audience.[137] Tribute was offered during the succeeding decades,[138] indeed until the dissolution of the empire put an end to all payments.

The term tribute well expresses the political relations of this border people with the Ch'i-tan rulers who for generations tried in vain to transform the stubborn semi-independence of the Five Nations into the complete submission expected of a fully assimilated, tax-paying inner tribe.

d. THE ACCEPTANCE OF OFFERINGS FROM ABROAD

The presentation of gifts and tributes by foreign states and tribes to the Liao government was made within the frame of diplomacy rather than fiscal policy. Messengers from the various countries were lodged in special quarters at the southwestern corner of the Supreme Capital,[139] but according to SS 166, 9b the bearers of tribute were taken care of by the officials of the Guest Council. Together with these officials, the *Liao Shih* lists those of the reception places.[140] It may well have been their function to serve the envoys during court visits.

Even when the emperor was in residence at his seasonal tent palaces, tributes were still brought to him personally for inspection. The *Liao Shih* reports that he received tribute from Sung and other countries while staying at his winter camp.[141] The scene was probably not unlike the one observed in the thirteenth century by Carpini at the tent court of the great Mongol ruler, Kuyuk. Such quantities of gifts were presented to the khan by the envoys "that it was a marvel to see."[142] Evidently they were placed before the khan himself who accepted and then distributed them. Carts that could not be taken into the audience tent or into the enclosure studded a hill nearby. Carpini saw "more than five hundred carts, all full of gold and silver and silken gowns, all of which was divided up between the Emperor and the chiefs; and the various chiefs divided their shares among their men as they saw fit."[143] The procedure at the more southerly urban court differed in form but not in

---

[124] XI (15).

[125] XI (15).

[126] LS 69, 10b speaks of another tribute paid by the Ao-li tribe in 1003. Ao-li is the name of one of the Hsi tribes (see I, 2 (5), no. 11). Of course, the presentation of an occasional contribution is not at all impossible, even after the discontinuation of the payment of the regular tributes. But it seems more probable that this record really refers to one of the Five Nations tribes, Ao-li-mi, which, according to LS 70, 11a and 14, 4a, paid tribute to Liao in the year 1003. The Ao-li-mi, the Yüeh-li-tu, and Yüeh-li-chi are erroneously classed with the states for the year 1003 (see note to table).

[127] See XIII, introduction.

[128] See I, 2, no. 34.

[129] Cf. LS 69, 14a ff.; see also X, 1 (53) (59).

[130] LS 33, 9a.

[131] LS 69, 14a.

[132] LS 33, 9b.

[133] LS 69, 16a.

[134] Op. cit., 16b.

[135] Op. cit., 17b.

[136] Op. cit., 18a

[137] Loc. cit.

[138] Op. cit., 18b ff.

[139] XI (5).

[140] XIV, 2 (5), LS 47, 11a–b.

[141] II, 1 (27).

[142] Carpini 00, 23.

[143] Op. cit., 24.

essence. In Cambaluc the "presents" were brought to the palace and "seen by the emperor."[144]

We may assume that the Liao court in the Supreme Capital accepted tributes in its seasonal camps or urban palaces in much the same way as did its more powerful and more famous Mongol successors. An attendant who was the first to tell the emperor of the arrival of a gift of fine horses was appropriately rewarded;[145] offerings of this kind must have been particularly acceptable. The tribal delegations were usually led by their chieftains[146] or some other dignitaries whose position might[147] or might not[148] be definitely stated. At times their representation was sizable; in 1012 as many as thirty Jurchen chieftains appeared at a single audience.[149] When several delegations arrived simultaneously, they might be presented to the emperor by the head of the strongest tribe or state among them, such as the king of the Tsu-pu.[150]

Whether the missions from China Proper, Korea, or Hsia were expected on a fixed date, we do not know. Evidently some tribes did pay tribute at a set time (perhaps on a certain day or within a certain month), and, if their officials put in a later appearance, they were liable to punishment. This procedure, however, was in all probability more formal than real; in 1043 two tribal envoys who failed to arrive at the proper time were "pardoned and sent back."[151]

5. TRIBUTES AND "TRIBUTES"

Tributes may have been offered by semi-independent inner tribes; they may have been presented as gifts of respect by certain districts within the empire or by certain dignitaries; but generally the term denotes payments made by dependent or pseudo-dependent foreign countries and tribes to the Liao court. The old Chinese idea that their emperor ruled "all-under-heaven" (t'ien-hsia 天下), and that all foreign countries were tributary to them, was taken over by the Liao emperors, but with an interesting modification; China Proper was not classified among the subordinate states except occasionally.[152] Even when the Southern Court[153] paid "tribute," its em-

peror was treated by the Liao sovereign as a relative rather than as a vassal.[154]

The non-Chinese states were all listed as subordinate countries (shu kuo 屬國),[155] but their actual status differed greatly.[156] The presents which their envoys offered though generally called tribute, kung 貢, and only occasionally p'in 聘 or pi 幣, gifts, were often nothing but the courteous accessories of diplomatic visits or an exchange of objects under the cloak of politics.

The political and economic functions might overlap as indeed they often did. In such cases the actual "rate of exchange"[157] would be determined by the relative strength of the Liao empire on the one hand and considerations of prestige on the other. The balance of this diplomatic trade can be determined only by a comparison between the "tributes" received and the presents made. Since our texts are more eloquent about the first, we have to confine ourselves primarily to a survey of the tributes paid to the Liao government.

a. DIPLOMATIC OFFERING

The "tributes" offered by the Lion Country (Shih-tzŭ Kuo),[158] Persia,[159] and Japan[160] were evidently courtesy gifts, easily recognizable as such even though designated as "tributes" in the records. In 924 and again in 1020 and 1021 missions arrived from Ta-shih, the first to pay homage to the new man of destiny in Eastern Asia, T'ai-tsu, the second to negotiate a marriage with the Liao court.[161] The embassy of 924 may well have come from the capital of the Arabian Caliphate, Baghdad. The delegations of 1020 and 1021, however, were probably dispatched by the Qarā-Khānid ruler, Qadir-khan.[162]

Shêng-tsung's letter to Sultan Mahmūd does not mention any presents sent by him to Qadir-khan, but the Arabic source in which the letter is given enumerates certain gifts made by the Ch'i-tan emperor to the ruler of Ghazna in the hope of "establishing the custom of mutual donations." The "Khitāy" envoy, Qalitunkā, carried with him twenty-one suits, fifteen of which were "of raw silk, (each) of 2 pieces," furs of sable martens "(for) pelisse (*yāqū)," two hundred

---

[144] Marco Polo 03 I, 392.

[145] X, 2 (44).

[146] X, 2 (72) (78) (90) (93).

[147] X, 2 (80).

[148] X, 2 (52) (75).

[149] X, 2 (66).

[150] X, 2 (78).

[151] X, 2 (76).

[152] XVI, 942, LS 4, 8b.

[153] For this term see CTKC 8, 4b.

[154] Cf. XVI, 937, LS 3, 10b; X, 2 (61).

[155] See I, 2 (10).

[156] See I, introduction.

[157] A formula suggested in a personal communication by George E. Taylor.

[158] X, 2 (49).

[159] X, 2 (10).

[160] See below.

[161] X, 2 (11) (71).

[162] See I, introduction, note 108, and I, 2 (10), no. 46.

sable martens, one thousand gray squirrels, thirty vesicles of musk, one bow with ten arrows.[163]

The mission of 1020 offered, among other products, 象, "ivory" or "elephants." Elephants were known in Turkestan and in the adjacent southern regions,[164] and their use as official presents is documented in the contemporary history of Eastern Asia. Sung received many elephants from its southern neighbors,[165] and in 1055 Sung sent an elephant to the Liao court.[166] But, since great deserts separated Turkestan and the Liao capital, it may be doubted whether in 1020 a live elephant was actually sent from "Ta-shih."

"Tributes" (read: "presents") from Japan are reported for the year 925 and again for 1091 and 1092.[167] Compared with the Japanese visits to China Proper and the beauty of the "tributes" offered, the Japanese missions to Liao were few in number and the gifts probably inconspicuous since they were not specified. Relations between the two countries remained reserved, but what may seem surprising in view of a common Buddhist tradition is understandable in the light of the political situation. The interests of Liao and Japan clashed in Korea, and the threatened expansion of the Liao empire in the east could be contemplated only with uneasiness by her island neighbor.

b. TRIBUTES FROM SILLA AND KOREA

The astonishing military success of the first Liao emperor probably had something to do with the arrival of the first Japanese delegation in the year 925. During that same year tribute was paid by Korea and Silla. The latter country soon ceased to exist as a sovereign state. After its conquest by Korea in 936[168] the name Silla still appears in contemporary documents, now as another designation for Korea.[169] The Ch'i-tan Kuo Chih records a tribute which at an unspecified date was rendered by "Silla." In view of the size and value of the presents offered they probably originated from Korea rather than from Silla.

According to CTKC 21, 3a, the tribute included the following items:

gold objects	200 taels [in value]
a gold belly-cover	50 taels [in value]
a gold gong	50 taels [in value]
a gold saddle and a horse	50 taels [in value]
soft flowered silk	100 bolts
soft white silk	500 bolts
fine cloth	1000 bolts
plain cloth	5000 bolts
bronze articles	1000 catties
wine and vinegar	100 jars
tea	10 catties
rattan furniture	50 pieces
fine ginseng	amount uncertain
swords	10
fine paper and ink	amount uncertain
hard rice	500 piculs
soft rice	500 piculs
embroidered gowns for the emperor[169]	

The Korean tributes to Liao were few until the end of the tenth century.[170] But the Liao campaigns against Korea, although not completely successful, intimidated the peninsula kingdom: in 994 the Korean government, which from 963 on had used the Sung calendar, adopted the Liao calendar instead;[171] in 1002 the Korean court, while still maintaining friendly relations with Sung, submitted a map of its country and offered tribute to Liao.[172] The congratulations offered in 1005 by Korea to Liao upon the latter's victory over Sung[173] were an overt recognition of Liao supremacy, but this supremacy was again challenged during the second decade of the eleventh century when open warfare interrupted the accepted relations between the two northern countries. In 1015 Korea offered tribute to Sung China; in 1016 she adopted the Sung calendar;[174] but the defeat of Korean arms by Liao quickly put an end to this rapprochement. In 1020 the Korean court again declared itself ready to pay tribute to the Liao government, and two years later the Liao calendar was reintroduced.[175] The Pohai rebellion of 1029–1030 encouraged Korea to undertake an expedition against the Liao border territory along the Yalu River.[176] This feeble attack which was easily crushed led to an amusing calendric war—if it may be so called—during which Korea, disregarding

---

[163] Marvazī 42, 20.

[164] See appendix V: C, 5, b and Marvazī 42, 2.

[165] For instance, in 970 (SS 489, 4a), in 983 (SS 4, 18b), in 1055 (SS 12, 10a), in 1061 (SS 489, 9a), in 1063 (SS 488, 14a), and in 1082 (SS 488, 15b).

[166] X, 2 (89).

[167] X, 2 (12) (99). The delegation of 1091 included a Buddhist monk, the only person mentioned by name in the record. Students of Buddhism had been sent to China from the time of the Sui dynasty on (WHTK 324, 2552). After 1072 the Japanese missions to Sung were always entrusted to Buddhist monks.(op. cit., 2553). The appearance of a religious envoy in Shang-ching is therefore quite in keeping with the tradition which the Japanese had established during previous centuries.

[168] KRS 2, 24. Cf. VII, 2, note 82.

[169] Cf. Marvazī 42, 27.

[170] Cf. LS 70, passim.

[171] KRS 86, 724; see X, 2, note 37.

[172] WHTK 325, 2558–2561.

[173] X, 2 (62).

[174] KRS 86, 725.

[175] Loc. cit.

[176] Op. cit. 93, 63; 94, 80; see XIII, note 101.

the current Liao reign title, continued to use the previous one.[177] After 1030 Korea sent no official mission to the Sung court for forty-three years.[178] During the latter part of the eleventh century the power of Liao waned, and diplomatic relations between Korea and Sung were resumed. But the inner dissolution of the Liao empire progressed more rapidly than the collapse of its international prestige. Korea continued to pay tribute until the middle of the last emperor's reign. The final break was solemnly expressed in calendric terms: in 1116, when the Liao military situation became desperate, the Korean court again discarded the Liao calendar and established a neutral system which employed the sixty-year cycle.[179]

c. TRIBUTES FROM VARIOUS STATES AND TRIBES

The translated texts in X, 2 deal for the most part with tributes and presents that are specifically described as to content or that are of interest because of their country of origin. Most of these data are given in the *pên chi*, the first part of the *Liao Shih*. With only a few omissions and additions, they appear again in the third part of the *Liao Shih* which is composed of lists and tables. Supplemented by some political and military information LS 69 and 70 give chronologically the tributes from the outer tribes and the dependent states. These sections have been examined to determine the frequency of tribute payments and gifts made by foreign missions to the Liao court. In table 12 a column is given to each of the states and tribes that presented frequent tribute payments. Those that made only a few are listed together in a single column. The time of the visits is always noted. In the individual columns their frequency is indicated by a numeral; in the joint tabulation a number is affixed only when more than one visit occurred during the year in question.

The data in LS 69 and 70 exhibit certain discrepancies which the accompanying notes attempt to explain. Furthermore these records are not entirely identical with those in other chapters of the *History* from which, nevertheless, they were compiled; yet the similarities are sufficient to warrant the exclusive use of the former in constructing our table 12.

The classification used in LS 69 and 70 is obviously arbitrary. In the time of the Liao dynasty the Jurchen and Tsu-pu were tribes rather than states, and similar objections may be raised in a number of other cases. But such criticism does not invalidate the importance of the tabulated data for the political history of Inner Asia during the tenth and eleventh centuries. It goes without saying that a purely quantitative list does not accurately express the political weight of the various items included. However the number of the recorded missions seems to be causally related to the rise and decline of Liao power. The frequency curve of figure 32 rises strikingly before and after the great international achievements of the Liao empire—the victorious wars against Later T'ang and Chin during the first part of the tenth century, the war against Sung before 1005, and the diplomatic success which led to the increase of the Sung tributes in 1042. The tributary status of the Five Nations is clearly demonstrated. Less permanent evidently was the control exercised by the Liao government over a number of other tribes along the empire's northern border.

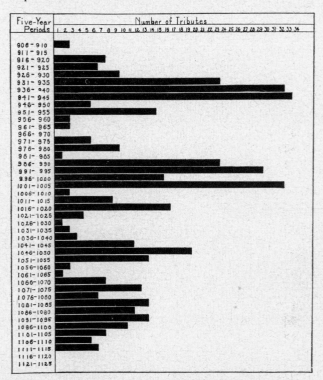

FIG. 32.　Tribute paid by subordinate states and tribes.

The T'ieh-li tribes (in modern Kirin[180]) paid tribute most frequently in the tenth century; after that time the offerings became fewer and fewer. The Ti-lieh and Wu-ku began to pay tribute during the early part of T'ai-tsung's reign; the names of both disappeared from the list of tribute payers around 1050. The Pi-ku-tê ceased offering regular tribute at an even earlier date. Hsiao Han-chia-nu describes the growing difficulties which beset the Liao government in its attempts to control the northern and northwestern border regions in the middle of the eleventh century.[181]

---

[177] KRS 86, 726.
[178] SS 487, 11*b*; *cf*. also WHTK 325, 2559.
[179] KRS 86, 730.

[180] I, 2 (10), no. 30.
[181] See XV, 1 (51).

TABLE 12

Tribute Paid by Subordinate States and Tribes

Date	STATES										TRIBES				
	Uighurs	Jurchen	T'ieh-li	Tsu-pu	Korea	Tang-hsiang	A-sa-lan Uighurs	Hsi Hsia	T'u-fan	Others	Pi-ku-tê	Wu-ku	Five Nations	Ti-lieh	Others
908															
909															Wu-niang-kai
910															
911															
912															
913															
914															
915															
916															
917															
918	2			1	2	1				Po-hai					
919															
920															
921															
922															
923										Persia					
924	1									Ta-shih, P'a-li					
925	1									Japan, Silla					
926			1							Wei-mo, Mo-ho					
927															
928		1								Ta-lu-ku, Turks	1				
929															
930													1	1	
931			1								1	1	1	1	
932		1		1								1		1	
933		1	1	4		1	1			T'u-hun, Chu-pu-ku (2)					
934		1				1					1				
935						1				T'u-hun					
936		1								T'u-yü-hun, T'u-hun	1				Yü-chüeh-li
937	1	1	1								1				
938		2	1							Mo-ho, T'u-yü-hun (2), Wu-sun					Shih-wei, Black-cart Shih-wei
939		1		1						T'u-yü-hun					
940		2	1	3						Lin-lieh, Tun-huang		1			Chu-pu-ku, Black-cart Shih-wei
941		1	1	1								1			Yü-chüeh-li, A-li-ti, Chu-pu-ku, Jurchen
942			1	2						Su-sa	3	1			Chu-pu-ku, Yü-chüeh-li
943		2													Ch'u-po-tê (a Hsi tribe)
944										Lin-lieh, Yao-li	1				Black-cart Shih-wei
945	1		1							T'u-yü-hun, Yao-li, Jên-mo-li	2				Black-cart Shih-wei
946	1	2								T'u-hun		1			
947															
948															
949															
950															
951															
952	1	1	2							Khirghiz	1		1		

TABLE 12—*Continued*

	STATES										TRIBES				
Date	Uighurs	Jurchen	T'ieh-li	Tsu-pu	Korea	Tang-hsiang	A-sa-lan Uighurs	Hsi Hsia	T'u-fan	Others	Pi-ku-tê	Wu-ku	Five Nations	Ti-lieh	Others
953			1						1	T'u-yü-hun	1	1		1	
954															
955											1				
956											1				
957											1				
958															
959															
960															
961															
962		1													
963										Wo-lang-kai					
964															
965															
966															
967															
968															
969															
970															
971	1									T'u-yü-hun	1				
972											1				
973							1								
974															
975															
976											1				
977	1	2								Khirghiz					
978		1					1								
979		1												1	
980															
981															
982															
983															
984															
985															I-shih Lao-wei
986				1		1									
987															
988							1								
989	1					1	1		1	Hsia-lieh, Khotan (3), Shih-tzǔ Kuo					
990	2	4		1			1			Khotan					
991	1	2					1			Turks	1				
992	1		3							Wu-jo					
993	1														
994	2	1	1	1	1	1				T'u-yü-hun					
995	1	2	1		1		1	1		Pi-ku-tê	1				
996	3	1	1												
997		1	1			2				Wu-jo					
998		1	1					1			1				
999															
1000															

TABLE 12—*Continued*

	STATES										TRIBES				
Date	Uighurs	Jurchen	T'ieh-li	Tsu-pu	Korea	Tang-hsiang	A-sa-lan Uighurs	Hsi Hsia	T'u-fan	Others	Pi-ku-tê	Wu-ku	Five Nations	Ti-lieh	Others
1001	2									Ta-lu-ku, Pi-ku-tê	1				Ta-lu-ku
1002		1	1		1										
1003		1	1			1				Wu-jo, Yüeh-li-tu, Yüeh-li-chi, Ao-li-mi*a*, Po-hai		1			Ao-li*b* ⎫ All Five Na- P'ou-a-li, P'u-nu-li ⎭ tions Tribes
1004		1				1									
1005	1	2	1			1	1			Wu-shê (jo)*c*	1	1			
1006										Sha Prefecture Uighurs					
1007															
1008				1											
1009															
1010															
1011															
1012															
1013															
1014	1	1	1	1						Sha Prefecture Uighurs					T'ieh-li
1015		1								Khotan					
1016											1				
1017															
1018															Yüeh-li-tu, P'ou-a-li, Ao-li-mi, P'u-nu-li (2), T'ieh-li, Hui-po (2), Ho-su-kuan (2)
1019			1	1											
1020										Ta-shih, Sha Prefecture Uighurs					
1021				1		1								1	
1022		1													
1023															
1024															
1025															
1026															
1027															P'u-lu-mao-to
1028															
1029															
1030															
1031															
1032														1	
1033		1													
1034															
1035															
1036															
1037				1											
1038					1			1							
1039															
1040															
1041	1							1							
1042															Chu-pu-ku

a The Yüeh-li-tu, Yüeh-li-chi, and Ao-li-mi are here erroneously listed as states. They belong to the Five Nations which are classed among the tribes. See I, 2 (5), no. 34, and LS 69, *passim*.

b See note 126.

c I, 2 (9), no. 26.

TABLE 12—*Continued*

	STATES										TRIBES				
Date	Uighurs	Jurchen	T'ieh-li	Tsu-pu	Korea	Tang-hsiang	A-sa-lan Uighurs	Hsi Hsia	T'u-fan	Others	Pi-ku-tê	Wu-ku	Five Nations	Ti-lieh	Others
1043	1			1				1							Wo-to[d], P'u-lu-mao-to
1044					1										
1045					1		1								
1046					1										
1047		1	1	1											
1048				1	1										Hui-po, Ch'ang-pai Mountains [Jurchen], P'u-lu-mao-to
1049				1						Kao-ch'ang					
1050				1	1										P'u-lu-mao-to (2), Hui-po, Ho-su-kuan, Pa-ssŭ-mu[e]
1051									1						
1052							1				1	1	1	1	
1053			1	1											
1054			1	1				2	1						
1055															
1056				1											
1057													1		
1058															
1059															
1060															
1061															
1062															Wu-t'u-wan
1063															
1064															
1065															
1066	1			1											
1067															
1068						1									
1069								1	1						
1070				1									1		
1071		1			1				1						
1072	2				1										
1073	1														
1074				1	2				1						
1075									1						
1076	1														
1077															
1078	1			1									1		
1079				1											
1080		1													
1081		1		1	1					Yü-ku-nan			1		
1082			1	1									1		
1083				1									1		
1084		1		1											

[d] According to LS 19, 4*a*, Wo-to is an error for Wo-lu. See also I, 2 (9), no. 56.

[e] In the year 1050 Korea and Pa-ssŭ-mu are listed together twice: first under the states and then again under the tribes. We have put the Pa-ssŭ-mu under the heading of the tribes (see I, 2 (9), no. 4) and Korea under that of the states (see I, 2 (10), no. 22).

TABLE 12—*Continued*

	STATES										TRIBES				
Date	Uighurs	Jurchen	T'ieh-li	Tsu-pu	Korea	Tang-hsiang	A-sa-lan Uighurs	Hsi Hsia	T'u-fan	Others	Pi-ku-tê	Wu-ku	Five Nations	Ti-lieh	Others
1085													1		
1086		1											2		
1087		1		1											Po-hai of the Ssŭ-pei tribe (*cf.* X, 2, note 73)
1088													1		
1089	1			1											
1090		1		1											
1091	2									Japan					
1092			1							Japan					
1093															
1094															T'i-tê (2), Ho-lieh-ko
1095		2		2	1										Eight P'o-li tribes
1096				1	1										Eight P'o-li tribes
1097													1		P'u-lu-mao-to
1098															
1099				1									1		T'i-tê
1100				1									1		
1101		1	2	1											
1102															
1103									1						
1104									1		1				
1105															
1106				1											
1107															
1108															
1109													1		
1110				1	1								1		
1111													1		
1112				1						Ho Prefecture Uighurs			1		
1113										Wo-lang-kai					
1114	1														
1115															
1116															
1117															
1118															
1119															
1120															
1121															
1122															
1123															
1124															
1125															

The Jurchen, who later overthrew the Liao empire, had maintained tributary relations with its rulers after T'ai-tsu's victory over the neighboring country of Po-hai, an event which obviously influenced relations between Liao and the T'ieh-li. The Jurchen paid heavy horse tribute to the end of the eleventh century; but this period of dependence was followed by one of intense conflict which ushered in the final collapse of the Liao dynasty.

The southwestern and western lines of contact and power were evidently more easily maintained than those north of the great desert. The Tsu-pu paid tribute to the Liao court during the greater part of the tenth and eleventh centuries. Their support of Yeh-lü Ta-shih's conquest of Eastern Turkestan cannot be taken as an expression of political subordination, for a number of other tribes, such as the Wu-ku, Ti-lieh, and Pi-ku-tê who had ceased paying taxes long before, also assisted in this lucrative adventure.[182] The western and more particularly the southwestern countries seem to have remained within the empire's orbit of influence until the close of the epoch. The remote A-sa-lan (Kao-ch'ang) Uighurs cultivated friendly diplomatic relations with the Liao court. However, the closer contact maintained by the Kan Prefecture Uighurs is shown by the frequency of their tribute. Perhaps the strong Ch'i-tan garrisons in Hsi-ching Circuit and beyond inspired the respect shown the Liao sovereign; they certainly made the Tang-hsiang tribes[183] and the Hsi Hsia[184] more willing to pay tribute to the northern court.

The data on the tributary relations of Liao, although laconic and incomplete, reflect more of the contemporary history of Central and Eastern Asia than can be commented on here. The exchange of envoys with T'u-fan (Tibet) probably had its religious as well as its political significance, particularly in the eleventh century after the restoration of Buddhism in Tibet. Intriguing possibilities are suggested by records relating to the Turks, the proto-Mongol Shih-wei, and other regional groups, but the exact political position of all these people can only be determined by more detailed investigation.

d. CHINA PROPER (THE SMALLER COUNTRIES)

The presents made to Liao by the South Chinese states of Nan T'ang and Wu Yüeh mirror the uncertain political status of the various Chinese countries which along with the Five Dynasties flourished during the early and middle part of the tenth century. Nan T'ang, an independent state until 975, maintained "brotherly" relations with Liao to the definite disadvantage of Later T'ang and Chin.[185] The Nan T'ang government repeatedly conveyed secret intelligences to the Liao court, in 940, in 941, in 943, and again in 957.[186] In 938 Liao bestowed a coronation title upon the first independent Nan T'ang ruler, sending at the same time presents and goods to be marketed to its southern ally.[187] Nan T'ang, not

unexpectedly, offered tribute to the Ch'i-tan court in 938 and in 940[188] and on several occasions in the fifties[189] when the armies of the Later Chou dynasty seriously threatened the existence of the southern state.[190]

Wu Yüeh also developed under the shadow of the Ch'i-tan empire. The coastal country offered tribute to Liao during the Later Liang and T'ang dynasties;[191] during the Later Chin dynasty Wu Yüeh even used the Liao calendar.[192] Under such conditions the continuation of tribute payments was only natural. Those recorded[193] may well represent a mere fraction of what was actually offered.

e. CHINA PROPER (THE FIVE DYNASTIES)

The full significance of the tributary relations between the Liao empire and the so-called Five Dynasties is revealed in the military and political developments of this period. While vigorously expanding their territorial power in every direction, the Ch'i-tan sugared their policy of aggression with periodic gestures of good will. Later Liang (907–923) sent a delegation to the Ch'i-tan court as early as 906, that is, before Liang had achieved dynastic status. During the following years the Ch'i-tan subdued many tribal neighbors; they alternately negotiated with and fought against local centers of power in North China. During the political gamble that ensued, A-pao-chi dispatched four delegations to the court of Liang, one with horses, sable coats, and silk.[194]

The changing fate of the Later T'ang dynasty (923–936), like that of the Later Liang, is less clearly depicted in the *Liao Shih* than in the *Wu-tai Shih*. The T'ang government took advantage of T'ai-tsu's campaign against the Po-hai kingdom to fall upon its hated neighbor and, in 926, achieved a temporary success.[195] In 927, according to the *Chiu Wu-tai Shih*, T'ai-tsung sent a mission to the south which offered tribute to the T'ang emperor.[196] In 928 the Chinese emperor responded by presenting the Liao ruler with a jade flute.[197] But a few years later, in 932, the T'ang court sent an impressive gift of silver vessels and silk to the Liao capital, evidently hoping to buy off the impending attack.[198]

---

[182] *Cf.* LS 30, 4b–5a; 69, 24b. *Cf.* also Bretschneider 88 I, 212 ff.

[183] *Cf.* I, 2 (10), no. 20.

[184] *Op. cit.*, no. 21.

[185] HTS 69, 596. See I, 1, note 13.

[186] XVI, 940, LS 4, 6a; 941, LS 4, 6b; 943, LS 49, 9a; 957, LS 6, 4a.

[187] MSNTS 1, 5a; LSNTS 15, 3a. See X, 2, note 18.

[188] X, 2 (23) (26).

[189] X, 2 (37) (41) (42)

[190] WTS 62, 5a–15b.

[191] X, 2 (4), and *passim.*

[192] CKC 5, 45; *cf.* also I, 1, note 12.

[193] X, 2 (27) (31) (33).

[194] WTS 2, 1a–b, 2b, 3a, 4b, 5b; and particularly 72, 3b.

[195] WTS 46, 9a–b.

[196] CWTS 38, 11b–12a.

[197] X, 2 (14).

[198] CWTS 43, 10b.

The bribe did not prevent the blow from falling. T'ang collapsed, succeeded by the Later Chin dynasty (936–946) which, having been set up with the help of the Liao emperor, remained completely dependent upon him. An attempt in 937 to regain the occupied northern territories from the Liao government failed. On this occasion the emperor of China offered his northern neighbor an annual tribute of three hundred thousand bolts of silk,[199] a quantity that was destined to play an important role in the financial relations of the Liao court and Sung China. The sixteen prefectures remained in the possession of Liao,[200] and annual tribute which included gold and silk as well as money[201] was paid in addition.[202] But an unending stream of miscellaneous offerings[203] supplemented the regular payments. The *Chiu Wu-tai Shih* tells of return-gifts made by the Liao court—silk, a few horses, and once a thousand sheep.[204] Compared with the thousands and tens of thousands of horses which the Liao emperors received as tribute,[205] a gift of twenty horses was only a matter of etiquette.

After the second Chin emperor's unsuccessful resistance and the great loot of 946, the Later Han (947–951) and Chou (951–960) dynasties struggled desperately to maintain their political independence. The seriousness of their short-lived efforts is well demonstrated by the almost complete absence of records concerning payments of tribute to Liao. Only Eastern Han (951–979), the reduced offspring of the Later Han dynasty, was in close political contact with the Liao empire. The little country (approximately modern Shansi province) temporarily received strong economic and military support in its fight against the Sung empire. It showed its gratitude by offering frequent, though modest, tribute to its powerful northern ally.

f. CHINA PROPER (SUNG)

The Sung dynasty, which again unified the greater part of China, was a close neighbor of Liao for a century and a half. The relationship between the two empires was, in the main, one of balanced hostility, neither being strong enough to subjugate the other. An initial advance by the Sung armies culminated in the conquest of Eastern Han in 979.[206] Then the tide turned. The *Sung History* records victory after

victory[207] but, in spite of temporary successes, the Sung government was unable to assist the Jurchen when they asked for help in 991. As a result, the Jurchen submitted to Liao.[208] The loss of prestige by the southern court can easily be imagined.

With only a few interruptions, the warfare between Liao and Sung lasted until 1005. A serious defeat of the Sung armies ended it, and a peace treaty guaranteed Liao an annual tribute of a hundred thousand taels of silver and two hundred thousand bolts of silk. The agreement is recorded not only in the *Liao Shih*,[209] but also in the *Sung Shih*.[210] The Sung emperor called the mother of the young Liao ruler his junior aunt,[211] and the Liao officials placed the two empires on the same level by speaking of the Northern and Southern Dynasties.[212]

LS 96, 1*b* insists that in 1042 the term "tribute" was used again. The statement implies that it had been used earlier, namely during the period 1005–1042. LS 19, 3*a* and 86, 2*b* designate the payments made by Sung as tribute, *kung* 貢. A present given by one state to another of equal status is generally called *p'in* 聘 or *pi* 幣, whereas *kung* is offered to a country of superior rank. The Sung literature does not use the term *kung*, but neither does it record a number of other unpleasant facts, such as the military defeats suffered in the war against Liao. The details which are admitted are sufficiently damaging to make the *Liao Shih* statement quite plausible. A recently discovered Liao inscription carved in 1031 shows that the northern court boasted of receiving tribute (*kung*) from the Sung empire at a time when relations between the two countries were peaceful and polite and when Sung envoys regularly visited the Liao emperor.[213]

But, whatever the terminology, the facts are clear. From the year 1005 on, as fixed by agreement, the "presents" from Sung arrived annually. The *Liao Shih* says so explicitly,[214] and the *Sung Shih* confirms it. In a discussion held at the Sung Court the wisdom of bribing the Liao barbarians instead of fighting them was questioned.[215] The argument implies that the bribe was being paid. Such payments are effective if the side that is being bribed is not strong enough to take advantage of the weakness which the bribes reveal. The Liao court accepted the huge offerings of the southern country and was temporarily

[199] X, 2 (19).
[200] XVI, 938, LS 4, 2*a–b*.
[201] X, 2 (25).
[202] *Loc. cit.*
[203] *Loc. cit.* and *passim.*
[204] CWTS 81, 5*a*.
[205] See II, 1 (3).
[206] SS 4, 10*a*

[207] SS 4, 10*a* and *passim.*
[208] SS 5, 13*b*.
[209] X, 2 (61).
[210] SS 7, 6*a* ff.; 281, 9*a* and 20*b*.
[211] See X, 2, note 44.
[212] See X, 2, note 59.
[213] Torii 36 II, pl. 125 ff.; see also X, 2, note 45.
[214] X, 2 (62).
[215] SS 315, 1*b*.

appeased. When the Hsia began to press the north-western provinces of China Proper,[216] the Liao court again pursued a more active policy; it asked Sung for additional tribute which was paid from 1042 on.[217]

After 1005 great politeness marked the relations of Liao and Sung, but at times this was forced into the background by unresolved political and military antagonisms. The portrait exchanges between the emperors of the two countries reveal the eager but unrewarded friendliness of Liao: Hsing-tsung sent his likeness to the Sung emperor, Jên-tsung (1023–1064), begging his "brother's" in return.[218] Apparently unconcerned, the southern emperor only complied with the request years later when the next Liao emperor, Tao-tsung, again asked for a portrait.[219] However, the annual payment of two hundred thousand taels of silver and three hundred thousand bolts of silk was an open wound; it kept reminding the Sung court of the ever-present military danger from the Liao-occupied North Chinese territory. The great Sung statesman, Wang An-shih (1021–1086), grew up under this menace. His reforms may have been initiated by more complex factors than considerations of foreign policy, but there can be no doubt that the threat of a barbarian invasion by the Hsi Hsia and, even more so, by the dreaded Liao armies loomed large in his thinking. In his famous Memorial of Ten Thousand Words he spoke of "the pressure of hostile forces on the borders,"[220] of "the constant anxiety about the situation on the borders,"[221] which made military affairs an issue "of the most vital importance to the country."[222] His reference to an earlier period when "for over two hundred years China was in the grip of barbarian tribes"[223] was as politically significant as his warning about "the menace of invasion."[224]

Wang's reforms did not succeed in removing the Liao armies from the soil of northern China; yet the inner consolidation that they effected enabled the Sung empire to undertake important defence measures in the northeastern border region. Wang's endeavor to increase the Sung cavalry[225] continued a military policy which had proved highly successful during the earlier years of the dynasty.[226]

The reconquest of the Hsi-ho 熙河 territory in the west of modern Kansu, which Wang An-shih fostered,[227] was a prerequisite for the control of the Hsi Hsia.[228] Such an advance would weaken the southwestern flank of the Liao empire. That the Sung attack against Hsi-ho and the fortification of captured towns in that region aroused the suspicion of the Liao emperor was openly stated at the Chinese court.[229] Elms and willows were planted in the border regions, apparently to impede the movements of hostile mounted forces. The strengthened defences of the northern border towns, the improved arms of the troops, and the concentration of thirty-seven divisions of soldiers in the north—all suspicious measures—were promoted under Wang An-shih's leadership.[230] The Liao delegation of 1074, led by Hsiao Hsi 禧, arrived at the Sung capital with definite demands for the destruction of the new border fortifications.[231] Wang An-shih's enemies accused him of being a warmonger and demanded the withdrawal of the thirty-seven divisions. A few months later Wang was removed from his dominant position as associate administrator of affairs for the Secretarial and Court Councils (t'ung-p'ing chang-shih 同平章事). Drought and famine were the ostensible reasons for his fall; in reality it was due to the attacks of his opponents who proposed policies more conservative internally and less militant externally.[232]

After 1074 the Chinese policy toward the Liao empire was a mixture of maneuver and compromise;[233] the southern country continued to fulfill its tribute obligations until the second decade of the twelfth century.[234] In 1115, when the Sung envoys presented silver and silk for the Liao army,[235] they supported a military machine that was already beginning to disintegrate. After a few years, the Sung empire concluded its pact with the rising Jurchen who were convenient allies against the common enemy, Liao, but terrifying enemies when they turned their victorious weapons against the Sung themselves.

6. THE TOTAL INCOME OF THE LIAO EMPIRE

The empire's income from taxes and tribute was complex and large—that much we may say with certainty. However, any attempt to determine the

---

[216] Cf. SS 11, 1a ff.

[217] X, 2 (74).

[218] X, 2 (87).

[219] X, 2, note 69; SS 318, 11b.

[220] See Williamson, WAS I, 49; for the Chinese original see LCHSWC 39, 1b.

[221] Williamson, op. cit., 64; cf. LCHSWC 39, 9a.

[222] Williamson, op. cit., 63; cf. LCHSWC 39, 8a.

[223] Williamson, op. cit., 77; cf. LCHSWC 39, 15b.

[224] Williamson, op. cit., 78; cf. LCHSWC 39, 15b.

[225] SS 15, 7b.

[226] See XV, introduction.

[227] Williamson, WAS I, 304

[228] Op. cit., 305.

[229] Op. cit., 278.

[230] Loc. cit.

[231] Op. cit., 277.

[232] Op. cit., 278–284.

[233] Op. cit., 354 ff.

[234] SS 351, 12b.

[235] X, 2 (106).

exact total meets with almost insurmountable difficulties.

In the time of the T'ang dynasty Tu Yu set down what he considered the main sources of the country's revenue and the main items of its expenditures.[236] The attempt, however, was none too satisfactory, in all probability more because of the inadequate data than because of the method used.[237]

The historical records of the Liao empire are decidedly inferior to those of T'ang. Not even an incomplete budget exists for the dual empire of the north. We know that certain goods and commodities were collected and distributed more or less regularly, but only in a few cases is the annual amount known; often the data refer only to a single circuit; sometimes we are not sure whether the collection was made each year. The presentation that follows cannot therefore be considered even a tentative budget for Liao. It is simply an enumeration of what have been the chief items of revenue and expenditure.

a. GRAIN

The empire controlled some 480,000 Chinese and 90,000 Po-hai households.[238] Neither figure includes the ordo families. Since the fiscal status of the ordo soldiers is obscure, it seems advisable to disregard them altogether—a procedure which fortunately affects the present analysis but little, for according to our estimates[239] this group probably comprised no more than 30,000 Chinese and 20,000 Po-hai households at the close of the dynasty. Of the 480,000 Chinese families counted, 400,000 lived in the old southern territories, the majority (about 283,000) in Nan-ching Circuit.[240]

Taxes paid in grain were gathered primarily from the rural sector of the population which probably included eighty to eighty-five per cent of the Chinese nationals[241] and a smaller proportion of the Po-hai, who in part were still nomads. Thus there may have been in the neighborhood of four hundred thousand Chinese and possibly fifty thousand to sixty thousand Po-hai farmsteads. Among the Nan-ching Chinese perhaps two hundred and forty thousand households delivered their "land and other taxes" in kind. How large were the farms of these Liao peasants and how

much grain did they pay? In T'ang China in 786 a farmstead of fifty mou was considered a poor one.[242] In Sung China in 989 a hundred mou was mentioned as the standard for farms of former soldiers, and a suggestion to establish smaller farms of fifty mou was made but not accepted.[243] In 1074 a soldier was given a farm of a hundred mou.[244] General figures of this kind do not differentiate between irrigated and dry fields, a practice still observable today; but this is less arbitrary than might appear at first glance, for many farmsteads include both kinds of fields and the law of large numbers establishes a crude balance between them.

If the available data on average farms during the T'ang and Sung periods are considered with this in mind, then Tu Yu's assumption of seventy mou as the size of an average farm during the time of T'ang[245] is not unreasonable. During the latter part of the T'ang period (in 780) the tax rates for the region around the capital were fixed at between seven and eleven pints per mou, and in the middle of the Sung period (1133) they ranged from seven to fifteen pints.[246] In general the Liao territory was located north of China Proper. Today the smaller crops produced in the north per mou are compensated for by the increased size of the farms;[247] in former times this was probably also true. We may, therefore, assume that the average Liao farm was somewhat larger, let us say, ninety mou in the regions south of the mountains and a hundred or more farther to the north. On the basis of these hypothetical figures we shall endeavor to determine in a general way how much grain tax was paid in Nan-ching, the most important agricultural circuit and the only one for which we have concrete data.

In 1123, as the dynasty was collapsing, the Jurchen (Chin) army invaded and occupied the Southern Capital. The Sung government, which for obvious political and military reasons wished to gain possession of this old Chinese territory, offered in return to hand over annually a part of the revenues collected there. After prolonged negotiations the payments were fixed in accordance with reports made by two Liao bureaus, the Triple Office and the Control Office. The final statement, which is translated below,[248] contains a number of terms whose meanings are still open to question. The main points, however, are sufficiently clear to permit an analysis of the whole.

---

[236] TT 6, 33–38.
[237] See Balázs 31 BWT, 57 ff.
[238] See I, introduction: Population.
[239] Loc. cit.
[240] Loc. cit.
[241] This percentage is given by "most observers" for the rural sector of modern China (Buck 37a, 363). In view of the fact that modern China contains the germs of modern industrialization, it may be assumed that its rural sector is not larger, but in all probability smaller, than that of T'ang, Liao, or Sung China.

---

[242] CTS 153, 5a.
[243] SS 176, 2b.
[244] Op. cit., 7b.
[245] TT 6, 34.
[246] CTS 48, 5b; SS 173, 16b.
[247] Buck 37a, 209 and 287.
[248] See X, 1, note 48.

TABLE 13
The Revenue of Nan-ching Circuit in 1123

| REVENUE | OFFICES | | TOTAL |
	Triple Office	Control Office	
k'o-ch'êng money	1,158,798	Source undefined: 49,248	1,208,416 strings[249]
	Salt monopoly: 390,000 Other sales: 433,212 [House taxes and other dues: 335,586]		[1,208,046]
Regular taxes	Land tax and other taxes 3,754,442	Tax paid by "government people" 530,438	4,284,860 strings and 800 coins [4,284,880]
Total	4,913,120 [4,913,240]	579,687 [579,686]	Grand total 5,492,906 strings and 800 coins [Combined revenues: 5,492,926; Both Offices: 5,492,807]

With certain interpolations and modifications made by us and enclosed in brackets, we present in table 13 the revenue of Nan-ching Circuit as defined in the document of 1123.

The money values for the year 1123 cited in table 13 were said to have been ten times as great as those prevailing during the preceding two hundred years.[250] Consequently during these two hundred years the regular taxes (*shui fu*) brought in something over four hundred thousand strings. The land and other taxes may, at that time, have yielded the equivalent of 375,444 strings.

The taxes on agriculture in Nan-ching Circuit are said to have been several times as high as those in Sung China.[251] If the Liao government increased the T'ang rate of seven to eleven pints per *mou* several times, the new land tax must have yielded twenty or thirty pints per *mou*, a very considerable amount. Accepting the increase as fact—particularly since it would be consistent with the policy of a conquest government—but hesitating to take the formula "several times" at face value, we suggest a rate of fifteen pints per *mou* as the starting point for further calculations, fifteen being one hundred and fifty per cent above the lowest and less than fifty per cent above the highest tax rate of the late T'ang period, and slightly more than one hundred per cent above

the lowest and equal to the highest Sung rate of the year 1123.

If the average farm of ninety *mou* included eighty *mou* that were cultivated and taxed,[252] the owner would have had to pay twelve hundred pints, the equivalent of one hundred and twenty pecks or twelve bushels of grain. Similarly, 240,000 farms would have had to pay 288,000,000 pints, the equivalent of 28,800,000 pecks or 2,880,000 bushels. (See appendix III.) At the conversion rate of six cash per peck, the land rent of Nan-ching Circuit would have approximated 172,800 strings of money. Compared with a total of 375,444 strings for land and other taxes, this figure is well within the range of possibility, if somewhat low. Either the land tax was actually several times the Sung rate or else the combined "other taxes" were more than the entire land tax.

Our conservative figures, whatever their inadequacies, convey a certain idea of the size of the land tax collected in the Liao empire as a whole. If 240,000 farms in Nan-ching Circuit yielded 2,880,000 bushels of grain, and if larger farmsteads compensated for a less intensive cultivation in the northern regions, a total of over four hundred and fifty thousand peasant households may have paid something under twice the Nan-ching share, let us say, five million bushels. During the middle period of the T'ang dynasty five million households with eight million two hundred thousand taxpayers delivered some twenty-five million

---

[249] All items were evaluated in strings, though a great part of the revenue was paid in kind.

[250] SCPMHP 13, 7a.

[251] HCLY 77, 5b.

[252] *Cf.* Buck 37a, 173.

bushels of grain in taxes.[253]   In other words, more than ten times as many T'ang farmsteads yielded only five times the estimated Liao revenue.   If these figures in any way reflect the actual conditions that prevailed in the two periods, then the Liao village paid indeed a much higher grain tax than did its T'ang prototype.

Another set of figures may be used to check our estimate.   A surplus of two hundred thousand bushels of grain was handed over by the Liao government to its ally, the Eastern Han country.[254]   The military granaries of Tung-ching Circuit kept a store of two hundred thousand to three hundred thousand bushels of grain.[255]   The peasant soldiers of a northwestern army accumulated a surplus of several hundred thousand bushels of grain in fourteen harvests.[256]   In Chung-ching Circuit a hundred and fifty thousand bushels of tax grain were collected in one year.[257]

The last figure is most significant for our calculations.   Analyzing the Liao population, we have submitted that something over twenty-five thousand households in Chung-ching Circuit was "probably a conservative guess."[258]   At the tax rate of twelve bushels per farmstead, twenty-five thousand households would yield three hundred thousand bushels. In the light of this hypothetical figure, an actual tax total of one hundred and fifty thousand is possible, but low. Two alternatives are suggested: either the farming families of Chung-ching Circuit numbered considerably under twenty-five thousand or the revenue from Chung-ching's agriculture was far less than that of the Southern Capital.   Both factors may have played their part.   If the second weighed heavily in the "central" region, it may also have done so in other territories beyond Nan-ching Circuit and the total grain tax of the Liao empire may then have fallen well below the above estimate of five million bushels.

b. MONEY

The statement of Nan-ching revenue in 1123 cites payments in kind for the bulk of the territory's "land and other taxes," but payments in cash for the k'o-ch'êng income of the Triple Office, accruing from salt and sundry government sales, from house and miscellaneous taxes.   The small k'o-ch'êng revenues of the Control Office are not specified.

In the introduction to section VI the average money total collected annually by the fiscal offices of the Liao empire has been estimated at around five hundred thousand strings.   This estimate, however, needs to

be qualified.   According to the *Liao Shih*, the salt and iron tax in Nan-ching Circuit was converted from money into silk.[259]   No further comment clarifies this important record, but the existence of a number of special Offices of Money and Silk[260] suggests that the payment of silk along with money was customary, at least during a considerable part of the Liao period.

c. TEXTILES

SILK

Besides the silk offered as salt and iron tax, the valuable tissue was paid instead of other taxes by the inhabitants of such prefectures as Chin 錦 and Hsien 顯 which specialized in sericulture.[261]   Silk of the finest quality was probably bought mostly from Sung merchants who traded it against salt, pastoral products, and other Liao goods.[262]   In addition, large quantities of tribute silk were offered by Sung China from 1005 on.   A great part of this, without doubt, was utilized directly by those receiving it in government grants but, more than probably, some of it found its way into the hands of Liao traders who either resold it at a profit or presented it in payment of taxes.

LINEN

After 926 the conquered territories of Po-hai offered a hundred and fifty thousand *tuan* of cloth per year.[263]   Was this tribute converted into a tax when the financial system of Tung-ching became coordinated with Nan-ching and Hsi-ching?   LS 13, 4a shows that a *tiao* 調 tax was paid.   Traditionally this was a levy raised in textiles, either in silk or in linen.   Since Liao produced but little silk, the major part of the *tiao* tax must have been paid in linen.

d. PRECIOUS METALS

Armor was offered on occasion as tribute,[264] but silver and gold were paid in annually by all sections of the country.[265]   Chin 晉 presented silver,[266] and Sung paid as much as a hundred thousand taels annually between 1005 and 1042, and two hundred thousand taels until the end of the Liao dynasty.[267]   Some copper flowed across the border,[268] but the greater part of the Liao demand for this metal was evidently satisfied by local production.

---

[253] Balázs 31 BWT, 57–58.
[254] II, 2 (7).
[255] XII (119).
[256] II, 2 (8).
[257] X, 1 (66).
[258] See I, introduction: Population.

[259] X, 1 (2).
[260] XIV, 2 (10).
[261] HCLY 77, 9a; X, 1 (16).
[262] See V, introduction.
[263] X, 1 (4).
[264] X, 2 (37) (45).
[265] X, 1 (58).
[266] X, 2 (25).
[267] X, 2 (61) (74).
[268] V (13).

e. MISCELLANEOUS PRODUCTS

Certain groups of metal workers paid iron as tax.[269] This statement is not inconsistent with the report made by the Nan-ching Control Office for 1123 which claimed a small *k'o-ch'êng* income paid in money and, juxtaposed to it, a much larger sum from the "government people,"[270] obviously paid in kind. Similar payments in kind may also have satisfied government needs for salt and coal. The Liao sources are particularly vague concerning this form of revenue, perhaps because it presented no major fiscal problems.

f. HORSES

The sedentary regions provided the Ch'i-tan government with grain, salt, metal, cash, and textiles. The countries of Inner Asia and the inner and outer tribes made a very different contribution. Most important were the horses which were offered annually by the empire's officials.[271] Whether these horses were selected with an eye to quality is not specified, but the records frequently note the fine breeding of the steeds presented by the diplomatic envoys of the Inner Asiatic States.[272] Levies on rich herd-owners[273] for military purposes were certainly more concerned with number than with grade; for the Ch'i-tan tribal commoner, this must have been equally true.[274]

The taxes imposed on the inner tribes were limited, for their economic and military strength had to be maintained. No such considerations restricted the tributes demanded from the outer tribes and states. Any transfer of horses from a neighboring territory to the Liao armies increased the weakness of the former and the power of the latter. War loot and annual tribute were two sides of the same predatory process. T'ai-tsu seized more than a hundred thousand oxen, sheep, camels, and horses when he victoriously invaded the northern border zone of China.[275] In 986 horses were also included in the huge war booty.[276] Wang An-shih was fully aware of the relation between animal loss and reduced military strength; he therefore made every effort to conserve China's horse power.

T'ai-tsu's victories against such western tribes as the Turks, T'u-hun, and Tang-hsiang were followed by the seizure of large numbers of horses, oxen, and sheep.[277] Three years later the northern Wu-ku tribes were deprived of two hundred thousand oxen, horses, carts, and tents, a not unexpected corollary to their temporary loss of political independence.[278] In the east the powerful Jurchen were plundered in the same way. After a crushing military defeat and the loss of two hundred thousand horses,[279] an almost unbelievable number, they agreed to join the Liao army against the Sung empire. The frequent demands for horse tributes continued. Herds of three hundred to ten thousand, and even twenty thousand, head were offered by at least eleven tribes, the Jurchen, Chih-pu-ku, and Tsu-pu being credited with particularly heavy payments.[280] Five tribes presented an annual tribute of three hundred horses;[281] the former Po-hai, whose large population was in part agricultural, paid a thousand head annually.[282] The extraordinary payments of ten thousand or twenty thousand head can only have been made occasionally: the Jurchen offered ten thousand horses and then joined the campaign against Korea in 1010;[283] the Tsu-pu, who once paid twenty thousand head, presented seventeen hundred annually.[284] The Tangut people, the Tang-hsiang tribes and the Hsi Hsia kingdom, are known to have paid horses as well as other animals.[285] No exact estimates can be made from our incomplete textual data, but the economic and military effect of such large horse payments is obvious.

g. OTHER ANIMALS

In addition to horses, camels,[286] sheep,[287] and oxen[288] were demanded as tribute from the various tribal peoples. These payments reflected not only the economic but also the prestige values that the Ch'i-tan masters had established.[289]

h. FURS

Garments of fur and fur trimmings were traditional in the tribal life of the Ch'i-tan. While Chinese dress was adopted to a limited degree,[290] the high Ch'i-tan aristocracy dressed in dark sable and white ermine.

---

[269] III (3).
[270] SCPMHP 13, 11*b*.
[271] X, 1 (15).
[272] X, 2 (24) and *passim*.
[273] X, 1 (29).
[274] See above.
[275] II, 1 (3).
[276] XVI, 986, LS 11, 2*a*.
[277] XVI, 916, LS 1, 9*a*.

[278] XVI, 919, LS 2, 1*a–b*.
[279] XVI, 986, LS 11, 1*a*.
[280] II, 1 (3).
[281] X, 2 (69). Among them four divisions of the Five Nations (I, 2 (5), no. 34), and the T'ieh-li, who, though not one of the inner tribes, had a more or less similar status (see I, 2 (10), no. 30).
[282] X, 1 (4).
[283] X, 2 (66).
[284] X, 2 (70).
[285] *Cf.* X, 2 (18) and *passim*.
[286] X, 2 (18) (25) (57) (75) (80) (81) (83) (86) (88) (91).
[287] X, 2 (83).
[288] X, 2 (48) (97).
[289] II, introduction.
[290] VII, introduction.

The lower nobles arrayed themselves in "the furs of the sable, sheep, mole, and corsac."[291] The large demand could be satisfied, for many of the tributary tribes still indulged in hunting as a subsidiary means of support. The Wu-wei Yü-ch'üeh may have gradually changed from hunting to herding for, in 988, they were permitted to replace their former fur tribute by oxen and horses.[292] Other tribes asked for some alleviation of their tribute obligations which included furs, without however suggesting a change in kind.[293] The Tsu-pu contributed ten thousand ermine and twenty-five thousand gray mole-skins regularly;[294] the northeastern tribes, which paid three hundred horses annually, had to present sixty-five thousand ermine skins at the same time.[295] The fur tribute fluctuated for political as well as natural reasons, but the fact that such large payments were expected indicates the importance of this particular item in the Liao budget.

i. FELT

Felt was needed in the construction of tents and tent-carts, necessary adjuncts in both the military and civil life of the Ch'i-tan. It was brought from the border tribes[296] and, for a time, was considered too precious to be sold to Sung.[297] This being so, it is possible that felt was one of those "local products" that the Liao government obtained from both the inner and outer tribes.

j. MISCELLANEOUS TAXES AND CONTRIBUTIONS

Many minor items are mentioned in the financial records. Almost without exception, they are articles desired particularly by the emperor, the court, the higher nobility, and officials. Deer[298] (for the imperial park), eagles, and falcons[299] for the imperial hunt and for the emperor's aviaries were included in the tribute payments with great regularity. Curios were offered by the territorial officials,[300] and fresh produce by remote regions of the empire.[301] Foreign drugs[302] —and doctors[303]—were a welcome addition to the traditional medicine. Grape wine was presented on occasion;[304] so was Chinese tea.[305] However, kumiss and

the native wine made from grain remained the common beverages.

Other items such as silver ornaments, precious silk, and special suits, which were also presented or exchanged, have more cultural than financial significance. Politically interesting are the gifts presented by the Sung court to the Liao emperor on his birthday. They included:

> 37 gold utensils
> 5 suits
> 1 gold belt
> 1 jade belt
> 1 pair of black leather boots
> 1 pair of white leather boots
> 1 set of musical instruments
> 2 horses with bridles, saddles and whips
> 30 silver objects with gold flowers
> 20 silver objects
> 2,000 bolts of silk of different varieties
> 2,000 bolts of colored silk
> 30 jars of imperial wine
> 10 catties of tea
> 5 catties of a different variety of tea
> 30 jars of preserved fruit
> 30 baskets of dried fruit

The presents for New Year's Day consisted of:

> 60 silver objects with gold flowers
> 2,000 bolts of silk of different varieties
> 2,000 bolts of colored silk.[306]

k. ADDITIONAL REVENUES

In addition to its income from taxes and tribute, the government received certain other revenues, some occasional, some regular. Labor services might be converted into money payments.[307] The interest from official grain loans might augment the grain reserves.[308] Government industries[309] produced iron and copper for the workshops and mints; they furnished textiles for the court and perhaps for the army. Such revenues reduced national expenditures or added directly to the state treasury.

7. GOVERNMENT OUTLAY

These then were the main sources of the empire's income. The various items were collected through thousands of local and territorial agencies and transported to regional and metropolitan storehouses. However, the huge government machine had to be maintained, not only occasionally, but permanently;

---

[291] VII, 1 (48).
[292] X, 2 (48).
[293] X, 2 (55).
[294] X, 2 (70).
[295] X, 2 (69).
[296] V (4).
[297] V (10).
[298] X, 2 (18) and *passim*.
[299] X, 2 (77) and *passim*.
[300] X, 1 (61).
[301] X, 1 (64).
[302] X, 2 (25) (40).
[303] IX (13).
[304] X, 2 (39) (47) (both times from Eastern Han).
[305] X, 2 (25—from Chin) (40—from Eastern Han).

[306] CTKC 21, 1b–2a.
[307] XI (26).
[308] VI, 2 (5).
[309] See III and VI, *passim*.

the stream of taxes and tribute payments which filled the coffers of the empire, both regional and central, flowed outwards again to support the court, the officialdom, the army, and the needy. No quantitative estimate can be made of government expenditure, but the text gives some idea of its more important items and functions.

a. THE IMPERIAL HOUSE

Theoretically the emperor as the country's overlord was free to dispose of government possessions and income at will. Hsing-tsung's suggestion that his brother-in-law, Hsiao Hui, might "take whatever treasures he desired"[310] clearly expresses the unlimited power of the sovereign. Hui's polite refusal did not imply any criticism of the emperor's attitude; it merely indicated his satisfaction with the status quo.

Within the frame of the emperor's uncontested overlordship, however, custom and expediency had established a division between expenditures for the court and those for the administration and the army. The imperial treasury[311] evidently handled expenditures of the first class, but the *Liao Shih* gives no systematic account of their nature. We know that the emperor and his entourage lived well; we know that at first they dressed in Ch'i-tan clothes and only later substituted Chinese silk garments on occasion; we know that they ate well and drank plentifully, using the country's best foodstuffs, both Ch'i-tan and Chinese. Yet we look in vain for exact figures.

Silver went to the court;[312] silver and gold ornaments were worn and generously distributed.[313] Huge sums of money were at the disposal of the emperor and his consort, and their cash gifts to a Buddhist temple at times almost matched the cash income of Chung-ching Circuit in its most impressive fiscal year. The princes and princesses who held "entrusted prefectures" had control over all revenues collected in their territories with the exception of the wine tax.[314] And certain illegitimate drains were common enough; the princesses who appropriated valuable property from the government storehouses met with little criticism.[315]

After the conclusion of the new and advantageous tribute agreement with the Sung empire in 1042, poor members of the Three Patriarchal Households received special benevolences.[316] In all probability, these were made through a government grant, but, as in most records of this kind, no precise description is given. What concrete information is available refers to social groups below the imperial family.

b. THE OFFICIALDOM

The officials received monthly salaries,[317] an arrangement confirmed by a Sung report.[318] Hsiao Wu-na speaks of the cash he received,[319] but it is doubtful whether this was the usual or even the expected way for the government to reward its officers. Sheep[320] and grain[321] are known to have been given as salary; theoretically these payments were made by the treasury, but at times they were squeezed directly from the people.[322]

The gifts offered to officials on special occasions were taken from the government surplus. Included were money,[323] grain,[324] silk,[325] precious metals,[326] and tributes.[327] Twice a year officers of the imperial army were entertained at the expense of the government,[328] and occasionally other great festivities were held. Envoys to foreign courts were not infrequently the recipients of presents of considerable value which, while designated gifts of courtesy, approached the status of attempted bribes. A few figures indicate how far a wealthy state might go in its desire to please a Liao emissary,[329] but no precise data discuss the relation of such emoluments to the salaries of the officials, or, if the emoluments were taxed,[330] to the budget of the Liao government.

When not even official salaries are known, there is little possibility of determining real income. In three months Li Ch'u-wên acquired seventy thousand strings of cash plus other property of equal value.[331] To accumulate any such sum, the prime minister must have dipped into the resources of the empire rather heavily. In his case the underground drain was stopped, but for political not financial reasons;

---

[310] VIII (7).

[311] See above and XIV, 2 (5), LS 47, 14a.

[312] X, 1 (58).

[313] *Cf.* the description of the imperial carriages (in section IV) and the record of presents made to the Sung court (III, introduction).

[314] See above.

[315] X, 1 (57).

[316] X, 1 (46).

---

[317] X, 1 (37).

[318] X, 1, note 57.

[319] X, 1 (65).

[320] V (4).

[321] SHYK 196, 23b.

[322] X, 1 (32).

[323] X, 1 (21) (40).

[324] X, 1 (21).

[325] X, 1 (16).

[326] X, 1 (11) (12).

[327] X, 1 (5).

[328] X, 1 (55).

[329] For the impressive presents given to Liao envoys by the Sung court see SS 119, 11b; CTKC 21, 2a–b; SHYK 196, 36b–38a.

[330] The Chin 金 dynasty taxed its envoys heavily (CS 46, 1b); whether it followed a Liao precedent, we do not know.

[331] VIII (11).

indeed, the financial angle might have escaped official attention altogether. Any realistic study of the expenditures of Liao must make liberal allowance for these underground drains upon the public funds which began with the petty thieveries of a few strings[332] and culminated in the embezzlement of thousands and tens of thousands of cash.

c. THE ARMY

The expenditures of Liao, like those of T'ang, were in large part directed toward meeting the needs of the army; and the number of horses levied was frequently determined by these needs.[333] Since one soldier might have three horses,[334] the total government supply must have been large.

Two passages state that the soldiers provided their own food,[335] but this could only have occurred in times of war. In times of peace some troops of the standing army lived primarily on meat secured by their own hunting,[336] while others subsisted for the most part on grain from the fields cultivated by the garrison or for it;[337] but all depended on supplies made available to them from public resources. Sometimes special granaries were maintained by the army, and the grain was purchased from the farming population.[338] Salt was also necessary,[339] and so were all kinds of leather, metal, and wooden equipment.[340] While many commodities were distributed directly, certain expenses were met in money; at times cash was allotted to a particular army.[341] Relief was also given to the soldiers of a damaged cantonment in money, grain, and horses.[342]

d. GOVERNMENT CONSTRUCTION

Although the construction work undertaken by the Liao government was extensive,[343] no information on costs is available.

e. RELIEF

Expenditures for relief played a considerable role in the economy of the Liao empire. Their relation to the country's regular income and disbursements will be discussed in section XII.

f. GIFTS

In addition to gifts bestowed upon the Liao officialdom, contributions of importance were made to re-

ligious institutions, to their leaders, to persons of merit—such as virtuous widows[344]—and to the old.[345] But the steadily increasing donations to Buddhist temples and priests[346] put a much greater strain on the country's budget than did the special honorific grants or spontaneous gifts made by a hilarious Ch'i-tan emperor in mufti to the bewildered owners of the metropolitan wine shops.[347]

g. DIPLOMATIC PRESENTS

Presents probably accompanied most official missions to foreign capitals, but they are less carefully recorded by the *Liao Shih* than those brought to the Liao court. While the birthday gifts sent to the Sung ruler in 1005[348] are not mentioned in the *Liao Shih*, those dispatched to a neighboring country when its ruler died were noted.[349] At times no reason for the presentation is given; the *History* only states that sheep were offered to Korea in 1093.[350] The political significance of all diplomatic presents far outweighs their economic importance; they are included here to indicate the general structure if not the exact total of government expenditure.

8. CONCLUSION

The financial system of a state such as the Liao empire cannot be measured by the standards of a modern industrial society. It must be interpreted in the light of its own possibilities, traditions, and functions. Yet the general idea of a state budget must have existed; it is suggested by the concreteness of many of the requisitions and appropriations. Indeed, it is likely that, at least in the later years of the dynasty, some kind of a written budget was prepared by the clerks in the Ministry of Revenue.

The budget presented to the emperor was certainly crude and disorderly, and probably unreliable in many of its details. Such as it was, it records two centuries of growth, prosperity, crisis, and dissolution. We do not say that it was a good budget because it lasted so long, nor do we say that it was a bad budget because it lasted no longer. It was as good and as bad as the socio-political order of which it was the fiscal marrow. When the spine broke, the marrow decayed. The breakdown of the Liao budget was the expression rather than the cause of the empire's general disintegration.

[332] XIV, 4 (12).
[333] See below.
[334] XV, 2 (1).
[335] II, 1 (2); XV, 2 (1).
[336] II, 1 (5).
[337] II, 2 (8).
[338] VI, 2 (6).
[339] III (4).
[340] XV, 2 (1).
[341] X, 1 (22).
[342] X, 1 (56).
[343] See XI, *passim*.

[344] X, 1 (14).
[345] X, 1 (18) (33) (41).
[346] See IX, *passim*.
[347] X, 1 (12).
[348] See III, introduction.
[349] X, 2 (101).
[350] X, 2 (100).

TRANSLATION

1. TAXES

1. TRADE TAX

907–926   The system of taxing trade began when T'ai-tsu set up Yang City[1] north of Mount T'an[2] and established a government monopoly in order to open up trade with the various regions.[3] When T'ai-tsung obtained Yen, he founded the Southern Capital. In the northern section of the city was a market in which all kinds of goods were piled up. Officials were ordered to take charge of their taxation. Wherever there was trade in goods and products in the four remaining capitals and in the other prefectures and counties, the arrangement was the same.   60, 1a

2. THE TAXATION OF LIAO

After 907   In general all market taxes went to the entrusted [territories];[4] only the tax on wine[5] was paid to the Supreme Capital.[6] Thus the taxes of the entrusted commandery-prefectures were divided into two classes.[7]

Previously, in the newly submitted regions of Liao-tung,[8] the liquor trade was not monopolized by the government, and the restrictions concerning salt and yeast for fermenting liquor were also lenient.[9] Fêng Yen-hsiu,[10] and after him Han Shao-hsün,[11] in casting about for revenue, wanted to

---

[1] Yang 羊 City, corresponding to modern Pain Tsaghan Nor, Chahar (Yanai 30, 828), was built in 909 (LS 1, 3b).

[2] Probably northwest of Hei-lung Mountain in Chahar (Yanai 30, 834).

[3] Here the term tao 道 cannot signify the "circuit" of Shang-ching Circuit, Tung-ching Circuit, and so forth, for this administrative unit came into being only after 928. As the rest of the text proves, the chüeh-wu 榷務 in this case does not mean a government monopoly of the manufacture of commodities, but an impost levied upon their sale.

[4] Cf. I, 1 (3).

[5] The Chin emperor, Shih-tsung (1161–1187), once remarked that under the Liao dynasty the liquor monopoly was controlled by the yin officials (CS 7, 17a).

[6] The real capital of the empire.

[7] Yüan Hao-wên 元好問 (1190–1257) describes how

the Ch'i-tan acquired their subjects and distributed them among the nobles and meritorious officials, who in turn used them to establish one or two new prefectures. Since these bondsmen paid taxes to the government and to their masters, they were called "double-tax payers" (二稅戶) (CCC 2, 24a).

[8] Present Liaoning Province.

[9] A parallel passage in LS 17, 6b reads, "There was no government control over the liquor trade, and the laws concerning salt and yeast for fermenting liquor and the taxes on trade at the passes were also very lenient."

[10] There is no biography of this man in the Liao Shih. Probably he was one of the special envoys who visited the Sung court on a mission of courtesy in 1022 (LS 16, 6b).

[11] The grandson of Han Yen-hui, the first Chinese who, according to tradition, advised T'ai-tsu to build cities, towns, and villages for the Chinese captives (cf. LS 74, 3b).

impose restrictions after the example of the Yen[12] and P'ing-shan[13] districts.   Its people considered this an affliction, and presently the rebellion of Ta Yen-lin[14] broke out.   After decrees were issued suspending their land tax for several years, the people began to quiet down.

In the Southern Capital the annual payment of money taxes on salt and iron to the Triple Office was converted into [a payment of] lustring.   In Ta-t'ung[15] the annual payment of money taxes to the Triple Office was converted into [a payment of] grain.   According to the old precedent in K'ai-yüan Commandery,[16] in the payment of the annual tax by the people one peck of millet was made equivalent to five cash.   Yeh-lü Mo-chih,[17] who was in charge of the commandery, suggested in a memorial that a peck be made equivalent to six cash.   These also were enlightened government measures which benefited the people.[18]   59, 4a–b

3. SALT

907–926   The system of salt permits originated with T'ai-tsu.   Because he had secured many Chinese [subjects], he set apart from the eight tribes the ancient Chinese City and made it into another tribe to govern it.   The city, situated south of Mount T'an, enjoyed the advantages of a salt lake.   This was the Hua-yen County of Later Wei.   All eight tribes extracted [the salt] and ate it.

Then, after the expedition to Yu and Chi, [T'ai-tsu] returned and halted at Ho-la Lake where he ordered salt to be taken to supply the army.   Afterwards the amount of salt from the lake increased so much that both the government and the people were fully provided.

938–947   In the beginning of the Hui-t'ung period T'ai-tsung was very benevolent toward Chin.   Chin offered sixteen prefectures, among which were Ying and Mo.   Now for the first time they obtained the benefits of evaporating water [for salt] in Ho-chien.   A Salt Monopoly Department was set up in Hsiang-ho County.   As a result, the people to the north of Yen and Yün were temporarily provided with the salt of Ts'ang.   At this time the Offices of the Accountants of the five capitals for such salt-producing areas as Po-hai, Chên City, Hai-yang, Fêng Prefecture, Yang-lo City, and Kuang-chi Lake each controlled its own region.   As to the method of evaporating salt and the amount of the annual output, no details are known.[19]   60, 1b–2a

4. THE TRIBUTE OF PO–HAI

926   In the first year of T'ien-hsien, [Pei[20]] participated in the punitive campaign against Po-hai. . . . The country was renamed Tung-tan and its [Capital] city was called T'ien-fu.   Pei was appointed Prince Jên-huang to rule it. . . . It offered an annual tribute of one hundred and fifty thousand *tuan*[21] of cloth and a thousand horses.   72, 1a–b

5. TRIBUTES DISTRIBUTED AMONG THE OFFICIALS

939   [On the day *i-ssŭ* of the fifth month in the second year of Hui-t'ung], Nan T'ang sent envoys to pay tribute.   On the day *ting-wei* the articles of tribute were bestowed upon the officials.   4, 3b

---

[12] In this region, equivalent to modern Peiping, Liao was able to collect the highest amount of taxes.   See below, note 48.

[13] 平山 is equivalent to modern Lu-lung 盧龍 County, Hopei.   In Liao times it was a wealthy region.

[14] A descendant of the founder of the Po-hai kingdom. He rebelled in 1029 and was made prisoner in 1030 (PHKC 3, 20b; cf. also XIII (38)).

[15] The capital of Hsi-ching Circuit in the northern part of modern Shansi.

[16] Northwest of the Urot Banner, Suiyuan.

[17] Yeh-lü Mo-chih 抹只, who was of noble descent,

played an important role in the battle of 979 against Sung. In 980 he attained the position of vice-chancellor and was transferred to the post of commanding prefect of K'ai-yüan Commandery in the beginning of the T'ung-ho period (983–1012).   He died at the end of this period (LS 84, 1b–2a).

[18] The last story is told with slight variations in LS 84, 2a.

[19] For notes to this passage see section III.

[20] The eldest son of T'ai-tsu.

[21] One *tuan* 端 was equal to about 61.2 feet (see appendix III).

6. ABUSES OF THE SYSTEM OF TAXATION

939   On the day *kuei-wei* of the intercalary [seventh] month [in the second year of Hui-t'ung] the great king of the I-shih,[22] who was found guilty of an inequitable assessment of taxes, was beaten on his back with a wooden cudgel[23] and then released. The contributions made by the people of the Southern and Northern Administrations to the emperor and the taxes and services rendered to the prime ministers and commanding prefects which were not in accordance with the old system were also discontinued.   4, 3*b*

7. DEER OFFERED

943   [In the sixth month of the sixth year of Hui-t'ung] the Ch'u-po-tê tribe of Hsi presented white musk deer.   69, 5*b*

943   On the day *chi-wei* [of the sixth month in the sixth year of Hui-t'ung] the Ch'u-ku-li tribe[24] of Hsi offered white musk deer.   4, 9*a*

8. A LIBERAL REWARD

951–969   According to the law of Liao, a stag with antlers could be shot only by the Son of Heaven. It happened that in the autumn hunt a man skilled in imitating the cry of a deer attracted a stag by his call. [Yeh-lü] I-la-ko was ordered to shoot; it fell immediately. The emperor was greatly delighted and granted him a hundred taels of gold, a hundred taels of silver, a hundred famous horses, and land in Mo-chên east of the Black Mountain.[25]   78, 1*b*

9. BLACK HARES

952   On the day *chi-mao* [of the eleventh month in the second year of Ying-li] . . . the people of Shuo Prefecture[26] offered black hares.   6, 2*a*

10. SPOTTED DEER

963   On the day *jên-hsü* of the fifth month [in the thirteenth year of Ying-li] a spotted deer offered by the country of Wo-lang-kai gave birth to fawns.   6, 6*a*

11. GRANTS TO OFFICIALS

964   On the day *ping-wu* of the tenth month [in the winter of the fourteenth year of Ying-li] the imperial close attendant, Wu-ku-chê, who offered a whetstone, was granted two hundred and fifty taels of silver.

On the day *ping-ch'ên*, because Yin-ssŭ, who was keeper of the deer, had replaced Wo-li as *cha-sa-yüeh*,[27] he was granted a gold belt, a gold goblet, and two hundred taels of silver.   7, 1*b*

12. PRESENTS TO WINE DEALERS

966   On the day *chia-shên*[28] [of the first month in the sixteenth year of Ying-li] the emperor walked incognito in the market and bestowed silver and lustring upon the wine dealers.   7, 2*b*

---

[22] According to LS 33, 2*b*, the great king of the I-shih tribe was stationed southwest of the Supreme Capital (Boro Khoton, Jehol) and its minister over the masses stayed at Yüan-yang Lake 鴛鴦泊 (near modern Ch'ih-ch'êng 赤城 County, Chahar). The whole tribe therefore probably lived nearby.

[23] Literally, "wooden sword." Actually this was a wooden cudgel, a weapon used to administer punishment to high officials for certain crimes which normally would have been differently treated (LS 61, 2*b*).

[24] The Ch'u-ku-li 鋤骨里 tribe is probably identical with the Ch'u-li 楚里 tribe, which lived north of T'an 潭 Prefecture (modern Kara Khotun on the upper Ta-ling River, Jehol) (MRC II, 66).

[25] In northern Chahar and Jehol.

[26] Modern Shou 朔 County, Shansi.

[27] See XIV, introduction.

[28] The day *chia-shên* fell on the eighteenth day of the first month. Therefore, the passage refers to the end of the Lantern Festival (see VII, 2 (27)).

13. CONTRIBUTIONS TOWARD A MAUSOLEUM

983   [On the day *jên-wu* of the first month in the spring of the first year of T'ung-ho]
Concubine Chao, Princess Hu-ku-tien,[29] Prince Ch'ou-ning of Hsi, Prime Minister
An-ning, Northern Great King P'u-nu-ning, the *t'i-yin* Ch'ü-lieh, Prince Shao[30] of Wu, Prince
Chih-mo[31] of Ning, the Horizontal Tents, the Imperial Maternal Uncles, and the Ch'i-tan and Chinese
camps all contributed to cover the expenditure for the mausoleum [of Ching-tsung].   On the day
kuei-wei the Princess of Ch'i[32] led the titled ladies of the inside and outside of the palace to make
similar offers.   **10, 2a–b**

14. HONORED WIDOWS

983   On the day *kuei-ssŭ* [of the fourth month in the first year of T'ung-ho] an imperial
decree ordered that the titled ladies who were widows be given presents.   **10, 3b**

15. CONTRIBUTIONS BY OFFICIALS

983   On the day *i-wei* [of the tenth month in the first year of T'ung-ho] the vicegerent
of Yen-ching, the *yü-yüeh* [Yeh-lü] Hsiu-ko, suggested that the annual contributions
of the commanding prefects be limited, as in the case of the Ch'i-tan officials, to offers of saddled
horses. This was approved.   **10, 5b**

16. GIFTS OF SILK

984   On the day *ting-hai* [of the twelfth month in the first year of T'ung-ho] the annual
offering of damask and brocade from Hsien Prefecture[33] was distributed among [the
emperor's] personal attendants.   **10, 6a**

17. SILK IN LIEU OF A MONEY TAX

986   On the day *jên-tzŭ* [of the sixth month in the fourth year of T'ung-ho] the vicegerent
of the Southern Capital memorialized that the lustring which the people paid annually
to the Triple Office in lieu of the money tax on salt and iron did not accord with the value.   A decree
ordered it increased.   **11, 5a**

18. FURS

986   On the day *jên-hsü* [of the tenth month in the fourth year of T'ung-ho] ermine,
grey moles, and various [other] goods were granted to the officials of the capitals, to
Buddhist monks and Taoist priests, and to the old people.   **11, 7b**

19. UNLAWFUL TAXATION

986   On the day *jên-shên* [of the eleventh month in the fourth year of T'ung-ho], because
the unlawful taxation exacted at Ku-pei, Sung-t'ing, and Yü Pass[34] seriously interfered with the traveling merchants, an emissary was sent to investigate the case.   **11, 7b**

20. LAND TAX PAID IN GRAIN INSTEAD OF IN MONEY

988   In the sixth year [of T'ung-ho][35] there was frost and drought. The calamity-
stricken people faced starvation.   It was decreed to the Triple Office that, because in
previously converting the money tax into grain the valuation [of the grain] did not conform to the
real value, its price was to be increased in order to benefit the people.   **59, 2b**

---

[29] The first daughter of Shih-tsung.
[30] The third son of Pei 倍.
[31] The second son of Shih-tsung.
[32] The eldest daughter of Ching-tsung (see VII, 1 (12) and note).

[33] Modern Pei-chên 北鎮 County, Liaoning.
[34] These three places were passes located north and northeast of present Peiping.
[35] LS 12, 2b states that this event occurred in the sixth year of T'ung-ho.

21. BESTOWAL OF AN HONORARY GIFT

989   On the day *chia-hsü* [of the sixth month in the seventh year of T'ung-ho] the amanuensis of Hsüan-chêng Hall, Ma Tê-ch'ên,[36] died.   The rank of junior guardian of the heir apparent[37] was posthumously conferred upon him by imperial decree, and a hundred thousand cash and a hundred bushels of grain were bestowed [upon his family].   12, 6*b*

22. MONEY GIVEN TO AN ARMY

993   On the day *ping-wu* [of the third month in the eleventh year of T'ung-ho] money was taken from the imperial treasury and given to the army of the Office of Military Control of the Southern Capital.   13, 3*b*–4*a*

23. DIFFERENT KINDS OF TAXES

994   On the day *mou-wu* [of the first month in the twelfth year of T'ung-ho], I Prefecture[38] was exempted from paying the *fu* and *tiao* taxes.[39]   13, 4*a*

24. SUBSTANTIAL REWARDS

994   [On the day *jên-hsü* of the first month in the twelfth year of T'ung-ho] a native of Pa Prefecture, Li Tsai-yu, who was one hundred and thirty-three years old, was granted a bundle of silk,[40] a variegated silk robe, and a silver girdle.   He was given sheep and wine every month, and his family was exempted from labor service.[41]   13, 4*b*

25. ANNUAL PAYMENT OF SHEEP BY THE TRIBES

994   On the day *chia-wu* [of the second month in the twelfth year of T'ung-ho] the annual tribal payment of sheep and duties levied at the passes were suspended.   13, 4*b*

26. WAS TAXATION EQUITABLE?

994   On the day *i-ssŭ* [of the tenth month in the twelfth year of T'ung-ho] it was decreed that an equitable system of taxation be established.[42]   13, 5*b*

27. MONEY TAX ON AGRICULTURAL IMPLEMENTS

994   Because [the regions of] the Southern Capital and P'ing Prefecture[43] had a poor harvest this year, [Yeh-lü Lung-yün[44]] memorialized for exemption of the people from payment of the money tax on agricultural implements[45] and for stabilization of market prices in all prefectures.   All this was approved.   82, 2*a*

28. TAXES INCREASED

995   On the day *ting-ssŭ* [of the first month in the thirteenth year of T'ung-ho] the taxes of the counties of T'ai Prefecture[46] and Sui City[47] were increased.   13, 6*a*

---

[36] Ma Tê-ch'ên 馬得臣, a native of the Southern Capital, was skilled in the composition of essays and poetry. He occasionally drew up the imperial edicts (LS 80, 2*b*–3*b*).

[37] According to LS 80, 3*b*, the title conferred upon Ma Tê-ch'ên was that of grand guardian of the heir apparent.

[38] I 宜 Prefecture, a territory near modern I 義 County, Liaoning.

[39] See introduction.

[40] According to ILCS 4, 4*b* ff., in ancient China the *shu-po* 束帛 was a gift of five bolts of silk. Each bolt was two *tuan* (twenty feet) long. The five bolts were tied together into a bundle.

[41] See XI, introduction.

[42] Whether the measure of 994 was directed against the unequal taxation of officials and commoners or whether it was only aimed at a more equitable taxation of the commoners is not clear. If it was meant to remove the social stratification of taxation, then it failed completely, for

such stratification continued until after the foundation of the Chin dynasty. In 1132 the Chin emperor decreed, "Formerly the Liao people were divided into gentlemen (士) and commoners (庶) and taxes were levied unequally on them. Hereafter the system should be equalized" (CS 3, 15*b*).

[43] Modern Lu-lung 盧龍 County, Hopei.

[44] His original name was Han Tê-jang.

[45] Probably Liao followed the Five Dynasties in taxing agricultural implements. According to SS 186, 1*b*, the commanding prefects of the T'ang period used to impose taxes upon the people without restriction, and the government under the Five Dynasties also taxed the people very heavily. In 1013, under Emperor Chên-tsung of Sung, the tax on agricultural implements was abolished.

[46] Southwest of modern Nung-an 農安 County, Kirin.

[47] Sui City 遂城 probably refers to Sui Prefecture, southwest of modern K'ang-p'ing 康平 County, Liaoning.

29. HORSES FOR THE ARMY

995   On the day *i-hai* [of the fifth month in the thirteenth year of T'ung-ho] three Administrations—the Northern, Southern, and I-shih—asked permission to requisition rich people's horses in order to supply the needs of the army. This was not approved. Government horses were provided [instead].   13, 6a

30. TAXES REDUCED

997   On the day *chia-yin* of the twelfth month [in the fourteenth year of T'ung-ho], because the newly established system of taxation in Nan-ching Circuit[48] was too burdensome, it was reduced.   13, 7b

31. HSI "TRIBUTE" DISCONTINUED

997   On the first day *i-wei* of the fourth month in the summer [of the fifteenth year of T'ung-ho] the annual tribute of hornless deer paid by the Five Tribes[49] of Hsi was discontinued.   13, 8b

---

[48] HCLY 77, 5b calls the taxation of the Southern Capital extremely heavy; after a calamity no reduction was granted; the taxes collected were several times larger than those levied in Sung China. This statement is evidently exaggerated, for the *Liao Shih* relates a number of cases in which Nan-ching Circuit was given tax exemptions in times of hardship (see X, 1 and XII, *passim*); but although the claim is not altogether correct, it is not wholly without foundation. The Southern Capital was severely taxed; the Liao government employed more tax-collectors in that region than in all the old Ch'i-tan territories together (*cf.* XIV, 2 (6), LS 48, 1a).

Some idea as to the amount of taxes paid by the population of the Southern Capital may be gained from a Chin document which was submitted to the Sung government in 1123. This document is highly significant because it contains concrete information on financial conditions in Nan-ching Circuit and gives considerable insight into certain aspects of Liao taxation not available from any other source known to us. The statement is therefore translated in full despite the difficulties offered by its peculiar, elliptical style.

"According to the results arrived at by the investigation on the different items provided by the prefectures and counties under the jurisdiction of Yen-ching, the *k'o-ch'êng* 課程 money, together with the various taxes from individuals and households [temporarily] suspended or [actually] paid and converted according to their approximate present value and market price [collected] by the departments and bureaus under the control respectively of the capital's Triple Office and Control Office, amounts to a total of 5,492,906 strings and 800 coins. The *k'o-ch'êng* money amounts to 1,208,416 strings and the money [equivalent] of the *shui wu* 稅物 [tax in kind ?] to 4,284,860 strings and 800 coins.

"The Triple Office has a total income of 4,913,120 strings. Therein the house tax and miscellaneous taxes, amounting to 1,158,798 strings, are *k'o-ch'êng* money [collected by] the departments and bureaus. The two Yung Salt Monopoly Departments 榷永兩鹽院 together evaporate 220,000 piculs (石) of salt, which are sold for 390,000 strings of money. The *k'o-ch'êng* money from miscellaneous items, sold by the various departments and bureaus, amounts to 433,212 strings. The regular taxes (正錢), land and others, paid by individuals and families, amount to 3,754,442 strings.

"The Control Office has a total income of 579,687 strings and 800 coins. Of this, 49,248 strings are *k'o-ch'êng* money and 530,438 strings and 800 coins are the money paid as tax by the government people (官民)" (SCPMHP 14, 11a–b).

The historical background of the document was this: In 1121 the Chin and Sung governments agreed that the region of the Liao Southern Capital with six prefectures and twenty-four counties should be handed over to the Sung government. Early in 1123 the Southern Capital was seized by the Chin invaders who demanded that the region's taxes should now go to the Chin government (*op. cit.*, 12, 9a–11b). But the Sung government held that the taxes should follow the land which, as previously agreed, was destined to be given to the Sung government. The Chin and Sung representatives met several times and discussed the matter. The Chin envoy presented two documents: The first stated that the annual income of Yen for two hundred years had amounted to four hundred thousand strings; later the sum increased to over four million strings. The second, which included the *k'o-ch'êng* tax, spoke of a total of approximately six million strings annually (*op. cit.* 13, 7a).

The Sung representative doubted the reasonableness of the increase. He ascribed it to the tenfold rise in the grain price, caused by the adversities of the recent war. The Chin representative, a Jurchen who was not familiar with the conditions, insisted that the Sung government should pay his government one-fifth or one-sixth of the annual income of the region (*op. cit.*, 7b). Finally, the Sung representative agreed to pay annually various goods worth one million strings as compensation for the old Liao Southern Capital in addition to the traditional annual amount (*op. cit.* 15, 11a; *cf.* also TCTFL 1, 5b).

[49] Hsi formerly consisted of five tribes. In 923, when the Hsi were subdued by T'ai-tsu, they were subdivided into six tribes (LS 2, 3b; 33, 4b). Whenever the old designation of "Five Tribes" occurs after that date it seems to refer to the original tribes of Hsi.

997   [On the first day *jên-ch'ên* of the tenth month in the fifteenth year of T'ung-ho] the payment of tribute by the tribes of the king of Hsi was abolished.   13, 9*a*

32. WHO PAYS THE SALARIES?

998   On the day *ting-wei* [of the fourth month in the sixteenth year of T'ung-ho] the payment of salaries of officials by the people was stopped.   They were provided by the imperial treasury.   14, 1*a*

33. NONAGENARIAN WOMEN RECEIVE PRESENTS

998   On the day *i-yu* [of the fifth month in the sixteenth year of T'ung-ho] the emperor returned to the Supreme Capital.   Women over ninety years of age were granted presents.   14, 1*a–b*

34. TAXES LEVIED AT THE PASSES

1002   On the day *chi-wei* [of the intercalary eleventh month in the nineteenth year of T'ung-ho] the duties levied in the markets and at the passes were reduced.   14, 3*a*

35. REMISSION OF TAXES

1002   On the day *kêng-ch'ên* of the twelfth month [in the nineteenth year of T'ung-ho the regions of] the Southern Capital and P'ing Prefecture were exempted from the land tax and other taxes.   14, 3*a*

36. TRADE TAX

1013   The tax on trade in the seven prefectures of Kuei-tê,[50] Lung-hua,[51] I-k'un,[52] Shuang,[53] Liao,[54] T'ung,[55] and Tsu[56] was levied for the first time now by imperial decree.   15, 5*b*

37. MONTHLY SALARIES OF OFFICIALS

1014   On the day *mou-wu* of the second month [in the third year of K'ai-t'ai] an imperial decree ordered that the monthly salaries[57] of the officials from the chancellors down be increased.   15, 7*b*

38. FAMILIES OWNED BY A PRINCE MUST ALSO PAY TAXES

1015   On the day *ping-yin* [of the fourth month in the fourth year of K'ai-t'ai] the Ho-su-kuan tribe[58] requested that a census be made of the households owned by the Nü-chih prince, Shu-chih-ni, which had previously been unregistered, and that their adults be listed for taxes and services.   This was approved.   15, 8*b*

39. REGISTRATION OF HORSES OWNED BY CHINESE

1020   On the day *i-hai* [of the ninth month in the ninth year of K'ai-tai] . . . the horses of Chinese in all circuits were requisitioned for distribution to the eastern expeditionary army.   16, 4*b*–5*a*

---

[50] Southeast of T'ieh-ling 鐵嶺 County, Liaoning.

[51] A region between the Shira Muren and the Lao-ha River, Jehol.

[52] A region between the Shira Muren and modern Boro Khoton, Jehol.

[53] West of modern T'ieh-ling County, Liaoning.

[54] Modern Liao-pin-t'a 遼濱塔 of Hsin-min 新民 County, Liaoning.

[55] A region between T'ieh-ling County and K'ai-yüan 開原 County, Liaoning.

[56] A region southwest of modern Boro Khoton, Jehol.

[57] In 998 Ma Shou-yü 馬守玉 reported that the annual salary for a *yü-yüeh* was only a hundred bushels of grain (SHYK 196, 23*b*).   According to Lu Chên, a Sung envoy sent to Liao, the court officials of Liao were given monthly allowances.   A palace gentleman in the Ministry of Works received ten thousand cash (ten strings), seven bushels of wheat, and seven bushels of millet.   Local officials were given 利潤莊, or Profitable Farmsteads (*cf.* HCLY 77, 10*b*).   Lu does not state whether the local officials received allowances from the government; probably they did not.   The Profitable Farmsteads presumably belonged to the government and were assigned to officials as long as they held office.   Perhaps instead of receiving allowances from the government they were temporarily placed in control of these properties, the profits from which accrued to them.

[58] The Jurchen captives taken by T'ai-tsu were shifted to the modern Liaotung Peninsula in order to separate

40. HIGH OFFICIALS RECEIVE PRESENTS

1022 On the first day *kuei-mao*[59] of the tenth month in the winter [of the second year of T'ai-p'ing] the prime minister, Lü Tê-mou, the associate director of political affairs, Wu Shu-ta, the vice-chancellor, Yang Yu-hsüan, and the right prime minister, Ma Pao-chung, were given money and goods according to their ranks.[60] 16, 7*a–b*

41. FOOD TO THE OLD PEOPLE AT A FESTIVAL

1024 On the day *mou-tzŭ* of the third month [in the fourth year of T'ai-p'ing] on the Thousand Year Festival[61] an imperial decree ordered that food be given to the old people of all the palaces. 16, 8*b*

42. CONTRIBUTIONS FOR AN HEIR APPARENT'S MARRIAGE

1028 On the day *kuei-ssŭ* [of the sixth month in the eighth year of T'ai-p'ing] the acting great king of the Northern Division, Yeh-lü Chêng-liu, memorialized that, in view of the coming marriage of the heir apparent in the eleventh month of this year, the various lineages should prepare tents for the gathering of the relatives. It was decreed that thirty wealthy families should pay the expenses. 17, 5*a*

43. THE WEALTHY EVADE TAXATION

1031 At the time of Hsing-tsung's accession[62] emissaries were sent out to inspect the crops of all circuits. In this year a general census was taken.

An imperial decree said, "From earlier years We learned that in husbandry those who are affluent extend their undertakings in the cultivation of land and are rarely heard of as paying [taxes], while those who have to live off their families are entirely lacking in [opportunities for] sowing and planting and often reach the point where they run off. Therefore a general census[63] should be taken in order to achieve a general equalization."[64] 59, 2*b*–3*a*

44. FOOD PROVISIONS FOR THE ARMY

1031 On the day *i-mao* [of the seventh month in the first year of Ching-fu], in view of the good harvests in recent years, an end was made to providing food supplies for the Office of Military Control of the Eastern Capital. 18, 2*a*

45. EMBEZZLEMENT

1041 On the day *jên-hsü* of the seventh month in the autumn [of the tenth year of Ch'ung-hsi] an imperial decree ordered that the officials who appropriated to themselves articles belonging to the government were to be punished according to [the laws for] actual robbery. 19, 1*b*

---

them from their original tribes. The transplanted people were called Ho-su-kuan by the Ch'i-tan (WHTK 327, 2570). For the term *ho-su-kuan* see I, 2 (10), no. 4.

[59] LS 44, 21*b* and the present passage agree in assigning the cyclical sign *hsin-ch'ou* (no. 38 in the sexagenary cycle) to the first day of the second month in the second year of T'ai-p'ing. Hoang 10, 442 disagrees slightly in giving the cyclical sign no. 37 (*kêng-tzŭ*). All three agree on *ping-yin* (no. 3) for the first day of the first month in the third year of T'ai-p'ing. But for the fifth and tenth months in the second year LS 16, 7*a* has *i-hai* (no. 12) and *kuei-mao* (no. 40) respectively for the first days, while LS 44, 21*b* and Hoang 10, 442 have *chi-ssŭ* (no. 6) and *ting-yu* (no. 34).

[60] Another record indicates concretely the character of the presents to high Liao officials. According to the tomb inscription of Han Ch'un, after his return from a mission to the Uighur country in 1005, he was granted two hundred taels of gold, eighty pieces of plush, and a hundred bolts of silk. In 1028 he was rewarded with a hundred taels of silver vessels and a suit of fine clothing because of his merit in fighting the Po-hai rebellion (MCCSC 2, 4*b* ff.).

[61] The Thousand Year Festival 千齡節 was given in celebration of Shêng-tsung's birthday. The festival was inaugurated under this name by officials in 983 (LS 10, 5*b*).

[62] He ascended the throne in 1031, but his mother actually held the reins of government until 1034.

[63] This is the same census referred to in the first paragraph.

[64] We follow the Palace edition in reading 爲 for the 遂 of our text.

46. RELIEF FOR POOR IMPERIAL CLANSMEN

1042   On this day [*kuei-wei* of the intercalary ninth month in the eleventh year of Ch'ung-hsi[65]] the poor persons of the Three Patriarchal Households were given relief.

19, 3a

47. TRIBAL TAXATION

1043   On the day *hsin-hai* [of the twelfth month in the eleventh year of Ch'ung-hsi] it was decreed that the taxes [imposed] on the tribes in preparation for the campaign against Sung be suspended for one year.   19, 3b

48. HORSES REQUISITIONED

1046   On the day *chi-hai* [of the eleventh month in the fifteenth year of Ch'ung-hsi] there was a general requisition of army horses among the [Po-] hai[66] tribes[67] in accordance with the procedure among the Ch'i-tan households.   19, 8a

49. SALARY OF A HIGH OFFICIAL

1046–1055   Each month [the emperor] granted money, grain, and attendants[68] to [Yang Chi[69]], and during the four seasons sent emissaries to inquire after his health.   89, 4b

50. HORSES REQUISITIONED

1048   On the first day *i-wei* of the eleventh month [in the seventeenth year of Ch'ung-hsi] emissaries were sent out to requisition horses.   20, 2b

51. MONEY AND SILK OFFICE

1053   On the day *kuei-ssŭ* [of the intercalary seventh month in the twenty-second year of Ch'ung-hsi] the Office of Money and Silk[70] was established in Ch'ang-ch'un Prefecture.   20, 7b

52. OFFICERS SENT TO EQUALIZE TAXES

1056   On the day *i-yu* [of the sixth month in the second year of Ch'ing-ning] emissaries were sent to different circuits to equalize taxes, repair the military equipment, encourage agriculture and mulberry-culture, and take precautionary measures against robbers and thieves.[71]   21, 4a

53. FIVE NATIONS TRIBE

1057   On the day *i-wei* [of the first month in the third year of Ch'ing-ning] the chieftains of the Five Nations tribe came to offer local products as tribute.   21, 4b

54. EMBEZZLING OF GOVERNMENT MONEY

1058   On the day *hsin-ssŭ* of the seventh month in the autumn [of the fourth year of Ch'ing-ning] it was prescribed that officials in charge of the imperial treasury[72] who stole two or more strings of money might be denounced by their slaves.   21, 5b

---

[65] This was the same day on which the emperor celebrated with his officials the new advantageous treaty concluded with Sung (XVI, 1042, LS 19, 3a).

[66] The word *po* 渤 is missing in our text. We follow other editions in adding it.

[67] After the kingdom was destroyed by T'ai-tsu in 926 several tribes were set up in the old territory of Po-hai (see I, 2 (9), no. 10).

[68] 傔隸 is probably equivalent to 傔從 which means "followers" or "attendants" (LS 89, 3a). According to CS 42, 13b, there were several special categories of these followers. The number possessed by an official depended upon his position and rank.

[69] Yang Chi 楊佶 (T. 正叔), a native of the Southern Capital, had the highest standing in the *chin-shih* examinations of 1006. He obtained the position of president of the Ministry of Civil Appointments and was concurrently associate administrator of affairs for the Political and Court Councils (LS 89, 3b–4b).

[70] According to his tomb inscription, Wang Lin 王隣 was appointed chief supervisor of the Office of Money and Silk of Yü 蔚 Prefecture in 1000, and in 1003 chief supervisor of the Department of the Commercial Tax at the Supreme Capital (MCCSC 1, 36a).

[71] We follow other editions in reading 賊 for the 賦 of our text.

[72] Under the Chin dynasty this treasury had four subdivisions: the treasury for jewels and valuables, the treasury for silk and brocade, the treasury for gold and silver, and the treasury for miscellaneous objects (CS 56, 5b).

55. PUBLIC FUNDS USED TO FEAST THE OFFICERS

1064   [On the day *kêng-ch'ên* of the eleventh month in the tenth year of Ch'ing-ning] orders were given to the Triple Office of the Southern Capital to feast the military officers every year in the spring and autumn with government money.   22, 3a

56. GRANT MADE TO A MILITARY UNIT

1067   On the day *ting-hai* of the intercalary [third] month [in the third year of Hsien-yung] the cantonment of the imperial bodyguard caught fire.   They were given money, grain, and horses according to their rank.   22, 4b

57. PRINCESSES TRY TO "BORROW" MONEY

1074–1121   [Ta Kung-ting[73]] was transferred to the post of chief intendant of money and silk at Ch'ang-ch'un Prefecture.[74]   When the emperor went to the Ch'un River, the princesses, as was their wont, came to borrow money [from this office.   Ta] Kung-ting remarked, "How can government expenditures be suspended out of personal considerations?"   He refused them. Hearing many spiteful remarks, he said, "This is my duty.   I dare not neglect it."   105, 1b–2a

58. TRIBUTE OF GOLD AND SILVER

1077   On the day *i-mao* [of the first month in the third year of Ta-k'ang] the spring tribute of gold and silk paid by all circuits was suspended and the annual offering of silver to the imperial workshop[75] was stopped.   23, 5a

59. FIVE NATIONS

1085   On the day *kêng-hsü* [of the first month in the first year of Ta-an] the chieftains of the Five Nations came to offer fine steeds as tribute.   24, 6a

60. SILK DONATED TO AN ORDO

1087   On the day *ting-ssŭ* [of the seventh month in the third year of Ta-an] odds and ends of silk were granted to the poor people of Hsing-shêng Palace.[76]   25, 1b

61. CONTRIBUTIONS OF CURIOS STOPPED

1087   On the day *jên-ch'ên* [of the tenth month in the third year of Ta-an] the offering of precious curios by the officials from the commanding prefects down was discontinued.   25, 1b

62. THE REGULAR TRIBUTE

1088   On the day *i-yu* [of the fourth month in the fourth year of Ta-an] the regular offering of imperial equipment for horses and chariots made by all routes was reduced.   25, 2a

63. HORSES REQUISITIONED

1094   On the day *chia-yin* of the fifth month [in the tenth year of Ta-an] horses were requisitioned.   25, 6b

64. OFFERINGS OF FRESH THINGS STOPPED

1097   On the day *chia-shên* of the sixth month [in the third year of Shou-lung] an imperial decree ordered all routes to discontinue offering fresh things by mounted couriers.[77]
                                                                                    26, 3a

---

[73] Ta Kung-ting, a Po-hai, was an able administrator of financial affairs.   For his attitude toward the embankment system of Liao-tung see XI (22).

[74] Northwest of Po-tu-na 伯都訥, Kirin.   Ch'ang-ch'un Prefecture was near the Ch'un 春 River (modern T'ao-êrh 洮兒 River, Heilungkiang) which the emperor, with his officials and family, visited annually on a hunting trip.

[75] According to CS 56, 11a, the imperial workshop made gold and silver objects, tents, carts, beds, curtains, mats, saddles, reins, umbrellas, fans, etc.   The director was an official of the sixth rank.

[76] Shêng-tsung's ordo (XV, 1 (12)).

[77] Probably because it was very burdensome and the population began to show signs of restlessness (see XIII, introduction).

65. SALARY OF A PRIME MINISTER

1101–1110   Because Wang Hua, a servant in Buddha's Hall, falsely accused [Hsiao] Wu-na[78] of borrowing rhinoceros horn from the imperial treasury, an imperial decree ordered that he be examined. [Hsiao] Wu-na memorialized, "When I served in the court of the deceased emperor,[79] it was decreed that I might take daily a hundred thousand cash[80] from the treasury for my private use. I never misappropriated a single cash. Would I have been willing to borrow rhinoceros horn?"   98, 1b–2a

66. FEATURES OF THE FINANCIAL ADMINISTRATION

[Ma Jên-wang] was transferred to the post of financial commissioner of the Central Capital. When he first arrived the treasury and granaries were completely empty. After he had looked after things for half a year, one hundred and fifty thousand bushels of grain and two hundred thousand strings of cash were accumulated. . . . Before long he was appointed associate director of political affairs[81] and concurrently commissioner of the Triple Office in the Southern Capital.

1114   At this time the abuses in paying and receiving cash and grain were particularly bad in Yen.[82] [Ma] Jên-wang made a calendric schedule [written on] heavy silk and had the disbursements and receipts of the treasuries separately listed. This was called *lin k'u*.[83] None of the corrupt persons and scheming officials were able to interfere in the matter, so they spread stories about his senility everywhere.[84] Court opinion had no understanding of the matter. He was transferred to the position of master of court etiquette in the Southern Division in order to show respect for his old age.   105, 4a–b

67. EMERGENCY LEVY OF HORSES

1120   On the day *chi-yu* of the third month [in the tenth year of T'ien-ch'ing] the people who had herds of horses were required to give one out of ten to supply the armies of the Eastern Route.[85]   28, 7b

2. TRIBUTE

1. Liang   2. Wu-niang-kai   3. Uighurs   4. Silla, Korea, and Wu Yüeh   5. Ta-tan   6. Many missions "pay tribite"   7. Koreans and Uighurs   8. Wu Yüeh   9. Liang and Wu Yüeh   10. Persia   11. Ta-shih   12. T'ang, Japan, Korea, and Silla   13. A white wolf offered   14. T'ang   15. Wu Yüeh   16. T'ang   17. Tsu-pu   18. Tang-hsiang   19. Chin   20. China Proper   21. Shih-wei and T'ieh-li   22. Weapons as Tributes   23. T'u-yü-hun, Jurchen, and Nan T'ang   24. Black-cart Shih-wei   25. Chin   26. Nan T'ang   27. Chin   28. Jurchen and Wu Yüeh   29. Chin   30. Chin   31. Wu Yüeh   32. Chin   33. Wu Yüeh   34. Chin   35. Uighurs and others   36. Han   37. Nan T'ang   38. T'ieh-li   39. Grape wine and pheasants   40. Han   41. Nan T'ang   42. Chou and Nan T'ang   43. Jurchen   44. Silver bestowed   45. Han   46. Han supported by grain   47. Han   48. The Wu-wei Yü-chüeh tribe   49. Khotan and others   50. Extraordinary presents   51. Korea   52. Korea and T'ieh-li   53. Hsia   54. T'ieh-li   55. Tributes too heavy   56. Korea   57. Hsia   58. Jurchen   59. Korea   60. Barbarian tribes   61. Sung   62. Repercussions of the new treaty with Sung   63. Sung   64. Uighurs   65. Korea   66. Jurchen   67. Hsia   68. Uighurs   69. Northeastern tribes   70. Tsu-pu   71. Ta-shih   72. Ti-lieh   73. Hsia   74. Sung   75. Hsia   76. Tribal tribute must be paid on time   77. Sung sends special gifts   78. A high tribal visitor   79. P'u-lu-mao-to   80. Tsu-pu and others

---

[78] Hsiao Wu-na 兀納 was promoted to the position of prime minister of the Northern Administration in 1095, but he was degraded to the rank of commanding prefect when T'ien-tsu ascended the throne, since he had offended the latter before he became emperor (LS 98, 1a–2b).

[79] Tao-tsung.

[80] This figure was doubtless an exaggeration. Had this been his regular allowance, it would have amounted to three thousand strings per month or thirty-six thousand strings per year. In the Sung and Chin 金 systems the allowance of the highest official was only three hundred strings per month (SS 118, 1a ff.; CS 58, 4b).

[81] Ma Jên-wang was appointed to this post in 1114 (LS 27, 7b).

[82] An ancient name for the Southern Capital.

[83] The term simply means that receipts and expenditures were recorded after checking.

[84] Literally, "in the circuits and routes."

[85] At this time the Liao soldiers had been defeated on several occasions by the Jurchen; new soldiers were raised according to the economic capacity of the people. Three hundred thousand cash were collected from the rich to supply a detachment. A very rich family might support one or two hundred soldiers. If the sons of rich families offered three million cash, they were given a special *chin-shih* rank (CTKC 10, 4b; 11, 1b).

81. Tsu-pu 82. Tribes offer horses 83. Hsia 84. Gray falcons 85. Uighurs 86. All tribes offer horses and camels 87. Portraits exchanged 88. Hsia 89. Sung 90. Tsu-pu 91. Wu-tu-wan 92. Jurchen 93. Tsu-pu 94. Jurchen 95. The Mongols 96. Jurchen 97. Po-hai 98. Uighurs 99. Japan 100. Sheep bestowed upon Korea 101. Funeral presents offered to Korea 102. Jurchen 103. P'o-li 104. Sung 105. Wo-lang-kai 106. Sung

1. LIANG

906   In the second month of the next year [the third year of the reign period T'ien-yu of Emperor Ai of T'ang[1]] . . . Chu Ch'üan-chung[2] of Pien Prefecture[3] sent envoys by sea with credentials, silks, clothing, belts, and precious curios to pay a courtesy call.[4]   1, 2a–b

2. WU–NIANG–KAI

909   [On the day chi[5]-ssŭ of the tenth month in the winter of the third year of T'ai-tsu's accession] the Wu-niang-kai tribe[6] of the northwest offered cart-pullers.   1, 3b

3. UIGHURS

913   On the day mou-yin [of the tenth month in the seventh year of T'ai-tsu's accession] the Uighurs of Ho Prefecture[7] came to pay tribute.   1, 7a

4. SILLA, KOREA, AND WU YÜEH

915   [On the day mou-shên of the tenth month in the ninth year of T'ai-tsu's accession] Silla sent envoys to offer local products as tribute. Korea sent envoys to present a precious sword. The king of Wu Yüeh,[8] Ch'ien-liu, sent T'êng Yen-hsiu to pay tribute.   1, 8b

916   On the day kêng-yin of the sixth month [in the first year of Shên-ts'ê] the king of Wu Yüeh sent T'êng Yen-hsiu to pay tribute.   1, 9a

916–922
924
927   Beginning with the reign period Shên-ts'ê of Emperor T'ai-tsu, Korea sent envoys to present a precious sword; in the third year of T'ien-tsan [the country] offered tribute; and in the second year of T'ien-hsien of T'ai-tsung it offered tribute.[9]   115, 1a

---

[1] The last emperor of the T'ang dynasty. He ruled from 904 to 907.

[2] The founder of the first of the Five Dynasties, Liang 梁 (907–922). He ruled from 907 to 912.

[3] Modern K'ai-fêng, Honan.

[4] In the Liao Shih the term lai p'in 來聘 is generally used for the visits of emissaries from independent states, while the term lai kung 來貢 is applied to the visits of emissaries from dependent countries. Kung refers to the tribute paid by subordinates. P'in, on the other hand, is really a courtesy call, usually between equals and always accompanied by offerings of presents which sometimes are of considerable value. Such presents generally call for return gifts of more or less equal value.

The Liao Shih uses p'in for visits from Liang and T'ang; it applies kung to Korea, Hsi Hsia, Chin 晉 and many tribes. P'in is also used for the Ta-tan 達旦 (Tatars) and Mêng-ku 萌古 (Mongols) by the Yüan historians out of respect for the ancestors of the Yüan dynasty.

[5] We follow other editions in reading 巳 for the 紀 of our text.

[6] See section IV (1) and note.

[7] Equivalent to modern Ko-la-ho-cho 哈剌和卓, southeast of Turfan, Sinkiang. See I, 2 (10), no. 19.

[8] See I, 1, note 12.

[9] In 922 A-pao-chi sent envoys with camels, horses, and felt to Korea (KRS 1, 16). In 942 T'ai-tsung sent Korea thirty men and fifty camels, but the founder of Korea, who resented the annexation of Po-hai, banished these men to an island in the sea and tied the camels to a bridge so that they starved (KRS 2, 26). From 1043 on Liao gave Korea either carriages or leather-decorated chariots whenever a new king was invested (KRS 72, 477–478). In 1088 Korea was given two thousand sheep, twenty-three carts, and three horses (KRS 10, 148).

CTKC 21, 3a–b lists return presents given by the Liao government to Korea: two girdles decorated with rhinoceros horn and jade, two sets of fine garments, two horses with saddles and reins decorated with gold, five horses with plain saddles and reins, fifteen horses, two sets of bows, arrows, and other weapons, two hundred bolts of various kinds of silk, one thousand bolts of lustring, two hundred sheep, wine, and fruit.

The Liao government also presented the following gifts: to the Korean envoys, two belts decorated with silver and gold, two suits, thirty bolts of fine silk, one hundred bolts of colored lustring, two horses with saddles and reins, five horses, a set of bow and arrows and other weapons, wine and fruit; to each of the distinguished aides of the envoys, a white silver belt, a suit, twenty bolts of lustring, a horse; and to each of the lower officials, a suit, ten bolts of lustring, a long robe of purple damask (CTKC 21, 3b).

The enumeration of Korean tributes, given in the Liao Shih, is supplemented by data contained in the Korean

5. TA–TAN

918   In the second month [of the third year of Shên-ts'ê] the country of the Ta-tan came to pay a courtesy call.   1, 10*a*

6. MANY MISSIONS "PAY TRIBUTE"

918   [On the day *kuei-hai* of the second month in the third year of Shên-ts'ê], Liang sent envoys to pay a courtesy call.   Chin,[10] Wu Yüeh, Po-hai, Korea, the Uighurs, Tsu-pu, and Tang-hsiang,[11] and the prefectures of Yu, Chên, Ting, Wei, and Lu all sent envoys to pay tribute.   1, 10*a–b*

7. KOREANS AND UIGHURS

918   [In the third month of the third year of Shên-ts'ê], Korea and the northwestern barbarians all sent envoys to offer tribute.   The Uighurs offered coral trees.   70, 1*b*

8. WU YÜEH

920   On the day *ping-yin* of the fifth month in the summer [of the fifth year of Shên-ts'ê], T'êng Yen-hsiu, who had been sent again by the king of Wu Yüeh to offer a tribute of rhinoceros horn and coral, was granted an official title and sent back.   2, 1*b*

9. LIANG AND WU YÜEH

923   On the day *chi-yu* of the fourth month in the summer [of the second year of T'ien-tsan], Liang sent envoys to pay a courtesy call.   The king of Wu Yüeh sent envoys to pay tribute.   2, 3*b*

10. PERSIA

923   On the day *hsin-ch'ou* of the sixth month [in the second year of T'ien-tsan] the country of Persia came to offer tribute.   2, 3*b*

11. TA–SHIH

924   On the day *kuei-hai* [of the ninth month in the third year of T'ien-tsan] the country of Ta-shih came to offer tribute.   2, 4*b*

12. T'ANG, JAPAN, KOREA, AND SILLA

925   On the day *ting-mao* of the tenth month in the winter [of the fourth year of T'ien-tsan], T'ang[12] came to report the overthrow of Liang.   Immediately envoys were sent to return the courtesy call.   On the day *kêng-ch'ên* the country of Japan[13] came to offer tribute. On the day *hsin-ssŭ* the country of Korea came to offer tribute. . . . On the day *chi-yu* [of the eleventh month] the country of Silla came to offer tribute.   2, 5*b*

History and contemporary Chinese sources.   For instance, in 1038 Korea offered Liao drugs in gold and silver vases, hats, gauze, cloth, tea, paper, ink, and *lung-hsü* 龍鬚 mats (KRS 6, 85).   Some of the objects presented to Liao originally came from Sung China as Su Shih claims (TPCL 3, 21*b*).   In 1093 a Sung envoy, Fêng Chi 豐稷, noticed in a magnificent Liao Buddhist temple a number of sacrificial utensils, all of which had formerly been given to Korea by the Sung emperor, Shên-tsung (1068–1085) (SKTP 2, 7*b*).

In addition to the official tribute, the Korean envoys also made personal presents to Liao functionaries in charge of their reception.   This custom began toward the end of the Liao dynasty when Mun Kong-in 文公仁 gave white brass objects, books, paintings, fans, vases, and curios. Thereafter, the Liao officials took this as a precedent and demanded that similar gifts be presented to them regularly (KRS 125, 557).

[10] Chin 晉 refers to the region in what is now Shansi, which was under the control of Li Ts'un-hsü 李存勖, the founder of Later T'ang.

[11] Further information on these groups may be found by consulting the index.   Note especially the material in section I, 2.

[12] The Later T'ang 後唐 (923–936), the second of the Five Dynasties.

[13] The contacts between the Japanese and the Ch'i-tan seem originally to have taken place via the old territory of Po-hai with which Japan had such close relations that diplomatic missions had frequently been exchanged. PHKC 3, 27*b* states that in 929, four years after the conquest of Po-hai by the Ch'i-tan, the kingdom of Tung-tan, which had been created from Po-hai territory by the Ch'i-tan, sent P'ei Ch'iu 裴璆 and ninety-two other messengers to Japan to make a courtesy call.

13. A WHITE WOLF OFFERED

928   On the day *chi-hai* [of the second month in the third year of T'ien-hsien] the *t'i-yin*, Nieh-li-kun, offered a white wolf.   3, 2a

14. T'ANG

928   [On the day *chi-yu* of the tenth month in the third year of T'ien-hsien], T'ang sent envoys to present a jade flute.   3, 3a

15. WU YÜEH

932   On the day *jên-shên* of the second month [in the seventh year of T'ien-hsien] the *i-la*,[14] Ti-tê, who had been sent as an envoy to Wu Yüeh, came back.   With him came an envoy who had been sent by the king of Wu Yüeh to offer precious objects.   An envoy was again sent there with return presents.   3, 5b

16. T'ANG

932   On the day *jên-ch'ên* [of the seventh month in the seventh year of T'ien-hsien], T'ang sent emissaries to present a musical instrument[15] made from red ivory.   3, 6a

17. TSU–PU

932   On the day *ting-wei* [of the eleventh month in the seventh year of T'ien-hsien] the Tsu-pu offered as tribute thirty gray falcons from east of the sea.   3, 6a–b

18. TANG–HSIANG

934   On the day *ping-shên* [of the first month in the ninth year of T'ien-hsien] the Tang-hsiang offered camels and deer as tribute.   3, 7a

19. CHIN

937   On the day *chia-shên* of the sixth month [in the twelfth year of T'ien-hsien], Chin sent the president of the Ministry of Revenue, Nieh Yen-tsu, and others to ask that they be permitted to offer an honorific title to the emperor and get back the area north of Yen-mên and the region of Yu and Chi, in return for which Chin would pay an annual tribute of three hundred thousand bolts of silk.   This was rejected by an imperial decree.[16]   3, 11b

20. CHINA PROPER

937   On the day *kêng-yin* [of the eighth month in the twelfth year of T'ien-hsien], Chin, and Liu Chih-yüan[17] of T'ai-yüan, and Li Pien[18] of Nan T'ang each sent envoys to pay tribute.   3, 12a

---

[14] According to LS 46, 12a, a foot soldier was called *i-la* 拽剌 in the Ch'i-tan language.   Ti-tê was most likely an officer in charge of a detachment of these soldiers.

[15] The *shêng* 笙 is a small musical instrument consisting of a number of pipes of different lengths.   It has a spout through which the player sucks the air while fingering the keyholes.

[16] This ambiguous passage has two possible interpretations.   It may mean that Chin offered to present an honorific title, territory, and silk to Liao; or it may mean that Chin offered an honorific title and silk to Liao in return for the Chin territory temporarily occupied by Liao at the beginning of 937 when the Ch'i-tan gave military aid to Chin against Later T'ang.

The second interpretation seems the more plausible. In the first place, the word 歸, which is applied to the territories, means "to return."   In the second place, the regions were first offered to Liao in the beginning of 937 when they were already occupied by the Ch'i-tan troops (TCTC 280, 6b).   But the date of our passage is the middle of 937.   Perhaps Chin, after an initial offer at the beginning of 937, repented of its generosity and asked that the territories be returned.   This would explain the Liao refusal of the offer.   The territories were formally presented to Liao at the end of 938 (LS 4, 2b).

[17] He became emperor of Later Han in 947, ruling until 948.

[18] He made himself emperor of Nan T'ang in 937 and reigned until 943.   In 938 he received the investiture title Ying-wu Ming-i Huang-ti 英武明義皇帝 from Liao (MSNTS 1, 5a).   In 937 the Liao government sent envoys with gifts of sheep and horses to Nan T'ang.   It also exchanged thirty thousand sheep and two hundred horses for silk, tea, and medicine (LSNTS 15, 3a).

21. SHIH–WEI AND T'IEH–LI

938   On the day *jên-wu* [of the second month in the first year of Hui-t'ung] the Shih-wei offered white single-horned deer.

On the day *mou-tzŭ* the T'ieh-li came to offer tribute.   4, 1a

22. WEAPONS AS TRIBUTES

938   [In the fourth month of the first year of Hui-t'ung] the country of the Nü-chih sent envoys to present bows and arrows.[19]   70, 4b

23. T'U–YÜ–HUN, JURCHEN, AND NAN T'ANG

938   On the first day *ping-tzŭ* of the sixth month [in the first year of Hui-t'ung] the T'u-yü-hun and the Nü-chih came to pay tribute.   On the day *hsin-mao* Nan T'ang came to pay tribute.   4, 1b

24. BLACK–CART SHIH–WEI

938   On the day *kêng-hsü* of the ninth month [in the first year of Hui-t'ung] the Black-cart Shih-wei offered famous steeds as tribute.   4, 1b

25. CHIN

938   On the day *jên-yin* [of the tenth month in the first year of Hui-t'ung], Chin sent envoys to express gratitude for the investiture ceremony.[20]   On the same day other envoys came to offer dromedaries and famous steeds.   4, 2a

939   On the day *mou-shên* [of the first month in the second year of Hui-t'ung], Chin sent the grand general of the gendarmery,[21] Ma Ts'ung-pin, and the palace gentleman in charge of scrutiny,[22] Liu Chih-hsin, to offer precious gifts.   These were ordered to be distributed among the officials.

On the day *ping-ch'ên* Chin sent envoys to express gratitude for suspending the money and silk payments of four prefectures along the frontier.   4, 3a

On the day *mou-shên* of the seventh month in the autumn Chin sent envoys to offer a belt [decorated with] rhinoceros [horn].   4, 3b

On the day *i-ch'ou* of the eighth month Chin sent envoys to offer the annual tribute[23] and to report in a memorial that the gold and silk for the two years *hsü* and *hai*[24] had been delivered in Yen-ching.[25]

4, 3b

940   On the day *ping-ch'ên* of the fourth month [in the third year of Hui-t'ung], Chin sent envoys to offer tea and drugs.   4, 4b

26. NAN T'ANG

940   On the day *i-ch'ou* [of the fourth month in the third year of Hui-t'ung], Nan T'ang offered a white tortoise.   4, 4b

---

[19] The Chinese text does not indicate the number of weapons offered. On certain occasions the gift was purely symbolic; then probably one bow with a few arrows was presented (see XVI, 1004, LS 14, 5b). It is possible that the tribute recorded in our passage had the same meaning. According to the official *History of Korea*, however, in 1030 certain Jurchen tribes offered to Korea not less than 117,600 *hu* 楛 arrows, and through another delegation, 58,600 arrows made from the same hard straight wood of the *hu* tree (KRS 5, 72). In view of this fact, it seems possible that, under the unspecified conditions of 938, arrows were offered, not symbolically, but because of their real military value. If that was the case, they probably were accompanied by a number of bows.

[20] The investiture of the Chin 晉 emperor took place under the auspices of the Ch'i-tan (LS 4, 1b).

[21] This official was in charge of protecting the palace and court and of patroling the roads and rivers (TS 49A, 3b).

[22] This official had to investigate the merits and demerits of the central and the regional government officials (TS 46, 7a).

[23] According to CTKC 2, 7b and WHTK 345, 2703, Chin annually paid a total of three hundred thousand taels of gold, silk, and other precious things. In addition, presents had to be made on special occasions, such as festivals and birthdays.

[24] The years 938 and 939.

[25] Present Peiping.

27. CHIN

940   On the day *kêng-ch'ên* [of the fifth month in the third year of Hui-t'ung], Chin sent envoys to offer bows and arrows.   4, 5*a*

940   On the day *ping-hsü* [of the ninth month in the third year of Hui-t'ung], Chin sent envoys to offer famous steeds as tribute.   4, 5*b*

28. JURCHEN AND WU YÜEH

940   On the day *mou-tzǔ* [of the ninth month in the third year of Hui-t'ung] the Nü-chih and the king of Wu Yüeh sent envoys to pay tribute.   4, 5*b*–6*a*

29. CHIN

940   On the day *kêng-shên* [of the tenth month in the third year of Hui-t'ung], Chin sent envoys to present plain cloth as tribute and to request that [its ruler] be permitted to offer sacrifice personally to the Southern Sacred Mountain.   This was approved.   4, 6*a*

30. CHIN

941   On the day *chia-ch'ên* [of the second month in the fourth year of Hui-t'ung], Chin sent envoys to offer perfumes and drugs.   4, 6*b*

On the day *kuei-yu* [of the third month], because they had been allowed to offer sacrifice at the southern altar,[26] Chin sent envoys to express thanks and to offer ten *i*[27] of gold.   4, 6*b*

On the day *chi-mao* of the fourth month in the summer Chin sent envoys to offer cherries.   4, 6*b*

On the day *jên-shên* [of the seventh month in the autumn] Chin sent envoys to present a crystal inkstone.   4, 7*a*

On the day *kêng-tzǔ* [of the eighth month] Chin sent envoys to offer a bow [decorated with] rhinoceros [horn] and bamboo arrows.   4, 7*a*

31. WU YÜEH

941   On the day *kuei-mao* [of the tenth month in the fourth year of Hui-t'ung] the king of Wu Yüeh sent envoys to pay tribute.   4, 7*a*

32. CHIN[28]

942   On the day *ping-tzǔ* [of the fourth month in the fifth year of Hui-t'ung], Chin sent envoys to offer saddled horses for [the ceremony of] Shooting at Willows.   4, 8*a*

---

[26] This sacrifice was a customary ceremony undertaken only by the emperor himself for the worship of Heaven. Since at this time Chin was a dependency of the Liao empire, its ruler could not perform the ceremony without the latter's permission.

[27] One *i* 鎰 equals twenty-four taels (*liang* 兩).

[28] Among the documents discovered in Tun-huang by Sir Aurel Stein there are thirteen letters and proclamations written in the tenth century (Giles 40, 317). The editor and translator of "Dated Chinese Manuscripts in the Stein Collection" presents a photostatic copy of one of these items which he classes as a "Letter from the Emperor Ch'u Ti [出帝 of Later Chin] to the Khitan Emperor in A.D. 942" (*op. cit.*, pl. 1; see fig. 33).   According to Dr. Giles, in this letter Ch'u Ti announces "his predecessor's decease" (*op. cit.*, 339).

Reinvestigation of the document leads to a somewhat different conclusion.   The "letter" is written in an informal style, suggesting an exercise in writing rather than an official draft.   The first column introduces it as the Chin emperor's will (遺書).   The sovereign in question is obviously the first ruler of Later Chin, Kao-tsu, who died in the sixth month of 942.   Being seriously ill, he prepared a mission to the Liao emperor concerning the succession of his eldest son, Prince of Ch'i, the later Ch'u-ti.

In its preserved form, the will cannot have been sent to the "northern court" for it contains phrases (致 and 足下) which place the Chin ruler on an equal footing with the Liao emperor, while actually Chin Kao-tsu accepted Liao T'ai-tsung as his father and superior (CWTS 75, 9*a*; LS 3, 10*b*).   The open conflict which led to the down-

33. WU YÜEH

943   On the first day *chi-mao* of the third month [in the sixth year of Hui-t'ung] the king of Wu Yüeh sent envoys to pay tribute.   4, 9a

34. CHIN

943   On the day *hsin-yu* [of the sixth month in the sixth year of Hui-t'ung], Mo Prefecture[29] offered white magpies.   Chin sent envoys to offer gold.
On the first day *ting-wei* of the eighth month in the autumn Chin again offered gold as tribute.
                                                                              4, 9a–b

35. UIGHURS AND OTHERS

945   [In the sixth month of the eighth year of Hui-t'ung] the Uighurs and T'u-yü-hun brought tribute.   The countries of Jên-mo-li and Yao-li offered local products as tribute.   70, 5b

36. HAN

952   On the day *chia-ch'ên* of the twelfth month [in the first year of Ying-li], Han[30] sent envoys to offer bows, arrows, and saddled horses.   6, 1a

---

fall of the Later Chin dynasty was caused by Ch'u-ti's refusal to be addressed as "subordinate" (臣), though he was willing to be called Liao T'ai-tsung's "grandson" (CWTS 88, 1b–2a; WTS 29, 4b–5a).

[29] Modern Jên-ch'iu 任邱 County, Hopei.
[30] See II, 2, note 13.

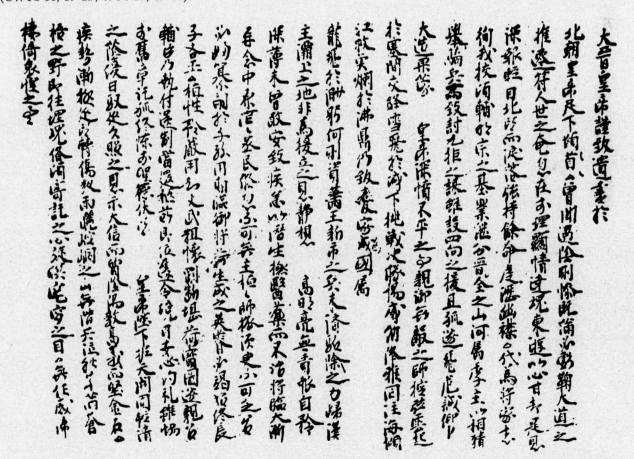

FIG. 33.   Draft of a letter to the Liao emperor T'ai-tsung containing the will of the first emperor of the Later Chin dynasty, found at Tun-huang.   Reproduced by permission of Luzac and Co. from an article by Lionel Giles in the *Bulletin of the School of Oriental Studies*, vol. 10, part 2, facing p. 339.

37. NAN T'ANG

952   On the first day *mou-wu* of the first month in the spring of the second year [of Ying-li], Nan T'ang sent envoys to present a document incased in wax[31] and to offer ten thousand sets of rhinoceros [hide] armor.[32]   6, 1*b*

38. T'IEH–LI

952   On the day *chi-hai* [of the fourth month in the second year of Ying-li] the T'ieh-li offered eagles and falcons.   6, 1*b*

39. GRAPE WINE AND PHEASANTS

952   On the first day *chia-shên* of the tenth month in the winter [of the second year of Ying-li], Han sent envoys to offer grape wine.

On the day *chia-wu* the minister over the masses, Lao-ku, and others offered white pheasants.
6, 2*a*

40. HAN

953   On the day *ting-yu* [of the third month in the third year of Ying-li], Han sent envoys to offer clothes and horses for polo.   6, 2*b*

On the day *kêng-tzŭ* of the ninth month [in the third year of Ying-li], Han sent envoys to offer medicine as tribute.   6, 2*b*

954   On the day *ping-ch'ên* [of the second month in the fourth year of Ying-li], Han sent envoys to offer tea and medicine.   6, 3*a*

41. NAN T'ANG

955   On the day *kêng-yin* [of the tenth month in the fifth year of Ying-li], Nan T'ang sent envoys to pay tribute.   6, 3*b*

42. CHOU AND NAN T'ANG

957   On the day *ping-ch'ên* of the sixth month [in the seventh year of Ying-li], Chou sent envoys to pay a courtesy call.   Nan T'ang sent envoys to pay tribute.[33]   6, 4*a*

43. JURCHEN

962   [In the eighth month in the twelfth year of Ying-li] the country of the Nü-chih offered as tribute a boy with hair on his nose.   70, 6*a*

44. SILVER BESTOWED

965   On the day *hsin-hai* of the sixth month [in the fifteenth year of Ying-li], Yü-lu-ku offered fine horses and was granted two thousand taels of silver.   An imperial close attendant, Hu-la, who was the first to report that the horses were coming, was granted a thousand taels of silver.   7, 2*b*

45. HAN

966   On the day *ting-yu* of the eighth month [in the sixteenth year of Ying-li], Han sent envoys to offer gold objects and armor.   7, 3*a*

969   On the day *chia-tzŭ* [of the third month in the nineteenth year of Ying-li], Han sent envoys to offer a white single-horned deer.   7, 5*a–b*

---

[31] Documents were wrapped in balls of wax in order to protect them against water as well as against theft.

[32] We follow the Palace edition in reading 甲 for the 申 of our text.

[33] According to MSNTS 3, 7*a*, the Liao emperor Mu-tsung sent his maternal uncle to Nan T'ang in 954.   The Liao envoy was assassinated in his lodge; thereafter his country refused to send another envoy to Nan T'ang (*cf.* also LSNTS 15, 5*b*).

46. HAN SUPPORTED BY GRAIN

977 On the day *mou-ch'ên* [of the third month in the ninth year of Pao-ning] an imperial decree ordered the aiding of Han by a grant of two hundred thousand bushels of grain.[34] 9, 1*a*

47. HAN

977 In the eighth month [of the ninth year of Pao-ning], Han sent envoys to offer grape wine. 9, 1*b*

48. THE WU-WEI YÜ-CHÜEH TRIBE

988 On the day *chia-yin* [of the intercalary fifth month in the sixth year of T'ung-ho] the Wu-wei Yü-chüeh tribe,[35] because the sable and gray mole furs which they annually offered as tribute were not produced locally but were all purchased from other places for presentation, requested that the tribute be changed. An imperial decree ordered that from then on they should offer only oxen and horses. 12, 2*a*

49. KHOTAN AND OTHERS

989 On the day *chia-yin* [of the second month in the seventh year of T'ung-ho] the countries Uighur, Khotan, and Shih-tzŭ came to offer tribute. 12, 5*a*

50. EXTRAORDINARY PRESENTS

991 On the day *mou-yin* [of the eighth month in the ninth year of T'ung-ho] the Nü-chih offered deer-callers.[36]

On the day *jên-wu* a crow with three feet was presented by the Eastern Capital. 13, 3*a*

51. KOREA[37]

995 In the twelfth month [of the twelfth year of T'ung-ho], Wang Ch'i[38] presented singing girls. An imperial decree declined them. 115, 1*b*

In the thirteenth year [of T'ung-ho, Wang] Ch'i sent Ngi Chu-chöng to bring tribute and to present eagles. 115, 1*b*

---

[34] The date of this event is given as the seventh year of Pao-ning (975/6) in LS 59, 2*a*, which is almost certainly incorrect. According to SS 3, 11*b*, Sung invaded Han in the eighth month of the ninth year of the reign period K'ai-pao 開寶 (976). LS 8, 5*b* records that Sung again attacked Han and looted the country's food supplies, whereupon Han sent emissaries to her military ally, Liao, to ask for a grain subsidy. The same passage dates this attack very precisely as the day *ting-wei* of the twelfth month in the eighth year of Pao-ning. In Western chronology this day would fall into the year 977. The date of the subsidy must have been in 977, as our text states, and not before, as is asserted in LS 59, 2*a* (see II, 2 (7)).

[35] Also written Wu-wei Wu-ku-li 烏隈烏古里 (LS 46, 30*a*). They probably lived in modern Outer Mongolia (*cf.* I, 2 (8), no. 6).

[36] These men were skilled in luring deer from hiding by blowing horns and bugles (II, 1 (26)).

[37] Although during the greater part of the Liao period Korea called herself the subordinate of her western neighbor, she did not blindly pursue a course of submission. The changes in the Korean calendar are a noteworthy reflection of the country's changing political attitude.

938—Korea uses Chin 晉 calendar.
948—Korea uses Han calendar.

952—Korea uses Chou calendar.
963—Korea uses Sung calendar.
993—Liao invades Korea; Korea asks for peace.
994—Liao calendar adopted for the first time.
1015—Korea offers tribute to Sung and complains about recent Liao attacks.
1016—Sung calendar adopted.
1020—Korea sends envoys to Liao, who promise payment of tribute and suggest designation of the Koreans as "barbarians."
1022—Liao calendar re-introduced.
1031—Conflict over Yalu bridge(s). Korea uses reign title of deceased Liao emperor, instead of the current, Ch'ung-hsi.
1032—Liao envoy not received by Korean court.
1038—Korean mission pleads for Liao friendship. Korea accepts current Liao reign title, Ch'ung-hsi.
1116—Informed that the Chin 金 invasion has put Liao in a critical position, Korea discards Liao calendar and instead counts the years by means of the sixty-year cycle (KRS 14, 205; 86, 724–730).

[38] 王治 the sixth king of the newly established kingdom of Korea (918–1892), ruled from 982 to 997.

52. KOREA AND T'IEH–LI

995   [In the fifth month of the thirteenth year of T'ung-ho], Korea presented eagles. In the twelfth month T'ieh-li sent envoys to offer eagles and horses as tribute.

70, 9a

53. HSIA

995   On the day *ping-tzŭ* [of the eighth month in the thirteenth year of T'ung-ho] the country of Hsia sent envoys to present horses.   13, 6b

54. T'IEH–LI

995   On the day *chi-mao* of the twelfth month [in the thirteenth year of T'ung-ho], T'ieh-li sent envoys to offer eagles and horses as tribute.   13, 7a

55. TRIBUTES TOO HEAVY

997   On the day *kêng-yin* [of the third month in the fifteenth year of T'ung-ho], Wu-chao-tu[39] of Wu-jo, because of the remoteness of his country, requested a remission of the seasonal offerings of eagles, horses, and sable skins.   An imperial decree ordered that it pay the tributes for the [imperial] birthday[40] and New Year's day as before but that it be exempted from the rest.   13, 8b

56. KOREA

997   On the day *ping-tzŭ* [of the seventh month in the fifteenth year of T'ung-ho], Korea sent Han Ön-kiöng with gifts to mourn at the funeral of the Princess of Yüeh.[41]

13, 8b–9a

57. HSIA

1002   On the day *chia-yin* [of the first month in the twentieth year of T'ung-ho] the country of Hsia sent envoys to offer horses and camels[42] as tribute.   14, 3b

58. JURCHEN

1002   On the day *hsin-yu* [of the first month in the twentieth year of T'ung-ho] the prime minister of the Nü-chih, I-li-ti, came to offer tribute.   14, 3b

59. KOREA

1002   On the day *hsin-ch'ou* [of the seventh month in the twentieth year of T'ung-ho], Korea sent envoys to offer maps of their country as tribute.   14, 3b

60. BARBARIAN TRIBES

1004   On the day *chi-ch'ou* of the third month [in the twenty-second year of T'ung-ho] there was a remission of the tribute paid by the barbarian tribes for the celebration of the emperor's birthday, the Winter Solstice, and the Double-Fifth Festival.[43]   14, 4b

61. SUNG

1005   On the day *mou-tzŭ* [of the twelfth month in the twenty-second year of T'ung-ho], Sung sent Li Chi-ch'ang to ask for a truce.   They acknowledged the mother of the [Liao] emperor as a junior aunt[44] [of the Sung emperor] and expressed their willingness to make an annual

---

[39] The last part of his name is sometimes written *tu* 度 and sometimes *ch'ing* 慶.

[40] The conversion of the emperor's birthday into a national festival can be dated back in China to the seventeenth year of K'ai-yüan of the T'ang dynasty (729). The officials then offered gifts and enjoyed three days of rest.   After that time the emperor's birthday was generally celebrated each year.   Under the Liao dynasty the tributary states and tribes offered large birthday gifts which constituted a considerable addition to the regular income of the government (JCL 14, 88–91).

[41] The third daughter of Ching-tsung (LS 65, 2b).

[42] Hsi Hsia once paid the following tribute to Liao: twenty fine horses, two hundred ordinary horses, one hundred camels, three hundred rolls of silk brocade, five sets of woven silk mattresses and coverlets, one thousand catties of salt, one thousand fox skins, five falcons for catching hares, ten dogs (CTKC 21, 3b).

[43] See VII, 2 (83), and note 158.

[44] According to a study by Nieh Ch'ung-ch'i, the courtesy titles of "elder brother" and "younger brother" were applied between a Sung emperor and a Liao emperor of the

payment of a hundred thousand taels of silver and two hundred thousand bolts of lustring.   Consent was given to this.   Then Ting Chên, the commissioner of court ceremonies, was immediately dispatched with an official communication to return the courtesy.[45]   14, 6a

62. REPERCUSSIONS OF THE NEW TREATY WITH SUNG

1005   On the day *ping-yin* [of the fifth month in the twenty-third year of T'ung-ho], Korea offered congratulations on the peace made with Sung. . . . On the day *chia-wu* [of the sixth month] the Tsu-pu chieftain, T'ieh-la-li, sent envoys to offer congratulations on the peace made with Sung.   On the day *chi-hai* nine tribes of the country of Ta-tan sent envoys to pay a courtesy call.   14, 6b

63. SUNG

1005   On the day *kuei-mao* [of the tenth month in the twenty-third year of T'ung-ho] the annual presents of Sung arrived for the first time; thereafter they came regularly.
14, 6b

64. UIGHURS

1006   In this month [the eighth month of the twenty-fourth year of T'ung-ho] the Tun-huang King[46] of Sha Prefecture, Ts'ao Shou,[47] sent envoys to offer Ta-shih[48] horses and beautiful jade.   He was presented in return with a pair of garments and silver objects.   14, 7a

65. KOREA

1008   On the day *ping-yin* [of the fifth month in the twenty-sixth year of T'ung-ho], Korea offered mats made of the *lung-hsü* plant.[49]   14, 7b

[In the fifth month in the twenty-sixth year of T'ung-ho], Korea provided the Wên-hua and Wu-kung Halls with floor mats made of the *lung-hsü* plant.   70, 12b

In the twenty-sixth year [of T'ung-ho] mats made of the *lung-hsü* plant were presented and compliments were offered on the building of walls for the Central Capital.   115, 2a

66. JURCHEN

1010   On the first day *ping-wu* of the tenth month in the winter [of the twenty-eighth year of T'ung-ho] the Nü-chih offered ten thousand fine horses and asked permission to join the punitive expedition against Korea.   This was approved.   15, 2a

---

same generation according to their ages. If the Sung emperor had been a generation lower than the Liao emperor, he would have called the Liao emperor either "junior uncle" or "senior uncle" and his wife either "junior aunt" or "senior aunt," depending upon whether the Liao emperor was older or younger than the Sung emperor's father. It happened, however, that the Sung emperors were always older than the Liao emperors of the same generation; therefore, they were always called "elder brothers." Consequently the Sung emperor looked upon the mother of the Liao emperor as "junior aunt" (Nieh CC 40, 12–13).

[45] The story of the agreement between Liao and Sung in 1005 is confirmed by two newly discovered inscriptions from Tsaghan Khoton. The first, an epitaph (哀册文) of Shêng-tsung carved in 1031, states with probable exaggeration that Sung begged for the continuation of peace (懇求繼好) and offered a tribute of money and silk (貢奉金幣) (LLSKCL 3, 1b–2a). The second, a fractured stone tablet, which is supposed to have been carved in the time of Hsing-tsung (1031–1055), describes the invincibility of the Liao armies and states that just as a Liao force was pressing hard against T'an-t'ing (southwest of present P'o-yang 濮陽 County in southern Hopei), a Sung official, Ts'ao Li-yung 曹利用, took the initiative in presenting an offer of capitulation (首以誓書), whereupon a truce was concluded (see fig. 34 and Torii 36 II, pls. 125–129).

The humiliating term *kung* 貢, which is not applied to Sung in the *Sung Shih*, is used in the first inscription and also in LS 19, 3a; 86, 2b; and 96, 1b. As for the initiative in seeking peace, LS 14, 5b attributes it to Sung while CTKC 7, 4a and SS 7, 5b attribute it to Liao. After this agreement the embassies of both empires traveled back and forth on special missions or to exchange routine courtesies until the end of Liao. (For a detailed report of the diplomatic relations see Nieh CC 40.)

[46] A title conferred upon the chieftains of the Uighurs by Liao.

[47] According to WHTK 135, 2632, the full name of Ts'ao Shou was Ts'ao Tsung-shou 曹宗壽. Because Hsing-tsung's personal name was Tsung-chên 宗眞, the word *tsung* was omitted by the Liao historiographers.

[48] Arabian? See I, introduction, note 108.

[49] A kind of rush, probably *juncus effusus*, L, used in making mats (Giles 12, 7479).

Fig. 34. Chinese inscription from an octagonal stone found at Ch'ing-chou,
recording the signing of the Sung-Liao treaty of 1005 by Ts'ao Li-yung
(Torii 36 II, pl. 130).

1012   On the day *kuei-wei* [of the first month in the first year of K'ai-t'ai] the chieftains of thirty Nü-chih tribes of the Ch'ang-pai Mountains came to pay tribute and to ask that they be given ranks and degrees.   15, 3*b*

67. HSIA

1012   On the day *jên-yin* [of the fourth month in the first year of K'ai-t'ai] the country of Hsia sent envoys to offer fine horses.   15, 4*a*

In the first year of K'ai-t'ai, [Li] Tê-chao[50] sent envoys to present fine horses.   115, 7*b*

68. UIGHURS

1016   On the day *ting-ch'ou* [of the sixth month in the fifth year of K'ai-t'ai] the Uighurs offered peacocks.   15, 10*b*

69. NORTHEASTERN TRIBES

1018   On the day *hsin-ch'ou* of the third month [in the seventh year of K'ai-t'ai] the five northeastern tribes of Yüeh-li-tu, P'ou-a-li, Ao-li-mi, P'u-nu-li,[51] and T'ieh-li[52] were ordered to render an annual tribute of sixty-five thousand ermine furs and three hundred horses.   16, 1*a*

70. TSU–PU

1019   On the day *kuei-hai* [of the seventh month in the eighth year of K'ai-t'ai] the Tsu-pu were ordered by edict to pay as of old a tribute of seventeen hundred horses, four hundred and forty camels, ten thousand ermine furs, and twenty-five thousand gray mole furs.   16, 3*b*

71. TA–SHIH

1020   On the day *jên-yin* [of the tenth month in the ninth year of K'ai-t'ai] the country of Ta-shih sent envoys to offer ivory[53] and local products and to ask for a wife for [the ruler's] son, Ts'ê-ko.[54]   16, 5*a*

72. TI–LIEH

1021   On the day *ting-wei* of the tenth month in the winter [of the first year of T'ai-p'ing] the Ti-lieh chieftain, P'o-pai, came to offer horses and camels.   16, 6*a*

73. HSIA

1031   In the eleventh year [of T'ai-p'ing], Shêng-tsung died. When the sad news was announced to Hsia, [Li] Tê-chao sent envoys to present funeral gifts.   115, 7*b*

74. SUNG

1042   In the eleventh year [of Ch'ung-hsi, Yeh-lü Jên-hsien[55]] was promoted to the post of a vice-chancellor of the Northern Division. At this time Sung asked to increase the annual payment of silver and lustring in order to compensate for the land property of the ten

---

[50] Li Tê-chao 李德昭 was the king of Hsia. He ruled from 1003 to 1032.

[51] Same as P'ên-nu-li.

[52] The location of these five tribes is ascribed to the northeastern part of modern Kirin (TSSTS 14*a*–15*a*).

[53] Or an elephant. See introduction, note 164.

[54] Arguments given above (I, introduction, note 108 and I, 2 (10), no. 46) make it all but certain that this mission came from the energetic Qarā-Khānid ruler, Qadir-khan Yusuf, who from 1013 on extended his control over Khotan, Yarkand, and Kashghar—that is, over all of Eastern Turkestan (Barthold 28, 281). Shêng-tsung's letter to Sultan Mahmūd, written in 1024, boasts of "an alliance with Qadir-khan through a noble lady from the bosom of

my house who became married to his son *Chaghrï-tegin" (Marvazī 42, 20). LS 16, 5*b* relates that in 1021 the court of Ta-shih again sent messengers to ask for a Liao bride. A daughter of a noble family was allowed to marry a Ta-shih prince.

Does LS 16, 5*a* refer to the son of Qadir-khan whose name Minorsky reconstructs as Chaghri-tegin? Minorsky's transliteration is closer to the Chinese Ts'ê [Ch'ê or Ch'ai]-ko 册割 than either of the names which Barthold gives for the Khan's two eldest sons: Bughrā-tagïn Sulaymān and Yaghān-tagïn (Barthold 28, 284, text and note 7 and 295).

[55] Yeh-lü Jên-hsien 仁先, a descendant of the First Patriarchal Household of the imperial clan. He first became

counties.[56] [Yeh-lü] Jên-hsien and Liu Liu-fu[57] were sent to Sung to negotiate further the documentary use of the term "tribute." Sung balked at it.

[Yeh-lü] Jên-hsien explained, "Formerly the Shih [family of] Chin[58] showed its gratitude to our country[59] by ceding the territory as a present. [Then] Chou took possession of it. The right and wrong, benefit and injury can be clearly perceived."

Sung had no argument in reply. Then an agreement was concluded to increase [the annual contribution] by a hundred thousand taels of silver and a hundred thousand bolts of silk and also to call it "paying tribute."[60]   96, 1a–b

---

known in 1042 for his part in the preparation of the treaty with Sung. In 1063 he helped the emperor to crush the rebellion of the imperial clan headed by Ch'ung-yüan 重元, whereupon he was promoted to the post of chancellor of the Northern Division and granted the highest honorary title, that of yü-yüeh. In 1069 he subdued the northwestern tribes. He died in 1072 (LS 96, 1a–3a).

[56] These ten counties were occupied in 959 by the Later Chou and in 960 came under the control of Sung. In 1042 Hsing-tsung, supported by Hsiao Hui 惠 (981–1056), desired to reconquer the region. The negotiations mentioned in our text are the diplomatic countermoves of the Sung.

[57] 劉六符. This Chinese statesman in the service of Liao played a leading role in the negotiations between Liao and Sung.

[58] See I, 1, note 10.

[59] The word ch'ao 朝, which usually is rendered "court," sometimes also has the connotation of dynasty or country. In the above passage "country" seems a more adequate equivalent than "court."

The terms pei ch'ao 北朝, Northern Country, and nan ch'ao, 南朝 Southern Country, first appear in 1005 in Liao and Sung documents (CTKC 20, 2a ff.; SS 310, 12b). The officials of both governments used them in speech as well as in writing though some Sung officials were reluctant to accept the compound formula because of its political implications. In the middle of the eleventh century the Liao court suggested the use of the two terms instead of "Ch'i-tan" or "Liao" and "Sung" in the official documents of both governments. After critical opposition the Sung officials accepted the proposed innovation. The compound formula appears not only in Sung and Liao documents but also in the official writings of states that were subordinate to Liao. Cf. HWKC 12, 188 ff.; JLKI 2, 31; HYC 37, 496; LYCWC 5, 61; TSCH 4.

[60] The present text speaks of Sung as "paying tribute" (kung 貢), but SS 313, 4b gives a different version. According to this source, in 1042 Liao demanded that the terms hsien 獻 (to offer) or na 納 (to pay) be applied to the Sung contributions. Sung refused at first, but consented to the use of the word na, when Liao threatened to use force.

In 1005 Sung agreed upon the payment to Liao of one hundred thousand taels of silver and two hundred thousand bolts of lustring. The added payment of one hundred thousand taels and one hundred thousand bolts raised the total to two hundred thousand taels of silver and three hundred thousand bolts of lustring. According to PCP 10, 4b, the annual payment in silver was three hundred thousand taels.

Besides this regular annual payment and the various kinds of gifts listed in CTKC 21, 1b and offered on the occasion of New Year's Day and the emperor's birthday, the Sung court gave Liao four thousand bolts of silk and two thousand taels of silver objects on New Year's Day, and five thousand bolts of silk and five thousand taels of silver objects annually on the Liao emperor's birthday (PCP 10, 4b). The Sung government furthermore was put to heavy expense on behalf of the Liao envoys dispatched to the southern court. On the occasion of the first interview with the emperor the Chinese hosts made the following presents:

1) To each of the two envoys (one sent by the emperor, the other by his mother): one hat decorated with gold and silver, one felt hat, eight suits of clothing, one belt, one pair of leather boots, two hundred taels of silver objects, one hundred bolts of colored silks, one saddled horse.

2) To each of the two vice-envoys (one sent by the emperor, the other by his mother): one towel, seven suits of clothing, one gold belt, an ivory tablet, a pair of leather boots, one hundred taels of silver objects, one hundred bolts of colored silks, one saddled horse.

3) To the suite: (a) Officials of the first class (eighteen men) each received four silk-lined coats, one belt, a pair of shoes, twenty taels of silver objects, thirty bolts of colored silks; (b) Officials of the second class (twenty men) each received three lined coats, one belt, a pair of shoes, ten taels of silver objects, twenty bolts of colored silks; (c) Officials of the third class (eighty-five men) each received four lined coats, one belt, ten taels of silver objects, twenty bolts of colored silks.

When they said farewell to the emperor, the Sung court again presented gifts, as follows:

1) To each of the envoys: seven suits of tight-fitting robes, two hundred taels of silver objects, two hundred bolts of colored silks, a belt, one hundred bolts of various kinds of silk.

2) To each of the vice-envoys: six suits of tight-fitting robes, two hundred taels of silver objects, two hundred bolts of colored silks.

3) To each of the suite: different articles according to rank (SHYK 196, 36b–38a).

In addition to these gifts, the Sung emperor personally gave fifteen hundred taels of silver to each of the Liao envoys and thirteen hundred taels of silver to each of the vice-envoys (HML 23b).

During their sojourn in the Sung capital the envoys each received ten bushels of rice and millet, twenty bushels of flour, fifty sheep, and twenty jars of wine of various kinds;

75. HSIA

1043   On the day *kêng-tzŭ* [of the fourth month in the twelfth year of Ch'ung-hsi] the country of Hsia sent envoys to present horses and camels.   19, 4a

76. TRIBAL TRIBUTE MUST BE PAID ON TIME

1043   On the day *hsin-mao* of the fifth month [in the twelfth year of Ch'ung-hsi] two envoys of the Wo-lu and P'u-lu-mao-to tribes who came to pay tribute missed the proper time.   They were pardoned and sent back.   19, 4a

77. SUNG SENDS SPECIAL GIFTS

1044   On the day *mou-ch'ên* of the ninth month [in the thirteenth year of Ch'ung-hsi], because the [Liao] emperor had himself headed the punitive campaign against the state of Hsia, Sung sent Yü Ching[61] to present him with parting gifts.   19, 6a

78. A HIGH TRIBAL VISITOR

1047   On the day *ting-ssŭ* [of the sixth month in the sixteenth year of Ch'ung-hsi] the great king of the Tsu-pu, T'un-t'u-ku-ssŭ, came to the court to offer local products.
                                                                          20, 1a

79. P'U–LU–MAO–TO

1048   [In the fourth month of the seventeenth year of Ch'ung-hsi] the great king of the P'u-lu-mao-to tribe, P'u-lien, presented shipbuilders.   69, 16a

80. TSU–PU AND OTHERS

1048   On the day *kêng-ch'ên* of the sixth month [in the seventeenth year of Ch'ung-hsi] the Tsu-pu offered twenty thousand horses and camels.   On the day *hsin-mao* Grand Preceptor[62] Ch'ai-ko of the Ch'ang-pai Mountains [tribes][63] and Grand Preceptor Sa-la-tu of the Hui-po tribe came to offer local products as tribute.   20, 2a–b

81. TSU–PU

1049   On the day *kêng-ch'ên* [of the sixth month in the eighteenth year of Ch'ung-hsi] the Tsu-pu came to offer horses, camels, and precious curios as tribute.   20, 3b

82. TRIBES OFFER HORSES

1050   [On the day *jên-shên* of the sixth month in the nineteenth year of Ch'ung-hsi] the Hui-po, Ho-su-kuan, and P'u-lu-mao-to tribes each sent envoys to offer horses.
                                                                          20, 4b

83. HSIA

1051   On the day *kuei-ch'ou* of the fifth month in the summer [of the twentieth year of Ch'ung-hsi], Hsiao Yu-k'uo[64] and others returned from a mission to Hsia.   The mother of Li Liang-tsu[65] submitted a memorial asking that like the Tang-hsiang they be temporarily allowed to present horses,[66] camels, oxen, and sheep.   20, 5b

---

the vice-envoys each received seven bushels of rice and millet, fifteen bushels of flour, thirty sheep, and twenty jars of wine (CTKC 21, 2b).

The Liao diplomatic mission to Sung usually consisted of more than a hundred persons.   The Sung government kept more than a thousand men at each prefecture along the road to provide food and help of all kinds.   For instance, Hsing 邢 Prefecture gathered 1203 men for the service of the Liao mission which passed through the region.   On a rainy day when the Liao carts got stuck in the mud, between twenty and thirty oxen and mules and between forty and fifty men were employed to move a single cart (CTC 5, 60).

[61] This Sung envoy, who spoke the Ch'i-tan language (CTKC 24, 3a), lived from 1000 to 1064.

[62] An assistant to the great king.   For various uses of this title see XIV, 1 (9), LS 45, 5a–b and VI, 1, note 1. It was often bestowed upon tribal chieftains.   See I, 2 (6), no. 5.

[63] See I, 2 (6), no. 9.

[64] The word *yu* 友 in the *Liao Shih* is sometimes written *yao* 爻. *Yu* is probably the correct form.

[65] The king of Hsia.

[66] We follow other editions in reading 馬 for the 之 of our text.

84. GRAY FALCONS

1052   [In the seventh month of the twenty-first year of Ch'ung-hsi] agents were sent to four tribes of the Five Nations, and to the Pi-ku-tê, Wu-ku, and Ti-lieh to catch the gray falcons from east of the sea.   69, 17*a*

85. UIGHURS

1052   On the day *chia-tzŭ* [of the eleventh month in the twenty-first year of Ch'ung-hsi the emperor] halted at the Chung-hui River.[67]   The Uighur Arslan[68] sent envoys to offer famous steeds and leopards.   20, 7*a*

86. ALL TRIBES OFFER HORSES AND CAMELS

1053   On the day *chi-yu* of the seventh month in the autumn [of the twenty-second year of Ch'ung-hsi] the great king of the Tsu-pu, T'un-t'u-ku-ssŭ, led the chieftains of the tribes to offer horses and camels.   20, 7*b*

87. PORTRAITS EXCHANGED

1054   On the day *jên-tzŭ* [of the twelfth month in the twenty-second year of Ch'ung-hsi] an imperial decree was issued to the high officials, saying, "Since We and the ruler of Sung agreed to be as older and younger brothers there have been many years of friendship. We now desire to see his portrait.[69]   The envoys coming [from Sung] may be so instructed."   20, 8*a*

88. HSIA

1054   On the day *mou-tzŭ* [of the first month in the twenty-third year of Ch'ung-hsi] the country of Hsia sent envoys to offer local products as tribute.   20, 8*a*

On the day *chi-ssŭ* of the fifth month Li Liang-tsu requested [that Hsia be allowed] to present horses and camels.   An imperial decree ordered that these be offered as tribute annually.   20, 8*a*

89. SUNG

1055   On the day *hsin-ssŭ* [of the first month in the twenty-fourth year of Ch'ung-hsi], Sung sent envoys to offer congratulations[70] and to present a tame elephant.[71]

20, 9*a*

90. TSU–PU

1056   On the day *hsin-yu* [of the sixth month in the second year of Ch'ing-ning] the chieftains of the Tsu-pu came to court to offer local products as tribute.   21, 3*b*

91. WU–TU–WAN

1062   In the summer of the fifth month [in the eighth year of Ch'ing-ning] the *t'i-yin* of Wu-tu-wan, T'un-t'u-ko, and others begged permission to offer an annual tribute of horses and camels.   This was approved.   22, 1*a*

---

[67] Hsing-tsung and Tao-tsung used to make stops at this river, especially during the winter. Shêng-tsung's wife, Ch'in-ai, died here in 1058.   The place was probably not far from the Supreme Capital.

[68] The word *arslan* means "lion."   It was probably used as a title, sometimes preceding and sometimes following the name Uighur (see I, 2 (10), no. 15).

[69] The portrait of the Sung emperor was sought repeatedly by Liao.   Hsing-tsung sent portraits of himself and his father to Sung in the hope of receiving one of the Sung emperor in exchange, but the negotiations were interrupted when Hsing-tsung died in 1055.   In 1057 Tao-tsung repeated the request.   Some Sung officials were opposed to granting the request on the ground that the Ch'i-tan might use the portrait for the purpose of averting evil.   Others like the great historiographer, Ou-yang Hsiu, strongly recommended the sending of the portrait.   The Sung emperor, overriding all objections, sent an envoy with a portrait to Liao in 1058 (OYWCCC 111, 2*a*–3*a*; TYL 27*a*; SSWCHL 1, 4).

[70] The congratulations were probably called forth by the presentation of an honorific title to the emperor and empress in the preceding month (LS 20, 8*b*).

[71] According to HTCCP 177, 5*b*, the Sung court sent Liao two tame elephants at the close of 1054.

92. JURCHEN

1071   On the day *i-ch'ou* of the second month [in the seventh year of Hsien-yung] the Nü-chih offered horses.   22, 7*a*

93. TSU–PU

1078   On the day *chia-yin* of the sixth month [in the fourth year of Ta-k'ang] the chieftains of the Tsu-pu presented fine steeds.   23, 6*b*

94. JURCHEN

1081   On the day *chia-yin* [of the first month in the seventh year of Ta-k'ang] the Nü-chih offered fine steeds as tribute.   24, 3*a*

95. THE MONGOLS

1084   On the first day *kêng-wu* [of the second month in the tenth year of Ta-k'ang] the country of Mêng-ku[72] sent envoys to make a courtesy call.   24, 5*b*

96. JURCHEN

1084   On the day *ting-ch'ou* of the fourth month in the summer [of the tenth year of Ta-k'ang] the Nü-chih offered fine steeds as tribute.   24, 5*b*

1086   On the day *i-yu* of the third month [in the second year of Ta-an] the Nü-chih offered fine steeds as tribute.   24, 7*a*

1087   On the day *kêng-ch'ên* [of the third month in the third year of Ta-an] the Nü-chih offered fine steeds as tribute.   25, 1*a*

97. PO–HAI

1087   [In the seventh month of the third year of Ta-an] the Po-hai of the Ssŭ-pei tribe[73] presented oxen.   69, 19*a–b*

98. UIGHURS

1089   On the day *kuei-ssŭ* [of the fifth month in the fifth year of Ta-an] the Uighurs sent envoys to offer fine steeds as tribute.   25, 3*a*

1091   On the first day *mou-wu* of the seventh month [in the autumn of the seventh year of Ta-an] the Uighurs sent envoys to offer rare objects as tribute.   These were not accepted.   [The envoys] were given generous presents and sent back.   25, 4*a*

99. JAPAN

1091   On the day *chi-hai* [of the ninth month in the seventh year of Ta-an], Japan sent twenty-eight persons—Teigen, Teishin, the Buddhist monk Ohan, and others—to offer tribute.   25, 4*b*

1092   On the day *ting-wei* [of the ninth month in the eighth year of Ta-an], Japan sent envoys to pay tribute.   25, 4*b*

100. SHEEP BESTOWED UPON KOREA

1093   On the day *jên-yin* [of the seventh month in the ninth year of Ta-an] envoys were sent to Korea with a gift of sheep.   25, 5*b*

---

[72] The term Mêng-ku 萌古 refers to the Mongol tribes who, in the T'ang histories in the seventh, eighth, and ninth centuries, are called Mêng-wa 蒙瓦 or Mêng-wu 蒙兀 (CTS 199*B*, 10*a*; TS 219, 7*a*).   From the time of Chingis Khan on, the term Mêng-ku is applied to the newly established Mongol nation.

[73] Ssŭ-pei Pu Po-hai 四北部渤海 (the Po-hai of the Ssŭ-pei tribe) may be an error for Hsi-pei 西北 Po-hai Pu, the Northwestern Po-hai tribe (*cf.* I, 2 (9), no. 11).

101. FUNERAL PRESENTS OFFERED TO KOREA

1094   In the summer [of the tenth year of Ta-an] the king of the country of Korea, Un, died. His son, Uk, sent envoys to report this. Envoys were immediately sent to make a donation toward the funeral.   25, 7a

102. JURCHEN

1095   On the day *ping-shên* of the eleventh month [in the first year of Shou-lung] the Nü-chih sent envoys to offer horses.   26, 2a

103. P'O–LI

1096   [In the eighth month of the second year of Shou-lung] the Eight P'o-li Tribes[74] presented horses.   69, 21b

104. SUNG

1098   On the day *hsin-wei* [of the first month in the fourth year of Shou-lung], Sung sent envoys to offer embroidered and variegated silk presents.   26, 3b

105. WO–LANG–KAI

1113   On the day *i-mao* of the sixth month [in the third year of T'ien-ch'ing] the country of Wo-lang-kai sent envoys to offer fine dogs as tribute.   27, 7b

106. SUNG

1115   On the day *hsin-wei* of the seventh month in the autumn [of the fifth year of T'ien-ch'ing], Sung sent envoys to convey silver and silk for the support of the army.[75]

28, 1b

---

[74] P'o-li was one of the many northwestern tribes, which also included the Tsu-pu, Wu-ku, Ta-li-ti, Pa-ssŭ-mu, Ch'a-cha-la, Mei-li-chi, Nien-pa-ko, and Ti-lieh, that rebelled against Liao at the end of the eleventh century.

[75] Diplomatic intercourse between Liao and Sung formally ceased in 1122 when the Liao emperor, T'ien-tsu, fled to the Western Capital and the throne was usurped by Ch'un 淳 in the Southern Capital. The latter sent Hsiao Ta-pu-yeh 撻不也 and Wang Chü-yüan 王居元 as envoys to Sung, but when they reached the Sung border the Sung emperor refused to receive them on the ground that Ch'un's usurpation could not be recognized by the Sung government (CTKC 11, 4b).

It is not clear when the Sung government stopped the payments of silk and silver. The date of the last payment mentioned in our texts is 1115.

SECTION XI

LABOR SERVICE

INTRODUCTION

1. THE ADOPTION OF THE CHINESE CORVÉE

Cooperative action was no Chinese monopoly. The tribes dispersed to herd their animals; yet they united for the communal hunts and for serious warfare. Even after the establishment of the empire the Ch'i-tan continued to organize their tribal manpower for military purposes, for big hunts, and for tribal labor service.

But the conquest raised new technical problems whose solution depended upon mobilizing the subdued sedentary masses. The degree to which the victorious Ch'i-tan utilized their Chinese officials to coordinate the labor power of the Chinese commoners determined both the character and the extent of their public works.

2. TERMS

In our texts, Chinese terms are applied to the labor service, no matter whether it was rendered by the country's pastoral or agricultural population. The compulsory labor service is called *yao i* 徭役,[1] or more briefly, just *i* 役.[2] In numerous passages, taxes and labor service, *fu i* 賦役,[3] are both mentioned. Service rendered as a kind of "aid," not to the government itself, but to the imperial tribes is called *chu i* 助役,[4] "subsidiary service." Criminals sentenced to hard labor, *i t'u* 役徒,[5] also worked for the state. But the corvée was mainly performed by free subjects who paid taxes and served the government part-time. Various terms, *fu* 復,[6] *mien* 免,[7] and *pa* 罷,[8] indicate the "suspension," either temporary or permanent, of the required services.

3. THE LABORERS

The government "exacted labor from the people" (*i ch'i min* 役其民).[9] The word *min* reveals the social structure of the corvée: only commoners were subjected to it. Labor service certainly was not demanded from the Ch'i-tan nobility; it was not demanded from officials, candidates for office, or students preparing for a public career.[10] To be sure, members of the noble lineages might serve as bodyguards and attendants of high dignitaries,[11] and court nobles might perform duties even more honorific.[12] But the privileged position of the Ch'i-tan officials and the Chinese scholarly bureaucracy is evident. Theoretically, Chinese merchants were expected to participate in the corvée; actually they were able to avoid it by hiring poor persons as substitutes.[13] By the middle of the eleventh century even the nominal services expected of the Ch'i-tan nobility were performed by substitutes or suspended altogether.[14]

The Chinese rural population was assigned to one of three categories depending upon the amount of property owned.[15] Each household was expected to provide an adult male for frontier service, though under certain conditions a substitute could be hired.[16] Similar regulations may also have governed the corvée.

Labor service, therefore, fell unequally upon different strata within Liao society, a situation commented upon by Chin 金 critics.[17] The rigid military structure of the conquest society of Liao blocked any thoroughgoing change. Measures such as those taken after 951 and 1039 were not expected to democratize the corvée; they merely served to reduce taxes and service for the hard pressed.[18]

4. SEASONAL DISTRIBUTION

Oriental statesmanship has always understood that mobilization for labor service should not conflict with work in the fields. In the Liao empire sowing and planting began in the second or third month, that is by April.[19] The harvesting of barley, wheat, and peas

---

[1] XI (19).
[2] XI (15) and *passim*.
[3] XI (8—tribal) (13—Chinese).
[4] XI (20).
[5] XI (24).
[6] XII (78).
[7] XI (20).
[8] XII (3).
[9] XI (25).

[10] CS 47, 15*a*.
[11] XI (20).
[12] *Loc. cit.*
[13] VI, 2 (1).
[14] See notes 11 and 12.
[15] LWT 4, 17*a*; TCCSPI 2–3.
[16] XV, 1 (51).
[17] CS 47, 15*a*.
[18] XI (8) (19).
[19] See II, introduction.

usually began in June. The country's staple crop, millet, was harvested then as now in the seventh and eighth months, that is in August and September.[20]

In the eighth month the government turned its attention to the village altars,[21] the local centers for taxation and mobilization of manpower. According to our records, it was in the following month, before the cold weather set in,[22] that most of the public construction work was undertaken. The seat of Lung-hua Prefecture was walled in 902 in the ninth month,[23] that is between October 5 and November 3; in 908 the Great Wall was extended some time about or after October 28;[24] the walls of the Supreme Capital were repaired in (or after?) October in the year 931;[25] and large-scale road work was done in the autumn of 984.[26]

The cold months from the end of November to the beginning of March seem to have been a good time of year for military training and warfare,[27] though not for construction work. A few exceptions that have been noted occurred either at the beginning or end of the winter season. In 1018[28] in the tenth month two newly built halls were named in the Central Capital,[29] but the actual work was manifestly completed prior to that time. In the first month of 994, "in the spring,"[30] old canals in Nan-ching Circuit were dredged, the work obviously being done at the end of the cold season or just before the spring sowing. At the same time of year in 1019 Ching-tsung's temple was built in the Central Capital.[31] On March 26 of the year 983[32] artisans were rewarded for work done inside a tomb[33] during the cold season or on the warmer days at the winter's end—the text does not say. The building of a fortified city on the shores of the Sungari River was commenced in the second month of 1026[34] (February/March). An imperial decree urged the officials in charge to utilize the weeks between agricultural activities for construction.[35]

[20] This is the general picture that emerges from a survey of the *Liao Shih*. A more detailed analysis of local differences must be left to special studies.
[21] XI (12).
[22] *Cf.* Hosie 01, 152 ff.; North-Manchuria 24, 4.
[23] XI (1).
[24] XI (2).
[25] XI (6).
[26] XI (10).
[27] *Cf.* XV.
[28] XI (17).
[29] *Loc. cit.*
[30] XI (14).
[31] XI (17).
[32] XI (9).
[33] For the shape of the tombs of later Liao emperors see Torii 36 III, pl. 173, *passim.*
[34] XI (18).
[35] *Loc. cit.*

This was the general aim but it was not always the practice. It might be disregarded when a harsh ruler insisted that some task be completed without delay. The building of the Supreme Capital was begun some time in 918;[36] the commissioner of construction was appointed on April 3;[37] work on the temples was initiated on June 14.[38] The whole undertaking was completed within a hundred days.[39] Even if this round number is viewed with scepticism, there can be little doubt that the capital was built with excessive speed during the better part of the growing season. A similar disregard for the demands of a rural economy was shown when work was done in the Central Capital in 1009,[40] and again when the southwestern border fortifications were constructed in 1077.[41] In the latter case the task must have been completed by early summer, for the head official was rewarded for his achievement on July 26.[42]

5. ORGANIZATION

Little is known concerning the organization of the empire's labor service. The sedentary populations were under the jurisdiction of the government of the Southern Region whose administrative offices included a Ministry of Works, a Board of Imperial Construction, and a Board of Waterworks.[43] However, it is difficult to say how these various offices were coordinated with the territorial, regional, and local administrations.

No departments like those of the central government are recorded for the circuits, prefectures, or counties. The village altars seem to have been the controlling centers of the rural communities,[44] and the village heads were persons of importance, acting as intermediaries between the local magistrates and the individual peasants; but the texts do not state how these local agents were fitted into the larger bureaucratic machine.

Organization in the settled regions was rather complex; among the tribes it was immeasurably simpler. The tasks of the tribal corvée were relatively limited, and the tribal officials probably had little difficulty in executing them. The list of officials includes a minister of works for all the smaller tribes and a minister over the masses for all the tribes;[45] but whether these

[36] XI (3).
[37] *Loc. cit.*
[38] XI (4).
[39] XI (3).
[40] XI (15).
[41] XI (23).
[42] LS 23, 6a.
[43] See XIV, 2 (5), LS 47, 2b and 14b.
[44] *Cf.* XIV, introduction.
[45] XIV, 1 (23) (24).

officials dealt exclusively, or even primarily, with questions of the corvée (and of taxation) is open to doubt.

6. THE CORVÉE OF THE EMPIRE'S SEDENTARY SUBJECTS

The great agricultural societies of Asia required the organized services of thousands of men because of the nature of their economy—more specifically because of their dependence on irrigation and flood control. The corvée, once established, could readily be called upon to solve important problems of military defense and transportation or to satisfy the court's need of personal protection, pleasure, or prestige. But the original function of the corvée was never lost; in the hour of economic or political emergency it was vigorously asserted.[46]

The Ch'i-tan conquerors took over the Chinese technique of large-scale corvée, but they could not completely accept the economic philosophy in which this technique was rooted. Too familiar with agriculture to destroy the Chinese fields, they were still not familiar enough with the Chinese mode of cultivation to understand the secret of its productivity. In the great typically Chinese dynasties of Ch'in and Han, Sui and T'ang, Sung and Ming[47] government policy depended upon the corvée for the construction and maintenance of their large-scale waterworks, but such undertakings are rarely mentioned among the public works initiated by the Liao government.

The Ch'i-tan rulers used the forced labor of their subject peasants to construct cities in former grazing grounds and wastelands.[48] Fortifications were erected in and around Shang-ching Circuit;[49] walls and ramparts were built at strategic places in the North,[50] the Southwest,[51] and the South;[52] majestic tombs were raised,[53] and impressive palaces, temples, and towers were constructed. The whole male population might be rallied to repair the roads,[54] and local manpower might be strained by government transportation.[55] But the great machine of organized labor was rarely used to increase the country's agricultural strength by building productive or protective waterworks.

It is true a great part of the Liao territory lay beyond the realm of rivers and of irrigated agriculture. But in Nan-ching Circuit and along the Liao River there were canals[56] and embankments,[57] indicating that construction work of the Chinese type had been previously undertaken. In 994 the "old canals" near Kuo-yin were dredged, but the repair of the river dikes of Shên Prefecture (modern Liaoning) was not considered urgent.[58] No doubt the peasants were pleased to be exempted from this service, but no compassion for its hard-working subjects would have persuaded a strong Chinese government to curtail the construction of any waterworks deemed necessary for agricultural, fiscal, or military reasons. Nor did pity deter the Liao government from mobilizing its people for the building of cities and palaces during the busiest months of the agricultural year. The Ch'i-tan court approved the extension of rice farming only during the latter part of the eleventh century, and even then with characteristic military reservations.[59] Not until 1103, when its political power was rapidly waning, did the Liao government overcome its narrow economic philosophy and relax the existing restrictions on reservoirs and "marshes."[60]

7. THE TRIBAL CORVÉE

A mechanical consideration of social status may lead to a false equating of members in a conquering nation with those in similar groups or strata in a subject nation. As long as the conquest situation persists, the victors will enjoy a relatively better status.

But this difference, important as it is, must not be exaggerated. The commoners of a master people may be exempted from many obligations imposed upon the commoners of a subdued nation; yet they are not necessarily free from all public duties. The members of the inner Ch'i-tan tribes paid fewer taxes than the Chinese and Po-hai, but they did pay taxes. They served as elite troops of the Liao army, but they did serve. They were not required to suffer the drudgery and exhaustion of urban construction work, but they had to participate in the tribal corvée.

When Rubruck visited the pastoral regions of the Mongol empire, he found that all tribes, no matter how destitute, had to pay labor service to their Mongol masters. "For it was a commandment of Chingis that no one man should be free from service, until he be so old that he cannot possibly work any more."[61]

---

[46] Cf. Wittfogel, OS (ms).
[47] And even in the dynasty of conquest of the Manchus who were agriculturists before they set their foot on Chinese soil.
[48] Cf. XI (5) (15) (18) and *passim*. See also Torii 36 I, pl. 7 ff.; IV, pl. 306 ff.
[49] See I, 1 (3) (5).
[50] Torii 36 II, pl. 161 ff.
[51] XI (23).
[52] XI (2).
[53] See Torii 36 III, pl. 173 ff., 241 ff.; IV, pl. 254 ff.
[54] XI (10).
[55] XI (21).

[56] XI (14).
[57] XI (22) (28).
[58] XI (22).
[59] Considerations for the movements of the Liao cavalry! See II, 2 (31).
[60] XII (110).
[61] Rubruck 00, 199.

Carpini found that the tribes were responsible for the traveling messengers, supplying them with "horses and other necessaries"; political envoys were furnished with carriages as well as horses.[62]

The nature of the tribal corvée within the Liao empire is not clearly described, but a number of records reveal that labor service was exacted; they even note some of the tasks assigned to the tribal commoners, the care of courier posts and government-owned horses and oxen[63] among them. Since the greater part of the imperial herds grazed in the tribal region, they must have been the responsibility of local tribes and sub-tribes. Similarly, transportation services depended upon local cooperation in this region; tribes were ordered to send carts when the local trade required it,[64] and government grain was transported by native tribesmen.[65]

Skilled horsemen that they were, the tribesmen were also called upon to participate in the imperial hunts. While these semi-military expeditions assured the meat supply of the court and the army,[66] they interfered so seriously with the normal life of the tribal hunters[67] that, in times of weakened discipline, the harassed subjects fled their homes in great numbers.[68]

According to LS 10, 7b, most Ch'i-tan families were required to render labor service, even those belonging to T'ai-tsu's old tribes. In fact the duties imposed on two of these tribes in 985 were so onerous that the government interfered.[69] Members of the imperial tribes were not exempted from the corvée, but they enjoyed a privileged position and, for a considerable

time, succeeded in getting other tribes to do subsidiary service for them.[70]

8. THE CHANGING FORM OF THE LIAO CORVÉE

The burdens of the tribal corvée were eased by the government's desire to protect the tribes and to retain their loyal support. The sedentary peoples were accorded much harsher treatment. No diary or inscription evaluates the corvée from a Chinese or Po-hai point of view; nor are the official documents interested in playing up this aspect. But on several occasions the veiled language of the *Liao Shih* itself indicates the human sufferings involved. The people who built the imperial capital in a few months[71] faced a task hardly less gruelling than the construction of the Egyptian pyramids. It is doubtful whether the goal was achieved more humanely. The labor service demanded of the Chinese people who lived beyond the southern frontier of the Liao empire in Sung China, hard though it was, must have seemed relatively mild to the men who were building the walled cities and towers in the pastoral regions of the north.

In the years 982 and 983, in spite of government disapproval,[72] the hiring of substitutes continued, a device probably inherited from the T'ang dynasty.[73] A decree in 1012 reveals that some small remuneration was given at that time for "troublesome and onerous" labor service.[74] Near the close of the dynasty, a money tax was substituted for corvée service.[75] As in other fields, the Ch'i-tan rulers adopted this Chinese measure, not at the peak of the empire's power, but only during the period of final dissolution.

[62] Carpini 28, 20.
[63] XI (26).
[64] V (4).
[65] V (18).
[66] II, 1 (7) and XI (27).
[67] *Loc. cit.*
[68] *Loc. cit.*
[69] XI (11).

[70] XI (20).
[71] XI (3).
[72] VI, 2 (1).
[73] TS 52, 2b.
[74] XI (16).
[75] XI (26).

TRANSLATION

LABOR SERVICE

1. A walled city built 2. The Great Wall extended 3. The Supreme Capital built 4. Temples built 5. The Supreme Capital 6. The walls of the capital repaired 7. Serving travelers 8. Tribal taxes and labor service 9. Work at a mausoleum 10. Two hundred thousand people construct roads 11. Labor service exhausts the Ch'i-tan commoners 12. Village altars 13. Recalcitrance during Sung war 14. Canals dredged 15. The Central Capital 16. Onerous labor service 17. Additions to the Central Capital 18. A city built 19. Equalization of labor services 20. Privileged position of noble groups 21. Unequal distribution of transport services 22. Repair of river dikes 23. Southern frontier fortifications 24. Convict laborers 25. Construction of dwellings 26. Local services converted into money payments 27. Hunting service 28. A dike

1. A WALLED CITY BUILT

902   In the seventh month of the autumn of the next year [T'ai-tsu] led four hundred thousand soldiers to attack Ho-tung[1] and Tai[2]-pei.   He conquered nine commanderies and captured alive[3] ninety-five thousand persons and innumerable camels, horses, oxen, and sheep. In the ninth month Lung-hua Prefecture, south of the Huang River, was built up as a walled city,[4] and the construction of the Temple of the Commencement of Teaching was begun.[5]   **1, 1b**

2. THE GREAT WALL EXTENDED

908   On the first day *chi-hai* of the tenth month in the winter [of the second year of T'ai-tsu's accession] the Ming-wang Tower[6] was erected.   The Great Wall was extended to the sea-mouth of Chên-tung.[7]   **1, 3a**

3. THE SUPREME CAPITAL BUILT

918   On the day *kuei-hai* [of the second month in the third year of Shên-ts'ê] for the building of the Imperial Capital[8] the president of the Ministry of Rites, K'ang Mo-chi,[9] was appointed commissioner of construction.   **1, 10a**

In the third year of Shên-ts'ê the Imperial Capital was placed under construction.   [K'ang] Mo-chi was in charge of the work.   The people all exhorted each other to join in.   Within a hundred days the work was finished.   **74, 1b**

4. TEMPLES BUILT

918   On the day *i-hai* of the fifth month [in the third year of Shên-ts'ê] an imperial decree was issued ordering the construction of Confucian, Buddhist, and Taoist temples.   **1, 10b**

5. THE SUPREME CAPITAL

The Supreme Capital was the place where T'ai-tsu founded the empire.   It had mountains in the rear and embraced the seas.[10]   The natural barriers sufficed to make it an impregnable place.

---

[1] In T'ang times Ho-tung 河東 was the region east of the great bend of the Yellow River.   It corresponds to modern Shansi.

[2] We follow LS 34, 1b, in reading *tai* 代 for the *fa* 伐 of the present text.   Tai-pei 代北 corresponds to modern northern Shansi.

[3] In written Chinese the term 生口 (living mouths) is used to indicate living captives as opposed to dead enemies' heads (首級) brought back from the battlefield.

[4] This work was begun by Han Yen-hui.

[5] See IX (1).

[6] In the [Supreme] Capital.   The tower was destroyed in 913 in the course of internal strife (LS 1, 5b).

[7] The phrase *chên-tung hai-k'ou* 鎮東海口, which occurs only once in the *Liao Shih*, is difficult to explain. Chên-tung was probably the military name of T'ung 同 Prefecture (*cf.* LS 38, 12b).   If this is correct, it corresponds to the region between K'ai-yüan 開原 County and T'ieh-ling 鐵嶺 County in Liaoning.   The sea-mouth would then be the mouth of the Liao River.

[8] The Supreme Capital, for a fuller description of which see below.   See figs. 35 and 36.

[9] K'ang Mo-chi 康默記, whose original name was K'ang Chao 照, was a collaborator of Han Yen-hui who advised T'ai-tsu to build cities and towns for the Chinese captives. He died in 926.

[10] This may refer to the Shira Muren, for in literary Chinese the word 海 (sea) sometimes refers to rivers.

FIG. 35.   Site of the Liao Supreme Capital, ruins of western wall and gate (Torii 36 I, pl. 8).

FIG. 36.   Ruins of the city wall of the Liao Supreme Capital, built with unbaked bricks
(Torii 36 I, pl. 7).

The soil was fertile and suitable for cultivation; the water and grass were suitable for raising animals. An arrow with a golden auger laid the foundation for two hundred years.[11]   It was indeed magnificent!

926   In the first year of T'ien-hsien, after returning from the subjugation of Po-hai, [T'ai-tsu] extended the suburbs of the city and built a palace which was named T'ien-tsan.   He built three great halls, called K'ai-huang, An-tê, and Wu-luan, in which were placed the images of the emperors of all reigns.   On the first and fifteenth days of each month and on [imperial] birthdays and death-days all the civil and military officials who were in the capital went there to offer sacrifice.   In the southeastern corner of the inner city he also built the Temple of Celestial Heroes in which he placed the image of his illustrious father, Emperor Hsüan-chien.

During this year T'ai-tsu died.   Empress Ying-t'ien cut off her hand[12] in the I-chieh Temple and placed it in T'ai-tsu's mausoleum.   In this temple a Tower of the Severed Hand was built and a stone tablet was set up in it.

927–947   As T'ai-tsung had assisted in its founding, Chin dispatched the prime ministers Fêng Tao, Liu Hsü, and others bringing credentials of office and imperial equipage. On arriving here they invested T'ai-tsung and Empress Ying-t'ien with honorific titles.   T'aitsung ordered the barbarian tribes also to follow the Chinese rules.   He presided at K'ai-huang Hall, opened the Ch'êng-t'ien Gate, and received salutations.   Then he changed the name of the Imperial Capital to Supreme Capital.

The walls were twenty feet high.   No watch-towers were built.   The area was twenty-seven *li*. The east gates were called Ying-ch'un and Yen-êrh, that of the south was named Shun-yang, and those of the west were called Chin-fêng, Hsi-yen-êrh, and Nan-fu.

The northern part, called the Imperial City, was thirty feet high and had watch-towers.   As to the gates, the eastern was called An-tung; the southern Ta-shun; the western Ch'ien-tê; and the northern Kung-ch'ên.   Inside was the Great Interior.   Its southern gate, called Ch'êng-t'ien, had a tower and a pavilion.   The eastern gate was called Tung-hua.   The western gate was called Hsi-hua. These were the entrances and the exits for communication with the Interior.

On the eastern side of the main street which led directly south was the office of the vicegerent, then the Salt and Iron Office, and then Dragon Temple Street near the southern gate.   To the south was Lin-huang Administration; next to it was Lin-huang County.[13]   To the southwest was Ch'ung-hsiao Temple, built by Empress Ch'êng-t'ien.   West of the temple was Ch'ang-t'ai County. Further west was T'ien-ch'ang Temple.[14]   To the southwest was the Imperial Academy.   North of the academy was the Confucian Temple.   To the east of this was Chieh-i Temple and to the northwest was An-kuo Temple, built by T'ai-tsung.   East of the temple was the old residence of Empress Ch'i-t'ien.[15]   East of the residence was the first imperial concubine's residence, built by Empress Fa-t'ien.[16]   South of the residence were Pei-shêng-ni Temple, the silk brocade workshop, the Office of Internal Administration, the Yeast Department,[17] and two granaries of the Administrative Office for Supplying the Country.   All were situated southwest of the Great Interior.   The Office of the Eight Trades faced the Temple of Celestial Heroes.

The southern city was called the Chinese City.   In the southern part were transverse streets with storied buildings facing each other.   Below spread the market place.   North of the East Gate was Lu County; to the southeast was Hsing-jên County.   East of the South Gate was the Uighur settlement.   The Uighur merchants who remained in the Supreme Capital established a settlement and lived there.

---

[11] Legend has it that in 920 T'ai-tsu shot a dragon at the foot of I-la 抴刺 Mountain.   The dragon was five feet long, had one horn, a long tail, short feet, and a tongue two and a half inches long.   It was preserved from the time of Liao down to Chin (*cf.* LS 68, 1*b*–2*a*; ICCC 1, 5; HICC 2, 9*b*).

[12] See VII, 2 (12).

[13] The location of this and several other counties mentioned in the course of the description of the city must refer to the offices of the surrounding counties.   These

offices were obviously situated within the Supreme Capital which constituted their urban center.

[14] This temple is described as a *kuan* 觀, indicating that it was a Taoist edifice.

[15] Shêng-tsung's first wife.

[16] Shêng-tsung's second wife.   See LS 18, 3*b*.

[17] This office obviously administered the taxation of yeast, the basic raw material for making Chinese "wine." *Cf.* X, 1 (2).

In the southwest was the T'ung-wên courier station. The envoys from foreign countries lodged there. Southwest of the courier station was the Lin-huang courier station. It was used for receiving messengers of the state of Hsia. West of the courier station was the Fu-hsien Temple.

West of the temple was Hsüan-hua County and southwest was Ting-pa County. West of this county was Pao-ho County. North of the West Gate was I-su County and east of this county was Ch'ien-liao County.   37, 4a–5a

6. THE WALLS OF THE CAPITAL REPAIRED

931   On the day *chia-wu* of the ninth month [in the sixth year of T'ien-hsien] an imperial decree ordered that the walls of the [Supreme] Capital be repaired.   3, 5b

7. SERVING TRAVELERS

938   On the day *ting-wei* [of the second month in the first year of Hui-t'ung] a decree ordered that the households furnishing provisions for passing Chin envoys be increased in number.[18]   4, 1a

8. TRIBAL TAXES AND LABOR SERVICE

951–969   In the beginning of the reign period Ying-li, [Yeh-lü Ta-lieh],[19] on being promoted to the position of great king of the Southern Division,[20] equalized the taxes and labor services and encouraged cultivation. Consequently, the tribesmen were transformed by him and the population flourished.   78, 7a

9. WORK AT A MAUSOLEUM

983   On the day *ping-shên* [of the second month in the first year of T'ung-ho] the empress dowager,[21] while visiting the mausoleum [of Ching-tsung] to offer a sacrifice, ordered the portraits of his intimate courtiers to be painted in the hall of the late emperor's image.[22] She bestowed upon the artisans who worked at the tomb rewards befitting their positions.   10, 2b

10. TWO HUNDRED THOUSAND PEOPLE CONSTRUCT ROADS

984   In the autumn [of the second year of T'ung-ho] an imperial decree ordered the building of mountain roads. [Shih] Fang mobilized two hundred thousand people and finished the work in one day.   79, 1b

11. LABOR SERVICE EXHAUSTS THE CH'I-TAN COMMONERS

985   On the first day *i-ssŭ* of the third month [in the third year of T'ung-ho] the chancellor memorialized that most of the Ch'i-tan households which supplied labor service were exhausted and asked that rich families[23] be used in their place. The emperor therefore examined the registers of the tribes, discovering that the number of households in the two tribes of Nieh-la and Wu-wei were few but that their labor service was heavy. Both were exempted, to a certain extent, from their labor services.   10, 7b–8a

---

[18] Hung Hao reports that the Jurchen provided Liao envoys with lodgings in certain private families with unmarried girls. Later the envoys stopped wherever they desired without first inquiring if the female members of the families in question were married or not (SMCW 9b). The story indicates the problems involved in this sort of enforced hospitality. Our text does not give us any information on this point.

[19] Yeh-lü Ta-lieh 撻烈, a noble from the Six Divisions lineage, was ordered by the Liao government to protect Eastern Han 東漢 from the inroads of its neighbors. It was partly through his efforts that the little kingdom was not destroyed until 979 by Sung.

[20] This high dignitary "shared control of the military and civil affairs of the tribes." See XIV, 1 (9), LS 45, 6a.

[21] Ching-tsung's powerful widow who was empress dowager for twenty-seven years.

[22] The emperor's coffin was placed here. In 1933 and 1935 Torii discovered some frescoes in the Liao tombs with figures accompanied by Ch'i-tan characters. These probably designated the names of the court officials (Torii 36 III, pl. 181 ff.; 37, 183).

[23] A decree issued by T'ai-tsung of Chin in 1132 reveals that during the Liao period the different classes of the population contributed unequally to the services required by the government. Chin tried to abolish this system but failed. Officials, *chü-jên* 舉人, and students were exempted from all services for life (CS 47, 15a).

12. VILLAGE ALTARS

985   On the day *chia-shên* [in the eighth month of the third year of T'ung-ho the emperor] ordered the officials of the Southern and Northern Regions to inspect individually the forests and groves of the mausoleums. He also ordered that the two prefectures of Ch'ien[24] and Hsien[25] report to the court the number of their village altars.[26]   10, 8*b*

13. RECALCITRANCE DURING SUNG WAR

991   In the ninth year [of T'ung-ho, Yeh-lü Lung-yün[27]] again said, "The people of Yen are tricky and cunning and evade the taxes and labor services; for this reason the noble families fill their bags. The master of court etiquette of the Northern Division, Chao Chih, should be sent out to admonish them." This was approved.   82, 1*b*–2*a*

14. CANALS DREDGED

994   On the first day *kuei-ch'ou* of the first month in the spring of the twelfth year [of T'ung-ho] the market town of Kuo-yin[28] suffered from flood, and more than thirty villages were inundated. An imperial decree ordered the old canals dredged.[29]   13, 4*a*

15. THE CENTRAL CAPITAL

Before 1006   Once, when Shêng-tsung in passing Ch'i-chin Mountain along the T'u River gazed off to the south, the clouds presented a vision of city suburbs and storied buildings. Consequently, the establishment of a capital was discussed. Fine artisans selected from Yen[30] and Chi[31] directed the work for two years. The suburbs, palaces, towers, treasuries and depots, market places, and galleries followed the arrangement of the Divine Capital.[32]

1006   In the twenty-fourth year of T'ung-ho the Five Tents Division offered the land where of old the imperial tent of the kings of Hsi stood.[33] In the twenty-fifth year it was walled and filled up with Chinese households. It was named the Central Capital, the administration being called Ta-ting. In the Imperial City was an [imperial] ancestral temple and a hall with the images of Ching-tsung and Empress Ch'êng-t'ien.

The city was low and damp. Many wells were dug to drain off the water. The people then found it convenient.   39, 1*b*

1007   In the first month of the spring in the twenty-fifth year [of T'ung-ho] the Central Capital was established.[34]   14, 7*b*

1009   On the first day *ping-hsü* of the fourth month in the summer [of the twenty-seventh year of T'ung-ho] the emperor halted at the Central Capital. Palaces were constructed [there].   14, 8*a*

Fan Chên 范鎮 tells us that a Ch'i-tan envoy to Sung, on being urged by his Chinese hosts to drink more, politely refused with the remark that men should drink according to their capacity just as people should render government service according to the social status (等) of their family. From this remark Fan concludes that the Liao policy was very different from that of his own country (TCCSPI 2–3).

A Liao inscription describes how a certain magistrate named Liu 劉 divided the people of San-ho 三河 County according to their property into three classes for government service (LWT 4, 17*a*).

[24] Southeast of modern Pei-chên 北鎮 County, Liaoning.

[25] Pei-chên County, Liaoning.

[26] Implied in the term 里社 is the village practice of using a temple or public building for religious purposes, sacrifices, and also for the assignment of government services.

[27] Yeh-lü Lung-yün was the Ch'i-tan name of Han Tê-jang.

[28] Southwest of modern T'ung 通 County, Hopei. First it was a town (鎮) and later it was elevated to the rank of a county.

[29] We follow other editions in reading 疏 for the 數 of our text.

[30] The Southern Capital.

[31] Chi 薊 County, Hopei.

[32] The Supreme Capital.

[33] This evidently means that the headquarters of the former kings of Hsi were presented to the Liao government and made part of the Central Capital.

[34] See XIV, 4, note 10.

16. ONEROUS LABOR SERVICE

1012   In the first year of K'ai-t'ai an imperial decree declared, "We regard the labor service[35] imposed upon the people as troublesome and onerous. Therefore, more remuneration should be given for their work. If the year's crops do not flourish, the granaries should be opened in order to lend [grain to the people]. Those whose farms and gardens are lying waste should be granted oxen and seeds to assist them."   *59, 2b*

17. ADDITIONS TO THE CENTRAL CAPITAL

1018   In the tenth month in the winter [of the seventh year of K'ai-t'ai] two newly built halls in the Central Capital were named Yen-ch'ing and Yung-an.   *16, 2a*

1019   [On the day *jên-hsü* of the first month in the spring of the eighth year of K'ai-t'ai] the temple of Ching-tsung was built in the Central Capital.   *16, 2b*

18. A CITY BUILT

1026   On the day *chi*[36]-*yu* of the second month [in the sixth year of T'ai-p'ing], Mi-li-chi was appointed as co-director of affairs for the Chancellery, Huang P'ien as chief military controller, Ta-ku-chih as his assistant, and Ho-shih as chief supervisor, to direct the army in building a city between the Hun-t'ung and Shu-mu Rivers.[37] Huang-lung Administration[38] requested permission to construct three ramparts and ten beacon platforms. An imperial decree ordered them built by using the time between agricultural activities.   *17, 2b*

19. EQUALIZATION OF LABOR SERVICES

1039   In the eighth year [of Ch'ung-hsi, Hsiao Hsiao-mu] sent up a memorial suggesting that the population of the empire be registered in order to equalize the labor services. He also pointed out the advantages and disadvantages of the tribal and Shê-li armies. This was approved. Henceforth the taxation was somewhat equalized. The masses were delighted.

87, 1b–2a

20. PRIVILEGED POSITION OF NOBLE GROUPS

1041   On the day *chia-shên* [of the second month in the tenth year of Ch'ung-hsi] the northern chancellor said, "[The members of] the administrations of the northern and southern kings, the commanding prefects of various tribes, imperial guardsmen and attendants, all come from noble lineages. Since they are exempt from the frontier garrison service of the common people,[39] I beg that, for their service as attendants also, their retainers may be substituted for them." This request was granted by imperial decree.   *19, 1a*

1044   In the thirteenth year [of Ch'ung-hsi], during the punitive campaign against Hsia, [Yeh-lü] Jên-hsien was left behind to guard the frontier. Not long afterward he was summoned to be chief controller of the Ch'i-tan traveling camps. In a memorial he suggested to exempt from miscellaneous services the court nobles of princely standing and the various palaces.

1047   In the sixteenth year, on being transferred to the position of great king of the Northern Division, he suggested in a memorial that, since the population of the two Divisions was prosperous, the assistance [rendered to them] as labor service by other tribes should be suspended. This was approved.   *96, 1b*

---

[35] We follow other editions in reading 傜 for the 搖 of our text.

[36] We follow other editions in reading 己 for the 巳 of our text.

[37] Two sections of the same watercourse, the modern Sungari River.

[38] Modern Nung-an 農安 County, Kirin.

[39] We follow the Palace edition in reading 民 instead of the 戊 of our text.

21. UNEQUAL DISTRIBUTION OF TRANSPORT SERVICES

1065–1075   During the reign period Hsien-yung, [Ma-Jên-wang] received the *chin-shih* degree and was appointed to the post of magistrate of Sung-shan County.[40]   As the task of yearly transporting government coal[41] from Tsê Prefecture[42] devolved upon Sung-shan alone, [Ma] Jên-wang sent a petition to the vicegerent of the Central Capital, Hsiao T'u-hun, requesting an equalization of the service with other counties.   [Hsiao] T'u-hun became furious and detained him in prison for almost a hundred days.   When he was called in again and questioned, Jên-wang refused to give in.

Hsiao [T'u-hun] was pleased and said, "Since you are so devoted to the people, later on you will certainly be of great service."

The case was reported to the court, and all that was requested was granted.   105, *3a–b*

22. REPAIR OF RIVER DIKES

1074   In the tenth year of Hsien-yung, [Ta Kung-ting][43] obtained the rank of *chin-shih* and was appointed supervisory assistant of Shên Prefecture.[44]   At this time the harvest in Liao-tung had been damaged by rain.   The northern chancellor [ordered] large-scale mobilization of the able-bodied men along the river in order to complete the river dikes.   The authorities who received the order considered it exceedingly urgent, but [Ta] Kung-ting alone said, "Since the frontier regions have just been pacified, starting large-scale works is not the way to benefit the state or to promote the interests of the peasants."   He therefore sent up a memorial on the matter.   The imperial court approved it and discontinued the work.   Nor did the river cause a calamity.   Along the shores of the river for a thousand *li* there was not a person who was not highly pleased.   105, *1b*

23. SOUTHERN FRONTIER FORTIFICATIONS

1077   In the third year [of Ta-k'ang, Hsiao Han-chia][45] marked out the course of the old moat of T'ien-ch'ih[46] on the southwestern frontier where he set up ramparts and strongholds, defined the border,[47] and made inscriptions on stone tablets.   Then he went back.   92, *3b*

24. CONVICT LABORERS

1088   On the day *ting-ch'ou* [of the first month in the fourth year of Ta-an] the convict laborers of the Western Capital[48] were pardoned by special action of the emperor.

25, *2a*

On the day *chia-wu* [of the second month in the fourth year of Ta-an] the convict laborers of Ch'un Prefecture[49] were pardoned by special action of the emperor.   The life term convict laborers were set free after five years.

On the day *chi*[50]-*hai* [the emperor], on a visit to Ch'un Prefecture, pardoned the convict laborers of T'ai Prefecture.[51]   25, *2a*

On the day *ting-ssŭ* [of the fifth month in the fourth year of Ta-an] an imperial decree announced that life-term convict laborers were to be released after five years.   25, *2a*

---

[40] Southwest of modern Ulan Khada, Jehol.

[41] See III, note 72.

[42] North of modern P'ing-ch'üan 平泉 County, Jehol.

[43] An official of Po-hai descent.

[44] Modern Shên-yang 瀋陽, Liaoning.

[45] In 1077 Hsiao Han-chia 韓家 headed the Liao delegation to a joint commission which fixed the boundary between Liao and Sung (LS 92, *3a–b*).

[46] T'ien-ch'ih 天池 corresponds to a place sixty *li* southwest of modern Ning-wu 寧武 County, Shansi.

[47] The southwestern part of border between Liao and Sung started from Tao-ma 倒馬 Pass, went westward through P'ing-hsing 平型 Pass, paralleled the Great Wall to a place west of Yen-mên 雁門 Pass, turned southward to Kuan-ts'ên 管涔 Mountain, and then went north-westward to Ho-ch'ü 河曲 in the northwestern part of Shansi (*cf.* MHPT 24, 162; LTLCT).

Under Tao-tsung the Liao government demanded from Sung the cession of certain territories along the Hsi-ch'ing border. After four years of negotiation the southern empire yielded a strip of land which covered several hundred *li* from east to west (*cf.* JCWP 1, *3a–b*; CWCW 2, 25–27).

[48] Modern Ta-t'ung 大同, Shansi.

[49] Probably southwest of modern Po-tu-na 伯都訥, Kirin.

[50] We follow other editions in reading 己 for the 巳 of our text.

[51] Southwest of modern Nung-an 農安 County, Kirin.

25. CONSTRUCTION OF DWELLINGS

1097   On the day *ping-hsü* [of the sixth month in the third year of Shou-lung] it was decreed that in localities where the emperor stopped on his winter journeys [the officials] from the prime minister down were not to exact labor from the people for the construction of their dwelling-places.   26, *3a*

26. LOCAL SERVICES CONVERTED INTO MONEY PAYMENTS

1101–1125   At this time what the people were deeply disturbed about were the services for the courier post, horses and oxen, banners and drums, village heads,[52] official attendants, and granary offices.   They had reached a state of bankruptcy and were unable to fulfil the obligations.   [Ma] Jên-wang had the people pay money and the government itself engage [men] for the services.   This was then considered convenient.   105, *4b*

27. HUNTING SERVICE

1102   In the seventh month of the autumn [of the second year of Ch'ien-t'ung the emperor] hunted on the Black Mountain.[53]   Because it rained continuously, the huntsmen were supplied with horses.   27, *2b*

1103   On the day *mou-tzŭ* of the fifth month in the summer [of the third year of Ch'ien-t'ung], because many of the huntsmen fled, severe restrictions were set up.   27, *3a*

1113   On the day *ping-tzŭ* [of the first month in the third year of T'ien-ch'ing, when the emperor] hunted in the Kou-ya Mountains, it was bitterly cold and many huntsmen died.   27, *7a*

28. A DIKE

Along the Ling River[54] stones were built up to form a dike.   39, *6b*

---

[52] *Cf.* XIV, 2, notes 28 and 29.
[53] In the northwestern part of modern Jehol.   The region belonged to the administration of Ch'ing 慶 Prefecture (modern Tsaghan Khoton, Jehol).

[54] Modern Ta-ling 大凌 River.   It ran near the I 宜 Prefecture of Liao (modern I 義 County, Liaoning).

SECTION XII

CALAMITIES AND GOVERNMENT RELIEF

INTRODUCTION

1. THE HISTORICAL ASPECT OF NATURAL CALAMITIES

The degree to which natural calamities, such as floods and droughts, extreme cold, and insect pests, influence the course of human events varies with historic circumstance. Both time and place are decisive factors in determining the gravity of any calamity that may befall a people.

Too much rain may affect but little the life of a modern mining community, of an oceanic fishing tribe, or of certain stock-breeders and rainfall agriculturists,[1] but it may so completely ruin the embankment system of a territory dependent on irrigation for its crop that the whole economy would be disorganized and undermined. Lack of rain may be of little economic importance in a modern industrial center or in a coastal fishing village, but it may destroy the grazing grounds of a pastoral tribe and threaten the food-supply of agriculturists whose crops depend upon the local rainfall.[2] Excessive winter cold may do little harm to an agricultural economy if the fields are buried under a heavy snow; but the heavier the snow, the more disastrous it is for the herds of a nomadic people. Locusts reduce the vegetable diet of a fishing tribe, but they do not threaten the main food supply, as they do in a predominantly agricultural community.

The historical setting, therefore, of even a "natural" calamity must be carefully examined before the effect of that calamity on the economic and political life of a people can be properly understood.

2. THE ECONOMIC AND POLITICAL BACKGROUND OF CALAMITIES IN THE LIAO EMPIRE

a. THE CALAMITIES

Within the Liao empire the two main economic divisions, animal husbandry and agriculture, responded in different degree and also in different ways to the calamities suffered. Floods and locusts threat-

ened the crops; droughts endangered both stock-breeding and cultivation; severe cold brought disaster to the herds, particularly if it occurred in the late spring or summer; but, on occasion, it benefited agriculture by putting an end to the destructive locusts.

b. LIMITED UNDERSTANDING

To combat calamities and to give relief was the natural concern of a government that wished to maintain its subjects' ability to pay taxes and to render labor and military service. Yet even an interested government might not act, either because it was not fully aware of the situation or because it was too weak or too poor to pursue a vigorous protective policy.

The Liao government established by conquest had basic difficulties in understanding the sufferings of its conquered peoples and in combating their calamities. The construction of a system of new dikes and canals would have strengthened Liao agriculture; it would have lessened the disastrous effects of droughts and floods. But the mounted Ch'i-tan overlords failed to appreciate the economic advantage of waterworks, although they were quick to recognize that such works interfered with the free movement of the core of their army, the cavalry. Ways of preventing floods and combating droughts were, therefore, neglected rather than promoted. No important waterwork constructions are recorded for the Liao dynasty.[3] In 1074 Ta Kung-ting, an official of Po-hai provenience, argued before the court and presented his reasons for not undertaking any large-scale repairs on river dikes in Liaotung. His decision not to act was upheld, although local officials considered the work most urgent.[4]

Similarly the reluctance of the Ch'i-tan masters to allocate any part of the tax revenue to projects they did not completely understand is evidenced by their failure to deal effectively with the locust pest, although they had before them the example of the Chinese government of the Sung empire which fought the plague aggressively. During the years of the Liao dynasty the voracious insects visited the two empires a number of times, either simultaneously or in close succession. Early in 1017 unfledged locusts were dis-

---

[1] For this term see Wittfogel, OS (ms).

[2] The Egyptians pitied the Greeks because of their dependence upon rainfall instead of river inundation (Herodotus 42, 96 ff.). From their point of view they were right, for they saw little of actual rainfall, their river bottomlands benefiting only from rain that fell on the upper courses of the Nile.

[3] See XI, introduction.

[4] XI (22).

375

covered in many Sung regions, some bordering on southern Liao.[5] A short time later, in the sixth month, mature locusts devastated "all routes" of Sung causing a famine.[6] In the same month they appeared in the southern part of Liao.[7] The famine that followed necessitated large shipments of relief grain to Nan-ching Circuit.[8] In 1102–1103 the locusts destroyed the Sung crops[9] and a year later the plague again reached Liao territory.[10] From 1073 to 1083 the dreaded insects attacked both empires as shown by table 14.

TABLE 14

MOVEMENTS OF LOCUSTS BETWEEN 1073 AND 1083

LOCUSTS IN LIAO	REFERENCE	LOCUSTS IN SUNG	REFERENCE
1073	LS 23, 2a	1073	SS 62, 13b
		1074	SS 62, 13b
		1075	SS 62, 13b
1076	23, 4b	1076	SS 62, 13b
1077	23, 5a		
1081	24, 3a	1081	SS 62, 13b
		1082	SS 62, 13b
		1083	SS 62, 13b

Between 1073 and 1077 the locusts traveled back and forth between the two countries concentrating in 1074 and 1075 in the southern region, after their spectacular departure from the northern empire in the fall of 1073.[11] From 1077 to 1081 nothing is said concerning the plague, but such an omission does not necessarily mean its complete eradication; a short interlude also occurred in Cyprus after a campaign to destroy locust eggs in 1881.[12] Dry and barren heights like those of the border hills of modern Hopei and Shansi offer an ideal breeding ground for the insects.[13] It is therefore probable that some locusts survived in this southern zone of the Liao empire where they had last conspicuously appeared in 1077. After 1081 they again attacked the crops of China Proper until nature, in 1082 and 1083, put a temporary stop to their disastrous visits. In the late fall of 1082 a heavy blizzard swept the traveling camp of the Liao emperor[14] and in 1083 an unseasonable summer snow fell in the northern empire.[15] Since summer is the grow-

ing season of young locusts in China,[16] this snow must have put a quick end to their possible increase; for a number of years no serious locust blight is recorded for either country. What insects appeared in 1088 in three districts of Nan-ching were evidently not too threatening, for they were adequately taken care of by the birds.[17] Others, noted in one Sung locality in 1098, died while hatching.[18] The first disastrous descent after the summer snows of 1083 is recorded twenty years later, in 1102 in Sung China[19] and in 1104 in the Liao empire.[20]

Thus locusts appeared in both empires, sometimes simultaneously, sometimes in alternating attacks. How did the two governments react? Even though locusts are difficult to combat, some few measures can be taken to check their increase. Paramount among them is the gathering and destroying of the larvae while they are still unwinged.[21]

This method, considered most effective by the Chinese,[22] was employed by the Sung administration in 1074 and 1075.[23] No such measures are reported by Liao officials. At the close of the dynasty, when the benevolent Ch'i-tan, Hsiao Wên, was advised, probably by his Chinese underlings, to exterminate the locusts by catching them, he refused to act and instead recommended critical self-examination: "The locusts are a visitation from heaven. What benefit can be gained from catching them?"[24] The reference to self-examination sounds very Chinese, but it must not be forgotten that even Lao Tzŭ's saints resorted to action when necessary, and that Confucius recommended inaction only for the ruler, not for his officials. The Chinese Sage, himself, did not fail to act when action was needed; and the Sung administrators, who were certainly as well versed in the classics as their Ch'i-tan contemporary, Hsiao Wên, were not afraid to take practical measures against the locusts, no doubt quoting the classics while so doing.

It was therefore not a Chinese way of thinking that induced Hsiao Wên to remain passive. Rather it was his lack of understanding that made him unwilling to act and led him to misinterpret Chinese thought. He did not hesitate to take strong measures against abuses familiar to him, but he was loathe to drain the government treasury for a program that was alien to his tribal tradition. On another occasion the officials in charge of a locust-ridden region failed to

---

[5] SS 62, 13a ff.

[6] SS 8, 16a; 62, 13a.

[7] XII (37).

[8] XII (38).

[9] SS 19, 9b, 11b; 62, 13b.

[10] XII (112).

[11] XII (63).

[12] See Locusts, 858.

[13] Locusts, 857 and 859. *Cf.* also a Chinese description of the phenomena in question in CHCF 1, 2a ff.

[14] XII (84).

[15] *Loc. cit.*

[16] CHCF 1, 3b.

[17] XII (95).

[18] SS 62, 13b.

[19] SS 62, 13b.

[20] XII (112).

[21] Locusts, 859.

[22] CHCF 1, 3a.

[23] SS 62, 13a.

[24] XII (107).

report any action against them; it was enough to hope for the disappearance of the insects across the Sung border or to watch their destruction by the wasps.[25]

c. LIMITED MEANS OF SUPPORT

Although the Ch'i-tan rulers did not fully understand the country they had conquered, they did not hesitate to offer aid when they thought it was seriously threatened. Depending as they did upon the grain produced in the agricultural sector, they had every reason to combat the recurring calamities with all relief measures known to them. After paying little attention in the first decades to the sufferings of its new subjects, the Liao government suddenly became sympathetically aware of their destitution and despair. During the Liao-Sung war the conquered Chinese in the North saw the armies of Sung China meet and at times even defeat the armies of their Ch'i-tan conquerors. The political situation then was as tense as it was provocative; in 991 Yeh-lü Lung-yün complained of the recalcitrant behavior of the population of Nan-ching;[26] in 995 charity granaries were set up,[27] and the government's relief policy was institutionalized.

It remained institutionalized but, as elsewhere, the amount of relief actually distributed depended upon more than a general political attitude and the establishment of public storehouses. The administration needed to understand the mechanics of calamities and crises; this it did only to a limited degree. It had to have adequate means; and here the Liao government was hampered by those same difficulties that interfered with an effective relief policy—difficulties rooted either in the dual administrative and political structure of Liao society or in the growing crisis within the agricultural sector. The dual structure of the Liao administration reduced the effectiveness of government measures even when these measures were eagerly implemented. Economically speaking, government action was considerably weakened by the dual drain which decreased the country's public reserves of grain and money. The Ch'i-tan officials secretly or openly appropriated funds urgently needed to meet government expenses.[28] In addition, the Chinese officials, inadequately checked by their incompetent masters, carried to excess the traditional misappropriation of government property.[29]

The complete history of the inefficiency and corruption of the Liao administration will probably never be known. But with the passing years, the inefficiency seems to have decreased, at least temporarily, while the corruption or "drain" increased. More funds were appropriated privately when the government faced a shrinkage in tax income and a diminution in available labor power. At such times an increasing number of people and an increasing amount of land and money were accumulated by the country's powerful families and by the Buddhist temples. Rich individuals[30] and temples[31] strove hard, and probably often with success, to avoid taxation and corvée for their retainers as well as for themselves. In general, the wealthy land owners were "rarely heard of as paying taxes" at all.[32] More persons entered the "tenancy sector,"[33] fewer taxpayers were subject to government control, and less manpower was available for labor and military service.

As the inner resources of the country decreased so did its tribute income from abroad. Aggressive warfare and military success were greatest before the middle and at the end of the tenth century. Then a political and economic saturation point seems to have been reached, and the Ch'i-tan rulers, unable to conquer China Proper, settled down to enjoy the fruits of partial victory.[34] Looting decreased as did the income from "subordinate" peoples beyond the border. The treaty of 1042 once again swelled the tributary revenue of the Liao government, but the political history of the period shows clearly that the Ch'i-tan were already "going soft"; they preferred negotiations to war and a comfortable income to risk and hardship. As might be expected, the visits of tributary missions were most frequent in the middle and at the end of the tenth century. They then decreased conspicuously; after a minor upsurge in the middle of the eleventh century they continued to decline, not paralleling so much as following upon the inner decay of the empire.[35]

The shrinkage of the taxable sector and the decline of the tributary income resulted in more pressure on those whose surplus and labor power were still accessible to the government. The efficient officials, Yang Tsun-hsü, who collected four hundred million cash in back taxes, Liu Shên, who submitted an additional annual revenue of three hundred million

---

[25] XII (63).
[26] See XI (13).
[27] XII (20) (21).
[28] See VIII and X, 1, *passim.*
[29] *Cf.* Gabelentz 77, 56.

[30] See VIII (3). In this case the government took action after approximately thirty years, but whether effectively we do not know.
[31] *Cf.* CS 96, 4*b.* In the case reported in this passage the government did not interfere until the end of the dynasty. See also IX, introduction.
[32] X, 1 (43).
[33] Wittfogel, OS (ms).
[34] See XIII.
[35] See X, introduction.

cash,[36] and Ma Jên-wang, who quickly filled a completely empty treasury,[37] all functioned toward the end of the Liao dynasty. Their efficiency increased the funds available for relief, but the ways in which the relief funds were augmented weakened the very people who were economically most vulnerable and who would be hit hardest by any serious calamity.

3. FORMS OF GOVERNMENT RELIEF

a. FISCAL AND CHARITY MEASURES

In spite of the psychological and economic limitations inherent in its structure, the Liao government developed a number of devices for combating calamities and mitigating their effect. When the inhabitants of a county or prefecture suffered from a disastrous drought or flood, or from the visitation of locusts, they often were unable to fulfill their fiscal obligations. In such a situation, tax exemption for the year would be a natural alleviating measure. It is doubtful whether this was always granted even when it was necessary, and it is equally doubtful whether, once granted, it was always properly administered. But it is certain that this was a measure which the government would favor, for it involved no disbursement of official funds, only the renunciation of a none too sure income. In administering relief the Liao government frequently suspended annual tax payments or cancelled back taxes;[38] at times the amount paid was reduced by raising the price of the grain accepted for the land tax in lieu of money.[39]

When the calamities were severe, such negative measures as tax exemption or reduction had to be supplemented by positive acts of relief. The starving were given food.[40] Peasants or tribesmen who had lost their draft animals or herds received a grant in kind.[41] The destitute, whether sedentary or nomadic, were supplied with textiles[42] and money.[43] It is probable that when the records speak of "relief" without any further qualification[44] it falls into these categories, with gifts of grain the most usual. Suspension or mitigation of the corvée[45] did not bring immediate aid to the starving villagers, but it did permit them to

devote themselves to their own farmwork without interruption. Recourse to this form of relief is proof that the corvée tended to restrict the productive activity of the people for their own needs.

b. THE GRANARIES

Relief grain was kept in granaries—public storehouses similar to those reported for other politically centralized "Oriental" countries.[46] The importance of such storage places to an organized system of governmental relief has often been noted, but they served other purposes as well. The Liao texts emphasize their various functions and clarify, at least to some degree, the relation between government grain, government storehouses, and Charity Granaries.

As soon as the Liao empire established control over large agricultural areas, it must have begun to store grain. Tax grain was kept in storehouses which, like the treasury, constituted part of the country's fiscal machinery. Revenue grain might be issued for relief,[47] but this was not its main use. It was paid out by the government to meet the regular expenditures of the court, the officials, and the army. The Fair Purchase Granaries (ho ti ts'ang 和糴倉), which are described in LS 59 for Tung-ching Circuit, were military and not charitable.[48] Following the pattern of the T'ang dynasty,[49] their officials were expected to buy grain from the people in a "harmonious" or "fair" way (ho), and to maintain a considerable grain reserve for possible military campaigns. The Fair Purchase Granaries of Tung-ching evidently fulfilled this purpose, for they remained well stocked "in spite of frequent military expeditions."[50] Whether the purchases were concluded more "harmoniously" than during the T'ang period, we do not know. In the latter dynasty the military authorities acquired their grain stores with increasing ruthlessness; near its close the peasants were lucky to obtain any payment at all.[51]

The military granaries along the eastern frontier of the Liao empire had their counterpart in the northwest. There the grain was produced by soldier farmers rather than by peasants.[52] The regulation prohibiting the lending of grain to the people "without authority"[53] indicates that abuses of this kind actually occurred. Yet the grain loans granted by the Fair Purchase Granaries of Tung-ching at an official rate

---

[36] VI, 1 (1) 1055–1101.

[37] X, 1 (66).

[38] XII (1) (9—remission of back taxes) (80—taxes reduced) and passim.

[39] XII (8). See also X, introduction.

[40] XII (70) (85) (87).

[41] XII (10) (103).

[42] XII (89) (90) (96) (102) (108).

[43] XII (35—money or possibly grain) (50) (70) (101) (102) (117).

[44] XII (2) (4).

[45] XII (3) (15—two records pertaining to two different prefectures) (78); XI (16).

[46] See Wittfogel, OS (ms).

[47] XII (91).

[48] XII (119).

[49] Cf. Balázs 32 BWT, 69.

[50] See note 48.

[51] Balázs 32 BWT, 70.

[52] II, 2 (8) (9).

[53] Loc. cit.

of twenty per cent show that, when authorized, this was a legitimate practice.[54]

Price Equalization Granaries (*ch'ang p'ing ts'ang* 常平倉) of the traditional Chinese type[55] are not reported for Liao. The Ch'i-tan government might well have continued the economic policy of the preceding dynasty, but while clearly recognizing the value of government granaries for military needs it was less receptive to a program of buying and selling grain to maintain a normal price level. Here again, as in the construction of waterworks or in the fight against locusts, the tribal rulers were reluctant to use the government machine for purposes alien to their traditional economy.

Whatever objections might have been raised to the establishment of relief granaries were overruled by the pressures of the Sung war. In 995 "Charity Granaries" (*i ts'ang* 義倉) were set up. The word *i* implies both duty and communal welfare, as does the English word "public." These granaries were local institutions connected with the village altar (社), the center of all local public affairs.[56] Contributions to them were obligatory[57] and constituted an additional tax. Grain that had been stored might be distributed without charge;[58] during the great war against Sung relief of this kind was customary. After the war granary grain was loaned out.[59] In general, the lending of grain and money increased in the latter part of the Liao dynasty.[60]

c. OTHER FORMS OF RELIEF

The diverse measures for relief mentioned in the texts indicate the complexity of the economic tasks which faced the Liao government. If the people felt threatened by forced registration of their fields, the measure might be suspended;[61] if duties levied at the passes interfered with the importation of grain into a starving region, they might be temporarily discontinued;[62] if a heavy snow made it difficult to locate fuel, permission might be given to gather it from lands usually reserved to the emperor;[63] if rich people were able to aid their poor neighbors, the administration might press them to do so.[64] In 1013, when a serious calamity had forced the destitute everywhere

to sell their relatives into bondage, the government made it possible for those who had been pledged to regain their freedom.[65] This entailed no basic condemnation of slavery,[66] for during the famine of 1088 the government officially sanctioned the right of a subject to sell himself into slavery as a means of meeting an emergency.[67]

d. MIGRANTS, REFUGEES, AND RESETTLEMENT ON THE LAND

The government, however, was directly concerned with the fate of those individuals who were forced to abandon land and home because of unfavorable economic or political conditions. The Ch'i-tan treated the large Chinese populations that had fallen under their rule in a typically Chinese way. Newcomers were frequently settled on abandoned lands, but the graduated penalties for flight encouraged fugitives to return and again cultivate their fields.

An order of the Liao government issued in 982 has been preserved by a local gazetteer: "Barbarians as well as Chinese may take over the deserted land as tenants, paying to the government land tax and other taxes (*tsu shui* 租稅). If the migrant returns to his property within five years, two-thirds of it shall be given back to him. If he returns within ten or fifteen years, he may regain one-half or one-third respectively."[68] This law is similar to a decree issued in 955 by the last of the Five Dynasties, the Later Chou, which penalized a migrant who returned within three years by withholding one-half of his property; if he returned within five years, he lost two-thirds; after an absence of five years he forfeited all his cultivated fields and mulberry trees. His only hope was to regain possession of those lands that had not been farmed during his absence.[69]

Abandoning his land, the migrant also refused to recognize his civil obligations; he evaded his tax payments and avoided military and labor service. The government, therefore, took strong measures against such deserters. Refugees of war, however, fell into a different category and were differently treated; the "floating people" (流民) were resettled[70] and temporarily exempted from taxation,[71] a procedure not dissimilar to the granting of wasteland to ordinary settlers who were also exempted from land

[54] XII (119).
[55] *Cf.* Balázs 32 BWT, 67.
[56] XI (12); XII (21).
[57] XII (21) (28).
[58] XII (27).
[59] XI (16).
[60] See VI, 2 and introduction.
[61] XII (11).
[62] XII (4).
[63] XII (62).
[64] XII (25) (116).

[65] XII (34).
[66] See VII, introduction.
[67] XII (93).
[68] *Hsüan-hua Fu Chên Chih* = LSSI 6, 8a.
[69] WTHY 25, 14a.
[70] XII (23).
[71] XII (24).

tax[72] and, in one case, even from labor service for ten years.[73]

e. MAGIC DEVICES

Although the governments of the more advanced agricultural societies recognized the need for combating the ever present threat of drought or flood by such realistic measures as the construction of waterworks, they never completely relinquished their faith in the efficacy of magic performance. However, the magic "relief" of the Ch'i-tan rulers of Liao, most frequent in the early years of the dynasty,[74] reflected in no small degree their tribal interests and traditions. The pastoral economy of Inner Asia was more at the mercy of drought than of flood, and it is not surprising to find that the magic of the Ch'i-tan was directed mainly toward insuring a more abundant rainfall. They were less well prepared to deal magically with too much water, and little prepared to meet either calamity realistically in an agricultural society.

During the first period of the Liao dynasty rain magic was eagerly resorted to in fighting drought, but government relief to the suffering agricultural regions was slight indeed until the close of the tenth century. Then the long and difficult war against the powerful Sung empire created such poverty and restlessness among the Chinese subjects of Liao that the government could no longer afford to fight a calamity by occasional measures or by magic ceremonies, such as the pouring of water by one official upon another or by imperial prayers offered in a pool.

Magic practices did not disappear when the Charity Granary system was established in 995; still compatible with the existing civilization, they continued with full solemnity.[75] However, after the outbreak of the great Sung war the realistic Chinese forms of relief were quickly instituted, culminating, it would seem, in the granary edicts of the year 995. From that time on both magic and practical measures were employed as in the typically Chinese dynasties,[76] but with one significant difference: the Ch'i-tan rulers retained their confidence in the rain magic of their former and purely pastoral society.

4. THE RISE AND FALL OF INSTITUTIONALIZED RELIEF IN THE LIAO EMPIRE

An examination of the changing attitudes of the Liao government toward impending or actual disasters

during the course of the dynasty is revealing for any historical analysis of the period. The social and psychological biases of the tribal conquerors and the Chinese bureaucracy, the economic and political antagonisms within the empire, the Sung war, and the development of an inner crisis, all affected the country's relief policy.

During the first period of victorious expansion few relief measures are recorded, not because there were no calamities, but because the war-intoxicated Ch'i-tan paid little attention to them. Their mounted warriors enriched themselves from the huge booty seized from neighboring tribes and China's Five Dynasties. The conquered agricultural peoples were too crushed by the horrors of war and by the mass deportations that followed to offer any serious political resistance. The lack of organized relief persisted even in the face of great disasters which the Liao rulers still preferred to cure by magic rather than by practical measures.

The war against Sung was not as simple as the campaigns against the preceding "dynasties." With several interruptions it lasted from 979 to 1005, that is, longer than the reign of any of the Five Dynasties. For the first time the Liao armies were confronted by a united Chinese empire which, instead of yielding territory upon territory, endeavored to regain what had been lost over generations of weakness and disintegration. Sung China did not win the war; the lost border regions of the North remained in the hands of the Ch'i-tan who, in addition, collected a large annual "tribute." But the Liao empire, although successful, achieved no full victory such as made the Jurchen masters of North China and the Mongols inheritors of the whole Sung empire. The difficult war taxed the resources of the Liao government to the utmost; and it was at this very time that the unrest in the Chinese sector was most threatening. The government was quick to recognize the critical situation and quick to counteract it; taxes were remitted, relief was distributed, and in 983 labor service was discontinued "in order to aid the hungry and the poor."[77] Reports reached the capital that the peasants had dropped their work and deserted their crops and homes.[78] The Chinese of Nan-ching Circuit in general displayed a tricky and uncooperative attitude.[79] In the light of this situation we have to understand the government's resettlement program,[80] the interruption of the land survey in 991,[81] the

[72] II, 2 (16) and *passim*.
[73] II, 2 (20).
[74] VII, 2 (26) (71).
[75] XII (107); see also VII, 2 (71).
[76] Hsiao Wên, under the influence of Chinese etiquette and education, did not engage in the Ch'i-tan ceremonies of spilling water, shooting at trees, and standing in water; he prayed instead (XII (107)).

[77] XII (3).
[78] XII (6).
[79] XI (13).
[80] *Cf.* II, 2 (11) (16); XII (23).
[81] XII (11).

numerous tax remissions,[82] and the various individual relief measures.[83] The new government policy was climaxed by the establishment of the Charity Granaries in the year 995. The peasants were often unable to contribute their share, but failure to do so was treated with indulgence;[84] enough grain had been concentrated to make distribution over all Nan-ching possible.[85] Government-owned grain was given to the destitute as a grant, not as a loan. In all probability the new granary system hastened the successful conclusion of the campaign against Sung, for by stabilizing conditions at home it enabled the Liao government to promote its military and political aims abroad.

The war against Korea which ended in 1020 retarded but did not block the empire's return to normalcy. Calamities continued to be the concern of the government, and relief was liberally distributed, but with an important modification: now the granaries made grain loans, not grain gifts, to the people.[86] The improved situation explains the victorious government's ability to utilize the economic strength of the peasantry. Sung China, besides making its annual contribution of silk and silver, was forced to aid the northern empire's consolidation still further: in 1009 and 1010, when both countries suffered from floods,[87] the southern government had to sell its powerful neighbor two hundred thousand bushels of grain, at what price we do not know.[88] The victory over Sung did not make the Liao administration more waterwork-conscious. After 1005 the emperor treated himself to a new capital, Central Capital, but no great strengthening of the country's river dikes is recorded. The inundation of 1011 caused such distress that a mass sale of people into slavery followed. Neither in that year nor in 1031 did the government prevent disaster from flood; however, it acted vigorously, and probably with some success, to mitigate the inevitable devastation.

Except for a few campaigns such as that against Korea and Hsia, the period after 1005 was a time of peace and consolidation. The calamities were less frequent and less severe. The golden age of Liao had come. The agricultural population relaxed; its importance within the economy of the empire grew and with it grew the social, political, and cultural influence of the Chinese sector. But this golden age was of short duration. The Liao empire was poorly protected against those inner contradictions which were intensified as the consolidation of its agrarian economy advanced. The rapid growth of banditry after the "thirties" reveals a rapidly deteriorating economic situation.[89]

The new calamities that befell the empire after 1068 were met by a government still active and resourceful, but this resourcefulness was a symptom not of a growing but of a declining power. The increasingly impoverished population was increasingly sensitive to the recurring national disasters. Was the reduction of the herds by the summer frost of 1083 compensated for by 1086?[90] No answer is possible until we know how many horses the empire possessed before 1083. However, it is interesting to note that the tribes needed and received all kinds of relief after 1086. Suffering severely from malnutrition and oppression, the rural population disintegrated with amazing speed. Migrants, this time not refugees of war but of peace, became a serious problem which the government made great effort to solve[91] but without success. In 1087 "a large number of people had wandered off and become scattered." The severe regulations concerning migrants could no longer be upheld.[92] Two months after their cancellation another edict ordered the Office of the Ministry of Revenue to give out tax grain for relief. The fiscal granaries had to be opened; the Charity Granaries were no longer able to cope with the emergency.

The history of the last decades of the dynasty is filled with reports of calamities and relief measures taken to meet them. While the government's strength waned, adversity stalked the country with unabated, nay, with increased fury. The final records have much to say about disasters and little or nothing about relief. In 1119, when the people in the richest agricultural circuit, Nan-ching, ate the bark of trees and finally resorted to cannibalism, the relief system of Liao was completely bankrupt. Its collapse coincided with the collapse of the administrative and political order of the empire itself.

---

[82] XII (7) (9) and *passim*.
[83] XII (8) and *passim*.
[84] XII (26) (28).
[85] XII (27).
[86] XII (119).
[87] Liao: XII (31). Sung: SS 61, 9a; 91, 6a–b; 93, 20b.
[88] SS 7, 24a.

[89] XIII, introduction.
[90] II, 1 (20).
[91] XII (58) (65) (78).
[92] XII (88).

TRANSLATION

CALAMITIES AND GOVERNMENT RELIEF

1. Remission of land tax 2. Relief for the lonely and poor 3. Bad crops and locusts 4. A disastrous year 5. The people of the Southern Division 6. War relief 7. Relief for war and famine 8. Rate of conversion changed 9. Remission of taxes 10. Frontier people receive livestock 11. Tribes in distress 12. Calamities in Nan-ching 13. An earthquake 14. Remission of taxes 15. Refugees from the war zone 16. Floods destroy crops 17. Land near imperial residences untaxed 18. Remission of taxes 19. Flood in Nan-ching 20. Granaries 21. Local granary system centered at village altar 22. Large-scale remission of taxation 23. Settlement of refugees 24. Remission of taxes 25. Rich people urged to support poor tribesmen 26. Remission of taxes and grain 27. Granary grain distributed 28. Agriculture aided 29. Flood relief in Shang-ching 30. Famine relief 31. A flood in the central region of Liao 32. Relief for Nan-ching 33. Famine relief 34. People given into bondage 35. The interest of an ordo used for relief 36. Relief 37. Locusts in Nan-ching 38. Famine in Nan-ching 39. Famine relief and other charities 40. An earthquake 41. A flood in Nan-ching 42. A big flood 43. Famine relief 44. Relief to a tribe 45. Peaceful times 46. The P'in tribe 47. Remission of taxes 48. Nan-ching 49. A kindhearted and popular official 50. Military funds used to support the poor 51. Locusts in Chung-ching 52. An earthquake 53. A drought 54. Calamities in Nan-ching 55. Famine relief 56. Rain and earthquake 57. A flood in Nan-ching 58. Remission of land-tax 59. Remission of taxes 60. Relief given 61. Famine relief 62. Various forms of relief 63. Locusts in Nan-ching 64. The traveling route of the emperor 65. Returned refugees rewarded 66. A drought 67. Famine relief 68. A conflagration 69. Famine relief 70. Relief measures for Nan-ching 71. Famine relief 72. Remission of taxes 73. An earthquake in Nan-ching 74. A famine in Liao-tung 75. No imperial inspection tour 76. Locusts in southern Liao 77. Famine relief 78. Relief for Nan-ching 79. Returned refugees rewarded 80. Remission or reduction of taxes 81. Locusts in Nan-ching 82. Relief for ordos and frontier guards 83. Floods in Nan-ching 84. Blizzards decimate animals 85. Acting and retired officials organize relief 86. Relief in Nan-ching 87. Famine relief 88. Regulations concerning refugees abolished 89. Grants and remissions 90. Silk for poor tribespeople 91. The grain of the Ministry of Revenue 92. Remission of taxes 93. Free persons may sell themselves 94. Relief 95. Birds destroy locusts 96. Oxen and cloth as relief 97. Relief for the Northwestern Route 98. Relief 99. Increased storage 100. Relief to refugees of Nan-ching 101. Relief money for the northwest 102. Several kinds of relief 103. Relief for tribes and frontier troops 104. Flood relief in Nan-ching 105. Poor tribesmen resettled 106. Relief for Liao Prefecture and for *Chiu* units 107. Magic help for all kinds of distress 108. Relief silk 109. Remission of taxes 110. Flood relief 111. Rain and hail 112. Locusts in Nan-ching 113. A frost 114. Remission of taxes 115. A great famine 116. Relief for unruly tribesmen 117. Money for the poor of Nan-ching 118. Famine raises grain prices 119. The granary system of Tung-ching

1. REMISSION OF LAND TAX

953   Because Nan-ching suffered from a flood, a decree ordered the remission of the land tax for this year. 6, 3a

2. RELIEF FOR THE LONELY AND POOR

976   On the day *hsin-wei* of the third month [in the eighth year of Pao-ning] five commissioners were sent to investigate the empire's widowers, widows, orphans, and single old people as well as the poor and jobless in order to give relief to them. 8, 5a

3. BAD CROPS AND LOCUSTS

983   In the fifth year of the reign period Ch'ien-hêng of Shêng-tsung[1] an imperial decree declared, "As the five crops have not ripened, tax-paying by the people shall be replaced by opening up the national treasury.[2] As caterpillars and locusts have caused distress, forced labor shall be discontinued in order to aid the hungry and the poor." 59, 2a

---

[1] See V, note 22.

[2] We follow other editions in reading 藏 after the word 帑.

4. A DISASTROUS YEAR

983   On the first day *kuei-ch'ou* of the ninth month [in the first year of T'ung-ho], because the Eastern Capital and P'ing Prefecture[3] suffered from drought and locusts, an imperial decree ordered that relief be given to them.   10, 5a

On the day *ping-ch'ên* [of the ninth month in the first year of T'ung-ho] the vicegerent of the Southern Capital memorialized that continuous autumn rains had ruined the crops, and requested that the duties levied at [Chü-yung] Pass[4] be temporarily discontinued so as to open a way for the purchase of grain from Shan-hsi.   This was approved.   10, 5a

5. THE PEOPLE OF THE SOUTHERN DIVISION

986   On the day *mou-wu* [of the tenth month in the fourth year of T'ung-ho], because of a suggestion made by the great king of the Southern Division, Liu-ning,[5] the tribespeople of the Southern Division were exempted from this year's land tax and other taxes.   11, 7b

6. WAR RELIEF

986   The grand preceptor, Han Tê-jang,[6] said, "Since the war[7] began the refugees have been giving up their occupations.   The crops remain in the fields.   Men should be enlisted to harvest them and should in return be given[8] half of [the yield]."

The chief of the Political Council, Shih Fang, also said, "Since the various prefectures of Shan-hsi[9] began to supply the army the people's strength has been dissipated[10] and most of the grain in the fields has been trampled down by the frontier troops."   He requested the remission of this year's land tax.   59, 2a–b

7. RELIEF FOR WAR AND FAMINE

986   [Han Tê-jang] memorialized, "The prefectures of the west[11] have repeatedly suffered from wars, and in addition there is a famine this year.   Therefore it is advisable that the taxes be lightened so as to induce the refugees to return."   This was approved.   82, 1b

8. RATE OF CONVERSION CHANGED

988   [On the day *ting-ch'ou* of the eighth month in the sixth year of T'ung-ho] the commanding prefect of Ta-t'ung Commandery,[12] Yeh-lü Mo-chih, memorialized that this year, because of frost and drought, there was a scarcity of food, and asked that the price for the conversion of grain be increased in order to benefit the poor people.[13]   This was approved by imperial decree.   12, 2b–3a

9. REMISSION OF TAXES

989   On the day *chi-ch'ou* [of the third month in the seventh year of T'ung-ho] a decree ordered the remission of the taxes owed by Yün Prefecture.[14]   12, 5b

10. FRONTIER PEOPLE RECEIVE LIVESTOCK

989   On the day *i-hai* [of the sixth month in the seventh year of T'ung-ho] a decree ordered that various kinds of animals should be taken out and given to the poor people of the frontier regions.   12, 6b

---

[3] Modern Lu-lung 盧龍 County in the northeastern corner of Hopei.

[4] Northwest of the Southern Capital.   *Cf.* V (4).

[5] Liu-ning 留寧 was the style of Yeh-lü Hai-li 海里. He occupied the office of great king of the Southern Division for more than ten years (LS 84, 3b–4a).

[6] Han Tê-jang made this statement in 986 (LS 11, 6a–b).

[7] The war between Liao and Sung started in 979 and ended in 1005.

[8] We follow the Palace edition in reading 給 for the 拾 of our text.

[9] *Cf.* V, note 25.

[10] After 凋 other editions have the word 敝 which is omitted in our text.

[11] Northern Shansi.

[12] Modern Ta-t'ung 大同 County, Shansi.

[13] This evidently means that the tax burden of the people was to be lightened by raising the money price of the grain which they turned over to the government, thus actually reducing the amount of grain to be paid.

[14] Modern Ta-t'ung County, Shansi.

11. TRIBES IN DISTRESS

990　　　　　On the day *kêng-wu* [of the fourth month in the eighth year of T'ung-ho] all tribes which, because of the year's drought, had difficulty in feeding themselves were given relief.　　13, 1*a*

990　　　　　On the day *kêng-yin* of the eleventh month [in the eighth year of T'ung-ho], because the T'u-yü-hun[15] people suffered from famine, they were given relief.　　13, 2*a*

991　　　　　On the day *hsin-mao* [of the first month in the ninth year of T'ung-ho] an imperial decree ordered a remission of the taxes of the circuits of the three capitals.[16]　The registration of the fields was also discontinued.　　13, 2*a*

12. CALAMITIES IN NAN–CHING

991　　　　　During this month [the sixth month of the ninth year of T'ung-ho] continuous rain damaged the crops in Nan-ching.　　13, 2*b*

13. AN EARTHQUAKE

991　　　　　[On the day *chi-yu* of the ninth month in the ninth year of T'ung-ho] there was an earthquake in Nan-ching.　　13, 3*a*

14. REMISSION OF TAXES

992　　　　　On the day *jên-wu* [of the second month in the tenth year of T'ung-ho], Yün Prefecture was exempted from the land tax and other taxes.　　13, 3*b*

On the day *hsin-mao* the refugees of Yün Prefecture were granted exemption from their regular obligations.[17]　　13, 3*b*

15. REFUGEES FROM THE WAR ZONE

992　　　　　On the first day *kuei-ssŭ*[18] of the fifth month [in the tenth year of T'ung-ho] the refugees of Shuo Prefecture[19] were granted exemption from their regular obligations for three years.　　13, 3*b*

16. FLOODS DESTROY CROPS

993　　　　　In the sixth month [of the eleventh year of T'ung-ho] heavy rains fell.　On the day *chi-ch'ou* of the seventh month in the autumn the Sang-ch'ien and Yang Rivers[20] overflowed.　West of the Chü-yung Pass[21] the crops were almost completely ruined and most of the inhabitants' dwellings in Fêng-shêng[22] and the Southern Capital[23] were submerged.　　13, 4*a*

17. LAND NEAR IMPERIAL RESIDENCES UNTAXED

994　　　　　[On the day *chia-yin* of the first month in the twelfth year of T'ung-ho] an imperial decree ordered the remission of the land tax within fifty *li* of the emperor's traveling residences.[24]　　13, 4*a*

---

[15] See I, 2 (10), no. 25.

[16] Probably the Southern, Western, and Eastern Capitals, for the inhabitants of these regions were particularly affected by the war with Sung and Korea. These were also the predominantly agricultural areas.

[17] That is, from the ordinary taxes and labor services.

[18] LS 44, 16*b* and Hoang 10, 439 give *chia-wu* (no. 31 in the sexagenary cycle) for the first day, in place of the *kuei-ssŭ* (no. 30) of our text.

[19] Modern Shuo 朔 County, Shansi.

[20] In modern Chahar and Hopei.

[21] Northwest of Peiping.

[22] Modern Cho-lu 涿鹿 County, Chahar.

[23] Modern Peiping.

[24] When the emperor went on his seasonal hunting tours, he was accompanied by a retinue of several thousand persons. This cavalcade, which also included numerous horses, hunting birds, etc., might remain at one place for a whole season. The many supplies required in such cases generally had to be furnished by the people of nearby regions. The measure described in the present passage was obviously calculated to keep the population along the imperial routes in a friendly spirit.

18. REMISSION OF TAXES

994   On the day *mou-wu* [of the first month in the twelfth year of T'ung-ho] there was a remission of the *tiao* and other taxes[25] of I Prefecture.[26]   13, 4a

19. FLOOD IN NAN–CHING

994   On the day *chia-shên* of the second month [in the twelfth year of T'ung-ho] the flood-stricken families of Nan-ching were exempted from the land tax and other taxes.

13, 4b

20. GRANARIES

995   On the day *i-hai* of the tenth month in the winter [of the thirteenth year of T'ung-ho] Charity Granaries[27] were established.   13, 6b

21. LOCAL GRANARY SYSTEM CENTERED AT VILLAGE ALTAR

995   In the thirteenth year [of T'ung-ho] it was decreed that all routes should establish Charity Granaries.   In the autumn of each year each family belonging to a village altar was to provide grain in accordance with its harvest for storage in the granaries.   The office of the altar was to keep a record of the amounts.   When the year's harvest was poor, the grain was to be given out to relieve the people.   59, 2b

22. LARGE–SCALE REMISSION OF TAXATION

996   On the day *ting-ssŭ* [of the first month in the fourteenth year of T'ung-ho] there was a remission of the taxes of the three capitals[28] and all the prefectures.   13, 7a

23. SETTLEMENT OF REFUGEES

996   On the day *chia-tzŭ* [of the third month in the fourteenth year of T'ung-ho] an imperial decree ordered the refugees of Shuo Prefecture to be settled.   13, 7a

24. REMISSION OF TAXES

997   On the day *i-wei* [of the first month in the fifteenth year of T'ung-ho] there was a remission of taxes for refugees.   13, 8a

25. RICH PEOPLE URGED TO SUPPORT POOR TRIBESMEN

997   On the day *mou-hsü* [of the second month in the fifteenth year of T'ung-ho] the rich people of the P'in tribe[29] were urged to donate money for the support of the poor.

13, 8a

26. REMISSION OF TAXES AND GRAIN

997   On the day *jên-wu* [of the third month in the fifteenth year of T'ung-ho] a general census of individuals and families in the ordos was made.   There was a remission of the taxes owed by Nan-ching and of the grain for the Charity Granaries.   13, 8a–b

27. GRANARY GRAIN DISTRIBUTED

997   On the day *jên-yin* [of the fourth month in the fifteenth year of T'ung-ho] the grain of the Charity Granaries was given out to relieve the people of the various counties in Nan-ching.   13, 8b

---

[25] The term *tiao* 調 means the tax paid in textiles.

[26] Near present I 義 County, Liaoning.

[27] This kind of granary was first set up in A.D. 583 under the Sui dynasty by Chang-sun P'ing 長孫平 (T. 處均; d. 601–604). In view of frequently occurring famines, he ordered the establishment of local granaries to which millet and wheat had to be contributed by the people every autumn according to their status.   In case of drought or flood the grain was distributed among the poor (Sui 46, 6a ff.).

[28] See above, note 16.

[29] See I, 2 (4), no. 4.

28. AGRICULTURE AIDED

997   In the fifteenth year of T'ung-ho an imperial decree ordered the remission of the grain long in arrears to the Charity Granaries in Nan-ching. The military officers were also forbidden to hinder agriculture by engaging in hunts or grazing cattle at improper seasons.

59, 2b

29. FLOOD RELIEF IN SHANG–CHING

998   On the day *kuei-mao* of the fourth month in the summer [of the sixteenth year of T'ung-ho] the flood-stricken people of the prefectures and counties controlled by Ch'ung-tê Palace[30] were given relief.   14, 1a

30. FAMINE RELIEF

1008   On the day *chi-yu* of the twelfth month [in the twenty-fifth year of T'ung-ho] the famine-stricken people of Jao Prefecture[31] were given relief.   14, 7b

31. A FLOOD IN THE CENTRAL REGION OF LIAO

1009   On the first day *chia-yin* of the seventh month in the autumn [of the twenty-seventh year of T'ung-ho], because of incessant rain, four rivers, the Huang,[32] T'u,[33] Wo-la,[34] and Yin-liang,[35] overflowed. They swept away and sank the people's dwellings.   14, 8a

32. RELIEF FOR NAN–CHING

1010   On the day *mou-shên* of the eighth month [in the twenty-eighth year of T'ung-ho] the famine-stricken people of P'ing Prefecture were given relief.   15, 1b

1011   On the day *kêng-yin* [of the third month in the twenty-ninth year of T'ung-ho] the Southern Capital and P'ing Prefecture suffered a flood. They were given relief.

15, 2b

33. FAMINE RELIEF

1013   On the day *jên-shên* [of the twelfth month in the first year of K'ai-t'ai] the famine-stricken people of Fêng-shêng Prefecture[36] were given relief.   15, 5a

34. PEOPLE GIVEN INTO BONDAGE

1013   On the day *chia-shên* [of the twelfth month in the first year of K'ai-t'ai] it was decreed that in cases where males or females were pledged[37] by flood- and famine-stricken people throughout the country, starting from the first month of the coming year, each day [of servitude] was to be counted as [the equivalent of] a wage of ten cash. When the full value was repaid, the servitude was to end, and they were to be sent back to their families.   15, 5a

35. THE INTEREST OF AN ORDO USED FOR RELIEF

1013   On the day *mou-shên* [of the seventh month in the second year of K'ai-t'ai] an imperial decree ordered that the interest of Tun-mu Palace[38] be used to relieve the poor people.   15, 6b

---

[30] This is the Chinese name of the ordo of Empress Dowager Ch'êng-t'ien. It was situated near the Supreme Capital (see XV, 1 (11)).

[31] On the upper Shira Muren.

[32] The present Shira Muren, Jehol.

[33] The present Lao-ha River, Jehol.

[34] No details are known about this river, but since the other streams are situated in modern Jehol, we may assume the same for the Wo-la River.

[35] A river in the region of the Supreme Capital (LS 37, 2b).

[36] Modern Cho-lu 涿鹿 County, Chahar.

[37] The word 質, translated here as "to pledge" for want of a better rendition, has in the present context the idea of placing a person in bondage in return for a loan.

[38] The ordo of Shêng-tsung's brother near the region of modern Pei-chên 北鎮 County, Liaoning. See XV, 1 (16).

36. RELIEF

1016   On the day *i-hai* of the fourth month [in the fifth year of K'ai-t'ai] the people of Chao Prefecture[39] were given relief.   15, 10a

37. LOCUSTS IN NAN–CHING

1017   In this month [the sixth month of the sixth year of K'ai-t'ai] various counties in Nan-ching suffered from locusts.   15, 11b

38. FAMINE IN NAN–CHING

1017   On the day *ting-mao* of the tenth month in the winter [of the sixth year of K'ai-t'ai], because of famine in Nan-ching Route, grain was transported from the prefectures of Yün, Ying, Shuo, and Hung[40] for relief.   15, 11b–12a

39. FAMINE RELIEF AND OTHER CHARITIES

1018   On the day *ping-yin* [of the fourth month in the seventh year of K'ai-t'ai], Ch'uan Prefecture[41] and Jao Prefecture[42] were given famine relief.

On the day *hsin-wei* the poor and distressed of the Central Capital[43] were given relief.   16, 1a

40. AN EARTHQUAKE

1022   During this month [the third month of the second year of T'ai-p'ing] there was an earthquake.   In Yün and Ying Prefectures buildings were destroyed, and the ground caved in.   Wei-po Mountain[44] was split by a crevice several hundred paces deep, and a spring gushed forth, forming a stream.   16, 6b–7a

41. A FLOOD IN NAN–CHING

1026   On the day *chi-ssŭ* [of the second month in the sixth year of T'ai-p'ing] there was a flood in Nan-ching.   Emissaries were sent to give it relief.   17, 2b

42. A BIG FLOOD

1031   In the fifth month of the summer [of the eleventh year of T'ai-p'ing] heavy rains caused a flood.   The rivers overflowed and all left their old courses.   17, 8b

43. FAMINE RELIEF

1031   On the day *kêng-hsü* [of the seventh month in the first year of Ching-fu] the famine-stricken people of Chi Prefecture[45] were given relief.   18, 1b

On the day *ting-mao* [of the intercalary tenth month in the first year of Ching-fu] the famine-stricken people of Huang-lung Administration[46] were given relief.   18, 2b

44. RELIEF TO A TRIBE

1034   On the day *chia-yin* of the fourth month [in the third year of Ch'ung-hsi] the Yeh-mi-chih tribe[47] was given relief.   18, 4b

---

[39] The walled city of this frontier prefecture was built in 1014 by Yeh-lü Shih-liang 世良 (d. 1016).   The place was probably located in the eastern part of Outer Mongolia, for its founder "pacified" the northwestern tribes from 1012 to 1015 (LS 94, 4b).

[40] Respectively modern Ta-t'ung 大同 County, Ying 應 County, and Shuo 朔 County, Shansi; and Yang-yüan 陽原 County, Chahar.

[41] A city sixty-seven *li* northeast of modern Ch'ao-yang 朝陽 County, Jehol.

[42] Near the upper course of the modern Shira Muren, Jehol.

[43] Modern Tsaghan Suburghan, Jehol.

[44] This mountain is mentioned only this once in the *Liao Shih;* hence its precise location cannot be defined. But, since the other places all lie in present Shansi, we may assume the same location for Wei-po Mountain.

[45] Modern Chi 薊 County, Hopei.   No calamity is recorded in the *Liao Shih* for 1029.   However, according to LYCWC 4, 48, in this year a serious famine occurred in the Liao territory.   Refugees who crossed the Sung border were each given two pints of millet.   They were assigned to various prefectures and provided with unused arable land.

[46] Modern Nung-an 農安 County, Kirin.

[47] This tribe was probably identical with the Yeh-mi-chih-li 耶迷只里 which was visited by Hsing-tsung in the first month of 1035 (LS 18, 5a).

45. PEACEFUL TIMES

1037   On the first day *hsin-ch'ou* of the seventh month in the autumn [of the sixth year of Ch'ung-hsi], because the prisons of the Northern and Southern Chancelleries were empty, rewards were granted according to ranks.   18, 7a

46. THE P'IN TRIBE

1039   On the day *mou-hsü* [of the first month in the eighth year of Ch'ung-hsi] the P'in tribe was given relief.   18, 9a

47. REMISSION OF TAXES

1043   On the day *ting-hai* [of the eleventh month in the twelfth year of Ch'ung-hsi], because the year's harvest in Shang-ching was poor, the people were exempted from the land tax and other taxes.   19, 5a

48. NAN–CHING

1046   On the day *i-ssǔ* [of the eleventh month in the fifteenth year of Ch'ung-hsi] the poor people of Nan-ching were given relief.   19, 8a

49. A KINDHEARTED AND POPULAR OFFICIAL

1046   In the fifteenth year [of Ch'ung-hsi, when Yang Chi] was sent out as commanding prefect of Wu-ting Commandery,[48] fierce drought occurred in the region and the sprouting crops were about to dry up.   On the night that he assumed office rain fell and [the soil] became sufficiently soaked.   In a song the people said,

> What was it that saved us?
> The rain sent down by heaven.
> Who was it that helped us?
> Lord Yang who was our master.

As the Lei-yang River[49] had left its old course and yearly caused harm to the people, he used his own salary to build a long bridge so that the people were no longer troubled about crossing the river. Later, when he was recalled, the people of the prefecture grasped the shafts of his carriage and tearfully bade him farewell.   89, 4a

50. MILITARY FUNDS USED TO SUPPORT THE POOR

1049–1052   [Yeh-lü I-hsien[50]] requested in a memorial that interest should be derived from the money of the Office of Military Control[51] in order to aid the poor people.   In less than a year[52] the military equipment was completed and the people were able to have a respite.   90, 2a

51. LOCUSTS IN CHUNG–CHING

1056   On the day *i-hai* [of the sixth month in the second year of Ch'ing-ning] winged and unfledged locusts caused a calamity in Chung-ching.   21, 3b

52. AN EARTHQUAKE

1057   On the day *chia-shên* [of the seventh month in the autumn of the third year of Ch'ing-ning] there was an earthquake in Nan-ching.   An amnesty was proclaimed in this region.   21, 4b

---

[48] The military designation of Fêng-shêng 奉聖 Prefecture (modern Cho-lu 涿鹿 County, Chahar) (LS 41, 5b).

[49] The ancient name of the Sang-ch'ien 桑乾 River which flows through Shansi, Chahar, and Hopei to the Gulf of Po-hai.

[50] Yeh-lü I-hsien 義先 achieved merit during the punitive campaign against the P'u-nu-li tribe in 1048 to 1049. On his return he was honored by being given the post of commissioner of military control in the Southern Capital (LS 20, 3a; 90, 2a).

[51] The Office of Military Control was the regional military headquarters for the defense of the borders.   Such offices existed in the Southern Capital and other regions (LS 46, 15b–23b).

[52] The memorial must have been submitted between 1049 and 1052.   Cf. LS 20, 3b–4a.

53. A DROUGHT

1066   [On the day *ting-mao* of the seventh month in the second year of Hsien-yung], because of this year's drought, emissaries were sent to give relief to the poor people behind the mountains.[53]   22, 4*a*

54. CALAMITIES IN NAN–CHING

1067   During this year Nan-ching suffered from drought and locusts.   22, 5*a–b*

55. FAMINE RELIEF

1068   On the day *hsin-mao* [of the first month in the fourth year of Hsien-yung] emissaries were dispatched to relieve the famine-stricken people of Hsi-ching.   22, 5*b*

On the day *chia-shên* [of the third month] relief was given to the famine-stricken people of Ying Prefecture.   22, 5*b*

On the day *kêng-yin* relief was given to the famine-stricken people of Shuo Prefecture.   22, 5*b*

56. RAIN AND EARTHQUAKE

1068   During this month [the seventh month in the fourth year of Hsien-yung], Nan-ching had continuous rain and an earthquake.   22, 6*a*

57. A FLOOD IN NAN–CHING

1068   [On the day *hsin-hai* of the tenth month in the fourth year of Hsien-yung], because the counties of Yung-ch'ing, Wu-ch'ing, An-tz'ŭ, Ku-an, Hsin-ch'êng, Kuei-i, and Jung-ch'êng[54] had all suffered from floods, they were exempted from the land tax for one year.
                                   22, 6*a*

58. REMISSION OF LAND TAX

1071   On the day *mou-tzŭ* of the eleventh month [in the seventh year of Hsien-yung] there was a remission of the land tax for the refugees of Nan-ching. On the day *chi-ch'ou* the famine-stricken people of Jao Prefecture were given relief.   22, 7*b*

59. REMISSION OF TAXES

1072   On the day *mou-ch'ên* [of the second month in the eighth year of Hsien-yung], because of this year's famine, the people of Wu-an Prefecture[55] were exempted from paying the land tax and other taxes. The people of the prefectures of Ên,[56] Yü,[57] Shun,[58] and Hui[59] were given relief.   23, 1*a*

60. RELIEF GIVEN

1072   On the day *jên-tzŭ* of the fourth month in the summer [of the eighth year of Hsien-yung] the people of I Prefecture[60] and Jao Prefecture were given relief.   23, 1*b*

On the day *chia-ying* of the sixth month [of the eighth year of Hsien-yung] the poor people of I Prefecture[61] were given relief.

---

[53] This refers to what is now Chahar and northern Shansi.

[54] For the exact location of these places, all of which were in present Hopei, see I, 1 (8).

[55] West of modern Fou-hsin 阜新 County, Jehol.

[56] Sixty *li* north of present Tsaghan Suburghan, Jehol.

[57] Modern Yü 蔚 County, Chahar.

[58] During the Liao period there were two Shun 順 Prefectures. The first was located in Nan-ching in what is now Shun-i 順義 County, Hopei; the other, an entrusted commandery-prefecture in Shang-ching, was probably situated 120 *li* northeast of modern Pei-chên 北鎮 County, Liaoning. It was built by people from the first Shun Prefecture. The Shun Prefecture of our passage is apparently the first one, in Nan-ching (LS 37, 13*a*; 40, 4*a–b*).

[59] Modern Berke 博羅科, 340 *li* north of Chien-ch'ang 建昌, Jehol.

[60] No I 義 Prefecture is recorded in the geographical section of the *Liao Shih*. It must be an error for I 宜 Prefecture (modern I 義 County, Liaoning) which in Chin times was designated by the character 義.

[61] I 易 Prefecture, modern I 易 County, Hopei.

On the day *chi-wei* Chung-ching [Circuit] was given relief.

On the day *chia-tzŭ* Chung-hsing[62] Administration was given relief.   23, 1*b*

61. FAMINE RELIEF

1072   On the day *ping-shên* [of the seventh month in the eighth year of Hsien-yung] the famine-stricken people of Jao Prefecture were given relief.   23, 1*b*

62. VARIOUS FORMS OF RELIEF

1072   On the day *kêng-hsü* of the eleventh month [in the eighth year of Hsien-yung], Tsu Prefecture[63] was exempted from taxes.

On the day *ping-ch'ên* there was a heavy snow.   The people were allowed to gather fuel in forbidden regions.

1073   On the day *ting-mao* money was given to the poor families of Yen-ch'ang Palace.[64]

23, 1*b*–2*a*

63. LOCUSTS IN NAN–CHING

1073   On the day *ping-yin* [of the seventh month in the ninth year of Hsien-yung], Nan-ching reported in a memorial to the throne that the locusts of the two counties of Kuei-i[65] and Lai-shui[66] had flown away into the territory of Sung and that the remainder had been eaten by wasps.   23, 2*a*

64. THE TRAVELING ROUTE OF THE EMPEROR

1073   On the day *mou-wu* of the eleventh month [in the ninth year of Hsien-yung] a decree ordered that the places through which the emperor traveled and where he halted were to be exempted from the land tax for one year.   23, 2*b*

65. RETURNED REFUGEES REWARDED

1074   On the day *kuei-wei* of the second month [in the tenth year of Hsien-yung] the people of P'ing Prefecture who had returned to their occupations were exempted from the land tax and other taxes.   23, 2*b*

66. A DROUGHT

1074   In the fourth month of the summer [of the tenth year of Hsien-yung] there was a drought.   23, 2*b*

67. FAMINE RELIEF

1075   On the day *jên-ying* [of the first month in the first year of Ta-k'ang] relief was given for the famine in Yün Prefecture.   23, 3*a*

68. A CONFLAGRATION

1075   On the day *ting-mao* of the second month [in the first year of Ta-k'ang] there was a conflagration in Hsiang Prefecture.[67]   Emissaries were sent to alleviate the distress.

23, 3*a*

69. FAMINE RELIEF

1075   On the day *ping-tzŭ* of the fourth month in the summer [of the first year of Ta-k'ang] relief was given for a famine in P'ing Prefecture.   23, 3*a*

---

[62] Chung-hsing 中興 is probably an error for Hsing-chung 興中 (modern Ch'ao-yang 朝陽 County, Jehol).

[63] Southwest of modern Boro Khoton, Jehol.

[64] The ordo of Mu-tsung (951–969). See XV, 1 (9).

[65] This city was originally situated thirty-five *li* northwest of modern Hsiung 雄 County, Hopei.

[66] Present Lai-shui 淶水 County, Hopei.

[67] North of modern Nung-an 農安 County, Kirin.

On the day *ping-wu* of the intercalary [fourth] month relief was given for a famine in P'ing Prefecture and Luan Prefecture.[68]   23, 3a

On the day *ping-yin* [of the seventh month] relief was given to the poor people of Nan-ching.

23, 3b

70. RELIEF MEASURES FOR NAN-CHING

1075   On the day *chi-mao* [of the ninth month in the first year of Ta-k'ang], in view of the famine in Nan-ching, there was a remission of the land tax and other taxes for one year.   Money and grain were also given out for relief.   23, 3b

71. FAMINE RELIEF

1076   On the day *mou-tzŭ* of the second month [in the second year of Ta-k'ang] relief was given for a famine in Huang-lung Administration.   On the day *kuei-ch'ou*, because Nan-ching Route suffered from famine, it was exempted from the land tax and other taxes for one year.   23, 4a

72. REMISSION OF TAXES

1076   On the day *mou-wu* of the ninth month [in the second year of Ta-k'ang], because Nan-ching was attacked by locusts, it was exempted from the land tax and other taxes for the next year.   23, 4b

73. AN EARTHQUAKE IN NAN-CHING

1076   During this month [the eleventh month in the second year of Ta-k'ang] there was an earthquake in Nan-ching.   Most of the people's homes were destroyed.   23, 4b

74. A FAMINE IN LIAO-TUNG

1076   In the second year of Ta-k'ang the famine-stricken people of Liao-tung[69] died in great numbers.   [Wang T'ang[70]] asked that relief be given.   This was granted.

105, 6a

75. NO IMPERIAL INSPECTION TOUR

1077   On the day *hsin-mao* [of the second month in the third year of Ta-k'ang], because of a famine in Chung-ching, the imperial tour of inspection was called off.   23, 5a

76. LOCUSTS IN SOUTHERN LIAO

1077   On the day *ping-ch'ên* [of the fifth month in the third year of Ta-k'ang] locust grubs damaged the crops at Yü-t'ien and An-tz'ŭ.[71]   23, 5a

77. FAMINE RELIEF

1078   On the day *chia-wu* [of the first month in the fourth year of Ta-k'ang] relief was given for a famine in Tung-ching.   23, 6b

78. RELIEF FOR NAN-CHING

1079   On the day *kuei-wei* [of the eleventh month in the fifth year of Ta-k'ang] the refugees of Nan-ching were exempted from labor services for three years, and the families which had suffered from conflagrations were exempted from taxation for one year.   24, 2a

---

[68] Respectively present Lu-lung 盧龍 County and Luan 灤 County in Hopei.

[69] The name of a prefecture which during the Han dynasty covered nearly half of the region of present Liaoning.   The term has been employed by the literati from the time of Han to the present day.

[70] Wang T'ang 王棠 obtained his *chin-shih* degree in 1046.   He asked for aid to Liao-tung in his capacity as commissioner of the Ministry of Revenue.

[71] Respectively modern Yü-t'ien 玉田 County and An-tz'ŭ 安次 County in Hopei.

79. RETURNED REFUGEES REWARDED

1080   On the day *jên-shên* of the fifth month [in the sixth year of Ta-k'ang] the people of
P'ing Prefecture who had returned to their occupations were exempted from the land
tax and other taxes for one year.   24, 2a

80. REMISSION OR REDUCTION OF TAXES

1081   On the day *kêng-wu* [of the twelfth month in the sixth year of Ta-k'ang] the refugees
of Hsi-ching were exempted from the land tax and other taxes for one year.
On the day *chia-hsü* the taxes paid by the people were reduced.   24, 2b

81. LOCUSTS IN NAN–CHING

1081   On the day *kuei-ch'ou* [of the fifth month in the seventh year of Ta-k'ang] the
officials reported to the throne that locusts had attacked the three counties of Yung-
ch'ing, Wu-ch'ing, and Ku-an.[72]   24, 3a

82. RELIEF FOR ORDOS AND FRONTIER GUARDS

1081   On the day *i-yu* of the eleventh month [in the seventh year of Ta-k'ang] an imperial
decree ordered that government money be provided annually as relief for the various
ordos and also for the poor households of the frontier guards.   24, 3b

83. FLOODS IN NAN–CHING

1082   On the day *chia-wu* of the seventh month in the autumn [of the eighth year of Ta-
k'ang] . . . as continuous rains had fallen in Nan-ching, the Sha River[73] overflowed
and damaged the crops in the six counties of Yung-ch'ing, Kuei-i, Hsin-ch'êng, An-tz'ŭ, Wu-ch'ing,
and Hsiang-ho.[74]   24, 4a

84. BLIZZARDS DECIMATE ANIMALS

1082   On the day *ting-wei* [of the ninth month in the eighth year of Ta-k'ang] a blizzard
struck Ou-ssŭ-tien[75] during a stop of the emperor.   Many of the oxen and horses
died.   He bestowed clothes and horses upon his retinue, from the escorting officials down, in accordance with their ranks.   24, 4b

1083   On the first day *ping-wu* of the fourth month in the summer [of the ninth year of
Ta-k'ang] a heavy snow fell to a depth of more than ten feet on level ground.   Six
or seven out of ten horses died.   24, 4b

85. ACTING AND RETIRED OFFICIALS ORGANIZE RELIEF

Before 1086   When the people in Yen and Chi became famine-stricken, [Liu] Shên and the retired
officials, Chao Hui and Han Tsao-jih, provided relief by distributing gruel.   Innumerable lives were thereby saved.   98, 4b

86. RELIEF IN NAN–CHING

1087   On the day *chia-hsü* [of the first month in the third year of Ta-an] money and
grain were given out to relieve the poor people of Nan-ching.   They were also exempted from the land tax and other taxes.   25, 1a

---

[72] Respectively modern Yung-ch'ing 永清 County, Wu-
ch'ing 武清 County, and Ku-an 固安 County, all in
Hopei.

[73] In modern Hopei.

[74] For the exact location of these places, all of which
were in what is now Hopei, see I, 1 (8).

[75] According to the *Liao Shih*, the last two emperors of
Liao frequently chose this place for a rest during the
winter.   The exact location of the place is not known,
but it cannot have been far from the modern Shira Muren,
for the emperor used to travel in that region during this
time of year.

87. FAMINE RELIEF

1087   On the day *ping-hsü* of the second month [in the third year of Ta-an] grain was distributed to relieve the famine in Chung-ching.   25, 1a

88. REGULATIONS CONCERNING REFUGEES ABOLISHED

1087   On the day *chia-ch'ên* [of the second month in the third year of Ta-an], because a large number of people had wandered off and become scattered, the regulations for punishments[76] and rewards for the settlement of these refugee families were abolished.   25, 1a

89. GRANTS AND REMISSIONS

1087   On the day *mou-tzŭ* of the fourth month [in the third year of Ta-an] silk was bestowed upon the poor people of Chung-ching and there was a remission of half the tribute due from the various routes.   25, 1a

90. SILK FOR POOR TRIBESPEOPLE

1087   On the day *ping-shên* [of the fourth month in the third year of Ta-an] the poor people of the Wei Wu-ku tribe were granted silk.   25, 1a

91. THE GRAIN OF THE MINISTRY OF REVENUE

1087   On the day *i-ssŭ* [of the fourth month in the third year of Ta-an] an imperial decree ordered that the grain of the Office of the Ministry of Revenue be distributed in order to provide relief for the refugees of the various routes and for the famine of I Prefecture.[77]
25, 1b

92. REMISSION OF TAXES

1088   On the day *kêng-wu* [of the first month in the fourth year of Ta-an] the refugees and poor families of Shang-ching were exempted from the land tax and other taxes.
25, 1b

93. FREE PERSONS MAY SELL THEMSELVES

1088   On the day *chia-hsü* [of the first month in the fourth year of Ta-an], because of the famine in Shang-ching and Nan-ching, free persons were permitted to sell themselves.   25, 1b–2a

94. RELIEF

1088   On the day *chi-ssŭ* [of the third month in the fourth year of Ta-an] relief was given for the famine in Shang-ching and in P'ing,[78] Chin,[79] and Lai Prefectures.[80]

On the day *chi-mao* of the fourth month in the summer the poor people of the five prefectures of Su,[81] Chi,[82] Fu,[83] Lu,[84] and T'ieh[85] were given relief and were exempted from the land tax and other taxes.

On the day *chia-shên* the poor people of Ch'ing Prefecture[86] were given relief.   25, 2a

On the day *i-mao* [of the fifth month in the fourth year of Ta-an] the poor people of Tsu Prefecture[87] were given relief.   25, 2a

On the day *chi-wei* the poor people of Ch'un Prefecture[88] were given relief.   25, 2a

---

[76] The use of the word 徵 in place of 懲 is frequent in Yüan literature.

[77] See note 60.

[78] Present Lu-lung 盧龍 County, Hopei.

[79] Modern Chin 錦 County, Liaoning.

[80] Near Hsing-ch'êng 興城 County, Liaoning.

[81] Modern Chin 金 Prefecture, Liaoning.

[82] The present location of this region is not clear. It may possibly have been on the Liaotung Peninsula.

[83] Modern Fu 復 Prefecture, Liaotung Peninsula.

[84] Present Lin-chiang 臨江 County, Liaoning.

[85] Modern T'ang-ch'ih-pao 湯池堡, Liaoning.

[86] Modern Tsaghan Khoton, Jehol.

[87] Southwest of modern Boro Khoton, Jehol.

[88] Roughly corresponding to the northwestern part of modern Po-tu-na 伯都訥, Kirin. See I, 3, note 11.

95. BIRDS DESTROY LOCUSTS

1088   On the day *kêng-ch'ên* [of the eighth month in the fourth year of Ta-an] officials memorialized that the locusts of Wan-p'ing and Yung-ch'ing had been eaten up by flying birds.   25, 2*b*

96. OXEN AND CLOTH AS RELIEF

1091   On the day *jên-yin* [of the second month in the seventh year of Ta-an] an imperial decree ordered the poor people of Wei Prefecture[89] to be given oxen for ploughing, cloth, and lustring.   25, 4*a*

97. RELIEF FOR THE NORTHWESTERN ROUTE

1092   On the day *ping-ch'ên* [of the tenth month in the eighth year of Ta-an] relief was given for the famine in the Northwestern Route.[90]   25, 4*b*

98. RELIEF

1092   On the day *ting-yu* [of the eleventh month in the eighth year of Ta-an], because a flood in T'ung Prefecture[91] had damaged the crops, emissaries were sent to carry out relief work.   25, 5*a*

1093   On the day *kuei-mao* of the ninth month [in the ninth year of Ta-an] the poor people of the Northwestern Route were given relief.   25, 5*b*

99. INCREASED STORAGE

1093   On the day *chi-ssŭ* [of the tenth month in the ninth year of Ta-an] an imperial decree ordered increased storage of supplies to prepare for flood and drought.   25, 6*a*

100. RELIEF TO REFUGEES OF NAN–CHING

1094   On the day *chi-ssŭ* [of the fourth month in the tenth year of Ta-an] the refugees of Yü-t'ien and Mi-yün[92] were exempted from the land tax and other taxes for one year.   25, 6*b*

101. RELIEF MONEY FOR THE NORTHWEST

1094   On the day *kêng-tzŭ* of the intercalary [fourth month in the tenth year of Ta-an] the poor people of the Northwestern Route were given money.   25, 6*b*

102. SEVERAL KINDS OF RELIEF

1095   On the day *i-mao* [of the first month in the first year of Shou-lung] the poor people of Fêng-shêng Prefecture were given relief.

On the day *mou-ch'ên* of the second month the poor people of the Left and Right P'i-shih [Armies][93] were given money.   26, 1*a*

On the day *ping-wu* of the third month the poor people of the Northeastern Route were given lustring.   26, 1*a*

103. RELIEF FOR TRIBES AND FRONTIER TROOPS

1096   On the day *hsin-yu* [of the first month in the second year of Shou-lung] oxen were purchased and given to the poor people of the Wu-ku, Ti-lieh,[94] and Wei Wu-ku[95] tribes.

---

[89] This entrusted commandery-prefecture, built by Hsiao Ch'ang-i 昌裔, roughly corresponds to the southwestern part of modern Chang-wu 彰武 County, Liaoning.

[90] Near the Kerulen River in modern Outer Mongolia. Liao garrison soldiers were settled in this area.

[91] Southwest of Nung-an 農安 County, Kirin.

[92] Respectively modern Yü-t'ien 玉田 County, and Mi-yün 密雲 County in Hopei.

[93] See XV, 1 (25) and notes.

[94] The Wu-ku and Ti-lieh were originally two separate tribes which dwelt in the region of the modern Kerulen River in Outer Mongolia, but, after their removal in 1096 to the west of the modern Nonni River, Heilungkiang (LS 26, 2*a*), they were formed into one political unit (Yanai 30, 132–137).

[95] The military detachments stationed in the region of the Wei Wu-ku, Wu-ku, and Ti-lieh tribes are frequently mentioned together. They are, for example, enumerated

On the day *kuei-hai* of the second month the Ta-ma-li-pieh-ku tribe[96] was given relief.

On the day *chi-mao* of the fourth month in the summer the frontier troops of the northwest were given relief.   26, 2a

104. FLOOD RELIEF IN NAN-CHING

1097   On the first day *ping-ch'ên*[97] of the second month [in the third year of Shou-lung] there was a flood in Nan-ching. Emissaries were sent to administer relief.   26, 2b

105. POOR TRIBESMEN RESETTLED

1098   On the day *chi-ssŭ* [of the first month in the fourth year of Shou-lung] the poor people of the Tsu-pu[98] and other tribes were moved to the region in front of the mountains.   26, 3b

106. RELIEF FOR LIAO PREFECTURE AND FOR *CHIU* UNITS

1099   On the day *mou-ch'ên* [of the tenth month in the fifth year of Shou-lung] relief was given for the famine of Liao Prefecture[99] and there was a remission of the land tax and other taxes for one year.

On the day *chia-hsü* of the eleventh month the Southern and Northern *Chiu*[100] were given relief.
26, 4b

107. MAGIC HELP FOR ALL KINDS OF DISTRESS

Ca. **1100**   Toward the end of the reign period Shou-lung, [Hsiao Wên][101] administered I Prefecture[102] and was concurrently pacification commissioner of the Southwestern Region. Although the soil of Kao-yang[103] was fertile and the people rich, because those who held office in this town were inveterately acquisitive, the people suffered greatly. As soon as Wên arrived he eradicated all the old abuses. He devoted attention to agriculture and mulberry-culture and promoted education in propriety so that all the people were transformed.

During this time, when there was a great drought and the people were greatly worried, Wên offered up prayers and immediately it rained. Again, when locusts appeared in the subordinate counties and a discussion was held on how to catch and exterminate them, Wên said, "The locusts are a visitation from heaven. What benefit can be gained from catching them? We should only reflect upon ourselves and examine our own faults." The locusts all flew away and even those remaining did not eat the sprouting crops. They scattered over the grass and bushes and were devoured by crows and magpies.

Once a heavy rain fell without stopping. When Wên again prayed the sky became clear. During this year there was a great harvest.   105, 2b–3a

108. RELIEF SILK

1100   On the day *kuei-ch'ou* [of the second month in the sixth year of Shou-lung] lustring was given out to the poor people of the Five Divisions.   26, 5a

109. REMISSION OF TAXES

1100   On the day *chia-ying* [of the tenth month in the sixth year of Shou-lung], because of the famine in P'ing Prefecture, it was exempted from the land tax and other taxes for one year.   26, 5b

---

in close succession in the list of the tribal troops (LS 35, 9a–b). We may therefore assume that these tribes were neighbors.

[96] Same as Ta-ma Pi-ku-tê. See I, 2 (5) no. 33.

[97] LS 26, 3a agrees with LS 44, 34a in giving the first day of the seventh month as *jên-tzŭ*. We follow the latter in correcting *chia-chên* of our text to *ping-chên* for the first day of the second month.

[98] In 1097 a Liao general defeated these tribes which were then removed from their original territory in present Outer Mongolia to Heilungkiang.

[99] Modern Liao-pin-t'a 遼鑌塔, northwest of Hsin-min 新民 County, Liaoning.

[100] The *Chiu* 糺 is said to have been the name of certain bodies of troops stationed in the northwestern part of the Liao empire. Their main function was the protection of the country against the invasion of hostile tribes. See II, 2, note 20.

[101] Hsiao Wên 文 (T. 國華), a descendant of the Imperial Maternal Uncles, achieved the position of prefect (LS 105, 2b–3a).

[102] Modern I 易 County, Hopei.

[103] The military name for I 易 Prefecture.

110. FLOOD RELIEF

1103   On the day *kêng-wu* of the second month [in the third year of Ch'ien-t'ung], in view of the great flood in Wu-ch'ing County,[104] the restrictions on reservoirs and marshes were relaxed.[105]   27, *3a*

111. RAIN AND HAIL

1103   In the seventh month in the autumn [of the third year of Ch'ien-t'ung] rain and hail damaged the crops in Chung-ching.   27, *3a*

112. LOCUSTS IN NAN–CHING

1104   In the seventh month in the autumn [of the fourth year of Ch'ien-t'ung], Nan-ching suffered from locusts.   27, *3b*

113. A FROST

1109   In the seventh month in the autumn [of the ninth year of Ch'ien-t'ung] a frost damaged the crops.   27, *5b*

114. REMISSION OF TAXES

1109   On the day *ting-ch'ou* [of the tenth month in the ninth year of Ch'ien-t'ung] an imperial decree ordered the remission of the land tax and other taxes for this year.

27, *5b*

115. A GREAT FAMINE

1110   During this year [the tenth year of Ch'ien-t'ung] there was a great famine.   27, *6a*

116. RELIEF FOR UNRULY TRIBESMEN

After 1111   In the beginning of the reign period T'ien-ch'ing the Wu-ku and Ti-lieh tribes rebelled. [Yeh-lü T'ang-ku] was summoned and appointed commanding prefect of the Wu-ku tribe. On arriving in the tribe he persuaded them to submit. Then he expended his own money and requisitioned the hoards of wealthy people to relieve the exhaustion and distress. The tribespeople were greatly delighted.   100, *1a*

117. MONEY FOR THE POOR OF NAN–CHING

1113   On the day *ping-yin* of the first month in the spring of the third year [of T'ien-ch'ing] the poor people of Nan-ching were given money.   27, *7a*

118. FAMINE RAISES GRAIN PRICES

1118   At this time the various routes in front of the mountains[106] suffered a great famine. In the regions of Ch'ien, Hsien, I, Chin, and Hsing-chung[107] one peck of grain cost several [bolts of] lustring. The people stripped the bark from elm trees and ate it. Later men even ate each other.   28, *6b*

---

[104] Modern Wu-ch'ing 武清 County, Hopei.

[105] Does the order simply refer to the restriction of fishing rights? This is not impossible, but in view of the government's negative policy toward dikes and waterworks another explanation seems more plausible. The flood must have clearly demonstrated the danger of neglecting embankments. Increased attention given to devices which drained off excess water or restricted lakes and marshes in all probability facilitated future flood control.

[106] The designation refers to the present Peiping area southeast of the Great Wall. This was the most fertile region of Nan-ching. Here the people reaped the richest crops and paid the highest taxes. The existence of famine in this part of the Liao empire indicates the sad state of its economic foundations.

[107] Respectively: southwest of modern Pei-chên 北鎮 County; Pei-chên County; near I 義 County; Chin 錦 County, Liaoning; and Ch'ao-yang 朝陽 County, Jehol.

119. THE GRANARY SYSTEM OF TUNG–CHING

Among the more than fifty cities in Tung-ching, such as Hsien,[108] Hsin,[109] Su, Fu, Ch'ên, Hai,[110] T'ung,[111] Yin,[112] Wu,[113] Sui,[114] Ch'un,[115] and T'ai,[116] each of the prefectures situated along the frontier had a Fair Purchase Granary. Following the ancestral system, the stale grain was taken out and replaced with a new supply. The people were permitted of their own accord to borrow [the grain] at an interest of twenty per cent. There were [in the granaries] not less than two to three hundred thousand bushels. In spite of frequent military expeditions it was never exhausted. But during the reign period T'ien-ch'ing[117] the Chin troops made a great invasion and seized all [the granaries].[118]

59, 3a–b

---

[108] Modern K'ai-yüan 開原 County, Liaoning. The cities mentioned in the text, all of which were located in Tung-ching or Shang-ching, seem also to have suffered famine, which explains the high cost of grain.

[109] In the vicinity of present Huai-tê 懷德 County, Liaoning.

[110] Respectively: modern Chin 金 Prefecture and Fu 復 Prefecture, on the Liaotung Peninsula; Kai-p'ing 蓋平 County and Hai-ch'êng 海城 County in Liaoning.

[111] A city between modern T'ieh-ling 鐵嶺 County and K'ai-yüan County, Liaoning.

[112] Modern T'ieh-ling County, Liaoning.

[113] According to LS 31, 7a and 48, 15b–16a, there were two Wu 烏 Prefectures, one in Shang-ching and the other in Tung-ching. The geographical section, however, lists only one Wu Prefecture, under Shang-ching (LS 37, 8b) which corresponds to a city northwest of Aro Korchin.

[114] Southwest of modern K'ang-p'ing 康平 County, Liaoning.

[115] Northwest of modern Po-tu-na 伯都訥, Kirin.

[116] Southwest of modern Nung-an 農安 County, Kirin. The above three prefectures are listed under Shang-ching in the geographical section (LS 37, 8a–b, 13a); evidently they did not belong to Tung-ching. The mistake of the Yüan historiographers is possibly due to the fact that these three prefectures were controlled by the headquarters of the Northeastern Route.

[117] This period lasted from 1111 to 1121. In 1112 clashes between the Ch'i-tan and Jurchen broke out. In 1114 the war started in earnest, and in 1116 the Eastern Capital and several prefectures were seized by the Jurchen army (LS 27, 7a, 8a–b; 28, 4a).

[118] The same record is mentioned in CTKC 10, 11a, except that the number of stored bushels is given as from "three to five hundred thousand bushels."

SECTION XIII

REBELLIONS

INTRODUCTION

1. THE MORPHOLOGY OF REBELLIONS

A country's political crises dramatically express the contradictions and conflicts inherent in its social and national configurations. The fact that the Liao empire rested upon conquest is of paramount importance to an understanding of its rebellions, for only by examining the status of various groups within their national segment and the relation of these segments to the Liao empire as a whole can its smouldering revolts and open rebellions be fully comprehended.

When a rebellion occurred among the Ch'i-tan proper, it was usually confined to members of the ruling families and the tribal nobility who sought new leadership either in the person of the emperor or among the high officialdom. The Ch'i-tan commoners, less powerful and for that reason less overtly ambitious, were content to improve their plebian position by more moderate action.

The revolts of the conquered peoples, besides differing from the struggle for power within the ruling Ch'i-tan groups, varied also according to the position of the rebels within the subdued sector. The conquest situation affected their fighting strength. Furthermore, it determined the degree of coordination and the chance of ultimate success.

2. CH'I–TAN REBELLIONS

a. STRUGGLE FOR IMPERIAL POWER

The first victorious rebel of the Liao dynasty was its founder. When A-pao-chi refused to submit his mandate as khaghan to the tribal council for approval, he violated his people's unwritten constitution which held that the supreme chieftain had to be elected (or confirmed) "every three years."[1] In 907, when A-pao-chi established himself as permanent ruler,[2] he not only violated the former political order; he destroyed it. In cementing his new position he resorted to the same ruthless methods that Machiavelli recommended some six centuries later to the autocrats of the Italian Renaissance.[3] He killed all rival chieftains[4] and, by means unknown but probably no less

brutal, reduced to a shadow the Yao-lien lineage, which had furnished the head chieftain of the tribes for a considerable time.[5]

b. THE DYNAMICS OF CH'I–TAN SUCCESSION (THE TRIBAL PATTERN)

A-pao-chi's new monarchic power did not go unchallenged. A series of attacks was made against him, not by the independent heads of independent Ch'i-tan tribes (he evidently had succeeded in completely removing this threat), but by members of his own Yeh-lü lineage and by rebel supporters belonging to the consort lineage, Hsiao. These noble conspirators had probably contributed whole-heartedly to the overthrow of the old tribal order by A-pao-chi, for all of them profited greatly from the establishment of a monarchy that perpetuated the privileged position of their families. What they objected to was A-pao-chi's determination to arrogate to himself and his sons control in perpetuity over the seat of power—a procedure which ignored the traditionally recognized right of all branches of a family to leadership.

Like other Inner Asiatic peoples, the Ch'i-tan subscribed to a pattern of succession which had little in common with the system of primogeniture prevailing in China from the days of the Chou dynasty on. While the latter principle had not always operated with success, the political stability it fostered was so advantageous to a complex agricultural society of the Chinese type that it was not easily disregarded. Wilful overriding of the eldest son's claim to rulership violated the magic order of life and was bound to result in discord, turmoil, and eventual disaster.[6]

The fluid conditions of nomadic life suggested a more flexible system of succession. A family might well be strong enough to maintain political supremacy for a number of generations, but, in order to do so, effective rather than fixed leadership was necessary. The eldest son was not always the best qualified; and, not infrequently, a ruler died (or was killed) at a relatively early age. In such an emergency brothers were

---

[1] XIII (1).

[2] WTS 72, 2b ff.; cf. III, introduction.

[3] Machiavelli 40, 28; also idem 40a, 406 ff.

[4] See note 2.

[5] XIV, 1 (1), LS 63, 7b and 8a–b; cf. also XIV, introduction.

[6] For the elaboration of the principle during the Chou period see SC 33, 9a; 39, 2b; 42, 2b (Chavannes, MH IV, 104, 252–253, 452–453); CCTCCS 12, 9a–10a (Legge, CC V, 5).

THE CHIEFTAINSHIP WITHIN THE I–LA TRIBE AS HELD BY SU–TSU AND HIS DESCENDANTS
(According to LS 37, 5a, 6b; 64, 2a ff.; 73, 1b, 3a, 5b; 75, 1a, 5a; 112, 1b, 2b)

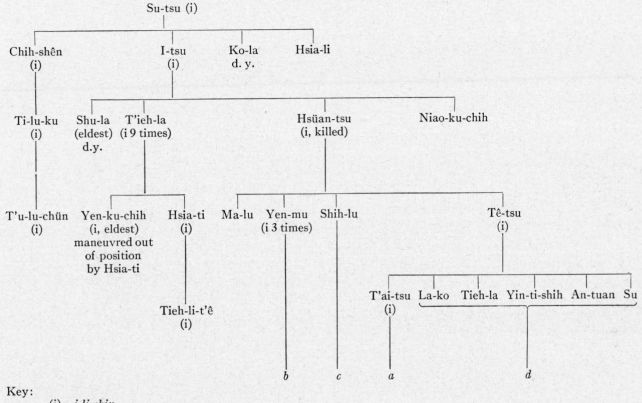

Key:

 (i)—*i-li-chin*
 d.y.—died young
  a—Hêng-chang: the imperial lineage
 b–d—the Three Patriarchal Households

FIG. 37.

often called upon to succeed the deceased chieftain before power descended to his sons or nephews, all of whom were considered legitimate candidates for his position.

Such was the pattern of succession which prevailed with certain modifications among China's Inner Asiatic neighbors and invaders. Analysis of the T'o-pa shows that political leadership frequently oscillated between brothers and sons.[7] Among the Shih-wei the deceased chieftain's position was inherited either by a son or a brother.[8] Succession in both the collateral and direct line was traditional to the Jurchen founders of the Chin 金 dynasty.[9] In the early days of Mongol rule primogeniture was not a consideration, though the choice of the heir apparent remained in the direct line. After Chingis Khan's death supreme power was given, not to his official wife's eldest son, Juchi, but to her third, Ogotai, because he was his father's choice.[10] The General Assembly, the *kurultai*, favored the youngest son, Tului. However, the deceased khaghan's will prevailed. According to Vladimirtsov, "the *kurultai* had no power to change the decision of the Kagan; so it could only accept Chingis's choice of an heir."[11] Similar trends found expression among the Manchus. At no time during the dynasty did primogeniture determine succession nor, despite certain feeble attempts, was the designation of an heir apparent institutionalized.[12]

Among the Ch'i-tan, chieftainship frequently descended to the brothers of a deceased leader before it passed to members of the next younger generation. Though many details are obscure, the *Liao Shih* enables us to reconstruct in a general way the pattern

---

[7] WS 1, *passim.*
[8] Sui 84, 20b.
[9] CS 1, *passim.*

---

[10] D'Ohsson 1834 II, 9 ff.; *cf.* also Vladimirtsov 30, 150; and Howorth, HM I, 116.
[11] Vladimirtsov 30, 151.
[12] See General Introduction.

of chiefly tenure in the I-la tribe from the time of A-pao-chi's great-great-grandfather, Su-tsu, until the establishment of the dynasty.

Of Su-tsu's sons, at least two, the first and the second, Chih-shên and I-tsu, held the post of *i-li-chin* as their father had done before them. In the next generation one of Chih-shên's sons and two of I-tsu's became chieftains. I-tsu's eldest son, Shu-la, died while young; his second, T'ieh-la, was "elected" *i-li-chin* nine times; his third, Hsüan-tsu, who occupied the position once, was murdered—most probably by his brother, T'ieh-la.[13] In the subsequent generation, that of T'ai-tsu's father, representatives of several branches within the larger family secured the reins of leadership: the post of *i-li-chin* was held by Chih-shên's grandson, T'u-lu-chün; in I-tsu's line, by two sons of T'ieh-la, Yen-ku-chih and Hsia-ti, and by two sons of Hsüan-tsu, Yen-mu and Tê-tsu. The uncertainty of succession is well illustrated by the behavior of Hsia-ti who, in the political struggle to become *i-li-chin*, physically shoved his elder brother aside.[14]

Succession from Su-tsu to Tê-tsu was determined by neither the principles of primo- nor ultimogeniture. An eldest son might be made chieftain, as the careers of Chih-shên and Yen-ku-chih show, but the latter was readily abandoned in favor of his younger brother; and Chih-shên's senior lineage (the later Five Divisions) exercised much less power than that of his younger brother (the later Six Divisions), which seems to have provided most of the tribal leaders. A youngest son might also become *i-li-chin*, as Tê-tsu did, but in the period under discussion it was the "middle" sons who were more frequently chosen to fill the highest office.

c. CONTESTED PRIMOGENITURE (THE STRUGGLE FOR THE THRONE)

In view of this pattern of succession, it is not surprising that, during the formative years of the dynasty, the power of the new monarch was challenged by a number of serious "rebellions." A-pao-chi's brothers and cousins readily accepted his rule for the first three years—the traditional period of tenure—but after this "term" had expired they no doubt expected him to seek reelection or replacement in the usual way, permitting the choice to rest with his relatives—if not with those non-Yeh-lü chieftains who survived the purge of 907.

The *Liao Shih* speaks of no gesture of this kind. More than probably none such was ever made. Im-

mediately after A-pao-chi's accession to power in 907 he appointed his cousin in the senior line, Tieh-li-t'ê, *i-li-chin* of the I-la tribe;[15] in 908 he made his next younger brother, La-ko (Sa-la), *t'i-yin* of the Yeh-lü clan.[16] But these assignments emphasized rather than fulfilled his political obligations. When A-pao-chi entered upon his second term without offering the throne to his Yeh-lü relatives and, instead, entrusted to his wife's brother the highest political office, that of prime minister of the Northern Administration,[17] he created a situation that inevitably led to dissatisfaction and unrest. All of A-pao-chi's brothers except the youngest joined in a conspiracy against him. When it was discovered, the ruler did not have the rebels killed, but after a great ceremonial sacrifice he solemnly pardoned them[18] and further conciliated his brother, La-ko, by appointing him chieftain of the I-la tribe.[19]

But these efforts brought no lasting peace. In 912 La-ko, with Tieh-la, Yin-ti-shih, and An-tuan, prepared an armed attack on his eldest brother. The attempt was again uncovered and again pardoned[20]—only to be repeated on a larger scale the following year. In 913 at the close of T'ai-tsu's second "term"[21] La-ko openly expressed his determination to become supreme ruler,[22] supported this time by two leading members of the senior line, his uncle, Hsia-ti, and his cousin, Tieh-li-t'ê. After A-pao-chi had crushed this insurrection and seized the leaders, Hsia-ti, in a dramatic dialogue, admitted that he had participated in the plot, not in the interest of his weak nephews, but to secure power ultimately for his own house.[23] The accuracy of the dynastic record cannot be checked, but the attitude which it reveals was certainly not in conflict with the traditional political mores of the Ch'i-tan.

This time all the rebels were threatened with death and most of them suffered it. Many were torn to pieces, publicly executed, or strangled,[24] the last being the fate of Hsia-ti and his son, Tieh-li-t'ê.[25] Only T'ai-tsu's brothers escaped severe punishment: after experiencing the questionable pleasure of a last day's feast, they were set free.[26]

---

[13] According to LS 71, 2*a*, Hsüan-tsu was killed by Hên-tê. The sound of 狠得 is equivalent to 痕得, the childhood name of T'ieh-la (*cf.* LS 64, 2*a*).

[14] VII, 2 (4).

[15] XVI, 907, LS 1, 2*b*.

[16] XIV, 1 (3).

[17] *Loc. cit.*

[18] VII, 2 (6).

[19] XIII (5).

[20] XIII (6).

[21] For further discussion of this point see XIII, note 50.

[22] XIII (8).

[23] XIII (9).

[24] XIII (10).

[25] XIII (9) (10).

[26] XIII (10).

THE STRUGGLE FOR THE THRONE

(Liao emperors and main contestants)

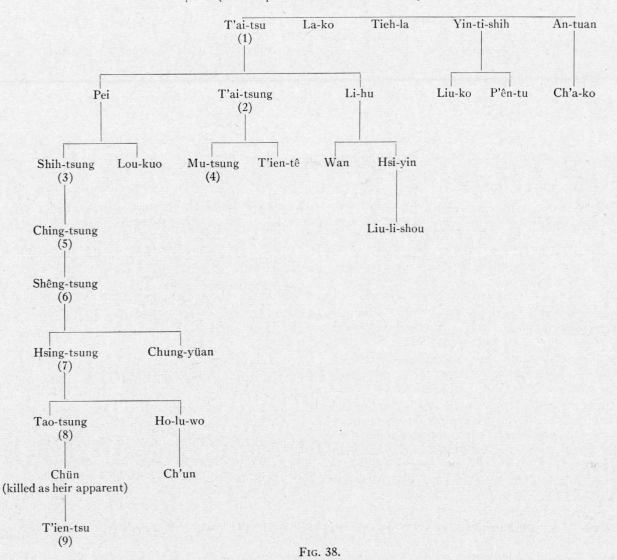

Fig. 38.

In the crystallization of the Liao empire the year 916, like 907, was a crucial date. A-pao-chi had succeeded in retaining supreme power for three times three years. Again Ch'i-tan custom must have demanded that he offer his throne to his brothers, but instead he took deliberate measures to establish himself in the eyes of the world as the founder of an imperial dynasty of the orthodox Chinese type. He set up his own reign title;[27] he designated his eldest son, Pei, his successor;[28] and he proclaimed Confucius the greatest sage, preferring him even to Buddha whose religious tenets were considered non-Chinese.[29] It was no accident that in the decisive court session Pei anticipated his father's choice;[30] it was no accident either that in 916 T'ai-tsu founded the first Confucian temple.[31] The revered teacher obviously served as an austere symbol of Chinese political tradition which postulated permanency of tenure for the ruler and succession to his eldest son.

A-pao-chi's constitutional reforms simultaneously reflected and bulwarked his growing power. Following closely one upon the other, the historic events of 916 must have provoked his brothers to the utmost;

[27] LS 1, 9a.
[28] Loc. cit.

[29] IX (3).
[30] Loc. cit.
[31] IX (3).

they must also have discouraged ambitious intrigue, for T'ai-tsu's career had raised him to a level where revolt had little hope of success. In 917 La-ko and his son conspired once again,[32] and in 918 Tieh-la plotted anew,[33] but the quick failure of both efforts merely confirmed the strength of the emperor's position.

Internal peace prevailed until 926. Then, at the moment of T'ai-tsu's death, it was blatantly demonstrated that the Chinese pattern of succession had by no means been accepted by even those nearest the throne. The empress dowager wanted her husband's mantle to rest upon her second son, citing the dead ruler's "will" to justify her choice.[34] But it is doubtful whether the observant father had actually considered his "accomplished" second son more capable than the "clever" elder Pei.[35] Whatever T'ai-tsu may have thought or said in private, in 916 he solemnly proclaimed Pei the heir apparent; and no passage in the *Liao Shih* indicates that he altered this decision. Pei's spokesman, therefore, stood on firm ground—theoretically. Practically, he was confronted not only by the dowager's personal desires which carried great weight, but also by a still unbroken national tradition which settled questions of succession according to concrete political needs rather than by a rigid and alien principle of primogeniture. Pei's supporter was executed, and the prince himself yielded the throne to his younger brother, ending his political career in exile and dying by violence on foreign soil.[36]

The old Ch'i-tan ideas of succession still survived. In 930 T'ai-tsung's younger brother, Li-hu, was designated heir apparent.[37] Another record states that in this year he was given the title "the emperor's great younger brother" 皇太弟,[38] a title which may well have expressed the collateral right to succession. In 947 after T'ai-tsung's death, when Pei's eldest son, the later Shih-tsung, made himself emperor, Li-hu objected bitterly: "While I am alive, how can Wu-yü ascend the throne."[39] His indignation expresses the Ch'i-tan attitude to succession as consistently as the argument of Shih-tsung's pleader presents the traditional Chinese ideas of propriety (*li* 禮): "According to propriety, whenever there is an eldest son by the principal consort, the succession is not passed to any younger brother. Even the former enthronement of Ssǔ-shêng [T'ai-tsung] is considered to have been

wrong."[40] Shih-tsung emerged victorious, perhaps not so much because the Ch'i-tan nobles shared his Chinese theory of succession, but because they preferred him for personal reasons to the unpopular Li-hu.[41] Nevertheless, the legitimacy of Li-hu's claim must have impressed itself strongly on the later Liao rulers, for he was posthumously honored with the title "emperor."[42]

Li-hu's defeat did not settle the controversy. In 948, the second year of his reign, Shih-tsung was faced with a conspiracy organized by one of T'ai-tsung's sons, T'ien-tê. The plot failed, and the ringleaders were executed.[43] Three years later, another intrigue got under way, this time initiated by the sons of T'ai-tsu's younger brothers, An-tuan and Yin-ti-shih, who asserted the claims of other junior branches of the imperial house. The rebels murdered Shih-tsung without, however, profiting from their bloody deed. They were summarily executed, and a scion of the most powerful junior line—T'ai-tsung's eldest son, Mu-tsung—was declared emperor.[44]

Mu-tsung's accession, which implied a new defeat for the principle of primogeniture, encouraged other relatives of T'ai-tsu to make a bid for imperial power. In 952 Lou-kuo, Shih-tsung's younger brother, and thus a member of a collateral line of the senior branch, conspired against his imperial cousin and persuaded a considerable number of supporters to further his cause. But his plans were discovered and his followers arrested.[45] Li-hu's sons harbored similar ambitions and met with a similar fate. In 953 Li-hu's second son, Wan, was arrested;[46] in 960 Wan's elder brother, Hsi-yin, was seized.[47] In both cases their subversive efforts were quickly ended.

In 969, when Mu-tsung was assassinated, the junior branches had evidently spent their energies. Imperial succession swung back to the senior line. Shih-tsung's eldest son had died, but his claim was recognized nevertheless, for, when the second son, Ching-tsung, ascended the throne, he honored his dead elder brother by bestowing on him the posthumous title "heir apparent."[48] In 981 Hsi-yin, this time supported by his son, Liu-li-shou, challenged Ching-tsung. During the revolt a group of Chinese soldiers hailed Liu-li-shou as emperor. The new attempt to assert the claim of

---

[32] XIII (12).
[33] XIII (13).
[34] LS 7 , 2a and XIII (16).
[35] XIII (3).
[36] See VII, 2, note 29.
[37] LS 3, 4b.
[38] LS 64, 8b and 72, 4a.
[39] XIII (20).

[40] *Loc. cit.*
[41] *Loc. cit.*
[42] LS 64, 8b–9a.
[43] XIII (21).
[44] XIII (23) and LS 112, 3b.
[45] XIII (25).
[46] XIII (26).
[47] XIII (27).
[48] LS 64, 13a ff.

the junior line failed[49] as had previous ones. The two distinguished ringleaders were put to death, the son by execution, the father by government-"permitted" suicide.[50]

Ching-tsung's eldest son, Shêng-tsung, was never proclaimed heir apparent, but after his father's death he was made emperor. Collateral claims were still put forth, but Shêng-tsung's mother succeeded in breaking up the coalition of paternal uncles, cousins, and other relatives which threatened the young emperor.[51] Shêng-tsung's younger brother, Lung-ch'ing, was posthumously called "the emperor's great younger brother,"[52] a title conferred in an earlier time upon another distinguished imperial Liao sibling, Li-hu. Perhaps unjustifiably, the *Ch'i-tan Kuo Chih* refers to Lung-ch'ing as "emperor,"[53] but without doubt he exercised exceptional power. He had his own ordo,[54] and the splendor of his menage in the Southern Capital is said to have been rivaled only by the court.[55] In view of this it is all the more significant that the distinguished prince made no attempt to overthrow his brother's rule, but vigorously defended it during the great Sung war.

Shêng-tsung's two sons by his empress died before they reached maturity. He was succeeded by Hsing-tsung, one of his concubine-sons, though not the eldest.[56] The new emperor's position was threatened by his own mother who sought to place his younger brother on the throne, obviously in the hope of gaining more power for herself. The plan failed, and the dowager was exiled to her husband's mausoleum until 1037. A Sung report reveals that as late as 1054 Ch'in-ai still clung to her design; but her un-Chinese ideas concerning the merits of fraternal succession remained without practical consequence.[57]

Tao-tsung's accession to the throne in 1055 seemed to demonstrate that the principle of primogeniture was unshakably established, for the new emperor was Hsing-tsung's eldest son. But the rebellion of 1063 revealed that this was not so. Chung-yüan, Hsing-tsung's "great younger brother,"[58] had not forgotten his mother's earlier attempt to install him in the seat of supreme power. After accepting the new reign for a number of years, Chung-yüan and his sons, among whom Nieh-lu-ku was the most active, planned the

emperor's destruction. In 1063 the rebels gathered an armed force which attacked Tao-tsung's traveling camp. Although the first onslaught, which cost Nieh-la-ku his life, did not achieve its avowed purpose, the insurrectionists acclaimed Chung-yüan emperor. His "reign," however, did not last long: on the following day his army was dispersed and he, himself, committed suicide.[59] Tao-tsung had every reason to uphold the principle of primogeniture, on the basis of which he had attained his position. After the execution of his eldest son, Chün,[60] he considered appointing his nephew, Ch'un, heir apparent,[61] but in the end he bestowed the title on Chün's eldest son, the later T'ien-tsu.

At the close of the dynasty the Ch'i-tan attitude toward collateral succession, which had never been completely suppressed, asserted itself again. In 1115 a rebellious Ch'i-tan army sought to replace the emperor by his uncle, Prince Ch'un. The prince refused to cooperate in their plans, and the rebels were annihilated.[62] But seven years later this same prince ascended the throne, establishing an ephemeral rule over the northern and eastern parts of the empire, while T'ien-tsu's authority was still acknowledged—at least nominally—in the remaining territories.[63]

The struggle for the throne touches on many aspects of Liao society, such as the changing social background and the important role of the empress dowager;[64] but at this point in our discussion attention has been focused on the political conflicts arising from two antagonistic concepts of succession. The violence of these numerous conflicts did not result from ideological differences alone, though the attack on established tradition certainly stirred up considerable feeling. Primarily, the fires were kindled by those whose interests were legitimatized by the old patterns but challenged by the new. The gradual, if imperfect, victory of the new principle was achieved by a ruling Ch'i-tan group, which in many other situations piously maintained the old tribal customs, but in this, as in the setting up of the two clans, eagerly adopted a Chinese institution as a convenient device for establishing their superiority over their own nationals.

The role of the Hsiao clan in these Yeh-lü feuds was determined by its position as consort family. The great rebellion of 913 was put down by T'ai-tsu with the assistance of his brother-in-law, Ti-lien.[65] This was to be expected. Since the power of the Hsiao

[49] XIII (31).
[50] *Loc. cit.*
[51] CTKC 18, 2a–b.
[52] LS 64, 14b.
[53] CTKC, table 1.
[54] XV, 1 (16).
[55] See XIII, note 50.
[56] *Loc. cit.*
[57] *Loc. cit.*
[58] LS 64, 15b.

[59] *Loc. cit.*, and XIII (41).
[60] XIII (43).
[61] SCPMHP 5, 3a.
[62] XIII (47).
[63] XIII (58).   (See appendix V, B, 1.)
[64] See VII, introduction and XIII, note 50.
[65] XIII (9).

clan depended upon the marriage of one of its women to the emperor, it was natural for its members to support the ruler when a conflict arose. Yet certain Hsiao followed their rebellious Yeh-lü in-laws.[66] One, the husband of a Yeh-lü princess, actually led an independent conspiracy.[67] But the advantage of maintaining good relations with the throne was so obvious that the great majority of the Hsiao clansmen preferred to defend it rather than risk an uncertain fight for individual benefit.

The open dissolution of the dynasty's power eventually weakened the loyalties that had prevailed for more than two centuries. True, there were Hsiao nobles who fought faithfully for T'ien-tsu until the end,[68] but, when even Yeh-lü clansmen were deserting the imperial cause,[69] members of the Hsiao family actively participated in the final assault against the crumbling dynasty.[70]

d. CH'I–TAN COMMONERS, AMENABLE EVEN WHEN DISCONTENTED

If we can trust the record, the struggles for the throne were organized by dissatisfied members of the ruling lineages. The lesser nobility did not lead any major rebellion, probably because its strength was not great enough to insure a reasonable chance of success.

This was even more true for the Ch'i-tan tribal commoners. Their political position was weak; their occasional discontents were readily dissipated. The government, which depended to a large extent upon the loyalty of these tribesmen, did not relieve them of all public obligations—they paid taxes[71] and rendered services in transportation, herding, hunting,[72] and war[73]—but it tried to keep its demands moderate. And, if these demands happened to strain the resources of the inner tribes, then the government was willing to listen to criticism and to accept suggestions for modifying its policy. So considerable were the privileges, both real and potential, that fell to the mass of the Ch'i-tan commoners because of the conquest situation that, as a rule, they were satisfied to make their complaints to the administration through their tribal spokesmen and officials. The tribes' dissatisfactions growing out of unequal and burdensome taxes and services would more than probably receive a hearing.[74] The government tried eagerly to ameliorate the situation by enacting various measures of relief.[75]

Only when the dynasty approached its close did the tribesmen cease to be "reasonable" and obedient. At that time, they openly showed their discontent by deserting the imperial hunts.[76] They expressed their loss of confidence in the government, not by turning their weapons against it, but by mounting their horses and carts and joining the new tribal upstarts in the northeast, the Jurchen.[77] The winter cold had always been biting; now suddenly the chill in the air and the strain of the hunt became unbearable. The government had always been imperfect and, in a way, demanding; now its deficiencies were conspicuous and its usefulness less apparent. Under the changing political conditions the old grievances, which were indeed aggravated, appeared in an entirely new light. The end of the tribesmen's loyalty bluntly signals the end of the glory and advantage that the conquest situation brought to the Ch'i-tan people.

3. SUBJECT AND DEPENDENT PEOPLES

During the period of political prosperity the Ch'i-tan tribes profited from the imperial rule, whereas the Po-hai, the Chinese, and the subdued tribes were its victims. The Ch'i-tan people, naturally, abstained from revolting against the conquest government. The subject peoples, no less naturally, tried to fight it whenever an appropriate opportunity arose.

a. SEDENTARY PEOPLES: THE PO-HAI

Among the subdued sedentary peoples the Po-hai were treated with particular harshness. Unlike China Proper, their country was not in a state of dissolution when A-pao-chi crossed its borders. The Ch'i-tan did not come to them as bringers but as breakers of the peace. Their government capitulated in the first month of the year 926,[78] and a part of the population rebelled in the third[79] and in the seventh month,[80] thus protesting directly against the conquest, and indirectly against the quick submission of their former rulers. The Ch'i-tan, hardened by conflict and costly success on other fronts, dissolved all possible centers of resistance. They radically reduced the kingdom's ruling house;[81] they exiled the aristocracy to the Central Capital;[82] they ruthlessly weakened the common people by mass deportations to Shang-ching and Chung-ching Circuit.[83]

---

[66] XIII (9) (21).
[67] XIII (22).
[68] XIII (48) (53).
[69] XIII (48) (50).
[70] XIII (44).

[71] X, 1, *passim*.
[72] XI, introduction.
[73] XV, introduction.
[74] XI (8) (11).
[75] XII, *passim*.
[76] XI (27).
[77] XIII (50) (57); *cf.* also CS 2, 16a.
[78] XVI, 926, LS 2, 6a.
[79] XIII (17).
[80] XIII (18).
[81] XIV, introduction.
[82] VIII (2).
[83] I, 3 (2) and I, 1, *passim*.

The remaining population was treated with great suspicion. The rate of conscription for militia service in this eastern territory was only half that of the country at large.[84] Even polo, an old national ball game, was temporarily forbidden,[85] obviously because it was played on horseback and offered an opportunity for military training. Such measures partly provoked, partly countered the numerous Po-hai rebellions recorded in the *Liao Shih*. A serious revolt occurred in the former eastern kingdom in the year 975; the movement was directed by a Po-hai general who eventually was defeated, but not captured, by the Liao army.[86]

The outbreak of 1029–1030 was a revolution rather than a rebellion. The immediate issue was economic, but the final aim was political. The Liao governors tried to impose upon the former Po-hai regions the same rigid system of taxation which they maintained in the southern (Chinese) sections.[87] The new measures led to violent revolt; a number of important Ch'i-tan nobles and officials were imprisoned or killed. The Po-hai leader of the revolution established an independent state, Hsing-liao, and declared himself emperor.[88] It is doubtful whether his regime could have withstood the onslaught of the Liao armies even if Yang Hsiang-shih had not deserted him,[89] for the foundations upon which the new state rested were none too secure and the resources of the Liao empire were unexhausted. Probably Yang's treason only precipitated an inevitable catastrophe. More significant than its collapse is the fact that the rebellion lasted for some months, and that even after it had been put down the Liao treasury was compelled to treat the population with special leniency "for several years."[90]

Whether the suppression of polo dated from the conquest of Po-hai in 926, or whether the measure was introduced only after the revolution of 1029–1030, we do not know. But we do know that the prohibition was lifted at the very moment when the people of Tung-ching Circuit became amenable.[91]

Several decades of relative calm followed. The growing inner difficulties probably affected Tung-ching too, but no serious outbreak is recorded for the second half of the eleventh century. When, however, increasing disintegration weakened the iron grip of the government, the Po-hai were among the first to take up the fight against their hated oppressors. In 1116 the old territory of Po-hai flared in open revolt inspired by political resentment rather than by liquor, as LS 28, 3a ff. would have us believe. Wine had always been drunk in Tung-ching, and intoxication was probably not uncommon, but only in this final period did the consumption of alcohol lead to significant political action. A Po-hai officer proclaimed himself emperor[92] (there were generally more emperors than empires when a great dynasty collapsed). From that time on Tung-ching remained a breeding ground of rebels and rebellions until the new Chin empire gradually "pacified" and consolidated the turbulent political situation.

b. SEDENTARY PEOPLES: THE CHINESE

The specific circumstances that attended the subduing of the Chinese and the specific role they played within the Liao empire determined their specific attitude toward the conquest situation. The Chinese colonists who voluntarily turned to A-pao-chi settled down peacefully and "had no further thought of returning,"[93] at least not during the period covered by this record. The population of China Proper was less acquiescent. Before the region around modern Peiping fell into the hands of the Ch'i-tan, its peasants openly supported the imperial Chinese armies in their fight against the northern barbarians. In 926 the villagers in a kind of guerilla warfare siezed hoes, rakes, and sticks, attacked the scattered Ch'i-tan troops while they were retreating, and killed anyone they caught.[94]

After the conquest was effected the Chinese found it difficult to offer open resistance to a regime which had cleverly divided its new Chinese subjects by resettling many families in the northern circuit and by assigning a junior administrative partnership to their bureaucracy. The block formed by the Ch'i-tan rulers and influential members of the Chinese officialdom consolidated the Liao empire in time of peace and made it possible for it to endure through the long years of the war against Sung China.

It is certainly true that the attitude of the Chinese subjects of the Liao dynasty cannot be measured by the standards of Chinese morale of today. In earlier times the concept of national loyalty was much more elastic than now; but to say that it was different does not mean that it was absent. The *Liao Shih*, composed and supervised by members of the scholarly bureaucracy and learned deputies of the tribal rulers, gave little space to the hostile attitudes of the un-

[84] See I and XV, introductions.
[85] VII, 1 (31).
[86] XIII (30).
[87] X, 1 (2).
[88] XIII (38).
[89] *Loc. cit.*
[90] LS 59, 4b.
[91] See notes 89 and 90.

[92] XIII (48).
[93] WTS 72, 2b ff.; *cf.* III, introduction.
[94] WTS 46, 9a–b.

reconciled Chinese sections of the empire. Such attitudes, however, existed. They were translated into conspicuous acts of political aggression during periods of crisis, such as the Sung war, the economic depression in the eleventh century, and the final decades of Liao rule.

In 979 the Liao defenders of the Southern Capital could not fully rely upon the metropolitan population, for their loyalties were divided;[95] in 981 two hundred Chinese soldiers after their surrender to the Ch'i-tan were inducted into the Liao army and stationed at the Supreme Capital. Here they staged a rebellion which, short-lived though it was, succeeded in proclaiming a new "emperor."[96] In 989 the Liao government had to take action because of the slanderous writings circulated anonymously by certain *chü-jên*.[97] The rising tide of war evidently aroused more ill-feeling among the Chinese subjects of the empire. In 991 in Nan-ching Circuit the avoidance of taxation and labor service was so widespread that Han Tê-jang complained about it in an alarmed report to the court. His request for a representative from the central government was heeded.[98] But the situation was too serious to be met exclusively by "admonitions"; disquieted by the mass abandonment of land by the peasants, the government inaugurated a comprehensive relief policy in the orthodox Chinese style.[99]

The successful completion of the war strengthened the conformist tendencies among the Liao Chinese; it bulwarked the alliance between the Ch'i-tan masters and the Chinese literary bureaucracy. In earlier days, this alliance, based on Ch'i-tan power and incompetence and Chinese experience and cunning, had led to oppressive treatment of the Chinese masses, so oppressive in fact that robber bands were formed which assaulted officials and townspeople in sanguinary battle.[100] The consolidation of the Liao

empire during the second half of the tenth century made a working adjustment possible between the two most important national groups in the government and between each of them and the common people. After 1005 calm prevailed for a few decades, but pressure continued to be imposed by the dual administration. With growing economic distress, these pressures were more keenly felt. The public services demanded were excessive, and poverty grew by leaps and bounds; the people, driven by destitution, thieved, robbed, and rebelled. Murdering without regard for law, the malcontents gathered in the mountains and swamps and instigated revolts.[101] Hsiao Han-chia-nu is careful not to say who was murdered by the rebels, but developments, described in that classic of Chinese banditry, the *Shui Hu Chuan*,[102] suggest that many of the victims had probably been oppressive local officials.

The Chinese revolts which occurred during the later period of the Liao dynasty must be viewed against this background of rural unrest and banditry. In 1043 the population of the old Chinese territories were forbidden to possess bows and arrows.[103] In 1066 a certain Yang Ts'ung tried to set up officials of his own, but his enterprise which lacked adequate support failed miserably.[104] Five years later an edict prohibited the Chinese from hunting.[105] Evidently the government did not wish to give its Chinese subjects any pretext for bearing weapons.

When the empire disintegrated, some Chinese revolutionaries joined the Po-hai fighters,[106] while others acted alone or in conjunction with Sung China.[107] Tung P'ang-êrh assembled more than ten thousand Nan-ching rebels.[108] An Shêng-êrh and Chang Kao-êrh led twenty thousand men against the crumbling Liao government.[109] Other Chinese groups broke away from Liao and surrendered to the rising power of Chin.[110] In 1122 the Chinese inhabitants of the Southern Capital aided the Sung army in an attack upon the Ch'i-tan and the Hsi[111] which succeeded in killing about ten thousand of them. The size and aggressiveness of the rebellious Chinese forces indi-

---

[95] Gabelentz 77, 79.

[96] XIII (31).

[97] XVI, 989, LS 12, 5*a*; XIV, 3, note 25.

[98] XI (13).

[99] XII (20).

[100] The Manchu version of the *Liao History* gives a detailed account of the economic and social conflict that followed the conquest of the Chin capital by T'ai-tsung in 947. The northern ruler wished to reward his victorious soldiers well, and in addition he installed his relatives and trusted followers in important government posts. These high-placed Ch'i-tan nobles "understanding nothing of administration, relied on the fawning and deceitful Chinese, who, under the cloak of promoting their power and happiness, squeezed to the extreme the property of the people so that they could barely satisfy their vital needs. Therefore, bandit gangs sprang up everywhere, the larger ones boasting a membership of many thousands. These seized Dsheosiyan, killed the

officials and the remaining inhabitants and stole the silver and other goods" (Gabelentz 77, 56).

[101] XIII (39).

[102] *Cf.* the novel's English version by Mrs. Buck (Buck 33, *passim*).

[103] XV, 2 (14).

[104] XIII (42).

[105] XV, 2 (21).

[106] XIII (49).

[107] *Cf.* LS 46, 24*b*.

[108] XIII (53).

[109] XIII (55).

[110] *Loc. cit.*

[111] See SCPMHP 11, 2*a*.

cates that the mass of the Chinese population were moved by bitterness against, rather than by loyalty toward, the alien dynasty that had ruled them for more than two hundred years.

c. ADJUSTED AND SEMI-ADJUSTED TRIBES

The peoples of the pacified inner tribes differed from the Chinese both in their relative position within the empire and in their attitude toward its overlords. Their complete subjugation made it possible to class them with the other Ch'i-tan tribes. Their economic and political situation was not without occasional hardship, but the government endeavored to right conspicuous wrongs and to maintain their goodwill by granting them minor privileges.

According to the official classification, the Five Nations belonged to those peoples who, under Shêng-tsung, were added to the empire's inner tribes. Actually, however, the independence of these northeastern border tribes, although temporarily curbed, was never fully destroyed.[112] The establishment of a Liao prefect to control the Five Nations did not secure complete submission; their tributes were never replaced by taxes—a step that would have followed naturally if they had really been equated with the inner tribes. Although the rebellions of these northeastern peoples did not bring them full freedom, they nevertheless prevented as complete an acceptance of the imperial order as the master minds of Liao desired.

Imperial strategy was more successful in dealing with the Hsi people. Each abortive rebellion brought them one step nearer submission to the rule of their powerful Ch'i-tan cousins. The process had already begun by the close of the T'ang period when A-pao-chi's father defeated them and transplanted seven thousand Hsi households to Jao-lo.[113] But whether the Wu-ma Mountain Hsi, who "revolted" in 910,[114] had really been subdued before is not clear. The Western and Eastern Hsi, whom the Ch'i-tan "pacified" in 911, are not designated as rebels by the *Liao Shih*.[115]

Although the Five Tribes of Hsi were added to T'ai-tsu's inner tribes,[116] they did not immediately become loyal Ch'i-tan. When A-pao-chi's brother, Tieh-la, planned his revolt in 913, he was prepared to make himself king of the Hsi people,[117] most probably because he counted upon their hatred of his autocratic relative. Yet whatever hopes he had vanished that same year when the conspiracy collapsed.

In 923 the Hsi were on the war-path again. This time the infuriated emperor was at the end of his patience. Again victorious, he publicly executed the ringleader and three hundred of his followers. The remaining rebels were organized into a separate unit, adding one more to what had been the Five Tribes of Hsi.[118] The Western Hsi had preserved their independence by maintaining good relations with China Proper but, after the cession of the sixteen prefectures by Chin China, their southern support ceased to exist.[119]

From then on the Hsi peoples accepted a semi-independent position, paying tribute—not taxes[120]—to the Liao government whose superiority they no longer challenged. The war against Sung China was not complicated by any serious unrest among the Hsi, for with few exceptions[121] they loyally supported the Ch'i-tan cause. The emergency changed what had been a semi-independent status to complete integration. The tribute payments were discontinued in 994; the Hsi king, now an official of the central government, relied solely upon his regular emolument; and the old Hsi capital became the Central Capital of the empire in 1007, a few years after peace had been concluded with Sung China.[122]

During the second half of the Liao reign the Hsi continued faithfully to support the Ch'i-tan regime. Only at the end of the dynasty, when revolts occurred everywhere, did rebellion rear its head again in Chung-ching Circuit. Some part of a rebel force of ten thousand men had been recruited from this district[123] but whether this included Hsi insurgents is not clear. When the Liao empire disintegrated, the old inner tribes, which had enjoyed special privileges within the conquest situation, were fearful and bewildered. Disinclined to take up arms against the crumbling Ch'i-tan government, they either remained quietly in their own territory or moved away to avoid being drawn into the struggle. The fact that the Po-hai were specifically mentioned as ringleaders in this rebellion[124] makes the participation of Hsi tribesmen still more doubtful, for it is difficult to imagine that they would cooperate with a group of settlers with whom they shared neither language nor culture nor political position. In the same year, in another revolt, this time in the Liao capital in the old Po-hai territory, Hsi (and Chinese) soldiers acted as the military police

---

[112] For an account of the changing relations of the Five Nations and the Liao government see X, introduction.

[113] LS 1, 2a.

[114] XVI, 910, LS 1, 3b.

[115] XIII (4).

[116] LS 1, 4a.

[117] XIII (8).

---

[118] XIII (14); I, 2 (4), no. 10.

[119] WTS 74, 1b.

[120] X, 1 (7); cf. also X, introduction.

[121] A Hsi officer, Ai-li-hsia 隘離轄, deserted to Sung in the year 986 (LS 11, 3b).

[122] See X, introduction.

[123] XIII (49).

[124] Loc. cit.

of the government, arresting and killing the recalcitrant Po-hai rebels.[125]

The "bandit," Chang Sa-pa, who led a revolt in the Chung-ching region and made himself emperor in 1119,[126] may have been a Hsi tribesman. Hui-li-pao, a high Liao official, certainly was of Hsi descent. His attempt to establish a new Hsi empire which included representation for the Chinese and Po-hai neither proves nor disproves the loyalty of the Hsi people to the Ch'i-tan government. This government had practically ceased to function when Hui-li-pao established his reign which lasted "altogether eight months."[127]

d. DEPENDENT AND SEMI-DEPENDENT TRIBES

Formally, the Five Nations were classed with the empire's inner tribes, and the Hsi, after a period of resistance, actually were coordinated. No such claim can be made for the numerous border peoples who, although dependent in one way or another upon the Liao government, never became completely integrated in its "inner" tribal system. Their revolts were a mixture of border conflicts and civil wars. But, since the *Liao Shih* calls them rebellions and since they were indeed attacks against the authority of the Liao empire, they may well be discussed in this category.

Whenever the Liao government gained control over a border people it tried to maintain its power either with the aid of the old tribal leader or through a new man of their choice who, in accordance with his formal position, might be given an official Liao ranking, such as great king, *hsiang-wên*, or prefect.[128] Hsiao Han-chia-nu, in his brilliant exposé, emphasized two ways of insuring successful domination over the border tribes: (1) by appointing a chief for each tribe, (2) by making each tribe pay its tribute annually.[129]

Obviously, the Liao government was not always in a position to appoint its own tested officials, but that it was eager to do so is clearly indicated by its refusal to permit the Hua-li tribes to choose their *hsiang-wên* from among their own members.[130] A number of other passages record the installation of Liao-appointed officials as heads of the border tribes.[131] Similarly, the government strove to make the barbarian peoples pay tribute and, in addition, render labor and military service. Again the reality fell short of the goal, but our survey of the tribute and

services given to the empire shows how heavy a burden could be placed on a border tribe, if that tribe happened to be held under the control of the Liao empire.[132]

As might be expected, the official records of the dynasty do not fully reveal the cruel treatment meted out to the border peoples, but the annals of the southern courts are less reserved. The *Wu-tai Shih* has preserved certain accusations levelled at the Liao government by embittered tribal spokesmen who had fled from Liao territory to China Proper. The Ch'i-tan, they complained, oppressed them by brutally seizing their people, their sheep and horses, and by mobilizing their men and arms for military campaigns. The tribal emissaries "all wept when speaking of their hardship and wanted to take revenge."[133]

Small wonder, then, that the border tribes engaged in anti-Liao activity whenever the political situation permitted. If their chieftain was ready to lead the fight, they accepted his leadership.[134] But often the initial step in a revolt was the assassination of the tribal chieftain[135] or the appointed Liao official,[136] evidently because the tribespeople considered these men their enemies. The discontented tribes either fought their oppressors openly—and this happened frequently[137]—or they tried to avoid their obligations by changing their pastoral residence, sometimes taking refuge in neighboring tribes or states such as Hsi Hsia and the great empire of China Proper. When those who gave asylum were strong, no demand for the return of the deserters might be made; or, if made, it might not meet with compliance.

The tribes whose complaints are registered in the *Wu-tai Shih* and the forty households that fled to the Wu-ku in 965[138] belong in this last category. So do the five tribes that escaped to the Hsi Hsia in 1044. The population of the border zone from which they fled was normalized by settling other families there.[139] But in most instances recorded in the *Liao Shih*, the demands for the return of tribal deserters were met;[140] the fugitives were returned to their former residences[141] where they resumed their occupations,[142] forced, no doubt, to fulfill again all the financial and service obligations implicit in their dependent status.

---

[125] XIII (48).
[126] XIII (56).
[127] XIII (59).
[128] For this title *cf*. XIV, 1 (23) (24); see also XIV, introduction.
[129] LS 103, 3a.
[130] XIII (33).
[131] *Cf*. LS 69, 14b; 70, 15b ff.

---

[132] See X, XI, and XV, *passim*.
[133] WTS 51, 13b–14a.
[134] XVI, 1000, LS 14, 2a; 70, 10b.
[135] LS 69, 7a.
[136] XVI, 965, LS 7, 1b; *cf*. also LS 69, 10a, 11b, 18a ff.
[137] See LS 69, *passim*.
[138] LS 69, 7a.
[139] LS 69, 15a–b.
[140] *Cf*. LS 69, 13b.
[141] *Cf*. LS 69, 11a and 70, 7a.
[142] *Cf*. LS 69, 14a–b.

e. WHO REBELLED WHEN?

The numerous rebellions against the Liao empire were neither aimless nor accidental. They followed trends in the country's growth and decline, revealing and accenting specific difficulties and conflicts which derived from specific historical situations. Thus the first decades of the dynasty bristled with court rebellions, for then the new order of succession had not yet been accepted by the rival Yeh-lü lineages. The wars against Sung China encouraged disaffection and sabotage among the Chinese subjects and increased hostility in the tribal border regions. Tribal unrest continued to smoulder during the war against Korea, while the Chinese population remained amenable, evidently resigned after peace had been concluded with Sung in 1005. Isolated revolts, such as that in the old Po-hai territory in 1029–1030, and local uprisings led by discontented Chinese bandit-rebels indicated that the society of conquest had not overcome its inner contradictions although it could control them, at least for a time.

The empire's general decay led to an outburst of open rebellion in its agrarian as well as in its pastoral sector. As in the past, the different ethnic groups within the empire behaved differently. The Po-hai and Chinese rebels desired the overthrow of the Liao government, while the Ch'i-tan nobles and tribesmen contributed to the empire's dissolution more by resignation and passivity than by aggressive action. When leading Ch'i-tan (and Hsi) attempted to establish new "empires" of their own, the old empire had already disintegrated beyond hope of survival.

f. A–KU–TA REFUSES TO DANCE

In the turmoil of the last decades the border tribes played an accessory rather than a leading role—with one exception, that of the "savage" Jurchen. As their name implies these tribes had never been fully subdued by the Liao government. Living beyond the eastern borders, they rendered their powerful neighbor only as much respect as was required by military and political necessity.

Like other semi-dependent border peoples, the Jurchen paid tribute. Their chieftains were given the opportunity—and the duty—of appearing before the Liao emperor when he came to fish once each year in the frontier rivers. He feasted the visiting chieftains who, in turn, might be asked to dance before him, a request that expressed ceremonially the power of the ruler of Liao over his tributary guests.[143] Their willingness to comply was a tacit acknowledgment of their political inferiority.

It would seem that the head chief of the "savage" Jurchen had in former times danced before the emperor, as had the other chieftains. But by 1112 the political prestige of Liao was rapidly waning. The imperial armies had lost their old striking power; they now feared those very tribes that formerly they had intimidated. Prominent among the suspect peoples were the Jurchen whose political unity was growing with their military success.

Thoughtful Liao statesmen understood the revolutionary changes occurring beyond the northeastern border. Not so the emperor, T'ien-tsu, who still expected reverence and obedience as usual. In 1112, at the winter's end, when the Jurchen chieftains assembled in the imperial camp to participate in the traditional First Fish Feast, the emperor, half drunk as were his guests, ordered the mighty Jurchen chief, A-ku-ta, to dance before him.[144]

The scene was picturesque, the action dramatic. On the sandy tracts that surrounded the favorite northeastern fishing ground,[145] the tents of the imperial winter camp stood out theatrically against a background of elm, willow, and apricot trees.[146] There in his dragon-ornamented chariot, was seated T'ien-tsu, the ruler of an empire which had terrorized the Far Eastern world for two hundred long, bitter years. He called upon the head chieftain of a dangerous border tribe to step into the space opened by the spectators, Liao nobles and soldiers, tribal leaders and warriors. A-ku-ta was to pay homage to the glory of Liao by dancing for her intoxicated emperor.

The great Jurchen chieftain refused. Again the emperor asked. Again his request was refused. On the surface this was merely a breach of etiquette. Actually it was much more. A-ku-ta's deliberate effrontery announced to the startled onlookers that the time was over when Liao could order and the world would dance. His bold refusal was a breach of etiquette that initiated a revolution. The obstinate chieftain who signaled the political decay of the Liao empire was the founder of the next great Chinese dynasty of conquest, Chin.

---

[143] VII, 2 (19).

[144] XIII (45).

[145] At the Hun-t'ung River, which was actually the Duck River Lake, formed by what today is the Sungari River (see II, 1, note 54).

[146] II, 1 (24).

TRANSLATION

REBELLIONS

1. A-pao-chi overthrows the old tribal order 2. Yao-lien replaced 3. Personality tests 4. The Hsi "pacified" 5. The emperor's brothers rebel 6. The brothers rebel again 7. The brothers "repent" 8. The brothers rebel once more 9. Capture of the rebels 10. Treatment of the rebels 11. Rebellion affects the people 12. La-ko's last rebellion 13. Tieh-la rebels again 14. A rebellion of the Hsi 15. La-ko's death 16. Shall the eldest son succeed? 17. The Po-hai not yet pacified 18. Another Po-hai rebellion 19. Opposition to Shih-tsung's accession 20. The eldest son should succeed his father 21. Punishment for rebellious Ch'i-tan nobles 22. A Hsiao noble conspires 23. Shih-tsung murdered 24. A high dignitary rebels 25. Shih-tsung's brother and others plan treason 26. Li-hu's second son, Wan, rebels 27. Li-hu's first son, Hsi-yin, rebels 28. An emperor murdered by his servants 29. Hsi-yin pardoned by Ching-tsung 30. A territorial official rebels 31. Hsi-yin rebels against Ching-tsung 32. Tribes difficult to control 33. Request for indigenous *hsiang-wên* refused 34. Northern tribes rebel 35. They return to their old regions 36. Fugitive tribesmen 37. Revolt of the Tsu-pu tribes 38. The Po-hai revolt of 1029–1030 39. Growing misery, growing banditry 40. Fugitive tribesmen brought back 41. Revolt of Tao-tsung's uncle 42. A Chinese rebellion suppressed 43. Tao-tsung's son, the heir apparent, killed 44. The rebellion of Hsiao Hai-li 45. A-ku-ta refuses to dance 46. Revolt of the Jurchen 47. Defeat and death of the rebel Chang-nu 48. The old territory of Po-hai in rebellion 49. Rebellion in the central region 50. Imperial clansmen surrender to the Jurchen 51. Another Po-hai rebellion 52. The army breaks up 53. Rebellion in the southern parts of Liao 54. Banditry and cannibalism 55. Further dissolution 56. Another "emperor" in Chung-ching 57. Intrigue and dissolution 58. The empire split between two emperors 59. A Hsi "emperor"

1. A–PAO–CHI OVERTHROWS THE OLD TRIBAL ORDER

907   The chieftains of the eight tribes [of the Ch'i-tan] according to the rule were regularly replaced every three years. When Yeh-lü A-pao-chi of the I-la tribe set up the drums and banners,[1] established an independent tribe, and, unwilling to accept replacement, announced himself as king,[2] he came into possession of the entire Ch'i-tan state. The Yao-lien family thereupon came to an end.   63, 8a–b

2. YAO–LIEN REPLACED

907   On the day *kêng-tzŭ* [of the first month in the first year of T'ai-tsu's accession] it was decreed that the imperial clan was to succeed the nine tents of the Yao-lien lineage as the tenth tent.[3]   1, 2b

3. PERSONALITY TESTS

907–926   Once, when T'ai-tsu looked at his sons in their sleep and saw Li-hu[4] lying with his neck drawn in, he remarked that he would be inferior to all the other sons.

On another occasion, during a severe cold, he ordered the three sons to gather firewood. T'ai-tsung[5] gathered the wood indiscriminately and returned first. Prince Jên-huang[6] gathered dry wood, tied it up in bundles, and returned last. Li-hu gathered least and lost most. On returning he put his hands in his sleeves and stood there.

T'ai-tsu[7] said, "The eldest son is clever and the second accomplished; the youngest cannot come up to them."

But the mother loved Li-hu devotedly.   72, 4a

---

[1] Drums and banners were the symbols of supreme tribal power, as the seal was the symbol of the imperial rank in China Proper. Almost three hundred years before the above event, in 629, a Ch'i-tan chieftain, Mo-hui 摩會, visited the T'ang court and was honored by the bestowal of a drum and a large banner (LS 63, 4a).

[2] The title *wang* 王 (king) was bestowed upon the supreme chieftain of the Ch'i-tan by the T'ang government (XIV, 1 (2)). The position which A-pao-chi created for himself was that of a supreme ruler.

[3] For the explanation of the formula "the tenth tent" see VII, introduction.

[4] T'ai-tsu's third son. He unsuccessfully competed with Shih-tsung for the throne in 947.

[5] T'ai-tsu's second son, who became emperor in 926.

[6] T'ai-tsu's eldest son.

[7] We follow other editions in reading 祖 for the 子 of our text.

4. THE HSI "PACIFIED"

911 On the day *ping-shên* [of the first month in the fifth year of T'ai-tsu's accession] the emperor personally led an attack on the Western Hsi. . . . The Eastern Hsi were also pacified.[8]   1, 4*a*

5. THE EMPEROR'S BROTHERS REBEL

911 In the fifth month [of the fifth year of T'ai-tsu's accession] the emperor's younger brothers, La-ko,[9] Tieh-la,[10] Yin-ti-shih,[11] and An-tuan,[12] planned to rebel. Through An-tuan's wife, Nien-mu-ku, who knew of it and gave information, the truth was obtained. The emperor, who could not bear to kill them, climbed to the top of a mountain with his brothers, killed animals as a sacrifice, made an oath to Heaven and Earth, and pardoned their crime. La-ko was made *i-li-chin* of the I-la tribe, and Nien-mu-ku was granted the rank of Lady of Chin.[13]   1, 4*a*

6. THE BROTHERS REBEL AGAIN

912 On the day *mou-yin* of the tenth month in the winter [of the sixth year of T'ai-tsu's accession] La-ko, after conquering P'ing Prefecture,[14] returned and again rebelled with Tieh-la, Yin-ti-shih, and An-tuan.   1, 4*b*

7. THE BROTHERS "REPENT"

912 On the day *jên-ch'ên* [of the tenth month in the sixth year of T'ai-tsu's accession] T'ai-tsu on his way back stopped at Northern A-lu Mountain where he learned that his brothers had blocked the roads with soldiers. At the head of an army he rushed south to the Shih-ch'i Lakes.[15] On this day firewood was burned.[16] The next day, when T'ai-tsu halted at the Ch'i-tu River,[17] the brothers all sent messengers to apologize. The emperor still[18] had compassion on them and permitted them to reform.   1, 4*b*

8. THE BROTHERS REBEL ONCE MORE

913 On the day *kuei-ch'ou* of the third month [in the seventh year of T'ai-tsu's accession], when T'ai-tsu halted at the Lu River, his younger brother, Tieh-la-ko,[19] plotted to make himself king of Hsi. With An-tuan he rushed up more than a thousand horsemen, pretending that he had come to visit the emperor. The emperor said angrily, "When you fellows first plotted rebellion, We gave you a special pardon so that you might repent and reform. But you are still unreliable and would do harm to Us."

Thereupon he put them under arrest and had their subordinates distributed under the control of the various armies. La-ko, however, led his band to I-shih-chin-tien. He made ready the banners

---

[8] From the fifth century down to the middle of the ninth century the Hsi were a powerful people who resided in the territory of modern Jehol. In 847 a T'ang general, Chang Chung-wu 張仲武 (d. 849), defeated the Hsi and was alleged to have burned two hundred thousand tents. Whatever the real figure was, this defeat manifestly weakened the Hsi to a very high degree. For the gradual subjugation of the Hsi people by the growing Liao power see LS 73, 1*b*; WTS 74, 1*a–b*; WHTK 344, 2700.

[9] The eldest of T'ai-tsu's younger brothers (T. 剌懶 or 撒剌). He was appointed to the post of *t'i-yin* of the imperial clan in 908.

[10] T'ai-tsu's second younger brother.

[11] The third younger brother of T'ai-tsu. A simple and unsophisticated character, he was murdered in 926 while on his way to assist his nephew, Pei, to rule Po-hai (LS 64, 5*b*).

[12] The fourth younger brother of T'ai-tsu. He was appointed *t'i-yin* of the imperial clan in 918 (LS 64, 6*a*).

[13] The *Liao Shih* does not discuss this title. Under the Chin 金 dynasty the wife of a prince was granted the title of *fu-jên* 夫人 of the first rank (CS 55, 11*b*). The formula *chin kuo* 晉國 *fu-jên* was applied to an honorary position of the first rank. It seems possible that the Liao system, in this respect as in many others, was similar to that of Chin.

[14] Modern Lu-lung 盧龍 County, Hopei.

[15] See below, note 109.

[16] Probably as a sacrifice.

[17] The Ch'i-tu 七渡 River is the Ch'i-tu 度 or Ch'ao-li 朝鯉 River (CTKC 24, 1*b*) which corresponds to a river near modern Ku-pei-k'ou 古北口, north of Peiping.

[18] We follow other editions in reading 上猶 for the 止蘅 of our text.

[19] The same as Tieh-la 迭剌, the second of T'ai-tsu's younger brothers. The word *ko* 哥 was probably a Ch'i-tan suffix. The *Liao Shih* mentions many personal names ending in *ko*.

and drums of a Son of Heaven and was about to make himself emperor. The empress dowager secretly dispatched a messenger to advise him to make his escape.   1, 5a

9. CAPTURE OF THE REBELS

913   [When T'ai-tsu] personally headed an attack against the tribes of the southwest, Hsia-ti[20] induced La-ko and others to rebel. Those who did not follow were killed. When the emperor returned to Ch'ih-shui City,[21] Hsia-ti became frightened and together with La-ko fled north to the Yü River,[22] where they were captured by the pursuing soldiers.

T'ai-tsu asked, "Previously, when We ascended the throne, We offered to yield the country to you, Our uncle, but you refused it. Why do you now rebel and want to place Our younger brother on the throne?"

Hsia-ti replied, "At first I did not realize how exalted a Son of Heaven is. Then Your Majesty ascended the throne. With your guard of attendants you were extremely dignified and in a different class from the common run of people. Once, when I reported a matter to the throne, my heart was stirred, and I began to have the idea of looking around [for an opportunity]. I reasoned that Your Majesty, being resolute and courageous, certainly could not be ensnared, but that, since your younger brothers are weak, once they had taken over [the throne] it would be easy to plot against them. After the affair had been accomplished, how could I have tolerated them?"

T'ai-tsu addressed his younger brothers, saying, "Do you follow the words of this man?"

Tieh-la replied, "Those who plan great enterprises must utilize such persons. After the thing has been accomplished, then they must be done away with."

Hsia-ti made no further reply. He was kept prisoner for several months and then strangled to death.   112, 2a

913   On the day *kuei-ch'ou* of the fifth month [in the seventh year of T'ai-tsu's accession] the northern prime minister,[23] Ti-lien,[24] was sent in command of daring horsemen to cross [the Cha-tu River][25] first. On the day *chia-yin* he reported the capture of La-ko, Nieh-li-kun,[26] and A-po at the Yü River. The former northern prime minister, Hsiao Shih-lu,[27] and Yin-ti-shih tried to cut their own throats but failed to kill themselves.[28] Then black and white sheep were sacrificed to Heaven and Earth.[29]   1, 6a

10. TREATMENT OF THE REBELS

913   On the day *chi-mao* of the eighth month [in the seventh year of T'ai-tsu's accession] the emperor went to Lung-mei Palace. Twenty-nine rebels were torn to pieces by carts. Their wives and daughters were given to meritorious generals and officers. The valuables and animals which had been seized by them were returned to the original owners. In cases where the original articles were lost the families [of the rebels] were ordered to make compensation. Those who could not make compensation were ordered to give up their retainers.   1, 7a

---

[20] See introduction.

[21] Ch'ih-shui 赤水 City probably corresponds to modern Ch'ih City, Chahar.

[22] Probably a river in central Chahar.

[23] This outstanding hereditary position was generally granted to members of the clan of the empress.

[24] Ti-lien 迪輦 was the style of Hsiao Ti-lu 敵魯, a younger brother of T'ai-tsu's wife. He assisted T'ai-tsu in crushing several rebellions and in expanding the Ch'i-tan territory. He died in 918 (LS 73, 4a–b).

[25] The Cha-tu 札塔 River was probably the Ch'i-tu River. See note 17.

[26] After his capture, Nieh-li-kun 涅里袞, an *i-li-chin*, was ordered to commit suicide by throwing himself from a cliff (LS 1, 7a).

[27] Hsiao Shih-lu 室 (or 實) 魯 or Hsia-la 轄剌 was the brother of Empress Ch'un-ch'iu. He married a daughter of T'ai-tsu; later one of his daughters was married to T'ai-tsung. Being of very high rank, he was appointed prime minister of the Northern Administration in 907, but was replaced by Hsiao Ti-lu in 910 (*cf.* LS 1, 2b, 3b; 65, 1b).

[28] Both survived and were released by T'ai-tsu (LS 64, 5b).

[29] Probably to celebrate the capture of the rebels.

914   The rebellious group examined by the officials numbered more than three hundred
persons. When the trial was completed,[30] the emperor, considering that human life
was of the utmost importance and that once ended it could not be restored, granted them a feast in
which for one day they were permitted to follow their ordinary desires. When they became intoxicated, some sang, some danced, and some practised shooting or wrestling. Everyone satisfied his
own wishes. The next day sentences were meted out according to the seriousness [of the crimes].
La-ko was pronounced the chief offender, the next being Tieh-la-ko.[31] The emperor, who still kept
his brotherly love for them, could not bear to apply the law and so released them after a beating.
Because Yin-ti-shih and An-tuan were mediocre and weak by nature, so that they had been made
use of by La-ko, the crimes of both were pardoned. The former *yü-yüeh* Ho-ti-li,[32] his son, Hsieh-li,[33]
and the wife of La-ko, Hsia-la-ssŭ, who had actually participated in the plot to revolt, were ordered
killed by strangulation. The wife of Yin-ti-shih, Nieh-li, who had been coerced into taking part,
and the wife of An-tuan, Nien-mu-ku,[34] who had shown her loyalty by disclosing [the plot], were
both acquitted.   1, 7b–8a

11. REBELLION AFFECTS THE PEOPLE

914   On the first day *ping-shên* of the seventh month in the autumn [of the eighth year
of T'ai-tsu's accession] the officials presented to the throne a verdict of guilty for more
than three hundred persons from various camps and lineages[35] who had plotted rebellion. They
were all publicly executed. The emperor sighed, "How could putting people to death be what We
desire? If they had revolted only against Ourself, they might still have been shown mercy. But
these men have acted unrestrainedly and inhumanly. They have committed outrages against loyal
and good persons. They have caused great distress to the people and have looted them of their
property. Those among the people who formerly had ten thousand horses must now all walk on
foot. Since We have come into possession of the state this has never happened before. We really
had no alternative but to kill them."[36]   1, 8a–b

12. LA–KO'S LAST REBELLION

917   [On the day *i-ssŭ* of the sixth month of the second year of Shên-ts'ê], La-ko and his
son, Sai-pao-li, rebelled and entered Yu Prefecture.[37]   1, 10a

13. TIEH–LA REBELS AGAIN

918   On the day *i-ssŭ* of the fourth month [of the third year of Shên-ts'ê] the emperor's
younger brother, Tieh-lieh-ko,[38] plotted a rebellion. The affair was discovered.
Knowing that he was guilty and deserved death, he built a tomb beforehand. But his relatives
asked that he be pardoned.

The emperor, who had a hatred for Nieh-li-kun, the wife of his younger brother, Yin-ti-shih,
thereupon said, "If Nieh-li-kun is willing to take his place in death, We will agree." Nieh-li-kun
strangled herself in the grave. Together with her, the slave Nü-ku and the rebel Ho-lu-chih were
buried alive in it. Then Tieh-lieh-ko was pardoned.   1, 10b

---

[30] Some time between the first and seventh months in 914.

[31] See above, note 19.

[32] According to LS 112, 1b–2b, Ho-ti-li 赫底里 is iden-tical with Hsia-ti 轄底. The divergence in the two names is caused by two different transcriptions of the original Ch'i-tan words. Hsia-ti suggested the division of the I-la tribe into two parts just before his death in 914.

[33] Hsieh-li 解里 is another transcription for Hai-lin 海隣, the style of Tieh-li-t'ê 迭里特 (LS 112, 2b).

[34] In 911, when the emperor's brothers first rebelled, she divulged the plot to T'ai-tsu (LS 1, 4a).

[35] Besides the emperor's brothers, descendants of the imperial clan had also participated in the plot (LS 112, 1b–2b; 5b–6a).

[36] In 916, after this revolt had been crushed, the first reign period of Liao, Shên-ts'ê 神册, was fixed. The Sung literature, therefore, takes this year to be the begin-ning of the Liao dynasty.

[37] Modern Peiping. At this time the territory of Yu was held by the Prince of Chin 晋, Li Ts'un-hsü, who in 923 founded the Later T'ang dynasty.

[38] Another name for Tieh-la.

14. A REBELLION OF THE HSI

923　　　　On the day *mou-yin* of the third month [in the second year of T'ien-tsan, T'ai-tsu] led an army to the Chien-ko Mountain,[39] crushed Hu-sun of the rebellious Hsi and captured him. He was executed by being shot with "devil arrows"[40] and his three hundred partisans were drowned in the Kou River.[41] The [rest of the rebellious] Hsi were set up as the To-kuei tribe,[42] Po-lu-ên[43] being temporarily placed in charge of its affairs.　　　2, 3b

15. LA-KO'S DEATH

923　　　　[La-ko], while fleeing south from Yu Prefecture, was killed by someone.[44]　　　64, 3a

16. SHALL THE ELDEST SON SUCCEED?

926　　　　After the death of T'ai-tsu,[45] Empress Ch'un-ch'in assumed the reins of government and wanted the grand commander in chief[46] to succeed to the throne. [Yeh-lü] Tieh-li[47] suggested that the emperor's position should be given first to the eldest son of the principal consort, and that, since the Prince of Tung-tan[48] had arrived at the court, he should be made emperor. He thus offended the imperial will. Accused of forming a clique in support of the Prince of Tung-tan he was ordered to be imprisoned and to be cross-examined with the hot pillar,[49] but as he did not confess he was killed and his family seized and their property confiscated.[50]　　　77, 5a

---

[39] Modern Ch'a-p'ên 茶盆 Mountain, seventy *li* northwest of Lin-yü 臨渝 County, Hopei.

[40] See VII, 2, note 141.

[41] Probably a river north of the Great Wall in Jehol.

[42] Probably located in the northeastern part of modern Hopei.

[43] One of Po-lu-ên's 勃魯恩 descendants, Hsiao Han-chia-nu, suppressed a rebellion in 1063 and was promoted to the rank of prince (LS 96, 4b–5a).

[44] This statement contains two errors: La-ko was not killed while fleeing south from Yu, and he was not put to death by an unknown hand. After his flight to Yu, he was well received by the Prince of Chin 晉 who even raised him to the rank of prefect (TCTC 270, 10a). But in 923, after having made himself the first emperor of the Later T'ang dynasty, the erstwhile prince killed the exile, officially "because he had rebelled against his elder brother, deserted his mother, and betrayed his country" (TCTC 272, 9a), but more probably because he hoped thus to win the favor of the Liao ruler.

[45] He died in the seventh month of 926.

[46] This title was bestowed upon T'ai-tsu's second son, the later T'ai-tsung, who became emperor in 927 (LS 3, 1a).

[47] Yeh-lü Tieh-li 迭里 was the *i-li-chin* of the Southern Division (LS 2, 7b).

[48] T'ai-tsu's eldest son, Pei.

[49] What the torture of the hot pillar 炮烙 really entailed is not quite clear. The malefactor was forced either to embrace a hollow cylindrical pillar in which a fire had been kindled or to walk across a greased metal column which was placed horizontally above a fire (see Chavannes, MH I, 201).

[50] Chao I observes that the eldest sons of the Liao emperors usually met with an unhappy end. As proof of his thesis he cites the following facts:

T'ai-tsu's eldest son, Pei, was compelled to yield the throne to his younger brother, T'ai-tsung, and Shih-tsung, Pei's son, succeeded his uncle. Mu-tsung, T'ai-tsung's son succeeded his cousin, Shih-tsung. Ching-tsung, Shih-tsung's second son succeeded his uncle, Mu-tsung. Shêng-tsung, though Ching-tsung's eldest son, was not made heir apparent during his father's lifetime. When Hsing-tsung and Tao-tsung were born, their mothers were not yet empresses. Tao-tsung's eldest son, Chün, was killed; Chün's wife was delivered of her eldest son, the later T'ien-tsu, before she was named empress (NESCC 27, 9a–b).

The facts presented do not always substantiate the thesis, but Chao I has rightly called attention to certain striking peculiarities in the pattern of Liao succession. This pattern was evidently rooted in a tribal tradition of fraternal succession which strongly asserted itself during the early part of the Liao dynasty, and which, even during the later period, led to numerous conflicts and disturbances. To judge from the available facts, it would seem that at the close of the predynastic period the chieftainship of the I-la tribe moved in the collateral in preference to the direct line. LS 2, 8b gives only one *i-li-chin* for each generation, but the concrete historical records clearly indicate that several members in the collateral line held this office before it descended to the next generation (*cf.* XIII, introduction, fig. 37). Thus the tribal Ch'i-tan, like the Po-hai, Koreans, Jurchen, and Mongols, recognized fraternal claims to succession (PHKCCP 6, 4b; CLLS 1a; CHHC 18, 217; HNYL 84, 1387; MAC 24, 5b).

A-pao-chi's conflicts with his brothers arose most probably out of his determination to rule for life and to assure the throne to his sons, substituting direct succession with emphasis on primogeniture for the traditional tribal pattern. Chinese sources claim that A-pao-chi, unwilling to be "replaced" after a khaghanate of nine years, killed the rival chieftains (WTS 72, 2b–3a; CTKC 23, 2a). No reference is made to these purges in the older sections of the *Liao Shih*, but the *History* offers abundant testimony on the frequent struggles for power between A-pao-chi and his brothers in the early days of his rule.

T'ai-tsu became khaghan in 907. His brothers rebelled in 911, that is, after his first three-year "term" had expired. To appease them La-ko was appointed *i-li-chin* of the I-la tribe. In 912, evidently discontented with his rank, he again joined with his brothers in rebellion. In 913, in the first year of A-pao-chi's third term, La-ko tried to establish himself as emperor (for data on this and the following points see XIII and XVI, *passim*). The attempt failed, and in 916, the first year of his fourth term, A-pao-chi, like the emperors of China, assumed a reign title and proclaimed his eldest son, Pei, the heir apparent. La-ko, deprived of his traditional prerogative, rebelled again in 917; the following year his brother Tieh-lieh-ko also rebelled. After T'ai-tsu's death the struggle for the throne flared up time and again. Usually, brothers, uncles, and cousins of the new emperor asserted their claim in line with the tribal tradition of fraternal succession.

Within the direct line primogeniture was frequently contested. T'ai-tsu's widow forced her eldest son, Pei, to resign in favor of his brother, T'ai-tsung (CTKC 14, 1a ff.). In 930 T'ai-tsung's brother, Li-hu, was made heir apparent (LS 3, 4b and CTKC 14, 2a; according to LS 64, 8b; 72, 4a; and 113, 3a he was made "the emperor's great younger brother 皇太弟"). After T'ai-tsung's death in 947 the empress dowager endeavored to place T'ai-tsung's brother, Li-hu, on the throne. The plan met defeat because of the military strength of Pei's son, Shih-tsung. Interestingly, the title "emperor" was given posthumously to T'ai-tsung's two brothers (LS 72, 2b and 4b). From the Chinese standpoint the honoring of Pei is appropriate for he was the original heir apparent and his son eventually became emperor. In the case of Li-hu the distinction can only be understood as an open recognition of the legitimacy of the collateral claim.

Shih-tsung was assassinated by Ch'a-ko 察割 and P'ên-tu 盆都, sons of T'ai-tsu's younger brothers, An-tuan and Yin-ti-shih, respectively (LS 5, 3a; 112, 3a; 113, 3b). Mu-tsung's imperial position was challenged first by Pei's son, Lou-kuo (LS 112, 4b) and Li-hu's sons, Wan and Hsi-yin. The latter as well as Li-hu's grandson, Liu-li-shou, also contested the claim of the next emperor, Ching-tsung, and Liu-li-shou temporarily succeeded in usurping the throne. Shêng-tsung faced a strong political coalition, controlled by a number of paternal uncles, cousins, and other relatives. Their power was eventually broken by the Empress Dowager Ch'êng-t'ien, who skillfully used the Liao Chinese troops led by Han Tê-jang (CTKC 18, 2a).

Hsing-tsung was the eldest son of his mother, the Empress Dowager Ch'in-ai, who originally was a concubine (the empress' two sons died early), but he was not the eldest concubine-son of Shêng-tsung. An elder concubine-half-brother of Hsing-tsung attained important offices before or shortly after his birth (*cf.* LS 15, 6b, 10a; 64, 16b). In 1034 the Empress Dowager Ch'in-ai tried to replace her eldest son, Hsing-tsung, by his brother, Chung-yüan. The effort failed and she was ordered to live near her husband's mausoleum until 1037 (LS 71, 6a). In 1054, in the course of a conversation with the Sung envoy, Wang Kung-ch'ên, Ch'in-ai noted with approval that the first two Sung rulers had been brothers, while her son, the emperor, underlined the propriety of the relationship which existed between the second and third Sung rulers who had been father and son. Alone with the foreign visitor, Hsing-tsung added that, should his younger brother seize the Liao throne, the Sung empire would not be able to live in peace (HTCCP 177, 5a). In 1063 Chung-yüan and his son, together with T'ieh-pu 貼不, a son of Shêng-tsung's second younger brother, and certain other rebels would have defeated Tao-tsung had it not been for the aid of his Yeh-lü and Hsiao relatives (LS 112, 5a ff.; 22, 1b). Tao-tsung, after having imprisoned his son, Chün, first considered choosing Chün's cousin, his nephew, Ch'un, heir apparent before he appointed Chün's son, the later T'ien-tsu (SCPMHP 5, 3a).

During T'ien-tsu's reign continued internal strife hastened the collapse of the Liao empire. In 1115 a rebellious Ch'i-tan group urged Ch'un, an uncle of T'ien-tsu, to seize power. He refused to do so at this time, but seven years later he replaced his unfortunate nephew, ascending the throne at the Southern Capital (XIII (47) (58)). After Ch'un's death T'ien-tsu's fifth son, the Prince of Ch'in, who previously had contested his elder concubine-brother's (Prince of Chin) candidacy, was made emperor under the regency of Ch'un's wife (LS 29, 1a–2a, 4b). In 1123 Ya-li 雅里, the second son of T'ien-tsu, was made emperor in the northwest region. After his death Chu-lieh 朮烈, a descendant in the fourth generation of Wu-ko 吳哥, a brother of Hsing-tsung, became emperor (LS 29, 6b; 64, 16b).

These many facts indicate how ardently succession in the direct line was contested throughout the Liao period. Before Ching-tsung's reign the collateral claim was often successful. From that time on succession in the direct line prevailed, but not without repeated struggle. Within the direct line, and despite the not disinterested efforts of the empress dowagers to oppose it, primogeniture was also victorious.

In indirect recognition of their claim, collateral relatives were usually given high positions. After Pei became heir apparent, his brother, the later T'ai-tsung, was made grand commander in chief (LS 3, 1a). Li-hu was offered the same honor in 930; and, when his imperial brother was engaged in a distant campaign, he guarded the Supreme Capital (LS 64, 8b; 72, 4a). Shêng-tsung's brother, Lung-ch'ing 隆慶, was appointed vicegerent of the Southern Capital and the grand commander in chief, and Lung-yu 隆佑 was placed in charge of the Eastern Capital (LS 64, 14b–15a). Lung-ch'ing, like the emperor, was permitted to possess an ordo of his own. His whole manner of living rivaled the court in the Southern Capital in splendor and extravagance. (HCLY 77, 4a). According to CTKC (table 1), he even obtained the [posthumous] title "emperor" (CTKC 14, 2b and LS 64, 14b call him "the emperor's great younger brother"). Hsing-tsung's brother, Chung-yüan, held a number of important offices, such as that of chancellor, vicegerent of the Southern Capital, and after Tao-tsung ascended the throne, grand commander in chief of the armies of the empire (LS 64, 15b; 112, 5a; MHPT 25, 166). Ho-lu-wo 和魯斡, Tao-tsung's younger brother, was first appointed vicegerent of the Supreme Capital and then of the Southern Capital. In 1101 he was made grand commander in chief (LS 27,

17. THE PO-HAI NOT YET PACIFIED

926   On the day *chi-ssŭ* [of the third month in the first year of T'ien-hsien], because the three administrations of An-pien, Mo-chieh, and Ting-li[51] rebelled, An-tuan was sent to attack them.   2, 6*b*

18. ANOTHER PO-HAI REBELLION

926   On the day *ping-ch'ên* of the seventh month [in the first year of T'ien-hsien] the prefect of T'ieh Prefecture,[52] Wei Chün, rebelled.   2, 7*a*

19. OPPOSITION TO SHIH-TSUNG'S ACCESSION

947   When Shih-tsung ascended the throne[53] in Chên-yang,[54] the empress dowager became furious and sent Li-hu with an army to attack him.[55]   On reaching T'ai-tê-ch'üan,[56] [Li-hu] was defeated by An-tuan and Liu-ko.[57]   The empress dowager and Shih-tsung disposed their troops on opposite sides of the Huang River.[58]   Each explained the reason for raising

---

1*b*; 64, 17*a*).   After his death, his son, Ch'un, was raised to the same post (LS 30, 2*a*).

Among those factors that shaped Ch'i-tan succession, the extraordinary influence exercised by the rulers' wives and mothers was particularly significant.   The prominent part played by the first empress during her husband's lifetime and for many years following his death has already been described (*cf.* above and VII, introduction). Under the pretext of carrying out T'ai-tsu's will, his widow shifted the succession from Pei to his younger brother, T'ai-tsung; again in 947 she sought to be a "king-maker." Empress Jui-chih exerted great power while her husband lived; she maintained her regency until her death which occurred in the twenty-seventh year of her son Shêng-tsung's reign (LS 71, 4*b*).   Hsing-tsung's mother, although unsuccessful, did everything to place Hsing-tsung's younger brother on the throne (LS 71, 6*a*).   Tao-tsung's mother personally directed her guard in putting down the rebellion of 1063 (LS 71, 6*b*).   After Ch'un's death in 1122 his wife seized power and fought vigorously against the invading Sung troops (LS 29, 4*b* ff.; CTKC 11, 8*a* ff.).

The unusually strong position of women among the Ch'i-tan found continued expression in the state of Western Liao.   Here also the empress dowagers frequently acted as regents.   Empress Kan-t'ien 感天 maintained her power for seven years, Empress Ch'êng-t'ien 承天 for fourteen (LS 30, 7*a*).   At the close of the Chin 金 dynasty a Ch'i-tan general made himself king of Liao in present Liaoning, and after his death in 1220 his wife inherited his position.   In 1226 she traveled westward to meet Chingis Khan in what is now Inner Mongolia.   The Mongol ruler exclaimed in surprise, "Even a strong eagle cannot fly to this place, but you, a woman, were able to get here!"   He accepted her aid in the war against the Tanguts and in recognition of her services he presented her with nine prisoners, nine horses, and nine gold ingots (YS 149, 4*a* ff.).

Contrary to the Ch'i-tan, the T'o-pa rulers of the Wei dynasty (386–556) purposely restricted the influence of the emperors' wives.   The lady who bore him the first male child was killed either before or after her son had been officially nominated heir apparent (WS 13, 5*a*, ff.).   The practice, which is said to have institutionalized the policy pursued by Emperor Wu of Han (WS 3, 1*a*),

is also described as based upon an old Wei custom (WS 13, 5*a*, 13*a* and 20*a*).   Whatever its root, it was intended to eliminate the political influence of the future emperor's mother (WS 3, 1*a*; *cf.* also WS 13, 25*a*).   Under these circumstances, no powerful consort clan arose. The noble families hesitated to offer their daughters to the imperial harem, and the T'o-pa ruler had to take captive girls to insure the dynastic succession, or else he chose unsuspecting brides from distant countries.

[51] These administrations were probably situated in the present Ussuri Province of the Soviet Far East.

In the first month of 926 the Po-hai capital, Hu-han 忽汗 City (modern Tung-ching 東京 City), had been captured by Liao, and in the second month all the prefects had come to surrender.   But now in the third month these three regions rebelled again.

After 926 many Po-hai officials and commoners fled to Korea.   The Po-hai heir apparent Ta Kuang-hsien 大光顯 with several tens of thousands of people fled to Korea. He was given the Korean imperial name, Wang Kie 王繼, and attached to the imperial clan.   His followers were assigned residences and land according to their rank (KRS 2, 23; *cf.* also TKTK 12, 341–342).   The *Korean History* dates the flight in 934, but according to PHKCCP 19, 41*a*, the event took place in the year of the conquest, 926.

[52] Modern T'ang-ch'ih-pao 湯池堡, Liaoning.

[53] In the fourth month of 947, while on a military expedition in Honan, T'ai-tsung died.   In the same month Shih-tsung, who had accompanied T'ai-tsung on the campaign, ascended the throne.

[54] Modern Chêng-ting 正定 County, Hopei.

[55] The Empress Dowager Ying-t'ien, T'ai-tsu's wife, had three sons, namely Pei, Tê-kuang (T'ai-tsung), and Li-hu. On the death of T'ai-tsung the empress dowager backed a campaign against Pei's son who had already ascended the throne.   He was Shih-tsung, the third emperor.

[56] Probably in the middle of Jehol where the great king of the Six Divisions tribe spent the spring and summer (LS 32, 2*a*).

[57] The son of T'ai-tsu's third younger brother, Yin-ti-shih (LS 113, 2*b*).

[58] The modern Shira Muren, Jehol.

his army. . . . After a peaceful settlement was reached, they quickly proceeded to the Supreme Capital.   72, 4*b*

20. THE ELDEST SON SHOULD SUCCEED HIS FATHER

947   Li-hu exclaimed, "While I am alive, how can Wu-yü[59] ascend the throne?"

[Yeh-lü] Wu-chih[60] explained, "According to propriety, whenever there is an eldest son by the principal consort, the succession is not passed to any younger brother.   Even the former enthronement of Ssŭ-shêng[61] is considered to have been wrong.[62]   How much more so for you, who are tyrannical and cruel, so that most persons hate and resent you and are unanimous in saying that they prefer Prince Yung-k'ang as emperor.   There is no help for it!"

The empress dowager[63] looked at Li-hu and said, "Did you too hear these words?   In truth you yourself brought this about!"   Then she consented to let Yung-k'ang have the throne.   77, 2*b*–3*a*

21. PUNISHMENT FOR REBELLIOUS CH'I-TAN NOBLES

948   In the first month of the spring of the second year [of T'ien-lu], T'ien-tê,[64] Hsiao Han,[65] Liu-ko, and P'ên-tu[66] plotted rebellion.   T'ien-tê was executed, Hsiao Han was beaten, Liu-ko was exiled to the frontier, and P'ên-tu was sentenced to go as an envoy[67] to the Khirghiz state.[68]   5, 2*a*

22. A HSIAO NOBLE CONSPIRES

949   In the first month of the spring of the third year [of T'ien-lu], Hsiao Han and [his wife] Princess A-pu-li[69] plotted rebellion.   [Hsiao] Han was put to death and A-pu-li starved to death in prison.   5, 2*a*–*b*

23. SHIH-TSUNG MURDERED

951   On the day *kuei-hai* of the ninth month in the fifth year of T'ien-lu, Shih-tsung was murdered.[70]   The rebels, Ch'a-ko[71] and others, suffered capital punishment.

6, 1*a*

24. A HIGH DIGNITARY REBELS

952   On the day *jên-hsü* [of the first month in the second year of Ying-li] the grand commandant,[72] Hu-ku-chih, who had plotted rebellion, suffered capital punishment.

6, 1*b*

25. SHIH-TSUNG'S BROTHER AND OTHERS PLAN TREASON

952   On the day *i-hai* of the seventh month in the autumn [of the second year of Ying-li] the chief of the political council, Lou-kuo,[73] the scribe, Ti-lieh,[74] the inner chamberlain, Shên-tu, and the court noble, Hai-li, who had plotted rebellion, were arrested.   6, 1*b*–2*a*

---

[59] The style of Shih-tsung.   Before ascending the throne he had the title of Prince Yung-k'ang.

[60] Yeh-lü Wu-chih 屋質, a descendant of the First Patriarchal Household, reached the rank of *yü-yüeh*, the highest honorary position.   He died in 972 (LS 77, 1*a*–4*a*).

[61] T'ai-tsung.

[62] See introduction.

[63] Ying-t'ien, the powerful widow of T'ai-tsu.   She was Shih-tsung's grandmother.

[64] The third son of T'ai-tsung, and therefore a cousin of the emperor, Shih-tsung (LS 64, 11*a*).

[65] A nephew of T'ai-tsu's wife; he was married to Shih-tsung's sister (LS 113, 1*b*).

[66] A brother of Liu-ko (LS 113, 3*b*).

[67] According to the Ch'i-tan custom, nobles who were guilty of crimes could be sentenced to be sent as envoys to distant countries.   See VII, 1 (25); and also LS 61, 1*b*.

[68] Northwest of modern Outer Mongolia, on the upper Yenisei River.

[69] A sister of Shih-tsung.

[70] Four days later T'ai-tsung's eldest son, who was also a cousin of Shih-tsung, ascended the throne.   His temple name was Mu-tsung.

[71] A son of T'ai-tsu's fourth younger brother, An-tuan (LS 112, 3*a*).

[72] One of the Three Dukes, the highest dignitaries of the Southern Region of the empire.

[73] A son of Pei, that is a brother of the deceased emperor, Shih-tsung (LS 112, 4*b*).

[74] His descent is unknown.

26. LI–HU'S SECOND SON, WAN, REBELS

953   On the day *chi-yu*[75] of the tenth month in the winter [of the third year of Ying-li] . . . a son of Li-hu, Wan,[76] and the court noble, Hsi-kan, and Ti-lieh[77] plotted rebellion. The affair was discovered. Because their testimony involved the Prince of T'ai-p'ing, Yen-sa-ko,[78] the scribe, Hua-ko, and the court noble, Hsin-lo, these were all arrested.   6, 2b–3a

27. LI–HU'S FIRST SON, HSI–YIN, REBELS

960   During the Ying-li [period Hsi-yin[79]] plotted rebellion. When the affair was discovered, the emperor personally made an investigation and found him guilty, but because of his relationship [to the emperor] he was released. Soon afterwards he rebelled again and was imprisoned.   72, 5a

28. AN EMPEROR MURDERED BY HIS SERVANTS

969   This night [of the day *chi-ssŭ* of the second month in the nineteenth year of Ying-li] six men, including a personal attendant, Hsiao-ko, a bath attendant, Hua-ko, and a cook, Hsin-ku, rebelled and assassinated the emperor.[80]   7, 5b

29. HSI–YIN PARDONED BY CHING–TSUNG

969   When the reign title was changed to Pao-ning,[81] [Hsi-yin] was pardoned.   72, 5a

30. A TERRITORIAL OFFICIAL REBELS

975   In the autumn of the seventh month [in the seventh year of Pao-ning] the general of the guards at Huang-lung Administration,[82] Yen-p'o,[83] starting a rebellion, killed the chief supervisor, Chang Chü. The directing secretary, Yeh-lü Ho-li-pi,[84] was sent to punish him. In the ninth month he defeated Yen-p'o at the Chih River[85] and sent his younger brother, An-t'uan, to pursue him. Yen-p'o fled and sought refuge in Wu-jo City,[86] whereupon An-t'uan withdrew. The remnants of his faction, numbering more than a thousand households, were used to build the city wall of T'ung Prefecture.[87]   8, 4b

31. HSI–YIN REBELS AGAINST CHING–TSUNG

981   On the day *ping-wu* of the fifth month [in the third year of Ch'ien-hêng] the Chinese soldiers in the Supreme Capital revolted and tried by force to place Hsi-yin on the throne, but without success, whereupon they made his son, Liu-li-shou, the emperor. The vicegerent of the Supreme Capital, Ch'u-shih, captured him.   9, 4b

981   [Hsi-yin] again induced a band to plot a rebellion. The emperor ordered his hands and feet to be fettered and a dungeon to be built in Tsu Prefecture[88] to imprison him. More than two hundred surrendered Sung soldiers plotted to enthrone Hsi-yin by force, but, as they were unable to get in owing to the strength of the walls, they placed his son, Liu-li-shou, on the throne. The vicegerent of the Supreme Capital, Ch'u-shih, captured him. Liu-li-shou was put to death and Hsi-yin was granted permission to commit suicide.   72, 5a–b

---

[75] We correct the *i* 巳 of our text to *chi* 己.

[76] The second son of Li-hu, and therefore a cousin of the emperor, Mu-tsung, who had just ascended the throne.

[77] The fourth son of T'ai-tsung (LS 64, 12a).

[78] The eldest of Mu-tsung's younger brothers and the second son of T'ai-tsung (LS 64, 10b).

[79] Hsi-yin 喜隱, the first son of Li-hu, was a cousin of the emperor Mu-tsung. According to LS 6, 5a, he plotted rebellion in the tenth year of Ying-li (960).

[80] The text incorrectly ascribes the day *chi-ssŭ* to the third month. We follow LS 8, 1b in correcting it to the second month.

[81] On the same day that Ching-tsung ascended the throne.

[82] Modern Nung-an 農安 County, Kirin.

[83] A Po-hai.

[84] 曷里必 a descendant of the imperial clan. His given name is also written Ho-lu-pu 何魯不 (LS 77, 4b).

[85] A river near modern Nung-an County, Kirin.

[86] *Cf.* I, 2 (9), no. 26.

[87] Forced labor was used to build the walls around this city which was located southwest of present Nung-an County, Kirin.

[88] Southwest of modern Boro Khoton, Jehol.

32. TRIBES DIFFICULT TO CONTROL

984   On the day *i-ssŭ* [of the second month in the second year of T'ung-ho] the commanding prefect of the Five Nations and Wu-wei Yü-chüeh tribes, Yeh-lü Wei-wa, in view of the fact that the tribes under his control were difficult to govern, asked to be granted a decree and a sword[89] so that he could dispose of matters at his own discretion.   This was approved.

10, 6b

33. REQUEST FOR INDIGENOUS *HSIANG-WÊN* REFUSED

984   On the day *i-mao* of the third month [in the second year of T'ung-ho] the Hua-li tribe requested that hereafter the *hsiang-wên* should be selected and appointed only from his own tribe.   The emperor said, "In the matter of tribal officials, the only thing is to obtain the right men.   How can they be limited to their own tribe?"   He refused consent.   10, 6*b*

34. NORTHERN TRIBES REBEL

1013   [On the day *chi-wei* of the first month in the second year of K'ai-t'ai] the Wu-ku and Ti-lieh rebelled.   The *hsiang-wên* of the Right P'i-shih [Army],[90] Yen-shou, led a force to attack them.   15, 5*b*

35. THEY RETURN TO THEIR OLD REGIONS

1013   On the day *jên-ch'ên* of the seventh month in the autumn [of the second year of K'ai-t'ai] the Wu-ku and Ti-lieh all returned to their old regions.   15, 6*a*

36. FUGITIVE TRIBESMEN

1026   [In the fourth month of the sixth year of T'ai-p'ing], because within the P'u-lu-mao-to tribe there were many Wu-jo households, an imperial decree demanded them.

69, 13b

37. REVOLT OF THE TSU-PU TRIBES

1026   In the eighth month [of the sixth year of T'ai-p'ing], Hsiao Hui attacked Kan Prefecture,[91] but as he was unable to take it his army was withdrawn.   After this the Tsu-pu tribes all rebelled; the Liao armies which fought them were all defeated.   Nieh-li-ku, the inspector of the army,[92] and Ho-pu-lü, the grand guardian of the tents of the Imperial Maternal Uncles, lost their lives.   An imperial order sent the *t'i-yin*, Yeh-lü Hung-ku,[93] and the scribe, Hua-ko, to lead an army to punish them.   17, 3*a*

38. THE PO-HAI REVOLT OF 1029–1030

1029   On the day *chi-ch'ou* of the eighth month [in the ninth year of T'ai-p'ing] the *hsiang-wên* of the Shê-li Troop[94] in the Eastern Capital,[95] Ta Yen-lin,[96] imprisoned the vicegerent and imperial son-in-law chief commandant, Hsiao Hsiao-hsien,[97] and the Princess of Nan-yang.   He

---

[89] The decree was probably to certify that he was fully authorized to execute matters without reporting to the emperor beforehand.   The sword may have been a symbol of permission to carry out summary punishment.

[90] See XV, 1 (25) and note 79.

[91] The failure of the Liao attack against the Uighur stronghold of Kan Prefecture (in present Kansu) encouraged the Tsu-pu to rebel against Liao.

[92] The position of inspector of the army (監軍) is mentioned only for the Northwestern Route (LS 46, 19*a*).

[93] After his return to the court, Yeh-lü Hung-ku 洪古 was promoted to the post of prime minister of the Southern Administration.   Later he became the vicegerent of the

Supreme Capital.   In 1043 the honorary title of *yü-yüeh* was conferred upon him (LS 19, 4*b*; 95, 1*a*).

[94] See XV, introduction.

[95] Modern Liao-yang 遼陽 County, Liaoning.

[96] Ta Yen-lin 大延琳 was a Po-hai.   According to TKTK 16, 418–419, he organized the administration after the pattern of the former Po-hai kingdom.   See also note 101.

[97] Hsiao Hsiao-hsien 孝先 was later promoted to the post of prime minister of the Northern Administration.   He also held the post of northern chancellor at the beginning of the Ch'ung-hsi period (1032–1055).   He married the Princess of Nan-yang, the fourth daughter of Shêng-tsung (LS 65, 4*a*).

killed the commissioner of the Ministry of Revenue, Han Shao-hsün,[98] the vice-commissioner, Wang Chia, and the chief commanding commissioner[99] of the Ssŭ-chieh Army,[100] Hsiao P'o-tê. [Ta] Yen-lin thereupon usurped the throne, designating his dynasty as Hsing-liao and his reign period as T'ien-ch'ing.[101]   17, 6b

1030   On the day *ping-wu* of the eighth month [in the tenth year of T'ai-p'ing] a bandit general of the Eastern Capital, Yang Hsiang-shih, secretly communicated friendly terms [to Liao]. At night he opened the south gate and received the Liao army. [Ta] Yen-lin was seized and Po-hai was pacified.   17, 8a

39. GROWING MISERY, GROWING BANDITRY

1035–1044   "Your majesty's servant has also heard that from ancient times on no ruler has ever been free from banditry. During recent years the people, being in distress, seek gain in plundering. Good persons often become cruel and ruthless. The worst murder people without any fear and even flee to the mountains and swamps to start rebellions and to lead revolts. What has been said of the people because of poverty all becoming robbers and thieves is just as Your Majesty fears.

"Now, in order to exterminate the roots [of banditry], I hope that Your Majesty will lighten the forced labor and reduce the services so that the people may devote themselves to agriculture. When their clothes and food are sufficient, the people will peacefully submit to reforming influences and will consider it a serious matter to transgress the laws. Then the people will press on toward proper conduct, and punishments will seldom be used.

"I have heard that, when T'ai-tsung of T'ang asked his courtiers how to deal with banditry, all answered that the penalties should be made stern and the laws should be made strict. But T'ai-tsung smiled and said, 'The reason why banditry flourishes is that the taxes are limitless so that the people have nothing to live on. Now I will within the palace decrease my desires and outside will give up my travels. When the empire is made tranquil, then banditry and theft will automatically come to an end.'

"Looked at from this point of view, the amount of banditry depends entirely upon whether clothes and food are abundant or scarce and forced labor and services heavy or light."[102]   103, 4a

40. FUGITIVE TRIBESMEN BROUGHT BACK

1041   On the first day *kêng-ch'ên* of the second month [in the tenth year of Ch'ung-hsi] an imperial decree ordered the P'u-lu-mao-to tribe to return the Ho-su-kuan families[103] who had fled there and to let them return to their occupations.   19, 1a

---

[98] The grandson of Han Yen-hui (LS 74, 3b).

[99] These officers were in command of the various armies (*cf.* LS 46, 15b).

[100] According to the glossary (LS 116, 10b), Liao organized two special armies of former Sung soldiers captured during the war. One was called the Ssŭ-chieh 四捷 Army, the other the Kuei-shêng 歸聖 Army.

[101] According to the official *Korean History*, in the ninth month of 1029 Ta Yen-lin, a descendant in the seventh generation of the founder of the Po-hai kingdom, sent a messenger, Kao Chi-tê 高吉德, to Korea, who announced the establishment of the country of Hsing-liao 興遼 and the creation of a reign title, T'ien-hsing 天興 (instead of T'ien-ch'ing 天慶). The Korean court was asked for help, but refused and even prepared to take a stand against

a possible invasion of the rebel ruler. In 1030 Ta Yen-lin several times sent messengers to ask military assistance, but again the Korean Court remained unresponsive. Many Po-hai, Ch'i-tan, and Hsi fugitives, who had crossed the Yalu River, were settled in the southern part of Korea (KRS 5, 71–73).

During this period some Korean officials suggested the reconquest of the regions east of the Yalu River which Liao had taken. After some argument the idea was put into practice, but the attacking Koreans were defeated by the Liao frontier guards (KRS 93, 63; 94, 80).

[102] This passage is a paragraph from Hsiao Han-chia-nu's long memorial, the remainder of which is given in XV, 1 (51).

[103] Jurchen tribesmen.

41. REVOLT OF TAO–TSUNG'S UNCLE

1063   [Hsiao] Hu-tu,[104] together with Nieh-lu-ku, the son of Chung-yüan,[105] had previously made plans for high treason and was eager to carry them out quickly. When the emperor happened to be hunting at the T'ai-tzǔ Mountains,[106] he, with Nieh-lu-ku, compelled a force of crossbowmen to attack the emperor's traveling camp. After the fighting had begun, Nieh-lu-ku was struck by a stray arrow and killed. The troops all fled and dispersed. At that moment a fellow-partisan, Yeh-lü Sa-la-chu,[107] who happened to be at the hunting ground and had learned of the revolt, led hunters to bring help to his adherents and addressed Hu-tu and the others, saying, "Our army is very large, and if we take advantage of their being unprepared and launch a decisive battle at midnight, we can hope for success in the matter. If we wait until tomorrow, who will follow us?"

Hu-tu said, "In our haste we will not be able to see anything,[108] and if the [emperor's] soldiers inside and outside [the camp] support each other our cause will be lost. If we begin at early dawn, how can that be late?"

Chung-yüan, who agreed with Hu-tu's plan, issued an order to patrol the four directions and to wait for the morning. During that night the partisans set up Chung-yüan to usurp the throne and title. Hu-tu appointed himself to the post of chancellor. The next day they were defeated in battle. Hu-tu was wounded and fled alone on horseback to Shih-ch'i Lakes[109] where he threw himself into the water and died. His five sons were executed together in one day.   114, 1b–2a

42. A CHINESE REBELLION SUPPRESSED

1066   On the day mou-shên of the sixth month [in the second year of Hsien-yung] the officials reported that a native of Hsin-ch'êng County,[110] Yang Ts'ung, had plotted rebellion and had set up officials on his own authority. The emperor said, "The people are ignorant; this is only child's play!" Only the ringleaders were banished. The rest were set free.   22, 4b–5a

43. TAO–TSUNG'S SON, THE HEIR APPARENT, KILLED

1077   During the eleventh month [of the third year of Ta-k'ang] the chancellor of the Northern Division, Yeh-lü I-hsin, sent his close followers to assassinate the commoner,[111] Chün,[112] in the Supreme Capital.   23, 6a

44. THE REBELLION OF HSIAO HAI–LI

1102   On the day i-mao of the tenth month in the winter [of the second year of Ch'ien-t'ung], Hsiao Hai-li rebelled[113] and robbed the Ch'ien Prefecture[114] armory of its mili-

[104] The rebellion of Hsiao Hu-tu started on the day *mou-wu* of the seventh month in the ninth year of Ch'ing-ning (1063) (LS 22, 1b–2a).

[105] Chung-yüan 重元 was a brother of the deceased emperor, Hsing-tsung, and an uncle of the then emperor, Tao-tsung. After the defeat related in this passage he committed suicide (LS 64, 15b).

[106] LS 22, 1b; 96, 2a; and 114, 1b state that the place where Tao-tsung hunted was in the T'ai-tzǔ 太子 Mountains, but LS 112, 5a and 114, 3a locate it near the Luan River where the rebellion took place. Apparently the T'ai-tzǔ Mountains were located near the Luan River, or somewhere in the southwestern part of Jehol. Cf. note 15.

[107] A descendant of the First Patriarchal Household (LS 114, 3a).

[108] Literally, "black and white will be indistinguishable."

[109] According to LS 112, 5a, Hsiao Hu-tu's attempt to overthrow the emperor took place near the Luan 灤 River (in the southwestern part of Jehol) where the

emperor had halted for an autumn hunt. The place to which Hsiao Hu-tu fled must have been near present Dolo-Nōr, Chahar, where there are still many marshes. Shih-ch'i Lakes 十七濼, the seventeen Lakes, apparently correspond to these marshes in Chahar.

[110] Modern Hsin-ch'êng 新城 County, Hopei.

[111] The term *shu-jên* 庶人 was given to a dignitary who was deprived of his official position because he had committed a crime.

[112] Tao-tsung's heir apparent. He had been deposed and degraded in the sixth month of 1077 because of a false accusation of treason (LS 23, 5b).

[113] According to CS 1, 14a–b, this event strongly encouraged the Jurchen to attack the Liao empire. Although the Jurchen had refused to join Hsiao Hai-li in his rebellion against the Liao, they nevertheless began to consider the matter very seriously after his venture. They then secured metal weapons and other equipment and prepared for the coming struggle for power.

[114] Southeast of modern Pei-chên 北鎮 County, Liaoning.

tary equipment.   The scribe of the Northern Region, Ho-chia-nu, was ordered to arrest him.   Hsiao Hai-li escaped to the A-tien tribe[115] at the P'ei-chu River.[116]   *27, 2b*

45. A–KU–TA REFUSES TO DANCE

1112   On the day *ting-yu* of the second month [in the second year of T'ien-ch'ing] the emperor went to Ch'un Prefecture[117] and halted at the Hun-t'ung River,[118] where he fished.   The chieftains of the Savage Nü-chih beyond the border who lived within a thousand *li* had all come to court for an audience in accordance with the old tradition.   It happened that at this time a First Fish Feast was given.   When the serving of the wine reached a certain point, the emperor mounted his carriage and ordered all the chieftains one after the other to get up and dance.   A-ku-ta[119] alone refused on the grounds of inability.[120]   He was ordered repeatedly but refused to the end.

27, 6a–b

46. REVOLT OF THE JURCHEN

1114   In the first month in the spring of the fourth year [of T'ien-ch'ing] the emperor went to Ch'un Prefecture.   Previously, when the Nü-chih had mobilized their soldiers, as A-shu, a Ho-shih-lieh[121] tribesman, did not follow [the order], they sent Sa-kai[122] of their tribe to attack him.   When A-shu's younger brother, Ti-ku-pao, came and reported this, an imperial decree ordered [the Nü-chih] not to attack him.   But, as they did not obey, A-shu fled [to Liao].   Now the Nü-chih sent emissaries to demand him, but he was not handed over. . . .

In the seventh month in the autumn the Nü-chih again sent emissaries to get A-shu.   The emperor did not hand him over, but sent an imperial coachman, A-hsi-pao, to inquire why they were building fortifications on the frontier.[123]   The Nü-chih contemptuously replied, "If you return A-shu, we will present tribute as before.   If not, we cannot stop building fortifications."

Thereupon [Liao] dispatched the armies north of the Hun River[124] to reinforce the Office of Military Control of the Northeastern Route.   A-ku-ta and his younger brothers, Nien-han[125] and Hu-shê,[126] made plans, with Yin-chu-ko, I-lieh, Lou-shih, and Shê-mu as commanders, to bring together the soldiers of all the Nü-chih tribes to seize the Liao officials in charge of catching falcons.[127]   When Ning-chiang Prefecture[128] was attacked, the Office of Military Control of the Northeastern Route reported it.   The emperor, who at this time was at Ch'ing Prefecture[129] hunting deer, heard of it but did not give it much attention.   He sent the prefect of Hai Prefecture,[130] Kao Hsien-shou, at the head of a Po-hai army to render assistance.   Hsiao Ta-pu-yeh[131] encountered the Nü-chih east of Ning-chiang and was utterly defeated.   *27, 8a–b*

---

[115] Same as the Hsi-an Nü-chih A-tien 係案女直阿典 tribe, which was located in the northern part of present Liaoning.   *Cf*. CS 1, 14*a*.

[116] Probably a tributary of the Liao River.

[117] Northwest of modern Po-tu-na 伯都訥, Kirin.

[118] The Sungari River.

[119] The supreme chief of the Savage Nü-chih who soon became the first emperor, T'ai-tsu, of the succeeding Chin 金 dynasty (1115–1235).

[120] Another passage describes A-ku-ta's attitude as very disrespectful toward the emperor: "Standing erect and looking straight [at the emperor] he refused on the ground of inability" (LS 54, 2*a*).

[121] This tribe lived in Kirin.

[122] A cousin of A-ku-ta.   He died in 1121 (CS 70, 3*a*).

[123] We follow other editions in reading 境 before 上.

[124] A branch of the Liao River in Tung-ching Circuit.

[125] Nien-han 粘罕, the eldest son of Sa-kai, assisted A-ku-ta to overthrow Liao and later helped in the defeat of Northern Sung.   He died in 1136 (CS 74, 1*a*–7*b*).

[126] Nien-han and Hu-shê 胡舍 (or Ku-shê 骨捨) were actually cousins of A-ku-ta (CS 74, 1*a*–7*b*; TCKC 27, 2*a*).

[127] These officials were probably charged with providing falcons for the imperial hunts.   They were apparently located in or near the territory of the Jurchen.

[128] Modern Shih-t'ou Ch'êng-tzǔ 石頭城子, southeast of Po-tu-na 伯都訥, Kirin.

[129] Modern Tsaghan Khoton, Jehol.

[130] Modern Hai-ch'êng 海城 County, Liaoning.

[131] Another name for Hsiao Wu-na 兀納 who belonged to the Six Divisions.   He became prime minister of the Northern Administration in 1095 and was made commissioner of military control in the Northeastern Route in 1111 (LS 98, 1*a*–2*b*).

47. DEFEAT AND DEATH OF THE REBEL CHANG–NU

1115   On the day *i-ssŭ* [of the ninth month in the fifth year of T'ien-ch'ing], Yeh-lü Chang-nu[132] rebelled and hastened to the Supreme Capital. He planned to welcome and set up the Prince of Wei, Ch'un,[133] as emperor. . . .

Chang-nu, on realizing that the Prince of Wei was not acquiescent, led his followers to plunder the prefectures of Ch'ing, Jao, Huai, and Tsu,[134] and also joined up with the many Po-hai bandits, so that the forces amounted to several tens of thousands in number. They rushed to Kuang-p'ing-tien[135] and attacked the imperial traveling camp. But A-hu-ch'an of the Obedient Nü-chih with three hundred horsemen was victorious in a single battle. He captured more than two hundred people of [Chang-nu's] noble families, cut off their heads, and displayed them publicly. Their wives and sons[136] were punished by forced labor in the Embroidery Workhouse[137] or by distribution among the personal attendants of the emperor as slaves. Those of the rest who were able to escape all fled to the Nü-chih. Chang-nu tried to flee to the Nü-chih by posing as a messenger, but was arrested by the patrol and sent in fetters to the emperor's residence. He was cut in two at the waist in the market-place. His heart was cut out and offered to the ancestral temples. He was dismembered and displayed in the five routes.[138]   28, 2b–3a

48. THE OLD TERRITORY OF PO–HAI IN REBELLION

1116   On the first day *ping-yin* of the first month in the sixth year [of T'ien-ch'ing] in the Eastern Capital during the night more than ten young ruffians, under the influence of liquor, seized broadswords and, jumping over the walls, entered the office of the vicegerent. Inquiring where the vicegerent, Hsiao Pao-hsien,[139] was, [they shouted], "The army is rebelling. Get ready!" When Pao-hsien came out, they stabbed him to death. The commissioner of the Ministry of Revenue, Ta Kung-ting,[140] on hearing of the rebellion, at once assumed the position of temporary vicegerent. Together with the assistant vicegerent, Kao Ch'ing-ming,[141] he gathered a thousand Hsi and Chinese soldiers, arrested the whole band, and decapitated them, thus quieting the people.

Tung-ching was the old territory of Po-hai. T'ai-tsu had fought more than twenty years before he got it. And now, because Hsiao Pao-hsien had been very oppressive and the Po-hai had suffered, this rebellion occurred.

[Hsiao Pao-hsien's] subordinate general, Kao Yung-ch'ang,[142] a Po-hai man, usurped the title of emperor and proclaimed [this year as] the first year of [the new reign period] Lung-chi. Hsiao I-hsieh[143] and Kao Hsing-shun were sent to ask him to submit, but he refused. On the day *chi-hai*

---

[132] A descendant of the Third Patriarchal Household.

[133] 淳 a cousin of Emperor T'ien-tsu's father, Chün. In 1122 he was made emperor in the Southern Capital. His coronation title was Emperor T'ien-hsi 天錫; the name of his reign was Chien-fu 建福. He died in the same year and was buried in Hsiang 香 Mountain, west of modern Peiping at a place not far from Hsiung Hsi-ling's 熊希齡 summer home.

[134] Respectively located at modern Tsaghan Khoton; on the upper Shira Muren; southwest of Boro Khoton; and southeast of Boro Khoton, all in Jehol.

[135] Near the juncture of the Shira Muren and the Lao-ha River, Jehol. The emperors used to spend their winters there (LS 32, 3a).

[136] CTKC 10, 6b has daughters 女, not sons 子.

[137] A kind of prison in which female prisoners did sewing or embroidery.

[138] That is, in all regions. The five routes or directions are the north, east, south, west, and center.

[139] A brother of T'ien-tsu's wife.

[140] A Po-hai whose family had long before taken up residence in the Central Capital (modern Tsaghan Suburghan, Jehol) (LS 105, 1a–2b).

[141] CTKC 10, 7b and SHYK 196, 71b read *ch'ên* 臣 for the *ming* 明 of our text. Since Ching-tsung's childhood name was Ming-i 明扆, these words should have been tabooed, as indeed is the case in the Liao inscriptions.

[142] Kao Yung-ch'ang 高永昌 was the leader of two thousand Po-hai soldiers recruited by the emperor in 1116 (SHYK 196, 71a).

According to the *Korean History*, on the day *jên-yin* of the third month of the same year, a Korean official, Chöng Ryang-chik 鄭良禝, was imprisoned upon his return from the Liao Eastern Capital because he had presented to Kao Yung-ch'ang a forged Korean document and gifts, placing his country in a subordinate position to Kao's new kingdom of Ta-yüan 大元. In return Kao had made him presents of considerable value (KRS 14, 204).

[143] Hsiao I-hsieh 乙薛 a descendant of the Junior Patriarchal Household of the Imperial Maternal Uncles. He became the vicegerent of the Supreme Capital and was killed by Yeh-lü Ta-shih in 1124 (LS 101, 3a–b).

of the intercalary [first] month Hsiao Han-chia-nu and Chang Lin[144] were dispatched to punish him. On the day *mou-wu* Yeh-lü Yü-tu,[145] the general guarding Kuei-tê Prefecture,[146] rebelled with the Po-hai people of Kuang Prefecture[147] and joined [Kao] Yung-ch'ang. Our army attacked and defeated him.   28, 3a–b

49. REBELLION IN THE CENTRAL REGION

1116   On the day *mou-tzǔ* [of the second month in the sixth year of T'ien-ch'ing], Chang Chia-nu[148] induced more than ten thousand people—the Po-hai of Jao Prefecture[149] and the bandit, Hou-kai, and others of Chung-ching—to attack and capture Kao Prefecture.[150]   In the third month the vice-commander of the campaigning army in the Eastern Region, [Hsiao] Ch'ou-wo,[151] and others captured Hou-kai at Ch'uan Prefecture.[152]

On the day *mou-ch'ên* of the fourth month in the summer the emperor personally headed a punitive campaign against Chang Chia-nu. On the day *kuei-yu* he defeated him. On the day *chia-hsü* the participants in the rebellion were put to death and the Po-hai [people] of Jao Prefecture were pacified. On the day *ping-tzǔ* the generals and soldiers who had participated in the pacification of the bandits were rewarded in accordance with their merit. But Hsiao Han-chia-nu, Chang Lin, and others were again defeated by the bandits.[153]   28, 3b–4a

50. IMPERIAL CLANSMEN SURRENDER TO THE JURCHEN

1116   [In the fifth month of the sixth year of T'ien-ch'ing], Nü-chih troops attacked and captured Shên Prefecture.[154]   They also took the Eastern Capital and seized Kao Yung-ch'ang.   In the prefectures and counties of Tung-ching thirteen [imperial] clansmen, including Hên-po, To-la, Wu-shih, Ta-pu-yeh, Tao-la, and Ch'ou-wo, all surrendered to the Nü-chih.[155]

28, 4a

51. ANOTHER PO-HAI REBELLION

1116   In the seventh month in the autumn [of the sixth year of T'ien-ch'ing, while the emperor] was hunting in the Ch'iu Mountains,[156] more than two thousand Po-hai households in Ch'un Prefecture[157] rebelled.   The commissioner of military control of the North-eastern Route led a force in pursuit and brought them all back.   28, 4a

---

[144] A native of Shên 瀋 Prefecture (modern Shên-yang 瀋陽, Liaoning). He died in 1122 (LS 102, 3a).

[145] See below, note 182.

[146] Southeast of modern T'ieh-ling 鐵嶺 County, Liaoning.

[147] Modern Chang-i-chan 彰驛站, Liaoning.

[148] Perhaps the same person who traveled back and forth between the Liao court and the Jurchen in an attempt to negotiate an agreement. The negotiations collapsed in 1115 (LS 28, 1a).

[149] On the upper Shira Muren, Jehol.

[150] In the vicinity of the juncture of the Lao-ha River and the Ying-chin 英金 River, Jehol.

[151] A descendant of the Junior Patriarchal Household of the Imperial Maternal Uncles. He died in 1116 (LS 100, 3a).

[152] Sixty-seven *li* northeast of modern Ch'ao-yang 朝陽 County, Jehol.

[153] Toward the end of the Liao dynasty numerous Ch'i-tan, Hsi, Po-hai, Chinese, and "civilized" Jurchen of the Eastern Capital fled to Korea because their houses, tents, and fields had been destroyed by the Jurchen invaders (KRS 14, 205 and 208). In 1117, when the Korean king visited his Southern Capital, the Ch'i-tan

who were settled there welcomed him by singing, dancing, and performing Ch'i-tan plays in his honor (KRS 14, 210).

A number of Ch'i-tan officials and commoners who lived near the Sung border fled into the Sung territory after the fall of the Liao empire. Some were distributed over various Sung prefectures (FHC 28, 354), others later returned to the north upon the request of the Chin government. Still others, well-fed and probably well-paid, were utilized by Chinese generals as guides in the Chin territory during the Sung campaign. For instance, Tsung Tsê 宗澤 (1059–1128) had Ch'i-tan nationals do espionage work for him (HCTL 1b; LCCWP 8, 157).

[154] See note 144.

[155] In 1115 the Liao government several times sent officials to Korea, asking the "subordinate" state to recruit soldiers for the campaign against the Jurchen. The Korean government discussed the matter in several conferences without reaching a decision. At the end of the year the leading Liao envoy, Yeh-lü I 義, realized the failure of his efforts and left Korea for Liao (KRS 14, 203–204).

[156] Probably near the juncture of the Shira Muren and the Lao-ha River, Jehol.

[157] Probably northwest of Po-tu-na, Kirin.

52. THE ARMY BREAKS UP

1117   In this month [the first month of the seventh year of T'ien-ch'ing] the Nü-chih
army attacked Ch'un Prefecture.   The armies of the Northeastern Region dispersed
without fighting.   Four divisions of the Nü-ku P'i-shih,[158] along with the Po-hai people, all surrendered [to the Nü-chih].   They also took T'ai Prefecture.[159]   28, 4b

53. REBELLION IN THE SOUTHERN PARTS OF LIAO

1117   In the second month [of the seventh year of T'ien-ch'ing] a bandit of Lai-shui
County,[160] Tung P'ang-êrh,[161] assembled a troop of more than ten thousand men.
The vicegerent of the Western Capital, Hsiao I-hsieh, and the chief supervisor of military control
of the Southern Capital, Ch'a-la, fought a battle with them at the I River[162] and routed them.   In
the third month the partisans of [Tung] P'ang-êrh reassembled, but [Hsiao] I-hsieh attacked and
routed them again at Fêng-shêng Prefecture.[163]   28, 4b

54. BANDITRY AND CANNIBALISM

1118   [In the eighth year of T'ien-ch'ing] bandits and thieves arose like bees in the various
prefectures of the Eastern Route.   The captured people were made to follow them in
order to serve as food.[164]   28, 5b

55. FURTHER DISSOLUTION

1118   On the day *kêng-yin* [of the first month in the eighth year of T'ien-ch'ing] the commanding prefect of Pao-an Commandery,[165] Chang Ch'ung, surrendered to Chin with
two hundred households of Shuang Prefecture.[166]   28, 5b

During this month [the fifth month] the emperor arrived at Na-ko Lake.[167]   The bandits, An
Shêng-êrh and Chang Kao-êrh, gathered a horde of two hundred thousand men.   Yeh-lü Ma-ko and
others beheaded [An] Shêng-êrh in Lung-hua Prefecture.[168]   [Chang] Kao-êrh escaped to I Pre-

---

[158] According to LS 46, 11a–b, T'ai-tsu originally divided
the P'i-shih Army (see XV, 1, note 79) into five sections,
the Left (Eastern), Right (Western), South, North, and
Yellow.   The Nü-ku P'i-shih was perhaps identical with
the Yellow P'i-shih.   According to LS 116, 18a, the Ch'i-
tan called gold *nü-ku* 女古.   Since gold is yellow, the
word *nü-ku* possibly meant both gold and yellow.

[159] Southwest of modern Nung-an 農安 County, Kirin.

[160] Modern Lai-shui 淶水 County, Hopei.

[161] Also called Tung Ts'ai 董才 and Chao Hsü 趙詡
(SCPMPH 1, 9a).   T'ung P'ang-êrh's revolt marks the
beginning of revolutionary movements conducted by Liao
Chinese.   A Ch'i-tan spokesman expected this group to
be loyal to their masters because they had served them
for over two hundred years (HSC 1, 9).

A Sung writer specifically mentions the lack of personal
reminiscences among the younger generation at the beginning of the eleventh century and their prolonged adjustment to the new rule as reasons for the Liao Chinese
attitude toward the Ch'i-tan, an attitude, which, according to him, implied more respect for the Ch'i-tan than for
their own people, the Liao Chinese (JLKI 2, 30).   The
political bias of the Ch'i-tan spokesman is manifest; the
Sung observer probably gained his impression essentially
from the Liao Chinese officials, among whom there were
indeed many convinced adherents of Liao power.   But
the question of the political psychology of the Liao Chinese
must be judged in the light of the historical situation as a
whole, which never lost its basically antagonistic character.

The Ch'i-tan might closely cooperate with a limited number of Chinese officials and professional soldiers; the mass
of the Liao Chinese remained untrustworthy.   This is
shown by the Liao policy which prevented the bulk of the
Chinese from possessing arms, from hunting, and from
participating in important military matters (XV, 2 (14)
(21) (26)).   The many expressions of dissatisfaction
which the Liao Chinese gave vent to in the days of the
great Sung war, and again during the last decades of
Ch'i-tan rule, confirm the technical correctness of the
Ch'i-tan policy toward the Liao Chinese, which was
based on distrust and apprehension rather than on confidence.

[162] Near present I 易 County, Hopei.

[163] Modern Cho-lu 涿鹿 County, Chahar.

[164] After 1114 several great battles were fought between
the Ch'i-tan and the Jurchen.   The Ch'i-tan were routed
each time, and the defeated soldiers spread over the
countryside robbing and killing.   Because they were short
of food, "at each meal they slaughtered several thousand
people" (CTKC 10, 9b–10a).   Our passage seems to refer
to this instance of cannibalism.

[165] West of modern T'ieh-ling 鐵嶺 County, Liaoning.

[166] In the same region.

[167] Probably near the juncture of the Shira Muren and
the Lao-ha River, Jehol.

[168] Southeast of the juncture of the Shira Muren and the
Lao-ha River.

fecture[169] and joined forces with Ho Liu-ko. . . . [In the sixth month] Ho Liu-ko seized Hai-pei Prefecture[170] and rushed to I Prefecture.[171]   The military leader, Hui-li-pao,[172] and others attacked and defeated him.   The people of the four prefectures of T'ung,[173] Ch'i,[174] Shuang,[175] and Liao,[176] numbering more than eight hundred households, surrendered to Chin.   28, 6a

In the tenth month in the winter . . . four persons, including Chang Ying-ku of Lung-hua Prefecture,[177] led the people to surrender to Chin.   28, 6b

1119   On the day *chia-shên* of the twelfth month . . . the commanding prefect of Ning-ch'ang Commandery,[178] Liu Hung, surrendered to Chin with three thousand households of I Prefecture.[179]   28, 6b

56. ANOTHER "EMPEROR" IN CHUNG–CHING

1119   During the second month [of the ninth year of T'ien-ch'ing] the emperor arrived at Yüan-yang Lake.[180]   The bandit, Chang Sa-pa, won over the *shê-liang* army[181] at Chung-ching and usurped the imperial title.   The military leader, [Yeh-lü] Yü-tu,[182] captured [Chang] Sa-pa.   28, 6b

57. INTRIGUE AND DISSOLUTION

1121   [Hsiao] Fêng-hsien[183] inveigled someone into falsely accusing the imperial son-in-law, Hsiao Yü, and [Yeh-lü] Yü-tu, and others of a conspiracy to make the Prince of Chin the emperor.   When this became known, [Hsiao] Yü, [Yeh-lü] Ta-ho-li, and others were executed and the imperial concubine[184] was permitted to commit suicide.   Only upon the Prince of Chin [the emperor] could not bear to inflict punishment.   [Yeh-lü] Yü-tu, on learning of this while with the army, became greatly alarmed and immediately led more than a thousand horsemen[185] to rebel and to join Chin.   29, 1a–b

---

[169] I 懿 Prefecture, modern Chang-wu 彰武 County, Liaoning.

[170] Forty *li* south of I 義 County, Liaoning.

[171] I 義 Prefecture, modern I County, Liaoning.

[172] Hui-li-pao 回離保, a native of Hsi who was in charge of the Hsi soldiers, was one of those who, in 1122, helped Ch'un seize the throne in the Southern Capital. When the Jurchen soldiers entered the Southern Capital in 1122, he made himself emperor of Hsi, but was soon afterwards killed by his followers (LS 114, 3b–4a).

[173] Southwest of Nung-an 農安 County, Kirin.

[174] Ch'ing-yün-i 慶雲驛, fifty *li* northwest of T'ieh-ling County, Liaoning.

[175] West of present T'ieh-ling County, Liaoning.

[176] Present Liao-pin-t'a 遼鑌塔, northeast of Hsin-min 新民 County, Liaoning.

[177] Southeast of the juncture of the Shira Muren and the Lao-ha River, Jehol.

[178] Modern Chang-wu County, Liaoning.

[179] See note 169.

[180] Modern Ang-ku-li Lake 昂古里湖 in Ch'ih-ch'êng 赤城 County, Chahar (LSTLCK 8138).

[181] According to the glossary in LS 116, 12b, the word *shê* 射 means "to request" 請.   Thus the term *shê-liang chün* 射糧軍 could mean "the food-requesting army." During the Chin period the term was applied to young men who were tatooed as retainers of nobles and were given food supplies as soldiers (see CS 42, 13b and 44, 7b).

[182] Yeh-lü Yü-tu 余覩 was a descendant of the imperial clan.   His wife was a younger sister of one of T'ien-tsu's concubines.   In 1121, after a quarrel with chancellor Hsiao Fêng-hsien, he fled to the Jurchen.   The surrender of so important a person strongly encouraged the Jurchen, as stressed in CS 2, 16a.   Yü-tu took three thousand families with him to the Jurchen, along with five thousand carts and several tens of thousands of cattle (CS 133, 5a). Furthermore, being chief commander of the Eastern Route, he had a thorough knowledge of the military situation of Liao.   After his surrender the Jurchen soldiers swiftly destroyed the military strength of Liao and chased Emperor T'ien-tsu from modern Jehol to Chahar and from Suiyuan to Shansi until they captured him in 1125.   In 1133 Yü-tu was put to death by the Chin government for treason.   *Cf.* appendix V, B, 2, *passim*.

[183] Hsiao Fêng-hsien 奉先 was an elder brother of emperor T'ien-tsu's first concubine.   He was inept but ambitious.   His false accusation concerning T'ien-tsu's eldest son, the Prince of Chin 晉, caused bloodshed in the palace and a revolt led by members of the imperial clan, such as Yeh-lü Yü-tu.   Fêng-hsien was put to death in 1122 (LS 102, 1a–2a).

[184] The concubine (*wên-fei* 文妃) was the mother of the Prince of Chin.

[185] CS 133, 5a gives more precise figures for the number of people, carts, and livestock surrendered by Yeh-lü Yü-tu to Chin (see above, note 182).

58. THE EMPIRE SPLIT BETWEEN TWO EMPERORS

1122   In the second year of Pao-ta, when T'ien-tsu entered Chia Mountain,[186] the king of Hsi, Hui-li-pao, and the scribe, Yeh-lü Ta-shih, citing the earlier occurrence at Ling-wu during the T'ang period,[187] discussed their desire to place Ch'un on the throne. Ch'un would not consent. His subordinate officials urged him to ascend the throne, saying, "The emperor has taken flight and the empire is in turmoil. If we do not enthrone you, where will the people turn? This should be given careful consideration."

Then he ascended the throne. The officials offered him the title of Emperor T'ien-hsi and changed the second year of Pao-ta to be the first year of Chien-fu. A general amnesty was proclaimed. Nineteen persons, including Li Pao-hsin, were made *chin-shih*. T'ien-tsu was degraded in absentia to be the king of Hsiang-yin. The six routes of Yen, Yün, P'ing, Shang-ching, Chung-ching, and Liao-hsi[188] were under the rule of Ch'un, while [the regions] north of the desert, the two Chief Punitive Administrations of the Northern and Southern Routes, and the barbarian tribes were still controlled by T'ien-tsu. Hereafter the Liao empire was split up.   30, 2a–b

59. A HSI "EMPEROR"

1122   In this year [the second year of Pao-ta] the Chin soldiers entered [Yen] from Chü-yung Pass.[189] Hui-li-pao, while director of affairs for the chancellor of the Northern Division, placed himself on the throne at Chien-ko Mountain,[190] called himself emperor of the Hsi empire and changed the reign title to T'ien-fu. He set up three chancelleries for the Hsi, Chinese, and Po-hai, changed the eastern and western commanding prefects to be two kings and split up the offices and set up officials. . . . His partisan, Yeh-lü A-ku-chih, with his nephew, I-shih-pa-chin, and others killed him. He usurped the throne in all for eight months.[191]   114, 3b–4a

---

[186] The location of Chia 夾 Mountain has been disputed. According to TSFYCY 44, 14b, Chia Mountain is situated three hundred and forty *li* north of Shuo 朔 County, Shansi; CCITC 543, 5b locates it sixty-five *li* southeast of Tso-i Ch'ien-ch'i 左翼前旗 in the modern Ordos region. LSTLCK 8138 identifies it with a mountain outside Pien-ch'iang 邊牆 northeast of Yu-yü 右玉 County, Shansi. According to SHTC 54, 61b, it corresponds to modern Wu-tang-ku 五當谷, west of Sa-la-chi 薩拉齊.

[187] Ling-wu 靈武, northwest of the modern city of Ning-shuo 寧朔 in southeastern Ninghsia. It was there that in 756, after the rebellion of An Lu-shan, Emperor Su-tsung of T'ang ascended the throne, replacing his father, Hsüan-tsung, who abdicated in his favor.

[188] Respectively modern Peiping, Hopei; Ta-t'ung 大同 County, Shansi; Boro Khoton, Jehol; Lu-lung 盧龍 County, Hopei; Tsaghan Suburghan, Jehol; and Ch'ao-yang 朝陽 County, Jehol.

[189] A strategic pass northwest of Yen (modern Peiping).

[190] See note 39.

[191] Hui-li-pao's soldiers, though suffering from lack of food, were directed to move to the south where a Sung force defeated them. His followers thereupon turned against him (LS 114, 4a; CS 67, 15a–b). They decapitated him, sending his head to a Sung temple; the people called it "the head of the king of Yen" 燕王頭 (PSLH 2, 55).

GOVERNMENTAL ORGANIZATION

INTRODUCTION

1. POLITICAL AND MILITARY ORGANIZATION

When a society is compounded of strongly conflicting elements, political domination is largely tied to military power. This is particularly apparent in societies of conquest. However, even under such circumstances the political machine is not identical with the army. A number of civil and military functions may overlap in techniques, even in personnel; yet the duties of the tax collector, the granary inspector, the judge, or the supervisor of the calendar and agriculture differ fundamentally from the coercive tasks of the armed forces. Whatever the relation between the army and the civil government (and this relation manifestly changes with the changing social configuration) it is necessary to distinguish between the political organization which steers, supervises, and administers, and the military machine which conquers, intimidates, and defends.

2. FROM TRIBAL CHIEFTAINSHIP TO DYNASTIC RULE

a. FROM CHIEFTAINSHIP TO KHAGHANATE

The power that built the Liao empire was the organized might of the Ch'i-tan people. Although its success was contingent upon the economic advantage derived from the control of Chinese settlers and Chinese industry, this formative political factor remained tribal in root and character.

The term "tribal" does not necessarily mean primitive. When the ambitious A-pao-chi was making his bid for leadership, the Ch'i-tan were already a complex confederation. Their political structure, like that of other Inner Asiatic tribes, had not evolved simply from a single origin, but resulted from a repeated process of agglomeration and disintegration of tribal components in accordance with the changing historical situation. Their national antecedents, the Hsien-pei, seem to have been a powerful political complex before they broke up, in the fourth century, into three independent units, of which the Ch'i-tan were one.[1]

For several centuries, the newly established Ch'i-tan people enjoyed only a limited prestige; their leaders were merely chieftains, mo-fu-ho 莫弗賀,[2] and later,

ssŭ-chin or i-chin 俟斤.[3] The title khaghan which, during this period, was used by tribal rulers of extraordinary power[4] does not appear in the early history of the Ch'i-tan. Only during the later part of the T'ang dynasty did it become the official designation of the supreme chieftain of the Ch'i-tan confederation.[5]

b. A COMPLEX TRIBAL NOMENCLATURE

The Ch'i-tan khaghanate developed in a setting which at times stimulated, at times impeded, the growth of a strong northeastern state. The T'ang dynasty in the south and the Eastern Turks and Uighurs in the west and northwest pressed upon the Ch'i-tan with varying intensity and success. None of these countries was able to maintain permanent control, but they had sufficient influence to leave their mark on the nomenclature and perhaps even on the character of the Ch'i-tan officialdom. At the close of the seventh century the T'ang court conferred the title of prince or king (wang 王) on the khaghan of the northeastern tribal confederation. Thereafter, the Ch'i-tan "began to have the titles and ranks of T'ang."[6] Having observed the bureaucratic terminology current in the Chinese border zone and found it to their liking, they applied a number of Chinese titles to their own officials; the Liao Shih mentions the "grand preceptor," the "grand guardian," the "minister over the masses," and the "minister of works."[7]

The adoption of the Turkic-Uighur designations is not as clearly described. We learn that the Turks, while asserting their supremacy over the Ch'i-tan people, bestowed on their ruler the rank of 俟斤.[8] The two Chinese characters whose modern romanization is ssŭ-chin[9] have been tentatively transcribed by

---

[1] XIV, 1 (1), LS 63, 2a.
[2] XIV, 1 (1), LS 63, 2b.

[3] XIV, 1 (1), LS 63, 4a.
[4] Shiratori 26, 5–8 and 16.
[5] Cf. LS 45, 20a; 63, 4a and 7b. It may be doubted that these supreme chieftains were actually called khaghan during the years when the Orkhon Turkic and Uighur empires dominated Inner Asia. After 842, however, there was no tribal power which could prevent the Ch'i-tan rulers from officially assuming the majestic title.
[6] XIV, 1 (2).
[7] Loc. cit.
[8] XIV, 1 (1), LS 63, 4a.
[9] The authors of the K'ang-hsi Dictionary suggest i 矣 as a possible pronunciation of 俟, basing themselves on a passage in the Shih Ching [Odes of Yung, no. 8]. Karl-

Hirth as *i-kin* [*i-chin*]. On this basis, he suggests an affinity to a Turkic numeral *äkin*, "the second," and when used as a title, the possible meaning "*secundus a rege*" or "second to the khaghan."[10]   Hirth evidently based himself upon Radloff's interpretation of a passage in the Chinese part of the Orkhon inscriptions.[11] Here *äkin* may indeed have had the meaning "the second," but the form is unusual,[12] and Thomsen questions the numeral without, it is true, refusing it altogether.[13]   Pelliot agrees with Hirth's transcription of 俟 in the Orkhon inscriptions but considers this case exceptional and, on the basis of an extended argument, suggests instead the reading *ch'i* for the first part of the problematic expression.[14]   But, whatever the transcription, the semantic intent of the term is clear.   Among the early Turks it designated a high official[15] whose status among the Western Turks was that of a "Statthalter"[16] (governor).

In many cases it is difficult to establish the provenience or the time of adoption of the Ch'i-tan tribal titles used either before or during the dynastic period. Nevertheless, we have listed below a number of titles whose Mongol, Tungus, or Turkic (Uighur) equivalents can be indicated with some degree of certainty. Whenever these equivalents were taken from the studies of such scholars as Shiratori, Hirth, or Pelliot, the appropriate reference is made.   All other analyses were made by Dr. K. H. Menges who generously permitted us to include here the first tentative results of what may eventually be a more comprehensive investigation of the Ch'i-tan language.   The modern Chinese transliterations of the Ch'i-tan titles have been given according to the Wade-Giles system; Karlgren's Sui-T'ang equivalents are referred to only in a limited number of cases.   His analysis seeks to establish the Chinese pronunciation used in the north (in Ch'ang-an) in A.D. 601, that is under the Sui dynasty, and perhaps in early T'ang time.[17]   If the Chinese tran-

scriptions of Altaic words contained in the *Liao Shih* are given the phonological values reconstructed by Karlgren, sharp discrepancies appear in many instances between Sui-T'ang Chinese and Altaic forms. Frequently the final consonant of Sui Chinese finds no correspondence in early or modern Altaic, whereas the modern Chinese forms, because of their loss of the final consonants (except *-n* and *-ng*), do not present this difficulty.   For instance:

TABLE 15

CHINESE TRANSCRIPTIONS OF ALTAIC WORDS

Chinese Transcription	Sui-T'ang Chinese Pronunciation	Modern Chinese Pronunciation	Altaic Prototype
閘撒	.*ap-* or *kâp* ˍ*sât* (Karlgren 23, 344, 767)	*cha-sa*	*džasaq*
葛兒罕	*kât-* ˍ*ńźię-* ᶜ*xân* (*op. cit.* 73, 12, 296)	*ko-êrh-han*	*gorxan*
撻馬	*d*ᶜ*ât-* ᶜ*ma* (*op. cit.,* 956, 592)	*ta-ma*	*taman*
特滿	*d*ᶜ*ək-* ᶜ*muân* (*op. cit.,* 811, 597)	*t'ê-man*	*tuman*

Examples of this type suggest that the post-T'ang Chinese phonology as reflected in the Liao transcription of Altaic words had gone a long way in abandoning the final consonants characteristic of earlier Chinese.

Shiratori claims that the Hsien-pei, a proto-Mongol people, used the term khaghan before it appeared among the Turks,[18] and that the T'o-pa, another proto-Mongol group, were the first to call the wife of a khaghan *kasun*.[19]   If this is so, then the proto-Mongol Ch'i-tan may have taken both titles from their ethnic antecedents.   On the other hand, they may have received the designations from the Turks, even if they were current among proto-Mongol groups at an earlier time.   During the eighth century, when the Ch'i-tan first called their supreme chieftain khaghan, this title was used by the head of the greatest

---

gren, however, assumes a Chou pronunciation **dz'i̯əg* for the word as used in the *Shih Ching* (Karlgren 40, 93) and a Sui pronunciation **dz̦'i̯əg/dz̦'i* (*op. cit.,* 384, no. 976m).

[10] Hirth 99, 111 ff.

[11] See Radloff 95, 193; *idem* 97, 141; for Radloff's grammatical interpretation see 97, 90.

[12] *Cf.* Radloff 97, 70; see also Brockelmann (28, 65): *ikinč*, "second." *Iki* is a variant of *äki*, the Turkic numeral "two," which Radloff gives as *äki* for Orkhon-Turkic (Radloff 97, 162), but as *äki, äkki, iki, ikki, igi* for other Turkic languages (*idem,* WB I, 678, 682, 1417, 1421, 1426).

[13] Thomsen 96, 180, note 97.

[14] Pelliot 29a, 225–229.

[15] TS 215A, 3a; *cf.* also Chavannes 03, 21.

[16] Hirth 99, 112.

[17] The dictionary *Ch'ieh-yün* 切韻 was completed in 601, in the middle of the Sui dynasty (A.D. 581–618).

Along with the rediscovered part of the *Ch'ieh-yün*, Karlgren uses also its enlarged T'ang version, the *T'ang-yün* 唐韻 (Karlgren 40, 7).

Although the pronunciation thus restored was that of the Sui "and early T'ang time" (*op. cit.,* 3; *cf.* also *idem* 23, 4), more exactly speaking it is the Sui "projection" of ancient Chinese (*idem* 40, 3 ff.), the language spoken between A.D. 500 and 600 (*idem,* PC, 32), that is, in the sixth century (*idem* 40, 5).

[18] Shiratori 26, 17; *cf.* also Boodberg 36, 171–172.

[19] Shiratori 26, 34; Boodberg 36, 169 ff. In this form the title is purely hypothetical. The texts offer only *qatun. Cf.* note 21.

contemporary Inner Asiatic state, the Orkhon Turkic empire.[20]   It is equally interesting that the wife of the Orkhon Turkic khaghan was called *qatun*,[21] a term that appears among the Ch'i-tan as *k'o-tun* 可敦.[22] After the establishment of the Liao empire both titles, khaghan and *k'o-tun*, disappeared from the recorded nomenclature although they may well have been retained in the vocabularies of the Ch'i-tan tribesmen.[23] Other tribal titles, evidently of predynastic origin, continued to be employed officially: in a number of cases their early origin is expressly stated.[24]

Variants of the terms *mo-hu* 抹鶻, "official of a *wa-li* 瓦里,"[25] and *mo-fu-ho* 莫弗紇 (or 賀), "chieftain,"[26] occurred in the titular nomenclature of other tribes of the proto-Mongol Hsien-pei group from which the Ch'i-tan originated.   The Wu-lo-hou 烏洛侯, a branch of the Hsien-pei people, called their hereditary chief *mo-fu* during the time of the Wei dynasty (fourth to sixth century);[27] the Ch'i-fu 乞伏, another branch of the Hsien-pei people, had the word *mo-ho* 莫何 as part of the title of their ruler.[28]   The T'u-yü-hun word *mo-ho* 莫賀, which is reported for the same period, is equated in the *Sung Shu* with "father."[29]   The Shih-wei called their great chieftain *mo-ho-tu* 莫賀咄, and the three chiefs of an individual tribe, *mo-ho-fu* 莫何弗.[30]   In the fifth century *mo-fu-ho*, and in the sixth century *mo-ho-fu*, refers to a tribal leader of the Ch'i-tan.[31]   No such title is recorded for a Ch'i-tan chieftain during the dynastic period.   Only the tribal subdivision, called *wa-li*, was still headed by a *mo-hu*.[32]   Is the proto-Mongol *mo-hu* etc. related to the Old-Turkic *baγa*, a word that in the Orkhon inscriptions designated a tribal dignitary?[33]   The reciprocal substitution of *m* for *b* is common to all Altaic languages; Altaic *γ* is often rendered by *h* in Chinese transcriptions.   However, Shiratori's attempt[34] to

connect *mo-hu* etc. with *abaga*, "uncle" (Altai-Mongol dialect), or *aba*, "father" (Tungus dialect), or with Mongol *baγa* ["small"[35]] is unconvincing, partly for linguistic, partly for semantic, reasons. Orkhon-Turkic *baγa* is derived from the same Iranian base as the later term *beg*.[36]   *Beg* was as widely used among the Altaic peoples of Western and Central Asia as *baγa*, *mo-hu*, etc. seem to have been by the Altaic tribes of Central and eastern Central Asia from the fifth to the eighth century.

Cha-sa 閘撒, a small tribal unit,[37] suggests affinity to Jurchen *hāh-ša*, "village,"[38] and other Tungus designations for "village": Goldi *gasa, gasan;* Orochi *gasa;* and Negidal *gasin*.[39]   LS 45, 25*a* lists a *cha-sa-yüeh* as the title of the official in charge not of a *cha-sa*, but of a *mei-li* 抹里.   It is strange that the *cha-sa* is not mentioned in LS 45, for the list of the officials of the ordos given in this section follows in general the more detailed description given in LS 31, 2*a*, and here the *cha-sa* is mentioned after the *mo-li*.   Is the version given in LS 45, 25*a* a mutilation of an earlier list? And in the original manuscript did the title *cha-sa-yüeh* precede the word *cha-sa*?   Taking the text as it stands, there is a probability that *cha-sa-yüeh* derived not from the Tungus word for "village," but from Mongol *džasaq*, "office, law, government, commander."[40]   The Chinese syllable *yüeh* 獄 (Sui pronunciation *xịwăt*[41]) may indicate the Altaic plural suffix (vowel + *-t*), as it possibly does in the word *ta-ma-yüeh* 撻馬獄.[42]   If *cha-sa-yüeh* is a Chinese transliteration of a Ch'i-tan word for "official" related to Mongol *džasaq* (plural: *džasaγut*), and if *cha-sa* actually meant "village," then the two terms transcribed as *cha-sa* and *cha-sa-yüeh*, although phonetically identical, were of different origin and meaning.

The Ch'i-tan word transcribed as *mo-li* 抹里,[43] *mei-li* 抹里,[44] or *mi-li* 彌里[45] (Karlgren 23, 13 and 529: ˛*mjịĕ-ᶜlji*), "a small tribal settlement," suggests relationship to the Mongol appellative "horse."   The

---

[20] Radloff 95, 360 ff.; *idem* 97, 167 ff.; *idem* 99, 92 and 93; Thomsen 96, 97 ff.

[21] Radloff 95, 361; *idem* 97, 168; *idem* 99, 93; Thomsen 96, 101, 106, 108.   The Turkic *qatun* derives from Soghdian *xwatēn*, "lady."

[22] VII, 2 (84).

[23] See Shiratori 12 TMK, 1265.

[24] XIV, 1 (23).

[25] LS 45, 25*a*; *cf.* also LS 116, 17*a*.   It seems that *mei* 抹 is an error for *mo* 抹, since in all other cases the Altaic syllable in question is transcribed by the character *mo* 莫.

[26] XIV, 1 (1), LS 63, 2*a–b*.

[27] WS 100, 16*b*.

[28] Chin 125, 1*a*.

[29] Sung 96, 3*b*.

[30] Sui 84, 21*b*.

[31] See above, note 26.

[32] LS 45, 25*a*.

[33] Radloff 97, 46 and 179.

[34] Shiratori 11 TMK, 603.

[35] Kovalevskij 1844, 1055.

[36] The different forms *baγa* and *beg* may be explained by the fact that Old-Iranian has two terms, *baγa-* (Āvestā) and *baga-* (Old Persian), both meaning "god."   Later the word was also used as a title for a king.   Middle-Iranian: *baγ, baγē* (Sasanid inscriptions); Pahlavī: *baγ*. (The Iranian terms have been kindly contributed by Professor B. Geiger.)

[37] XV, 1 (3).

[38] Grube 96, 92.

[39] Schmidt 23, 16 ff.; *cf.* also Shiratori 13 TMK, 17.

[40] Kovalevskij 1844, 2272.

[41] Karlgren 40, no. 303f.

[42] LS 116, 2*a*.

[43] XV, 1 (7), *passim*.

[44] XV, 1 (3), *passim*.

[45] XIV, 1 (23).

divergencies in Chinese rendering may be due to some early copyist's mistake; they may, however, reflect genuine proto-Mongol dialectal variants. (Literary Mongol: *morin;* Buryat and modern Mongol dialects: *mörin;* also as loan-word in Russian: *merin.*)

It is interesting to note that all these terms which exhibit Mongol affinity refer to smaller tribal divisions and their officials. However, some few do refer to larger tribal units and their leaders. Besides the debatable proto-Mongol titles, khaghan and *qatun*, the *Liao Shih* uses the Ch'i-tan designation *t'ê-li-chien* 忒里蹇 or 腯俚寋[46] (Karlgren 23, 178, 529, and 773 [?]: *tʿək - ᶜlji - ᶜki̯än*) for empress, a word reminiscent of the Mongol *terigün*, "the head, origin, the first, principle."[47]

The Ch'i-tan also called an empress *nou-wo-mo* 耨斡麼,[48] which according to the *Liao Shih* is a composite of *nou-wo*, "deity of the earth," and *mo*, "mother."[49] This suggests Tungus affinity. The word *nou* in *nou-wo* may possibly be a transliteration of the Jurchen *náh*[50] (other Tungus languages *na*[51]), "land," while *mu* is evidently related to Manchu *mama*, "grandmother," or to Manchu *eme*, "woman, wife, female."[52] A few other titles also seem to have Jurchen or Manchu affinity. *A-tien* 阿點 (Karlgren 23, 414 and 1162: *ᴄ·â - ᶜtiem*), "noble,"[53] suggests Mongol *erdem*[54] and Manchu *erdemu*, "capability, virtue, achievement, virtuous";[55] and *ch'u-ku* 楚古 (Karlgren 23, 904 and 421: *ᴄtṣʿi̯ʷo - ᶜkuo*), "title of an official,"[56] may be related to Jurchen *čʿáo-hāh*, "army," and Manchu *čoxa*, "army, war, warrior."[57]

The title *ko-êrh-han* 葛兒罕 adopted by Yeh-lü Ta-shih when he made himself the first emperor of the newly established Hsi Liao[58] state (Qarā-Khitāy), evidently is the title of the Qarā-Khānid rulers,[59] *gür-xān* or *gōr-xān*, which hitherto has not been explained etymologically. The first two syllables of *ko-êrh-han* may well be identical with Mongol *gür*, "large, wide, general, common," as found in the *Secret History of the Yüan Dynasty*.[60] The same root seems to be present in the Turkic word *kür*, "brave," as recorded by Mahmūd al-Kāshgharī,[61] and in Osman *gür*, "abundant, rich, good luck;"[62] it may also be related to Manchu *goro*, "far, far-reaching."[63] A *gōr-xān* then would be a khan with far-reaching power, a supreme ruler.

---

[46] LS 71, 1*a*; 116, 22*b*.

[47] Kovalevskij 1844, 1770.

[48] LS 71, 1*a*.

[49] LS 116, 22*b*.

[50] Grube 96, 96.

[51] Manchu, Goldi, Olcha, Orochen, etc. (see Shiratori 13 TMK, 24).

[52] These equations were already suggested by Shiratori (13 TMK, 24), who, however, does not clearly distinguish between the different roots.

[53] LS 116, 3*b*–4*a*.

[54] Kovalevskij 1844, 260.

[55] Gabelentz 64, 56; Zakharov 75, 90. Shiratori (12 TMK, 1145) links up *a-tien* with the designation *a-lu-tun* 阿魯敦 or *a-lu-to-li* 阿廬朵里 given in LS 73, 3*b* and 116, 5*b*. The affinity of these two words to *a-tien* is linguistically problematic. *A-tien* may be connected with Mongol *altan*, since in a number of cases the final *-l* of a syllable may not be rendered in Chinese transcriptions, as in *ta-la-kan* and *ta-kan* < *tarqan*, *darxan* (SS 490, 9*a*), *i-li-chin* and *i-chin* < *ilig*, *wo-lu-to* and *ou-t'o* < *ordo* (see XV, introduction), and since cases are known where the sound *a* of proto-Mongol seems to have undergone palatalization in Ch'i-tan, as in *nieh-la* = Mongol *nara*(*n*), "sun" (I, 2 (4), no. 7). However, this palatalization is rare and seems to be limited to the first syllable.

But composition with Mongol *altan*, "gold," may be expected in analogy with Turkic (Kāshgharī) *altun tarym* as a title of the khaghan's wives (see below, text and note 131). This is in full accord with our text, LS 116, 4*a* giving *a-tien i-li-ti* 夷离的 (the variant of *i-li-chin* 堇), "wife of a high official of noble rank." Distinction of gender has not been developed in Ural-Altaic, but in a few cases gender-suffixes are found in the three Altaic groups. Thus we may see a gender-suffix in the word rendered in Chinese as *i-li-chin* or *i-li-ti* which could either be an Altaic **ilig-in* with a feminine suffix **-in*, possibly identical with *-um*/*-ym* in Turkic (Kāshgharī) *tarym*, Chaghatai *xan-um*, *beg-üm*, "lady, princess, noblewoman." The word would then be split up into the syllabic groups *i-li-gin* for notation in Chinese, the syllable *-gin* = *chin* deriving from *ki̯ən*<**ki̯ən* (Karlgren 40, 248, no. 480*t*) or from *chien* < *kăn* < **kɛn* (*op. cit.*, 247, no. 480*e*). A Chinese form *i-li-ti*, *ti* being < *tiek* < **tiok* (*op. cit.*, 418, no. 1120*h* and *i*), however, might represent an older form of the Mongol feminine suffix *-džin* < **-dyn*/**-din*, which in modern Mongol is mainly found in the designation of female animals. A form related to the above postulated feminine suffix *-ym* is found in the Tungus (Evenki) suffix *-m̆ni* for female tribespeople. But *a-tien* may also be related to Jurchen *ʾa-tīh*, "rank" (Grube 96, 89).

[56] LS 116, 21*b*.

[57] Grube 96, 91; Gabelentz 64, 34; Zakharov 75, 942 ff.

[58] LS 30, 6*a*.

[59] Barthold 28, 366 ff.

[60] Transcribed as *ku-êrh* 古兒 in YCPS 8, 29*b*, 30*a*, and *passim*, and explained by the Chinese word *p'u* 普, "great, universal, all-pervading, all." *Cf.* Haenisch 37, 65 and Kozin 41, 278 and *passim*. In his glossary (*op. cit.*, 618) Kozin erroneously connects *gür* (*ḱur*) with Mongol *kegür* > *kūr*, "forward, smash, attack," and Kalmyk *körö-*, "to become furious, enraged," while he lists *gür-ijer* and *gür deere-in džarγu* (*loc. cit.*) separately; actually the *gür* in these two instances is identical with the *gür* (*ḱur*) quoted above.

[61] Brockelmann 28, 117.

[62] Radloff, WB II, 1637; *cf.* also *kür* (*op. cit.*, 1447).

[63] Gabelentz 64, 84; Zakharov 75, 345 ff.

The designation for a tribal subdivision, *wa-li*,[64] evidently is related to Mongol *ajil*,[65] "tents, tent-camp, tent-village," Turkic *aɣyl*, "fence, manure;"[66] in modern Turkic *ajyl*, *aul* means "tent-camp, nomadic settlement." The Ch'i-tan word has an initial labial going back to a proto-Altaic initial labial which is lacking in the Turkic group; it is replaced by *h-* in Old-Mongol (**hajyl*), and is preserved in the Tungus-Manchu group and in Finno-Ugrian: *cf.* Manchu *falga*, "village," Hungarian *falu*, stem *falv-*, "village." *Wa-li* may therefore be considered one of the few genuine Tungus words in the *Liao Shih* whose etymology can be definitely established.

A number of Ch'i-tan titles suggest Turkic affinity. Shiratori[67] and Pelliot connect the word *i-li-chin* 夷离堇 (Karlgren 23, 186, 533 and 389: ₜ*i* - ₜ*ljie̯* - ₜg*ᶜi̯ən⁾* or g*ᶜie̯n* or *ᶜki̯ĕn*) with the Turkic-Mongol titles, *irkin* or *erkin*,[68] the latter obviously thinks of Mongol *ärgin*, *ärgim*, "superior, principal, master, chief."[69] Equally plausible seems its relation to the Uighur designation for ruler, *ilig*.[70] The high honorific appelation *yü-yüeh* 于越 (Karlgren 23, 1317 and 1348: ₜ*ji̯u* - *ji̯ᵂ̯vt*) resembles the term *ögüt*, "counsel," which appears in Kāshgharī's Turkic dictionary[71] and in Uighur texts.[72] Its meaning may possibly have changed from counsel to councillor. The title *yü-yüeh*, which is prominent in the Ch'i-tan hierarchy, was also used by the Uighurs.[73] Did the latter accept it from the Ch'i-tan, or was the process reversed, or did both peoples receive it from an earlier common source? Since the word is old,[74] it may well have been derived from the Orkhon Uighurs, whose influence on their eastern neighbors is well documented.[75]

The Ch'i-tan *t'i-yin* 惕隐 evidently is the Turkic *tegin* or *tigin*, a term which in the Orkhon inscriptions designates a prince of royal blood, a son or brother of the khan.[76] Hirth believes that the old Turkic word

äl, *el*, or *il*, "people" [Radloff: "tribe"],[77] was transcribed by the Chinese in a number of different ways: as 頡 [*chieh*],[78] 頡利 [*chieh-li*],[79] 伊利 [*i-li*].[80] The Ch'i-tan *i-li-pi* 夷離畢 might then mean the *pi* [from *beg*, "lord," "official," "hero,"] of the tribe or people, just as the early *Äl-* or *Il-Xan* (*i-li-k'o-han*) probably meant "the khan of the people, tribe."[81]

The designation *hsien* 賢, "worthy," "virtuous," was the fifth Liao emperor's given name; it was also the first part of his Ch'i-tan style.[82] It occurs in many Turkic and Uighur titles. According to Pelliot it must be a Chinese "equivalent of the Turkic *bilgä*"[83] ["wise].[84] The *ti-lieh-ma-tu* 敵烈麻都 possibly is the Chinese transcription of a Turkic word **tirämät*, an old plural in *-t* of a verbal noun in *-mä* of *tirä-*, "to support"; **tirämät* may mean "the pillars of the empire."[85]

The old Yao-lien title *a-cha-ko-chih* 阿札割只[86] (Karlgren 23, 414, 206, 57 and 1213: ₜ*â* - *ṭṣat* - *kát* - *ᶜt'śie̯*) evidently contains the Turkic word *ačqu*, "key"; the *ačqučy* would be "the holder of the key," the treasurer. The office was later absorbed by the [Northern] Chancellery,[87] whose southern department among other things administered the tribal taxation.[88] In all probability the Hsi title *t'u-li* 吐 (or 禿) 里[89] (Karlgren 23, 1129 and 529: ₜ*t'uo* - ₜ*lji*) also originated in predynastic times. The word may be the Chinese transliteration of the Turkic *törä*, "prince," a term which occurs in the Uighur texts.[90] The latter part of the Ch'i-tan designation of a supreme chieftain in the eighth century, Ti-lien-tsu-li 迪輦俎里[91] (*tsu-li* was Sui ₜ*tṣi̯ᵂ̯o* - ₜ*lji*[92]), may be the transcription of the Turkic title *čur*. In the Orkhon inscriptions this word indicating an honorific position of unspecified character[93] frequently occurs as the second part of a compound.

---

[64] XV, 1 (3).
[65] Kovalevskij 1844, 3.
[66] Brockelmann 28, 3. *Cf.* also Shiratori 13 TMK, 17 ff.
[67] Shiratori 11 TMK, 1406 ff.
[68] Pelliot 30, 44.
[69] Kovalevskij 1844, 268.
[70] Bang and Gabain 31, 479.
[71] Brockelmann 28, 132.
[72] Bang and Gabain 31, 479.
[73] In the year 941 (LS 4, 6*b*); in 983–984 for the Kao-ch'ang Uighurs (SS 490, 9*a*), and in 990 for the Arslan Uighurs (LS 13, 1*b*).
[74] A-pao-chi held the rank of *yü-yüeh* under the last Yao-lien khaghan (LS 1, 2*a*); so did his uncle Shih-lu (LS 64, 3*a*).
[75] See General Introduction.
[76] Radloff 97, 175; *idem*, WB III, 1034; Thomsen 96, 59, note 1, and 73. In the Orkhon inscriptions it has the form *teggin*.

[77] Radloff 97, 163; *idem*, WB I, 803–805, 1471 ff.
[78] Pelliot: *hsieh* (Pelliot 29*a*, 210).
[79] Hirth transcribes *hit*, *hit-li*, and *i-li* respectively.
[80] Radloff 95, 375.
[81] Hirth 99, 110.
[82] See appendix II.
[83] Pelliot 29*a*, 210.
[84] Radloff 95, 378; *idem* 97, 180.
[85] LSYC 5, 3*a* suggests the equation of *ti-lieh-ma-tu* with Manchu *dorolon*, "proper behavior, ceremonies," and *muten*, "skill"; the *dorolon muten* would be ritual skill. The equation, although semantically possible, is phonologically improbable.
[86] XIV, 1 (9), LS 45, 9*b*.
[87] *Loc. cit.*
[88] *Op. cit.*; LS 45, 3*a–b*.
[89] LS 46, 3*a*; 25, 4*b*.
[90] Radloff, WB III, 1250.
[91] XIV, 1 (1), LS 63, 7*b*.
[92] Karlgren 23, 1070 and 529.
[93] *Cf.* Radloff 95, 372; *idem* 97, 177; *idem*, WB III, 2172. *Cf.* also Thomsen 96, 155, note 39*a*.

Ta-la-kan 達剌干, the old title of the second highest official of the Ch'i-tan subtribe, *shih-lieh*,[94] is doubtless a transcription of the term *tarqan* which appeared in the Orkhon inscriptions[95] and occurred again in the Uighur texts as *tarqan* and *tarxan*.[96] The word is also found in Mongol vocabularies in the form *darxan*, with the meaning "worker, artist, exempt from taxation, smith, privileged artisan,"[97] and possibly as a Juan-juan title at the time of the Western Wei[98] (sixth century). Laufer claims an Old-Turkic origin for it.[99] According to him, "whenever the Chinese mention the title, it regularly refers to Turkic personages."[100] However, Bang and Gabain contest its Altaic provenience. They consider the term a loanword from Chinese.[101] Originally the term designated a military commander;[102] in the Uighur texts it means a minister.[103] Its latest semantic development[104] cannot concern us here.

The Ch'i-tan *ta-ma* 撻馬 (Karlgren 23, 956 and 592: *dᶜât - ᶜma*), "a person who acts as an escort,"[105] is probably identical with the *ta-mo-chi* 答摩支 of the Western Turks,[106] the *taman* of the Orkhon Turks,[107] and the Mongol *tamači*.[108]

The Ch'i-tan word for a subtribe, *shih-lieh* 石烈[109] may be related to Turkic *tirä*, "part of a tribe,"[110] originally *tir-ä*, "a gathering," from *tir-*, "to gather." The change of the sound groups *ti* and *di* to *či* and *dži* is a regular phonological shift in Mongol, and it has also been noted in Tungus. Turkic *tir-ä*, in accordance with Osman forms such as *der-lä-*, goes back to the proto-Turkic **dir-ä*, which suggests also a proto-Altaic **dir-ä*. This early term could be expected to develop into **džirä* in Mongol and a

similar form in Tungus-Manchu. Indeed Manchu contains the word *dzira*[111] or *džira*,[112] "close together, following in close sequence, densely settled, containing many people." Relation between these words and the Ch'i-tan designation transcribed as *shih-lieh* seems probable phonologically as well as semantically.

In *ch'ao-wu-êrh* 炒伍㑧 "to fight,"[113] which is also transcribed *ch'ao-li* 杪離,[114] the Turkic noun of the aorist *čab-yr*, *čab-ur*, might be related to *čab-*, *čap-*, "to beat, cut off, swing, ride fast, gallop."[115] This root is found in Mongol *čab-či-* and its derivatives, "to cut, slaughter, mow."[116]

The first part of the compound T'ê-man Army,[117] *t'ê-man* 特滿, obviously refers to an Inner Asiatic pre-Altaic word "very many, ten thousand" which appears in the Orkhon inscriptions as *tümän*.[118] Jurchen has *t'ù-man*,[119] Manchu *tumen*,[120] Mongol *tümen*.[121] In the form *toman* the word became known in the West through Marco Polo's description of the Mongol army.[122] The term *k'o* 怯 also had a predominantly military connotation;[123] it either designated a group of people, or a specific military detachment, or its officer.[124] Chinese *k'o* may be a transcription of at least three Turkic words: *qoł*, *qur*, and *qat*. Various Turkic people, including the Uighurs, call an army or a wing of an army, *qoł*.[125] From the Orkhon period on, the Turks had the word *qur*, "a situation, step, degree, rank, position."[126] *Qat* is a general Turkic appellation for "stratum, row, side."[127] The word *k'o* may be a variant of Mongol *γoł*, which in the *Secret History of the Yüan Dynasty* appears in combination with *čerig*, "army": *γoł-čerig*, "the main force."[128] If the term transcribed as *k'o* in the *Liao Shih* is related to one of these Turkic or Mongol

[94] XIV, 1 (23).

[95] Thomsen 96, 59, 131, 185; Radloff 95, 369; *idem* 99, 174.

[96] Bang and Gabain 31, 501. Mahmūd al-Kāshgharī also has *tarxan* (Brockelmann 28, 198). LS 13, 1*b* mentions the occurrence of the title *ta-la-kan* among the Arslan Uighurs.

[97] Kovalevskij 1844, 1676 ff.

[98] Han JL 37, 86.

[99] Laufer 19, 592.

[100] *Op. cit.*, 593.

[101] Bang and Gabain 31, 501.

[102] Hirth 99, 56.

[103] Bang and Gabain 31, 501.

[104] Laufer 19, 593 ff.

[105] XVI, 979, LS 9, 2*a* and LS 116, 2*a*. *Cf.* also I, 2 (5), no. 33.

[106] Pelliot 29*a*, 220.

[107] Radloff 95, 125; *idem* 97, 174; *idem*, WB III, 996.

[108] Pelliot 29*a*, 221.

[109] *Cf.* I, introduction.

[110] Chaghatai Turkic (see Radloff, WB III, 1365). The word also occurs in the Özbek dialects of modern Afghanistan (Jarring 39, 41 ff., 48, 77).

[111] Gabelentz 64, 121.

[112] Zakharov 75, 990.

[113] VII, 2 (83).

[114] CTKC 27, 3*b*.

[115] Uighur and later Turkic (Radloff, WB III, 1916 ff.).

[116] Kovalevskij 1844, 2092 ff.

[117] LS 46, 13*a* and 19*b*.

[118] Thomsen 96, 114; Radloff 97, 177; *idem*, WB III, 1602–1603.

[119] Grube 96, 101.

[120] Gabelentz 64, 206; Zakharov 77, 758 ff.

[121] Kovalevskij 1844, 1924–1925.

[122] Marco Polo 03 I, 261, 263, note 2; II, 192, 217, note 2.

[123] LS 116, 7*a*.

[124] XIV, 1 (20), LS 45, 21*a*; (21).

[125] Radloff, WB II, 581 ff.

[126] *Op. cit.*, 916 ff.

[127] *Op. cit.*, 274 ff.

[128] YCPSHC 1, 2*a*; *cf.* Kozin 41, 298 and 497. The Chinese transcription is *huo-lo* 豁勒; the second syllable is placed in the margin in small script to indicate final *-l* as an aid to the reader. (For an explanation of these auxiliary symbols, see Haenisch 31, 51 ff.)

words, then it must have lost its final consonant either when borrowed by the Ch'i-tan, or more probably when transcribed into Chinese.

The title *t'a-lin* 闥林, the original designation for one of the officials of the "subordinate states,"[129] linguistically resembles the Uighur Turkic designation *tarym*. In Uighur this title refers to women only;[130] in the Turkic language of the eleventh century, according to Mahmūd al-Kāshgharī, it is a title given to a ruler; combined with the epithet *altun*, "golden," it becomes a title of the khaghans' wives.[131]

A number of other Ch'i-tan titles that are manifestly military in character may be Altaic forms of originally Chinese words. The title *hsin-kun* 辛袞 (Karlgren 23, 802 and 464: ₜsi̯ěn - ᶜkuən), the designation of the head of a *mi-li*, replaced the earlier—and still more enigmatic—title *ma-t'ê-pên* 馬特本.[132] The term *hsin-kun* is perhaps related to the Old Turkic *säŋün*,[133] which according to Thomsen may be a Turkicized form of the Chinese title *chiang-chün* 將軍, "general."[134] Pelliot discusses three other Liao titles, *hsiang-wên* 詳穩, *ch'ang-kun* 常袞, and *ch'ang-wên* 敞穩. He assumes that all of them had the same Chinese root, probably *hsiang-kung* 相公, rather than *chiang-chün*,[135] thus, it seems, arriving independently at the same conclusion reached by Ch'ien Ta-hsin more than a century earlier.[136]

c. A COMPLEX TRIBAL HIERARCHY

Our survey has not attempted to identify all the tribal titles contained in the *Liao Shih*, nor has an explanation been offered for each term identified. Furthermore, certain equations are admittedly open to question. Yet, in spite of all this, the validity of the greater number seems to be well enough established to permit a few tentative conclusions.

Titles with a Turkic affinity, which were particularly conspicuous within the upper ranks of the Ch'i-tan hierarchy, underline the dominant role of the Orkhon and Uighur Turks in Inner Asia during the last centuries before the establishment of the Liao empire. These titles designate a number of tribal units as well as certain lower and higher tribal officials. This would seem to indicate that, at the close of the T'ang period, the Ch'i-tan had already developed a political order comparable with, if not as complex as, that of the Huns and Turks at the height of their

political power. Favored by the historical situation, the Ch'i-tan had grown into a confederation of socially stratified tribes with a fixed nobility and a relatively stable ruling house, whose head, the khaghan, might be offered a Chinese princess in marriage.

The positions of the tribal officials were, in general, designated by terms that found their origin in Inner Asia. Certain titles were, however, taken over from the alien but impressive Chinese bureaucracy by a process of creative misunderstanding which is as typical in the selective diffusion that operates between dissimilar groups and cultures as it is in the play of children.

To be sure, the opportunity of transforming a tribal society into an imperial state depended to a large degree upon external factors, above all, upon the crisis and temporary decay of China's economic and political order at the end of the ninth and during the first half of the tenth century. But, while all the border tribes were aware of the dissolution of T'ang China, only the Ch'i-tan ruler was able to take advantage of it. Evidently he could profit so uniquely, because during these years his people had achieved a degree of political and military integration far beyond that of China's other barbarian neighbors.

3. THE GOVERNMENT OF THE NORTHERN REGION

The great political revolution of 900–950 that transformed the tribal state of the Ch'i-tan into the Liao empire is but vaguely indicated in the *Liao Shih*. However, considerable space is devoted to the resulting bureaucracy. The basic data of LS 45 and 46 consist in the main of extensive lists of titles. Explanatory details in this section are few, but valuable. Additional information has been gleaned from a number of other passages and texts which describe the origin, development, and function of certain tribal Liao offices.

a. "NORTH" AND "SOUTH"

From its inception, A-pao-chi's state included two main cultural groups: the pastoral tribes, mainly Ch'i-tan, in the north and the sedentary population, mainly Chinese, in the south. Small wonder, therefore, that the terms "north" and "south" soon became important elements in the country's administrative terminology.

While no statement specifically defines a regional division of the empire before 947, the presence of a northern and a southern prime minister, when A-pao-chi ascended the throne,[137] suggests that such a dichotomy was recognized, at least functionally. According to LS 45, the northern prime minister was

---

[129] XIV, 1 (25).
[130] Bang and Gabain 31, 501.
[131] Brockelmann 28, 197.
[132] XIV, 1 (23).
[133] Radloff 97, 177; *idem*, WB IV, 449.
[134] Thomsen 96, 149; *cf.* also Pelliot 30, 46, note 3.
[135] Pelliot 30, 46, note 3.
[136] NESKI 83, 9a.

[137] LS 1, 2b.

drawn from the distinguished lineages of the imperial clan, while his southern counterpart belonged to the family lines of the Maternal Uncles.[138]   In the light of the concrete data of the *Liao Shih* this assertion is untenable.   Actually, the situation was reversed: members of the Yeh-lü clan held the southern office, while Hsiao clansmen filled the northern ministry.[139] The trend was established at the founding of the empire in 907, when Hsiao Hsia-la was the northern prime minister and Yeh-lü Ou-li-ssŭ controlled the southern office.[140]

The reasons for the directional alignments of the clans are not stated, but in all probability they reflected some geo-historical connection.   A-pao-chi's power over the tribes derived from his control of the southern "Chinese City" and the all-important salt-lake nearby.[141]   Although reluctant to admit it publicly, he is said to have spoken the Chinese language.[142] The second Liao emperor began to wear Chinese clothes on certain occasions, while his empress, drawn from the Hsiao clan, continued to dress in the customary tribal attire.[143]   It is possible that the Yeh-lü clan considered itself southern in comparison with the Hsiao whose traditions suggest a Uighur, i.e. northerly, origin; it is beyond question that the head of the Yeh-lü clan, in fact and symbol, acted as the middleman for the Ch'i-tan people and the "southern" world.

The basic concepts of "north" and "south" found application in various spheres of Ch'i-tan life.   Within the imperial I-la tribe A-pao-chi's subtribe, the Six Divisions, became the Southern Division, reaffirming again the emperor's link to the south.   The remoter branch, the Five Divisions, was called the Northern Division.[144]

In 947 the extension of the Liao state southward necessitated the reorganization of its political structure.   The empire was now clearly divided into two primary sections, the Northern and the Southern Regions (面) or Divisions (院).[145]   These geographical designations were in general correspondence with the cultural and ethnical divisions within the empire.   The Southern Region comprised the Chinese and other sedentary groups, whereas the Northern Region comprehended the tribal population.   The bulk of the country's agriculturists (most of whom were Chinese or Po-hai) lived in Nan-ching, Hsi-ching, or Tung-ching; the tribes, for the most part, dwelt in

the northern regions.   But the mass deportations and colonizations settled many Chinese and Po-hai in the old tribal territories of the north, Shang-ching and Chung-ching, while a number of tribes moved into certain sections of the eastern circuit, Tung-ching.[146] The Liao rulers, aware of this fact, gave the government of the so-called Southern Region jurisdiction not only over the old Chinese territories of the south but also over the sedentary populations of the northern circuits.   Similarly, the Northern Region controlled not only the tribes of the North but also those of the East and West.

Thus, in the new imperial order the terms "north" and "south" lost, to some degree, their geographical significance, and acquired, instead, an ethnical and cultural emphasis, a process that was repeated within the tribal world in the Yeh-lü and Hsiao clans.   The country's military organization revealed a further modification of the concept.   The two branches of the imperial tribe, which were controlled by the Yeh-lü clan, saw to the defence of the southern area within the Northern Administration, while the I-shih tribe, which may have been controlled by the Hsiao clan, held the corresponding key position in the southwestern area of the Southern Administration.[147]

Variations of this kind obscured but did not eliminate the fundamental dichotomy within the Liao empire and the basic significance of the terms "north" and "south" which reflected it.   The political reorganization in 947 carried the concept to its logical conclusion.   But the dual arrangement of political functions was so deeply rooted, and the balance of power between the two ruling clans evidently so delicate, that, in addition, the earlier dichotomy was duplicated and elaborated within the Northern Region.   The "northern" government now had a Ch'i-tan Northern Chancellery and a Ch'i-tan Southern Chancellery, controlling a Northern and a Southern Division respectively; it had northern and southern prime ministers and great kings.   These two Divisions must be confused neither with the tribal unit of the same name nor with the two main Regions themselves which, as stated above, are occasionally also thus designated.   Furthermore the northern and southern prime ministers must be carefully distinguished from their counterparts in the southern government whose functions were completely different, although at times their titles were almost identical.   The authors of the *Liao Shih*, well aware of the confused nomenclature, introduce their survey of the Liao hierarchy with the statement that the officials of the tribal government "all were divided into North and South.   In reality, however, they

[138] XIV, 1 (9), LS 45, 4*b* and 4*b*–5*a*.
[139] *Cf.* XIV, 1, notes 61 and 64; see also LTCNP 8045 ff.
[140] LS 1, 2*b*.
[141] III, introduction; WTS 72, 2*b* ff.
[142] CWTS 137, 6*a*.
[143] VII, 1 (7).
[144] LS 46, 3*a*; see also 11*b*.
[145] XIV, 1 (4); XIV, 2 (1).

[146] See I, 1, *passim*.
[147] XV, 1 (33).

governed only the affairs of the north. This must be clearly understood by those who discuss the political system of Liao."[148]

b. THE COURT

The center of an absolutistic government is the court, the ruler, and his entourage. This was as true for the Liao empire as for the more typically Chinese dynasties in spite of specific features deriving from the tribal origins of its rulers. Controlling a partly pastoral, partly agricultural population, the Liao emperors had fixed capitals and city palaces in the classic Chinese manner.[149] The imperial city of the Supreme Capital harbored the important bureaus of both central governments.[150] But the emperors, perpetuating the nomadic habits of their ancestors,[151] spent much time in their seasonal camps, the na-po 捺鉢. If the picture drawn in LS 32 can be trusted, an emperor set out for his spring camp during the first ten days of the first month, spending sixty days on the way to Duck River Lake. There he fished and hunted until the end of spring.[152] Shortly after his return to the capital he set out again. In the middle of the fourth month the emperor "moved his tent," traveling until the end of the fifth month. For fifty days he remained at his cool summer na-po, departing again in the middle of the seventh month.[153] In the instance described he went directly from his summer camp to hunt deer and tigers in the mountains.[154] The length of his sojourn at the autumn na-po is not stated, but the account goes on to say that he generally spent the winter months at the somewhat warmer winter camp.[155]

Such a routine was not always feasible. Matters of military or political importance might necessitate changes in the schedule, and a serious campaign would completely upset it, at least for the duration. It is also possible that the later emperors spent more time in the capitals than did the first rulers of the state. Yet, although a certain softening was apparent from the eleventh century on, the interest in hunting and fishing continued until the end of the dynasty,[156] and with it probably the maintenance of the traveling routine. Moving from place to place, en route at times for as long as sixty days, the emperor had ample opportunity to receive regional officials and to keep in touch with local conditions. It is, therefore, not

surprising that these peregrinations are designated in the Liao Shih as "quarterly tours of inspection."[157]

On his travels to his seasonal residences the ruler was accompanied by a rump government of Ch'i-tan and Chinese officials. As a rule, dignitaries of the Southern Region did not participate in the early fishing and hunting activities. Instead, during the first month of the year, they went to the Central Capital, which geographically was the natural link between the Supreme Capital and the southern centers of administration. There they promoted all matters concerning the Chinese,[158] no doubt in accordance with decisions reached at the winter assembly. Twice each year the emperor summoned the officials of the Northern and Southern Regions in what seems to have been the supreme political council of the empire, first during the fifth or sixth month in the summer na-po,[159] and again during the tenth month in the winter na-po.[160] Problems of special significance, particularly those dealing with military affairs, were withheld from the Chinese bureaucracy and only discussed with close and trusted tribal officials.[161] Many major routine problems, including the official nominations, were considered at the emperor's seasonal residences,[162] probably at the semiannual conferences. It is obvious that an emperor who spent so much time traveling, hunting, and fishing could not give full attention to the details of administration. But it is equally obvious that he, his court, and his councillors determined the empire's over-all civil and military policy.

c. COURT OFFICIALS

The records mention numerous court officials. Those listed as members of the "northern" government evidently constituted the tribal element in the new ("third") Liao culture. Within this government, both its Northern and Southern Divisions (院) served the emperor through the respective Northern and Southern Departments of the Master of Court Etiquette.[163] Judging from the context, the two Divisions in question were the tribal and not the regional units of this name.

The Department of the Master of Court Etiquette of the Southern Region was set up by T'ai-tsung in 938.[164] Manifestly, this was an effort to institutionalize official Chinese manners at the Liao court, but, in all probability, it exercised only a limited influence

[148] XIV, 1 (6).
[149] See XI (5) (15); I, 1 (8).   (See also CTKC 22, 6b ff.)
[150] See below.
[151] See II, 1 (23).
[152] II, 1 (24).
[153] II, 1 (25).
[154] II, 1 (26).
[155] II, 1 (27).
[156] See XI (27); cf. also XIII (41) (45) (46) (51).

[157] XIV, 2 (4).
[158] Loc. cit.; cf. also II, 1 (25) (27).
[159] II, 1 (25).
[160] II, 1 (27).
[161] See XV, 2 (26).
[162] XIV, 2 (4).
[163] XIV, 1 (9), LS 45, 7a and 7b.
[164] XIV, 2 (5), LS 47, 9b ff.

in a government whose rulers preferred the felt tent to the stone palace and the bow to the brush. Unlike its Ch'i-tan counterpart, this department held a relatively inferior rank in the bureaucratic hierarchy of the Southern Region.[165] Its officials, in the main, must have been Chinese, for they would know best how to present the traditional Chinese court ceremonial.

The Department of the Northern Region must have been manned primarily by Ch'i-tan dignitaries.[166] But practice did not always conform to expectation. At the beginning of the twelfth century the too successful Chinese fighter against financial corruption, Ma Jên-wang, was removed from his influential administrative office in the Southern Region and installed as master of court etiquette of the Southern Division.[167] If the authors of the *Liao Shih* did not confuse the Southern Region 南面 with the Southern Division 南院, then a "northern" position, which traditionally was reserved for members of the imperial clan, was given to a Chinese official. Inconsistencies are not infrequently recorded for the earlier periods; it is therefore not surprising that they should also occur in the year 1114, shortly before the empire's collapse.

The daily routines of court life were the concern of the numerous attendants and servants attached to the emperor, whether he stayed in one of his capitals or set out on a military campaign, a tour of inspection, or a hunting and fishing expedition. A description of the minor court offices is beyond the scope of our analysis. The titles enumerated in our text are largely self-explanatory; they give some idea of the needs of the court and its ways of satisfying them.

No sharp distinction existed between those offices and "bureaus" which served the emperor personally and those which served the central government. LS 46, 6a ff. classes the superintendent of the eagle aviaries and hunting grounds with the heads of iron smelteries, arsenals, and herds. No particular consistency is apparent, but consistency was perhaps not the aim of the authors; the emperor being the absolute political head, any distinction between his private and public activities would have been formal rather than real.

Special officials were assigned to the empress dowager, the empress, the imperial concubines, and the heir apparent.[168] A powerful empress dowager might have military detachments, guards, armies, and camps of her own.[169] The heir apparent, who had

his own palace, was surrounded by dignitaries of both Chinese and Ch'i-tan nationality, the bi-national composition of this entourage clearly foreshadowing the dual task ahead of him.

The crown prince's household, his "tent(s)," was in the charge of a *t'i-yin*, an official of the northern government[170] who evidently represented the traditional Ch'i-tan way of life. Supervised by him and served by "northern" attendants,[171] the heir apparent learned the military lore of his tribal people. Even that pious patron of Buddhism, Tao-tsung, had his eldest son educated in the spirit of his imperial ancestors, past masters in riding and shooting, who had made the world tremble with their power.[172]

But the future ruler of a large Chinese population had to be trained in Chinese ways as well. Numerous officials of the Southern Region were assigned to his service, some as teachers whose main duty was to familiarize their young charge with the Chinese classics and the equally important Chinese ceremonial.[173] Their southern classification did not necessarily imply Chinese origin; among the five outstanding tutors of the heir apparent listed as officials of the Southern Region in LS 47, 15b–16a three bear Chinese, and two Ch'i-tan names.

d. OFFICIALS OF THE DISTINGUISHED LINEAGES

All the difficulties which regularly confront the analyst of Liao bureaucracy appear when an attempt is made to integrate the data concerning the officials of the distinguished lineages. The authors of the *Liao Shih* have lumped together in a single list the titles of officials of the court, of the central government, and of a number of eminent families and lineages. The tendency to arrange the titles according to political position is complicated by an equally strong desire to arrange them according to social rank. The task is further aggravated by the fact that rival dignitaries not infrequently belonged to different complexes of power and prestige, such as an important section of the civil service or an honored branch of a former ruling family. In the absence of any single reliable criterion their relative position had to be weighed in accordance with tradition, expediency, or the personal judgment of the compiler. The translated passages offered in XIV, 1 and 2, clearly reveal the mixed character of the original Chinese list.

The *Liao Shih* indicates that the outstanding families and lineages of the tribal world of the Liao empire were placed in the charge of special officials who, acting both in administrative and judicial ca-

[165] See preceding note.
[166] See LTCNP *passim*.
[167] X, 1 (66).
[168] XIV, 1 (12).
[169] See XV, 1 (3) (23); *cf.* also VII, introduction.

[170] XIV, 1 (10).
[171] See note 168.
[172] XV, 2 (20).
[173] XIV, 2 (5), LS 47, 15b–19a.

pacities, seem to have been responsible for the political and private conduct of their group. The system was extended to the families of defeated and displaced former rulers; it was also applied to the distinguished lineages of the Yeh-lü and Hsiao clans.

The official who controlled the four most prominent lineages ("tents") of the Yeh-lü clan was the Grand Imperial *t'i-yin*.[174] Each of these lineages in turn was under the immediate leadership of special officials: a grand *ch'ang-kun* controlled the Horizontal Tents,[175] and three *ch'ang-kun*, the three Patriarchal Households respectively.[176] The heads of the distinguished Hsiao lineages were also called *ch'ang-kun*,[177] while the patriarch of the former ruling house, the Yao-lien, like the head of the ruling Yeh-lü lineage, was designated grand *ch'ang-kun*,[178] apparently indicating a rank above that of the Hsiao clan and the other non-ruling Yeh-lü lineages. The way in which these titles were applied suggests interesting hierarchic differences as well as historical relationships.

Honorific though the designation *ch'ang-kun* was, its possibly Chinese origin[179] may account for its application to positions of lesser rank than the title *t'i-yin*, a genuinely Altaic and therefore probably older word. The term *t'i-yin*, the Ch'i-tan equivalent of the old Turkic *tegin*[180] (brother of the khaghan, royal prince), was given to the head officer of the four imperial lineages and to the chief of the family of the heir apparent or future ruler. In another context, this time as grand *t'i-yin*, it appears near the top of the hierarchical pyramid of the Northern Region, listed directly below the grand *yü-yüeh*, the elder statesman of the northern tribal government.[181] It is possible that this grand *t'i-yin* is identical with the grand imperial *t'i-yin* who, as the representative of the four outstanding imperial lineages, joined the grand *yü-yüeh* as a second elder statesman.

Those who bore the title *t'i-yin* were dignitaries of high status, probably men of wealth as well as power. A *t'i-yin* was included among the nation's leading functionaries who were responsible for securing the wherewithal to construct an imperial mausoleum;[182] a *t'i-yin* joined the highest official of the central government in revising the Liao legal code;[183] a *t'i-yin* was one of two commanders-in-chief during a serious frontier war.[184] But high as the position of *t'i-yin* was, his sphere of power was restricted for the most part to clan affairs, a situation that did not always satisfy the desires of a politically ambitious man. La-ko, T'ai-tsu's brother, shortly after receiving the title of *t'i-yin* of the imperial clan, participated in a court rebellion.[185]

Other officials, whose titles were less time-honored, but whose power was more substantial, dominated the political machine of the rapidly expanding central government. First among these were the two prime ministers, and later the two chancellors who superseded them.[186] The two great kings of the Northern and Southern Division, who headed the two branches of the I-la tribe, also exercised more real power, particularly in the military field. The traditional attitude was succinctly expressed by Yeh-lü P'o-tê when he stated that "the rank of the great kings of the Northern and Southern Divisions is higher than that of the *t'i-yin*."[187] Under T'ai-tsung an attempt to elevate the imperial lineage above the great kings failed.

Subtle considerations of this kind were of obvious importance in maintaining the hierarchy of prestige which paralleled or penetrated the hierarchy of power. Whoever wishes to understand Liao society must be aware of the terminological distinctions which reflect the concepts underlying hierarchic rank and station. The order in which the dignitaries who contributed to Ching-tsung's mausoleum were listed indicates that even in such situations social status was recognized. Aside from several close personal relatives the donors appear as follows: a prime minister, a northern great king, a *t'i-yin*, the Horizontal Tents, and the Imperial Maternal Uncles.[188]

A special office represented the principalities of the imperial princes;[189] another managed the affairs of the princesses' residences;[190] a third took care of "all tents of the imperial descendants."[191] The functions of these three bureaus are not clearly defined, a fact that is of particular interest as the fief-like territories of the princes and princesses, the "entrusted commandery-prefectures," are fully treated in the geographical survey of the *Liao Shih*. Was their administrative organization unknown? This seems highly improbable, for the territories entrusted to the princesses and their husbands were headed by officials of

[174] XIV, 1 (13).
[175] XIV, 1 (14).
[176] XIV, 1 (15).
[177] XIV, 1 (21).
[178] XIV, 1 (20).
[179] See above.
[180] See above.
[181] XIV, 1 (9), LS 45, 7b–8a.
[182] X, 1 (13).
[183] VII, 1 (45).

[184] XIII (37).
[185] XIV, 1 (3), and XIII (5); cf. also XIII, introduction.
[186] XIV, 1 (9), LS 45, 2a–5a.
[187] VII, 1 (5).
[188] X, 1 (13).
[189] XIV, 1 (16).
[190] XIV, 1 (19).
[191] XIV, 1 (18).

the central government.[192] Were they politically insignificant? This seems equally improbable, for the administrative units of much smaller complexes were noted in LS 45 and 46. We are inclined to believe that organizationally the principalities more or less resembled other territories of similar size which were directly controlled by the central government. The authors of the *Liao Shih* may well have assumed that their description of certain of these in LS 48 covered the structure of all of them.

e. THE OFFICIALS OF FORMER RULING FAMILIES

Besides the distinguished lineages of the Yeh-lü and the Hsiao clans, remnants of former ruling houses, such as the Yao-lien tents and the royal families of the former Po-hai kingdom and the Hsi people, were also duly recognized.

According to LS 63, the Yao-lien, the line of the former Ch'i-tan Khan, "came to an end" after A-pao-ch'i's usurpation of the throne.[193] This statement is correct if real power is being considered. But a revolution rarely destroys the whole structure of the earlier society; in the case of the Yao-lien family the loss of its preeminent political position did not lead to complete liquidation. After 907 members of the nine Yao-lien tents were deprived of their tribal support,[194] and some were probably purged; but those who survived the period of transition were still accorded considerable respect. By continuing to honor the former ruling family, the Liao emperors may have been giving symbolic emphasis to their ideas regarding the permanency of power and the sacredness of its personnel. The Yao-lien had their lineage officials, as did the Yeh-lü and the Hsiao. As shown above, the rank of their leader, the grand *ch'ang-kun*, placed their line above the other non-ruling families and equated them with the imperial lineage.

The experts on rank and etiquette must have found it difficult to express these subtle differentiations in their tables. In the *Liao Shih*, the problem is solved by listing the Yao-lien officials after those of the imperial clan but before those of the Hsiao.[195] The bureaucratic positions conceded to the family administration of the Yao-lien were relatively numerous. The roster of their civil and military functionaries approximates that of a small court—probably the well-considered intent of the Liao rulers.

Unlike the Yao-lien, the royal family of the former Po-hai kingdom was not of Ch'i-tan nationality. Before their land was conquered they had wielded considerable power as leaders of an independent and frequently hostile state. Together with the Po-hai masses, they were probably severely disciplined after their country's defeat. The *Liao Shih* gives no detailed account of their positions. What few officials are mentioned are placed after those of the Hsiao lineages.[196]

The status accorded the ruling family of the Hsi people differed again. Ethnically and culturally, they were close relatives of the Ch'i-tan;[197] they had struggled valiantly to maintain their independence, but finally accepted the inferior position imposed upon them by their stronger Ch'i-tan cousins.[198] In the reorganization that followed, their head ("king") continued to be drawn from the former ruling family.[199]

Apparently, the authors of the *Liao Shih* were not certain where to list the Hsi kings and their officialdom. In LS 45 they are mentioned after the officials of the Po-hai "tents,"[200] and before the king of the I-shih tribe. In the following chapter, LS 46, which deals with the tribal governments, the four "great tribes" of the empire are listed as the Five and Six Divisions, the I-shih, and the Hsi.[201] The administrative offices of the Five and Six Divisions, the "Departments of the Northern and Southern Great King," are referred to here but not discussed in detail, probably because in the preceding chapter they were treated as one of the high-ranking bureaus of the northern government. Mention of the I-shih tribe before the Hsi in LS 46 gives added confirmation to the assumption that in some way this tribe was associated with the consort clan, Hsiao. A laconic reference in LS 46, 3a to the office of commanding prefect, preceded by the obscure word *ti-ku-li* 迪骨里, throws little light on the administrative organization of the I-shih.

The Administration of the King of the Six Tribes of Hsi, however, is described in some detail. Besides the king, it included two *ch'ang-kun* (not mentioned in the list of officials of the great tribes), two prime ministers, a *t'u-li*,[202] and a number of other officials whose functions were partly military.[203] The presence of the two *ch'ang-kun* gives the Hsi "court" a rank more or less similar to that of the two ruling Ch'i-tan clans. Although the Hsi kings had no "grand" *ch'ang-kun*, they were closer to the sources of real power. They had not been separated from their

---

[192] I, 1 (3).

[193] XIII (1).

[194] See I, 2 (1) and note 9.

[195] XIV, 1 (20), LS 45, 20a–21a. *Cf.* the preceding and subsequent texts concerning the Yeh-lü and their officials.

[196] XIV, 1 (22).

[197] *Cf.* LS 1, 2a.

[198] See XIII, introduction.

[199] LS 32, 4b.

[200] LS 45, 23a.

[201] LS 46, 3a.

[202] See above, note 89 ff. and pertinent text.

[203] LS 46, 3a.

people nor removed from their traditional residences like the ruling family of the Yao-lien. Yet their might was not left unchecked; the I-shih tribe was honored in order to counterbalance that other "great" tribal complex, the Hsi.[204]

f. THE "NORTHERN" CENTRAL GOVERNMENT

The emperor and his court were the center of Liao political power. This center included representatives of the country's distinguished lineages which, in various ways, maintained permanent contact with and exerted influence over their ruler. But, however strong such influence may have been in shaping the emperor's political decisions, these decisions once made required for their execution a medium completely different from the semi-personal atmosphere of the court with its noble families and powerful personalities. They required an organized political machine with an effective central government as its core and territorial, regional, and local administrations as its agents.

Of course, even the central government of an absolutistic regime must take into account the experience of its lesser administrative units made available through routine reports and intelligence. But the technical direction, as well as the political, remains the task of the central government. Following the presentation in the *Liao Shih*, our survey first discusses the central government of the Northern Region, then its regional organization.

The central government of the Northern Region, as constituted after 947, had developed in accordance with the needs of an expanding state and the internal reorganizations that accompanied its growth. The official hierarchy of A-pao-chi's monarchy was headed by the northern and southern prime ministers who were chosen from the two leading clans respectively, the Hsiao and the Yeh-lü. The arrangement implies that these tribal groups supported A-pao-chi's rule, but it also indicates that because of their tribal status and tradition they might challenge the new dynastic head, if not the dynastic principle itself. The attitudes of the two clans toward the regime differed. For obvious reasons,[205] most members of the consort clan supported the emperor, even protecting his power from the machinations of his kinsmen. A-pao-chi therefore had every reason to allow the Northern Prime Ministry to remain in the hands of the Hsiao. The leaders of the Yeh-lü, however, who revolted time and again, could not be equally trusted. After the appointment of a Yeh-lü clansman, Ou-li-ssŭ, to the Southern Prime Ministry,[206] the emperor transferred

the important office to loyal outsiders, members of the Ch'u-tê tribe,[207] until, at the death of La-ko in 917 and the failure of Tieh-lieh-ko's rebellion in 918,[208] he felt sufficiently secure to install a close relative as southern prime minister. With the nomination of A-pao-chi's youngest brother, Su, in 921 the claim of the Yeh-lü clan to the office was definitely established.[209]

The following year T'ai-tsu, disturbed by the increasing strength of his own tribe, split it into two parts.[210] The single chieftain (*i-li-chin*) was now replaced by two leaders whose loss in real power was mitigated by their new and august title, great king.[211]

During the reigns of T'ai-tsu and his son, T'ai-tsung, the growing Chinese population required increasing political attention. But not until the reorganization of 947 was the administration, which had charge of the Chinese people, recognized as an independent government, that of the Southern Region. It need not be stressed again that the supreme power remained with the government of the Northern Region.

The Ch'i-tan Northern Chancellery of the Northern Region held a key position second only to the throne. Like its southern namesake, it dealt with "Ch'i-tan," that is, tribal affairs. The northern chancellor controlled the traditional wealth and strength of the Ch'i-tan people,[212] their soldiers and their herds. In addition, he selected the military officers.[213] Together with the emperor, he determined the country's general policies; on many occasions he personally supervised their execution.

It was a chancellor of the Northern Division who, in 986, assisted in subduing the dangerous Jurchen;[214] in 1015 it was the northern chancellor, Yeh-lü Shih-liang, who decisively defeated the Eight Tribes of Ti-lieh;[215] it was the successive heads of the Northern Chancellery who fought against Sung before 1005,[216] and who again in 1042 organized a military campaign against the great southern empire.[217] A chancellor of the Northern Division suppressed the clan rebellion of 1063;[218] another planned the mobilization of great

---

[204] See I, 2 (4), no. 3; cf. LS 45, 19b.
[205] Cf. XIII, introduction.
[206] LS 1, 2b.

[207] XIV, 1 (5).
[208] XIII (12) (13).
[209] XIV, 1 (5).
[210] XV, 1 (25).
[211] XIV, 1 (6). It seems that the division was made in 922, whereas the head of the two subtribes received the title "king" only in 938. See XVI, 938, LS 4, 2b.
[212] Cf. II, 1 (2).
[213] XIV, 1 (9), LS 45, 2a.
[214] II, 1 (10).
[215] VII, 2 (49).
[216] Cf. II, 1, note 12.
[217] XVI, 1042, LS 19, 2a–b.
[218] XIII (41); cf. also X, 2, note 55.

masses of the population to repair the river dikes in Tung-ching.[219]   And while he was northern chancellor, the powerful and sinister Yeh-lü I-hsin, a member of the Five Divisions of the imperial clan, revised the laws of the nation,[220] cunningly discredited the heir apparent, and finally engineered his assassination.[221]

The prestige of the Chancellery is strikingly illustrated by two episodes which occurred during the later rebellions against the Liao government: in 1063 the rebel, Hsiao Hu-tu, set up a new emperor and had himself appointed chancellor;[222] in 1122 the director of affairs for the Northern Chancellery, Hui-li-pao, a Hsi, made himself emperor and bulwarked his short-lived dignity with chancellors for the Hsi, Chinese, and Po-hai.[223]

The choice of the northern chancellor does not seem to have been limited by clan or lineage until 1077, when the scheming Yeh-lü I-hsin succeeded in having the hereditary claim to this and several other positions granted to his family.[224]   Before 1077[225] and a few years after,[226] Yeh-lü and Hsiao[227] nobles held the key position; in a time of great emergency it was even offered to a Chinese.[228]   What was the exception in the Northern Chancellery almost became practice in its southern counterpart: an experienced Chinese was often placed in charge of the Ch'i-tan Southern Chancellery which dealt with civil affairs, particularly taxation.[229]

The Northern Prime Ministry, for the most part, remained in the hands of Hsiao dignitaries.   While at times it was entrusted to Chinese officials, it does not seem to have been held by any member of the Yeh-lü clan.[230]   During the tenth century the post of southern prime minister was, in the main, filled by Yeh-lü clansmen, but later the situation changed. During the second half of the eleventh century the office of southern prime minister was generally held by members of the Hsiao clan,[231] thus giving the consort families temporary control over the ministries

of both the Northern and Southern Administrations. In the first decades of the twelfth century Yeh-lü clansmen continued to hold offices of secondary importance but, during the last years of the dynasty, the two prime ministries were filled by Hsiao nobles and Chinese officials.[232]

The great kings of the Northern and Southern Divisions continued to be drawn from the Yeh-lü clan.   Although officially entrusted with civil matters, the main field of their activity seems to have been the organization of tribal warfare and border defence. Their functions will therefore be more fully discussed in section XV.

Below the chancellors, the two prime ministers, and the two great kings are listed the offices of those dignitaries who belonged either to the northern central government or to its glamorous center, the court. The two masters of court etiquette obviously fall into the second category.   The *yü-yüeh* was a high political official before 907.   A-pao-chi's uncle, Shu-lan, and later A-pao-chi himself, held the office under the last Yao-lien khaghan.   The descriptions of Shu-lan's achievements indicate that they were both military and civil, but whether or not they were connected with his position as *yü-yüeh* is not clear.[233]   Regarding A-pao-chi's official duties, the *Liao Shih* leaves no doubt.   When he became *yü-yüeh*, he was given control in military and political affairs.[234]

However, after the dynasty was established, the growing power of the emperor and his newly created bureaucracy left no room for a tribal *major-domo*. The office of the *yü-yüeh* now became purely honorific; it was awarded to men of great political achievement and loyalty.   Yeh-lü Jên-hsien, who played a leading part in the events of 1042 and who in 1063 crushed Ch'ung-yüan's rebellion, was made chancellor of the Northern Division and concurrently honored with the title of *yü-yüeh*.[235]   As elder statesmen, the holders of this office might advise as well as assist the emperor.   The *yü-yüeh*, Yeh-lü Hsiu-ko, after reporting on the great Sung attack of 986,[236] participated with noteworthy success in the ensuing campaign.[237]

Like most Ch'i-tan dignitaries, the *t'i-yin* (or grand *t'i-yin*) conferred on military matters if the situation demanded it.[238]   But more especially he was the administrative head of the imperial clan.   Leading his Yeh-lü kinsmen and accompanied by his wife as clan mother, the *t'i-yin* formally welcomed a new empress

---

[219] XI (22).
[220] VII, 1 (45).
[221] XVI, 1077, LS 23, 5*b* and XIII (43).
[222] XIII (41).
[223] XIII (59).
[224] XIV, 3 (23).
[225] LTCNP 8048 ff.
[226] *Op. cit.* 8064 ff.
[227] Hsiao Ho-cho was a member of one of T'ai-tsu's old tribes, the T'u-lü-pu (see XVI, 1017, LS 15, 11*b* and note). Whether he really descended from the Hsiao clan or whether he was a T'u-lü-pu noble who was made a Hsiao *honoris causa*, we do not know.
[228] See below.
[229] LTCNP 8048 ff.
[230] *Op. cit.* 8045 ff.
[231] *Op. cit.* 8059 ff.

[232] *Op. cit.* 8066 ff.
[233] See II, 2 (1) and note 1; III (1).
[234] XVI, 903, LS 1, 2*a*.
[235] X, 2 (74) and note 55.
[236] XVI, 986, LS 11, 1*b*.
[237] XVI, 986, LS 11, 2*a* and 987, LS 11, 8*b*.
[238] XVI, 973, LS 8, 3*b*.

on her wedding day.[239]   Together with the imperial couple, a shaman and the prime minister of the Northern Administration, a *t'i-yin* participated in the great sacrifice to Mu-yeh Mountain.[240]   Here, again, he probably acted as the representative of the imperial clan, while the northern prime minister may have fulfilled a similar function for the consort family.

The next five offices were apparently concerned with the affairs of the Northern Region.   The *i-li-pi* headed what seems to have been a high court for tribal litigants.[241]   Being an important northern official, he also participated conspicuously in several of the more tribal state ceremonies;[242] and in 1119 a director of affairs in his department was sent as an envoy to the Jurchen court to proclaim A-ku-ta emperor of the new eastern state.[243]

The Department of Grand Scribe supervised official writings of various kinds, most particularly the imperial edicts.[244]   The orders and announcements of the Southern Region were prepared in the Han-lin Academy in Chinese;[245] but the edicts of the Northern Region, destined for the tribespeople, were no doubt issued in the Ch'i-tan language.   The Ch'i-tan mouthpiece of the emperor obviously held a position of great political significance.   It is, therefore, not surprising to find that a grand scribe suggested such far-reaching reforms as those contained in Yeh-lü Shu-chên's memorial of 1074.[246]   But, reflecting the Ch'i-tan military tradition, the scribe might also lead an army to victory,[247] suppress a rebellion,[248] or initiate a revolution.[249]   A right and a left scribe assisted the regular commander in chief in directing the army on the march.[250]   Yeh-lü Ta-shih, who after the collapse of the empire escaped westward with a handful of daring tribesmen, finally founding the new state of Hsi Liao in Turkestan, originally held the post of scribe of the Northern Region of the Liao empire.[251]

The functions of the *ti-lieh-ma-tu*, ceremonial though they were, differed from those of the masters of court etiquette.   The realm of court etiquette was essentially secular; the ceremonies supervised by the *ti-lieh-*

ma-tu were religious.   It should be noted that he acted specifically in ceremonies of a tribal character, such as the solemn winter hunt[252] and the sacrifice to Mu-yeh Mountain.[253]

The functions of the Office of the Secretariat are not explained in the *Liao Shih*,[254] but they seem self-evident.   If the "northern" government wanted to maintain regular contact with its tribal subjects, some kind of routine correspondence was necessary between the tribal officials and their copyists, on the one hand, and a central secretarial bureau, on the other.   The Office of the Secretariat, like the Department of the Grand Scribe, must have used the Ch'i-tan script.

The office of *a-cha-ko-chih*, a mere shadow of its historical self, soon faded completely from the scene.[255] Under the Yao-lien rulers, a "holder of the key" may have been the khaghan's treasurer,[256] but the new dynastic government needed a different and more complex financial organization.   The archaic office is interesting only in so far as it seems to indicate the existence of a rudimentary financial center in the Ch'i-tan government during the later years of the predynastic period.

Besides these offices, the central government of the Northern Region included a series of technical bureaus which supervised the government herds, the smelting of iron, the arsenals, mints, and workshops.   Their titles,[257] like those of the Minor Court Bureaus,[258] are listed without comment, probably not because the authors of the *Liao Shih* were unfamiliar with the functions of these offices, but because a knowledge of their character was taken for granted.

The designations of the various officials of the central government of the Northern Region exhibit an interesting linguistic stratification; the higher dignitaries, from the emperor down to the great kings of the Northern and Southern Divisions, bore Chinese titles, while the next lower group continued to be known by tribal designations, *yü-yüeh*, *t'i-yin*, *i-li-pi*, *ti-lieh-ma-tu*, and the archaic *a-cha-ko-chih*.   Two exceptions, however, occurred within this group.   The titles, Department of the Grand Scribe and Office of the Secretariat, as might be expected, are Chinese rather than Altaic.   It would seem that the new dynastic bureaucratic top of the new conquest state required new designations which naturally enough were taken from the Chinese, first, because the tribal governments of the inner tribes did not possess such offices, and second,

---

[239] VII, 2 (89).

[240] VII, 2 (85).

[241] XIV, 1 (9), LS 45, 8a.

[242] VII, 2 (85) (the *i-li-pi* "prepared the ceremonies," possibly as the head of a ceremonial police); VII, 2 (91).

[243] XVI, 1119, LS 28, 6b–7a.

[244] XIV, 1 (9), LS 45, 8b ff.

[245] XIV, 2 (5), LS 47, 8b–9a.

[246] VII, 2 (67).

[247] See XVI, 967, LS 7, 3b; VII, 2 (37); II, 1 (10); XVI, 1010, LS 15, 1b; 1050, LS 20, 4a; 1115, LS 28, 3a.

[248] XIII (37) (44).

[249] XIII (25).

[250] XV, 2 (2).

[251] II, 1 (3).

[252] VII, 2 (93).

[253] VII, 2 (85).

[254] XIV, 1 (9), LS 45, 9a.

[255] *Loc. cit.*

[256] See above.

[257] XIV, 1 (26).

[258] XIV, 1 (11).

because the adopted Chinese terms carried with them the quasi-magic prestige which an imperial government had acquired in the course of a long and essentially successful political history. But the Northern Region remained tribal. So did many functions of its central government. This fact is evidenced by the retention of numerous tribal titles from the *yü-yüeh* down.

The Chinese designations for the two secretarial departments may be explained by the novelty and "Chinese" nature of their tasks. Even if, before 907, a few Ch'i-tan tribesmen knew how to write Uighur or Chinese, writing as an integral part of government routine originated only with, or after, the founding of the empire. Although the Uighur script influenced the form of the "smaller" Ch'i-tan script, the "larger" script was created under Chinese stimulus, and writing as a government institution had no more impressive model than China.

In our translations English equivalents have been given for the Chinese and quasi-Chinese titles. The tribal titles have been romanized to make them as conspicuous in our English version as they are in the Chinese original. The stratification established by the four categories of titles within the "northern" central government confirms linguistically what institutional analysis has revealed regarding the peculiar character of the new Ch'i-tan government.

g. THE TRIBAL OFFICIALDOM

The nomenclature of the tribal officialdom fell into strata not dissimilar to those of the northern central government. A survey of the titles of the officials of both the "great" and small tribes demonstrates again that Chinese designations prevailed in the tribes' general government, whereas the officials of the tribal subdivisions, except for the "copyist," either bore Altaic titles or titles whose Altaic (tribal) equivalents were still remembered.

The reason for this is obvious. The political revolution, which created the centralized imperial state, also created new tasks for its tribal components. The tribes' political status changed; they lost in independence, but they gained in wealth and military importance. Closer political and military integration required a tribal government strong enough to mobilize its manpower quickly and effectively for warfare, transport duties, and, when necessary, for taxation.

As early as the T'ang dynasty Chinese designations had appeared among the Ch'i-tan titles, but this predynastic trend could only receive limited encouragement from the not-yet-centralized tribal state. The political revolution inaugurated by A-pao-chi gave greater meaning to the Chinese titles already adopted, and in all probability extended their use. It led to the acceptance of additional Chinese designations for

the ruler of a great tribe, who now became a "great king," for his lieutenants, the two "prime ministers," and for the "commanding-prefect."[259] This last official delegated by the Ch'i-tan government to rule the dependent border tribes appears also in the bureaucracies of the small and great tribes of the empire, but whether or not the commanding-prefect of these Ch'i-tan tribes was directly responsible to the central government, as were his colleagues in the border tribes and the commanding-prefects of the entrusted-commanderies, is not known.

Two offices of the over-all government of the great tribes have titles whose former Altaic equivalents are given: the tribal chief was originally called *i-li-chin*, the minister over the masses, *t'i-yin*[260] Thus, before the adoption of the Chinese designations, the head of a more important tribe was evidently an *i-li-chin* (*ilig ?*) who was supported, among others, by a *t'i-yin* (*tegin*). Although the smaller tribes in the dynastic period were governed by a minister over the masses, it seems doubtful whether in their case this official replaced a former *t'i-yin*. LS 46, 2b ff. does not comment on the point, but LS 46, 1a–2a shows that even a subdivision of a great tribe was headed by an *i-li-chin*.

h. THE *SHIH–LIEH* AND *MI–LI*

According to the survey made in LS 46, the great as well as the small tribes of the empire were subdivided into *shih-lieh* and *mi-li* (or *mo-li*[261]). Internal evidence indicates that the *shih-lieh* is larger than the *mi-li*. The former is always mentioned first in the hierarchic lists which in general proceed from the more inclusive items to the lesser ones; in the descriptions of the various ordos the *shih-lieh* is always tabulated before the *mo(mei)-li*, just as the prefectures (*chou*) are always noted before the counties (*hsien*).[262] A-pao-chi's background is described as follows: Ch'i-tan I-la tribe, Hsia-lai-i *shih-lieh*, Yeh-lü *mi-li*.[263] In this passage as well as in the glossary[264] the authors of the *Liao Shih* have added the term *hsiang* 鄉[265] to *shih-lieh* to clarify the unusual designation. The same term also appears with *mi-li* in LS 46, 2a, but in LS 116, 2a a *mi-li* is more specifically defined as a smaller *hsiang*. The relative size of the *shih-lieh* is again indicated in LS 45, 24b where it is equated with a county (*hsien*), an administrative unit definitely larger than a *hsiang*.

---

[259] See XIII, introduction.
[260] XIV, 1 (23).
[261] Shiratori 13 TMK, 18.
[262] XV, 1 (3); and LS 31, 2b ff.
[263] LS 1, 1a.
[264] LS 116, 2a.
[265] The word is given as 卿 in our edition; this evidently is a misprint for *hsiang*. The glossary, LS 116, 2a, has *hsiang*.

The Chinese term *hsiang* may refer either to a single village or to a somewhat larger rural complex comprising a group of individual hamlets.[266] Such a designation seems out of place for any subdivision of a pastoral tribe, no matter what its size. But it must not be forgotten that pastoral groups, even if nomadic, do not move about aimlessly; their residence has been defined as "a mobile village."[267] Among the modern Qazaqs, the *aul* (their "mobile village") is a compact unit during the winter months when many households gather at the same well-sheltered and well-watered spot.[268] After the coming of spring the large winter encampments split up into smaller groups for convenient herding. Until recently "these smaller groups consisted of perhaps half a dozen *kibitkas* [households], usually belonging to one family, while half a mile or a mile away would be another such group of *kibitkas*, with numerous other similar clusters of habitations scattered over the whole area customarily occupied by the *urū* ['clan'] group."[269] An *aul* might include several hundred households—two or three hundred—and several thousand people.[270]

The modern pastoral institutions described by Hudson and other contemporary observers[271] should not be identified uncritically with those recorded for Inner Asia a thousand years ago. Yet Hudson's claim that "the practice of spending each winter in the same place is very ancient and general among all the Central Asiatic nomadic groups"[272] is borne out by the historical evidence. Rubruck in 1253–1255 found a definite order in the seasonal movements of the Mongol tribes of his time,[273] and similar rhythms have been noted for other nomadic peoples of Asia for an even earlier period.[274] In view of these facts, it seems reasonable to visualize the *shih-lieh* of the *Liao Shih* as large tribal subdivisions, the size and number of which may have been determined by the character of their winter encampments. The changing needs of pastoral life, which had their military as well as physical causes, inevitably affected the development of the tribes' subdivisions.

No developments of this kind are recorded by the *Liao Shih* except for the I-la tribe, and even here the data are few. During the lifetime of A-pao-chi's great-granduncle, Chih-shên, the I-la tribe had five

shih-lieh and six *chao* 爪.[275] In 922 these two designations were replaced by the single Chinese word, *yüan* 院,[276] which suggests great similarity, if not identity, between the older terms. That *chao* referred to some type of pastoral encampment may be inferred from the names of two Hsi tribes, Yao-chao and Nou-wan-chao, both of which had, at an earlier time, been "camps" (*ying* 營).[277] These camps may not have differed greatly from the *shih-lieh* from which other tribes developed.[278] *Chao* means "hundred";[279] originally the term may have indicated the number of families living in an encampment; but in its later usage it merely designated a tribal subdivision containing, perhaps, "hundreds" of families.

During the time of Chih-shên, a period of unusual prosperity, the five *shih-lieh* of the I-la tribe were reorganized into seven, and its six *chao* into eleven.[280] The decades just prior to 907 must have witnessed a further growth of the I-la tribe, but no corresponding reorganization is recorded. After the founding of the empire, a large but undefined number of Ch'i-tan tribesmen were assigned to the ordos which, in the course of the dynasty,[281] had control over twenty-three *shih-lieh* and ninety-eight *mei-li*.[282] Whether the reduction of tribal strength was balanced in part by the tribes' privileged position and growing prosperity is difficult to say.[283] One fact is known, whatever its value: the four imperial tribes now had only four *shih-lieh* each,[284] instead of the original five and six, or the later seven and eleven; each of the other old tribes of T'ai-tsu was credited with only two *shih-lieh* apiece.[285]

Regarding the subdivisions of the rest of the Ch'i-tan tribes, little information is available. In a few cases we hear that a tribe grew from a *shih-lieh* or *chao*,[286] and two Hsi tribes possessed three and six *shih-lieh* respectively,[287] but this information reveals little about the actual organizational changes. Even less meaning can be derived from the mere names of the Ti-lieh of the Eight Shih-lieh and the Nine Shih-lieh tribes or peoples.[288] Obviously the *shih-lieh* and the *chao* were important tribal subdivisions, smaller

[266] KHTT, sub 鄉.
[267] Hudson, quoting Levshin (Hudson 38, 24).
[268] *Op. cit.*, 24 and 30.
[269] *Op. cit.*, 24.
[270] *Op. cit.*, 24 ff.
[271] *Cf.* Lattimore 30, 242 ff.; *idem* 40, 73 ff.
[272] Hudson 38, 30.
[273] Rubruck 00, 53.
[274] *Op. cit.*, 53; *cf.* notes 1 and 2 by Rockhill. *Cf.* also II, introduction.

[275] LS 64, 2a.
[276] LS 33, 1b.
[277] I, 2 (5), nos. 2 and 3.
[278] *Op. cit.*, nos. 6 and 7.
[279] LS 116, 21b.
[280] LS 64, 2a.
[281] See XV, introduction.
[282] See XV, 1 (3).
[283] *Cf.* I, introduction.
[284] I, 2 (4), nos. 1 and 2.
[285] *Op. cit.*, nos. 3–9.
[286] See above, notes 277 and 278.
[287] I, 2 (5), nos. 8 and 9.
[288] I, 2 (9), nos. 24 and 32.

than a tribe but larger than a *mi-li* (*mo-li*). The term *chao*, "hundred," is a clue to the possible (minimum ?) size of these units; the recorded numbers of *shih-lieh*, however, do not reveal the principles—if there were any—which dictated the actual partition.

The officialdom of the *shih-lieh* and the *mi-li* was simple. The *shih-lieh* of the great tribes were ruled by a chieftain (*i-li-chin*) whose assistant originally bore the title *ta-la-kan*, a term evidently identical with the Uighur word *tarqan* or *tarxan*, a minister.[289] The later designations, *ma-p'u* 麻普 or *ma-pu* 馬步, are not explained in the glossary of the *Liao Shih*. Like the term *ling-wên* 令穩, they may be Chinese loan-words that were Altaicized. The Liao titles of the tribal *hsiang-wên* and *hsin-kun* probably also belong in this category.[290]

4. THE GOVERNMENT OF THE SOUTHERN REGION

a. ITS GROWTH

The incorporation of the first substantial Chinese settlement into the growing Ch'i-tan empire was the first step toward the creation of a separate Chinese or "southern" government. No concrete data describe the birth of this new administration, but, whatever its initial shape, in general it followed the T'ang model, inspired perhaps by the organization of the old Chinese city[291] and its political hinterland. Certain offices in the government of the Southern Region can actually be traced to T'ai-tsu's time, while others, although the sources do not expressly say so, were without doubt also set up in this early period.

T'ai-tsu established a special Chinese Bureau 漢兒司 which later developed into the Chinese Chancellery.[292] According to the *Liao Shih*, this Chancellery "originally had the functions of a Ministry of War."[293] Although explicit data are lacking, it is not unlikely that this statement refers to an early form of the office. The Political Council (later, the Secretarial Council) and the Presidential Council were also set up under T'ai-tsu.[294] It seems that at first the Presidential Council controlled, in the main, the civil affairs of the Southern Region.[295] This may have been so even before 947, while the Political Council[296] acted as a general steering committee.

The acquisition of sixteen prefectures from Chin

(晉) China in 937–938,[297] led to the establishment of a new political center, the Southern Capital,[298] and to the creation of numerous Chinese government offices. The *Ch'i-tan Kuo Chih* claims that the Chinese Chancellery was established in 938.[299] The question of the time of the change in name is unimportant when compared with the increasing political significance of the office about which there can be little doubt.

Between 938 and 947 many Chinese titles appear for the first time in the Liao records: the grand tutor and the grand guardian in 938,[300] the head officials of the Court Council in the Hui-t'ung reign period[301] (938–946), a special section of this Council in 938,[302] the Censorate in the same year[303] (a chief censor is known to have held office in 946),[304] the (Chinese) Department of the Master of Court Etiquette in 938,[305] and also the Guest Council. The latter bureau, however, was staffed with Yeh-lü, Hsiao, and even Uighurs[306]—probably because it was concerned with the reception of tribal visitors.

The development in nomenclature shows that the political reorganization of 947, basic though it was, did not create a completely new administrative set-up. It merely brought to a conspicuous climax a process of institutional development which, initiated by A-pao-chi, had led to the formation of a rather elaborate Chinese administrative system almost a decade before that year.

The reforms of 947 immediately followed the taking of the Chinese capital P'ien by the Liao armies. The northern ruler who seized the Chinese emperor and, for a time, controlled millions of new Chinese subjects felt with increasing intensity the weight and importance of the Chinese sector within his empire. Now the dynastic name, Liao came to the fore, either for the first time, or with renewed emphasis;[307] the official paraphernalia of the Chinese emperor were taken to the Supreme Capital;[308] and an elaborate calendar was introduced,[309] the symbol of Chinese imperial authority and statesmanship.[310] The division between the pastoral north and the agricultural

---

[289] See above, notes 94–103.

[290] See above, notes 132–136.

[291] *Cf.* WTS 72, 3a.

[292] XIV, 2 (5), LS 47, 2b–3b.

[293] *Loc. cit.*

[294] *Op. cit.*, LS 47, 3b–4b and 7a.

[295] XIV, 2, note 13.

[296] XIV, 2, note 8.

[297] X, 2 (19) and XVI, 938, LS 4, 2a ff.

[298] I, 1 (1).

[299] CTKC 16, 3b.

[300] LS 47, 2a.

[301] *Op. cit.*, 5a.

[302] *Op. cit.*, 6a.

[303] *Op. cit.*, 7b.

[304] *Op. cit.*, 8a.

[305] *Op. cit.*, 9b.

[306] *Op. cit.*, 11a.

[307] XVI, 947, LS 4, 15a; *cf.* Technical Introduction: Chinese Dynasties, Emperors, Reign Periods.

[308] VII, 2 (22).

[309] XIV, 4 (4).

[310] See below.

south, which had become increasingly conspicuous during the preceding decade, was formulated in definite political terms by coordinating the agricultural sections of the empire under the government of the Southern Region.

b. THE CENTER

The officialdom of the new "southern" government, as it developed after 947, is outlined in LS 47 and 48. The Supreme Capital was the seat of the central governments of both the Southern and the Northern Regions. "Southern" court officials are listed with the political staff of the "southern" central government,[311] just as "northern" court officials are included in the official list of the central government of the Northern Region.

Most of the "southern" court officials were Chinese, but some tribal dignitaries were included among them. Those who represented the Southern Region at court must have seen to it that correct Chinese behavior prevailed during imperial receptions and banquets. The officials of the harem of the Southern Region[312] probably supervised the emperor's domestic arrangements in the urban centers, but they were chiefly concerned with the imperial harem.

Far more important than the Chinese court administration was the political organization of the Southern Region which included the wealthiest territories of the empire and the greater part of its population. The *Liao Shih* stresses the T'ang background of the Chinese institutions of Liao, the central[313] as well as the regional[314] and local.[315] This emphasis seems justified, particularly for the formative period of the Liao empire. It is true, the Ch'i-tan in 938 acquired the sixteen prefectures and in 947 carried off the paraphernalia of imperial power from the Later Chin, but this short-lived dynasty had itself fed upon the cultural inheritance of the T'ang dynasty, which it modified only slightly. A number of recently discovered inscriptions reveal that T'ang elements penetrated the bureaucratic system of the northern state.[316] The new titles, which in some cases reappear in the nomenclature of the succeeding Chin (金) dynasty,[317] are not found in the official lists of the *Liao Shih*. According to this source, the bulk of the Liao empire's Chinese offices were established during the first half of the tenth century and followed, directly or indirectly, the T'ang pattern.

The T'ang emperor assembled about him two groups of elder statesmen, the "three teachers" and the "three dukes."[318] Besides the elder statesmen of the Northern Region, the grand *yü-yüeh*, the Liao ruler had at his disposal six elder statesmen of the Southern Region whose titles were identical with those of their T'ang predecessors. However, while enjoying considerable social prestige, the southern dignitaries exercised little political influence. A grand preceptor might suggest an emergency measure to aid the agricultural section of the country;[319] a grand commandant might instigate a rebellion,[320] but neither the "teachers" nor the "dukes" seem to have participated in making the empire's great political decisions.

The heads of the executive branch of the T'ang government, the Three Councils (三省), also appear in the "southern" hierarchy of the Liao empire. Under the T'ang dynasty the chief of the Presidential Council was the highest official of the central government;[321] by controlling the Six Ministries[322] he directed the country's executive activities. The Chinese Chancellery of Liao, probably established in 947 as an office of the Southern Region, was at first combined with the Presidential Council.[323] Although primarily charged with the military affairs of the sedentary population,[324] the Chancellery contained certain offices, whose functions apparently corresponded to those of five of the Six Ministries. Some of these offices were in charge of edicts of the Sections of Civil Appointments, and War and Punishments which were probably liaison offices between the Chancellery and the Ministries of Nominations, War, and Punishments. Furthermore, the Chancellery had another bureau which seems to have fulfilled a similar function in relation to the Ministry of Revenue, and a fifth department described as the Ministry of Works.[325] No such bureau existed in the Chancellery for the Ministry of Rites, an organization administered concurrently with the Secretarial Council.[326]

The *Liao Shih* places the Six Ministries immediately after the Presidential Council. It seems more than probable that, following the T'ang model, the Liao Ministries were originally supervised by the Presidential Council, and only later came under the direct jurisdiction of the new over-all office of the Southern Region, the Southern Chancellery.

---

[311] XIV, 2 (6), LS 48, 1a.
[312] LS 47, 10a ff.
[313] LS 47, 2a.
[314] LS 47, 2b.
[315] XIV, 2 (9), LS 48, 9b.
[316] CYTPW 6, 17a ff.; MCCSC 1, 41b–45b.
[317] See MCCSC 1, 41b ff.

[318] TS 46, 2b.
[319] XII (6).
[320] XIII (24).
[321] Cf. Franke, GCR II, 532 ff.
[322] TS 46, 1a ff.
[323] XIV, 2 (5), LS 47, 3a.
[324] Loc. cit.
[325] XIV, 2 (5), LS 47, 2b–3b.
[326] LS 47, 1b.

At the beginning of the Liao dynasty the Political Council was the key office in the Chinese civil administration. Han Yen-hui, T'ai-tsu's Chinese advisor, headed it.[327] The establishment of the Chinese Chancellery, together with the Presidential Council, apparently deprived the Political Council of many of its original functions, but their exact nature remains indefinite. In 1044 the Political Council became the Secretarial Council, and it is so listed in LS 47, 3b–4a.

The third council of Liao, the Court Council, fulfilled a great variety of court duties. The T'ang office of this name was mainly concerned with the preparation of imperial edicts and the supervision of court ceremonies.[328] The latter function cannot have been too significant at the Liao court which stuck tenaciously to its tribal ceremonies; the former, however, was as important as the complex administrative system of the Chinese regions.

The *Liao Shih* gives no clear picture of the activities of any of the three councils. In 986 a president of the Political Council suggested a lenient fiscal policy for Shan-hsi,[329] indicating some, though not too great political influence; in 1022 an official of this same council was honored by a special gift from the emperor.[330] In 975 a leading Buddhist dignitary was given the post of inner chamberlain, an office in the Court Council.[331] Ma Jên-wang, who as commissioner of finance of the Central Capital successfully reorganized the tax system, was honored by a high appointment in this Council,[332] again demonstrating the considerable prestige attached to its membership.

Continuing the T'ang tradition, the Southern Region included a special censorate.[333] This office played an important role in the purely Chinese dynasties, but in the conquest dynasty of Liao the government probably depended more directly on its military machine to keep itself informed about conditions in the Southern Region.

Descriptive details regarding the offices of the Six Ministries are few,[334] owing perhaps to the belief that their structure was too familiar to warrant lengthy discussion, or that their functions and personnel were too insignificant. The latter seems improbable, for the general list includes many titles of minor court officials and harem attendants. But the fact remains that LS 47, 7b, mentions only four of the Six Ministries, the Ministries of Civil Appointments, of War, of Works, and of Rites. The Ministries of Punishments and of Revenue are referred to in LS 47, 1b, the latter also in other passages.[335]

Under the heading "the palace gentlemen of such and such a ministry," LS 47, 7b speaks of the "palace gentlemen" of the *yü-pu* 虞部. Under the T'ang dynasty this office, which among other things regulated the hunt, was a division of the Ministry of Public Works. In the *T'ang Shu* it is listed just before the Department of Waterworks (水部[336]), a department which receives no mention in records covering the Liao Ministry of Works.

Many passages, such as LS 48, 2b, indicate that the regional sub-sections of the Ministry of Revenue were extremely active. Lack of corresponding information regarding the other ministries may reflect their relative unimportance.

The Han-lin Academy, the center of Chinese learning, was naturally a part of the government of the Southern Region.[337] Its officials, unlike the heads of the Ch'i-tan Department of the Grand Scribe, were dedicated essentially to scholarly pursuits. The fact that the Ch'i-tan had a non-Chinese script and a "northern" grand scribe did not cause them to underestimate the value of Chinese literacy. Although the national history of Liao in the main chronicled events in the lives of its Ch'i-tan rulers, and numerous Ch'i-tan acted as recorders, the Department of National Historiography belonged, not to the Northern (tribal) Region, but to the government of the Southern (Chinese) Region.[338]

Directly after the Department of National Historiography, LS 47 lists a number of institutions whose names indicate a general interest in matters of learning.[339] During the T'ang dynasty such institutions served as libraries and centers for literary study.[340]

The nine "halls" of the T'ang dynasty[341] were reduced to eight under the Liao,[342] the Government Treasury being designated as a "board" 監.[343] The T'ang Council (省) of Imperial Archives also became a board under the Liao.[344] The smelteries which had been supervised by a board in the T'ang period were now, however, controlled by the government of the Northern Region,[345] in all probability because the Ch'i-tan looked to them for their military equipment.

[327] *Op. cit.*, 4a.
[328] TS 47, 1a.
[329] XII (6).
[330] X, 1 (40).
[331] IX (8).
[332] X, 1 (66).
[333] XIV, 2 (5), LS 47, 7b–8a.
[334] *Op. cit.*, LS 47, 7b.

[335] VI, 1 (1) 1055–1101; XII (91); XIII (38) (48).
[336] TS 46, 13a.
[337] XIV, 2 (5), LS 47, 8b–9a.
[338] *Op. cit.*, LS 47, 9a.
[339] LS 47, 9a–b; cf. XIV, 2, note 16.
[340] TS 47, 5a.
[341] TS 48, 4a ff.
[342] XIV, 2 (5), LS 47, 12a–13a.
[343] *Op. cit.*, LS 47, 13a–14b.
[344] *Loc. cit.*
[345] XIV, 1 (26).

The separate administrations of the Government and the Imperial Treasuries continued the T'ang tradition. In the T'ang dynasty the former had been a "hall,"[346] the latter a "board."[347] During the Liao period each was considered a "board" in the government of the Southern Region which still sought to distinguish between the needs of the government and those of the imperial household. The Ministry of Works does not seem to have been concerned with water-control, but activities of this kind are recorded for the region along the Liao River and in Nan-ching.[348] Their supervision probably fell to the jurisdiction of the Board of Waterworks, which is mentioned in LS 47, 14b.

c. THE GOVERNMENT OF THE FIVE CAPITALS

Modelling themselves upon the administrative organization of the Po-hai,[349] the Ch'i-tan divided their empire into several large territories or "capitals." Eventually five such units were established, equalling the number of "capitals" that had existed in the Po-hai state. The Chinese names of the individual regions refer either to the capital city or to the territory or circuit of which it was the urban center. For the sake of clarity, English equivalents, such as Supreme Capital, Central Capital, etc., are used in the translations when reference is made to the city, and Chinese terms, such as Shang-ching, Chung-ching, etc., when the circuit is being discussed.[350]

Each metropolis had its own city government, administered by two sets of offices, the civil and the military. The Eastern, Central, and Southern Capitals were under the immediate direction of a left and right prime minister.[351] The vicegerent, who headed the individual circuit, usually also acted as mayor (府尹) of its capital.[352] This powerful official might be called upon to conduct a military campaign, like that against Korea in 993,[353] or to quell a rebellion.[354] He and his assistants supervised such important civil tasks as the taking of the census,[355] the mobilizing of the labor service,[356] the collecting of customs duties[357] and taxes,[358] and the implementing of relief

measures.[359] That the office represented a key position is evident from a study of certain local revolts: during the rebellion of 1029 the vicegerent of Tung-ching was seized,[360] and in the revolt of 1116 the first attack of the Po-hai rebels was directed against him.[361]

The economic offices of the five capitals or circuits are listed before the offices of the vicegerent and the metropolitan bureaucracy.[362] Such an arrangement possibly reflected not only the vital importance of their functions[363] but also the extended field of their activities. They had jurisdiction over varied economic aspects in each circuit, while the offices of the five mayors[364] supervised only the five capital cities and perhaps their immediate environs.

d. THE REGIONAL GOVERNMENT

Each of the five circuits controlled a number of prefectures, which, in turn, administered several counties. Certain irregularities, discussed in section I, occasionally complicated but did not destroy the general scheme.[365]

The prefectures were headed by officials whose title changed with the size and importance of their territory. The commanding prefect (節度使), who exercised enormous power during the later part of the T'ang dynasty,[366] administered the largest Liao prefectures. The supervisory prefect (觀察使), trainband prefect (團練使), defence prefect (防禦使), and prefect (刺使) controlled territories of lesser importance, not a few of them subordinate to the large prefectures and their chiefs, the commanding prefects.[367] The subdivision of the various prefectures into units of a superior, middle, and lower class[368] makes a total of fifteen categories. These subtle gradations within the bureaucratic pyramid were probably of greater interest to the ambitious officials of the Liao empire than they need be to the modern investigator.

The prefects are listed by LS 48, 10a ff. as commanders of regional armies; this indicates the significance of their military tasks.[369] But the prefectures had important civil functions as well: they received taxes[370] and made standard contributions to the

---

[346] TS 48, 13b.
[347] TS 48, 15b.
[348] XI (14) (22) (28).
[349] LS 37, 2a.
[350] Cf. I, introduction.
[351] XIV, 2 (6).
[352] XIV, 2 (8).
[353] XVI, 993, LS 13, 3b.
[354] XIII (31) and also (53).
[355] I, 3 (6).
[356] XI (21).
[357] V (4).
[358] X, 1 (15) (17).

[359] XII (4).
[360] XIII (38).
[361] XIII (48).
[362] XIV, 2 (7).
[363] See X, introduction.
[364] XIV, 2 (8).
[365] See I, introduction.
[366] Cf. Franke, GCR II, 539.
[367] XIV, 2 (9), LS 48, 9b–15b.
[368] LS 37, 2b ff.
[369] For a concrete example see XIII (46).
[370] X, 1 (6).

court.[371] In a number of territories the financial administration, though supervised by the prefects, was actually controlled by the Offices of Money and Silk. Such offices are also mentioned for several "routes" (路),[372] but no explanation clarifies the relation between the two centers of taxation. Special transportation offices are reported for one route, Shan-hsi, and for five of the prefectures[373]—four belonging to Hsi-ching and one to Tung-ching. Again there is no way of determining how these regional bureaus resembled the territorial transportation office of Nan-ching.

Entrusted commandery-prefectures were bestowed, in the main, on distinguished members of the imperial and consort lineages.[374] These territories were governed by a commanding prefect, who received his orders from the court. Eventually they "reverted to the royal administration,"[375] which obviously means to the administration of the central government.

e. THE LOCAL GOVERNMENT

Below the leading offices of the central government and the important territorial and regional administrations were many local administrative units called *hsien* 縣, "counties." They were governed by a magistrate and his assistant. These two, together with some other officials whose positions are qualified in LS 48[376] and various lower officials (吏)[377] mentioned occasionally in the text but not included in the official lists, formed the base of the empire's bureaucratic pyramid.

The magistrates and their subordinates were closer to the real life of the people than any of their metropolitan colleagues. Through the village heads they were in touch with the individual peasant, the backbone of the country's sedentary population. And it was the village heads who mobilized the peasants for labor service and who controlled the local granaries and the village "altars," the centers of rural activity. Through these smallest administrative units the will of the central government was made known to the remotest village. As long as the "altars" functioned, the administration of the agricultural regions of the Liao empire could continue to collect taxes, commandeer laborers, and mobilize militiamen. When the local cells "reached a state of bankruptcy,"[378] when they were "unable" (that is unwilling) to fulfill

the government demands, then the administrative order of Liao had reached a critical phase in its development. The only passage which reports such a crisis[379] significantly refers to the last years of the dynasty.

f. CONCLUDING REMARKS

The lists of officials translated in XIV, 1 and 2 represent only a part of the data contained in LS 45–48. The *History*, based in the main on routine government records, treats the bureaucratic hierarchy in much greater detail than, for instance, the country's general economy. To give a more rounded view, we have tried to include as much information as possible on the economic aspect, while limiting the space devoted to descriptions of the officialdom. Therefore, not all the names of offices and minor titles appearing in LS 45–48 have been translated. The omitted data might further embellish our picture, but they would probably add little to a better understanding of the organization of the Liao state. The translated texts and our analysis endeavor to reveal the basic structure of the Liao government, inconsistent and changing though it was.

We are fully aware of the limitations of our study, but it is hoped our readers will recognize that certain of these limitations are the consequence of unsatisfactory material. Any cursory survey of the lists contained in LS 45–48 shows that its authors, except in a few instances, failed to describe the functions attached to the various offices, that they failed to explain how the more important offices were integrated in the larger pattern or what their relationship was to the many lesser offices in the central government and outside it. An analysis such as ours should not be judged by a utopian standard of perfection, but by the results achieved in comparable studies, faced with comparable difficulties in the field of historical and institutional research.

The history of the Chinese Chancellery presents many of the difficulties just indicated. The *Liao Shih* leaves no doubt as to the existence of this office. Its staff is enumerated in considerable detail in LS 47, 2b–3b; and in a description of the emperor's escort on his seasonal tours representatives of the Chinese Chancellery are mentioned directly after the Ch'i-tan officials.[380] Both statements make it clear that the Chinese Chancellery was an independent office of the Southern Region, unrelated to the Ch'i-tan Southern Chancellery of the Northern Region, which managed "the selection of civil officials and the taxation of the tribes and lineages" and controlled "all the Ch'i-tan people."[381]

---

[371] X, 1 (15).

[372] XIV, 2 (10).

[373] *Loc. cit.*

[374] XIV, 2 (9), LS 48, 9b.

[375] *Loc. cit.*

[376] XIV, 2 (9), LS 48, 16a.

[377] VII, 1 (43).

[378] XI (26).

[379] *Loc. cit.*

[380] XIV, 2 (4).

[381] XIV, 1 (9), LS 45, 3a.

Such passages also indicate that there must have been not only two chancellors of the Northern Region, a northern and a southern one,[382] but also a Chinese chancellor of the Southern Region, at least during the formative period of Liao rule. The *Liao Shih* does not refer directly to any subsequent reorganization, but certain texts imply that a radical change did occur and that in some way the Chinese Chancellery of the Southern Region merged with the Southern Chancellery of the Northern Region.

Individual records frequently mention the Southern,[383] but not the Chinese Chancellery. Perhaps the most important textual evidence is the following: in 1043 the northern chancellor, Hsiao Hsiao-chung, based his reform plan on the fact that the Ch'i-tan and the Chinese were governed by the northern and southern chancellors respectively. The text makes no reference to the southern chancellor of the Northern Region, but speaks of the southern chancellor as the head of the Chinese administration. Of course, this may have been a mistake, but it does not seem plausible to assume such negligence in an important statement whose aim was the unification of the offices in question. The decisive sentence, which is given in direct speech, points specifically to the number of chancellors. Hsiao Hsiao-chung says: "The reason why the customs are different is that the same country has two chancellors."[384] The proposal to unite the two chancelleries was not accepted, but the original tripartite arrangement does not reappear. In 1123, when the Jurchen set up a special chancellery for their new Chinese subjects, they patterned it after the Southern Chancellery of Liao.[385] As explained above, the office of the Southern Chancellery was not infrequently held by a Chinese. In addition, from 1031 on there is regular reference to the position of vice-chancellor (樞密副使) which was always held by a Chinese; in many instances the positions of vice-chancellors of the Southern and Northern Divisions are mentioned for the same years as that of the vice-chancellor (1056–1058, 1071–1075, 1102).[386] It may be assumed therefore that the position designated only as vice-chancellor referred to the vice-chancellor of the Chinese Chancellery. This arrangement harmonizes well with the fusion of the position of Chinese chancellor of the Southern Region and the southern chancellor of the Northern Region. The continuance of the Chinese influence in the second highest position expresses clearly the importance of Chinese matters in the Chancellery's sphere of activity. It may also be noted that the position of vice-chancellor of the Southern Division was almost always held by a Chinese.

The Chinese Chancellery was originally concerned with military affairs, but later only one of its contact offices seems to have retained military significance. The civil tasks assigned to the Chinese Chancellery in all probability resembled those of the Southern Chancellery of the Northern Region which administered the tribes' civil affairs in general and their taxation in particular. Whether or not the desire to coordinate the country's financial organization led to the unification of the Chinese Chancellery and the Ch'i-tan Southern Chancellery cannot be definitely stated, but it is not beyond the range of possibility. That such a conjecture need be ventured at all clearly indicates how inadequate the information is on even one of the highest political offices. If descriptions at the bureaucratic top are so unsatisfactory, detailed and dynamic data can hardly be expected for less prominent offices and officials. This may explain to some degree why certain titles of Sung provenience, which are preserved in Liao inscriptions, never found their way into the hierarchic lists of the *Liao History*.

5. THE SELECTION OF OFFICIALS

a. HEREDITARY PREROGATIVE AMONG THE CH'I–TAN

Since the time of the Huns[387] and probably even earlier, the tribes of Inner Asia have had "hereditary officials." Hereditary officials are recorded for the Wu-lo-hou,[388] the Shih-wei,[389] and the Turks.[390] The *Liao Shih* indicates that the Ch'i-tan followed a pattern of succession more or less similar to that of other Inner Asiatic peoples, but radically different from that current in imperial China or mediaeval Europe.

The instances of hereditary succession in the pre-dynastic period are given in rather general terms. In the eighth century an ancestor of Hsiao T'a-lieh-ko is supposed to have received a high tribal office for himself and his descendants.[391] Another Hsiao was awarded a "hereditary" position as judge during the Yao-lien rule.[392] Within the tribal confederacy the post of khaghan remained for generations first in the line of the Ta-ho, then in that of the Yao-lien family.[393] Within the I-la tribe leadership seems to have been confined to a single lineage, the Yeh-lü. The position

---

[382] See, for instance, the very emphatic assertion in XIV, 1 (6).

[383] LTCNP 8048 ff.

[384] XIV, 2 (3).

[385] CS 55, 1b.

[386] LTCNP 8056 ff.

[387] SC 110, 9b; HS 94B, 7a.

[388] WS 100, 16b; PS 94, 23b.

[389] PS 94, 21b.

[390] Chou 50, 4b; Barthold 97, 16 ff.

[391] LS 85, 5b.

[392] LS 73, 4a.

[393] TS 219, 2a; LS 45, 20a.

of chieftain (*i-li-chin*) descended either in the direct or the collateral line.[394]   The relatively detailed data of the *Liao Shih* reveal that succession followed no rigid system of descent within the biological (or small) family.   Instead, members of an entire kin group held what may be called a permanent ("hereditary") claim on the office in question.

This principle of hereditary prerogative, while it may have been modified, was certainly not abandoned after the founding of the dynasty.   The desire to maintain political power within the noble Ch'i-tan lineages led the new rulers to assign specific offices to specific families: the "hereditary officials" (*shih kuan* 世官)[395] were appointed according to a rule of hereditary selection (*shih-hsüan* 世選).[396]

This prerogative could be established in a number of ways; sometimes it was granted to several related lineages; sometimes it was bestowed on the head of a small family.   Occasionally the claim might designate a particular post, but more frequently it referred to a class of office.

How valid were the claims established by the *shih-hsüan* system?   Since the answer to this question may be relevant to an understanding of the forms of Inner Asiatic political organization, it seems desirable to examine carefully a Liao office whose history is relatively well documented.   For this purpose, the Northern Prime Ministry of the Northern Region has been chosen.   The list of its head officials is not complete, but enough information is available to indicate the trend of succession.

The ministry was "hereditarily" reserved for members of the five distinguished lineages of the Hsiao clan.[397]   This regulation implied, first that the post was not open to non-Hsiao, and second that every member of the afore-mentioned lineages had an equal claim on the office.   Actually neither intent was rigidly enforced: one Yeh-lü clansman, Wu-li 兀里, is reported[398] to have held the northern post; a number of Chinese were admitted to the position of northern prime minister in a time of emergency (the Sung war)[399] and during the second half of the eleventh century.[400]

Still more significant, among the Hsiao clansmen accession to the office was on occasion restricted to members of a few selected families.

The privilege within the privilege was no matter of accident; it was granted to several powerful individuals obviously with the understanding that their descendants would be considered first whenever the important position had to be filled.   When Ti-lu, the first empress' elder brother,[401] became northern prime minister in 910, "his position was made hereditary."[402] A similar statement records the bestowal of the Northern Ministry on the empress' younger brother, A-ku-chih, in 919.[403]   Under Mu-tsung the special prerogative was granted to two of the emperor's most prominent supporters, Hsiao Hai-li[404] and Hsiao Hu-ssŭ.[405]   The formula was repeated once again in 969 when the staunch defender of Ching-tsung's cause, Hsiao Ssŭ-wên, was installed in the northern post.[406]

Does the wording of these five records merely re-emphasize the general principle that the ministry was "inheritable" by any member of the distinguished Hsiao lineages?   It is difficult to reconcile such an interpretation with the only discussion of the formula given in the *Liao Shih*.   Hu-ssŭ declined the ministerial office because he was not certain whether his descendants (literally "sons and grandsons") would be sufficiently qualified to fill it.   The argument implies that the prerogative was offered him for his direct descendants.   A similar inference may be drawn from the story of Hsiao T'a-lieh-ko's nomination in 1051:[407] in the eighth century, according to the *Liao Shih*, one of his ancestors was made northern prime minister "hereditarily."[408]   In one respect the statement seems somewhat inaccurate: there is no evidence of a "Northern" Prime Ministry in the tribal government of the Ch'i-tan.   However, the presence of a hereditary officialdom in predynastic times is amply recorded, and the genuineness of T'a-lieh-ko's

---

[394] See XIII, introduction.

[395] VII, 1 (1) and *passim*.

[396] *Cf*. LS 73, 4a, and *passim*.

[397] For the number and character of the distinguished Hsiao lineages see VII, 2, note 3.

[398] LS 85, 2a.   The uniqueness of the record does not necessarily imply its incorrectness.   Yet it seems legitimate to ask whether in this instance the authors of the *Liao Shih* did not confuse the Northern and Southern Prime Ministries as they did in their list of the officials of the Northern Region (LS 45, 4b).

[399] Shih Fang in 975 (LS 79, 1a ff.); Han Tê-jang in 994 (LS 82, 2a).

[400] See LTCNP 8060 ff.

[401] According to LS 73, 4a the empress was older than Ti-lu (其女兄), but according to the *pên chi* (LS 1, 3b) he was her senior (后兄).

[402] 世其官 (LS 73, 4b; *cf*. also LS 1, 3b).

[403] 世其職 (LS 73, 5a; *cf*. also LS 1, 10b).

[404] 世爲北府宰相 (LS 6, 3b).   The formula, although unmistakable, is not as complete as those quoted below. The term *shih* 世, "hereditary," is present, but not its complement *hsüan* 選, "selected."   The second word is used in Hai-li's biography, but there the term *shih* is lacking; 命預北府宰相選 "It was ordered that there be bestowed upon him the prerogative of the selection for the post of northern prime minister" (LS 78, 1b).

[405] 命世預宰相選 (XIV, 3 (3)).

[406] 命世預其選 (LS 78, 3a).

[407] LS 20, 5b.

[408] 世預其選 (LS 85, 5b).

claim is not questioned by those who nominated him; in fact, they based their decision on this very point.[409]

A survey of the northern prime ministers mentioned in the *Liao Shih* shows that the restricted hereditary claims, once awarded, were seriously considered. Immaturity of a son might make immediate succession impossible; expediency or political emergency might make it undesirable, but over a period of time perceptible efforts were made to satisfy the pledge given to a meritorious forefather.

Ti-lu was the first to receive the hereditary prerogative, but at the time of his death in 919 his two sons were not yet fitted to fill their country's highest office: Kan was still a child,[410] his brother, Han, a youthful officer who only won his first laurels several years later, in 922.[411] Ti-lu's younger brother, A-ku-chih, who succeeded him, was also granted the hereditary privilege, but his son did not become prime minister either; instead he was made *hsiang-wên* in the P'i-shih Army.[412]

After a short notice recording the appointment of a certain Hsiao Hsia-ti as northern prime minister[413] little is heard of the incumbents of this office until the turbulent times of Shih-tsung and Mu-tsung. The position was then successively offered to a number of "outsiders," T'a-la-ko, a tribesman of unknown provenience who was made an honorific member of the Hsiao clan under Shih-tsung,[414] Hsiao Hai-li, whose father held a minor tribal office,[415] and Hsiao Hu-ssŭ, another "honorific" Hsiao, who accepted the Prime Ministry neither for himself nor for his descendants, but requested a hereditary claim to a lower office[416]— perhaps because he considered his children unequal to the task of competing with the more prominent members of the Hsiao nobility.

After Hai-li's death a first attempt was made to honor one of the promises given in T'ai-tsu's time. Ti-lu's son, Kan (the elder brother Han had been killed as a rebel in 949),[417] was finally appointed northern prime minister, but the record notes that later he became commanding prefect of the T'u-lü-pu tribe.[418] The principle of special (family) prerogative found increasing recognition[419] with Ching-tsung's

accession to the throne. In 969 Hsiao Ssŭ-wên was granted the hereditary claim to the Northern Prime Ministry by his son-in-law, Ching-tsung, and in this case fulfillment followed soon upon the promise: in 986 Ssŭ-wên's adopted son, Chi-hsien, was assigned to the northern office where he remained until his death in 1010. For a short interlude, 1001–1005, he actually became prime minister; during the other years he was assistant to Shih Fang, Han Tê-jang, and Hsiao P'ai-ya who held the supreme office.[420] Manifestly his fellow-clansmen, as well as the two Chinese dignitaries, were better qualified to fill the post than Hsiao Chi-hsien who, although a protegé of the court, achieved little personal distinction. This being so, the government's persistent efforts to keep him attached to his "hereditary" office are all the more noteworthy.

Hsiao P'ai-ya's incumbency returned the office to the Junior Patriarchal Tent,[421] Hsiao A-ku-chih's direct line according to LS 65.[422] From then on until late in the eleventh century the Northern Prime Ministry was occupied, with but few interruptions, by members of the Junior Patriarchal line. Five brothers of Empress Ch'in-ai were all northern prime ministers, Hsiao-mu 孝穆,[423] Hsiao-chung 孝忠,[424] Hsiao-hsien 孝先,[425] Hui 惠,[426] and Hsiao-yu 孝友.[427] Even in the succeeding generations the line continued to fill the northern office: two sons of Hsiao-mu, Sa-pa 撒八[428] and A-la 阿剌,[429] and A-la's son, Yü-li-yeh 余里也,[430] were northern prime ministers, as were Hsiao-chung's son, A-su 阿速,[431] and a son[432] of Hsiao-mu's brother, Kao-chiu 高九.[433] From 1005 to 1077 the Junior Patriarchal Tent provided eleven northern prime ministers, while all other Hsiao lines together furnished only eight.[434]

Information on the last decades of the dynasty is less detailed, but it seems that during this final period

---

[409] "He was made northern prime minister because of the hereditary prerogative" (*loc. cit.*).

[410] He died in 986 (LS 84, 2b).

[411] LS 113, 1a.

[412] LS 73, 5a.

[413] LS 2, 3a; *cf.* LTCNP 8046.

[414] LS 90, 4a.

[415] LS 78, 1b.

[416] XIV, 3 (3).

[417] XIII (22); *cf.* also LS 113, 1b.

[418] LS 84, 2b.

[419] LTCNP 8049 dates Kan's tenure of office from 967–969, which would be between Hai-li's death (LS 7, 3b) and

Ching-tsung's accession to the throne and Hsiao Ssŭ-wên's nomination (LS 8, 1b).

[420] LS 78, 3a–b; LTCNP 8052 ff.

[421] LS 88, 2b–3a.

[422] LS 67, 2b.

[423] LS 87, 1a.

[424] LS 81, 2b.

[425] LS 18, 2a; *cf.* also LS 87, 3a–b.

[426] LS 93, 2a.

[427] LS 19, 8a; *cf.* LS 87, 4a.

[428] LS 18, 8b; *cf.* LS 87, 2b ff.

[429] LS 90, 1a.

[430] LS 111, 1b.

[431] LS 21, 6a.

[432] Chu-chih 朮哲 (LS 91, 3a).

[433] The authors of the tables of the Hsiao clan state in LS 67, 5a that they do not know where to place Kao-chiu genealogically. According to LS 91, 2b Kao-chiu was Hsiao Hsiao-mu's younger brother.

[434] See LTCNP 8052 ff.

many Hsiao "outsiders" succeeded in obtaining the office. Still more significant is the increasing number of Chinese.[435]

The events taken as a whole assert the hereditary right of the distinguished Hsiao lineages to the Northern Prime Ministry. At times circumstances necessitated the thrusting aside of all inherited claims and the appointment of a complete outsider—a Chinese—to the post. More often, and at least as significantly, the general principle was restricted, the prerogative being limited to certain outstanding Hsiao nobles and their direct descendants.

Even then the principle was handled flexibly. While one or more descendants of an illustrious prime minister might occupy the post that he had worthily filled, the promise of privilege might at times be completely disregarded. For instance, Hai-li, although a member of the Hsiao clan, was in all probability something of a social outsider; no other prime minister can be traced to his family line. The strength of the restricted prerogative seems, therefore, to have depended on a number of factors—status, personality, the favor of the court, or the exigencies of the moment.

The Southern Prime Ministry of the Northern Region was "hereditarily" assigned to the Yeh-lü clan, more particularly to its distinguished lineages.[436] The prerogative is definitely stated, but its actual operation is none too clear. No individual, as in the Northern Ministry, seems to have been awarded the restricted privilege, and many "outsiders," Hsiao as well as Chinese, filled the important office.

In referring to offices held by "hereditary families," the Liao Shih conspicuously couples the two Prime Ministries with the post of commanding prefect.[437] LS 85, 3a relates that the last office was given "hereditarily" to a meritorious official, Yeh-lü Hsieh-li. Another record, though less complete, seems to have the same meaning.[438]

As discussed above, the office of commanding prefect is mentioned for at least four types of political unit: two tribal (the Ch'i-tan and the subordinate border tribes) and two sedentary (the prefectures of the five circuits and the fief-like entrusted command-ery-prefectures). In all four the office was significant, either because it served as a direct agent of the central government, or because it controlled regional key positions. The vagueness of the material makes it difficult to say how the hereditary prerogative functioned in the various types of prefecture, or even whether it operated in all of them. Within the Ch'i-tan tribes it was easy enough to give a particular family a specific office. In other instances the hereditary claim may have pertained to the post of commanding prefect in general, the immediate situation determining the form of the eventual assignment. The prefectures of the five circuits belonged to the government of the Southern Region. Frequently they were headed by Chinese officials,[439] whose appointments certainly did not depend on any shih-hsüan system. But these "southern" positions were also given to many Ch'i-tan nobles, sometimes with the emphasis placed on the civil,[440] but more often on the military function.[441] Whether the Ch'i-tan commanding prefects of "southern" territories obtained their offices because of a hereditary claim cannot be decided on the basis of the Liao Shih.

The history is equally laconic regarding other "hereditary" offices held by Ch'i-tan nobles. Both the hereditary grand physician[442] and the hereditary commissioner of the Guest Council[443] were evidently attached to the court; the hereditary member of the staff of the Punitive Office[444] probably belonged to a territorial military organization in the northwest of the empire. Certain tribal positions that had existed in predynastic times continued to be filled according to the shih-hsüan system; some seem to have been more or less identical with the early offices, while others were somewhat modified. During the time of the Yao-lien khaghanate the office of i-li-chin was "hereditarily" held by A-pao-chi's father.[445] In the dynastic period Ko-lu was given the post of "hereditary" i-li-chin of a subtribe (shih-lieh).[446] Yeh-lü Chieh-li was appointed his tribe's ling-wen,[447] a term used temporarily for i-li-chin.[448] "This post was made hereditary."[449] Other tribal offices, less clearly de-

---

[435] Op. cit. 8063 ff.

[436] XIV, 1 (9), LS 45, 4b. The four distinguished Yeh-lü tents are described as having been attached to the Northern Ministry. Actually they had the hereditary claim to the Southern Region (see XIV, 1 (5) and passim).

[437] VII, 1 (21) and XIV, 4 (13).

[438] According to LS 23, 6a Yeh-lü Ch'a-la 查剌 (we follow the Palace edition in reading 剌 instead of 次) was given the prerogative of selection to the post of commanding prefect of the T'u-lü-pu tribe. Chao I interprets this as referring to the hereditary prerogative (NESCC 27, 10b). For a similar abbreviation of the same general formula see above, note 409 (cf. LS 6, 3b and 78, 1b).

[439] LS 74, 3b and 5a; 83, 3a; 86, 2b (several instances); 97, 4a; 98, 2b; 105, 3a.

[440] LS 10, 3b; 17, 5b; 18, 8b.

[441] LS 4, 15a; 10, 3a and 8b; 12, 2b; 15, 9b; 16, 1a, 7a, 9a, 9b; 17, 1b, 2a, 8a, 8b; 21, 6b; 22, 7a; 23, 3b and 6b; 24, 2b, 4b, 7a, and passim.

[442] XIV, 3 (7); cf. XIV, 1 (26).

[443] XIV, 3 (3); cf. XIV, 2 (5), LS 47, 11a–b.

[444] LS 101, 2a.

[445] LS 2, 8b.

[446] LS 6, 1b.

[447] LS 76, 1b.

[448] LS 33, 2b.

[449] 世其職 (LS 76, 1b).

fined (one is merely referred to as "small")[450] might also be "hereditary."[451] Certainly many positions were filled by elders of individual tribes whose claim to hold office hereditarily was confirmed by the decree of 1047.[452]

Numerous passages note appointments to the post of *t'i-yin, i-li-pi,* or *hsiang-wên* without reference to inherited right. Lack of evidence does not necessarily imply the actual absence of all hereditary prerogatives to such offices; it is possible that the early historiographers did not consider it necessary to repeat a formula that, at least to them, was self-evident.

The all-important post of the northern chancellor of the Northern Region was held by members of the two ruling clans. Both Chao I and Ch'én Shu include this office and its southern counterpart in their lists of the hereditary Liao offices.[453] Their references to Yeh-lü I-hsin, who according to the *Liao Shih* had the Northern and the Southern Chancellery hereditarily granted to himself and his brother,[454] are not convincing. Yeh-lü I-hsin was a "wicked official,"[455] a usurper, who contrary to tradition had seized extraordinary power, even engineering the death of the heir apparent. But the general pattern—which I-hsin tried to constrict—suggested indeed the existence of a hereditary claim shared by the empire's most powerful clans.

For the office of *yü-yüeh* individual considerations seem to have prevailed. How frequently in predynastic times this method superseded the assertion of hereditary prerogative it is difficult to say. But this much is certain: the tribal system of "hereditary officials," as revealed in the Ch'i-tan institutions, did not assign a position to a specific heir. Like the general pattern of nomadic pastoral life and like its kinship organization, the selection of political functionaries according to the principle of hereditary prerogative was extremely flexible, permitting considerable scope for the evaluation of personal differences and qualifications within a general frame of stratification and privilege.

b. THE SELECTION OF CHINESE OFFICIALS (BY EXAMINATION)

The largest and most important group among the empire's non-tribal officeholders were the Chinese. Chinese played a prominent role in the government of the Southern Region: they even held a number of high positions in the "northern" government. The

selection of these functionaries was not determined by any Ch'i-tan system of hereditary prerogative: like many other "southern" institutions it followed a pattern set by the last great Chinese dynasty, T'ang. According to the *Chin History* the Liao government "chose its men by means of the *chin-shih* system of T'ang."[456]

The *chin-shih* degree was part of the general examination system inaugurated under the Sui dynasty[457] and elaborated in the time of T'ang. A candidate who passed a particularly difficult examination[458] was designated *chin-shih* 進士, "accomplished scholar";[459] if he also fulfilled the relatively simple requirements of a civil service test,[460] he could obtain a position in the ninth (or lowest) rank,[461] and thus enter the realm of officialdom. Another degree, that of *hsiu-ts'ai* 秀才, entitled the holder to apply for an office of the eighth rank,[462] but by the middle of the T'ang dynasty this degree had already lost its significance;[463] in the ninth century the examination for *chin-shih* was far and away the most important.[464] Top-government positions were open to candidates who had passed this metropolitan test,[465] while those who only succeeded in the regional examinations generally had to be content with a restricted official career.[466]

Under Liao rule the acquisition of the sixteen Chinese prefectures in 938 seems to have inspired the establishment of examinations modelled after the T'ang pattern. The first Chinese recorded as having taken the traditional examination in the newly acquired territory was Shih Fang 室昉, who is said to have received the degree of *chin-shih* in the later part of T'ai-tsung's rule, sometime between 938 and 947.[467] No further details are given, but, to judge from the *Liao Shih*, no significant developments in the general

---

[450] LS 76, 1a.

[451] XIV, 3 (3).

[452] XIV, 3 (12).

[453] NESCC 27, 10a; Ch'ên S 39, 182.

[454] XIV, 3 (23).

[455] Yeh-lü I-hsin is classed as 姦臣 (LS 110, 1a).

[456] CS 51, 1b.

[457] TT 14, 81; TS 44, 5b.

[458] TS 44, 2b.

[459] "Lettré accompli" (Des Rotours 32, 27).

[460] TS 45, 1a.

[461] TS 45, 2a. Offices of the same rank were open to those who had passed the legal examination, the *ming fa* 明法 (loc. cit.).

[462] Loc. cit.

[463] See Des Rotours 32, 28 and 40 ff.

[464] Cf. TS 44, 5a.

[465] TCY 1, 4b; cf. also TKSP 3, 9b.

[466] According to T'ang tradition, it was not considered appropriate for an official to rise to the top of the hierarchical pyramid without a *chin-shih* degree (TCY 1, 5a). This statement is somewhat vague, for, as it stands, it may refer also to persons who held office by virtue of the *yin* prerogative or through special appointment. But, whatever its intent, it probably also included individuals who did not obtain the metropolitan degree, though they may have passed the regional examination.

[467] LS 79, 1a.

system took place until 977 when the Ministry of Rites restored the old (T'ang ?) examination hall in the Southern Capital.[468] This constructional step seems to have prepared for rather than inaugurated the holding of regular examinations. The first imperially decreed *chin-shih* examination reported by the *Liao History* was given eleven years later, in 988.[469] From this year on, the official tests were held more or less regularly until the end of the dynasty.

Following the T'ang pattern, three different examinations were offered: one in the candidate's immediate locality (*hsiang* 鄉), one in the next larger regional administration (*fu* 府), and the highest in the capital. The last was called *shêng* 省 because it was held under the auspices of the Ministry of Rites, a subdivision of the Secretarial "Council" (*shêng*). The persons who succeeded in the local examinations were called *hsiang-chien* 鄉薦, in the regional examinations, *fu-chieh* 府解, and in the metropolitan or final examinations, *chi-ti* 及第.[470]

Interestingly, the *Ch'i-tan Kuo Chih*, and not the *Liao Shih*, contains the fullest information on the examination system. But valuable as this information is, its complete trustworthiness must be questioned. According to CTKC 23, 5a, the candidates were originally examined in poetry and the classics, and from Shêng-tsung's time on—that is, during the period when the examination system was fully developed—the required subjects were poetry and law, the former remaining the major topic. This statement is at variance with a Chin 金 description which claims that the subjects demanded in the Chin dynasty were, as they had been in the Liao dynasty, the classics, their commentaries, the philosophies of the different schools, and history.[471]

It is impossible to decide in this case which source has the greater validity, but it may be said that the Southern author of the *Ch'i-tan Kuo Chih* was, in all probability, neither as well informed as his Chin colleague nor as eager to admit that the Liao empire had so elaborate an examination system. The *Liao Shih*, while recording the creation of a hierarchy of colleges in 1059, mentions as their aim the dissemination of the classics and their commentaries.[472] The state colleges would surely not have emphasized these two topics, if, after Shêng-tsung's time, they were without importance in the examinations.

Even more to be questioned is the *Ch'i-tan Kuo Chih's* claim that the Liao examinations were held every three years. The giving of the *chin-shih* exami-

nations triennially was introduced by the Sung government in 1066, after many years of irregularity and the temporary establishment of a two year interval in 1057.[473] No known edict proclaimed such a fixed pattern in the Liao empire. The Imperial Annals (*pên chi*) of the *Liao Shih* contain more than fifty individual entries concerning the holding of the metropolitan examinations. These fifty-odd statements, despite a few deficiencies, provide an unusually comprehensive picture of the development of the institution. Similar to, and no doubt in imitation of, T'ang and early Sung policy, the Liao government in 988 began to hold the *chin-shih* examinations more or less regularly every year. After the year 1000 this interval was gradually—and irregularly—lengthened to two, three, or four years, at times even to five.[474]

How many ranking *chin-shih* were provided by these examinations? During the first decade after 988 an average of two or three successful candidates is recorded. In the first quarter of the eleventh century the number increases gradually, reaching a first peak of twenty-three in 1006[475] (the year after the conclusion of the peace treaty with Sung) and rising still higher after 1013 to thirty-one (in 1014), forty-eight (in 1016), thirty-seven (in 1019), forty-five (in 1021), and forty-seven (in 1022 and 1024).[476] In the second quarter the figures oscillate between twenty-two and seventy-two, attaining this maximum once in 1025. After 1055 they frequently pass the hundred mark, the all-time high being one hundred and thirty-eight in 1070.[477] Dividing the total number of ranking *chin-shih* according to periods by the number of years over which the degrees were obtained, the annual average of persons thus distinguished would be as follows:

2 persons per year from 988 to 999
13 persons per year from 1000 to 1024
20 persons per year from 1025 to 1049
25 persons per year from 1050 to 1073
20 persons per year from 1074 to 1099[478]
27 persons per year from 1100 to 1120.[479]

The men who were fortunate enough to pass the metropolitan examinations were eligible for official

---

[468] XIV, 3 (5).

[469] XIV, 3 (6).

[470] CTKC 23, 5a.

[471] YTCH 5, 6a.

[472] XIV, 3 (16).

[473] SS 12, 13a; 13, 7a.

[474] A full list of all chronological records contained in the *Liao Shih* is given in XIV, 3, note 4.

[475] LS 14, 7b.

[476] LS 15, 8a, 10b; 16, 2b, 5b, 7b.

[477] LS 17, 1b; 22, 6b.

[478] For the two years, 1050 and 1076, the holding of the *chin-shih* examination is recorded, but the number of successful candidates is not noted (LS 20, 4b; 23, 2b). In both cases, we have substituted figures computed from the period's known averages.

[479] The last examination is recorded for 1118, but according to the existing pattern the next examination was due only two or three years later.

position. But eligibility implied no legal claim. The government was expected to give serious consideration to the successful *chin-shih* candidates, but it was under no obligation to place them in office. The coefficient of appointment for holders of the *chin-shih* degree varied with the socio-historical circumstances. A Chin survey of the pre-Chin regulations claims that the Liao government employed only two or three out of every ten persons who had passed the final tests.[480]

If the Chin statement is accepted as more or less correct—it was made for comparative purposes and without any obvious polemical intent—then only from three to seven ranking *chin-shih* were annually taken into the imperial administration during the eleventh century, some few more after the year 1100, and considerably less before the year 1000. If the Chin statement is somewhat exaggerated and if, let us say, thirty-five or forty per cent instead of twenty-five per cent of the successful candidates were employed—the revised averages of four to eight, and eventually ten, persons are still unimpressive. When viewed in relation to the large number of government positions occupied by Chinese nationals within the many regional administrations, in the metropolitan centers, and in the central government of the Southern Region,[481] the figures seem surprisingly small.

They were small indeed. A survey of the biographies of Chinese officials given in the *Liao Shih* reveals that only a fraction of the officials mentioned held the *chin-shih* degree. Our data include some short notes (1–3 lines), some biographies of medium length (4–7 lines), and a number of rather long life histories (8 lines to several pages). Twenty-two long biographies omit all mention of a *chin-shih* degree,[482] whereas five medium-length histories[483] and even a few short notes do not fail to record their protagonists' scholarly success.[484] To be sure, the length of a note is no absolute criterion for possible omissions; but it is reasonable to assume that the short notes were more apt to ignore the examination, and that possibly more officials held the degree than these notes reveal. In the longer biographies reference to the degree may on occasion have been omitted because of lack of information or because of editorial error, but willful exclusion seems improbable in view of the high prestige which the title attained in the scholarly bureaucratic world. Thus, among the Chinese officials of the Liao

dynasty there were perhaps more holders of the *chin-shih* degree than the *Liao Shih* indicates; when omissions occurred, they were probably due in the main to the brevity of the individual record, not to a lack of esteem for the title. The absence of any reference to the degree in many long and medium-length biographies, however, suggests that within the Liao empire a considerable number of Chinese officials obtained office by means other than the *chin-shih* examination.

If this assumption is correct then the questions must be asked: by what other means could a Chinese enter the empire's bureaucratic hierarchy?

c. THE SELECTION OF CHINESE OFFICIALS (THROUGH THE *YIN* SYSTEM)

Was "purchase of office" (as it has been called incorrectly) or recommendation or simplified examination the easy way to join the bureaucratic hierarchy? Such procedures which time and again occur in Chinese history appear also under the Liao dynasty: purchase of the right to apply for an office was permitted by law in 1088;[485] and persons of literary attainment might be employed either on the basis of official recommendation[486] or after having passed a simple examination,[487] according to decrees announced in the second half of the eleventh century.

But these methods, which were given legal sanction in the later years of the Liao dynasty, do not explain the great number of Chinese officials who occupied important positions in the tenth as well as in the first half of the eleventh century, apparently without holding a *chin-shih* degree. In some families, few if any members in high positions are credited with having passed the metropolitan (*chin-shih*) or even a regional examination.[488]

Did some kind of hereditary prerogative, comparable to the tribal *shih-hsüan* principle, enable a Chinese in the Liao empire to enter upon an official career without fulfilling the examination requirements? Many writers in discussing imperial China have considered the elaborate examination system, which impressed Western visitors in the seventeenth, eighteenth, and nineteenth centuries, a permanent feature of its political organization. For the early period of the empire's history such a theory is patently

---

[480] CS 51, 1*b*.

[481] See I, introduction, note 16 and XIV, 2, *passim*.

[482] LS 74, 1*b*, 2*a*, 4*a*; 75, 4*a*; 76, 2*b*, 5*b*, 6*b*; 79, 3*b*; 80, 2*a*, 2*b*; 81, 1*b*, 3*a*; 82, 1*a*, 2*b*, 3*a*; 83, 3*b*; 85, 4*a*; 86, 1*b*; 102, 2*a*, 3*a*; 103, 6*a*; 105, 3*a*.

[483] LS 88, 6*b*; 97, 2*b*, 3*a*, 4*b*; 105, 5*b*.

[484] Liu San-chia and Liu Ssŭ-tuan (both LS 86, 2*b*).

[485] XIV, 3 (27).

[486] XIV, 3 (15).

[487] XIV, 3 (20) (21).

[488] No member of Han Tê-jang's family who held office in Liao time is reported to have obtained the *chin-shih* degree (LS 74, 4*a* ff. and 82, 1*a* ff.). A descendant in the ninth generation of Tê-jang's grandfather passed the metropolitan examination at the close of the Liao dynasty, but he achieved a leading position only under the subsequent Chin government (CS 78, 8*a*; see below, note 546).

incorrect; for the later period it needs serious qualification.

Under the Han dynasty (207 B.C.–A.D. 220) a person could, as a rule, enter the government career only if he was recommended by a leading central or regional official or if he was sponsored by his father who himself held an official post. The second method was called *jên-tzǔ* 任子, "to sponsor a son." Certain recommended candidates were made to answer written questions, but there existed no institutionalized opportunity to apply for an examination and thus for an office.[489] During the four centuries of political disruption that followed, the nine ranks (*p'in* 品) of officialdom were set up and elaborated.[490] Positions in these ranks were to a large extent occupied by members of the upper groups (*shang p'in* 上品), the "hereditary families" (*shih chia* 世家).[491] The *jên-tzǔ* system was modified and restricted, but not abandoned.[492] During this era of disunion and open conflict the states preferred a stable bureaucracy to a more liberally recruited officialdom which might be more efficient, but perhaps less reliable.

The reunified China of the Sui and T'ang dynasties presented new administrative problems which could not be satisfactorily solved by a hereditary officialdom. Additional intellectual resources were opened up by the creation of an elaborate examination system which, in spite of many interruptions and changes, continued to flourish until the end of the Manchu dynasty.

However, those who installed the new examination system did not find it incompatible with the old concept of a self-perpetuating bureaucracy; they pointedly adopted a number of measures that limited the effectiveness of the new and more flexible method of official selection. T'ang regulations dealing with application for office threatened to punish "the sons of families with a criminal record, artisans and merchants, [who belong to] groups other than [the literati and peasants],"[493] and those with false

documents,—obviously if they sought government posts.[494]

In classifying the artisans and merchants as undesirable outsiders, the T'ang government followed its Sui predecessor which specifically prohibited these groups from holding office.[495] Whether the T'ang laws actually closed the examinations to artisans and merchants is not clear. The Sung government seems to have permitted them to participate, but it did so with reservations: the "artisans, merchants [being] outside groups"[496] and former Buddhist and Taoist monks were warned not to falsify their family or personal status in their examination documents.[497] Marked as social outsiders, the artisans and merchants were obviously suspect, and, in all probability, were discriminated against.

The restriction governing outsiders was only one way of interfering with the democratic functioning of the examination system. Protective measures were also taken to strengthen and maintain the power of the bureaucratic in-group. The Sui and T'ang dynasties which established and elaborated the world's greatest system of competitive examinations were careful to insure access to office to the direct descendants of the acting bureaucracy without examination. This solicitude, and the privilege that resulted from it, technically resembled the Han institution of "sponsoring sons," *jên-tzǔ*. But in its new social context—the examination system—the old institution assumed a new significance, and not surprisingly, a new name, *yin*. *Yin* 蔭 or 廕 means "shade, shelter, to protect." The son of an official who entered the civil service through the *yin* (以廕) prerogative was indeed, thanks to his father's position, "protected" against the hardships and pitfalls of the regular examinations. The earlier phrase, *jên-tzǔ*, did not completely disappear, but the new term *yin*, which had been used on occasion under the Northern Chou dynasty,[498] the last pre-Sui dynasty, acquired increasing importance when, under the Sui[499] and particularly under the T'ang dynasties, the prerogative was systematically elaborated.

---

[489] For cases of selection through official recommendation see HS 56, 1a ff.; 58, 1a ff.; 64A, 1a; 75, 6b; 77, 7a; 86, 17b; 88, 8a. For the "sponsoring of sons" see HS 11, 3b; 74, 8a and *passim*. A fuller treatment of the institutional development involved will be given in HCS, Ch'in and Han, XIV.

[490] At the beginning of the Three Kingdoms, the nine ranks were established according to the suggestion of Ch'ên Ch'ün 陳羣 of the state of Wei 魏 in A.D. 220 (SKC, Wei 22, 5a; *cf.* also TT 14, 77).

[491] WHTK 34, 324.

[492] See Chin 2, 6b; 7, 3b; WS 6, 3a; Chou 6, 13a.

[493] 刑家之子工賈異類 (TS 45, 1a). Des Rotours (32, 215) translates the term *i-lei* 異類 as "[autres personnes] étrangères à la classe des lettrés" (Des Rotours' brackets). This interpretation, which treats the *i-lei* as a coordinated

noun, would indicate a still stronger social bias. Our translation, suggested by Mr. Ch'ü T'ung-tsu, places the difficult term in apposition.

[494] This is Des Rotours' (32, 215) opinion, which is supported by the context.

[495] 工商不得入仕 (TT 14, 81).

[496] 工商異類 (SS 155, 3a). Semantically, the formula is like the one used in TS 45, 1a, except that the term *ku* 賈 is replaced by *shang* 商, a word which also means "merchant," perhaps a man engaged in more extensive business than the *ku*.

[497] SS 155, 3a.

[498] Chou 6, 13a.

[499] According to the *Sui Shu* (3, 12b), the Sui government in 607 decreed that the officials of the former dynasties,

According to regulations in force before 650[500] and confirmed in 717,[501] the sons of officials in the first three ranks (p'in) might apply for positions in the seventh rank; those whose fathers held offices in the fourth or fifth ranks could apply for positions in the eighth rank. But the holder of a chin-shih degree could only ask for a position in the ninth rank, second class, upper grade, if he had attained top honors, or, if he had achieved minor distinction, for a post in the ninth rank, second class, lower grade.[502] Thus the son of a high official, without submitting to any difficult examination, had considerable advantage at the start of his official career over the well-equipped but not "protected" holder of a chin-shih degree.

The establishment of the exact percentage of T'ang officials who are known to have entered upon a bureaucratic career on the basis of the yin prerogative must be left to a comprehensive analysis of T'ang society. However, two preliminary samplings have been made from biographical data contained in the New History of the T'ang Dynasty. First, the names of one hundred and eleven leading officials (mostly prime ministers) who held office at different periods during the dynasty were chosen from the chronological tables of the Chung-kuo Ta-shih Nien-piao;[503] then their life histories as recorded in the T'ang Shu were investigated. The second sampling was obtained from an examination of one hundred and fifty-three biographies of officials of different rank who lived during the dynasty's middle period, when T'ang institutions were in full flower.[504] The two surveys yielded the results as shown below:

TABLE 16

WAYS OF BEGINNING AN OFFICIAL CAREER IN THE T'ANG PERIOD

Categories	Officials of top rank (all periods of T'ang dynasty)		Officials of all ranks (middle period of T'ang dynasty)	
	Number	Percentage	Number	Percentage
Examination recorded	86	77.5	42	27.4
No record of either examination or yin	18	16.2	93	60.8
Yin privilege	7[505]	6.3	18[506]	11.8
Total	111	100	153	100

The number of officials in the second category who benefited from the yin privilege is impressive; it is even more impressive when seen in relation to the number of degrees recorded, 18 to 42. The picture among the leading functionaries is somewhat different. Here the ratio of yin officials to those who held the degree is 7 to 86. While, of course, no definite statement is possible at this point, it may be hazarded that appointment to the empire's leading offices was determined in the main by considerations of personal qualification. Officials hardened in competition and of tested ability seem to have had a better chance of achieving the highest positions than the privileged sons who more often obtained posts in the middle or upper middle brackets.

An instructive illustration of the functioning of the yin privilege is found in the biographical sketches in TS 166, 2a ff. These cover several generations of officials of the Tu 杜 family, and show how the high position of a member, Tu Hsi-wang 希望, opened the door to office for his son, Yu 佑.[507] Yu's position benefited his son, Shih-fang 式方, who also possessed the yin privilege.[508] Having attained high office, the latter again paved the way for his yin son, Ts'ung 悰,[509] who climaxed the family's service record by

---

Wei and Chou, should not have the yin privilege (不得爲蔭). For an instance of application of the yin principle see Sui 47, 7a.

[500] CTS 42, 13b. Detailed regulations governing access to the imperial bodyguard by means of the yin privilege were established during the first decades of T'ang rule (TS 49A, 2a).

[501] THY 81, 1499.

[502] CTS 42, 13b; TS 45, 2a; cf. also THY 81, 1499.

[503] Selection was confined to the more important T'ang officials mentioned in the chronological tables of the CKTSNP, 189 ff.

[504] This material was taken from eighteen chapters of the T'ang Shu dealing with officials of the middle period: TS 129, 6a ff.; 130–134; 136, 4b ff.; and 137–147. The influence of the barbarian element in T'ang society is not unimportant, and any detailed study has to take it into account. But in tracing the typically Chinese trend, the biographies of non-Chinese (Turkic, Korean, etc.) officials, given in TS 135 and in various parts of the preceding and succeeding chapters have been omitted.

While some of the officials discussed lived at the end of the seventh century or during the first part of the ninth, the majority held office in the eighth century.

[505] Lu Ch'i 盧杞, prime minister in 781 (TS 223B, 1a); Tou Ts'an 竇參, prime minister in 789 (TS 145, 12a); Li Chi-fu 李吉甫, prime minister in 807 and 811 (TS 146, 2b); Chang Hung-ching 張弘靖, prime minister in 814 (TS 127, 4b); Li Tê-yü 李德裕, prime minister in 833 (TS 180, 1a); Chêng T'an 鄭覃, prime minister in 835 (TS 165, 4a); Tu Ts'ung 杜悰, prime minister in 844 (TS 166, 5b).

[506] TS 129, 7a; 132, 2b, 3a, 7b; 138, 5b, 6b; 139, 1a, 2b; 140, 3a, 4a, 4b; 142, 1a; 143, 5b, 6b; 144, 2b; 145, 12a; 146, 2b; 147, 2a.

[507] TS 166, 2b.

[508] TS 166, 5a.

[509] TS 166, 5b.

achieving the post of prime minister. Two other sons of Shih-fang also rose to office; for one, Tao 慆,[510] the method of entry is not specified; Mu 牧 held the *chin-shih* degree.[511]

While revealing the obvious advantages of the *yin* privilege for achieving a distinguished governmental career, the biographies of the Tu family also indicate its limitations. The prerogative did not carry the holder automatically to the bureaucratic level of his father; furthermore, the number of those who enjoyed the *yin* status seems to have been definitely restricted.[512] These facts explain why many sons and grandsons[513] of officials entered upon a bureaucratic career by way of the *chin-shih* or some similar examination. It also explains why the non-privileged sons of high officials were prone to consider the examination an unmitigated nuisance. The T'ang statesman, Li Tê-yü, voiced the discontent of this group when in 840 he said: "The outstanding officials of the court ought to be the sons of the highest officials. Why? Because from childhood on they are accustomed to this kind of position; their eyes are familiar with court affairs; even if they have not been trained in the ceremonial of the palace, they automatically achieve perfection. Scholars of poor families, even if they have an extraordinary talent, are certainly unable to accustom themselves to it."[514] Obviously pleased with his own *yin* status, which had enabled him to become prime minister twice without the usual examination worries,[515] Li Tê-yü proudly pointed to other leading officials who also had never exposed themselves to the exacting tests.[516]

Neither Li Tê-yü's plea nor Chêng T'an's[517] earlier demand caused the abolition of the examination system. Yet the two attacks show how articulate the enemies of that system were in the ninth century. The author of the *T'ang Shu* accuses Li Tê-yü of bias;[518] nevertheless he concludes his survey of the

T'ang examination system with a detailed report of the prime minister's critical utterance.

In T'ang times the emphasis placed on hereditary privilege was strong indeed, but under the Sung dynasty the trend assumed still greater vigor. During this fateful period of Chinese history, the *yin* privilege was bestowed at the great triennial *chiao* 郊 sacrifice, on the emperor's birthday,[519] after the death of a distinguished official,[520] and on a number of other occasions.[521]

Under the T'ang dynasty the possession of the *yin* privilege was automatic with certain official positions. The beneficiaries, whose number was restricted to one or two persons, were usually the official's son or grandson. In the Sung period the potential beneficiaries included all male kin within the *wu fu* 五服 (the five degrees of mourning),[522] as well as relatives bearing a different surname,[523] and even such persons as an attendant and physician who might boast neither blood nor affinal tie.[524] The significance of these extensions becomes quickly apparent when it is understood that, under Sung rule, one individual might have several *yin* claims bestowed on him simultaneously. In addition, the honor might be conferred on the same individual on a number of different occasions. Fan Chung-yen 范仲淹 estimated that if a man was an amanuensis (學士) for twenty years, he might start some twenty of his relatives on an official career by virtue of the *yin* prerogative.[525] After 1182, when energetic efforts were made to restrict the system, a prime minister might still receive the *yin* privilege for ten individuals.[526]

This policy of repeated honorings greatly increased the total number of *yin* beneficiaries. During the reign of Kao-tsung, that is, in the years following the collapse of the northern part of the Sung empire in 1127, as many as four thousand *yin* prerogatives are said to have been distributed on the occasion of a single *chiao* sacrifice.[527] The figure becomes particularly impressive when it is viewed against the number of successful *chin-shih* candidates in the same critical

[510] TS 166, 6b.
[511] TS 166, 7a.
[512] TS 45, 2a ff. Des Rotours (32, 229 ff.) assumes that the one or two persons who were selected (選) were chosen for court colleges. But TS 45 deals with selection for office and here mentions the students of the court colleges as graduates who were ready to begin their official careers. The colleges themselves are discussed in the preceding *chüan*, TS 44, 1b.
[513] The *yin* privilege also applied, with certain modifications, to a grandson or even a great-grandson, if the forefather's position was sufficiently high (CTS 42, 13b; TS 45, 2a; THY 81, 1499).
[514] TS 44, 7a. See also Des Rotours 32, 205.
[515] *Loc. cit.; cf.* TS 180, 1a.
[516] TS 44, 7a.
[517] TS 44, 6b. Chêng T'an also held the *yin* privilege (TS 165, 4a).
[518] TS 44, 7a.

[519] SS 159, 7a–b; WHTK 34, 324 and 325. The survey of the *yin* system in the Sung period and the subsequent dynasties has, in the main, been prepared by the social historian, Ch'ü T'ung-tsu, who in 1945 joined the staff of the Chinese History Project.
[520] SS 170, 25a–b; WHTK 34, 324.
[521] SS 159, 7a–8a; WHTK 34, 324–325; HTT 21, 1247.
[522] SS 159, 8b; 170, 23a–24b. The descendants of "ego's" great-great-grandfather (see de Groot, RSC I, 546 ff.).
[523] SS 159, 10b and 12b, 170, 23a–25a; WHTK 34, 326; HTT 21, 1247.
[524] SS 170, 23a and 25a; 159, 16b.
[525] FKCFTI 4b; *cf.* also SS 159, 14b.
[526] WHTK 34, 324.
[527] SS 159, 14b.

decade. These successful candidates only averaged between three hundred and four hundred persons, with a maximum of five hundred and thirty-eight in 1128.[528] Even before 1127 the *chin-shih* total rarely rose above six hundred, the all-time high for Northern Sung being eight hundred and five in 1124.[529]

At the end of the twelfth century successful *chin-shih* candidates averaged in the neighborhood of four hundred persons triennially.[530] To be sure, *yin* claims at this time were conspicuously reduced by the reforms of 1182; yet at the *chiao* sacrifices some three to four hundred individuals still received the *yin* privilege.[531] On the basis of the material just cited and with due allowance for possible exaggeration, it seems fair to say that at best in Sung times the number of persons who might claim office by virtue of the *yin* principle approximated the number of those who succeeded in passing the *chin-shih* examinations. Under emergency conditions the first group seems to have strikingly outnumbered the second.

We cannot enter here into a detailed account of the Sung policy for selecting officials, nor can we dwell upon the intense criticism directed against it.[532] But from the standpoint of the history of the Liao dynasty it is highly significant that the *yin* privilege, which influenced the structure of T'ang officialdom to no inconsiderable degree, continued to flourish, and to flourish more fully, under the aegis of Sung power. After the fall of the T'ang dynasty the Liao government adopted a number of Chinese administrative institutions, but only later, when the Sung empire was established, did these institutions reach their fullest development. Small wonder, then, that when the Liao rulers set up their examination system, they restricted its effectiveness, as did the T'ang and Sung rulers by social discrimination on the one hand and the *yin* prerogative on the other.

No Chinese official of the Liao dynasty is known to have risen from the ranks of doctors, diviners, butchers, peddlers, slaves, unfilial children, or criminal fugitives, all of whom were excluded from participating in the examinations by the edict of 1050. The divergence from the T'ang formula is clear. Artisans are not mentioned in the Liao list and the tradesmen who were discriminated against were called *fan* 販, peddlers, not *ku* 賈 or *shang* 商 as in the analogous Sui, T'ang, and Sung laws.[533] Was the Liao measure actually confined to peddlers, or was the term *fan*

used contemptuously to designate the whole merchant class? The order of 1105 was less ambiguous; it marked as undesirable the families of the more or less substantial merchants (*shang ku*).[534] Thus, in certain details the Liao government modified the earlier formula, but in principle it accepted the T'ang policy of excluding social outsiders from the *chin-shih* examinations. By implication it also excluded them from the offices to which the examination led.

The existence of the *yin* privilege can be clearly demonstrated from the pages of the *Liao Shih*,[535] but the *Standard History* provides little concrete information on its form and operation. Additional data are available in the *Ch'i-tan Kuo Chih* whose Sung author, at the close of his description of the Liao examination system, writes: "As to the regulations concerning the sponsoring of sons, both civil and military officials had to present a request to the throne for the *yin* prerogative, and the number [of those who might receive the privilege] was fixed."[536]

This privilege, implicit in the biographies of many outstanding Liao Chinese officials, persisted until the end of the dynasty. According to the great Chin 金 scholar, Yüan Hao-wên 元好問, the new Chin government inherited from the preceding dynasties an "extremely broad" principle of selection. Those who began their careers as sponsored sons (*jên-tzŭ*) were very numerous. "The sponsored sons frequently became high officials, and those who did not achieve this were still placed [socially] on equal footing with the high officials."[537] Since the *yin* prerogative was important before the establishment of Chin power, the new government had to adopt special measures for dealing with the inherited situation. In 1165 it was decreed that the descendants of former Sung officials who had possessed the *yin* privilege should receive the same treatment as that accorded to former Liao officials who had been employed because they held this privilege.[538]

Did the *yin* privilege assume unusual importance in the Chinese administration of the Liao government?

---

[528] WHTK 32, 306.

[529] *Loc. cit.*

[530] *Op. cit.*, 307.

[531] JCSaP 6, 8a.

[532] WHTK 34, 325; SS 159, 13a ff.; LCHSWC 39, 12b (*cf.* Williamson, WAS I, 71–72).

[533] XIV, 3 (13); see above, note 496.

[534] XIV, 3 (30).

[535] See XIV, 3 (14) (22).

[536] 若夫任子之令不論文武並奏蔭亦有員數 (CTKC 23, 5a–b). Stein (39, 109) in his translation of this passage erroneously coordinates, and thus erroneously juxtaposes, officials who were "sponsored sons" with those who were employed because of their fathers' or grandfathers' merit. The error arises from his misunderstanding of both the institutional and terminological problems involved. The *yin* privilege did not rest upon a father's merit, but upon his official position. Reporting a *yin* son was not another method of selection, but only one step in the process of selecting (and employing) a privileged son.

[537] ISHSC 27, 12a–b.

[538] 制亡宋官當廕子孫者並同亡遼官用蔭 (CS 52, 2b).

Was its role as great under Liao rule as under the contemporary Sung dynasty? The Chin critics thought so, and an examination of the available records tends to confirm their impression. Obviously, the Ch'i-tan masters were even less inclined than were their southern rivals to award high-ranking positions to successful *chin-shih* candidates. The reasons for this policy can easily be imagined. The Liao empire was dominated by a tribal nobility which traditionally considered political positions in terms of hereditary prerogatives—highly flexible, it is true, but prerogatives nevertheless. The presence of a Chinese system of official privilege probably attracted more than it repelled the Liao rulers. While personal ability was always a consideration, it could be determined by more pragmatic methods than an examination system. The scholarly bureaucracy's desire to maintain the cherished *chin-shih* tradition came into conflict with the Ch'i-tan predisposition not to take the examination system too seriously—although its value for Chinese administration was not denied.

The closer the family of a Chinese official came to Ch'i-tan life and power, the less did its individual members seem to consider it necessary to take the examinations. Li Yen 李儼 began his career as a *chin-shih*,[539] but once he had attained great honors, including the Ch'i-tan name Yeh-lü, few if any other distinguished members of his family appear to have obtained the degree. His nephew, Li Ch'u-wên 李處溫, never became an honorific Yeh-lü, yet his long biography[540] fails to mention a *chin-shih* degree, probably because he never bothered to seek it; nor are any of the descendants of the first famous Liao Chinese, Han Yen-hui, known to have held a *chin-shih*.[541] In Liu Ching's 劉景 family, few holders of top offices obtained the *chin-shih* degree.[542]

An analysis of Han Tê-jang's family from the point of view of the present study leads to still more negative results. Tê-jang, son of the chancellor Han K'uang-ssŭ 韓匡嗣, obtained office apparently without passing an examination. His unique career, which made him the mightiest man in the empire and an honorific Yeh-lü as well, opened the way for many of his relatives[543] to achieve leading positions in the various branches of the northern and southern governments. Two nephews "went so tribal" that

they were made *t'i-yin*;[544] another became great king of the Southern Division,[545] and, if the record can be trusted, neither they nor any other of Han Tê-jang's many relatives in official places were distinguished by a *chin-shih* degree,[546] except one—Han Ch'i-hsien 企先. Ch'i-hsien, a descendant in the ninth degree of Han Chih-ku, passed the metropolitan examination under the last Liao emperor; he achieved outstanding official success only in the Chin dynasty. Logically enough, his life is described not in the *Liao Shih*, but in the *Chin Shih*.[547]

As stated above, access to office was possible through other means than the *yin* prerogative or the examinations. Appointment and subsequent promotion played a not insignificant part. But the edict of 1086 suggests that the appointees were frequently, if not primarily, chosen from among the sons and brothers of office holders,[548] a practice not very different from that which operated in regard to *yin* designations. The proclamation of 1086 implies the existence of earlier restrictions, probably in relation to the official status of the family concerned; and the conflict among Wang Pang-yen's sons[549] reveals the presence of certain limitations also among the claimants of the *yin* privilege. Yet, despite such restrictions, the chances of a member of a Liao Chinese official family to enter the hierarchy without an examination degree were evidently very good. The *yin* prerogative was nothing but an institutionalized formulation of these chances.

The differences between the *shih-hsüan* and the *yin* privileges are obvious. The former, an institution of a relatively simple tribal state, gave members of a specific family a claim over generations to a specific office or class of office. The latter, the product of a complex bureaucratic government, granted a limited number of direct descendants (not a family) access without examination to an official career (not to a specific office). The *shih-hsüan* system, although not applied directly to the Liao Chinese officialdom, may well have promoted the growth of corresponding trends in the existing Chinese government institutions.

The *yin* concept, on the other hand, also influenced the development of the tribal hereditary principle within the conquering nation. The complexity of the conquest society necessarily increased the flexibility of the Inner Asiatic pattern. To be sure, under

---

[539] LS 98, 3a.

[540] LS 102, 2a–3a.

[541] LS 74, 3b.

[542] LS 86, 1b ff. Several members of the Liu family who passed the examination attained less outstanding offices; two of them married imperial princesses.

[543] These relatives did not automatically become Yeh-lü, but kept their Chinese family name, Han. The reference to Han Chih-hsin as Yeh-lü Chih-hsin in LS 15, 2a is probably an error.

[544] Han Hsieh-shih 謝十 and Han Ti-lu 滌魯 (LS 82, 3a).

[545] Han Chih-hsin 制心. He was an expert in taming eagles (LS 82, 3b).

[546] *Cf.* LS 74, 4a ff. For more data concerning the extraordinary career of the Han family under the Liao regime see VII, 1, note 17 and VII, 2, note 21.

[547] CS 78, 8a ff.

[548] XIV, 3 (26).

[549] XIV, 3 (22).

the conditions of the Liao empire, the pattern never lost its functional significance, and its perpetuation (in a modified form) is well expressed in the special designation, *shih-hsüan*. Occasionally, however, the term *yin* is applied to a tribal holder of the hereditary prerogative, as in the case of Yeh-lü Yin-chi.[550]

In the subsequent dynasties of conquest members of the ruling nationality were fitted into a unified political machine, although, as a group, they continued to maintain their control over it. Under these conditions master nationals were often appointed to office without recourse to examination. Others, with a bow to the system, enjoyed hereditary exemption, while those who exposed themselves to competition found their tests considerably simplified. The tribal holders of hereditary privilege usually enjoyed advantages denied their Chinese rivals, but, interestingly, their prerogative in imitation of the old Chinese institution was called *yin*.[551] In this form the *yin* privilege manifests itself in all post-Liao conquest societies of China—in Chin,[552] in Yüan,[553] and Ch'ing.[554] In each of them, however, it is only one aspect, although a significant aspect, of the larger *yin* institution as it operated in all post-Liao and post-Sung dynasties.

In the northern and southern sections of their newly established empire the Jurchen found a pattern of selection which permitted hereditary claims to play almost as important a role as competitive examinations. According to a Chin scholar, Yüan Hao-wên, four out of ten officials came from the ranks of the "sponsored sons."[555] Such an extension of the *yin* system bothered the Chin rulers considerably—however, not so much because it curtailed the chances of successful *chin-shih* candidates, as because it increased the number of potential Chinese office holders.

It is well to remember that the semi-Sinicized Jurchen, who found it unnecessary to set up a separate

"northern" government, filled many leading positions in their monistic political organization with their own nationals. However, despite this very natural bias, they readily bestowed official favors upon trusted Chinese dignitaries. After the year 1202 an official of the first rank still had the right to place six persons in office because of his *yin* privileges; and the fortunate beneficiaries might still be drawn either from the direct or the collateral line.[556]

The Mongols, like the Ch'i-tan, followed a pastoral way of life; but they exhibited much less understanding of Chinese civilization than had their nomadic predecessors. Their distrust of a politically independent Chinese leadership was consistently expressed by their recourse to methods other than the examination system when selecting Chinese for office. In 1237, shortly after the collapse of Chin power, Yeh-lü Ch'u-ts'ai urged the introduction of competitive examinations. The first attempt at realization produced more than four thousand successful candidates (儒士),[557] but the plan was soon abandoned as "not convenient."[558] From then on until the time of Kublai Khan, Chinese officials in the service of the Mongol government achieved their positions primarily on the basis of appointment. In 1267, however, when the Great Khan came to regard himself as the overlord of the entire Chinese world, the value of establishing an examination system was again discussed, again without lasting practical results.[559] Instead the government carefully formulated the *yin* principle which in the forty-six years that followed[560] constituted the sole rival to position by appointment. During the middle period of Yüan rule a blue print for a new examination system was worked out,[561] but it was accepted only in 1313. Two years later the much-debated plan was put in operation and, except for a short interlude between 1335 and 1340, it continued to function until the close of the dynasty.[562] The restored examinations, far from putting an end to the *yin* claim, emphasized its importance in a new way: a *yin* beneficiary, who passed the *chin-shih* examination, might enter the official hierarchy one rank higher than his less favored colleagues.[563]

The Liao rulers had been none too eager to adopt the Chinese examination system. The Mongol masters were considerably less so. Even when they took the "democratic" step, the number of successful *chin-shih* candidates remained extremely small: one hun-

---

[550] XIV, 3 (14). Of course, the use of the word *yin* in this passage may be an error: a thoughtless scribe may have confused it with the term *shih-hsüan*, which usually refers to the hereditary prerogative of distinguished Liao tribesmen. However, we have no right to exclude the possibility of the text's accuracy. An occasional extension of the term *yin* to the tribal rulers—no matter whether purposeful or unconscious—is evidently based on the social, if not the technical, similarity of the two types of prerogatives.

[551] Other forms of privilege, such as the perpetual or temporary inheritance of noble titles, will be treated in connection with those periods during which they assumed institutional significance.

[552] CS 52, 2*b* ff.

[553] YTC 8, 15*a* ff.; HWHTK 40, 3182.

[554] CSK 116, 4*a*–8*a*; CCWHTK 54, 5359 ff. Even members of the imperial family held the *yin* privilege (YSTKCL 甲辰 [1904]—Li-fang 立方).

[555] ISHSC 27, 12*a-b*.

[556] HWHTK 40, 3182.

[557] *Op. cit.* 34, 3150.

[558] YS 81, 3*a*.

[559] *Op. cit.*, 3*a*–4*a*.

[560] YTC 8, 15*a*.

[561] YS 81, 4*a* ff.

[562] HWHTK 34, 3152–3153.

[563] YS 81, 5*b*.

dred and eighty constituted the all-time high, but averages totalled not more than seventy (including a number of "barbarians"),[564] and this within a territory easily larger than the Sung domain and many times larger than the Chinese regions of the Liao empire.

The *chin-shih* figures clearly reveal the Mongol tendency to limit the number of high Chinese officials. The same tendency is disclosed by the regulations dealing with the hereditary claim to office, a claim that otherwise was held in great esteem. During the Yüan period the *yin* privilege could only be bestowed on one son or grandson, or, if there was no direct descendant, on one male collateral.[565] But, as if to compensate for the numerical restriction, the Mongols raised the level of entry into the official hierarchy for *yin* claimants from the seventh to the fifth rank,[566] a level higher than during the T'ang dynasty.

At the outset the Ming dynasty accepted their predecessor's policy of official selection;[567] but, in the changed political climate, the *yin* principle assumed a markedly different functional significance. Under the Mongols the limiting of the number of *yin* claims to one was part of a general effort to restrict the number of Chinese in official positions. Under the Ming government the same device greatly enhanced the opportunities of the successful *chin-shih* candidates who, freed from Yüan oppression and suspicion, again totalled several hundred persons triennially.[568] Furthermore, in the year 1467 the Ming rulers limited the claim to the *yin* prerogative to officials within the three highest ranks, a policy that contrasted sharply with the Mongol precedent of granting the hereditary privilege to members of all ranks above the two lowest.[569] But most important, those who possessed the *yin* prerogative could no longer reach the apex of the hierarchical pyramid, as indeed they had been able to do until the close of the Yüan dynasty. In Ming times the *yin* prerogative assured the holder access only to a minor position in the central government or to the post of prefect in the provincial administration.[570] Occasional appointments to high office excepted,[571] persons eager to attain top-ranking positions had to pass through the gates of the regular examination system.

The Manchus, willing to utilize as many Chinese institutions as political expediency permitted, adopted the *yin* policy of the Ming dynasty with minor restrictions. The *yin* beneficiaries might still fill the office of assistant prefect or magistrate, but they could not become prefects; in the main, they were confined to secondary positions in the central government.[572]

Our comparative survey of the two Liao types of inherited privilege, the tribal *shih-hsüan* and the Chinese *yin* prerogative, draws attention to three important points:

1. The Ch'i-tan *shih-hsüan* system ingeniously combined inherited privilege and individual ability. A comparative study of other Inner Asiatic peoples may reveal, either for some or for all of them, a similarly flexible policy governing their "hereditary" officialdom.

2. The *yin* prerogative was a corollary to the developing examination system. Study of either must include the other; it must also include a consideration of policies that discriminated against undesirable social outsiders.

3. A special problem arises in dynasties of conquest. As long as the tribal conquerors maintained a dual political order, their hereditary claims to office tended to assert themselves in a form more or less similar to the traditional tribal pattern. However, when the political organization was unified, the prerogatives were adjusted in large degree to the existing Chinese institutions (examinations and *yin*). Thus, the *yin* privilege must be seen as a specific aspect of the Chinese examination system not only in such essentially Chinese dynasties as T'ang, Sung, and Ming, but also in the great periods of conquest, Liao, Chin, Yüan, and Ch'ing.

d. THE FUNCTIONS OF THE CHINESE OFFICIALS

The *Ch'i-tan Kuo Chih*, in its meager references to the Liao examination system, claims that the candidates for the *chin-shih* degree were examined only in two subjects—poetry and the classics—the second, under Shêng-tsung (982–1031) being replaced by law, while poetry remained the major requirement.[573] Independent Chin sources, confirmed by the *Liao Shih*, enable us to correct the narrow and partially incorrect picture drawn by the Sung work. Obviously, under Liao rule, the candidates were supposed to have received a well-rounded training in the Chinese humanities. This being so, there can be little doubt as to the essentially literary character of their education. A Ch'i-tan ruler who made the Chinese candidates write a poem on such an unacademic subject as

---

[564] HWHTK 34, 3152–3153.
[565] YTC 8, 15*a–b*.
[566] *Op. cit.*, 19*a*.
[567] HWHTK 40, 3183.
[568] *Op. cit.*, 35, 3159 ff.
[569] MS 69, 8*a*.
[570] MS 71, 5*b*–6*a*; HWHTK 40, 3184; MHY 48, 4*a–b*.
[571] MS 69, 8*b* and HWHTK 40, 3184.

---

[572] CSK 116, 4*a–b*; CCWHTK 56, 5360. Certain exceptions to the rule, which occurred particularly during the later part of the Ch'ing period will be discussed separately in our detailed survey of Ch'ing institutions.
[573] CTKC 23, 5*a*.

"Shooting Thirty-six Bears in One Day"[574] did not consider these candidates experts in riding and marksmanship. But the versatile, though bookish, applicants were expected to clothe their ignorance of wild life in learned quotations from ancient songs and stories set down in immaculate calligraphy.

The studies required included neither military science nor any practical administrative training. The first defect could have been overcome; it often was in the typical Chinese dynasties. But the Liao rulers did not wish to see their Chinese subjects too proficient in a field which they rightly considered the very basis of their own political power. The military key office of the empire, that of the northern chancellor of the Northern Region, was entrusted to a Chinese only once—during the final phase of the great Sung war and in the years immediately thereafter (999–1011). But, although Han Tê-jang's (Yeh-lü Lung-yün's) leadership successfully aided Ch'i-tan interests, the experiment was never repeated. As soon as the political strength of the empire was fully consolidated, the key military office was again reserved for members of the two ruling clans.

The Chinese Chancellery of the Southern Region, which was merged with the Southern Chancellery of the Northern Region, originally exercised military functions; but later, no matter whether a Chinese or a Ch'i-tan filled the office, attention remained concentrated on those civil affairs which had been its chief concern after 947. Within the Southern Region the military power rested in the hands of various territorial and regional officers who in the main were of Ch'i-tan nationality.

The second defect, lack of practical training in administration, presented no serious obstacle to the Chinese aspirant to office. The technique of government was relatively simple. Stripped of its decorative unessentials, it required only a knowledge of reading, writing, calculating, and certain elementary facts of bureaucratic organization. An educated Chinese learned most of these techniques early in life; the rest were readily acquired in the congenial atmosphere of office routine and secretarial practice.

A large part of the civil administration of the Liao government, therefore, fell to the Chinese masters of script and number. Although Ch'i-tan officials were assigned to various offices of the Southern Region,[575] the great majority of government positions in that sector were held by Chinese officials. Chinese officials even filled certain offices in the Northern Region, but most of these, as might be expected, were purely administrative in character.[576]

e. EUNUCHS

In the complex absolutistic society of imperial China the emperor employed eunuchs as political foils to counteract the influence of a high and sometimes centrifugal officialdom,[577] for inevitably they supported the throne which was the sole source of their power and wealth. A dynasty of conquest, such as Liao, relied primarily, not upon the bureaucracy of its sedentary population, but upon the strength and loyalty of its tribal herdsmen and warriors.

Eunuchs therefore were marginal men in Liao society. The educated Wang Chi-ên enjoyed Shêng-tsung's confidence,[578] and Chao An-jên succeeded in eventually obtaining a military position.[579] But no real political influence was ever concentrated in the hands of any Liao eunuch mentioned in the historical records.

f. PO–HAI OFFICIALS

Compared to that of the Chinese, the number of Po-hai in government positions seems insignificant. This is not surprising, for Po-hai nationals, the second most important conquered people, were never fully subdued and therefore never fully trusted. A qualified Chinese was an acceptable candidate for office as long as he was not labelled a rebel; a Po-hai was suspect until his loyalty was proved.

The first Po-hai who achieved a distinguished official career, Kao Mu-han, repeatedly demonstrated his devotion on the battlefield before he was awarded the highest post in his native territory, Tung-ching.[580] Little is known of Ta K'ang-i's early career, but after having obtained a number of high offices, the Southern Prime Ministry among them, he successfully administered the eastern border tribes.[581] Hsia Hsing-mei earned his first laurels during the great Po-hai revolt in 1029, when, as commander of a Po-hai army, he supported the Liao cause against his rebelling country-man, Ta Yen-lin.[582] The last famous Po-hai official in the Liao government, Ta Kung-ting, was the scion of a distinguished Po-hai family which had been transferred to Chung-ching. His great-grandfather and his father had held minor offices; he, himself, passed the chin-shih examination and occupied a number of civil and military posts. Ta Kung-ting is pictured as a benevolent administrator,[583] but his particular claim to distinction seems to have derived from his

---

[574] XIV, 3 (10).

[575] LS 8, 4a; 10, 2a; 14, 1a; 15, 3a; 16, 1b; 17, 2a; 22, 3a; 28, 7b and *passim*.

[576] See above.

[577] See Wittfogel 35, 55.

[578] LS 109, 2a.

[579] LS 109, 2b.

[580] LS 76, 4a–5b.

[581] Ta K'ang-i reached the peak of his career between 1016 and 1020 (LS 88, 7a).

[582] See LS 87, 5b and XIII (38).

[583] See XI (22).

skill in checking the rising tide of "bandits" (read: rebels) who attacked the tottering dynasty.[584]

The fate of the Po-hai officials is not dissimilar to that of certain tribal chieftains who, after their peoples were defeated, collaborated with the Liao victors. This collaboration either came to an abrupt end because temporary submission was followed by renewed struggle, or else, if permanency was achieved, it led to personal conflict and political degradation which increased as the inner antagonisms of the conquest situation approached their climax.

6. SPECIAL FUNCTIONS OF THE LIAO GOVERNMENT

Directly or indirectly political supervision or control penetrated almost every aspect of Liao society. It made its influence felt in agriculture and stock-breeding, in industry and commerce. The Liao state forced its subjects to pay taxes, to serve in the corvée and in the army. This it accomplished by means of a government organization which, though clumsy and wasteful, succeeded in mobilizing, coordinating, and utilizing the empire's many human and material resources. The methods it employed grew out of the special needs of production and circulation, taxation, labor service, and relief.

But to execute its tasks effectively the state also had to provide a modicum of stability in the country's political and cultural life. It had to maintain "peace and order"; it had to administer certain proto-scientific and literary activities (astronomy, historiography, publication, and translation) which could not be advantageously left in the hands of private individuals.

a. LAWS, CH'I–TAN AND LIAO

Many laws of the early dynastic period conspicuously reflected the tribal traditions and customs of the Ch'i-tan peoples. Those mentioned in the *Liao Shih* were for the most part formulated under T'ai-tsu, that is, during the formative period of the empire.[585] Some few concerned with adultery and the stealing of government horses,[586] while first noted at a later date, obviously also arose in a tribal setting. In their Liao form they may well have originated concurrently with T'ai-tsu's laws; in any case, they are an interesting, if fragmentary, supplement to them.

To appreciate the historical value of the legal data contained in the *Liao Shih*, it is important to re-

member that T'ai-tsu proclaimed his laws centuries before Chingis Khan composed his Yasa (code), the first "pan-Mongol written law."[587] Riasanovsky calls Chingis Khan's great Yasa the "most ancient of the records of Mongol law that have come down to us."[588] His claim is correct only if the word Mongol is understood in its narrower sense; the *Liao Shih* contains "laws" formulated almost three hundred years earlier by a proto-Mongol people.[589]

The difference between the living conditions of the Ch'i-tan and Mongols expresses itself in the contents of their respective laws; it is apparent even in a number of accessory features. The Ch'i-tan practice of hurling a rebellious prince from a cliff[590] indicates the mountainous character of the terrain occupied by the early Ch'i-tan as clearly as certain Mongol prohibitions reflect the water scarcity of the arid Central Asiatic desert and steppe.[591] Significantly the Ch'i-tan, who dwelt in a relatively well-watered territory, either had no water laws of the Mongol type, or, if they originally possessed any, felt no need to stress them in the early days of the dynasty.

Mongol law punishes sodomy, a common practice among pastoral peoples, with death.[592] The Ch'i-tan explicitly forbid incest,[593] while the Yasa does not mention it. Adultery is condemned in both codes.[594] Mongol law imposes the death penalty when disrespect is shown to the old,[595] and obedience to state and family are sternly demanded in A-pao-chi's regulations: a person who insults a superior or disobeys his parents is threatened with death by torture.[596]

Among the Mongols the punishment for horse-stealing affected the rich and poor in different degree: the rich man paid the nine horses demanded in restitu-

---

[584] LS 105, 1a–2b.
[585] XIV, 4 (1).
[586] Tampering with the property marks of government horses (XIV, 4 (15)) is a typically tribal crime. In LS 62, 1b (XIV, 4 (13)) adultery is discussed only in relation to the hereditary Ch'i-tan nobility.
[587] Riasanovsky 37, 35.
[588] *Loc. cit.*
[589] These fragments of Ch'i-tan laws have come down to us through records that in their present form were written not during Liao T'ai-tsu's reign, but later. The same is true, however, for Chingis Khan's Yasa which though "supposed to have been written down during his life" is "known to us only through later chroniclers." (Vernadsky 38, 337. For a discussion of the main sources of our information concerning the Yasa see *op. cit.*, 339–343; *idem* 39, 33 ff.)
[590] XIV, 4 (1).
[591] Don't call anything unclean (Yasa no. 16; Riasanovsky's numbering); don't wash your clothes until they are completely worn out (no. 15); don't dip your hands into water, but use a vessel (no. 14); don't urinate into water (no. 4)—punishment for the last crime: death. See Riasanovsky 37, 83–85.
[592] Yasa no. 2 (Riasanovsky 37, 83).
[593] XIV, 4 (1).
[594] XIV, 4 (13); Yasa no. 1 (Riasanovsky 37, 83).
[595] Yasa no. 31 (*op. cit.*, 85).
[596] XIV, 4 (1).

tion; the poor paid with his children, "and if he have no children, he himself shall be slaughtered like a sheep."[597] The Liao laws only refer to the theft of government horses; as late as 1036 both the dishonest herdsman and the receiver of the stolen horses were killed.[598]

Generally speaking, the Yasa reveals a far more primitive ("purely nomadic") way of life than the Ch'i-tan laws. The Mongol code metes out the death penalty to most offenders,[599] but the punishment itself is not specified. The Ch'i-tan lawgivers offer a relatively detailed list of methods by which a criminal could be disposed of. A Ch'i-tan who was guilty of a serious infraction of the law might be pulled to pieces by five chariots; he might have his mouth pierced with a hot iron; he might be decapitated; he might be shot full of "devil arrows"; he might be buried alive or used as a catapult.[600] Compared with such penalties beating seems considerably less horrible. But three hundred lashes or more is no light penalty either; that anyone could survive the maximum of five hundred strokes[601] is more than doubtful.

The gradual growth and stabilization of the Liao empire not only modified the laws but also mitigated the terroristic practices of T'ai-tsu's time. A first step in this direction was made by the founder of the dynasty himself; in 921 he promulgated two laws, one for his Ch'i-tan subjects, one for the Chinese,[602] the two most important nationalities within his state. Different treatment does not necessarily imply discrimination, but in this instance it did.[603] As long as the murderer or thief and his victim were members of the same national group, the old laws of that nationality still applied; but, when the offender and the victim belonged to different groups, then the might of the conquerors made right, and punishment was imposed according to the national status of the offender. The Liao Shih does not describe the exact nature of the laws of the tenth century, but, judging by the inequalities that persisted after the recodification of Liao law in 994,[604] the earlier regulations must have discriminated harshly against the Chinese (and Po-hai).[605] Chingis Khan frankly distinguished between his subjects of different nationality. The penalty for murdering a Mohammedan was forty golden coins, for a Chinese, a donkey.[606]

The "equalization" of Liao law undertaken during the Sung war was part of the government's general policy to appease its restless and obstructive Chinese subjects.[607] In 983 representatives of the government of the Southern Region provided the court with a law code which had to be translated[608]—obviously it was written in Chinese. In 994 it was solemnly announced that a Ch'i-tan who committed any of the "ten crimes" enumerated in the Chinese code should be punished according to Chinese law.[609]

Details of the code are few, and it is therefore difficult to establish to what extent it covered crimes usual among hunters and herders. The Chinese regulations probably took little note of such matters. The only case cited concretely in the Liao Shih is concerned with a brawl between Ch'i-tan and Chinese.[610] A Sung writer, describing legal conditions in the Liao empire about the middle of the eleventh century, notes that crimes committed by a member of any one of the four main nationalities against an individual belonging to any other group were punished according to Chinese law, whereas crimes within a national group were punished according to the law of that group.[611]

Such judicial procedures reasonably resolved certain national difficulties, but peculiarly enough the code never clearly defined how conflicts between the Ch'i-tan and the Chinese, who set the standard for all other groups, should be handled.[612] If the Ch'i-tan and the Chinese were treated equally under the new law—as the edict of 1070 implies[613]—how did the political superiority of the Ch'i-tan express itself in case of a legal clash? Whatever the solution, for a number of decades other problems seem to have occupied the court's attention. Once the Sung war was successfully ended, the Liao government asserted its increased authority by introducing a number of new measures, some less discriminatory, some more. In 1006 an edict forbade owners of slaves to kill them without official authorization.[614] For the first time, all Ch'i-tan might be tatooed. This put the privileged families in the same category as the commoners,[615] at least as far as this method of punishment was concerned. However, the fact that a sentence might be commuted from hard labor to a diplomatic

[597] Yasa no. 29 (Riasanovsky 37, 85).
[598] XIV, 4 (15).
[599] Vernadsky 38, 356.
[600] XIV, 4 (1).
[601] Loc. cit.
[602] VII, 1 (3).
[603] VII, 1 (17).
[604] See VII, introduction.
[605] VII, 1 (3).
[606] Yasa no. 28 (Riasanovsky 37, 85; Vernadsky 38, 356).

[607] See XII, introduction.
[608] XIV, 4 (6).
[609] VII, 1 (17); XIV, 4 (9).
[610] Loc. cit.
[611] Wu Hsi Chi = LSSI 15, 15b.
[612] See VII, 1 (3).
[613] XIV, 4 (24).
[614] VII, 1 (20).
[615] VII, 1 (21).

assignment with subsequent pardon continued to benefit the Ch'i-tan nobles.[616]

The old laws were revised and a code of five hundred and forty-seven items was set up in 1036,[617] a year that is as significant for the golden period of the empire[618] as is 994 for the emergency created by the Sung war. One year after the publication of the modified code, the country's officials were rewarded "because the prisons of the Northern and Southern Chancelleries were empty."[619] Few details of the new laws are given, but the vivid legal discussions of the "thirties" and the new regulations concerning the theft of government horses[620] show clearly that the state felt sufficiently secure to reduce the severity of the punishment for certain crimes.

Lesser punishments than those established by law had been meted out to high officials ever since the days of T'ai-tsung and Mu-tsung; a distinguished culprit might be let off after a beating with a wooden sword or a sandbag,[621] or, later, with a large stick.[622] From Shih-tsung's time on, members of the distinguished lineages and the "hereditary" officialdom, when guilty of crime, were confined to special camps[623] or banished to the tribes;[624] this probably took the place of the more usual death penalty. In 1032 officials were permitted to make restitution for former acts against the government.[625] For commoners as well as nobles, tatooing on the neck replaced tatooing on the face.[626] Another order further restricted the authority of the slave-owners; a slave might be tatooed on the face only with official approval.[627]

Shortly before the middle years of the eleventh century, the antagonisms of the two main nationalities again flared in the open. The Ch'i-tan dissatisfied with the decisions of the Chinese judges wanted their cases to be tried by Ch'i-tan officials. Their demand was granted in 1044,[628] certainly to the disadvantage of the Chinese litigants.

The Ch'i-tan must have been gratified by the benefits guaranteed them by this decree, but evidently

not completely so. In 1070 the emperor again ordered a revision of the code, based this time on the differences in Ch'i-tan and Chinese customs.[629] Thus, national discrimination, which the codes of 994 and 1036 sought to minimize, was wilfully and formally reintroduced into Liao law.

The new code created an impossible situation. Although the *Liao Shih* does not clearly state what people suffered from its application, it seems safe to surmise that it discriminated against the Chinese masses rather than their Ch'i-tan rulers. The Chinese, who under continued economic stress increasingly avoided their fiscal duties and fled from their homes, were only too ready to question the government's judicial fairness. After almost twenty years of embarrassed experiment and two years after the breakdown of the rigid regulations against destitute families,[630] the revised code was discarded.[631]

But administrative and legal concessions which had strengthened a robust regime in the time of the Sung war had a contrary effect when made by a disintegrating government at the end of the eleventh century. After 994 the Chinese masses, whatever the intensity of their national feelings, accepted the orders of the imperial government; after 1089 the Chinese participated in rapidly swelling numbers in active rebellion against the hated regime.[632]

b. ASTRONOMY AND CALENDAR–MAKING

The judicial activities of the Liao state were directed to its pastoral as well as agricultural populations. Other government functions were more particularly a response to the special needs of its sedentary subjects. Although eventually applied throughout the empire, they remained essentially Chinese in character.

Agricultural societies of the "Oriental" type require reliable devices for defining the seasonal limits that determine when public works may be most satisfactorily undertaken and when the individual peasant may best engage in productive pursuits for his own benefit.[633] The Ch'i-tan were not as well prepared to rule the Chinese people as were their successors, the Jurchen and Manchus, but they were sufficiently familiar with the ways of their southern and eastern agricultural neighbors to take over such all-important Chinese functions as astronomy and calendar-making.

The technical details of the Liao calendar which fill the greater part of LS 42–45 are not the concern of this study, but their general significance as well as

---

[616] VII, 1 (25).
[617] XIV, 4 (14).
[618] See XII, and XVI, introductions.
[619] XII (45).
[620] XIV, 4 (15).
[621] LS 61, 2*b*; see also YPL 18*b*.
[622] VII, 2 (56); VIII (6).
[623] VII, 1 (1).
[624] VII, 2 (69).
[625] XIV, 4 (12). The lenient policy had to be replaced by a more severe one, probably because it had too strongly encouraged the bureaucratic greed and dishonesty (see X, 1 (45) (54)).
[626] XIV, 4 (13).
[627] *Loc. cit.*
[628] VII, 1 (35).

[629] XIV, 4 (24).
[630] XII (88).
[631] XIV, 4 (30).
[632] See XIII.
[633] *Cf.* Wittfogel 31, 457 ff.; *idem* 38, 98.

their limitations may be deduced from the short introduction (LS 42, 1b–2a) that precedes the astronomical tables. Even during the first decades of the tenth century the officials of the Chinese regions of the Liao empire must have depended upon some kind of calendar. The calculations of the Later Liang and Later T'ang astronomers, based on the T'ang calendar,[634] were available to them. But in 939, when the Chin 晉 court adopted a new calendar, the northern emperor was placed in an embarrassing position; he either had to accept the calendar of a politically inferior ruler (his "son"),[635] or continue to use a T'ang calendar discarded by the Chin court, which retained possession of the numerous charts and calculations of the T'ang dynasty.

The emperors of China Proper, and not the barbarian rulers of the north, had inherited the technical personnel and the astronomical paraphernalia of the great T'ang state. In 947, when the victorious Liao emperor carried the calendar, the charts, the observatory, and even the "specialists" of the Chin court to his own country,[636] "then Liao for the first time had a calendar."[637] The practical benefits were as important as the political success. The Liao emperor could now fulfill a function which the Chinese masses considered the privilege and duty of every legitimate ruler.

But, although "the northern court" endeavored to establish a national calendar, its attitude toward astronomy remained conservative and imitative. The calendar offered by two Liao astronomers in 961 is said to have been the T'ang calendar which T'ai-tsung seized in Pien in 947; and Chia Chün's presentation to the throne in 994, greeted as Liao's "own calendar," proved to be merely a resurrected pre-T'ang product.[638]

c. HISTORIOGRAPHY

The chief aim of Chinese historiography has been the transmission of political, administrative, and military experience from one generation of statesmen and officials to the next. The Ch'i-tan rulers never became "real" Chinese, but they did achieve sufficient insight into Chinese political organization and techniques to appreciate the advantages of a written history. Hsing-tsung visualized the task of history rather narrowly; to him it merely put on record "the glory of the nation."[639] Yeh-lü Mêng-ch'ien understood its functions differently; he emphasized the need for truthful recording: because the written

word is followed "by a hundred generations"[640] the historiographer faces a most serious responsibility; he must be careful and always critical.[641] Other historians had vigorously taken the same position: Hsiao Han-chia-nu restored a deleted passage commenting on the sinister effects of an imperial hunting expedition. His insistence was praised by Hsing-tsung, the emperor under fire, who finally admitted, "This is what historiography should be like."[642]

Such then was the ideal; but the political climate of the Liao court did not favor the development of ideal historians or an ideal historiography. Hsiao Han-chia-nu's experience reveals that Hsing-tsung read the daily records openly, thus violating one of the basic rules of official Chinese historiography; and he did not hesitate to order a critical passage deleted. Tao-tsung went even further than his father. When the two recorders, Pu-tien and Hu-t'u-chin, refused to show him the *Diaries of Activity and Repose*, he ordered both severely beaten and the scribe, Hsiao Yen-shou, banished to a remote border tribe.[643]

These stories are illuminating in several respects. The presence of many Ch'i-tan among the recorders indicates that the Department of Historiography was manned by a staff of Ch'i-tan as well as Chinese officials; and the former were probably responsible for the Ch'i-tan biases shown in the records. The behavior of the two emperors indicates that, until the end of the Liao dynasty, its rulers did not feel called upon to conform to the traditional Chinese attitudes toward historiography.

The order of 1003, suggesting that it was unnecessary to bother with "trifling matters,"[644] may have been dictated by a sincere desire to improve the quality of the records, but it is equally possible that it was an attempt to cover certain too revealing personal and political actions of the court. The exclusion of the historiographers from court discussions ordered in 1056[645] was possibly an act of political prudence to lessen the dangers of espionage from unreliable Chinese officials, but it inevitably affected the accuracy of the daily entries which recorded political arguments, not as they were presented, but as they were retold by the prime ministers.[646]

In view of these many factors, it is not surprising that the *History of the Liao Dynasty* is relatively short and crude,[647] even when compared to the histories of

---

[634] XIV, 4 (4).

[635] XVI, 937, LS 3, 10b.

[636] VII, 2 (22); XIV, 4 (4).

[637] *Loc. cit.*

[638] *Loc. cit.*

[639] XIV, 4 (16).

[640] XIV, 4 (26).

[641] *Loc. cit.*

[642] XIV, 4 (18).

[643] XIV, 4 (27).

[644] XIV, 4 (10).

[645] XIV, 4 (21).

[646] *Loc. cit.*

[647] For the technical aspect of the composition of the *Liao Shih* see appendix IV.

the Chin and Yüan dynasties. What may cause astonishment is that it contains much more concrete cultural information than the histories of the smaller pre- and post-T'ang dynasties. Obviously this is owing to the power and duration of the Liao state, which made it possible for its historians not only to record political events and biographical data, but also to describe at considerable length its political and cultural institutions. Those same conquerors who might conceal the more personal political and military secrets of their power did not hesitate to record fully the unique features of their civilization which they considered "not inferior to that of the Chinese."[648]

d. LITERARY PURSUITS

The antagonistic trends which characterized Liao historiography are also revealed in the dynasty's attitude toward literacy and literary pursuits. The Ch'i-tan, who "made the world tremble" with their superior horsemanship and shooting skill,[649] were none too eager to engage in literary activities, even when they recognized the fundamental need for reading and writing in government administration. The empire's widely-spread population, mostly Chinese and sedentary, could only be properly ruled by a literate bureaucracy. While the Ch'i-tan rulers took great pains to establish their own system of writing, which may have been equal to the demands of tribal adminis-tration, it could not replace the Chinese script which boasted a long and rich history and an extended use throughout Eastern Asia. Literacy, whether Ch'i-tan or Chinese, was the oil that lubricated the wheels of the administrative organization of the Liao govern-ment. To maintain and encourage some degree of literacy was more than a cultural ambition; it was a political necessity.

Books had to be provided before they could be read.

LS 72 proudly comments on the many volumes col-lected by T'ai-tsu's eldest son, Pei.[650] The presence of learned proofreaders and collators in the Ch'ung-wên and Chien-wên Libraries[651] suggests that the num-ber of books was increased by copying no less than by purchase.

Ch'i-tan writers are said to have produced poetry of extraordinary beauty and profundity in their mother-tongue; unfortunately none of it survives in the original.[652] In Chinese, Liao scholars made outstanding contributions only in the field of Buddhist literature. Ordered and supported by the court, the new critical edition of the Canon and similar publica-tions were prepared by Buddhist monks.[653] Private individuals, particularly in Nan-ching, must have pro-duced some books other than the Buddhist Canon, but no fragment of any important Liao work has come down to us. In 1064 the private publication of books was forbidden altogether.[654]

A few translations of Taoist and historical Chinese works into Ch'i-tan, and the publication (or transla-tion ?) of the two earliest dynastic histories[655] illus-trate the poverty rather than the wealth of the dy-nasty's intellectual achievement. As for the Con-fucian classics: in 1086 Tao-tsung ordered their "general principles expounded"; in 1088 a few selected chapters from the Documentary Classic (Shu Ching) were discussed or copied.[656] These unspectacular con-tributions were made by the Liao intelligentsia at a time when outstanding Sung philosophers, poets, his-torians, and statesmen were creatively reshaping many vital features of China's cultural heritage.

---

[648] SMCW 9a; see VII, 1 (41) and note.
[649] XV, 2 (20).

[650] XIV, 4 (2).
[651] XIV, 3 (8); XIV, 4 (23).
[652] See VII, 2, note 25.
[653] See IX, introduction, passim.
[654] XIV, 4 (22).
[655] XIV, 4 (20) (25).
[656] XIV, 4 (24) (25).

TRANSLATION

1. THE NORTHERN REGION

1. From tribal chieftainship to dynastic state   2. Infiltration of T'ang elements   3. Further developments   4. Division into North and South   5. Imperial clansmen become southern prime ministers   6. Subdivision of the Northern Region   7. Direct appeal to the emperor   8. A Ch'i-tan police bureau   9. Officials of the Northern Region   10. A special office for the heir apparent   11. Minor court bureaus   12. Minor attendants of the imperial relatives   13. Office of the four imperial lineages   14. The office of the imperial lineage   15. Administration of the Three Patriarchal Households   16. Officials of the imperial princes   17. A temporary Tung-ching office   18. The imperial descendants   19. The residences of the princesses   20. Officials of the Yao-lien lineage   21. Officials of the Imperial Maternal Uncles   22. The former royal family of Po-hai   23. Administration of the great tribes   24. Administration of the small tribes   25. Administration of the subordinate states   26. Miscellaneous officials of the Northern Region.

1. FROM TRIBAL CHIEFTAINSHIP TO DYNASTIC STATE[1]

209–174 B.C.   Mao-tun Khaghan[2] attacked the eastern barbarians[3] with an army and annihilated[4] them. The remnants of their people sought refuge in the Hsien-pei Mountains.[5] Hence they were called the Hsien-pei.

233–236   During the Ch'ing-lung period[6] the tribal chieftain Pi-nêng, who was somewhat tyrannical and unrestrained, was killed by the prefect of Yu Prefecture,[7] Wang Hsiung. [The tribe] dispersed and migrated [to the region] south of the Huang River[8] and north of Huang-lung.[9]

A descendant of Ko-wu-t'u[10] of the Hsien-pei was called P'u-hui. P'u-hui had a son, Mo-na, who migrated south from the Yin Mountains[11] and was the first to settle down in Liao-hsi.[12] After

337–345   nine generations the mass of the Hsien-pei, upon being destroyed[13] by Mu-jung Kuang,[14] broke up into the Yü-wên,[15] K'u-mo-hsi,[16] and Ch'i-tan.

The country of the Ch'i-tan was situated east of the K'u-mo-hsi. They comprised different lineages but were of the same stock, a branch of the eastern section of the Hsien-pei. Now for the first time they called themselves Ch'i-tan.[17]

---

[1] The survey of the tribal history of the Ch'i-tan given in LS 63 is based on a number of earlier sources, such as the *Wei Shu, Pei Shih, Sui Shu,* and *T'ang Shu,* whose data have been used in various parts of this publication.

[2] After a short survey of the predynastic history of the Ch'i-tan, LS 63 describes the "ancestors" of the Ch'i-tan in somewhat greater detail. Since the genealogical position of the earliest legendary chieftains like Ch'i-shou 奇首 "cannot be investigated," the report begins with the time of the Early Han dynasty. In that period the great Hunnish ruler, Mao-tun 冒頓 (209–174 B.C.), fought and defeated the ancestors of the Ch'i-tan, who are called *tung hu* 東胡, "eastern barbarians" (*cf.* SC 110, 8a ff.). The word *khaghan* of our text is anachronistic. During the Han period the supreme chieftain of the Huns was called *shan-yü* 單于.

[3] For the relation of the "eastern barbarians" to the Tungus see I, introduction.

[4] Terms such as "annihilate" or "destroy" are used frequently to describe the complete defeat of a pastoral people. But the "destruction" was rarely total. Often, after a certain period of time the "annihilated" people emerged again, evidence of the fluidity of pastoral nomadism.

[5] The exact location of these mountains is not known. They were probably situated in the northwestern part of modern Jehol.

[6] The second reign period of Emperor Ming 明 of the Wei 魏 dynasty (220–265).

[7] Modern Peiping.

[8] The present Shira Muren in Jehol.

[9] The two geographical names, Huang-lung 黃龍 and Ho-lung 和龍, are used in the *Liao Shih* with different significance. When they refer to a place which existed before the time of Liao (LS 63, 2a–b), both correspond to modern Ch'ao-yang 朝陽, Jehol, but when they refer to places which existed in the Liao period, Huang-lung indicates modern Nung-an 農安, Kirin, while Ho-lung indicates modern Ch'ao-yang, Jehol.

[10] An early ancestor of the Northern Chou dynasty; he is described as a wise man who ruled twelve Hsien-pei tribes (Chou 1, 1a).

[11] A mountain range covering part of Suiyuan and Chahar. Liao-hsi was southeast rather than south of the Yin Mountains.

[12] Modern Jehol.

[13] See note 4.

[14] The second emperor of Early Yen 前燕 (285–370).

[15] One group of this people, under the dynastic name of Chou 周, controlled North China from 557 to 581.

[16] See I, 2, note 4.

[17] *Cf.* General Introduction, note 9.

Upon being routed by the Mu-jung family they all fled to the region of Sung-mo.[18]   During the

386-396   Têng-kuo[19] period Emperor Tao-wu defeated them severely, whereupon they split off
from the K'u-mo-hsi.   After several decades they multiplied somewhat and spread
out.   They had tribes several hundred *li* north of Ho-lung.[20]

440-450   From the T'ai-p'ing Chên-chün period of Emperor T'ai-wu, they annually presented
famous steeds [as tribute].   At the time of Hsien-wên, when the *mo-fu-ho*,[21] Ho-ch'ên,
came to pay tribute, [the Ch'i-tan] for the first time were classified among the last of the [vassal]
states.   *63, 2a-b*

553   In the ninth month of the fourth year of T'ien-pao[22] the Ch'i-tan invaded the border.
Emperor Wên-hsüan personally headed a punitive campaign against them. . . .   The
emperor himself crossed the mountain ranges and launched a vigorous attack, capturing more than a
hundred thousand men and women and several hundred thousand animals of different kinds.   [P'an]
Hsiang-lo[23] also severely defeated another [Ch'i-tan] tribe in the Ch'ing Mountains[24] and distributed the captives among various prefectures.   On being also harassed by the Turks, they temporarily
resided with ten thousand families within the territory of Korea.   *63, 3a*

581-600   Towards the end of the K'ai-huang period[25] more than four thousand households of
another tribe deserted the Turks and came to surrender [to Sui].   Kao-tsu gave them
provisions and ordered them back, but they stubbornly refused to leave.   The tribes, gradually
increasing in population, then migrated northward in pursuit of water and grass.   They settled
down two hundred *li* due north of Liao-hsi along the Ho-ch'ên River,[26] covering an area five hundred
li from east to west and three hundred *li* from north to south.   They were divided into ten tribes,
those with the most soldiers having three thousand, and those with the least having over a thousand.
In case of a military operation the chieftains discussed it together.   In mobilizing troops, tallies
were matched.[27]   *63, 3b*

The territory of the Ch'i-tan, which was located more than five thousand *li* directly northeast of
the [T'ang] capital,[28] reached Korea in the east, the Hsi in the west, Ying Prefecture[29] in the south,
and the Mo-ho[30] and Shih-wei[31] in the north.   They relied upon the Lêng-hsing Mountains[32] for their
protection.   The places where they hunted or lived were not permanent.   Their ruler, of the Ta-ho[33]
family, had forty thousand valiant soldiers.   He divided [his people] into eight tribes and submitted
to the Turks, who made him an *i-chin*.[34]   During mobilizations or military enterprises the tribes all
gathered together; in hunting each tribe could act independently.   [The relations] with the Hsi
were not peaceful.   Whenever a conflict turned out to be disadvantageous, they fled and sought
refuge in the Hsien-pei Mountains.   *63, 4a*

Li Huai-hsiu, whose name was given to him by the T'ang [government], had the Ch'i-tan designation of Ti-lien-tsu-li.   He was originally the supreme chieftain of the eight tribes.   In the fourth

---

[18] The northern region of modern Jehol.

[19] The first reign period of Emperor Tao-wu 道武 of
Northern Wei (386-535).   The present passage mentions
the names of two other emperors of Northern Wei, T'ai-wu
太武 and Hsien-wên 獻文.

[20] See note 9.

[21] See introduction.

[22] The reign title of Emperor Wên-hsüan 文宣 of Northern Ch'i 北齊 (550-577).

[23] P'an Hsiang-lo 潘相樂 was minister over the masses
of Northern Ch'i.

[24] Probably in southeastern Jehol.

[25] The first reign period of the first emperor, Wên 文
(temple title Kao-tsu), of the Sui dynasty (581-618).

[26] The present Lao-ha 老哈 River, Jehol.

[27] The messenger presented one part of the tally to the
local group which held the remaining part.   The tally
thus served as a watchword or code.

[28] Modern Sian 西安, Shensi.

[29] Modern Ch'ao-yang 朝陽 County, Jehol.

[30] The Mo-ho were a tribal complex from which the
Po-hai and Jurchen later derived.   During the T'ang
period they lived in modern Kirin and the Russian Maritime Provinces.   *Cf.* I, 2 (10), no. 31.

[31] *Cf.* I, 2, note 5.   During the T'ang period the many
branches of the Shih-wei spread over modern Heilungkiang
and the adjacent regions.

[32] Probably in the eastern part of Jehol.

[33] The first ruling family of the Ch'i-tan people.

[34] See introduction, note 9.

745 year of T'ien-pao[35] he surrendered to T'ang and was installed as governor-general of Sung-mo. . . . Thus it is clear that [Li] Huai-hsiu, actually the first chieftain of the Yao-lien family, was Tsu-wu Khaghan.   *63, 7b*

885–887 Ch'in-tê, king of the Ch'i-tan, who belonged to the clan of Hsi-êrh-chih,[36] became Hên-tê-chin Khaghan. During the Kuang-ch'i period he plundered the Hsi and Shih-wei tribes and subdued all of them. Several times he and Liu Jên-kung[37] attacked each other. In his last years his government fell into decay.

The chieftains of the eight [Ch'i-tan] tribes as a rule were regularly replaced every three years. But, when Yeh-lü A-pao-chi of the I-la tribe set up the banners and drums and established an independent tribe, unwilling to accept replacement, he announced himself as king and came into possession of the entire Ch'i-tan state. The Yao-lien family thereupon came to an end.[38]   *63, 8a–b*

2. INFILTRATION OF T'ANG ELEMENTS

From the time when T'ang T'ai-tsung established governors-general and prefects, Empress Wu conferred kingships, and Hsüan-tsung set up controlling commissioners,[39] the Ch'i-tan state began to have the titles and ranks of T'ang. Later, on hearing frequently of the regional military governors of Ho-pei[40] receiving the official titles of T'ang, [the Ch'i-tan] thereupon applied the titles of grand preceptor, grand guardian, minister over the masses, and minister of works[41] in their tribes. T'ai-tsu followed this policy.   *47, 1a*

3. FURTHER DEVELOPMENTS

908 On the day *hsin-ssŭ* [of the first month in the second year of T'ai-tsu's accession] the *t'i-yin* was established for the first time.[42] He had charge of the imperial clan. The emperor's younger brother, Sa-la, was given the position.   *1, 3a*

910 On the first day *mou-tzŭ* of the seventh month in the autumn of the fourth year [of T'ai-tsu's accession] the empress' elder brother, Hsiao Ti-lu,[43] was appointed prime minister of the Northern Administration. The appointment of [members of] the empress' clan as prime ministers began at this time.   *1, 3b*

919 On the day *mou-wu* [of the twelfth month in the third year of Shên-ts'ê], Han-li-chên a younger brother of the *yü-yüeh*, [Yeh-lü] Ho-lu,[44] was made *i-li-chin* of the I-lieh[45] tribe, and Hsiao A-ku-chih[46] was appointed prime minister of the Northern Administration.[47]
1, 10b

---

[35] T'ien-pao 天寶 (742–756) and Kuang-ch'i 光啓 (885–887), which is mentioned below, were both reign periods of the T'ang dynasty.

[36] We follow TS 219, 4b in reading *chih* 之 as the final syllable of the name of Hsi-êrh-chih. He was the predecessor of Ch'in-tê as king of the Ch'i-tan.

[37] Liu Jên-kung 劉仁恭 was the military overlord of Lu-lung 盧龍, the northern part of modern Hopei, during the end of the ninth and the beginning of the tenth century.

[38] *Cf.* XIII, notes 1 and 2.

[39] T'ai-tsung's action referred to above can be definitely dated in 629 (LS 63, 4b) and that of Hsüan-tsung in 716 (LS 63, 6a), but the establishment of the rank of king among the Ch'i-tan by Empress Wu can only be said to have occurred within her reign (684–705).

[40] During T'ang times Ho-pei 河北 covered the area north of the Yellow River from present Honan and Shantung up to the Great Wall. The term 藩鎮, "regional military governor," designates a political institution which assumed great significance during the T'ang period.

[41] In the early Chinese dynasties these terms were applied only to men of the highest ministerial ranks. Subsequently they became honorary titles which were also

bestowed upon persons of great merit. Their use to designate tribal positions is one of the early instances of acculturation in the history of the Ch'i-tan people.

[42] "For the first time"—as an office of the imperial clan. As a designation for a tribal office the term *t'i-yin* 惕隱 existed long before, as is shown by a record which mentions it as preceding the later Chinese title of minister over the masses (*cf.* LS 46, 1b).

[43] According to LS 73, 4a, Hsiao Ti-lu 敵魯 was a younger brother of the empress. He aided T'ai-tsu in suppressing the rebellion of the emperor's brothers. He died in 919 (LS 1, 10b).

[44] Yeh-lü Ho-lu 曷魯 was a member of the imperial clan who together with twenty other officials helped T'ai-tsu to ascend the throne (LS 73, 1a ff.).

[45] 迭烈, another transcription for I-la, the name of the imperial tribe.

[46] The brother of Empress Ch'un-ch'in. He aided T'ai-tsu in crushing the rebellion of the emperor's brothers (LS 73, 4b–5a).

[47] Hsiao A-ku-chih succeeded to this position upon the death of his brother Hsiao Ti-lu. *Cf.* note 43.

4. DIVISION INTO NORTH AND SOUTH

In the old Ch'i-tan way of life their affairs were simple, their official duties specific, and their government system plain and unsophisticated and not confused by terminology.   Their rise was **921** rapid indeed.   In the sixth year of the Shên-ts'ê period of T'ai-tsu an edict was issued concerning the regularization of grades and ranks.   When T'ai-tsung came **927–947** to rule over China, he divided the government into North and South.   The Ch'i-tan were governed according to their national system,[48] while the Chinese were governed according to their own system.   The national system was simple and plain.   In the Chinese system the usage of the traditional terminology was preserved.

The government system of the Liao state was divided into a Northern and a Southern Division. The Northern Region[49] administered the affairs of the camps, tents, tribes, lineages, and tributary states, while the Southern Region administered the taxes and the military affairs of the Chinese prefectures and counties.   To govern according to custom is indeed to achieve what is proper.

45, 1a–b

5. IMPERIAL CLANSMEN BECOME SOUTHERN PRIME MINISTERS

921   On the day *ping-wu* of the first month in the spring of the sixth year of Shên-ts'ê the emperor's younger brother, Su,[50] was appointed prime minister of the Southern Administration. . . .

With regard to the prime minister of the Southern Administration, in view of the fact that with the revolts of T'ai-tsu's younger brothers[51] most of the distinguished lineages of the Administration suffered from the turmoil, this position had been vacant for a long time.[52]   It was occupied temporarily by Hsia-tê-li and Chih-li-ku of the Ch'u-tê tribe.[53]   Within the Administration the request was made repeatedly to fill the office from the imperial house.   The emperor considered that the old system could not be changed abruptly.   As the requests were made incessantly, the emperor, after reporting to the ancestral temple, then appointed him.[54]   The appointment of [members of] the imperial house as prime ministers of the Southern Administration began at this time.   2, 2a

6. SUBDIVISION OF THE NORTHERN REGION

922   In the beginning T'ai-tsu divided [the position of] the *i-li-chin* of the I-la [tribe] into [the positions of] the two great kings, the northern and southern, calling [their territories] the Northern and Southern Divisions.[55]   From the prime ministers, chancellors, masters of court etiquette, and scribes down to the court nobles and guardsmen, all were divided into North and South.   In reality, however, they governed only the affairs of the north.   This must be clearly understood by those who discuss the political system of Liao.   45, 1b

---

[48] The Ch'i-tan "national system" implied the preservation of many tribal titles, as is shown in the translated passages of this section.   It seems that not all "national" titles have been recorded in the *Liao Shih*.   The Ch'i-tan *Kuo Chih* mentions the titles *ho-pa-chih* 賀跋支, *tu-nu-ku* 都奴古 or *t'u* (徒) *-nu-ku*, which cannot be found in the *Liao Shih*'s list of northern officials.   The Sung work equates *ho-pa-chih* with the Chinese title of commissioner of court ceremonies and the other terms with directing secretary (CTKC 23, 3a; 24, 3a).

[49] The word *mien* 面, which we render as "region," designates exclusively the two main administrative units of the Liao empire.   The word *yüan* 院, "division," is, in this passage and in XIV, 2 (1) and (2), equated with "region"—a most confusing usage, for usually it is applied either to the two complexes of imperial tribes or to the two subdivisions of the Northern Region.

[50] The fifth of T'ai-tsu's younger brothers.   In reality he was T'ai-tsu's half-brother (*cf.* LS 85, 3a).   He did not participate in the early rebellions against the emperor, perhaps because he was still too young. He assisted T'ai-tsu in the conquest of Po-hai in 926 and died in the same year.

[51] See XIII (5) to (13).

[52] Prime ministers were first appointed in the Northern and Southern Administrations in 907, the first year of T'ai-tsu's accession.

[53] Probably identical with the Ch'u-t'ê 楮特 tribe whose territory was northwest of modern Boro Khoton.

[54] That is, Su.   The preceding sentences give the background of Su's appointment, which was mentioned in the first paragraph.

[55] This was done in 922 (LS 2, 3a).

7. DIRECT APPEAL TO THE EMPEROR

1039   On the day *chia-wu* of the eleventh month [in the eighth year of Ch'ung-hsi] an imperial decree ordered that those who complained against unjust treatment in legal decisions by the Northern Administration and appealed [to the emperor] by striking the bell or intercepting the emperor should all be reported.   18, 9a

8. A CH'I-TAN POLICE BUREAU

1044   In this month [the third month of the thirteenth year of Ch'ung-hsi], a Police Department for the Ch'i-tan was set up.[56]   19, 5b

9. OFFICIALS OF THE NORTHERN REGION

The Ch'i-tan Northern Chancellery[57] was in charge of the administration of military affairs, selection of officers, and stockbreeding. All the Ch'i-tan armies and horses were under its control.
. . .

Chancellor of the Northern Division[58]
Director of affairs for the chancellor of the Northern Division.[59]   45, 2a

The Ch'i-tan Southern Chancellery was in charge of the administration of the selection of civil officials and the taxation of the tribes and lineages. All the Ch'i-tan people were under its control.
. . .

Chancellor of the Southern Division
Director of affairs for the chancellor of the Southern Division.[60]   45, 3a–b

The Northern Prime Ministry assisted in managing the important military and state affairs. The four tents of the imperial family had the hereditary prerogative of selection to it.[61]

Left[62] prime minister of the Northern Administration
Right prime minister of the Northern Administration.[63]   45, 4b

The Southern Prime Ministry assisted in managing the important military and state affairs. The five tents of the Imperial Maternal Uncles had the hereditary prerogative of selection to it.[64]

Left prime minister of the Southern Administration
Right prime minister of the Southern Administration.[65]   45, 4b–5a

---

[56] See VII, 1 (35).

[57] The Northern Chancellery, partly replacing the Northern Ministry (see note 61), was established by Shih-tsung in 947. A few Chinese, such as Han Tê-jang, held this post, but in general only Ch'i-tan nobles had access to it.

[58] In this as in the succeeding cases our translation gives the titles of the leading official and of a few others which follow in the text. We have endeavored to include all titles mentioned in our various translations, but not all the titles listed in the *Liao Shih*, and this for two reasons: (1) the titles listed in LS 45 and 46 apparently are not complete; and (2) the titles, listed as a whole, do not convey any idea of the functions of the title-holder. In the introduction to this section we have sought to explain the functions of the more important offices.

[59] The Chinese text lists in all seventeen titles for the Northern Chancellery.

[60] Seventeen titles listed.

[61] Before the establishment of the Northern Chancellery in 947 this office was the most powerful of the whole state, second in significance only to the position of the emperor himself. According to LS 45, 4b–5a, the Northern Prime Ministry was controlled by members of the emperor's family, while the Southern Prime Ministry was controlled by the Hsiao clan. Actually, the reverse was true. For a fuller discussion see below, note 64 and introduction.

[62] "Left" indicates a higher position than "right."

[63] Four titles listed.

[64] See note 61. The position of northern prime minister was really held by an Imperial Maternal Uncle, while that of southern prime minister was held either by members of the emperor's family or by reliable Chinese officials. In 907, when T'ai-tsu ascended the throne, the position of northern prime minister was bestowed on a member of the Hsiao clan, whereas the post of southern prime minister was given to a member of the emperor's clan (LS 1, 2b). In 910 T'ai-tsu appointed the eldest brother of the empress to the post of prime minister of the Northern Administration (LS 1, 3b). In 921 T'ai-tsu appointed his younger brother, Su, to the post of prime minister of the Southern Administration. See XIV, 1, *passim;* also Fêng CS 33, 122 ff.; LTCNP 8045–8068.

[65] Four titles listed.

The Department of the Northern Great King shared control of the military and civil affairs of the tribes.[66]

> Great king of the Northern Division . . .
> Director of affairs for the great king of the Northern Division
> Grand preceptor of the Northern Division
> Grand guardian of the Northern Division
> Minister over the masses of the Northern Division
> Minister of works of the Northern Division. . . .   45, 5a–b

The Office of the Military Control of the Northern Division was in charge of the administration and orders in regard to all conscription for the Northern Division.

> Commissioner of military control of the Northern Division
> Vice-commissioner of military control of the Northern Division
> Chief supervisor of military control of the Northern Division.

The Office of the *Hsiang-wên* of the Northern Division was in charge of the administration and orders in regard to the armies and horses of the tribes of the Northern Division.

> *Hsiang-wên* of the Northern Division
> Chief supervisor of the Northern Division
> General of the Northern Division
> Minor general of the Northern Division.

The Office of the Chief Controller of the Northern Division was in charge of military and civil affairs of the tribes of the Northern Division.

> Chief controller of the Northern Division
> Assistant controller of the Northern Division.   45, 5b–6a

The Department of the Southern Great King shared control of the military and civil affairs of the tribes.

> Great king of the Southern Division[67]
> Director of affairs for the great king of the Southern Division
> Grand[68] preceptor of the Southern Division
> Grand guardian of the Southern Division . . .
> Minister over the masses of the Southern Division
> Minister of works of the Southern Division.[69]   45, 6a–b

The Northern Department of the Master of Court Etiquette[70] . . . had charge of the personal services rendered to the emperor by the Northern Division.

> Master of court etiquette of the Northern Division
> Director of affairs for the master of court etiquette of the Northern Division.[71]   45, 7a

---

[66] In 1008 a Liao prefect of T'an 檀, Ma Shou 馬壽, told the Sung envoy, Lu Chên, that the northern great king and the southern great king were both members of the Yeh-lü family, and that each commanded four strong armies of ten thousand bowmen. They controlled an area of more than eight hundred *li* in and around the modern province of Chahar. Not infrequently, they disobeyed government orders concerning taxation and the recruiting of soldiers (HCLY 77, 9b).

[67] The Palace edition reads 面 for the 而 of our text.

On the basis of the formula 北院 we should expect 南院. We therefore give the latter rendering.

[68] The 大 of our text should be read as 太.

[69] The titles of the military officers of the Southern Division are the same as those listed for the Northern Division. See above, LS 45, 5b–6a.

[70] The Northern and Southern Departments of the Master of Court Etiquette were both established in 938 (LS 45, 7a).

[71] Four titles listed for this office as well as for the following one.

The Southern Department of the Master of Court Etiquette . . . had charge of the personal services rendered to the emperor by the Southern Division.

> Master of court etiquette of the Southern Division
> Director of affairs for the master of court etiquette of the Southern Division.   45, 7b

The Administration of the Grand *Yü-yüeh*, who had no official duties and was ranked above the ordinary officials, was granted only to those who had great merit and virtue.   It was an honorary rank of the Liao state similar to the Three Dukes[72] in the Southern Region.[73]   45, 7b

The Office of the Grand *T'i-yin*, which was established by T'ai-tsu, was in charge of the administrative and educational affairs of the imperial family. . . .

> *T'i-yin* . . .
> Director of affairs for the Office of the *T'i-yin*
> Chief supervisor for the *t'i-yin*.   45, 8a

The Department of the *I-li-pi* was in charge of punishments.

> *I-li-pi*
> Left *i-li-pi*
> Right *i-li-pi*.[74]   45, 8a-b

The Department of the Grand Scribe was in charge of literary matters.[75]

> Chief scribe of the Northern Region
> Scribe of the Northern Region in charge of edicts
> Scribe of the Northern Region
> Left scribe
> Right scribe.   45, 8b-9a

The Office of the *Ti-lieh-ma-tu* was in charge of ceremonies.

> *Ti-lieh-ma-tu*
> General director of court ceremonies
> General manager of ceremonial affairs.   45, 9a

As regards the Office of the Secretariat, of what it was in charge there are no details.

> Grand guardian of the secretariat
> Scribe of the secretariat.[76]   45, 9a

As regards the *a-cha-ko-chih*, of what it was in charge there are no details.   It was an old Yao-lien office which was later incorporated into the Chancellery.

> *A-cha-ko-chih*.[77]   45, 9b

---

[2] See XIV, 2 (5), LS 47, 2b.

[73] No subordinates mentioned.

[74] Seven titles listed.   CTKC 23, 3a explains the *i-li-pi* as an official whose duties parallel those of the associate director of political affairs (參知政事).

[75] The Department of the Grand Scribe bears a certain resemblance to the Han-lin Academy of the Southern Region, which was modelled after the traditional Chinese institution of the same name.   The literary activities of the Department were, however, carried on in the Ch'i-tan language (see VII, 2, note 25).   The term *lin-ya*, "scribe," also appears in connection with other sections of the Liao goverment.   The offices of the Northern Region included a number of "scribes" (XIV, 1 (26)), and in the southern hierarchy, the leading officials of the Han-lin Academy were also thus designated (XIV, 2 (5)).

[76] Four titles listed.

[77] No subordinate mentioned

10. A SPECIAL OFFICE FOR THE HEIR APPARENT

The Office of the *T'i-yin* of the Imperial Heir Apparent was in charge of the affairs of the tents of the imperial heir apparent.

> *T'i-yin* of the imperial heir apparent.   45, 13a

11. MINOR COURT BUREAUS

Bureau of Stationery . . .
Bureau of Tablets and Seals . . .
Bureau of Rugs and Bedding . . .
Bureau of Lamps and Candles . . .
Bureau of Bed Curtains . . .
Bureau of Court Tents . . .
Bureau of Carriages . . .
Bureau of Imperial Cups . . .
Bureau of *Pên-pan*.[78]   45, 14b–15b

12. MINOR ATTENDANTS OF THE IMPERIAL RELATIVES

Office of Attendants of the Empress Dowager . . .
Office of Attendants of the Emperor's Father's Concubines
Office of Attendants of the Empress
Office of Attendants of the Imperial Concubines
Office of Attendants of the Imperial Heir Apparent
Office of Attendants of the Imperial Princes.   45, 15b–16a

13. OFFICE OF THE FOUR IMPERIAL LINEAGES

The Office of the Grand Imperial *T'i-yin* was in charge of the administration and education of the four tents of the imperial clan.   45, 17a

14. THE OFFICE OF THE IMPERIAL LINEAGE

The Office of the Grand *Ch'ang-kun* of the Horizontal Tents was in charge of the affairs of the imperial lineage of the nine tents of Emperor T'ai-tsu's descendants.   45, 17b

15. ADMINISTRATION OF THE THREE PATRIARCHAL HOUSEHOLDS

The Office of the *Ch'ang-kun* of the Tents of the First Patriarchal Lineage managed the affairs of the household of Yen-mu, Prince of Shu.[79]

The Office of the *Ch'ang-kun* of the Tents of the Second Patriarchal Lineage managed the affairs of the household of Shih-lu, Prince of Sui.[80]

The Office of the *Ch'ang-kun* of the Tents of the Third Patriarchal Lineage managed the affairs of the three households of Emperor Tê-tsu.[81]   45, 17b–18a

16. OFFICIALS OF THE IMPERIAL PRINCES

A detailed description of the bureaucratic system in the principalities of the imperial princes[82] is not given.   45, 18b

---

[78] The meaning of the term *pên-pan* 本班 is not clear. The *pên-pan lang-chün* 郎君, who is mentioned in LS 82, 4b; 91, 3b; 95, 2a; 97, 1a; and 100, 1a, may have been a court noble in charge of miscellaneous items not previously mentioned.

[79] An uncle of T'ai-tsu.
[80] An uncle of T'ai-tsu.
[81] Father of T'ai-tsu.
[82] This term refers to the "entrusted commandery-prefectures" described in I, 1.

17. A TEMPORARY TUNG–CHING OFFICE

926   The Council of Presidents of the Great Tung-tan Kingdom was established in the first year of T'ien-hsien of T'ai-tsu. It was abolished by Shêng-tsung in the first year of Ch'ien-hêng.[83]   45, 19a

18. THE IMPERIAL DESCENDANTS

The Department of Imperial Descendants was in charge of the affairs of all tents of the imperial descendants.   45, 19a

19. THE RESIDENCES OF THE PRINCESSES

The Administration of the Imperial Son-in-Law Chief Commandant was in charge of the affairs of the tents and residences[84] of the princesses.   45, 19b

20. OFFICIALS OF THE YAO–LIEN LINEAGE

The Office of the Grand *Ch'ang-kun* of the Nine Yao-lien Tents managed . . . the affairs of the palaces of nine reigns of the Yao-lien khaghans. . . .

> Grand *ch'ang-kun* . . .
> Grand preceptor of Yao-lien
> Grand guardian of Yao-lien
> Grand commandant of Yao-lien
> Minister over the masses of Yao-lien
> Minister of works of Yao-lien
> Inner chamberlain of Yao-lien . . .
>> Directing secretaries
>> Directors of affairs.   45, 20a–b

The Office of the Commanding Prefect of the Yao-lien Tents

> Commanding prefect
> Vice-commanding prefect

The Office of the *Hsiang-wên*[85] of the Yao-lien *Chiu*[86]

> *Hsiang-wên* of the Yao-lien *Chiu*
> Chief supervisor of the Yao-lien *Chiu*
> General of the Yao-lien *Chiu*
> Minor general of the Yao-lien *Chiu*

Officials of the Yao-lien *K'o*.[87]   No details on their names.   45, 20b–21a

21. OFFICIALS OF THE IMPERIAL MATERNAL UNCLES

The Office of the Grand Imperial Maternal Uncles managed the affairs of the two tents of I–shih-ssŭ and Pa-li of the Imperial Maternal Uncles . . . .

> *Ch'ang-kun* of the I-shih-ssŭ Senior Elder's Tent of the Imperial Maternal Uncles. . .
> *Ch'ang-kun* of the I-shih-ssŭ Junior Elder's Tent of the Imperial Maternal Uncles
> *Ch'ang-kun* of the Pa-li Senior Patriarchal Tent of the Imperial Maternal Uncles
> *Ch'ang-kun* of the Pa-li Junior Patriarchal Tent of the Imperial Maternal Uncles
> Grand Preceptor of the Imperial Maternal Uncles
> Grand Guardian of the Imperial Maternal Uncles

---

[83] According to PHKCCP 19, 44b–45b, the "first year" is an error for the fourth year of Ch'ien-hêng. For this reign period see V, note 22.

[84] Or "tent residences"?

[85] A Ch'i-tan term designating some sort of military officer.

[86] A military unit. *Cf*. II, 2, note 20.

[87] See II, 2, note 3.

    Grand Commandant of the Imperial Maternal Uncles
    Minister over the masses of the Imperial Maternal Uncles
    Minister of works of the Imperial Maternal Uncles
        Directing secretaries . . .

Office of the *Hsiang-wên* of the I-shih-ssŭ Senior Elder's Tent of the Imperial Maternal Uncles

    Hsiang-wên of the Imperial Maternal Uncles
    Chief supervisor of the Imperial Maternal Uncles
    General of the Imperial Maternal Uncles' own clan
    Minor general of the Imperial Maternal Uncles' own clan . . .

Office of the *Hsiang-wên* of the I-shih-ssŭ Junior Elder's Tent of the Imperial Maternal Uncles
Office of the *Hsiang-wên* of the Pa-li Senior Patriarchal Tent of the Imperial Maternal Uncles
Office of the *Hsiang-wên* of the Pa-li Junior Patriarchal Tent of the Imperial Maternal Uncles
Office of the *I-li-pi* of the Imperial Maternal Uncles

    I-li-pi of the Imperial Maternal Uncles
    Left *i-li-pi* of the Imperial Maternal Uncles
    Right *i-li-pi* of the Imperial Maternal Uncles
        Directing secretaries

K'o of the Tents of the Imperial Maternal Uncles

Separate lineage of the Imperial Maternal Uncles, set up by Shih-tsung.   No details on the system of its officials.   45, 21a–22b

22. THE FORMER ROYAL FAMILY OF PO-HAI

Office of the Tents of Po-hai.   No details on the system of their officials.

    Prime minister of Po-hai
    Grand guardian of Po-hai
    Escorting officials of Po-hai
    Office of the *Hsiang-wên* of the Attendants of Po-hai.   45, 22b–23a

23. ADMINISTRATION OF THE GREAT[88] TRIBES

The great tribes

    Great king of the tribe.[89]   Originally called *i-li-chin*
    Left prime minister of the tribe
    Right prime minister of the tribe
    Grand preceptor of the tribe
    Grand guardian of the tribe
    Grand commandant of the tribe
    Minister over the masses of the tribe.   Originally called *t'i-yin*

Office of the Commanding Prefect of the tribe

    Commanding prefect of the tribe
    Vice-commanding prefect of the tribe
    Assistant to the commanding prefect of the tribe

---

[88] These "great" tribes (大部族) must not be confused with the "large" tribes (大部) of LS 46, 29b (see I, 2 (8)). The latter were important non-Ch'i-tan tribes of doubtful political allegiance. The "great" tribes, the cream of the inner Ch'i-tan tribes, were only four in number: (1) the Five Divisions, (2) the Six Divisions, (3) the I-shih tribe, and (4) the six Hsi tribes (LS 46, 3a). See I, 2 (4), nos. 1 and 3.

[89] Literally, "of such-and-such tribe" (某部). Similar formulas are repeated throughout the lists of officials of the great and small tribes and the subordinate states.

Office of the *Hsiang-wên* of the tribe

> *Hsiang-wên* of the tribe
> Chief supervisor of the tribe
> General of the tribe
> Minor general of the tribe

The *shih-lieh*

> *I-li-chin* of the *shih-lieh*
> *Ma-p'u* of the *shih-lieh*.   Also called *ma-pu*.   Originally called
> > the *ta-la-kan* of the *shih-lieh*
> *Ya-shu* of the *shih-lieh*

The *mi-li*.   *Mi-li* means "village."

> *Hsin-kun*.   Originally called *ma-t'ê-pên*.   46, 1a–2a

24. ADMINISTRATION OF THE SMALL TRIBES[90]

The small tribes

Administration of the Minister over the Masses of the tribe

> Minister over the masses of the tribe
> Minister of works of the tribe

Office of the Commanding Prefect of the tribe
Office of the *Hsiang-wên* of the tribe
The *shih-lieh*

> *Ling-wên*
> *Ma-p'u*
> *Ya-shu*

The *mi-li*

> *Hsin-kun*.   46, 2b–3a

25. ADMINISTRATION OF THE SUBORDINATE STATES[91]

A general list of the titles of officials of the subordinate states

> Great king of the state
> *Yü-yüeh* of the state
> Left prime minister of the state
> Right prime minister of the state
> *T'i-yin* of the state.   Also called minister over the masses
> Grand preceptor of the state[92]
> Grand guardian of the state
> Minister of works of the state.   Originally called *ta-lin*.

Office of the Commanding Prefect of such-and-such tribe of the state

> Commanding prefect of such-and-such tribe of the state
> Vice-commanding prefect of such-and-such tribe of the state

---

[90] For the names of the small tribes see LS 46, 3a–5b.

[91] Such "subordinate states" as Japan, Persia, and Ta-shih were, of course, organized according to their own traditions and needs.

[92] In 1036 the chieftain of the Northeastern Jurchen, A-tao-hsien 阿道閒, who with fifty-eight tribesmen surrendered to Korea bore a title which the Korean officials transcribed as *t'ai-shih* 太史.   They called it a Ch'i-tan title and suggested its replacement by a Korean one (KRS 6, 82).   The latter is not in the Ch'i-tan list of officials; the Koreans seem to have used this transcription for the term *t'ai-shih* 太師, grand preceptor of the state.

Office of the *Hsiang-wên* of the state

> *Hsiang-wên* of the state
> Chief supervisor of the state
> General of the state
> Minor general of the state.   46, 23*b*–24*a*

26. MISCELLANEOUS OFFICIALS OF THE NORTHERN REGION

The first ancestor of Liao, Nieh-li,[93] devoted his attention to the matters of agriculture and industry; T'ai-tsu paid still more attention to them.   Stock-raising, hunting, and fishing were highly esteemed practices.[94]   The officials of the workshops, hunting ground, herds, and stables were as follows:[95]

A general list of the titles of officials in the various workshops

> Commissioner of the workshop
> Vice-commissioner of the workshop

Office of the *Hsiang-wên* of the Workshop

> *Hsiang-wên* of the workshop
> Chief supervisor of the workshop

Eagle aviary
Iron workshop
The Five Animal Quarters.[96]   No details.
The eight workshops.   Includes an arsenal.   Others not specified.

The above were officials of the workshops.

Hunting grounds

> Chief grand preceptor of the hunting grounds
> Chief official of the hunting grounds
> Commissioner of the hunting grounds
> Vice-commissioner of the hunting grounds

The above were officials of the hunting grounds.

A general list of the titles of officials in the bureaus

> Commissioner of the bureau
> Vice-commissioner of the bureau

Bureau of Visiting Guests
Bureau of Implements
Bureau of Grand Physician
Veterinary Bureau.   There were chief scribes for the four bureaus.

---

[93] In Ch'ên Ta-jên's 陳大任 *Liao Shih*, written in 1207, the name is given as Ya-li 雅里.   In the much earlier *Veritable Records* the name is Nieh-li 涅里 (LS 63, 7*a*–*b*). According to LS 2, 8*a* and 59, 1*b* T'ai-tsu's grandfather was the first to teach farming to the Ch'i-tan, but LS 48, 17*a* (see XIV, 2 (10)) says "Nieh-li taught them tilling and weaving."   Nieh-li probably lived in the eighth century.

[94] *Cf.* II, introduction.

[95] The original text offers little evidence on order and less explanation.   Our presentation follows the original closely in the arrangement of the material.

[96] The emperor's eagles and falcons were housed in these quarters (see VII, 2 (61); *cf.* also II, 1 (24)), along with other animals.   LS 61, 3*b* and 4*a* speak of wardens "who took care of the animals (掌獸) of the five quarters." These men were probably trained huntsmen.   LS 6, 6*a* mentions several animal attendants who were treated cruelly by Mu-tsung.   Their resentment may possibly account for the rebellion of forty households in the Five Animal Quarters in 965, two years later (LS 7, 2*a*).

The above were officials of the bureaus.

Five smelteries.   No details
    Grand preceptor

The above were officials in the smelteries.

A general list of titles of officials for the herds

Office of the Commissioner of Herds of such-and-such route[97]

    Grand guardian of the herd
    Inner chamberlain of the herd
    Directing secretary of the herd

Office of the General Commissioner of the Herds

    General commissioner of registers of the herds
    Chief scribe of the herds

Office of such-and-such herd

    Commissioner of the herd
    Vice-commissioner of the herd

Office of the Commissioner of Herds in the Western Route
Office of the Commissioner of Herds in the Western Route of Tao-t'a-ling
Office in charge of the Horse Herds North of the Hun River
Office in charge of the Horse Herds South of the Desert
Office in charge of the Horse Herds in the Hua River Region North of the Desert
Office of the Herds of Oxen

The above were officials for the herds.

Imperial stables

    Commissioner of imperial stables
    Vice-commissioner of imperial stables

Department of Flying Dragons[98]

    Commissioner of flying dragons
    Vice-commissioner of flying dragons

Office of the General Director of Horses in All[99] Stables

    General director of horses in all stables

The above were stable officials.

A general list of titles of officials in the Office of the *Hsiang-wên* Supervising Birds and Animals

    Hsiang-wên supervising such-and-such birds or animals
    Chief supervisor supervising such-and-such birds or animals

        Supervisor of such-and-such birds
        Supervisor of such-and-such animals

---

[97] See I, 3, note 18.

[98] 飛龍 was a figurative way of referring to the best horses (*cf.* TS 47, 6*b*).

[99] Literally, "inner and outer," referring to all the stables inside and outside the Supreme Capital.

Office of the *Hsiang-wên* supervising deer
[Office of the *Hsiang-wên*] supervising pheasants

The above were officials who supervised the raising of birds and animals.[100]   46, 6a–9a

2. THE SOUTHERN REGION

1. Offices of the Southern Region set up under Shih-tsung   2. The administration must be differentiated but just
3. Should the two chancelleries be combined?   4. The dual government in action   5. Officials of the Southern Region
6. Officials of the five capitals   7. Economic offices of the five capitals   8. Miscellaneous officials of the five capitals
9. Regional and local government of the Southern Region   10. Financial officials of various regions

1. OFFICES OF THE SOUTHERN REGION SET UP UNDER SHIH–TSUNG

947   In the first year of Ta-t'ung, Shih-tsung for the first time set up a chancellor of
            the Northern Division. In the next year Shih-tsung appointed Kao Hsün as chan-
cellor of the Southern Division.[1] Thus the establishment of the posts of chancellors originated after
950   T'ai-tsung entered Pien.[2] In the fourth year of T'ien-lu the Political Council[3] was
set up. Hence it is possible to write of the officials of the Southern Region.   47, 1a–b

2. THE ADMINISTRATION MUST BE DIFFERENTIATED BUT JUST

1026   In the sixth year of the T'ai-p'ing period an imperial decree was issued, saying,
            "We, taking into consideration the fact that our country comprises Ch'i-tan and
Chinese, therefore administer them separately through the two Divisions of North and South. This
has the aim of doing away with greed and injustice and getting rid of vexations and annoyances.
If there are different laws for the high and the low, grievances are sure to arise. The common people
who commit crimes are quite unable to have the authorities make a report to the court, while the
imperial lineages and the consort lineages often depend on favoritism and offer bribes in the hope of
undeservedly escaping punishment. Thus the laws are flouted. Hereafter, whenever important
imperial relatives are accused of anything, whether it be big or small, an inquiry shall be conducted
by the local officials and a complete report made to the Northern and Southern Divisions, which
shall carry out a reexamination and secure the truth in order to present a memorial to the throne.
Those who make reports without an inquiry and present memorials [on someone's behalf] after
accepting requests for favors shall be punished according to the offence of the original culprit."
                                                                                        61, 6b

3. SHOULD THE TWO CHANCELLERIES BE COMBINED?

1043   Because, according to the national system, the Ch'i-tan and the Chinese were
            administered separately by the northern and southern chancellors, [Hsiao] Hsiao-
chung memorialized, "The reason why the customs are different is that the same country has two
chancellors. If [these offices] were combined into one, the empire would be greatly benefited."
Before this could be brought about he died.   81, 2b

4. THE DUAL GOVERNMENT IN ACTION

When the emperor made his quarterly tours of inspection, the Ch'i-tan high and low and inner and
outer officials, the persons of various classes who provided service, and the offices controlled by the

---

[100] For two reasons this list has been given in full: first, the emphasis on the possession of horses and stockbreeding, which was a significant feature of predynastic Ch'i-tan society, remained so even during the dynastic period; and second, although the introductory note speaks of agriculture as well as of industry, etc., the list itself includes many items related to stockbreeding and some data on handicraft, but no reference to agriculture.

[1] The appointment of Kao Hsün as chancellor of the Southern Division (here equivalent to Region) occurred in the ninth month of the first year of T'ien-lu (LS 5, 2a) that is, still in the same Western year, 947.

[2] The capital of Chin 晉 (936–946), corresponding to present K'ai-fêng, Honan. It fell to Liao in 947.

[3] Nominally this office stood very high. In reality only a few civil affairs were under its control.

Chinese Department of the Master of Court Etiquette all went along.   From the Chinese Chancellery and the Secretarial Council there were selected only one prime minister, the chief and the associate in charge of edicts (two persons) and ten secretarial workers of the Chancellery, and one secretarial worker of the Secretarial Council; and from the Censorate and the Hall of Judicature and Revision one person was selected to go along.

During the first ten days of the first month of every year, when the emperor started out, the officials from the prime ministers down returned to the Central Capital where they remained on duty dispatching all matters concerning the Chinese and appointing officials simply by orders[4] for temporary commissions.   They awaited receipt of orders after discussions in the emperor's temporary residence and then issued the imperial certificates of appointment.   Civil officials from county magistrates and recorders down were permitted to be selected by the Secretarial Council without informing the throne by memorials.   Military officials had to be reported to the emperor.

During the fifth month, when the emperor enjoyed the coolness in his temporary residence, conferences were held with southern and northern officials.   During the tenth month, when the emperor spent the winter in his temporary residence, conferences were similarly held.   32, 3b–4a

5. OFFICIALS OF THE SOUTHERN REGION

The Administration of the Three Teachers[5] . . .

> Grand preceptor . . .
> Grand tutor . . .
> Grand guardian . . .
> Junior preceptor . . .
> Junior tutor
> Junior guardian.   47, 2a–b

The Administration of the Three Dukes . . .

> Grand commandant . . .
> Minister over the masses . . .
> Minister of works.   47, 2b

The Chinese Chancellery originally[6] had the functions of a Ministry of War. . . . At the beginning of T'ai-tsu's [reign] there was a Chinese Bureau.   Han Chih-ku was the general director of affairs for the Chinese Bureau.   When T'ai-tsung entered Pien, he followed Chin in setting up a Chancellery to have charge of the military affairs of the Chinese.   At first it was held concurrently with the Presidential Council.

> Chancellor . . .
> Director of affairs for the chancellor
> Director of affairs for the Chancellery
> Vice-chancellor . . .
> Co-director of affairs for the Chancellery . . .
> Director of affairs for the vice-chancellor . . .
> Assistant amanuensis of the Chancellery . . .

---

[4] The term 堂帖 or 堂帖子 refers to a kind of document issued by the Secretarial Council during the T'ang period. It was the same as the 堂剳子 of the Sung dynasty.   The documents consisted of four sheets signed by the prime minister, who was the chief of the Secretarial Council, and by his subordinate officers (MHPT 1, 3–4).

[5] The titles of the Three Teachers and the Three Dukes and their functions underwent several changes during the first millennium A.D.   By the time of the T'ang dynasty they had completely lost their former impor-tance.   The holders of these titles assisted the emperor in executing his religious functions and discussed the principles of government with him (TS 46).   During the Liao period the positions of the Three Teachers and the Three Dukes were purely honorary.   The historical changes in these titles, which the text reports, are omitted in our translation.

[6] CTKC 16, 3b claims that the Chinese Chancellery was formed as early as 938.

Chief in charge of edicts of the Chancellery . . .
Associate in charge of edicts of the Chancellery . . .
Official in charge of edicts of the Section of Civil Appointments
Official in charge of edicts of the Section of War and Punishments
Superintendent of the Section of Revenue
Superintendent of the Section of the Main Hall; the same as the Ministry of Works.[7]

47, 2b–3b

907–926
950
1044

The Secretarial Council[8] was first called the Political Council.   T'ai-tsu set up the office.   Shih-tsung in the fourth year of T'ien-lu established the Political Council, and Hsing-tsung in the thirteenth year of Ch'ung-hsi changed this name to the Secretarial Council.

Chief of the Secretarial Council[9] . . .
Grand prime minister . . .
Left prime minister . . .
Right prime minister . . .
Director of affairs for the Secretarial Council . . .
Palace chamberlain of the Secretarial Council . . .
Associate administrator of affairs for the Secretarial and Court Councils[10] . . .
Associate director of political affairs.[11]   47, 3b–4b

The Court Council

Inner chamberlain . . .
Permanent chamberlain.[12]   47, 5a

The Presidential Council.   T'ai-tsu at one time set up left and right presidents.

Chief of the Presidential Council[13] . . .
Left lord high chamberlain . . .
Right lord high chamberlain.[14]   47, 7a

A general list of the titles of officials of the Six Ministries . . .

President of such-and-such Ministry . . .
Palace chamberlain of such-and-such Ministry . . .
Palace gentleman of such-and-such Ministry . . .
Supernumerary gentleman of such-and-such Ministry.   47, 7b

---

[7] Some explanation of these titles is attempted in the introduction to this section.

[8] At first this was perhaps the most powerful office of the Southern Region. Gradually, however, it lost its importance, until finally positions in the bureau were merely honorary ranks bestowed on great officials (LTCNP 8045–8068).

[9] This official, reflecting the earlier name of his office, was originally called the chief of the Political Council (政事令).

[10] This official was originally called the associate administrator of affairs for the Political and Court Councils (同政事門下平章事). The title was established in 634 when the high chamberlain, Li Ching 李靖, was ill and resigned. He was ordered to administer the affairs of the Secretarial Council every two or three days after his recovery (TS 46, 1b).

[11] Thirteen titles listed.

[12] Five titles listed.

[13] T'ai-tsung, the second emperor of the T'ang dynasty, had once borne this title. Therefore the T'ang officials did not dare to accept it, and it was replaced by the title of lord high chamberlain (TS 46, 1b). The Liao government, not restrained by the taboo, used both terms.

The titles of left and right president may have been set up only temporarily by T'ai-tsu. They do not appear in the list of officials under the Presidential Council.

Liao, imitating T'ang, had three leading ministers, the chief secretary, inner chamberlain, and chief president. The last two were inferior to the first. During the early part of the Liao dynasty the chief secretary largely controlled the civil affairs of the Southern Region.

[14] Nine titles listed.

The Censorate . . .

    Chief censor . . .
    Assistant censor.   47, 7b–8a

The Han-lin Academy was in charge of the literary affairs of the emperor.

    Chief scribe[15] of the Han-lin . . .
    Scribe of the Southern Region . . .
    Amanuensis of the Han-lin in charge of edicts . . .
    Amanuensis of the Han-lin . . .
    Libation officer of the Han-lin . . .
    Director of decrees . . .

Han-lin Painting Department . . .
Han-lin physicians.   47, 8b–9a

The Department of National Historiography

    Supervisor of national history . . .
    Amanuensis in the Bureau of Historiography . . .
    Editor in the Bureau of Historiography . . .
    Compiler in the Bureau of Historiography.[16]   47, 9a

The Department of the Master of Court Etiquette[17] was established by T'ai-tsung in the first year of the Hui-t'ung period.

    Master of court etiquette
    Director of affairs for the Department of the Master of Court Etiquette . . .
    Vice-master of court etiquette.   47, 9b–10a

The Guest Council[18] was established by T'ai-tsung in the first year of the Hui-t'ung period.

    Chief of the Guest Council . . .
    Commissioner of the Guest Council . . .

Hostels for the Four Quarters[19]

    Commissioner of Hostels for the Four Quarters . . .
    Vice-commissioner of Hostels for the Four Quarters.   47, 11a–b

A general list of the titles of officials of the Halls

    Chief executive . . .
    Junior executive . . .

Hall of Sacrificial Worship . . .
Hall of Banqueting . . .
Hall of Imperial Equipment . . .
Hall of the Imperial Clan . . .

---

[15] See above, XIV, 1, note 75.

[16] After this section the *Liao Shih* also lists a number of halls and libraries, the Hsüan-chêng 宣政 Hall, the Kuan-shu 觀書 Hall, the Chao-wên Library 昭文館, the Ch'ung-wên Library 崇文館, and the Ch'ien-wên Library 乾文閣, which were generally staffed with poets and writers. According to PCKT 2, 25, Chu Yü 朱彧 declared that many features of the Liao administration were imitations of Sung institutions. For instance, after the Sung government had entrusted the Lung-t'u Library 龍圖閣 with the preservation of the emperor's writings, the Liao government established the Ch'ien-wên Library for scholars who were charged with definite literary tasks.

[17] This office was in charge of court banquets during the Chin period (CS 56, 3a). It was possibly the same in the Liao dynasty.

[18] *Cf.* X, introduction.

[19] That is, hostels for guests coming from all directions.

Hall of the Imperial Stud . . .
Hall of Judicature and Revision . . .
Hall of State Ceremonial
Hall of Granaries.   47, 12a–13a

A general list of the titles of officials of the Boards

        Grand supervisor . . .
        Junior supervisor . . .

Board of Imperial Archives . . .
Board of Astronomy . . .
Imperial Academy . . .
Board of the Government Treasury
Board of the Imperial Treasury
Board of Imperial Construction
Board of Waterworks.   47, 13a–14b

The Administration of the Three Teachers of the Heir Apparent . . .

        Grand preceptor of the heir apparent . . .
        Grand tutor of the heir apparent . . .
        Grand guardian of the heir apparent . . .
        Junior preceptor of the heir apparent. . .
        Junior tutor of the heir apparent. . .
        Junior guardian of the heir apparent . . .

Department of the Heir Apparent's Guests . . .
Department of the Heir Apparent's Superintendents . . .
Office of the Heir Apparent's Overseers . . .
Left Palace of the Heir Apparent . . .

    Hall of Literary Studies . . .
    Bureau of Classics . . .
    Bureau of Ceremony . . .
    Bureau of Palace Gates . . .

Right Palace of the Heir Apparent . . .

    Hall of the Heir Apparent's House-master . . .
    Hall of the Heir Apparent's Time-keeper . . .
    Hall of the Heir Apparent's Stud . . .

Administration of the Retinue of the Heir Apparent   47, 15b–18b

Administration of the Tutors of the Princes . . .
Administration of the Personal Secretaries of the Imperial Princes . . .

    Hall of Literary Studies of the Princes.   47, 18b–19a

6. OFFICIALS OF THE FIVE CAPITALS

Liao had five capitals. At the Supreme Capital, which was the imperial capital, there were officials of the court and officials of the capital. In the other four capitals officials were set up according to circumstances. The system was not uniform. In general the Western Capital possessed mainly officials for frontier defense, while the Southern Capital and the Central Capital possessed mainly officials for finance and taxation.   48, 1a

A general list of titles of officials in the Administrations of the Prime Ministers of the three capitals[20]

> Left prime minister
> Right prime minister
> Left administrator of political affairs
> Right administrator of political affairs.   48, 1a–b

Administration of the Prime Minister of the Eastern Capital . . .
Administration of the Prime Minister of the Central Capital
Administration of the Prime Minister of the Southern Capital.   48, 1b

7. ECONOMIC OFFICES OF THE FIVE CAPITALS

Office of the Salt and Iron Commissioner of the Supreme Capital
Office of the Commissioner of the Ministry of Revenue of the Eastern Capital
Office of the Financial Commissioner of the Central Capital
Office of the Commissioner of the Triple Office of the Southern Capital
Office of the Transportation Commissioner of the Southern Capital.   Also called the Office of the Transportation Commissioner of Yen-ching
Office of the Accountant of the Western Capital.   48, 2b

8. MISCELLANEOUS OFFICIALS OF THE FIVE CAPITALS

Offices of the Vicegerents of the five capitals who were concurrently mayors . . .

> Vicegerent of a capital managing the affairs of a mayor . . .
> Assistant vicegerent of a capital.   48, 2b

Administrations of the Chief General Officers[21] of the Five Capitals.   48, 3b

Offices of the Chief Commissioners of Investigation[22] of the Five Capitals.   48, 4a

Police Departments of the Five Capitals.   48, 4b

Offices of the Commissioners of Habitations of the Five Capitals.   48, 5a

Office of the Guardian Commissioner of the Supreme Capital.   Also called the commissioner of the imperial city of the Supreme Capital.[23]   48, 5b

9. REGIONAL AND LOCAL GOVERNMENT OF THE SOUTHERN REGION

East and west of the Liao [River] commanderies and counties had already been set up and official posts established during the time of Yen,[24] Ch'in, Han, and T'ang.   Korea and Po-hai followed this. At the time of the Liao dynasty five capitals were established; they embraced all the territory of Yen and Tai[25] and all became imperial domains.   For more than two hundred years[26] walled cities and suburbs were in sight of each other and the wilderness was increasingly cultivated.   The main

---

[20] These offices were limited to the Eastern, Central, and Southern Capitals. Their administrations were taken from both the Chinese and Po-hai systems.

[21] Under the Chin dynasty this office was concurrently held by the mayor. The office, which existed in the capital and other large cities, was in charge of the city's soldiers, horses, armor, and weapons (CS 57, 10a).

[22] In ancient times the 虞候 had charge of mountains, marshes, and rivers, but later he became a military official.

[23] This official had charge of opening and closing the gates (cf. SS 166, 6b) and seems to have acted as some sort of guardian of the city.

[24] The administrative organization of the country into 郡 and 縣 (commanderies and counties), as opposed to the ancient feudal system, spread to northeast China at the time of King Chao 昭王 of the feudal state of Yen.   King Chao was well known for his administrative achievements. He seems to have been the first ruler to set up commanderies in the region north and northeast of Hopei (Fêng CS 35, 12 ff.).

[25] Corresponding to present northern Hopei and northern Shansi.

[26] This refers to the period of the Liao empire, from 907 to 1125.

[prefectures] were headed by commanding prefects, the lesser ones by supervisory prefects, defence prefects, and trainband prefects, and the subdivisions by prefects and county magistrates. In general the T'ang system was taken over.

Among these [prefectures] the families of the emperor's relatives, the empress' relatives, and the high officials built cities which were given names by the emperor. They were called "entrusted prefecture-commanderies." The commanding prefects alone were appointed by the court. Later all gradually reverted to the royal administration.   48, 9b

Commanding prefects[27] . . .

> Commanding prefect of a prefecture or commandery
> Vice-commanding prefect of a prefecture or commandery
> Co-director of affairs for the commanding prefect.   48, 9b–10a

Supervisory prefects . . .

> Supervisory prefect of a prefecture or commandery
> Vice-supervisory prefect of a prefecture or commandery
> Supervisory assistant of a prefecture or commandery.   48, 13a–b

Trainband prefects . . .

> Militia trainband of a prefecture
> Vice-trainband prefect of a prefecture.   48, 14a–b

Defence prefects . . .

> Defence prefect of a prefecture
> Vice-defence prefect of a prefecture.   48, 14b

Prefects of prefectures . . .

> Prefect of a prefecture
> Co-director of affairs for a prefecture.   48, 15a–b

A general list of the titles of county officials

> Magistrate of a county
> Assistant magistrate of a county
> Registrar of a county . . .
> Commandant of a county.   48, 16a

In the counties there were [exacted] services for the courier post, for [supplying] horses and oxen, for banners and drums,[28] for the village heads,[29] for the official attendants, for granaries and others.
48, 16b

10. FINANCIAL OFFICIALS OF VARIOUS REGIONS

To the Liao state, herding, hunting, and fishing were like agriculture. The financial officialdom was at first very simple, but after tilling and weaving were taught by Nieh-li and after [it obtained] the salt and iron bounties [its wealth] increased day by day. When Yen and Tai were taken over, it became much wealthier.

---

[27] The term for this office was taken over from the T'ang dynasty, but the power of the commanding prefect of T'ang was much greater. Toward the end of the T'ang period the post developed into that of an independent governor-general. During the Liao dynasty, however, the commanding prefect was merely the leading official in a first-class prefecture. The text gives a list of the prefectures for which commanding prefects and similar officials were appointed.

[28] The duties of the special officers responsible for banners and drums are not clearly defined.

[29] This term is the only item of local government mentioned in the text. A local gazetteer reports that the man who owned the most property in his village was selected as the head of the village. He was responsible for holding discussions on distributing fields from the rich to the poor (LWT 2, 5a).

A general list of the titles of officials in the Offices of Money and Silk

Chief superintendent[30] of money and silk in such-and-such prefecture . . .

Office of Money and Silk of Ch'ang-ch'un Route[31] . . .
Office of Money and Silk of Liao-hsi Route[32]
Office of Money and Silk of the Route of P'ing Prefecture[33]

A general list of the titles of officials in the Transportation Offices

> Commissioners of transportation
> Vice-commissioners of transportation
> Co-director for commissioners of transportation
> Assistants in transportation

Office of the Chief Commissioner of Transportation of Shan-hsi Route[34] . . .
Office of the Commissioner of Transportation of Fêng-shêng Prefecture[35]
Office of the Commissioner of Transportation of Yü Prefecture[36]
Office of the Commissioner of Transportation of Ying Prefecture[37]
Office of the Commissioner of Transportation of Shuo Prefecture[38]
Office of the Commissioner of Transportation of Pao Prefecture[39] . . .
Commissioner of Transportation of Hsi-shan.   48, 17a–18a

3. SELECTION OF OFFICIALS

1. A predynastic hereditary position   2. Appointment of Liao nobles   3. Various hereditary positions   4. Hereditary offices   5. The examination hall of the Southern Capital   6. The *chin-shih* examination   7. Hereditary imperial doctor   8. After successfully passing the examinations   9. Ch'i-tan may not take the Chinese examinations   10. Topics for the *chin-shih* examination   11. Transfer of officials   12. Selection of tribesmen   13. Groups ineligible for the *chin-shih* degree   14. A Ch'i-tan enjoys the *yin* privilege   15. Capable scholars to be recommended   16. Colleges established   17. Fraudulent registration   18. Imperial Academy established   19. A disputed office   20. The rank of the worthy and good   21. Examination questions   22. The *yin* prerogative contested   23. I-hsin attempts to establish new prerogatives   24. Transfer and placement of officials   25. Transfer and promotion of officials   26. Officials' relatives appointed   27. Buying positions with grain   28. *Chü-jên* selected   29. Selection of officials by throwing dice   30. Merchants may not become *chin-shih*

1. A PREDYNASTIC HEREDITARY POSITION

About 800   Hu-mu-li, ancestor of the fifth generation [of Hsiao Ti-lu], was once, in the time of
                 Yao-lien reign, sent as envoy to T'ang.[1]   He was detained at Yu Prefecture by T'ang.
One night he broke through the passes and fled home.   Henceforth [the members of his family]
held the hereditary position of judges.[2]   73, 4a

2. APPOINTMENT OF LIAO NOBLES

928   On the day *ting-wei* [of the twelfth month in the second year of T'ien-hsien, T'ai-
                 tsung] ordered the selection of the descendants of the Nine Tents of the Yao-lien
family who were able to assume office.   3, 2a

---

[30] To illustrate the existence of the position of chief superintendent (都點檢) the text mentions Ta Kung-ting as holding the office of chief intendant (都提點). Obviously the second term was either considered identical with the first or else it was mentioned in error.

[31] Roughly the region west of the Sungari River.

[32] Roughly the region of eastern Jehol.

[33] Roughly the northeastern part of Hopei.

[34] Approximately Suiyuan and northern Shansi.

[35] Modern Cho-lu 涿鹿 County, Chahar.

[36] Modern Yü 蔚 County, Chahar.

[37] Modern Ying 應 County, Shansi.

[38] Modern Shuo 朔 County, Shansi.

[39] Modern Wiju 義州, Korea.

[1] Since Hsiao Ti-lu flourished at the beginning of the tenth century, his ancestors of the fifth generation may have lived around 800.   This would place him well within the period of the Yao-lien rule, which began in the middle of the eighth century.

[2] The term 決獄官 (judge) probably is a Chinese equivalent of the Ch'i-tan title *i-li-pi*.

3. VARIOUS HEREDITARY POSITIONS

951–969   Hsiao Hu-ssŭ's style was Yen-ning.   For generations the members of his family had been minor officials of the Northern Division. . . .   At this time, because they were being accused, many of the princes were thrown into prison.   The emperor, feeling that Hu-ssŭ was talented, ordered him to make a thorough investigation.   Accordingly this was done.   [Therefore] his position was changed to that of chancellor of the Northern Division.   An order was also issued that [his descendants] might have the hereditary prerogative of selection to the post of prime minister.   But Hu-ssŭ refused, saying, "Whether or not my sons and grandsons will be qualified is not known.   It is sufficient if I may have the position of commissioner of the Guest Council."   This was approved.   78, 2a

4. HEREDITARY OFFICES

Yeh-lü Hsieh-li whose style was P'o-tan was a native of the T'u-lü-pu tribe.   [The members of his family] hereditarily held the position of low functionaries. . . .

951–969   In the beginning of the Ying-li period the position of ling-wên was set up in his tribe.   Hsieh-li was given this position as hereditary [for his family].[3]   76, 1a–b

5. THE EXAMINATION HALL OF THE SOUTHERN CAPITAL

977   On the day mou-wu [of the twelfth month in the eighth year of Pao-ning] an imperial edict ordered the Southern Capital to restore the examination hall of the Ministry of Rites.[4]   8, 5b

---

[3] According to a report given to the Sung court in the eleventh century by Fu Pi, the Ch'i-tan kings, generals, and prime ministers were generally chosen from close relatives of those in power (HSSS 5b).

[4] Shih Fang is said to have obtained the chin-shih degree between the years 938 and 947 (LS 79, 1a), but only after 977 is concrete information on the Liao examination system available.   The restoration of the examination hall in the Southern Capital evidently marked the commencement of a growing interest in this important Chinese institution. The first examination for the chin-shih after 977 is said to have been held eleven years later (see the subsequent translated passage no. 6).   After 988 the holding of the metropolitan (chin-shih) examinations is reported in the Liao Shih at intervals of one to several years.   The Ch'i-tan Kuo Chih, in a general description of the Liao examination system, mentions that poetry and the classics were required topics.   From Shêng-tsung on, law replaced the classics (CTKC 23, 5a).   An account of the examination system of the Chin dynasty notes that the following subjects were identical with those demanded in Liao time: the classics, commentaries to the classics, philosophy, and history (YTCH 5, 6a).

From 988 on, the chronological section (pên chi) of the Liao Shih contains regular statements concerning the holding of the chin-shih examinations and the number of successful candidates.   These data provide a detailed picture of the development of the institution in the middle and the later part of the dynasty.

YEAR	NUMBER OF chin-shih	REFERENCE IN Liao Shih
988	1	12, 4a
989	2	12, 7a
990	2	13, 2a
991	1	13, 3a
993	2	13, 4a
994	2	13, 5b
995	2	13, 7a
996	3	13, 7b–8a
997	2	13, 9b
998	2	14, 1b
999	4	14, 2a
1000	3	14, 2a–b
1002	6	14, 4a
1004	3	14, 6a
1006	23	14, 7b
1008	13	14, 8a
1009	3	14, 8a
1011	2	15, 3b
1012	19	15, 4a
1013	6	15, 7b
1014	31	15, 8a
1016	48	15, 10b
1019	37	16, 2b
1021	45	16, 5b
1022	47	16, 7b
1024	47	16, 9b
1025	72	17, 1b
1028	57	17, 6a
1029	22	17, 7b
1031	57	18, 1b

6. THE *CHIN-SHIH* EXAMINATION

988   In this year [the sixth year of T'ung-ho] an imperial edict ordered that examinations [for the *chin-shih* degree] be held.   One candidate attained the degree.   12, 4*a*

7. HEREDITARY IMPERIAL DOCTOR

1005   During the T'ung-ho period the prime minister, Han Tê-jang, was honored and favored.   [Hsiao] Ti-lu to please the emperor suggested that [Han] Tê-jang should be given a national name and registered in the Horizontal Tents.   Henceforth he [and his family] enjoyed the hereditary prerogative of selection to the post of grand physician.   As for his descendants who had the same privilege, many of them entered government service.   101, 3*b*

8. AFTER SUCCESSFULLY PASSING THE EXAMINATIONS

1025   On the day *kêng-tzŭ* of the eleventh month [in the fifth year of T'ai-p'ing], when the emperor attended a banquet in the inner orchard, the people of the capital[5] thronged to look on.   He was seeking for [holders of] the *chin-shih* degree and obtained seventy-two persons.   They were ordered to compose poems in order to grade their capabilities.   Fourteen persons, Chang Yü and others, were appointed proofreaders to the heir apparent, and the other fifty-eight persons, Han Luan and others, were appointed proofreaders in the Ch'ung-wên Library.

17, 1*b*

9. CH'I-TAN MAY NOT TAKE THE CHINESE EXAMINATIONS

1032–1055   During the Ch'ung-hsi period [Yeh-lü P'u-lu][6] tried to obtain the *chin-shih* degree, but the director of the examination,[7] holding that the national statutes contained no regulation permitting a Ch'i-tan to take the *chin-shih* examination, reported the case to the emperor. Because Shu-chên had allowed his son to enter the examination illegally, he was punished by two hundred lashes with a whip.   89, 2*a–b*

10. TOPICS FOR THE *CHIN-SHIH* EXAMINATION

1036   On the day *jên-tzŭ* [of the tenth month in the fifth year of Ch'ung-hsi the emperor] presided at the Yüan-ho Hall[8] and gave as [topics for] the *chin-shih* examination in

YEAR	NUMBER OF *chin-shih*	REFERENCE IN *Liao Shih*
1032	57	18, 4*a*
1036	49	18, 6*a*
1038	55	18, 8*a*
1042	64	19, 2*b*
1046	68	19, 7*b*
1050	No number given	20, 4*b*
1055	44	21, 3*a*
1059	115	21, 6*a*
1062	93	22, 1*a*
1066	101	22, 4*b*
1070	138	22, 6*b*
1074	No number given	23, 2*b*
1079	113	24, 1*b*
1083	51	24, 5*b*
1086	26	24, 7*a*
1090	72	25, 4*a*
1092	53	25, 5*a*
1095	130	26, 2*a*
1100	87	26, 6*a*
1103	103	27, 3*b*
1107	100	27, 5*a*
1109	90	27, 5*b*
1112	77	27, 7*a*
1118	103	28, 6*b*

The legitimate Liao government held the last metropolitan examination in 1118.   In 1122 and 1122/3, the rebel "emperor," Ch'un, and his widow bestowed the *chin-shih* degree upon nineteen and one hundred and eight persons respectively (LS 30, 2*b*), evidently as a demonstration of their loyalty to the established tradition.

The institutional meaning of these figures is discussed together with other aspects of the Liao examination system in the introduction to this section.

[5] The Southern Capital where the emperor arrived in the ninth month.

[6] Yeh-lü P'u-lu was a son of Yeh-lü Shu-chên.   The latter and his brother, Shu-ch'êng, were Ch'i-tan scholars who were well-known for their prose writings and poetry. In their political careers they attained the rank of scribes (LS 89, 1*a*–2*b*).

[7] The term 主文, which may designate a document based upon a legal decision, was also used for a person in charge of the *chin-shih* examination.

[8] In the Southern Capital.

the court a *fu*, "Shooting thirty-six bears in one day," and a *shih*, "An imperial visit to Yen."   He granted the *chin-shih* degree to forty-nine men, including Fêng Li and Chao Hui. . . . The conducting of the *chin-shih* examination by the emperor himself began at this time.   18, 6a

11. TRANSFER OF OFFICIALS

1042   [On the first day *jên-yin* of the seventh month in the autumn of the eleventh year of Ch'ung-hsi it was ordered] that the regional officials who worked hard and honestly should be given another position after the completion of their office assignments had been verified. Those who did not devote themselves to their duty should be replaced immediately.   19, 3a

12. SELECTION OF TRIBESMEN

1047   [On the day *hsin-yu* of the second month in the sixteenth year of Ch'ung-hsi] it was decreed that, as regards hereditarily selected officials, from the elders of each tribe those who had ability should be chosen and employed.   20, 1a

13. GROUPS INELIGIBLE FOR THE *CHIN-SHIH* DEGREE

1050   On the day *jên-shên* [of the sixth month in the nineteenth year of Ch'ung-hsi] it was decreed that doctors, diviners,[9] butchers, peddlers, slaves, unfilial children, and criminal fugitives were not to be permitted to take the examination for the *chin-shih* degree.   20, 4b

14. A CH'I-TAN ENJOYS THE *YIN* PRIVILEGE

1055–1062   [Yeh-lü] Yin-chi[10] was held in awe; he was inclined toward righteousness.   Through the *yin* privilege, he was appointed to office.[11]   97, 2b

15. CAPABLE SCHOLARS TO BE RECOMMENDED

1056   On the day *ting-ssŭ* of the sixth month [in the second year of Ch'ing-ning] an imperial decree ordered the prime ministers to recommend gifted and capable scholars.[12]

21, 3b

16. COLLEGES ESTABLISHED

1059   A general list of the titles of officials in the colleges of the five capitals.[13]   In the fifth[14] year of Ch'ing-ning of Tao-tsung an edict was issued to establish colleges to

---

[9] The Liao government followed the Chinese in discriminating against the Chinese doctors and diviners. Ch'i-tan diviners and doctors, however, were treated differently.   They might even be granted high positions (*cf.* LS 108, 2a–b).

[10] See I, 3, note 13.

[11] The nature of the office is not disclosed.   The possible significance of this record is discussed in the introduction to this section.

[12] Talented descendants of Ch'i-tan and Chinese officials were urged to study Chinese calligraphy, the classics, and history.   After 1005 the Liao envoys and reception officials were selected from persons versed in Chinese literature and history (HCLY 77, 10b).   When Ou-yang Hsiu, in 1055, went to the Liao court, the Liao reception officials were selected from among the educated nobles, and the Liao emperor told Ou-yang Hsiu that he was treated with special honor because of his scholarly attainments (MSYTL 2, 11).

From 1111 to 1118 a Sung official, Tu Ch'ung 杜充, acted as an envoy to Liao.   Just prior to this time the Sung titles for prime ministers, the left and right *p'u-yeh* 左右僕射, had been changed to *t'ai-tsai* 太宰 and *shao-tsai* 少宰.   A member of the Liao escort inquired about the

origin of the new terms.   Tu countered with the impolite question: "Have you ever read the *Chou Li?*"   The Liao official replied ironically that the chapter of the *Chou Kuan* (*Chou Li*) dealing with this subject mentioned only one *t'ai-tsai*, who assumed the post of prime minister, while two *shao-tsai* assisted him.   Hence the two offices evidently could not have been equal in status.   Tu was embarrassed and did not know how to answer (CSP 2, 111). Obviously the Liao spokesman implied that the Sung system did not follow the classical pattern.

The episode shows that certain officials at the Liao court were thoroughly familiar with the standard Chinese writings.   Their nationality is not revealed, but it may be assumed that at least a considerable number of them were Chinese.

[13] At the old site of the Central Capital the fragment of a stone tablet has been discovered, on which the term, 學宮 is still recognizable.   Whether the imperial princes only were taught in this "School-palace," or whether it was open also to the descendants of officials we do not know. *Cf.* Torii 36 IV, pl. 335.

[14] This date is probably wrong, as information similar to that in our present passage is placed by LS 21, 3a in the twelfth month of the first year of Ch'ing-ning (1055/6).

train scholars and to disseminate the classics and their commentaries. There were set up [for each college] one erudit and one assistant. 48, 5*a*

The college of Huang-lung Administration[15]

Erudit
Assistant   48, 8*b*–9*a*

The college of Hsing-chung Administration[16]

Erudit
Assistant   48, 9*a*

Prefectural colleges

Erudit
Assistant   48, 13*b*

County colleges . . .

Erudit
Assistant.   48, 16*a*–*b*

17. FRAUDULENT REGISTRATION

1060   On the day *jên-hsü* of the twelfth month [in the fifth year of Ch'ing-ning] . . . the associate director of political affairs, Wu Chan, who had fraudulently registered the name of his brother [Wu] Hsün, in the list of officials, was deprived of his rank and made a commoner. 21, 6*a*

18. IMPERIAL ACADEMY ESTABLISHED

1060   On the day *ping-yin* [in the sixth month of the sixth year of Ch'ing-ning] the Imperial Academy was inaugurated in the Central Capital. Former sages and teachers were ordered to be worshipped at the proper season. 21, 6*b*

19. A DISPUTED OFFICE

1069   On the day *ting-mao* of the eleventh month [in the fifth year of Hsien-yung] it was decreed that the post of vice-commissioner of Hostels for the Four Quarters[17] was to be filled only by a Ch'i-tan.[18] 22, 6*b*

20. THE RANK OF THE WORTHY AND GOOD

1070   On the day *chia-yin* [of the fifth month in the sixth year of Hsien-yung] the rank of the worthy and good[19] was inaugurated. It was decreed that those who intended to acquire this rank should first submit a hundred thousand words of their writings. 22, 6*b*

21. EXAMINATION QUESTIONS

1074   On the day *mou-ch'ên* of the sixth month [in the tenth year of Hsien-yung] the emperor himself chose the subjects for the *chin-shih* examination. On the day *jên-shên* he decreed that courtiers and commoners should discuss the accomplishments and shortcomings

---

[15] Modern Nung-an 農安 County, Kirin.

[16] Modern Ch'ao-yang 朝陽 County, Jehol.

[17] Meaning the four directions of the Liao world.

[18] The Hostels for the Four Quarters belonged to the Guest Council whose principal officials were Uighur and Ch'i-tan (*cf.* LS 47, 11*a*).

[19] The term *hsien liang* 賢良, the worthy and good, is short for *hsien liang fang chêng* 方正, the worthy, good, foursquare, and upright. Both versions go back to the Han dynasty when they were used to designate persons who, because of their outstanding qualifications, were likely to be recommended to governmental positions. These men might be private individuals of only local reputation. Others who were already in office might be promoted to higher posts (*cf.* HS 49, 16*a*; 56, 1*a*; 58, 1*a*; 64*A*, 1*a*; 72, 3*a*; 77, 1*a*; see also HHHY 44, 1*a*–3*b* and NESKI 2, 19*b*–20*a*). Our text does not offer a definition of "the worthy and good," but both LS 22, 6*b* and 23, 2*b* point to men of high literary training.

[of the government].   On the day *ping-tzǔ* the emperor presided in the Yung-an Hall and gave the examination questions to the worthy and good.   23, 2*b*

22. THE *YIN* PREROGATIVE CONTESTED

1075   The sons of Wang Pang-yen contended for the *yin* prerogative.   For several years [the dispute] could not be settled.   The officials responsible reported to the throne. The emperor ordered [Hsiao] Wên to make an inquiry.[20]   The case was immediately decided.

105, 2*b*

23. I-HSIN ATTEMPTS TO ESTABLISH NEW PREROGATIVES

1077   On the day *chia-shên* [of the second month in the third year of Ta-k'ang] it was decreed that the chancellor of the Northern Division, the Prince of Wei, Yeh-lü I-hsin, his elder brother by the same mother, Ta-nu, and his younger brother by the same mother, A-ssǔ, had the hereditary prerogative of selection to the positions of northern and southern chancellors, and that his other brothers by different mothers had the hereditary privilege of selection to the positions of *i-li-chin*.   23, 5*a*

24. TRANSFER AND PLACEMENT OF OFFICIALS

1083   On the day *chi-wei* [of the eleventh month in the ninth year of Ta-k'ang] the different ranks for the transfer and placement of secretarial workers and translators were fixed.[21]   24, 5*b*

25. TRANSFER AND PROMOTION OF OFFICIALS

1085   On the day *i-wei* of the eleventh month [in the first year of Ta-an] an imperial decree said, "Recently, the officials outside the capital[22] have been promoted in rank for good reputations.   But if they hold office for a long time without being transferred, their misconduct would cause the people to suffer.   From now on, they should be transferred according to their qualifications."   24, 6*b*

26. OFFICIALS' RELATIVES APPOINTED

1086   On the day *jên-tzǔ* [of the sixth month in the second year of Ta-an] the brothers and sons of officials from the highest[23] down to the county magistrates and record keepers were all made eligible for official appointment.   24, 7*b*

27. BUYING POSITIONS WITH GRAIN

1088   On the day *ting-yu* [of the fourth month in the fourth year of Ta-an] the law that eligibility to official positions might be obtained by offering grain was established.

25, 2*a*

28. *CHÜ-JÊN* SELECTED

1089   On the day *kuei-yu* of the third month [in the fifth year of Ta-an] an imperial edict ordered Hsi-chin Administration and Ta-ting Administration[24] to select the *chü-jên*[25] carefully and to make a report.   25, 3*a*

---

[20] We follow the Palace edition in reading 詰 for 誥.

[21] No description of this system is given in the *Liao Shih* account of the government organization.   We can therefore only assume that the positions mentioned had a special regional and hierarchical order according to which the officials were shifted and promoted.

[22] Those holding official posts outside the five capitals were usually not so easily promoted as those in the capitals, since the chances of obtaining information and of exerting influence were stronger in the latter.

[23] The glossary of LS 116, 12*a* explains 高墩 as a term applied to the highest officials who stood, according to their positions, on the beacon-mound during the official ceremonies.

[24] Respectively the Southern Capital, corresponding to modern Peiping, and the Central Capital, corresponding to modern Tsaghan Suburghan in central Jehol.

[25] The term *chü-jên* 舉人 was differently used before and after the Ming dynasty.   During the T'ang, Sung, and Liao periods the term loosely designated a student

29. SELECTION OF OFFICIALS BY THROWING DICE

Before 1101   During his last years the emperor[26] became old and languid.   In appointing officials, as he could not select them himself, he had each of them throw dice in order to select the winners and make them officials.   Once [Yeh-lü] Yen[27] won.   The emperor exclaimed, "This is a sign of a prime minister!"   He was promoted to the position of director of affairs for the Chancellery,[28] granted the honorific title of meritorious dignitary managing the country and aiding the imperial mandate, and enobled as Duke of Yüeh.   98, 3b

30. MERCHANTS MAY NOT BECOME *CHIN-SHIH*

1105   On the day *mou-hsü* of the eleventh month [in the fifth year of Ch'ien-t'ung] the families of merchants were forbidden to participate in the competition for the *chin-shih* degree.   27, 4b

4. SPECIFIC GOVERNMENT FUNCTIONS

1. Punishments 2. Books and paintings 3. Early traditions compiled 4. Calendars 5. Biographies composed 6. Laws translated 7. *Veritable Records* presented 8. *Veritable Records* 9. Formal equalization of the law 10. Material for *Daily Records* 11. *Daily Records* 12. Punishments 13. Grades of punishment 14. Revision of the laws 15. Horse-stealing 16. Aim of national historiography 17. Compilation of history 18. Duty of a good historiographer 19. History, Rituals, Laws 20. Books translated 21. Historiographers omitted from court discussion 22. Ban on private publications 23. Library supplemented 24. Changes in the laws 25. Publication of *Shih Chi* and *Han Shu* 26. Bureau of historiography 27. Emperor disregards secrecy of the *Diaries* 28. *Veritable Records* presented 29. The classics studied 30. Old laws restored 31. Offensive historiography 32. *Veritable Records* ordered compiled 33. *Veritable Records* compiled

1. PUNISHMENTS

After 907   In the early years of T'ai-tsu everything was in an initial stage.   Those who committed a crime were punished according to its seriousness.   Afterwards, when his brothers and rebels were to be punished, laws were temporarily set up.   Imperial princes[1] who joined the rebels were not[2] strangled by the huntsmen, but were killed by being thrown from a cliff. Those who committed incest and treason were pulled to pieces by five chariots.   Those who turned against their parents were punished in the same way.   Those who offended against superiors by slander and vilification were killed by having a hot iron[3] awl thrust into their mouths.

Accomplices were punished by beatings in accordance with the seriousness of the crime.   Beatings were of two degrees: the heaviest was of five hundred lashes and the lightest of three hundred lashes.

There were also the punishments of decapitation, hacking into pieces, burial alive, shooting by devil arrows, being hurled from catapults, and dismembering.   These belonged to the most severe punishments.   They were a precaution against rebellion by the people.   61, 2b–3a

2. BOOKS AND PAINTINGS

Before 930   Previously Pei purchased up to ten thousand *chüan* of books.[4]   These books were preserved in Wang-hai Hall at the summit of I-wu-lü Mountain.[5]   He was versed in

---

who was admitted to the examination for the *chin-shih* degree.   Later it was applied to a person who had passed the examination for the second degree (JCL 16, 35).

[26] Tao-tsung, who died in 1101.

[27] Yeh-lü Yen 儼 (T. 若思), a native of the Southern Capital, was the last compiler of the *Veritable Records* of the Liao dynasty (LS 98, 2b–3b).

[28] Presumably in the Southern Region (LS 98, 3b).

[1] We follow other editions in reading 王 for the 主 of our text.

[2] We would expect the text to read: "If imperial princes joined a rebellion, they were strangled by huntsmen

親王從逆則磬諸旬人," parallel to the *Li Chi* 公族其有死則磬于旬人 (LCCS 20, 12b).   Perhaps 不 is an error for 則, in which case 或 should be translated as "or" instead of "but."   The former *yü-yüeh*, Ho-ti-li 赫底里, and his son, Hsieh-li 解里, who joined a rebellion, were strangled (*cf.* XIII (10) and LS 112, 2a–b).

[3] We change the 熟鐵 (wrought iron) of our text to 熱鐵 (hot iron), for the latter seems more appropriate in making the punishment fit the crime.

[4] Pei was the eldest son of T'ai-tsu.   His book collecting was done previous to his flight from Liao in 930.

[5] Northwest of modern Pei-chên 北鎮 County, Liaoning.

the principles of *yin* and *yang*,[6] understood music, was skilled in medicine, acupuncture, and cauterizing, and was proficient in composing Liao[7] and Chinese essays. He once translated the *Secret Charm Scripture*[8] [into Ch'i-tan]. He was adept at painting the national [Ch'i-tan] figures; and such pictures as the Shooting Cavalry, Hunting Cavalry,[9] Snow Cavalry, and One Thousand Deer were all included in the Imperial Museum of Sung.   72, 2b–3a

3. EARLY TRADITIONS COMPILED

941   On the day *ting-ssŭ* [of the second month in the fourth year of Hui-t'ung] an imperial decree ordered the officials to compile the traditions concerning the first ancestor, Ch'i-shou Khaghan.   4, 6b

4. CALENDARS

947   In the first year of Ta-t'ung, when Emperor T'ai-tsung took from Pien, the capital of Chin, the officials of all offices, the specialists, the calendar, and the observatory and transferred them to the Central Capital,[10] then Liao for the first time had a calendar. Previously [Later] Liang and [Later] T'ang had used the Ching-fu and Ch'ung-hsüan Calendars of T'ang,[11] but in the fourth[12] year of T'ien-fu of [Later] Chin the chief of the Astro-

939   nomical Board, Ma Ch'ung-chi,[13] had presented to the emperor the I-wei-yüan[14] Calendar, which was entitled the T'iao-yüan Calendar. This was what T'ai-tsung took away from Pien.

961   In the eleventh year of Ying-li of Mu-tsung, the astronomical officials, Wang Pai and Li Chêng, offered a calendar which was probably the I-wei-yüan Calendar.

994   In the twelfth year of T'ung-ho of Shêng-tsung the prefect of K'o-han Prefecture,[15] Chia Chün, offered a new calendar which was the Ta-ming Calendar.[16] The *Ta Liao Ku-chin Lu*, which was presented[17] by Korea, says that in the twelfth year Liao for the first time issued its own calendar. This is proof that they had changed calendars.   42, 1b–2a

5. BIOGRAPHIES COMPOSED

Before 949   At this time someone selected contemporary distinguished persons and wrote the *Biographies of the Seven Worthy Persons*, [Yeh-lü] Hou[18] being one among them.

77, 4b

---

[6] For a discussion of these principles and the magic practices based on them see Fung 37, 159 ff., 165 ff. and de Groot 18, 364 ff.

[7] Ch'i-tan.

[8] A Taoist book.

[9] According to the *Hsüan-ho Hua-p'u* 宣和畫譜, fifteen paintings done by Pei were preserved in the Imperial Museum of Sung. Among these were the *Shê-ch'i-t'u* 射騎圖, *Lieh* (獵) *-ch'i-t'u*, and *Hsüeh* (雪) *-ch'i-t'u*. Therefore we read the word *ch'i* after the *lieh* of our text.

When Pei took refuge in the territory of Later T'ang, he carried with him a large library. He delighted in painting Ch'i-tan nobles who held spears and crossbows. The figures in his pictures wore barbarian clothes; their saddles and bridles were strange and differed from those used by the Chinese. He did not paint Chinese clothes. Connoisseurs found his horses heavy. In general, they considered his style lacking in vigor (HHHP 8, 230–232).

For some specimens of Liao art see figures 1, 6, 8, 39, 40, and 41.

[10] In 947 Chên 鎮 Prefecture was set up as the Central Capital. This place, which corresponds to modern Chêng-ting 正定 County, Hopei, was afterwards lost by Liao. In 1007 another Central Capital was created by Shêng-tsung (see XI (15)). According to LS 4, 15a, the

booty was taken to the Supreme Capital; this seems highly probable.

[11] That is, the two calendars used in the T'ang period (*cf.* CWTS 96, 10a; HCLY 33, 9a).

[12] According to CWTS 96, 10a and WTS 57, 13b, the calendar was presented to the Chin emperor in the third year of T'ien-fu (938), and in the next year it was issued by the emperor. Owing to its inaccuracies, it was discontinued after a few years.

[13] Ma Ch'ung-chi 馬重績 (T. 洞微) worked out the T'iao-yüan Calendar on the basis of two T'ang calendars, the Hsüan-ming 玄明 and Ch'ung-hsüan 崇玄 Calendars (CWTS 96, 10a).

[14] I-wei 乙未 refers to the year 755, the year with which the calendar started.

[15] Modern Huai-lai 懷來 County, Chahar.

[16] As this calendar was presented in the sixth year of Ta-ming 大明 of Emperor Hsiao-wu 孝武 of Sung (462), it was designated the Ta-ming Calendar. The author was Tsu Ch'ung-chih 祖冲之 (T. 文遠, 429–500). This calendar is contained in Sung 13 and LS 42.

[17] We follow LS 44, 39a in reading 進 for the 志 of our text.

[18] A descendant of the Six Divisions who assisted Shih-tsung to ascend the throne in 947. He died in 949 (LS 77, 4a–b).

FIG. 39. Flowers and birds painted by Hsiao Yung, a Liao artist (KKSHC, fasc. 3).

6. LAWS TRANSLATED

983 [On the day *jên-tzŭ* of the fourth month in the first year of T'ung-ho] the chancellors asked that an edict command the minister over the masses of the Northern Administration, [Yeh-lü] P'o-tê, to translate[19] the code of laws which had been offered by the Southern Capital. This was approved.   10, 3*b*

7. *VERITABLE RECORDS* PRESENTED

991 On the day *i-yu* [of the first month in the ninth year of T'ung-ho] the chancellor and supervisor of national history, Shih Fang, and others presented the *Veritable Records*.[20] They were awarded gifts according to their ranks.   13, 2*a*

8. *VERITABLE RECORDS*

991 [Shih Fang] memorialized on presenting twenty *chüan* of the *Veritable Records* which had been compiled. The emperor personally wrote a decree to praise him, promoted him to be the chief of the Political Council, and granted him six hundred bolts of silk.

79, 1*b*

9. FORMAL EQUALIZATION OF THE LAW

994 On the day *kêng-wu* [of the seventh month in the twelfth year of T'ung-ho] it was decreed that those Ch'i-tan who committed one of the ten crimes should be [punished] according to Chinese law.   13, 5*a*

10. MATERIAL FOR *DAILY RECORDS*

1003 On the day *jên-ch'ên* of the third month [in the twenty-first year of T'ung-ho] it was decreed that the officials who compiled the *Daily Records*[21] were not to record trifling matters.   14, 4*a*

11. DAILY RECORDS

1011 On the first day *chia-hsü* of the fifth month [in the twenty-ninth year of T'ung-ho] an imperial decree ordered that the events which had been reported should be sent to the office concerned to be placed in the *Daily Records*.   15, 3*a*

12. PUNISHMENTS

1032 In the first year of Ch'ung-hsi an imperial decree ordered that officials in service who committed a public offence were allowed to make redemption. Those who committed a personal crime were subject to the regular law. If their descendants and kinsmen received bribes without the knowledge of the officials, then only the culprits were subject to punishment.

Previously the Triple Office of the Southern Capital [ordered] that those who made three catties of utensils by melting coins, took ten strings of cash out of Nan-ching, or stole property worth five strings from a house which was on fire were to be sentenced to death. Now the death penalty was applied to those who melted over three catties of bronze or took away cash or stolen goods [valued at] twenty strings and more.   62, 1*b*

13. GRADES OF PUNISHMENT

1033 In the second year [of Ch'ung-hsi] the officials,[22] memorializing on a decree of the first year, said, "A person who commits a serious crime and is sentenced to hard

---

[19] The translation was presumably from Chinese into Ch'i-tan.

[20] The *Veritable Records* (*shih lu* 實錄) are the first draft of the collected data of the Office of National Historiography. They are particularly valuable to the later historian because they are close to the original documents. They form the main material for the later *Dynastic Histories*, the *chêng-shih* 正史 (*cf*. Gardner 38, 91 ff.).

[21] The *jih-li* 日曆 (*Daily Records*), written day by day by special court historians, were the material for the first draft of the later *Veritable Records*, from which the dynastic history was written.

[22] We follow other editions in reading 司 for the 可 of our text.

labor for life in addition is given a beating and moreover is tatooed on the face. That is, he commits one crime but suffers three punishments. The tatooing should be eliminated. In the case of the officials in service and the families of prime ministers and commanding prefects who have the hereditary prerogative to selection, if their descendants are given sentences up to hard labor for unlawful acts, are they to be exempted from tatooing or not?"

The emperor instructed, "Transgressors who have repented and reformed are sometimes useful persons too. Once tatooed on the face they are disgraced for life. We greatly pity them. Hereafter criminals sentenced to hard labor for life shall be tatooed only on the neck. In the case of escaped slaves who have stolen their masters' possessions, the masters may not tatoo their faces without authorization, but are permitted to tatoo the arms and necks. In the case of people who commit theft or robbery, the first time they are to be tatooed on the right arm, the second time on the left arm, the third time on the right side of the neck, and the fourth time on the left side of the neck. After the fifth offence they are to be sentenced to death."[23]   62, 1b–2a

14. REVISION OF THE LAWS

1036   In the fifth year [of Ch'ung-hsi] the revision of the regulations was completed. An imperial decree ordered the authorities to decide upon the audience day for their presentation;[24] then they were issued and put into use in all circuits. They included laws and orders from T'ai-tsu down and embodied the foregoing regulations.[25] The punishments were of five[26] kinds, namely death, banishment, beating, and hard labor in three degrees.[27] In all there were 547 items.

62, 2a

15. HORSE-STEALING

1036   At this time herdsmen who stealthily altered the government's brand and turned over a horse to someone else were, according to the law, to be punished by death. The emperor[28] said, "Is it not excessive to kill two[29] men for one horse?" The punishment was made one degree less than death.   62, 2a

1042   On the first day *jên-yin* of the seventh month in the autumn [of the eleventh year of Chung-hsi] it was ordered that those who stole or exchanged the government horses should be punished one degree less than death.   19, 2b–3a

16. AIM OF NATIONAL HISTORIOGRAPHY

Before 1044   [Hsiao Han-chia-nu] was promoted to be chief scribe of Han-lin and concurrently the compiler of national history. The emperor instructed him, saying, "The task of literary writing is the glory of the nation. An ungifted person would not be employed. Because of your literary knowledge you are a great scholar of the present, and you are therefore given the post of Han-lin. Our daily life[30] should all be recorded accurately."   103, 4b

17. COMPILATION OF HISTORY

1044   On the day *ping-shên* [of the sixth month in the thirteenth year of Ch'ung-hsi] an imperial decree ordered the former great king of the Southern Division, Yeh[31]-lü

---

[23] According to NKCML 13, 9a, under the Liao dynasty a man who committed theft for the first time was tatooed (or branded ? 文) with the word thief (賊) on his wrist, the second time on his arm, the third on his elbow, the fourth on his back; the fifth time he was decapitated.

[24] Reading 摯 for the 執 of our text.

[25] This refers to the regulations of the Ch'ung-hsi period mentioned in the *Liao Shih* before the present passage.

[26] The text speaks of five penalties, but like LS 61, 1b enumerates only four. The Chinese had five kinds of punishment. Whether in our text one of the five Chinese

penalties, light beating (笞), has been omitted, or whether 五 (five) is an error for 四 (four) we do not know.

[27] According to LS 61, 1b, the three degrees were life, five years, and one and a half years.

[28] We follow other editions in reading 帝 for the 常 of our text.

[29] Presumably the two men were the herdsman who stole the horse and the person who received it.

[30] Literally, "rising and resting," or, as Gardner translates, "activity and repose" (Gardner 38, 88).

[31] We follow the Palace edition in reading 耶 for the 即 of our text.

Ku-yü,[32] and the chief scribe of the Han-lin, Yeh-lü Shu-ch'êng,[33] to compile the history of the country from previous generations down to the present day.   19, 6a

1044   [Yeh-lü Ku-yü] received an imperial decree to collaborate with the scribes, Yeh-lü Shu-ch'êng and Hsiao Han-chia-nu, in compiling the history of the early[34] generations and the *Veritable Records* of all the emperors of the Liao empire.   Before it was completed, he died.

104, 4b

1044   [Hsiao Han-chia-nu], together with Yeh-lü Shu-ch'êng, was ordered to record the traditions from the Yao-lien Khaghans down to the period of Ch'ung-hsi.   These were compiled in twenty *chüan* and presented to the emperor.   103, 5b

18. DUTY OF A GOOD HISTORIOGRAPHER

1044   [Hsiao] Han-chia-nu, whenever he saw the emperor go out hunting, never failed to reprove him.   It happened[35] that the officials reported that during the hunt in the autumn mountains[36] several tens of men were killed by bears and tigers.   [Hsiao] Han-chia-nu wrote it into the records.   On seeing it the emperor ordered it to be deleted.   After [Hsiao] Han-chia-nu had come out [of the palace],[37] he wrote it in again.   Later, when the emperor saw it, he remarked, "This is what historiography should be like!"   103, 5a

19. HISTORY, RITUALS, LAWS

After 1044   [Yeh-lü Shu-ch'êng] collaborated with the scribe, Hsiao Han-chia-nu, and others in compiling the *Veritable Records* and the *Book of Ceremonies*, and with the vice-chancellor, Yeh-lü Tê, in revising the laws.   The emperor issued a decree to Yeh-lü Shu-ch'êng, saying, "At present the laws are inequitable, being too heavy or too light.   Laws, being primary in government and concerned with man's life, should not be handled carelessly.   You should weigh the light and the heavy in order to revise them in accordance with expediency."

Yeh-lü Shu-ch'êng, consulting the past and the present and correcting the errors, completed a book, and presented it.   The emperor read and praised it.   89, 1a–b

20. BOOKS TRANSLATED

Ca. **1046**   When the emperor again ordered the translation of books, Hsiao Han-chia-nu, desiring the emperor to know about successes and failures in the past and present, translated the *T'ung Li*,[38] *Chên-kuan Chêng-yao*,[39] and *Wu-tai Shih*.[40]   103, 5b–6a

21. HISTORIOGRAPHERS OMITTED FROM COURT DISCUSSION

1056   On the day *hsin-wei* [of the sixth month in the second year of Ch'ing-ning] the participation of the historiographers in court discussions was abolished.   They were to ask the prime ministers [what to put down] and then do the writing.   21, 3b

---

[32] This Ch'i-tan noble was well versed in composing essays.   He was one of the literary friends of Hsing-tsung (LS 104, 4a–b).

[33] A man who mastered the Chinese language as well as that of his own people.   He wrote poetry and translated books from Chinese into Ch'i-tan (LS 89, 1a).

[34] That is, predynastic.

[35] In 1044, according to LS 103, 4b.

[36] This is probably a general term for whatever mountains the emperor happened to hunt in during the autumn (LS 32, 2b).

[37] Presumably the deletion was ordered in the presence of Hsiao Han-chia-nu, who waited until he was out of sight of the emperor before again placing the notice of the event in the records.

[38] 通曆 a simple general history originally written by Ma Tsung 馬總 of the T'ang dynasty and later revised. The existing book is incomplete.

[39] 貞觀政要 a dialogue about administration between T'ang T'ai-tsung and his courtiers, written by Wu Ching 吳兢 (670–749).

[40] LS 103, 1b says Hsiao Han-chia-nu first became an official in the fourteenth year of T'ung-ho (996), and LS 103, 6a adds that he died at the age of seventy-two.   His translation of the works mentioned above was made about 1046 (*cf.* LS 103, 5b).   The *New History of the Five Dynasties* was not published until after the death of the author, Ou-yang Hsiu, in 1072 (SKTY 46, 36–37).   Hence the *Wu-tai Shih* translated by Hsiao Han-chia-nu must have been the "old" version.

22. BAN ON PRIVATE PUBLICATIONS

1064   On the day *mou-wu* [of the tenth month in the tenth year of Ch'ing-ning] the people were forbidden to publish literature privately.[41]   22, 3a

23. LIBRARY SUPPLEMENTED

1064   On the day *ting-ch'ou* [of the eleventh month in the tenth year of Ch'ing-ning] an imperial decree ordered a search for books lacking in the Ch'ien-wên Library and commanded the scholarly courtiers to collate them.[42]   22, 3a

24. CHANGES IN THE LAWS

1070   In the sixth year [of Hsien-yung] the emperor, considering that the customs of the Ch'i-tan and the Chinese were not the same and that the national law should not be applied indiscriminately, therefore ordered the *t'i-yin* Su and Chancellor [Yeh-lü] I-hsin to revise the regulations. Those which were in harmony with the laws and orders were all recorded, and those which were not were separately preserved.

At this time the revision officials in going over the old Ch'ung-hsi regulations[43] changed the item that the theft, burglary, or embezzlement of twenty-five strings of money was to be punished by death, increasing the amount to fifty strings before applying the death penalty. They also took out two items which were duplications,[44] leaving 545 items. They adopted 173 items of law and created in addition 71 items, making a total of 789 items. Adding the newly formulated ones, the total reached more than a thousand items. These were listed according to classifications.

1075–1085   The [additional laws] decided on during the Ta-k'ang period were also compared with the [previous] laws and regulations, and 36 items were again added. Later, as matters came up, they referred continuously [to the new laws], until the third year of Ta-an, when 67 items were added.

1087

Since the items were numerous, the officials responsible for litigation were unable to learn them, and the ignorant people could not know how to avoid [punishment]. The people who violated laws became numerous, and the officials were able to cooperate in doing evil. Therefore, in the fifth year an imperial decree was issued, saying, "Law must give the people confidence if the country is to be peaceful. It should be as simple as heaven and earth and as permanent as the four seasons, so that the people may avoid [punishment] but may not violate [the laws].

1089

"When the officials were ordered to compile the penal law, they were unable to understand Our purpose clearly. They made many items to trap people in crime. We highly disapprove of this. Hereafter the old laws should be used again, and the rest should all be cancelled."   62, 3a–b

---

[41] The Liao and Sung governments strictly forbade writings composed by their respective subjects to be exported to the other country. The Liao prohibition was particularly severe: a man who sold or exported Liao books or writings to Sung territory was executed (MHPT 15, 100). In 1006 the Sung government announced that except for the Nine Classics the sale of books abroad was prohibited (SS 186, 23b). It is more than probable that both governments sought to protect their political and military secrets by such measures.

Envoys, however, were exempted from the restrictions; it was through them that writings of the prohibited type were carried across the border. About 1036 a poem, *Ssŭ Hsien I Pu-hsiao* 四賢一不肖, which dealt with the achievements and the disreputable deeds of contemporary Sung officials, was written by a Sung official, Ts'ai Ching 蔡靖. A Ch'i-tan envoy bought it secretly. In 1059, when Chang Chung-yung 張中庸 came as an envoy to the Liao territory, he found the poem pasted on the wall of his lodge in the Southern Capital (FWCKWC 6, 71; MSYTL 2, 12).

[42] Bibliographies compiled by Ch'ing and modern scholars contain not more than two hundred books written, edited, preserved, and compiled under the Liao government. This figure, however, does not indicate the number which existed within the Liao empire, but only our fragmentary information on the point. T'ai-tsu's eldest son, Pei, owned a library which totalled some ten thousand *chüan* (see above, (2); CTKC 14, 2a). If so much reading matter was accumulated by one prince at the beginning of the dynasty, it may be taken for granted that the number of books in all imperial libraries must have been considerably greater later on.

[43] These regulations refer to the law code of the Ch'ung-hsi period. See above, (14).

[44] 復 is used in the same sense as 複 (double).

25. PUBLICATION OF *SHIH CHI* AND *HAN SHU*

1074 On the day *ting-ch'ou* [of the tenth month in the tenth year of Hsien-yung] an imperial decree ordered the officials to publish the *Shih Chi* and *Han Shu*. 23, 3a

26. BUREAU OF HISTORIOGRAPHY

1075–1084 [Yeh-lü Mêng-chien] visited the court and presented a memorial saying, "It has been almost two hundred years since the establishment of our dynasty. We should have a national history to transmit to later generations."

Then he made a compilation of the deeds of Yeh-lü Ho-lü, Yeh-lü Wu-chih, and Yeh-lü Hsiu-ko and presented it.

The emperor ordered the setting up of a bureau to compile [the national history]. [Yeh-lü] Mêng-chien said to the other officials. "Historical writing is the great truth of the world. Whether a word is true or not, it will be followed by a hundred generations. If you do not possess prudence, and if you are personal in your likes and dislikes, disaster may come unexpectedly. Thus Tso, Ssǔ-ma Ch'ien, Pan Ku, and Fan Yeh all suffered misfortune.[45] How can you not be careful?"

104, 3b–4a

27. EMPEROR DISREGARDS SECRECY OF THE *DIARIES*

1076 On the day *chia-hsü* of the eleventh month [in the second year of Ta-k'ang], when the emperor wanted to see the *Diaries of Activity and Repose*,[46] the recorders, Pu-tien and Hu-t'u-chin, did not present them. Each was given two hundred lashes and discharged, and the scribe, Hsiao Yen-shou, was banished to the Wu-wei tribe. 23, 4b

28. *VERITABLE RECORDS* PRESENTED

1085 On the day *hsin-hai* [of the eleventh month in the first year of Ta-an] the historiographers presented [to the throne] the *Veritable Records* of the seven emperors from T'ai-tsu down. 24, 6b

29. THE CLASSICS STUDIED

1086 On the day *kuei-ch'ou* [of the first month in the second year of Ta-an the emperor] summoned the acting amanuensis of the Han-lin, Chao Hsiao-yen, and the associate composer of imperial edicts, Wang Shih-ju, to expound the general principles of the Five Classics.[47]

24, 7a

1088 On the day *kuei-mao* [of the fourth month in the fourth year of Ta-an], while on a journey to the west, the emperor summoned the assistant amanuensis of the Chancellery, Yeh-lü Yen, to expound the Great Plan from the *Documentary Classic*. 25, 2a

On the day *hsin-hai* of the fifth month [in the fourth year of Ta-an], Prince of Yen, Yen-hsi,[48] was ordered to copy the Songs of the Five Sons from the *Documentary Classic*. 25, 2a

30. OLD LAWS RESTORED

1089 On the day *i-ssǔ* of the tenth month [of the fifth year of Ta-an], because the newly established laws were too complicated,[49] the old laws were put into effect again.

25, 3b

31. OFFENSIVE HISTORIOGRAPHY

1096 In the second year of Shou-lung, [Liu Hui][50] again submitted a memorial to the throne. It said, "Ou-yang Hsiu[51] of Sung in compiling the *History of the Five*

---

[45] These historians all suffered personal punishments. Ssǔ-ma Ch'ien was castrated, Pan Ku was thrown into prison and died there, and Fan Yeh was executed. Tso, presumably Tso Ch'iu-ming, was said to have become blind.

[46] *Cf.* Gardner 38, 88.

[47] The *Book of Changes, Documentary Classic, Book of Odes, Spring and Autumn Annals*, and *Book of Rites*.

[48] The later T'ien-tsu.

[49] See VII, 1, note 70.

[50] Liu Hui 劉輝 obtained the *chin-shih* degree in 1079 and was made librarian of the heir apparent at the end of the Ta-an period.

[51] Ou-yang Hsiu 歐陽修 (T. 永叔, 1007–1072), the great Sung scholar and writer, among other things, aided in compiling the *Hsin T'ang Shu*.

Dynasties attached our country to [the section on] the 'Four Barbarians.' In it he rabidly heaps contumely upon us.[52]   Yet the Sung people, who thanks to the generosity of our country are permitted to enjoy peace, should practice the courtesy which is proper between brothers.[53]   Now, on the contrary, a subordinate official is allowed to write history thoughtlessly and with blissful ignorance.   Your servant requests permission to append a detailed early history of the Chao family[54] to the history of our own country."

The emperor praised his words.   104, 3*a*

32. *VERITABLE RECORDS* ORDERED COMPILED

1103   [On the day *i-ssŭ* of the eleventh month in the third year of Ch'ien-t'ung the emperor] summoned the supervisor of national history, Yeh-lü Yen, to compile the *Veritable Records* of T'ai-tsu and the other emperors.   27, 3*b*

33. *VERITABLE RECORDS* COMPILED

[Yeh-lü Yen] was promoted to be director of affairs for the Chancellery, granted the honorific title of meritorious minister managing the country and aiding the imperial mandate, and ennobled as Duke of Yüeh.   He compiled the *Veritable Records* of the imperial dynasty in seventy chapters.[55]

98, 3*b*

---

[52] The present *Wu-tai Shih* 五代史 consists of seventy-four *chüan*.   The seventy-second and seventy-third *chüan* have a special section on the Ch'i-tan in which they are described as very primitive, brutal, and savage.   In 1207 the "old" history of the Five Dynasties, the *Chiu Wu-tai Shih* 舊五代史, was put aside by the Chin emperor, Chang-tsung, and the *Wu-tai Shih* from then on became the standard history of that period (SKTY 46, 35 ff.).

[53] In the treaty concluded in 1005 the emperors of Liao and Sung addressed each other as brothers.

[54] The imperial family of the Sung dynasty.   The motive for appending the history of Sung to the history of Liao was to indicate the inferiority of Sung to Liao and to give the story of the infamous seizure of the throne from the young emperor of Later Chou.   Perhaps they also wished to record the sudden death of the founder of the Sung dynasty who, according to contemporary rumors, was murdered by his brother, T'ai-tsung.

[55] This work was still extant in four incomplete manuscript copies in the Ming dynasty (SSTML 1, 24).

SECTION XV

ARMY AND WARFARE

INTRODUCTION

1. THE ARMY—WEAPON OF CONQUEST AND DOMINATION

a. THE MILITARY ASPECT OF CONQUEST SOCIETY

Conquest is a matter of armed force. The military is employed (or its use threatened) when an invader attacks and seizes a country. The military is employed (or its use threatened) when a conqueror seeks to transform temporary victory into permanent domination. A conqueror's army may not be the sole cause of his success; but, no matter what the socio-political frame, the military base of conquest cannot be questioned. An institutional study of any society that neglects the organization of the army and warfare is incomplete; an institutional study of a society of conquest that disregards the military factor is misleading.

b. AN ERA OF CAVALRY SUPERIORITY

The next to last Liao emperor claimed that the Ch'i-tan "made the world tremble with [their] power," because they "surpassed others in riding and shooting."[1] Superiority in horsemanship and archery indeed brought to the fore a new type of mounted warrior, whose attacks, from the middle of the first millennium A.D. on, challenged the traditional balance of power in all parts of the Old World. The revolutionary rise of the cavalry occurred after many centuries of experiment with saddle and harness; but most particularly it was the improved stirrup that made the horse a military weapon of extraordinary effectiveness.

As early as 852 B.C. a crude board supported the foot of a royal Assyrian rider,[2] and in the last centuries before the turn of the era a leather foot sling was depicted on certain Scythian[3] and Indian[4] monuments.

The "true stirrup"[5] may have been carried from Inner Asia to China sometime between A.D. 200 and 400[6]; it was in general use by 477[7] according to a biography of a Chinese officer of the Liu Sung and Southern Ch'i dynasties;[8] it appears in a T'o-pa Wei relief dated 554.[9] At approximately the same time it is documented for western Asia and southern Europe: Byzantium,[10]

---

[5] Term used by Coomaraswamy (loc. cit.).

[6] Pelliot 26, 262. According to Pelliot, the nomads of Central Asia, who taught the Chinese the art of riding, may also have invented the stirrup (loc. cit.). Le Coq (25, 22) thinks that the innovation was probably made by a people of good horsemanship who roved far, or by a non-riding people who quickly learned how to ride in order to combat their mounted enemies.

[7] NS 45, 11a. The incident in which the stirrup (馬鐙) is mentioned is undated, but the very next sentence which continues the story places the action consequent on its receipt in the winter of 477. In his discussion Hirth (90, 209) dates the reference before 477; Pelliot (26, 259) about 477. Pelliot's formulation seems preferable.

[8] Chang Ching-êrh 張敬兒, the protagonist of the biography, grew up in the region of modern Têng-chou 鄧州 (southern Honan) where the natives at the close of the Liu Sung dynasty (420–479) were known to have excelled in mounted archery 風俗出騎射 (NS 45, 9b). Chang, a superior horseman and brilliant officer, was given a stirrup as a signal for military action. The story indicates, as Hirth and Pelliot have noted, that the stirrup must have been in general use at that time; otherwise its appearance would have caused suspicion (Hirth 90, 209; Pelliot 26, 259). Laufer's attempt to prove the presence of the stirrup in China in the Han period (Laufer 09, 230, note 2) is rejected by Pelliot because of the spurious nature of the evidence (Pelliot 26, 260 and 261, note 1).

[9] Chavannes 14, 20–25 and pls. XL and XLI; see also Pelliot 26, 261.

[10] The stirrup is mentioned in [Pseudo-] Mauricius' Strategikon (see Oman 24 I, 187; Lammert 29, 2239; Schrader 29). Obviously the work was not written by the Byzantine emperor Mauricius himself, but, according to Lingenthal (94, 441), during his reign. The attempts by Vári (06, 80 ff.) and others to place the origin of the Strategikon in the eighth century have been rejected as "quite perverse" by Bury (31 II, 75, note 2), who considers it "quite clear that it was composed after the reign of Justinian and before the institution of the system of Themes. . . . Thus we get as outside limits A.D. 565–615" (similarly Ensslin 30, 2394). Other internal evidence makes Oman (24 I,

---

[1] XV, 2 (20).

[2] Unger 27, 30, fig. 41. Unger (28, 392) calls this device "the oldest stirrup of antiquity," but the arrangement seems to have been casual and improvised. Later representations of Assyrian horsemen do not show any stirrup-like equipment. See idem 27, fig. 60, 65, 76, 98.

[3] According to Hellenistic Scythian objects in Russian collections (Arendt 34, 206 ff.).

[4] Lefebvre des Noëttes 31, 231 and fig. 263; confirmed by Coomaraswamy (32, 85).

Persia,[11] Hungary,[12] and Arabia;[13] and somewhat later for western[14] and northern[15] Europe.

---

174) ascribe the composition of the *Strategikon* to the year 579. Several wooden panels in the Coptic Church of Abu Sargah in Alexandria show horsemen, Byzantine style, with stirrups. Originally Butler (84 I, 191) dated the carvings eighth century, but several decades later he redated them "sixth century" (*idem* 25, 28), evidently because of the change in Coptic art from figure-carving to "flat geometrical and arabesque designs" after the Arab conquest (*loc. cit.*). This seems indeed to suggest the sixth or the early part of the seventh century as the latest possible date for the figure panels in the Church of Abu Sargah.

[11] A mounted hunter is depicted on a Sassanid silver bowl found in South Russia and tentatively placed in the fourth or fifth century by Hampel (85, 90); Pope and Ackerman (38, 217) ascribe the piece to the Sassanid or Parthian period. But the absence of stirrups on other Sassanid objects of art (*op. cit., passim;* Ettinghausen and Schroeder 41, fig. 0417–0420, 0422 and 0424) supports Lefebvre des Noëttes (31, 235, fig. 291) in ascribing it to the seventh century, that is, to the close of the dynasty.

[12] According to archeological finds, the stirrup appears in Hungary as early as the "Avaric" epoch, in the seventh century (Hampel 85, 181; *cf. idem* 05 I, 217 and II, 344 ff., and III, table 265).

[13] The Arabs possessed saddles for camels and horses when the great era of conquest began (see Mufaddalīyāt 18, 10, 12, 18, 21, 26 and *passim;* see also Ṭufail 27, 4, 8, 13, 19, and 27; Ibn Ishak 64 II, 222, 227, 287, 323, 324; and Tabari 71, 63, 168, 169, 247 and *passim*). They maintained close contact with their Byzantine and Persian neighbors (O'Leary 27, 110 ff., 153 ff., 179 ff.) who used the stirrup before the Arab attacks of the seventh century (see above). Arabs fought in the ranks of the Byzantine and the Persian armies of the sixth century (see Procopius 14 I, 159, 161 ff., 181, 261, 421 ff., 511). Small wonder therefore that they "copied the Romans [Byzantines] in most of their military practices, both in arms and in strategy" (Leo, *Tactica* 18, 120 = Oman 24 I, 209). In the second half of the sixth century the poet al-Muthaggib (Brockelmann 37, 56) speaks of the camel's *gharz* (Mufaddalīyāt 18, 105, poem 28, verse 10). According to Lyall, the word may have meant "stirrup," but Lyall follows an Arabian commentator in explaining *gharz* as "girth," because "the camel-saddle . . . has no stirrup (see description by Euting in *Orientalische Studien* pp. 393–398), nothing but a cushion for the foot to rest on" (Mufaddalīyāt 18, 108, note). If Euting's assertion is correct for the Arabian world (it does not hold for Central Asia, where a camel stirrup similar to the horse stirrup was employed), then the Arab camel rider supported his foot by a device which, though different in form from the horse stirrup, fulfilled the same function. Jacob (97, 69) does not hesitate to translate the word *gharz* in the passage under discussion as "camel stirrup." The oldest known biography of Mohammed mentions the *gharz* twice as part of a camel's trapping in an incident that occurred around A.D. 630. Weil renders the word as "stirrup,"

which translation fully agrees with the context (Ibn Ishak 64 II, 267). Dr. G. E. von Grunebaum is convinced that in all these quotations "*gharz* means camel stirrup" (letter of April 12, 1943; in a second letter, dated April 1, 1944, Dr. Grunebaum draws our attention to a passage in al-Mubarrad's *Kāmil* [ed. W. Wright, Leipzig 1864–1892, 509, 1.4] in which the prophet is described as riding "with his feet in his stirrup (*gharz*);" the recorded event occurred in the year 625).

Arabian horses in the seventh century seem to have been equipped with wooden stirrups; around A.D. 700 al-Muhallab replaced them with iron stirrups (al-Mubarrad, *Kāmil* [675] = Yusuf 43, 2).

During the period of the conquest and afterwards the saddle and fighting weapons were closely associated. The dating of the records which state that 'Umar I (634–644) forbade the subjugated Christians to own riding saddles and weapons (Kremer, CO I, 103; Tritton 30, 7) has been disputed (*op. cit.*, 115). Other texts incontestably dated early in the next century depict the Arabs as extremely saddle-conscious. The poet Aṭ-Ṭirimmāh (d. before 734) sings of horse and camel saddles, describing in some detail their general appearance and ornamentation (Aṭ-Ṭirimmāh 27, 32, 73, and particularly 40). In 712 the first Arabian invaders of India are said to have upheld laws that denied the use of the saddle to certain national groups in northwestern India (Chach-náma 67, 151 and 187). 'Umar II (719–720) did not permit his Christian subjects to have riding saddles (Bar Hebraeus 32 I, 109) or horses. Similar restrictions were announced by the chief judge Abū-Yūsuf (d. ca. 798) and by Hārūn in 813 (Tritton 30, 116). Later, saddles of special design were permitted but the stirrup had to be made of wood (Bar Hebraeus 32 I, 184; Tritton 30, 118, and 120).

Pictorial documentation for the history of the saddle is practically non-existent for the first century of the Arab empire, probably because of the negative attitude of the Arabs to this kind of expression (see Ibn Khaldoun, PH II, 365). Figure-carving in which the Egyptians had excelled in the fifth and sixth centuries "fell out of favor at the Arab conquest" (Butler 25, 28). Nevertheless, the earliest artistic evidences of the saddle with stirrup in western Europe are Arabian in origin or influence. An ivory set of chessmen presented to Charlemagne by Hārūn al-Rashīd contained knights with saddles and stirrups (Lefebvre des Noëttes 31, 236 and figs. 366–368); the same equipment is pictured in a drawing of the apocalypse in a Latin manuscript composed about 840 in Valencia, that is, in Arab-controlled Spain (*op. cit.*, 237 and fig. 294).

[14] Having presented the evidence discussed above (*cf.* note 12), Lefebvre des Noëttes concludes his survey of the ninth to twelfth centuries by saying: "To judge from the pictorial documents, the diffusion of the new elements of the harness, particularly of the stirrup, was very slow in the Occident" (*op. cit.*, 238). The statuette of Charlemagne reproduced by Lefebvre des Noëttes (31, fig. 277) shows the emperor seated in a saddle without stirrups.

But, if the new cavalry techniques spread slowly to western Europe, they were accepted still more slowly on English soil. Oman (24 I, 149) calls the battle of Hastings

For the Chinese of the seventh, eighth, and ninth centuries there is abundant evidence for the use of the stirrup; artists drew it,[16] and statesmen referred to it in their social regulations.[17]   Turkic and Khirghiz tombs of the seventh and eighth centuries contain iron stirrups[18] as well as bronze effigies of horsemen so accoutered.[19]   A painting from the seventh or eighth century[20] found in Turkestan near Khotan depicts a camel-rider using a "true" stirrup[21] and—less distinctly—a horseman similarly equipped.[22]   In Korea the stirrup is documented from the seventh century on.[23]

Many aspects of the spread of the stirrup still need clarification, but there can be no doubt that the invention made the cavalryman "far more formidable,"[24] for it provided him with "the support which was almost indispensable for exerting force in attack."[25] A mounted archer supported by a saddle with stirrups could aim better and pull harder than a stirrup-less horseman.   A horseman seated on a saddle with stirrups could wield his sword with greater accuracy and strength.   The lance, formerly used chiefly

as a missile, became a dangerous weapon of shock attack.[26]

The potentialities of the new invention[27] were quickly recognized.   In the middle of the sixth century the Byzantine historian, Procopius, refuting conservative critics, defended the mounted bowman, that product of "modern improvements," who was able to shoot in all directions and could "draw the bowstring along the forehead about opposite the right ear, thereby charging the arrow with such an impetus as to kill whoever stands in the way, shield and corcelet alike having no power to check its force."[28]   In the Far East the second Sui emperor, Yang (605–618), stated categorically: "The reason for the superiority of the Turks is that they rely primarily on mounted archers."[29]

An era of cavalry superiority began,[30] in the course of which the old centers of higher agricultural civilization either accepted the new technique and used it successfully, or else were over-run and conquered by their powerful mounted neighbors.   The history of military innovation reveals that an initial one-sided advantage is frequently only temporary: the value of

---

"the last great example of an endeavor to use the old infantry tactics of the Teutonic races against the now fully-developed cavalry of feudalism" (see also Delbrück, GK III, 153 ff.).   The Tapestry of Bayeux, the most authoritative contemporary document on the Norman side, pictures the Normans as predominantly horsemen, the Saxons as predominantly footsoldiers (Belloc 14, figs. 48, 55 ff., 60 ff.).   Both the invaders and the Saxons had stirrups (op. cit., fig. 13 and passim), but the disparity in the number of their horsemen is evident.   While many Norman bowmen fought on foot, some were mounted (op. cit., fig. 75).

[15] Forrer 07, 775; Olshausen 90, 207–209.

[16] Lefebvre des Noëttes 31, fig. 282 ff., 287.

[17] The T'ang government prescribed iron stirrups for those who held no office, while officeholders were permitted to use stirrups made of a special and more precious metal. But merchants, [other] commoners, and Buddhist and Taoist monks were forbidden even to ride a horse (TS 24, 12a–b).

[18] For iron stirrups in Turkic graves, see Radloff 93 II, 110, 118, 122, 126, 132, and 134 and fig. 10; for the date of these finds see Zakharov 25, 52 ff.

[19] Salmony 43, 73, 82, and fig. 6.

[20] Lefebvre des Noëttes (31, fig. 289) dates the panel in question seventh century; Stein (07 I, 284) not later than the eighth century and not appreciably earlier than 790.

[21] Stein 07 II, pl. LIX.   Le Coq (25, 22) is emphatic about the camel stirrup, but less certain about the horse stirrup.

[22] Stein (07 I, 298) does not mention the camel stirrup, but notes stirrups for the horseman.

[23] Lefebvre des Noëttes 31, fig. 286.

[24] Nickerson 37, 270.

[25] Yusuf 43, 2.

[26] Lefebvre des Noëttes 31, figs. 308–310.

[27] Horsemen equipped with stirrups "were far more formidable" (Nickerson 37, 270).

[28] Procopius 14 I, 7–9.

[29] CYCCC 2a.

[30] Bury (31 II, 4–42) does not connect the "change in military theory" with a change in military equipment, yet he clearly recognizes the general transformation of the Roman army that occurred before and around the middle of the first millennium: "The conquests of Rome had always been due to her infantry, the cavalry had always been subsidiary, and down to the second half of the fourth century and the successful campaigns of Julian on the Rhine, experience had consistently confirmed the theory that battles were won by infantry, and that squadrons of horses were only a useful accessory arm." Then came the great change: "the gradual degradation of the infantry until it became more or less subsidiary to the cavalry on which the generals depended more and more to win their victories.   In the sixth century . . . the battles are often fought and won by cavalry only."   Nickerson (37, 270) states that, during the critical period, "only one new thing is to be found, the use of stirrups."   To him "the tactical importance of stirrups is self-evident" (loc. cit.).

For descriptions of the era of cavalry superiority in Europe, see Delbrück, GK II, 429 ff.; III, 273 ff.; Oman 24 I, 24–30, 56, 76, and passim; also Nickerson 37, 271, 297, and 368.   No special reference is needed for the Arabs and the Turks of western Asia, because the role played by the cavalry arm in their conquests is evident.

For India, see Elliot and Dowson, HI I, 434 ff.; II, 12, 19, 23, 25, and passim.

For Eastern Asia, see further development of the argument in this chapter.

a new device is quickly understood and, if possible, imitated. In the long run the center of military gravity will rest with those peoples who, for geographical and historical reasons, can produce the new weapon in superior quality and quantity.

These conditions were strikingly fulfilled on the vast steppes of the Near East (Arabia) and Inner Asia (Mongolia and its western and eastern extensions). Their broad plains became the breeding ground of the new mounted warrior whose swelling armies, from the middle of the first millennium on, assaulted and overwhelmed the agrarian countries of Western and Central Asia, advancing ultimately to North Africa and Spain, Asia Minor, Persia, and India. Within this historical framework occurred the Arabian, and later the Turkic attacks upon Byzantium, and the invasions of China by the T'o-pa and the Turks, the Ch'i-tan and the Mongols. The spirit of the age is magnificently expressed by a Mongol general who exhorted his great ruler, Chingis Khan, to proceed to victory and glory, to give no thought to his last days "as long as boys are born and grow into men and as long as an iron stirrup hangs together."[31]

c. TWO ASPECTS OF LIAO MILITARY HISTORY

The foregoing considerations define the military history of the Ch'i-tan as part of a general development which deeply affected the political and cultural history of the Old World. To be sure, cavalry supremacy in the period under discussion assumed different forms in Europe, the Near East, India, and Eastern Asia. In each of these regions, the original situation was modified by innumerable experiments in the field of cavalry equipment and organization, and, no less important, in the way of combating the terrifying new force. At the end of the T'ang period, when the Ch'i-tan mounted warriors made Inner Asia and China "tremble with their power," they drew upon experiences gained over centuries of "modernized" nomadic cavalry warfare. Their methods of attack had no doubt improved since the early days of the stirrup, but their strongest opponents, the army of China Proper, had also gained new insight in countless battles with their "barbarian" enemies. Although unable to protect their soil from destructive invasions, their strategists succeeded in confining

occupation to the northern border territories. The military events of the period offer, therefore, not only a significant illustration of Inner Asiatic conquest warfare; they also illuminate an important phase in the military history of China Proper.

2. THE LIAO MILITARY MACHINE
a. THE ORDO

The importance of the military in Liao society is readily apparent in the arrangement of the *Liao Shih:* a full description of the empire's army and warfare precedes the discussion of all other Liao institutions.[32]

First among the organizations for defence was the *wo-lu-to* 斡魯朵 or ordo, backbone of the Liao military system. From the Mongol conquest on, the Altaic term *orda*,[33] *ordu*,[34] *ordo*[35] became part of the vocabularies of many invaded countries;[36] as *orda* (Russian and Italian), *horda* (Polish, Spanish, Portuguese), *horde* (German, Danish), and *hord* (Swedish)[37] it penetrated the whole of Europe when the Tatar "hordes" bore down upon the western continent and struck terror to the hearts of its bewildered people.

i. PRE-LIAO ORDOS

In Inner Asia the ordo was known long before the Mongol period, even long before the Liao dynasty. During the time of Early Han (207 B.C.–A.D. 9) there were settlements (or places ? or stations ?) called *ou-t'o* 甌脫 on both sides of the vast desolate border which separated the Huns and the Tung-hu.[38] Early Chinese commentators have offered various explanations, some describing them as earthen houses, some as subterranean caves, some as frontier observation posts or border patrols.[39] Shiratori, claiming a con-

---

[31] Ssanang Ssetsen 1829, 85. The Mongol historian also tells of an attempt on Chingis Khan's life; to insure against his escape his left stirrup was cut by a woman (*op. cit.*, 81). The role of the stirrup among the Mongols spread to the westernmost limits of their conquest. Bar Hebraeus (32 I, 352) relates that in predynastic times a Mongol dignitary "when riding . . . had feet-cases (i.e. stirrups) made of iron, whilst for every one else they were made of wood."

[32] Only the official history of the subsequent Chin 金 dynasty followed this example.

[33] Mongol: Carpini 00, 17; Rubruck 00, 57, note 1.

[34] Turkic: Thomsen 96, 113; Radloff 97, 15, 32; Brockelmann 28, 128.

[35] *Loc. cit.*

[36] Indian *urdu* is the "language of *urdu*" or *ordu* (SOED II, 2323).

[37] NED, 383. The prothetic *h* appears first in Polish, whence it spread into central, western and northern Europe.

[38] SC 110, 8b; *cf.* also HS 54, 20a and 94A, 6a.

[39] SC 110, 8b, note. The earliest commentary, that given by the Later Han author, Fu Ch'ien 服虔, defines the *ou-t'o* as a *t'u shih* 土室, an earthen house (*loc. cit.*). At the same period certain tribes of the northeast lived in *t'u shih*, tomb-like underground houses (HHS 85, 6b and 15a). We cannot say, however, whether the Hunnish "earthen houses" resembled these earlier dwellings. A recent scholar completely rejects the idea of the *ou-t'o* as a house and claims instead that it is a "desert," or a "desolate place" (HSHNKC 1, 23b–24b).

nection between the term and such Altaic words as *oda, odu, odar, otak,* which signify "cave, stable, refuge for sheep, living room," translates it as "cave."[40] De Groot feels certain that *ou-t'o* is the Turkic *ordu,* which later designated "the camp or residence of Mongol princes; doubtless the word also meant the inner territory administered by the prince himself, as opposed to the feudal states."[41]

The linguistic side of Shiratori's and de Groot's interpretation cannot be discussed here, but several passages of the *Han Shu* seem to support the latter's conclusions. After a great victory the Han armies captured a Hunnish "*ou-t'o*" king,[42] whose frightened followers withdrew "to the northwest" where they established an *ou-t'o* garrison.[43] Later the *ou-t'o* garrison successfully withstood the attack of thousands of tribesmen and inflicted severe losses on them.[44]

Thus, under the eyes of the Chinese chroniclers, the Hunnish *ou-t'o* developed from a frontier post (or place, or garrison) into an armed camp of considerable size and great political significance. If such a camp became the center of a reorganized Hunnish state, as HS 94A suggests, it no doubt also served, at least at times, as the residence of the ruler, the shan-yü. Indeed, Liao records tell of an old settlement in Inner Asia called Wo-lu-to 窩魯朵 which formerly was the city of a [Hunnish[45]] shan-yü.[46]

The first mention of the *ordu* in an authentic Altaic text occurs in the Orkhon inscriptions where it is described as a place that sheltered the khan's wife and other female relatives; when attacked by the enemy, it was defended by the khan's brother.[47] Thomsen considers the *ordu* a camp or capital,[48] an interpretation that fits the context.

It is certain, therefore, that the *ordu* was known in the Eastern Turkic empire during the eighth century, and it seems that an organization similar in name was reported for the Huns and Tung-hu at the end of the first millennium B.C. But this does not justify the loose application of the word "horde" by Western scholars in their translations of T'ang and pre-T'ang writings on Inner Asia.[49] Nor does it indicate a clear

understanding of the Turkic and the pre-Turkic ordo: the details given in the Han and Orkhon texts are few and vague. As far as we know, the first extended description of an ordo is contained in the *Liao Shih.*[50] Even here the data do not clarify all aspects of organization, but they are substantial enough to convert the ordo of the pre-Mongol period from a historical shadow to an institutional reality.

ii. THE GROWTH OF THE LIAO ORDOS

According to LS 35, A-pao-chi created an ordo only after the division of the I-la tribe in 922.[51] The statement seems to imply that before that date the monarch had looked to warriors of this tribe for protection. Actually, however, he seems to have assembled a "belly and heart" guard[52] of more than two thousand braves "from all [Ch'i-tan] tribes" before his brothers rebelled.[53] This bodyguard protected his "palace," which was then identical with his traveling camp.[54] Thus the desire for a personal standing army led the first emperor to create an intertribal Ch'i-tan guard, which after 922 became the nucleus of his enlarged guard camp, the ordo.[55]

別為部落" (KCTSCC, sub 方輿, 130, 1*a*). Hirth (99, 32) speaks of the *ordus* of the Khirghiz and the Uighurs. The passages quoted (TS 217*B*, 10*b* and 217*A*, 1*b*) contain no transcription for the term *ordu*; they merely refer to the ruler's tent. Schlegel (96, 188) translates in the same way. Chavannes (03, 44 and 46) in his distinguished monograph on the Turks gives the word "horde" as an equivalent for *chung* 種 and for *pu-lo* 部落 (CTS 194*B*, 7*b*–8*a*). The difficulties inherent in the translation of the term *chung* have been discussed in VII, introduction, note 220. De Groot (21, 82, translation of SC 110, 9*b* and 17*a*) renders it as "tribe." "Tribe" certainly is the most satisfactory equivalent for *pu-lo*.

[50] XV, 1, *passim.*

[51] XV, 1 (2).

[52] The formula "heart and belly" (心腹) or "belly and heart" is a standard expression in Chinese literature. It already occurs in one of the oldest sections of the *Shang Shu* (SSCS 9, 9*a*; *cf.* Legge, CC III, 1, 244) and in the *Shih Ching* (MSCS 1: 3, 2*a*; *cf.* Legge, CC IV, 1, 14), and is frequently used thereafter (see, for instance, MTCS 8*A*, 2*b* and SC 31, 17*b*; 41, 4*a*; 43, 21*b*).

In LS 31, 2*a*, the phrase "heart and belly" is given as the translation of a Ch'i-tan word which is probably related to an old Altaic noun meaning "thought" (see XV, 1, note 10). No matter what the order of its components, the Chinese formula refers to man's vital organs. In combination with the word "guard" it seems justifiable to translate it "bodyguard."

[53] LS 73, 3*a*; *cf.* also 73, 4*b*.

[54] LS 73, 3*a*. Obviously the organization is identical with the imperial 宿衛 (LS 73, 4*a*), the "guard of the emperor's nocturnal rest."

[55] XV, 1 (5).

---

[40] Shiratori 02, 3–4.

[41] De Groot 21, 52.

[42] HS 94*A*, 31*b*.

[43] *Op. cit.,* 32*a*.

[44] *Op. cit.,* 36*b*.

[45] Marquart 14, 195. Translation and interpretation of the *Liao Shih* passage was provided by de Groot.

[46] LS 93, 5*a*–6*b*.

[47] Thomsen 96, 113; Radloff 97, 147.

[48] Thomsen 96, 113.

[49] Such usage is at variance with the Chinese terms actually employed. Julien (64, 326) translates: The Turks "formèrent une horde à part." Actually the sentence in questions says, "they formed a separate tribe

Each subsequent emperor had an ordo; and in addition, two exceptionally powerful empresses and one high-ranking dignitary enjoyed the extraordinary privilege. The *Liao Shih* ascribes Ch'ang-ning Palace to Empress Dowager Ying-t'ien,[56] and Ch'ung-tê Palace to Empress Dowager Ch'êng-t'ien, Ching-tsung's wife.[57] Ying-t'ien's ordo is listed after her son's and grandson's, whereas Ch'êng-t'ien's ordo is mentioned immediately after that of her husband. Perhaps Ch'êng-t'ien's camp was established after the death of her husband, but while her son was still living.

The political constellations created by the Sung war were reflected in the formation of one non-imperial ordo and one tomb camp modelled "after the pattern of the ordos."[58] The former was attached to "the emperor's great younger brother," Hsiao-wên, who served with distinction in several campaigns and held a number of military and political key positions;[59] the latter was established in honor of the famous Chinese northern chancellor, Yeh-lü Lung-yün, who succeeded beyond all others in coordinating the empire's forces in the struggle against China Proper. In spite of his unusual achievements, he was not permitted to set up an ordo during his lifetime. Only after his death was a "mansion" attached to his funeral temple.[60]

When an emperor died, his ordo garrison was assigned as a guard to his mausoleum. At some later date certain households might be transferred to other ordos or incorporated in the country's tribal[61] or agricultural administration.[62]

iii. THE COMPOSITION OF THE ORDOS

In its survey of the twelve ordos LS 31 frequently notes the national provenience, the geographical background, or the former military status of various groups in each individual camp. It always records the number of "regular," barbarian, and Chinese households and the size of the cavalry arm. Finally, it adds a

list of the administrative districts and tribal units attached[63] to each ordo.

In most cases the attached districts are more numerous than the places of recruitment, but, to add to the dilemma, not all of the latter are reported among the attached districts, although correspondence is high. The discrepancies are too conspicuous to be accidental; they may well arise from a standardized system of place reference depending on methods of disposing ordo soldiers. The principle of arrangement may have been as follows: when households selected for ordo service remained in their original homes, the old region was noted; when they were transferred to the ordo camp, no attached place of residence was mentioned; when they were settled in a new district, this new district was recorded. Such an interpretation, tentative though it is, lends value to the incomplete and inconsistent data in LS 31. Supplemented by the geographical chapters and sundry scattered passages, the material indicates in a general way the complex composition and intricate organization of the Liao ordos.

Judging from the available records, the ordo households were recruited in the main from the following sources and agencies:

(1) *Bodyguards and retainers.* The core of T'ai-tsu's ordo was his "heart and belly guard." Later emperors, such as Shih-tsung and Ching-tsung, and the statesman Hsiao-wên bulwarked their ordos with the bodyguards and retainers of deceased members of the imperial house. Such transfers not only provided trained soldiers for the new camps; simultaneously, they disposed of the potential threat of independent military forces.

(2) *Prisoners of war* were included in a number of ordos. Po-hai captives are mentioned in three instances;[64] Tsu-pu tribesmen in one;[65] prisoners of unspecified origin in another.[66]

(3) *Transferred subjects: Chinese and others.* The vast majority of all Chinese attached to the ordos lived in the northern regions of the empire where they had been settled by government action. The geographical records frequently describe these resettled Chinese as "prisoners of war," but they are not so designated in the survey of the ordos.[67] Through

---

[56] XV, 1 (8).

[57] XV, 1 (11). See also VII, introduction.

[58] XV, 1 (17).

[59] XV, 1 (16); Of course, it is possible that other princes of the imperial family also had ordos, as was customary under the Mongols. But no such minor ordos are mentioned either in LS 31 or elsewhere in the *History*. In all probability, therefore, during Liao time possession of an ordo was still reserved to rulers or individuals of almost imperial status.

[60] A bodyguard of one hundred men (CTKC 18, 2b) may have been the nucleus of his posthumous ordo-like "mansion."

[61] See I, 2 (5), nos. 6 and 7.

[62] See I, 1 (6): Ch'ang-ch'ing County and Yen-ch'ang County; (7): Ên County, Hui-ho County, Fou-su County, and Ch'ien Prefecture.

---

[63] In LS 31 the districts and tribal units are listed after the ordos without any explanation. However, the geographical chapters generally state that these various units are "attached to" (隸) the ordo in question.

[64] T'ai-tsu's, T'ai-tsung's, and T'ien-tsu's ordos.

[65] Mu-tsung's ordo.

[66] Shih-tsung's ordo.

[67] For instance, Chin 錦 Prefecture was set up "with Chinese captives" (LS 39, 7a; see I, 1 (7)). But the description of T'ai-tsu's ordo (LS 31, 2a) speaks only of

enlistment, they manifestly achieved the status of ordinary subjects, regardless of how they or their forefathers had fallen under Liao sway.

Po-hai and other nationals were treated similarly. The ordo of Ching-tsung's wife controlled a number of administrative districts which included not only Chinese,[68] but—as is evident from particular passages[69] as well as from the general context of the geographical survey[70]—also many Po-hai. These Po-hai are not referred to as prisoners of war, probably because they too had already been accepted as ordinary subjects in the victor-nation. Nor do the texts treat as prisoners of war the four hundred and fifty tribal households that, in 971, submitted voluntarily to Liao rule and were then assigned to three different ordo camps.[71] As ordinary subjects, they receive no special mention in the ordo lists.

(4) *Households recruited through the Control Bases.* In the tenth century, during the time of conquest and consolidation, these offices served as recruiting centers: in Huai Prefecture for T'ai-tsung's ordo, in Yüan Prefecture (Hsi-ching) for Shih-tsung's, and in Chung-ching for Mu-tsung's. No such function is recorded either for the period of the Sung war or afterward. However, throughout the years of the dynasty these offices mobilized the ordo soldiers not garrisoned at the main camp.

(5) *The Control Office of the Southern Capital* recruited fighters for Mu-tsung's ordo. Since this office was responsible for the defence of the southern frontier,[72] it must have had at its disposal well-trained and dependable soldiers, in the main probably Ch'i-tan tribesmen.

(6) *Soldiers from old ordos.* Four emperors, Mu-tsung, Hsing-tsung, Tao-tsung, and T'ien-tsu, all drew upon the manpower of former ordos for their personal armies.

(7) *Tribal offenders.* A Ch'i-tan who was convicted of crime might be forced to serve as a camp attendant, whether in an ordo or a traveling camp is not clear. However, in the only story that mentions the place of detention, the political offender (Yeh-lü Nu) was sent to an ordo.[73] Furthermore, the accounts

dealing with camp attendants, both noble and common,[74] follow immediately on the discussion of the Liao ordos; the traveling camps are described in a later chapter.

(8) *Ch'i-tan tribesmen.* This most important source of recruitment is never mentioned in the passages concerned with the origin of the ordo garrisons, obviously because the Ch'i-tan tribesmen, though politically a privileged stratum, were considered ordinary Liao subjects. However, in another context considerable light is thrown on the status of the Ch'i-tan contingent in the ordo armies.

iv. REGULAR, BARBARIAN, AND CHINESE HOUSEHOLDS

In the general survey of the "various ordos" as well as in the detailed notes on the individual camps there is always a concluding statement in which the ordo households are classified as regular, barbarian, or Chinese. In our discussion of the Liao population[75] "regular" has been tentatively equated with Ch'i-tan. This identification is based on the following considerations:

The Chinese word *chêng* 正 means "proper, regular, principal, real." "Principal" or "regular" may at times be used to express a technical distinction, and when combined with such a word as "soldiers" could be interpreted as shock troops or *triarii*. But in LS 31 the "regular" households are juxtaposed to two ethnic groups, the barbarians and the Chinese. If consistency may be assumed, the third category, like the other two, must also designate an ethnic group. Within Liao society the "principal" people were most certainly the Ch'i-tan; significantly in LS 31 the *chêng* always precede the barbarians and the Chinese.

The term "barbarians" (*fan*) as used in the *Liao Shih* sometimes refers to all non-Chinese people, the Ch'i-tan included. More often, however, it designates only non-Ch'i-tan "barbarians."[76] The latter would seem to be the intended meaning in the ordo lists.

The description of T'ai-tsu's ordo offers an unusual opportunity for testing our hypothesis. Set up with a "close guard," Po-hai captives, and households from Chin 錦 Prefecture, this ordo, like others, comprised regular, barbarian, and Chinese households. According to LS 39, 7a, Chin Prefecture was settled with Chinese, and, according to LS 46, 11a, T'ai-tsu's close guard was recruited "from the braves of all tribes." This evidently refers to members of the Ch'i-tan tribes both old and new, who formed the very marrow of the empire's tribal population. A general state-

---

"households" from Chin Prefecture, while the Po-hai are referred to as "prisoners of war."

[68] Chinese settlers are noted for Shuang Prefecture, for one subdivision of Ch'ien Prefecture, Hai-pei, and for Lu County, (I, 1 (6) (2)).

[69] I, 1 (2), Lu County.

[70] All places of recruitment and most of the attached districts were old Po-hai regions which only in part were settled with Chinese colonists. The rest of the population was evidently Po-hai.

[71] VII, 1 (11).

[72] See XV, 1, note 35.

[73] VII, 2 (69). Eventually, he was sent still farther away, to the Wu-ku tribe.

[74] VII, 1 (1).

[75] See I, introduction.

[76] *Loc. cit.*

ment in LS **32**, *3b* designates all the soldiers in the imperial close (tent) guard at the winter *na-po* as Ch'i-tan.[77] Hence it seems legitimate to equate the households from Chin Prefecture tentatively with the Chinese element in T'ai-tsu's ordo, and the tribal "close guard" with its regular soldiers.

Besides the Chinese retainers, T'ai-tsu's ordo contained numerous Po-hai. Among the attached districts was the old Po-hai Silver Prefecture, Yin;[78] and in Yen Prefecture Chinese were settled among the indigenous inhabitants[79] who were probably Po-hai. A final equation, therefore, between Po-hai and barbarians seems possible.

The real situation in T'ai-tsu's ordo may have been more complex than the texts disclose: non-Chinese elements other than Po-hai may have been included among the barbarians; and the Chin households may not have been exclusively Chinese. But since no such complicating factors are mentioned, it seems justifiable to assume that the *Liao Shih* statements reflect the basic composition of this camp.

Data on other ordos are less revealing, but they also throw some light on the history of these organizations. Even when no direct mention is made of the nationality of the households incorporated in a new ordo garrison, the fact that the texts later describe this garrison as composed of regulars, barbarians, and Chinese adds to our understanding of the process of recruitment. The Liao ordos differed in many respects from the Manchu banners, but they had this in common: both contained auxiliary tribal and Chinese elements which were coordinated with a powerful and distinguished nucleus of the ruling people.

V. STATUS AND TREATMENT OF THE ORDO HOUSEHOLDS

The barbarians and Chinese who joined an ordo garrison were automatically raised in status. No doubt the "transferred" (*chuan* 轉)[80] families were still considered inferior to the "regular" households, but most certainly they rose above the level of their subdued co-nationals.

To be sure, no ordo soldier was free, not even the tribal Ch'i-tan. A government that could arbitrarily mobilize its civilian population had little reason to hesitate when it wanted to shift well-disciplined shock troops. Ordo households were sometimes given to meritorious dignitaries,[81] in one case because the

beneficiary, a Chinese official, "had no slaves."[82] The wording of the record suggests an unfree status, at least for the transferred ordo families. But, in accepting such an interpretation, we must keep in mind that within the Liao empire, as elsewhere, the term "slave" covered a wide range of social conditions. The Turkic Janissaries were the sultan's "slaves," *qul*; but this designation, rather than being an epithet of disgrace, "was felt to be an honor. . . . It carried marked distinction and secured deference everywhere."[83] Although supposed to be poor,[84] the Janissaries were paid regularly,[85] and had unexpected revenues from gifts and loot.[86] Whatever they acquired was theirs without restriction, for they were exempted from taxation.[87] At times they might even marry.[88] They cannot therefore be counted as full slaves.[89]

This consideration is equally valid for the transferred ordo families. Their right to property is revealed by a decree in 1043 which regulated the disposition of the "permanent property" of childless Chinese camp families,[90] and by a relief measure in 1087 which granted silk to "the poor people" of Shêng-tsung's ordo.[91] The transferred families may also have been exempted from taxation, for this privilege was even extended to the less distinguished farmer-soldiers in the frontier service.[92]

Marriage was taken for granted in the Liao armies. The soldiers were always registered in households; in 997, in a general camp census, the government recorded both individuals and families,[93] and in 989 special steps were taken to redeem Chinese prisoners that they might join their relatives who were attached to various camps.[94] Thus the transferred ordo

---

[77] In the winter *na-po* the emperor's tent was guarded by four thousand Ch'i-tan soldiers (II, 1 (27)).

[78] *Cf.* III (5).

[79] See I, 1 (7).

[80] XV, 1 (3) and *passim*.

[81] VII, 1 (30). The "ten camp households" given to Yeh-lü Chüeh (VII, 1 (44)) probably fall into this category.

[82] VII, 1 (19).

[83] Lybyer 13, 114.

[84] *Op. cit.*, 92.

[85] *Op. cit.*, 114; Hammer, GOR I, 93 ff.

[86] Lybyer 13, 92 ff.; Hammer, GOR III, 45.

[87] Lybyer 13, 114.

[88] *Op. cit.*, 95.

[89] See VII, introduction; *cf.* also Wittfogel 31, 394 ff.; *idem* 32, 601 ff. Toynbee (SH III, 28–47) has given a suggestive survey of the employment of "slaves" in a number of dynasties of the Near East. We do not question the correctness of the bulk of his information, but it seems extremely doubtful whether the word "slave," even if used in the original record, is a scientifically adequate designation for men who had the chance to rise to the rank of minister of state (*op. cit.*, 33 ff.), who were paid for their services (*op. cit.*, 36), and who might marry the rulers' daughters (*op. cit.*, 33).

[90] VII, 1 (34).

[91] X, 1 (60).

[92] II, 2 (9).

[93] I, 3 (3).

[94] VII, 1 (16).

soldiers, who remained with their families and received some little material reward, evidently enjoyed more freedom than the well-paid Janissaries in the armies of the Turks.

Contingents of "transferred" and Ch'i-tan warriors served in the same ordos. The Janissaries were separated from the older and more distinguished cavalry regiments.[95] Yet such technical and social differences must not obscure the similarities in methods of recruitment and in function. Both groups were enlisted from nations that had been or still were enemies of the ruling people; both served in elite corps close to the person of the sovereign; both were formally unfree but enjoyed a status which, at times, equalled or was even superior to that of the country's "free" men.

vi. ORDO ECONOMY

In 1013 the interest of Tun-mu Palace (Hsiao-wên's ordo) was used "to relieve the poor people."[96] The payment of interest implies special camp property. This property, "money and silk," which was in the main accumulated war loot, bolstered the Imperial Treasury.[97] But in times of need the camps instead of providing a surplus might require help. In 1081 the government ear-marked annual money relief "for the various ordos."[98] Unfortunately the record does not state whether the money was allocated to the camp fund or paid directly to needy ordo households. Another passage is somewhat more revealing: in 1067, when the cantonment of the imperial bodyguard caught fire, its members received grants of money, grain, and horses "according to their rank."[99] It is readily understandable that the ordo soldiers who lived away from the main camp should retain their private property, but evidently even the most reliable troops, the permanent camp garrison, maintained a "private" (household) economy of their own.

vii. THE LOCATION OF THE ORDOS AND MAUSOLEUMS

More definite information is available regarding the original location of the ordo camps and the mausoleums to which they were later transferred. It is possible in a general way to place seven of the twelve Liao ordos;[100] all of them seem to have been situated either in Shang-ching or Chung-ching Circuit, that is, in or near the grazing grounds of the

Ch'i-tan and the Hsi. The mausoleums of most ordo overlords were erected in Shang-ching Circuit.[101] Shih-tsung and his son, Ching-tsung, were buried in Tung-ching Circuit;[102] the site of Hsiao-wên's mausoleum is in doubt.[103] Even those ordo garrisons which had been stationed in Chung-ching Circuit returned to Ch'i-tan territory after their masters' death.

viii. ATTACHED PREFECTURES AND COUNTIES

In an introductory statement the *Liao Shih* first enumerates the twelve ordos (and Yeh-lü Lung-yün's "mansion"); it then lists without comment the administrative districts and tribal units (category and number) that were attached to them. Including the Control Bases which appear after the administrative districts, the list is as follows:[104]

Prefectures	38
Counties	10
Control Bases	41
Shih-lieh	23
Wa-li	74
Mei-li	91
Tê-li	2
Cha-sa	19

The organizational units mentioned in this statement were irregularly distributed among the twelve ordos. Frequently, the standardized presentation reports more prefectures and counties for each ordo than are noted in the texts describing their origins. In discussing T'ai-tsu's ordo, for instance, only one prefecture, Chin, is mentioned as a place of origin for its Chinese element, and no comparable information is to be found for the Po-hai captives. The appendix, however, lists five prefectures[105] and one county. By utilizing the regional descriptions, it is possible to show that several of these districts were inhabited by Po-hai, and that Chinese were settled in regions other than Chin Prefecture. The records on subsequent ordos present similar discrepancies, but there seems little need to labor the point here. However, some consideration should be given to the status of the counties listed after the attached prefectures.

---

[95] Lybyer 13, 98; Hammer, GOR I, 95 ff.

[96] XII (35).

[97] *Wu Hsi Chi* = LSSI 15, 15a.

[98] XII (82).

[99] X, 1 (54).

[100] We have not been able to identify the sites of Mu-tsung's, Shêng-tsung's, and T'ai-tsung's ordos from the available geographical data. For Hsiao-wên's ordo there are none at all.

[101] T'ai-tsu was buried in Tsu Prefecture; T'ai-tsung and Mu-tsung in Huai Prefecture; Shêng-tsung, Hsing-tsung, and Tao-tsung in Ch'ing Prefecture (see I, 1 (2)); T'ien-tsu finally in Ch'ien Prefecture in Tung-ching Circuit (LS 30, 1b).

[102] See I, 1 (6).

[103] According to LS 31, he was buried southwest of Tsu Prefecture; according to two other passages, this mausoleum was situated in Tung-ching Circuit (see XV, 1 (16) and note 6).

[104] XV, 1 (3).

[105] One of these prefectures, Yen, was actually a subdivision of Chin Prefecture.

The *Liao Shih* mentions ten counties attached to ordos; all were controlled by camps established during the early period of the dynasty. Fu-i, the only county attached to T'ai-tsu's ordo, was situated in the western part of Shang-ching Circuit, not far from Tsu Prefecture. Like this district, it was relatively close to the seat of the central government—closer in fact than any of the attached prefectures which were all under the jurisdiction of Tung-ching Circuit. According to LS 37, 8a, the district was set up by T'ai-tsung; its soldiers may at times have assisted the transferred garrisons of T'ai-tsu's ordo which guarded his mausoleum in Tsu Prefecture.

T'ai-tsung's ordo controlled two counties. One, Luan-ho, was located in Chung-ching Circuit, in the same region that harbored the ordo. The four attached prefectures also lay beyond the borders of Shang-ching Circuit. Only one county, Pao-ho, was close to the Supreme Capital; its administrative office was probably within the city precincts.[106] Such an arrangement had obvious advantages when T'ai-tsung resided in the capital.

Considerations of expediency may also have led to the assignment of suburban counties to the ordos of T'ai-tsu's and Ching-tsung's empresses.[107] Shih-tsung's ordo controlled one county, Shan-tung, which was situated in Tung-ching Circuit, formerly his father's domain; and in this circuit Shih-tsung was buried. Ching-tsung's ordo had two attached counties, both in Chung-ching Circuit, where troops were massed for the campaigns against Sung. In a number of cases a functional explanation may be given for the location of the attached counties; in others this is not possible. The absence of attached counties from the ordos organized after the close of the tenth century is equally inexplicable.

---

[106] XI (5) and note 13. In the geographical survey of the *Liao Shih* the history of this county, like that of several others, is given in abbreviated form. Nothing is said concerning the attachment of the county to T'ai-tsung's ordo, which is asserted in LS 31, 3a. But other facts in LS 37, 3a confirm the correctness of that passage. According to the geographical record, T'ai-tsu settled the region of Pao-ho with Po-hai natives; later, in 990, "the population of the Control Bases of various ordos was assigned to Ching-tsung's ordo [mausoleum]." These sentences make sense only if Pao-ho County before 990 was attached to a Control Base, and through it to another ordo.

[107] T'ai-tsu's wife controlled three counties, two located in Tung-ching Circuit, the third, Ting-pa, under the walls of the Supreme Capital. The ordo of Ching-tsung's wife had only one county, Lu, which, like Ting-pa, was suburban (XV, 1 (8) (11); see also XI (5)).

ix. THE CONTROL BASES

The great majority of the Control Bases were situated in Nan-ching and Hsi-ching Circuits,[108] the old Chinese territories where the ordos had few attached prefectures or counties. The ordo planners chose strategically important places for the new military units. Situated in the none too dependable Chinese regions, the Base garrisons, Ch'i-tan, barbarians, and Chinese, must have been selected with special care. They maintained contact with all neighboring ordo troops and, according to LS 35, in a military emergency "the Control Bases of the five capitals and the two prefectures" mobilized all ordo cavalry.[109] The statement, in this form, is not completely accurate, for no Control Bases are noted for Tung-ching Circuit, and only a few of relatively late origin are mentioned for Shang-ching and Chung-ching.[110] The participation of the Bases in troop mobilization must, therefore, have been confined in the main to the old Chinese territories.

x. ATTACHED TRIBAL DIVISIONS

After the Control Bases, the *Liao Shih* notes five administrative units that are connected with the ordos: the *shih-lieh*, the *wa-li*, the *mo-li* (*mei-li*), the *tê-li*, and the *cha-sa*. Of these, the *shih-lieh* and *mo-* (*mei-*) *li* are clearly established as tribal subdivisions.[111] Contextual and linguistic considerations lead to similar conclusions regarding the character of the *wa-li* and *cha-sa*.

Wa-li resembles the Mongol, Turkic, Tungus, and Finno-Ugrian words for "tent, tent-camp, village"; its initial labial is preserved in Manchu.[112] The affinity of *cha-sa* to another Tungus word for "village" (Jurchen: *hāh-šā*, Manchu and other Tungus languages: *gasa, gasan, gasin*[113]) is equally evident. Such similarities suggest some ethno-historical relation to the Tungus cultures of eastern Asia. The words may well have become part of the Ch'i-tan language before the dynastic period; or they may have entered along with other Tungus elements during the time of the empire.

The Liao empire included a considerable number of Tungus peoples, certain Jurchen tribes,[114] and many Po-hai. This perhaps accounts for the great number of what may be tentatively called Tungus tribal divisions within the ordo organization. It perhaps also explains why the *wa-li* were commonly used as places

---

[108] LS 36, 4b ff.
[109] XV, 1 (2).
[110] LS 35, 6b–7a.
[111] See XIV, introduction.
[112] *Loc. cit.*
[113] *Loc. cit.*
[114] See I, 2 (5), nos. 17 and 18.

of punishment. Safely detained among a group of well-disciplined aliens who spoke a foreign language, the Ch'i-tan criminal or political offender would no longer threaten the rulers of the nation. Curiously, the "Tungus" *wa-li* is listed before the Ch'i-tan *mo-li*; whether this arrangement reflects the superior status of a relatively old complex, or only its greater size, or both, we do not know.

The *wa-li* is noted as a component of the earliest Liao ordo, T'ai-tsu's Hung-i Palace. The ordo also controlled two *tê-li*, puzzling units that later completely disappear from the record.[115] The *cha-sa* is first mentioned in references to T'ai-tsung's ordo, and again in descriptions of Shêng-tsung's, his mother's and his brother's camps, all of which were probably created during the great Sung war. The word *wa-li*, which appears in various forms in most Altaic languages, may have been incorporated by the Ch'i-tan in pre-dynastic times; the more exclusively Tungus term *cha-sa* possibly emerged during the dynastic period, perhaps along with other eastern elements. The two Liao tribes whose Jurchen origin is definitely established are both classified with Shêng-tsung's tribes.[116]

xi. LOCATION OF THE ORDO TROOPS

Data on the attached districts and tribal units reveal the ordos as centers of an organizational network that spread out over many regions of the Liao empire. The exact nature of this network is not adequately exposed, but what information we have makes a discussion of at least a number of basic points possible.

The *Liao Shih* gives the locale of each ordo, with the exception of the last emperor's and Hsiao-wên's, thus indicating that the camps had a fixed place of residence.[117] However, no statement reveals how many ordo families actually lived in and around the camps or how many were garrisoned in other districts. T'ai-tsu's ordo is reported to have numbered 15,000 households; Shêng-tsung's and T'ai-tsung's not less than 30,000. If a household averaged five members, these ordo garrisons must have comprised at least 75,000 and 150,000 persons respectively. To concentrate so many people in the camp and its environs would have created most serious economic and administrative problems. Such problems, however, never arose for, according to LS 35, 1*b*, the ordo soldiers were disposed over a large territory beyond the boundaries of the ordo camp. Faced with a military emergency, the government would notify its ordo fighters through "the Control Bases of the five capitals and the two prefectures,"[118] and perhaps through other channels. The quickly massed ordo troops were ready to strike before the common soldiers of the Northern and Southern Regions could be mobilized.[119]

While the text is definite regarding the presence of ordo soldiers in distant regions, details of organization remain obscure. We do not know whether the scattered households formed the greater part of the total ordo garrison; neither do we know how or where these troops were "assembled" when called to arms. But one thing is certain: the ordo system was expedient. It provided the Liao rulers with an army that could be quickly mobilized, and once mobilized, quickly moved—for it was an army of mounted shock troops. Furthermore, it was an army of considerable size; according to LS 35, before the militia and the tribes could gather their forces, "an army of a hundred thousand horsemen was already in existence."

xii. THE SIZE OF THE ORDO ARMIES

The above statement evidently refers to the total number of ordo horsemen at the close of the dynasty. Adding the members of all twelve ordos and Yeh-lü Lung-yün's Mansion, the authors of the *Liao Shih* arrive at the following maximums:

households	adult males	mounted soldiers
203,000	408,000	101,000
(LS 31, 2*a*)	(LS 35, 7*a*)	(LS 35, 7*a*)

These totals reflect the fact that the "old" ordos did not break up when their masters died: according to LS 35, 1*b*, their garrisons continued as tomb guards. As such, they might carry on generation after generation. Shêng-tsung's ordo is mentioned in 1077[120] and again in 1087;[121] it existed at the end of the century as it had at the beginning.

But, while giving full consideration to the ordos' continuity, the authors of the *Liao Shih* have not taken into account the government policy which tended to limit the size of the total ordo army. The first move in this direction was made when Mu-tsung's ordo was set up,[122] but not until Shêng-tsung's reign did the policy have any serious numerical effect.

In establishing Shêng-tsung's ordo, all reservoirs of manpower excepting old ordos were disregarded; the 30,000 households of the new camp were recruited

---

[115] But each of these later ordos, those of Hsing-tsung, Tao-tsung and Hsiao-wên, still had a *wa-li* called *tê-li* (LS 31, 7*b*, 8*a*, and 9*a*).

[116] See note 114.

[117] Modern geographical equivalents have been established in seven of eleven cases. See above.

[118] XV, 1 (2).

[119] *Loc. cit.*

[120] VII, 2 (69).

[121] X, 1 (60).

[122] XV, 1 (9).

exclusively from the camps of T'ai-tsung, Shih-tsung, and Empress Dowager Ying-t'ien, which were accordingly reduced. Therefore the combined armies of the ordos up to and including Shêng-tsung's still comprised the same number of households as before, namely, 89,000, with 178,000 adult males and 46,000 horsemen.[123]

The ordos of the last three emperors recruited the bulk of their troops from "various ordos." Only for Hsing-tsung's camp is a non-ordo source mentioned—Jao Prefecture, which had all told 6,000 households.[124] The figure implies that almost two-thirds of this ordo garrison was also enlisted from established ordo camps. It may then be conservatively assumed that the non-ordo component of all three ordos was less than half, or not more than the 30,000 households with 60,000 adult males and 15,000 horsemen.

While no soldiers from existing camps were included in Hsiao-wên's ordo, Yeh-lü Lung-yün's mausoleum had attached Ch'uan Prefecture, a district that had formerly belonged to Empress Dowager Ch'êng-t'ien's ordo.[125] The two outsiders' camps together comprised a total of 21,000 households with 42,000 adult males and 15,000 horsemen.

If it is assumed that the birth and death rates more or less compensated each other, and, if no unusual factors appeared, the ordo garrisons of the Liao empire were constituted approximately as shown in table 17.

TABLE 17

ORDO GARRISONS

Date	Historical Situation	Households	Adult males	Mounted Soldiers
926	T'ai-tsu's death	15,000	30,000	6,000
951	Shih-tsung's death	51,000	102,000	24,000
969–83	After establishment of Ch'ing-tsung's ordo and before that of his wife	73,000	146,000	36,000
Before 1031	Including culmination of Sung war and creation of three ordos plus one "mansion" under Shêng-tsung	110,000	220,000	61,000
1101–25	T'ien-tsu	140,000	280,000	76,000

These are maximum estimates.[126] Whatever the peacetime increase in population may have been, it was probably more than balanced by the later separation of certain prefectures and counties from the ordos

to which they had been attached, a change which was as clear a gain for the government of the Southern Region as it was a loss to the ordos. In view of the relatively large number of these re-normalized districts and the conservativeness of our estimate of intra-ordo shifts, it seems safe to say that the ever-ready ordo army not only never reached a total of 100,000 horsemen, but that it even fell short of 75,000, the reduced maximum. During the critical period of the Sung war all Liao ordos taken together may have put an army of 50,000–60,000 mounted soldiers in the field.

xiii. FUNCTIONS OF THE ORDO ARMIES

The primary function of the ordo guard was to protect the person of the ruler. "When the emperor entered his residence, it settled down to protect him, and when he went out it escorted him."[127] Such guard service was rendered all sovereigns, and it probably followed strictly defined rules and regulations. The emperor's winter na-po, for instance, had four thousand Ch'i-tan soldiers who watched the imperial tent in shifts of one thousand men.[128] The record indicates that in the ordo troops, the Ch'i-tan were definitely considered the most trustworthy element; and it also indicates that only a limited number of elite soldiers attended the emperor. Even if the Ch'i-tan "tent guard" of four thousand was supplemented by a less distinguished camp guard of several thousand men, the ordo escort was small in terms of the total ordo army.

Considered historically, the Liao ordos developed from a personal body-guard into a "guard" army, elite troops similar to the garde regiments of Napoleon, imperial Germany, or Russia. Although called to arms before the tribes or militia, the ordo soldiers did not fight alone. In 994 an expedition to the western frontier region was undertaken by tribal soldiers of the Northwestern Route and T'ai-tsung's ordo army;[129] in 1015, during the war against Korea, the Liao government raised an army of fifty-five thousand trained soldiers who were recruited from the Supreme and Central Capitals "and the various ordos."[130] Both times the ordo soldiers were accompanied by less distinguished troops who probably attacked the enemy before the precious "guard" was engaged. In the great campaigns against China Proper an imperial bodyguard of thirty thousand elite fighters was established. This guard, which functioned as a special army, was not drawn exclusively from the ordo troops, but "from the various armies."[131] The record suggests

[123] XV, 1 (5–12).
[124] I, 1 (2).
[125] I, 1 (7).
[126] See I, introduction.

[127] XV, 1 (2).
[128] II, 1 (27).
[129] XV, 1 (48).
[130] XV, 2 (12).
[131] XV, 2 (3).

that those warriors who participated in the action were distributed among the four main bodies of the invasion army, most certainly to build up fighting morale.

The relation between the Ch'i-tan, barbarians, and Chinese ordo soldiers is not clearly defined. The Ch'i-tan troops, who provided the emperor's tent guard in the winter *na-po* and probably elsewhere, evidently held the more responsible and distinguished positions; but the subjugated barbarians and Chinese, who had been "transferred" to the emperor's "palace" guard, also participated in the prestige—and the material advantages—of this unique organization. They all were under the jurisdiction of the chief controller of the various traveling camps.[132]

The ultimate effectiveness of the entire ordo army was tested at the moment of emergency. Then the Control Bases and other agencies rallied the scattered warriors whose united strength embodied the empire's quickest and most terrible striking power. Although the mounted ordo troops never numbered as many as a hundred thousand men, as LS 35 claims, an elite force of fifty, sixty, or seventy thousand horsemen presented a military potential that, in its best days, probably was not equalled by the cavalry arm of any Far Eastern state.

xiv. CONTEMPORARY AND POST-LIAO ORDOS

The Liao ordos were camps for the imperial guard or shock army. As places of fixed locale, they must be clearly distinguished from the emperor's traveling camps or "palaces" (*hsing kung*); and as military centers, they must be differentiated from the civil administrations of the five capitals. Other peoples of Inner Asia used the term "ordo" according to their need and desire; at the end of the tenth century the Turkic ruler named the town where he resided *Ordu*.[133] Mahmūd al-Kāshgharī's dictionary (1066) defines the Turkic word "*ordu*" as "the camp of a ruler"[134] or "the lair of an animal."[135] The Turkic idea of "residence" was accepted even by that heir of Ch'i-tan tradition, Yeh-lü Ta-shih, who deserted the collapsing Liao empire and founded Western Liao, calling his capital Hu-ssŭ Wo-êrh-to.[136] A hundred years later, when Yeh-lü Ch'u-tsai visited the country, the transcription had been changed to Hu-ssŭ Wo-lu-to, but the city still existed.[137]

None of these ordos is described in any detail. Much more is known about the Mongol *ordu*. In the fluid world of Chingis Khan and his successors the traditional Altaic term again acquired a different meaning. Chingis Khan had "four great ordos,"[138] which were piously preserved by later rulers until the close of the dynasty.[139] Apparently these "great" ordos were not identical with the khan's "traveling palaces" (*hsing kung*), although they were also referred to as *wo-li-to*.[140] Certain *ordus* were controlled by the khan's wives and female relatives;[141] Mongol princes, such as Hulagu, had their own *ordus*,[142] and even "rich Mongols" without any other distinction are reported to have possessed ordus "like a large town."[143]

Among the Mongols, then, the term is no longer restricted to the ruler's camp or residence. A detailed analysis of the many new applications need not concern us here; suffice it to note that they indicate a considerable change in usage from the time of the Orkhon inscriptions and the Liao empire. In all probability Chingis Khan's headquarters were called *ordu*, as Vladimirtsov suggests,[144] and a "great *ordu*" served as the temporary seat of the empire's supreme government and council;[145] but not all *ordus* fulfilled such extraordinary military or political functions.

Contemporary travelers have presented us with impressive descriptions of the size and splendor of the city-like Mongol ordos.[146] None discusses the ethnic composition and administrative organization of any of them; in this respect the records of the *Liao Shih* are unique. One point, however, is clear: the Mongol *ordu* was always a camp,[147] never a tribe or "a great company, esp. of the savage, uncivilized, or uncultivated; a gang, troop, crew."[148] This meaning of the word "horde" developed later in Europe, the result of a historical process, in which the Tatar (Mongol) invasion of the West was probably the decisive factor.

b. TRIBAL ARMIES

The other components of the Liao army can be surveyed more briefly; fewer facts are known concern-

---

[132] XV, 1 (19).

[133] Barthold 28, 234; *idem* 35, 81.

[134] Brockelmann 28, 128.

[135] *Loc. cit.*

[136] 虎思斡耳朵 (LS 30, 6a).

[137] 虎司窩魯朵 (HYLC 8).

[138] YS 29, 2a.

[139] Rashīd ad-Dīn = d'Ohsson 1834 I, 383; *cf.* also Blochet 10, 2 and 77.

[140] 窩里朵 (HYCCC 1, 17b–18a). Another transliteration is *wu-li-to* 兀里朵 (*op. cit.*, 3a).

[141] HYCCC 1, 17b; *cf.* also Rashīd ad-Dīn 1836, 95 and Carpini 00, 17; *idem* 28, 38.

[142] Rashīd ad-Dīn 1836, 139 and 145.

[143] Rubruck 00, 57.

[144] Vladimirtsov 30, 59.

[145] Rashīd ad-Dīn 1836, 21–25.

[146] HYCCC 1, 17b–18a (for translation see Bretschneider 88 I, 58 and, more complete, Waley 31, 71); Carpini 00, 19–25; Rubruck 00, 122 and 165 ff.; Ibn Batoutah 77, 380 ff.

[147] See Ibn Batoutah and other sources quoted above; *cf.* also Aboulfeda 1848 II, 2, 153–154; Hammer-Purgstall 1840, 32 and *passim;* and Curtin 08, 250 ff.

[148] NED, 383.

ing them, and the problems involved seem to be less intricate. Besides the ordo troops, the empire mustered two main categories of armed forces, the tribes and the militia.[149] The troops of the "subordinate states," which in LS 36, 9*b* are noted as a fourth group, were in large part independent of the Liao government; the border tribes, that acted as auxiliaries in numerous campaigns, were considered subdivisions of the Liao tribal armies for the duration.

i. THEIR ORGANIZATION

The tribes were economic, political, and military organizations. The commanding prefects of the empire's great and small tribes carried out the policies of the central government, probably in all spheres of tribal life. The *hsiang-wên*, however, fulfilled a purely military function; his subordinates as listed in LS 46, 2*a* all had military titles.[150]

The tribal subdivisions, the *shih-lieh* and the *mi-li* (or *mo-li* or *mei-li*),[151] were not only herding and camping units, but, as suggested in passages describing the ordos, military as well. In the great tribes, the *shih-lieh* was controlled by a chieftain, *i-li-chin;* the leader of the *mi-li* bore the title *hsin-kun,* a Ch'i-tan variant of the Chinese word *chiang-chün,* general.[152] The authority of these officials was apparently both military and civil.

Each tribe possessed a special detachment called *chiu* 紀.[153] Each "palace," whatever the word may connote in this passage, had a "*Chiu* Troop"; and the "twelve traveling *Chiu* Troops"[154] may have been elite ordo soldiers who attended their overlords when they resided in traveling camps. The traveling *Chiu* Troops had on their staff a "minister over the masses" and certain other officers who were usually attached to the *hsiang-wên.*

No exact equivalent of the ordo guard is noted for the tribes, but it is possible that the tribal chieftains and leaders assembled small detachments (*chiu*) for permanent guard and police duties. Two *Chiu* Troops are mentioned in relation to the [government] herds;[155] police functions in this connection are more than probable.[156]

ii. THEIR SIGNIFICANCE

In the general description of Liao warfare in LS 34 little space is devoted to the role of the country's

tribal forces, but innumerable passages in various parts of the *History* leave no doubt of the tribes' military significance. At the beginning of the tenth century, during the empire's formative years, the Ch'i-tan had practically no Po-hai and few Chinese subjects; T'ai-tsu's continual campaigns must have been fought almost exclusively by the armed manpower of the Ch'i-tan confederation. The creation of the ordo armies and the militia decreased the importance of the tribal contingents, but nevertheless they remained essential military adjuncts. The tribes participated in the wars against the independent peoples of Inner Asia; they joined in the great campaigns against China Proper and Korea; and they constituted a vital element in the empire's frontier defence.

In 983 two border tribes were mobilized to strengthen the attack against the Western Turks;[157] in 994 Wu-ku soldiers and other tribesmen fought shoulder to shoulder with an ordo army on the western frontier.[158] Wu-ku and other tribal troops engaged in a victorious northern campaign in 1072;[159] and in 1092 tribal soldiers warred against Mo-ku-ssŭ, the powerful chieftain of the Tsu-pu tribes.[160] In 1093 the Liao government gave three thousand horses to the Wu-ku,[161] whose commanding prefect in the following year reported a successful fight against the Ch'a-cha-la.[162]

The empire's forces against China included "the troops of the southern, northern, and Hsi kings,"[163] tribal soldiers who held key positions in the national defence.[164] Their mobilization orders, therefore, had to be confirmed by special gold tallies from the emperor before they went into action.[165] When possible, semi-independent tribesmen were used as auxiliary warriors; after suffering a crushing defeat at the hands of the Liao army, the Jurchen in 986 "asked permission for their soldiers to join the southern expedition."[166] In 1010 the Jurchen were again under pressure; they "offered ten thousand fine horses and asked permission to join the punitive expedition against Korea." The *History* adds laconically, "This was approved."[167]

In the empire's defence system, the tribes were

---

[149] XV, 1 (2).
[150] XIV, 1 (23).
[151] *Loc. cit.* and XIV, 1 (24).
[152] See Thomsen 96, 149.
[153] LS 46, 13*b*.
[154] XV, 1 (31).
[155] *Loc. cit.*
[156] In post-Liao times the term *chiu* seems to have been applied essentially to detachments of frontier guards (see II, 2, note 20).

[157] XVI, 983, LS 10, 4*a*.
[158] XV, 1 (48).
[159] XVI, 1072, LS 23, 1*a*.
[160] XVI, 1092, LS 25, 4*b*–5*a*.
[161] XVI, 1093, LS 25, 5*b*.
[162] XVI, 1094, LS 25, 6*b*. In 1100 the Wu-ku achieved another victory over this tribe (XVI, 1100, LS 26, 5*a*).
[163] XV, 2 (3).
[164] See below.
[165] See XV, 2, note 7.
[166] XVI, 986, LS 11, 7*b*.
[167] X, 2 (66).

second only to the ordo troops, which they matched in political reliability if not in military effectiveness. The defence of Shang-ching Circuit was in part entrusted to the king of the Hsi tribes, to the offices of the two imperial tribes, and to a few high officials, the *t'i-yin* (of the imperial family),[168] representatives of the lineages of the Maternal Uncles and the grand *ch'ang-kun*,[169] all leading tribal dignitaries. The defence of the empire's frontier included practically all of T'ai-tsu's and Shêng-tsung's tribes; their geographical and military disposition is outlined in LS 35.[170] The great kings of the Five and Six Divisions, who "shared control of the military . . . affairs of the tribes" and who employed a large military staff,[171] were stationed within the southern border;[172] the offices of the two kings and the I-shih tribe are listed as part of the border defences of the southwest.[173] The organization of the northwestern border included among others the offices of the *Shê-li* Troops of the Administration of the Hsi King and offices of the *hsiang-wên* of the Ch'i-tan, T'u-[yü]-hun, and Shu-lü armies.[174] During the period of Liao rule various inner tribes changed their locale, in part for military reasons. In 942 Ch'i-tan households were spread along the southern frontier for garrison service.[175]

The inner ring of frontier defence was reenforced by a loose fringe of remote outposts consisting of semi-independent border tribes; the Chu-chê Ta-lu-kuo and the Po-ssŭ Pi-ku-tê "did garrison service within the border, but lived outside of it."[176] A number of non-Liao tribes are said to have been "under some sort of obligation to the Northeastern Route."[177] Since this Route, like all others, was part of the defence system,[178] the service expected was probably also military in character.

c. THE MILITIA

The arming of the Ch'i-tan tribes offered no serious problem to the Liao government, for essentially their political loyalty was guaranteed by their privileged status in the conquest society. The subdued sedentary populations, the Chinese and the Po-hai, could not be equally trusted. In 1043 the Chinese south of the passes, the inhabitants of the old Chinese

territories, were "forbidden to possess bows and arrows";[179] in 1071 the Chinese "were forbidden to . . . hunt animals."[180] Similar restrictions were imposed on the Po-hai: before 1038, they were not even permitted to play polo;[181] and the absence of hunting grounds in Tung-ching Circuit[182] implies that, for the native population, participation in an organized semi-military hunt was not encouraged.

Such precautions, however, did not preclude calling up these vast reservoirs of manpower for military purposes. The Ch'i-tan rulers had Chinese and Po-hai and even captives of war in their ordo troops; they selected groups of Chinese soldiers for training as catapultiers,[183] crossbowmen,[184] and swordsmen;[185] and they merged all commoners of the Southern Region into one large auxiliary army, the militia.

i. SIZE AND COMMAND

This army which was drawn from the "five capitals" was the country's "district army" (鄉兵);[186] its members were the "district men" (鄉丁)[187] or territorials; it functioned as a militia, an auxiliary "citizens' army," distinct from the regular army.[188]

Every able-bodied adult male commoner (丁) was expected to fulfill his military obligations, just as he was expected to render labor service and pay taxes. LS 36 states that two "men" were demanded from each individual household,[189] except in Tung-ching Circuit where the rate of conscription was lower.[190] The total strength of the militia was "roughly speaking" well over a million men,[191] that is, several times the combined manpower of all ordos at the moment of their greatest numerical strength.[192]

Command over this mass army rested in the hands of the officials of the "five capitals" who were charged with both the military and civil affairs of the sedentary population. Each capital had its "chief general officers" and a "chief commissioner of investigation."[193] However, the regional troops were more immediately

---

[168] *Cf.* XIV, 1 (13).

[169] LS 46, 14*b*–15*a*. The grand *ch'ang-kun* represented "the imperial lineage of the nine tents of Emperor T'ai-tsu's descendants" (XIV, 1 (14)).

[170] XV, 1 (33).

[171] XIV, 1 (9), LS 45, 5*a*–6*b*.

[172] LS 33, 1*b*–2*a* (*cf.* I, 2 (4), nos. 1 and 2).

[173] LS 46, 18*b*–19*a*.

[174] LS 46, 19*a*–*b*.

[175] XVI, 942, LS 4, 7*b*.

[176] I, 2 (5), nos. 22 and 32.

[177] I, 2 (9), nos. 18–20 and, possibly, 21.

[178] LS 46, 16*b*.

[179] XV, 2 (14).

[180] XV, 2 (21).

[181] VII, 1 (31).

[182] *Loc. cit.*

[183] XV, 2 (9) (15) (22).

[184] XIII (41).

[185] XV, 2 (15).

[186] XV, 1 (34). The "district" was a subdivision of a county composed of a number of villages.

[187] LS 36, 1*a*.

[188] For this definition see SOED I, 1250.

[189] *Cf.* LS 36, 1*a* ff. and LS 37, 39, 40, and 41. The figures for Chung-ching Circuit are fragmentary.

[190] *Cf.* LS 36 and LS 38, *passim* (see also I, introduction).

[191] XV, 1 (34).

[192] See above.

[193] XIV, 2 (8)

controlled by the prefects, who are listed as the commanders of the militia armies, trainbands,[194] and defence guards,[195] units which, it seems, differed more in number than in function.

ii. RECRUITMENT AND SCOPE

When a campaign was to be initiated, the militia soldiers were conscripted from the public registers,[196] and officials estimated the "ability" of an individual household, probably according to the number, age, and fitness of its male members. Whether the men received any military training in peacetime is not clear, but after mobilization the draftees were organized, lined up for inspection, and equipped with arms "from the military headquarters."[197] The last statement implies that, unlike the tribesmen, the conscript soldiers did not commonly own weapons.

The *Liao Shih* does not explain the relation of the "district soldiers" to those who served in the frontier garrisons. The frontier armies were drawn from the sedentary populations as well as from the nomad peoples.[198] Draftees were permitted to hire substitutes, but there still were rich men at the side of, or perhaps behind, the poor: "The rich join the army; the poor become patrols."[199] Did a similar system prevail in the regular militia service?

Ethnically, the bulk of the militia was Chinese; technically, it was an infantry army. There were Chinese horsemen among the ordo troops, in the Shu-shan Army,[200] and even among the "district men,"[201] but basically the militia remained an organization of footsoldiers.[202] Catapultiers and crossbowmen formed special detachments[203]—whether or not these belonged to the militia, we do not know.

Within its home territory, the militia supplemented the elite ordo troops and the tribal armies. During the greater part of Liao rule few hostile armies reached

the heart of the empire's sedentary regions, and the reliability of the militia soldiers was, therefore, rarely tested. In 979, when a Sung army besieged the Southern Capital, the inhabitants betrayed symptoms of unrest, but the Ch'i-tan armies repelled the invaders before any serious revolt occurred.[204]

In an emergency district troops were used even against tribal enemies of the dynasty. In 1114 a "mobilization of soldiers in all circuits" against the Jurchen was suggested,[205] and in 1117 an army of twenty-eight thousand men was raised from various prefectures for the defence of the eastern border.[206] But more important by far was the role played by the militia in the wars against the empire's great sedentary neighbors.

In 1015 Korea was attacked by ordo troops and well-trained soldiers selected by the Supreme Capital and the Central Capital.[207] The homeland of the Po-hai, Tung-ching Circuit, is not mentioned in this record, but promotions granted in 1019 to Po-hai generals and officers for merit in the war against Korea[208] indicate that Po-hai troops of some kind also participated. The ordos' horsemen were rallied before "the prefectures, countries, and tribes," but the militia and the tribal armies were not overlooked in a general mobilization. For the great campaigns against China Proper, all regions were ordered to conscript soldiers. Certain tribal troops,[209] the Po-hai of Tung-ching and the armies controlled by the Southern Capital, had to wait for a special signal: only when the goldfish tally arrived and was found genuine "the soldiers were put into motion."[210]

The tribal elite troops were mobilized reluctantly, probably because they held vital defence positions; the Po-hai of Tung-ching and the Chinese of Nan-ching presented political problems of a different order. They might be armed and used with safety as long as the empire was strong, but their loyalty remained uncertain and the Liao government was none too eager to put it to the test.

In their expeditions against China Proper the northern invaders employed a number of typically Chinese techniques and devices; they used ladders, poles, and rattan shields when attacking cities,[211] and the necessary weapons and implements were prepared by "the troops of the various circuits."[212] Large Chinese militia detachments accompanied the Liao armies for

---

[194] XIV, 2 (9).

[195] *Loc. cit.*

[196] XV, 2 (3).

[197] *Loc. cit.*

[198] XV, 1 (51).

[199] *Loc. cit.*

[200] XV, 1 (25).

[201] LS 48, 10*b*. Eighteen thousand Chinese horsemen who were stationed in the Nan-ching Circuit in eight cantonments (WHTK 346, 2708) may have been drawn from the militia. But the fact that they were provided with food by the government (HCLY 77, 5*a*) points to greater permanency. Perhaps they were the southern counterpart of the Chinese guards of the northwestern frontier.

[202] In 945, when T'ai-tsung attacked China Proper, the infantry army was under the command of the Chinese general, Chao Yen-shou 趙延壽 (LS 4, 13*a*).

[203] LS 46, 12*a*.

---

[204] Gabelentz 77, 79.

[205] XV, 2 (23).

[206] XV, 2 (27). *Cf.* also LS 46, 14*a–b*.

[207] XV, 2 (12).

[208] XV, 1 (50).

[209] See above.

[210] XV, 2 (3).

[211] SHYK 196, 30*a*.

[212] LS 12, 2*a*.

the express purpose of cutting down trees and repairing roads.[213]   These auxiliary services, which strengthened the oppressors' hitting power against the armies of China Proper, must be counted among the perversities of war, as tragic for one side as they were expedient for the other.

d. SPECIAL ARMIES

The three pillars of the Liao military system, the ordos, the tribes, and the militia, were supplemented by a number of secondary armed forces.   Outstanding among them were (1) the Shu-shan and P'i-shih Armies; (2) the personal armies of high Liao dignitaries; (3) the Shê-li Troops.

i. THE SHU-SHAN AND P'I-SHIH ARMIES

The same situation which brought about the organization of the first imperial guard led to the installation of *p'i-shih* officials and the creation of the Shu-shan Army.   A-pao-chi entrusted his personal protection to a "belly and heart" guard[214] which was headed by officials called *p'i-shih hsiang-wên* 皮室詳穩.[215]   To add to its security, the empress organized two hundred thousand valiant "barbarians" (tribesmen) and Chinese into the Shu-shan Army.[216]   The figure seems very large; other sources speak of only twenty to thirty thousand men.[217]

Whatever the new army's numerical strength, its general organization is of considerable interest.   The tribal sector of the Shu-shan Army may have been divided according to tribe or kin groups, but it was integrated in a super-tribal whole which included Chinese soldiers.   This pattern was so appealing that T'ai-tsung created another super-tribal organization, the P'i-shih Army, which is said to have numbered either three hundred thousand[218] or thirty thousand horsemen.[219]   LS 46, 11*b* claims that the P'i-shih Army existed in the early days of the dynasty, for *p'i-shih hsiang-wên*[220] were in command of A-pao-chi's bodyguard.   But this guard became the nucleus of the first ordo army,[221] not of the P'i-shih Army, which peculiarly preserved the old name.   The P'i-shih Army outlived its creator by many decades.   In the survey of Liao officers LS 46 enumerates the Offices of the *Hsiang-wên* of the Left, Right, Northern, Southern, and Yellow P'i-shih Armies,[222] and frequent references are made to their commanders in other parts of the History.[223]   Yet the P'i-shih Army remained one among many; the Shu-shan Army played no role in the military history of the Liao empire.   The concept of a super-tribal armed force seems to have been more successfully realized in the elite ordo troops.   As they grew in importance, the other more or less similar military organizations were either eliminated or, at least, seriously restricted.

ii. PERSONAL ARMIES

The personal armies of the imperial princes and high dignitaries were significant for political rather than military reasons.   The larger detachments numbered not much more than a thousand horsemen, the smaller ones, a few hundred—and even these modest units could not be disposed at will by their overlords; their members were listed by the central government, which might "borrow" three or five thousand horsemen when it so desired.[224]

The status of the warriors of the personal armies was probably not unlike that of the soldiers of the entrusted prefectures whose commanding prefect was an official of the central government,[225] and whose men were part of the general militia.[226]   Within the strongly centralized Liao state there was no place for an independent and genuinely feudal army.

iii. THE SHÊ-LI TROOPS

The word *shê-li*, probably meaning "turban," was used to designate individuals of distinguished status;[227] in a military context it obviously referred to military detachments of noble warriors.   A Shê-li Troop comprised the inner group of imperial clansmen, namely those belonging to the Horizontal Tents and the Three Patriarchal Households; the Shê-li Troops of the two great kings included imperial clansmen of the Five and Six Divisions.[228]   Another Shê-li Troop was attached to the Administration of the Hsi King,[229] and each tribe had a *Shê-li* Office, which "managed the military administration of the tribe's [noble ?] descendants."[230]

Whether the Shê-li Troops were always soldiers of noble rank is a question which the texts do not satis-

---

[213] XV, 2 (3).

[214] XV, 1 (26).

[215] LS 73, 6*a*.

[216] XV, 1 (25).

[217] CTKC 23, 3*a–b* and SHYK 196, 14*b*.

[218] XV, 1 (25).

[219] See note 217.

[220] XV, 1 (26).

[221] See above.

[222] LS 46, 11*a–b*.   See XV, 1, note 79.

---

[223] *Cf.* XV, 1 (47); XII (102).   See also LS 7, 3*b*; 10, 8*b*; 16, 2*b*; 21, 3*a*; 69, 17*b*.

[224] XV, 1 (32).

[225] XIV, 2 (9), LS 48, 9*b*.

[226] LS 46, 3*a–b*.

[227] VIII (12), and notes.

[228] LS 46, 11*b*.

[229] LS 46, 19*b*.   In 1027 a Hsiao clansman was the *hsiang-wên* of the Hsi Shê-li Troop (LS 17, 4*b*; *cf.* also LS 17, 2*b*).

[230] LS 46, 12*a*.

factorily answer. In 1029 a Shê-li Troop in the Eastern Capital was commanded by a Po-hai, Ta Yen-lin, who later organized a rebellion against the state.[231] Were the soldiers who served under him Ch'i-tan nobles or less favored nationals?

In 1039 the advantages and disadvantages of the tribal and Shê-li armies were discussed in relation to problems of unequal labor service and taxation.[232] The record is vague, but the issue of unequal privilege is conspicuous. The military significance of the (turban-wearing ?) Shê-li warriors seems to have been slight; nevertheless, the institution has importance for it illustrates again the complexity of organization within the tribal sector of Liao society.

e. THE FRONTIER GARRISONS

The defence of the empire's frontier is described at considerable length in the *Liao Shih;* yet the frontier garrisons present problems that are more easily noted than solved. LS 36 contains a detailed survey of the garrisons stationed on the Korean border; LS 37 enumerates the fortified cities of the northwest; and some memorials throw additional light on the military situation along the northwestern and western frontiers. The defences of the eastern border, which the *Liao Shih* regards as typical,[233] were concentrated in two cities and seventy fortified places. Their garrisons numbered a few hundred to five or ten thousand "regular" soldiers; their maximum, given in an undated passage, is said to have been twenty-two thousand men.[234]

The garrison soldiers are referred to as "regulars" (*chêng* 正). If the term has the same meaning in this context that it presumably had in the descriptions of the ordos, then the eastern border defence units were mustered exclusively from reliable (Ch'i-tan) tribesmen. Such an assumption seems to be reenforced by the fact that the only fortified city of the northwest whose numerical strength was specifically noted, Chên, was garrisoned by over twenty thousand horsemen selected from all tribes.[235]

Other records state with equal certainty that the frontier service was drawn from the sedentary populations as well as from the nomadic peoples of the empire;[236] and discussions of the hardships involved note that certain soldiers were expected to provision themselves from their own grain, and that some in their distress had been forced to sell their children and their fields.[237]

Po-hai, Jurchen, and Chinese nationals were "settled" in the fortified border cities of the northwest.[238] Yet the highest total reported is seven hundred households, among which the Chinese were quite inconspicuous.[239] This leads us to conclude that either the conscripted Chinese soldiers were included among the "regulars," or that the garrison lists count only the tribal shock troops. The record concerning Chên Prefecture supports the latter alternative.

But whichever hypothesis is preferred, neither explains the relation of the frontier "regulars" to the main components of the Liao army, the ordo troops, the tribes, and the militia. Was frontier service a duty required of all or only some members of these three armed forces? Ch'i-tan commoners were obliged to serve in the border garrisons, but Ch'i-tan nobles were exempted from this onerous duty;[240] and among the sedentary peoples, the rich could buy themselves off by hiring substitutes.[241] For different reasons, then, both the tribal nobility and the bureaucratic upper class were exempted from military obligation; among the commoners, those with some means were preferred, for they could provide their own grain and oxen during the trek to the border.

Once recruited, everyone had to serve unless he secured a substitute. The combined permanent frontier detachments must have mustered a considerable total. Taking the figure for the eastern frontier as a starting point, we may conservatively estimate that all the garrisons along the Liao borders together numbered somewhere between seventy-five and one hundred thousand regular soldiers.

f. OVER-ALL COMMAND

All the components of the Liao military machine were coordinated in an over-all organization which maintained absolute control in the hands of the sovereign and his close associates. The major decisions rested with the emperor alone. He reviewed the nomination of each army officer;[242] he sent out the two hundred silver tablets which guaranteed the genuineness of the total mobilization order; he accepted these tablets in person when they were brought back by his couriers from the empire's outposts.[243] In particularly vital areas the troops were mobilized only after golden tallies confirmed previous orders;

[231] XIII (38).
[232] XI (19).
[233] XV, 1 (43).
[234] *Loc. cit.*
[235] I, 1 (5).
[236] XV, 1 (51).
[237] *Loc. cit.*

[238] I, 1 (5).
[239] *Loc. cit.*
[240] XI (20). A member of the imperial house, Liu-ko, was exiled to the frontier (XIII (21)); this was evidently considered a severe punishment.
[241] See above.
[242] XIV, 2 (4).
[243] IV (16).

and it was the emperor himself, who entrusted these fateful symbols to high and dependable generals for delivery.[244] When a campaign was imminent, the emperor inspected his officers and selected meritorious relatives or reliable officials to act as chief and vice-commanders.[245] The big invasion armies were led personally by the monarch, while an imperial prince designated by him administered both civil and military affairs at home.[246]

The survey of the Liao military hierarchy does not include the emperor; his preeminence was self-evident. The imperial high command, which was part of the government of the Northern Region, was shared by two grand commanders in chief, the heir apparent or some other imperial prince holding one office,[247] the northern chancellor the other.[248] LS 46, 9b ff. lists certain other commanders without, however, explaining their functions. One title may be translated "deputy acting according to circumstances,"[249] a designation that implies great power in times of emergency. The *hsiang-wên* was a tribal officer; the grand *hsiang-wên* may have been concerned with the command of the (united ?) tribal armies.

Special officers were in charge of larger or smaller divisions of the empire's military organization, the East, the West, or the individual armies;[250] frontier defence was administered from regional headquarters.[251] The militia armies of the Southern Region were led by officials who exercised both military and civil authority.[252] The vicegerents and their territorial subordinates, the commanding prefects, took their orders originally from the Chinese chancellor of the Southern Region, but when this office was merged with the Southern Chancellery of the Northern Region[253] the command of the southern armies seems to have been shifted to the Northern Chancellery. Only one chancellor is mentioned in LS 46, 21b as supreme commander of the Liao fighting forces, and undoubtedly he was the northern chancellor of the Northern Region.

3. EQUIPMENT AND TRAINING

a. EQUIPMENT

The horseman being the backbone of the Liao army, his equipment is treated fully in the *Liao Shih*. This description furnishes the basis for a comparison with the armaments of the Mongol warrior which may be both illuminating and profitable in view of the unusual interest expressed today in the mounted soldiers of Chingis Khan and his successors.[254] LS 34 and Carpini are the two main sources of our information, but a few additional facts drawn from other duly noted texts have been included:

LIAO HORSEMAN	MONGOL HORSEMAN[255]
3 horses per "regular" soldier	A horse which was used for one day was not ridden for three or four days thereafter.[256] (Marco Polo, ed. Ramusio: an average of eighteen beasts to every man.[257])
armor: 9 pieces	helmets, coats of mail
saddle-cloths, bridles	stirrups, bits, saddles[258]
horse armor of leather and iron	armor for the horses' shoulders and breasts; some horses had leather jackets
4 bows	2 long bows or, at least, one good one
400 arrows	3 quivers full of arrows Marco Polo: 60 arrows, 30 light and 30 heavy ones[259] 1 file for sharpening the arrowheads
2 spears, 1 long, 1 short	
1 club	1 mace[260]
1 ax	1 ax
1 halberd	1 lance (sometimes with a hook at the end)
1 small banner	
1 hammer	
1 awl	
1 knife	
dried food	dried milk[261]
1 grappling hook	
1 umbrella	1 little tent[262]
200 feet of rope for tying the horses	rope to draw engines of war
swords[263]	swords[264]

[254] See Oman 24 II, 316 ff.; Morel 22; Liddell Hart 27; Sheppard 29; Walker 39.

[255] If not otherwise stated, the data for Liao are taken from XV, 2 (1); for the Mongol horseman: Carpini 28, 25 ff.

[256] This implies a total of four or five horses per warrior.

[257] Marco Polo 03 I, 264. The editor, Yule, places a question mark after the figure, which indeed seems absurdly high.

[258] Rubruck 00, 76.

[259] Marco Polo 03 II, 460.

[260] *Op. cit.* I, 260.

[261] *Op. cit.* I, 262.

[262] *Op. cit.* I, 261.

[263] VII, 1 (40).

[264] Carpini (28, 25) mentions single-edged swords for the richer; Marco Polo (03 I, 260 and II, 460) classes the sword among the regular weapons of the Mongol warrior.

[244] XV, 2 (3).

[245] *Loc. cit.*

[246] *Loc. cit.*

[247] XV, 1 (24).

[248] XIV, 1 (9); see also XV, 2 (2).

[249] XV, 1 (24).

[250] *Loc. cit.*

[251] See XV, 1 (42) and notes.

[252] See above.

[253] See XIV, introduction.

The Liao mounted "regular" so accoutered needed at least three horses, particularly if he wanted to keep his battle horse fresh. This equipment must have been greatly superior to that of the Hunnish soldier in the Han period, who may have possessed some kind of saddle,[265] but certainly had inferior bows[266] and no stirrup.[267] The Ch'i-tan warriors exploited the technical proficiency of their Chinese subjects; they were also better equipped than the Turks of the T'ang period,[268] although the great development in the saddle and stirrup had occurred in pre-T'ang time, and no basically new elements emerged in the Ch'i-tan arsenal. The stirrup, already an integral part of the saddle, is not mentioned separately in LS 34 or by Carpini. Rubruck notes its presence, not in discussions of warfare but in his descriptions of tribal industry: the average commoner made his own bows, arrows, stirrups, bits, and saddles.[269]

If the data in our two lists approximately reflect actual conditions, then the Mongol warrior possessed the finer armor and superior headwear. Upper-class Ch'i-tan usually wore caps[270] even with military dress,[271] and the archaeological finds show guards equipped with headgear[272] that bears little if any resemblance to the elaborate casque which protected the Mongol soldier's head and neck.[273] Swords are mentioned in a number of passages in the Liao Shih; they are also found on Liao reliefs and sculptures,[274] but in LS 34 the sword is not listed, perhaps because it was not part of a Liao horseman's regular equipment. The Liao bow was a powerful weapon; archaeology has disclosed two varieties, one simple[275] and

one composite.[276] According to the two lists, the Mongol soldiers carried fewer bows and arrows, but these were probably more effective than those of the Ch'i-tan. It is apparent that the Mongols simplified certain weapons of war: while the Ch'i-tan boasted a separate spear and grappling hook, the Mongols combined both devices in their lance.

There is no need here to compare the two lists item by item. The Ch'i-tan of the tenth and eleventh centuries evidently possessed a great variety of fighting weapons, some less developed, some more intricate, but none very different from those of the Mongol conquerors in the thirteenth century. The armed superiority of both peoples depended upon the archery of soldiers seated in dependable saddles. "The Ch'i-tan by ancient customs found it convenient to use saddled horses."[277] The saddle is mentioned many times in the Liao Shih. Saddled horses are listed before the bows and arrows in the survey of Liao armament; they are offered as gift or tribute by China Proper;[278] and even tribal officials and commanding prefects presented "saddle horses."[279] With bows and arrows, the saddle occupied a most conspicuous place in the country's great ceremonies. Saddled horses were used by the emperor and his mother during the great sacrifice to Mu-yeh mountain;[280] a newly-wed empress walked over a saddle.[281] Saddled horses were first on the list of precious gifts offered to a deceased emperor;[282] and among the highly valued objects burned in the funeral hall were "bows, arrows, saddles and bridles."[283] The recently discovered Liao reliefs of a saddled elephant[284] and a saddled lion[285] give a curiously distorted picture of Ch'i-tan life. Yet they confirm pictorially what the historical records assert in writing: the elaborate saddles and trappings used by this nation on horseback.

b. EVALUATION OF HANDICRAFT

A complex equipment for riding and fighting is no natural phenomenon like growing grass or running water; it must be produced by man's ingenuity. The development of a more advanced horsemanship had as its corollary the development of a more advanced tribal industry.

The Turks, who attained a dominant military posi-

---

[265] The Chinese horsemen of the Han period who fought the Huns used saddles, as is apparent from the description of an event which occurred before 141 B.C. (SC 109, 2b; cf. also SWCTC 3B, 12–13). In view of the permanent military and economic contact between the two peoples, it is very probable that the Huns imitated the Han saddle, if they did not possess the device before their settled neighbors.

[266] HS 49, 8a–11b.

[267] See above.

[268] Chou 50, 4b; CYCCC, 2a.

[269] Rubruck 00, 76.

[270] II, 1 (24); VII, 1 (39) and note. For pictorial presentations of Liao caps see Torii 36 III, pl. 191 ff.

[271] VII, 2 (94).

[272] Torii 36 III, pl. 184 ff.

[273] Carpini 28, 25.

[274] Torii 36 II, pls. 105, 106, 107, 108, 113; a monumental stone image of a man shows his two hands resting on a heavy sword (op. cit., pl. 152).

[275] A guardsman in a relief on the southern side of the White Tower of Ch'ing Prefecture holds a simple Chinese bow (Torii 36 II, pl. 105).

[276] A dignified figure painted on the wall of a Liao tomb carries a composite bow in a case (see fig. 41).

[277] IV (14).

[278] X, 2 (32) (36).

[279] X, 1 (15).

[280] IV (14).

[281] VII, 2 (89).

[282] VII, 2 (91).

[283] VII, 2 (54).

[284] Torii 36 II, pl. 113A.

[285] Op. cit., pl. 113B.

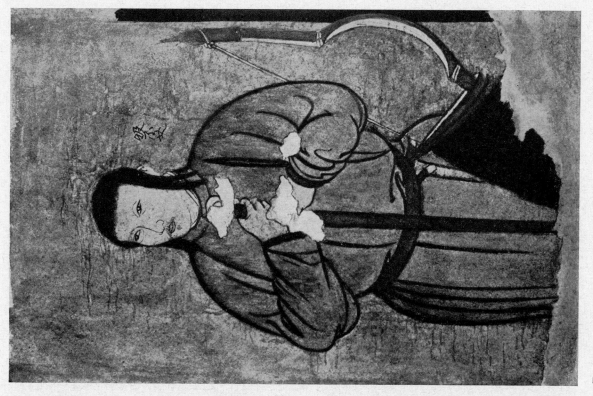

FIG. 41. Ch'i-tan dignitary holding a bow. Drawing on the wall of Hsing-tsung's tomb. Sketched by Miss Midorii Torii (Torii 36 III, pl. 196).

FIG. 40. The front and back of a Liao stone "screen" (IHC, fasc. 1).

tion in Inner Asia for a considerable period of time, were renowned metal workers.[286]   The Ch'i-tan paved the way to conquest and power by establishing iron smelteries[287] and settling Chinese in a region which "enjoyed the advantages of salt and iron."[288]   In the early period of Liao history T'ai-tsu's wife aided her husband by selecting prisoners with technical skills and transferring them to the centers of military activity, the camps.   These specialists were called *shu-shan*, "coral."[289]   The seemingly contradictory policy of the Mongol conquerors, who after capturing a city frequently annihilated its entire population with the exception of the technical (and religious) experts,[290] is completely consistent when examined in the light of the conqueror's needs.

c. TRAINING (CULTURAL CONDITIONING)

The Ch'i-tan tribesmen who herded and hunted in eastern Mongolia and western Manchuria received an elementary military training while pursuing their normal way of life.   Riding was the usual means of getting about,[291] and endurance was a necessary aid in combating a severe climate and periodic food shortages.   The intricacies of archery had to be learned early in a society that had to defend its herds and depended on wild game for part of its diet.

Descriptions of Ch'i-tan life naturally include both civil and military aspects,[292] for these were well integrated in the same over-all pattern.   The economic section of the *Liao Shih* states: "They bent the powerful [bow] and shot living [animals] in order to provide for their daily needs."[293]   The military section concludes: "They were skilled in fighting and could endure the cold.   This is why their military force was so powerful."[294]

d. TRAINING (MORAL AND MILITARY)

Trekking, camping, and hunting by their very nature encourage discipline and obedience.   But these social attitudes are fully developed only when they are consciously shaped by a society's educational will. The Huns crassly favored the young and strong as compared to the old and decrepit.[295]   Ch'i-tan law, however, made considerable effort to assert the authority of the elders; it condemned to death those who

turned against their parents.[296]   The same law safeguarded its officials by threatening the insertion of a hot iron awl into the mouth of anyone who dared to slander or vilify his superior.[297]

All the elements of warfare, skill in riding and shooting, discipline and endurance were coordinated in the great hunts whose semi-military character was well recognized by the Ch'i-tan themselves.   T'ai-tsung makes the point clearly: "Our hunting is not simply a pursuit of pleasure.   It is a means of practising warfare."[298]   Military officials were told what to avoid during a hunt,[299] and the emperor and his tribal and Chinese officials might wear military dress while following the game.[300]   Chinese and Po-hai were not permitted to engage in such exercises,[301] but tribal horsemen on occasion hunted by the thousands.[302]   In 1115 all the military units of the eastern army "were named after hunting grounds."[303]

The order in T'ai-tsu's army startled the Chinese general, Li Ts'un-hsün, who, in 922 after a victorious battle, entered the barbarian camp and found the straw piled neatly and carefully.   "Such discipline," he exclaimed, "the Chinese can never attain it."[304] In battle the Ch'i-tan soldiers formed organizational units of five and ten men.   In case any one member of the team failed to follow the leader during an attack on the enemy the whole group was put to death.[305]

The empire's technical troops were also submitted to systematic training and official inspection.   In 1036 a decree stated that "the catapultiers, crossbowmen, and swordsmen of all the armies should be periodically reviewed."[306]   In 1046 Hsing-tsung watched the Chinese catapultiers and swordsmen display their skills.[307]   No data describe the training of the militia, but the Chinese and Po-hai ordo soldiers were probably exposed to the same routine drill and discipline as were their Ch'i-tan comrades.

4. SUPPLIES

"Men and horses were not provided with supplies."[308]   The horses depended on water and grass,

---

[286] Chou 50, 2a; Sui 84, 1a; cf. also Barthold 97, 2.
[287] III (1).
[288] WTS 72, 2b–3a (see III, introduction).
[289] III (2) and note.
[290] D'Ohsson 1834 I, 239, 269, 286, and *passim*. Cf. also Vladimirtsov 30, 107 and Rubruck 00, 137 and 177.
[291] IV (14).
[292] II, 1 (2).
[293] *Loc. cit.*
[294] XV, 2 (3).
[295] SC 110, 2a.

[296] XIV, 4 (1).
[297] *Loc. cit.*
[298] XV, 2 (6).   Of course, many hunts were engaged in on a smaller scale for the exclusive pleasure of the distinguished hunters.
[299] II, 1 (12).
[300] VII, 2 (94).
[301] See above.
[302] II, 1 (7).   See also II, 1 (5).
[303] XV, 2 (24).
[304] CWTS 137, 4a.
[305] JLKI 2, 30.
[306] XV, 2 (13).
[307] XV, 2 (15).
[308] XV, 2 (1).

and the men on kumiss, game, and, when possible, plunder.[309] The Ch'i-tan, like the Turks[310] and the Mongols,[311] fought in cavalry armies that were essentially self-supporting. This factor, which contributed so much to the terrifying mobility of Mongol warfare,[312] similarly affected the military movements of the Ch'i-tan. In Inner Asia where the Ch'i-tan had to overcome what Napoleon called the most difficult of all obstacles for an army on the march, the desert,[313] their success depended primarily on their soldiers' self-sufficiency and endurance. During the campaigns in China Proper plunder became the preferred technique for maintaining the army. This technique, which does not draw upon the resources of the occupied country as a whole,[314] quickly exhausts the immediate environment of the invading forces.[315] While unsuited to stationary warfare, it is well adapted to mobile action.[316]

In peacetime a completely different situation demanded a completely different policy. The tribesmen who returned to their grazing grounds were again self-sufficient stockbreeders and hunters. Those ordo troops who lived in the attached districts probably also supported themselves. However, the provisioning of the guards stationed in the main camps and the numerous frontier garrisons presented serious problems. The Fair Purchase Granaries which had supplied the army during the T'ang period were reestablished on a large scale in the eastern frontier prefectures of the Liao empire.[317] The statement that they were never exhausted "in spite of frequent military expeditions"[318] indicates that they continued to function in the traditional manner. Funds assigned to the ordo camps[319] may in part have been used to feed the standing camp troops. The soldiers along the southern border were easily supported because they protected an agricultural hinterland that yielded the country's largest grain surplus and, incidentally, its most substantial land tax. It is certainly no accident that the two southern circuits had a particularly elaborate system of government transportation.[320]

Other conditions prevailed along the northwestern border; the "west," speaking more narrowly, was almost completely protected by the Gobi Desert.

North of the desert and remote from the centers of agriculture, the frontier garrisons were maintained only with great effort. It seems that the families of some tribal troops lived nearby, but the men remained with the army while "the work of grazing and herding devolves upon their wives and children." Exposed to predatory raids and deprived of their adult males, these insecure frontier households needed rather than provided food.[321]

Under such conditions, the system of pastoral self-sufficiency was inevitably strained, and the government had to look to other sources of supply. Food was transported to the northwestern border from the interior, but the routes were long and the people suffered in the effort.[322] The nearer, therefore, that civilian grain production could be shifted to the frontier, the better.[323] Soldiers from the agricultural regions were asked to carry their own provisions, but "by the time the garrison stations are reached, the supplies are already more than half consumed," and "hardly an ox or a cart returns."[324]

There remained the system of soldier farming which had long been successfully tested in China Proper.[325] According to LS 59, at the end of the tenth century garrison fields were set up "along each of the borders"; the fields were tilled by the soldiers themselves "to provide food for the army."[326] Effectively controlled, the garrison farmers produced abundant crops,[327] but such a dual task did little to lighten the frontier service, which was considered particularly onerous in the northwest where the soldier farms prevailed. In the middle of the eleventh century long-term benefit was expected, not by maintaining the northwestern system, but by radically withdrawing troops from the troublesome defence line, so that "the remote garrisons and the exhausted soldiers" might return home and compulsory services be decreased.[328] Hsiao Han-chia-nu's bold proposals do not seem to have been accepted, but his frank criticism of the frontier situation shows clearly that the maintenance of the empire's Inner Asiatic border garrisons was far more than a matter of endurance and pastoral self-sufficiency.

5. LIAO WARFARE

Composition, equipment, training, and the system of supply, all reveal an army's technical potential,

[309] See II, 1 (2) and note 308.
[310] CYCCC 2a.
[311] Marco Polo 03 I, 260.
[312] Loc. cit.
[313] Napoleon 40, 730.
[314] Cf. Clausewitz 57 II, 90 ff.
[315] Op. cit., 89.
[316] Op. cit., 87 ff.
[317] XII (119).
[318] Loc. cit.
[319] See above.
[320] XIV, 2 (7) (10).

[321] XV, 1 (45).
[322] XV, 1 (53).
[323] Loc. cit.
[324] XV, 1 (51).
[325] Cf. HS 7, 3a; 69, 12b–13b; 79, 6a; 96A, 3a; 96B, 13a, 18b, 19a; TT 2, 19; CTS 139, 16a; and 161, 8a.
[326] II, 2 (9). See also XV, 1 (45).
[327] XV, 1 (44).
[328] XV, 1 (51).

but they do not explain its actual achievement. The Ch'i-tan military machine, like others, operated in response to changing conditions, both internal and external. These changes ultimately determined the success as well as the limitations of Liao warfare.

a. WARS AGAINST THE TRIBES

The lengthy descriptions of Ch'i-tan warfare given in the military sections of the *Liao Shih* do not dwell on the empire's campaigns against its tribal neighbors. Compared with the great attacks launched against China Proper, the tribal wars must have appeared relatively insignificant to the Mongol conquerors who ordered the *Liao Shih* to be compiled and to the Manchu ruler who requested its partial translation.[329] Yet these wars played a decisive role in the military history of Liao, particularly during the first decades of the dynastic period. Early in his energetic career, A-pao-chi clashed with the Chinese armies of the border zone,[330] but he achieved his most important victories against the Jurchen,[331] Hsi,[332] Shih-wei,[333] Chu-pu-ku,[334] Wu-ku,[335] and against the Turkic and Tibetan peoples to the west. In 916 he "pacified" the Turks, T'u-hun, and Tang-hsiang,[336] and in 924, in his greatest western campaign, he defeated the T'u-hun, Tang-hsiang, and Tsu-pu.[337]

In 908 the Ch'i-tan extended the Great Wall,[338] that is, they set up a defence against their southern neighbors. In 917 A-pao-chi besieged the capital of Yu Prefecture for two hundred days, without being able to take it.[339] Local gains were made,[340] and a number of Chinese districts were seized or robbed of their manpower,[341] but the only agricultural country conquered was the Po-hai kingdom,[342] between the former Ch'i-tan territory and Korea. The founder of the Liao dynasty subdued and coordinated the tribes of eastern and middle Inner Asia; he secured a goodly number of Chinese subjects, whom he disposed shrewdly; but his armies never struck deeply into China Proper nor closely approached her capital.

This task fell to the second emperor, T'ai-tsung, who because of his father's northern victories was free to throw his armed forces southward into the key area of Later Chin. But even this mighty ruler had to be on guard against the tribes of Inner Asia,[343] who seemed meek and obedient enough when the empire's power was not being contested, but who rose in arms as soon as the Liao forces were seriously engaged. The Liao wars against Sung[344] and Korea,[345] the Po-hai rebellion of 1029,[346] and the conflict with Hsi Hsia,[347] all encouraged the border tribes to "rebellious" acts against their oppressors. The progressive decay of the dynasty became apparent in the long and sanguinary fight against the Tsu-pu tribes;[348] its final collapse was sealed in the struggle against the great tribal power of the east, the Jurchen confederation.[349]

The wars against the tribes were but the military expression of an unstable political situation.[350] Minor conflicts were settled by the local defence troops,[351] sometimes with the aid of loyal tribes.[352] A campaign against a powerful tribe or tribal confederation required greater effort. In 942 "soldiers from all circuits" were mobilized for an attack against the Tang-hsiang.[353] In 985 the empire's highest official, the northern chancellor, led an army against the Jurchen.[354] The extensive booty seized, one hundred thousand captives and two hundred thousand horses,[355] suggests the strength of the attacking Liao forces. In 1014 a huge army was sent against the "rebellious" Eight Tribes of Ti-lieh.[356]

The Liao troops were technically superior in a number of ways. They were equipped with metal weapons, whereas the sale of iron to their potentially dangerous neighbors was discouraged or even forbidden.[357] They used "war horses,"[358] probably protected by armor, which the tribes could produce only with difficulty. They carried a reserve of dried food

---

[329] The abridged Manchu version of the *Liao Shih* presents in full the description of the Liao campaigns against China Proper given in LS 34, but no attempt is made to reconstruct the history of the Ch'i-tan wars against the tribes (see Gabelentz 77, 189–194).

[330] XI (1); II, 1 (3) and *passim*.

[331] XVI, 903, LS 1, 1*b*; 906, LS 1, 2*b*.

[332] XVI, 903, LS 1, 2*a*; 906, LS 1, 2*b* and *passim*.

[333] XVI, 904, LS 1, 2*a*; 905, LS 1, 2*a*; 907, LS 1, 2*b* and 3*a*; and *passim*.

[334] XVI 912, LS 1, 4*b*.

[335] XVI, 915, LS 1, 8*a*; 919, LS 2, 1*a–b*.

[336] XVI, 916, LS 1, 9*a*.

[337] XVI, 924, LS 2, 4*b*.

[338] XI (2).

[339] XV, 2 (4); XVI, 917, LS 1, 10*a*.

[340] XVI, 902, LS 1, 1*b* and *passim*.

[341] XVI, 905, LS 1, 2*a*; 921, LS 2, 2*a–b*.

[342] XVI, 926, LS 2, 5*b* and 6*a*.

[343] I, 3 (2); XVI, 933, LS 3, 6*b*; 942, LS 4, 9*a*.

[344] XVI, 960, LS 6, 5*a* and *passim*.

[345] XVI, 1012, LS 15, 4*a* and *passim*.

[346] XIII (38).

[347] X, 2 (77).

[348] XVI, 1092, LS 25, 4*b*–5*a* and *passim*.

[349] XIII (45); XVI, 1113, LS 27, 7*a–b* and *passim*.

[350] See X, XI, and XIII, introductions.

[351] XVI, 997, LS 13, 8*a* and *passim*.

[352] XVI, 983, LS 10, 4*a*.

[353] XVI, 942, LS 4, 9*a*.

[354] XVI, 985, LS 10, 7*b*.

[355] II, 1 (10).

[356] XVI, 1014, LS 15, 8*a*.

[357] V (9) (15).

[358] XVI, 1093, LS 25, 5*b*.

with them, and they fought in well-organized disciplined units.

To some degree, the hostile tribes compensated for a less effective equipment and organization by their extraordinary ability to endure hardships and by their expert knowledge of techniques of evasion and retreat. However, as long as the empire was strong, the tribes of the outer border zone could not stand indefinitely against its superior military machine. Cornered and forced to fight, they finally had to yield. Their submission often involved more than a temporary military defeat. Whenever possible, the hostile tribal leader was replaced by an official whose collaboration could be relied on. But even more effective in preventing any resurgence of power was the seizure of the defeated tribes' herds. From one point of view, many Ch'i-tan forays were mere cattle wars, which increased the annual wealth of the Liao empire and weakened their potential enemies. The immediate advantage derived from capturing herds after victory[359] was multiplied by liens established on the herds of the future, the annual tributes demanded by the Liao government.[360]

Significantly, at the end of the eleventh century, serious tribal wars were again the concern of the tottering empire, but aggressor and victim had changed places. In 1094 the Tsu-pu and other tribes "stole" all the Liao horses in close-lying regions, and in 1095 the Ti-lieh made a similar raid. Whether or not the Liao troops succeeded in recovering all the lost animals, as the *Liao Shih* claims,[361] is less important than the mechanics of war revealed by the records. When the Liao empire collapsed, Yeh-lü Ta-shih escaped to Turkestan with all the horses herded north of the desert.[362] The conquering Jurchen showed little concern for the individual herds; when they occupied the Liao country, they automatically acquired all that remained of its animal wealth.

b. CAMPAIGNS AGAINST CHINA PROPER

The campaigns in "the south," that is, against China Proper, called for very different military ways and means. In Inner Asia wars might be fought and won by cavalry alone. Even against the Chinese empire, cavalry remained the most important weapon of Liao aggression.[363] But while the Ch'i-tan horsemen were successful in the open field, they were less so when attacking heavily fortified cities whose resistance could be more effectively broken by the use of technical troops and footsoldiers. This was quickly recognized, and such troops reenforced the Ch'i-tan cavalry in its fight against the enemy mass armies.

LS 34 does not clearly describe the development of the Ch'i-tan military machine during the first half of the tenth century, but other records leave no doubt that at the close of T'ai-tsung's reign a composite army was employed which, though still relying on its cavalry strength, was far different from the predominantly cavalry troops of A-pao-chi's early campaigns. Liao strategy mobilized both military arms in defence of the empire; it employed both with considerable expertness in maneuver, siege, and battle.

i. ORGANIZATION (COMMAND)

Organization was fundamental to the success of Liao warfare. In peacetime, the military machine was coordinated by a centralized command and a rigid discipline. Both these factors were heightened to the extreme when the country massed its armed manpower for a great campaign of invasion and conquest. At such times the emperor himself held the supreme command.[364] Under him, and somewhat modified, the dual peacetime command functioned: the chancellor with his staff of two "scribes" and a councillor on the one hand, and on the other the chief commander whose office included a number of top-ranking dignitaries, supervisors of the campaigning army.[365] In all probability, these supervisors belonged to that group of meritorious grandees who were nominated to their positions of commander and vice-commander by the emperor.[366]

Each chief commander acted as a check on the other.[367] But, since the chancellor's position was permanent and supreme, the establishment of a joint military command in time of war primarily restricted his power. Other imperial appointees who temporarily assumed significant military posts obviously fulfilled a similar function.

The division of an invasion army into a vanguard, two wings, a center, and an imperial guard was logically expressed in the hierarchy of its commanders.[368] The military police[369] in all probability maintained rigid discipline and threatened with death any soldier who did not blindly follow the orders of his immediate superior, or who failed to cooperate completely with the movements of his unit.[370]

[359] See X, introduction.

[360] *Op. cit.* The practice of seizing the defeated enemy's horses and cattle is a typical feature of the military history of Inner Asia. See TS 215A, 11a; Radloff 97, 138, 141, 144, 146; *cf.* also Barthold 97, 30.

[361] XVI, 1094, LS 25, 7a; 1095, LS 26, 1a.

[362] II, 1 (3).

[363] LS 4, 9b ff.

[364] XV, 2 (3).

[365] XV, 2 (2).

[366] XV, 2 (3).

[367] XV, 2 (2).

[368] XV, 2 (3).

[369] XV, 2 (2).

[370] JLKI 2, 30.

ii. ORGANIZATION (SUBDIVISIONS)

The "natural" groupings of kin and tribe were not the determining factors in Liao army organization although the smaller units may well have been filled with members of such groups. Long before Chingis Khan and long before A-pao-chi, the great tribal powers of Inner Asia had begun to arrange their troops in numerically determined divisions. The Huns are said to have had units of ten thousand men whose leaders exercised control over the chiefs of lesser commands of ten, a hundred, or a thousand warriors.[371]

The Liao armies were organized similarly. Groups of five or ten soldiers are mentioned;[372] enemy cities were guarded by units of a hundred horsemen;[373] larger divisions, "regiments," comprised between five and seven hundred men;[374] "ten regiments formed a column and ten columns a side."[375] Depending on the figure chosen, the next two higher units must have numbered either five or seven thousand and fifty or seventy thousand soldiers respectively. The indefiniteness of these figures is manifest; yet equally manifest is the effort to arrange the huge Liao fighting machine in multiples of ten. The precise organization of a war machine, counted by modern strategists among Chingis Khan's greatest achievements,[376] was clearly visualized, if not completely realized, by the military master-minds of Ch'i-tan glory.

iii. SCOUTS, VANGUARDS, SIGNALS

Another aspect of Mongol warfare that has received recent attention is the excellent system of intelligence.[377] Intelligence in general, and scouting in particular, were indeed important in the Mongol and pre-Mongol art of war, but like other factors they have to be seen in relation to the whole military and cultural pattern of which they are a part. Frederick II's small compact infantry army used few scouts or vanguards,[378] and in the positional warfare of 1914–1918 scouting was completely subordinated to other strategic devices.

The mounted tribesmen of Inner Asia, however, had developed a highly flexible system of intelligence as a necessary adjunct in their struggle for existence. The mobility of their pastoral life made a surprise attack an ever-present possibility; disaster could be avoided only by super-mobile scouting techniques.

In inter-tribal warfare, the use of these techniques was not too terrifying, for both sides were familiar with them. In a campaign against a sedentary enemy, the mounted scouts of the steppe added appreciably to the general impression of the fiendish omnipresence and unpredictability of the great barbarian armies.

The Liao invaders used scouts to guide and protect their movements. A small scouting force of a hundred dare-devils moved ahead of a vanguard of three thousand picked fighters.[379] The three main armies were flanked on all sides by "vanguard" troops, who in turn were "preceded and followed . . . at a distance of more than twenty li" by scouting forces of over ten men each.[380] The scouts were well armored; they were trained to the sound of men and horses moving through the night. If they met a few of the enemy, they made every effort to capture them; if many, they appealed to the vanguard to assist in the attack. Thus the enemy's tentacles were destroyed and the main forces quickly uncovered.[381] The three armies which invaded China Proper employed an unbelievably large number of scouts: each of them, it is claimed, disposed over ten thousand scouts who moved within a radius of ten to a hundred li. Smaller units were sent wherever need arose; mobile patrols were posted at night on both sides of the paths, mountain roads, highways, and river ferries.[382]

Within the main body of the army numerous devices speedily relayed orders and information. Soldiers were selected "to bring in troops and to dispatch messages";[383] but certain military orders reached the commanders of remote detachments more quickly if conveyed by signal.

The Liao armies had a large arsenal of signals well adapted to need and circumstance. At the border stations they were directed by beacons placed on special platforms;[384] on the march by visual and acoustic devices which could be easily transported or shifted about. Three rolls on the drum were the final signal for getting under way; the sound of horns announced a halt and rest.[385] During the day Ch'i-tan warriors were directed by banners;[386] if an army split during a fight the sections would try to give information to, and reestablish contact with, each other by shouting Ch'i-tan place names,[387] obviously in accordance with a pre-arranged code. During the

---

[371] SC 110, 9b and 10b.
[372] JLKI 2, 30.
[373] XV, 2 (3).
[374] Loc. cit.
[375] Loc. cit.
[376] Liddell Hart 27, 9 ff.
[377] Walker 39, 204.
[378] Clausewitz 57 II, 39 ff.

[379] XV, 2 (3).
[380] Loc. cit.
[381] Loc. cit.
[382] Loc. cit.
[383] Loc. cit.
[384] XI (18).
[385] XV, 2 (3).
[386] JLKI 2, 30.
[387] XV, 2 (3).

night signals were given by gongs and conches, and by imitating the calls of birds and animals.[388]

Whether the military leaders relied completely on the information provided by scouts, guides, and spies,[389] or whether they also depended upon maps is not stated in the military sections of the *Liao Shih*. It is more than probable, however, that maps were valued not only as symbols of domination, but as sources of administrative and topographical information. In 938 the Chin government, when ceding the sixteen prefectures to T'ai-tsung, delivered at the same time "maps and documents";[390] in 947 the Ch'i-tan troops seized the "maps and books"[391] which they found at the Chinese court; in 1002, impressed by a great Liao victory over Sung China,[392] Korea presented the Liao government with "maps of their country."[393] In the numerous campaigns against China Proper and Korea these maps must have proved most useful to the Ch'i-tan aggressors.

iv. ORGANIZATION OF INVASION—TACTICS OF BATTLES

The Liao army was able to move with great speed as long as it was composed entirely of cavalry units. The addition of infantry troops established an inverse ratio between mobility and coordination. Combined forces were not always employed, particularly not on the steppe, but in such great campaigns as those of 944 and 946 both branches were effectively engaged. In 944 T'ai-tsung himself led an army which consisted in part of Hsi infantry.[394] In 946 Chao Yen-shou's footsoldiers, who at times fought separately, cooperated closely with the mounted force of the invading army.[395]

The Liao government issued orders forbidding its troops to damage the empire's crops.[396] Such a measure was superfluous when a campaign fell within the preferred fighting season, which began in the fall and ended "not later than the twelfth month," but military movements were not always confined to this schedule.[397] On Chinese soil the troops proceeded

ruthlessly; "the infantry, cavalry, and tent-carts did not follow roads and paths," and the destruction of crops and orchards was systematically encouraged.[398]

The organization of the invading troops imitated certain time-honored Chinese features and foreshadowed the Mongol pattern.[399] The central army, led by the emperor, was flanked by two wing armies. These, like the imperial guard, a force of considerable size (not identical with the ordo troops), kept their separate columns and followed separate routes.[400] The idea of preserving an elite reserve recommended itself from the military as well as from the political point of view.

If the northern troops had been similar in composition to the Sung armies, they would have had little chance of success, for the latter were far superior in manpower and material resources. Only a more effective cavalry force enabled the Ch'i-tan emperors to defeat the armies of China Proper. Ch'i-tan tactics were designed to bring to the fore the specific strength of their mobile archers. Men and horses had to be fresh when they entered battle: the Ch'i-tan mounted their war horses only when they were closing in on the enemy,[401] and at times they even transported their armor in carts.[402]

When nearing the enemy, the Ch'i-tan employed methods of nomadic warfare that had been familiar to the Scythians[403] and the Huns[404] and that were used with increased effectiveness by the Turks[405] and, at a later period, by the Mongols.[406] Combat at close range was avoided until such moment when the enemy was exhausted or his massed force loosened. To weaken morale and fighting power supply lines were cut, fires set at night, and annoying dust clouds raised. Volleys of arrows were shot from the bows of mounted warriors who withdrew as quickly as they advanced, only to return again and again until the enemy forces were worn out by wounds, hunger, and general fatigue.[407] The light cavalry which had no armor was placed in the van, the partly armored warriors followed, and the heavily mailed fighters were kept in the rear.[408] Such an arrangement al-

---

[388] JLKI 2, 30.

[389] According to SS 326, 17a, during the last years of the Sung-Liao war, inhabitants of the border zone "frequently acted as local guides for the Ch'i-tan."

[390] XVI, 938, LS 4, 2a–b.

[391] VII, 2 (22).

[392] XVI, 1002, LS 14, 3b.

[393] X, 2 (59).

[394] CWTS 95, 9b.

[395] LS 4, 13a.

[396] XV, 2 (3).

[397] The campaigns of 908, 924, 928, 982, 983, and 1014 began or were continued in the warm season (see XVI, *passim*), but many more military actions were undertaken either in the fall or in the spring. Months of particularly

high frequency were the tenth (early winter) and the first (winter's end).

[398] XV, 2 (3).

[399] See Howorth, HM I, 115.

[400] XV, 2 (2); *cf.* also XV, 2 (3).

[401] *Loc. cit.*

[402] IV (12).

[403] *Cf.* Herodotus 42, 269 ff.; Neumann 55, 303.

[404] SC 110, 2a.

[405] CYCCC 2a.

[406] Hyathon, *Livre de la Fleur de l'Orient* = Strakosch-Grassmann 93, 27; d'Ohsson 1834 I, 399 ff.

[407] XV, 2 (3).

[408] NKCML 13, 9a.

lowed for maximum mobility during the initial stages of the battle, and for maximum vigor and protection at the moment of shock attack.

The assault is said to have been undertaken with great "clamor" (譟),[409] but it may be questioned whether such a statement refers to organized shouting or to the unavoidable noise of onrushing horsemen. The Mongol attacks seemed most terrifying to the European soldiers because they were made silently.[410] The Ch'i-tan also recognized the value of such an attack of nerves: in battle their warriors "had to hold a piece of wood in their mouth and must not make noise."[411]

Camping was simple.[412] A cavalry troop which was protected by a cordon of scouts had little need to erect cumbersome fortifications.[413] Being highly mobile, the nucleus of the Liao army felt comparatively safe from any surprise attack unleashed by a slow-moving enemy.

The hit-and-run tactics of the open battle and its corollary, the ambush, which appeared savage, unnatural, and fiendish to the Chinese strategists, were completely natural and rational from a barbarian point of view. The nomadic herders and hunters of Inner Asia continued to use them to their advantage until new inventions reasserted the military superiority of their agrarian and industrial neighbors.

v. SIEGES

When invading China Proper, the Liao armies were hampered by trees and ditches and by innumerable fortified cities. These were serious obstacles for the northern horsemen whose pastoral training included little or no experience in military engineering. Faced with them, the Ch'i-tan strategists called upon their Chinese militia and the sedentary populations of the occupied areas. Special Chinese troops were ordered to hack down the trees and orchards and repair roads. The mounted foragers also engaged in the auxiliary tasks, but more particularly it was they who rounded up the civilian population, both young and old, and compelled them to fill the moats and ditches with wood and soil.[414] These poor creatures were given

noteworthy assistance in destroying their home defences by their fellow-Chinese catapultiers, who battered and demolished the walls and towers of the beleaguered cities.[415] When the defences were sufficiently shaken, typically Chinese weapons—ladders, long poles, rattan shields—were brought into action.[416] Then, gruesome spectacle, the Chinese civilians were compelled to lead the way. They and not the Liao soldiers bore the brunt of the defending forces' missiles, arrows, stones, and rolling logs.[417] This mode of advance must have been as devastating to the morale of the fighting Chinese of the tenth century as it was two hundred years later when Chingis Khan employed it against the fortified cities of North China: then the defenders on the wall recognizing their own brothers and fathers did not dare to use their arms against their cunningly protected Mongol aggressors.[418]

The Ch'i-tan were able to encircle and take Chinese cities, but sieges remained a cumbersome task for an army that had to move fast because it lacked an organized system of supply and because it was eager to complete its winter campaigns before the beginning of the next growing season. The advancing Liao troops might threaten to encircle a strongly walled town; they might make a feint attack, and they might leave a scouting force to report on the garrisons' movements, but whenever possible they were eager to avoid a long continued siege.[419]

vi. TWO PRE-MONGOL ACHIEVEMENTS OF LIAO WARFARE

The difficulties which the Liao armies encountered when they attacked fortified Chinese cities must not obscure the fundamental fact that the Ch'i-tan concluded a number of highly successful campaigns against the great southern country, campaigns which culminated in the temporary seizure of its capital and in the permanent acquisition of sixteen rich prefectures and numerous strategically important mountain passes.

Contrary to the opinion of Delbrück and others that a general history of war may neglect the great Mongol campaigns,[420] writers on military affairs have recently paid increasing attention to them[421] and to the tactical lessons they offer. In 1927 a study of "the period of the great raids of the Mongols" was recommended by the chief of the British Imperial General Staff, significantly, to the officers of the Mechanized Bri-

---

[409] LS 34, 5a.

[410] Thomas Spalatinus, *Historia Salonitana* = Strakosch-Grassmann 93, 28.

[411] JLKI 2, 30.

[412] XV, 2 (3).

[413] The Sui emperor, Yang, noticed the absence of any camping technique among the Turks (CYCCC 2a). It is an interesting parallel that with the growing predominance of cavalry within the Byzantine army the old Roman tradition of camping also fell into decay (*cf.* Grosse 20, 305 ff.).

[414] XV, 2 (3).

[415] XV, 2 (9) (10).

[416] SHYK 196, 30a.

[417] XV, 2 (3).

[418] D'Ohsson 1834 I, 141.

[419] XV, 2 (3).

[420] Delbrück, GK III, 487.

[421] *Cf.* the sketch of Mongol warfare in Oman 24 ii, 316–323.

gade;[422] and a textbook of the World's Military History for American Officers devotes about as much space to Chingis Khan as to Alexander the Great or Caesar.[423]

Authors have differed in their emphasis on one or another aspect of Mongol warfare: organization, discipline, mobility, striking power, the scouting system.[424] Liddell Hart has singled out three factors as essential to its success: simplicity of the military system (the use of a single arm, cavalry), superior mobility, and hitting-power.[425] "The Mongol tactics were to avoid closing with the adversary until he was weakened and disorganized by fire."[426] "For the first time in military history" fire was "employed systematically to pave the way for the assault."[427] The success of this mode of attack "proved that mobility is the king-pin of tactics, as of strategy; that lightly armed troops can beat more heavily armed ones if their mobility is sufficiently superior, demonstrating that the 'weight' of a force is weapon-power *multiplied* by its mobility, and that this mobility is a far better protection than armour or any such form of negative defence."[428]

Liddell Hart's analysis, which has been frequently quoted and reprinted, offers a key, not only to an understanding of the military career of Chingis Khan, but to the whole epoch of cavalry warfare which culminated in him. Mobility plus hitting-power is certainly a more acceptable formula than one that stresses only mobility. But while the Orientalist gratefully acknowledges the contribution of this military expert, whose technical authority cannot be questioned, he must qualify certain historical assertions.

Chingis Khan did not "for the first time in military history" combine superior mobility and hitting-power. As early as the middle of the first millennium A.D., this combination was known; it resulted no doubt from the rise of the cavalry arm which in turn followed upon great changes in nomadic industry and, more particularly, upon the invention of a saddle with stirrups. To the great distress of their Chinese contemporaries, the Turks in Inner Asia had recognized the value of the new technique for centuries before the Mongol conquest. But the Turkic assaults against the Middle Kingdom did not result in the "unbroken run of victory" which Liddell Hart ascribes to the Mongol armies.[429] The Turks had both mo-

bility and hitting-power, but it would seem little else. The same Sui emperor, who acknowledged the superiority of their mounted archery, added, no doubt with relief, that "their troops were not drawn up in orderly ranks" (隊不列行).[430]

The Turks of the early seventh century evidently lacked the clock-like coordination of tactical movements which Liddell Hart admiringly noted in the Mongol armies. The introduction of the saddle with stirrups was only an important first step in the growth of Inner Asia's military potential. A second had to follow: the welding of the floating mass of mounted archers into an integrated fighting machine. This development may well have begun after the fall of the Sui dynasty, when the Turks, Uighurs, and Ch'i-tan came in increasingly close contact with the organized Chinese armies, at times even serving in their ranks; but it gained full momentum only with the rise of Liao power. It would probably be an oversimplification to say that A-pao-chi or his successors "invented" the disciplined arrangements of their armed forces, yet there can be little doubt that this new type of military organization became historically conspicuous for the first time in the Ch'i-tan (Liao) army.[431] The combination of superior mobility and great hitting-power with a clock-like organization (and perhaps improved armaments) prepared a new military potential which was fully utilized, but not conceived, by Chingis Khan.

A second qualification concerns the claim that "the use of a single arm," cavalry, was "the secret" of the unbroken run of Mongol victory.[432] Pure cavalry attacks were extremely successful in open battle and against a weak enemy, but they were much less effective when directed against the massive fortifications of strong and large countries. At the beginning of the thirteenth century the single arm of Mongol horsemen bogged down between the walled cities of the Yellow River basin; and Chingis Khan died without having achieved his most desired goal, the conquest of China. Only after adding an infantry troop and an engineering corps to their cavalry force did the Mongol aggressors succeed in gradually breaking the resistance of a disunited China.

By proceeding thus, the Mongol armies utilized

---

[422] Sheppard 29, 304.

[423] Mitchell 40, 219–242, 38–68, 101–125.

[424] See Morel 22, 358 ff.; Sheppard 29, 313 ff.; Walker 39, 204 ff.; Mitchell 40, 221 ff.

[425] Liddell Hart 27, 32 ff.

[426] *Op. cit.*, 31.

[427] *Op. cit.*, 28.

[428] *Op. cit.*, 31 ff.   Italics in the original.

[429] *Op. cit.*, 32.

[430] CYCCC 2a.

[431] Early Turkic laws severely punished the rebel, but the "old" fared badly compared with the "strong" (Chou 50, 5a and 4a). The Ch'i-tan sanguinarily enforced respect for the old and for their superior officers (see XIV, 4 (1)). No unilineal development is claimed by this juxtaposition, yet whatever the earlier Ch'i-tan tradition, A-pao-chi's "laws" like Chingis Khan's Yasa strikingly coincide with the growing power of the Ch'i-tan and Mongol military machines.

[432] Liddell Hart 27, 32.

and extended a pattern of attack familiar to the Ch'i-tan several centuries earlier. The need for this technique indicates that mobility, though an extremely powerful weapon, was not always "the king-pin of tactics, as of strategy."[433] There existed in China Proper, as in other Asiatic countries, non-mobile forms of what Liddell Hart calls "negative defence,"[434] which could be overcome only by "complex" armies—if they could be overcome at all.

vii. THE GREAT STUMBLING BLOCK

The fight of agricultural China against northern hunters and herders has passed through several phases. Before the middle of the first millennium B.C. the horse, which was bred by both groups and ridden by neither, was a military asset to the charioteering Chinese. The formula, "they [the barbarians] are footmen, we [the Chinese] have chariots,"[435] properly describes a situation that lasted until some time around 500 B.C., when the tribes of Inner Asia learned to ride on horseback.[436]

The increased mobility of tribal warfare that resulted seriously threatened the safety of the Chinese border states; in the fourth century their rulers hastened to build walls, not only against their sedentary neighbors, but also against the mounted barbarians of the north.[437] In 307 B. C. King Wu-ling 武靈 of Chao 趙 ordered his army to adopt the enemy's military techniques as the only hope for successful resistance.[438]

---

[433] Op. cit., 31.

[434] Op. cit., 32.

[435] CCTCCS 4, 8b [714 B.C.]; 41, 10a [536 B.C.].

[436] Erkes 40, 55.

[437] SC 43, 17a, 19a; 110, 5b and 6a. Cf. also Wang KL 31, 22 ff. and 27 ff.

[438] SC 43, 22a ff. Ch'i Ssŭ-ho and Erkes have discussed the date of the introduction of horseback riding in China, arriving at the conclusion that the technique appeared in China during the period of the Warring States, that is, between 403 and 221 B.C. (Ch'i SH 38, 191) or somewhat before 307 B.C. (Erkes 40, 49–55). The two scholars reject certain earlier dates with arguments which are plausible, though perhaps not altogether conclusive. Another passage suggesting a slightly earlier beginning for the art of riding in China should be mentioned. In the Ch'un-ch'iu the word an 鞍 appears as part of a place name in an incident that occurred in 590 B.C. (CCTCCS 25, 2b). The Han dictionary, Shuo Wên, defines an as a device to ride on a horse (SWCTC 3B, 12). Through the years it has always meant "saddle" (TH sub 鞍, Couvreur 11, 594; Giles 12, 47).

Of course, an may originally have had a somewhat different meaning. But whatever the final decision in this and similar cases may be, the assertion that riding horseback spread in the Far East around the middle of the first millennium B.C. may be considered valid, if reasonable allowance is made for a period of incubation and for

The new Chinese system of defence reached its peak of effectiveness when the first Ch'in emperor, after having unified "all-under-heaven," merged the several frontier walls into one Great Wall,[439] and when, somewhat later, the Han emperors bulwarked their complex and well-armed war machine[440] by a semi-military border zone of considerable depth and elasticity.[441]

These measures created a temporary equilibrium between the two opposing civilizations; but the balance again favored the steppe when the introduction of the stirrup added increased hitting-power to the barbarians' superior mobility. This technical development, which probably occurred somewhere between A.D. 220 and 400[442] was reflected in the growing importance of the barbarian cavalry. Having entered the empire as guests, fugitives, settlers, or paid mercenaries, they soon used their military strength to establish "infiltration states" and even "infiltration dynasties." Among the former dynasties the Hunnish Early and Later Chao 趙 (304–351) deserve particular attention; among the latter, the T'o-pa Wei (386–556) are most noteworthy.

The growing barbarian aggressiveness intensified the Chinese strategy of defence. In the following centuries Turkic and Uighur invasions shook the reunified empire repeatedly, but Chinese strategy, supported by a daring and flexible diplomacy, succeeded in preventing the permanent occupation of any essential part of Chinese territory. During the very period in which Arab cavalry overran the greater part of Byzantium's Near Eastern possessions and the whole of Persia, China resisted all barbarian attacks and, in the eighth century, temporarily extended its dominion over large sections of Central Asia. In more than three hundred years of violent warfare the Sui and T'ang dynasties had proven that the Chinese military machine could cope with this new type of barbarian mobility plus hitting-power.

The post-T'ang period demonstrated again what the pre-Sui epoch had shown earlier: the mounted northern aggressors had great difficulty in combating

---

regionally diversified diffusion. The date of the origin of the great Chinese military classic, Sun Tzǔ 孫子, is still debated. L. Giles (10, xxviii) assumes that the book was written between 505 and 496 B.C. There is no need here to enter into the argument, but it may be noted that the Sun Tzǔ does not discuss cavalry warfare, but only movements of footsoldiers and chariots.

[439] SC 6, 22a.

[440] Hunnish archery could not match the Chinese crossbow and long lance. The well-organized and well-armed Chinese infantry, supported by light chariots and shock cavalry, was superior to the mounted Huns "in the plain and on even terrain" (HS 49, 8a–11b).

[441] HS 49, 11b–14b.

[442] See above.

the Chinese defence in depth. The recognized bearers of Chinese national tradition and sovereignty might lose considerable territory; yet, because they could fall back upon many well-protected and well-provisioned cities, they were able to wear down their oppressors and maintain their independence in the great Central and South Chinese regions except twice: in the thirteenth and seventeenth centuries when inner disunity paralyzed their resistance to the invading Mongol and Manchu armies.

The tenth century seemed to offer a similar opportunity for total conquest. The decay of the T'ang empire encouraged the growth of Ch'i-tan power, but, as happened in the early days of the Mongols, it took the founders of the Liao state several decades to consolidate their empire and to prepare for an all-out assault against their strong southern neighbor. Ogotai's attacks exposed the inner weakness of the Chin 金 conquest dynasty and the chasm between the Chin north and the Sung south. The thrust of the Liao armies against the Chinese capital, Pien, in 946–947, while it overthrew the Chin 晉 regime, actually paved the way for the reunification of China Proper.

The Liao rulers lost out in the race between inner consolidation and further conquest. After the establishment of the Sung dynasty in 960 the southern country entered upon an era of renewed political, economic, and military might. During the later part of the tenth century the Liao armies learned in a series of sanguinary campaigns what the Turks had realized centuries earlier—that even a powerful army of nomads should think twice before attacking a united and prosperous China.[443] After a thirty-year war against Sung the Liao rulers were forced to abandon the hope they had had of controlling "the Southern Countries";[444] they had to be satisfied with the territory acquired by the first two Liao emperors. For more than one hundred and fifty years the Sung armies successfully defended their country against the Ch'i-tan military machine with its terrifying mobility, hitting-power, rigid discipline, and organization.

As the Chinese had done from the days of King Wu-ling on, the Sung generals opposed the mounted barbarians with a well-trained cavalry force of their own. In 979, when a showdown with Liao was imminent,[445] the Sung government ordered the purchase of one hundred and seventy thousand horses for the army;[446] in 1008, three years after peace was concluded,

it boasted more than two hundred thousand horses;[447] and in the second half of the eleventh century Wang An-shih again introduced special measures to increase the cavalry mounts.[448]

Even so, the Sung horsemen were no match for the Liao cavalry which was superior in numbers as well as skill. Alone, the mounted Sung soldiers could not stop the barbarian invaders; success against their ruthless attack could be achieved only by complex armies, bulwarked by a strategy different from that of mobile warfare. The Mongol fighter, as Oman correctly notes, "was essentially a conqueror of the steppe and plainland."[449] His movements were seriously, and sometimes hopelessly, impeded by woodlands and swampy terrain and by fortified cities, particularly when their walls were strong and their granaries filled.

The Sung strategists, fully aware of the importance of these various factors, utilized them as the basis of their defence system. After the fall of the T'ang empire important mountain passes in the north of modern Hopei and Shansi were lost to A-pao-chi and his son, but many southwestern mountain regions were still occupied either by Sung or Hsi Hsia troops. The Chinese rulers did everything in their power to keep these military key positions from falling into the hands of their dreaded Liao enemies. In addition, they systematically built posts and fortresses in the northern border zone; and along a frontier of 800 *li*, they planted three million elm and willow trees, and dug canals, ditches, and artificial lakes— some one hundred *li* long, fifty *li* broad, and ten feet deep.[450] This elaborate defence system was manned by large garrisons which numbered about 28,000 soldiers in Ting 定 Prefecture; 45,000 in Shun-an 順安 Commandery; 42,000 in Ying 瀛 Prefecture; 10,000 in Mo 莫 Prefecture;[451] and 73,000 in Ping 并 Prefecture (or Ho-tung Lu).[452] The Liao troops who broke through the outer defence cordon found behind it innumerable walled cities and, supporting these "porcupines" of the interior, large standing armies which were later augmented by militia. The equipment of the Sung armies may frequently have been inadequate, their military quality uneven, and at times poor; but they fought bravely in battle and,

---

[443] *Cf.* Radloff 99, vi.

[444] I, 3 (2).

[445] XVI, 979, LS 9, 2a.

[446] SS 198, 3a. Cavalry warfare is comprehensively discussed in the military writings of the Sung dynasty (see WCTY 4, 4b ff. and 5, 6b ff.). The whole chapter 198

of the *History of the Sung Dynasty* is devoted to a survey of the country's cavalry.

[447] SS 198, 3a.

[448] SS 15, 7b; 198, 26b. *Cf.* also Williamson, WAS I, 256 ff.

[449] Oman 24 II, 323.

[450] WCTY 16A, 1a ff.

[451] *Loc. cit.* and *passim*.

[452] *Op. cit.* 17, 1a–17b. The principles of the Sung defence strategy, which included a scorched earth 清野 policy, are outlined by Sung Ch'i 宋祁 (T. 子京, 998–1061) in seven essays (CWC 44, 547–562).

aided by the country's defence in depth, with considerable success.

The Liao rulers fully realized the difficulties presented by such a system of defence to any invading cavalry army. Suspicious of irrigated fields in their own territory,[453] they were particularly sensitive to the ditches and moats, some of which were dug by their Sung neighbors expressly "to ward off the Liao people."[454] In 1042, when the Sung government was busily engaged in improving passes and waterways, moats and ditches, the Liao court, not without reason, felt that an outbreak of hostilities was imminent.[455] In 1074, in the time of Wang An-shih, a Liao mission visited the Sung capital to protest their unfriendly activities in the border regions; among other things the northern state resented the building of city fortifications, the planting of trees, and the increase of border garrisons.[456]

The apprehension of the Liao government hardly justifies the opinion of a modern scholar who, in an otherwise well-argued study, contemptuously describes the Sung standing army of 1070 as "generally inefficient"[457] and who traces the "military weakness" of the Sung defence system to "the very beginning of the dynasty."[458] The critic fails to explain how this "inefficient" army succeeded in holding at bay for more than a century and a half the most powerful machine of aggression then existing in the eastern part of Asia. It is true, the Sung government suffered numerous defeats and agreed to render annual "tribute" to the Liao court. But such offerings were commonly made by Chinese statesmen who at times found it more expedient to pay their threatening neighbors than to fight them.[459]

In some ways, the Chinese military situation was similar to that of the Byzantine empire whose defence system has been subjected to equally damning criticism. Oman counters Gibbon's claim that "the vices of Byzantine armies were inherent, their victories accidental,"[460] by asserting that "it would be far more correct to call their defeats accidental, their successes well-deserved."[461] The English military historian does not overlook the disastrous defeats suffered by certain Greek generals, nor does he deny the basically defensive character of their strategy and their un-

chivalrous tactics.[462] But he insists that the Byzantine army, which after its reorganization in the sixth century for "five hundred years held back the Slav and Sarazen from the frontier of the Eastern empire . . . was in its day the most efficient military body in the world."[463]

Oman's thesis is not unreasonable, but it is easier to uphold if a few qualifications are made. During the period of conquest to which Oman refers, the most efficient armies of the world evidently developed in the great centers of horse-breeding, Arabia and Inner Asia. Exploiting the revolutionized technique of cavalry warfare in its most devastating form, these armies overran huge territories and occupied proud countries. Syria fell; Egypt fell; so did Persia, Spain, and Turkestan. India in the extreme south succumbed, weakened beyond relief by her political disunity. Within the range of the great centers of expansion only two important states weathered the storm, Byzantium in the extreme west and China in the extreme east.

The comparison between the two "stumbling blocks" must not be unnecessarily pressed. Neither the forces of Byzantium nor those of the Arabian and Osman Turkic world can be mechanically equated with the forces of China and her Inner Asiatic neighbors. But, whatever the differences in certain specific features of aggression or defence, the socio-economic and military similarities are so obvious that any general statement on Byzantium must by necessity also consider China.

The Chinese soldiers, like the men of Byzantium, "received scant justice at the hands of the modern historians."[464] Byzantium suffered staggering territorial losses, but until the eleventh century it successfully maintained its inner line of defence, Asia Minor. During more than three hundred years of Sui and T'ang rule China lost none of her key territories; in the first half of the tenth century the northeastern

---

[453] II, 2 (6) (30) (31).

[454] SS 95, 13a.

[455] XVI, 1042, LS 19, 2a–b.

[456] Williamson, WAS I, 278; see X, introduction.

[457] Williamson, WAS I, 178.

[458] Op. cit. II, 73.

[459] SC 110, 19a–20b; Chou 50, 7b; TS 215B, 2a. Cf. also Radloff 97, 151; idem 99, 22.

[460] Gibbon, DFRE II, 430.

[461] Oman 24 I, 172.

[462] Op. cit., 200 ff.

[463] Op. cit., 171.

[464] Thus Oman (loc. cit.) in his vindication of "the men of the lower empire." He continues: "their manifold faults have thrown the stronger points of their character into the shade. . . ."

In a recent study, O. Lang (39, 22) has shown that the Chinese attitude toward the military has not been as uniformly negative as is usually assumed; and that "with something to fight for, the Chinese have always been good soldiers" (op. cit., 36). The prevalent underestimation of the military value of the old Chinese army is caused by the failure to differentiate between social status and professional achievement. For centuries in England weavers, miners, and sailors occupied a low social position; nevertheless, their work laid the material foundation for their country's industrial and commercial greatness.

border zone had to be yielded to the Ch'i-tan invaders, but after 960 Sung China again withstood Liao pressure for more than a century and a half. Byzantium undoubtedly had one of the most efficient defence systems of the time. But China because of its unique defence in depth survived these five hundred years of nomadic terror with still greater success. The Chinese army, manifestly, was at least as successful a fighting force as its great Near Eastern counterpart. It may even be that for some time it was the most efficient military defence body in the world.

6. STAGNATION AND DECAY OF THE LIAO ARMY

a. THE STANDSTILL

In the year 929 the statesman Yeh-lü Yü-chih unfolded before his young emperor, T'ai-tsung, his vision of a Liao world-empire. Supported by their Inner Asiatic subjects, Po-hai, Turks, Tang-hsiang, and Shih-wei, the Ch'i-tan could "control the Southern Countries [and] unify the whole world. . . ."[465] The dream which approached realization in the following decades vanished irrevocably after the rise of Sung China. In the course of innumerable battles, duly noted by the historians of both empires,[466] Liao aggressiveness lost its momentum. The Inner Asiatic borders, originally maintained by military prestige and a fluid defence system, congealed into a zone of fixed posts and fortified cities.[467] The Ch'i-tan rulers who in the first half of the tenth century hoped to conquer the world now withdrew behind walls of mud and stone and looked with suspicion on neighbors whose hatred they had so well earned. The authors of the *Liao Shih* properly describe the scene: "Surrounded on the four sides by militant peoples, [Liao] crouched in their midst like a tiger whom no one dared to challenge."[468]

Some consolation could be derived from the fact that the beast of prey, though cornered, was still feared.[469] The careful organization of the southern border defence,[470] the numerous garrisons in the East, and the far-flung girdle of Inner Asiatic fortified cities, all revealed the crisis: a mighty machine of aggression, after a vigorous start, had been forced to a standstill. An equilibrium of power might strengthen the government of an agricultural society whose inner potential increased as its military efforts decreased. But a conquest society such as Liao was differently affected; a static international situation endangered its very foundation, the fighting value of its military machine.

b. DECAY OF THE FIGHTING SPIRIT

Within the orbit of the empire the Ch'i-tan rulers were not harassed by the independent attitude of poorly trained, albeit courageous, volunteers,[471] for their state did not rest on the democratic spirit of pioneering colonists, nor on the predilection for autonomy of mediaeval knights[472] and burghers.[473] Liao society was authoritarian and centralized; its warriors had to submit to a military training which they had no means of questioning. The militiamen received as much instruction as the government deemed desirable; its elite troops acquired the status of professionally disciplined experts, "ascetics," as Xenophon calls this type of soldier in contradistinction to the amateur or private, the *idiōtēs*.[474]

The fighting spirit of the Liao army had its professional as well as political aspect. A prolonged period of stagnation tended to soften the military morale of the standing army; the gradual disintegration of the country's economy, power, and prestige weakened the loyalty of all troops, but most particularly it weakened the loyalty of the non-Ch'i-tan nationals.

---

[465] I, 3 (2).

[466] A special study of the military records contained in the *Liao Shih* and *Sung Shih* would considerably refine the picture of Liao warfare given in LS 34. Such a study, however, must be left to the military historian who will find an investigation of this period, like that of other epochs of Chinese history, highly rewarding. Our survey follows LS 34 in neglecting the Liao government's occasional struggles against enemy battleships and ephemeral efforts in building and utilizing a navy of its own (*cf.* IV (10) (11)). These efforts are interesting from the standpoint of the spread of military techniques; their role in the history of Liao warfare is insignificant.

[467] XV, 1 (51).

[468] XV, 1 (42).

[469] *Loc. cit.*

---

[470] *Cf.* WCTY 16*A* and 17 *passim*.

[471] The independent spirit of the American colonists in 1775 forced Washington to consider severe disciplinary measures (see Washington 1834 II, 194 ff.; III, 279 ff.; IV, 131, 203 ff.; *cf.* also Mitchell 40, 420 ff.). The fact that, despite these difficulties, the American troops achieved great things (Clausewitz 57 I, 186) clearly shows the flexibility of the military categories concerned.

[472] At the time of A-pao-chi's struggle for political power the Byzantine emperor, Leo, expressed his contempt for the Franks and Lombards who, compared with the Eastern Romans, had "neither organization nor drill" and were "destitute of all respect for their commanders . . . they will deliberately disobey orders when they grow discontented" (Leo, *Tactica* 18 = Oman 24 I, 204–205).

[473] At the close of the Middle Ages, Machiavelli found the German burghers similarly reluctant to take orders from above: "The cities of Germany are absolutely free . . . and obey the emperor when they choose, and they do not fear him or any other potentate that they have above them" (Machiavelli 40, 40).

[474] Xenophon 25, 278–279.

i. THE FIGHTING SPIRIT OF THE ELITE TROOPS

The professional Ch'i-tan warrior was the backbone of the Liao army. He set the pattern for other groups in the imperial camp guards; he influenced his non-professional fellow-tribesmen, for, in time of peace, he joined them in communal hunts and maneuvers, and, in time of war, in military action. A-pao-chi feared the demoralizing effect of Chinese contact on his men. A Chinese envoy, Yao K'un 姚坤, reports that the aging ruler, though familiar with the Chinese language, was reluctant to use it: "I am afraid the tribesmen may imitate me, which would make the soldiers timid and weak."[475]

The failure of the Liao armies to occupy China Proper reduced the opportunities for culture contact. In the main, such contact was confined to the court and a few upper-class Ch'i-tan groups. The mass of Ch'i-tan tribesmen were less directly affected, although the conquest of the Chinese border zone gave them a privileged political status and an increased economic security. The rations allotted to distressed tribes were occasionally of inferior quality,[476] but the expectation of such benefits must have had a considerable influence on the psychology of the recipients. At an earlier time their well-being depended completely on their effectiveness as herders and fighters; under the dynasty, pressure on government officials might bring equal satisfaction. In the time of Shêng-tsung, Yeh-lü Chao significantly suggested that booty should be distributed to the border tribes to build up the morale of the frontier troops.[477]

Two other factors added to the softening process: the Sung war and the period of relative peace that followed it. Success in battle heightens the confidence of any armed force;[478] it is essential to the morale of an army of invasion. (An adversary may actually gain in self-assurance by skillful retreats to stronger lines of defence.[479]) The Liao empire derived some advantage from the Sung war: after the treaty of 1005 it received large annual payments from the southern government; but it lost in aggressiveness what it gained in silver and silk. The Ch'i-tan soldiers, who "surpassed others in riding and shooting"[480] and who, according to their national history, "held the upper hand and encountered no opposition wherever they went,"[481] were no longer called upon to display their military efficiency.

In 1042 the government did not attack the Sung forces—it preferred bribe to battle. A few years later the Liao troops gave a poor account of themselves in their fight against Hsia,[482] and in 1049 a Liao spokesman admitted publicly that his country's army could lose battles as well as win them.[483] The wars against the border tribes were fought with increasing emphasis on defence. Between 1035 and 1044 the frontier troops seemed exhausted, and a realistic statesman pleaded for the withdrawal of the whole northwestern line of defence.[484]

Most of the Liao troops stationed inland or along the southern and eastern frontiers were immobilized during the greater part of the eleventh century. Lack of battle experience is a serious handicap to any army, even one that cherishes glorious memories;[485] it is most serious when an army's recent performance has been none too convincing. The gradual decay of the morale of the Ch'i-tan troops during the eleventh century cannot be documented in detail. Certain facts, however, are suggestive. Except for the campaigns against Hsia, the Liao armies engaged in no major effort after 1020. Buddhism boasted a rapidly increasing membership: by 1078 the empire counted more than three hundred and fifty thousand Buddhist votaries,[486] not a few of whom must have been tribesmen and potential warriors, for the creed enjoyed great prestige among the Ch'i-tan people. Tao-tsung's praise of his eldest son for not having lost the martial spirit of his ancestors[487] may well have implied the fear that others in the nation were not exhibiting as much courage. And in 1103 "many of the huntsmen fled,"[488] openly rejecting their semi-military obligations.

The full significance of these separate acts is mercilessly revealed when the Liao armies were called on to fight the united Jurchen forces. The first battles proved disastrous; and in 1114 a high Ch'i-tan dignitary confessed: "Our soldiers have not been trained for a long time. If they were to meet a strong enemy and should be somewhat unsuccessful, all the tribes would become disloyal and could not be controlled at all."[489] The statement, though still veiled in the polite language of the court, actually announced the beginning of the end of Liao power. The growing military crisis encouraged even the empire's subject people to show openly their long-hidden hostility.

---

[475] CWTS 137, 6a.

[476] XV, 1 (45).

[477] Loc. cit.

[478] Cf. Xenophon 25, 273; Vegetius 41, 152 and 172; Washington 1834 IV, 136; Napoleon 40, 738; Clausewitz 57 I, 189.

[479] Clausewitz 57 II, 160 ff.

[480] XV, 2 (20).

[481] II, 1 (2).

---

[482] XVI, 1044, 19, 6a–b; 93, 2a–b.

[483] XV, 2 (17).

[484] XV, 1 (51).

[485] Clausewitz 57 I, 188 ff.

[486] IX (36).

[487] XV, 2 (20).

[488] XI (27).

[489] XV, 2 (23).

ii. LOYALTY AMONG THE NON-CH'I-TAN SOLDIERS

A soldier's loyalty to a cause that he does not understand, or does not consider his own even when he understands it, presents a problem as old as complex societies and complex armies.[490] The issue can be completely resolved if the social and political differences at its root are eliminated. More often, however, it is settled by discipline and training,[491] and the creation of an *esprit de corps*[492] which makes the regiment a "home"[493] or a "military fatherland."[494]

The Liao rulers who depended to a large degree on non-Ch'i-tan nationals for their manpower were fully cognizant of the doubtful loyalty of these under-privileged subjects. Innumerable political measures dealt with the matter. While Ch'i-tan tribesmen were permitted to carry arms on any occasion, the militia received weapons from the government arsenals only at the time of mobilization. In 1043 the Chinese south of the passes were officially forbidden to own bows and arrows;[495] Chinese and Po-hai civilians were given no opportunity to hunt;[496] and to the end of the dynasty Chinese officials were denied access to the empire's military secrets.[497]

But such precautions did not prevent the Liao government from conscripting Chinese, Po-hai, and non-Ch'i-tan tribesmen into the imperial army as militiamen, tribal fighters, or ordo troops. The militia soldiers were held together primarily by rigid discipline and considerations of safety for themselves and their families. The non-Ch'i-tan ordo soldiers, however, may well have been imbued with an *esprit de corps*, for they were members of the empire's most distinguished standing army.

The results achieved fully justified the government's military policy. During the greater part of the Liao rule, national dissatisfactions were frequently voiced by the civilian population; they were rarely echoed in the armed forces. The Chinese soldiers, who in 981 supported Hsi-yin's rebellion, were Sung captives,[498] not Liao Chinese. The Po-hai rebellion of 1029–1030 was led by a Po-hai officer,[499] but the attempt was confined geographically as well as nationally. Symptoms of growing discontent, such as banditry and desertions from the frontier service,[500] foreshadowed the deterioration in non-Ch'i-tan morale; yet the tradition of discipline and compliance persisted. The Chinese revolt in 1066 was not taken seriously; the emperor dismissed it as childish.[501]

More significant was the gradual loss of Liao military prestige. The soldiers in the frontier garrisons watched the growing ineffectiveness of the empire's defence against the border tribes. The war against the Tsu-pu tribes, which lasted from 1094 to 1100, was won only after great effort. The Jurchen chieftain A-ku-ta insulted the emperor, Tien-tsu, in full view of an entourage which certainly included some Chinese and Po-hai soldiers.

From this moment on, the disintegration of the Ch'i-tan military spirit was joined to the breakdown of loyalty among the empire's subjugated peoples. The open challenge to Liao authority was initiated by Po-hai and Chinese civilians[502] who, like the border tribes, could move more easily than their brothers in the armed forces. It is significant that the first "civilian" rebellions were opposed by the imperial troops which, on one occasion, even included Chinese soldiers.[503]

But the growing decay atomized the foundations of the Liao state. In 1117 the northeastern armies, faced by a new Jurchen invasion, broke all military discipline and "dispersed without fighting."[504] Within every national sector, including the Ch'i-tan, rebellious groups defied imperial authority and surrendered either to the Jurchen or to the Sung Chinese.[505] Tien-tsu's unorthodox suggestion that the supreme command of the army be given to a Chinese prime minister[506] admitted the final bankruptcy of the country's military tradition and might.

---

[490] The problem arose in a dramatic way when the Greek mercenaries of the Persian king faced a Greek army that fought the king (Xenophon 42 [1, 3 and 2, 1] 228 and 252; Arrian 42 [1, 16] 421 ff.). Vegetius (41, 100) expected little from hired corps of foreigners who were "without any tie of affection."

[491] Frederick II, whose regiments were composed half of citizens and half of mercenaries (Frederick 41, 311), relied on rigid discipline (*loc. cit.*) to make "the soldier fear his officer more than the dangers to which he is exposed." "Goodwill never binds the vulgar [man] in such dangers; fear must do it" (Friedrich 20, 147).

[492] *Cf.* Friedrich 20, 147; Clausewitz 57 I, 185 ff.

[493] Saxe 41, 201.

[494] *Op. cit.*, 224.

[495] XV, 2 (14).

[496] See above.

[497] XV, 2 (26).

[498] XIII (31).

[499] XIII (38).

[500] XIII (39); XV, 1 (51).

[501] XIII (42).

[502] XIII (48) (49) (51) (55), and *passim*.

[503] XIII (48).

[504] XIII (52).

[505] XIII (47) and *passim*.

[506] XV, 2 (26).

TRANSLATION

1. THE ARMY

1. THE ORDOS (GENERAL STATEMENT)

According to the law of the Liao state, when a Son of Heaven ascended the throne an ordo guard was established, its prefectures and counties laid out, its tribes and clans divided, its government offices set up, its people registered, and its army prepared. After the death of an emperor [the guard] followed the palaces and tents of the empress and concubines to serve at his mausoleum. In case of a military mobilization its able-bodied adults engaged in active military service, while the old and weak remained behind on guard.   31, 1b

2. THE ORDOS (ORIGIN AND TASK)

T'ai-tsu, after ascending the throne through the I-la tribe, split his own tribe into the Five Divisions and the Six Divisions which were governed by the imperial clan. But a personal guard was lacking. Therefore the ordo system was established, the prefectures and counties were divided, and the households and individuals were parted so as to strengthen the trunk and to weaken the branches. This device was transmitted to posterity; an ordo guard was set up for each reign. When the emperor entered [his residence] it settled down to protect him, and when he went out it escorted him. After his burial it then guarded his mausoleum. In case of military activities the Control Bases of the five capitals and the two prefectures[1] quickly sent out notices and assembled [the troops] so that it was unnecessary to wait for the mobilization of the prefectures, counties, and tribes, for an army of a hundred thousand mounted soldiers was already in existence.   35, 1b

3. THE VARIOUS ORDOS

T'ai-tsu: Hung-i Palace; Empress Ying-t'ien:[2] Ch'ang-ning Palace; T'ai[3]-tsung: Yung-hsing Palace; Shih-tsung: Chi-ch'ing Palace; Mu-tsung: Yen-ch'ang Palace; Ching-tsung: Chang-min Palace; Empress Dowager Ch'êng-t'ien:[4] Ch'ung-tê Palace; Shêng-tsung: Hsing-shêng Palace; Hsing-tsung: Yen-ch'ing Palace; Tao-tsung: T'ai-ho Palace; T'ien-tsu:[5] Yung-ch'ang Palace. In addition the

---

[1] Fêng-shêng 奉聖 Prefecture (modern Cho-lu 涿鹿, Chahar) and P'ing 平 Prefecture (modern Lu-lung 盧龍 County, Hopei) (LS 35, 5b ff.). These two prefectures were important military centers where the soldiers assembled in case of need.

[2] Ying-t'ien 應天 was the honorific title of T'ai-tsu's wife.

[3] We follow other editions in reading 太 for the 大 of our text.

[4] Ch'êng-t'ien 承天 was the honorific title of Ching-tsung's wife. The troops under her direct control were very numerous. It was she who personally directed the Liao army against Sung in the final campaign before the peace treaty of 1005.

[5] T'ien-tsu, the last Liao emperor, was captured by Chin 金 in 1125. He therefore had no temple title but only the honorific title offered to him by the officials in 1101.

emperor's great younger brother, Hsiao-wên,[6] had Tun-mu Palace, and Prime Minister Yeh-lü Lung-yün[7] had the Mansion of Prince Wên-chung. They had altogether thirty-eight prefectures, ten counties, forty-one Control Bases, twenty-three *shih-lieh*, seventy-four *wa-li*, ninety-eight *mei-li*, two *tê-li*, and nineteen *cha-sa*.[8] The regular households numbered eighty thousand and the barbarian and Chinese transferred households one hundred and twenty-three thousand, the total being two hundred and three thousand households.   31, 1b–2a

4. THE CONTROL BASES

The twelve palaces and one mansion each set up Control Bases at places of strategic significance from the Supreme Capital to the Southern Capital. In important places each palace established [one]. In the inner territories there were only one or two. T'ai-ho and Yung-ch'ang Palaces were identical with Hsing-shêng and Yen-ch'ing. In the old history[9] no Control Bases can be found. It seems that the text was incomplete.   35, 4b

5. HUNG–I PALACE

Suan Ordo was established by T'ai-tsu. In the national language "heart and belly" was called *suan*,[10] and "palace" was called *ordo*. This was Hung-i Palace, which was set up with a close guard,[11] to which were added prisoners of war from Po-hai and households from Chin Prefecture.[12] His ordo was located in Lin-huang Administration,[13] and his mausoleum was located twenty *li* southeast of Tsu Prefecture.[14]

It had 8,000 regular households and 7,000 barbarian and Chinese transferred households. It furnished 6,000 mounted soldiers.

Five prefectures: Chin, Tsu, Yen, Ch'i, Yin
One county: Fu-i
Four Control Bases: Southern Capital, Western Capital, Fêng-shêng Prefecture, P'ing Prefecture
Two *shih-lieh* . . .
Four *wa-li* . . .
Four *mei-li* . . .
Two *tê-li*.   31, 2a–b

---

[6] Hsiao-wên 孝文 is the posthumous title of this prince, the second son of Ching-tsung and the younger brother of Shêng-tsung. His personal name is not given in the *Liao Shih*, but in CTKC 14, 3a it is recorded as Lung-ch'ing 隆慶. His possession of an ordo was probably due to his strong political and military position (see XIII, note 50). In LS 64, 14b the site of his mausoleum is given as I-wu-lü 醫巫閭 Mountain in Hsien 顯 Prefecture (modern Pei-chên 北鎮 County). LS 31, 8b–9a places it in Tsu 祖 Prefecture. It seems very probable that the first passage is correct, for the mausoleum of Lung-ch'ing's parents was located not very far from this place.

[7] Yeh-lü Lung-yün 隆運 is the Ch'i-tan name of the Chinese official, Han Tê-jang 韓德讓, who contributed a great deal to the success of the Liao war against the Sung empire under Shêng-tsung (XIV and XV, introductions).

[8] For a discussion of these tribal subdivisions see introduction. In the present passage as in a number of others (LS 31, 2b, 3a, 6b; 45, 25a and 25b) the word *mei-li* 抹里 appears, whereas in many other instances the form *mo-li* 抹里 is given (see LS 31, 4a, 4b, 5a, 5b, 7a, 8a, 8b, 9a and 116, 17b); on occasion even a third variant is found, *mi-li*

彌里 (LS 46, 2a). Theoretically such inconsistency may well be the result of one or several copyists' blunderings, but the frequency of the two main variants makes this explanation somewhat problematic. Perhaps the deviations in the transliteration were caused by dialectical divergencies, divergencies which can be noted today in the Mongol word for horse: *morin, mörin;* as loanword in Russian: *merin* (see XIV, introduction).

[9] Probably the history of Liao written by Ch'ên Ta-jên 陳大任 (see appendix IV).

[10] *Suan* 算 may well be related to the Mongol *saba*, "vessel, receptacle; (as medical term:) stomach, intestines, gall bladder, vesica, testiculi" (Kovalevskij 1844, 1302). Shiratori's (13 TMK, 27) equations cannot be maintained. Equivalents seem to be lacking in Jurchen and Manchu.

[11] Literally a "heart and belly" guard. For the term "belly and heart" see XV, introduction, note 52.

[12] In Chung-ching Circuit.

[13] That is, in the metropolitan region of the Supreme Capital.

[14] Tsu Prefecture is recorded as the birthplace of the Liao ancestors. It is located at modern Monchok Ola, west of Boro Khoton, Jehol.

16,000 regular adult males[15]
14,000 barbarian and Chinese transferred adult males
6,000 mounted soldiers. 35, 2*a*

6. YUNG–HSING PALACE

Kuo-a-lien Ordo was established by T'ai-tsung. "To rule the country"[16] was called *kuo-a-lien*.[17] This was Yung-hsing Palace, previously called Ku-wên[18] Ordo, which was set up with households captured when T'ai-tsu pacified Po-hai and with households from the Control Bases of Huai Prefecture in Tung-ching,[19] from Huai-jên County in Yün Prefecture,[20] and from Luan-ho County in Tsê Prefecture.[21] His ordo was located in the vicinity of the Yu-ku River,[22] and his mausoleum was thirty *li* south of Huai Prefecture.

It had 3,000 regular households and 7,000 barbarian and Chinese transferred households. It furnished 5,000 mounted soldiers.

Four prefectures: Huai, Ch'ien, K'ai, Lai
Two counties: Pao-ho, Luan-ho
Four Control Bases: Southern Capital, Western Capital, Fêng-shêng Prefecture, P'ing Prefecture
One *shih-lieh* . . .
Four *wa-li* . . .
Thirteen *mei-li* . . .
Seven *cha-sa*. 31, 2*b*–3*a*

6,000 regular adult males
14,000 barbarian and Chinese transferred adult males
5,000 mounted soldiers. 35, 4*a*

7. CHI–CH'ING PALACE

Yeh-lu-wan Ordo was established by Shih-tsung. "Prosperity" was called *yeh-lu-wan*.[23] This was Chi-ch'ing Palace, which was set up with the guards of Emperor Wên-hsien,[24] households captured by T'ai-tsu, and households from the Control Bases of Yün Prefecture and from Kao[25] and I[26] Prefectures. His ordo was located east of the T'u River,[27] and his mausoleum was north of Ch'ang-ning Palace.[28]

---

[15] *Ting* 丁, literally "adult males," here refers to the men available for various kinds of military service. Except for Yung-ch'ang Palace the number of adult males is twice as large as that of the families mentioned for the different ordos.

[16] The first character 抆 in the phrase appears in some editions as 牧 or 收. The latter is probably correct, for 收國 is the reign title of T'ai-tsu of the Chin dynasty.

[17] For *kuo-a-lien* 國阿輦 *cf.* Mongol derivatives of *qara-*, "to look, protect," and *qory-*, "to fence in, protect" (Kovalevskij 1844, 831 ff., 954 ff.). *Cf.* also Jurchen *kuôh-lûn* (Grube 96, 95) and Manchu *gurun*, "empire, state" (Gabelentz 64, 88–89).

[18] LS 116, 18*a* explains the Ch'i-tan term *ku-wên* 孤穩 as meaning "jade." The Jurchen word *kù-wēn* 古温 had the same meaning (Grube 96, 94).

[19] Huai Prefecture did not belong to Tung-ching, but to Shang-ching. As there is no such name connected with Tung-ching, *tung* 東 must be a misprint for *shang* 上.

[20] Yün Prefecture had received its name by 758, i.e. in the T'ang dynasty. In 1044 it was raised to the rank of Western Capital by Hsing-tsung (LS 41, 1*b*–2*a*). Its location corresponds to that of Ta-t'ung in Shansi.

[21] Tsê Prefecture was located in the vicinity of modern P'ing-ch'üan 平泉 Prefecture, Jehol.

[22] The location of this river is not clear. If, as seems likely, it was identical with the Yu-ku 遊古 River of CS 90, 9*b*, it was probably a little south of Sung-shan 松山 County (west of modern Ulan Khada 赤峯, Jehol). It may have been a branch of the Lao-ha River.

[23] *Yeh-lu wan* 耶魯盌 may be equated to Mongol *urγu-*, "to grow, to bud," as Shiratori (13 TMK, 45) suggests; however, a relationship with Jurchen *'oh-léh-hēi-hûŋ*, "content" (Grube 96, 96) and Manchu *elehun* (Gabelentz 64, 53) from the base *ele-*, "to satisfy" seems more plausible.

[24] Emperor Wên-hsien 文獻 was the posthumous title given in 1051 to T'ai-tsu's eldest son, Pei, who did not actually come to the throne but yielded the crown to his younger brother, the later T'ai-tsung. He was therefore called Jang-kuo Huang-ti 讓國皇帝, "The Emperor who yielded the Country" (LS 72, 1*a*–3*a*).

[25] Kao Prefecture was perhaps situated north of modern Ulan Khada, Jehol (JHC 60, 11*a* ff.).

[26] I 宜 Prefecture was located in the vicinity of present I 義 County, Liaoning.

[27] The T'u 土 River is the present Lao or Lao-ha 老哈 River in Jehol. The name may be related to the Mongol word *toγosu(n)* "dirt, mud, earth" (*cf.* Shiratori 10 TMK, 1008).

[28] In Kao 高 Prefecture (*cf.* note 32 below). However, according to LS 5, 3*a* and 38, 8*a*, Shih-tsung's mausoleum was in Hsien 顯 Prefecture (modern Pei-chên 北鎮 Liaoning).

It had 5,000 regular households and 8,000 barbarian and Chinese transferred households. It furnished 8,000 mounted soldiers.

> Three prefectures: K'ang, Hsien, I
> One county: Shan-tung
> Four Control Bases
> One *shih-lieh* . . .
> Eight *wa-li* . . .
> Ten *mo-li*.   31, 3b–4a

10,000 regular adult males
16,000 barbarian and Chinese transferred adult males
8,000 mounted soldiers.   35, 2b

8. CH'ANG–NING PALACE

P'u-su-wan Ordo was established by Empress Dowager Ying-t'ien. "Development" was called *p'u-su-wan*.[29]   This was Ch'ang-ning Palace, which was set up with households from Liao Prefecture[30] and Hai-pin County.[31]   Her ordo was located in Kao Prefecture,[32] and her mausoleum was a hundred *li* east of Lung-hua Prefecture[33] . . . .

It had 7,000 regular households and 6,000 barbarian and Chinese transferred households. It furnished 5,000 mounted soldiers.

> Four prefectures: Liao, I-k'un, Liao-hsi, Hsien
> Three counties: Fêng-hsien, Kuei-i, Ting-pa
> Four Control Bases
> One *shih-lieh* . . .
> Six *wa-li* . . .
> Thirteen *mo-li*.   31, 4a–b

14,000 regular adult males
12,000 barbarian and Chinese transferred adult males
5,000 mounted soldiers.   35, 2a

9. YEN–CH'ANG PALACE

To-li-pên Ordo was established by Mu-tsung. This was Yen-ch'ang Palace. "To pacify" was called *to-li-pên*.[34]   It was set up with households from the Kuo-a-lien Ordo, captured Tsu-pu households, and households from the Control Bases of the Central Capital, from the Control Office[35] of the Southern Capital and from Hsien,[36] Hsin,[37] and Han[38] Prefectures.   His ordo was south of Chiu-ya-li Mountain,[39] and his mausoleum was south of the capital.[40]

It had 1,000 regular households and 3,000 barbarian Chinese transferred households. It furnished 2,000 mounted soldiers.

---

[29] *P'u-su-wan* 蒲速盌 probably equivalent to Manchu *fusen*, "propagation, increase" (Gabelentz 64, 72). Shiratori's (12 TMK, 1255) suggestion of a Korean word *p'ö-tifi* seems problematical.

[30] Liao Prefecture is now Liao-pin-t'a 遼賓塔, sixty *li* northeast of Hsin-min 新民 County in modern Liaoning.

[31] Hai-pin 海賓 County corresponds to modern Ch'ien-t'un-wei 前屯衞 in Liaoning.

[32] Near the juncture of the Lao-ha River and the Ying-chin 英金 River in Jehol.

[33] The modern equivalent of Lung-hua Prefecture is the region southeast of the junction of the Shira Muren and the Lao-ha River, in present Jehol. However, according to LS 6, 3a and 71, 3b, this mausoleum was identical with that of T'ai-tsu, which was located in Tsu Prefecture (see note 14).

[34] *To-li-pên* 奪里本 may be related to Mongol and Manchu *daj-la-*, "to attack" (cf. Shiratori 12 TMK, 1244).

[35] The Control Offices (制置司) were common during the Southern Sung period. They had charge of military affairs on the frontiers (SS 167, 2b).

[36] Hsien 咸 Prefecture was located northeast of K'ai-yüan 開原 County in modern Liaoning.

[37] Modern Huai-tê 懷德 County in Liaoning.

[38] Han 韓 Prefecture is the present Pa-mien 八面 City, southeast of Fêng-hua 奉化 County in Liaoning.

[39] The character 紕 is very rare; it is probably the same as *chiu* 紸.

[40] The text simply says "south of the capital," but which capital is meant? LS 7, 5b and 37, 7a note that Mu-tsung was buried beside the mausoleum of T'ai-tsung in Huai Prefecture (southeast of Boro Khoton), thus indicating that the capital in question was the Supreme Capital.

Two prefectures: Sui, Han
Three Control Bases: Central Capital, Southern Capital, P'ing Prefecture
One *shih-lieh* . . .
Four *wa-li* . . .
Four *mo-li.*   31, 4*b*–5*a*

2,000 regular adult males
6,000 barbarian and Chinese transferred adult males
2,000 mounted soldiers.   35, 2*b*–3*a*

10. CHANG–MIN PALACE

Chien-mu Ordo was established by Ching-tsung. This was Chang-min Palace. "To transmit" was called *chien-mu*. It was set up with the guards of Emperor Chang-su[41] and households from Wu-an Prefecture.[42] His ordo was near the Ho-lu River,[43] and his mausoleum was south of Tsu Prefecture.[44]

It had 8,000 regular households and 10,000 barbarian and Chinese transferred households. It furnished 10,000 mounted soldiers.

Four prefectures: Yung, Lung-hua, Chiang-shêng, T'ung
Two counties: Hsing-t'ang, Fou-su
Four Control Bases
Two *shih-lieh* . . .
Seven *wa-li* . . .
Eleven *mo-li.*   31, 5*a*–*b*

16,000 regular adult males
20,000 barbarian and Chinese transferred adult males
10,000 mounted soldiers.   35, 3*a*

11. CH'UNG-TÊ PALACE

Ku-wên Ordo was established by Empress Dowager Ch'êng-t'ien. This was Ch'ung-tê Palace. "Jade"[45] was called *ku-wên*. It was set up with households from the three prefectures of Ch'ien,[46] Hsien,[47] and Shuang.[48] Her ordo was located east of the T'u River,[49] and she was entombed in the same mausoleum as Emperor Ching-tsung.

It had 6,000 regular households and 10,000 barbarian and Chinese transferred households. It furnished 10,000 mounted soldiers.

Four prefectures: Ch'ien, Ch'uan, Shuang, Kuei-tê
One county: Lu
Three Control Bases: Southern Capital, Western Capital, Fêng-shêng Prefecture
Three *shih-lieh* . . .

---

[41] Emperor Chang-su 章肅 was the posthumous title bestowed in 1052 upon T'ai-tsu's third son, whose personal name was Li-hu 李胡 or Hung-ku 洪古. The prince, who never actually became emperor, died in prison, where he had been confined for treason (LS 64, 8*b*–10*a*; 72, 4*a*–5*a*; *cf*. also XIII, introduction).

[42] Wu-an 武安 Prefecture, originally named Hsin 新 Prefecture, was established with Chinese prisoners captured by T'ai-tsu. It was located in the region west of Fou-hsin 阜新 County in modern Jehol.

[43] The location of the Ho-lu 合魯 River is not clear, but, judging from the location of Ching-tsung's mausoleum and his wife's ordo, it would seem to correspond to the Chiao-lai 叫來 River, east of the Lao-ha River, Jehol.

[44] In LS 37, 6*a*–*b*, under Tsu 祖 Prefecture, there is no mention of the tomb of Ching-tsung and his wife. According to LS 10, 2*b*; 31, 9*b*, and 38, 9*a*, Ching-tsung and his wife were buried in Ch'ien 乾 Prefecture and their mausoleum was called Ch'ien-ling. Hence the 祖 of our text seems to be a misprint for 乾.

[45] We follow LS 116, 18*a* in reading 玉 for the 王 of our text.

[46] Southeast of present Pei-chên County, Liaoning.

[47] East of present Pei-chên County, Liaoning.

[48] West of modern T'ieh-ling 鐵嶺 County, Liaoning.

[49] In modern Jehol. *Cf.* note 27.

> Seven *wa-li* . . .
> Eleven *mei-li* . . .
> Five *cha-sa*.   31, 6a–b

12,000 regular adult males
20,000 barbarian and Chinese transferred adult males
10,000 mounted soldiers.   35, 3a

12. HSING–SHĔNG PALACE

Nü-ku Ordo was established by Shêng-tsung.   This was Hsing-shêng Palace.   "Gold" was called *nü-ku*.[50]   It was set up with households from the Kuo-a-lien, Yeh-lu-wan, and P'u-su-wan Ordos. His ordo was in Nü-hun-huo-chih, and his mausoleum was in Nan-an[51] in Ch'ing Prefecture.[52]

It had 10,000 regular households and 20,000 barbarian and Chinese transferred households.   It furnished 5,000 mounted soldiers.

> Five prefectures: Ch'ing, Hsi, Wu, Wu,[53] Pa
> Four Control Bases
> Four *shih-lieh* . . .
> Six *wa-li* . . .
> Nine *mo-li* . . .
> Five *cha-sa*.   31, 6b–7b

20,000 regular adult males
40,000 barbarian and Chinese transferred adult males
5,000 mounted soldiers.   35, 3b

13. YEN–CH'ING PALACE

Wo-tu-wan Ordo was established by Hsing-tsung.   This was Yen-ch'ing Palace.   "Propagation" was called *wo-tu-wan*.[54]   It was set up with households from various ordos and from Jao Prefecture.[55] His ordo was west of Kao Prefecture, and his mausoleum was in Ch'ing Prefecture in Shang-ching.

It had 7,000 regular households and 10,000 barbarian and Chinese transferred households.   It furnished 10,000 mounted soldiers.

> Three prefectures: Jao, Ch'ang-ch'un, T'ai
> Four Control Bases
> Two *shih-lieh* . . .
> Six *wa-li* . . .
> Six *mo-li*.   31, 7b–8a

14,000 regular adult males
20,000 barbarian and Chinese transferred adult males
10,000 mounted soldiers.   35, 3b

---

[50] *Nü-ku* 女古 suggests a relationship with Jurchen *nén* (*nún*)-*kiāŋ*, "green" (Grube 96, 96), Manchu *niowanggiyan* etc., "greenish, light blue" (Gabelentz 64, 158 ff.), Mongol *noγo-qan*, "green" (Kovalevskij 1844, 679).

[51] No such name as Nan-an 南安 appears either in the geographical section of the *Liao Shih* or elsewhere, but from the 1930 excavations of the tombs of Shêng-tsung, Hsing-tsung, and Tao-tsung we judge that the present location of this place corresponds to War-Manha (or War-in-Manha), north of Pai-t'a-tzŭ 白塔子, Barin, Jehol (Torii 36 III, foreword).

[52] Present Tsaghan Khoton, Jehol.

[53] Wu 烏 Prefecture in Tung-ching.   But, according to the geographical section of the *Liao Shih*, Tung-ching has no Wu Prefecture.   See XII, note 113.

[54] *Wo-tu-wan* 窩篤盌 can hardly be connected with Mongol *üs-*, "to grow," as Shiratori (12 TMK, 1256) suggests, but rather with Manchu *ete-*, "to conquer, rule, grow, be able, resist."   Identical with Jurchen *ote-* in *'oh-tʻéh-hēi* (Grube 96, 97).

[55] In the region of the upper Shira Muren in present Jehol.

14. T'AI–HO PALACE

A-ssŭ Ordo was established by Tao-tsung. This was T'ai-ho Palace. "Extensive" was called a-ssŭ.[56] It was set up with imperial retainers from the various ordos and households from Hsing-chung Administration.[57] His ordo was at the Hao-shui Lake,[58] and his mausoleum was in Ch'ing Prefecture in Shang-ching.

It had 10,000 regular households and 20,000 barbarian and Chinese transferred households. It furnished 15,000 mounted soldiers.

> Two shih-lieh . . .
> Eight wa-li . . .
> Seven mo-li.   31, 8a

20,000 regular adult males
40,000 barbarian and Chinese transferred adult males
15,000 mounted soldiers.   35, 3b–4a

15. YUNG–CH'ANG PALACE

A-lu-wan Ordo was established by Emperor T'ien-tsu. This was Yung-ch'ang Palace. "To assist" was called a-lu-wan.[59] It was set up with imperial retainers from the various ordos and households from Ch'un[60] and Hsüan[61] Prefectures.

It had 8,000 regular households and 10,000 barbarian and Chinese transferred households. It furnished 10,000 mounted soldiers.

> Two shih-lieh . . .
> Eight wa-li . . .
> Eight mo-li.   31, 8b

14,000[62] regular adult males
20,000 barbarian and Chinese transferred adult males
10,000 mounted soldiers.   35, 4a

16. TUN–MU PALACE

Tun-mu Palace of the emperor's great younger brother, Hsiao-wên, was called Ch'ih-shih-tê-pên Ordo. "Filial piety" was called ch'ih-shih-tê-pên.[63] It was set up with retainers of Emperor Wên-hsien, prisoners of war from Po-hai, and households from the three prefectures of Chien,[64] Shên,[65] and Yen.[66] His mausoleum was thirty li southwest of Tsu Prefecture.[67]

It had 3,000 regular households and 5,000 barbarian and Chinese transferred households. It furnished 5,000 mounted soldiers.

---

[56] A-ssŭ 阿思 suggests affinity with Turkic jasy (Kāshgharī), "large, plain, extent," but not with Tungus agdy, ägdi, "large, big," as assumed by Shiratori (12 TMK, 1146–1147).

[57] Present Ch'ao-yang 朝陽 County, Jehol.

[58] The location of this place is not known.

[59] A-lu-wan 阿魯盌 is related to Manchu al-, "to take, provide, support, lift, erect, put up" (Gabelentz 64, 8) and Turkic al-, "to take, buy, seize, do." Shiratori's equations (12 TMK, 1146) are erroneous.

[60] No such name appears in the geographical section of the Liao Shih. It is probably the same as Ch'ang-ch'un 長春 Prefecture northwest of modern Po-tu-na, Kirin.

[61] In the vicinity of present I 義 County, Liaoning. Yung-ch'ang Palace belonged to the last Liao emperor, T'ien-tsu. Unlike the foregoing descriptions, the present text gives no data for the location of his ordo.

[62] If the ordo had 8,000 regular households, then, according to the general principle, we would expect 16,000 adult males rather than 14,000.

[63] The term ch'ih-shih-tê-pên 赤寔得本 resists all attempts at etymologization. Shiratori's (13 TMK, 29–30) equation of the first two syllables with Mongol čisun, "blood," is highly improbable.

[64] Chien 建 Prefecture was originally located south of the Ta-ling River in present Jehol. During the time of Shêng-tsung (982–1031) it was moved north on account of frequent floods.

[65] Present Mukden, Liaoning.

[66] Yen 巖 Prefecture (Tung-ching Circuit) is the present Shih-ch'êng-shan 石城山, fifty-seven li northeast of Liao-yang 遼陽 County, Liaoning.

[67] See above, note 6.

Three prefectures: Chien, Shên, Yen
One Control Base: Southern Capital
Two *shih-lieh* . . .
Six *wa-li* . . .
Two *mo-li* . . .
Two *cha-sa*.   31, 8b–9a

6,000 regular adult males
10,000 barbarian and Chinese transferred adult males
5,000 mounted soldiers.   35, 4a

17. MANSION OF PRINCE WÊN–CHUNG

The grand prime minister and Prince of Chin, Yeh-lü Lung-yün, whose original surname was Han and whose given name was Tê-jang, was granted the national surname because of his merit. He left the ordo registers[68] and became attached to the Third Patriarchal Household of the Horizontal Tents. He was granted the posthumous title of chief of the Presidential Council and the posthumous name of Wên-chung. He had no sons, so Yeh-lu, son of the Prince of Wei, T'ieh-pu,[69] of the imperial clan was made his heir. As Yeh-lu died young, Emperor T'ien-tsu again had an imperial prince, Ao-lu-wo,[70] succeed him.[71]

The government presented the funeral equipage, erected a temple alongside Ch'ien Mausoleum,[72] and set up the Mansion of Prince Wên-chung after the pattern of the ordos.[73]

It had 5,000 regular households and 8,000 barbarian and Chinese transferred households. It furnished 10,000 mounted soldiers.

One prefecture
Six Control Bases: Supreme Capital, Central Capital, Southern Capital, Western Capital, Fêng-shêng Prefecture, P'ing Prefecture.   31, 9a–b

10,000 regular adult males
16,000 barbarian and Chinese transferred adult males
10,000 mounted soldiers.   35, 4b

18. SUMMARY OF THE ORDOS

All the ordos together had 408,000 adult males. They furnished 101,000 mounted soldiers.

35, 7a

19. OFFICES OF THE TRAVELING CAMPS

After Liao established the various palaces or ordos, the tribal and barbarian households were put under the control of the following ordo offices of the Northern Region:

The Department of the Chief Controller of the Various Traveling Camps had general control over the Ch'i-tan and Chinese affairs of the imperial traveling camps. . .

The Office of the Chief Controller of the Ch'i-tan Traveling Camps had general control over the military movements of the imperial traveling residences and the administration of the ordos. . .

---

[68] See VII, 1, note 23.
[69] Son of Shêng-tsung's brother, Lung-yu 隆祐. Cf. LS 64, 15a.
[70] The eldest son of T'ien-tsu.
[71] According to CTKC 18, 3a, the successor of Yeh-lü Lung-yün was a nephew of Shêng-tsung, Tsung-yeh 宗業, who was succeeded by his younger brother, Tsung-fan 宗範, both sons of Shêng-tsung's younger brother, Lung-yu.

[72] The mausoleums of Ching-tsung and his wife, Empress Jui-chih. It was located fifty-five *li* southwest of present Pei-chên County, Liaoning.
[73] The term *fu* 府, which we have translated "mansion," was applied to the only "ordo" not belonging to a Ch'i-tan, that of Han Tê-jang. CTKC 18, 2b notes that during his lifetime Yeh-lü Lung-yün was permitted to have a personal guard of one hundred men, called 護位, similar to the Liao emperor's personal guard.

The Office of the Chief[74] Controller of the Traveling Camps had control over the administration of the palaces of the imperial traveling residences.   45, 23a–b

20. AN OFFICE OF THE CHINESE TRAVELING CAMPS

The Department of the Chief Controller of the Chinese Traveling Camps was also called the Office of the Chief Controller of the Traveling Camps of the Southern Region. . .

    Chief controller of the Chinese traveling camps . . .
    Assistant controller of the Chinese traveling camps.   47, 19b

21. GUARDS OF THE TRAVELING CAMPS

The Office of Strongholds[75] was in charge of the spear-stockades, the establishment of outposts, and the communication by bells for the Forbidden Enclosures.[76]

    Grand preceptor of the strongholds.   45, 13a

22. PROVISIONS FOR TRAVELING CAMPS

The Office of the *I-li-pi* in charge of the Baggage Trains of the Traveling Camps took care of matters concerned with the imperial suite and the baggage trains during the imperial tours to all the ordos.   45, 25b

23. HONORARY GUARDS

The Administration of the Northern Guard was in charge of the guards of the Northern Division. In the ordos of the empress dowagers there were left and right guards.

    Grand preceptor of the northern guard
    Grand guardian of the northern guard
    Minister over the masses of the northern guard

Office of the General Director of the Left and Right Guards. . . .

The Administration of the Southern Guard was in charge of the guards of the Southern Division.

    Grand preceptor of the southern guard
    Grand guardian of the southern guard
    Minister over the masses of the southern guard

Office of the General Director of the Left and Right Guards.   45, 10b–11b

24. MILITARY COMMANDERS OF THE NORTHERN REGION

The Liao palaces and tents, tribes, capitals and prefectures, and the subordinate states, each had its own army. The organizations were correlated; the system was uniform. This is the reason why the power [of Liao] lasted for more than two hundred years.   That which is known about it may be examined as follows:

The Administration of the Grand Commander in Chief of the Armies of the Empire: the heir apparent and imperial princes had control of its military affairs.

    Grand commander in chief of the armies of the empire
    Vice-commander in chief

The Administration of the Grand Commander in Chief: the high dignitaries had control of its military affairs.

    Grand commander in chief
    Vice-commander in chief

---

[74] Reading 都 for the 諸 of our text in conformity with the repeated formulas in this passage.

[75] This office had charge of the Forbidden Enclosures

(禁圍), in which the emperor resided during his travels or hunts.

[76] See II, 1 (27).

The Administration of the General Commander in Chief: the grand general had control of its military affairs.

> General commander in chief of the army
> Vice-commander in chief
> Co-director of affairs for the Administration of the Commander in Chief

The Administration of the Plenipotentiary: also called the deputy acting according to circumstances. . .

The Office of the Grand *Hsiang-wên* . . .

The General Council of the East shared control of the military administration.

> Grand preceptor of the General Council of the East

The General Council of the West shared control of the military administration.

> Grand preceptor of the General Council of the West

The Administrations of the Grand General: each was in charge of the military administration concerning the army under its control . . .

The Office of Defence Army . . .

The Office of the Guards . . .

The Control Office of the Armies of the Various Routes

> General controller of the armies of the various routes
> Assistant controller of the armies of the various routes.   46, 9a–11a

25. SPECIAL ARMIES

Liao T'ai-tsu, because the imperial house had flourished and become strong, divided the I-la tribe into two parts. Internally the palace guard was weak, for while occupied with the pacification of the four directions he had no time to collect it. The empress née Shu-lü, while remaining behind on guard, selected well-trained and valiant barbarians and Chinese to form the Shu-shan Army.[77] T'ai-tsung again chose the best soldiers of the empire as his claws and teeth[78] and created the P'i-shih Army.[79] There were altogether 500,000 horsemen, so that the power of the nation was indeed great.

The P'i-shih Army of the Imperial Tent

Set up by T'ai-tsung.   Altogether 300,000 horsemen.

The Shu-shan Army

Set up by the Empress of the Earth.[80]   200,000 horsemen.[81]   35, 1a–b

26. THE P'I–SHIH ARMY

Formerly, when T'ai-tsu transformed his traveling camp into a palace, he selected over a thousand brave and strong men from all the tribes and established a "belly and heart" detachment. Yeh-lü Lao-ku,[82] because of his merit, was appointed *hsiang-wên* of the Right P'i-shih. Consequently the

---

[77] This term is found also on a Liao inscription which states that Li Nei-chên 李内貞, who surrendered to T'ai-tsu in Huai-lai 懷來 County, was appointed *shu-shan tu-t'i-chü shih* 屬珊都提舉使 (LWT 5, 22b). The inscription confirms the claim made in one passage that the Shu-shan Army was in part composed of Chinese.

[78] A literary expression for close followers.

[79] According to the glossary the P'i-shih Army consisted of five detachments: the Northern, Southern, Left, Right, and the Yellow (LS 116, 16b). Yü-ching 余靖 (T. 安道 1000–1064) states that the Ch'i-tan called a diamond *p'ai-shih* 牌室, *pei-shih* 北室, or *pi-shih* 比室. This army was likened to a diamond to indicate its firmness

(*Wu Hsi Chi* = LSSI 13, 2b). Cf. Manchu *palta wexe* and *paltari* "diamond" (Gabelentz 64, 167). *Palta* and *paltari* are loanwords in Manchu.

[80] T'ai-tsu's wife.

[81] The figures given here are different from those offered by other sources, such as CTKC 23, 3a–b and SHYK 196, 14b. According to these two sources, the P'i-shih Army numbered only thirty thousand mounted soldiers and the Shu-shan Army only twenty thousand.

[82] Yeh-lü Lao-ku 老古, a nephew of Empress Ch'un-ch'in, was highly considered by T'ai-tsu because of his military ability (LS 73, 5b–6a).

P'i-shih Army was already in existence in the time of T'ai-tsu: it was the Belly and Heart Detachment. T'ai-tsung increased the number [of its soldiers] to 300,000.   46, 11a–b

27. MILITARY AFFAIRS OF THE FOUR DISTINGUISHED LINEAGES

The Office of the Chief *Hsiang-wên* of the Four Tents[83] was in charge of the military affairs of the Four Tents.   45, 18a

28. MILITARY AFFAIRS OF THE IMPERIAL CLAN

The *Shê-li*[84] Office was in charge of the military administration of the imperial clan.   45, 18b

29. VARIOUS *HSIANG–WÊN* OFFICES

The Office of the *Hsiang-wên* of the Shê-li Troops had control of those imperial relatives who had joined the army: the Horizontal Tents and the Three Patriarchal Households belonged to it.

The Office of the *Hsiang-wên* of the Shê-li Troops of the Administration of the Northern King: the imperial clansmen of the Five Divisions belonged to it.

The Office of the *Hsiang-wên* of the Shê-li Troop of the Administration of the Southern King: the imperial clansmen of the Six Divisions belonged to it.

The Office of the General *Hsiang-wên* of the Imperial Guard was in charge of the affairs concerning all the troops of the imperial guard.

The *Shê-li* Office of each tribe was in charge of the military administration of the [noble] descendants of each tribe.

The Office of the *Hsiang-wên* of the Army of Court Nobles was in charge of the military affairs concerning the noble camp attendants.

The Office of the *Hsiang-wên* of the I-la Army: the foot-soldiers were called *i-la*.

The Office of the *Hsiang-wên* of the *I-la* of the Banners and Drums was in charge of the affairs concerning the banners and drums.

The Office of the *Hsiang-wên* of the Thousand *I-la*

The Office of the *Hsiang-wên* of the Fierce *I-la*. . .

The Office of the *Hsiang-wên* of the Catapultiers was in charge of the affairs concerning the flying catapults.

The Office of the *Hsiang-wên* of the Crossbowmen was in charge of the affairs concerning the strong crossbows.[85]   46, 11b–12a

30. THE *K'O* TROOPS

The Office of the *Hsiang-wên* of the Southern *K'o* Troop of the Hsi King.   All the tents also had a *k'o* officer who was its head.   As for the rest [of its organization] it was similar to that of the Office of the *Hsiang-wên*.

The Office of the *Hsiang-wên* of the Northern *K'o* Troop of the Hsi King

The *K'o* Troop of the tents of the Imperial Maternal Uncles

The Three *K'o* Troops

The P'in-pi *K'o* Troop

The Nine *K'o* Troops.   46, 13b

31. THE *CHIU* TROOPS

The twelve traveling *Chiu* Troops.   All the *Chiu*, moreover, had a minister over the masses. For the rest [of the organization] it was similar to that of the Office of the *Hsiang-wên*.

The *Chiu* Troop of each palace

---

[83] The Horizontal Tents and the Three Patriarchal Households.

[84] See VIII (12) and note.

[85] Subsequently twenty-one *hsiang-wên* offices of dif-ferent armies are listed (LS 46, 12a–13a), among them the offices of one Ti-lieh army, one Ti-lieh P'i-shih Army, two Hsi armies, and one P'o-hai army.

The Yao-lien *Chiu* Troop
The *Chiu* Troop of each tribe
The two *Chiu* Troops of the [government] herdsmen.   46, 13b–14a

32. PRIVATE ARMIES OF HIGH DIGNITARIES

The imperial princes and high officials of Liao treated the state as their family.   During expeditions they often set up private armies in order to pursue imperial affairs.   The large ones consisted of more than a thousand horsemen, and the small ones of several hundred men.   They were entered upon the register of the imperial administration so that, when the state was engaged in military activities, it would, depending upon its needs, borrow three or five thousand horsemen.   The remaining troops were always left behind as the foundation of the tribes.

Army of the heir apparent[86]
Army of Prince Wei[87]
Army of Prince Yung-k'ang[88]
Army of the *yü-yüeh*[89]
Army of Ma-ta[90]
Army of Wu-ya.[91]   35, 7a–b

33. TRIBAL ARMIES

The tribes and lineages, which were variously subordinate to the Southern or Northern Administrations, guarded the four frontiers.   Each belonged to an office, as follows:[92]

The Northern Administration with a total of twenty-eight tribes

[Office of] the Imperial Attendants of the Palaces and Tents

Tribe of the Administration of the King of Hsi

[Office of] Stabilization of the Southern Area

Five Divisions tribe
Six Divisions tribe

Punitive Office of the Northeastern Route

Wu-wei tribe

Military Control Office of the Northeastern Route

Yao-li tribe
Po-tê tribe
Ao-li tribe
Southern K'o tribe
Northern K'o tribe
T'u-lu tribe

---

[86] Probably the later Mu-tsung, for during T'ai-tsung's reign he led an army against Sung.

[87] This title refers to Li-hu, the third son of T'ai-tsu (*cf.* LS 64, 8b–10a; CTKC 4, 2a).

[88] This title was conferred by T'ai-tsung upon his elder brother's eldest son, the later Shih-tsung (LS 5, 1a).

[89] We follow CTKC 23, 2b in omitting the 王 of our text.   The word makes no sense in this context.   It must be an erroneous interpolation.

[90] Same as Pa-li-tê 拔里得.   He was a son of La-ko and therefore a cousin of T'ai-tsung (*cf.* CTKC 17, 1b ff.; LS 76, 1b).

[91] LS 46, 18a mentions a Wu-ya Punitive Office of the Southwestern Region.   However, SHYK 196, 23a suggests that Wu-ya was a personal name.   According to this source, in 996, the chieftains of the I-tang 佗黨 people informed the Sung prefect that in the spring they had succeeded in defeating a Ch'i-tan general, Han Wu-ya 韓五押.   At this time, Han Tê-wei 韓德威 was the punitive commissioner of the Southwestern Region (LS 82, 2b).   Whether the latter is related to or identical with Han Wu-ya, we have no means of determining.

[92] For the tribes, see I, 2.

Chu-chê Ta[93]-lu-kuo tribe
Ho-hsi tribe

Punitive office of the Northwestern Route

T'u-lü-pu tribe
Ao-yen Nü-chih tribe
Shih-wei tribe

Punitive Office of the Southwestern Route

Nieh-la tribe
Wu-ku [Nieh ?]-la tribe
Nieh-la Yüeh-wu tribe
Mei-ku-hsi tribe
Chieh-ti tribe
Ni-ch'i Tangut tribe
Ho-la Tangut tribe

Office of the Chief Controller of Huang-lung Administration[94]

Wei-yen Turkic tribe
Ao-yen Turkic tribe
Northern Tangut tribe
Five Nations tribe

Military Control Office of the Wu-ku and Ti-lieh[95]

Tieh-lu Ti-lieh tribe

[Office of] the Garrison in the Wei Wu-ku Tribe[96]

Northern Ti-lieh tribe

The Southern Administration with a total of sixteen tribes

[Office of] Stabilization of the Southwestern Area

I-shih tribe

Punitive Office of the Southwestern Route

P'in tribe
Tieh-ta Tieh-la tribe[97]
P'in Ta-lu-kuo tribe
I-tien Nü-chih tribe

Punitive Office of the Northwestern Route

Ch'u-t'ê tribe

Military Control Office of the Northeastern Route

Ta-ma Pi-ku-tê tribe

Office of the Nü-chih Troops of the Northeastern Route

I-shih Ao-wei tribe

---

[93] We follow LS 33, 8a in reading ta 達 for the wei 違 of our text.

[94] Corresponding to modern Nung-an 農安 County, Kirin.

[95] These two tribes are frequently mentioned in the text. Yanai assumes that they lived a nomadic life near the Nonni River, Heilungkiang (Yanai 30, 135).

[96] This tribe probably lived near the Wu-ku and Ti-lieh, for Hsiao Han-chia-nu once memorialized the throne to the effect that K'o-tun City should be shifted nearer to the Wu-ku, Ti-lieh, and Wei Wu-ku (see below, (51)).

[97] According to LS 33, 5a, the name of this tribe is Tieh-la Tieh-ta.

Office of the Chief Controller of the Eastern Capital

    Ch'u-t'ê Ao-wei tribe
    Yao-chao tribe
    Shao-wa tribe
    Ho-chu[98] tribe

[Office of] the Garrison at Tao-t'a-ling

    Ê-p'u-kua tribe

[Office of] Garrisons in Native Regions

    Sa-li-ko tribe
    Southern Tangut tribe
    Hsieh-t'ê tribe.   35, 7b–10b

34. MANPOWER OF THE FIVE CIRCUITS

Liao established five capitals. Lin-huang was the old territory of the Ch'i-tan. Liao-yang, the Liao-tung of the Han [dynasty], was the former state of Po-hai. Chung-ching, the region of Liao-hsi during the Han [period], had been occupied by the Ch'i-tan since T'ang [times]. The list of adult males in these three capitals, so far as it can be given, amounted to 226,100, in the main transferred barbarian and Chinese households. Hsi-chin and Ta-t'ung, old Chinese territories, registered 806,700 adult males. The Ch'i-tan themselves generally belonged to camps and tribes. The rest of the barbarian and Chinese people, those who were attached separately, are not included here.   36, 1a

Roughly speaking, the adult males of the five capitals, so far as can be reckoned, numbered 1,107,300. They were the militia.   36, 9b

35. SHANG–CHING

T'ai-tsu established the imperial capital at Lin-huang Administration. When T'ai-tsung set up Chin, the prince of Chin, Shih Ching-t'ang, came and offered sixteen cities. Then the four [other] capitals were established and the imperial capital was changed to the Supreme Capital. There were 167,200 adult males.   36, 1b

36. TUNG–CHING

The Eastern Capital was originally Po-hai. Its territory[99] was made the Southern Capital. Liao-yang Administration controlled six counties and had jurisdiction over twenty-six commanderies, administrations, prefectures, and cities. There were 41,400 adult males.[100] In the thirteenth year of T'ien-hsien,[101] T'ai-tsung renamed it the Eastern Capital.   36, 3b–4a

37. NAN–CHING

The Southern Capital (Hsi-chin Administration) controlled ten counties and had jurisdiction over nine commanderies, administrations, prefectures, and cities. There were 566,000 adult males.
36, 5a

38. HSI–CHING

The Western Capital (Ta-t'ung Administration) controlled seven counties and had jurisdiction over seventeen commanderies, administrations, prefectures, and cities. There were 322,700 adult males.   36, 7a

---

[98] We follow LS 33, 6b in reading chu 朮 for the mu 木 of our text.

[99] We follow other editions in reading 地 for the 他 of our text.

[100] See I, introduction.

[101] According to the pên chi there was no thirteenth year of T'ien-hsien. The next reign period, Hui-t'ung, was made retroactive to the first month (see appendix I). However, on occasion, the period from the first to the eleventh month of the year 983 is called the thirteenth year of T'ien-hsien.

39. CHUNG–CHING

In the twenty-third year of T'ung-ho,[102] Shêng-tsung built a city at Ch'i-chin Mountain and founded Ta-ting Administration which was called the Central Capital. It controlled nine counties and had jurisdiction over twenty-three commanderies, administrations, prefectures, and cities. Since it was newly created and not yet well-founded, the number of its adult males cannot be investigated. Only [that of] one county is known.

Kao Prefecture
    San-han County—10,000 adult males.   36, 9b

40. ARMIES OF THE SUBORDINATE STATES

The subordinate states of Liao, so far as can be reckoned, numbered fifty-nine. They did not come regularly to court to pay tribute. In case of war, envoys were sent out to request soldiers, or orders were issued to undertake their own punitive expeditions.[103] Those who disobeyed were punished. The number of assisting troops was decided by each country according to its convenience. There was no fixed number.   36, 9b

41. SUBORDINATE STATES

According to the Liao system of officials for the subordinate states and tribes, the large ones were given titles equal to that of king, and the small ones ranks similar to that of tribal commanding prefect, in order to distinguish the native chieftains from the Ch'i-tan officials. And benevolence and awe were both used to control them. Thus a way was found to win the good will of the distant peoples.   46, 23b

42. OFFICERS OF FRONTIER DEFENCE OF THE NORTHERN REGION

The territory of Liao in the east adjoined Korea. In the south it valiantly rivaled the six dynasties of Liang, T'ang, Chin, Han, Chou, and Sung. In the north it was close to about ten important states, such as Tsu-pu and Chu-pu-ku. In the west it controlled about a hundred strong states, such as Hsi Hsia, T'ang-hsiang, T'u-hun, Uighur, and others.

Surrounded on the four sides by militant peoples, [Liao] crouched in their midst like a tiger whom no one dared to challenge. This was because it had a method for controlling them. By an examination of the officials of the frontier defence, the audacious plans of T'ai-tsu and T'ai-tsung can be understood.

The Office of the Chief Commissioner of Investigation of the Various Armies

    Chief Commissioner of Investigation

The Administration of the King of Hsi: see the tribal officials
The Office of the Grand *T'i-yin*: see the tent officials
The Office of the Grand Imperial Maternal Uncles
The Office of the Grand *Ch'ang-kun*
The Office of the Five Divisions: see the tribal officials
The Office of the Six Divisions
The Office of *T'a-wên*: no details

The above mentioned were all offices of the Shang-ching Route, and had control of all the Hsi.[104]

                                        46, 14b–15a

---

[102] From this passage and XI (15) and XVI (1007, LS 14, 7b), it seems that the building of the city was begun in the twenty-third year (1005), but it was evidently not set up as the Central Capital until the twenty-fifth year (1007).

[103] How different the relation of most of these subordinate states to Liao really was is seen from the fact that countries like Japan and Ta-shih were mentioned as states which were expected to support Liao in case of war.

[104] The *Liao Shih* furthermore lists all the military offices of (1) the Liao-yang Route to control Korea, (2) the Ch'ang-ch'un Route to control all the northeastern countries, (3) the Southern Capital to resist the Sung country; also under the Administration of the Commander in Chief, (4) the Western Capital to control the Hsi Hsia, (5) Northwestern Route, (6) the Southeastern Route, (7) the Eastern Route, (8) the Southwestern Border, and (9) the Western Route (LS 46, 15a–21b).

43. TROOPS GUARDING THE FRONTIER

Moreover,[105] the *Ta Liao Shih Chi*, which gives a record of the eastern frontier garrisons on duty against Korea, Nü-chih, and other states, was obtained from Korea. From it the scheme of national defence which was outlined simply but with all essentials can be grasped. By taking one [frontier as an example], the [situation at the other] three borders can be understood.

In Tung-ching the boundary extended to the Northwestern Mountain on the Yalu River.

> Huang-lung Administration[106] had 5,000 regular soldiers
> Hsien Prefecture[107] had 1,000 regular soldiers

In Tung-ching [garrisons] fringed the Nü-chih frontier to the Yalu River.

> Seventy[108] military fortifications each with a guard of twenty men, making a total of 1,400 regular soldiers

There were eight cantonments at Lai-yüan City[109] and Hsüan-i Commandery.[110]

> Heir Apparent Cantonment with 300 regular soldiers
> Great Cantonment with 600 regular soldiers
> P'u Prefecture Cantonment with 200 regular soldiers
> Hsin Cantonment with 500 regular soldiers
> Chia-t'o Cantonment with 300 regular soldiers
> Wang-hai City [Cantonment] with 300 regular soldiers
> Liu-pai Cantonment with 400 regular soldiers
> Wo-yeh Cantonment with 1,000 regular soldiers

Shên-hu-chün City,[111] which had 10,000 regular soldiers, was founded in the tenth year of the Ta-k'ang period.[112]

One administration, one prefecture, two cities, seventy fortresses, and eight cantonments together with 22,000[113] regular soldiers [are listed] above.   36, 13a–14a

44. PROBLEMS OF THE WEST

982–1013   In the court there was a discussion of the plan to expand the southwestern territory, which was to extend several thousand *li* west of the Black Mountain.[114] [Yeh-lü] T'ang-ku said, "If the garrison fortresses are too remote, in case of a sudden emergency the rescue forces cannot arrive in time. This is not a good arrangement." This was approved.

---

[105] We follow the Palace edition in reading 又 for the 人 of our text. LS 42, 1b says that Korea presented the *Ta Liao Ku-chin Lu* 大遼古今錄, which was probably the same book.

[106] North of modern Nung-an 農安 County, Kirin.

[107] Modern K'ai-yüan 開原 County, Liaoning.

[108] We follow the Palace edition in reading 七 "seven" for the first 十 "ten" of our text.

[109] Present Kimchong 黔定 Island in the Yalu River. The military significance of Lai-yüan 來遠 City may be seen from the role it played during the last years of the Liao dynasty. In the third month of 1116 the king of Korea offered one thousand bushels of grain to Lai-yüan and Pa 把 Prefecture (identical with Pao 抱 or 保 Prefecture), which were short of food because of the previous Jurchen siege. The Liao commander rejected the offer (KRS 14, 204), probably fearing that Korea might try to acquire possession of the places involved. In 1117 the same Liao officer was compelled to ask for a loan of fifty thousand bushels of grain from Korea. The eastern court,

after a heated discussion, promised to give the grain in exchange for the two cities. Before the Liao had time to acquiesce, the Jurchen armies attacked Lai-yüan City and the cantonments of Ta-fu 大夫, Ch'i-ta 乞打 (Chia-t'o 加陀?) and Liu-pai 柳白, burning many Liao warships and seizing the guards. Thereafter the Liao commander, Yeh-lü Ning 寧, and the prefect of Lai-yüan, Ch'ang Hsiao-sun 常孝孫, fled with their followers in one hundred and forty boats from the mouth of the Yalu River, requesting that the two cities be turned over to Korea and that the people who had sought refuge in Korea be given relief (KRS 14, 209; 58, 276).

[110] According to LS 38, 5a, Hsüan-i 宣義 Commandery was the military name for Pao 保 Prefecture (modern Wiju 義州, Korea).

[111] Probably near the Yalu River.

[112] That is, in 1084.

[113] But addition of the preceding figures gives only 21,000.

[114] Probably in Suiyuan.

As the western barbarians[115] were making incursions, an imperial decree ordered a discussion of defence plans.   [Yeh-lü] T'ang-ku was ordered to take charge of the cultivation so as to supply the soldiers in the west.   The cultivation was carried on along the Lu-ch'ü River.[116]   This year the harvest flourished exceedingly well.   In the next year the garrison was transferred to Chên Prefecture[117] where, in the course of fourteen harvests, several hundred thousand bushels of grain were accumulated.   [As a consequence] one peck of millet cost not more than a few cash.   91, 2a

45. SERVICES AND DUTIES IN THE NORTHWEST

983-1012   "In the northwestern regions,[118] during the agricultural seasons for each person engaged in patrol service, another cares for the public land and two render service to the *chiu* officers.   Generally none of the four adult males lives at home.   The work of grazing and herding devolves upon their wives and children.   Once robbed or plundered they immediately become impoverished.   During the summer and spring they are relieved by compassionate actions [of the government].   The officials, however, frequently mix [the government grain] with chaff, thus adding to their exploitation so that after a few months they again face distress.

"Moreover, animal husbandry is the foundation of a prosperous country.   But the officials, to guard against concealment [of the animals], herd them together in one place and do not permit them to scatter in places where water and grass are plentiful.   Further, because of desertions and deaths, the soldiers on guard at the frontier are continually being replaced by persons who are not accustomed to the natural conditions of the region.   Thus the deterioration goes on day after day, and the inroads continue month after month, so that they are gradually reaching complete exhaustion.

"As a plan for the present there is nothing better than to succor the poor, to reduce their taxes, and to provide them with oxen and seeds so as to induce them to engage in tilling and harvesting. Roving patrols should be created to guard against stealing and robbing.   Booty should be distributed [among the people] in order to help them through the summer and winter.   The herds should be scattered so that they can reach good pastures.   We can then look forward to wealth and power within a few years.   Then, if a picked force is trained and selected so as to build up the ranks of the army, how can it stand on the defensive without being firm?   How can it take the offensive without conquering?

"But the people who are hard to control must first be eliminated.   The rest will then automatically be intimidated.   If big things are neglected and little ones pored over, if the strong are avoided and the weak attacked, then not only will money and energy be wasted, but it will also be impossible to win them over completely.   These two [policies] are the devices which make for advantages and disadvantages.   They should not be ignored."[119]   104, 2a–b

46. AN ARMY OF SUNG SOLDIERS

991   On the day *mou-tzŭ* [of the first month in the ninth year of T'ung-ho] five hundred of the Sung soldiers who had surrendered were selected and organized into the Hsüan-li Army.   13, 2a

47. OVER-AGE SOLDIERS

994   On the day *chia-yin* of the fifth month [in the twelfth year of T'ung-ho] an imperial decree ordered that those in the Northern P'i-shih Army who could not perform their duties because of old age were to be exempted from services.   13, 4b

---

[115] Various tribes in Outer Mongolia.

[116] The modern Kerulen River in Outer Mongolia.

[117] On the modern Orkhon River in Outer Mongolia.

[118] Here the word *pu* 部 obviously designates not a "tribe" but a geographical division.   A parallel passage refers to "the people of the northwest" (see II, 2 (9)). The above description of the northwestern regions was written by Yeh-lü Chao who died about 1016.

[119] Yeh-lü Chao's suggestions were favorably received.

48. A WOMAN MILITARY LEADER

994 On the first day *kêng-ch'ên* [of the eighth month in the twelfth year of T'ung-ho] the emperor's grandaunt[120] was ordered to direct the soldiers of Wu-ku and other tribes of the Northwestern Route as well as the armies of Yung-hsing Palace[121] to pacify the western frontiers.[122] Hsiao Ta-lin[123] was to supervise military affairs.   13, 5a

49. THE EASTERN FRONTIER

997 On the day *ping-yin* [of the ninth month in the fifteenth year of T'ung-ho] the garrison soldiers on the eastern frontiers were withdrawn.   13, 9a

50. PO–HAI TROOPS

1019 On the day *chi-mao* [of the third month in the eighth year of K'ai-t'ai] an imperial decree ordered promotions in ranks[124] for the Po-hai generals and officers who had achieved merit in the punitive campaign against Korea.   16, 3a

51. PROBLEMS OF FRONTIER SERVICES

1035–1044 [Hsiao] Han-chia-nu replied,[125] "In my humble opinion, since during recent years Korea has not submitted and the Tsu-pu[126] have remained strong, preparations for offence and defence certainly cannot be allowed to cease. Recently we have been selecting for the protection of the frontiers wealthy individuals who supply their own provisions of grain. The way is long and difficult, so that the trip takes a long time. By the time the garrison stations are reached, the supplies are already more than half consumed. Consequently hardly an ox or a cart returns.

"The families without adults [capable of military service] offer double prices for hired [substitutes], but these men fear the hardships and run off in the middle of the journey, so that provisions for the frontier troops frequently cannot be supplied. If they seek a loan from a person, tenfold interest has to be paid. Things go so far that repayment is impossible even if both children and fields are sold. Whenever there are permanent desertions from the service or deaths in the army, replacements are made with young and able-bodied men. Such in general is the frontier garrison service east of the Yalu River.

"Furthermore the Po-hai, Nü-chih, and Koreans form alliances. Punitive expeditions are always taking place.[127] The rich join the army; the poor become patrols. Besides, the occurrence of floods and droughts and the fact that beans and millet are not flourishing increase the distress of the people daily. This is because circumstances make it so.

"Nowadays no service is heavier than that of the garrisons at the western frontier. Without the garrison service at the western frontier, even in an excessively bad year, the hardships would not come to such a point. If the western garrisons could be shifted slightly closer, then the journey would not be arduous and the people would not be deeply distressed.

---

[120] Hu-lien 胡輦, the grandaunt of Shêng-tsung, an elder sister of Empress Dowager Ch'êng-t'ien. She was a powerful personality who directed the "pacification" campaign in the west and initiated the garrison system, but the *Liao Shih* does not devote a special biography to her. She was married to Yen-sa-ko 罨撒葛, Prince of Ch'i, the second son of T'ai-tsung and Shêng-tsung's granduncle. After the prince's death she led a punitive campaign in 994 against the Tsu-pu. In 1004 K'o-tun 可敦 City was built near the Orkhon River (Outer Mongolia) under her direction. In 1006 she was arrested and imprisoned in Huai 懷 Prefecture (southeast of Boro Khoton, Jehol) for political conspiracy. In 1007 she was put to death in prison (see LS 14, 5a, 7a–b; 37, 14a; 64, 10b; 85, 1b; CTKC 13, 3b–4a; SHYK 196, 27a).

[121] T'ai-tsung's ordo.

[122] That is, to fight Hsi Hsia (LS 85, 1b).

[123] Hsiao Ta-lin 撻凜 in 986 captured the famous Sung general, Yang Chi-yeh 楊繼業. In 994 he was chief *hsiang-wên* of the Tsu-pu tribes (LS 85, 1a–b).

[124] We follow other editions in reading 官 for the 宮 of our text.

[125] The long memorial translated here must have been presented between 1035 and 1044 as it is preceded and followed in the *Liao Shih* by passages bearing these dates.

[126] See I, 2 (10), no. 8.

[127] Three times Liao conducted huge military campaigns against Korea as well as against other countries east of Liao. The first began in 992 and ended in 993; the second in 1010, ending in 1012; and the third in 1015, ending in 1020 (LS 115, 1a–4b).

"Some critics may hold that the shifting of [these garrisons] would by no means be advantageous—firstly, because of the loss of prestige; secondly, because it would give rise to invasion and insults; thirdly, because it would mean the abandonment of cultivated land and pastures.

"I say that this is not so. The Tsu-pu tribes, which have long since dwelt there, formerly extended as far north as the Lu-ch'ü River[128] and as far south as the border [of Liao[129]] where most of them lived dispersed and disunited. They simply went back and forth stealing and plundering. When T'ai-tsu made a western expedition into the desert, the Tsu-pu all quickly submitted, and all the various states of the western regions became willing to pay tribute. He then moved the [Tsu-pu] tribesmen into the interior and reorganized them into three tribes in order to enlarge our country. No walled cities were constructed. Neither were garrison troops set up. And yet for generations the Tsu-pu did not dare to make incursions.

994 "During the T'ung-ho period the emperor's grandaunt[130] directed an expedition into the western regions. As the territory[131] was extended still farther, the people who surrendered and were subjugated also increased in number. From then on, if one tribe rebelled, the neighboring tribes punished it in order that they might act as a check on each other with an equality of power. This is precisely the way to manage distant people.

1003 "But since the walling of K'o-tun[132] and the expansion of the frontier by several thousand *li*, day by day the compulsory services of the northwestern people have increased, and day by day their productive occupations have declined. In case of emergency deliverance is impossible. And acts of revolt and surrender are unpredictable. Nominally we have expanded our territory, but in reality we have gained nothing from the land. If the greed for territory is not ended, gradually a state of exhaustion will be reached. The disaster will be indescribable. . . .

"Formerly, when the system of replacements for [garrison] service was begun, everyone, whether he lived in a permanent residence or led a nomadic life, was generally well off. So for generations it was easy to arrange for replacements to serve at the frontier. But during recent years trouble has arisen at the frontier on several occasions, and most of the people have become impoverished. Consequently they are unable to fulfill their obligations. As soon as a replacement is made another vacancy occurs. If there are no upper class families,[133] then middle class families take their place. As time goes on their poverty grows worse, so that getting replacements is difficult. Such is the case not only with getting the replacements for conscripted service. The same is true for the frontier garrison troops. How can a double handful of earth, as it were, fill a ditch eight or ten feet deep?[134]

"If it is desired to create long-lasting benefits, it would be best to have the remote garrisons and the exhausted soldiers return home and to decrease the compulsory services so as to enable everyone to have a sufficiency. Then the system of replacements for [garrison] service can be restored as of old. . . .[135]

"Right now, K'o-tun City should be moved to a closer place to support and be in touch with the Wu-ku, Ti-lieh, and Wei Wu-ku[136] tribes under the vice-controller of the Southwest. The two armies of Hei-ling[137] should be abolished. K'ai Prefecture[138] and Pao Prefecture should both be controlled by the Eastern Capital.[139] The frontier troops in the northeast and the soldiers of the

---

[128] The modern Kerulen River in the eastern part of Outer Mongolia.

[129] The original border between the Liao empire and the Tsu-pu tribes was probably the northeastern part of the Gobi Desert. Later, after K'o-tun City had been established (see note 120) near the Orkhon River in Outer Mongolia, the Liao frontier stretched further north beyond the Kerulen River.

[130] See note 120.

[131] We follow other editions in correcting the word 士 of our text to 土.

[132] Another name for Chên 鎭 Prefecture (see I, 1 (5)).

[133] The passage refers, of course, to the economic status of the families.

[134] We follow other editions in reading 丈 for the 文 of our text.

[135] The passage omitted here is given in XIII (39).

[136] See I, 2 (6), nos. 1–3.

[137] A mountain in the northwestern part of modern Jehol.

[138] Respectively Fêng-huang 鳳凰 City, Liaoning, and Wiju 義州, Korea.

[139] Modern Liao-yang 遼陽 County, Liaoning.

general officer[140] of the Southern Capital should be increased. Walls and ramparts should be increased and repaired, and outposts should be in sight of each other. Look-out towers should be repaired, and city moats dredged for the defence of the frontier. This is the pressing need of the moment. I pray that Your Majesty will decide on this."[141]   103, 2a–4b

52. SOLDIERS REGISTERED

1056   On the day *mou-wu* [of the sixth month in the second year of Ch'ing-ning] the authorities were ordered to register soldiers in order to supplement the garrisons at the frontiers.   21, 3b

53. MILITARY SUPPLY

1085–1095   Toward the end of the Ta-an [period, Liu Hui[142]], the librarian of the heir apparent, memorialized, "Because the barbarians of the western frontier are making trouble, our soldiers are in remote garrisons. The people of the Middle Kingdom[143] are worn out by the urgent transportation. This is not a long-range policy. As a plan for the present it would be best to establish a city at Yen-p'o[144] and fill it with Chinese so that they may cultivate the soil and accumulate grain for the expenses of the northwest."
Though his statement was not acted upon, those cognizant thought it was right.   104, 3a

2. WARFARE

1. Equipment of a "regular" soldier 2. Commanders of the campaigning armies of the Northern Region 3. Organization of a campaign 4. Incendiary warfare 5. Fighting the southwestern tribes 6. Hunting as military practice 7. Military registration 8. Summer uniforms 9. Catapult soldiers 10. Technical preparations for attack 11. Surrendered soldiers of Sung 12. Partial mobilization 13. Military training 14. Southern Chinese to be unarmed 15. Training of the Chinese army 16. Military registration 17. Victory no longer certain 18. Investigation of military registers 19. Additional military registration 20. The old Ch'i-tan spirit 21. Chinese forbidden to hunt 22. Military instruction 23. The Jurchen menace 24. Specific military measures 25. Stock-owning soldiers conscripted 26. Military secrets kept from Chinese 27. Regional organization of a big army

1. EQUIPMENT OF A "REGULAR" SOLDIER

Under the military system of the Liao empire, all persons between fifteen and fifty years of age were placed on a military register. Each regular soldier had three[1] horses, one forager, and one orderly.[2]
Each man had nine pieces of iron armor along with saddle-cloths, bridles, armor of leather and iron for the horses according to their strength, four bows, four hundred arrows, a long and a short spear,

---

[140] See XIV, 2, note 21.

[141] After having made this critical statement, the author was promoted to another honorific position, but nothing is said about the effect of his bold proposals. Obviously they were not accepted, for the frontier continued to be the sore spot that it had been previously.

[142] Liu Hui 劉輝, a *chin-shih* of 1079, suggested appending a section on Sung at the end of the national history of Liao (*cf.* XIV, 4 (31)).

[143] The term 中國 (Middle Kingdom) was claimed by Liao and Chin for the areas under their control.

[144] Probably in the northern part of modern Suiyuan.

[1] The word 三 (three) of our text may be a misprint. In WHTK 346, 2712 the word 二 (two) is used. The providing of a soldier with two horses was common among the Inner Asiatic peoples. The Sung writer, Ma Yung-ch'ing 馬永卿, who first doubted this fact, became convinced of it when watching the Jurchen during a battle. He quotes an old verse which ascribes to each Uighur soldier two horses:

Five thousand soldiers were sent 送兵五千人
They drove [rode] ten thousand horses 驅[騎]馬一·萬匹
                                    (LCT 3, 38).
Two horses were probably the minimum number required for efficient fighting.

Another contemporary work, the *Yang-wang Chiang-shang Lu* 煬王江上錄, states that in 1610, when the Jurchen carried out a campaign against the Sung empire, ditties like the following were circulated:

A regular soldier [rides] three horses 正軍三匹馬
A conscript [wears] two pairs of shoes 簽軍兩量鞋
                                    (SCPMHP 243, 5a).

According to a Sung observer, Hsü T'ing 徐霆, a Mongol officer rode one horse and was followed by three, four, or even five or six horses (HTSLCC 14b).

[2] The term 家丁 seems to be used in composition with 打草穀 (to gather fodder and grain—translated as forager) and 守營舖 (to take care of the camp position—translated as orderly).

a club,[3] axe, halberd, small banner, hammer, awl, knife and flint, a bucket for the horse, a peck of dried food,[4] a bag for the dried food, a grappling hook, a [felt] umbrella,[5] and two hundred feet of rope for tying up the horses. All this was furnished by the men themselves.

Men and horses were not provided with supplies. Mounted foragers were instead dispatched daily in all directions to get supplies by plundering.[6]   34, 2b–3a

2. COMMANDERS OF THE CAMPAIGNING ARMIES OF THE NORTHERN REGION

With regard to the Liao campaigning army staff, the offices of the chancellor, the chief commander, and the chief controller were mutually interlinked from the highest to the lowest. The vanguard [stretched out] two wings, while the central army remained cautious and steady. Great care was extended to the distant scouts and patrols. When the battle started, responsibility was in the hands of the supervisor of the battle.

The offices had their regular pattern. Their orderly arrangement was set up in ordinary times. This was the way in which victory was assured.

The Chancellery of the Campaigning Army had right and left scribes and a councillor.

The Office of Chief Commander of the Campaigning Army comprised the supervisor of the army, the chief supervisor of the various sections of the campaigning army, and the supervisor of the battle.

> Chief commander of the campaigning army
> Vice-commander of the campaigning army
> Chief supervisor of the campaigning army

The Office of the General Police of the Campaigning Army had a chief police officer and an assistant police officer.

The Office of the Chief Controller of the Campaigning Army
The Office of the Commissioner of the Vanguard
The Board of the Chief Commander of the Vanguard
The Board of the Chief Commander of the Army of the Left Wing
The Board of the Chief Commander of the Army of the Right Wing
The Board of the Chief Commander of the Central Army
The Board of the Chief Commander of the Imperial Cantonment.   46, 21b–22b

3. ORGANIZATION OF A CAMPAIGN

Goldfish tallies[7] were cast for mobilizing the troops. For requisitioning horses and dispatching orders there were two hundred silver tablets.[8]

---

[3] According to a similar version in WHTK 346, 2712, the word 鎈 is a simplified form of 錁. The term 錉錁 is also written 骨朵. It was the name of a military weapon made of iron or wood with a ball at one end for striking (WPC 104, 13b–14a).

[4] The usual meaning of *sha* 粆, "sugar," can hardly be applied here. According to CTKC 24, 2b, one kind of Ch'i-tan food was called *sha-pi* (糒). The word *pi* means "dried food" (LKSC 2, 51a; *cf.* also TCTCSW 26, 9a). LS 59, 1a (see II, 1 (2)) mentions dried food as part of the provisions of a Ch'i-tan soldier.

[5] The word 毪 is not to be found in dictionaries. Our text is clarified by a parallel version in WHTK 346, 2712, which reads 搭鉤氈傘, "a grappling hook and a felt umbrella."

[6] The Ch'i-tan troops were largely self-supporting for they did not, like the Chinese armies, depend entirely on government supplies. When a Chinese general, Chao Yen-shou 趙延壽 (d. 948), in the service of Liao, asked T'ai-tsung for food supplies, T'ai-tsung replied that the Ch'i-tan made no such provision and that the soldiers should go out and loot as did the Ch'i-tan foragers 打草穀 (CTKC 3, 6b). This could be done only in the densely populated Chinese territory. It was impossible in the sparsely populated regions of what is now Outer Mongolia. There the Ch'i-tan drove sheep along with them as their main food supply and augmented this by hunting. Thus in 924, when T'ai-tsu led an expedition into this region, several thousand wild animals were caught (see II, 1 (5)). HCLY 77, 10a notes that at the beginning of the eleventh century only the Chinese soldiers of the Liao armies were given food and clothes, while the Ch'i-tan and other tribal fighters were not so provided.

[7] Before the time of T'ai-tsu only wooden tallies were used for mobilizing the troops. The "goldfish" tallies introduced after his accession were six inches long, made of gold, and shaped like a fish. Each had two halves; one was given to a general, and the other was retained by the imperial court. At times of military mobilization an imperial messenger was sent to summon the general and his troops by presenting the emperor's half of the tally, which was checked against the general's half before the troops were permitted to move (LS 57, 3a). Several illustrations of these tallies with Ch'i-tan characters are given in LTFPTL 1, 19b–20a. See figure 3.

[8] These tablets were a foot long and engraved with

Wherever the army camped, there were scouting *lan-tzŭ* forces[9] whose duty it was to listen for the sounds of men and horses at night.

Whenever a military campaign was undertaken, the emperor led the corps of barbarian and Chinese civil and military officials to sacrifice a grey ox and a white horse and to report to the gods of Heaven, Earth, and the Sun. The moon, however, was not worshipped. Intimate officials were variously ordered to make a report to the mausoleums of the emperors from T'ai-tsu down and to the god of Mu-yeh Mountain.[10]

Then an imperial decree ordered all regions to conscript soldiers. However, as regards the troops of the southern, northern, and Hsi kings, those of the Po-hai of Tung-ching, and the troops under the military control of Yen-ching, even though the imperial decree was received they did not rashly dispatch their troops. They had to report to the emperor, who then dispatched grand generals with the goldfish tallies. If the tallies matched, the soldiers were put into motion.

As soon as notice was received of a [mobilization] edict, the conscripts were brought together, household properties estimated, registers examined, and the masses organized as preparation.

Officers from sergeants up inspected the army in regular order and took weapons and tallies from the military headquarters. Imperial emissaries could not interfere with them. After a joint inspection of the army a report was made again to the emperor. According to the number of troops the emperor sent further orders for emissaries to assume the posts of military leaders. They and the military headquarters maintained a check on each other. The banners and drums of the five directions were also brought forth.

Then the emperor personally inspected the generals and officers. He also selected meritorious relatives and officials of high rank as the chief commander, vice-commander, and chief supervisor of the troops of the imperial traveling cantonments. From the various armies thirty thousand special elite troops were chosen as the imperial guard, three thousand valiant men were picked as a vanguard, and more than a hundred quick daredevils were selected as a *lan-tzŭ* scouting force. Each of the above armies had its own commander. From each section of the armies were selected, according to the number of men, five to ten men, who were brought together in a company with a special commander and were used to bring in troops and to dispatch messages.

For expeditions against the South the soldiers were reviewed for the most part at Yüan-yang Lake,[11] a thousand *li* north of Yu Prefecture.[12] On the march they took the routes via the passes of Chü-yung,[13] Ts'ao-wang,[14] Pai-ma,[15] Ku-pei,[16] An-ta-ma,[17] Sung-t'ing,[18] and Yü.[19] When they approached the territory of P'ing Prefecture[20] and Yu Prefecture, [the emperor] sent messengers along the different routes to urge[21] them to move on and not tarry long for fear that the crops would be trampled. The departure of the army took place not later than the ninth month, and its return not later than the twelfth month.[22]

Ch'i-tan characters. In important developments the emperor personally gave a tablet to a special courier who could travel five to seven hundred *li* in a day and a night. Wherever he went the messenger was treated as if the emperor himself were present (IV (16)).

[9] The *lan-tzŭ-ma* 攔子馬, also called *lan-tzŭ chün* (軍) or simply *lan-tzŭ*, was a military group whose function was to scout the movements of the enemy (*cf.* LS 116, 20*b*-21*a*; CTKC 23, 2*b*).

[10] *Cf.* VII, 2 (82).

[11] Corresponding to An-ku-li 昂古里 Lake in Chahar.

[12] Present Peiping.

[13] A pass northwest of Peiping.

[14] 曹王峪. Possibly identical with the Ts'ao-wang Mountains, north of Shun 順 Prefecture (modern Shun-i 順義 County, Hopei) (*cf.* Matsui 18, 125).

[15] Modern Pai-ma-kuan-k'ou 白馬關口, west of Ku-pei-k'ou 古北口 (*loc. cit.*).

[16] North of Ch'ang-p'ing 昌平 County, Hopei.

[17] Probably, like the other passes, located north of Peiping.

[18] North of Hsi-fêng-k'ou 喜峯口, Hopei.

[19] 榆. Near modern Shan-hai-kuan 山海關, Hopei.

[20] Modern Lu-lung 盧龍 County, Hopei.

[21] We follow other editions in reading 催 for the 惟 of our text.

[22] See XV, introduction, note 397. The late autumn was the ideal season for the start of a campaign, for then the horses were well fed (*cf.* SC 110, 10*b*) and the crops harvested. The climate of North China was also a not insignificant factor for a people accustomed to living in the somewhat cooler region of Jehol. When T'ai-tsung left K'ai-fêng, the capital of the Later Chin dynasty, in the spring of 947, he complained, "If Pien Prefecture were cooler and the climate more suitable, the conquest of the empire could be easily achieved in less than a year." It

Along the roads[23] priests, nuns, and persons in funeral dress were not allowed to be seen. When the emperor personally undertook an expedition, a prince of the imperial family was left in Yu Prefecture to take temporary charge of important military and civil affairs.

Upon passing the southern frontier they went separately via three routes, Kuang-hsin Commandery,[24] Hsiung Prefecture,[25] and Pa Prefecture[26] each having one. The emperor had to take the middle route, while the armies of the chief military commander and of the imperial bodyguard each took an individual route. When the troops encountered a county or town, they attacked it at once. If it was a large prefecture or commandery, the actual situation had first to be appraised. If it could be attacked, then the soldiers were advanced in succession. The houses, gardens, parks, mulberry trees, and silkworm thorn trees[27] of the people along the line of march had to be destroyed and set afire. On reaching the Northern Capital[28] of Sung, the soldiers from the three routes met together to discuss the attack. The same was true when they withdrew.

To the front and rear, left and right of the troops of the three routes there were vanguard forces. Scouting *lan-tzŭ* forces of over ten men each preceded and followed the vanguards at a distance of more than twenty *li*. They were fully dressed in armor. During the night at each five or ten *li* of the march they stopped briefly and dismounted to listen for the sounds of men and horses. If these were heard, they captured [the men and horses]. If the enemy could not be overpowered, they quickly notified the vanguards to attack with united force. If there was a great army, they hastened to notify the commanding officer. The actual situation among the enemy had to be ascertained immediately.[29]

When the army was on the march, if the walls of the prefecture cities along the way were firmly guarded and could not be attacked, the army was led past them. Lest the enemy come out of the cities and intercept [the soldiers], they encircled and shot at [the city], beat the drums, and shouted to feign making an attack. When the enemy closed the gates of the city and maintained a strong defence, there being no obstacles on the road ahead, the soldiers would be led forward.

The army was split up for attacking and blockading in order to leave the cities of the prefectures everywhere cut off without contact and standing alone without reenforcements. As regards the larger and smaller cities of the prefectures which were passed, because it was feared that during the night soldiers might come out to launch a surprise attack and to plan a rendezvous with troops of neighboring prefectures, when it was dusk a hundred horsemen for each city were dispatched to within about a hundred paces to the left and right of the city gates. Clad in armor and holding weapons, they stood their horses and waited. If an enemy force emerged and could not be beaten off, they galloped back and summoned reenforcements to join the fighting. Soldiers were also sent on patrol during the night to the left and right of the highways, paths, mountain roads, and ferries.

---

is even said that his death was due to the hot weather which he encountered in this relatively southern territory (LS 4, 15b–16a; TCTC 286, 8a, 11a).

[23] We follow the Southern Academy and Northern Academy editions in reading 在 for the 正 of our text.

[24] Twenty-five *li* west of modern Hsü-shui 徐水 County, Hopei.

[25] Present Hsiung 雄 County, Hopei.

[26] Modern Pa 霸 County, Hopei.

[27] Read 36, no. 599 gives the scientific name of *chê* 柘 as *Cudrania triloba*.

[28] Modern Ta-ming 大名 County, Hopei.

[29] After having taken the Chin 晉 capital, T'ai-tsung used to say to the Chinese officials, "I know everything about your country, but you know nothing of ours" (TCTC 286, 3b).

Preparatory espionage work was conducted by Liao agents even in peacetime. In the year of the establishment of the Sung dynasty, 960, two Liao spies were caught. The Sung emperor personally questioned them. He said, "What you want to find out is only the number of soldiers and officers and the amount of our provisions. Can you spy out the plans in my heart?" The men were set free by special order (LYCWC 1, 4). About 1007, when the Sung emperor toured the eastern part of his country, Liao spies reported to their court that the Sung soldiers were mobilized against Liao. When the story proved false, the spies were arrested and handed over to the Sung government (HCLY 77, 10b–11a).

At the beginning of the eleventh century Liao agents burned the arsenal of Hsiung 雄 Prefecture. The able Sung general, Li Yün-tsê 李允則, who was aware of the origin of the fire, showed no excitement, but secretly provided military weapons from an adjacent prefecture (HTPKC 4, 43b–44a).

In 1042, when war between Sung and Liao seemed imminent, the Sung general, Wang Tê-yung 王德用, caught a number of Liao spies. Instead of executing them, he had them watch a splendid review which he had carefully prepared (SS 278, 20a; SLYY 9, 83–84).

In the middle of the eleventh century, when the birthday of Hsing-tsung's sister was being celebrated, a Chinese

The foragers wore armor and carried weapons. From groups they formed companies.[30] They had first to cut down orchards and trees and later to herd together the old and the young, who carried earth and wood to fill up the moats and ditches[31] and who, when a city was attacked, were forced to advance first, so that the arrows, stones and rolling logs would, when coming down, injure only the old and the young. Ten thousand Chinese militia, who had been raised in the prefectures and counties of the Liao country, followed the armies for the special purpose of cutting down orchards and trees and filling up roadways.

For the palisades of the imperial stronghold and the various cantonments, only mulberry, silk-worm thorn, pear, and chestnut[32] trees were used. When the army was withdrawn, they were burned.

When the enemy force was drawn up in battle formation, consideration was given to the amount of its strength, the position of hills and streams, the roads for coming and going, the short-cuts for reinforcements, and the places for transporting provisions. There were means of taking care of each of these.

Then, on the four sides of the battle array, the horsemen were formed into regiments, each of five to seven hundred men. Ten regiments formed a column and ten columns a side. Each had its commanding officer.

The first regiment of troops galloped their horses and with a great uproar assaulted the enemy's formation. If an advantage was gained, all regiments advanced together. If no advantage was gained, [the first] withdrew and a second regiment took over. Those who withdrew rested their horses and partook of water and dried food. The same was true of all the columns. Withdrawals alternated with advances. If the enemy's formation refused to budge, the struggle was not pushed with full strength. They waited two or three days until the enemy became worn out.

Commands were also given to the foragers to drag[33] pairs of brooms on horseback, while following the wind at a gallop, so as to stir up a dust in the enemy formation. They went back and forth continuously. At this time [the enemy troops], already hungry and tired out, could not see each other. Thus victory might be obtained. If the southern part of the formation gained success and the northern part failed, while the commanding officer in between had no way of knowing about it, they used the names of mountains and rivers located in the four directions of their country as sound signals to give information to each other and to make it possible to aid each other.

If the expedition was not undertaken by the emperor personally, but by a high official with not less than a hundred and fifty thousand men, then the going and returning was via three routes and the troops assembled at the Northern Capital.[34] The advance took place in the ninth month and the return in the twelfth month. The order of the military actions remained the same. If [for an expedition] during the first month in the spring to the ninth month in the autumn a chief commander was not appointed, only sixty thousand mounted soldiers were sent out. They were not allowed to

---

actor who was performing was discovered to be a Sung spy. Evidently the man was harmless, for after an examination he was released (LS 62, 2b).

In order to prove the effectiveness of their work within Sung China, Liao spies often offered conspicuous pieces of evidence to their superiors. Daring agents stole the heavy lock of the gate of Hsiung Prefecture; on another occasion they wounded some people and fled. If they were unable to prove that they had achieved what they had claimed, they were executed (HTPKC 4, 43b).

In 1081 a Sung official stated that the Liao court was very well informed about the Sung empire, whereas the Sung government obtained only scanty information about Liao from its frontier officials. He suggested that the prefect of Hsiung Prefecture, Liu Shun-ch'ing 劉舜卿, should be put in charge of the espionage work. The Triple Office was ordered to provide Liu Shun-ch'ing with one thousand taels of silver and one hundred taels of gold for this purpose (SHYK 196, 65b ff.).

[30] This ambiguous passage presumably means that from haphazard groups engaged in the various activities of the camps the foragers formed companies for military purposes when the need arose.

[31] The Sung people resisted the Liao horsemen by digging artificial lakes, which, all told, measured two thousand li in circumference (CTC 5, 61). For the same purpose, trees were planted along the borders. During the eleventh century one single section of the border west of T'iao 跳 Mountain (in modern Shansi) was covered with three million willow and elm trees (PSHC 34, 3a). The Liao soldiers used to cut down the trees in order to facilitate the movement of the horses (CKCCC 3, 6b–7a).

[32] We follow other editions in reading 栗 for the 粟 of our text.

[33] Reading 拖 for the evidently incorrect 施 of our text.

[34] See above, note 28.

penetrate deeply [into enemy territory], to attack [places with] walls and moats, nor to cut down forests and trees,[35] but only to devastate and depopulate the land[36] within a zone of three hundred *li* beyond the frontier so as to prevent the cultivation of land and the raising of animals.

When the army penetrated into the southern regions, the infantry, cavalry, and tent-carts did not follow roads and paths. The generals of the three routes each led ten thousand *lan-tzŭ* scouts who, dispersed over a distance of ten to a hundred *li*, were to patrol alternately. At dusk horns were blown[37] as a signal, and all halted around the imperial tent. Here and there branches were broken off trees and bent to make bow-like resting places for a covering.[38] No preparations were made for spear-cantonments[39] or moated stockades. Whenever the troops got under way, the drums were beaten three times. No matter whether it was day or night, all started at the same time.

Before an encounter with a major enemy the war horses were not ridden. When the enemy army was approached, newly bridled horses with fresh strength were mounted. Enemies in battle array were not engaged, but when they retreated, the opportunity was seized. In the main [the strategy was] to place soldiers in ambush, to cut supply roads, to set fires at night, and to drag brush-wood to windward. Food supplies were provided by the individual. [The troops] came together after scattering. They were skilled in fighting and could endure the cold. This is why their military force was so powerful.   *34, 3a–5b*

4. INCENDIARY WARFARE

907–926   The ruler[40] of Wu,[41] Li Pien,[42] offered fierce-burning oil.[43] If water was poured on it, it burned even more furiously. When T'ai-tsu selected thirty thousand horse-

---

[35] Trees were cut down only on large expeditions.

[36] In 947, when the Ch'i-tan seized Hsiang 相 Prefecture of Chin 晉, they killed all males, herded the women to the north, and threw the little children into the air, catching them on their swords. Only seven hundred persons survived the ordeal. When later the city was cleaned up, more than one hundred thousand skeletons were found and buried (TCTC 286, 9a). At the end of the Liao period the Jurchen behaved in the same way when they captured Ta-t'ung. They pursued the young boys who had escaped the soldiers and killed them with large clubs (HICC 4, 7a).

[37] In 995 two men of Silla fled to Sung from Liao, carrying with them two conches, each of which was as large as a five pint measure. The fugitives said that they had lived in the Liao territory for eleven years, during which time they were trained to use these instruments. According to them, their group comprised fifty men. Whenever the army advanced, they blew their conches (SHYK 196, 22b–23a).

[38] The 弓子舖, as the text indicates, were the simplest shelters for soldiers in wartime (*cf.* LS 116, 21a). YLMC 6, 180, which records this and the following paragraphs, has 三丫舖, "shelters made of three V-shaped [branches]." They were probably some sort of lean-to.

[39] The spear-cantonment was so called because the imperial tent was usually surrounded by spears planted in the ground in order to protect it from stampeding horses (*cf.* II, 1 (27)).

[40] CTKC 13, 1b reads 王 instead of the 主 of our text.

[41] This small kingdom existed from 902 to 937 in the southeastern part of China.

[42] The founder of Nan T'ang 南唐 (in South China) who usurped the throne in 937 from Emperor Jui 睿 of Wu. This kingdom lasted until 975. The passage evidently contains an anachronism, for T'ai-tsu died in 926

before the usurpation. Li Pien may have offered the oil when he was an official of Wu.

[43] The fierce-burning oil, *mêng-huo-yu* 猛火油, apparently is petroleum. The passage translated here is the only one of its kind in the *Liao Shih*; a similar story appears in CTKC 13, 1b.

In Chinese literature petroleum is mentioned under various designations, such as *shih-ch'i* 石漆, *shih-chih* 石脂, *shih-chih shui* (水), *chih-shui* 脂水, *shih-chu* 石燭, *shih-yeh* (液), *shih-yu* (油), and *mêng-huo-yu*. The substance was known to the Chinese at a very early date. They used it for the making of lacquer, medicine, ink, and candles; on occasion they greased their cuts with it. It was also employed for military purposes. As fuel in lamps oil had very little popularity, perhaps because of the smell and smoke.

According to HS 28B, 5a, in the vicinity of Kao-nu 高奴 County there was a river, the Yu 洧, whose water "could be burnt." The *Shui-ching Chu* 水經注 notes that the water of the Yu River was "fat" and ignitible (HCSCC 3, 28b–29a). The T'ang work *Yu-yang Ts'a-tsu* 酉陽雜俎 and the Sung work *T'ai-p'ing Kuang-chi* 太平廣記 both speak of "stone-lacquer," the *shih-chih*-water, which floated on the surface of this river "like lacquer." It was used to grease carts; when used as fuel for lamps it burned with a bright flame (YYTT 10, 74; TPKC 399, 2b).

According to a Sung work, *shih-yu* ("stone oil") was produced in the region of Fu 鄜 and Yen 延 (modern Fu-hsien 鄜縣 and Yen-an 延安, Shensi). The oil mixed with sand gushed from a spring. The natives gathered it into a jar with a pheasant's tail. It looked like pure lacquer. It burned like hemp but with a heavier smoke which blackened the curtains. The Sung scholar, Shên K'uo 沈括, realizing the usability of the material for writing, made it into ink by collecting the soot. He called his

men to attack Yu Prefecture,[44] the empress said, "Where is there a case of attacking a country by experimenting with oil?"[45]

She pointed to a tree in front of the tent and asked, "Could it live without bark?"

T'ai-tsu replied, "Of course not."

The empress said, "Yu Prefecture having land and people is like[46] this.   If we use three thousand horsemen to plunder its surrounding suburbs, within a few years it will become distressed and fall to us.   Why must we act like that?[47]   In case of failure it would make us the laughing-stock of the Middle Kingdom.   Would not our tribes also go adrift?"   71, 2b–3a

5. FIGHTING THE SOUTHWESTERN TRIBES

922   In the sixth month [of the first year of T'ien-tsan] the Eagle Army was dispatched to attack the tribes of the southwest.   The booty was granted to the poor people.
                                                                              2, 3a

6. HUNTING AS MILITARY PRACTICE

940   On the day kêng-wu of the ninth month [in the third year of Hui-t'ung] the inner chamberlain, Ts'ui Ch'iung-ku, said, "The Chin ruler has heard that Your Majesty frequently goes hunting and wishes to beg that you would moderate it."

The emperor replied, "Our hunting is not simply a pursuit of pleasure.   It is a means of practising warfare."

Then he issued an edict to inform him.   4, 5b

7. MILITARY REGISTRATION

946   [In the first month of the ninth year of Hui-t'ung] the Pi-ku-tê [tribe] made a report on military registration.   69, 6a

---

product Yen-chou shih-yeh, "the stone juice of Yen Prefecture."   In a poem he says:

Beneath Êrh-lang Mountain	二郎山下
The snow swirls in clouds . . .	雪紛紛 . . .
The "stone smoke" is heavy	石煙多
Like the Lo-yang dust	似洛陽塵

(MHPT 24, 155; cf. also HCLY 58, 6b–7a).

Another place in the Northwest, Chiu-ch'üan 酒泉 County in modern Kansu, also produced oil.   A Chin 晉 work, Po-wu Chih 博物志, written by Chang Hua 張華, says that south of Yen-shou 延壽 County there was a spring from which came forth a yellow greasy substance similar to gravy.   When it was put in a vessel it turned black.   It burned with a bright flame.   It could be used to grease carts and water mills, and to make jars watertight, but it could not be eaten.   The natives called it shih-ch'i, "stone lacquer" (PWC 9, 55; cf. also HHC 23, 12b and HCSCC 3, 29a).

The oil mentioned in our passage was sent by the ruler of Wu.   Wu possibly obtained it from the Malayan Archipelago, which from early times enjoyed communications with South and Southeastern China.   In 958 Chan-ch'êng 占城 (Malaya ?) paid eighty-four jars of fierce-burning oil as tribute to Later Chou.   It is said that this oil burned with increasing fury if water was thrown on it (WTS 74, 17a; SS 489, 3b).   In 971 the country of San-fu-ch'i 三佛齊 (in Sumatra) also offered oil as tribute to Sung (SS 489, 13a).

During the Northern Sung period (960–1127) reservoirs about ten feet long were dug for the storage of this oil at border cities of strategic importance.   Before the end of a month, when the earth of the reservoir became yellowish-red, the oil had to be transferred to another reservoir; otherwise, a fire would start and destroy the houses.   West of Chung-shan 中山 City (modern Chên-ting 眞定, Hopei) there was a large lake, at which the Sung troops held maneuvers.   Once the writer, K'ang Yü-chih 康譽之, watched them.   The attackers burned oil and destroyed the "enemy's" camp, as well as the seaweed.   The fish and turtles which were exposed to the flames died immediately (TML 1b).

The comprehensive Sung work on military affairs, Wu-ching Tsung-yao 武經總要, devotes a special section to "fierce-burning oil," which was used among other things for burning bridges and warships, and for repelling a besieging army.   Illustrations show the type of receptacles in which the powerful liquid was kept (WCTY 12, 66a–69a).

According to our text, the Ch'i-tan knew oil from the days of T'ai-tsu, experimenting with it even for military purposes.   In contrast to the Sung armies, however, the Liao troops do not seem to have counted petroleum among their standard weapons, most probably because their home territory lacked easily accessible oil deposits.

[44] Present Peiping.

[45] The word 艜 being meaningless here, we follow CTKC 13, 1b in reading 油 (oil) instead.

[46] We follow CTKC 13, 1b in reading 猶 for the 由 of our text.

[47] This refers to the use of the oil.

8. SUMMER UNIFORMS

986   On the day *chi-wei* [of the fourth month in the fourth year of T'ung-ho, when Yeh-lü] Hsiu-ko and P'u-ling[48] came to receive an audience, an imperial decree ordered the Triple Office to provide cloth for summer uniforms for the soldiers at the front.   11, 4a

9. CATAPULT SOLDIERS

986   On the day *chia-ch'ên* [of the sixth month in the fourth year of T'ung-ho] an imperial decree ordered the vicegerent of the Southern Capital, [Yeh-lü] Hsiu-ko, to send catapultiers to assist [Yeh-lü] Hsieh-chên in the west.[49]   11, 5a

10. TECHNICAL PREPARATIONS FOR ATTACK

988   On the day *i-ch'ou* [of the sixth month in the sixth year of T'ung-ho] an imperial mandate issued to the troops of the various circuits ordered the preparation of implements for attacking city walls on the expedition to the south.   12, 2a

11. SURRENDERED SOLDIERS OF SUNG

990   On the day *mou-tzǔ* of the fifth month [in the eighth year of T'ung-ho] the Sung troops who had surrendered were split up and were distributed to various armies.

13, 1a–b

12. PARTIAL MOBILIZATION

1015   On the day *kêng-shên* [of the eleventh month in the fourth year of K'ai-t'ai] an imperial decree ordered that the Buddhist monks of the Eastern Capital be reduced in number.   The Supreme Capital, the Central Capital, and the various ordos were ordered to select fifty-five thousand well-trained soldiers in order to prepare for an eastern expedition.[50]   15, 9b

---

[48] These men were commanders of troops engaged at the time in fighting Sung.

[49] In early Chinese literature *p'ao* 砲 or 礮 is designated in various ways.   The *Shuo Wên* mentions a catapult, the device called *kuei* 䈹, made of large logs, which was used to hurl rocks upon the enemy (SWCTC 7*A*, 35–36). At the close of the Later Han dynasty, in A.D. 200, Ts'ao Ts'ao 曹操 employed a *p'i-li ch'ê* 霹靂車, or *fa-shih ch'ê* 發石車, or *p'ao ch'ê* 拋車 for the same purpose in a battle with Yüan Shao 袁紹 (HHS 74, 30*b*; SKC, Wei 6, 24*b*).   The term *p'ao* 礮 seems to have become popular in the third and fourth centuries.   It appeared in a poem 閑居賦 of the Chin poet, P'an An-jên 潘安仁 (WH 16, 5*a*).   In 573 a Ch'ên 陳 general, Huang Fa-ch'ü 黃法㷬 made a *p'ao ch'ê*; his *p'ao* catapults hit the towers of the enemy's cities (NS 66, 17*b*).   From the sixth century on, the *p'ao* was a major device in sieges.   For a detailed study of the early use of the weapon see KYTK 30, 16*b* ff.; Matsui 11; Lu MT 28.

From the eighth to the eleventh and twelfth centuries the device underwent great improvement.   In the middle of the eighth century Li Ch'üan 李筌 describes in detail the making of a catapult.   The frame consisted of large logs which moved on four wheels.   A long pole on the top had a receptacle for holding the stone missiles.   When the soldiers pulled [?] the opposite end of the pole, the rocks were discharged (SCTPYC 4, 78).

A Sung work on military affairs gives a very systematic description of various kinds of catapults used in the eleventh century.   See figure 42.   Of the sixteen types enumerated, some were high, others low, some had wheels, others did not.   One complex catapult was served by one hundred men; another, still larger, was put into action by one hundred and fifty men.   The largest had a crew of two hundred and forty men; the smallest was handled by "only" forty.

Besides these complex machines, there were also simple catapults.   The "hand catapult" which threw stones weighing two catties required only two men.   The "fire catapult" (*huo p'ao* 火砲) resembled the other machines in its construction, but it threw gunpowder balls and other inflammable matter.   The *chin chih* (金汁) *p'ao* threw molten metal.   The "manure catapult" (*fên* 糞 *p'ao*) threw dirt and poisonous matter (WCTY 12, 38*b* ff.).

No record dwells upon the character of the Liao catapult.   In all probability the northern strategists imitated the Chinese pattern which in this field was without rival in the eastern part of Asia.   In 1004 the Liao troops who invaded Ying 瀛 Prefecture are said to have used a technical device of marvelous quality.   The catapult is not especially mentioned in these records, but since catapults were part of the Liao armies' regular equipment, it seems safe to assume that the formidable machines were employed on this occasion (*cf.* SHYK 196, 30*a*).

[50] The punitive campaign against Korea started in 1014 and ended in 1020.   As a result the king of Korea sent an envoy to sue for peace and to ask that he be permitted to resume the payment of tribute as a subordinate (*cf.* LS 16, 4*a*).

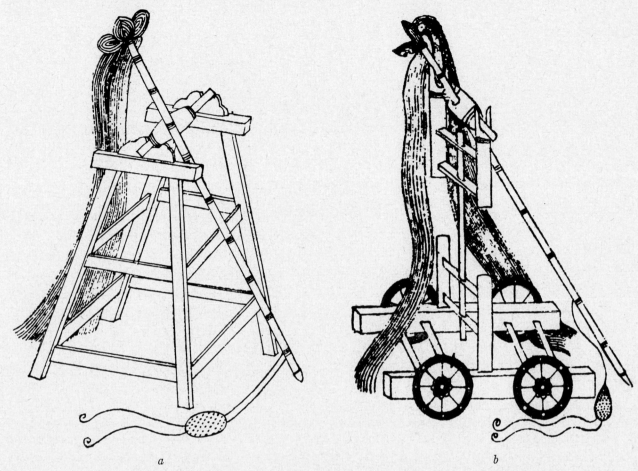

FIG. 42.   Two Sung catapults: (a) simple type, (b) machine on wheels (WCTY 12).

13. MILITARY TRAINING

1036   On the day *kuei-ch'ou* of the twelfth month [in the fourth year of Ch'ung-hsi] an imperial decree ordered that the catapultiers, crossbowmen, and swordsmen of all the armies should be periodically reviewed.   18, 5*b*

14. SOUTHERN CHINESE TO BE UNARMED

1043   On the day *jên-yin* of the second month [in the twelfth year of Ch'ung-hsi] the Chinese south of the passes[51] were forbidden to possess bows and arrows.[52]   19, 4*a*

15. TRAINING OF THE CHINESE ARMY

1046   On the day *kuei-ch'ou* of the twelfth month [in the fourteenth year of Ch'ung-hsi] the emperor reviewed the Chinese troops as they practised shooting[53] with catapults and thrusting [with swords and spears].   19, 7*a*

16. MILITARY REGISTRATION

1046   On the day *ping-shên* [of the seventh month in the fifteenth year of Ch'ung-hsi] the soldiers of all routes were registered.   19, 8*a*

---

[51] This probably refers to Chü-yung 居庸, Sung-t'ing 松亭, and Yü-lin 楡林, which correspond to the passes along the Great Wall north of Peiping.

[52] A Liao imperial decree sent to Korea in 1043 reveals that in this year the Liao army was mobilized for an attack against Sung (TKTK 16, 428).   The attack, however, was not carried out.

[53] We follow other editions in reading 射 for the 謝 of our text.

17. VICTORY NO LONGER CERTAIN

After 1049   Having been appointed envoy for the birthday of the Sung [emperor, Yeh-lü Ho-li-chih[54]] lodged at the Pai-kou Station.[55]   During a feast given by Sung an actor poked fun at Hsiao Hui's defeat at Ho-hsi.[56]   Ho-li-chih said, "Victories and defeats are common matters among military men.   Our Emperor Ssŭ-shêng[57] captured Shih Ch'ung-kuei.[58]   To the present day there is still a Shih Family Stronghold in Hsing-chung.[59]   How is one defeat of Hui comparable?"

The Sung officials were shamed and overcome.

The emperor, on hearing of this, said, "Because an actor made a slip, why should the friendship of the countries be injured?"

[Ho-li-chih] was punished with two hundred lashes with the whip and was discharged from his position.   86, 5*b*

18. INVESTIGATION OF MILITARY REGISTERS

1051   On the day *chi-mao*, the first day of the tenth month in the winter [of the twentieth year of Ch'ung-hsi] the military registers of the various circuits were investigated.

20, 6*a*

19. ADDITIONAL MILITARY REGISTRATION

1058   On the day *mou-yin* of the third month [in the fourth year of Ch'ing-ning] the brave and alert adults of T'ien-tê,[60] Chên-wu,[61] and Tung-shêng[62] were enrolled and registered as soldiers.   21, 5*a*

20. THE OLD CH'I–TAN SPIRIT

1064   Shun-tsung, whose given name was Chün and childhood name Yeh-lu-wo, was the eldest son of Tao-tsung. . . . At the age of six he was given the title of Prince of Liang.   The next year,[63] while accompanying the emperor on a hunt, his arrows thrice in succession found a mark.   The emperor looked at his followers and said, "Since the time of our ancestors, we have surpassed others in riding and shooting and we have made the world tremble with our power. This boy, though still very young, has not lost the spirit."   Later, on encountering ten deer, [Shun-tsung] shot nine of them.   The emperor was delighted and gave a feast.   72, 6*a*

21. CHINESE FORBIDDEN TO HUNT

1071   On the day *hsin-yu* [of the twelfth month in the sixth year of Hsien-yung], Chinese were forbidden to hunt.   22, 7*a*

---

[54] Yeh-lü Ho-li-chih 合里只, a descendant of the imperial clan.   He attained the position of great king of the Northern Division (LS 86, 5*b*).

[55] Near the Chü-ma 巨馬 River, Hopei.

[56] Hsiao Hui 惠 was defeated by Hsi Hsia soldiers in 1049 (IV (12)), but according to his biography this happened at Ho-nan and not at Ho-hsi.   In the latter place he was victorious over the Hsi Hsia in the year 1044 (LS 93, 2*b*).

[57] T'ai-tsung.

[58] The name of the last emperor of Chin 晉.   He was captured by Liao in 947.

[59] In 947 the Chin emperor, with his mother, wives, and relatives, was captured.   In the eighth month of 948, when Shih-tsung returned from his summer residence, the Chin emperor's mother requested land from the Liao ruler for cultivation and for herding near a Chinese city.   In 949 the distinguished captives were moved to Chien Prefecture where they received more than five thousand *mou* of land.   Within this area, referred to as the Stronghold of the Shih Family (Shih 石 was the name of the Chin ruling family,) the Chin courtiers erected buildings and tilled the land.   It was in Hsing-chung Administration (modern Ch'ao-yang 朝陽 County, Jehol).   In 950 the Chin empress dowager died, and about 964 the Chin emperor followed her (CWTS 85, 6*a*–8*a*; WTS 17, 4*a*–6*a*: LS 39, 7*b*).

[60] In the territory of Urot Banner 吳喇忒旗, Suiyuan.

[61] The word 鎮 may be a misprint for 振.   Chên-wu 振武 is mentioned in LS 41, 4*b*.   It corresponds to modern Ho-lin-ko-êrh 何林格爾 in Suiyuan.

[62] Probably modern T'o-k'o-t'o 托克托, Suiyuan.

[63] According to LS 21, 6*a*, Shun-tsung 順宗 was born in 1058.   He was therefore six years of age (by the Chinese method of counting) in 1063, and seven years of age in 1064 when he exhibited his skill.   Considering that he was only six years old by the Western system, the story may well have been considerably embellished or even invented.

22. MILITARY INSTRUCTION

1095   On the day *ping-ch'ên* [of the ninth month in the first year of Shou-lung] an imperial decree ordered the catapultiers and crossbowmen of Hsi-ching to teach the Chinese army of the Northwestern Route.   26, 1*b*

23. THE JURCHEN MENACE

1114   [Hsiao] T'ao-su-wo[64] said, "Although the country of the Nü-chih is small, yet its people are brave and skilled in archery.   Since it seized our rebel, Hsiao Hai-li,[65] its force has become stronger.   Our soldiers have not been trained for a long time.   If they were to meet a strong enemy and should be somewhat unsuccessful, all the tribes would become disloyal and could not be controlled at all.   As a plan for the present it would be best to bring about a great mobilization of soldiers in all circuits in order to intimidate them into submission.   Then they may become obedient."   101, 1*b*

24. SPECIFIC MILITARY MEASURES

1115   In the fifth year [of T'ien-ch'ing, Hsiao Hu-tu[66]] followed T'ien-tsu on the eastern expedition as chief commander of the vanguard.   In a crisis he was indecisive.
All the military units were named after hunting grounds.
Advancing to the La-li River,[67] he fought with the Chin army and was badly defeated.   The main force retreated.   During the punitive campaign against Yeh-lü Chang-nu,[68] owing to his requisitioning private slaves as soldiers, he was transferred to the post of director of affairs for the chancellor of the Northern Division.   101, 4*a*

25. STOCK–OWNING SOLDIERS CONSCRIPTED

1116   On the day *i-ch'ou* of the sixth month [in the sixth year of T'ien-ch'ing] the soldiers of all routes were registered.   Whoever owned ten or more animals of any kind had to join the army.   28, 4*a*

26. MILITARY SECRETS KEPT FROM CHINESE

1116   Previously, when T'ien-tsu was defeated by the Nü-chih, he thought that Hsiao Fêng-hsien[69] was ignorant of tactics.   Therefore he summoned [Chang] Lin[70] and entrusted him with the affairs of the eastern expedition.   [Chang] Lin, considering that under the old system Chinese did not participate in the important military and state policies, refused the post. The emperor would not consent to his refusal.   102, 3*b*

27. REGIONAL ORGANIZATION OF A BIG ARMY

1117   In the ninth month [of the seventh year of T'ien-ch'ing] the emperor went from Yen to the Yin-liang River[71] and organized eight cantonments of the Avenging Army.[72]

---

[64] Hsiao T'ao-su-wo 陶蘇斡 came from the T'u-lü-pu tribe.   His highest office was that of grand tutor.   He was an intelligent Ch'i-tan fully aware of the deteriorating position of Liao (LS 101, 1*a* ff.).

[65] Hsiao Hai-li 海里 was probably a member of the imperial consort clan.   He looted the arsenal of Ch'ien Prefecture and fled to the Jurchen (XIII (44)).   His revolt supplied the Jurchen with military weapons and made them realize the extent of the Ch'i-tan weakness (CS 1, 14*b*).

[66] Hsiao Hu-tu 胡篤, who came from a medical family, was notorious for his flattery of Emperor T'ien-tsu (*cf.* LS 101, 3*b* ff.).

[67] Probably the modern La-lin 拉林 River, Kirin.

[68] Yeh-lü Chang-nu 章奴 revolted in 1115 during the expedition against the Jurchen.   As a result the Liao army lost the campaign.

[69] Hsiao Fêng-hsien 奉先, an elder brother of the first concubine of T'ien-tsu, was in charge of the military affairs of Liao at this time (*cf.* LS 102, 1*a*–2*a*).

[70] Chang Lin 張琳, a Chinese who was a native of Shên 瀋 Prefecture (modern Mukden, Liaoning), attained the position of prime minister of the Southern Administration (*cf.* LS 102, 3*a*–4*a*).

[71] According to LS 37, 2*b*, it was located in Shang-ching.

[72] The Avenging (怨) Army was so called because it avenged Jurchen raids in Liao territory (CTKC 11, 2*a*). In 1122 this army was renamed the Ever-Victorious (常勝) Army (SCPMHP 5, 3*b*).   Because it was made up mainly of Chinese, it surrendered to Sung after revolting.

The ones drawn from I Prefecture[73] were called the Front I and the Rear I, those from Chin Prefecture[74] were called the Front Chin and the Rear Chin, and those from Ch'ien[75] and Hsien[76] [Prefectures] were called the Ch'ien and the Hsien.   They also included the Great Cantonment of Ch'ien and Hsien and the Cantonment of Yen Prefecture.   In all there were more than twenty-eight thousand men. They were stationed in the Chi-li Mountains of Wei Prefecture.[77]   28, 5a

---

[73] 宜.   In the vicinity of modern I 義 County, Liaoning.

[74] Modern Chin 錦 County, Liaoning.

[75] Southwest of modern Pei-chên 北鎮 County, Liaoning.

[76] Pei-chên County, Liaoning.

[77] No Wei 衞 Prefecture is mentioned in the geographical section of the *Liao Shih*.   The Chinese traveler, Hu Chiao 胡嶠, notes in his narrative that he journeyed from Fu 福 Prefecture (near modern Chang-wu 彰武 County, Liaoning) eastward to the Shih-san 十三 Mountains and thence proceeded still further to Wei Prefecture (CTKC 25, 2a).   The Shih-san Mountains were in Hsien 顯 Prefecture (east of modern Pei-chên County) (LS 38, 8a). Hence Wei Prefecture must have been located east of present Pei-chên County, Liaoning.

THE MAIN EVENTS IN LIAO HISTORY TABULATED CHRONOLOGICALLY

INTRODUCTION

1. A CHRONOLOGICAL SURVEY OF THE MAIN EVENTS IN LIAO HISTORY

In the preceding pages the history of Liao society has been presented from several angles—the geographic, economic, social, administrative, and military; but, for the reader's convenience, it seems desirable to collate the main events in a chronological survey. Events referred to in our texts will receive brief mention. More space will be given to certain political and military facts which do not directly affect the structure of Liao society and which, therefore, do not appear in our selected passages.

2. THE FIVE MAIN PERIODS OF LIAO HISTORY

In the introduction to section XII we have examined the attitude of the Liao government to the country's economic crises. The changes revealed by our analysis marked off the main periods of Liao history. The following survey which seeks to integrate internal developments with external events modifies, but in no way negates, the earlier statement.

The predynastic history of the Ch'i-tan reveals them as a pastoral people dwelling in the eastern regions of Inner Asia. For centuries they participated in tribal struggles and migrations in Manchuria and Mongolia, sometimes as active, sometimes as passive, agents in a changing political and military scene. China and, to a lesser degree, other neighboring agricultural countries influenced the course of these tribal movements. Powerful nomadic neighbors, the Turks, the Uighurs, the Hsi, and the Shih-wei, also pressed upon them. But, when their power failed, the confederation of the rising Ch'i-tan was strengthened. Both the collapse of the Uighur empire in 840 and the dissolution of T'ang China contributed to the consolidation of Ch'i-tan might. The newly acquired Chinese centers of agriculture and industry made A-pao-chi master of his nation, and his nation master of Inner Asia. It is true, A-pao-chi fought a number of wars in North China to safeguard his southern flank, but frequent and important expeditions led him into the tribal regions of the East, North, and West. Only after the defeat of his tribal neighbors could A-pao-chi subdue the Po-hai kingdom;

only then could his son, T'ai-tsung, establish a firm foothold in Chinese territories south of the Great Wall.

(1) The *first period* of Liao history deals with the consolidation of Liao supremacy in Inner Asia and the recognition of A-pao-chi's direct line as hereditary rulers of the new state.

(2) The conquest of the Po-hai country, the successful campaigns against China Proper, and the establishment of a special agricultural ("southern") sector besides the tribal ("northern") one may be considered the most significant events of the *second period*, a time of territorial expansion and institutional growth. The temporary occupation of the Chinese capital, Pien, the seizure of the Chinese court, and the proclamation of the dual organization of the country which now formally was called "Liao," terminate the second phase.

(3) The *third period* saw the final consolidation of the Liao empire. A dual organization was definitely set up, experimented with, and expanded. The war against Sung China provided a crucial test of the country's inner strength and external striking power. Under pressure from a frequently uncertain military situation, the Liao rulers, contrary to the course pursued during the earlier part of the century, were forced to utilize certain Chinese economic methods previously neglected. Despite the successful battles fought in the tribal border regions and in the Chinese theater of war, the fortifications in the north and the military difficulties in the south indicate the limits of the empire's ability to expand.

(4) The decades after the peace of 1005—a peace that followed upon partial success and not complete victory—may be called the *fourth period* of Liao history. Minor wars against Korea and Hsia confirmed the experience gained in the Sung war: the military strength of Liao was unbroken, but the country had reached the peak of its power. This was a time of cultural borrowing and change; it was a time of peaceful evolution of existing institutions. From many points of view it was the golden age of the Liao dynasty. In the year 1037 the officials received imperial rewards "because the prisons of the Northern and Southern Chancelleries were empty."[1] The behavior

---

[1] XII (45).

of the kindly prefect, Yang Chi[2], who heaped benevolences upon his people, which they duly appreciated, is entirely in keeping with the trend of the times.

But below the unruffled surface discontent smoldered and spread. In 1046, when Yang Chi took office, banditry and local rebellion were already a serious problem.[3] The increase of large-scale landownership meant an increase of the country's tenancy sector and with it a decrease of taxes and labor power available for the government.[4] The shrinkage of the taxable agrarian sector, the decline of military prowess, and the diminution of tributary income necessarily led to more pressure on those whose surplus and labor power was still accessible to the government.[5] Many symptoms[6] indicate that it was this vicious circle which induced the peasants in ever growing numbers to give up houses and fields and to "wander about" in despair. It was this vicious circle which, by its merciless advance from bad to worse, brought about in 1087 the open breakdown of the repressive government policy against the peasant fugitives.[7] It was this vicious circle which so weakened the power structure of the conquest state that it was unable to exact labor service from its subjects[8] or obedience from the border peoples.[9]

(5) The *fifth period* was a time of rapid political decay and, finally, of open rebellion. Its contributions to the institutional and cultural history of Liao are insignificant; its contributions to the morphology of political disintegration many. From 1112 on, internal rebellion and attack from without combined to break down and destroy what for two hundred years had been the Great Liao Empire.

[2] XII (49).
[3] XIII (39).
[4] XII, introduction.
[5] *Loc. cit.*
[6] *Loc. cit.*

[7] XII (88).
[8] XI (26).
[9] XIII (45).

THE TABLES

TECHNICAL NOTE

The following table lists the main events of Liao history in chronological order. The first column gives the year, the second the month in which the event occurred. It has been pointed out in our technical introduction and in appendix I that the Liao year and the Julian year are similar but not identical. The Liao year begins somewhat later and ends somewhat later, overlapping the beginning of the succeeding Western year.

The month dates are taken from the *Liao Shih;* they follow the Liao calendar. The year dates follow the Julian calendar, but for the sake of conformity we have placed the Liao year, which is figured according to its position within the reign period, below the Julian year. The names of the various reign periods are not inserted. They occur many times in the texts and are listed systematically in appendix I.

Adjustment between the two calendars may frequently be of little moment. Occasionally, however, it is illuminating. The twelfth Liao month, which overlaps the January of the Western year 926, definitely inaugurated the "natural" year. The winter solstice was over, and the increasing length of the days invited new military activity. The great mobilization recorded for this twelfth month initiated the conquest of the Po-hai kingdom which occurred during the first month of the succeeding Liao year.

The *Liao Shih* reference is given in the last column. If the tabulated event has been recorded in one of our translated passages, the section and passage number are given.

YEAR	MONTH	MAIN EVENTS	REFERENCE
872		A-pao-chi born.	1, 1*a*
901		Hên-tê-chin,[1] khaghan of the Yao-lien lineage, became chieftain of the Ch'i-tan tribes.	1, 1*b*
		A-pao-chi made *i-li-chin* of the I-la tribe.	1, 1*b* II, 1 (3)
902	7	A-pao-chi led 400,000 soldiers to attack Ho-tung and Tai-pei.[2] Captured 95,000 people and more than 100,000 camels, horses, oxen, and sheep.	1, 1*b* XI (1) II, 1 (3)
	9	Lung-hua Prefecture[3] walled and the Temple of the Commencement of Teaching built.	1, 1*b* IX (1) XI (1)
903		In the spring of the year, A-pao-chi attacked the Jurchen and captured 300 households.	1, 1*b*
	9	A-pao-chi took several cities in Ho-tung.	1, 1*b*
	10	A-pao-chi led soldiers to attack and loot the region north of Chi.[4]	1, 1*b*
		The I-la 迭剌 of Hsi 奚 set up with 7,000 Hsi households. A-pao-chi appointed as *yü-yüeh* in charge of military and political affairs.	1, 2*a*
904	9	The Black-cart Shih-wei 黑車子室韋 and Chao Pa 趙霸, the foster son of Liu Jên-kung,[5] were badly defeated and Chao Pa was captured by A-pao-chi.	1, 2*a*
905	7	A-pao-chi again attacked the Black-cart Shih-wei. Li K'o-yung sent an envoy to request an alliance with the Ch'i-tan.	1, 2*a*
	10	A-pao-chi with 70,000 horsemen held a conference at Yün 雲 Prefecture[6] with Li K'o-yung. Both promised to be as brothers to each other.[7]	1, 2*a* VII, 2 (3)

[1] Same as Ch'in-tê 欽德 (LS 63, 8*a*; TS 219, 4*b*).
[2] Both in what is now Shansi.
[3] Between the Shira Muren and Lao-ha River, Jehol.
[4] Modern Chi 薊 County, Hopei.
[5] Liu Jên-kung 劉仁恭 was the commanding prefect of Lu-lung 盧龍 Commandery of Yu 幽 Prefecture in 895.
[6] Ta-t'ung County, Shansi.
[7] Some sources date this conference in 904, others in 907. The *Liao Shih* puts it in 905 which, according to Ch'ên Shu's study, is correct (*cf.* Ch'ên S 36, 82).

Year	Month	Main Events	Reference
		A-pao-chi attacked Liu Jên-kung, captured several prefectures, and took the inhabitants back to the Ch'i-tan territory.	1, 2a
906	2	Liu Jên-kung attacked again. The Hsi "north of the mountains" were routed by the Ch'i-tan soldiers. Chu Ch'üan-chung 朱全忠[8] sent messengers with gifts by sea.	1, 2b X, 2 (1)
	11	The Hsi 奚, Hsi 霫, and Jurchen were attacked.	1, 2b
907 (1)	1	On the day kêng-yin, A-pao-chi (T'ai-tsu), declared himself emperor of the Ch'i-tan. He was given the honorific title of Emperor of Heaven 天皇帝 and his wife that of Empress of Earth 地皇后.	1, 2b
	2	T'ai-tsu's cousin from the senior line, Tieh-li-ti 迭栗底 (or Tieh-li-t'ê), was appointed i-li-chin of the I-lieh [I-la] Administration 迭烈府.	1, 2b
		T'ai-tsu attacked the Black-cart Shih-wei and subdued their eight tribes.	1, 2b
	4	Chu Ch'üan-chung deposed the T'ang emperor and made himself emperor of Liang 梁.	1, 2b–3a
		Liu Jên-kung imprisoned by his son, Liu Shou-kuang 劉守光, who assumed the post of commanding prefect of Lu-lung Commandery of Yu Prefecture.	1, 3a
	10	T'ai-tsu attacked the Black-cart Shih-wei and routed them.	1, 3a
907 to 926		Mining and smelting "begun."	III (3)
		Salt permits introduced.	III (4)
		Captured artisans taken to Ch'i-tan residential centers.	III (2)
		Taxation of trade established.	X, 1 (1)
907 to 947		Dual system of dress established.	VII, 1 (2)
908 (2)	1	The office of t'i-yin of the imperial clan was established and entrusted to emperor's younger brother, Sa-la 撒剌.[9]	1, 3a XIV, 1 (3)
	5	T'ai-tsu's younger brother, Sa-la, was ordered to attack the Wu-wan 烏丸 and Black-cart Shih-wei.	1, 3a
	10	The Great Wall extended.	1, 3a XI (2)
909 (3)	3	Liu Shou-kuang defeated by Hsiao Ti-lu at Hêng-hai 橫海 Commandery.[10]	1, 3b
910 (4)	7	The appointment of the emperor's brother-in-law, Hsiao Ti-lu, as prime minister of the Northern Administration initiated the selection of members of the empress' lineage as prime ministers.	1, 3b XIV, 1 (3)
	10	The K'u-chih 庫支, Ch'a-la-ti 查剌底, and Ch'u-po-tê 鋤勃德 of the Wu-[11] ma Mountain Hsi 烏馬山奚, who had revolted, were pacified.	1, 3b
911 (5)	1	The Western Hsi[12] and Eastern Hsi[13] were pacified.	1, 4a XIII (4)

---

[8] The founder of the first of the Five Dynasties, Later Liang.

[9] This was the style of La-ko 剌葛 (cf. LS 64, 3a).

[10] Forty li southeast of modern Ts'ang 滄 County, Hopei.

[11] We follow other editions in reading 烏 for the 鳥 of our text.

[12] Probably in the region of modern Huai-lai 懷來 County, Chahar.

[13] The capital of this tribal confederation later became the Central Capital of Liao.

YEAR	MONTH	MAIN EVENTS	REFERENCE
	5	The imperial brothers, La-ko, Yin-ti-shih, and An-tuan, rebelled, but failed.	1, 4a XIII (5)
	8	Liu Shou-kuang made himself emperor and called his empire Yen 燕 in Yu Prefecture.	1, 4a
	10	Iron smelteries established.	1, 4a III (8)
912 (6)	2	The emperor personally led an attack against Liu Shou-kuang.	1, 4b
	7	The emperor personally attacked the Chu-pu-ku 尤不姑 tribe and subdued it.	1, 4b
	10	The emperor's brothers again rebelled.	1, 4b
913 (7)	1	The Prince of Chin 晉, Li Ts'un-hsü 李存勗, took Yu Prefecture and captured Liu Shou-kuang. The emperor's brothers surrendered.	1, 4b–5a
	3	The emperor's brothers burned the imperial traveling camp, military provisions, and various tents and also sent soldiers to loot and kill the people.	1, 5a–b
	5	The emperor's brothers and other rebels were captured.	1, 6a XIII (9)
915 (9)	1	The Wu-ku 烏古 tribe, which had rebelled, was pacified.	1, 8a
916 (1)	3	Temple of Confucius founded in the spring of the year. The emperor established his son Pei as heir apparent.	1, 9a IX (3)
	7	The emperor personally attacked the Turks, T'u-hun 吐渾, Tang-hsiang 黨項, Hsiao-fan 小蕃, and Sha-t'o 沙陀 and pacified them. 15,600 households, more than 100,000 weapons of war and sets of armor, and numerous horses, oxen, and sheep were captured.	1, 9a
917 (2)	3	Yu Prefecture was attacked and its commanding prefect, Chou Tê-wei,[14] was defeated east of Hsin 新 Prefecture.	1, 9b–10a
	4	Yu Prefecture besieged by Ch'i-tan soldiers.[15]	1, 10a XV, 2 (4)
	6	La-ko's last rebellion.	1, 10a XIII (12)
918 (3)	1	The emperor's brother, An-tuan, was sent to attack Yün Prefecture and the near-by tribes.	1, 10a
	2	The imperial city was built.	1, 10a XI (3)
	4	The emperor's brother, Tieh-lieh-ko 迭烈哥 (Tieh-la), plotted rebellion but was found out.	1, 10b
	5	An imperial decree ordered the building of Confucian, Buddhist, and Taoist temples.	1, 10b IX (4) XI (4)
	7	Yeh-lü Ho-lu 曷魯, who had helped T'ai-tsu to ascend the throne, died.	1, 10b
919 (3)	12	Empress Ch'un-ch'in's brother, Hsiao Ti-lu, died.	1, 10b

[14] Chou Tê-wei 周德威 (T. 鎮遠), a native of Ma-i 馬邑 (modern Ma-i County, Shansi), was a capable general who flourished at the beginning of Later T'ang (cf. WTS 25, 1a ff.).

[15] The seat of Yu Prefecture, which at this time was under the control of one of Li Ts'un-hsü's subordinates, was besieged for two hundred days. Later the Ch'i-tan soldiers withdrew in the face of strong reenforcements sent by Li Ts'un-hsü (TCTC 269, 9b; 270, 1a–b).

Year	Month	Main Events	Reference
919 (4)	8	T'ai-tsu visited the Temple of Confucius.	2, 1a IX (5)
	10	The Wu-ku tribe was routed. 14,000 persons and more than 200,000 oxen, horses, carts, and tents were taken. Henceforth the whole tribe was subdued.	2, 1a–b
920 (5)	1	The larger Ch'i-tan script created.	2, 1b VII, 2 (11)
	8	The emperor personally attacked the rebellious Tang-hsiang tribes.	2, 1b
921 (6)	1	The emperor's younger brother, Su, appointed prime minister of the Southern Administration. Henceforth this position was given to the imperial lineage.	2, 2a XIV, 1 (5)
	5	Different laws for Ch'i-tan and "all barbarians" on the one hand and Chinese on the other.	3, 2a VII, 1 (3)
	10	The emperor directed a large army to enter Chü-yung Pass.	2, 2a
	11	Ku-pei Pass was taken. More than ten cities of Yu Prefecture were looted, and their people were moved to the interior.[16]	2, 2a–b
922 (1)	4	Chi 薊 Prefecture taken.	2, 3a
	10	The I-la tribe was split into the Northern and Southern Divisions.	2, 3a XIV, 1 (6) XV, 1 (25)
923 (2)	1	P'ing 平 Prefecture taken.	2, 3b
	3	Hsi rebellion crushed.	2, 3b XIII (14)
	4*[17]	The Prince of Chin, Li Ts'un-hsü, made himself emperor. His empire was called Later T'ang 後唐.	2, 3b
	10	The Liang dynasty was overthrown by the T'ang forces.	2, 4a
924 (3)	5	The Po-hai killed the prefect of Liao Prefecture,[18] Chang Hsiu-shih 張秀實, and captured its inhabitants.	2, 4a
	6	The emperor carried out a large-scale expedition against the T'u-hun, Tang-hsiang, and Tsu-pu.[19]	2, 4b
	9	The emperor arrived in the old Uighur city.[20] He ordered that the old stone tablet of Bilgä Khaghan 關遏可汗 be erased and reinscribed in Ch'i-tan, Turkic,[21] and Chinese to commemorate his meritorious deeds.	2, 4b–5a
		Under Uighur influence, a smaller Ch'i-tan script created.	VII, 2 (11)
925 (4)	11	T'ai-tsu visited a Buddhist temple and presented food to monks.	2, 5b IX (6)
926 (4)	12	The army was mobilized, and the emperor personally headed a punitive campaign against Po-hai.	2, 5b
926 (1)	1	The Po-hai capital, Hu-han 忽汗 City, was taken, and the ruler, Ta Yin-chuan 大諲譔, was captured.	2, 6a

[16] Of the Ch'i-tan country.

[17] The asterisk indicates that the month in question was an intercalary one.

[18] Modern Liao-pin-t'a 遼濱塔, Liaoning.

[19] All these tribes probably lived originally in Inner Mongolia. Later they were driven either northward or westward.

[20] On the Orkhon River in Outer Mongolia.

[21] This passage implies that the Turkic language was still familiar to the Ch'i-tan in the tenth century even though the Turkic empire had perished long before.

Year	Month	Main Events	Reference
	2	The Po-hai kingdom was renamed the Tung-tan kingdom, and Hu-han City was renamed T'ien-fu 天福 City. Prince Jên-huang[22] was made the ruler of this state.	2, 6b X, 1 (4)
		Po-hai iron workers introduced.	III (9)
	7	On the day hsin-ssŭ the emperor died in Fu-yü 扶餘 Administration.[23] His wife assumed control of military and political affairs.	2, 7a–b VII, 2 (12) 3, 1b
		T'ai-tsu's widow refused to be buried with her deceased husband.	VII, 2(12)
927 (2)	11	On the day jên-hsü A-pao-chi's second son, Tê-kuang 德光, was made the emperor. He was the later T'ai-tsung.	3, 1b
928 (3)	5	The scribe, T'u-lü-pu,[24] was ordered to attack the Wu-ku tribes.	3, 2b
929 (3)	12	Yeh-lü Yü-chih 羽之 was ordered to move the people of Tung-tan to Tung-p'ing 東平[25] Commandery. Tung-p'ing Commandery was made the Southern Capital.	3, 3a I, 3 (2)
929 (4)	10	The emperor's brother, Li-hu, was ordered to lead soldiers against Yün-chung 雲中[26] to attack those regions which had not submitted.	3, 4a
930 (5)	11	Prince Jên-huang went by sea to T'ang.[27]	3, 5a
931 (6)	4	The Council of Presidents was established in the Southern Capital.	3, 5a XIV, 2 (5)
933 (8)	1	The emperor's brother, Li-hu, was ordered to lead soldiers against Tang-hsiang.	3, 6b
934 (9)	4	Li Ts'ung-k'o 李從珂[28] killed the emperor of Later T'ang and ascended the throne himself. Prince Jên-huang dispatched a memorial to the Liao emperor requesting an invasion of T'ang territory.	3, 7a–b
935 (10)	3	The two lineages of the Imperial Maternal Uncles established.	3, 8a VII, 2 (16)
936 (11)	7	The commanding prefect of Ho-tung 河東 of T'ang, Shih Ching-t'ang 石敬瑭, was attacked by the T'ang emperor. He sent messengers to Liao to ask for aid.	3, 8b
	8	The emperor personally led armies to aid Shih Ching-t'ang.	3, 8b
	9	The Liao soldiers entered Yen-mên 雁門 Pass and defeated the T'ang forces near T'ai-yüan 太原.	3, 9b
	11	Shih Ching-t'ang was made the emperor of Chin by the Liao emperor.	3, 9b
937 (11)	11	The Liao emperor and Shih Ching-t'ang agreed to call each other father and son in Lu 潞 Prefecture.[29] Prince Jên-huang was killed by T'ang.	3, 10b I, 1 (1)
937 (12)	6	Chin 晉 offered an annual payment of three hundred thousand bolts of silk for the return of the region of Yu and Chi 薊. Liao rejected the offer.	X, 2 (19)

[22] T'ai-tsu's eldest son.

[23] Modern Nung-an 農安 County, Kirin.

[24] Yeh-lü Tu-lü-pu 突呂不, who aided in devising the larger Ch'i-tan script, died in 942.

[25] Modern Liao-yang 遼陽 County, Liaoning.

[26] Modern Ta-t'ung 大同 County, Shansi.

[27] He fled to Later T'ang with forty followers. T'ang granted him a high official status and gave him the Chinese name of Li Mu-hua 李慕華 (later changed to Li Tsan-hua 贊華). He was killed in 937 (cf. LS 72, 1a ff.; TCTC 277, 7a; 8b).

[28] An adopted son of Ming-tsung of Later T'ang.

[29] Modern Ch'ang-tzŭ 長子 County, Shansi.

YEAR	MONTH	MAIN EVENTS	REFERENCE
938 (1)	11	Chin offered sixteen prefectures with maps and documents to Liao.	4, 2a–b
		The Imperial Capital was called the Supreme Capital; the seat of Yu Prefecture was called the Southern Capital; and the Southern Capital was named the Eastern Capital.	I, 1 (1) III (4) XV, 1 (35)
		The *i-li-chin* of the Northern Division, Southern Division, and I-shih tribe were raised to the rank of kings.	4, 2b
		Imperial Chinese carriages and robes introduced.	III (10)
938–947		The emperor's mother and officials of the Northern Region wore Ch'i-tan clothes; the emperor and the officials of the Southern Region dressed according to the Chinese style.	VII, 1 (7)
939 (2)	5	The shan-yü of the Uighurs sent envoys to Liao to request titles. His officials were given titles, such as prefects and magistrates, according to their status.	4, 3b
940 (2)	12	The servants of the Uighur envoy, who had used swords in a quarrel, were ordered to be taken to the envoy for punishment.	4, 4a
940 (3)	1	Uighur emissaries asked permission to watch ceremonies connected with the reception of foreign envoys.	4, 4a
	4	The emperor made his first ceremonial visit to Yen.	4, 4b VII, 2 (18)
	8	The city established by An-tuan[30] was named Pai-ch'uan 白川 Prefecture.[31] Cultivable land given to imperial tribes.	4, 5b II, 2 (2)
	11	Nan T'ang sent an envoy to submit a letter in a ball of wax with information about the secret affairs of Chin. Sororate abolished.	4, 6a VII, 2 (20)
941 (3)	12	Ch'i-tan officials holding Chinese offices might intermarry with the Chinese.	VII, 1 (8)
941 (4)	2	The emperor ordered officials to compile the history of the first Ch'i-tan ancestor, Ch'i-shou Khaghan.	4, 6b XIV, 4 (3)
	7	Nan T'ang sent an envoy to offer a document in a wax ball.	4, 6b
	8	Nan T'ang offered a document in a wax ball.	4, 7a
942 (5)	1	Ch'i-tan households were ordered to do garrison service at the southern frontier	4, 7b
	6	The Chin ruler, Shih Ching-t'ang, died; his son, Ch'ung-kuei 重貴, ascended the throne. Food granted to fifty thousand Buddhist monks.	4, 8b IX (7)
	7	Chin sent two officials to present thanks.[32] The document referred to the Chin emperor as "grandson," not as "subordinate." A Liao official was sent to remonstrate against this.	4, 8b
		Ching Yen-kuang[33] replied, "The previous emperor was crowned by your court, but the present sovereign was set up by our own country. He might be your neighbor or grandson, but to present a memorial calling him your subordinate is impossible."[34]	

[30] T'ai-tsu's brother.

[31] The city was later renamed Ch'uan 川 Prefecture. Its location corresponds to a place 67 *li* northeast of Ch'ao-yang 朝陽 County, Jehol.

[32] That is, for the many presents sent by Liao for the funeral ceremony of their emperor, Shih Ching-t'ang (*cf.* CWTS 81, 5a).

[33] Ching Yen-kuang 景延廣 (T. 航川) was a powerful Chin general. He died in 946 as a prisoner of the victorious Liao army (*cf.* WTS 29, 4a ff.).

[34] According to WTS 29, 5a, he taunted Liao with the boast that Chin was waiting for the Liao emperor with a hundred thousand sharp broad swords.

YEAR	MONTH	MAIN EVENTS	REFERENCE
		When the Liao official returned and reported this, the Liao emperor began to consider making a military expedition against Chin.	
	10	Soldiers from all circuits were conscripted for the attack against Tang-hsiang.	4, 9a
943 (6)	3	Nan T'ang sent an envoy to offer a document in a wax ball.	4, 9a
944 (6)	12	The emperor went to the Southern Capital to discuss the campaign against Chin. Chao Yen-shou 趙延壽,[35] Chao Yen-chao 趙延昭, An-tuan,[36] and Yeh-lü Hsieh-li 解里[37] were ordered to march by separate routes from Ts'ang,[38] Hêng,[39] I,[40] and Ting.[41] The main army of Liao was to follow them.	4, 9b
944 (7)	8	The Uighurs sent an envoy to ask that a girl from the Liao court be given to them in marriage. This was refused.	4, 10b
945 (8)	3	The Liao army was defeated by the Chin soldiers at Pai-t'uan-wei 白團衞 Village. The Liao emperor fled on a camel.	4, 11b IV (3)
947 (9)	12	The Chin generals, Tu Ch'ung-wei 杜重威, Li Shou-chên 李守貞, and Chang Yen-tsê 張彥澤, surrendered with 200,000 soldiers.	4, 13b
947 (1)	1	The emperor, riding in a specially prepared carriage, entered the Chin capital, Pien 汴, and presided at the Ch'ung-yüan Hall, where he received congratulations from the officials.	4, 14a
947 (1)	1	The Chin ruler and his mother, wife, concubines, relatives, and some officials were sent to Huang-lung Administration.[42]	4, 14b
	2	On the first day ting-ssŭ the country was named Great Liao.[43] Liu Chih-yüan 劉智遠, the founder of the Later Han dynasty, made himself emperor and named his country Han 漢.	4, 15a
	3	Members of the Chin court and all imperial paraphernalia taken from Pien to the Supreme Capital.	4, 15a VII, 2 (22)
		The first elaborate calendar introduced.	XIV, 4 (4)
	4	1,090,118 families of Chin came under the control of Liao. Chên 鎮 Prefecture[44] was renamed the Central Capital.	4, 15b
		The emperor died in Luan City.[45]	4, 16a; 5, 1a II, 1 (9)
		Prince Jên-huang's son, Yüan 阮, made himself emperor in Chên Prefecture. He was the later Shih-tsung. Empress Dowager Ying-t'ien, on hearing that her grandson had become emperor, sent her third son, Li-hu, with troops to bar his return to the Supreme Capital.	5, 1a XIII (19)
	7	Li-hu resisted the imperial army at a ferry on the Huang 潢 River for several days. Finally they came to terms through the mediation of Yeh-lü Wu-chih.	XIII (19) (20)

[35] The chancellor and son-in-law of Ming-tsung of the Later T'ang dynasty. He had surrendered to Liao in 936. He was later authorized to take charge of the Chinese soldiers and of the civil affairs south of the Great Wall. T'ai-tsung promised to make him emperor after the fall of the Chin capital, but the plan failed. Chao Yen-shou died in 948 (cf. LS 76, 2b ff.).

[36] T'ai-tsu's brother.

[37] Yeh-lü Hsieh-li defeated the Chin general, Tu Ch'ung-wei, in 946. After entering the Chin capital, he allowed the Ch'i-tan soldiers to loot and to destroy the city (LS 76, 1a).

[38] Near modern Ts'ang 滄 County, Hopei.

[39] Modern Chêng-ting 正定 County, Hopei.

[40] Modern I 易 County, Hopei.

[41] Modern Ting 定 County, Hopei.

[42] Modern Ch'ao-yang 朝陽 County, Jehol.

[43] For a discussion of the various changes in the name of the empire see technical introduction.

[44] Modern Chêng-ting County, Hopei.

[45] North of modern Luan-ch'êng 欒城 County, Hopei.

YEAR	MONTH	MAIN EVENTS	REFERENCE
	8	The Northern Chancellery was set up for the first time. The establishment of the Southern Chancellery followed.	5, 1*b* XIV, 2 (1)
947–951		Chinese weavers established in Tung-ching Circuit.	III (12)
948 (2)	1	Some members of the imperial clan and of the maternal clan plotted treason but were found out.	5, 2*a* XIII (21)
	4	Nan T'ang sent envoys to discuss an attack against Han.[46]	5, 2*a*
	10	The vicegerent of the Southern Capital, Chao Yen-shou, died.	5, 2*a*; 76, 4*a*
		The empress dowager of defeated Chin asked the emperor for fifty *ch'ing* of land forty *li* south of Chien 建 Prefecture[47] to provide food for her family. She also asked that buildings be constructed for the worship of their ancestors.	39, 7*b*
950 (4)	2	The Political Council was set up.	5, 2*b* XIV, 2 (1)
951 (5)	1	Kuo Wei 郭威 killed the ruler of Later Han and made himself emperor, calling his kingdom Chou 周. Liu Ch'ung 劉崇 made himself emperor of Eastern Han in T'ai-yüan 太原.[48]	5, 2*b*–3*a*
	6	Liu Ch'ung, on being attacked by Chou, humbly designated himself as "nephew" and sent an envoy to the Liao court to beg for aid and to be invested as emperor.	5, 3*a*
	9	The emperor Shih-tsung was murdered by Ch'a-ko.[49] T'ai-tsung's son, Ching 璟, was made emperor. He was the later Mu-tsung.	5, 3*a*
952 (2)	6	Eastern Han, on being attacked by Chou, sent an envoy to ask for aid from Liao. Kao Mu-han 高模翰 was ordered to give it.	6, 1*b*
953 (3)	5	Eastern Han sent an envoy to report that the *shêng-tê shên-kung* 聖德神功 stone tablet of T'ai-tsung, which had been erected by Chin, was destroyed by Chou, and requested that it should be rebuilt.	6, 2*b*
	6	Empress Dowager Ying-tien died.	6, 2*b*
	10	Li-hu's son, Wan, rebelled.	6, 2*b* XIII (26)
957 (7)	2	Nan T'ang sent an envoy bearing a document in a wax ball.	6, 4*a*
959 (9)	4	Chou captured I-chin 益津,[50] Wa-ch'iao 瓦橋,[51] and Yü 淤[52] Passes.	6, 4*b*
	5	Ying 瀛 Prefecture[53] and Mo 莫 Prefecture[54] fell to Chou. The Chou army withdrew.	6, 4*b*
	6	The Chou ruler, Jung 榮, died. His son, Tsung-hsün 宗訓, ascended the throne.	6, 4*b*
	6	Han Yen-hui died.	74, 3*a*
960 (10)	1	The chief palace superintendent of Chou, Chao K'uang-yin 趙匡胤, deposed the ruler and made himself emperor. His dynasty was named Sung 宋.	6, 5*a*

[46] Nan T'ang sought an alliance with Liao against Later Han.

[47] Wu-shih-chia-tzŭ 五十家子, south of Ch'ao-yang County, Jehol.

[48] See II, 2, note 13.

[49] The son of An-tuan.   He was killed by one of his followers.

[50] In modern Pa 霸 County, Hopei.

[51] South of Hsiung 雄 County, Hopei.

[52] Fifty *li* east of Pa County.   These three places were of very great military importance.

[53] Modern Ho-chien 河間 County, Hopei.

[54] 30 *li* north of Jên-chiu 任邱 County, Hopei.

YEAR	MONTH	MAIN EVENTS	REFERENCE
963 (13)	7	Eastern Han sent an envoy to report on the invasion by Sung.	6, 6a
964 (14)	2	The punitive commissioner of the Southwestern Route, Yeh-lü Ta-lieh 撻烈, brought troops to the aid of Han.	7, 1a
965 (14)	12	The Wu-ku tribe rebelled and looted the people. The Liao *hsiang-wên*, Sêng-yin 僧隱 and I-shih 乙實, were killed in the battle.	7, 1b
965 (15)	3	The chieftain, Yin-ni-chi 寅尼吉, of the Big Yellow Shih-wei rebelled. Forty families of the Five Animal Quarters rebelled and entered the Wu-ku tribe.	7, 2a
	4	The Small Yellow Shih-wei rebelled and repulsed an attack from the Liao army.	7, 2a
	5	The Shih-wei chieftain fled to the Ti-lieh tribe.	7, 2b
	6	The Ti-lieh tribe surrendered to Liao.	7, 2b
	7	The Wu-ku looted the settlers of Yü-lin Yü 楡林峪 north of the Supreme Capital.	
967 (17)	1	The scribe, Hsiao Wo 斡,[55] and the court noble, Yeh-lü Hsien-shih 賢適,[56] were honored for their victory over the Wu-ku.	7, 3b; 79, 2a; 84, 2a–b
	2	As Sung was attempting to place a barrier at the I-chin Pass, Liao soldiers were sent out to thwart them.	7, 3b
969 (19)	2	The emperor, Mu-tsung, was murdered by his servants. Shih-tsung's son, Hsien 賢, became emperor. He was the later Ching-tsung.	7, 5b; 8, 1a XIII (28)
971 (3)	6	Eastern Han began to send envoys to pay courtesy calls to the emperor every month.	8, 2b
973 (5)	1	The *t'i-yin*, Yeh-lü Hsiu-ko 休哥, routed the Tang-hsiang.	8, 3b
	5	Yeh-lü Wu-chih died. The Jurchen encroached upon the frontier, killed Liao officials, looted, and captured part of the population.	8, 3b
974 (6)	3	Sung sent an envoy to ask for a truce, so the prefect of Cho 涿 Prefecture, Yeh-lü Ch'ang-chu 昌朮, was empowered to negotiate the terms.[57]	8, 4a
976 (8)	1	Sung sent an envoy to pay a courtesy call on the emperor.	8, 4b
	8	The Jurchen invaded the eastern part of Kuei-tê 貴德 Prefecture.[58]	8, 5a
	9	The Jurchen attacked Wu-chai 五寨 of Kuei 歸 Prefecture[59] and withdrew after capturing some booty. Eastern Han, on being invaded by Sung, sent an envoy to ask for aid. The emperor ordered the prime minister of the Southern Administration, Yeh-lü Sha 沙[60] and the Prince of Chi 冀, Ti-lieh 敵烈, to give aid.	8, 5a II, 2 (7) X, 2 (46)
977 (8)	12	Examination hall restored.	8, 5b XIV, 3 (5)

[55] Hsiao Wo, also written as Hsiao Kan 斡, was a son of Empress Ch'un-ch'in's brother, Hsiao Ti-lu. He died in 986.

[56] He attained the position of northern chancellor.

[57] According to CTKC 6, 1b, in the eleventh month of this year (974) the prefect of Hsiung 雄 Prefecture of Sung, Sun Ch'uan-hsing 孫全興, received a letter from a Liao official in which a truce was solicited. This letter is preserved in TPCCTL 2, 3a–b. It was written by Yeh-lü Ts'ung 琮 who is probably identical with the Yeh-lü Ch'ang-chu of our text.

[58] Southeast of T'ieh-ling 鐵嶺 County, Liaoning.

[59] 90 *li* southwest of Kai-p'ing 蓋平 County, Liaoning.

[60] He lost several battles in the war with Sung and would have been executed had it not been for the intervention of Empress Jui-chih. He died in 988 (*cf.* LS 84, 1a ff.).

YEAR	MONTH	MAIN EVENTS	REFERENCE
977 (9)	7	Sung sent an envoy to pay a courtesy call. Eastern Han sent an envoy to report on the invasion by Sung. Envoys were sent to give war-horses to Eastern Han.	9, 1a–b
979 (1)	1	The *ta-ma*, Ch'ang-shou 長壽, was sent to Sung to inquire why it had attacked Eastern Han. Ch'ang-shou returned from Sung, bearing the message that there might be a continuation of peace if Liao gave no assistance to Eastern Han; otherwise there would be war.	9, 2a
	3	Yeh-lü Sha led a force against the Sung army at the Pai-ma Mountains 白馬嶺.[61] The Liao troops suffered great losses.	9, 2b
	6	The emperor of Eastern Han, Liu Chi-yüan 劉繼元, surrendered to Sung. Han fell. The Sung ruler personally came to attack Liao and besieged the Southern Capital.	9, 2b
	7	Yeh-lü Hsiu-ko and Yeh-lü Hsieh-chên 斜軫 seriously defeated the Sung army at the Kao-liang River. The Sung ruler escaped alone to Cho Prefecture. Many Sung soldiers were killed; the weapons, provisions, and money acquired by the Liao soldiers were beyond calculation.	9, 3a 83, 1a ff., 3b ff.
980 (2)	10	The emperor personally directed a southern military campaign against Sung. Wa-ch'iao Pass was encircled.	9, 4a
	11	Yeh-lü Hsiu-ko defeated the Sung soldiers east of Wa-ch'iao Pass.	9, 4a
981 (2)	11	The Liao soldiers withdrew, and the emperor returned to the Southern Capital.	9, 4b
981 (3)	5	Two hundred surrendered Chinese soldiers revolted at the Supreme Capital and forced Liu-li-shou 留禮壽 to usurp the imperial throne. This revolt was put down by the vicegerent, Ch'u-shih 除室.	9, 4b; 72, 5a XIII (31)
982 (4)	4	The emperor personally directed soldiers to fight the Sung army, but the result was unfavorable.	9, 5a
	5	The soldiers withdrew.	9, 5a
	9	The emperor died at Chiao 焦 Mountain. His eldest son, Lung-hsü 隆緒, ascended the throne. He was the later Shêng-tsung. The empress dowager was made regent by order of the deceased emperor.[62]	9, 5a; 10, 1a
982–983		Measures against interest exceeding the capital.	VI, 2 (1)
983 (5)	1	The punitive commissioner of the Southwestern Region, Han Tê-wei 韓德威,[63] reported that fifteen Tang-hsiang tribes which had invaded the frontier were repulsed.	10, 2b; 82, 2b
		An imperial decree praised Su-sa 速撒 for defeating the Tsu-pu. He and Ta-han 大漢 were ordered to attack the Tang-hsiang tribes.	10, 2b
	2	Favorite courtier buried with the deceased emperor.	10, 2b VII, 2 (34)
	4	As the empress dowager had become the regent, high officials requested that she receive honorific titles. The minister over the masses of the Northern Administration, Yeh-lü P'o-tê 頗德, was ordered to translate the code presented by the Southern Capital.	10, 3b XIV, 4 (16)
	5	The punitive commissioner of the Southwestern Route requested that the Western Turkic tribes be attacked with a greater number of soldiers. The	10, 4a

---

[61] 70 *li* northeast of Yü 盂 County, Shansi.

[62] Ching-tsung's widow was very powerful. She not only dominated her husband, but also had great influence over her son, Shêng-tsung (*cf.* VII, introduction).

[63] Brother of Han Tê-jang.

YEAR	MONTH	MAIN EVENTS	REFERENCE
		emperor ordered that soldiers of the Ti-pi 敵畢 and I-lieh 迭烈 tribes be dispatched against them.	
983 (1)	7	The empress dowager managed the administration. Han Tê-wei sent the *hsiang-wên*, Hsia-ma 轄馬, to present a number of Tang-hsiang captives including the son of an *i-li-chin*.	10, 4*b*
After 983		Highest "northern" officials wore Chinese clothes at big ceremonies.	VII, 1 (7)
983–1012		Land system described: three main categories.	II, 2 (9)
984 (2)	2	Hsiao P'u-ning 蒲寧 reported a victory against the Jurchen.	10, 6*b*
	3	The Hua-li tribe requested that the *hsiang-wên* be selected from its own tribesmen. The emperor disapproved on the ground that the tribal officials should be selected according to qualification.	10, 6*b* XIII (33)
	8	Yeh-lü Mo-chih memorialized that the eight lineages of Chu-pu-chih 朮不直 and Sai-li 賽里 of the Jurchen had asked to submit to Liao.	10, 7*a*
	11	Su-sa and other generals attacked the Tsu-pu and killed the chieftain, Ta-la-yü 撻剌于 (*ta-la-kan* 干?).	10, 7*b*
		Two hundred thousand men worked on mountain roads during the autumn.	IV (4)
985 (3)	8	Chancellor Yeh-lü Hsieh-chên and the scribe, Hsiao K'ên-tê 懇德,[64] led soldiers against the Jurchen.	10, 7*b*
986 (4)	1	Yeh-lü Hsieh-chên and Hsiao K'ên-tê presented more than 100,000 Jurchen captives, more than 200,000 horses, and other booty.	11, 1*a* II, 1 (10)
	2	The king of Hsi Hsia, Li Chi-ch'ien 李繼遷, rebelled against Sung and came to submit to Liao.[65]	11, 1*b*
	3	The *yü-yüeh*, Yeh-lü Hsiu-ko, reported that Sung was sending Ts'ao Pin 曹彬, Ts'ui Yen-chin 崔彥進, and Mi Hsin 米信 to attack from the region of Hsiung Prefecture, T'ien Ch'ung-chin 田重進 from the region of Fei-hu 飛狐, and P'an Mei 潘美 and Yang Chi-yeh 楊繼業 from the region of Yen-mên 雁門.	11, 1*b*
		The commissioner of military control, Yeh-lü P'o-tê, defeated the Sung army at Ku-an 固安.[66] Yeh-lü Hsiu-ko intercepted its military supplies. Many generals and officials as well as horses, oxen, and weapons were captured. The Liao army suffered a defeat in the battle of Fei-hu.	11, 2*a*
	4	The Sung general, P'an Mei, captured Yün Prefecture.[67]	11, 3*a*
	5	The Liao army seriously defeated the soldiers of Ts'ao Pin and Mi Hsin at Ch'i-kou 岐溝 Pass[68] and pursued them to the Chü-ma 拒馬 River.	11, 4*a*
	7	The Sung general, Yang Chi-yeh, was captured at Lang-ya 狼牙 Village, 30 *li* south of Shuo Prefecture.	11, 6*a*
	11	The Jurchen asked permission for their soldiers to join the southern expedition. All soldiers were allowed to destroy the mulberry trees and fruit trees in the southern regions.	11, 7*b*, 8*a*
987 (4)	12	Yeh-lü Hsiu-ko defeated the Sung army at Wang-tu.[69] Li Chi-ch'ien, the Hsia ruler, asked to marry a Liao girl. The daughter of a commanding prefect, Yeh-lü Hsiang 襄, was ordered to marry him. 3,000 horses were given as a wedding gift.	11, 8*b*, 9*a*–*b* 115, 6*b*

---

[64] Identical with Hsiao Ch'in-tê 勤德. See II, 1, note 40.

[65] This was the first time that Hsi Hsia subordinated itself to Liao (*cf.* LS 115, 6*b*).

[66] Modern Ku-an 固安 County, Hopei.

[67] Modern Ta-t'ung 大同 County.

[68] 30 *li* southwest of Cho 涿 Prefecture, Hopei.

[69] Modern Wang-tu 望都 County, Hopei.

YEAR	MONTH	MAIN EVENTS	REFERENCE
988 (6)	10	The Sung soldiers who had surrendered were named "the army that submitted to the sage" (歸聖軍). Seven men were appointed to control them.	12, 3a
		Examinations for *chin-shih* degree held. One candidate successful.	12, 4a XIV, 3 (6)
989 (7)	2	The *chü-jên* 舉人 were forbidden to slander the court in unsigned statements.	12, 5a
	3	Seventeen Sung *chin-shih* 進士 who had brought their families to Liao were examined. Those who passed the examination were appointed officials in the state schools; the rest were appointed secretaries and military aides to the magistrates.	12, 5a
	6	Farm land distributed.	12, 6b II, 2 (11) (13)
990 (8)	5	The Sung soldiers who had surrendered were distributed among the various armies.	13, 1a XV, 2 (11)
991 (9)	5	The private city of the Prince of Ch'in 秦, Han K'uang-ssŭ 韓匡嗣,[70] was granted the name of Ch'üan 全 Prefecture.[71]	13, 2b
	7	General census taken.	13, 2b I, 3 (3)
		Chinese subjects tried to evade taxes and labor service.	XI (13).
992 (9)	12	Because the Hsia king, Li Chi-ch'ien, had secretly submitted to Sung, the punitive commissioner, Han Tê-wei, was sent with imperial instructions to reprove him.	13, 3a
992 (10)	2	Han Tê-wei memorialized that Li Chi-ch'ien refused to see him on the pretext of being ill. He looted Ling 靈 Prefecture[72] and returned.	13, 3a–b
992/3 (10)	12	The vicegerent of the Eastern Capital, Hsiao Hêng-tê 恆德,[73] and others were ordered to attack Korea.[74]	13, 3b
993 (11)	3	The Korean king, Wang Ch'i 王治, sent Pok Ryang-yu 朴良柔 to ask pardon for his misconduct. The emperor granted him several hundred *li* of land east of the Yalu River which had been taken from the Jurchen.	13, 4a
994 (12)	6	The prefect of K'o-han 可汗 Prefecture,[75] Chia Chün 賈俊, presented a new calendar.[76]	13, 5a XIV, 4 (4)
	7	Any Ch'i-tan committing one of the ten crimes was to be punished in the same way as a Chinese.	13, 5a XIV, 4 (9) VII, 1 (17)
	8	Sung sent an envoy to ask for peace. The offer was not accepted.	13, 5a
	9	Sung again sent an envoy to ask for peace, again in vain.	13, 5a–b
	11	Among the Sung captives, the high and minor officials, the talented scholars, and the meritorious military officers were to be made known by name to the emperor.	13, 5b

[70] Han Tê-jang's father.
[71] Its location is not known.
[72] Southwest of Ling-wu 靈武 County, Ninghsia.
[73] Husband of a daughter of Ching-tsung.
[74] A much earlier plan to attack Korea did not materialize. The Korean envoy, Hak Kwang-yun 崔光胤, who was sent to the court of the Later Chin dynasty, learned that after the fall of the Chin regime Liao prepared to invade Korea. The subsequent mobilization of three hundred thousand Korean troops probably made the Liao rulers change their minds (TKTK 13, 364–365). In 992/3 the situation seemed more promising because of the internal unrest which followed the death of the Korean king.

[75] Modern Huai-lai 懷來 County, Chahar.

[76] The Ta-ming Calendar.

Year	Month	Main Events	Reference
995 (12)	12	The Jurchen came to report that Sung had offered bribes to them and to the Wu-jo to rebel against Liao.	13, 5*b*
995 (13)	10	Charity granaries established.	13, 6*b* XII (20) (21)
	11	Korea sent ten young men to study the Ch'i-tan language.	13, 6*b*–7*a* VII, 2 (44)
996 (14)	1	Large-scale remission of taxation ordered.	13, 7*a* XII (22)
	3	Korea again sent ten young men to study the Ch'i-tan language.	13, 7*a*
996/7 (14)	11	The Uighur Arslan sent an envoy to request a girl from the Liao court in marriage. The request was rejected.	13, 7*b*
997 (14)	12	Taxation in Nan-ching Circuit reduced.	13, 7*b* X, 1 (30)
997 (15)	1	The Ho-hsi Tang-hsiang 河西黨項 rebelled, so Han Tê-wei was ordered to launch an attack against them.	13, 8*a*
	3	The Ho-hsi Tang-hsiang begged to submit.	13, 8*b*
	5	The Eight Tribes of Ti-lieh killed the *hsiang-wên* and rebelled. Hsiao Ta-lin 撻凜 attacked them and captured half of the tribesmen.	13, 8*b*
	7	T'u-yü-hun forbidden to sell horses to Sung.	13, 8*b* V (6)
	9	Hsiao Ta-lin reported victory over the Tsu-pu.	13, 9*a*
998 (16)	12	Yeh-lü Hsiu-ko died.	14, 1*b*
999 (17)	7	All circuits were informed of the punitive campaign against Sung.	14, 1*b*
1000 (18)	6	The rebellious Tsu-pu chieftain, Hu-nien 鶻碾, was executed.	14, 2*a*; 70, 10*b*
1001 (19)	3	The Punitive Office of the Southwestern Region reported a victory over the Tang-hsiang.	14, 2*b*
	9	The Punitive Office of the Southwestern Region reported a victory over the T'u-yü-hun.	14, 3*a*
1002 (20)	2	The Jurchen chieftain sent his son on a visit to the Liao court. Korea sent envoys to congratulate Liao on its victory over Sung.	14, 3*b*
	7	Korea offered a map of the country.	14, 3*b* X, 2 (59)
1003 (20)	12	The Five Tents of the Administration of the king of Hsi offered the region of the Ch'i-chin 七金 Mountain and the T'u 土 River	14, 4*a*
1003 (21)	6	T'ieh-la-li 鐵剌里 of Tsu-pu led various tribes to submit. K'o-tun 可敦 City walled.	14, 4*a*-*b*
1004 (22)	6	K'o-tun City was renamed Chên 鎮 Prefecture.	14, 5*a*
	8	The request of the Tsu-pu chieftain, T'ieh-la-li, to marry a girl from the Liao court was refused.	14, 5*a*

YEAR	MONTH	MAIN EVENTS	REFERENCE
	11	The great king of the Southern Division, Yeh-lü Shan-pu 善補,[77] reported to the throne that Sung had sent an emissary to present a bow and arrows[78] to Wang Chi-chung 王繼忠[79] and to ask secretly for peace. An imperial decree ordered Wang Chi-chung to meet the envoy to negotiate peace.	14, 5b
1005 (22)	11	The emperor halted at T'an-yüan 澶淵,[80] where Hsiao Ta-lin was killed by an arrow shot from ambush.	14, 5b
	12	Sung sent Li Chi-ch'ang 李繼昌 to ask for peace. The Sung emperor agreed to look upon the mother of the Liao emperor as a "junior aunt"[81] and to pay annually 100,000 taels of silver and 200,000 bolts of silk.	14, 6a X, 2 (61)
1005 (23)	4	The Tang-hsiang invaded the Liao frontier.	14, 6b
1007 (25)	1	Central Capital established.[82]	14, 7b; 39, 1b XI (15)
	9	The punitive commissioner of the Northwestern Route, Hsiao T'u-yü 圖玉, routed the Tsu-pu.	14, 7b
1008/9 (26)	12	Hsiao T'u-yü memorialized that in his punitive expedition against the Uighurs of Kan 甘 Prefecture[83] he had subdued the Uighur king, Yeh-la-li 耶剌里.[84]	14, 8a; 70, 12b
1009 (27)	12	Empress Dowager Ch'êng-t'ien died.	14, 8a
1010 (28)	5	Hsiao T'u-yü attacked the Uighurs of Kan Prefecture, took Su 肅 Prefecture,[85] and captured its people. Because the vicegerent of the Western Capital[86] of Korea, Kang Cho 康肇, killed the king, Wang Chong 王誦, and replaced him with the king's brother, Wang Sun 詢, without reporting to Liao, Shêng-tsung ordered that preparations be made for an eastern military campaign.	15, 1b
	8	Shêng-tsung personally directed a military expedition against Korea. Envoys were sent to inform Sung. The emperor's younger brother, Lung-yu 隆祐,[87] Prince of Ch'u, was left in charge of the capital.[88] Hsiao P'ai-ya 排押 was made the chief commander and the scribe, Sêng-nu 僧奴, was made the chief supervisor.	15, 1b
1010/1 (28)	11	The Liao army crossed the Yalu River and besieged the Western Capital of Korea. Hsiao P'ai-ya and Yeh-lü P'ên-nu 盆奴[89] captured Kê-kiong 開京[90] and burned it.[91]	15, 2a–b
1011 (29)	1	The Liao army withdrew from Korea. The cities of Korea which had surrendered to Liao rebelled again. When the emperor reached a deep mountain valley south of Kwi 貴 Prefecture,[92] a heavy rain fell incessantly for several	15, 2b; 115, 2b

[77] A descendent of the First Patriarchal Household of the imperial clan. He lost several battles in the war against Sung, but was nevertheless made great king of the Southern Division (cf. LS 84, 3a–b).

[78] The offer of the bow and arrows was a sign of respect. In this case it was also a plea to stop fighting.

[79] In 1003 this former Sung official was made prisoner on the battlefield by a Liao general, Yeh-lü Nu-kua 奴瓜. He was appointed commissioner of the Ministry of Revenue of Liao. The empress and the emperor both appreciated his high intelligence and skill; the Sung government therefore communicated the peace proposals to him (LS 81, 1b ff.).

[80] Southwest of P'u-yang 濮陽 County, Hopei.

[81] See X, 2, note 44.

[82] See XIV, 4, note 10.

[83] Modern Chang-yeh 張掖 County, Kansu.

[84] Also transcribed as Ya-lan 牙懶 (LS 93, 5a).

[85] Modern Chiu-ch'üan 酒泉 County, Kansu.

[86] P'ing-jang 平壤, Korea.

[87] The third son of Ching-tsung and a younger brother of Shêng-tsung. He died in 1012.

[88] The Supreme Capital.

[89] A descendant of the imperial clan. He reached the position of great king of the Northern Division (cf. LS 88, 2a–b).

[90] Modern Kê-s'öng 開城 in the center of Korea.

[91] In the same month Kang Cho was captured by the Liao army, and tied up in a felt blanket. Later he was put to death (KRS 127, 599).

[92] Present Kwi-s'öng 龜城 in northwestern Korea (Tsuda 13 II, 32).

YEAR	MONTH	MAIN EVENTS	REFERENCE
		days. The horses and camels being worn out, most of the armor and weapons were discarded.	
	3	Yeh-lü Lung-yün died.	15, 2b
1012 (1)	4	Korea sent Ch'ae Chung-sun 蔡忠順 to ask that Korea be permitted again to become subordinate to Liao. An imperial decree ordered the Korean king, Wang Sun,[93] to appear in person at court.[94]	15, 4a
	11	The grand preceptor of the seven Tsu-pu tribes, A-li-ti 阿里底, killed the tribal commanding prefect, Pa-an 霸暗, and his family and then fled to Wo-lu-to 窩魯朵 City.[95] The tribes along the border all revolted.	15, 5a; 93, 5a–b
1013 (2)	1	A Ta-tan army besieged Chên Prefecture, but as the defenses were very strong it withdrew.	15, 6a
	7	The Tang-hsiang tribes which had revolted fled to the north of the Yellow River. The emperor ordered the army to purchase horses. Yeh-lü Hua-ko 化哥[96] and others routed the soldiers of the Tsu-pu chief, Wu-pa 烏八.	15, 6b
1014 (3)	1	The Tsu-pu chief, Wu-pa, came to the Liao court and was given the title of king.	15, 7b
	6	Yeh-lü T'uan-shih 團石 attacked Korea.	15, 8a
	9	The Eight Tribes of Ti-lieh killed their hsiang-wên, Shao-wa 稍瓦, and rebelled. Yeh-lü Shih-liang 世良 led a huge army against them to force them into submission.	15, 8a; 94, 4b
1015 (4)	4	Yeh-lü Shih-liang routed the Ti-lieh and killed all the Wu-ku adults. The survivors were forced to build a walled city on the Lu-ch'ü River in order to settle them there.	15, 9a; 69, 12a 94, 4b
1016 (5)	1	Yeh-lü Shih-liang and Hsiao Ch'ü-lieh 屈烈 routed a Korean army west of Kwak 郭 Prefecture[97] and killed several tens of thousand of soldiers.	15, 10a; 115, 3a
1017 (6)	9	Hsiao Ho-cho 合卓[98] and others having attacked Korea without success, the troops withdrew.	15, 11b; 115, 3a
1018 (7)	10	Hsiao P'ai-ya and others attacked Korea.	16, 2a
1019 (7)	12	A Liao army was defeated by Korean soldiers.	16, 2b
1019 (8)	8	Ho-pu-lü 曷不呂 led a huge army in an attack on Korea.	16, 3b–4a
1020 (9)	5	King Wang Sun of Korea asked to become subordinate to Liao.	16, 4b; 115, 3b
1021 (1)	3	The king of Ta-shih again[99] sent messengers to request a marriage alliance. K'o-lao 可老, the daughter of Hu-ssǔ-li 胡思里, a court noble of princely rank, was given the title of princess and was married to him.	16, 5b

[93] The eighth Korean king of the Wang house. He reigned from 1010 to 1031.

[94] Although the Liao court made this demand very urgently, the king of Korea himself never came to the Liao court.

[95] On the Orkhon River in Outer Mongolia.

[96] A member of the imperial clan who was the northern chancellor at this time.

[97] Present Kwak Mountain in northern Korea (Tsuda 13 II, 32).

[98] A member of the T'u-lü-pu tribe who was promoted to the position of northern chancellor (LS 81, 3b).

[99] The first request was made in 1020 (cf. X, 2 (71)).

YEAR	MONTH	MAIN EVENTS	REFERENCE
	4	The chiefs of the thirty tribes of the Jurchen requested that their sons be sent to the court as imperial attendants. A decree replied that the fathers and sons should all come.	16, 5b–6a
1022 (2)	12	King Wang Sun of Korea died and his son, Wang Kim 王欽, sent an envoy to report the death. Wang Kim was approved as king of Korea by Liao.[100]	16, 7b
1026 (6)	2	Huang P'ien 黃翩 and others led soldiers into the territory of the Jurchen, where they captured numerous people, horses, oxen, and pigs. 270 Jurchen soldiers surrendered.	17, 2b
	3	An imperial decree ordered that a Ch'i-tan commanding prefect be set up to govern the sub-tribe T'a-hsi 塌西 of the Tang-hsiang.	17, 2b
1027 (6)	12	The Ho-su-kuan tribe was permitted to set up its own banner and drums.	17, 3b; 69, 13b VII, 2 (53)
1027 (7)	3	The Tsu-pu invaded Liao territory but were defeated by Hsiao Hui.	17, 2b–3a
	5	Hsiao Hui led troops against the Uighurs of Kan Prefecture.	17, 3a
	8	Hsiao Hui, having besieged Kan Prefecture for three days without breaking into the city, finally withdrew. On his way back he was attacked by some Tsu-pu tribes and badly defeated. Thereafter all the Tsu-pu tribes rebelled.	17, 3a; 93, 1b
1028 (8)	1	The Tang-hsiang who had invaded the frontier were routed.	17, 4b
	9	The commanding prefect Yeh-lü Yen-shou 延壽 of the Northern Ti-lieh tribe asked the emperor to check on the loyalty of the tribes and to grant banners and drums to those which were loyal.	17, 5a–b
1029	8	Great Po-hai rebellion.	17, 6b
(9)		The Southern and Northern Jurchen made an alliance with Ta Yen-lin and Korea to hold back on its tribute to Liao.	17, 7a XIII (38)
1030 (10)	3	Hsiao Hsiao-mu 孝穆 encircled the Eastern Capital with a wall five li from the capital.	17, 7b; 87, 1b
	8	The Po-hai pacified.	17, 8a XIII (38)
1031 (11)	6	Shêng-tsung died. Tsung-chên 宗眞 became emperor. He was the later Hsing-tsung.	17, 9a; 18, 1a
		General census taken.	I, 3 (3)
1032 (1)	12	Empress Ch'in-ai 欽哀 administered the government affairs.	18, 3a
1032 (2)	3	Empress Ch'i-t'ien 齊天 was falsely accused of a crime and was put to death by Empress Ch'in-ai.[101]	18, 3a–b
1034 (3)	4–7	Empress Ch'in-ai retired to the mausoleum of Shêng-tsung, and Hsing-tsung assumed complete power.	18, 3a–b
1036 (5)	10	The emperor conducted the *chin-shih* examination.	18, 6a XIV, 3 (10)

---

[100] LS 115, 3b incorrectly places this event in 1021.

[101] Empress Ch'i-t'ien, the wife of Shêng-tsung, had no son, whereas Empress Ch'in-ai, the first concubine of Shêng-tsung, bore Hsing-tsung. After the death of Shêng-tsung, Ch'in-ai became jealous of the empress dowager, Ch'i-t'ien, and in alliance with her close attendants and brothers planned to kill her. She went so far as to usurp the imperial power, but her son, Hsing-tsung, supported by certain high officials, forced her to retire. Many of the plotters were killed. At the time of her recall in 1039 Ch'in-ai had lost most of her earlier influence (CTKC 8, 1a–2b).

YEAR	MONTH	MAIN EVENTS	REFERENCE
		Law code revised.	XIV, 4 (14)
1037 (6)	7	Prisons in the north and south empty. Officials rewarded.	18, 7a XII (45)
	8	Because of the unscrupulousness of the leader of the Yüeh-chi 越棘 tribe, the office of chieftain in this tribe and that of the Five Nations tribe was abolished. A Ch'i-tan commanding prefect was appointed to control them.	18, 7a
1038 (7)		Po-hai allowed to play polo.	VII, 1 (31)
1039 (7)	12	Hsing-tsung accepted Buddhist commandments.	IX (18)
1040 (9)	11	The Jurchen invaded the frontier. The T'ieh-li 鐵驪 army of Huang-lung Administration was sent to resist them.	18, 9b
1042 (10)	12	The emperor, on hearing that Sung was improving passes and waterways and repairing moats and ditches, feared that frontier troubles were about to develop. Together with the northern chancellor, the Prince of Wu, Hsiao Hsiao-mu, and the southern chancellor, the Prince of Chao, Hsiao Kuan-ning, he planned to seize the ten counties south of the passes previously taken by Sung.[102] Then he sent Hsiao Ying and Liu Liu-fu[103] as envoys to Sung.	19, 2a–b
1042 (11)	4	The orders concerning rewards and punishments for the southern military campaign were made public.	19, 2b
	9	Yeh-lü Jên-hsien sent men to report to the emperor that Sung was willing to pay annually an additional tribute of 100,000 taels of silver and 100,000 bolts of silk. The written document phrased it "to pay tribute." The silver and silk were conveyed to Pai-kou.[104] The emperor was pleased and gave a feast for his courtiers in the Chao-ch'ing Palace.	19, 3a X, 2 (74)
1043 (11)	12	Killing of oxen and horses in funerals forbidden.	19, 3b VII, 2 (58)
1043 (12)	7	Hsiao Hsiao-chung 孝忠 died.	19, 4b XIV, 2 (3)
	8	Yeh-lü Hung-ku 洪古 died.	19, 4b
	10	Hsiao Hsiao-mu died.	19, 4b
		Suggestion to merge the Ch'i-tan and Chinese administrations not accepted.	XIV, 2 (3)
1044 (13)	3	Special police bureaus for the Ch'i-tan were set up.[105]	19, 5b XIV, 1 (8) VII, 1 (35)
	4–5	The Tang-hsiang tribes rebelled against Liao. Hsia aided them against the attacking Liao troops. The commanding prefect of the tribes of Shan-hsi, Ch'ü-lieh 屈烈, rebelled with five tribes and entered Hsia.	19, 5b
	9	The emperor personally directed a punitive campaign against Hsia.	19, 6a X, 2 (77)

[102] South of I-chin, Wa-ch'iao, and Yü Passes in the center of modern Hopei.

[103] The latter went back and forth several times between Liao and Sung. Finally in 1042 a new treaty was concluded between the two countries.

[104] Modern Chü-ma River in central Hopei.

[105] A Ch'i-tan commoner who committed a crime was examined by Chinese officials, an arrangement which did not please the Ch'i-tan people. Therefore, a special Ch'i-tan bureau was established in each of the five capitals.

YEAR	MONTH	MAIN EVENTS	REFERENCE
	10	King Li Yüan-hao 李元昊 of Hsia sent envoys to acknowledge his error in accepting the rebellious tribes.　He even came in person to admit his mistake. But the Liao officials were opposed to conciliation on the grounds that, since the government had mobilized a huge army, it would be advantageous if the war broke out.　So a surprise attack was made upon Hsia.　Several thousand Hsia soldiers were killed, but the emperor's brother-in-law, Hsiao Hu-tu 胡覩, was captured by Hsia, and many Liao soldiers died.	19, 6a–b 93, 2a–b
	11	The emperor withdrew the army from Hsia.[106] The emperor elevated Yün Prefecture to be the Western Capital.	19, 6b I, 1 (1)
1045 (13)	12	Hsiao Hu-tu returned from Hsia.	19, 6b
1046 (15)		Hsiao Han-chia-nu elaborated for all social strata a ritual which did not violate the past.	103, 5b
1047 (16)	12	The emperor went to the temple of T'ai-tsu and looked at the "Picture of T'ai-tsung taking over Chin."	20, 1b
1048 (17)	2	King Li Yüan-hao of Hsia died. Slaves allowed to present political advice only through their masters.	20, 2a VII, 1 (37)
	6	The Tsu-pu presented twenty thousand horses and camels.	20, 2a
		Warship built and successfully used against Hsia.	IV (11)
1049 (18)	7	The emperor personally directed a punitive campaign against Hsia.	20, 3b IV (12)
	9	Hsiao Hui 惠 was badly defeated by a Hsia force, the Liao troops suffering heavy casualties.	20, 3b; 115, 8b
1050 (19)	2	Hsia troops making an attack on Chin-su 金肅 City were repulsed and captured by Yeh-lü Kao-chia-nu 高家奴.	20, 4a
	3	Hsiao Tieh-li-tê 迭里得 defeated a Hsia force at San-chiao-ch'uan 三角川. The southwestern punitive commissioner, Hsiao P'u-nu 蒲奴, the great king of the Northern Division, Yeh-lü I-hsin 宜新, and the scribe, Hsiao Sa-mo 撒抹, led armies to attack Hsia.	20, 4a
	5	When Hsiao P'u-nu and others entered Hsia territory, no enemy soldiers were encountered.　They returned after permitting their soldiers to loot.	20, 4b
	9	Hsia soldiers invaded the frontier.　Hai-li 海里 repulsed them.	20, 5a
	10	The mother of King Li Liang-tsu of Hsia sent envoys to ask that her country again become subordinate to Liao.　An imperial decree said that, if a Hsia plenipotentiary were sent to the Liao court, this question would be considered.	20, 5a
1051 (19)	12	Hsia sent a plenipotentiary with a document asking subordination to Liao.	20, 5b
1051 (20)	6	One of Li Yüan-hao's wives and other Hsia captives were sent to Su 蘇 Prefecture.[107]	20, 5b–6a
1052 (21)	10	Li Liang-tsu of Hsia sent envoys to Liao to ask for the cessation of military preparations along the border.	20, 7a
1053 (22)	2	The Uighur Arslan, after the invasion of his territory by neighboring countries, sent envoys to beg for aid.	20, 7b; 70, 19b

[106] At first the Liao soldiers won a number of battles, but later when their horses were exhausted they suffered great losses (SS 485, 21a).　Hsia suggested an exchange of prisoners and the cessation of hostilities.　This was done and a temporary truce was concluded (LS 115, 8b).

[107] Modern Chin 金 Prefecture, Liaotung Peninsula.

YEAR	MONTH	MAIN EVENTS	REFERENCE
	3	Li Liang-tsu sent envoys to express gratitude for the imperial decree allowing Hsia to become subordinate to Liao.	20, 7b
	7	Various tribes headed by the great king of the Tsu-pu presented horses and camels.	20, 7b X, 2 (86)
	9	Li Liang-tsu sent envoys to offer his capitulation to Liao.	20, 7b
1054 (22)	12	On the day jên-tzŭ, an imperial decree was issued to the high officials saying, "Since We and the ruler of Sung agreed to be brothers, there have been many years of friendship. We now desire to see his portrait.[108] The envoys coming [from Sung] may be so instructed."	20, 8a X, 2 (87)
1054 (23)	7	Li Liang-tsu sent envoys to ask for a Liao girl in marriage.	20, 8b
1055 (24)	8	Hsing-tsung died, and his son, Hung-chi 洪基, ascended the throne. He was the later Tao-tsung.	20, 9a
After 1055		At big ceremonies all officials wore Chinese dress.	VII, 1 (7)
1056 (1)	12	The emperor issued an order to establish schools for training scholars and to disseminate the Five Classics and their commentaries.	21, 3a
1056 (2)	1	An imperial decree ordered the officials of prefectures and commanderies to punish prisoners in accordance with tribal procedure.	21, 3a
1057 (3)	1	The post of commanding prefect of Tao-t'a-ling 倒塌嶺 was set up.	21, 4b
1058 (3)	12	Empress Ch'in-ai died.	21, 5a
1059 (4)		Colleges set up for the five capitals.	XIV, 3 (16)
1060 (6)	5	Yeh-lü Pai 白 was ordered to write a preface to the emperor's verses which he had collected.	21, 6a–b
1063 (9)	7	The emperor's uncle, Chung-yüan, conspired against the emperor; the rebels were defeated and crushed. Chung-yüan committed suicide.	22, 1b–2a; 96, 2a XIII (41)
1064 (10)	10	The private publication of books was prohibited.[109]	22, 3a
	11	The style of dress for the officials and the people was defined. Slaughter of animals during six Buddhist fast days prohibited.	22, 3a IX (26)
1067 (3)	11	Uighur monks and Buddhist sūtra presented by Hsia.	22, 5a IX (28)
1068 (4)	2	King Li Liang-tsu of Hsi Hsia died. Tao-tsung composed a commentary on a sūtra.	22, 5b IX (29)
1069 (5)	3	The Tsu-pu rebelled. The Prince of Chin, Yeh-lü Jên-hsien, led the imperial guard against them.	22, 6a
	9	Yeh-lü Jên-hsien presented a memorial concerning the victory over the Tsu-pu.	22, 6a 96, 2b–3a
	11	The P'ou-a-li 剖阿里 tribe rebelled. Hsiao Su-sa 素颯 was ordered to put down the revolt.	22, 6b; 95, 3b

[108] See X, 2, note 69.
[109] There was also a law prohibiting the exportation of books to Sung. Violators were punished by death (MHPT 15, 100).

YEAR	MONTH	MAIN EVENTS	REFERENCE
1070 (5)	12	The Five Nations tribe came to surrender.	22, 6b; 95, 3b
1070 (6)	10	A captured Tsu-pu chieftain was presented to the court by the Punitive Office of the Northwestern Route.	22, 7a
		Because the Ch'i-tan and Chinese had different customs, the law was not to be applied indiscriminately. Revision of regulations was ordered.	XIV, 4 (24)
1072 (8)	1	The *hsiang-wên* of the tribe of Wu-ku Ti-lieh, Yeh-lü Ch'ao 巢, and others reported on the victory on the northern frontier.	23, 1a
	3	Three thousand persons permitted to become monks or nuns.	23, 1a–b IX (32)
	5	Yeh-lü Jên-hsien died.	23, 1b
1073 (8)	12	Buddhist sūtras granted to Korea.	23, 2a IX (34)
1073 (9)	7	The Ti-lieh Tribe of the Eight *Shih-lieh* killed the commanding prefect and rebelled. The army of the Wei Wu-ku tribe was ordered to attack them from two different routes.	23, 2a; 69, 18a–b
1074 (10)	10	Tao-tsung rejected proposal to introduce Chinese clan names and marriage system.	VII, 2 (67)
1075 (1)	11	Empress Hsüan-i 宣懿[110] was put to death because of alleged adultery with an actor.	23, 3b
1075–1084		Bureau of Historiography set up.	XIV, 4 (26)
1076 (2)	3	Empress Jên-i 仁懿, Tao-tsung's mother, died.	23, 4a
1077 (3)	5–6	Because the heir apparent, Chün 濬, was accused of high treason by Yeh-lü I-hsin's 乙辛 clique, Chün was flogged and imprisoned, and many high officials were sentenced to death.	23, 5b
	11	Yeh-lü I-hsin sent men to kill Chün at the Supreme Capital.	23, 6a XIII (43)
1078 (4)	4	Korea's request for the regions east of the Yalu River was rejected.	23, 6b
	7	Three hundred and sixty thousand monks and nuns were given food.	23, 6b IX (36)
1082 (7)	12	Yeh-lü Jên-chieh 仁傑[111] was degraded to the rank of commoner. Yeh-lü I-hsin was imprisoned at Lai Prefecture.[112]	24, 3b
1083 (9)	10	Yeh-lü I-hsin, who was planning to flee to Sung, was executed.	24, 5a
	11	Sūtras received from Korea published.	24, 5b IX (39)
1084 (10)	2	The country of Mêng-ku 萌古 sent envoys to pay a courtesy call.	24, 5b X, 2 (95)
	3	The distant country of Mêng-ku sent envoys to pay a courtesy call.	24, 5b
1086 (2)	1	Chao Hsiao-yen and Wang Shih-ju were summoned to expound the Five Classics.	24, 7a XIV, 4 (29)

[110] Tao-tsung's wife, a beautiful woman well versed in poetry and music. A Chinese inscription praises her virtue but only two sentences record her fate (LLSKCL 3, 8b–10a). The empress was accused of improper relations with a prominent actor, Chao Wei-i 趙惟一 (LS 71, 7a).

[111] A Chinese whose original name was Chang Hsiao-chieh. See VIII, note 11.

[112] 130 *li* southwest of Hsing-ch'êng 興城 County, Liaoning.

YEAR	MONTH	MAIN EVENTS	REFERENCE
	5	Horses reached a total of a million.	24, 7a II, 1 (20)
	6	The Prince of Yen, Yen-hsi 延禧, the later T'ien-tsu, was ordered to befriend the Tsu-pu chieftain, Yü-ku-nan 余古報, when the latter came to the court.	24, 7b
	9	The emperor took out the armor and weapons used by T'ai-tsu and T'ai-tsung, showed them to Yen-hsi, the Prince of Yen, and told him about the difficulties of the military campaigns for the founding of the empire.	24, 7b
1087 (3)	2	Because of the large number of fugitives the old regulations concerning refugees abolished.	25, 1a XII (88)
1088 (4)	4	Vacant official positions might be bought with grain.	25, 2a XIV, 3 (27)
	10	An imperial decree ordered the leading officials of all tribes to examine lawsuits personally.	25, 2b
1089 (5)		The Tsu-pu chieftain, Mo-ku-ssŭ 磨古斯, was appointed the chieftain of various tribes.	25, 3a
1090 (6)	4	An official in charge of martial law (掌法官) was appointed for the Office of Military Control of the Northeastern Route.	25, 3b
1092 (8)	10	Yeh-lü A-lu-sao-ku 阿魯掃古 attacked the Yeh-tu-kua 耶覩刮 tribe. He also attacked the Northern Tsu-pu, with the result that their chieftain, Mo-ku-ssŭ, rebelled. Yeh-lü Kuo-san 郭三 was ordered to lead tribal warriors to put down the revolt.	25, 4b–5a 94, 3a–4a
1093 (9)	2	Mo-ku-ssŭ invaded Liao.	25, 5a; 70, 23a–b
	3	The greater part of the Liao army was destroyed by Mo-ku-ssŭ.	25, 5a; 70, 23a–b
	10	Mo-ku-ssŭ launched a surprise attack upon the Liao army southwest of Chên Prefecture. The punitive commissioner of the Northwestern Route, Yeh-lü Ta-pu-yeh 撻不也, was killed. Wu-ku-cha 烏古札 of the Wu-ku rebelled. The Ta-li-ti 達里底 and the Pa-ssŭ-mu attacked Liao at Tao-t'a-ling. A Tsu-pu chief, Hsiao-ti, looted the herds of the Western Route.	25, 5b; 96, 3b
		The government ordered that the Wu-ku tribe be provided with three thousand war[113] horses.	25, 5b; 69, 20a
1094 (10)	1–2	The Ta-li-ti and Pa-ssŭ-mu tribes invaded the empire.	25, 6a
	4	Mêng-tê-ssŭ 萌得斯 and Lao-ku 老古 of the T'i-tê 惕德 led their tribes to submit. They were ordered to return to their original territories. The commanding prefect of the Wu-ku tribe, Yeh-lü Ch'ên-chia-nu 陳家奴, reported a victory over the Ch'a-cha-la. The Eight Tribes of P'o-li made an invasion but were eventually repulsed. The Ta-li-ti and Pa-ssŭ-mu tribes surrendered.	25, 6b
	5	The Ti-lieh and other tribes invaded and inflicted great losses on Liao.	25, 6b–7a
	7	The Tsu-pu and other tribes stole all the horses from the herds of the Western Route of Tao-t'a-ling and from the herds north of the Hun River,[114] but the commissioner of military control of the Northeastern Route, Yeh-lü Shih-liu 石柳, went in pursuit and retrieved them.	25, 7a
	9	The Ti-lieh chiefs came to surrender. Yeh-lü Wo-t'ê-la 斡特剌 routed Mo-ku-ssŭ.	25, 7a
1095 (10)	12	A report on the victory over Mo-ku-ssŭ was presented by the Office of Military Control of the Northwestern Route.	25, 7b

[113] LS 25, 5b speaks only of "horses."   [114] Probably the Orkhon River.

Year	Month	Main Events	Reference
1095 (1)	1	The Ti-lieh tribe looted horses from the Liao herds, but all were recovered by the Liao garrison soldiers.	26, 1a
	9	An imperial decree ordered the catapultiers and crossbowmen of the Western Capital to teach the Chinese army of the Northwestern Route.	26, 1b XV, 2 (22)
	11	Hsia offered a sūtra written on palm leaves.	26, 2a IX (41)
1096 (2)	12	Yeh-lü Wo-t'ê-la reported a victory over the Mei-li-chi.	26, 2b
1097 (3)	2	The Tsu-pu chief, Mêng-sa-ko 猛撒葛, the Nien-pa-ko chief, Sa 撒, and the Mei-li-chi chief, Hu-lu-pa 忽魯八, requested that their original territories be restored and that they be permitted to offer local products.	26, 2b
	6	Hsia envoys came to report that Sung was fortifying strategic places against Hsia. Liao sent envoys to persuade Sung to come to terms with Hsia.	26, 3a
1098 (4)	1	Impoverished Tsu-pu tribesmen were transferred to Nan-ching.	26, 3b
	5	Yeh-lü Na-yeh 那也 reported a victory on the northern frontier.	26, 3b
	6	Hsia, on being attacked by Sung, sent envoys to ask for aid.	26, 3b
	11	Yeh-lü Yen 儼 was sent to reprove Sung and to ask that it come to terms with Hsia.[115]	26, 4a
1099 (5)	1	An imperial decree ordered King Li Ch'ien-shun 李乾順 of Hsia to attack the Pa-ssŭ-mu.	26, 4a
	10	King Wang Ong 王顒 of Korea sent envoys to request a document of investiture.	26, 4b
1100 (6)	1	Yeh-lü Wo-t'ê-la captured the Tsu-pu chieftain, Mo-ku-ssŭ, and offered him to the court.	26, 5a
	2	Mo-ku-ssŭ was hacked to pieces in the market place.	26, 5a
	5	The Wu-ku tribe routed the Ch'a-cha-la.	26, 5a
	7	The Yeh-tu-kua and other tribes invaded the Northwestern Route.	26, 5b
	8	Yeh-lü Wo-t'ê-la defeated the Yeh-tu-kua and other tribes.	26, 5b
1101 (7)	1	Tao-tsung died, and his grandson, Yen-hsi, ascended the throne. He was the later T'ien-tsu.	26, 6a; 27, 1a
	2	An imperial decree ordered that those who had suffered because of the false accusations by Yeh-lü I-hsin were to be reinstated in their original positions. Those who had been imprisoned were released and those who had been banished were called back.	27, 1a–b
1101–1125		Labor services converted into money payments.	XI (26)
1102 (1)	12	Yang-ko 楊割 was appointed the commanding prefect of the Savage Nü-chih tribe.[116]	27, 2a

[115] Hostilities developed between the countries of Sung and Hsia because the Hsia government refused to return certain border territories which it had captured from the Sung empire after 1081.   In the subsequent dispute over the demarcation line, the Liao court took the position of mediator.   According to SS 486, 13a, besides Yeh-lü Yen, Hsiao Tê-ch'ung 德崇 was also sent to Sung a year after to mediate the quarrel.   However, hostilities did not cease.

[116] According to CS 1, 12a, Yang-ko or Ying-ko 盈歌 succeeded his brother, P'o-la-shu 頗剌淑, as commanding prefect in 1094.   The different dates are probably due to the fact that, while the succession occurred at this time, Yang-Ko did not receive his official appointment from the Liao government until 1102.

YEAR	MONTH	MAIN EVENTS	REFERENCE
1102 (2)	5	Yeh-lü Wo-t'ê-la reported a victory over the Yeh-tu-kua.	27, 2b
	6	King Li Ch'ien-shun of Hsia sent envoys to beg for aid against the attacking Sung armies.	27, 2b
	6	Yeh-lü Wo-t'ê-la defeated the Tsu-pu invaders.	27, 2b
	10	Hsiao Hai-li 海里 rebelled and stole weapons from the armory of Ch'ien 乾 Prefecture	27, 2b XIII (44)
1103 (3)	5	Huntsmen fled from the imperial hunts.	27, 3a XI (27)
	6	Hsia again sent envoys to beg for aid.	27, 3a
1104 (4)	6	Hsia sent Li Tsao-fu 李造福 and T'ien Jo-shui 田若水 to ask for aid.	27, 3b
1105 (5)	1	Hsia sent Li Tsao-fu and others to ask that Liao send aid and attack Sung. Liao sent Kao Tuan-li 高端禮 to persuade Sung to stop invading Hsia.	27, 4a
	3	A daughter from the imperial clan was married to Li Ch'ien-shun, the king of Hsia.	27, 4a
1106 (5)	12	Hsia again sent Li Tsao-fu and T'ien Jo-shui to ask for help. Sung sent Lin Chu 林洙[117] to discuss terms of peace between Sung and Hsia.	27, 4b
1106 (6)	1	The chancellor of the Northern Division, Hsiao Tê-li-ti 得里底, and the director of affairs for the chancellor of the Southern Division, Niu Wên-shu 牛温舒, were sent to persuade Sung to return the territory taken from Hsia.	27, 4b
1109 (9)	3	Hsia reported that Sung did not return the territory.	27, 5b
1110 (10)		A great famine.	27, 6a XII (115)
1112 (2)	2	During a fishing trip at the Hun-t'ung River all the Jurchen chieftains appeared before the emperor. In the course of a banquet the emperor ordered them to dance. The supreme chieftain, A-ku-ta 阿骨打, refused.	27, 6a XIII (45)
	9	A-ku-ta gradually gained control over the nearby tribes. He seized the family of a Jurchen chieftain, Chao-san A-hu-ch'an 趙三阿鵲產, for refusing to submit to him. A-ku-ta and Chao-san A-hu-ch'an appealed the case to the office of the *hsiang-wên* at Hsien 咸 Prefecture, but no settlement was made. Thereafter A-ku-ta did not come to court, although he was summoned several times.	27, 7a
1113 (3)	3	A-ku-ta led five hundred horsemen against the Liao officials at Hsien Prefecture, but he retreated at night in the face of superior forces.	27, 7a-b
1114 (3)	12	Yeh-lü Yen died.	27, 7b
1114 (4)	1	The Jurchen sent emissaries to demand A-shu 阿疎[118] of the Ho-shih-lieh tribe,[119] but the emperor refused to give him up.	27, 8a XIII (46)
	7	The attack on Ning-chiang 寧江 Prefecture[120] by A-ku-ta was not considered a serious matter by the emperor who sent only the prefect of Hai 海 Pre-	27, 8a XIII (46)

[117] According to CTKC 10, 1b, his name was Lin Shu 林攄.

[118] He was the chief of the Ho-shih-lieh 紇石烈 tribe who quarrelled with A-ku-ta and fled to Liao, whereupon his territory was occupied by A-ku-ta's followers. In 1122 he was captured by the Jurchen soldiers (CS 67, 13a–14a). After his flight to Liao, the Jurchen repeatedly demanded that he be given up, but the Liao government refused.

[119] This tribe lived near the Pu-êrh-ha-t'ê 布爾哈特 River, Kirin.

[120] The site of the Jurchen victory over Liao. Modern Wu-chia-chan 五家站, near the Sungari River.

Year	Month	Main Events	Reference
		fecture, Kao Hsien-shou 高仙壽, to reenforce the Liao troops. Hsiao Ta-pu-yeh 撻不也 was defeated east of Ning-chiang Prefecture.	
	10	The Jurchen crossed the Hun-t'ung River and made a surprise attack, routing a huge Liao army at Ch'u-ho-tien 出河店.[121]	27, 8b
	11	Hsiao Ti-li 敵里 and others were again defeated by the Jurchen at Wo-lin-p'o 斡鄰濼.[122]	27, 8b
1114/5 (4)	12	The prefectures of Hsien 咸, Pin 賓, and Hsiang 祥 and the tribes of T'ieh-li 鐵驪 and Wu-jo all revolted and went over to the Jurchen.	27, 9a
1115 (5)	1	An imperial decree announced that the emperor himself was to head the military campaign against the Jurchen.[123]	28, 1a
		The emperor sent Sêng-chia-nu 僧家奴 to negotiate peace with the Jurchen. A-ku-ta sent Sai-la 賽剌 to reply that, if A-shu were given up and the frontier post of Ning-chiang Prefecture demobilized, he would be willing to begin negotiations.	28, 1a
	2	Ku-yü 古欲, a Po-hai of Jao 饒 Prefecture, rebelled and assumed the title of great king.	28, 1a
	7	Yeh-lü Wo-li-to 斡里朵 and others were defeated by the Jurchen at Pai-ma 白馬 Lake.	28, 1b
	11	The imperial son-in-law, Hsiao T'ê-mo, and the scribe, Hsiao Ch'a-la, were dispatched in command of 50,000 mounted soldiers and 400,000 foot soldiers. The emperor himself led 700,000 men to T'o-mên[124] against the Jurchen.	28, 3a
	12	Yeh-lü Chang-chia-nu 張家奴 rebelled. The emperor personally led soldiers against him but was defeated at Hu-pu-ta-kan 護步答岡.	28, 3a
1116 (6)	1	The vicegerent, Hsiao Pao-hsien 保先, of the Eastern Capital was killed by the Po-hai. Kao Yung-ch'ang 高永昌 made himself the emperor, calling his reign period Lung-chi 隆基.	28, 3b XIII (48)
	5	The Jurchen captured the Eastern Capital and took Kao Yung-ch'ang prisoner.	28, 4a XIII (50)
1117 (7)	1	The army in the northeastern region dispersed without fighting.	28, 4b XIII (52)
		A-ku-ta established himself as emperor, set up the reign period T'ien-fu 天輔, and named his country Chin 金.[125]	28, 5b
1118 (8)	2	Yeh-lü Nu-ko 奴哥 returned from the Jurchen with a document saying that peace could be made if the Liao emperor would (1) consider A-ku-ta as an older brother; (2) pay an annual tribute; (3) cede to the Jurchen the routes of Shang-ching and Chung-ching and Hsing-chung Administration; (4) send a prince, princess, imperial son-in-law, and several sons of leading officials as hostages; (5) release the Jurchen emissaries together with their emblems of office; and (6) hand over to Chin the diplomatic documents that referred to the relations between Liao and Sung, Hsia, and Korea.	28, 5b

[121] West of the Sungari River, Kirin.

[122] West of Ch'u-ho-tien.

[123] The slow movement of the Liao forces against the Jurchen was one of the main causes of their final defeat. Although T'ien-tsu made the above announcement in the first month of 1115, it was not until the eleventh month of the year that the soldiers were really ready for action (LS 28, 1a–2a).

[124] Probably identical with Lo-t'o-k'ou 駱駝口 which, according to LSCSPM 33, 6b, is located at modern Cha-lai-t'ê 札賚特, Liaoning.

[125] According to CS 2, 8a–b, A-ku-ta became emperor and set up the reign title Shou-kuo 收國 in 1115. T'ien-fu, the second reign period of A-ku-ta, lasted from 1117 to 1123.

YEAR	MONTH	MAIN EVENTS	REFERENCE
	6	The diplomatic documents requested by the Jurchen were handed over to them.	28, 6a
		A great famine. People ate the bark of trees. Cannibalism was practised.	28, 5b, 6b XII (118) XIII (54)
1119 (9)	3	Hsiao Hsi-ni-lieh,[126] the director of affairs for the right i-li-pi, was sent to appoint the ruler of Chin as Emperor of the Tung-huai 東懷 State.	28, 6b–7a
	5	Pu-shu-chih 補疎只 of the Tsu-pu rebelled and captured the punitive commissioner, Yeh-lü Wo-li-to.	28, 7a
	7	Chin sent an envoy to Liao to complain that the style of the document investing A-ku-ta as emperor of the Jurchen was not acceptable.	28, 7a
	9	Yang Li-chung 楊立忠, carried the draft of a document of investiture to Chin to see if it was acceptable to the Jurchen.	28, 7a
1120 (10)	2	The Jurchen sent an envoy to reject the proposed draft of a document of investiture. They also protested because Liao had asked Korea for military assistance.	28, 7a–b
	3	As the term 大聖 (Great Sage) which was applied by Chin to its emperor had previously been applied to T'ai-tsu, the Liao emperor sent an envoy to ask Chin to refrain from using the term. The Chin ruler became angry and broke off diplomatic relations with Liao.	28, 7b
	5	The Chin ruler personally attacked the Supreme Capital. The vicegerent surrendered.	28, 7b
1121 (1)	1	Almost half of the Liao empire was captured by Chin soldiers after the outbreak of hostilities. Revolts occurred within the court, and the imperial concubine and several high officials were killed. A powerful high military official, Yeh-lü Yü-tu 余覩, surrendered to Chin.	29, 1a XIII (57)
1122 (2)	1	The Central Capital was captured by the Chin soldiers. The emperor fled to Yüan-yang Lake. The emperor killed his son, Ao-lu-wo 敖魯斡, because of a false accusation of treason made by Hsiao Fêng-hsien 奉先. The emperor fled to the Western Capital.	29, 2a; 72, 7a–b
	3	The emperor fled to the Chia 夾 Mountains, where Hsiao Fêng-hsien was executed. Ch'un 淳 was made emperor at the Southern Capital by some Chinese officials. His reign title was Chien-fu 建福.	29, 2b–3b XIII (58)
	6	Ch'un died. His wife née Hsiao took over the imperial power. The reign title was changed to Tê-hsing 德興.	29, 4b
	11	Ch'un's wife forced to flee through Ku-pei Pass, because the Chin soldiers had captured the Chü-yung Pass, northwest of Southern Capital.	29, 5a
1122/3 (2)	12	The Chin ruler entered the Southern Capital.	29, 5a XIII (59)
1123 (3)	1	Hui-li-pao 回離保 of Hsi made himself emperor with the reign title T'ien-fu 天復.	29, 5a XIII (59)
	5	T'ien-tsu's second son, Ya-li 雅里, fled to the Northwestern Region and was made emperor. His reign title was Shên-li 神曆. Hui-li-pao was killed by his followers.	29, 6b
	10	Ya-li died and was succeeded by Yeh-lü Chu-lieh 术烈.	29, 6b

[126] He was the main Liao envoy sent by the emperor to negotiate a peace treaty with the Jurchen. He failed in the end because the offers which he carried with him did not satisfy the demands of the Jurchen.

Year	Month	Main Events	Reference
	11	Yeh-lü Chu-lieh was killed by his followers.	29, 6b
1124 (4)	7	Yeh-lü Ta-shih 大石 led his followers westward, made himself king, and set up northern and southern officials.	29, 9a
	8	The Chin emperor, A-ku-ta, died.[127]	29, 9a
	10	Emperor T'ien-tsu married the wife of Ê-ko of the T'u-lü-pu tribe and made Ê-ko the commanding prefect of this tribe.	29, 9a
1125 (5)	2	Emperor T'ien-tsu, on reaching sixty *li* east of the New City of Ying 應 Prefecture,[128] was captured by the Chin general, Wan-yen Lu-shih 完顏婁室,[129] and others.	30, 1b
	8	T'ien-tsu was degraded to the rank of king of Hai-pin 海濱.[130]	30, 1b

[127] According to CS 2, 22b, A-ku-ta died in the eighth month of 1123.

[128] Modern Ying 應 County, Shansi. During the T'ang period the city was located a short distance east of the modern site. A later city, located on the modern site, was called the New City (新城).

[129] A member of the Wan-yen 完顏 tribe of the Jurchen who rose to a high military position. He seized the Liao emperor and conquered the regions of modern Shansi and Shensi. He died in 1130 (CS 72, 5a).

[130] Neither the *Liao Shih* nor the *Chin Shih* gives a date for the death of T'ien-tsu. According to the *Nan-tu-lu* 南渡錄, he was shot to death by order of the Chin emperor in 1161 (NTL 4, 248). If T'ien-tsu was born in 1075 (LS 27, 1a) and died "at the age of fifty-four" (LS 30 1b), his death would have occurred in 1128 according to the Chinese way of counting.

APPENDIX I

CHRONOLOGY OF THE LIAO DYNASTY

For several decades after 907 the Ch'i-tan rulers of Liao failed to set up a calendric system of the Chinese type.[1] In 947 they seized the T'iao-yüan 調元 Calendar of Chin; but even then they waited another fourteen years before they decided to have an official calendar of their own, apparently using for this purpose the T'iao-yüan Calendar.[2] In 994 Chia Chün 賈俊, the prefect of K'o-han Prefecture, suggested the public recognition of the so-called Ta-ming 大明 Calendar created under the Liu Sung 宋 dynasty (420–479). This proposal was accepted before the year ended, and the Ta-ming Calendar was employed from that time on until the close of the dynasty.[3]

Having different roots and different histories, the Liao and Sung calendars were not identical. At certain points the divergencies were significant. According to Sung calculations, the eleventh month of the year *i-hai*[4] (1035/6) numbered thirty days; according to the Liao calendar, only twenty-nine days. In the twelfth month the eclipse of the moon occurred at dusk on the fourteenth Sung day but at dawn on the fifteenth Liao day. In 1077[5] Su Sung 蘇頌 was sent as an envoy to the Liao court to celebrate a birthday, which according to the Sung calendar coincided with the winter solstice.[6] The Liao calendar set the feast one day later—a difference which caused an embarrassing situation. Su eventually suggested that both countries should follow their respective calendars.[7]

In the beginning of 1078 the Sung prefect, Hsüeh Hsiang 薛向, of Ting Prefecture presented a Liao almanac which placed the intercalary month after the twelfth month of the tenth year of the Hsi-ning period, whereas in the Sung almanac it appeared after the first month of the Yüan-fêng period. The difference between the two calendars affected the time of departure chosen by the envoys. After considerable discussion the Sung court decided to abide by its own calendar.[8]

The irregularities of the Liao calendar which troubled the acting officials also haunted the dynastic historiographers. In compiling the *Veritable Records* of the Liao dynasty, Yeh-lü Yen converted the dates originally given according to the T'iao-yüan Calendar into the Ta-ming Calendar. In compiling the *Liao Shih*, Ch'ên Ta-jên probably used the original Liao documents, with the result that many of his dates differ from those of Yeh-lü Yen.[9] On the basis of the notes made in the chapters on the calendar by the Yüan writers of the *Liao Shih*,[10] it is clear that the first days (朔) of the regular and intercalary months (閏) are sometimes identical with those of Yeh-lü Yen's *Veritable Records*, sometimes identical with those of Ch'ên Ta-jên's *Liao Shih*, and sometimes different from both but identical with those of the *Wu-tai Shih* and *Sung Shih*. Obviously the Liao government changed the calendar a number of times so that even the dates of the *Veritable Records* were not consistent. An accurate official chronology was therefore impossible.

This lack of accuracy has been a matter of concern to Chinese scholars. It also accounts for certain discrepancies in the histories of the Five Dynasties and the Sung empire. For instance, A-pao-chi's accession as a ruler is said by the *Veritable Records of Han Kao-tsu* 漢高祖實錄 and other contemporary works to have taken place between 874 and 903 instead of in 907.[11] The *Wu-tai Shih* omits the first reign title, Shên-ts'ê 神册, and lists T'ien-tsan 天贊 as the sole reign title for A-pao-chi.[12]

During the Ch'ing dynasty several general works on Chinese historical chronology were published, but most of them dealt inadequately and even inaccurately with the Liao period. For instance, the first year of Hui-t'ung is equated with the second year of T'ien-fu of Chin (937) instead of with the third year (938).

Even the most acceptable works on Liao chronology

---

[1] XIV, 4 (4).

[2] *Loc. cit.;* CWTS 96, 10*b*; WTS 57, 13*b*–14*a*.

[3] XIV, 4 (4); and LS 43, 1*b*.

[4] The year *chi-hai* 己亥 of the *Chia-yu Tsa Chih* 嘉祐雜志 = LSSI 15, 14*a* is probably either an error or a misprint for *i-hai* 乙亥.

[5] This date is given in his tomb inscription (SLYYP 3, 31).

[6] The winter solstice, according to the Sung calendar, fell on the day *mou-shên* 戊申 of the eleventh month in the tenth year of the Hsi-ning period (SSSJK 1, 12*b*).

[7] The story, which is given in detail in SS 340, 27*a*–*b*, MCML 2, 19, and SLYYP 3, 30–31 and 9, 84, places (probably erroneously) the Liao date one day before instead of after the Sung date; all other records are identical with Su's tomb inscription.

[8] NKCML 12, 16*a*.

[9] LS 44, 1*b*.

[10] LS 43 is a table of intercalary months; LS 44 is a table of first days of the months. Both note the differences between Ch'ên Ta-jên's and Yeh-lü Yen's works.

[11] *Cf.* the discussion in TCTC 266, 4*b*.

[12] WTS 72, 4*b*–5*a*.

have certain shortcomings. Some are incomplete; others suffer from minor errors. For instance, Ch'ien Ta-hsin's 錢大昕 *Sung Liao Chin Yüan Ssŭ Shih Shuo Jun K'ao* 宋遼金元四史朔閏考 (SSSJK),[13] Wang Yüan-sun's 汪遠孫 *Liao Shih Chi-nien Piao* 遼史紀年表 (in LSSI), and Huang Jên-hêng's 黃任恆 *Liao-tai Nien Piao* 遼代年表 (in 遼痕五種) all specially treat of Liao chronology, but the first begins only with the year 960, omitting the previous fifty-three years of the Liao dynasty; the second is complete but contains minor errors; the third has the disadvantages of both; it begins in 916 and is not entirely accurate.

In compiling the following tables we have therefore relied mainly on the *pên chi* 本紀 of the *Liao Shih* and have made use of Ch'ên Yüan's 陳垣 *Êrh-shih Shih Shuo Jun Piao* 二十史朔閏表 (ESSSJP), the most recent and most accurate work on the subject. In converting Chinese dates into the Julian calendar we have used Hoang's *Concordance des Chronologies Néoméniques Chinoise et Européenen*. For each year of the Liao dynasty we give the Western equivalent, noting also that part of the Liao year which fell in the succeeding year in the Julian calendar. Thus the first year of T'ai-tsu's accession is set within the years 907 and 908. The days of the eleventh month whose cyclical signs in the sexagenary system are numbered 35–40, as well as the whole of the twelfth month, fell in the year 908. An asterisk next to the number of the month indicates that this month is an intercalary one. A triangle indicates that an intercalary month of the same number follows. (See table C.)

TABLE A

LIAO EMPERORS

T'AI-TSU 907–926
> Ascended the throne on the day *kêng-yin* of the first month of his rule (February 27, 907) and died on the day *hsin-ssŭ* of the seventh month in the first year of T'ien-hsien (September 6, 926).

T'AI-TSUNG 927–947
> Ascended the throne on the day *jên-hsü* of the eleventh month in the second year of T'ien-hsien (December 11, 927) and died on the day *ting-ch'ou* of the fourth month in the first year of Ta-t'ung (May 15, 947).

SHIH-TSUNG 947–951
> Ascended the throne on the day *mou-yin* of the fourth month in the first year of Ta-t'ung (May 16, 947) and died on the day *kuei-hai* of the ninth month in the fifth year of T'ien-lu (October 7, 951).

MU-TSUNG 951–969
> Ascended the throne on the day *ting-mao* of the ninth month in the first year of Ying-li (October 11, 951) and died on the day *chi-ssŭ* of the second month in the nineteenth year of Ying-li (March 12, 969).

CHING-TSUNG 969–982
> Ascended the throne on the day *kêng-wu* of the second month in the first year of Pao-ning (March 13, 969) and died on the day *jên-tzŭ* of the ninth month in the fourth year of Ch'ien-hêng (October 13, 982).

SHÊNG-TSUNG 982–1031
> Ascended the throne on the day *kuei-ch'ou* of the ninth month in the fourth year of Ch'ien-hêng (October 14, 982) and died on the day *chi-mao* of the sixth month in the eleventh year of T'ai-p'ing (June 25, 1031).

HSING-TSUNG 1031–1055
> Ascended the throne on the day *chi-mao* of the sixth month in the eleventh year of T'ai-p'ing (June 25, 1031) and died on the day *chi-ch'ou* of the eighth month in the twenty-fourth year of Ch'ung-hsi (August 28, 1055).

TAO-TSUNG 1055–1101
> Ascended the throne on the day *chi-ch'ou* of the eighth month in the twenty-fourth year of Ch'ung-hsi (August 28, 1055) and died on the day *chia-hsü* of the first month in the seventh year of Shou-lung (February 12, 1101).

T'IEN-TSU 1101–1125
> Ascended the throne on the day *chia-hsü* of the first month in the seventh year of Shou-lung (February 12, 1101), was captured by the Jurchen on the day *jên-hsü* of the second month in the fifth year of Pao-ta (March 26, 1125), and died *ca.* 1128.

REIGN PERIODS

According to Chinese tradition a new emperor generally retained the reign title of his predecessor until the end of the calendar year, inaugurating a new reign period sometime during the year following.[14] The Ch'i-tan rulers of the Liao dynasty adopted the Chinese institution of the reign title but modified it in application. In general, the new reign title of a new Liao emperor was announced soon after his accession, becoming, as a rule, immediately effective. Delays in establishing new reign periods after the deaths of T'ai-tsu and Ching-tsung resulted in both instances from the desires of the powerful empress dowagers to preserve the status quo. When a reign title was changed by the emperor, it was usually made retroactive—that is, it was dated from the beginning of the current year. The only exceptions occurred under the two last emperors whose reign titles, omitting the first, were adopted either in the twelfth month of the preceding year or in the first month of the first year of the new reign period.

We note in table B the time when each reign title was adopted and when it went into effect, adding the Julian equivalent to clarify the Chinese dates.

---

[13] This work was completed by Ch'ien T'ung 錢侗.

[14] The typically Chinese dynasties very rarely changed the reign title for the remainder of the year in which an emperor died (see JCHP 10, 10*b* ff.).

TABLE B

Reign Periods

T'AI-TSU

Accession	907–916	on the 13th day *kêng-yin* of the first month (February 27, 907).
Shên-ts'ê	916–922	adopted on the 11th day *ping-shên* of the second month (March 17, 916). Made retroactive to the 1st day *ping-ch'ên* of the first month (February 6, 916).
T'ien-tsan	922–926	adopted on the 22d day *kuei-yu* of the second month (March 23, 922). Made retroactive to the 1st day *jên-wu* of the first month (January 31, 922).
T'ien-hsien	926–	adopted on the 5th day *jên-ch'ên* of the second month (March 21, 926). Made retroactive to the 1st day *mou-wu* of the first month (February 15, 926).

T'AI-TSUNG

T'ien-hsien	–939	reign title retained.
Hui-t'ung	938–947	adopted on the 23d day *ping-yin* of the eleventh month (December 17, 938). Made retroactive to the 1st day *mou-shên* of the first month (February 2, 938).
Ta-t'ung	947	adopted on the 1st day *ting-ssŭ* of the second month (February 24, 947). Made retroactive to the 1st day *ting-hai* of the first month (January 25, 947).

SHIH-TSUNG

T'ien-lu	947–951	adopted on the 16th day *ting-mao* of the ninth month (November 1, 947). Probably not made retroactive.

MU-TSUNG

Ying-li	951–969	adopted on the 8th day *ting-mao* of the ninth month (October 11, 951).

CHING-TSUNG

Pao-ning	969–979	adopted on the 23d day *kêng-wu* of the second month (March 13, 969).
Ch'ien-hêng	979–	adopted on the 25th day *hsin-ch'ou* of the eleventh month (December 19, 979). Made retroactive to the 1st day *hsin-ssŭ* of the first month (January 31, 979).

SHÊNG-TSUNG

Ch'ien-hêng	–983	reign title retained.
T'ung-ho	983–1012	adopted on the 10th day *chia-wu* of the sixth month (July 22, 983). Made retroactive to the 1st day *mou-wu* of the first month (February 16, 983).
K'ai-t'ai	1012–1021	adopted on the 1st day *chia-wu* of the eleventh month (December 16, 1012). Made retroactive to the 1st day *chi-ssŭ* of the first month (January 26, 1012).
T'ai-p'ing	1021–1031	adopted on the 12th day *kuei-wei* of the eleventh month (December 18, 1021). Made retroactive to the 1st day *ting-ch'ou* of the first month (February 15, 1021).

HSING-TSUNG

Ching-fu	1031–1032	adopted on the 15th day *hsin-mao* of the sixth month (July 7, 1031).
Ch'ung-hsi	1032–1055	adopted on the 11th day *chi-mao* of the eleventh month (December 16, 1032). Made retroactive to the 1st day *jên-shên* of the first month (February 13, 1032).

TABLE B—*Continued*

Tao-tsung

Ch'ing-ning 1055–1065 adopted on the 16th day *hsin-ch'ou* of the eighth month (September 9, 1055).

Hsien-yung 1065–1075 adopted on the 1st day *hsin-yu* of the first month (February 8, 1065). Put into effect on the same day.

Ta-k'ang 1075–1085 adopted on the 18th day *hsin-ssŭ* of the twelfth month in the tenth year of Hsien-yung (January 7, 1075). Put into effect on the 1st day *kuei-ssŭ* of the first month in the following year (January 19, 1075).

Ta-an 1085–1095 adopted in the twelfth month of the tenth year of Ta-k'ang (December 30, 1084–January 28, 1085). Put into effect on the 1st day *ping-shên* of the first month in the following year (January 29, 1085).

Shou-lung 1095–1101 adopted on the 18th day *i-yu* of the twelfth month in the tenth year of Ta-an (January 26, 1095). Put into effect on the 1st day *mou-hsü* of the first month in the following year (February 8, 1095).

T'ien-tsu

Ch'ien-t'ung 1101–1111 adopted on the 1st day *jên-chên* of the second month (March 2, 1101).

T'ien-ch'ing 1111–1121 adopted on the 15th day *chi-yu* of the twelfth month in the tenth year of Ch'ien-t'ung (January 26, 1111). Put into effect on the 1st day *chia-tzŭ* of the first month in the following year (February 10, 1111).

Pao-ta 1121–1125 adopted on the 1st day *ting-yu* of the first month (January 21, 1121). Put into effect on the same day.

TABLE C

Western Equivalents for Liao Dates

Emperor	Reign period	Year	Julian equivalent	Overlapping months	and days
T'ai-tsu: 太祖		1	907/8	11	35–40
		2	908/9	12	41–4
		3	909/10	11	46–58
		4	910/1	11	51–53
		5	911/2	12	56–16
		6	912/3	11	2–10
		7	913/4	12	7–34
		8	914/5	12	12–28
		9	915/6	11	17–23
	Shên-ts'ê 神册	1	916/7	12	23–47
		2	917/8	11	28–42
		3	918/9	11	33–36
		4	919/20	12	38–60
		5	920/1	11	44–54
		6	921/2	12	49–18
	T'ien-tsan 天贊	1	922/3	12	54–12
		2	923/4	11	59–6
		3	924/5	12	5–30
		4	925/6	12△	10–25
T'ai-tsu: } T'ai-tsung:} 太宗	T'ien-hsien 天顯	1	926/7	11	15–20
		2	927/8	12	20–44
		3	928/9	11	26–38
		4	929/30	11	31–32
		5	930/1	12	35–56

TABLE C—*Continued*

Emperor	Reign period	Year	Julian equivalent	Overlapping months and days	
		6	931/2	11	41–50
		7	932/3	12	47–14
		8	933/4	12	52–8
		9	934/5	11	57–3
		10	935/6	12	2–27
		11	936/7	11*	8–21
		12	937/8	11	13–15
	Hui-t'ung 會同	1	938/9	12	18–39
		2	939/40	11	23–33
		3	940/1	12	29–57
		4	941/2	12	34–52
		5	942/3	11	39–46
		6	943/4	12	44–10
		7	944/5	12△	50–5
		8	945/6	11	55–59
		9	946/7	12	60–23
T'ai-tsung: ⎫ Shih-tsung: ⎬ 世宗	Ta-t'ung 大同 T'ien-lu 天祿	1	947		
		1	947/8	11	5–17
		2	948/9	11	11–11
		3	949/50	12	16–35
		4	950/1	11	21–30
		5	951		
Mu-tsung: 穆宗	Ying-li 應曆	1	951/2	12	26–54
		2	952/3	12	32–48
		3	953/4	11	37–43
		4	954/5	12	42–7
		5	955/6	11	47–1
		6	956/7	11	53–55
		7	957/8	12	58–19
		8	958/9	11	3–13
		9	959/60	12	8–8
		10	960/1	12	14–32
		11	961/2	11	19–26
		12	962/3	12	24–50
		13	963/4	12△	29–45
		14	964/5	11	35–39
		15	965/6	12	40–3
		16	966/7	11	45–57
		17	967/8	11	50–51
		18	968/9	12	56–15
		19	969		
Ching-tsung: 景宗	Pao-ning 保寧	1	969/70	11	1–10
		2	970/1	12	6–34
		3	971/2	12	11–28
		4	972/3	11	17–23
		5	973/4	12	22–46
		6	974/5	11	27–40
		7	975/6	11	32–34
		8	976/7	12	38–58
		9	977/8	11	43–53
		10	978/9	11	48–48
	Ch'ien-hêng 乾亨	1	979/80	12	53–12
		2	980/1	11	59–6

TABLE C—Continued

Emperor	Reign period	Year	Julian equivalent	Overlapping months	and days
Ching-tsung: Shêng-tsung: 聖宗	Ch'ien-hêng T'ung-ho 統和	3	981/2	12	4–30
		4	982/3	12*	9–24
		1	983/4	11	14–18
		2	984/5	12	20–42
		3	985/6	11	25–36
		4	986/7	11	30–31
		5	987/8	12	35–55
		6	988/9	11	41–50
		7	989/90	12	46–14
		8	990/1	12	51–8
		9	991/2	11	56–2
		10	992/3	12	2–26
		11	993/4	11	7–20
		12	994/5	11	12–14
		13	995/6	12	17–38
		14	996/7	11	23–33
		15	997/8	11	28–28
		16	998/9	12	33–51
		17	999/1000	11	38–46
		18	1000/1	12	44–9
		19	1001/2	11*	49–3
		20	1002/3	11	54–58
		21	1003/4	12	59–22
		22	1004/5	11	5–16
		23	1005/6	11	10–11
		24	1006/7	12	15–35
		25	1007/8	11	20–29
		26	1008/9	12	26–53
		27	1009/10	12	31–47
		28	1010/1	11	36–41
		29	1011/2	12	41–5
	K'ai-t'ai 開泰	1	1012/3	11	47–60
		2	1013/4	11	52–54
		3	1014/5	12	57–18
		4	1015/6	11	2–13
		5	1016/7	12	8–37
		6	1017/8	12	13–31
		7	1018/9	11	18–25
		8	1019/20	12	23–49
		9	1020/1	12△	29–43
	T'ai-p'ing 太平	1	1021/2	11	34–37
		2	1022/3	12	39–2
		3	1023/4	11	44–56
		4	1024/5	11	50–51
		5	1025/6	12	55–15
		6	1026/7	11	60–9
		7	1027/8	12	5–33
		8	1028/9	12	11–27
		9	1029/30	11	16–21
		10	1030/1	12	21–45
		11	1031		
Hsing-tsung: 興宗	Ching-fu 景福	1	1031/2	11	26–40
	Ch'ung-hsi 重熙	1	1032/3	11	32–34
		2	1033/4	12	37–58
		3	1034/5	11	42–53

TABLE C—*Continued*

Emperor	Reign period	Year	Julian equivalent	Overlapping months and days	
		4	1035/6	11	47–47
		5	1036/7	12	53–10
		6	1037/8	11	58–4
		7	1038/9	12	3–28
		8	1039/40	12△	8–23
		9	1040/1	11	14–17
		10	1041/2	12	19–42
		11	1042/4	11	24–36
		12	1043/4	11	29–30
		13	1044/5	12	35–54
		14	1045/6	11	40–48
		15	1046/7	12	45–12
		16	1047/8	12	50–6
		17	1048/9	11	56–1
		18	1049/50	12	1–25
		19	1050/1	11*	6–20
		20	1051/2	11	11–14
		21	1052/3	12	17–38
		22	1053/4	11	22–32
		23	1054/5	12	27–56
		24	1055		
Tao-tsung: 道宗	Ch'ing-ning 清寧	1	1055/6	12	32–50
		2	1056/7	11	38–44
		3	1057/8	12	43–8
		4	1058/9	12△	48–3
		5	1059/60	11	53–57
		6	1060/1	12	59–21
		7	1061/2	11	4–16
		8	1062/3	11	9–10
		9	1063/4	12	14–33
		10	1064/5	11	20–28
	Hsien-yung 咸雍	1	1065/6	12	25–52
		2	1066/7	12	30–46
		3	1067/8	11	35–41
		4	1068/9	12	41–5
		5	1069/70	11*	46–59
		6	1070/1	11	51–53
		7	1071/2	12	56–17
		8	1072/3	11	2–11
		9	1073/4	12	7–35
		10	1074/5	12	12–29
	Ta-k'ang 大康	1	1075/6	11	17–24
		2	1076/7	12	23–48
		3	1077/8	12△	28–43
		4	1078/9	11	33–37
		5	1079/80	12	38–1
		6	1080/1	11	44–55
		7	1081/2	11	49–49
		8	1082/3	12	54–13
		9	1083/4	11	59–7
		10	1084/5	12	5–32
	Ta-an 大安	1	1085/6	12	10–26
		2	1086/7	11	15–21
		3	1087/8	12	20–45
		4	1088/9	12△	26–39

TABLE C—*Continued*

Emperor	Reign period	Year	Julian equivalent	Overlapping months	and days
		5	1089/90	11	31–33
		6	1090/1	12	36–57
		7	1091/2	11	41–51
		8	1092/3	12	47–15
		9	1093/4	12	52–10
		10	1094/5	11	57–4
	Shou-lung 壽隆[15]	1	1095/6	12	2–28
		2	1096/7	12	8–22
		3	1097/8	11	13–17
		4	1098/9	12	18–40
		5	1099/1100	11	23–34
		6	1100/1	11	29–29
		7	1101		
T'ien-tsu: 天祚	Ch'ien-t'ung 乾統	1	1101/2	12	34–53
		2	1102/3	11	39–47
		3	1103/4	12	44–12
		4	1104/6	12	50–6
		5	1105/6	11	55–60
		6	1106/7	12	60–24
		7	1107/8	11	5–18
		8	1108/9	11	11–12
		9	1109/10	12	16–36
		10	1110/1	11	21–31
	T'ien-ch'ing 天慶	1	1111/2	12	26–55
		2	1112/3	12	32–50
		3	1113/4	11	37–44
		4	1114/5	12	42–8
		5	1115/6	12	47–2
		6	1116/7	11	53–56
		7	1117/8	12	58–20
		8	1118/9	11	3–14
		9	1119/20	11	8–9
		10	1120/1	12	14–33
	Pao-ta 保大	1	1121/2	11	19–27
		2	1122/3	12	24–51
		3	1123/4	12	29–46
		4	1124/5	11	35–40
		5	1125		

[15] See VI, introduction, note 4.

APPENDIX II

NAMES AND TITLES OF THE LIAO EMPERORS

A Liao emperor was given a number of personal names and titles. The latter followed Chinese tradition: when ascending the throne, the ruler received an honorific title (*tsun hao* 尊號);[1] after his death he was given a posthumous title (*shih hao* 諡號); his temple title (*miao hao* 廟號) placed him officially in the sacred line of his imperial ancestors.

An emperor "typically" Chinese in background received a personal name (*hui* 諱). In addition he might receive a "style" (*tzŭ* 字) and a "fancy" name (*hao* 號). Liao designations did not entirely conform to this pattern. The authors of the *Liao Shih* have classed the Ch'i-tan names either as styles or as childhood names. Probably all the rulers had Ch'i-tan personal names, but the *Liao Shih* does not record the styles of Shih-tsung and Mu-tsung, or of Shêng-tsung whose Buddhist name[2] seems to have replaced his original national designation. The so-called style of the first ruler, A-pao-chi, was definitely his tribal name,[3] but whether this was normal procedure in other cases we do not know. The frequent use of the childhood name makes the Ch'i-tan emperors seem less aloof than their typically Chinese counter-parts. The documents of the Liao government also refer at times to Ch'i-tan officials by their childhood names,[4] using designations which would have appeared highly improper in a formal Chinese record.

The names which the *Liao Shih* classes as the emperors' *hui* are all Chinese names. In the case of A-pao-chi this given name was only the Chinese translation of the ruler's Ch'i-tan name, probably of his Ch'i-tan given name. Whether this was always so, or whether sometimes the Chinese personal name was chosen simultaneously and independently is not clear.

Our classification of names follows that of the *Imperial Annals* of the *Liao Shih*, in which the record of each emperor is preceded by a list of his names and titles. However, we only mention the first of the honorific titles bestowed when the new ruler ascended the throne. While others might be added later, it was the first title that was most significant and most frequently used on official occasions.

All Ch'i-tan names have been marked by an asterisk (*). The last emperor, T'ien-tsu, has neither a temple nor a posthumous title, for the imperial line was broken when he was dethroned.

---

[1] The custom of bestowing an honorific title upon a living emperor probably originated in 221 B.C. when the courtiers of the First Emperor of the Ch'in dynasty offered him the title of *t'ai-huang* 泰皇 (SC 6, 11*a*). According to Ssŭ-ma Kuang, the practice of adding further supplementary appellatives to the main title began perhaps with Empress Wu of the T'ang dynasty (SS 110, 3*a*). In the empires of the steppes the name of a supreme ruler was similarly embellished. The Huns, for instance, preceded the title of shan-yü 單于 with the honorific term *lao-shang* 老上 (SC 110, 15*b*). In the fourth and fifth centuries the powerful Shê-lun 社崙 of the Juan-juan nation called himself *chiu-tou-fa* khaghan 丘豆伐可汗 (WS 103, 3*b*). The rulers of the Orkhon Turks and of the subsequent Uighur empire were distinguished by an agglomeration of complimentary epithets (Thomsen 24, 127, 128, 140, and 144; Müller 12*a*, 9; Chavannes-Pelliot 13, 282, note 2). The Liao officials bestowed an honorific title upon the emperor on the occasion of his enthronement; further complimentary designations were created afterwards.

[2] See IX, introduction.

[3] See Ou-yang Hsiu's discussion of the problem (KTL 2, 2*a*).

[4] The *Liao Shih* usually mentions the Ch'i-tan given name (*ming* 名) and the style of a Ch'i-tan dignitary. This style may actually have been the person's childhood name, or occasionally, a second personal name, a Ch'i-tan style, adopted after the Chinese pattern. Sometimes the childhood name is mentioned too, and even in official documents this name may be used rather than the given name. T'ai-tsu's third son is generally called Li-hu 李胡 and not Hung-ku 洪古, although Hung-ku was his given name and Li-hu only his childhood name (LS 72, 4*a*).

If a Ch'i-tan adopted a Chinese name, he did not give up his Ch'i-tan name or names, but his Ch'i-tan given name was then called "style" and his Ch'i-tan style (which may have been either a childhood name or a style) was designated *hsiao tzŭ* 小字, "childhood name." Again the latter designation might be used in the official documents in place of the given name, Chinese or Ch'i-tan. A member of the imperial family who served as an envoy to Korea for six years (LS 88, 4*b*) was referred to by his Ch'i-tan childhood name, Chih-la-li 只剌里 (Ch'a-la 札剌), instead of by his Chinese name, Tzŭ-chung 資忠 (*cf.* LS 16, 4*b*).

APPENDIX II

TABLE D

THE DESIGNATIONS OF THE LIAO EMPERORS

PERSONAL NAMES				IMPERIAL TITLES	
Given name (*hui* 諱)	Style (*tzŭ* 字)	Childhood name (*hsiao tzŭ* 小字)	Honorific title (*tsun hao* 尊號)	Posthumous title (*shih hao* 諡號)	Temple title (*miao hao* 廟號)
I 億	A-pao-chi* 阿保機	Cho-li-chih* 啜里只	T'ien Huang-ti 天皇帝	Ta Shêng Ta Ming Shên-lieh T'ien 大聖大明神烈天 Huang-ti	T'ai-tsu 太祖
Tê-kuang 德光	Tê-chin 德謹	Yao-ku* 堯骨	Ssǔ-shêng 嗣聖 Huang-ti	Hsiao-wu Hui-wên 孝武惠文 Huang-ti	T'ai-tsung 太宗
Yüan 阮		Wu-yü* 兀欲	T'ien-shou 天授 Huang-ti	Hsiao-ho Chuang-hsien 孝和莊憲 Huang-ti	Shih-tsung 世宗
Ching 璟		Shu-lü* 述律	T'ien-shun 天順 Huang-ti	Hsiao-an Ching-chêng 孝安敬正 Huang-ti	Mu-tsung 穆宗
Hsien 賢	Hsien-ning* 賢寧	Ming-i 明扆	T'ien-tsan 天贊 Huang-ti	Hsiao-ch'êng K'ang-ching 孝成康靖 Huang-ti	Ching-tsung 景宗
Lung-hsü 隆緒		Wên-shu-nu 文殊奴	T'ien-fu 天輔 Huang-ti	Wên-wu Ta-hsiao Hsüan 文武大孝宣 Huang-ti	Shêng-tsung 聖宗
Tsung-chên 宗眞	I-pu-chin* 夷不菫	Chih-ku* 只骨	Wên-wu Jên-shêng Chao-hsiao 文武仁聖昭孝 Huang-ti[5]	Shên-shêng Hsiao-chang 神聖孝章 Huang-ti	Hsing-tsung 興宗
Hung[6]-chi 洪基	Nieh-lin* 涅鄰	Ch'a-la* 查剌	T'ien-yu 天佑 Huang-ti	Jên-shêng Ta-hsiao Wên 仁聖大孝文 Huang-ti	Tao-tsung 道宗
Yen-hsi 延禧	Yen-ning* 延寧	A-kuo* 阿果	T'ien-tsu 天祚 Huang-ti		

[5] This title, taken from LS 18, 3b, seems to be inaccurately recorded. First, the earliest titles offered to the other emperors are short, not more than four words; secondly, they begin with *t'ien* 天, except in the case of T'ai-tsung. Even the titles of Ch'un 淳 and the founder of Western Liao, Yeh-lü Ta-shih, begin with this word (LS 30, 2b, 6a); and thirdly, LS 18, 3b, which mentions the title under discussion, also gives a title for the emperor's mother which is at variance with that reported in LS 71, 6a.

In the chronological table of the Liao emperors in the *Ch'i-tan Kuo Chih* this honorific title reads *Wên-ch'êng* 文成 *Huang-ti*.

[6] According to the inscription, the Chinese name of Tao-tsung was written 弘基.

APPENDIX III

WEIGHTS AND MEASURES

The following list consists only of the weights and measures mentioned in our texts. As no direct Western equivalents are available, we offer those given for weights and measures in the T'ang dynasty. A number of Chinese measures of weight have been translated into Malayan words (tael, catty, picul), which are commonly employed by foreigners living in China; it seems expedient to use these terms instead of Western designations, such as ounce or pound, which are more remote and less accurate. For measures of capacity, however, no such treaty-port equivalents exist; in this case Western terms (pint, peck, bushel) are used, not because they refer to units of exactly the same size, but because the Western units at least indicate the approximate dimensions of the measures in question. We have followed the data given in Wu CL 37 for our calculations.

TABLE E

Length

1 *ch'ih* 尺 (foot) = 311 millimeters = 12.244 inches
5 *ch'ih* = 1 *pu* 步 (pace) = 1.555 meters = 5.1 feet
10 *ch'ih* = 1 *chang* 丈 = 3.11 meters = 10.2 feet
4 *chang* = 1 *p'i* 疋 (bolt) = 12.44 meters = 40.8 feet
6 *chang* = 1 *tuan* 端 = 18.66 meters = 61.2 feet
360 *pu* = 1 *li* 里 = .559 kilometer = .3478 mile

Weight

1 *lei* 絫 = .1554 gram = 2.398 grains
10 *lei* = 1 *shu* 銖 = 1.554 grams = 23.98 grains
24 *shu* = 1 *liang* 兩 (tael) = 37.3 grams = 1.315 ounces
16 *liang* = 1 *chin* 斤 (catty) = .5968 kilogram = 1.3129 pounds
24 *liang* = 1 *i* 鎰 = .8952 kilogram = 1.9694 pounds
120 *chin* = 1 *shih* 石 (picul) = 71.616 kilograms = 157.884 pounds

Capacity

1 *shêng* 升 (pint) = .5944 liter = 36.273 cubic inches
10 *shêng* = 1 *tou* 斗 (peck) = 5.944 liters = 362.73 cubic inches
10 *tou* = 1 *shih* 石 or *hu* 斛 (bushel) = 59.44 liters = 1.6869 U. S. bushels

Area

1 *mou* 畝 = 5.803 ares = .1434 acre
100 *mou* = 1 *ch'ing* 頃 = 580.3 ares = 14.34 acres

APPENDIX IV

HISTORY OF THE TEXT, EDITIONS, SUPPLEMENTARY RESEARCHES

A. HISTORY OF THE *LIAO SHIH*

The *Liao Shih* (LS), from which the translated texts of this publication have been selected, is one of the twenty-four Chinese dynastic histories. The importance of these histories as source material and the way in which they were compiled have already been indicated in the General Introduction. We shall therefore confine ourselves here to a discussion of the genesis of our basic source, the *Liao Shih*.

1. LIAO HISTORIOGRAPHY

The Liao government included a Department of Historiography whose essential task was to record official acts and statements. The Department was in charge of a supervisor who was usually chosen from among the high ministers. He, in turn, was supported by three compilers.[1]

The *Diaries of Activity and Repose*, which took note of important events at the court and in the country, were kept by special Liao officials.[2] The emperor was expected to refrain from reading these *Diaries* lest he intimidate the compilers and thus suppress the truth, but the Liao rulers did not hesitate to satisfy their curiosity, one even beating an official who obstinately upheld Chinese practice in this matter.[3]

The Liao dynasty possessed *Daily Records*[4] compiled chronologically from the *Diaries of Activity and Repose* and other sources. In 941 T'ai-tsung ordered an official history of the first Ch'i-tan ancestor, Ch'i-shou Khaghan, to be written down. This is the first known statement concerning Liao historiography.

From Shêng-tsung (982–1031) down to T'ien-tsu (1101–1125) each emperor considered it his special task to compile and edit the *Veritable Records* of his predecessor. In 991 twenty chapters of the *Veritable Records* were completed and presented to Shêng-tsung

by Shih Fang.[5] In 1044 Hsing-tsung (1031–1055) ordered the compilation of Shêng-tsung's *Veritable Records* as well as a general history of his lineage from the time of the Yao-lien Khaghanate on.[6] The latter assignment was carried out by Hsiao Han-chia-nu, who completed the work in twenty-chapters.[7] The fate of the former is unknown.

During the reign period Ta-k'ang (1075–1084), Yeh-lü Mêng-chien[8] memorialized that a national history of Liao should be written for the benefit of later generations. The emperor agreed and ordered the establishment of a bureau suitable to the work of compilation. In 1085 the *Veritable Records* of the seven preceding emperors were completed and presented to Tao-tsung by the historiographers.[9] This was probably the first time that these early records were systematically arranged and coordinated. The final compilation was completed in 1103 under the direction of Yeh-lü Yen. The whole comprised seventy chapters[10] and provided the main material for the *Liao Shih*, which frequently quotes directly from them. These records, either in whole or in part, were extant until Ming time.

At times, however, the *Liao Shih* differs from the *Records* of both Hsiao Han-chia-nu and Yeh-lü Yen, whose works, according to a Ming catalogue,[11] each comprised four volumes. Some statements in these works are said to have been at variance with those in the *Liao Shih;* others were not included in the *History* at all.

2. PROGRESS MADE UNDER THE CHIN DYNASTY

During Chin 金 times the compilation of a history of Liao was twice initiated but not completed. In 1148 Hsiao Yung-ch'i 永祺, a Ch'i-tan disciple of Yeh-lü Ku, wrote a brief history of the dynasty in seventy-five chapters.[12] From 1189 to 1206 thirteen historiographers were appointed to compile a history of Liao,[13] but the project was repeatedly held up while debate as to the orthodoxy of the dynasty con-

---

[1] The chapter on the governmental organization of Liao, LS 47, 9a, mentions the existence of a supervisor of national historiography in the ninth year of T'ung-ho (991). As a matter of fact, however, this office existed much earlier. A Ch'i-tan, Yeh-lü Lu-pu-ku 魯不古, was the supervisor of national historiography during the time of T'ai-tsu (LS 76, 2a).

[2] *Cf.* LS 47, 5b.   *Cf.* also Gardner 38, 88.

[3] XIV, 4 (27).

[4] WHTK 51, 466.

[5] *Cf.* XIV, 4 (7) (8).

[6] XIV, 4 (17).

[7] *Loc. cit.*

[8] XIV, 4 (26).

[9] XIV, 4 (28).

[10] XIV, 4 (33).

[11] SSTML 1, 24.

[12] CS 4, 12a; 89, 16a, 17b; 125, 7a.

[13] *Op. cit.*, 13a ff.

tinued.[14] Finally, however, in 1207 an incomplete history of Liao was presented to the emperor by Ch'ên Ta-jên 陳大任.[15]

3. COMPLETION UNDER THE MONGOL DYNASTY

The debate on orthodoxy was revived at different times during the Yüan period.[16] One group asserted that the Ch'i-tan were usurpers and that their history should be added to that of the Sung dynasty, just as the histories of several smaller dynasties had been appended to the *Chin Shu* 晉書. The other group maintained that Liao was an independent northern state and that, since it had repeatedly forced the Chinese emperors to accept a subordinate position, its history, like the *Pei Shih* 北史, deserved to be presented as an independent work.[17] So vigorously did the two factions argue their views that compilation was temporarily suspended. In 1343, however, a Mongol, K'uei K'uei 巎巎, urged that despite differences the histories of the three dynasties, Liao, Chin, and Sung, should be compiled lest the source material be lost.[18] The emperor agreed. Prime Minister T'o T'o 脫脫 was appointed to supervise the work of twenty-three specially designated compilers.[19] When the debate was revived, T'o T'o stilled all argument by insisting that the Liao, Chin, and Sung were all orthodox dynasties and that the history of each should be dated in accordance with its own calendar.[20] The *Liao Shih* was finished during the next year.[21]

The material in the *Liao Shih* was derived from three main sources: the *Veritable Records* compiled by Yeh-lü Yen, the *History of Liao* written by Ch'ên Ta-jên, and the *Ch'i-tan Kuo Chih* written by Yeh Lung-li.[22] Little other material was used.[23]

B. EDITIONS

The first edition of the *Liao Shih* was printed in 1345 according to the Yüan edict which introduces the *Chin Shih*, published that same year. In the fourth month of 1345 several high ministers memorialized that, since the compilation of the *Liao Shih* and *Chin Shih* had been completed in the previous year, a hundred sets of each history should be printed in the provinces of Chiang-chê 江浙[24] and Chiang-hsi 江西.[25] In the sixth month the emperor approved the memorial and appointed officials to supervise publication. The original edition printed in 1345 evidently comprised only one hundred sets.[26]

All the editions listed in table F omit two significant passages, namely one in LS 116, 19a (after 有) and another in 116, 23a (after 傍). These passages, however, are included in the original edition quoted by the Ming scholar, Ch'ên Shih-yüan 陳士元.[27] Strange as it may seem, while this original edition was still available, the Ming government relied on a less satisfactory version when it republished the *Liao Shih*.[28]

The thirty-four editions of the *Liao Shih* known to us are listed in table F. Included are a number of manuscript copies. Items 1–9, none of which is complete, may even in some cases be different copies of one printing rather than separate editions. Certain of the thirty-four editions are rare and difficult of access; others recently issued are in common use.

In the table below we have noted that in many editions certain names and terms are not rendered as in the earlier versions. To some degree this may be explained by the fact that the Manchu rulers, to avoid a real or fancied slight, ordered their historiographers to substitute less derogatory renderings. Though generally of minor significance, these changes occasionally result in marked modifications in meaning and the doctored editions must, therefore, be used with great caution.

The Po-na edition (no. 33), the best in circulation today, was photostated from a number of incomplete Yüan editions. It is not without copyists' errors and typographical misprints, but these are less serious than the textual emendations mentioned in table F. For this reason, we have chosen it as the textual basis of our publication, but the Palace edition of 1739 (no. 14), the Northern Academy edition of 1596 (no. 12), and the Southern Academy edition of 1529 (no. 11) have also been used.

---

[14] KCWL 45, 7a ff.

[15] CS 12, 16b; 125, 13b.

[16] YS 4, 15b; 159, 6b; CKL 3, 53.

[17] KCWL 45, 3a–7b.

[18] YS 143, 5b.

[19] YS 41, 1b; cf. also the imperial edict at the beginning of the *Liao Shih*.

[20] KSWS 1, 16a.

[21] See the imperial edict published as an introduction to the *Liao Shih*.

[22] Fêng CS 33, 51 ff.

[23] Op. cit., 45 ff.

[24] Approximately modern Fukien and Chekiang.

[25] Approximately modern Kiangsi.

[26] For this and the following statements cf. Fêng CS 33, 4–11.

[27] (T. 心叔). He was a *chin-shih* in the Chia-ching period (1522–1566) of Ming. His work, *Chu-shih I-yü* 諸史夷語, is quoted in LSSI 23, 8a, 10a.

[28] The official editions published in the Ming dynasty were the Southern Academy and Northern Academy editions. The latter was based on the Southern Academy edition, which in turn was based, not on the original edition, but on one of the late Yüan or early Ming editions listed below.

TABLE F

EDITION	DATE	REMARKS
1. Late Yüan or early Ming edition[29]	Yüan dynasty (1206–1368)	Thin dark brown paper. 22 characters per column and 10 columns per page. Chapters (卷) 1–47 and 58–70 only. 8 volumes. In Peiping National Library (國立北平圖書館).
2. Late Yüan or early Ming edition		Same style as no. 1. Chapters 31–44, 49–62, 71–96. 8 volumes. In Peiping National Library.
3. Late Yüan or early Ming edition		Same style as no. 1. Handwritten characters added in damaged places. Chapters 1–6, 24–56, 58–70, 71–97. 9 volumes. In Peiping National Library.
4. Late Yüan or early Ming edition		Same style as no. 1. Chapters 1–6, 24–44, 48–101. Some pages of introduction missing. 13 volumes. In Peiping National Library.
5. Late Yüan or early Ming edition		Same style as no. 1. 72 chapters. 5 volumes. In Peiping National Library.
6. Late Yüan or early Ming edition		Same style as no. 1. 35 chapters. 3 volumes. In Peiping National Library.
7. Late Yüan or early Ming edition		32 volumes. In Kiangsu Provincial Library.
8. Late Yüan or early Ming edition[30]		Owned by Mr. Fu Tsêng-hsiang 傅增湘.
9. Late Yüan or early Ming edition[31]		10 volumes. Owned by a private library, the Seika-dō 靜嘉堂, Japan.
10. Manuscript copy[32]	Ming dynasty (1368–1644) Early Ming	Bound in yellow silk. White paper. 109 chapters, namely 1–8, 15–116. 19 volumes. 10 columns with 20 characters each; only the columns of chapter 4 have 22 characters. In Imperial Palace Library (故宮圖書館), Peiping.
11. Southern Academy edition (南監本)	1529	22 characters to a column and 10 columns to a page. Complete in 10 volumes. Based on a Yüan edition. Many copies in existence.
12. Northern Academy edition (北監本)	1596	21 characters to a column and 10 columns to a page. Complete in 8 volumes. Based on no. 11. Many copies in existence.
13. Manuscript copy	Ch'ing (Manchu) dynasty, K'ang-hsi period (1662–1722)	White paper, good calligraphy, punctuated. 25 characters to a column and 12 columns to a page. Complete in 8 volumes. In Imperial Palace Library.

[29] The characters of this edition differ slightly in style from those of the following eight, but the misprints and omissions are the same. The description of the original Yüan edition indicates that it is not identical with any of the late Yüan or early Ming editions extant.

[30] It has been generally assumed that the editions nos. 1–8 were cut at the end of the Yüan dynasty and printed in early Ming time. Mr. Wang Chung-min 王重民, however, after a careful study of the material in question suggests a somewhat modified formula. He discovered the names of several cutters of the so-called "Yüan" editions of the *Liao Shih* in a book (大明清類天文分野之書) which was completed in 1385, that is seventeen years after the establishment of the Ming dynasty. Mr. Wang, therefore, holds that the editions nos. 1–8 were made at the very end of the Yüan dynasty or in the early days of the Ming period. Basing himself on the *Nan-yung Chih* 南雍志, he states that the Ming government collected the wood-blocks during the Huang-wu and Yung-lo reign periods (1368–1424); but various blocks were stolen by the cutters and printers, who copied them. Blocks that had been lost were restored and lost again. Finally the confusion became so great that the government decided to edit the *Liao Shih* anew. This led to the production of the Southern Academy Edition. (Personal communication of Mr. Wang Chung-min, temporarily in charge of the collection of rare Chinese books in the Library of Congress, Washington, D. C.)

[31] There was no opportunity to see this edition. The library catalogue dates it as Yüan, but it probably belongs to the set of editions listed by us as late Yüan or early Ming.

[32] Microfilm copies in the Library of Congress and in the Columbia University Library.

TABLE F—*Continued*

EDITION	DATE	REMARKS
14. Palace edition (殿本)	1739	Good white paper. 21 characters to a column and 10 columns to a page. Complete in 8 volumes. Based on Northern Academy edition (no. 12). Many copies in existence.
15. Ssǔ-k'u Ch'üan-shu[33] manuscript copy (四庫全書鈔本)	Ch'ien-lung period (1736–1795)	White paper. Good calligraphy. 21 characters to a column and 8 columns to a page. Complete in 116 chapters. In Peiping National Library. Many terms and names differently rendered from former editions.
16. Manuscript copy	1824	Punctuated. 21 characters to a column and 10 columns to a page. 115 chapters in 61 volumes. In Imperial Palace Library.
17. Palace edition	*ca.* 1824	Same style as no. 14. Chapters 1–30 and 33–70. 68 chapters in 58 volumes. Palace edition of 1739 with handwritten corrections and changes. Names and terms differently rendered from former editions. In Imperial Palace Library.
18. Palace edition	1824	21 characters to a column and 10 columns to a page. Complete. 115 chapters in 28 volumes. This is probably another printing of no. 17, with its handwritten corrections. In Imperial Palace Library.
19. Manuscript copy	1824	Same style as no. 14. Complete. 115 chapters in 10 volumes. Original manuscript contains later emendations. Terms and names differently rendered from former editions. In Imperial Palace Library.
20. Manuscript copy	Tao-kuang period (1821–1850)	White paper. Good calligraphy. Punctuated with red ink. Complete. 115 chapters in 63 volumes. In Imperial Palace Library.
21. Tso-ku-t'ang 茁古堂 edition	1869	21 characters to a column and 10 columns to a page. White paper. Complete. 115 chapters in 20 volumes. Based on 1824 Palace edition.
22. Kiangsu Province Bookstore 江蘇書局 edition	1873	Same style as no. 21. Complete. 115 chapters in 12 volumes. Based on no. 18. Provincial edition for general use.
23. San-wei Bookstore 三味書坊 edition	Kuang-hsü period (1875–1908)	
24. T'ung-wên 同文 Bookstore edition	1884	Same style as no. 14. Complete. 116 chapters. 8 volumes. First lithographed dynastic history. Lithographed from no. 14.
25. Chu-chien-chai 竹簡齋 edition	Kuang-hsü (1875–1908)	2 sizes of type. Complete in 116 chapters. Lithographed.
26. T'u-shu Chi-ch'êng 圖書集成 edition	1888	40 characters to a column and 13 columns to a page. Complete. 116 chapters in 8 volumes. Probably based on no. 14. Government edition for general use.
27. Shih-hsüeh Shê-hui 史學社會 edition	1902	45 characters to a column and 22 columns to a page. Complete. 116 chapters in 6 volumes. Very poor edition with many misprints.
28. Ssǔ-shih-chai 竢實齋 edition		Lithographed.
29. Tien-shih-chai 點石齋 edition	1903	50 characters to a column and 22 columns to a page. Small print. Complete. 115 chapters in 6 volumes. Terms and names differently rendered from former editions.

[33] The *Ssǔ-k'u Ch'üan-shu* was an important collection of 3461 works which were copied in manuscript form between 1773 and 1782 in the Ch'ien-lung period (see Têng and Biggerstaff 36, 23 ff.).

EDITION	DATE	REMARKS
30. Wu-chou T'ung-wên 五洲同文 edition	1903	21 characters to a column and 10 columns to a page. Complete. 116 chapters in 8 volumes.
31. Ssŭ-pu Ts'ung-k'an 四部叢刊 edition	1919–1922	Based on no. 30 and similar to it in format.
32. Ssŭ-pu Pei-yao 四部備要 edition		Based on no. 25.
33. Po-na 百衲 edition	1931	22 characters to a column and 10 columns to a page. Complete. 116 chapters in 16 volumes. Photostated from the fragments of several Yüan editions still extant.
34. K'ai-ming 開明 Bookstore edition	1934	Very small print. Complete in 116 chapters. Lithographed from Palace edition of 1739 (no. 14).

C. SUPPLEMENTARY RESEARCHES[34]

1. CHINESE STUDIES

There are frequent repetitions and contradictions within the *Liao Shih* which Chinese scholars have taken considerable pains to point out and resolve. Some have collected detailed data from numerous records concerning the Liao dynasty; some have examined inscriptions found in tombs and temples; and some have read the *History* again and again in an effort to establish an authentic text.

Li Ê 厲鶚 (T. 太鴻, 1692–1752), a pioneer in this field, compiled his *Liao Shih Shih-i* 遼史拾遺 (LSSI) from 358 sources, including diaries, notes, gazetteers, and the collected works of Sung and Yüan scholars, thus offering the most comprehensive collection of information to date since the completion of the *Liao Shih*.

Yang Fu-chi 楊復吉 (T. 慧樓, 1747–1820), using Li Ê's methodological approach, provided a "Supplement," the *Liao Shih Shih-i Pu* 遼史拾遺補 (LSSIP), which added valuable new material to the data collected by his predecessor.

Ch'ien Ta-hsin 錢大昕 (T. 曉微, 1728–1804) made a comparative study of the *Liao Shih, Chin Shih*, and *Sung Shih*, and was the first to call attention to certain diversities in these publications. His *Nien-êrh Shih K'ao-i* 廿二史考異 (NESKI), *Chu-shih Shih-i* 諸史拾遺 (CSSI), *Shih Chia-chai Yang-hsin Lu* 十駕齋養新錄 (SCCYHL), and *Sung Liao Chin Yüan Ssŭ-shih Shuo-jun K'ao* 宋遼金元四史朔閏考 (SSSJK), are important aids to the study of the dynastic histories in general and the *Liao Shih* in particular.

Chao I's 趙翼 (T. 雲松, 1727–1814) *Nien-êrh Shih*

Cha-chi 廿二史劄記 (NESCC) and *Kai-yü Ts'ung-k'ao* 陔餘叢考 (KYTK) lay particular emphasis on culture and institutions as revealed in the dynastic histories. Hence his discussion of the Liao period differs from that of Li Ê and Ch'ien Ta-hsin, who in the main concentrated upon textual criticism and the gathering of additional materials.

Li Yu-t'ang 李有棠 (T. 菶生, 1843–1902), quoting more than seven hundred sources, arranged his *Liao Shih Chi-shih Pên-mo* 遼史紀事本末 (LSCSPM) according to topic. Because the bulk of the material was taken from the works of Li Ê and Yang Fu-chi, interested scholars have frequently neglected this book, a procedure that is not altogether justified, since Li Yu-t'ang also cites other works and includes many of his own opinions and comments.

There are a few monographs dealing with specific aspects of Liao culture. Some, such as the *Liao Shih-hua* 遼詩話 of Chou Ch'un 周春 (1729–1815) (in 翠琅玕館叢書, 集部下), the *Liao Shih Chi-shih* 遼詩紀事 of Ch'ên Yen 陳衍, and the *Liao-tai Wên-hsüeh K'ao* 遼代文學考 of Huang Jên-hêng 黃任恆 (in 遼痕五種), treat the literature; others, such as the *Liao Ta-ch'ên Nien-piao* 遼大臣年表 (LTCNP) of Wan Ssŭ-t'ung 萬斯同 (1638–1702) and the *Liao Fang-chên Nien-piao* 遼方鎮年表 of Wu T'ing-hsieh 吳廷燮 (ESWSPP 6: 8069–8093), the system of officialdom; and most valuable is Li Shên-ju's 李慎儒 *Liao Shih Ti-li-chih K'ao* 遼史地理志考 (LSTLCK), which not only checks the geographical data contained in the *Liao Shih* but also gives modern locations for the cities, towns, tribes, rivers, lakes, and mountains. These publications are the products of laborious research. They constitute significant additions to our knowledge of the period.

Somewhat later a group of painstaking and patient scholars, Miao Ch'üan-sun 繆荃孫, Wang Jên-chün

---

[34] The following survey does not claim to exhaust the subject. It merely presents the main avenues of research and the most significant conclusions reached.

王仁俊, and Huang Jên-hêng 黄任恆 among them, examined inscriptions from old tombs and temples. Miao's *Liao Wên Ts'un* 遼文存 (LWT), Wang's *Liao Wên Ts'ui* 遼文萃, and Lo Fu-i's 羅福頤 *Liao Wên Hsü-shih* 遼文續拾 (in 待時軒叢刊) give the inscriptions in full; Huang's *Liao-tai Chin-shih Lu* 遼代金石錄 (LTCSL) only in abstract. Nevertheless, since this last also contains inscriptions on metal, Huang's contribution may be considered the most comprehensive. Lo Fu-i's *Man-chou Chin-shih Chih* 滿州金石志 (MCCSC), *Pieh-lu* 別錄 (MCPL), *Pu-i* 補遺, and *Wai-pien* 外編 (MCWP) are particularly scholarly, the major part of the material having been copied directly from the original inscriptions. Noteworthy comments are added by Lo Chên-yü 羅振玉.

In view of the many errors, misprints, and ambiguous passages in the *Liao Shih*, textual criticism is of the greatest importance. Fêng Chia-shêng 馮家昇 and Lo Chi-tsu 羅繼祖 have endeavored to clear up many moot points. Fêng's *Liao Shih Yüan-liu K'ao Yü Liao Shih Ch'u-chiao* 遼史源流考與遼史初校 (Fêng CS 33), published in 1933, compares similar passages in different editions of the *History*, different passages dealing with similar matters in the same edition, and the *Liao Shih* with contemporary works or those of an even earlier period. Lo's *Liao Shih Chiao-k'an Chi* 遼史校勘記 (LSCKC), published in 1938, follows Fêng in general method, incorporates his conclusions, and, in addition, discusses a number of newly discovered inscriptions.

Several articles deal with particular aspects of Liao society and culture. Wang Kuo-wei 王國維, during the later part of his life, investigated a number of tribes that had been part of the Liao world. His *Hei-ch'ê-tzŭ Shih-wei K'ao* 黑車子室韋攷 refutes Tsuda's belief that the Hei-ch'ê-tzŭ and Shih-wei were two separate tribes; instead he equates the composite name with Ho-chieh Shih-wei 和解室韋 and Hei-sha Shih-wei 黑沙室韋 tribes that originally dwelt at the Khulun-Nōr and later settled farther to the south in the neighborhood of the Ch'i-tan. In another study, *Ta-ta K'ao* 韃靼考, Wang Kuo-wei investigates the origin of the name Ta-ta, the location of the people so called, and the reason why they are only rarely mentioned in the *Liao Shih*. He discovered that the name occurred for the first time in the T'ang work, *Hui-ch'ang I-p'in Chi* 會昌一品集. In his *Liao Chin Shih Mêng-ku K'ao* 遼金時蒙古考, a brief history of the Mongols before Chingis Khan, he points out that the Yüan historiographers did not dare use the words "Ta-ta" and "Mêng-ku" 蒙古 freely in the *Liao Shih*. The article, *Hsi Liao Tu-ch'êng Hu-ssŭ-wo-êrh-to K'ao* 西遼都城虎思斡耳朵考, discusses the two capitals of Western Liao, one in Samarqand called Ho-chung Fu 河中府, the other Hu-ssŭ-wo-êrh-to 虎思斡耳朵, located at Beshbaliq. (For above articles, see KTCL.)

Influenced by Wang Kuo-wei's researches, Hsü Ping-ch'ang 徐炳昶 investigated the Ta-ta problem. In his *Tsu-pu Fei Ta-ta Pien* 阻卜非韃靼辨 (in 女師大學術季刊 **1** (1): 1–10, 1930) he points out that the name Ta-ta appears in the *Liao Shih* eight times, and not three as had been claimed by his predecessor. His *Tsu-pu Nien-piao* 阻卜年表 (*op. cit.*, **1** (2): 1–33) shows in the main the relations between the Liao government and the Tsu-pu tribes. He considers the Ta-ta and Tsu-pu as two different peoples. Wang Jih-wei's 王日蔚 study, *Ch'i-tan Yü Hui-hu Kuan-hsi K'ao* 契丹與回鶻關係考 (in YK **4** (6): 5–13, 1935), is an attempt to describe the relations between the Ch'i-tan and the Uighurs before and after the establishment of the Liao empire.

Fu I-ling's 傅以凌 *Liao-tai Nu-li K'ao* 遼代奴隸考 (in 食貨 **1** : 480–490, 1935) gives a brief survey of slavery in the Liao period. Yao Ts'ung-wu's 姚從吾 *Shuo A-pao-chi Shih-tai Ti Han-ch'êng* 說阿保機時代的漢城 (Yao TW 35) explains the Han-ch'êng ("Chinese City") as a general designation for places settled by the Chinese. Fu Lo-huan's 傅樂煥 *Sung-jên Shih Liao Yü-lu Hsing-ch'êng K'ao* 宋人使遼語錄行程考 (Fu LH 35) verifies the authenticity of a number of Sung travelogues; he also tabulates the stations used by the Sung envoys during their visits to Liao territory. His *Sung Liao P'ing-shih Piao Kao* 宋遼聘使表稿 (*AS* **10** (3): 433–527, 1942) contributes to the study of the diplomatic relations between Liao and Sung, and his *Liao-tai Ssŭ-shih Na-po K'ao Wu Pien* 遼代四時捺鉢考五篇 (*op. cit.* **10** (2): 231–346, 1942) to that of the *na-po*. Nieh Ch'ung-ch'i's 聶崇岐 *Sung Liao Chiao-p'ing K'ao* 宋遼交聘考 (Nieh CC 40), a comprehensive study of the diplomatic relations between Sung and Liao, is based upon a great wealth of Sung literary sources.

Among Ch'ên Shu's 陳述 articles on the Liao period, his investigation of the *t'ou-hsia* 頭下 system (Ch'ên S 39) deserves special mention. Ch'ên emphasizes the similarity between the Liao, Chin, and Yüan institutions. This similarity is also confirmed by a decree of 1343 in which the then Yüan emperor stresses the Liao origin of a number of Yüan institutions.

Before 1930 only five Ch'i-tan characters were identified from preserved literary fragments. Since the discovery of new inscriptions in the regions of Barin, Jehol, the zeal of the paleographers has been considerably stimulated. Lo Fu-ch'êng 羅福成 (LLSKCL), Li Ting-kuei 厲鼎煃 (熱河契丹國書碑, *KHCK* **3** (4): 563–572, 1932), and Wang Ching-ju 王靜如 (Wang CJ 33 and 契丹國字再釋, *AS* **5** (4): 538–543, 1935) have recently identified almost a hundred characters.

2. JAPANESE STUDIES

Japanese scholars interested for some forty years in Korea and Manchuria have, not unexpectedly, given increasing attention to the history of the Liao dynasty. Shiratori Kurakichi has in his *Tōko Min-zoku-kō* 東胡民族考 (Shiratori 10–13 TMK) made an ethnological study of the Tung-hu based on linguistic criteria. His monograph, using historical records, notes, collected works, and other sources, deals comprehensively with the Hsien-pei and their descendants down to and including the Ch'i-tan.

Matsui Hitoshi was the first Japanese to present Liao chronology, military organization, beliefs, customs, and political events in a systematic way. In his *Kittan no kokugun hensei oyobi senjutsu* 契丹の國軍編制及び戰術 (Matsui 18) he compares the Ch'i-tan, Jurchen, and Mongols. But while his field of inquiry is broad, he makes no clear distinction between the Ch'i-tan and other peoples of tribal provenience.

Tsuda Sokichi's philosophically weighted study of special Ch'i-tan features, *Ryō-dai no seido no nijū taikei* 遼代の制度の二重體系 (in *MCRKH* 5, 1918) is an important contribution to a more general understanding of Ch'i-tan society. Hashiguchi Kaneo, one of the younger Japanese scholars, has, in his *Ryō-dai kokkyu-chō ni tsuite* 遼代國舅張について (Hashiguchi 39), constructed a valuable table of the Maternal Uncles of the Liao ruling house.[35]

Of particular interest are the investigations of the topography of the Liao state north of the great wall made by Japanese scholars, investigations that combine the study of literary sources with observations on the spot. The results of their work were published annually in the *Mansen chiri rekishi kenkyū hōkoku* 滿鮮地理歷史研究報告.

Based on some of the aforesaid reports, the *Chi-lin T'ung-chih* 吉林通志, and *Jô-ho Chih* 熱河志, a new map was drawn and the *Manshu rekishi chiri* 滿洲歷史地理 (MRC I–II) was compiled under the direction of Shiratori Kurakichi. Though suffering from a number of inaccuracies, and covering only the Inner Asiatic regions of the Liao empire, this map is a great aid to students of Liao history.

In 1936 Torii Ryūzō, an anthropologist and archaeologist who traveled extensively in Manchuria, Jehol, and Siberia, produced the *Kōko-gaku-jō yori mitaru Ryō no bunka* 考古學上より見たる遼之文化 (Torii 36), a four volume work with 338 plates. The book is highly instructive, though of necessity the monuments that are described give a one-sided picture of Liao culture. Torii is reported to be working on another publication dealing with the same period.

3. WESTERN STUDIES

Only slowly did Western scholars become familiar with those sources which had been basic to the Liao

studies of the Chinese and, to a lesser degree, of the Japanese. Du Halde's *General History of China* (English edition 1736) does not even mention the Liao dynasty. Like the *T'ung-chien Kang-mu*, but much less satisfactorily than this famous secondary source, Du Halde presents the history of the tenth and eleventh centuries exclusively from the standpoint of the orthodox southern dynasties. The Liao empire is referred to as the Kingdom of Leao tong;[36] its "barbarous people"[37] are vaguely called Tartars,[38] Sie tan,[39] and occasionally Léao.[40] Deguignes includes a short survey of the "kingdom of the Ki-tan or Léao"[41] in his description of the Eastern Tartars. A good half of the survey is devoted to predynastic times, the history of the empire being condensed into a few sentences accompanying a chronological presentation of the nine emperors.[42]

De Mailla's translation of the *T'ung-chien Kang-mu* does not treat the history of the Liao dynasty independently, but occasionally the Ch'i-tan are mentioned in connection with earlier dynasties.[43] The Tartar Liao, in the days of their greatest glory, the tenth, eleventh, and twelfth centuries, merely serve as a dark northern background to high-light the civilization of the Five Dynasties and the Sung empire[44] which, in the opinion of the Sung author of the *Kang-mu*, were the only legitimate dynasties of the period.

Visdelou translates the earlier sections of the *Imperial Annals* of the *Liao Shih* which deal with T'ai-tsu[45] and T'ai-tsung.[46] In so doing, he presents the history of the two emperors in much more detail than Deguignes. Unfortunately he leaves it to two lists of Liao rulers[47] "to tell the rest."[48]

Klaproth, who in his *Tableaux Historiques de l'Asie* (1826) emphatically asserts the Tungus origin of the Ch'i-tan,[49] adds little to Visdelou. Some new data, however, are presented by Hyakinth (Bichurin) in a

---

[35] The genealogical table of the imperial maternal clan is incomplete and in some places incorrect.

[36] Du Halde 1736 I, 433.
[37] *Op. cit.*, 414 and 418.
[38] *Op. cit.*, 418.
[39] *Op. cit.*, 413 and 414.
[40] ". . . a barbarous People of the North, called *Sie tan* who afterwards were named Léao . . ." (*op. cit.*, 414).
[41] Deguignes, HGH I, 201–205.
[42] *Op. cit.*, 203.
[43] See de Mailla, HGC V, 393; VI, 168, *passim*.
[44] *Op. cit.*, VII, 118, *passim* and VIII, 3, *passim*. Cf. also XII, 189–190 (index, Léao), which show clearly that the Liao state is treated essentially in relation to the foreign policy of the contemporary southern dynasties.
[45] Visdelou 1779, 180–195.
[46] *Op. cit.*, 196–207.
[47] The second list (*op. cit.*, 212) includes A-pao-chi's ancestors back to Su-tsu.
[48] *Op. cit.*, 210.
[49] Klaproth 1826, 87 ff. and 159 ff.

work on the Mongols which was published in 1828 in Russian and in 1832 in German. Hyakinth's study also contains a survey of the main events of the later reigns of the Liao dynasty.[50]

The few pages of d'Ohsson's *Histoire des Mongols* (1834) which deals with the Ch'i-tan peoples[51] contribute little of note. The problematic theory of Tungus origin is repeated;[52] Liao is inaccurately translated as "iron," and an early statement mentions the introduction of Chinese "customs, ceremonies, and institutions" into the "empire khitan."[53]

Vasil'jev's treatment of the Ch'i-tan in his *History and Antiquity of Eastern Central Asia* (1859)[54] is more detailed. He devotes some seven pages to the predynastic history[55] and another ten pages to the history of the Liao empire,[56] using the *Liao Shih* as the source for the main political events in both periods[57] and the *Ch'i-tan Kuo Chih*[58] and the *Liao Chih*[59] for additional information on cultural aspects.

Vasil'jev's monograph was an important addition to Inner Asiatic historical studies, for Hyakinth's published material did not go beyond the close of the T'ang dynasty.[60] But the work, written in Russian, was little known to European students of Liao culture who relied more on H. C. von der Gabelentz's *Geschichte der grossen Liao* (1877), a translation from an abbreviated Manchu version of the *Liao Shih*. Except for a discussion of army organization, this version is more concerned with political events and wars than with institutions. Moreover, the usual difficulties of translation have led to numerous errors, and a lack of proper annotation[61] has made many passages unintelligible to the reader who is unfamiliar with things Ch'i-tan. Yet despite all these shortcomings the work is of utmost significance as the first detailed Western account of the Liao empire, which is, at least indirectly, based upon its official history.[62]

Depending little if at all on Gabelentz's *Geschichte*, Schott endeavors to establish by linguistic evidence the Tungus affinity of the Ch'i-tan.[63] In his researches he does not consult the glossary (*chüan* 116) of the *Liao Shih*, but takes his list of Ch'i-tan words from Howorth who had obtained them from Palladius, who in turn had recorded them "irgendwo" (somewhere).[64] Schott's conclusions suffer from the use of this inadequate material.[65]

Howorth's description of the Ch'i-tan people in Volume I of his *History of the Mongols* (1876) is laconic.[66] In an essay on *The Khitai or Khitans* published five years later,[67] he coordinates practically all the existing Western studies devoted to his topic. The result is a history of the predynastic period and of A-pao-chi's reign which, despite numerous limitations, shows the same skill in synthesis that characterizes his *History of the Mongols*. The final section of Parker's *A Thousand Years of the Tartars* (1895) is devoted to *The Empire of the Cathayans*. His discussion, which covers the entire dynastic period,[68] seems to be based on first-hand sources, primarily on the *Liao Shih*, although he fails to name any of them. A later article on *The Cathayans* (1900) deals with Ch'i-tan institutions and culture,[69] not exhaustively nor always accurately, but obviously using certain passages in the *Liao Shih* and the *Ch'i-tan Kuo Chih*.

Bretschneider's excellent *Mediaeval Researches* (1888) need only be mentioned in passing, for the *Notice of the K'i-tan and the Kara-Khitai* contained therein deals in the main with the history of the Hsi Liao or Qarā-Khitāy empire.[70] Far more significant for Western students of the Liao dynasty is Chavannes' translation of certain reports made by Chinese visitors to the northern country.[71] These translations, like his work on the early sections of the *Shih Chi*,[72] were accompanied by competent notes and

---

[50] Hyakinth 1832, 282–295.
[51] D'Ohsson 1834 I, 113–117.
[52] *Op. cit.*, 113.
[53] *Op. cit.*, 115.
[54] Vasil'jev 59. The whole monograph comprises 235 pages, out of which pp. 1–31, 37–40, and 171–196 are devoted to the history of the Ch'i-tan.
[55] *Op. cit.*, 1–14.
[56] *Op. cit.*, 15–24.
[57] *Op. cit.*, 7.
[58] *Op. cit.*, 25.
[59] *Op. cit.*, 171.
[60] *Op. cit.*, 3.
[61] The absence of systematic notes is emphasized by the few scattered explanations which the translator and the editor, his son, have attached to the German text.
[62] In 1636, while invading China, the Manchu emperor ordered the translation into Manchu of selections from the *Liao Shih*, the *Chin Shih*, and the *Yüan Shih*. Unneces-

sary details were to be omitted, but a full translation was to be made of the success of good and the failure of bad deeds, and of "the wars and the great hunts" (Gabelentz 77, 195).
[63] Schott 80, 6 ff.
[64] *Op. cit.*, 5.
[65] *Cf.* General Introduction.
[66] Howorth, HM I, 1–4.
[67] Howorth 81, 121 ff. Schott asserts that Howorth gave him a list of Ch'i-tan words collected by Palladius. Howorth in both writings quoted refers to his friend, Mr. Wylie, as the author of the list used by himself (Howorth, HM I, 1; *idem* 81, 123).
[68] Parker 95, 297–369.
[69] *Idem* 00, 343 ff.
[70] See below, appendix V, A.
[71] Chavannes 97–98 VC.
[72] *Cf.* Chavannes, MH.

commentaries, thus setting a precedent for Liao studies in general.

Mullie's researches in geography and his attempts to locate the sites of cities and tombs of the Liao empire (1922–1933)[73] have led to the translation of numerous passages of the *Liao Shih* relevant to his field of inquiry. Although not systematically annotated, the translations themselves are carefully done and in many cases the interpretations are based on the author's own archaeological investigations. Independent archaeological studies have been conducted by Gibert whose *Dictionnaire Historique et Géographique de la Mandchourie* (1934) combines the results of his field work with a comprehensive examination of the literary sources. Unfortunately, because of his failure to document his historical references, only a few Liao specialists are able to benefit fully from his rich data, and even they find considerable difficulty in checking his statements.

In his articles and notes on Inner Asiatic history[74] Pelliot has authoritatively discussed many linguistic as well as certain cultural aspects of pre-Liao, Liao, and post-Liao society. Kotwicz in *Les "Khitaï" et leur Ecriture* (1925) has also been concerned with the ethnic and linguistic affiliations of the Ch'i-tan. Agreeing with Rashīd-ad-Dīn's opinion, he arrives at conclusions similar to those of Shiratori and Pelliot.[75]

Stein, a student of Professors Pelliot and Granet, combines in his translation and analysis of the *Liao Chih* (1939) the linguistic approach of the former and the sociological method of the latter. The *Liao Chih* comprises the introduction and chapters (*chüan*) 23 and 27 of the famous Sung description of the Liao empire, the *Ch'i-tan Kuo Chih*.[76] Stein treats both the linguistic and cultural problems raised by the text with care and thoroughness. But, though his interpretations are based on a study of the *Liao Shih* and a number of supplementary sources, his method inevitably obscures the specific (dual) character of Liao society and culture during the dynastic period.

---

[73] See Mullie 22; 33; and 33*a*.

[74] See Pelliot 10; 12; 15; 15*a*; 20; 21; 29; 30; 30*a*; 31; 31*a*; 31*b*; and 34.

[75] Kotwicz 25, 249. His assumption that the Orkhon inscriptions contain a particularly old form of the name Ch'i-tan (*op. cit.*, 248–249) is erroneous, since the name is found in Chinese sources of a much earlier date (see General Introduction, note 9).

[76] Stein 39, 2.

APPENDIX V

QARĀ–KHITĀY

A. INTRODUCTORY REMARKS

1. THE SIGNIFICANCE OF HSI LIAO

To a student of the Liao dynasty this appendix needs little justification. It is concerned with the destiny of a small group of Ch'i-tan nationals who, led by Yeh-lü Ta-shih and supported by numerous tribes of Western Mongolia, established a new "Black" Ch'i-tan (Qarā-Khitāy) empire in the heart of Asia, Turkestan.

After the collapse of the Liao dynasty the major portion of the Ch'i-tan people fell under the sway of the victorious Jurchen; their fate will be dealt with in a special volume on the Chin period. The empire of the "Black" Ch'i-tan is topographically and functionally beyond the scope of any history of Chinese society, but since the development of Qarā-Khitāy power and civilization sheds light on important aspects of the political, military, and cultural history of Inner Asia on the eve of the Mongol invasion, and since this development occurred under the active direction of Ch'i-tan nationals, the present survey of the Qarā-Khitāy dynasty seems desirable both from the point of view of Asiatic conquest history in general and Ch'i-tan institutions and culture in particular.

The Qarā-Khitāy empire has been the subject of intensive scholarly investigation.[1] In the nineteenth century Bretschneider made an outstanding contribution by translating LS 30, 4a–7b[2] (the section dealing with the history of Hsi Liao), supplementary passages from CS 121,[3] and a number of travelogues describing conditions in Central Asia during the early days of Mongol rule.[4] He also included important Moslem sources taken, in the main, from d'Ohsson's *Histoire des Mongols* which treated of this same period and topic.[5] Bretschneider's material, more comprehensive than anything offered by his predecessors, was a great addition to Western knowledge on Qarā-Khitāy history. Since its appearance Iranists, Arabists, and Turkologists have frequently drawn upon his Chinese data, just as Sinologists have welcomed his convenient collection of Moslem texts.

In the twentieth century W. Barthold, utilizing primarily Persian and Arabic sources, wrote a history of Turkestan "down to the Mongol invasion"[6] —and after[7]—with considerable emphasis on the Qarā-Khitāy dynasty. For the political, military, and religious history of Central Asia, Barthold's work is a classic. The shortcomings of his institutional analysis will be discussed below in our examination of Qarā-Khitāy society and culture.

2. ARRANGEMENT OF SOURCES

The present survey deals with the Hsi Liao empire, first chronologically (B, 1–3), and then socio-culturally (C). The chronological data are given in three columns according to the sources cited: Column I takes its material exclusively from LS 30, Bretschneider's most important Chinese text; Column II includes information from other Chinese works, among them, CS 121, also translated by Bretschneider. But the bulk of the data in this column (from Sung, Chin, and Yüan sources, as well as parts of the *Liao Shih* not used by Bretschneider) has been assembled in China and America over a period of years by Mr. Fêng Chia-shêng in connection with his studies on the Liao dynasty.

Column II presents much new Chinese material, but no such claim can be advanced regarding the non-Chinese sources that appear in Column III. In this field, we, like Bretschneider, have drawn on the work of recognized specialists who sometimes translated, sometimes paraphrased, the original texts. Translations were naturally preferred, but whenever these were not available we have used the Persian and Arabic data appearing in such authoritative publications as Barthold, indicating both the original and the secondary source.

Fortunately, since the first publication of Bretschneider's investigations,[8] a number of important Moslem works of the eleventh, twelfth, and thirteenth centuries have been translated: Niẓām-al-Mulk's famous treatise[9] (1091) describing conditions in Persia

---

[1] See Bretschneider 88 I, 180–210.

[2] *Op. cit.*, 211–218.

[3] *Op. cit.*, 219–223.

[4] *Op. cit.*, 9–163.

[5] *Op. cit.*, 223 ff. and 233. Bretschneider's excerpt from Ibn al-Athīr's work is based on Grigorieff's Russian translation (*op. cit.*, 231).

[6] See particularly Barthold 28. His description of the rise of the Qarā-Khitāy dynasty, presented in Russian in the *Handbook of Semiryechye* [1898], was not available to us.

[7] *Cf.*, among other works, Barthold's numerous articles in the *Encyclopedia of Islam* dealing with both periods.

[8] Between 1874 and 1876 (Bretschneider 88 I, vi).

[9] French translation by Schefer: Nizam oul-Moulk 93.

and Turkestan some twenty years prior to the Black Ch'i-tan invasion; the *Chahār Maqāla* by Nidhāmī-i-'Arūdī (d. 1161);[10] an-Nasawī's account of the Mongol conquest (completed in 1269);[11] and aj-Jūzjānī's history of the conquest[12] (1260). References from two other basic Moslem works, Ibn al-Athīr and Juwaynī,[13] are taken from Barthold's paraphrased renderings, except for Juwaynī's chapter on Qarā-Khitāy. This most important West Asiatic record of the period attracted the attention of d'Ohsson who translated a considerable part in his *Histoire des Mongols*.[14] Dr. K. H. Menges has been kind enough to make a new and complete translation (cited as "Juwaynī 16"), which has enabled us to correct d'Ohsson's translation and Bretschneider's English version[15] at several points.

3. CHRONOLOGICAL PROBLEMS

a. DATING THE FIVE IMPERIAL REIGNS

The Moslem chroniclers give little information on the rulers of Hsi Liao whose names are rarely mentioned and whose number, sex, and sequence are incompletely and confusedly reported. The chroniclers are equally reticent regarding the length of the individual gurkhans' reigns.

Barthold, after commenting on the "scanty and contradictory" character of the Moslem sources, turns to the Chinese annals. These, he acknowledges, contain "a more accurate list," but, he adds, "their tradition also is obviously inaccurate, especially in its chronological data."[16] Barthold's rejection of the Chinese chronological data is understandable, for he bases himself not on the original Chinese texts, but on their incorrect interpretation by his Sinological authority, Bretschneider. With reason he prefers Marquart's chronology which takes as its starting point Ibn al-Athīr's date of the first gurkhan's death, Rağab 537 A.H., or according to the Western calendar January 20–February 19, 1143;[17] and then, using information on the length of each gurkhan's reign contained in the *Liao Shih*, he determines the respective dates of their accession and death or, in the case of the last, the date of dethronement.

Marquart's procedure is as simple as it is plausible.[18] His results are closer to the Chinese chronology than he realized. Marquart still considered most of the *Liao Shih* dates incorrect, "particularly the year of the dynasty's end, 1201."[19] However, by avoiding in large degree if not completely[20] Bretschneider's misinterpretations of the *Liao Shih*, he arrived at reign dates for each of the five gurkhans identical with those obtained by Chinese students who, previously and independently, made careful analyses of the decisive text, LS 30.

The great Ch'ing scholar, Ch'ien Ta-hsin (1727–1804), commenced his examination of Hsi Liao chronology[21] with the date *chia-ch'ên*, which LS 30, 6a gives as the year of Yeh-lü Ta-shih's accession to the throne. The passage from which this date is taken follows directly upon the account of Ta-shih's successful invasion of Turkestan: Having defeated his enemies at Hsin-ssŭ-kan (Samarqand), he advanced further to Karmīnīya where, most solemnly, the civil and military officials made him emperor.[22] Why he was so honored at this time remains an enigma, since, according to the same work and a number of parallel sources, Ta-shih had long before been made supreme ruler. If a reason must be found, it seems most plausible to assume that the gurkhan's overwhelming military successes culminated in a great ceremony, in the course of which his old as well as his new subjects joined in acclaiming him "emperor."

Ch'ien Ta-hsin obviously considered the passage containing the date *chia-ch'ên* a retrospective one; and indeed the record has meaning only if it is accepted as an added piece of information inserted from an independent source to emphasize and celebrate the peak of Yeh-lü Ta-shih's political career in 1141. In the Chinese cycle of sixty years, the *chia-ch'ên* of LS 30 must be the year 1124,[23] 1064 and 1184 in this context being manifestly absurd. The Sung official, Chao Tzŭ-ti, who resided in the Chin empire from 1126 to 1128, reported on returning to the Sung capital that Yeh-lü Ta-shih was known in the North as emperor.[24] Similar advices are preserved in the

---

[10] English translation by Browne: Nidhāmī-i-'Arūdī 99.

[11] French translation by O. Houdas: en-Nesawi 95.

[12] English translation by Raverty: Tabakat-i-Nasiri 81.

[13] For a discussion of the importance of these two and the afore-mentioned sources see Barthold 28, 25 ff. and 38–41.

[14] D'Ohsson 1834 I, 441–444.

[15] Bretschneider 88 I, 223–225.

[16] Barthold, KK, 739.

[17] Marquart 14, 237. *Cf.* Wüstenfeld 54, 23.

[18] Barthold (KK, 739) accepts it as "in general . . . successful."

[19] Marquart 14, 238.

[20] To his great disadvantage, Marquart (*op. cit.*, 125 ff.) in his discussion of the last gurkhan's reign uses Bretschneider's faulty dates, and while he challenges the fantastic sequence of events that results he does not, in this context, correct the underlying chronology.

[21] SCCYHL 8, 17b ff.

[22] B, 2, [1141], LS 30, 6a.

[23] Tchang 05, 367.

[24] B, 2, 1128, SCPMHP 98, 14a.

Chin records which, like LS 30, reckon Ta-shih's rule from 1124 on.[25]

According to LS 30, 6a, Yeh-lü Ta-shih reigned for twenty years. Proceeding in the Chinese way which counts the year of enthronement as the first, we must place his death in 1143, the self-same year recorded by Ibn al-Athīr. Small wonder, then, that basing himself on this Moslem date and accepting, as do the Chinese scholars, the number of reign years given in LS 30 for each of the five gurkhans, Marquart sets up a chronology in complete agreement with that established by Ch'ien Ta-hsin, and more fully by Wang Yüan-sun.[26] This chronology expressed in terms of the Western calendar is as follows:[27]

RULERS (Temple titles)	LENGTH OF REIGN (Years)	ABSOLUTE DATES From	To
Tê-tsung (Yeh-lü Ta-shih)	20	1124	1143
Empress Kan-t'ien	7	1144	1150
Emperor I-lieh	13	1151	1163
Empress Ch'êng-t'ien	14	1164	1177
Emperor Chih-lu-ku	34	1178	1211
Total	88	1124	1211

The data necessary to establish all imperial reign years are contained in LS 30, but this in no way detracts from the importance of the Moslem sources which confirm the Liao Shih at two vital points. Ibn al-Athīr's statement regarding the year of Yeh-lü Ta-shih's death is invaluable in bulwarking the first part of the Chinese chronology. West Asiatic texts also confirm the final date. The Chinese records

suggest 1211 as the last year of Chih-lu-ku's reign; Barthold, analyzing the Moslem histories, concludes that Chih-lu-ku's downfall occurred "not later than in the first half of 1211."[28]

b. THE TIME-TABLE OF YEH-LÜ TA-SHIH'S CONQUEST

In view of such evidence, there is little reason to question the accuracy of the Chinese time-schedule for the reigns of the five Hsi Liao rulers. More problematic are the data concerned with Yeh-lü Ta-shih's conquest of Turkestan. But passages in the Liao Shih, supplemented by a number of other sources, again enable us to determine, either exactly or approximately, the dates of at least some of the more significant events.

According to LS 30, 6b, Yeh-lü Ta-shih died in the tenth year of the reign period K'ang-kuo ("the country pacified"). This reign period must, therefore, have commenced in 1134. Furthermore, we learn that the designation K'ang-kuo was proclaimed in the third year of the preceding reign period, Yen-ch'ing, a fact which, if correct, would make 1131 the first year of this earlier period. The texts fail to mention a reign title for the first years of Yeh-lü Ta-shih's rule, that is, for 1124–1131, perhaps because there was none. In this connection it should be recalled that the early years of A-pao-chi's sovereignty were given no special designation either.

The year 1134 was decisive in the development of the Qarā-Khitāy state. The occupied regions of Eastern and Northern Turkestan were "pacified"; a capital was fixed, although, as it seems, with reservations, but after the unsuccessful campaign to reconquer the old Liao territory[29] Turkestan definitely became the new homeland. The year 1131 may also have been distinguished by important events, but these were obviously preparatory to the achievement of the larger goal.

Moslem sources mention 1128 as the year of the gurkhan's initial attack,[30] yet a letter written in 1133 implies that his defeat at Kāshghar occurred a few years after 1128.[31] Barthold assumes a southern Ch'i-tan thrust toward Kāshghar which failed, and

[25] See B, 2, [1124].
[26] Wang Yüan-sun's 汪遠孫 detailed chronology of Hsi Liao, which is based on Ch'ien Ta-hsin's analysis, was completed in 1828 (see the Chronological Tables of Hsi Liao in the Kuang-ya Shu-chü edition of the Liao Shih Shih-i). Liao custom differed from the orthodox Chinese usage in that a Liao emperor usually started his own reign period in the year of his accession, that is, in the year of his predecessor's death. The Hsi Liao gurkhans seem to have followed the regular Chinese pattern, according to which the reign period was changed only in the subsequent year (see appendix I, note 14). Such, at least, is the assumption which the Chinese scholars and also Marquart have made the foundation of their calculations. The coincidence of the last year of the Chinese chronology 1211 with the Moslem date for Chih-lu-ku's fall proves the correctness of this assumption. Why the gurkhans should have changed the Liao tradition we have no means of knowing. Perhaps they were less revolutionary than appears at first glance: the two last Liao emperors already deviated from their predecessors in changing their reign titles regularly every ten years and at the end of the last year of each reign period (see appendix I).
[27] See Marquart 14, 237.

[28] Barthold 28, 367.
[29] For a discussion of the possible background of this campaign see below, A, 4.
[30] See B, 2, 1128/9, column III.
[31] According to Ibn al-Athīr XI, 55 = Barthold, KK, 738, the gurkhan suffered complete defeat at the hands of the ruler of Kāshghar in 1128. However, in a letter sent in the name of Sultan Sanjar and written in the summer of 1133 this battle is mentioned "as a very recent event" (Barthold, KK, 738). Barthold concludes: "Perhaps it took place a few years later" than Ibn al-Athīr claims (loc. cit.).

a successful one "by a more northern route."[32] Actually, the southern expedition may have been only one part of a broader campaign, which began and finished along the northeastern borders of Turkestan. The Moslem sources mention many towns and regions assaulted by Qarā-Khitāy (Imīl, Balāsāghūn, Kāshghar, Khotan)[33], but it is difficult to set these places and those referred to by the Chinese historians (Pei-t'ing, Kao-ch'ang) into a meaningful whole of time and space. Pei-t'ing may have been the site of an old Uighur city near K'o-tun, in which case Yeh-lü Ta-shih must have remained in the vicinity of his first seat of power on the Orkhon River until he marched into the Uighur state of Kao-ch'ang.

This westward march was begun on the day *chia-wu* of the second month. The *Liao Shih* omits the year, but Liang Yüan-tung calculates that 1130 is the only reasonable date, since none of the five preceding years has a day in the second month so designated.[34] We believe, therefore, that the spring of 1130 may be considered the *terminus a quo* of Yeh-lü Ta-shih's invasion; 1131 a year of great achievement; and 1133 the conclusion of the successful campaign, at least as far as Eastern Turkestan was concerned.[35]

It must be left to further investigations to establish reliable dates for the war against the Khirghiz, the founding of Imīl, the attacks against Kāshghar, and the occupation of Balāsāghūn. The letter of 1133 indicates that the conquest of southeastern Turkestan had not yet been completed, but the creation of a first reign title in 1131 suggests a victorious progress, possibly in the northern and northwestern regions.

The conquest of Transoxania receives scant mention in the Chinese works. Moslem sources treat the subject in greater detail. They state clearly that the years 1137 and 1141 were milestones in establishing the gurkhan's victorious sway over Western Turkestan.[36]

c. SUNDRY PROBLEMS

The middle period of Qarā-Khitāy history is more or less adequately covered by the *Liao Shih* as far as the basic chronology is concerned. Otherwise both Chinese and Moslem sources treat the period lightly. The final period is more fully discussed by the Moslem historians who naturally showed a great interest in the momentous events leading up to the Mongol cataclysm. The Moslem reports are not infrequently supplemented or confirmed by Chinese and Mongol records collected or composed during the Yüan (Mongol) dynasty.

The dates of Wang-Khan's visit to Qarā-Khitāy given in a Hsi Hsia chronicle (composed by a Chinese) are incompatible with the recorded activities of Chingis Khan. We have, therefore, corrected them in our table following the work of certain Chinese writers who, avowedly or apparently, based themselves on the great Persian authority, Rashīd ad-Dīn.[37] Both the Moslem and the Chinese chronologies place the Uighur rebellion against Hsi Liao in the year 1209.[38] There is also general agreement on the dates of the last gurkhan's dethronement and death. As stated above, both categories of sources suggest the year 1211 for the first event; the second is said to have occurred one or two years later.[39] Again the difference is slight, the accord basic.

The dates cited in the survey of the Kirmān Qarā-Khitāy dynasty (B, 4) are taken in the main from one Persian source, the *Ta'rīḥ-i-Guzīda*, which gives them according to Islamic usage: A.H. The chronology in this source is often problematic though, on occasion, it stands up well against more recent claims.[40] When possible we have rejected the seemingly inaccurate dates and have, in their stead, accepted emendations made by the translator of our primary source, E. G. Browne, and, in some few cases, the independent calculations of S. Lane-Poole. Marco Polo's visits to Kirmān during the life of the Qarā-Khitāy dynasty are given in terms of the Christian calendar.

4. THE CAREER OF AN EMPIRE–BUILDER

The data in our chronological tables permit us to define the time-schedule of Qarā-Khitāy history in its main outlines. In addition, they throw considerable light on the birth of a Central Asiatic empire, on the military and political events preceding that birth, and on the personality of the man who organized and consolidated the conquest: Yeh-lü Ta-shih.

The passages of LS 30 translated by Bretschneider contain only a few references to Ta-shih before his arrival at Emperor T'ien-tsu's camp.[41] Other Chinese sources cited in our survey depict far more concretely the career, and particularly the early career, of this extraordinary individual.

A scion of the imperial family (the branch is un-

[32] *Loc. cit.*

[33] B, 2, 1128/9, column III.

[34] See B, 2, note 17.

[35] B, 2, 1133. It seems that Yeh-lü Ta-shih founded his capital and changed the reign title to K'ang-kuo at the end of the third year of Yen-ch'ing, for he had already started a campaign for the reconquest of the Liao empire in the third month of the first year of the new reign period.

[36] B, 2, 1137 and 1141.

[37] B, 3, note 21.

[38] B, 3, 1209.

[39] B, 3, 1213.

[40] *Cf.* B, 4, note 17.

[41] Bretschneider 88 I, 211.

specified), Yeh-lü Ta-shih received the "dual" education, Ch'i-tan and Chinese,[42] customarily given to members of the Liao aristocracy. As prefect and commanding prefect,[43] he no doubt learned the art of organizing for war as well as peace: officials in this category were in charge of both military and civil affairs within their territories.[44] In the critical year 1122 the ephemeral "Emperor" Ch'un[45] entrusted Ta-shih with the defence of the Southern Route against the approaching Sung armies, and the indomitable leader defeated superior Chinese forces in a number of battles.[46] Under Ch'un's widow, he shared the command with Hsiao Kan, chalking up further victories against the Sung invaders.[47] But valiant though these commanding officers were, they could not fight a two-front war. The eastern "barbarians," the Jurchen, soon succeeded in occupying the strategic Chü-yung Pass[48] in the mountainous region north of the Southern Capital.[49] In the ensuing political crisis Ta-shih refused to support a movement whose potential gains were temporary. Instead he joined the camp of the fugitive but legitimate Liao sovereign, T'ien-tsu, not as a lesser and insignificant noble, but as a distinguished military and political functionary.

The *Liao Shih*, which has little to say about Yeh-lü Ta-shih's early military career, is equally reticent about the events that followed his arrival at T'ien-tsu's camp, possibly because of the seemingly ambiguous role played by the future gurkhan. The Sung records, not inhibited by any considerations of loyalty, reveal him as an utterly ruthless man who, after capture by the Jurchen, agreed to guide them, under compulsion it is true, to his emperor's headquarters. The Liao emperor escaped, though most of his followers were seized. The power of Ta-shih's mind and arguments so deeply impressed his captors that, according to the *Pei Shih Chi* (KHCCL 6a), the Chin emperor gave him a wife. However, Yeh-lü Ta-shih did not attach himself to the cause of the victor. Some time later, after a dramatic game of Double Sixes with the Chin commander, he fled taking his five sons with him. His [Ch'i-tan?] wife remained behind, abandoned to the Jurchen, but she seems to have borne her ambitious husband no malice. Her behavior on the day following his flight provides perhaps the most moving episode in his life-story.[50]

Having refused to support a hopeless political enterprise, Yeh-lü Ta-shih displayed equally shrewd judgment when, after his return to T'ien-tsu's camp, he sharply and realistically criticized the emperor's fantastic plans. He must have felt that his allegiance to the Liao throne was at an end, for he did not join the abortive campaign. Left behind on plea of sickness, he killed two nobles who may have tried to detain him, just as on an earlier occasion he had killed a Hsiao clansman who opposed his will.[51] At the moment of departure he proclaimed himself "king," assuming a title which soon afterwards he changed to "gurkhan" and emperor.[52]

A great political leader may be recognized by his vision, superior insight, judgment, will-power, and resourcefulness—and by the mistakes which he makes and those which he avoids. Yeh-lü Ta-shih's temporary "play" with the enemy, sinister though it appears, obviously did not go so far as to discredit him with his own friends and followers. His support of "Emperor" Ch'un's government proved futile, but whether it can be called a political mistake is doubtful. At the time the successful organization of political resistance within the Liao empire still seemed a possibility. When the attempt failed—retrospectively assuming the appearance of an error of judgment—Yeh-lü Ta-shih did not repeat it. His refusal to join the Great Hsi adventure may have been motivated in whole or in part by dynastic considerations, yet his firmness in rejecting T'ien-tsu's plan demonstrated both his ability to learn from previous experience and his resolve not to make the same mistake twice. A crew's morale on a sinking ship is a complex phenomenon and does not concern the present analysis, but in fairness to Yeh-lü Ta-shih it must be said that, according to all records, he did not leave T'ien-tsu because the imperial "ship" was disabled (in fact he returned several times to his emperor's side). He left because the amateurish captain refused to take the only measures which would have assured the ship's ability to sail.

Ta-shih's progress after his final break with T'ien-tsu is striking evidence of his unusual perspicacity. Within the crumbling edifice of the Liao empire perhaps the only unexhausted reserve of military strength lay along the northwestern frontier with its well-trained veteran soldiers and ample horse herds. Yeh-lü Ta-shih went directly to the largest of all northwestern fortresses, K'o-tun, bringing new hope to its half-forgotten garrison who, in turn, provided a mass basis for his political ambitions.

No details are known concerning the following years of rest and reorganization. Ta-shih evidently suc-

---

[42] See B, 1, 1087 and 1115, LS 30, 4a and 6a.
[43] B, 1, N. D. [after 1115], LS 30, 4a–b.
[44] Cf. above, XIV, introduction.
[45] Cf. XIII (58).
[46] B, 1, 1122 (5), SCPMHP 7, 2b ff.
[47] B, 1, 1122 (6 and 10), SCPMHP 7, 7a ff.
[48] B, 1, 1122/3 (12), SCPMHP 12, 3b.
[49] B, 1, note 6.
[50] B, 1, N. D. [before 1124], SMCW 11b; CTKC 19, 4a.

[51] B, 1, 1122/3 (12), CTKC 12, 1b.
[52] B, 2, note 3.

ceeded in executing the plan which, without success, he had unfolded to T'ien-tsu: to create a well-trained army before undertaking a great military campaign. But responding to the special conditions at K'o-tun and probably stimulated by intelligences from scouts and spies, the self-made emperor gave new meaning and direction to his original plan. The countries west of the Desert boasted great wealth and considerable manpower. If one or more of them, if Turkestan in whole or in part could be seized, a mighty springboard would be provided for achieving the long-range aims of the conqueror. The new vision, realistically explained, acted as a magnet. In 1129, when Yeh-lü Ta-shih disclosed his intentions to the chieftains of seven "prefectures"[53] and eighteen tribes, he received more than academic approval. Over ten thousand experienced fighters joined his growing forces.[54]

Moslem sources speak of an invasion of the northern territory of the Khirghiz.[55] The attempt, after a rebuff, was resolutely abandoned, proving again that the new emperor had the ability to recognize a mistake and correct it. Within the Qarā-Khānid-controlled world of Central Asia, Balāsāghūn was, at this time, particularly attractive to the Ch'i-tan conqueror, for the local khan was unable to maintain his rule over the neighboring Turkic tribes. The situation was further aggravated by the arrival of numerous Ch'i-tan mercenaries (sixteen thousand "tents") who had deserted their ill-advised former master, the khan of Samarqand.[56] After residing for a time at Imīl, where he had firmly established himself, Yeh-lü Ta-shih seized Balāsāghūn without encountering any noteworthy resistance. The Qarā-Khānid khan submitted meekly, and the Ch'i-tan mercenaries quickly joined their victorious countryman. The snowball grew into an avalanche which soon gained sufficient momentum to sweep over the east of Turkestan and eventually also over the west.

A dramatic interlude occurred in 1134 when the gurkhan, perhaps under the pressure of his homesick Ch'i-tan followers,[57] prepared to reconquer the Liao homeland, thus fulfilling, at least in appearance, the promises he had given previously. The campaign itself, left completely in the hands of his generals, came to a discouraging end; and it is more than possible that the arch-organizer, Ta-shih, never seriously

intended to challenge the might of the consolidated Chin empire. "Heaven does not favor me. This is Its will," he announced sanctimoniously.[58] The Black Ch'i-tan had no choice but to accept Turkestan as their permanent home. Psychologically, the stage was now set for the great campaigns against the rulers of Soghdiana, Khwārazm, and Persia which culminated in the victories of 1137 and 1141 and which led to the establishment of the greater Qarā-Khitāy empire.

The military principles underlying Ta-shih's conquest are dealt with in the sub-section on the Hsi Liao army and warfare.[59] The limitations placed upon his success by certain basic factors operative in nomadic conquest are discussed in the concluding pages.[60] The present short biography of Yeh-lü Ta-shih emphasizes the subjective aspect of his career without any claim, to be sure, of being either exhaustive or final. But whatever the deficiencies of our sources or the shortcomings of our interpretation, one point emerges clearly from the texts at our disposal. Yeh-lü Ta-shih's success was not the result of a series of fortunate accidents. A specific constellation of objective factors made his amazing career possible; and a specific personality structure enabled him, firstly, to understand, and, secondly, to realize their potentialities.[61] Viewed in this light, the first gurkhan's life-story appears historically less miraculous—but sociologically more plausible. If sufficient data could be mustered it is more than probable that the life-story of many another empire-builder could be transformed as readily from an entertaining fairy tale into a scientifically meaningful order of events.

5. QARĀ–KHITĀY SOCIETY AND CULTURE

The Hsi Liao empire was also known as the empire of the Qarā-Khitāy. "Khitāy," as discussed above,[62] is an original Altaic form of the Chinese word "Ch'i-tan," and "*qara*" is the Turkic and Mongol term for "black." It is in this sense that the adjective occurs most frequently,[63] though not exclusively. A derived meaning, "low" or "common," was current as early as the Orkhon inscriptions.[64] In some contexts,

[53] B, 2, note 12.

[54] B, 2, 1129, LS 30, 4b–5a.

[55] Juwaynī 16, 88.

[56] B, 2, 1128, Ibn al-Athīr XII, 55–56 = Marquart 14, 164–165.

[57] Before dispatching an army of "seventy thousand men," the gurkhan in his address to his troops stressed his lack of attachment to the newly conquered land: "This is not a place where I and you shall stay permanently" (LS 30, 6a; cf. Bretschneider 88 I, 216–217).

[58] B, 2, 1134, LS 30, 6b.

[59] C, 5.

[60] C, 8.

[61] Yeh-lü Ch'u-ts'ai reports that the first gurkhan's greatness was still remembered at the time of his visit to Turkestan, that is, after the fall of the Qarā-Khitāy empire (CJCSWC 12, 170).

[62] See above, General Introduction, I.

[63] Cf. Radloff 95, 361; idem 97, 168; idem 99, 93; idem, WB II, 132–142.

[64] Radloff 95, 361. Until recent days, the "white bones" of certain Turkic tribes were superior in status to the "black bones" (cf. Czaplicka 18, 40).

FIG. 43. Picture of a "Black" Ch'i-tan, preserved in the Ming work, *San-ts'ai T'u-hui*.

"*qara*" has also acquired an honorific connotation.[65] Marvazī, who completed his work in 1120, believes that it was first used in this way by a somewhat legendary Ethiopian slave: "He assumed the title of QARĀ–KHĀN, which no one had held before him, for it means 'Black khaqan.' His dignity was great, so whenever the Turks after him wished to honour a king they addressed him as 'Qarā-khān.'"[66]

The Ch'i-tan were acquainted with this title as early as the first part of the eleventh century. In 1024 Shêng-tsung asked that friendly relations be established between him and "the amīr of Khurāsān Maḥmūd Qarā-khān."[67] When and how the formula Qarā-Khitāy originated is not clear.[68] Neither the Altaic designation nor its Chinese equivalent, "Black Ch'i-tan," occurs in the *Liao Shih*, though both appear occasionally in other Chinese texts of Sung, Yüan, Ming and Korean provenience.[69] The designation

may well have been suggested by the Turkic environment in which the Ch'i-tan established their western empire; the victors overcame a dynasty of no small prestige, that of the Qarā-Khānids. But whatever the specific meaning of the word "*qara*" in the compound Qarā-Khitāy, the name manifestly fulfilled two functions: it emphasized the ties of the new state to the Ch'i-tan of Liao and pre-Liao glory and, at the same time, it set off the "black" or western Ch'i-tan from their eastern [white ?] ancestors.

In a chapter on Qarā-Khitāy Society and Culture (C) we have tried to analyze the Chinese and Moslem records relating to the social and cultural history of Hsi Liao. Like its eastern predecessor, the Black Ch'i-tan empire was based on conquest; and also like Liao, it evolved institutions that reflected dual, and sometimes, multiple origins. Data on the culture history of Hsi Liao are scanty, but what information there is reveals a complex picture of intended, achieved, or frustrated acculturation, a not unexpected development under the existing complex conditions of power and tradition.

Barthold has clearly noted the resistance to cultural fusion in the conquest societies of Turkestan and Persia.[70] His understanding of Qarā-Khitāy life was, however, handicapped (1) by his limited interest in the social and cultural aspects of history which prevented him from drawing fully on the Moslem texts; (2) by his limited use of Chinese sources even when these were available in translation; and (3) by an erroneous identification of Liao and Chinese culture.[71] While fully appreciating Barthold's contribution to the political and military history of Central Asia in general and Qarā-Khitāy in particular, we deemed it necessary to reexamine the institutional and cultural problems presented by this empire with the aid of a more searching methodological approach and with the addition of new material. Not unexpectedly our analysis reveals a pattern of acculturation for Qarā-Khitāy civilization not dissimilar in principle to that observed by Barthold for certain Turkic dynasties of conquest in Central Asia.

---

[65] Hammer, GOR I, 79–80.

[66] Marvazī 42, 56.

[67] *Op. cit.*, 19.

[68] *Cf.* Bretschneider 88 I, 210; Rubruck 00, 109, note 2.

[69] A Sung work mentions the Chia-la Hsi-t'ai 呷辣吸紿 (HTSLCC 21b and 24a). The same source (*loc. cit*) and the *Hsi Shih Chi* (KHCCL 9b) speak of the Black Ch'i-tan 黑契丹. In two Yüan works reference is made to the Ho-la Ch'i-ta 合剌乞荅 (YCPS 6, 26a) and to the Ha-la Chi-ta-tai 哈剌吉荅歹 (CKL 1, 27). Two Ming works note Chin communications with the Black Ch'i-tan (STTH, sect. 人物, 13, 6b; see pl. 43; IYC 1, 7 ff.).

The Mongols, who in the early days of their rise to power were more concerned with the Black Ch'i-tan of Central Asia than with the Chin Ch'i-tan, tended to identify the second group with the first. In 1231 the successor of Chingis Khan in a letter to the king of Korea reminded him of the fact that in the year of the rat (1216) the Mongols had prevented the Black Ch'i-tan from conquering Korea (KRS 23, 343 ff.). He evidently referred to the two Ch'i-tan chieftains, Chin-shan 金山 and Chin-shih 金始, who in 1216 crossed the Yalu River and invaded Korean territory (KRS 22, 329 ff.).

[70] Barthold 35a, 6 ff.; *idem* 28, 306 ff.

[71] Barthold 35, 121.

6. KIRMĀN

At the end of our chronological table, we have placed a number of data concerned with the Qarā-Khitāy dynasty of Kirmān (B, 4). Further references to this dynasty appear in our discussion of Qarā-Khitāy society and culture.

The translator of the Ṭabaqāt-i-Nāṣirī, Major H. G. Raverty, objects to calling the Kirmān rulers in question "Qarā-Khitāy," for he claims that the first of them, Burāq,[72] "was in no way related to the Gur Khans, and was a mere successful adventurer."[73] The second part of Raverty's statement, even if true, seems irrelevant (the founders of many dynasties can be called "successful adventurers"); the first confuses rather than clarifies the issue.

Historically, it is of minor significance whether or not Burāq was related through ties of blood to the gurkhans; no West Asiatic or European historian known to us stresses this point. All of them, however, are emphatic regarding Burāq's political affinity to the masters of the Hsi Liao dynasty. Muḥammad an-Nasawī, who as a sympathizer with the defeated faction lived through Burāq's usurpation of power, states clearly that the new sovereign "had been chamberlain of the gurkhan, the Khitāy ruler."[74] Ḥamdu'llāh Muṣṭawfī of Qazwīn has a special chapter devoted to "the Qarā-Khitāy rulers of Kirmān," which he introduces by describing Burāq as "one of the *amīrs* of the Gur Khan of Qarākhitāy."[75] Basing themselves on the early Moslem sources, modern scholars have frequently stressed Burāq's Qarā-Khitāy background. Lane-Poole describes Burāq as "a native of Karā-Khitay";[76] Browne speaks of the "Ten Qarā-Khitā'īs who ruled over Kirmān";[77] Barthold, relying particularly on Ibn al-Athīr and Juwaynī,

states: "He was originally one of the Karā-Khitāy";[78] and Kramers calls him a man "who was descended from the Karā Khitāy."[79] A Chinese author in the Mongol period refers to a Black (黑) Ch'i-tan country, Ch'i-li-wan 乞里彎.[80]

Such unanimity of scholarly opinion brings into sharp relief the weakness of Raverty's objection which, in addition, is not supported by any documentary evidence. Such unanimity of opinion also strengthens us in our decision to treat the Qarā-Khitāy dynasty of Kirmān as a late and curious development of Ch'i-tan power, and one that is worth mentioning in the present survey of Qarā-Khitāy history and culture.

For our purpose, it does not matter whether Burāq was a member of the Yeh-lü or the Hsiao clan, or whether he was just one of a number of other Ch'i-tan nationals who could not claim descent from either of the two ruling families. It is even possible that his forbears belonged to a tribe or people other than the Ch'i-tan. But, if this was the case, we must assume that Burāq, or his ancestors, had been thoroughly Ch'i-tanized, for the early Moslem authors unreservedly considered him a Qarā-Khitāy.

The society of the Kirmān Qarā-Khitāy was not identical in structure with either of the two preceding Ch'i-tan conquest societies. The Liao empire included the whole Ch'i-tan people; the gurkhans' rule over Turkestan could at least rely on a fragment of Ch'i-tan nationals and a number of allied tribal forces. Nothing is known of any (Black) Ch'i-tan followers of Burāq. He may indeed have been a "successful adventurer," who, in the days of Mongol onslaught and with the aid of a handful of equally daring supporters, established control in the south of Persia over an alien mass of frightened peasants and townsmen. When Marco Polo visited Kirmān in 1271 and again in 1293–1294, he was not even aware that the country was ruled by a Qarā-Khitāy dynasty.[81]

---

[72] The value of the final syllable is uncertain. Barthold (BH, 793) renders the name as Burāk; Professor Pelliot suggests Barāq.

[73] Tabakat-i-Nasiri 81 II, 934, note.

[74] En-Nesawi 95, 157.

[75] Hamd-Allāh Mustawfī 13, 131.

[76] Lane-Poole 94, 179.

[77] Hamd-Allāh Mustawfī 13, 6.

---

[78] Barthold, BH, 793.

[79] Kramers 27, 1031.

[80] *Hsi Shih Chi* in KHCCL 9b; *cf.* Bretschneider 88 I, 147. According to Professor Pelliot, 彎 *wan* is "probably a faulty reading for 蠻 *man*."

[81] See below B, 4, 1271 (Marco Polo 03 I, 90).

B. MAIN EVENTS CHRONOLOGICALLY ARRANGED

1. THE BEGINNINGS OF YEH–LÜ TA–SHIH'S CAREER

Year	Month	LS 30	Additional Chinese Sources	Non-Chinese Sources
[1087][1]		Yeh-lü Ta-shih 大石 (T. 重德) born; a descendant in the eighth generation of T'ai-tsu (4a and 6a).		
1115		Ta-shih obtained *chin-shih* degree[2]; he was a "scribe" (*lin-ya*) of Han-lin Academy, and thoroughly familiar with Chinese as well as Ch'i-tan literature. He was an excellent horseman and a good archer (4a).		
N.D.		Was made prefect of T'ai and Hsiang Prefectures, and commanding prefect of Liao-hsing Commandery (4a–b).		
1122[3]	3	Ta-shih and other dignitaries acclaimed Ch'un emperor in Southern Capital (4b).	*Cf.* LS 29, 3a; TCKC 2, 1b.	
	5		As chief commander of the Southern Route, he led 2,000 Hsi and Ch'i-tan horsemen in Cho Prefecture (SHYK 175: 8, 16a; SCPMHP 7, 2b). Defeated Sung troops at Lan-kou-tien 蘭溝甸. Tried to cross Pai-kou River with 30,000 men (*op. cit.*, 4b). Meeting a Sung envoy, Ma K'uo 馬擴, he severely criticized the aggressive Sung policy: During conflict between Sung and Hsi Hsia, Liao behaved differently. Sent Ma back to commander with this message: "If you want peace, maintain the old situation. Otherwise — dispatch your soldiers!" (*op. cit.* 8, 6a–7b). The Sung troops sent against Ta-shih were routed by him and General Hsiao Kan 幹 (*op. cit.* 7, 5a–6b).	

[1] He was thirty-eight years old in the year *chia-ch'ên* 甲辰 (LS 30, 6a), that is, in 1124 (SCCYHL 8, 17b ff.).

[2] Since the Ch'i-tan did not participate in the Chinese examinations, this statement is somewhat puzzling. The author of LS 30 may have confused the Chinese term with the Ch'i-tan *lin-ya*. If, however, Ta-shih really received the *chin-shih* degree, he was honored by a procedure that was without precedent in recorded Liao history.

According to T'ang Ch'ang-ju, there is no record in the *pên chi* of Emperor T'ien-tsu of a *chin-shih* degree obtained by Ta-shih in the year 1115. T'ang also points out that Hsiang Prefecture, which Ta-shih governed as prefect after receiving his degree, was already lost to the Jurchen in 1114. Since according to the *pên chi* 103 persons obtained the *chin-shih* degree in the year 1112, he assumes that Ta-shih was among them (T'ang CJ 36, 14).

[3] Bretschneider (88 I, 211) has 1120 instead, which is erroneous. See above, A.

The beginnings of Yeh-lü Ta-shih's career (*continued*)

YEAR	MONTH	LS 30	ADDITIONAL CHINESE SOURCES	NON-CHINESE SOURCES
	6	After Ch'un's death, his widow was made regent (2*b*–4*b*).	At Hsiung Prefecture, Ta-shih again defeated the Sung army. Sung corpses covered the south of Hsiung and the north of Mo Prefectures (*op. cit.*, 7*a* ff.).	
	8		A Sung army of 100,000 men was organized for a campaign against Liao. While Ta-shih and Hsiao Kan were still in the Southern Capital, some Sung detachments crossed the Pai-kou River and captured many Liao soldiers (*op. cit.* 9, 4*a* ff.).	
	10		A Sung army of 500,000 men, including numerous Liao [Chinese ?] rebels attacked the Liao troops led by Ta-shih and Hsiao Kan (*op. cit.* 10, 11*b*–12*a*). The regent personally directed the Ch'i-tan and Hsi soldiers, who fought brilliantly; Hsiao Kan and Ta-shih were summoned back for support. The Sung army was completely routed.[4] Liao Chinese wrote poems which ridiculed the defeated Sung commander (*op. cit.* 11, 1*b*–4*a*).	
1122/3	12		Chin troops seized Chü-yung Pass. The regent and her two aides fled from Yen to Sung-t'ing Pass. Hsiao Kan suggested the establishment of a new regime among the Hsi people; Ta-shih suggested joining T'ien-tsu. The imperial son-in-law, Hsiao Tun-tieh 敦迭, who disagreed with Ta-shih was executed.	
1123	1		Hsiao Kan made himself emperor of Great Hsi [XIII (59)], while the regent and Ta-shih with 7,000 Ch'i-tan fighters joined T'ien-tsu at T'ien-tê[5] (CTKC 12, 1*b*–2*a*; LS 29, 5*a*; SCPMHP 12, 3*b* ff.).	
	2	The emperor had the regent executed. He reproached Ta-shih for having made Ch'un emperor while he, T'ien-tsu,	*Cf.* LS 29, 6*a*; CTKC 12, 2*a*; SCPMHP 12, 4*a*.	

[4] According to SS 357, 12*b*–13*b*, the Sung army suffered tremendous losses in equipment as well as in men. The provisions, which had been stored up from Wang An-shih's time on (1068), all fell into the hands of the Liao victors. See HNYL 1, 2–8.

[5] Modern Kuei-sui 歸綏 in Suiyuan.

The beginnings of Yeh-lü Ta-shih's career (*continued*)

YEAR MONTH	LS 30	ADDITIONAL CHINESE SOURCES	NON-CHINESE SOURCES
	was still alive. Ta-shih explained his action by pointing to T'ien-tsu's military failures and flight, which left the people in distress. By nominating Ch'un, the reign had been preserved for T'ai-tsu's descendants. The emperor gave a feast and pardoned Ta-shih (4b).		
4		Ta-shih took Fêng-shêng[6] and several other prefectures and established a position north of Chü-yung Pass. The Chin vanguard, led by Lou-shih 婁室 and Ma Ho-shang 馬和尚, seized him and all his troops twenty-five *li* east of Lung-mên 龍門[7] (CS 2, 21a–b; 72, 2b; LS 29, 6a).	
5		The Chin general, Wo-lu 斡魯, reported the capture of Yeh-lü Ta-shih and other Liao dignitaries to his sovereign (CS 2, 22a). The Chin soldiers got stuck in the swampy terrain of Ch'ing-chung 青塚.[8] A Chin prince, Tsung-wang 宗望, bound Ta-shih with a rope and ordered him to guide him to the Liao emperor. T'ien-tsu's concubines, sons, daughters, uncles, and officials, and many valuables were seized; the emperor, however, escaped to Ying 應 Prefecture (CS 74, 9b–10a).	
6–9[9]		The Chin emperor honored Ta-shih by an official decree: although he had not voluntarily surrendered, he had meritoriously acted as guide in Ch'ing-chung (CS 121, 4a).	
N.D.		The Chin emperor liked Ta-shih for his courage and ability in argument and gave him a wife. During the western campaign Ta-shih escaped	

[6] Cho-lu 涿鹿, Chahar.
[7] North of modern Ch'ih-ch'êng 赤城, Chahar. The story is confirmed in Lou-shih's inscription (MCWP 31a).
[8] South of modern Kuei-sui.
[9] CS 121, 4a places the story in the year 1122 (Bret-

schneider 88 I, 220 has 1121), but in view of the sequence of events recorded by the *Liao Shih* and *Chin Shih* the correct date seems to be 1123. This date is also supported by Shih Kuo-ch'i (CSHC 9, 39b).

The beginnings of Yeh-lü Ta-shih's career (*continued*)

Year	Month	LS 30	Additional Chinese Sources	Non-Chinese Sources
			with his sons to the region behind the mountain (*Pei Shih Chi* = KHCCL 6a). In the army camp at the Western Capital, Ta-shih aroused the anger of the Chin commander with whom he played the game of "Double Sixes." Fearing for his life, he escaped[10] with his five sons, leaving his wife behind. On the next morning the lady tried to explain her husband's flight, but the angry Chin general handed her over to one of the lowest tribesmen. She refused to yield, whereupon she was shot to death (SMCW 11b; CTKC 19, 4a).	
	9		Ta-shih returned to T'ien-tsu (LS 29, 6b).	
1124	7		T'ien-tsu, delighted by Ta-shih's arrival, planned a great campaign for the reconquest of the Western and Southern Capitals. But Ta-shih criticized him severely, saying that when the Chin troops invaded the eastern territory of Liao the emperor, instead of resisting, had withdrawn to the Central Capital; that after this region had been taken T'ien-tsu had fled first to Yün-chung and eventually to the Chia Mountain;[11] that the emperor, who headed all the armed forces, had not properly prepared the defence, and that consequently the whole empire, including its Chinese provinces, had fallen into the enemy's hands; that to insist upon a fight when conditions were desperate was not good strategy; and that it would be better to train soldiers and wait for an opportune moment. T'ien-tsu did not listen to this advice; he launched the campaign	

---

[10] A Sung scholar, Li Hsin-ch'uan, doubts the authenticity of the story concerning Yeh-lü Ta-shih's surrender to the Chin army as related by Hung Hao in the *Sung-mo Chi-wên* (CWCW 4, 52). His argument is evidently based on a confusion of Yeh-lü Ta-shih with his kinsman, Yeh-lü Ti-lieh who made the Prince of Liang emperor in 1123 (LS 29, 6b; 30, 3a–4a).

[11] See XIII, note 186.

The beginnings of Yeh-lü Ta-shih's career (*continued*)

YEAR MONTH	LS 30	ADDITIONAL CHINESE SOURCES	NON-CHINESE SOURCES
		and failed on the first attempt. Learning that the Chin commander had gone home, T'ien-tsu, supported by 50,000 Tatar warriors, started another attack. Ta-shih, who, under the pretext of illness, had not participated in the campaign, again tried to dissuade the emperor, but again without success (LS 29, 8*b* ff.; CTKC 12, 4*b*–5*a*; TCKC 3, 3*a*–*b*).	
	Ta-shih killed Hsiao I-hsieh[12] and Po-li-k'uo 坡里括, proclaimed himself king, and left by night with 200 horsemen, going in a northerly direction. After three days he crossed the Black River,[13] met Ch'uang-ku-êrh 牀古兒, the *hsiang-wên* of the White Tatars,[15] who presented him with 400 horses, 20 camels, and 1000 sheep. Proceeding westward through the Desert for three days and nights, he finally reached K'o-tun City [Chên Prefecture on the Orkhon River] (4*b*).	Ta-shih killed Hsiao I-hsieh and Po-li-k'uo, set up the offices of the Northern and Southern Regions, proclaimed himself king, and fled westward with his tribal followers (or partisans) (LS 29, 9*a*).[14]	
		[This place, the most important garrison of the northwestern Liao border, was defended by 20,000 horsemen. *Cf.* I, 1 (5) and XV, 1 (51).]	
		Ta-shih gained control over all the troops and over horse herds that numbered several hundred thousand head (II, 1 (3); CTKC 19, 4*b*).	He was followed by eighty people of his tribe;[16] another record speaks of a great number of people[17] (Juwaynī 16, 87).

[12] See XIII (48) (53). Ta-shih killed Hsiao I-hsieh probably because the latter opposed his rebellion.

[13] Not the "Etsina River" in modern Kansu, as Bretschneider (88 I, 159, note 428 and 212, note 544) suggests, but, according to Li Shên-ju, probably the modern Qara Muren, two hundred *li* north of the Ölöt Banner. A horseman could reach this river from the Chia Mountain in the Ordos region in three days (LSTLCK 8139).

[14] Of the two accounts of Yeh-lü Ta-shih's flight, that given in LS 29 obviously is an abbreviated and mutilated version. LS 30 offers a far more concrete and complex tale, which is confirmed by several parallel sources, such as CTKC 12, 4*b* and CWCW 4, 52.

[15] Same as Öngüt, a Turkic people who lived near the Yin Mountains of modern Suiyüan (Pelliot 29, 125 ff.).

[16] Literally, "eighty people of [his] tribe and his followers." The wording is ambiguous. It may mean: eighty followers, members of his own tribe and others; or: eighty members of his tribe and (in addition) other followers. The first interpretation seems suggestive since the figure eighty more probably refers to the whole

escort than to part of it; but the argument is by no means conclusive. The second interpretation implies the existence of additional followers beside the eighty tribesmen, which would bring the total closer to the number mentioned in the *Liao Shih*, i.e. two hundred.

D'Ohsson reads "seventy," whereas Mīrzā Muḥammad's standard edition (Juwaynī 16, 87) has eighty; no other version is mentioned in the notes. Bretschneider (88 I, 225), who follows d'Ohsson, speaks of "only sixty followers" apparently misreading *soixante* for *soixante-dix*.

[17] The two versions recorded by Juwaynī seem irreconcilable. However both make sense if we accept the Chinese record which notes that Yeh-lü Ta-shih reached K'o-tun with only a small group of followers, adding numerous new troops to this nucleus during his sojourn in the northern garrison. He soon had "ten thousand war horses" (see below, part 2). Juwaynī's seemingly contradictory versions possibly refer to these two phases of Yeh-lü Ta-shih's military career, which the Moslem historian, writing a hundred and fifty years after the event, failed to distinguish.

2. THE GROWTH OF THE QARĀ-KHITĀY EMPIRE

YEAR MONTH	LS 30	ADDITIONAL CHINESE SOURCES	NON-CHINESE SOURCES
[1124][1]	In the year *chia-ch'ên* 甲辰 in the second month,[2] on the fifth day, Yeh-lü Ta-shih ascended the throne. He was thirty-eight years old. He was called gurkhan [*ko-êrh-han* 葛兒罕]; in addition he had the supreme Chinese title, Emperor T'ien-yu 天祐[3] (6a).		
10		On the day *mou-ch'ên* the Chin acting chief commander of the Southwestern and Northwestern Routes, Wo-lu, conveyed to his emperor a statement made by the Liao *hsiang-wên*, Hsiao Ta-pu-yeh 撻不也,[4] after his surrender to the Chin forces, that Yeh-lü Ta-shih called himself king and had set up the officials of the Southern and Northern Regions. He had about ten thousand war horses. The Chin emperor instructed his commander to postpone the attack on Yeh-lü Ta-shih until further intelligence arrived (CS 3, 5a–b and 121, 4a).	
1125		The Chin commander, Lou-shih, reported to the court that the withdrawal of the Chin troops after the capture of the Liao emperor had encouraged Yeh-lü Ta-shih to ally himself with Hsi Hsia for the reconquest of the territories of Shan-hsi 山西. The Chin emperor ordered strict vigilance and preparation against this danger (CS 73, 14b and 121, 4a–b).	

[1] The reasons for putting this passage in the year 1124 are given above in the chronological discussion.

[2] If Yeh-lü Ta-shih ascended the throne in 1124, it could not have been in the second month since, according to numerous dated passages, he accepted T'ien-tsu's sovereignty until the seventh month of the year (see above, B, 1).

[3] LS 30, 4b says that Yeh-lü Ta-shih made himself king (see B, 1, 1124). According to LS 30, 6a, however, he was called gurkhan and emperor when he ascended the throne. It is possible that he assumed the more modest title, king, immediately before he fled from T'ien-tsu's camp, and that he appropriated to himself imperial dignity only after he had gained considerable support in men and

arms in the northern border fortress, K'o-tun. Our separation of the two acts is based on these considerations.

But it must be admitted that the two stories may actually describe one and the same event: perhaps Ta-shih made himself gurkhan and emperor at the start, only reaffirming in K'o-tun City his original proclamation. In this case the use of two different terms may be due to two different records which were indiscriminately thrown together by the Yüan authors of the *Liao Shih*. It is interesting that the Chin versions of Yeh-lü Ta-shih's enthronement also give his title as king, not emperor (see 1124 [10], CS 3, 5a–b and 121, 4a).

[4] He surrendered to the Chin army in the eighth month of 1124 (LS 29, 9a).

The growth of the Qarā-Khitāy empire (*continued*)

YEAR MONTH	LS 30	ADDITIONAL CHINESE SOURCES	NON-CHINESE SOURCES
1126		Chê K'o-ch'iu 折可求[5] of the Lin 麟 and Fu 府 Routes reported to the Sung government that north of Hsia the Prince of Liang 梁[6] and the *lin-ya*, Yeh-lü Ta-shih, had assembled an army of 100,000 soldiers. They claimed that the Sung emperor[7] repented having co-operated with Chin in the destruction of Liao. He therefore had yielded the throne to his successor.[8] If the Sung government were to attack Chin from the south, the new Liao government would forget the violation of the old treaties by the Sung government (SCPMHP 58, 6*b*; TCKC 4, 7*b*; HNYL 1, 16).	
1127		Yeh-lü Ta-shih established friendly relations with the Tatars who in consequence did not sell horses to the Chin army. When the Chin government inquired about the matter, the Tatars sent their heir apparent to Yün-chung, where he was detained (HNYL 181, 3017). According to a report of the Chin chief commander, Tsung-han 宗翰 (Nien-han 粘罕), to the court, Yeh-lü Ta-shih who was in the northwest maintained contact with Hsi Hsia (CS 74, 6*a*).	
1128		The Chin government dispatched Yeh-lü Yü-tu (I-tu 伊都) with an army to attack Yeh-lü Ta-shih. The Tatars promised to guide him if their heir apparent was sent back (HNYL 181, 3017). The Sung official, Chao Tzŭ-ti 趙子砥, who had been forced by the Jurchen to supervise the	N. D. The Khitāy who fled from China, called their leader and commander in chief gur-

[5] He later surrendered to Chin with Fêng 豐, Fu, and Lin Prefectures (the western part of Suiyuan and the northern part of Shensi) (CS 3, 12*b*).

[6] The Prince of Liang was made "emperor" by Yeh-lü Ti-lieh in the fifth month of 1123, and died in the tenth month. His successor was Yeh-lü Chu-lieh 朮烈, who

was killed in the eleventh month by his followers (LS 29, 6*b*). The Sung government, having learned of the events indirectly, believed that the Prince of Liang was alive in 1124 and for some time afterwards.

[7] Hui-tsung 徽宗 (1101–1125).

[8] Ch'in-tsung 欽宗 (1126–1127).

The growth of the Qarā-Khitāy empire (*continued*)

Year	Month	LS 30	Additional Chinese Sources	Non-Chinese Sources
			transportation of 1,700 wooden blocks of classical texts to Yen, returned to Sung after having stayed in the Chin territory from 1126 to 1128. He reported that Yeh-lü Ta-shih had become the ruler of a new state with the honorific title of Emperor T'ien-yu (*Yen-yün Lu* 燕雲錄 = SCPMHP 98, 14*a*).	khan after he left China (Juwaynī 16, 86) 1128–9 [?].[9] A prince of the destroyed empire of Qarā [*sic!*] Khitāy, Nushi Taifu, fled to the Khirghiz and then to the Uighurs. Finally he came to Turkestan which he conquered, thereupon [?] assuming the title gurkhan (Rashīd ad-Dīn = Bretschneider 88 I, 224–225). 1128 [?]. The gurkhan of China, called the "cripple," attacked Kāshghar but was defeated (Ibn al-Athīr, Chronicle XI, 55 = Barthold, KK, 738).
1129		While Yeh-lü Ta-shih stayed at Pei-t'ing Tu-hu Fu 北庭都護府,[10] he assembled the chiefs of seven prefectures: Wei-wu 威武, Ch'ung-tê 崇德, Hui-fan 會蕃, Hsin 新, Ta-lin 大林, Tzǔ-ho 紫河, and T'o 馳,[12] as well as from eighteen tribes: Big Yellow Shih-wei 大黃室韋, Ti-la 敵剌, Wang-chi-la 王紀剌 (Ongirat), Ch'a-ch'ih-la 茶赤剌 (Djadjirat), Yeh-hsi 也喜, Pi-ku-tê 鼻古德, Ni-la 尼剌, Ta-la-kuai 達剌乖, Ta-mi-li 達密里, Mi-êrh-chi 密兒紀 (Merkit), Ho-chu 合主, Wu-ku-li 烏古里, Tsu-pu 阻卜, P'u-su-wan 普速完, T'ang-ku 唐古 (Tangut), Hu-mu-ssǔ 忽母思, Hsi-ti 奚的, Chiu-êrh-pi 糺而畢. In his address Ta-shih frankly admitted the catastrophe that had occurred, the destruction of the Liao empire and the flight of the last emperor, T'ien-tsu.[14] He	P'o-lu-huo 婆盧火, chief commander of the route of T'ai Prefecture,[11] memorialized that Yeh-lü Ta-shih had already secured two camps among the northern tribes and therefore was hard to control. He was also near the herds. The general suggested that a garrison be set up [in the border regions]. The Chin emperor decided that it would be burdensome for the tribes to mobilize soldiers because of these two camps. It would be sufficient to attend seriously to patrolling and scouting (CS 121, 4*b*).	N. D. The gurkhan, who invaded the territory of the Khirghiz, withdrew after having met armed resistance and moved on to Imīl where he founded a city of this name. The Turks and other peoples together numbered 40,000 households. After an extensive rest, he moved into the region of Balāsāghūn whose khan was in conflict with the Turkic Qarluq and Qanqly tribes. The gurkhan deprived the [Iläk] Khan of his power,[13] confining him to the status of a "ruler of the Turks" (Juwaynī 16, 88). 1128. Various khans of Turkestan had taken into their service Khitāy tribesmen who had fled from their homeland before the gurkhan. The ruler of Samarqand, who controlled about 16,000 Khitāy tents, used

[9] This is probably too early a date for the conquest of Turkestan. Actually it seems to have begun a few years later (see above, A, 3, *b*).

[10] In T'ang time there was a place called Pei-t'ing in the western part of Eastern Turkestan on the site of modern Fu-yüan 孚遠 (LSTLCK 8139). It has, however, been suggested that the Pei-t'ing of LS 30, 4*b* was an old Uighur city, otherwise unknown, near K'o-tun (Liang YT 34, 21–24 and personal communication of Professor Pelliot). Since Yeh-lü Ta-shih appealed to a number of tribes who lived within the northwestern regions of the Liao empire,

the latter assumption seems the more plausible. (For further discussion of this meeting place see HLLKSM 1*a* ff.)

[11] West of the juncture of the Sungari and Nonni Rivers.

[12] According to Liang Yüan-tung, these seven prefectures were probably set up by Yeh-lü Ta-shih after he proclaimed himself king (Liang YT 34, 27).

[13] *Cf.* Barthold, KK, 738.

[14] T'ien-tsu was captured by the Chin soldiers in 1125 (LS 30, 1*b*), a fact which Yeh-lü Ta-shih either did not know or, more probably, tried to conceal from the tribes.

The growth of the Qarā-Khitāy empire (*continued*)

YEAR	MONTH	LS 30	ADDITIONAL CHINESE SOURCES	NON-CHINESE SOURCES
		proclaimed his intention of turning westward and rallying the various barbarian peoples (蕃) to his assistance in order to defeat the enemy and regain his old territory. In response to his moving appeal[15] he obtained more than 10,000 well-trained soldiers. Officials were installed and weapons and equipment were put in order (4*b*–5*a*).		Khitāy men as guards on his eastern frontier. When he, frightened by the prospect of their growing numbers, interfered with their marital life, they bound their supervisors, took their [native ?] wives, and trekked toward Balāsāghūn, upsetting the peace of its khan. When the gurkhan arrived, they all joined him, doubling his strength. With their aid he succeeded in conquering the whole of Turkestan (Ibn al-Athīr XII, 55–56 = Marquart 14, 164–165; *cf.* also Bretschneider 88 I, 232). While he stayed in Balāsāghūn, the gurkhan dispatched governors into the surrounding regions. His people lived well and his herds grew fat. He subdued the Qanqly[16] and sent troops to Kāshghar and Khotan; both towns were taken (Juwaynī 16, 88).
1130		(2) On the day *chia-wu*[17] Yeh-lü Ta-shih sacrificed a grey ox and a white horse to Heaven and Earth and to his ancestors, and the troops were made ready for the march to the west. A letter was dispatched to the Bilgä 畢勒哥 [Khaghan], king of the Uighurs,[19] explaining why his army had to pass through the Uighur territory on its way to Ta-shih 大食.[20] He reminded the	The Chin chief commander sent Yeh-lü Yü-tu, Shih-chia-nu 石家奴, and Pa-li-su 拔离速 to pursue Yeh-lü Ta-shih. An order was sent to various tribes to mobilize soldiers, but the tribal chieftains disobeyed them. Shih-chia-nu went as far as the Wu-na 兀納 River and returned. Yeh-lü Yü-tu reported to the headquarters of the chief com-	1129/30 The Arslan-Khan of Samarqand challenged by his mercenaries (Qarluq and Ghuz Turks) appealed to his sovereign, the Saljūqid Sultan of Persia, Sanjar,[18] for help. When Sanjar appeared at Samarqand the Qarluq fled (Ibn al-Athīr XI, 54–55 = Marquart 14, 165). 1130. According to Hamd-Allāh Mustawfī 1848, 336 [first

[15] For a full translation of his speech see Bretschneider 88 I, 213–214.

[16] Abūʾl-Ghāzī [seventeenth century] speaks of the many Turks, in the main Qanqly, who, camping near Balāsāghūn, incessantly plundered the country and destroyed the crops (Aboul-Ghāzi 74, 50; *cf.* also 37). Marquart (14, 164) believes that the author of *The History of the Mongols and Tatars* confuses them with the Qarluq who indeed together with the Türkmens lived in this region.

[17] According to the analysis of Haneda Toru, Yeh-lü Ta-shih departed from the Orkhon River region about 1130 (Haneda 16, 217 ff.). Liang Yüan-tung confirms this thesis by pointing to the fact that the second month of 1130 had a day *chia-wu*, whereas none of the preceding five years, 1125–1129, had such a date (Liang YT 34, 38 ff.).

[18] The sultan's name has been transcribed differently as Sanjar (Browne 28 II, 11 *passim*) and Sinjar (Barthold 28, *passim*). The problem arises out of the lack of vocalization in the original text. Professor Pelliot, in a personal communication, prefers Sanjar. We follow this suggestion, which, according to Dr. Menges, implies Turkic origin of the name: *sandž-ar*, nomen aoristi of *sandž-*, means "piercing with a lance." The transcription Sanjar is confirmed also by the Latinized form Samiardi or Saniardi (see below, note 33).

[19] The term *bilgä*, "sage," occurs early as part of the title of the Uighur rulers (see Chavannes-Pelliot 13, 189; Radloff, WB IV, 1767–1768).

[20] The gurkhan perhaps remembered the contacts established by the Liao emperor, Shêng-tsung, with the Qarā-Khānid country of "Ta-shih" by means of a political

The growth of the Qarā-Khitāy empire (*continued*)

Year	Month	LS 30	Additional Chinese Sources	Non-Chinese Sources
		Uighur ruler of the friendly relations that had existed between the Ch'i-tan and Uighurs from T'ai-tsu's time and asked him not to entertain any suspicions. The Uighur ruler welcomed Yeh-lü Ta-shih at his residence where the guests were feasted for three days. On the occasion of Yeh-lü Ta-shih's departure the ruler offered him 600 horses, 100 camels, and 3,000 sheep; he also delivered some of his descendants as hostages, thus expressing his subordination, and accompanied him beyond the borders of his country (5a–b).	mander that, according to the information received, Yeh-lü Ta-shih had gone to the territory of Ho-chou [Kao-ch'ang]. He might have formed an alliance with Hsi Hsia. Messengers should be sent there to demand his extradition. The Hsia government replied to the Chin request that its country did not border Ho-chou and that it was not informed of Yeh-lü Ta-shih's whereabouts (CS 120, 2a; 121, 4b).	version completed in 1330], the Arslan-Khan defied Sanjar, who took Samarqand, but afterwards re-instated the rebel (*cf.* also Hamd-Allāh Mustawfī 13, 101).
[1131][21]		Yeh-lü Ta-shih called his reign title Yen-ch'ing 延慶. He conferred honorific titles upon his ancestors, and upon his wife and the forefathers of forty-nine high dignitaries (6a).		
1131			(Spring) The Chin commander in chief, Nien-han, suggested the mobilization of 20,000 Chinese and Jurchen troops under Yeh-lü Yü-tu's experienced leadership for an attack on Yeh-lü Ta-shih (TCKC 7, 1b; CHHC 10, 123). Yü-tu planned to establish garrison fields at Ho-tung [K'o-tun] (SMCW 12a). When he advanced against this city, provisions had to be transported by people conscripted in Shan-hsi and Ho-pei; these men never returned (HNYL 43, 786).	
			(Fall) When Yeh-lü Yü-tu reached K'o-tun, Yeh-lü Ta-shih and his followers had left the place, going northward. Yü-tu withdrew because his reserves of food were exhausted[22] (HNYL 47, 854).	N. D. The gurkhan pacified Beshbalyq, and sent armies to Ferghāna and Transoxania; both territories were conquered (Juwaynī 16, 88).

marriage (see I, introduction, note 108; *cf.* also I, 2 (10), no. 46).

[21] See above, A, 3, b.

[22] A memorial ascribed to Tsung-han (Nien-han) says that the Chin soldiers fought Yeh-lü Ta-shih for three days and nights, but lack of food, the cold which killed soldiers and horses, and a mutiny so seriously affected the Chin army that it suffered defeat and had to withdraw (SCPMHP 178, 7a).

The growth of the Qarā-Khitāy empire (*continued*)

YEAR	MONTH	LS 30	ADDITIONAL CHINESE SOURCES	NON-CHINESE SOURCES
	9		The Uighurs of Ho-chou delivered to Chin some of Yeh-lü Ta-shih's fighters whom they had captured (CS 3, 15*b*).	
	10		A Sung official, Wang Tsao 汪藻, submitted a memorial to his emperor in which he suggested the establishment of friendly relations with Yeh-lü Ta-shih, who, as he had learned, was preparing in the northern region for the restoration of the Liao empire. Wang thought that, since Yeh-lü Ta-shih was still weak at this time, it would be easy to conclude an alliance with him against the Chin army. The Sung chief commander, Chang Chün 張浚, in Shensi might dispatch some courageous men with sizable gifts as envoys to Yeh-lü Ta-shih (SCPMHP 148, 8*b* ff.).	
N.D.			Yeh-lü Ta-shih summoned the *Chiu* 紇 Troops and went northward in search of grass and water. When he reached the Yin Mountains some years later, he could not proceed because of snow and rocks. He then used camels instead of carts. He entered the Hui-hu country, seized its territory, and established a kingdom there (*Pei Shih Chi* = KHCCL 6*a*).	
1132	9		Because Yeh-lü Yü-tu, during his advance to K'o-tun City, had lost the golden tablet[23] given to him by the Chin government, he was suspected of having secretly communicated with the enemy. Discontented with his treatment and embittered because members of his family were kept as hostages, he rebelled with other high Ch'i-tan dignitaries[24] (CS 3, 16*a*; SMCW 12*b*).	

[23] From 1116 on the Jurchen gave a gold tablet to a commander of ten thousand households (萬戶). It was a symbol of authority (*cf.* CS 58, 1*a*).

[24] The revolt and final execution of Yeh-lü Yü-tu and several other Ch'i-tan dignitaries are described in a number of works. The earliest and most detailed report is contained in SMCW 12*b* ff. and the inscription, *Wan-yen Kung Shên-tao Pei* 完顏公神道碑 (MCCSC 3, 13*b*), which confirm each other.

The growth of the Qarā-Khitāy empire (*continued*)

YEAR	MONTH	LS 30	ADDITIONAL CHINESE SOURCES	NON-CHINESE SOURCES
1133		Yeh-lü Ta-shih returned to the East, founded the capital, Hu-ssŭ Ordo 虎思斡耳朵, and changed his reign title to K'ang-kuo 康國 (6a–b).		
1134	3	He sent an army of 70,000 horsemen under the command of Hsiao Wo-li-la 斡里剌 eastward to the Desert to restore the glory of Liao, but the troops, who marched forward for 10,000 *li*,[25] suffered great losses in oxen and horses without achieving anything. When the exhausted soldiers returned, Yeh-lü Ta-shih sighed: "Heaven does not favor me. This is Its will!" (6b).[26]		
	7		A Chin Chinese, Yü-wên Hsü-chung 宇文虛中, in a confidential letter written with alum, advised the Sung commander, Chang Chün, to pursue an aggressive policy toward Chin in view of Yeh-lü Ta-shih's growing power (HNYL 78, 1279).	
			N. D. After the defeat of Liao by the Chin soldiers, Yeh-lü Ta-shih with several thousand men turned to the northwest where he settled down after more than ten years of wandering (HYCCC 1, 30a).	
			N. D. Someone told Ch'ang-ch'un that the Liao remnants had fled to Hsin-ssŭ-kan [Samarqand], the best territory of the Hui-ho,[27] setting up their capital there (HYCCC 1, 16b).	
1135/6				Sanjar fought the Khwā-razm-shāh Atsiz. In a treaty he finally recognized Atsiz's claim to his territory (Hamd-Allāh Mustawfī 1848, 336–337).
1137		N. D. Yeh-lü Ta-shih marching farther west conquered many countries and seized a rich booty of camels, horses, oxen, sheep, and valuable goods (5b).	Reports reached Sung that remnants of the Ch'i-tan led by Ta-shih and daily gaining in military strength, controlled a considerable territory. Hence the Liao empire	Muḥammad of Samarqand defeated by the gurkhan (Ibn al-Athīr = Bretschneider 88 I, 232).

[25] Probably figuratively for many *li*, i.e., very far.
[26] *Cf.* Bretschneider 88 I, 216–217.
[27] In the twelfth century Hui-ho 回紇 meant either Uighur or Moslem. But, since our passage mentions Samarqand, it would seem that the designation Hui-ho here has to be taken in the second sense.

The growth of the Qarā-Khitāy empire (*continued*)

YEAR	MONTH	LS 30	ADDITIONAL CHINESE SOURCES	NON-CHINESE SOURCES
			continued to exist (HNYL 114, 1854).	
1140	4		A member of the Liao consort clan, Hsiao Ho-ta 合達,[28] escorted a Liao princess, Ch'êng-an 成安, to Hsi Hsia, where she was married to the king. Disagreeing with the Hsia ruler concerning the policy of submission to Chin, he felt very uneasy when the Liao princess died. He dispatched messengers to the Western Regions in search of Yeh-lü Ta-shih, but they returned without locating him (HHSS 35, 9a; HKCCC 13, 2b).	
[1141]		Eventually he reached Hsin-ssŭ-kan 尋思干 where he met an army of 100,000, comprised of soldiers from various western countries under the command of Hu-êrh-shan 忽兒珊 [Khurāsān].[30] Ta-shih arranged his army in three parts and attacked the enemy. The western troops were completely defeated; their corpses covered the ground for ten *li*. The Moslem kings surrendered and offered him tribute. After a rest of ninety days he proceeded farther west to Ch'i-êrh-man 起兒漫 [Karmīnīya].[32]		[1141][29] In 1145 the Bishop of Gabula [Djebāl], Syria, during a visit to Italy, narrated that "a few years ago a certain John, who dwells beyond Persia and Armenia in the extreme Orient, a king and a priest and a Christian with his whole nation, though a Nestorian, conducted a war against the Kings of the Persians and Medes, brothers who were called Samiardi [or Samardi or Saniardi[31]]. . . . They fought for three days. . . . Presbyter Johannes, for thus they used to call him, yet having routed

[28] He was given the surname Li 李 by the king of Hsi Hsia. When he rebelled, he concluded an alliance with other Liao elements in what is now Suiyuan. He planned to restore the Liao empire, but was finally defeated and killed (HHSS 35, 9a–b).

[29] Otto von Freisingen, who completed his *Chronicon* in 1146, heard the bishop's story in 1145, but his record contains no exact date for the great battle: it is said to have taken place "not many years ago (*ante non multos annos*)." However, another contemporary history which leans heavily on Otto's *Chronicon* and which continues the *Annales Admuntenses* from 1140 on, places the battle in the year 1141: "Johannes presbyter rex Armeniae et Indiae cum duobus regibus fratribus Persarum et Medorum pugnavit, et vicit" (Annales Admuntenses, 580). Zarncke, who is fully aware of the later chronicle's dependence upon the former work, is puzzled by the accuracy of the date, which, despite the improbability of such an assumption, almost suggests an independent source (Zarncke 79, 850).

[30] Bretschneider finds "some resemblance" to Khwā-razm-shāh. But, whereas the Mohammedan historians do not record a battle between this ruler of the Saljuqs and

the gurkhan, "they mention . . . a great defeat of the Seldjuk Sultan *Sangiar* of Khorasan by the Gurkhan of Kara Khitai" (Bretschneider 88 I, 215, note 554). Haneda (16, 224) and Liang YT (34, 43) both take Hu-êrh-shan as referring to Khurāsān. Sanjar was indeed for twenty years governor of Khurāsān, before he "for forty years and four months" became the sultan of Persia (Hamd-Allāh Mustawfī 1848, 334). Marquart (14, 166), following de Groot, rejects Bretschneider's interpretation of the problematic word as designating a prince and takes it instead as an Arab term meaning volunteers who rob and kill on the path of Allah. Pelliot (20, 173) evidently does not accept this rendering as he states that Bretschneider's explanation is actually in conformity with that given in the old glossary attached to the *Liao Shih* (116, 13a), where Hu-êrh-shan is defined as 西域大將軍名, the name of the military commander of the Western Countries.

[31] For these textual variants see Ottonis Frisingensis Chronicon, 266, note *h*.

[32] Between Bukhārā and Samarqand (Barthold 28, 97).

The growth of the Qarā-Khitāy empire (*continued*)

YEAR	MONTH	LS 30	ADDITIONAL CHINESE SOURCES	NON-CHINESE SOURCES
		There he was proclaimed emperor (5b–6a).		the Persians, emerged victorious from the most atrocious slaughter" (Ottonis Frisingensis Chronicon, 266).[33]
				The *Chahār Maqāla* states: "The Gūr Khān of Khitā fought a battle with the King of the World Sanjar . . . at the gates of Samarqand, and so fateful was the day to the army of Islām that Transoxania passed into his power" (Nidhāmī-i-'Arūdī [d. 1161] 99, 650).
1140/1				Sanjar again supported the khan of Samarqand against the Qarluq, who, on their part, again appealed to the gurkhan for help.[34] The gurkhan, in a letter, declared himself protector of the Qarluq and asked Sanjar to forgive them. The sultan rejected these proposals, invited the gurkhan to adopt Islām and tried to impress him with the size and equipment of his troops. His army comprised soldiers from many Moslem countries; the gurkhan commanded Turks, soldiers from China and Khitāy.
1141				On September 9 or 10, Sanjar was disastrously defeated at Qaṭawān not far from Samarqand. Sanjar escaped, but his wife and many of his highest dignitaries were captured (Ibn al-Athīr XI, 54–67 = Marquart 14, 165; Bretschneider 88 I, 232; *cf.* also Barthold 28, 316).
1140/1				Sanjar set out to combat the gurkhan of Khitāy. He was defeated, and Transoxania fell into the hands of the non-

[33] The story of a "presbyter Johannes" is possibly foreshadowed by a tale told in 1122 concerning a fabulous Indian patriarch Johannes; but, according to our present knowledge, Otto von Freisingen is the first to mention the "presbyter" as the eastern ruler who defeated the kings of Persia, Samiardi, or Saniardi [actually Sanjar and his followers]. (For a detailed discussion of the origin of the legend of Prester John see Oppert 70, 100 ff. and with elaborate scholarly analysis, Zarncke 79, 847 ff.)

[34] In another version, Ibn al-Athīr (XI, 53 = Barthold 28, 327) tells that Atsiz invited the Qarā-Khitāy to attack Sanjar because of vindictiveness (Marquart 14, 165, note 3). Barthold considers this explanation merely a rumor, which arose because "Sinjar's defeat was so opportune for Atsiz." Obviously in order to show the absurdity of the story, he notes that, according to Juwaynī, Atsiz's territory was also plundered (Barthold 28, 327).

The growth of the Qarā-Khitāy empire (*continued*)

YEAR MONTH	LS 30	ADDITIONAL CHINESE SOURCES	NON-CHINESE SOURCES
			believers. Many soldiers of the sultan were killed. The gurkhan captured many distinguished persons whom he afterwards returned to Sanjar (Hamd-Allāh Mustawfī 1848, 337).
N.D.			At Qaṭawān, a battle took place "between the army of Islām and the infidels of the Qarā-Khitāy, when a great multitude of Moslems was martyred." The memory of this martyrdom was still alive in the fourteenth century (Hamd-Allāh Mustawfī 19, 238). After the conquest of Ferghāna and Transoxania, the ruler of the latter country began to obey the gurkhan's orders. He sent his general, Arbuz[?], to Khwārazm. After a devastating campaign, the ruler, Atsiz, submitted and agreed to pay an annual tribute of cattle, goods, and 30,000 dinars (Juwaynī 16, 88).
N. D.			After executing the Imām of the East Ḥusāmu'd-Dīn, the gurkhan bestowed Bukhārā on Alptägin (Nidhāmī-i-ʿArūdī 99, 650).
1141/2			The citadel of Bukhārā restored by Alptägin, the Qarā-Khitāy ruler of the town (Barthold 28, 100).
N. D.			After his victory over Sanjar, and before his departure, the gurkhan had entrusted the son of Bayānāni, the nephew of Atsiz Khwārazm-shāh, to the Imām Aḥmad b. ʿAbdu'l-ʿAzīz "who was the Imām of Bukhārā, and the leading man of his time, so that whatever he did he might do by his advice, and that he should not take any step without his instructions. Then the Gūr Khān turned back and retired to Barsjān.[35] . . . But

[35] The identity of Barsjān is uncertain (Nidhāmī-i-ʿArūdī 99, 651). Herrmann's map of 1141 has a town of Barskhan northeast of Kāshghar and east of Balāsāghūn (Herrmann 35, 46–47, C-2). Such a location makes sense in view of the "wide distance" which separated the gurkhan from Bukhārā when the mission arrived.

The growth of the Qarā-Khitāy empire (*continued*)

Year	Month	LS 30	Additional Chinese Sources	Non-Chinese Sources
				when Alptagīn saw a clear field, he turned his hand to oppression, and began to levy contributions on Bukhārā. So several of the people of Bukhārā went on an embassy to the Gūr Khān to seek redress. The Gūr Khān, after the way of good Muslims,[36] wrote a letter in Persian to Alptagīn as follows: '*In the Name of God, the Merciful, the Clement. Let Alptagīn know that, although wide distance separates us, our approval and displeasure are near at hand. Let Alptagīn do that which Aḥmad commands, and Aḥmad that which Muḥammad commands. Farewell*'" (Nidhāmi-i-'Arūdī 99, 650–651).
1143		In the tenth year of the reign period K'ang-kuo, the emperor, died. His temple title was Tê-tsung 德宗.[37] His rule had lasted twenty years (6*b*).	N. D. Tê-tsung died after having occupied the throne for more than thirty [*sic*!] years (*Pei Shih Chi* = KHCCL 6*a*).	1142/3. The gurkhan remained in Transoxania until his death which occurred early in 1143[38] (Ibn al-Athīr = Bretschneider 88 I, 233).
			N. D. Yeh-lü Ta-shih escaped from China, conquered several tens of countries, and established a country of several ten thousands of *li* in circumference in less than twenty years (CJCSWC 12, 170).	N. D. After the conclusion of the peace treaty with Atsiz, Arbuz[?] returned; the gurkhan died soon afterwards (Juwaynī 16, 88).
			N. D. The people of the West [Central Asia] remembered him at the time of the Mongol invasion because he promoted the development of culture (CJCSWC 12, 170).	N. D. After the defeat of Sanjar, the gurkhans controlled all the rulers of Turkestan; their power continued for about eighty years (Tabakat-i-Nasiri 81 II, 901).

Ibn al-Athīr says that the gurkhan remained in Transoxania until his death in 1143. Since the *Chahār Maqāla* was compiled by a contemporary writer who finished his work about one hundred years before Ibn al-Athīr's history, we do not dare to disregard his testimony in favor of the later writer. Perhaps the gurkhan "turned back" at least temporarily; or perhaps Barsjān is not Barskhan, but an undefined place somewhere in Transoxania.

[36] For the implications of this statement see below, C, 6, *b*.

[37] This title is also given in the *Pei Shih Chi* 北使記, a work written down by the Chin scholar, Liu Ch'i 劉祁, as told to him by Wu-ku-sun Chung-tuan 吾古孫仲端 in 1221 (KHCCL 6*a*). Bretschneider's remarks concerning the authorship of this book are incorrect.

[38] See above, A, 3.

3. QARĀ–KHITĀY FROM 1144 TO 1211

YEAR	MONTH	LS 30	ADDITIONAL CHINESE SOURCES	NON-CHINESE SOURCES
[1144]		Because of the youth of the heir apparent, I-lieh 夷列, Yeh-lü Ta-shih's wife, T'a-pu-yen 塔不煙, in accordance with her late husband's will, assumed power. Her honorific title was Empress Kan-t'ien 感天 and her reign title Hsien-ch'ing 咸清. She occupied the throne for seven years (7a).	1144. The Uighurs sent to Chin envoys who offered tribute and announced the death of Yeh-lü Ta-shih. According to their report, Ta-shih's people lived close to them (the Uighurs). Nien-k'o Han-nu was ordered to follow the envoys to obtain information regarding the Hsi Liao; he was never heard of again (CS 121, 4b).	N. D. The gurkhan was succeeded by his daughter, who died soon afterwards. She was succeeded by her mother; finally the son of the gurkhan[1] ascended the throne (Ibn al-Athīr = Bretschneider 88 I, 233).
1146			Nien-k'o Han-nu was killed by Ta-shih[2] (CS 4, 11a).	After the gurkhan's death, his wife, Göjüng, succeeded him (Juwaynī 16, 88).
			[From Sa-li-ya's report, in 1175/6]: Han-nu traveled via Ho-chou [Qočo]. When the envoy arrived, Ta-shih[3] was hunting. Asked why he did not dismount, Han-nu answered that, since he came as the messenger of the Son of Heaven, it was Ta-shih's duty to dismount and to listen to the imperial order. Thereupon he was pulled down from his horse and executed (CS 121, 5a–b).	N. D. When the Qarā-Khitāy "became supreme, the chief men [ministers ?] among them, in succession to each other, were several persons, and those who lived near unto my time, and of whom I have heard from narrators, were I-mā, Sunkam, Arbaz, Jūmā, and Bānīko [of Ṭāraz],[4] and their sovereign was a woman, and, at last, after that female, there was a man, and his title was the Gūr Khān" (Tabakat-i-Nasiri 81 II, 911).
[1151]		I-lieh ascended the throne. His reign title was Shao-hsing 紹興. Registering the people who were eighteen years and over, the government found 84,500 households[5] (7a).		
[1155]			Chingis Khan born (HYS 2, 6606).	
1156			The Chin general, P'o-lung-tun 婆隆敦, was appointed left general supervisor to direct troops in tilling the land at Ho-tung 曷董 City. Ta-shih's son Wu-lü 烏律 [I-lieh ?] sent sev-	Atsiz died (Juwaynī II, 13 and Ibn al-Athīr = Barthold 28, 331). The Qarluqs killed the ruler of Samarqand. His successor

[1] In the version used by Bretschneider the son's name is given as Muḥammad. According to Barthold (KK, 739), "the latter, of course, cannot have been called Muḥammad." For Marquart's attempt to solve the problem, see below, C, note 218.

[2] After Yeh-lü Ta-shih's death the tribes north and northwest of China continued to designate his successors as Ta-shih (CS 121, 5b). Chin and Sung writers followed this practice.

[3] According to CS 121, Han-nu left Chin after Yeh-lü Ta-shih's death in 1144, when Hsi Liao was ruled by Empress Kan-t'ien. If the story can be trusted, it must have been she, the new "Ta-shih," whom the envoy met. The story was told about thirty years later, and it is not impossible that the informants confused the empress either with her son, I-lieh, or a high dignitary who represented her on this occasion. But such an interpretation is scarcely necessary in view of the Ch'i-tan tradition that permitted empresses and princesses not only to participate in ceremonial hunts, but also to lead armies and to conduct independent military expeditions.

[4] Interpolation by the translator.

[5] That is, households that could provide adult males above eighteen for military and other service.

Qarā-Khitāy from 1144 to 1211 (continued)

Year	Month	LS 30	Additional Chinese Sources	Non-Chinese Sources
			eral hundred patrol horsemen to lead the army. They retired after having talked with the messengers of P'o-lung-tun (TCKC 14, 1a).	punished the Qarluqs, whose surviving chiefs fled to Īl-Arslan of Khwārazm (Ibn al-Athīr XI, 205 and Juwaynī II, 14 = Barthold 28, 333).
1158				The Khan of Samarqand appealed to the nomad Türkmens and the Qarā-Khitāy for help against Īl-Arslan. The Qarā-Khitāy dispatched 10,000 men led by Iläk-Türkmän; but, faced with Īl-Arslan's superior strength, their general concluded peace, using Samarqand dignitaries as mediators (Juwaynī II, 15 = Barthold 28, 333–334).
1161			A Ch'i-tan named Sa-pa 撒八 who had revolted against Chin was pursued by Chin soldiers. With a group of followers he fled westward along the Kerulen River, heading for Western Liao. Some of his companions objected and killed him (CS 132, 8b; 133, 6b).	
1163		I-lieh died. His temple title was Jên-tsung 仁宗. He had occupied the throne for thirteen years (7a).		
[1164]		Because I-lieh's son was still of tender age, the late emperor's younger sister, P'u-su-wan 普速完,[6] assumed power in accordance with her brother's expressed will. The reign title was changed to Ch'ung-fu 崇福. She was Empress Ch'êng-t'ien 承天 (7a).		
1171–1172[7]				The Qarā-Khitāy invaded Khwārazm, whose shāh had failed to pay tribute on the fixed date. The Khwārazm advance guard was defeated, but the destruction of the dams halted the Qarā-Khitāy attack. In March 1172 the shāh died in his capital (Ibn al-Athīr XI, 246 and Juwaynī II, 17 = Barthold 28, 336–337).

[6] Her surname was Kan 甘, according to *Pei Shih Chi* (KHCCL 6a).

[7] The sources differ concerning the date of Īl-Arslan's death, but Barthold (28, 336–337) plausibly explains his acceptance of Ibn al-Athīr's version which we also follow.

Qarā-Khitāy from 1144 to 1211 (*continued*)

Year	Month	LS 30	Additional Chinese Sources	Non-Chinese Sources
				[1172]. The shāh, Īl-Arslan, "is attacked by the Qarā-Khitāy, falls sick, and suffers defeat. He dies"[8] (Hamd-Allāh Mustawfī 13, 112).
1172				Īl-Arslan's eldest son, Takash [or Tukush[9]], seeing his younger brother raised to the throne through his mother's intervention, fled to the Qarā-Khitāy whose female ruler supported him. He then prevailed over his brother and, in December 1172, ascended the throne in his capital (Ibn al-Athīr XI, 247 and Juwaynī II, 17–19 = Barthold 28, 337–338; *cf.* also Hamd-Allāh Mustawfī 13, 112).
1175			Three I-hsi-lan 移習覽 [Islām ?] Hui-ho[10] came to the Southwestern Punitive Office of Chin in order to trade. They revealed that they belonged to the barbarian Tsou-k'uo 鄒括 tribe and that the town where they lived was called Ku-ssŭ O-lu-to 骨斯訛魯朵 [Ghuz-ordo].[11] Their elders had told them that when the Ch'i-tan came, the Hui-ho, unable to resist, submitted. During recent years the imperial son-in-law, A-pên-ssŭ 阿本斯 [wrong reading for 阿不斯 ? *Abuz = Arbuz ?],[12] led 50,000 soldiers to the north against the Yeh-pu-lien 葉不	

---

[8] The *Ta'rīkh-i-Guzīda* has the earlier date, A. H. 558 [= 1162]. The translator (Hamd-Allāh Mustawfī 13, 112, note 2) prefers Juwaynī's date, 560 [= 1164]. He also mentions Ibn al-Athīr's date, 1172. See preceding note.

[9] Or Tägiš (suggested by Professor Pelliot). Maḥmūd al-Kāshgharī (Brockelmann 28, 250) lists a Turkic name Täkiš, which evidently is identical with the name in question. The word is a verbal noun in -*iš* from *täg-* meaning in Orkhon-Turkic and Chaghatai "to attack, make an assault, assault," and in other Turkic languages, "to reach, arrive" (Radloff, WB III, 1028–1029, 1036).

[10] The Chinese text has 回紇, which Bretschneider (88 I, 222) transcribes phonetically "Hui-hu" without making an attempt to explain it. As already stated, Hui-ho in the twelfth century meant either Uighur or Moslem. The

traders mentioned in CS 121 called their home region Ku-ssŭ Ordo which obviously is Hu-ssŭ Ordo (*cf.* KTCL 14, 3*a*; Bretschneider 88 I, 22, note 571), the Qarā-Khitāy capital at or near Balāsāghūn. Balāsāghūn, like Kāshghar, was an old Turkic settlement which from the tenth century on "was regarded as a Mohammedan town" (Barthold, "Balāsāghūn," 615; *cf. idem* 28, 254 ff.; *idem* 35, 78; Marquart 12, 492 ff.). If the identification of Ku-ssŭ Ordo with Balāsāghūn is correct, then it is highly probable that in our story the term Hui-ho means Moslems rather than Uighurs.

[11] Personal communication from Professor Pelliot. See also note 38.

[12] Personal communication from Professor Pelliot. This reading would equate the name with Juwaynī's (16, 88) Arbuz. The form, however, is uncertain. For the various textual variants see *loc. cit.*, note 9.

Qarā-Khitāy from 1144 to 1211 (*continued*)

YEAR	MONTH	LS 30	ADDITIONAL CHINESE SOURCES	NON-CHINESE SOURCES

| | | | 輦 and other tribes, returning, however, without success. Fighting continued. | |

In the same year the chieftains of the Nien-pa-ên 粘拔恩 tribe,[13] leading the chieftain of the K'ang-li 康里[14] with more than 30,000 households, asked to submit to the Chin government. They handed over the tablets and seals which Yeh-lü Ta-shih had originally granted them (CS 121, 4*b*–5*a*; 7, 7*b*).

1177

The Chin emperor, Shih-tsung, sent officials to inspect the frontier. They secured four men who came from Western Liao. The emperor ordered that the [Chin] Ch'i-tan should be properly settled. If Western Liao influenced them, trouble might arise along the frontier (CS 88, 16*b*–17*a*).

[1177]

Empress Ch'êng-t'ien was married to Hsiao To-lu-pu 朵魯不, but maintained illicit relations with his younger brother, the *sha-li*[15] Hsiao P'u-ku-chih 朴古只沙里. After making her husband Prince of Tung-p'ing,[17] she had him murdered. The father [of the brothers], Hsiao Wo-li-la, put troops around the palace, and both the empress and her lover were shot to death. Ch'êng-t'ien had occupied the throne for fourteen years (7*a*).

N. D. The first gurkhan's widow ruled with the support of relatives. She indulged in a life of sensuality and was killed with her lover.[16] A brother of the gurkhan was chosen as ruler, although he was not the legitimate heir[18] (Juwaynī 16, 89).

[1178]

Chih-lu-ku 直魯古, I-lieh's second son, ascended the throne. His reign title was T'ien-hsi 天禧. He occupied the throne for thirty-four years (7*a*).

---

[13] Probably identical with Nien-pa-ko (*cf.* I, 2 (9), no. 6).

[14] The Qanqli, Qanqly, or Qangli of the Moslem sources (*cf.* Marquart 14, 78 ff.).

[15] The title *sha-li* occurs already in the early days of Liao history (LS 1, 1*b*). Obviously it is a Ch'i-tan word. LS 116, 2*a* equates it with the Chinese term *lang-chün* 郎君, court noble.

[16] Juwaynī evidently confuses Yeh-lü Ta-shih's widow with his daughter, Ch'êng-t'ien.

[17] In the Liao period this title was bestowed upon persons of great distinction (see LS 17, 8*a*; 88, 3*a*).

[18] The second part of Juwaynī's statement confirms, in some degree, the official Chinese record. I-lieh left orders that his younger sister was to rule as his "son" was immature. After her death his "second son" (次子) ascended the throne (see [1178], LS 30, 7*a*). Very possibly I-lieh had thought of another son (the eldest?) as his eventual successor.

Qarā-Khitāy from 1144 to 1211 (*continued*)

YEAR	MONTH	LS 30	ADDITIONAL CHINESE SOURCES	NON-CHINESE SOURCES
[–1181][19]				The Qarā-Khitāy envoy to the court of Khwārazm, who came to collect the tribute, behaved arrogantly. Takash had him killed. His younger brother, thereupon, tried to dethrone the latter with the gurkhan's aid. Takash, however, repelled the Qarā-Khitāy army by flooding the country. The gurkhan continued to support Takash's brother who succeeded in establishing his rule over a considerable territory, including Merv, Sarakhs, and Ṭūs (Ibn al-Athīr XI, 248 ff. and Juwaynī II, 19 = Barthold 28, 339).
1185	4		Sung spies reported that Ta-shih planned to attack Chin by way of Hsi Hsia. The emperor secretly ordered the chief commander, Wu T'ing 吳挺, and another high official, Liu Chêng 留正, to discuss the matter (SS 35, 17*a*; 486, 21*b*).	
			The report of Yeh-lü Ta-shih's intended expedition aroused the Sung court. The emperor discussed the matter with his courtiers orally and in writing. Some days afterwards the emperor received a report from Hsü-i 盱眙[20] that eight thousand Chin soldiers had crushed the Ch'i-tan. The emperor was alarmed, but some officials thought that the report had been deliberately fabricated by the Chin government (FCL 3, 9*a*–12*b*).	
1186	4		The Sung emperor directed Wu T'ing to conclude an alliance with Hsi Hsia (SS 35, 18*b*; 486, 21*b*; *cf.* also MKC 93, 27*b*).	
			The Sung emperor planned to send a messenger to Wu T'ing with an imperial letter instructing him to say that if the Hsi Hsia permitted Ta-shih to cross their territory, their	

---

[19] If Takash's brother incorporated certain territories after his victory of May 1181 (Barthold 28, 339), then the Qarā-Khitāy tax-collector cannot have been killed in 1192, as Sykes (30 II, 53) suggests.

[20] Modern Ssŭ 泗 County, Anhui.

Qarā-Khitāy from 1144 to 1211 (continued)

Year	Month	LS 30	Additional Chinese Sources	Non-Chinese Sources
			king would be made emperor with a status equal to that of the Sung ruler. Chou Pi-ta 周必大 suggested that the emperor be cautious since the Hsi Hsia were not trustworthy (FCL 4, 12a–b).	
1188			The Chin official, Wan-yen Hsiang 完顏襄, returned from a mission to the northern tribes. He presented a map to his emperor and developed a plan to control the dependent tribes and to keep the country of Ta-shih 大石 in check. His proposals were accepted (CS 94, 5b; for the date see CS 8, 24a).	
1190			A tribal chief of Western Liao offered to pay annual tribute to Chin, whereupon Wan-yen An-kuo 完顏安國 was dispatched to meet him. The chieftain respectfully received him in his tent (CS 94, 11b).	
1194[21]	2		The Kerait chieftain, Wang-Khan 汪罕, who was attacked by his brother and the Naiman chieftain, asked the Hsi Hsia king to permit him to travel through his territory to Western Liao. The king of Hsi Hsia gave him food and other provisions and allowed him to go to Western Liao through the country of the Uighurs (HHSS 38, 2a; YS 1, 6a–b; SWCCL 15a–b).	

[21] The earliest Mongol and Chinese histories of the period, the *Yüan-ch'ao Pi Shih* and *Shêng-wu Ch'in-chêng Lu*, report, but do not date, Wang-Khan's visit in Hsi Liao; nor does the *Yüan Shih* date it. According to Hsi Hsia records of late compilation, Wang-Khan departed for the [Black] Ch'i-tan country in the second month of 1173; he passed through Hsi Hsia on his way back in the tenth month of 1174 (HHSS 38, 2a–3b). This would place the event at a time when Chingis Khan was not yet twenty years old—if the statement concerning his birth is correct. In view of the role played by Chingis Khan in the story, this seems impossible.

Wang Kuo-wei in his commentary to the *Shêng-wu Ch'in-chêng Lu* bases himself on Rashīd ad-Dīn, who states that Wang-Khan was on his way from Qarā-Khitāy at the close of the year of the hare [A. H. 591 (YSIWCP 1A, 14b)—1195]. Wang Kuo-wei concludes

that Wang-Khan fled from his home country not later than the year of the tiger [1194], because the long two-way journey plus the sojourn in Hsi Liao must have lasted at least a year or two (SWCCL 15b). YSIWCP 1A, 15a gives 1196 as the date of Wang-Khan's return; this date, evidently taken from Rashīd ad-Dīn, coincides with that offered in HYS 2, 6606. If in accordance with the last named source we assume that Wang-Khan made the arduous voyage back in 1195, perhaps passing through Hsi Hsia in the tenth month, as HHSS 38 claims, and meeting the Mongol envoy early in 1196, we arrive at a chronology which coordinates practically all statements available, except the Hsi Hsia year dates and those in MWESC 2, 15a which claims that Wang-Khan went to Qarā-Khitāy in the autumn of 1196 and returned in the autumn of 1198.

Qarā-Khitāy from 1144 to 1211 (*continued*)

YEAR	MONTH	LS 30	ADDITIONAL CHINESE SOURCES	NON-CHINESE SOURCES
1195			The Kerait chieftain, Wang-Khan, who could not live peaceably with the people of Western Liao, returned to the territory of Hsi Hsia. His followers robbed the people. The Hsi Hsia expelled him (HHSS 38, 3*a–b*).	
N. D.			After a year's sojourn in Western Liao he rose against the gurkhan and fled. On his way through the Uighur and Tangut countries he suffered from lack of food. Chingis Khan sent men to welcome him (YS 1, 6*b*; YCPS 5, 12*b*).	
1196			Chingis Khan dispatched an envoy to welcome the returning Wang-Khan (HYS 2, 6606).	
1198				Balkh, which until this year had been ruled by a vassal of Qarā-Khitāy, came under the control of a Ghūrid partisan. When the Khwārazm-shāh, Takash, called for help, the gurkhan sent an army under the noble *tāyankū*.[22] After an initial success the army suffered a night attack by the Ghūrid forces. The gurkhan blamed Takash for this defeat and demanded 10,000 dinars for each of the 12,000 slain Qarā-Khitay soldiers.[23] The shāh preferred to join the Ghūrid camp, whereupon the gurkhan besieged his capital, without, however, being able to take it. After the retreat of the Qarā-Khitāy army Takash attacked Bukhārā. The town was courageously defended, but eventually it fell

[22] Browne spells *tāyangū* correctly, Barthold (28, 344, note 3) says, although he himself spells it Ṭāyankū. The word occurs several times in contexts which suggest that it is a title rather than a proper name. Marquart romanizes the word as Tājang Kōh and connects it with Chinese *t'ai-wang* 太 [大 ?] 王 [great king]. He treats it as a title and explains it as "regent" (Marquart 14, 126, text and note 4). Thus, Marquart leaves the word *kōh* unexplained. Professor Pelliot in a personal communication suggests an Altaic etymology for the title which is as as simple as it is plausible. He derives *tāyangū* from the Turkic verb *taja-n-*, "to lean on, to rely on"; the verbal noun in -γu would be *taja-n-γu*, "reliance, support." Barthold, though aware that the word "must be not a proper name but a title," nevertheless speaks of "the noble Tāyankū" (Barthold 28, 344, note 3 and text) in other passages (*op. cit.*, 350, 356, 358 ff., 363).

[23] The demand is extremely high. Barthold (28, 344–345, note 4) considers it "quite improbable." He says: "There were not, so far as is known to us, any cases of the payment of such a vast sum in the middle ages."

Qarā-Khitāy from 1144 to 1211 (*continued*)

Year	Month	LS 30	Additional Chinese Sources	Non-Chinese Sources
				into his hands (Ibn al-Athīr XI, 88 ff. = Barthold 28, 344, 345).
1200				After the death of Takash, his son, Muḥammad, was proclaimed Khwārazm-shāh (Juwaynī II, 47 = Barthold 28, 349). For a time he controlled, besides his native country, the whole of Persia and even ʿIrāq. On the eve of the Mongol conquest "among Muslim rulers the sultan had no rivals" (Barthold 28, 372).
1204				A strong Qarā-Khitāy army supported Muḥammad in his campaign against the Ghūrs, who were completely defeated (Ibn al-Athīr XII, 122 = Barthold 28, 350–351).
N. D.				Kāshghar rebelled, but was defeated, and the khan's son[24] was taken prisoner by the gurkhan (Juwaynī I, 48 = Barthold 28, 363).
1205/6				Tirmidh, which was seized by the governor of Balkh, was retaken by the Qarā-Khitāy, who were supported by Muḥammad of Khwārazm (Ibn al-Athīr XII, 135 = Barthold 28, 352 and 360).
1207				A rebellion temporarily made Sanjar, the son of a seller of shields, ruler of Bukhārā. He was captured by Muḥammad in the autumn of 1207 (Juwaynī II, 74 and ʿAwfī, *Lubāb* II, 393 = Barthold 28, 355 and 360).
				Before the spring of 1208 Qarā-Khitāy defeated Muḥammad and his ally, ʿOthmān, sultan of Samarqand (Ibn al-Athīr XII, 171–175 = Barthold 28, 359–360).
1208			Chingis Khan attacked and defeated the Merkits at the Irtysh River. The Naiman prince,	[1208].[25] When Chingis Khan's power increased, "the Naimans . . . and the people called

[24] From this statement Barthold (28, 363) concludes that the uprising occurred during the lifetime of Arslan Khan, who died in March 1205.

[25] Marquart (14, 126) places this battle in the year 1204,
but his dates are confused by Bretschneider's faulty chronology. According to Barthold (28, 361), the Naimans and Merkits were defeated by Chingis Khan on the bank of the Irtysh in 1208.

Qarā-Khitāy from 1144 to 1211 (*continued*)

YEAR	MONTH	LS 30	ADDITIONAL CHINESE SOURCES	NON-CHINESE SOURCES
			Ch'ü-ch'u-lü 屈出律, who had taken refuge there, eventually fled to the Ch'i-tan gurkhan (HYS 3, 6607; YS 1, 15a; SWCCL 47b).[26]	Kara-Cathay assembled and banded themselves at a certain valley where, after a battle fought, they were vanquished by the Mongols" (Carpini 28, 12; *cf*. d'Ohsson 1834 I, 87, text and note 1).
				Küchlük[27] became a close friend of the gurkhan, who bestowed great favor upon him (Juwaynī 16, 90–91).
1209			In the spring, hearing of Chingis Khan's prestige, the Uighur king killed the state supervisor and the junior supervisor installed by the Ch'i-tan (SWCCL 48a).	Shāwkam, Qarā-Khitāy representative in the Uighur village [?] of Qarā-Khodja, "was surrounded in a house, which they pulled down on top of him," thus killing him (Juwaynī I, 32 = Barthold 28, 362).
			The Uighurs submitted to the Mongols (YS 1, 15a).	The gurkhan sent Maḥmūd-bāy to Khwārazm whose ruler had not paid tribute for two or three years. According to Juwaynī (16, 90), the mission
N. D.			The junior supervisor of the Western Ch'i-tan embittered the king of Kao-ch'ang by his oppressive behavior. The king's soldiers attacked and killed the supervisor, throwing his head down from the high building in which they had caught him (KCWC 11, 5b; YS 124, 7b).	achieved its aim,[28] but the relations between the two courts remained tense and soon afterwards Muḥammad went to Bukhārā, taking up negotiations with 'Othmān of Samarqand and other discontented territorial rulers.
1210				Muḥammad and his allies attacked from the west. The eastern vassals also turned against the gurkhan, who permitted Küchlük to unite his scattered forces. An army of 30,000 Qarā-Khitāy soldiers took Samarqand, but were forbidden to sack it as the gurkhan considered it "his treasury." 'Othmān of Samarqand [now] was permitted to marry a daughter of the gur-

[26] All three sources give the date 1208.

[27] The sound values of this name vary. Barthold has Kūchluk (28, 356 *passim*) and Küčlük (KK, 739). LS 30, 7a writes Ch'ü-ch'u-lü 屈出律 and SWCCL 47b Ch'ü (曲)-ch'u-lü, both of which correspond to the vowel value of Barthold's second transcription; YCPS 8, 3b has Ku-ch'u-lu (k'o) 古出魯 (克). In accordance with the two first named Chinese sources we follow Barthold's second transliteration, which points clearly to the Turkic words küč-lüg,

küč-lük, "powerful." In spelling Kūchluk, Barthold merely transliterates the form as written in Arabic and Persian texts.

[28] Another record of the course of events that led to the last gurkhan's fall is given in Juwaynī 16, 75 ff. (*cf*. also Barthold 28, 355 ff.). Barthold (28, 359) prefers the version of our text as "nearer the truth, although it also contains some statements which evoke grave doubt."

Qarā-Khitāy from 1144 to 1211 (*continued*)

Year Month	LS 30	Additional Chinese Sources	Non-Chinese Sources
			khan, who previously had been refused to him (Juwaynī 16, 90 ff.).
			At Ṭarāz, an indecisive battle was fought against Muḥammad, but the Qarā-Khitāy commander *tāyankū*[29] fell into the enemy's hands. The inhabitants of Balāsāghūn, expecting the defeat of the gurkhan, rebelled against him, but, after a siege of sixteen days, their city was taken. The Qarā-Khitāy troops, which, after taking Ṭaraz, had plundered their own territory, now sacked Balāsāghūn, killing 47,000 townspeople. When the gurkhan's severe order turned his army against him, he submitted to Küchlük who outwardly treated him with the utmost respect, while actually seizing his power (Juwaynī 16, 93).
N. D.[30]			Bilgä-Khān, a vassal of Qarā-Khitāy, deserted to Muḥammad, who detained him for a year and then had him executed (en-Nesawi 95, 38 ff.).
[1211]	Chih-lu-ku was captured during the autumn hunt by the Naiman prince, Ch'ü-ch'u-lü, who used 8,000 soldiers to ambush him (7a). Ch'ü-ch'u-lü assumed the title gurkhan, adopted the dress and customs of Western Liao and made Chih-lu-ku the imperial father and his wife the empress dowager. As long as they lived he attended them every morning and evening [like a respectful son] (7a).	Because Chih-lu-ku mistrusted the officials, the country was badly administered. His regime was therefore destroyed by the Hui-ho (*Pei Shih Chi* = KHCCL 6a).	N. D. Küchlük and an allied khan seized the gurkhan at Kāshghar. The captured sovereign was still permitted to occupy the throne, Küchlük acting as chamberlain. He consulted the ruler about all matters, great and small, but he rarely followed his orders. Muḥammad reproached Küchlük and demanded the delivery of the gurkhan, his daughter, entourage, and treasures. Küchlük sent a number of valuable presents, but, moved by the gurkhan's vigorous objections, did not turn him and his daughter over to the Khwārazm-shāh (en-Nesawi 95, 13–15).

---

[29] See above, note 22.

[30] Barthold (28, 364) rejects the idea, suggested by Nasawī, that Bilgä-Khan remained master of his territory until 1217. He believes instead that he was probably deposed simultaneously with the other representatives of the Qarā-Khānid dynasty. 'Othmān of Samarqand, who was Bilgä-Khan's cousin, was killed in 1212 (*cf.* Barthold 28, 364 and 366).

Qarā-Khitāy from 1144 to 1211 (*continued*)

YEAR	MONTH	LS 30	ADDITIONAL CHINESE SOURCES	NON-CHINESE SOURCES
				N. D. 'Unk [Pelliot: 'Ung] Khan, John, King of the Christians,[31] ruler of a Hunnish barbarian tribe, called Krīth (Kerait), took "a wife from a tribe of one of the Chinese peoples which was called 'Ḳārā-ketā.' He forsook the Fear of his fathers and worshipped strange gods" (Bar Hebraeus 32 I, 352–353).
[1213]		N. D. When Chih-lu-ku died, Liao ceased to exist (7*a*).	Chih-lu-ku died two years after Ch'ü-ch'u-lü's seizure of power (HYS 118, 6860).	One or two years after his seizure by Küchlük, the gur-khan died (Juwaynī 16, 93).
				The gurkhan was captured by Küchlük, the king of the Naimans. He died two years later (Hamd-Allāh Mustawfī 13, 114).
1216			Chingis Khan ordered the Mongol general, Chê-pieh 者別 [or Chê-po 哲伯 (Djebe)], to attack Ch'ü-ch'u-lü (HYS 123, 6869).	
1217			Chê-pieh arrived at the Ch'ui 垂 River. One city after another surrendered. Ho-ssŭ-mai-li 曷思麥里, who had been the imperial close attendant of Chih-lu-ku and was now the *pa-ssŭ-ha* 八思哈[32] of K'o-san 可散 City, voluntarily surrendered to Chê-pieh, who made him vanguard-general. The village heads, responding to Ho-ssŭ-mai-li's appeal, killed the usurper's garrison soldiers. Ch'ü-ch'u-lü fled westward (YSIWCP 1*B*, 8*a*; YS 120, 15*b* ff.; HYS 3, 6608; 123, 6869).	
			Ch'ü-ch'u-lü's third son, Ch'ang-wên 敞温, whose Qarā-Khitāy wife was a member of the imperial clan, had died. His widow fled with her twelve year old son, Ch'ao-ssŭ 抄思,	

[31] Bar Hebraeus evidently confuses the Naiman chief, Küchlük, with the Kerait ruler, Wang-Khan. Both men are among those whom the Western world identified with the mysterious Prester John (see Rubruck 09, 110; Vladimirtsov 30, 25; Oppert 70, 101). It seems that Küchlük married either the former bride or the daughter of the gurkhan and became a bitter enemy of Islam.

He is said to have forced the Moslems to adopt Christianity or some other non-Islamic religion (perhaps Buddhism ?); at least the Mohammedans had to adopt the dress of the Qarā-Khitāy (Barthold, KK, 739; *idem* 28, 359; d'Ohsson 1834 I, 171).

[32] Representative or governor (see below, C, 4).

Qarā-Khitāy from 1144 to 1211 (*continued*)

Year	Month	LS 30	Additional Chinese Sources	Non-Chinese Sources
			and a wet nurse, but she finally surrendered to Chingis Khan's third wife[33] (CHWC 28, 12a ff.; YS 121, 21a).	
1218			Chê-pieh ordered Ho-ssŭ-mai-li to seize their common enemy, Ch'ü-ch'u-lü. Ho-ssŭ-mai-li pursued the usurper beyond the Ts'ung-ling 葱嶺. The people along the road refused to shelter the fugitive. At Sa-li-huan 撒里桓 [Saryqol[34] in the Pamirs ?], near Pa-ta-k'o-shan 巴達克山 [Badakhshān in modern Afghanistan ?], he was captured with the aid of a shepherd and executed. His head was displayed in the old Hsi Liao territory. Immediately afterwards, K'o-shih-ha-êrh 可失哈兒 (Kāshghar), Ya-êrh-ch'ien 押兒牽 (Yārkand), Wo-tuan 斡端 (Khotan ?), and other cities opened their gates to the Mongols (YCPS 10, 12a; SWCCL 60a; YS 120, 16a; YSIWCP 1B, 8a; HYS 3, 6608; 123, 6869).	Küchlük destroyed by the Mongols (en-Nesawi 95, 16–17).
1219[35]			A Chinese named Liu 劉, who followed Chingis Khan when he attacked the remnant of the Ch'i-tan called Hsi Liao, passed through the old city of Hsü-êrh-kuo O-i-to 古續兒國訛夷朶城[36] (ISHSC 28, 1b).	
1219[37]			Kuo Pao-yü 郭寶玉 participated in Chingis Khan's attack on what was left of the Ch'i-tan. He passed through the old city of Hsü-kuei[38]-kuo O-i-	

[33] YS 121, 21a gives no date for this event. According to the tomb tablet of the Ta-lu Naiman 答祿乃蠻氏先塋碑, Ch'ao-ssŭ was born in 1205. When he fled with his mother after the collapse of Qarā-Khitāy power he is said to have been twelve years old (CHWC 28, 12a ff.). According to this the flight must have taken place in or shortly after 1216. Judging from the advance of the Mongols, it may have occurred in 1217.

[34] Saryqol or Saryγ-Qoł (Radloff, WB II, 584), "Yellow Valley." Professor Pelliot draws our attention to the older form: Saryγ-Ɓoł.

[35] No source gives the date of this event. According to HYS 4, 6608, in the early part of 1219 Chingis Khan was still in Qaraqorum, and in the sixth month at the Irtysh River where he summoned his generals for a council of war. In the ninth month he was on his way to Bukhārā. Therefore, the event in question seems to have occurred in 1219.

[36] See below, note 38.

[37] The *Yüan Shih* puts this campaign in 1214 which is too early. The *Hsin Yüan Shih* dates it in 1219 which is in accordance with the reasons given in note 35 above.

[38] Wang Kuo-wei considers *kuei* 鬼 an error for *êrh* 兒. He refers to Ch'ien Ta-hsin's explanation relating *hsü-êrh* to *chü-êrh* 菊兒 of *chü-êrh-han* (汗), gurkhan (KTCL 14, 3a; SCCYHL 9, 6b–7a).

O-i-to manifestly means ordo. If the whole phrase *ku-hsü-êrh-kuo* 古續 (or 徐) 兒國 is taken as a name, it

Qarā-Khitāy from 1144 to 1211 (*continued*)

Year	Month	LS 30	Additional Chinese Sources	Non-Chinese Sources
			to 古徐鬼國訛夷朶城 where he defeated more than 300,000 of the enemy. He also seized Beshbalyq and Samarqand (YS 149, 12a; HYS 146, 6904).	
1220				Muḥammad died in hiding after the collapse of his power (Tabakat-i-Nasiri = Barthold 28, 426).
N. D.			A letter submitted to the Sung prime minister in the middle of the thirteenth century by a Yüan envoy refers to Huo [Ta ?]-shih Lin-ya 火 [大] 石 林牙 as the region which Western Liao had occupied (HWCKC 24, 6a).	

4. THE QARĀ–KHITĀY DYNASTY OF KIRMĀN[1]

Date A. D.	A. H.	Events
1210	607[2]	Kirmān conquered in the name of the Khwārazm-shāh (Kramers 27, 1030). Burāq taken to Khwārazm after battle on the Talas (Juwaynī = Barthold, BH, 794).
	N. D.	Burāq, a chamberlain of the gurkhan of Qarā-Khitāy court, was sent to the Khwārazm-shāh, Sultan Muḥammad, on the eve of the last war between the two rulers. The sultan, intending to use this able official, detained him. After the defeat of Qarā-Khitāy, Burāq first served Muḥammad and, later, his son, Ghiyāthu'd-Dīn,[3] to whom Muḥammad had assigned Kirmān among other territories. Burāq, dispatched to Kirmān, seized actual power by
1221–1222	end of 618[4]	military and diplomatic means and eventually was acknowledged as official ruler (en-Nesawī 95, 45, 47, and 157–158; Hamd-Allāh Mustawfī 13, 131).
	619	The Mongols gave Burāq-i-Ḥājib ("the chamberlain") the title Qutlugh Khan (*loc. cit.*).
	N. D.	Ghiyāthu'd-Dīn arrived with his mother in Kirmān. Burāq received him generously, but compelled the lady to marry him against her son's and her own will (en-Nesawī 95, 239; Hamd-Allāh Mustawfī 13, 116).
1230	627	Relatives of Burāq secretly planned to replace him by Ghiyāthu'd-Dīn. The khan, discovering the plot, accused his wife and her son of an attempt to poison him. The other conspirators

can perhaps be interpreted as another transliteration of Hu-ssŭ (Ku-ssŭ) Ordo. (See B, 2, 1134, LS 30, 6a–b and B, 3, 1175, CS 121, 4b–5a.)

Juwaynī (16, 87) reports that the first gurkhan went to Balāsāgūn [Balāsāghūn], "which the Mongols now call Ghur-Baliq." The editor of our edition, after giving various textual variants of the passage, refers to Marquart's suggestion to read it Ghuz-Balyq (Juwaynī 16, 87, note 5), that is, City of the Ghuz. The Chinese transliterations which all have "*ssŭ*" confirm the correctness of Marquart's emendation. Pelliot (29, 124) also writes "Ghuz-ordo."

[1] The chronology given in our main source, the *Ta'rīkh-i-Guzīda* by Ḥamdu'llāh Muṣṭawfī-i-Qazwīnī (Hamd-Allāh Mustawfī 13), is utterly confused; the translator, E. G. Browne, has corrected a number of obvious mistakes. We give the A. H. dates as corrected by Browne. Additional modifications and supplementary figures are explained in the notes.

[2] Kramers 27, 1030.

[3] This transliteration is used by Browne whom we follow because he is the translator of our main source (see note 1). Kramers (27, 1030) spells Ghiyāth al-Dīn and Barthold (28, 430) Ghiyāth ad-Dīn. Houdas (en-Nesawī 95, 45, *passim*) writes Ghyāts ed-Dīn.

[4] Barthold, BH, 794.

The Qarā-Khitāy dynasty of Kirmān (*continued*)

DATE A. D.	A. H.	EVENTS
		were publicly executed, the lady was secretly strangled, and her son was either strangled (*loc. cit.*) or, according to en-Nesawi's version (95, 239), imprisoned.
1234	632	After a reign of eleven years Burāq died, leaving a son and four daughters, one of whom, Khān Turkān, married her cousin (Burāq's nephew), Quṭbu'd-Dīn Tāyangū (Hamd-Allāh Mustawfī 13, 132).
	N. D	Tāyangū followed his father-in-law to the throne, reigning first for two years, when he was defeated and replaced by Burāq's son, Ruknu'd-Dīn Mubārak-Khwāja, whom Ogotai established as ruler of Kirmān.
1252	650[5]	After a reign of sixteen years, Mubārak-Khwāja was dismissed by Manggū Khān, and Tāyangū's power was restored. Four months after this event Tāyangū married Qutlugh Turkān, a former concubine of his uncle and father-in-law, Burāq, whose intelligent advice influenced him considerably.
	651	Mubārak-Khwāja again conspired. Tāyangū seized him and killed him with his own hands (*loc. cit.*).
1257	655	Tāyangū died.
1267	655[6] 666[7]	For fifteen years Qutlugh Turkān acted as regent during the minority of Tāyangū's son, Sulṭān Ḥajjāj, whom Mangū Khān had chosen as his father's successor. The grown Ḥajjāj and his [step-?] mother were in serious conflict. Eventually Ḥajjāj went to India, yielding his power to Qutlugh Turkān who continued to rule the country (*op. cit.*, 132–133).
1271		Marco Polo, on his way to the Far East, passed through Persia and visited "a fine kingdom which is called Kerman" (Marco Polo 03 I, 88). "Since the Tartars conquered the country the rule is no longer hereditary, but the Tartar sends to administer whatever lord he pleases"[8] (*op. cit.*, 90). In the south of Kirmān, in the region of Camadi [Jiruft],[9] the Venetian noticed great devastation brought about by the Tartars (*op. cit.*, 91 and 97), but, when departing from "the city of Kerman,"[10] he first traveled for seven days through pleasant scenery of "towns, villages, and handsome dwelling-houses" (*op. cit.*, 91).
		Qutlugh Turkān improved the country's economic condition by the construction of *qanāt's* (canals) (Kramers 27, 1031).
1282	681	After her death she was "buried at Kirmān by her daughter Bībī Turkān" (Hamd-Allāh Mustawfī 13, 133).
	681[11]	Qutlugh Turkān's daughter, Pādishāh Khātūn, quarreled with her brother, Sulṭān Jalālu'd-Dīn Sūrghatmush [Sūrghatmish] who reigned for nine years. She was married "in the Mongol

[5] Corrected by E. G. Browne; the manuscript has 605 (Hamd-Allāh Mustawfī 13, 132).

[6] Lane-Poole 94, 179. Kramers (27, 1031) says that "she reigned from 1258 to 1282."

[7] According to Lane-Poole (*loc. cit.*), Ḥajjāj was the titular ruler from 655 to 660.

[8] This evidently was the impression created by the Mongol khans' policy of dismissing old and appointing new rulers in Kirmān. Marco Polo's statement, however, does not make it clear (perhaps because the author was not aware of it) that the Kirmān rulers were connected through a dynastic tie, if only in a loose way.

[9] Identification suggested by Houtum-Schindler (81, 495). At the time of Ibn Ḥauqāl [tenth century], the territory of Jiruft was extremely fertile and well irrigated

(Aboulfeda 1848 II, 2: 103; *cf.* also Yaqout 61, 185; and Schwarz 12, 240 ff.).

[10] The capital of Kirmān, originally called Guvāshīr or Bardashīr (Hamd-Allāh Mustawfī 19, 139), was later frequently designated either as "the city of Kirmān" or still more briefly as "Kirmān." Ibn al-Athīr says that the Saljūqid ruler, Īrān Shāh, was expelled in A. H. 494 [1101] "from the city of Bardasīr, which same is the city of Kirmān" (Le Strange 01, 284). According to Mīrkhwānd, the founder of the Qarā-Khitāy dynasty in 1222 occupied "the city of Kirmān" (*loc. cit.*). For the description of Kirmān, the city and the territory, by an author of the thirteenth century, see Yaqout 61, 482–485; a comprehensive collection of Arabic sources is given in Schwarz 12, 211–230.

[11] Lane-Poole 94, 179.

The Qarā-Khitāy dynasty of Kirmān (*continued*)

Date A. D.	A. H.	Events
1292	[691][12]	fashion" to the Mongol prince Gay-Khātū who, when[13] he ascended the throne, made her ruler of Kirmān. She had her brother strangled.
1293	693	Pādishāh Khātūn had her brother strangled; she announced publicly that he had committed suicide.
1293/4[14]		Marco Polo, on his way home, arrived in Hormos [Hormus], a port then, as in 1271, under the sovereignty of the Sultan of Kirmān (Marco Polo 03 I, 110; II, 450).
1294	694[15]	In the following year Pādishāh Khātūn herself "was put to death."
1295	695[16]	A new ruler was appointed by order of the Mongol Khan of Persia, Ghāzān. "He died of drink," according to Hamd-Allāh Mustawfī (13, 133), "after a reign of eight years, in A. H.
1303	703	703." The same source (*op. cit.*, 131) consistently puts the end of the dynasty in the year 706
1306[17]	706	[1306], the last ruler, his predecessor's cousin, occupying the throne for "a little more than two years and a half" (*op. cit.*, 134).

C. QARĀ-KHITĀY SOCIETY AND CULTURE

1. THE SIZE OF THE QARĀ-KHITĀY EMPIRE

Data on the size of the Qarā-Khitāy empire differ considerably. Yeh-lü Ch'u-ts'ai, who visited Central Asia in 1219, speaks of a territory of "several ten thousand *li*";[1] his contemporary, Ch'ang-ch'un, of an area of "ten thousand *li* in every direction";[2] and recently Ting Ch'ien expressed the belief that the gurkhans exercised control over a land approximately six thousand *li* "wide" and seven thousand *li* "long."[3] The first two statements are somewhat indefinite; the third is obviously exaggerated. But all of them agree that the area covered by the Hsi Liao state was large. A survey of the empire's vassal countries confirms this impression, although the real figures are considerably smaller than those suggested by earlier writers.

The western limit of Hsi Liao imperial power was the Oxus River, for while Khwārazm paid tribute it was not a subordinate state.[4] Balkh,[5] Tirmidh,[6] and Khotan[7] were probably the southernmost vassal territories. In the east the empire approached Hsi Hsia, which bordered the Uighur dependencies of Qarā-Khitāy.[8] In the northeast, Hsi Liao sovereignty ended where the Naiman pastures began. The Khirghiz lived still farther north; they were definitely beyond the gurkhan's control.[9] Herrmann's map of 1141 does not indicate the country's maximal northern and southern extensions,[10] but taken as a whole it accords well with Chinese and Moslem sources. The greatest distance between the eastern and western

---

[12] He was killed in January 1295 (A. H. 694), after a reign of three years and seven months (Hamd-Allāh Mustawfī 13, 145).

[13] After? According to Lane-Poole (94, 179) her reign began in A.H. 693.

[14] Marco Polo 03 I, Yule Introductory Notices 23–24.

[15] Corrected by Browne; the manuscript has 664.

[16] Lane-Poole 94, 179: 694 = 1294.

[17] Lane-Poole (94, 179) dates the beginning of the last reign three years earlier. His final date, A. H. 703, is supported by Kramers (27, 1031), who also has the rule of the Qutlugh Khans last "until 1303." However, Ḥamdu-'llāh Muṣṭawfī's opinion follows closely the statement made by Rashīd ad-Dīn, from which it may well have derived (*cf.* YSIWCP 12, 1b).

[1] CJCSWC 12, 170.

[2] HYCCC 1, 30a; *cf.* Waley 31, 88.

[3] HLLKSM 4a.

[4] See below, C, 4.

[5] Barthold 28, 344 ff.

[6] *Op. cit.*, 352.

[7] See Stein 07 I, 183.

[8] The possibility of an alliance between Qarā-Khitāy and Hsi Hsia intrigued the statesmen of Chin and Sung (see B, 2, 1130, CS 120, 2a; 121, 4b; B, 3, 1185, SS 35, 17a; 486, 21b). In 1130 the Hsi Hsia government asserted its aloofness by saying that Hsi Hsia did not border Ho-chou (B, 2, *loc. cit.*), but this statement, made for diplomatic purposes, conceals rather than expresses the actual conditions. The oasis countries of eastern Turkestan and northwestern China are separated by a desert which establishes a kind of no-man's land between them. Thus, technically, the two countries did not touch each other; politically, however, they were neighbors. Wang-Khan's itinerary clearly demonstrates this. The Kerait ruler traveled from Hsi Hsia through the Uighur country to the gurkhan (see B, 3, 1194 and 1195).

[9] Juwaynī 16, 87.

[10] Herrmann (35, 46–47) draws the northern border south of the Naimans. In the south he does not include the city of Balkh which seems to have been seized by the Qarā-Khitāy only in 1165 (see Barthold 28, 336).

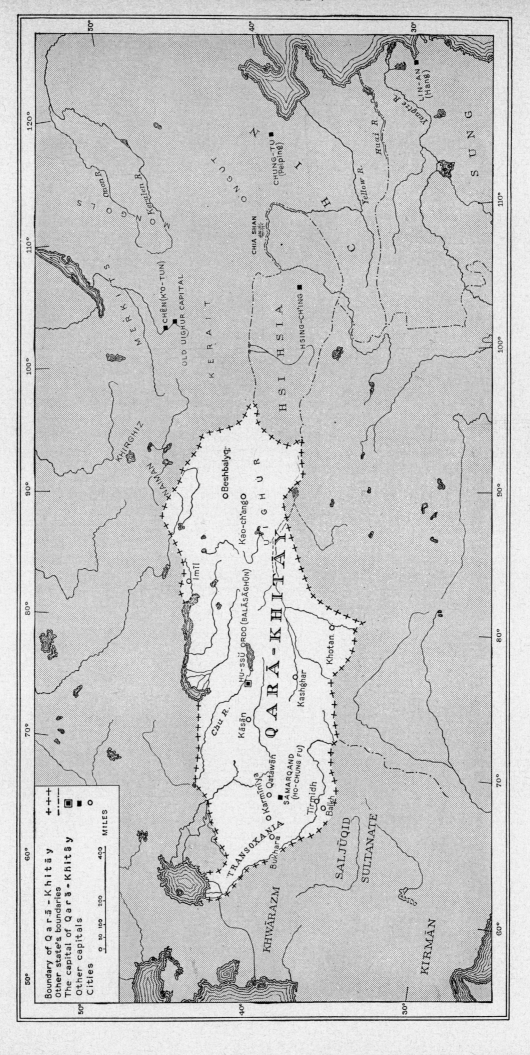

The Empire of Western Liao (Qarā-Khitāy).

limits of the Qarā-Khitāy empire was probably something under six thousand *li* (or two thousand miles), and between the northern and southern limits, something over two thousand *li* (or about seven hundred and fifty miles). Thus in size the Hsi Liao state is comparable to its two great contemporaries in the Far East, Chin and Southern Sung. But it differed fundamentally from both, first in density of population, and second in political and cultural homogeneity and integration.

2. POPULATION

a. NUMBER

Yeh-lü Ta-shih established his sovereignty over vast stretches of steppe and desert that supported only a relatively small number of pastoral tribesmen. A much larger population was settled in the heart of his empire, in the well-watered valleys and oases of Eastern and Western Turkestan.

The total number of the gurkhans' subjects is problematic. The *Liao Shih* mentions a census taken in 1151 under the gurkhan, I-lieh, which records 84,500 households with "persons" (men) eighteen years of age or over.[11] But since the capital of the vassal state of Samarqand alone is said to have comprised 100,000 households before the Mongol conquest,[12] the census of 1151 could have referred only to what may be called the empire's inner domain, territory under the immediate control of the gurkhan,—that is, the hinterland of Balāsāghūn (Hu-ssŭ Ordo).

Data on the increasing number of Yeh-lü Ta-shih's followers strengthen this hypothesis. Ta-shih left the collapsing Liao empire with a handful of fighting men, perhaps as few as eighty and certainly no more than a couple of hundred.[13] In K'o-tun he gained additional adherents. This famous frontier garrison, in all probability, could no longer muster 20,000 soldiers as it had in the days of Liao splendor, but the reports of 1124 state that Yeh-lü Ta-shih possessed 10,000 war horses.[14] After his conference with the eighteen tribes he was given 10,000 warriors.[15] Subsequently, the arrival of 16,000 tents of Ch'i-tan mercenaries at Balāsāghūn doubled his might.[16]

It is difficult to relate these facts to Juwaynī's statement that at Imīl, where Yeh-lü Ta-shih is supposed to have resided years before his sojourn in Balāsāghūn, the gurkhan had already under his control some 40,000 households, including many local Turks.[17] If this record is not disregarded—and there

is little justification for such action—we must conclude either that the "many" Turks of Imīl were left behind when the Ch'i-tan moved on or that the Moslem writer's figure actually refers to Balāsāghūn where the gurkhan is said to have controlled twice 16,000 households.

A population of 32,000 or 40,000 households might mobilize 64,000–80,000 soldiers if, following Liao tradition, an average family provided two men. The story that the eastern expedition of 1134 comprised 70,000 warriors[18] is therefore not outside the realm of possibility—at least technically. Politically it seems improbable, for it would imply that Yeh-lü Ta-shih left his new domain practically unprotected.

All armies after that time were smaller. In the glorious victory at Qaṭawān (near Samarqand) the gurkhan is said to have deployed only 2,500 soldiers in each of the two wings, a number suggesting a central army of perhaps only 10,000 or 20,000 men. To be sure, the gurkhan may have organized his force in an unorthodox manner, or national memory may consciously have minimized the strength of the Ch'i-tan in order to dramatize their triumph. But all known records dealing with the war of 1141 and later military events mention Qarā-Khitāy armies of moderate size: 10,000 men as a rule, and once 30,000[19] and 50,000[20] respectively. Such armies could be raised from 84,500 households or even from a considerably smaller number, let us say, 40,000 to 50,000 families.

These conclusions bear on the character of the census of 1151. Did that census register only Ch'i-tan and their tribal followers, or did it include the domain's sedentary population? In 1210, 47,000 inhabitants of the rebellious city of Balāsāghūn were killed by the Qarā-Khitāy. Since the city continued to exist (it surrendered a few years later to the Mongols),[21] the victims of 1210 can only have constituted a part of the total population, either a considerable part, or, if the figure is exaggerated, a lesser one. But in view of the small armies of the gurkhan, it seems legitimate to conclude that the 84,500 households included the native inhabitants of the towns and villages of Balāsāghūn as well as their tribal masters who, apparently, were the only ones customarily to bear arms.[22] If these tribesmen by the middle of

---

[11] See B, 3, 1151, LS 30, 7a.

[12] HYCCC 1, 32b.

[13] See B, 1, 1124, LS 30, 4b; Juwaynī 16, 87 and note 16.

[14] B, 2, 1124, CS 3, 5a–b and 121, 4a.

[15] B, 2, 1129, LS 30, 4b–5a.

[16] B, 2, 1128, Ibn al-Athīr XII, 55–56 = Marquart 14, 164–165.

[17] Juwaynī 16, 77; *cf.* Bretschneider 88 I, 226.

[18] B, 2, 1134, LS 30, 6a–b.

[19] B, 3, 1210, Juwaynī 16, 91.

[20] B, 3, 1175, CS 121, 4b–5a; 7, 7b.

[21] Barthold (28, 402), in accordance with an often repeated etymology, says that the Mongols called it Gobāligh, "fine city," because the city surrendered without offering resistance. The real Altaic name, however, was evidently Ghuz-Balyq (see B, 3, note 38).

[22] B, 3, 1175, CS 121, 5a. For a discussion of Bretschneider's differing interpretation of this passage, see below, note 175.

the twelfth century comprised about 40,000 to 50,000 households, they numbered something less than a third of the estimated strength of the Liao Ch'i-tan.[23]

b. COMPOSITION

The problems raised by the census figure of 1151 indicate the complex composition of the Hsi Liao populace. The "inner tribes," which Yeh-lü Ta-shih led into Turkestan, shared the not too homogeneous background of the Liao tribal world.[24] This conglomerate of proto-Mongol, Turkic, Tangut, and perhaps even Tungus elements, augmented by some Liao Chinese, conquered a territory that long before the twelfth century was one of the classic meeting grounds of alien peoples and cultures.

Turkestan still has within its cities a considerable old Iranian (Tādžik) population[25] which must have been even more numerous in the first centuries of the second millennium. The bearded urban Moslems who in 1220 startled the author of the *Pei Shih Chi*[26] probably belonged to this group. The army that in the same year opposed Chingis Khan at Samarqand is said to have included, besides Turks, Ghūrs, and others, a considerable number of Tādžiks—according to Juwaynī, not less than 50,000 out of a total of 110,000.[27] For our argument it matters little whether Juwaynī's total figure is inflated; other Moslem historians mention a considerably smaller number.[28] But in view of the general preference for Turks and other nomads in military affairs, the relatively high percentage of Tādžiks noted by Juwaynī remains significant.

Turkestan was settled by various branches of Turks who actively and passively participated in the historic changes brought about by Qarā-Khitāy power. Among their most primitive representatives may be counted the Qarluqs who were herding their flocks in the environs of Balāsāghūn when Yeh-lü Ta-shih arrived there[29] and who sometime later provoked sanguinary wars in Transoxania, while stubbornly resisting the attempts of Samarqand to pacify or resettle them.[30] The Qarā-Khānids were the leaders of a Turkic group that, perhaps under Uighur and Chinese (and Liao ?) influence,[31] had accepted more of sedentary life, without, however, fully mastering its techniques.[32] Despite the achievements ascribed to

certain Iläk- [Ilig-] Khans,[33] their rule "was without doubt a period of cultural retrogression for Transoxania."[34] After the partition of their ephemeral empire,[35] the Qarā-Khānids maintained power in Balāsāghūn, but Yeh-lü Ta-shih soon reduced them to insignificance.[36] In Bukhārā they were overthrown before 1141 by a rival within their gates.[37] In Samarqand, Khotan, and Kāshghar they were defeated,[38] but continued to rule as Qarā-Khitāy vassals until the end of the dynasty.

The Uighurs of Ho-chou (Kao-ch'ang) were among the first to bow before the gurkhan's growing might.[39] It is, however, difficult to ascertain how numerous the Turkic or Uighur elements were in the different countries or regions. In the nineteenth century about sixty per cent of all inhabitants of Samarqand were still Tādžiks (Iranians) and only ten per cent were Turks.[40] In Eastern Turkestan the most numerous sector of the population is composed even today of "mountain Iranians with a pronounced Turkish modification."[41] Stein assumes for Khotan, as for other Central Asiatic territories, a growth of Turkic influence after the victory of Satūq Bughrā-Khān, that is, the Qarā-Khānids. But the Turks, "nomads by origin and habits," were primarily soldiers, leaving agriculture and trade in the hands of their sedentary subjects: "Their numbers were far too small to affect fundamentally the racial character of the population."[42] Stein believes that this was equally true for the periods of Qarā-Khitāy and Mongol rule: "In view of what we know of the manner in which their temporary power was exercised in the settled portions of Turkestan, they could but slightly have strengthened the Turki element in so distant an oasis as Khotan."[43]

Other groups were still less significant numerically, but they may be mentioned because their presence indicates the complex constitution of the Turkestan population in the twelfth and early thirteenth centuries. Chinese officials served the Qarā-Khitāy government,[44] and Ch'ang-ch'un noted Chinese artisans

---

[23] See I, introduction.
[24] See I, introduction and I, 2, *passim*.
[25] *Cf.* Schuyler 77 I, 106 ff.; Le Coq 29, 40.
[26] KHCCL 6b; *cf.* Bretschneider 88 I, 30.
[27] *Cf.* Barthold 28, 411.
[28] *Loc. cit.*
[29] Juwaynī 16, 87.
[30] See B, 3, 1156 and 1158, Barthold 28, 333–334.
[31] Barthold 28, 304 and 311.
[32] *Op. cit.*, 17.

[33] Nidhāmī-i-'Arūdī 99, 781 ff.
[34] Barthold 28, 17.
[35] *Op. cit.*, 268 ff.; Lane-Poole 94, 135.
[36] See above B, 2, [1129] N. D., (Juwaynī 16, 87–88).
[37] Barthold 28, 326–327.
[38] See B, 2, *passim*.
[39] B, 2, 1130, LS 30, 5a–b.
[40] According to an estimate of Khorochkine (78, 225–226).
[41] Le Coq 29, 40. Le Coq's statement must be taken as referring to the ethnic background of the present population whose language is no longer Iranian, but Turkic.
[42] Stein 07 I, 146.
[43] *Loc. cit.*
[44] See below C, 4 and 7.

throughout Samarqand.[45] The flourishing Jewish community in this same city included "many wise and learned men."[46] The life and work of Nidhāmī-i-'Arūḍī of Samarqand and an-Nasawī show how readily upper-class natives of Persia and Turkestan shifted their residences from one country to the other. But, although Persians certainly played their part in the intellectual and economic life of the Hsi Liao empire, numerically they can have been little more important than the swarthy Hindu Moslems of low status who were employed as servants by their more favorably situated co-religionists.[47]

3. ECONOMIC FEATURES

a. THE TRADITIONAL INDIGENOUS PATTERN

When Yeh-lü Ta-shih arrived in Turkestan, he found there a well-established economic order which neither he nor his successors had much reason to modify. In the oasis regions village life depended primarily upon agriculture; in the cities and towns a great variety of crafts and trades flourished.

In 1175 three Hui-ho,[48] on arriving in Chin China, told of the native agriculture in the environs of the Qarā-Khitāy capital, Ku [Hu]-ssǔ Ordo.[49] Ch'ang-ch'un, who forty-six years later passed through this same region, confirms and elaborates the earlier report: in the surrounding plains the people tilled the soil, made grape-wine and bred silkworms. No rain fell in the summer and fall, but the necessary moisture was secured by means of canals which led the water from the river(s) to the fields.[50]

The irrigation system of the Zarafshān River is described in great detail by early Moslem geographers;[51] it also impressed contemporary eastern visitors. Singing the praise of Samarqand in one of his poems, Yeh-lü Ch'u-ts'ai notes the importance of canals to the country's welfare: the annual harvest never failed; there was no starvation; lakes and reservoirs everywhere provided the people with water to

bathe their feet and wash their clothes. For these reasons, he concludes, the capital city was given its name, Hsin-ssǔ-ch'ien 尋思虔.[52]

Among the agricultural products of Turkestan, the author of the *Pei Shih Chi* mentions particularly the "five grains" and mulberry trees resembling those of China, cotton,[53] grapes, brightly-colored apples, onions, melons, and gourds that weighed sixty catties.[54] Windmills ground the wheat and unhusked rice.[55] At the close of the eleventh century, land in the villages could be bought by wealthy townspeople,[56] and it is more than probable, although concrete evidence is lacking, that similar transfers were made in the twelfth.

In 1221 native economy, weakened but not destroyed by the Mongol onslaught,[57] continued to produce a variety of goods: among them, salt from the mountains [rock-salt], silver, and pearls. Windows and vases were made of clear glass, house-tops of clay. The weapons (arrows, bows, spears, mail), carts, clothes, and vessels, all seemed strange to the Chinese observer[58] who, in his survey of Central Asiatic industry, focused his attention on native production. Compared with this, Chinese handicraft,[59] however fine, obviously played a negligible role.

The gurkhans ordered coins cast after the Liao and Chinese pattern with the reign period inscribed in Chinese characters;[60] but the vassal states continued

---

[45] HYCCC 1, 32b; cf. Waley 31, 93.

[46] Benjamin 1840 I, 128–129.

[47] *Pei Shih Chi* = KHCCL 6b; cf. Bretschneider 88 I, 30.

[48] B, 3, 1175, CS 121, 4b–5a.

[49] For Wang Kuo-wei's discussion of the identity of Hu-ssǔ Ordo, Ku-ssǔ Ordo and Balāsāghūn, see KTCL 14, 3a–5b.

[50] HYCCC 1, 30a; cf. Bretschneider 88 I, 72 ff.; Waley 31, 88. According to the *Hsi Shih Chi*, when in 1259 Ch'ang Tê 常德 visited the Western Regions, he found in the plains between the I-tu 亦塔 Mountains many irrigation ditches and canals. The natives ascribed the old fortifications and dilapidated walls to the Hsi Liao dynasty (KHCCL 7b). In all probability, the irrigation system, like the walls, existed before the Mongol period.

[51] Cf. Barthold 28, 83 passim.

[52] CJCSWC 12, 170 and 174. Hsin-ssǔ-ch'ien is a transliteration of the Turko-Iranian name Sämiz-Kant, "Fat City," an alternate form due to Turkic popular etymology for the older Iranian word Samarqand. Ch'ang-ch'un's travelogue also describes the canals of Samarqand (HYCCC 1, 32b). Elevated terraces protected the people in case of flood (CJCSWC 6, 72).

[53] The wool that "grows in the soil" was evidently cotton (see III, note 74).

[54] KHCCL 6b. The grape wine of Hsi Liao was already famous in the Chin 金 period. According to a contemporary description, the gurkhans' subjects squeezed grapes and collected the juice in jars which they sealed and buried. After a while the liquid turned into wine. The longer the wine lay in the ground, the better its quality. There were people whose stores amounted to a thousand jars (ISHSC 1, 2a).

[55] CJCSWC 6, 72.

[56] Nizam oul-Moulk 93, 197.

[57] Thirty thousand artisans were handed over to members of the Mongol imperial family; others were employed in siege work. The remaining inhabitants who were allowed to re-occupy the city had to pay a large sum of money, two hundred thousand dinars (Barthold 28, 414).

[58] KHCCL 6b. For this and other quotations from the *Pei Shih Chi*, see Bretschneider 88 I, 30–31.

[59] HYCCC 1, 32b.

[60] See below, C, 3, c.

to mint a traditional Arab currency.[61] This local currency was recognized by the Qarā-Khitāy government, which assessed its taxes on tributary countries not in Liao but in Moslem money—the customary unit being the gold dinar.[62]

The herds of Turkestan included many animals familiar to the eastern steppes and even to China Proper, but the chronicler of Wu-ku-sun's mission noted particularly camels with only one hump (the Arab "African" type), a special variety of oxen, and sheep with "big" tails.[63] Horses were branded in Transoxania in pre-Hsi-Liao time,[64] and the practice was no doubt continued during the dynasty. An important noble might own eighteen thousand mares and as many colts.[65] Thousands of camels were gathered in a single caravan,[66] but when speed was the main consideration the horse was naturally preferred.[67] The proper traveling equipment of a person of rank included—besides his horse—a tent, a number of camels and slaves, wearing apparel, and carpets.[68]

Under the Qarā-Khitāy dynasty trade was carried on by men of various nationalities and creeds. The potentials of Moslem commerce may be gauged from the fact that a merchant prince, Maḥmūd-bāy, became the last gurkhan's vizier.[69] Uighur business men were as successful as they had been in the days of Great Liao. Traveling through Hsi Hsia to North China, they amassed great fortunes which made them attractive targets of the Tangut officials' squeeze.[70] The "very extensive commerce" that flourished around 1170 in the capital of Khwārazm, Giva (Khiwā), involved "traders of all countries and languages,"[71] including, without doubt and perhaps most importantly, those of the neighboring territories of Bukhārā and Samarqand. The eight thousand Jews of Khiwā,[72] as well as the larger Jewish community of Samarqand, probably participated in this activity— the only one mentioned by Benjamin of Tudela in his notes on the region.

In his invaluable treatise[73] Niẓām al-Mulk mentions

a number of traders without specifying their nationality; some came from Kāshghar;[74] others lived in Samarqand.[75] His story of the cunning Turkic slave girl[76] reveals that at the end of the eleventh century Turkic merchants who engaged in extensive enterprises were not an uncommon phenomenon. It also reveals the existence of trade-routes: one from Samarqand to Ghazna via Balkh;[77] another from Khotan to Khitāy; and still another from Khotan to Kāshghar and Samarqand.[78] Since the gurkhans did not interfere in the internal affairs of their subject countries, it may be assumed that the trade and commerce noted by Niẓām al-Mulk for the eleventh century continued to flourish during the subsequent Qarā-Khitāy period.

Designations such as "the seller of shields" (Bukhārā),[79] "the street of the Slave-sellers" (Balkh),[80] and the "Perfumers' Market" (Herāt)[81] suggest important categories of merchandise. Slave girls, curios, silk, and white felt were significant import items from Khitāy and (Sung) China.[82] The merchant who disposed of goods worth sixty thousand dinars was considered a very rich man at the court of Ghazna; and Niẓām al-Mulk's presentation makes it certain that the accumulation of such a fortune was not only possible but legitimate.[83]

The wealthy but anonymous protagonist of the above anecdote was being discussed by a group of international traders (he himself was probably similarly engaged), whose business was carried on in such widely separated places as Khitāy and (Sung) China in the east and Egypt and Maghrib in the west.[84] The number of these traders could not have been large but, in all probability, they were as well represented in the Qarā-Khitāy vassal countries—Bukhārā, Samarqand, Kāshghar, and Khotan—as they had been a century earlier in the mountainous capital of the Ghaznevid empire.

b. THE ECONOMY OF THE BLACK CH'I-TAN

Entering the steppes and oases of Turkestan, the Black Ch'i-tan encountered a dual economy which

[61] The existence of a mint in Samarqand is recorded for the year A. H. 558 = 1163 (Dorn 88, 65).

[62] Barthold, KK, 738.

[63] *Pei Shih Chi* = KHCCL 6b; *cf.* SHTYC 1, 21a.

[64] Nidhāmī-i-'Arūdī 99, 766 ff.

[65] *Op. cit.*, 766.

[66] *Op. cit.*, 630.

[67] Nizam oul-Moulk 93, 197.

[68] Nidhāmī-i-'Arūdī 99, 772.

[69] Juwaynī II, 89 = Barthold, KK, 738.

[70] SMCW 4b ff. Under the Mongols, Uighur merchants again traded all over North China (MTPLCC 3b and 11b).

[71] Benjamin 1840 I, 128.

[72] *Loc. cit.*

[73] "Niẓām al-Mulk's composition is incontestably the chief source for the study of the political structure of the

Eastern Muslim states [during the eleventh century]" (Barthold 28, 25).

[74] Nizam oul-Moulk 93, 194.

[75] *Op. cit.*, 197.

[76] *Op. cit.*, 194 ff.

[77] *Op. cit.*, 197.

[78] *Op. cit.*, 195.

[79] Juwaynī II, 74 = Barthold 28, 355.

[80] Nidhāmī-i-'Arūdī 99, 806.

[81] *Op. cit.*, 802.

[82] Nizam oul-Moulk 93, 194.

[83] *Op. cit.*, 303–304.

[84] *Op. cit.*, 304.

must have seemed comparatively familiar to them, for a basically similar economy had flourished for more than two hundred years in their Liao fatherland. Evidently, the mounted newcomers readily adjusted to the peculiarities of a Central Asiatic culture and society. But did they, like the majority of their Liao antecedents, still prefer a nomadic existence to the attractions of a settled life? Or did they abandon completely, or in part, their traditional pastoral economy for "civilized" agriculture?

A few records seem to indicate a trend toward agrarianism. The chronicler of Ch'ang-ch'un's journey states that in 1221 the Moslem inhabitants "were unable to manage (*chu* 主) their fields and gardens themselves, and had to depend upon Chinese, Ch'i-tan, and Ho-hsi [Tanguts]."[85] The arrangement here described was an obvious product of the Mongol conquest which had been completed in the previous year. The victors could not have distrusted their new Moslem subjects' competence in irrigation agriculture and gardening, tasks at which they were probably superior to the Ch'i-tan and Tanguts and, as Ch'ang-ch'un's recorder observes, at least the equal of the Chinese.[86] It is more conceivable that, having reduced the population of Samarqand by slaughter and mass deportation to a quarter of its former size,[87] the Mongols were still apprehensive regarding the cooperativeness of those who remained. In all probability, the aliens employed in 1221 were not agricultural technicians— of whom there was no dearth—but fiscal supervisors and agents (*chu* means "to manage," not "to cultivate").[88] Foreigners often acted as administrative agents for their Mongol masters.[89] In this context it does not matter whether the Ch'i-tan, who in 1221 assisted in organizing the "management" of Transoxanian agriculture, came from the east (from Chin China) or were Black Ch'i-tan who had joined Chingis Khan's forces. In either case, they fulfilled a function which made technical familiarity with the art of husbandry desirable but not imperative.

A further reference to Qarā-Khitāy agriculture is still less conclusive. Abū'l-Ghāzī asserts that the [Qarā-] Khitāy, after having founded Imīl, "devoted themselves to agriculture and soon made the country prosperous."[90] This late (seventeenth century)[91] record is not supported by any earlier Chinese or Persian-Arabic source known to us. Juwaynī, who mentions the founding of Imīl by the Qarā-Khitāy, does not comment on their economic pursuits. However, he observes that some time later, when they settled temporarily in Balāsāghūn, their "cattle grew fat. . . ."[92] This remark is in line with other early reports all of which stress Yeh-lü Ta-shih's efforts to increase his herds. The Uighur khan provided him with horses, camels, and sheep;[93] the booty acquired in Western Turkestan included camels, horses, oxen, and sheep;[94] and Atsiz of Khwārazm agreed to pay an annual tribute of money, goods, and cattle.[95]

The gurkhan's capital "camp" is described as extensive: half a day was needed to ride around it.[96] Such a statement is more suggestive of an ordo-like tent-city than a town in the usual sense. It seems possible that the gurkhans patterned themselves upon their semi-civilized predecessors, the Qarā-Khānid Iläk Khans. The first Iläk Khan of the western branch, Ibrāhīm, was "a wise, just, and sagacious ruler" who gained renown as "a great patron of poets."[97] His son, Shams al-Mulk (1068–1080),[98] famed as a just ruler and a builder of fine edifices in town and country, nevertheless, "continued to lead a nomadic existence and passed the winter only, together with his army, in the neighborhood of Bukhārā where he made it a strict rule that the soldiers kept to their tents and did not oppress the inhabitants. After sundown not one soldier dared remain within the town."[99] The Qarā-Khitāy may also have had their tent-camp beyond the limits of the city of Balāsāghūn, for otherwise it is difficult to understand how in 1210 the townspeople could close the gates to the gurkhan's troops without meeting with any conspicuous resistance from the inside.[100]

While discounting both references to Qarā-Khitāy agriculture, we do not claim that the Black Ch'i-tan

[85] HYCCC 1, 32b.

[86] *Op. cit.*, 34b.

[87] *Op. cit.*, 32b. *Cf.* also Barthold 28, 414.

[88] This point is not at all clear in Waley's translation, according to which the very numerous native Hui-ho [Moslems] were "quite unable to manage their fields and orchards for themselves, and are obliged to call in Chinese, Kitai and Tanguts" (Waley 31, 93). Bretschneider's translation of the passage is faulty in several ways, but it is superior in its emphasis on the legal aspect of the matter: the Mohammedans were not allowed to dispose of their fields and gardens, but were "obliged to manage their properties in conjunction with K'i-tan (i.e., Karakhitai), Chinese, and men from *Ho-si*" (Bretschneider 88 I, 78).

[89] YS 82, 19b; 110, 1a ff. (see General Introduction, note 125 ff.).

[90] Aboul-Ghāzi 74, 49.

[91] *Op. cit.*, 3.

[92] Juwaynī 16, 88.

[93] See above, B, 2, 1130, LS 30, 5a–b.

[94] B, 2, [1137], N. D., LS 30, 5b.

[95] Juwaynī 16, 88. Bretschneider (88 I, 229), who follows d'Ohsson 1834 I, 443, disregards the specific meaning of the passage and speaks only of a "large tribute."

[96] CS 121, 5a.

[97] Nidhāmī-i-'Arūḍī 99, 781–782.

[98] Barthold 28, 314 and 316.

[99] *Op. cit.*, 315.

[100] Juwaynī 16, 92.

were "pure" herdsmen. In Liao time a number of inner tribes seem to have engaged in agriculture of some kind;[101] their Hsi Liao successors may well have done likewise. But, judging from the behavior of other "semi-civilized" conquerors of Turkestan, the Qarā-Khitāy probably considered stockbreeding their basic economy. Both the Jurchen and Manchu experiences show that even agricultural conquerors shun the hardships of husbandry whenever their privileged position permits. Furthermore, the military tasks demanded by the political situation were in complete harmony with herding and its organic supplement, hunting. Hunting certainly was the tribal commoners' delight; it remained the rulers' great diversion. The Chin envoy, Nien-ko Han-nu, found the gurkhan engaged in a hunting expedition;[102] and Küchlük seized the last gurkhan in the autumn, when he was out hunting.[103]

After the collapse of the Hsi Liao state, Burāq and his descendants adjusted themselves to a highly urbanized culture in a southern province of Persia, Kirmān. The mass of the Black Ch'i-tan, however, embraced again a purely nomadic life, abandoning what agricultural interests they may have previously developed. A few decades after the last gurkhan's death Carpini and Rubruck[104] found the Qarā-Khitāy near the Naimans in the mountainous northern border regions of their old empire. Said the former: "These two nations do not till the soil, but like the Tartars live in tents."[105]

c. THE ECONOMIC POLICY OF THE HSI LIAO GOVERNMENT

The cornerstone of the gurkhans' economic policy seems to have been an attitude of non-interference in the internal affairs of their subject peoples. An occasional attempt to compel the roving Qarluq Turks to become agriculturists was evidently caused by military rather than economic considerations, for the plan mentions agriculture only as one alternative ("agriculture or some other work"[106]), and it frankly expects that the settled tribesmen "would cease to bear arms."[107]

In general, the Qarā-Khitāy rulers left the sedentary population to their traditional rural and urban pursuits—and the stockbreeders to their herds. Their main efforts were directed toward the collection of taxes and tributes. In 1175 three Moslem traders

reported that the natives in the regions surrounding the Hsi Liao capital camp paid one-tenth of their crop to the state.[108] Ibn al-Athīr states that the gurkhans imposed a tax of one dinar per family on the conquered peoples.[109] The different reports may well refer to different tax levies, one, in kind, collected in the domain; the other, in cash, gathered in the vassal states. A number of outlying countries, though technically independent, also paid tribute to the Hsi Liao court. Khwārazm made its contribution in money, goods, and cattle[110] on an annual basis ostensibly without any regard for the size of its population. Similar arrangements were probably concluded with other nations which flourished along the periphery of Qarā-Khitāy power.

The gurkhans issued special Hsi Liao copper money, which they moulded after the Chinese pattern. In a work, completed in 1149, the Sung scholar, Hung Tsun, mentions a coin, inscribed Kan-t'ien Yüan-pao 感天元寶, which he cannot identify. The coin was evidently cast in Hsi Liao where Empress Kan-t'ien had ascended the throne only five years before.[111] Another coin, inscribed K'ang-kuo T'ung-pao 康國通寶, was obviously cast under the founder of the Qarā-Khitāy dynasty.[112] The Hsi Liao state is said also to have issued paper money. But this claim has no validity, for it is based on an obviously spurious Hsi Liao banknote.[113]

4. THE POLITICAL ORGANIZATION

a. THE NEW TASK

The emperors of Great Liao established a dual system of government for the control of their nomadic and sedentary subjects. Under T'ien-tsu, Liao power dissolved; yet its basic principle of organization was not forgotten. When Yeh-lü Ta-shih in 1124 drew the blueprint for the new state, he set up, in accordance with the Liao pattern, "the offices of the Northern and Southern Regions."[114]

This step was taken before the long march westward. But in Turkestan the gurkhan encountered an administrative situation very different from that faced by his forefathers. To be politically successful, he had to be institutionally flexible. No record indicates the official rejection of the original plan, but none proves that it was put into operation. If a

---

[101] See II, 2 and introduction.
[102] B, 3, 1146, CS 121, 5a–b.
[103] B, 3, 1211, LS 30, 7a.
[104] Rubruck 00, 109 and 110.
[105] Carpini 00, 18.
[106] Barthold 28, 334, based on Ibn al-Athīr XI, 205.
[107] Loc. cit.

[108] CS 121, 5a.
[109] Ibn al-Athīr = Bretschneider 88 I, 232.
[110] B, 2, [ca. 1140/1], N. D., Juwaynī 16, 88.
[111] Ch'ing numismatists all agree upon the Hsi Liao origin of this coin (CL 12, 241, CSS, sect. 4; HWHTK 7, 2845).
[112] KCH 15, 17a ff.
[113] See VII, 2, note 25.
[114] B, 1, 1124 (7), LS 29, 9a; CS 3, 5a–b and 121, 4a.

dual government was maintained, it was certainly of less significance in a country whose chief components were not numerous "inner" tribes on the one hand and on the other a large and relatively uniform sedentary population, but a limited imperial domain surrounded by a vast agglomeration of vassal peoples, sedentary as well as nomadic.

b. THE SUPREME GOVERNMENT OF HSI LIAO

Hu-ssŭ Ordo, at or near Balāsāghūn, was the seat of the empire's supreme government. This government revolved around the gurkhan (emperor) and his court. Personal attendants (近侍)[115] served the sovereign, and officers of the guard (護衛)[116] protected him. It seems reasonable to assume that the Buddhist monk who bore the title of grand preceptor,[117] a mark of distinction under the Liao dynasty,[118] was being equally honored by the Hsi Liao, the more so since outstanding Buddhists were known to have received honorific titles of similar rank in the earlier empire.[119] The husband of the second female ruler of Qarā-Khitāy was designated *fu-ma*, "imperial son-in-law,"[120] a title bestowed on the husbands of imperial princesses in orthodox Chinese dynasties—and in the Liao empire. As in Liao days, the princes were educated by special tutors; the last gurkhan invited a Uighur judge to fill such a position.[121]

No list or survey reveals the over-all organization of the Qarā-Khitāy central government, but Chinese sources contain a few scattered references which, because of the paucity of our information on political institutions, are of particular value.

A general in the gurkhan's army during the battle of Samarqand (Qaṭawān), Hsiao Ch'a-la-a-pu 查剌阿不, was a right vice-chancellor;[122] later, this official appears as co-director of affairs for the Chancellery.[123] In Liao times the second title was given to the fifth highest official in the Chancellery of the Southern Region;[124] the first, except for the word "right" which is not attached to the original Liao title, is identical with that of the fourth highest functionary in this same bureau.[125] Both designations point to the existence of a chancellery of some sort, but whether this office was divided into a left (northern ?) and a right (southern ?) administration cannot be ascertained.

According to Chinese terminology, the head of this office was called a *shu-mi-shih* (chancellor);[126] the highest civil functionary of the Moslem hierarchy was the vizier. Juwaynī (II, 89) states that the last gurkhan was assisted by a vizier, Maḥmūd-bāy.[127]

Under the Liao government the prime ministers, while inferior to the chancellors, held positions of considerable importance. Yeh-lü Ch'u-ts'ai mentions a Chinese, Li Shih-ch'ang 李世昌,[128] whose grandfather acted as Yeh-lü Ta-shih's prime minister.[129] Li himself is called *chung-shu* 中書,[130] a title suggestive of one of the foremost positions in the Liao Secretarial Council.[131] But Yeh-lü Ch'u-ts'ai used the designation poetically; his teacher actually was a *chih-chêng* 執政, an assistant to the prime minister.[132]

In the Liao period the government of the Northern Region had as administrator of the Six Divisions the southern great king.[133] This great king, who was always a member of the Yeh-lü clan, "shared control of the military and civil affairs of the tribes."[134] Yeh-lü Ta-shih had among his prominent supporters a great king of the Office of the Six Divisions 六院司大王, but, contrary to Liao custom, this Hsi Liao functionary was a Hsiao clansman.[135] His title, however, was obviously of Liao provenience.

Fragmentary though these data are, they suggest the existence of Qarā-Khitāy government offices similar at least in name to such highly important Liao bureaus as the Chancellery, the Prime Ministry, and the Secretarial Council; but it is impossible to determine whether the former also had a "northern" or a "southern" affiliation, either because the records are deficient or because the dual administrative organization, though suggested, was never put into practice.

The great king of the Six Divisions, differing from his predecessors, had no I-la tribe over which to rule; but, like them, he may have exercised a general military and civil control over tribal matters.

c. THE VASSALS "SUPERVISED"

In the days of Qarā-Khitāy power Samarqand was called Ho-chung Fu 河中府,[136] "the *fu* (administration)

---

[115] YS 120, 15b.
[116] LS 30, 6b.
[117] YS 124, 7b.
[118] XIV, 2 (5), LS 47, 2a–b.
[119] See IX (21) (30).
[120] LS 30, 7a.
[121] YS 124, 4a.
[122] LS 30, 5b.
[123] LS 30, 6b.
[124] Cf. XIV, 2 (5), LS 47, 2b–3b.
[125] Loc. cit.

[126] Loc. cit.
[127] Barthold, KK, 738.
[128] His honorific title was 郡王; cf. CJCSWC 8, 109.
[129] Op. cit. 7, 94.
[130] Op. cit. 2, 21.
[131] XIV, 2 (5), LS 47, 3b–4b.
[132] Yeh-lü Ch'u-ts'ai's explanation is omitted in the Ts'ung-shu Chi-ch'êng edition (CJCSWC 2, 21); it is preserved, however, in the Ssŭ-pu Ts'ung-k'an edition (2, 13b), a photostatic reproduction of the Yüan original.
[133] LS 46, 3a.
[134] XIV, 1 (9), LS 45, 6a–b.
[135] LS 30, 6b.
[136] Cf. KTCL 14, 5b. This administration "between the rivers" must not be confused with Mā-warā-'n-Nahr,

between the rivers." The term has a number of meanings, but under the Liao dynasty it was used, in the main,[137] to designate "the metropolitan areas surrounding the five capitals."[138] Samarqand was considered a second capital within the Hsi Liao empire.[139]

But although the great city was held in high esteem by its overlords—the last gurkhan considered it "his own treasury"[140]—Samarqand was treated, not as a circuit or province, but as a vassal state. In such a state the native ruler was permitted to retain power, though the Qarā-Khitāy sovereign might replace a hostile individual by a more amenable one. As a symbol of submission, he was given a silver tablet[141] and a seal[142] by the gurkhan.

Qarā-Khitāy domination was expressed primarily in matters of finance. A Hsi Liao envoy permanently stationed at the vassal court saw to it that all fiscal obligations were satisfactorily fulfilled. Chinese sources record two terms for this official, *chien-kuo* 監國, "state supervisor," and *shao-chien* 少監, "junior supervisor,"[143] the latter evidently of somewhat lower rank than the former. Persian sources speak of a *šaḥnagān* or *šaḥangān*.[144] This title, according to Professor Pelliot,[145] probably reflects the Chinese term *shao-chien*.[146] At the close of the dynasty the town of K'o-san (Kāsān)[147] had a *pa-ssǔ-ha*,[148] obviously the Chinese transcription of the Turkic *basqaq*, a term already in use in our period. (The Khwārazm-shāh once sent a "*basqaq*" to Samarqand to represent him there.)[149] In a fourteenth century text the term "*basqaq*" designates a police-chief or tax-collector of a subdued people.[150] The Hsi Liao *pa-ssǔ-ha* in K'o-

san may well have fulfilled this same function, whatever were the duties of the Khwārazm envoy in Samarqand.

In 1134 Yeh-lü Ta-shih entrusted one of the leading positions in his expeditionary force to Yeh-lü Yen-shan 燕山, the *t'u-lu* 禿魯 of the Ch'a-ch'ih-la tribe.[151] The term *t'u-lu* bears close resemblance to *t'u-li* 吐 (or 禿) 里, a term which, in the Liao period, referred to an official of the Six Tribes of Hsi.[152] Did the Qarā-Khitāy control their tribal allies—for the Ch'a-ch'ih-la[153] fell within this category—by placing over them a representative of the central government? If so, they conformed to a pattern of domination that prevailed throughout the tribal sector of the Liao empire.[154]

d. VASSALAGE IN ACTION

Chinese and Persian sources report a few political incidents which reveal the character—and the limitations—of the gurkhans' control over their vassals.

Emphasis on cooperation: After the battle of Qaṭawān the gurkhan ordered the Imām of Bukhārā to be put to death, and appointed Alptägin to look after his interests. But he permitted the local government to remain in the hands of Īmām Aḥmad, "the leading man of his time." Alptägin, swollen with his new authority, levied untoward contributions on the people of Bukhārā, and delegates from the vassal country called in person upon the gurkhan to register their complaints. While retaining his officious functionary in office, the gurkhan ordered him to subordinate himself to Īmām: "Let Alptagīn do what Aḥmad commands, and Aḥmad that which Muḥammad commands."[155]

No Hsi Liao army stationed in a vassal state: In 1156 Samarqand fought a serious war with the Qarluqs, seemingly without aid from its overlord. The savage Turks killed the Iläk Khan whose successor retaliated by overwhelming the invaders. In 1158 the Qarluqs returned with a strong Khwārazm army. This time the khan of Samarqand, insufficiently supported by the nomad Türkmens, appealed to the gurkhan for aid. His request was heard and a detachment of ten thousand Qarā-Khitāy soldiers under Iläk-(Ilig)-Türkmän arrived in the Zarafshān valley. The Hsi Liao army prevented the seizure of Samarqand and their leader concluded a negotiated peace,[156] reasserting the power of Qarā-Khitāy through the

---

"[that] which [is] beyond the River": Transoxania (*cf.* Le Strange 05, 433).

[137] In a few cases the term *fu* was also applied to other territories (see I, 1 (7), Hsing-chung Administration) and several regions in Tung-ching Circuit that perpetuated the earlier Po-hai nomenclature.

[138] I, introduction, 4, *b*.

[139] KTCL 14, 5*b*.

[140] Juwaynī 16, 91.

[141] Ibn al-Athīr = Bretschneider 88 I, 232.

[142] B, 3, 1175, CS 121, 5*a*.

[143] YS 122, 2*a*; SWCCL 48*a*.

[144] *Cf.* Juwaynī 16, 88 and 89. A plural of *šaḥna* < older *šaḥnag*.

[145] Personal communication from Professor Pelliot.

[146] *Shao-chien*, transliterated as Shadkem, Shāwkam, or Schoukem, seems to have been considered a proper name (*cf.* Bretschneider 88 I, 260; Barthold 28, 362; d'Ohsson 1834 I, 109).

[147] In Ferghāna, between Samarqand and Balāsāghūn (Barthold 28, 164 ff.; *cf.* Herrmann 35, 49, C 2).

[148] YS 120, 15*b*.

[149] Juwaynī 16, 83.

[150] Radloff, WB IV, 1533.

[151] LS 30, 6*b*.

[152] LS 25, 5*a*; 69, 19*b*; 73, 1*a* and 7*a*; *cf.* LS 116, 23*b*. For its etymology see XIV, introduction.

[153] B, 2, 1129, LS 30, 4*b*; *cf.* Bretschneider 88 I, 213.

[154] See XIV, introduction.

[155] B, 2, [after 1141/2], N. D., Nidhāmī-i-'Arūdī 99, 651.

[156] Barthold 28, 333–334.

efforts, not of its regional "governor," but of a military force dispatched from the gurkhan's inner domain.

Overlordship—inconspicuous but real: The author of the *Chahār Maqāla*, who completed his book in 1160 while serving the house of Ghūr,[157] describes the loose and limited control which the great gurkhan exercised over Bukhārā. Benjamin of Tudela, the famous rabbi-traveler, when visiting Persia some ten years later, was completely unaware of any Qarā-Khitāy dominion over Transoxania. According to him, the empire of the sultan of Persia, Sanjar, extended "unto the city of Samarkand."[158] In another passage he repeats: ". . . on the frontiers of the kingdom [of Persia] stands Samarkand."[159]

In Benjamin's travelogue, as in Marco Polo's classic, it is not always clear whether regional descriptions are based on the writer's personal experience or on hearsay. Benjamin may have been in Samarqand, but his rather laconic statements about a place which at that time outdid in population and splendor most cities of Central and Western Asia[160] suggest that his information on Transoxania and Khwārazm was not based on direct observation.[161] In any event, a few years before 1173[162] the gurkhan's rule over Transoxania was so inconspicuous that a visitor to Persia [and Turkestan ?] might never be aware of it.

It is possible that the mass of the people in the vassal states of Qarā-Khitāy saw and heard little of their imperial overlord. Their native rulers, however, were better informed. They were too familiar with the gurkhan's military might to mistake remoteness for weakness. In the years following the completion of the *Chahār Maqāla* "all thoughts, not only of expelling the Qarā-Khitāys from Transoxania, but also of taking measures to safeguard the provinces situated to the south of the Amū-Daryā from their invasion were out of the question."[163] With little change, this attitude persisted until the beginning of the thirteenth century. The inhabitants of Bukhārā, who in 1209 exhibited such surprising loyalty to the gurkhan,[164] may have been motivated primarily by a hatred of their immediate neighbors; but their behavior makes sense only if they felt certain that Qarā-Khitāy was able to protect its faithful supporters. The Naiman chieftain, Küchlük, is said to have hesitated before

seizing the Hsi Liao state because of "the gurkhan's high position, the awe which he inspired, his great renown, and his glorious power."[165]

Rebellion (ḫuṭba and coinage): The gurkhans issued special Hsi Liao money, but vassal countries, such as Samarqand and Bukhārā, were permitted to use a currency of their own minting.[166] The sovereigns of Qarā-Khitāy offered no objection to this monetary independence as long as the inscriptions on these territorial coins bore only the name of the regional ruler; but when 'Othmān of Samarqand inscribed the name of the Khwārazm-shāh on his currency (and mentioned him in the formal Friday prayers, the *Ḫuṭba*),[167] he publicly renounced his allegiance to his Hsi Liao overlord.

Rebellion (the "supervisors" killed): According to a contested record concerning the last years of Qarā-Khitāy power preserved by Juwaynī,[168] the gurkhan's envoy to Khwārazm placed himself beside the shah. The ruler, incensed at this affront, had the Hsi Liao official thrown into the river.[169] True or not, the story has interesting implications, for, at least in the mind of the Persian historian, a Qarā-Khitāy delegate might behave thus at a tributary court, and this court could demonstrate its independence with violence and decision.

Information on the rebellion of the vassal king of Kao-ch'ang against the gurkhan in 1209 is more reliable. The uprising is mentioned in several Chinese sources and in one of the main Persian histories, that of Juwaynī. *The Chronicle of the Hsieh Family of Kao-ch'ang* (高昌偰氏家傳) tells of the overbearing behavior of the Hsi Liao "junior supervisor" in this Uighur city. The official, a Buddhist monk, arrogated to himself extraordinary authority and indulged in all manner of excess. Since the Uighurs could look to the rising Mongol power for refuge, their king dared to proceed against the hated "Western Ch'i-tan" delegate. Encircled by native troops, the supervisor fled into a high building (樓). But respite was short: the soldiers followed him up the stairs, cut off his head, and hurled it to the ground.[170] Two other Chinese sources place the incident in the year 1209, confirming the date given by Juwaynī.[171] According to SWCCL 48a, the gurkhan was represented not by one envoy, but two—a "state supervisor" and a "junior supervisor," both of whom were assassinated by the Uighurs. Juwaynī, who speaks of a single

[157] Nidhāmī-i-'Arūdī 99, 40 and 617.

[158] Benjamin 1840 I, 119; II, 170.

[159] *Op. cit.* I, 128.

[160] See Barthold 28, 83 ff.

[161] That Benjamin was not insensitive to the beauty of a great Eastern city is shown by his detailed description of Constantinople, a description manifestly based on personal observations (Benjamin 1840 I, 50–54).

[162] Benjamin (*op. cit.* I, 29) returned to Spain in 1173.

[163] Barthold 28, 335.

[164] *Op. cit.*, 345.

[165] En-Nesawi 95, 13.

[166] See Dorn 81, 734; *idem* 88, 65; Barthold 28, 353.

[167] Juwaynī 16, 91; *cf.* Barthold 28, 358.

[168] Juwaynī II, 74–84 = Barthold 28, 355.

[169] The reasons why Barthold, like d'Ohsson, prefers Juwaynī's second version are given in Barthold 28, 359.

[170] B, 3, 1209, KCWC 11, 5b.

[171] See B, 3, 1209, Juwaynī I, 32 = Barthold 28, 362.

delegate, gives a somewhat different account of his death, but one which also occurred inside a building: "He was surrounded in a house which they pulled down on top of him."[172]

No source mentions the representative's assistants and servitors, but, judging from traditional official decorum, it seems safe to say that the Liao envoy must have been accompanied by an appropriate retinue. Its members probably shared both the privileges and the disastrous end of their superior.

5. ARMY AND WARFARE

a. THE SIZE OF ARMIES

The largest Qarā-Khitāy armies mentioned in the Chinese texts numbered one hundred thousand,[173] seventy thousand,[174] and fifty thousand[175] soldiers respectively. The first figure was given by an informant who erroneously assumed that Yeh-lü Ta-shih had combined his forces with those of another Ch'i-tan enemy of Chin, the Prince of Liang. The second occurs in the description of a rather puzzling eastern expedition organized by Yeh-lü Ta-shih in 1134; the third was submitted by a group of Balā-sāghūn natives who entered Chin territory in 1175. All other statements on Qarā-Khitāy warfare speak of much smaller numbers. Armies of ten thousand men or a multiple of this figure are recorded several times.[176] In the greatest battle of his career, at Qaṭa-wān, Yeh-lü Ta-shih commanded an army whose two wings each comprised twenty-five hundred warriors. According to the rules of Chinese and Liao strategy, his main army should not have had more than ten or twenty thousand soldiers.

It is possible, though not probable, that the eastern expedition included seventy thousand soldiers, and that the battle of Qaṭawān was fought by Yeh-lü Ta-shih in an unorthodox manner, namely, with an unusually large central army. Even so, the maximal number of Hsi Liao troops remains small if compared with the recorded figures for the Liao armies. The number has meaning, however, if viewed in relation to the 84,500 households reported by I-lieh's census.[177]

Traditionally, each Liao household was expected to provide two soldiers. Accepting this as a basis for calculation, the potential manpower of the gurkhan's domain at the time of the census should have been about one hundred and sixty-nine thousand soldiers. But I-lieh's census may have included Balāsāghūn and other settlements whose inhabitants, though taxed and forced to render labor service, "customarily did not have arms (俗無兵器)."[178] In other words, the Hsi Liao warriors may have been recruited only from part of the 84,500 households. If this was the case—that is, if the Qarā-Khitāy troops were in the main drafted from an "inner" tribal population of, let us say, forty to fifty thousand households—then, with a proper allowance for reserve detachments and home defence, armies of ten thousand, thirty thousand, and even fifty thousand soldiers could have been placed in the field.

b. NOMENCLATURE AND ORGANIZATION

The sources give no systematic description of any Qarā-Khitāy army, but the titles of a few leading officials are mentioned in connection with the eastern expedition of 1134. We hear of a general commander in chief who was assisted by a vice-commander in chief. The text also refers to a chief supervisor and a chief controller.[179] All these titles occurred in the Liao army; the first two designated the top-ranking commanders who were subordinate only to the highest military dignitaries of the imperial family.[180] The chief supervisor ranked below the two chief commanders of the campaigning army.[181] The Office of the General Police was headed by a chief controller.[182] No other titles are mentioned in this connection, but the passage dealing with the battle of Qaṭawān speaks of three armies, the center, the right, and the left wings. Their leaders may be equated with the chief commanders of the right and left wings and of the central armies of Liao.[183]

Apparently much of the tradition of Liao warfare was preserved. The Liao armies arranged their fighting force in three divisions; Yeh-lü Ta-shih did likewise. The Liao generals organized their soldiers, predominantly if not entirely, according to the decimal system; the gurkhans seem to have followed the same principle. Both Chinese and Moslem sources speak of ten thousand or a multiple of ten thousand as the numerical standards of the Hsi Liao armies. Barthold mentions one hundred men as the maximal number that, under the first gurkhan, could be entrusted to a

---

[172] Loc. cit.

[173] B, 2, 1126, SCPMHP 58, 6b; TCKC 4, 7b; HNYL 1, 16.

[174] See B, 2, 1134, LS 6a–b.

[175] B, 3, 1175, CS 121, 4b–5a. Bretschneider (88 I, 222) has "10,000."

[176] B, 2, 1129, LS 4b–5a; B, 3, 1158, Juwaynī II, 15 = Barthold 28, 333–334; 1210, Juwaynī 16, 91. Cf. also Juwaynī 16, 89.

[177] B, 3, [1151], LS 30, 7a.

[178] CS 121, 5a. Bretschneider's translation "are not of a warlike character" (Bretschneider 88 I, 222) interpolates a meaning not justified by the text.

[179] LS 30, 6b.

[180] XV, 1 (24).

[181] XV, 2 (2).

[182] Loc. cit.

[183] Loc. cit.

[lower ?] officer.[184] The Liao Ch'i-tan horsemen, secure in their superior mobility, paid little attention to the art of camping;[185] the "Black" Ch'i-tan were equally negligent. Shortly before the end of the twelfth century they were overwhelmed by a night attack because "according to their custom"[186] they slept in tents without proper safeguards.[187] It is possible that in this last respect the Qarā-Khitāy were even less concerned than the Liao Ch'i-tan whose camps, while practically unfortified, were protected by a highly effective system of scouting.

Other deviations from the earlier pattern show that the gurkhans organized their armed forces under conditions that in some ways differed strikingly from those encountered by the "Great" Liao strategists. The Liao rulers augmented their mounted troops by a large infantry army recruited from the country's vast sedentary population. The Qarā-Khitāy, within their inner domain, had at their disposal a relatively small number of sedentary subjects. Though, in all probability, they had foot soldiers and, more particularly, technicians trained in the art of siege, they do not seem to have developed "complex" armies of the type that in the Liao period threatened the defences of the Five Dynasties and Sung China.[188] At the close of the dynasty, in the attack on the rebellious city of Balāsāghūn, elephants were used by the Hsi Liao,[189] further evidence of the effect of the new environment—Turkestan—on the armies of Qarā-Khitāy.

However, neither the introduction of elephants, which apparently occurred late in the history of the empire, nor other modifications which must have appeared earlier, fundamentally affected the character of the Hsi Liao armed force. This force was a cavalry troop built up by a brilliant general who had tested the principles of Ch'i-tan mounted warfare (machine-like organization plus high mobility) not only theoretically, but in a number of battles fought against Sung China and the Chin Jurchen. The transfer of Ch'i-tan strategy to Central Asia created a situation of great historical significance. According to both Chinese and Western sources, Yeh-lü Ta-shih challenged a huge Moslem army at Qaṭawān[190] with a relatively small number of warriors. Sanjar's catastrophic defeat which created an international sensation very possibly induced the chroniclers in both

camps to exaggerate the actual numerical differences. But other data on the size of Qarā-Khitāy, Turkestan, and Persian armies of the period strengthen the impression that Yeh-lü Ta-shih prevailed over an enemy vastly superior in numbers.

To many observers the battle of Qaṭawān was a contest between two religious systems; and there can be no doubt that Sanjar gathered around him in the main fellow-Moslems, whereas most of Yeh-lü Ta-shih's soldiers were "non-believers." But the religious factor played a very complex role in the contemporary history of Turkestan. The gurkhan's invasion of the western countries was motivated, not by religious zeal—he and his successors displayed the utmost religious tolerance[191]—but by the desire for land, power, and wealth. Even if the Moslems were fully conscious of the "heathenism" of their adversaries, militarily the battle of Qaṭawān remained a clash between two different concepts of cavalry warfare—the first great clash between the tactical principles of Western Asia and others conceived and developed during centuries of hostile contact with China's defence system in the vast deserts and steppes of Mongolia. A few generations later the clash of these two principles reached its historical climax when the armies of Turkestan and Persia were fatally crushed by the most accomplished exponent of Mongol warfare, Chingis Khan.

6. MISCELLANEOUS ASPECTS OF QARĀ–KHITĀY CULTURE

Our sources give no systematic picture of Qarā-Khitāy folkways and traditions, but a few scattered references shed light on certain cultural aspects such as language and script, religion, the pattern of marriage, and the position of women. Unsatisfactory though these data are, they provide valuable information concerning the kind of acculturation which occurred under the Qarā-Khitāy dynasties of Hsi Liao and Kirmān.

a. LANGUAGE AND SCRIPT

Yeh-lü Ta-shih was familiar with both the Chinese and the Ch'i-tan languages when he embarked upon his career of conquest. In intercourse with his "inner" (Ch'i-tan) followers, he doubtless preferred to use his native tongue. But even prominent Chinese at court must have found a knowledge of the Altaic language to their advantage: Yeh-lü Ch'u-ts'ai's teacher of the Ch'i-tan language, who had been assistant to the prime minister under the last gurkhan, was named Li;[192] possibly he was a Hsi Liao Chinese.

Archaeological finds and literary records reveal that

[184] Barthold, KK, 738.
[185] XV, 2 (3); see also XV, introduction, 5, b (iv) and note 413.
[186] Barthold 28, 344.
[187] Ibn al-Athīr XI, 88–91 = Barthold 28, 344.
[188] See XV, introduction, 5, b (vi).
[189] Juwaynī 16, 92.
[190] B, 2, [1141], LS 5b–6a and 1141, Ibn al-Athīr XI, 54–67 = Marquart 14, 165.

[191] See below, 6, b.
[192] CJCSWC 8, 109. See above, note 128.

Chinese was current in Turkestan from the days of the Han dynasty on.[193] The great Far Eastern language (and script) survived the breakdown of Han and T'ang control over Central Asia. Despite the difficulties arising from its complexities, difficulties that were duly recognized and, at times, even exaggerated in Western Liao,[194] the Chinese language played an important role during the tenth century in the cultural life of Kao-ch'ang and other cities of Turkestan. A story told by Nizām al-Mulk indicates that a hundred years later there were people in Persia who were known to speak and even write Chinese.[195]

Knowledge of Chinese evidently enhanced prestige in the oasis empire of Qarā-Khitāy. The gurkhan bestowed Chinese titles on himself, his court, and on his civil and military officials.[196] The Chinese nomenclature recorded in the Chinese sources does not necessarily prove that the titles were originally so designated, but the case for an extended official use of Chinese is strengthened by the fact that all the Hsi Liao coins that have been recovered are inscribed in Chinese only.[197] In addition, Persian authors have noted a few Qarā-Khitāy words, such as fu-ma (imperial son-in-law[198]) and paiza (token of office).[199]

But Chinese was not the only script employed officially. The Chahār Maqāla states that the first gurkhan reprimanded his representative in Bukhārā in a letter composed in Persian.[200] During the later part of the dynasty, an Uighur judge, Ha-la-i-hach'ih-pei-lu 哈剌亦哈赤北魯 (Qara-Jүγač Bujruq), was invited to teach the imperial princes,[201] probably because the Uighur language (and script) was an important means of communication in the eastern regions of Turkestan.

Thus the linguistic situation in Qarā-Khitāy was complex, much more so than is suggested by Barthold's assertion: "The language of the government seems to

have been Chinese."[202] The government did indeed use the Chinese script in its most solemn official documents; but in its dealings with the Moslem vassal states Persian was also employed, and in certain central or eastern territories possibly Uighur. The Ch'i-tan script, still popular in Chin China,[203] must also have persisted in the western regions ruled by a Ch'i-tan dynasty. If, at the close of this dynasty, a Hsi Liao Chinese gave. Yeh-lü Ch'u-ts'ai the instruction prerequisite to translating a Ch'i-tan text, it seems safe to assume that the Qarā-Khitāy themselves were still familiar with their own national script.

Barthold's hypothesis, which is highly problematic as far as the script is concerned, is even more so when the spoken language is under consideration. At the gurkhan's court the Chinese and Ch'i-tan who had received a thorough Chinese education must have been limited in number. In the Hsi Liao centers of power many Inner Asiatic nationals assembled who either spoke the Altaic languages (Ch'i-tan, Turkic) or some Iranian tongue. The need, therefore, to master Chinese was small, smaller no doubt than that which led the government officials of Mediaeval Europe to use Latin. The history of European civilization reveals that, for a considerable time, official documents might be written in Latin, while government officials transacted their verbal business in their native language.

The Moslems of Turkestan, according to the author of the Pei Shih Chi, wrote their legal documents in the Hui-ho 回紇 script.[204] The term Hui-ho as used in this passage does not seem to mean "Uighur," but, as in other parts of the same travelogue, "Moslem." In all probability, the script referred to was the Arabic, which, after the Arab conquest, spread into Persia and Turkestan, replacing in Persia Proper the Mediaeval Persian script (Pahlawī),[205] and in Turkestan, the Soghdian and Uighur scripts. In part, the Arabic alphabet may have been used for recording Iranian (Persian or Tādžik) texts. The "sacred books," however, which the Chinese visitor found unintelligible, were undoubtedly composed in Arabic, for this remained the language of Islam, even where for secular purposes national tongues such as Persian were commonly used.[206]

b. RELIGION

The records tell next to nothing about Qarā-Khitāy religion. At the beginning of his great trek, and again before the start of the eastern expedition of 1134, Yeh-lü Ta-shih sacrificed a grey ox and a white

---

[193] See Chavannes 13, passim.

[194] According to information gathered by the author of the Fihrist [completed in 988], it takes an intelligent person at least twenty years to master the Chinese script (Ferrand 13, 135–136).

[195] Nizam oul-Moulk 93, 194.

[196] See C, 4, b.

[197] See C, 3, c.

[198] The word fuma appears in Juwaynī; the word is also written farmā (Barthold, KK, 738).

[199] "So to be read for ba nayza" (loc. cit.). See also Barthold 35, 124. The Chinese term in question is evidently p'ai-tzŭ 牌子.

[200] B, 2, [after 1141/2], N. D., Nidhāmī-i-'Arūdī 99, 651.

[201] YS 124, 4a. Professor Pelliot, in his personal notes, recognizes in this unwieldly transliteration the name Qara-Jүγač Bujruq. This is indeed a very common Uighur designation, which literally means "the official 'Black Tree.'"

[202] Barthold, KK, 738.

[203] See VII, 2, note 25.

[204] KHCCL 7a.

[205] Browne 28 I, 9 ff.

[206] Op. cit., II, 4 ff.

horse,[207] thus indicating his continued reliance on Ch'i-tan tribal tradition. Buddhism, the "civilized" concomitant of Ch'i-tan shamanism during the Liao period, maintained its popularity among the Qarā-Khitāy until the end of the dynasty. The Naiman chief, Küchlük, who had been a Christian, adopted "idolatry" (Buddhism) after marrying a Qarā-Khitāy girl.[208] Later, in Eastern Turkestan, he displayed great intolerance toward the Moslem religion. Having forced the inhabitants of Kāshghar to become "idolaters," his soldiers compelled the people of Khotan to accept Christianity or Buddhism, or, at the very least, to don Qarā-Khitāy clothes.[209] "The cry of the Muazzin and the confession of the Unity of the God of Believers was no longer heard. The mosques were closed and the schools abandoned."[210] The choice offered to the Mohammedans of Khotan reveals a Küchlük more concerned with combating Islam than with spreading Buddhism. But there can be no doubt that he himself embraced this "idolatrous" religion.

Küchlük's ruthless aggressions against the Moslems of Kāshghar and Khotan contrast strikingly with the Hsi Liao attitude toward creeds other than their own. Under Qarā-Khitāy rule Christianity was practised in the empire's inner domain at the Chu River;[211] and a Nestorian bishop, Elias III, made his seat in Kāshghar.[212] Judaism flourished at Samarqand, as it did in a number of outlying cities.[213] Even Islam was generously treated, although resistance to Qarā-Khitāy conquest had been organized under its banner. The Moslem historian Jūzjānī, evaluating the first gurkhans' "equity and ability," observes that they "used to treat Mohammedans with great reverence, show respect unto ecclesiastics, and used not to consider tyranny and violence allowable towards any created being."[214]

This statement was probably based on a general impression of Qarā-Khitāy policy, inspired by such official acts as the upholding of the Imām of Bukhārā and the sending of an admonishing letter to the Hsi Liao representative, Alptägin.[215] The recorded version was composed "after the way of good Muslims."[216] Mohammedan historians of the thirteenth century must have read the *Chahār Maqāla*. Jūzjānī writes: "Some have related that this [the first] Gūr Khān had, secretly, become a Musalmān," but he adds cautiously, "God knows the truth in this matter."[217]

Hsi Liao policies in the final period clearly demonstrate that the Qarā-Khitāy never adopted the religion of Islam. According to an-Nasawī, who witnessed the collapse of pre-Mongol Turkestan, the last Khwārazm-shāh found "no difference" between the Mongol newcomers, the gurkhan, the Küchlük Khan, "for you are all given to idolatry."[218] The testimony of Juwaynī, Ibn al-Athīr, and an-Nasawī on the gurkhans' infidelity ("idolatry") is strengthened by a Christian statement: Bar Hebraeus lays it to the influence of a "Ķārāketā" woman that the ruler of the Krīth (the Naimans) "turned aside his heart from the fear of Christ His Lord" and "worshipped strange gods."[219]

c. THE PATTERN OF MARRIAGE

The only data available regarding marriage relations in Qarā-Khitāy refer to members of the two leading families, the Yeh-lü and the Hsiao. The two groups intermarried,[220] as they had in the time of Liao, but, since both must have been limited in number,[221] the arrangement was probably not as exclusive as it had been in the earlier empire.

Records on the Kirmān Qarā-Khitāy do not refer to either the Yeh-lü or the Hsiao clan. Apparently, the founder of the new dynasty did not find his close supporters among the Hsiao; it is even possible that he himself belonged to neither of the two former ruling houses. But, although the records give no clue to Burāq's family background, they suggest,

---

[207] B, 2, 1130, LS 30, 5a–b and LS 30, 6b.

[208] Barthold (01, 64), following Oppert's suggestion, interprets Juwaynī's record of Küchlük's conversion to "idolatry" as probably referring to Buddhism. The same conclusion had been reached previously by N. Elias (Mirza Haidar 98, 290, note 1).

[209] Juwaynī = Mirza Haidar 98, 291. We follow Barthold's (01, 64) slightly different interpretation of the passage.

[210] Juwaynī = Mirza Haidar 98, 291.

[211] Bathold, KK, 738.

[212] *Loc. cit.* See also Barthold 01, 58.

[213] Benjamin 1840 I, 128 ff.

[214] Tabakat-i-Nasiri 81 II, 912.

[215] B, 2 [after 1141/2], N. D., Nidhāmī-i-'Arūdī 99, 651.

[216] *Loc. cit.*

[217] Tabakat-i-Nasiri 81 II, 912.

[218] En-Nesawi 95, 18. In view of this, Ibn al-Athīr's remark concerning the first gurkhan's "son Muḥammad" (XI, 57 = Barthold, KK, 739) is puzzling. Barthold does not know how the text should be emended, but he feels sure that the son "cannot have been called Muḥammad." Marquart (14, 238) considers the traditional reading "nonsensical." He suggests a version which discards the word Muḥammad and instead makes the first gurkhan's wife his cousin. Barthold does not accept this correction because "it is nowhere stated that the wife of the Gurkhan was also his cousin."

[219] Bar Hebraeus 32 I, 353. See B, 3, note 31

[220] See LS 30, 7a.

[221] As in other "colonial" societies, there must have been a great numerical disproportion between the sexes, particularly at the beginning of the Hsi Liao period.

under a cover of Moslem names, a tendency to marry "upwards," that is, to take a spouse from a higher generation. After having usurped the throne, Burāq made the legitimate ruler's mother his wife, disregarding her own objections as well as those of her son.[222] The circumstances surrounding the marriage suggest that the step was taken in response to political rather than personal considerations; and the dramatic end of the alliance (the discovery of a plot and the subsequent execution of his suspected wife)[223] tends to confirm this assumption. The "upward" marriage of Burāq's nephew proved more fortunate. Tāyangū took as his wife one of his deceased uncle's concubines, the famous Qutlugh Turkān, "who guided him with wise councils."[224]

d. POSITION OF WOMEN

Under the Liao dynasty women, as revealed in the history of the empress dowagers, held positions of distinction both politically and ceremonially. Within the Hsi Liao state the matriarchal trend seems to have become even stronger. Two out of five times the imperial throne was officially occupied by a woman.

A similar development can be documented for the Qarā-Khitāy dynasty of Kirmān. During his second reign period Tāyangū was advised by his wife, Qutlugh Turkān. For a period of twenty-five years after his death she "became virtual ruler of Kirmān, governing in the name of her husband and of her two sons who in turn she allowed nominally to succeed to the throne."[225] In Kirmān City a tomb within "the magnificent Green (or blue) Dome," completed in 1242, preserves the memory of the "celebrated princess."[226] There in 1282 her body was laid to rest, not by her son, but by "her daughter, Bībī Turkān."[227]

The peace of mind of the next ruler was increasingly disturbed by his sister, Pādishāh Khātūn, who eventually seized power and had her brother strangled. She herself was killed in 1294,[228] nine years before the collapse of the Kirmān Qarā-Khitāy. Thus, female influence prevailed during the middle and later part of a dynasty which produced only two outstanding rulers—one, a man, Burāq, the other, a woman, Qutlugh Turkān.

The great importance of the Hsiao clan at the Hsi Liao court may explain why the first female gurkhan

was appointed to office, but it cannot account for the acceptability of the second who was a Yeh-lü princess; and no mention is made of the Hsiao clan in records dealing with the Kirmān Qarā-Khitāy. Historically speaking, consort families have often succeeded in covertly dominating a reign by placing their male members in key positions of power. The overt rule of women in the above instances may well reflect an old Ch'i-tan tradition—a tradition which found expression throughout the Liao empire, and which, with added force, asserted itself in the "Black" Ch'i-tan dynasties of Hsi Liao and Kirmān.

7. HOW CHINESE WERE THE QARĀ-KHITĀY?

In his article "*Karā-Khitāy*" in the *Encyclopedia of Islam* Barthold notes the progress of Christianity and Mohammedanism in the Hsi Liao empire. At the same time, he stresses the Chinese character of certain political usages and institutions: "The level of taxation was, as in China, fixed by the number of houses; a dinar was levied on every house. The language of the government seems to have been Chinese."[229]

Chinese titles were indeed conspicuous in the Qarā-Khitāy administration,[230] but these titles were frequently derived from the official nomenclature of the Liao empire. For instance, the use of the word "heaven" (天) as a component of Hsi Liao imperial titles is not a specifically Chinese formula, but an honorific designation peculiar to the Liao emperors.[231]

No doubt, Chinese formulas more or less unchanged remained prominent in Qarā-Khitāy official terminology, but they operated in an extremely complex linguistic milieu within which spoken Chinese probably played a very insignificant role. Still less satisfactory is Barthold's attempt to draw a parallel between the Hsi Liao a-dinar-per-house levy and Chinese fiscal procedure. Even if he had included the mode of taxation employed in the Balāsāghūn region under which ten per cent of the crop was surrendered to the government, his conclusions would still be open to question. A tax of ten per cent is recorded for ancient China, and throughout the ages the Chinese have paid a variety of poll-taxes. Yet, under the T'ang and Sung governments taxation was based primarily on the amount (and value) of *mou* cultivated.[232] A levy depending on the number of *mou* is also mentioned in one of the few concrete descriptions of Liao agriculture.[233]

On the other hand, Moslem law demanded that

[222] See B, 4, [before 1230], N. D., en-Nesawi 95, 239 and Hamd-Allāh Mustawfī 13, 116.

[223] B, 4, 1230, en-Nesawi 95, 239.

[224] Hamd-Allāh Mustawfī 13, 132.

[225] Le Strange 01, 287.

[226] *Loc. cit.*

[227] B, 4, 1282, Hamd-Allāh Mustawfī 13, 133.

[228] B, 4, 1294, Hamd-Allāh Mustawfī 13, 133.

[229] Barthold, KK, 738.

[230] See LS 30, 6a and 7a.

[231] See above, appendix II, note 5.

[232] See X, introduction, notes 245 and 246.

[233] II, 2 (9).

non-believers pay land and poll-taxes.[234] The poll-tax, according to one opinion, should be unrestricted; according to another, it should amount to at least one dinar.[235] The believers paid neither poll nor land tax,[236] but only ten per cent "alms."[237]

The two above-mentioned records concerning Hsi Liao taxation seem contradictory, but they may actually refer to two fiscal policies pursued in two different parts of the empire. The region around the capital was apparently treated according to the Chinese (and Liao) pattern, while in the rural territories a tax was levied which combined the Chinese preference for taxing "households" rather than individuals with the Islamic principle of extracting from the taxable subject a fixed sum of a dinar or more.

The Liao system of succession, which permitted two women and a younger son to wield supreme power, had little or no relation to orthodox Chinese tradition. Rather it conformed to principles which had validity for many nomadic peoples in Inner Asia and which operated also in predynastic and dynastic Ch'i-tan society.

Qarā-Khitāy civilization was obviously a compound of Liao Ch'i-tan elements (including a number of Liao Chinese features) and patterns and traits traditional in the new Central Asiatic (Turkic-Iranian) environment. The political organization of the gurkhans' empire was certainly not purely Chinese. Liao principles of administration, originally given recognition, were either discarded altogether or fundamentally modified under the influence of the natural and cultural landscape of Turkestan. The resulting set-up, a limited inner domain surrounded by a vast area of semi-independent vassal countries, resembles neither T'ang nor Sung China, nor even Liao; but it exhibits considerable affinity to those Central Asiatic conquest states which were ruled by semi- or full-nomads, such as the Qarā-Khānids of Balāsāghūn and Samarqand.

The Liao Ch'i-tan, though not unsympathetic to Chinese agriculture, paid little attention to one of its most important aspects, irrigation,[238] an aspect which was not particularly conspicuous in the northern part of their empire. If Turkān Khātūn (Qutlugh Turkān) achieved immortality because she improved the subterranean canals (qanāt's) of Kirmān,[239] she was obviously inspired by a policy that had long found

support in the classical irrigation regions of Turkestan as well as in Kirmān itself.[240] Most probably, the Qarā-Khitāy began to understand the value of irrigation only after they had departed from their eastern semi-Chinese homeland.

The similarity of the Hsi Liao system of taxation to Moslem fiscal practice has already been discussed. The employment of the "merchant-prince," Maḥmūd-bāy, as vizier has interesting religious and social implications. The first gurkhan was eager to have a Moslem religious leader at the helm of one of his great vassal states, Bukhārā; the last gurkhan appointed a Moslem to one of the highest, if not the highest, office in his government. Barthold does not elaborate his remark concerning Maḥmūd-bāy's background, but the formula "merchant-prince" seems to indicate that a business man could play a leading role in administrative affairs—a possibility excluded, it would seem, by law and custom in T'ang and Sung China as well as in the Liao empire.[241]

The Qarā-Khitāy army adopted Chinese titles and certain over-all features of organization from the Liao Ch'i-tan. However, its one-sided emphasis on cavalry warfare reflects the needs of Inner Asiatic strategy much more surely than the complex military system of Liao which was strongly influenced by the fight against its main enemy, China.

Chinese script was used in the official documents and announcements of the Qarā-Khitāy government. The gurkhan's reign titles inscribed on Hsi Liao coins were written in Chinese characters. But such preferences for the "Latin" of the Far East and the presence of Chinese officials at the gurkhan's court must not blind the investigator to the highly complex nature of Qarā-Khitāy culture. Elements of Liao Chinese tradition blended or co-existed with Central Asiatic patterns of power and economy coordinated by Ch'i-tan activists who, despite two hundred years of symbiosis with the Chinese, had not lost their national particularity. It is highly significant that, even according to the Chinese records of the Qarā-Khitāy dynasty, Yeh-lü Ta-shih, when obtaining supreme power, adopted the Chinese designation "emperor" only after (and in addition to) the blatantly Inner Asiatic, tribal, and barbarian title "gurkhan."

8. "ENLIGHTENMENT" AND LIMITATION OF QARĀ-KHITĀY RULE

The familiarity of the Ch'i-tan with the ways of sedentary peoples both facilitated and limited their expansion into the western countries. They conquered easily and ruled wisely. Though they were

[234] Mawerdi 15, 299 ff.
[235] Op. cit., 303 and note 4. The land tax was levied in accordance with the value of the land (op. cit., 309 and 315).
[236] Op. cit., 312.
[237] Op. cit., 239 and 310.
[238] See II, introduction
[239] See Kramers 27, 1031.

[240] See Schwarz 12, 220 ff., especially 238, 239, 243, 246, and 247.
[241] Cf. XIV, introduction, notes 493–496.

no saints (oppressive acts are recorded not only toward the close of the dynasty[242]), they resembled, and perhaps even out-did, other semi-acculturated nomad conquerors of Turkestan in their tolerance of alien cultures and ideas. Marquart's appraisal of Qarā-Khitāy culture as a shining exception in a depressing setting,[243] though perhaps an over-simplification of the actual picture, is in greater agreement with Moslem opinion of the twelfth and thirteenth centuries than Barthold's unconvincingly argued skepticism.[244]

Being well-equipped politically and militarily, the Qarā-Khitāy easily gained control over a considerable territory. However, their achievement is strikingly modest when compared with that of their successors, the Mongols. Why did Yeh-lü Ta-shih seize only the heart of Asia, whereas Chingis Khan and his descendants subdued almost the whole continent? The specific military and political reasons for the extraordinary success of the Mongol campaigns cannot be discussed here; nor can we analyze at this point the complex historical situation that encouraged and restrained the leader of the "Black" Ch'i-tan. Nevertheless, a few tentative comments may be made regarding the limitations of Qarā-Khitāy conquest.

Examining the various factors which determine the success or failure of nomad aggression, the great theoretician of Arab conquest, Ibn Khaldūn, emphasizes two which figure prominently also in the history of Qarā-Khitāy—the conquerors' ruthlessness and their number. The nomads, who preserve intact the spirit of the desert,[245] the "semi-savages," or "wild beasts," as they were considered by other peoples,[246] surpass in valor not only their sedentary enemies but also all their nomad rivals who, after victory, succumb to a life of plenty at the expense of their settled subjects: "If the two groups are equal in number and strength, those who are best suited for nomadic life, will prevail."[247]

Ibn Khaldūn's formula cannot be accepted without qualification. Lack of contact with the complex techniques of warfare traditional to urban civilization may so lower the efficiency of the "pure" nomads that even beastly ferocity cannot compensate for it. The struggle of T'ang China against the Turks and of the Liao armies against their tribal neighbors are cases in point. If, however, the nomads learn how to employ the sophisticated techniques of their "civilized" enemies without losing their "semi-savage" mentality then, *ceteris paribus*, they will prevail over their less savage opponents. It is in this last respect that the Mongols were crassly superior to the Qarā-Khitāy. The Ch'i-tan mind, mellowed by centuries of contact with Chinese civilization and, still more, by the pleasant experience of two hundred years of Liao rule, was less fierce—and more humane—than that of Chingis Khan who most devastatingly fulfilled Ibn Khaldūn's psychological requirements.

Discussing the size of invasion forces, the Arab historian says: "Expansion and power of an empire are directly related to the number of its founders."[248] This statement too needs qualifying. Other things being equal, a small army of superior organization and equipment may crushingly defeat a numerically stronger enemy: witness Yeh-lü Ta-shih's brilliant victories over his Moslem opponents. But, though quantitative inferiority may be compensated for by superior striking power, the inequality cannot be indefinitely increased. At a certain point the elite factor loses its strength and number becomes decisive. It is true that the small armies of Cortez and Pizarro overran two American empires, firstly, because their Indian enemies were unprepared to deal with strange European techniques, and secondly, because the Spanish elite could always draw new support from their homeland. However, Xenophon's Ten Thousand benefiting from neither factor could only achieve a heroic retreat.

The Hsi Liao soldiers, who apparently excelled in organization and training, were few in number, a fact that must not be viewed isolatedly, but in connection with the military mentality discussed above. A more ruthless manner of warfare might have attracted more followers, as it did in the case of Chingis Khan. But Ch'i-tan psychology being what it was at the end of the Liao dynasty, its Qarā-Khitāy heirs could act only in a semi-civilized (tolerant) way, attracting fewer supporters and establishing control only within the confines of a limited Central Asiatic empire.

Thus the military record of Hsi Liao is less impressive than that of the Mongols. From the standpoint of culture history, however, the dynasty remains highly significant—an "enlightened" variant of one of the two main types of Asiatic conquest society.

---

[242] It is possible that at the end of the Hsi Liao period oppression became more intense; it certainly was more resented (*cf.* B, 3, 1209, KCWC 11, 5*b*; see also *Pei Shih Chi* = KHCCL 6*a*). But the case of Alptägin proves that, on occasion, oppressive demands were made immediately after the establishment of Qarā-Khitāy sovereignty.

[243] Marquart 14, 209.

[244] Barthold, KK, 739.

[245] Ibn Khaldoun, PH I, 264.

[246] *Op. cit.*, 303.

[247] *Op. cit.*, 291.

[248] *Op. cit.*, 335.

BIBLIOGRAPHY

The books and articles quoted in this publication are listed below, the Chinese and Japanese works first and then all others subsumed for convenience under the heading "Western." An abbreviation by which the reference is cited precedes each title.

Our source material differs widely in character and arrangement, and this has determined the way in which our abbreviations have been formulated.

1. CHINESE AND JAPANESE WORKS

a. Chinese and Japanese writings which appeared before the introduction of modern ("Western") techniques of publication are cited by the initials of the key words in their titles. No more than six letters are used in any symbol and when possible fewer. Thus, SMCW stands for *Sung-mo Chi-wên.* When according to this method two or more abbreviations are identical, the author's initials are added to all but one. Thus PS stands for *Pei Shih,* PSHT for *P'u Shuang* by Hung Tsun. When the initials of the titles of dynastic histories are identical, only one is referred to by the standard abbreviation; the others are designated by the name of the dynasty. Thus LS stands for *Liao Shih,* Liang for *Liang Shu;* SS for *Sung Shih,* Sung for *Sung Shu,* and Sui for *Sui Shu.* Modern reprints of Chinese books (in traditional or modern pattern) are also quoted by initials.

b. Modern Chinese and Japanese books and articles are quoted by author and year of publication. Since Chinese family names are limited in number, the initials of the Chinese authors' personal names are added (Wang CJ 31 and Wang KL 31). Books of modern authors published in the traditional way are quoted like the old works.

Reference to Chinese sources, both old and new, usually include the *chüan* (chapter) before the page number, for instance, HHSS 35, 9*a*; or in a modern edition, HNYL 114, 1854. The Chinese subdivisions of a *chüan* 上, 下, and 上, 中, 下, are expressed by *A* and *B* or *A, B,* and *C* respectively (TS 221*A* and TS 221*B*).

If two different editions of the same work are used, the letter [A] is added to one of them, thus, SF and SF [A] distinguish two editions of the *Shuo Fu.*

The following equivalents are used to indicate smaller or larger units of Chinese publications:

vol. (volume)—册
ch. (chapter)—卷 or 帙
series—集 or 輯
coll. (collection)—編

2. WESTERN SOURCES

Reference to "Western" writings includes the family name of the author and the date of publication. The years before 1850 are given in full; from 1850 on only the last two figures are used (Remusat 1829, but Pelliot 04). If an author published two or more items in the same year, the letters *a, b,* etc. are added to the year (Pelliot 15 and Pelliot 15*a*).

Books of more than one volume appearing over a period of years are designated by author and title initials (Francke, GCR II), and articles published in installments over a period of years by author, year, and initials (Chavannes 97–98, VC).

In the bibliography the titles of periodicals and collections which appear more than twice are quoted according to the standard abbreviations listed below:

AA	American Anthropologist
AAW	Abhandlungen der [Königlichen] Preussischen Akademie der Wissenschaften zu Berlin, Philologisch-Historische Klasse
AS	Kuo-li Chung-yang Yen-chiu Yüan Li-shih Yü-yen Yen-chiu So Chi-k'an 國立中央研究院歷史語言研究所集刊 Academia Sinica: Bulletin of the Institute of History and Philology
BEFEO	Bulletin de l'Ecole Française de l'Extrême-Orient
CPTCTS	Chih-pu-tsu-chai Ts'ung-shu 知不足齋叢書 (preface dated 1776)
CYTCS	Ch'ien-yen-t'ang Ch'üan-shu 潛研堂全書 Lung-shih 龍氏 ed. 1884
Enc. Is.	Encyclopaedia of Islam
Enc. SS	Encyclopaedia of the Social Sciences, 1937 ed.
ESWSPP	Êrh-shih-wu Shih Pu-pien 二十五史補編 K'ai-ming 開明 ed. 1937
HCTY	Hsüeh-chin T'ao-yüan 學津討原 Han-fên-lou 涵芬樓 Comm. Press ed.
HJAS	Harvard Journal of Asiatic Studies
JA	Journal Asiatique
JAOS	Journal of the American Oriental Society
JRAS	Journal of the Royal Asiatic Society
KHCK	Kuo-hsüeh Chi-k'an 國學季刊 Journal of Sinological Studies, National University of Peking
LHTS	Liao-hai Ts'ung-shu 遼海叢書
MCRKH	Mansen chiri-rekishi kenkyū hōkoku: 滿鮮地理歷史研究報告

MRDTB Memoirs of the Research Department of the Toyo Bunko, Tokyo

PCHSTK Pi-chi Hsiao-shuo Ta-kuan 筆記小說大觀 Chin-pu 進步 ed., Shanghai

Po-na 百衲本 Comm. Press ed.

SAW Sitzungsberichte der [Königlichen] Preussischen Akademie der Wissenschaften zu Berlin, Philologisch-Historische Klasse

SCPS Ssǔ-ch'ao Pieh-shih 四朝別史 Sao-yeh-shan-fang 掃葉山房 ed.

SF Shuo Fu 說郛 Wan-wei-shan-t'ang 宛委山堂 ed.

SF [A] Shuo Fu 說郛 Han-fên-lou 涵芬樓 Comm. Press ed.

SL Ta Ch'ing Li-ch'ao Shih-lu 大清歷朝實錄 Tokyo 1937

SPPY Ssǔ-pu Pei-yao 四部備要 Chung-hua 中華 ed. Shanghai 1936

SPTK Ssǔ-pu Ts'ung-k'an 四部叢刊 Comm. Press ed.

SSKTS Shou-shan-ko Ts'ung-shu 守山閣叢書 Hung-wên 鴻文 ed. 1889

SZ Shigaku zasshi 史學雜誌

TP T'oung Pao

TSCC Ts'ung-shu Chi-ch'êng 叢書集成 Comm. Press ed.

WCHS Wu-ch'ao Hsiao-shuo 五朝小說

WKW Wang Chung-k'o-kung I-shu 王忠慤公遺書 1927

WYTCCP Wu-ying-tien Chü-chên-pan Ts'ung-shu 武英殿聚珍版叢書 Kuang-ya 廣雅 ed. 1899

YCHP Yen-ching Hsüeh-pao 燕京學報 Yenching Journal of Chinese Studies

YK Yü Kung 禹貢, The Chinese Historical Geography

CHINESE AND JAPANESE BIBLIOGRAPHY

AJCTC: *Ai-jih-chai Ts'ung-ch'ao* 愛日齋叢鈔 in *TSCC* no. 0325

CC: Hung Tsun 洪遵 *Ch'üan Chih* 泉志 in *HCTY* series 8

CCC: Yüan Hao-wên 元好問 *Chung-chou Chi* 中州集 in *Sung-fên-shih Ts'ung-k'an* 誦芬室叢刊 first coll. 1920

CCCW: Ho Yüan 何薳 *Ch'un-chu Chiu-wên* 春渚舊聞 in *HCTY* series 15

CCHT: Ch'ien K'ang-kung 錢康公 *Chih-chang Hsien-t'an* 植杖閒談 in *WCHS* ch. 80

CCITC: *Chia-ch'ing Ch'ung-hsiu Ta Ch'ing I-t'ung Chih* 嘉慶重修大清一統志 in *SPTK* second coll.

CCKCT: Li Yeh 李冶 *Ching-chai Ku-chin T'ou* 敬齋古今黈 in *TSCC* no. 0216

CCSLCT: Ch'ên Chên-sun 陳振孫 *Chih-chai Shu-lu Chieh-t'i* 直齋書錄解題 in *WYTCCP*

CCSSC: Tsung Lin 宗懍 *Ching Ch'u Sui-shih Chi* 荆楚歲時記 in *SF* ch. 96

CCTCCS: *Ch'un-ch'iu Tso Chuan Chu-shu* 春秋左傳注疏 in *SPPY*

CCWC: Wang Yün 王惲 *Ch'iu-chien Hsien-shêng Ta-ch'üan Wên-chi* 秋澗先生大全文集 in *SPTK* first coll.

CCWHTK: Hsi Huang 稽璜 and others *Ch'ing-ch'ao Wên-hsien T'ung-k'ao* 清朝文獻通考 Wan-yu Wên-k'u 萬有文庫 ed. Shanghai 1936

CCYL: Sun Ssǔ-miao 孫思邈 *Ch'ien-chin Yüeh-ling* 千金月令 in *SF* ch. 69

CFC: Chao Ju-k'uo 趙汝适 *Chu Fan Chih* 諸蕃志 in *TSCC* no. 3272

CHANG HL 30: Chang Hsing-lang 張星烺 *Chung-hsi Chiao-t'ung Shih-liao Hui-pien* 中西交通史料匯編 6 v. Peiping 1930

CHC: Wang Chi 王寂 *Cho-hsüan Chi* 拙軒集 in *Shih-lien-an Hui-k'o Chiu Chin Jên Chi* 石蓮盦彙刻九金人集 Wu-ying-tien Chü-chên 武英殿聚珍 ed. 1909

CHCF: Ku Yen 顧彥 *Chih Huang Ch'üan Fa* 治蝗全法 Yu-pai-yün-chai 猶白雲齋 ed. 1888

CH'ÊN MC 36: Ch'ên Mêng-chia 陳夢家 "Shang-tai Ti Shên-hua Yü Wu-shu 商代的神話與巫術 (Myths and Witchcraft during the Shang Period)," *YCHP* 20: 486–576, 1936

CH'ÊN S 36: Ch'ên Shu 陳述 "A-pao-chi Yü Li K'o-yung Mêng-chieh-hsiung-ti Chih Nien Chi Ch'i Pei-mêng-hsiang-kung Chih T'ui-ts'ê 阿保機與李克用盟結兄弟之年及其背盟相攻之推測 (Notes on the Date of Li K'ê-jung's Alliance with the Khitan Chieftain Apochi)," *AS* 7 (1): 79–88, 1936

—— 39: —— "T'ou-hsia K'ao 頭下考 (上) (Notes on 'T'ou-hsia,' Part I)," *AS* 8 (3): 387–398, 1939

—— 39a: —— "Ch'i-tan Shih-hsüan K'ao 契丹世選考 (On the Khitan System of Heir Selection)," *AS* 8 (2): 181–187, 1939

CH'ÊN Y 23: Ch'ên Yüan 陳垣 "Mo-ni Chiao Ju Chung-kuo K'ao 摩尼教入中國考 (History of Manichaeism in China)," *KHCK* 1 (2): 203–240, 1923

—— 23a: —— "Yüan Hsi-yü-jên Hua-hua K'ao 元西域人華化考 (The Sinicization of the 'Western People' during the Yüan Dynasty, Part I)," *KHCK* 1 (4): 573–653, 1923

CHHC: Hsiung K'o 熊克 *Chung-hsing Hsiao-chi* 中興小紀 in *TSCC* no. 3858–3860

CH'I SH 38: Ch'i Ssǔ-ho 齊思和 "Chan-kuo Chih-tu K'ao 戰國制度考 (Political, Economic and Social Institutions of the Chan-kuo Period)," *YCHP* 24: 159–219, 1938

CHIN: Fang Ch'iao 房喬 and others. *Chin Shu* 晉書 Po-na ed.

CHOU: Ling-hu Tê-fên 令狐德棻 and others. *Chou Shu* 周書 Po-na ed.

CHTSL: *Ta Ch'ing Shih-tsu Chang Huang-ti Shih-lu* 大清世祖章皇帝實錄 in *SL*

CHU H 36: Chu Hsieh 朱偰 "Liao Chin Yen-ching Ch'êng-kuo Kung-yüan T'u-k'ao 遼金燕京城郭宮苑圖考," *Wên-chê Chi-k'an* 文哲季刊 6 (1): 49–81, 1936

CHWC: Huang Chin 黃溍 *Chin-hua Huang Hsien-shêng Wên-chi* 金華黃先生文集 in *SPTK* first coll.

CJCSWC: Yeh-lü Ch'u-ts'ai 耶律楚材 *Chan-jan Chü-shih Wên-chi* 湛然居士文集 in *TSCC* no. 2053

CKC: Lu Chên 路振 *Chiu Kuo Chih* 九國志 in *TSCC* no. 3843–3844

CKCCC: *Ching-k'ou Ch'i-chiu Chuan* 京口耆舊傳 in *SSKTS*, *Shih Chi* 史集

CKL: T'ao Tsung-i 陶宗儀 *Cho-kêng Lu* 輟耕錄 in *TSCC* no. 0218–0220

CKTLHC: Yang Wên-hsün 揚文洵 and others *Chung-kuo Ti-li Hsin-chih* 中國地理新誌 Shanghai 1936

CKTSNP: Ch'ên Ch'ing-ch'i 陳慶麒 *Chung-kuo Ta-shih Nien-piao* 中國大事年表 Shanghai 1935

CL: Liang Shih-chêng 梁詩正 *Ch'ien Lu* 錢錄 in *TSCC* no. 0768–0769

CLCS: *Chou Li Chu-shu* 周禮注疏 in *SPPY*

CLLS: Sun Mu 孫穆 *Chi-lin Lei-shih* 雞林類事 in *WCHS* ch. 96

CLP: Chuang Ch'o 莊綽 *Chi-lei Pien* 雞肋編 in *TSCC* no. 2867

CMYS: Chia Ssǔ-hsieh 賈思勰 *Ch'i-min Yao-shu* 齊民要術 in *SPTK* first coll.

CP: Tung Yu 董逌 *Ch'ien P'u* 錢譜 in *Ts'ui-lang-kan-kuan Ts'ung-shu* 翠琅玕館叢書 Nan-hai Huang Jên-hêng 南海黃任恆 ed. 1916

CPMHPK: Ngi Wan-yung 李完用 and others *Ch'ing-po Mun-hön Pi-ko* 增補文獻備考 1865

CPTC: Mêng Lin 孟麟 *Ch'üan-pu T'ung-chih* 泉布統志 (Tao-kuang period, 1821–1850)

CS: T'o T'o 脫脫 and others. *Chin Shih* 金史 Po-na ed.

CSCSI: Liu Chih 劉摯 *Chung-su Chi Shih-i* 忠肅集拾遺 in *TSCC* no. 1926–1929

CSCSPM: Li Yu-t'ang 李有棠 *Chin Shih Chi-shih Pên-mo* 金史紀事本末 Li I-ê-lou 李彞鄂樓 ed. 1903

CSCW: Lu Yu 陸游 *Chia-shih Chiu-wên* 家世舊聞 in *SF* ch. 45

CSHC: Shih Kuo-ch'i 施國祁 *Chin Shih Hsiang-chiao* 金史詳校 1880

CSK: Chao Êrh-hsün 趙爾巽 and others *Ch'ing Shih Kao* 清史稿 1927

CSP: Hsü Tu 徐度 *Ch'üeh Sao Pien* 却掃編 in *TSCC* no. 2791

CSS: *Chin Shih So* 金石索 Tzǔ-yang-hsien 滋陽縣 ed. 1824

CSSC: Ch'ien Shih-chao 錢世昭 *Ch'ien-shih Ssǔ-chih* 錢氏私誌 in *SF* ch. 45

CSSI: Ch'ien Ta-hsin 錢大昕 *Chu-shih Shih-i* 諸史拾遺 in *CYTCS*

CSTC: Wang Kung 王鞏 *Chia-shên Tsa-chi* 甲申雜記 in *SF* ch. 50

CTC: Lü T'ao 呂陶 *Ching-tê Chi* 淨德集 in *TSCC* no. 1921–1925

CTKC: Yeh Lung-li 葉隆禮 *Ch'i-tan Kuo Chih* 契丹國志 in *SCPS*

CTS: Liu Hsü 劉昫 and others. *Chiu T'ang Shu* 舊唐書 Po-na ed.

CTYY: Chou Mi 周密 *Ch'i-tung Yeh-yü* 齊東野語 in *HCTY* series 14

CWC: Sung Ch'i 宋祁 *Ching-wên Chi* 景文集 in *TSCC* no. 1872–1883

CWCW: Li Hsin-ch'uan 李心傳 *Chiu-wên Chêng Wu* 舊聞證誤 in *TSCC* no. 3896

CWT: Chang Chin-wu 張金吾 *Chin Wên Tsui* 金文最 Yüeh-ya-t'ang 粵雅堂 ed.

CWTS: Hsieh Chü-chêng 薛居正 and others *Chiu Wu-tai Shih* 舊五代史 Po-na ed.

CY: Ting Tu 丁度 *Chi Yün* 集韻 in *SPPY*

CYCCC: Wên Ta-ya 溫大雅 *Ta T'ang Ch'uang-yeh Ch'i-chü Chu* 大唐創業起居注 in *SF* ch. 42

CYCW: Chu Pien 朱弁 *Ch'ü-yu Chiu Wên* 曲洧舊聞 in *TSCC* no. 2768

[CYIL . . .]: 建炎以來繫年要錄 see HNYL

CYTC: Li Hsin-ch'uan 李心傳 *Chien-yen I-lai Ch'ao-yeh Tsa-chi* 建炎以來朝野雜記 in *TSCC* no. 0836–0841

CYTPW: Ch'ien Ta-hsin 錢大昕 *Ch'ien-yen-t'ang Chin-shih-wên Pa-wei* 潛研堂金石文跋尾 in *CYTCS*

ESSSJP: Ch'ên Yüan 陳垣 *Êrh-shih Shih Shuo Jun Piao* 二十史朔閏表 Kuo-li Pei-ching Ta-hsüeh Yen-chiu So Kuo-hsüeh Mên 國立北京大學研究所國學門 ed. Peking 1925

FCL: Chou Pi-ta 周必大 *Fêng Chao Lu* 奉詔錄 in *Chou I-kuo Wên-chung-kung Chi* 周益國文忠公集 1848

FÊNG CC 39: Fêng Ch'êng-chün 馮承鈞 "Liao Chin Pei-pien Pu-tsu K'ao 遼金北邊部族考," *Fu-jên Hsüeh-chih* 輔仁學誌 8 (1): 15–26, 1939

FÊNG CS 32: Fêng Chia-shêng 馮家昇 "Ch'i-tan Ssǔ-t'ien Chih Su Yü Ch'i Tsung-chiao Fêng-su Chih Kuan-hsi 契丹祀天之俗與其宗教風俗之關係 (The Relation Between the Heaven-worship of the Ch'i-tan and their Religion and Customs)," *Shih-hsüeh Nien-pao* 史學年報 1 (4): 105–117, 1932

—— 33: —— "Liao Shih Yüan-liu K'ao Yü Liao Shih Ch'u-chiao 遼史源流攷與遼史初校 (The Sources of Liao Dynasty History and a Preliminary Textual Criticism)," *YCHP*, Monograph series (專號) no. 5, 1933

—— 33a: —— "Ch'i-tan Ming-hao K'ao-shih 契丹名號考釋 (The Origin of the Name Ch'i-tan)," *YCHP* 13: 1–48, 1933

—— 33b: —— "Man-chou Ming-ch'êng Chih Chung-chung T'ui-ts'ê 滿洲名稱之種種推測 (Conjectures on the origin of the name Manchuria)," *Eastern Miscellany*, *Tung-fang Tsa-chih* 東方雜誌 30 (17): 61–74, 1933

—— 34: —— "Liao Chin Shih Ti-li-chih Hu-chiao 遼金史地理志互校 (Textual Comparison of the Section on Geography in the Liao and Chin Histories)," *YK* 1 (4): 6–10, 1934

—— 34a: —— "Tung-pei Shih Chung Chu Ming-ch'êng Chih Chieh-shih 東北史中諸名稱之解釋 (Explanations of Names in the History of the Northeast)," *YK* 2 (7): 2–7, 1934

—— 35: —— "Chou Ch'in Shih-tai Chung-kuo Ching-ying Tung-pei K'ao-lüeh 周秦時代中國經營東北考畧 (A Brief Study of Chinese Administration of the Northeast during the Chou and Ch'in Periods)," *YK* 2 (11): 12–17, 1935

—— 36: —— "Ta-yüeh-chih Min-tsu Chi Ch'i Yen-chiu Chih Chieh-lun 大月氏民族及其研究之結論 (The Ta-yüeh-chih People and Conclusions on Studies about Them)," *YK* 5 (8/9): 1–18, 1936

—— 37: —— "Juan-juan Kuo-hao K'ao 蠕蠕國號考 (On the National Name of the Juan-juan)," *YK* **7** (8/9): 77–80, 1937

FHC: Wang Tsao 汪藻 *Fu-hsi Chi* 浮溪集 in *TSCC* no. 1958–1961

FIMIC: Fa Yün 法雲 *Fan-i Ming-i Chi* 翻譯名義集 in *SPTK* first coll.

FJHC: Niu Ch'ang-hsü 牛昶煦 and others *Fêng-jun-hsien Chih* 豐潤縣志 1921

FKCFTI: Fan Chung-yen 范仲淹 *Fan Wên-chêng-kung Chêng-fu Tsou-i* 范文正公政府奏議 in *Fan Wên-chêng-kung Chi* 范文正公集, *SPTK* first coll.

FTTT: Nien Ch'ang 念常 *Fo-tsu Li-tai T'ung-tsai* 佛祖歷代通載 in *Ta Jih-pên Hsü Ts'ang-ching* 大日本續藏經

Fu LH 35: Fu Lo-huan 傅樂煥 "Sung Jên Shih Liao Yü-lu Hsing-ch'êng K'ao 宋人使遼語錄行程考 (An Investigation into the Travelling Routes of Song Embassy to Liao as Seen from their Journals)," *KHCK* **5** (4): 165–194, 1935

Fujita 23: Fujita Toyohachi 藤田豐八 "Zenzen no kokugō oyobi Kakan-gō ni tsuite 蠕蠕の國號及び可汗號に就いて (On the State Name 'Juan Juan' and the Titles of their Kaghan)," *Tōyō gakuhō* 東洋學報 **13** (1): 55–70, 1923

—— 32: —— *Tōzai kōshō-shi no kenkyū* 東西交涉史の研究 Nankai-hen 南海篇 Tokyo 1932

—— 33: —— *Tōzai kōshō-shi no kenkyū* 東西交涉史の研究 Seiiki-hen 西域篇 Tokyo 1933

FWCKWC: Fan Chung-yen 范仲淹 *Fan Wên-chêng-kung Wên-chi* 范文正公文集 in *TSCC* no. 2359–2360

Han JL 37: Han Ju-lin 韓儒林 "Sui-pei Ti Chi-ko Ti-ming 綏北的幾個地名," *YK* **7** (8/9): 81–88, 1937

Haneda 16: Haneda Tōru 羽田亨 "Sei-Ryō kenkoku no shimatsu oyobi sono nenki 西遼建國の始末及び其の年記 (History of the Establishment of Western Liao and its Chronology)," *Shirin* 史林 **1**: 206–234, 1916

Hashiguchi 39: Hashiguchi Kaneo 橋古兼夫 "Ryō-dai kokkyū-chō ni tsuite 遼代國舅帳について (On the Imperial Maternal Uncles of the Liao Dynasty)," *SZ* **50**: 153–191, 326–357, 1939

HCCL: Wang Ming-ch'ing 王明清 *Hui-chu Ch'ien-lu* 揮塵前錄 in *TSCC* no. 2770

HCCSC: *Hêng-chai Chin-shih Chih-hsiao-lu* 衡齋金石識小錄 Compiled by Huang Chün 黃濬 Peiping 1935

HCKKFL: A Kuei 阿桂 and others, *Huang Ch'ing K'ai-kuo Fang-lüeh* 皇清開國方略 Kuang-pai-sung-chai 廣百宋齋 ed. 1887

HCLY: Chiang Shao-yü 江少虞 *Huang-ch'ao Lei-yüan* 皇朝類苑 in *Sung-fên-shih Ts'ung-k'an* 誦芬室叢刊 first coll. 1916

HCSCC: Li Tao-yüan 酈道元 *Shui-ching Chu* 水經注. Ed. by Wang Hsien-ch'ien 王先謙, entitled *Ho-chiao Shui-ching Chu* 合校水經注 1892

HCTL: Chiang Wan-li 江萬里 *Hsüan-chêng Tsa-lu* 宣政雜錄 in *SF* ch. 47

HFJL: Wang Ming-ch'ing 王明清 *Hsi-fêng Jih-li* 熙豐日曆 in *WCHS* ch. 12

HFT: *Han Fei Tzŭ* 韓非子 in *SPPY*

HHC: Ssŭ-ma Piao 司馬彪 *Hsü Han Chih* 續漢志 (also referred to as 後漢書志) Po-na ed.

HHHP: *Hsüan-ho Hua-p'u* 宣和畫譜 in *TSCC* no. 1652–1653

HHHY: Hsü T'ien-lin 徐天麟 *Hsi Han Hui-yao* 西漢會要 in *WYTCCP*

HHK: Hsieh Ch'i-k'un 謝啓昆 *Hsiao-hsüeh K'ao* 小學考 Chê-chiang Shu-chü 浙江書局 ed. 1888

HHS: Fan Yeh 范曄 *Hou Han Shu* 後漢書 Po-na ed.

HHSS: Wu Kuang-ch'êng 吳廣成 *Hsi Hsia Shu Shih* 西夏書事 Hsiao-hsien Shan-fang 小峴山房 ed. 1849, photostat ed., Peiping 1935

HICC: Yüan Hao-wên 元好問 *Hsü I-chien Chih* 續夷堅志 in *PCHSTK* series 4

HJC: Liu Ch'i 劉跂 *Hsia-jih Chi* 暇日記 in *WCHS* ch. 93

HKCCC: Lo Fu-ch'ang 羅福萇 *Sung Shih Hsia Kuo Chuan Chi-chu* 宋史夏國傳集註 in *Tai-shih Hsüan Ts'ung-k'an* 待時軒叢刊 1937

HLLKSM: Ting Ch'ien 丁謙 *Hsi Liao Li-kuo Shih-mo* 西遼立國始末 in *Ku-hsüeh Hui-k'an* 古學彙刊 Shanghai 1923

HLWC: Chou Lin 周麟 *Hai-ling Wai-chi* 海陵外集 in *Hai-ling Ts'ung-k'o* 海陵叢刻 1921

HML: Chang Shun-min 張舜民 *Hua Man Lu* 畫墁錄 in *SF* ch. 18

[HNSS . . .]: 河南邵氏聞見前錄 and 後錄 see SSWCCL and SSWCHL

HNT: *Huai-nan Tzŭ* 淮南子 in *SPPY*

HNYL: Li Hsin-ch'uan 李心傳 *Chien-yen I-lai Hsi-nien Yao-lu* 建炎以來繫年要錄 in *TSCC* no. 3861–3878

Ho SC 27: Ho Shih-chi 何士驥 "Pu-ch'ü K'ao 部曲攷 (On *pu-ch'ü*)," *Chinese Classical Review*, *Kuo-hsüeh Lun-ts'ung* 國學論叢 **1** (1): 123–162, 1927

HS: Pan Ku 班固 *Han Shu* 漢書 Po-na ed.

HSC: Wang Chih 王質 *Hsüeh-shan Chi* 雪山集 in *TSCC* no. 1990–1992

HSHNKC: Ting Ch'ien 丁謙 *Han Shu Hsiung-nu Chuan Ti-li K'ao-chêng* 漢書匈奴傳地理攷證 in *P'êng-lai-hsüan Yü-ti Ts'ung-shu* 蓬萊軒輿地叢書 series 1, Chê-chiang Shu-chü 浙江書局 ed. 1915

HSSS: Shên Shu 沈俶 *Hsieh Shih* 諧史 in *SF* ch. 35

HTC: Pi Chung-yu 畢仲游 *Hsi T'ai Chi* 西臺集 in *Shan-yu Ts'ung-shu* 山右叢書 first coll., Shan-hsi Shêng Wên-hsien Wei-yüan Hui 山西省文獻委員會 ed.

HTCCP: Li T'ao 李燾 *Hsü Tzŭ-chih T'ung-chien Chang-pien* 續資治通鑑長編 Chê-chiang Shu-chü 浙江書局 ed. 1881

HTPKC: Lu Shou 陸壽 *Hsü T'ai-p'ing Kuang-chi* 續太平廣記 Huai-tê-t'ang 懷德堂 ed. 1800

HTS: Ch'ên Chan 陳鱣 *Hsü T'ang Shu* 續唐書 in *TSCC* no. 3847–3849

HTSLCC: Wang Kuo-wei 王國維 ed. *Hei-ta Shih-lüeh Chien-chêng* 黑韃事略箋證 in *WKW* series 3

HTT: Hsi Huang 嵇璜 and others, *Hsü T'ung Tien* 續通典 Wan-yu Wên-k'u 萬有文庫 ed. Shanghai 1935

Hu S 35: Hu Shih 胡適 *Hu Shih Wên-ts'un* 胡適文存 Shanghai 1935

HWCKC: Ho Ching 郝經 *Ho Wên-chung-kung Chi* 郝文忠公集 in *Ch'ien-k'un Chêng-ch'i Chi* 乾坤正氣集 1848

HWHTK: Hsi Huang 嵇璜 and others, *Hsü Wên-hsien T'ung-k'ao* 續文獻通考 Wan-yu Wên-k'u 萬有文庫 ed. Shanghai 1936

HWKC: Han Ch'i 韓琦 *Han Wei-kung Chi* 韓魏公集 in *TSCC* no. 2363–2366

HYC: Wang Kuei 王珪 *Hua-yang Chi* 華陽集 in *TSCC* no. 1912–1916

HYCCC: Wang Kuo-wei 王國維 ed. *Ch'ang-ch'un Chên-jên Hsi-yu-chi Chiao-chu* 長春眞人西遊記校注 in *WKW* series 3

HYLC: Yeh-lü Ch'u-ts'ai 耶律楚材 with notes by Li Wên-tien 李文田 *Hsi-yu-lu Chu* 西遊錄注 in *TSCC* no. 3253

HYS: Ko Shao-min 柯劭忞 *Hsin Yüan Shih* 新元史 K'ai-ming 開明 ed. Shanghai 1935

ICCC: Hung Mai 洪邁 *I-chien Chia Chih* 夷堅甲志 in *TSCC* no. 2707–2708

ICLTC: Chu I 朱翌 *I-chüeh-liao Tsa-chi* 猗覺寮雜記 in *PCHSTK* series 4

ICPC: Hung Mai 洪邁 *I-chien Ping Chih* 夷堅丙志 in *TSCC* no. 2711–2712

IFCSWT: Miao Ch'üan-sun 繆荃孫 *I-fêng-t'ang Chin-shih Wên-tzǔ Mu* 藝風堂金石文字目 1906

IHC: *I-hsien Chih* 義縣志 1928

IKEUCHI, MSK: Ikeuchi Hiroshi 池內宏 *Mansen shi kenkyū* 滿鮮史研究 I, Tokyo 1933; II, Tokyo 1937

ILCS: *I Li Chu-shu* 儀禮注疏 in *SPPY*

INABA 32: Inaba Iwakichi 稻葉岩吉 "Kittan no ōsen ōshi no meishō 契丹の橫宣橫賜の名稱 (The Ch'i Tan Terms Ōsen and Ōshi)," *Shirin* 史林 17: 113–122, 1932

ISHSC: Yüan Hao-wên 元好問 *I-shan Hsien-shêng Chi* 遺山先生集 in *Shih-lien-an Hui-k'o Chiu Chin Jên Chi* 石蓮盦彙刻九金人集 Wu-ying-tien Chü-chên 武英殿聚珍 ed. 1909

IWC: Yang Fu 楊孚 *I Wu Chih* 異物志 in *Ling-nan I-shu* 嶺南遺書 series 5, Nan-hai Wu-shih 南海伍氏 ed. 1885

IYC: Chou Chih-chung 周致中 *I-yü Chih* 異域志 in *TSCC* no. 3273

JCHP: Hung Mai 洪邁 *Jung-chai Hsü Pi* 容齋續筆 in *SPTK* second coll.

JCL: Ku Yen-wu 顧炎武 *Jih-chih Lu* 日知錄 Shanghai 1935

JCSaP: Hung Mai 洪邁 *Jung-chai San Pi* 容齋三筆 in *SPTK* second coll.

JCSP: —— *Jung-chai Ssǔ Pi* (四筆) in *SPTK* second coll.

JCWP: —— *Jung-chai Wu Pi* (五筆) in *SPTK* second coll.

JHC: *Ch'in-ting Jô-ho Chih* 欽定熱河志 Darien 1934

JLKI: *Ju-lin Kung I* 儒林公議 in *TSCC* no. 2793

KAMIO 37: Kamio Kazuharu 神尾弌春 *Kittan Bukkyō bunka-shi-kō* 契丹佛教文化史考 1937

KCCL: Ni Mu 倪模 *Ku-chin Ch'ien Lüeh* 古今錢畧 Wang-chiang Ni-shih 望江倪氏 ed. 1877

KCH: Li Tso-hsien 李佐賢 *Ku Ch'üan Hui* 古泉匯 Li-shih Shih-ch'üan-shu-wu 李氏石泉書屋 ed. 1684

KCTSCC: Chiang T'ing-hsi 蔣廷錫 *Ku-chin T'u-shu Chi-ch'êng* 古今圖書集成 Chung-hua Shu-chü 中華書局 ed. 1934

KCWC: Ou-yang Hsüan 歐陽玄 *Kuei-chai Wên-chi* 圭齋文集 in *SPTK* first coll.

KCWL: Su T'ien-chüeh 蘇天爵 *Kuo-ch'ao Wên-lei* 國朝文類 in *SPTK* first coll.

KHCCL: Wang Kuo-wei 王國維 ed. *Ku Hsing-chi Ssǔ-chung Chiao-lu* 古行記四種校錄 in *WKW* series 3,

including *Pei Shih Chi* 北使記 6a–7a and *Hsi Shih Chi* 西使記 7a–10a

KHTSL: *Ta Ch'ing T'ai-tsu Kao Huang-ti Shih-lu* 大淸太祖高皇帝實錄 in *SL*

KHTT: *K'ang-hsi Tzǔ-tien* 康熙字典 Shanghai 1936

KKSHC: *Ku-kung Shu Hua Chi* 故宮書畫集 Peiping 1932

KLTC: Hsü Ching 徐兢 *Hsüan-ho Fêng-shih Kao-li T'u-ching* 宣和奉使高麗圖經 in *CPTCTS* series 16

KLTY: *Kuo-lao T'an-yüan* 國老談苑 in *TSCC* no. 2744

KRS: Chŏng Nin-chi 鄭麟趾 *Ko ryŏ sǎ* 高麗史 Tokyo 1909

KSC: Liu Ch'ang 劉敞 *Kung-shih Chi* 公是集 in *TSCC* no. 1899–1906

KSLK: Yü Chêng-hsieh 俞正燮 *Kuei-ssǔ Lei-kao* 癸巳類稿 in *An-hui Ts'ung-shu* 安徽叢書 third coll. Shanghai 1934

KSTK: Yü Chêng-hsieh 俞正燮 *Kuei-ssǔ Ts'un-kao* 癸巳存稿 in *TSCC* no. 0360–0364

KSTY: K'ung P'ing-chung 孔平仲 *K'ung-shih T'an-yüan* 孔氏談苑 in *TSCC* no. 2861

KSWS: Ch'uan Hêng 權衡 *Kêng-shên Wai-shih* 庚申外史 in *HCTY* series 6

KTCL: Wang Kuo-wei 王國維 ed. *Kuan-t'ang Chi-lin* 觀堂集林 in *WKW* series 1

KTL: Ou-yang Hsiu 歐陽修 *Kuei-t'ien Lu* 歸田錄 in *SF* ch. 40

KTLYK: Yüeh K'o 岳珂 *K'uei-t'an Lu* 愧郯錄 in *TSCC* no. 0842–0843

KY: Ch'ên P'êng-nien 陳彭年 *Kuang Yün* 廣韻 in *SPPY*

KYTK: Chao I 趙翼 *Kai-yü Ts'ung-k'ao* 陔餘叢考 in *Chao Ou-pei Ch'üan-chi* 趙甌北全集 Shou-k'ao-t'ang 壽考堂 ed. 1877

LC: Yeh Lung-li 葉隆禮 *Liao Chih* 遼志 in *SF* [A] ch. 86

LCC: Su Ch'ê 蘇轍 *Luan-ch'êng Chi* 欒城集 in *SPTK* first coll.

LCCS: *Li Chi Chu-shu* 禮記注疏 in *SPPY*

LCCWP: Wang Po 王柏 *Lu-chai Chi* 魯齋集 in *TSCC* no. 2402–2404

LCHSWC: Wang An-shih 王安石 *Lin-ch'uan Hsien-shêng Wên-chi* 臨川先生文集 in *SPTK* first coll.

LCIWC: Sung Ying 宋膺 *Liang-chou I Wu Chih* 涼州異物志 in *Chang-shih Ts'ung-shu* 張氏叢書 Êrh-yu-t'ang 二酉堂 ed. 1821

LCPC: Su Ch'ê 蘇轍 *Lung-ch'uan Pieh-chih* 龍川別志 in *SF* ch. 21

LCSY: Yao T'ung-shou 姚桐壽 *Lo-chiao Ssǔ-yü* 樂郊私語 in *SF* ch. 18

LCT: Ma Yung-ch'ing 馬永卿 *Lan Chên Tzǔ* 嬾眞子 in *TSCC* no. 0285

LCTY: Yang Yün-fu 楊允孚 *Luan-ching Tsa-yung* 灤京雜詠 in *CPTCTS* series 23

LCWC: Ch'ên Liang 陳亮 *Lung-ch'uan Wên-chi* 龍川文集 in *TSCC* no. 2394–2399

LCYHP: Chou Ch'un 周春 *Liao Chin Yüan Hsing-p'u* 遼金元姓譜 in *Chao-tai Ts'ung-shu* 昭代叢書 series 6, ch. 12, Shih-k'ai-t'ang 世楷堂 ed. 1833

LHAPC: Lu Yu 陸游 *Lao-hsüeh-an Pi-chi* 老學庵筆記 in *TSCC* no. 2766

LHKTI: Lu Chih 陸贄 *Lu Hsüan-kung Tsou-i* 陸宣公奏議 in *Lu Hsüan-kung Han-yüan Chi* 陸宣公翰苑集 in *SPTK* first coll.

LIANG: Yao Ssŭ-lien 姚思廉 and others, *Liang Shu* 梁書 Po-na ed.

LIANG SY 35: Liang Ssŭ-yung 梁思永 "Hsiao-t'un Lung-shan Yü Yang-shao 小屯龍山與仰韶 (Hsiao-t'un, Lung-shan and Yang-shao)," *Studies Presented to Ts'ai Yüan-p'ei on his Sixty-fifth Birthday by Fellows and Assistants of the National Research Institute of History and Philology* 慶祝蔡元培先生六十五歲論文集 II: 555–568, 1935. *AS*, special series (外編) no. 1

LIANG YT 34: Liang Yüan-tung 梁園東 *Hsi Liao Shih* 西遼史 Shanghai 1934

LKSC: Hsing Chün 行均 *Hsin-hsiu Lung-k'an Shou-chien* 新修龍龕手鑑 in *SPTK* second coll.

LLSKCL: Chin Yü-fu 金毓黻 *Liao-ling Shih-k'o Chi-lu* 遼陵石刻集錄 1934

LPL: Fan Ch'êng-ta 范成大 *Lan-p'ei Lu* 攬轡錄 in *CPTCTS* series 23

LS: T'o-t'o 脫脫 *Liao Shih* 遼史 Po-na ed. 1931

LSCC: *Lü-shih Ch'un-ch'iu* 呂氏春秋 in *SPPY*

LSCKC: Lo Chi-tsu 羅繼祖 *Liao Shih Chiao-k'an Chi* 遼史校勘記 1938

LSCSPM: Li Yu-t'ang 李有棠 *Liao Shih Chi-shih Pên-mo* 遼史紀事本末 Li I-ê-lou 李移鄂樓 ed. 1903

LSNTS: Lu Yu 陸游 *Lu-shih Nan T'ang Shu* 陸氏南唐書 in *SPTK* second coll.

LSP: Ling Yang-tsao 凌揚藻 *Li-shao Pien* 蠡勺編 in *TSCC* no. 0225–0230

LSSI: Li Ê 厲鶚 *Liao Shih Shih-i* 遼史拾遺 Kuang-ya Shu-chü 廣雅書局 ed. 1900

LSSIP: Yang Fu-chi 楊復吉 *Liao Shih Shih-i Pu* 遼史拾遺補 Kuang-ya Shu-chü ed. 1900

LSTLCK: Li Shên-ju 李慎儒 *Liao Shih Ti-li-chih K'ao* 遼史地理志考 in *ESWSPP* VI: 8095–8142

LSYC: *Ch'in-ting Liao Shih Yü-chieh* 欽定遼史語解 Chiang-su Shu-chü 江蘇書局 ed. 1878

LTCL: *Liao-tung Chih Lüeh* 遼東志畧 in *SF* [A] ch. 97

LTCNP: Wan Ssŭ-t'ung 萬斯同 *Liao Ta-ch'ên Nien-piao* 遼大臣年表 in *ESWSPP* VI: 8045–8068

LTCSL: Huang Jên-hêng 黃任恆 *Liao-tai Chin-shih Lu* 遼代金石錄 in *Liao-hên Wu Chung* 遼痕五種 1925

LTCYK: Chung Yüan-ying 鍾淵映 *Li-tai Chien-yüan K'ao* 歷代建元考 in *TSCC* no. 3456–3458

LTFPTL: Lo Chên-yü 羅振玉 *Li-tai Fu-p'ai T'u-lu* 歷代符牌圖錄 Tung-fang Hsüeh-hui 東方學會 ed. 1925

LTHPC: Wang Chi 王寂 *Liao-tung Hsing-pu Chih* 遼東行部志 in *LHTS* series 8

LTLCT: Yang Shou-ching 楊守敬 *Liao Ti-li-chih T'u* 遼地理志圖 in *Kuan-hai-t'ang Ti-li-shu* 觀海堂地理書 Hupei 1911

LTSCL: Kuei Fu 桂馥 *Li-tai Shih-ching Lüeh* 歷代石經略 1883

LTSS: Wên Wei-chien 文惟簡 *Lu-t'ing Shih-shih* 虜廷事實 in *SF* [A] ch. 8

LU MT 28: Lu Mou-tê 陸懋德 "Chung-kuo Jên Fa-ming Huo-yao Huo-p'ao K'ao 中國人發明火藥火礮考," *Tsing-hua Journal* 清華學報 5 (1): 1489–1499, 1928

LWKKC: Ting Ch'ien 丁謙 *Liao Shih Ko Wai-kuo Ti-li K'ao-chêng* 遼史各外國地理考証 in *P'êng-lai-hsüan Yü-ti Ts'ung-shu* 蓬萊軒輿地叢書 series 1, Chê-chiang Shu-chü 浙江書局 ed. 1915

LWT: Miao Ch'üan-sun 繆荃孫 *Liao Wên-ts'un* 遼文存 Lai-ch'ing-ko 來青閣 ed. (preface dated 1896)

LWTT: Chou Ch'ü-fei 周去非 *Ling-wai Tai-ta* 嶺外代答 in *PCHSTK* series 4

LYCS: *Lun Yü Chu-shu* 論語注疏 in *SPPY*

LYCWC: Lo Ts'ung-yen 羅從彦 *Lo Yü-chang Hsien-shêng Wên-chi* 羅豫章先生文集 in *TSCC* no. 2385–2386

MAC: Yao Sui 姚燧 *Mu-an Chi* 牧菴集 in *SPTK* first coll.

MATSUI 11: Matsui Hitoshi 松井等 "Shina no hō to hōseki 支那の砲と拋石 (Cannon and Catapult in China)," *Tōyō gakuhō* 東洋學報 1: 395–406, 1911

—— 15: —— "Kittan Katon-jō kō 契丹可敦城考," *MCRKH* 1: 295–333, 1915

—— 15a: —— "Kittan Bokkō shi 契丹勃興史 (History of the Rise of the Ch'i-tan)," *MCRKH* 1: 137–294, 1915

—— 18: —— "Kittan no kokugun hensei oyobi senjutsu 契丹の國軍編制及び戰術 (Ch'i-tan National Military Organization and Strategy)," *MCRKH* 4: 1–66, 1918

MCCSC: Lo Fu-i 羅福頤 *Man-chou Chin-shih Chih* 滿洲金石志 Man Jih Wên-hua Hsieh-hui 滿日文化協會 ed. 1937

MCML: Chang Pang-chi 張邦基 *Mo-chuang Man-lu* 墨莊漫錄 in *TSCC* no. 2864–2866

MCPL: Lo Fu-i *Man-chou Chin-shih Chih Pieh-lu* 滿洲金石志別錄 Man Jih Wên-hua Hsieh-hui ed. 1937

MCTL: Chin Yü-fu 金毓黻 and others, *Ch'in-ting Man-chou Chi-shên Chi-t'ien Tien-li* 欽定滿洲祭神祭天典禮 in *LHTS* series 9

MCWP: Lo Fu-i *Man-chou Chin-shih Chih Wai-pien* 滿洲金石志外編 Man Jih Wên-hua Hsieh-hui ed. 1937

MCYLK: A Kuei 阿桂 and others, *Ch'in-ting Man-chou Yüan-liu K'ao* 欽定滿洲源流攷 Pien-i Shu-chü 便益書局 ed. Hangchow 1893

MÊNG S 36: Mêng Shên 孟森 "Pa-ch'i Chih-tu K'ao-shih 八旗制度考實 (On the Origin and Growth of the System of the Eight Banners of the Manchus)," *AS* 6 (3): 343–412, 1936

MHPT: Shên K'uo 沈括 *Mêng-hsi Pi-t'an* 夢溪筆談 in *TSCC* no. 0281–0282

MHY: *Ming Hui Yao* 明會要 compiled by Lung Wên-pin 龍文彬 Yung-huai-t'ang Ts'ang-pan 永懷堂藏板 ed. 1887

MIKAMI 34: Mikami Tsuguo 三上次男 "Bokkai Jōkei Ryūsen-fu-shi no dai-nikai hakkutsu ni tsuite 渤海上京龍泉府址の第二回發掘に就いて (The Second Excavation at the Old Site of Lung-ch'üan Prefecture of Po-hai)," *Rekishi-gaku kenkyū* 歷史學研究 3: 73–78, 1934

—— 37: —— *Kin-tai Joshin no kenkyū* 金代女眞の研究 Hsinking 1937

MKC: Lou Yüeh 樓鑰 *Mei-kuei Chi* 玫瑰集 in *SPTK* first coll.

MLL: Wu Tzŭ-mu 吳自牧 *Mêng Liang Lu* 夢梁錄 in *PCHSTK* series 4

MRC I–II: Shiratori Kurakichi 白鳥庫吉 and others, *Manshu rekishi chiri* 滿洲歷史地理 2 v. Tokyo 1913

MS: Chang T'ing-yü 張延玉 and others, *Ming Shih* 明史 Po-na ed.

MSCS: *Mao Shih Chu-shu* 毛詩注疏 in *SPPY*

MSNTS: Ma Ling 馬令 *Ma-shih Nan T'ang Shu* 馬氏南唐書 in *SPTK* second coll.

MSYTL: Wang P'i-chih 王闢之 *Shêng-shui Yen-t'an Lu* 澠水燕談錄 in *TSCC* no. 0209

MTCS: *Mêng-tzŭ Chu-shu* 孟子注疏 in *SPPY*

MTPLCC: Wang Kuo-wei 王國維 ed. *Mêng-ta Pei-lu Chien-chêng* 蒙韃備錄箋証 in *WKW* series 3

MWESC: T'u Chi 屠寄 *Mêng-wu-êrh Shih Chi* 蒙兀兒史記 Chieh-i-i 結一宦 ed.

NAWA 31: Nawa Toshisada 那波利貞 "Ryōkin Nankin Enkei kojō kyōiki-kō 遼金南京燕京故城疆域攷," *Shina-gaku ronsō* 支那學論叢, Commemorative volume of the 61st birthday of Professor Takase 高瀨博士還曆紀念: 455–516, 1931

NCCS: Hsü Kuang-ch'i 徐光啓 *Nung-chêng Ch'üan-shu* 農政全書 Shu-hai-lou 曙海樓 ed. 1843

NCIY: Lo Fu-ch'êng 羅福成 *Nü-chên I-yü* 女眞譯語 Ta-k'u Chiu Tang Chêng-li-ch'u 大庫舊檔整理處 ed. 1933

NCS: Hsiao Tzŭ-hsien 蕭子顯 *Nan Ch'i Shu* 南齊書 Po-na ed.

NESCC: Chao I 趙翼 *Nien-êrh Shih Cha-chi* 廿二史劄記 in *Chao Ou-pei Ch'üan-chi* 趙甌北全集 1877

NESKI: Ch'ien Ta-hsin 錢大昕 *Nien-êrh Shih K'ao-i* 廿二史攷異 in *CYTCS*

NGJG: Ennin 圓仁 *Nitto guhō junrei gyōki* 入唐求法巡禮行記 in *Dai Nihon bukkyō zensho* 大日本佛教全書 113, Tokyo 1931

NIEH CC 40: Nieh Ch'ung-ch'i 聶崇岐 "Sung Liao Chiao-p'ing K'ao 宋遼交聘考 (Embassies between Liao and Sung)," *YCHP* 27: 1–51, 1940

NKCML: Ch'ien Hsi-tso 錢熙祚 *Nêng-kai-chai Man-lu* 能改齋漫錄 in *SSKTS*, Tzŭ Chi 子集

NS: Li Yen-shou 李延壽 *Nan Shih* 南史 Po-na ed.

NSCY: *Nung Sang Chi-yao* 農桑輯要 in *WYTCCP*

NTL: Hsin Ch'i-chi 辛棄疾 *Nan-tu Lu* 南渡錄 in *Chung-kuo Nei-luan Wai-huo Li-shih Ts'ung-shu* 中國內亂外禍歷史叢書 III, 1936

OYWCCC: Ou-yang Hsiu 歐陽修 *Ou-yang Wên-chung Ch'üan-chi* 歐陽文忠全集 in *SPPY*

PCC: Liu Pin 劉邠 *P'êng-ch'êng Chi* 彭城集 in *TSCC* no. 1907–1911

PCKT: Chu Yü 朱彧 *P'ing-chou K'o T'an* 萍洲可談 in *TSCC* no. 2754

PCP: Fang Shao 方勺 *Po-chai Pien* 泊宅編 in *Tu-hua-chai Ts'ung-shu* 讀畫齋叢書 series 4, Ku-shih 顧氏 ed. 1803

PCSIWC: Wên T'ing-shih 文廷式 *Pu Chin Shu I-wên-chih* 補晉書藝文志 in *ESWSPP* III: 3703–3795

PFTL: Tsêng Kung-liang 曾公亮 and others, *Pei Fan Ti-li* 北番地理 in *Ch'i-tan Chiao-t'ung Shih-liao Ch'i Chung* 契丹交通史料七種 Kuo-hsüeh Wên-k'u 國學文庫 ed. no. 47

PFYSL: *Pei-fêng Yang-sha Lu* 北風揚沙錄 in *SF* [A] ch. 25

PHHIWC: Tsêng P'u 曾樸 *Pu Hou Han Shu I-wên-chih Ping K'ao* 補後漢書藝文志幷考 in *ESWSPP* II: 2447–2566

PHKC: Huang Wei-han 黃維翰 *Po-hai Kuo Chi* 渤海國記 in *LHTS* series 1

PHKCCP: Chin Yü-fu 金毓黻 *Po-hai Kuo Chih Ch'ang-pien* 渤海國志長編 Ch'ien-hua-shan-kuan 千華山館 ed.

PHL: Tuan Kung-lu 段公路 *Pei Hu Lu* 北戶錄 in *TSCC* no. 3021

PLSIWC: Huang Jên-hêng 黃任恒 *Pu Liao Shih I-wên-chih* 補遼史藝文志 in *Liao-hên Wu Chung* 遼痕五種 1925

PS: Li Yen-shou 李延壽 and others, *Pei Shih* 北史 Po-na ed.

PSHC: Ch'êng Chü 程俱 *Pei-shan Hsiao Chi* 北山小集 in *SPTK* first coll.

PSHT: Hung Tsun 洪遵 *P'u Shuang* 譜雙 in *Li-lou Ts'ung-shu* 麗廔叢書 Ch'ang-sha Yeh-shih 長沙葉氏 ed. 1919

PSLH: Yeh Mêng-tê 葉夢得 *Pi-shu Lu-hua* 避暑錄話 in *TSCC* no. 2786–2787

PSTJSC: Chiang K'uei 姜夔 *Pai-shih Tao-jên Shih-chi* 白石道人詩集 in TSCC no. 2261

PTKM: Li Shih-chên 李時珍 *Pên-ts'ao Kang-mu* 本草綱目 Wei-ku-chai 味古齋 ed. 1885

PTL: Chao Yü-shih 趙與時 *Pin T'ui Lu* 賓退錄 in *Tsê-shih-chü Ts'ung-shu* 擇是居叢書 Wu-hsing Chang-shih 吳興張氏 ed. 1926

PWC: Chang Hua 張華 *Po-wu Chih* 博物志 in *TSCC* no. 1342

PYC: Hsü Ch'ien 許謙 *Pai-yün Chi* 白雲集 in *TSCC* no. 2080

SAEKI 35: Saeki Yoshio 佐伯好郎 *Keikyō no kenkyū* 景教の研究 Tokyo 1935

SC: Ssŭ-ma Ch'ien 司馬遷 *Shih Chi* 史記 Po-na ed.

[SCC]: 水經注 see HCSCC

SCCYHL: Ch'ien Ta-hsin 錢大昕 *Shih-chia-chai Yang-hsin Lu* 十駕齋養新錄 in *CYTCS*

SCHY: Yang Yü 楊瑀 *Shan-chü Hsin-yü* 山居新語 in *Wu-lin Wang-chê I-chu* 武林往哲遺著 1897

SCPMHP: Hsü Mêng-hsin 徐夢莘 *San-ch'ao Pei-mêng Hui-pien* 三朝北盟會編 Ssŭ-k'u Ch'üan-shu T'i-yao 四庫全書提要 ed. 1879

SCTPYC: Li Ch'üan 李筌 *Shên-chi Chih-ti T'ai-pai Yin-ching* 神機制敵太白陰經 in *TSCC* no. 0943–0944

SHIRATORI 98: Shiratori Kurakichi 白鳥庫吉 "Kittan, Joshin, Seika moji-kō 契丹女眞西夏文字考," *SZ* 9: 922–936, 1898

—— 10–13 TMK: —— "Tōko minzoku kō 東烏民族考 (On the Tung-hu Peoples)," *SZ* 21: 369–393, 741–762, 1003–1026, 1910; 22: 63–88, 589–606, 1265–1288, 1381–1407, 1911; 23: 117–142, 237–262, 1013–1030, 1133–1148, 1243–1269, 1912; 24: 17–45, 854–884, 1913

SHTC: Tsêng Kuo-ch'üan 曾國荃 and others, *Shan-hsi T'ung-chih* 山西通志 1892

SHTYC: Yeh-lü Chu 耶律鑄 *Shuang-hsi Tsui-yin Chi* 雙溪醉隱集 in *LHTS* series 6

SHYK: *Sung Hui-yao Kao* 宋會要稿 Ta-tung Shu-chü 大東書局 ed. Shanghai 1936 (the number following the symbol indicates the volume 册)

SKC, Wei: Ch'ên Shou 陳壽 *Wei Shu* 魏書 in *San Kuo Chih* 三國志 Po-na ed.

SKTP: Sun Shêng 孫升 *Sun-kung T'an-p'u* 孫公談圃 in *SF* ch. 15

SKTY: *Ssŭ-k'u Ch'üan-shu Tsung-mu T'i-yao* 四庫全書總目提要 Shanghai 1933

[SLCY . . .]: 宋遼金元四史朔閏攷 see SSSJK

SLYY: Yeh Mêng-tê 葉夢得 *Shih-lin Yen-yü* 石林燕語 in *TSCC* no. 2754–2755

SLYYP: —— *Shih-lin Yen-yü Pien* (辨) Notes by Wang Ying-ch'ên 汪應辰 in *TSCC* no. 0295

SMCW: Hung Hao 洪皓 *Sung-mo Chi-wên* 松漠紀聞 in *HCTY* series 6

SMCWPI: —— *Sung-mo Chi-wên Pu-i* (補遺) in *HCTY* series 6

SS: T'o T'o 脫脫 and others, *Sung Shih* 宋史 Po-na ed.

SSCS: *Shang Shu Chu-shu* 尚書注疏 in *SPPY*

SSHY: T'ao Tsung-i 陶宗儀 *Shu-shih Hui-yao* 書史會要 T'ao-shih I-yüan 陶氏逸園 ed.

SSKC: Ch'ên Yüan-ching 陳元靚 *Sui-shih Kuang-chi* 歲時廣記 in *TSCC* no. 0179–0181

SSSJK: Ch'ien Ta-hsin 錢大昕 *Sung Liao Chin Yüan Ssŭ Shih Shuo Jun K'ao* 宋遼金元四史朔閏攷 Kuang-ya Shu-chü 廣雅書局 ed. 1892

SSTML: Ch'ên Ti 陳第 *Shih-shan-t'ang Ts'ang-shu Mu-lu* 世善堂藏書目錄 in *TSCC* no. 0034

SSWCCL: Shao Po-wên 邵伯温 *Ho-nan Shao-shih Wên-chien Ch'ien-lu* 河南邵氏聞見前錄 in *TSCC* no. 2749–2750

SSWCHL: Shao Po 邵博 *Ho-nan Shao-shih Wên-chien Hou-lu* (後錄) in *TSCC* no. 2751–2752

STTH: Wang Ch'i 王圻 *San-ts'ai T'u-hui* 三才圖會 Huang Shêng 黃晟 ed. 1609

SUI: Chang-sun Wu-chi 長孫無忌 and others, *Sui Shu* 隋書 Po-na ed.

SUN CS 37: Sun Chung-shan 孫中山 *San Min Chu-i* 三民主義 Shanghai 1937

SUNG: Shên Yüeh 沈約 *Sung Shu* 宋書 Po-na ed.

SWCCL: Wang Kuo-wei 王國維 ed. *Shêng-wu Ch'in-chêng Lu Chiao-chu* 聖武親征錄校注 in *WKW* series 3

SWCTC: Tuan Yü-ts'ai 段玉裁 *Shuo-wên Chieh-tzŭ Chu* 說文解字注 Commercial Press ed. 1936

T'ANG CJ 36: T'ang Ch'ang-ju 唐長孺 "Yeh-lü Ta-shih Nien-pu 耶律大石年譜," *Kuo-hsüeh Lun-hêng* 國學論衡 1 (7): 12–26, 1936

T'AO and CHÜ 36: T'ao Hsi-shêng 陶希聖 and Chü Ch'ing-yüan 鞠清遠 *T'ang-tai Ching-chi Shih* 唐代經濟史 Shanghai 1936

TC: Yü Yü 虞裕 *T'an Chuan* 談撰 in *SF* ch. 35

TCC: Tonkin-jō 東京城 "Bokkai-koku Jōkei Ryūsen-fu-shi no hakkutsu chōsa 渤海國上京龍泉府址の發掘調查 (Report on the Excavation of the Site of the Capital of Po-hai)," *Archaelogia Orientalis* 東方考古學會叢刊 The Toa-koko-gakukwai 東亞考古學會 series A, 5, 1939

TCCL: *Ta Chin Chi Li* 大金集禮 in *TSCC* no. 1047–1048

TCCS: Fan Chên 范鎮 *Tung-chai Chi-shih* 東齋紀事 in *TSCC* no. 2744

TCCSPI: —— *Tung-chai Chi-shih Pu-i* (補遺) in *TSCC* no. 2744

TCHC: Yang Tu 楊篤 *T'ien-chên-hsien Chih* 天鎮縣志 1890

TCHL: Fan Chêng-min 范正敏 *Tun-chai Hsien Lan* 遯齋閒覽 in *SF* ch. 35

TCHT: *Chin-ting Ta Ch'ing Hui-tien* 欽定大清會典 Shang-hai Shu-chü 上海書局 ed. 1899

TCKC: Yü-wên Mao-chao 宇文懋昭 *Ta Chin Kuo Chih* 大金國志 in *SCPS*

TCP: Chao Shan-liao 趙善璙 *Tzŭ-ching P'ien* 自警篇 in *TSCC* no. 0993

TCTC: Ssŭ-ma Kuang 司馬光 *Tzŭ-chih T'ung-chien* 資治通鑑 Chi-shan Shu-chü 積山書局 ed. Shanghai 1902

TCTCSW: Shih Chao 史炤 *Tzŭ-chih T'ung-chien Shih-wên* 資治通鑑釋文 in *SPTK* first coll.

TCTFL: *Ta Chin Tiao-fa Lu* 大金弔伐錄 in *SSKTS*, *Shih Chi* 史集

TCTL: *Ta Ch'ing T'ung Li* 大清通禮 1824

TCY: Wang Ting-pao 王定保 *T'ang Chih-yen* 唐摭言 in *HCTY* series 17

TH: Shu Hsin-ch'êng 舒新城 and others, *Tz'ŭ-hai* 辭海 Shanghai 1936

THY: Wang P'u 王溥 *T'ang Hui-yao* 唐會要 Commercial Press ed. 1935

TKSP: Li Chao 李肇 *T'ang Kuo-shih Pu* 唐國史補 in *HCTY* series 8

TKTK: Sê Kö Chöng 徐居正 and others, *Tong Kuk T'ong Kam* 東國通鑑 1914

TLCY: Kao Shih-ch'i 高士奇 *T'ien Lu Chih-yü* 天錄識餘 in *Shuo-ling* 說鈴 series 1 (preface dated 1705)

TLKI: Jên Ta-ch'un 任大椿 *Tzŭ-lin K'ao I* 字林考逸 in *Yen-hsi-t'ang Wu Chung* 燕禧堂五種 Chiang-su Shu-chü 江蘇書局 ed. 1787

TLT: *T'ang Liu-tien* 唐六典 Kuang-ya Shu-chü 廣雅書局 ed. 1895

TML: K'ang Yü-chih 康譽之 *Tso-mêng Lu* 昨夢錄 in *SF* ch. 34

TMT: Yeh Tzŭ-ch'i 葉子奇 *Ts'ao Mu Tzŭ* 草木子 Pên-chia Ts'ang-pan 本家藏板 ed. 1786

TMTTT: Tsang Li-ho 臧勵龢 and others, *Chung-kuo Ku-chin Ti-ming Ta Tz'ŭ-tien* 中國古今地名大辭典 Shanghai 1933

TORII 37: Torii Ryūzō 鳥居龍藏 *Ryō no bunka o saguru* 遼の文化を探る Tokyo 1937

—— 40: —— "Ch'i-tan Hei-shan Hei-ling K'ao 契丹黑山黑嶺考 (A study of the Hei-shan and the Hei-ling of the Khitan Period)," *YCHP* 28: 161–174, 1940

—— 41: —— "Ch'i-tan Chih Chüeh-ti 契丹之角觝 (*Chio-ti* of the Khitans)," *YCHP* 29: 193–200, 1941

TPCC: Su Shih 蘇軾 *Tung-p'o Ch'üan-chi* 東坡全集 in *SPPY*

TPCCTL: P'êng Pai-ch'uan 彭百川 *T'ai-p'ing Chih-chi T'ung-lei* 太平治蹟統類 in *Shih-yüan Ts'ung-shu* 適園叢書 series 10, Chang Tiao-hêng 張鈞衡 ed. 1916

TPCL: Su Shih *Tung-p'o Chih-lin* 東坡志林 in *HCTY* series 15

TPHYC: Yüeh Shih 樂史 *T'ai-p'ing Huan-yü Chi* 太平寰宇記 (preface dated 1803)

TPKC: Li Fang 李昉 and others, *T'ai-p'ing Kuang-chi* 太平廣記 Wên-yu-t'ang Shu-fang 文友堂書坊 ed. Peiping 1934

TPTKSW: Lo Yung 羅邕 and Shên Tsu-chi 沈祖基 *T'ai-p'ing-t'ien-kuo Shih Wên Ch'ao* 太平天國詩文鈔 Shanghai 1935

TPYL: Li Fang and others, *T'ai-p'ing Yü-lan* 太平御覽 in *SPTK* third coll.

TS: Sung Ch'i 宋祁 and others, *T'ang Shu* 唐書 Po-na ed.

TSCH: *Tao-shan Ch'ing-hua* 道山清話 in *TSCC* no. 2785

TSFYCY: Ku Tsu-yü 顧祖與 *Tu Shih Fang-yü Chi-yao* 讀史方輿記要 T'ung-hua Shu-wu 桐華書屋 ed. 1879

TSSTS: Ts'ao T'ing-chieh 曹廷杰 *Tung-san-shêng Yü-ti T'u-shuo* 東三省輿地圖說 in *LHTS* series 7

TSUDA 13: Tsuda Sōkichi 津田左右吉 *Chōsen rekishi chiri* 朝鮮歷史地理 2 v. Tokyo 1913

—— 15: —— "Bokkai kō 渤海考 (On the Po-hai)," *MCRKH* 1: 106–136, 1915

—— 16: —— "Ryo-dai Ukotekiretsu kō 遼代烏古敵烈考 (On the Wu-ku and Ti-lieh of the Liao Dynasty)," *MCRKH* 2: 1–16, 1916

TSUKAMOTO 36: Tsukamoto Zenryū 塚本善隆 "Nihon ni isonseru Ryō bungaku to sono eikyō 日本に遺存せる遼文學とその影響 (On some Chinese Buddhist Texts of the Liao Dynasty preserved in Japan . . .)," *Tōhō gakuhō* 東方學報 7: 275–352, 1936 (Kyoto)

—— 36a: —— "Bukkyō shiryō to shite no Kin koku zōkyō 佛教史料としての金刻藏經 (The Newly Discovered *Chin* (金) Edition of the Tripitaka)," *Tōhō gakuhō* 6: 26–100, 1936 (Kyoto)

TT: Tu Yu 杜佑 *T'ung-tien* 通典 Wan-yu Wên-k'u 萬有文庫 ed. Shanghai 1935

TTSL: Wang Ch'êng 王偁 *Tung-tu Shih-lüeh* 東都事略 in *SCPS*

TWSTT: Ts'ai T'ao 蔡絛 *T'ieh-wei-shan Ts'ung-t'an* 鐵圍山叢談 in *CPTCTS* series 9

TYCH: Han Yüan-chi 韓元吉 *T'ung-yin Chiu-hua* 桐陰舊話 in *SF* ch. 45

TYHKL: Yü Chi 虞集 *Tao-yüan Hsüeh-ku Lu* 道園學古錄 in *SPTK* first coll.

TYL: Kung Ting-ch'ên 龔鼎臣 *Tung-yüan Lu* 東原錄 in *Han Hai* 函海 Wan-chüan-lou 萬卷樓 ed. 1782

WANG CJ 31: Wang Ching-ju 王靜如 "Lun Tsu-pu Yü Ta-tan 論阻卜與韃旦 (On the Tsu-pu and Ta-tan)," *AS* 2 (3): 296–301, 1931

—— 32: —— "Hsi Hsia Kuo-ming K'ao 西夏國名考," in *Hsi Hsia Yen-chiu* 西夏研究, *Shishiah Studies* Part I: 78–88, *AS* Monographs, series A, no. 8, 1932

—— 33: —— "Liao Tao-tsung Chi Hsüan-i Huang-hou Ch'i-tan Kuo-tzŭ Ai-ts'ê Ch'u-shih 遼道宗及宣懿皇后契丹國字哀册初釋 (Buried Stone Tablets in the Tomb of Emperor Tao-tsung and Empress Hsuen-yi of the Kitan Dynasty)," *AS* 3 (4): 467–478, 1933

—— 38: —— "T'u-chüeh Wên Hui-ho Ying-wu Wei-yüan Pi-chia K'o-han Pei I-shih 突厥文回紇英武威遠毗伽可汗碑譯釋," *Fu-jên Hsüeh-chih* 輔仁學誌 7 (1/2): 186–240, 1938

WANG JW 36: Wang Jih-wei 王日蔚 "Ting-ling Min-tsu Shih 丁零民族史 (A Brief History of the Ting-ling People)," *Shih-hsüeh Chi-k'an* 史學集刊 2: 83–114, 1936

WANG KL 31: Wang Kuo-liang 王國良 *Chung-kuo Ch'ang-ch'êng Yen-ko K'ao* 中國長城沿革攷 Shanghai 1931

WCTL: P'ang Yüan-ying 龐元英 *Wên-ch'ang Tsa-lu* 文昌雜錄 in *TSCC* no. 2792

WCTY: Tsêng Kung-liang 曾公亮 *Wu-ching Tsung-yao Ch'ien-chi* 武經總要前集 in *Ssŭ-k'u Ch'üan-shu Chên-pên* 四庫全書珍本 series 1, *Tzŭ-pu* 子部 *Ping-chia Lei* 兵家類 Shanghai 1935

WEI CH 37: Wei Chü-hsien 衛聚賢 *Chung-kuo K'ao-ku-hsüeh Shih* 中國考古學史 Shanghai 1937

WH: *Liu Ch'ên Chu Wên-hsüan* 六臣註文選 in *SPTK* first coll.

WHL: Shên K'uo 沈括 *Wang-huai Lu* 忘懷錄 in *WCHS* ch. 54

WHTK: Ma Tuan-lin 馬端臨 *Wên-hsien T'ung-k'ao* 文獻通攷 Wan-yu Wên-k'u 萬有文庫 ed. Shanghai 1936

WHTSL: *Ta Ch'ing T'ai-tsung Wên Huang-ti Shih-lu* 大清太宗文皇帝實錄 in *SL*

WKC: Hu Su 胡宿 *Wên-kung Chi* 文恭集 in *TSCC* no. 1884–1889

WPC: Mao Yüan-i 茅元儀 *Wu-pei Chih* 武備志 1621

WS: Wei Shou 魏收 *Wei Shu* 魏書 Po-na ed.

WSTL: Wang Chu 王洙 *Wang-shih T'an-lu* 王氏談錄 in *SF* ch. 24

WTHY: Wang P'u 王溥 *Wu-tai Hui-yao* 五代會要 1895

WTS: Ou-yang Hsiu 歐陽修 *Wu-tai Shih-chi* 五代史記 Po-na ed.

WU CL 37: Wu Ch'êng-lo 吳承洛 *Chung-kuo Tu-liang-hêng Shih* 中國度量衡史 Shanghai 1937

WU CT 33: Wu Chin-ting 吳金鼎 "Chai-chi Hsiao-t'un I-hsi Chih San Ch'u Hsiao Fa-chüeh 摘記小屯迤西之三處小發掘 (Notes on Minor Excavations at Three Localities West of Hsiao-t'un)," *Preliminary Reports of Excavations at Anyang* 安陽發掘報告 4: 627–633, Shanghai 1933

WWC: Yang Chieh 揚傑 *Wu-wei Chi* 無為集 in *Sung Jên Chi* 宋人集 series 2, Li-shih I-ch'iu-kuan 李氏宜秋館 ed. 1915

WWCPL: Wang Tsêng 王曾 *Wang Wên-chêng Pi-lu* 王文正筆錄 in *SF* ch. 16

YANAI 30: Yanai Watari 箭內互 *Mōkō-shi kenkyū* 蒙古史研究 Tokyo 1930

YANG CI 35: Yang Chung-i 楊中一 "Pu-ch'ü Yen-ko K'ao-lüeh 部曲沿革攷畧 (On the History of *pu-ch'ü*)," *Shih-huo* 食貨 1: 97–107, 1935

YAO TW 35: Yao Ts'ung-wu 姚從吾 "Shuo A-pao-chi Shih-tai Ti Han-ch'êng 說阿保機時代的漢城 (On the Hann-cherng at Ah Bao Ji's Time)," *KHCK* 5 (1): 53–78, 1935

YCPS: *Yüan-ch'ao Pi Shih* 元朝祕史 Yeh-shih Kuan-ku-t'ang 葉氏觀古堂 ed. 1908

YCPSHC: *Yüan-ch'ao Pi Shih Hsü-chi* (續集) in *Yüan-ch'ao Pi Shih*

YFL: Ch'êng Ta-ch'ang 程大昌 *Yen Fan Lu* 演繁露 in *Hsü Ku-i Ts'ung-shu* 續古逸叢書 *chung* 種 45, Shanghai 1939

YLMC: Chao Yen-wei 趙彥衞 *Yün-lu Man-ch'ao* 雲籚漫鈔 in *TSCC* no. 0297–0298

YPL: Wang I 王易 *Ch'ung-pien Yen-pei Lu* 重編燕北錄 in *SF* [A] ch. 38

YPTC: Wu Kuei 武珪 *Yen-pei Tsa-chi* 燕北雜記 in *SF* [A] ch. 4

YS: Sung Lien 宋濂 and others, *Yüan Shih* 元史 Po-na ed.

YSIWCP: Hung Chün 洪鈞 *Yüan Shih I-wên Chêng-pu* 元史譯文證補 1897

YSTKCL: *Kuang-hsü Yin-shêng T'ung-kuan Ch'ih-lu* 光緒醒生同官齒錄 year 甲辰 (1904)

YTC: *Yüan Tien-chang* 元典章 1908

YTCH: Wang Yün 王惲 *Yü-t'ang Chia-hua* 玉堂嘉話 in *SPTK* first coll.

YTCS: Wang Hsiang-chih 王象之 *Yü-ti Chi Shêng* 輿地紀勝 Wên-hsüan-lou 文選樓 ed. 1849

YTPCM: —— *Yü-ti Pei-chi Mu* 輿地碑記目 in *TSCC* no. 1580

YYC: Wu Lai 吳萊 *Yüan-ying Chi* 淵穎集 in *TSCC* no. 2269–2274

YYKYL: Chou Mi 周密 *Yün-yen Kuo-yen Lu* 雲煙過眼錄 in *TSCC* no. 1553

YYTT: Tuan Ch'êng-shih 段成式 *Yu-yang Tsa-tsu* 酉陽雜組 in *TSCC* no. 0276–0278

WESTERN BIBLIOGRAPHY

ABOUL-GHĀZI 74: *Histoire des Mongols et des Tatares par Aboul-Ghāzi Behādour Khan*, publiée, traduite et annotée par le Baron Desmaisons, II. St. Petersburg 1874

ABOULFEDA 1848: *Géographie d'Aboulféda*, traduite de l'Arabe en Français et accompagnée de notes et d'éclaircissements par M. Reinaud. 2 v. Paris 1848

ACKERMAN: See Pope and Ackerman

ANNALES ADMUNTENSES: Annales Admuntenses. In *Monumenta Germaniae Historica* IX: 569–593. Hannover 1851

ARENDT 34: W. W. Arendt. Sur l'Apparition de l'Etrier chez les Scyths. *Eurasia Septentrionalis Antiqua* 9: 206–208, 1934

ARISTOTLE 41: *The Basic Works of Aristotle*, ed. by Richard McKeon. New York 1941

AROSENIUS 18: Edvard Arosenius. The History and Organization of Swedish Official Statistics. In John Koren, *The History of Statistics*, 537–569. New York 1918

ARRIAN 42: The Anabasis of Alexander, tr. by Edward J. Chinnoch. In *The Greek Historians*, ed. by Francis R. B. Godolphin, II: 402–591. New York 1942

AT-ṬIRIMMĀH 27: *The Poems of Ṭufail Ibn 'Auf al-Ghanawī and At-Tirimmāh Ibn Ḥakīm At-Ṭā'yī*. Arabic text ed. and tr. by F. Krenkow. E. J. W. Gibb Memorial XXV. London 1927

BALÁZS 31–33 BWT: Stefan Balázs. Beiträge zur Wirtschaftsgeschichte der T'ang-Zeit (618–906). *Mitteilungen des Seminars für Orientalische Sprachen* 34: 1–92, 1931; 35: 1–73, 1932; 36: 1–62, 1933

BALES 37: W. L. Bales. *Tso Tsung-t'ang*. Shanghai 1937

BANG AND GABAIN 31: Willi Bang and Annemarie von Gabain. Analytischer Index zu den fünf ersten Stücken der Türkischen Turfan-Texte. *Sitzungsberichte der P. A. W. (Phil.-Hist. Klasse)* 17: 458–517. Berlin 1931

BAR HEBRAEUS 32: *The Chronography of Gregory Abū'l Faraj, the Son of Aaron, the Hebrew Physician commonly known as Bar Hebraeus*, tr. from the Syriac by Ernest A. Wales Budge. 2 v. London 1932

BARTHOLD, "Balāsāghūn": W. Barthold. Balāsāghūn. *Enc. Is.* I: 614–615

—— BH: ——. Burāk-Hādjib. *Enc. Is.* I: 793–794

—— KK: ——. Kara Khitai. *Enc. Is.* II: 737–739

—— 97: ——. Die historische Bedeutung der alttürkischen Inschriften. In W. Radloff, *Die alttürkischen Inschriften der Mongolei* n.f. St. Petersburg 1897

—— 01: ——. *Zur Geschichte des Christentums in Mittelasien*, ed. by Rudolf Stübe. Tübingen and Leipzig 1901

—— 28: ——. *Turkestan down to the Mongol Invasion*. London 1928

—— 35: ——. *12 Vorlesungen über die Geschichte der Türken Mittelasiens*. Berlin 1935

—— 35a: ——. Ulug Beg und seine Zeit. *Abhandlungen für die Kunde des Morgenlandes herausgegeben von der Deutschen Morgenländischen Gesellschaft* 21 (1). Leipzig 1935

BCP 22: Ph. Clement. La Pagode de la Croix; Lettre du P. Cheikho, S.J. sur l'inscription de la croix de Che-tze-seu. *Bulletin Catholique de Pékin*, 290–297 and 464–465. Peking 1922

—— 23: ——. Les Croix et les Stèles de Che-tze-seu. *Bulletin Catholique de Pékin*, 218–224. Peking 1923

—— 24: Charles Pieters. Croix d'un ancien cimetière chrétien. *Bulletin Catholique de Pékin*, 54–56. Peking 1924

BEARD 34: Charles A. Beard. *The Nature of the Social Sciences in Relation to Objectives of Instruction*. New York etc. 1934

BECK 16: Hermann Beck. *Buddhismus (Buddha und seine Lehre)*, I. Berlin and Leipzig 1916

BELL 31: Sir Charles Bell. *The Religion of Tibet*. Oxford 1931

BELLOC 14: Hilaire Belloc. *The Book of the Bayeux Tapestry*. New York 1914

BENEDICT 38: Ruth Benedict. Religion. In Franz Boas, *General Anthropology*, 627–665. Boston 1938

BENJAMIN 1840: *The Itinerary of Rabbi Benjamin of Tudela*, tr. and ed. by A. Asher. 2 v. New York 1840

BERGMAN 39: Folke Bergman. *Archaeological Researches in Sinkiang*. Stockholm 1939

BERNHEIM 14: Ernst Bernheim. *Lehrbuch der Historischen Methode und der Geschichtsphilosophie*. Munich and Leipzig 1914

BERR 11: Henri Berr. *La Synthèse en Histoire*. Paris 1911

BERR and FEBVRE 37: Henri Berr and Lucien Febvre. History and Historiography. *Enc. SS* VII: 357–368

BĒRŪNĪ 79: *The Chronology of Ancient Nations, an English Version of the Arabic Text of the Athār-ul-Bākiya of Albīrūnī*, collected and reduced to writing by the author in A. H. 390–391, A. D. 1000, tr. and ed. with notes and index by Dr. C. Edward Sachau. London 1879

BIGGERSTAFF: See Têng and Biggerstaff

BLOCHET 10: E. Blochet. *Introduction à l'Histoire des Mongols de Fadl Allah Rachid Ed-Din*. Leiden and London 1910

BLOOMFIELD 41: Leonard Bloomfield. *Language.* New York 1941

BOAS 21: Franz Boas. *Ethnology of the Kwakiutl.* Thirty-fifth Annual Report of the Bureau of American Ethnology 1913–1914. 2 v. Washington 1921

—— 35: ——. *Kwakiutl Culture as Reflected in Mythology.* New York 1935

—— 37: ——. Anthropology. *Enc. SS* II: 73–110

—— 40: ——. *Race, Language and Culture.* New York 1940

BODDE 36: *Annual Customs and Festivals in Peking* as recorded in the *Yen-ching Sui-shih-chi* by Tun Li-ch'ên, tr. by Derk Bodde. Peiping 1936

BOGHOLM 39: N. Bogholm. *English Speech from an Historical Point of View.* Copenhagen and London 1939

BOODBERG 34: Peter A. Boodberg. Ting-ling and Turks. *Sino Altaica* II (5). Berkeley 1934

—— 36: ——. The Language of the T'o-pa Wei. *HJAS* 1: 167–185, 1936

—— 39: ——. Marginalia to the Histories of the Northern Dynasties. *HJAS* 4: 230–283, 1939

BRÉAL 00: Michael Bréal. *Semantics. Studies in the Science of Meaning.* London 1900

BRETSCHNEIDER 88: E. Bretschneider. *Mediaeval Researches from Asiatic Sources: Fragments Towards the Knowledge of the Geography and History of Central and Western Asia from the 13th to the 17th Century.* 2 v. London 1888

BRITTON 38: *Seven Collections of Inscribed Oracle Bones,* drawn by Frank H. Chalfant, ed. by Roswell S. Britton. New York 1938

BROCKELMANN 28: C. Brockelmann. *Mitteltürkischer Wortschatz, nach Mahmud al-Kāšγarīs Dīvān Luγāt at-Turk.* Budapest and Leipzig 1928

—— 37: ——. *Geschichte der Arabischen Litteratur.* Leiden 1937

BROWNE 28: Edward G. Browne. *A Literary History of Persia.* 3 v. Cambridge 1928

BROWNE 33: Laurence E. Browne. *The Eclipse of Christianity in Asia* from the time of Muhammad till the Fourteenth Century. Cambridge 1933

BRUNNERT AND HAGELSTROM 12: H. S. Brunnert and V. V. Hagelstrom. *Present Day Political Organization of China.* Shanghai 1912

BUCK 30: J. L. Buck. *Chinese Farm Economy.* Chicago and Shanghai 1930

—— 37a: ——. *Land Utilization of China. Statistics.* Chicago 1937

—— 37b: ——. *Land Utilization of China. Atlas.* Chicago 1937

—— 37c: ——. *Land Utilization in China.* Chicago 1937

BUCK 33: *All Men are Brothers* (*Shui Hu Chuan*), tr. from the Chinese by Pearl S. Buck. 2 v. New York 1933

BUNZEL 38: Ruth Bunzel. The Economic Organization of Primitive Peoples. In Franz Boas, *General Anthropology,* 327–408. Boston 1938

BURY 31: J. B. Bury. *History of the Later Roman Empire* from the death of Theodosius I to the death of Justinian (A.D. 395 to A.D. 565). 2 v. London 1931

BUSHELL 80: S. W. Bushell. The Early History of Tibet. *JRAS,* n.s. 12, 32: 435–535, 1880

—— 95/96: The Hsi Hsia Dynasty of Tangut, their Money and Peculiar Script. *Jour. China Branch Royal Asiatic Soc.,* n.s. 30: 142–160, 1895/6

BU-STON 32: Bu-ston. *History of Buddhism.* Part II: *The History of Buddhism in India and Tibet,* tr. from Tibetan by Dr. E. Obermiller. Heidelberg 1932

BUTLER 84: Alfred J. Butler. *The Ancient Coptic Churches of Egypt.* 2 v. Oxford 1884

—— 25: ——. *Islamic Pottery.* London 1925

CARL 26: Katherine A. Carl. *With the Empress Dowager of China.* Tientsin 1926

CARPINI 00: *The Journey of William of Rubruck to the Eastern Parts of the World, 1253–55, as Narrated by Himself, with Two Accounts of the Earlier Journey of John of Pian de Carpine,* tr. from the Latin and ed. with an introductory notice by William Woodville Rockhill. London, The Hakluyt Society 1900

—— 28: The Journey of Friar John of Pian de Carpini to the Court of Kuyuk Khan, 1245–1247, as Narrated by Himself. In *Contemporaries of Marco Polo,* ed. by Manuel Komroff. New York 1928

CARTER 31: T. F. Carter. *The Invention of Printing in China and its Spread Westward.* Rev. ed. New York 1931.

CHACH-NÁMA 67: Sir H. M. Elliot and John Dowson. *The History of India as Told by its Own Historians,* I: 131–211. London 1867

CHAVANNES, "Khitans": Edouard Chavannes. Khitans ou Ki-tan. *Grande Encyclopédie* XXI: 511–513

——, "Kin": ——. Kin. *Grande Encyclopédie* XXI: 537–538

——, MH: ——. *Les Mémoires Historiques de Se-ma Ts'ien.* 5 v. Paris 1895–1905

—— 97: ——. Le Nestorianisme et l'Inscription de Kara-Balgassoun. *JA,* ser. 9, 9: 43–85, 1897

—— 97–98 VC: ——. Voyageurs Chinois chez les Khitans et les Joutchen. *JA,* ser. 9, 9: 377–422, 1897; ser. 9, 11: 361–439, 1898

—— 03: ——. *Documents sur les Tou-kiue (Turcs) Occidentaux.* St. Petersburg 1903.

—— 03a: ——. Voyage de Song Yun 宋雲 dans l'Udyāna et le Gandhāra. *BEFEO* 3: 379–441, 1903

—— 04: ——. Notes Additionnelles sur les Tou-kiue (Turcs) Occidentaux. *TP* 5: 1–110, 1904

—— 04–05 ICC: ——. Inscriptions et Pièces de Chancellerie Chinoises de l'Epoque Mongole. *TP* 5: 357–447, 1904; 6: 1–42, 1905

—— 07: ——. Les Pays d'Occident d'après le *Heou Han chou. TP* 8: 149–234, 1907.

—— 13: ——. *Documents Chinois Decouverts par Aurel Stein.* Oxford 1913

—— 14: ——. Six Monuments de la Sculpture Chinoise. *Ars Asiatica* 2 [Monograph], 1914

—— 16: ——. Le Royaume de Wou et de Yue 吳越. *TP* 17: 129–264, 1916

CHAVANNES-PELLIOT 13: Un Traité Manichéen retrouvé en Chine, traduit et annoté par Edouard Chavannes et P. Pelliot. *JA,* ser. 11, 1: 99–199; 261–383, 1913

CHUNG: See Moule and Chung

CLAUSEWITZ 57: Carl von Clausewitz. *Vom Kriege,* I–II. Berlin 1857

COLUMBUS 70: *Select Letters of Christopher Columbus* with other Original Documents, Relating to his Four Voyages to the New World, tr. and ed. by R. H. Major. London, The Hakluyt Society 1870

COOLE 36: Arthur Braddan Coole. *Coins in China's History.* Tientsin 1936

COOMARASWAMY 32: A. K. Coomaraswamy. Review of Lefebvre des Noëttes, *L'Attelage et le Cheval de Selle à travers les âges. JAOS* **56**: 84–86, 1932

COUVREUR 11: S. Couvreur. *Dictionnaire classique de la Langue chinoise.* 3d ed. Ho Kien Fou 1911

—— 13: ——. *Li Ki.* 2 v. 2d ed. Ho Kien Fou 1913

CREEL 37: H. G. Creel. *Studies in Early Chinese Culture. First series.* Baltimore 1937

—— 37a: ——. *The Birth of China.* New York 1937

—— 38: ——. *Literary Chinese by the Inductive Method,* I. *The Hsiao Ching.* Chicago 1938

CREIGHTON 07: Mandell Creighton. Introductory Note to the Cambridge Modern History. *The Cambridge Modern History.* Cambridge 1907

CROCE 15: Benedetto Croce. *Zur Theorie und Geschichte der Historiographie.* Tübingen 1915

CULIN 98: Steward Culin. Chess and Playing Cards. *Report of the U. S. National Museum, Under the Direction of the Smithsonian Institution, for the year ending June 30, 1896,* 665–942, 1898

CURTIN 08: Jeremiah Curtin. *The Mongols in Russia.* Boston 1908

CZAPLICKA 18: M. A. Czaplicka. *The Turks of Central Asia in History and at the Present Day.* Oxford 1918

DEGUIGNES, HGH: Jos. Deguignes. *Histoire Générale des Huns, des Turcs, des Mongols, et des autres Tartares Occidentaux, etc.* 5 v. Paris 1756–1758

DELBRÜCK, GK: Hans Delbrück. *Geschichte der Kriegskunst im Rahmen der politischen Geschichte,* I–III. Berlin 1900–1907

DEMIÉVILLE 25: Paul Demiéville. Les Versions chinoises du *Milindapañha. BEFEO* **24**: 1–258, 1924

DER LING 11: The Princess Der Ling. *Two Years in the Forbidden City.* New York 1911

DES ROTOURS 27: Robert Des Rotours. Les grands Fonctionnaires des Provinces en Chine sous la Dynastie des T'ang. *TP* **25**: 219–330, 1927

—— 32: ——. *Le Traité des Examens.* Bibliothèque de l'Institut des Hautes Etudes Chinoises II. Paris 1932

DORÉ, RSC: Henri Doré. *Recherches sur les Superstitions en Chine,* VI. Variétés Sinologiques, no. 39. Shanghai 1914

DORN 81: B. Dorn. Über die Münzen der Ileke oder ehemaligen Chane von Turkistan. *Mélanges Asiatiques tirés du Bulletin de l'Academie Impériale des Sciences de St. Petersbourg* **8**: 703–744. St. Petersburg 1881

—— 88: ——. Nachträge zu der Abhandlung über die Münzen der Ileke oder ehemaligen Chane von Turkistan. *Mélanges Asiatiques* etc. **9**: 55–73. St. Petersburg 1888

DOWSON: See Elliot and Dowson

DROYSEN 37: Johann Gustav Droysen. *Historik: Vorlesungen über Enzyklopädie und Methodologie der Geschichte.* Im Auftrage der Preussischen Akademie der Wissenschaften herausgegeben von Rudolf Hübner Munich and Berlin 1937

DUBS, HFH: *The History of the Former Han Dynasty,* A Critical Translation with Annotations by Homer H. Dubs. 2 v. Baltimore 1938–1941

—— 45: ——. Chinese Imperial Designations. *JAOS* **65**: 26–33, 1945

DU HALDE 1736: J. B. Du Halde. *The General History of China.* 4 v. London 1736

DUYVENDAK 28: J. J. L. Duyvendak. *The Book of Lord Shang.* London 1928

—— 35: ——. Review of J. K. Shryock, *The Origin and Development of the State Cult of Confucius. JAOS* **55**: 330–338, 1935

—— 39: ——. The True Dates of the Chinese Maritime Expeditions in the early 15th Century. *TP* **34**: 341–412, 1939

EBERHARD 42: W. Eberhard. *Liu Yüan ve Liu Ts'ung.* Dil ve Tarih-Coğrafya Fakültesi Sinoloji Enstitüsü Neşriyatı No. 4. (German translation). Ankara 1942

ELLIOT AND DOWSON, HI: Sir H. M. Elliot and John Dowson. *The History of India as told by its own historians,* ed. from the posthumous papers of the late Sir H. M. Elliot by Professor John Dowson. 8 v. London 1867–1871

ENSSLIN 30: Ensslin. Mauricius. *Real-Encyclopädie der Classischen Altertumswissenschaften,* ed. Pauly-Wissowa, XV: 2–394

ERKES 39: Eduard Erkes. Zur Sage von Shun. *TP* **34**: 295–333, 1939

—— 40: ——. Das Pferd im Alten China. *TP* **36**: 26–63, 1940

ETTINGHAUSEN AND SCHROEDER 41: Richard Ettinghausen and Eric Schroeder. Iranic and Islamic Art. *Oriental Art,* ser. 0, sec. 4 of the University Prints. Newton, Mass. 1941

FEBVRE: See Berr and Febvre

FERRAND 13: Gabriel Ferrand. *Relations de Voyages et Textes Géographiques Arabes, Persans et Turks Relatifs à l'Extrême-Orient du VIIIᵉ au XVIIIᵉ Siècles.* Paris 1913

FINK 07: Elias Fink. Über das angebliche fabelhafte Tier *adne has-sadeh* in der Mischna. *Monatsschrift für die Geschichte und Wissenschaft des Judentums* **51**: 173–182, 1907

FLÜGEL 62: Gustav Flügel. *Mani, seine Lehre und seine Schriften.* Leipzig 1862

FORRER 07: Robert Forrer. Steigbügel. *Reallexikon der praehistorischen, klassischen und frühgeschichtlichen Altertümer.* Stuttgart 1907

FRANKE, GCR: O. Franke. *Geschichte des chinesischen Reiches,* I–III. Berlin and Leipzig 1930–1937

—— 02: ——. *Beschreibung des Jehol-Gebietes in der Provinz Chihli.* Leipzig 1902

FRAZER 38: Sir James George Frazer. *The Native Races of Africa and Madagascar.* London 1938

—— 40: ——. *The Golden Bough.* New York 1940

FREDERICK 41: The Instruction of Frederick the Great for his Generals 1747, tr. by Major Thomas R. Phillips. In *Roots of Strategy,* 301–400. New York 1941

FRIEDRICH 20: *Die Politischen Testamente Friedrichs des Grossen,* ed. by Dr. Gustav Berthold Volz. Berlin 1920

FUNG 37: Fung Yu-lan. *A History of Chinese Philosophy. The Period of the Philosophers*, tr. by Derk Bodde. Peiping 1937

GABAIN: See Bang and Gabain

GABELENTZ 81: Georg von der Gabelentz. *Chinesische Grammatik.* Leipzig 1881

GABELENTZ 64: Hans Conon von der Gabelentz. *Sse-Schu, Schu-King, Schi-King in Mandschuischer Übersetzung mit einem Mandschu-Deutschen Wörterbuch.* Abhandlungen für die Kunde des Morgenlandes III, fasc. 1 and 2. Leipzig 1864

—— 77: ——. *Geschichte der Grossen Liao.* St. Petersburg 1877

GARDNER 38: Charles S. Gardner. *Chinese Traditional Historiography.* Cambridge 1938

—— 40: ——. India and China through the 18th Century. *An Encyclopedia of World History*, ed. by William L. Langner, 40–45, 128–137, 335–354, 535–548. Boston etc. 1940

GEORGE 09: H. B. George. *Historical Evidence.* Oxford 1909

GIBBON, DFRE: Edward Gibbon. *The Decline and Fall of the Roman Empire.* 2 v. New York, The Modern Library

GIBERT 34: Lucien Gibert. *Dictionnaire historique et géographique de la Mandchourie.* Hongkong 1934

GIFFORD 26: E. W. Gifford. Miwok Lineages and the Political Unit in Aboriginal California. *AA* **28**: 389–401, 1926

GILES 12: Herbert A. Giles. *A Chinese-English Dictionary.* 2nd ed. Shanghai 1912

—— 12a: ——. *China and the Manchus.* London 1912

GILES 10: *Sun Tzŭ on the Art of War, the oldest military treatise in the world*, tr. by Lionel Giles. London 1910

—— 15: Lionel Giles. A Census of Tun-Huang. *TP* **16**: 468–488, 1915

—— 33–35: ——. A Topographical Fragment from Tunhuang. *Bull. School Orient. Studies* **7**: 545–572. London 1933–1935

—— 40: ——. Dated Chinese Manuscripts in the Stein Collection, V (Plate I). *Bull. School Orient. Studies* **10** (2): 317–344. London 1940

GILMOUR 93: James Gilmour. *More About the Mongols.* London 1893

GINSBERG 25: Louis Ginsberg. *Legends of the Jews*, V. Philadelphia 1925

GOËS 16: The Journey of Benedict Goës to Cathay. In Yule, *Cathay and the Way Thither* IV: 198–254. London 1916

GOLDENWEISER 16: Alexander A. Goldenweiser. Sociological Terminology in Ethnology. *AA* **18** (3): 248–357, 1916

—— 22: ——. *Early Civilization.* New York 1922

GOODRICH 35: L. Carrington Goodrich. *The Literary Inquisition of Ch'ien-lung.* Baltimore 1935

—— 40: ——. A Note on the *Ta Ming Shih Lu. TP* **36**: 81–84, 1940

—— 43: ——. Cotton in China. *Isis* **34** (5): 408–410, 1943

GRANET 29: Marcel Granet. *La Civilisation Chinoise.* Paris 1929

DE GROOT, RSC: J. J. M. de Groot. *The Religious System of China.* 6 v. Leiden 1892–1910

—— SRP: ——. *Sectarianism and Religious Persecution in China.* 2 v. Amsterdam 1903–1904

—— 86: ——. Les Fêtes annuelles célébrées à Émoui (Amoy), *Annales du Musée Guimet* XI–XII, 1886

—— 18: ——. *Universismus.* Berlin 1918

—— 21/26: ——. *Chinesiche Urkunden zur Geschichte Asiens* I: Die Hunnen der vorchristlichen Zeit, 1921; II: Die Westlande Chinas in der vorchristlichen Zeit, 1926. Berlin and Leipzig

GROSSE 20: Robert Grosse. *Römische Militärgeschichte von Gallienus bis zum Beginn der byzantinischen Themenverfassung.* Berlin 1920

GROUSSET 39: René Grousset. *L'Empire des Steppes.* Paris 1939

GRUBE 96: Wilhelm Grube. *Die Sprache und Schrift der Jučen.* Leipzig 1896

GRÜNWEDEL 00: Albert Grünwedel. *Mythologie des Buddhismus in Tibet und der Mongolei.* Leipzig 1900

HAENISCH 31: Erich Haenisch. Untersuchungen über das Yüan-ch'ao Pi-shi, Die Geheime Geschichte der Mongolen. *Abhandlungen der Philologisch-Historischen Klasse der Sächsischen Akademie der Wissenschaften* **41** (4). Leipzig 1931

—— 37: ——. *Manghol un Niuca Tobca' an (Yüan-ch'ao Pi-shi).* Leipzig 1937

—— 41: ——. Kulturbilder aus Chinas Mongolenzeit. *Historische Zeitschrift* **164**, fasc. 1: 21–48, 1941

HAGELSTROM: See Brunnert and Hagelstrom

HAMD-ALLĀH MUSTAWFĪ 1848: Histoire des Seldjoukides, Extraite du *Tarikhi Guzideh*, ou Histoire choisie, d'Hamd-Allāh Mustaufī, traduite et accompagnée de notes par M. Defrémery. *JA*, ser. 4, **12**: 334–370, 1848.

—— 13: *The Ta'rīkh-i-Guzīda or "Select History" of Hamdu'llāh Mustawfī-i-Qazwīnī*, compiled in A. H. 730 (A. D. 1330) and now abridged in English from a Manuscript dated A. H. 857 (A. D. 1453) by Edward G. Browne. E. J. W. Gibb Memorial XIV (2). Leiden and London 1913

—— 19: *The Geographical Part of the Nuzhat-al-Qulūb composed by Hamd-Allāh Mustawfī of Qazwīn in 740 (1340)*, tr. by G. Le Strange. E. J. W. Gibb Memorial XXIII (2). Leyden and London 1919

HAMMER, GOR: Joseph von Hammer [-Purgstall]. *Geschichte des Osmanischen Reiches*, I–III. Pest 1827

HAMMER-PURGSTALL 1840: Joseph von Hammer-Purgstall. *Geschichte der Goldenen Horde in Kiptschak, das ist der Mongolen in Russland.* Pest 1840

HAMPEL 85: Joseph Hampel. *Der Goldfund von Nagy-Szent-Miklós.* Budapest 1885

—— 05: ——. *Altertümer des Frühen Mittelalters in Ungarn.* 3 v. Braunschweig 1905

DE HARLEZ 87: Ch. de Harlez. *La Religion Nationale des Tartares Orientaux: Mandchous et Mongols.* Mémoires Couronnés et autres Mémoires publiés par l'Académie Royale des Sciences, des Lettres et des Beaux-Arts de Belgique XL. Brussels 1887

—— 94: ——. *La Religion et les Cérémonies Impériales de la Chine Moderne d'après le cérémonial et les décrets officiels.* Mémoires de l'Académie Royale des Sciences, des Lettres et des Beaux-Arts de Belgique LII. Brussels 1893–1894

HAUER 26: *Huang-Ts'ing K'ai-Kuo Fang-Lüeh, Die Gründung des Mandschurischen Kaiserreiches*, tr. and interpreted by Erich Hauer. Berlin and Leipzig 1926

HCS: *History of Chinese Society, Ch'in* 秦 *and Han* 漢, *and Chin* 金, in preparation by the Chinese History Project.

HERBERSTEIN 52: Sigismund von Herberstein. *Notes upon Russia: being a Translation of the Earliest Account of that Country entitled Rerum Moscoviticarum Commentarii*, tr. and ed. by R. H. Major. 2 v. London, The Hakluyt Society 1852

HERODOTUS 42: Herodotus: The Persian Wars, tr. by George Rawlinson. In *The Greek Historians*, ed. by Francis R. B. Godolphin, II: 3–518. New York 1942

HERRMANN 35: Albert Herrmann. *Historical and Commercial Atlas of China.* Cambridge 1935

HERSKOVITS 38: Melville J. Herskovits. *Acculturation, The Study of Culture Contact.* New York 1938

—— 40: ——. *The Economic Life of Primitive Peoples.* New York and London 1940

——: See also Redfield, Linton, and Herskovits

HIRTH 85: F. Hirth. *China and the Roman Orient: Researches into their Ancient and Mediaeval Relations as Represented in Old Chinese Records.* Shanghai and Hongkong 1885

—— 90: ——. Note on the Chinese stirrup. *Verhandlungen der Berliner Gesellschaft für Anthropologie, Ethnologie und Urgeschichte: Zeitschrift für Ethnologie* **22**: 209–210, 1890

—— 99: ——. Nachworte zur Inschrift des Tonjukuk. In W. Radloff, *Die Alttürkischen Inschriften der Mongolei.* n.s. St. Petersburg 1899

HIRTH AND ROCKHILL 11: *Chau Ju-Kua: His Work on the Chinese and Arab Trade in the twelfth and thirteenth Centuries, entitled Chu-fan-chi*, tr. from the Chinese and annotated by Friedrich Hirth and W. W. Rockhill. St. Petersburg 1911

HOANG 10: P. Hoang. *Concordance des Chronologies Néoméniques Chinoise et Européenne.* Variétés Sinologiques no. 29. Shanghai 1910

HODOUS: See Soothill and Hodous.

HOSIE 01: A. Hosie. *Manchuria.* London 1901

HOUTUM-SCHINDLER 81: A. Houtum-Schindler. Notes on Marco Polo's Itinerary in Southern Persia. *JRAS* n.s. **13**: 490–497, 1881

HOWORTH, HM: H. H. Howorth. *History of the Mongols.* 4 v. London 1876–1927

—— 76: ——. The Northern Frontagers of China. Part III: The Kara Khitai. *JRAS* **8** (2): 262–290, 1876

—— 81: ——. The Northern Frontagers of China. Part V: The Khitai or Khitans. *JRAS* **13**: 121–182, 1881

HSIEH 25: Hsieh Pao Chao. *The Government of China (1644–1911).* Baltimore 1925

HU S 31: Hu Shih. The Literary Renaissance. In *Symposium on Chinese Culture*, ed. by Sophia H. Chen Zen, 129–141. Shanghai 1931

—— 34: ——. *The Chinese Renaissance.* Chicago 1934

—— 41: ——. The Exchange of Ideas between the Occident and the Orient. *Contemporary China* **1** (12), November 3, 1941

—— 43: ——. Preface to *Eminent Chinese of the Ch'ing Period*, ed. by Arthur W. Hummel. Washington 1943

HUDSON 38: Alfred E. Hudson. *Kazak Social Structure.* Yale University Publications in Anthropology, no. 20. New Haven 1928

HUDŪD AL-ʿĀLAM 37: *The Regions of the World*, a Persian geography, 372 A. H.–982 A. D., tr. and explained by V. Minorsky with the preface by V. V. Barthold, tr. from the Russian etc. London 1937

HUMMEL, ECCP: *Eminent Chinese of the Ch'ing Period*, ed. by Arthur W. Hummel. 2 v. Washington 1943–1944

HYAKINTH 1832: *Denkwürdigkeiten über die Mongolei*, tr. from the Russian by K. F. von der Borg. Berlin 1832

IBN BATOUTAH 77/79: *Voyages d'Ibn Batoutah*, texte Arabe, accompagné d'une traduction par C. De Frémery et B. R. Sanguinetti, II: Paris 1877; IV: Paris 1879

IBN BATUTA 16: Ibn Batuta's Travels in Bengal and China. In Yule, *Cathay and the Way Thither* IV: 80–150. London 1916

IBN ISHAK 64: *Das Leben Mohammed's nach Mohammed Ibn Ishak, bearbeitet von Abd el-Malik Ibn Hischam*, aus dem Arabischen, tr. by Dr. Gustav Weil. 2 v. Stuttgart 1864

IBN KHALDOUN, PH: *Prolégomènes Historiques d'Ibn Khaldoun*, tr. by M. G. de Slane. Notices et Extraits des Manuscrits de la Bibliothèque Impériale et autres bibliothèques, publiés par l'Institut Impérial de France, XIX, XX, XXI. Paris 1862–1868

JACKSON 32: A. V. Williams Jackson. *Researches in Manichaeism.* New York 1932

JACOB 97: Georg Jacob. *Altarabisches Beduinenleben nach den Quellen geschildert.* Berlin 1897

JARRING 39: Gunnar Jarring. *On the Distribution of Turk Tribes in Afghanistan.* Lunds Universitets Årsskrift N.F., Avd. l., Bd. 35, Nr. 4. Lund 1939

JESPERSEN 05: Otto Jespersen. *Growth and Structure of the English Language.* Leipzig 1905

JOCHELSON 28: Waldemar Jochelson. *Peoples of Asiatic Russia.* New York, Amer. Mus. Nat. Hist. 1928

JOHNSTON 34: Reginald F. Johnston. *Twilight in the Forbidden City.* New York 1934

JULIEN 1847: Stanislas Julien. Notices sur les Peuples Etrangers, tirées des géographies et des annales chinoises, . . . Les Oigours . . . Thien-tchou. *JA*, ser. 4, **9**: 50–66, 189–210; and **10**: 81–121, 1847

—— 64: ——. Documents Historiques sur les Tou-kioue (Turcs), extraits du *pien-i-tien*, et traduits du chinois. *JA*, ser. 6, **3**: 325–367, 490–549; and **4**: 200–242, 391–430, 453–477, 1864

—— 69: ——. *Syntaxe Nouvelle de la Langue Chinoise*, I. Paris 1869

JUWAYNĪ 16: *The Ta'rīkh-i Jahān-gushā of 'Alā'u-'d-Dīn 'Atā Malik-i-Juwaynī* (composed in A. H. 658–A. D. 1260), ed. with an introduction, notes, and indices from several old mss. by Mīrzā Muḥammad ibn 'Abdu'l Wahhāb-i-Qazwīnī, Part II, containing the History of the Khwārazm-shāh dynasty. E. J. W. Gibb Memorial XVI (2). Leiden and London 1916

KARAMISHEFF 25: W. Karamisheff. *Mongolia and Western China*. Tientsin 1925

KARLGREN, PC: Bernhard Karlgren. *Etudes sur la Phonologie Chinoise*. Archives d'Etudes Orientales XV, 1915–1926

—— 23: ——. *Analytic Dictionary of Chinese and Sino-Japanese*. Paris 1923

—— 40: ——. Grammata Serica, Script and Phonetics in Chinese and Sino-Japanese. *Bull. Mus. of Far Eastern Antiquities* **12**: 1–471, 1940

KENKYŪSHA: Kenkyūsha's *New Japanese-English Dictionary*. Tokyo 1931

KENNEDY 41: George A. Kennedy. Dating of Chinese Dynasties and Reigns. *JAOS* **61**: 285–286, 1941

KHOROCHKINE 78: A. P. Khorochkine. Itinéraires de l'Asie Centrale. In *Recueil d'Itinéraires et de Voyages dans l'Asie Centrale et l'Extrême-Orient*, 165–243. Paris 1878

KLAPROTH 1826: J. Klaproth. *Tableaux Historiques de l'Asie*. Paris 1826

KNIGHT 37: Frank H. Knight. Interest. *Enc. SS* VIII: 131–143, 1937

KOEPPEN 59: Carl Friedrich Koeppen. *Die Lamaische Hierarchie und Kirche. Die Religion des Buddha und ihre Entstehung*, II. Berlin 1859

KOTWICZ 25: W. Kotwicz. Les "Khitaï" et leur Ecriture. *Rocznik Orjentalistyczny* **2**: 248–250, 1925

KOVALEVSKIJ 1844: O. Kovalevskij. *Dictionnaire Mongol-Russe-Français*. 3 v. Kazan 1844

KOZIN 41: S. A. Kozin. *Sokrovennoje Skazanije*. Moscow and Leningrad 1941

KRAMERS 27: J. K. Kramers. Kirmān. *Enc. Is.* II: 1028–1031

KREMER, CO: Alfred von Kremer. *Culturgeschichte des Orients unter den Chalifen*. 2 v. Vienna 1875–1877.

KROEBER 23: A. L. Kroeber. *Anthropology*. New York 1923

—— 38: ——. Basic and Secondary Pattern of Social Structure. *Jour. Royal Anthrop. Inst.* **68**: 299–309, 1938

—— 39: ——. *Cultural and Natural Areas of Native North America*. Berkeley 1939

KULISCHER, AWMN: Josef Kulischer. *Allgemeine Wirtschaftsgeschichte des Mittelalters und der Neuzeit*. 2 v. Munich and Berlin 1928–1929

LAMMERT 29: F. Lammert. Steigbügel. *Real-Encyclopädie der Classischen Altertumswissenschaft*, ed. Pauly-Wissowa, ser. 2, **3**: 2236–2238, 1929

LANE-POOLE 94: Stanley Lane-Poole. *The Mohammadan Dynasties*. Westminster 1894

LANG 39: Olga Lang. The Good Iron of the New Chinese Army. *Pacific Affairs* **12**: 20–33, 1939

—— 40: ——. Recent Russian Literature on Buriat Mongolia. *Pacific Affairs* **13**: 45–62, 1940

LANGLOIS AND SEIGNOBOS, IEH: Ch. Langlois and Ch. Seignobos. *Introduction aux Etudes Historiques*. Paris n. d.

LATTIMORE 28: Owen Lattimore. Caravan Routes of Inner Asia. *Geog. Jour.* **72**: 497–528, 1928

—— 29: ——. *The Desert Road to Turkestan*. Boston 1929

—— 30: ——. *High Tartary*. Boston, Little, Brown, & Co., Atlantic Monthly Press, 1930[1]

—— 33: ——. *The Gold Tribe, "Fishskin Tatars" of the Lower Sungari*. Mem. Amer. Anthrop. Assn. **40**, 1933

—— 35: ——. *Manchuria, Cradle of Conflict*. New York 1935

—— 38: ——. The Geographical Factor in Mongol History. *Geog. Jour.* **91**: 1–19, 1938

—— 40: ——. *Inner Asian Frontiers of China*. New York 1940

—— 41: ——. *Mongol Journeys*. New York 1941

LAUFER 09: Berthold Laufer. *Chinese Pottery of the Han Dynasty*. Leiden 1909

—— 13: ——. Arabic and Chinese Trade in Walrus and Narwhal Ivory. *TP* **14**: 315–364, 1913

—— 16: ——. The Hsi-Hsia Language. *TP* **17**: 1–126, 1916

—— 16a: ——. Supplementary Notes on Walrus and Narwhal Ivory. *TP* **17**: 348–389, 1916

—— 19: ——. *Sino-Iranica*. Chicago, Field Museum of Natural History 1919

—— 27: ——. Methods in the Study of Domestications. *Sci. Monthly* **25**: 251–255, 1927

—— 30: ——. The Early History of Felt. *AA* **32**: 1–18, 1930

LE COQ 11, 19, 22. TMC: Albert von Le Coq. Türkische Manichaica aus Chotscho. *AAW*, Anhang, Nr. vi, 1911; Nr. 3, 1919; Nr. 2, 1922

—— 25: ——. *Bilderatlas zur Kunst und Kulturgeschichte Mittel-Asiens*. Berlin 1925

—— 29: ——. *Buried Treasures of Chinese Turkestan, An Account of the Activities and Adventures of the Second and Third German Turfan Expeditions*, tr. by Anna Barwell. New York 1929

LEE 87: Henry Lee. *The Vegetable Lamb of Tartary, A Curious Fable of the Cotton Plant*. London 1887

LEE: M. P. H. Lee. *Economic History of China*. New York 1921

LEFEBVRE DES NOËTTES 31: Richard Lefebvre des Noëttes. *L'Attelage et le Cheval de Selle à travers les âges*. 2 v. Paris 1931

LEGGE, CC: James Legge. *The Chinese Classics*. 5 v. Oxford 1893

LEONARD 94: Arthur Glynn Leonard. *The Camel*. London 1894

LE STRANGE 01: Guy Le Strange. The Cities of Kirmān in the time of Hamd-Allāh Mustawfī and Marco Polo. *JRAS*, n.s. **33**: 281–290, 1901

---

[1] We are obliged to Little, Brown & Co. and the Atlantic Monthly Press for permission to use the extended passage from Owen Lattimore's *High Tartary* on pages 117–118.

—— 05: ——. *The Lands of the Eastern Caliphate, Meso-potamia, Persia, and Central Asia from the Moslem conquest to the time of Timur.* Cambridge 1905

LEVASSEUR 89: E. Levasseur. *La Population Française*, I. Paris 1889

LIDDELL HART 27: B. H. Liddell Hart. *Great Captains Unveiled.* Boston 1927

LIN-LE 66: Lin-le. *Ti-ping Tien-kwoh; The History of the Ti-ping Revolution.* London 1866

LINGENTHAL 94: C. E. Zachariae von Lingenthal. Wissenschaft und Recht für das Heer vom 6 bis zum Anfang des 10 Jahrhunderts. *Byzantinische Zeitschrift* 3: 437–457, 1894

LINTON 33: Ralph Linton. *The Tanala.* Chicago, Field Museum of Natural History 1933

—— 36: ——. *The Study of Man.* New York 1936

—— 40: ——. Acculturation and the Process of Cultural Change; The Process of Culture Transfer; The Distinctive Aspects of Acculturation. In *Acculturation in Seven American Indian Tribes*, ed. by Ralph Linton, 463–520. New York and London 1940

—— 43: ——. Nativistic Movements. *AA* 45 (2): 230–240, 1943

——: See also Redfield, Linton, and Herskovits.

LIPSON 37: Ephraim Lipson. *The Economic History of England*, I. London 1937

LOCKE 1727: John Locke. Two Treatises of Government. In *The Works of John Locke* II: 101–227. London 1727

LOCUSTS: Locusts. *Encyclopedia Britannica* XV: 857–859. 11th ed.

LOWIE 19: Robert H. Lowie. Family and Sib. *AA* 21 (1): 28–40, 1919

—— 20: ——. *Primitive Society.* New York 1920

—— 24: ——. *Primitive Religion.* New York 1924

—— 37: ——. Kinship. *Enc. SS* VIII: 568–572, 1937

—— 40: ——. *An Introduction to Cultural Anthropology.* New York 1940

LYBYER 13: Albert Howe Lybyer. *The Government of the Ottoman Empire in the Time of Suleiman the Magnificent.* Cambridge 1913

LYND 39: Robert S. Lynd. *Knowledge for What?* Princeton 1939

MACHIAVELLI 40: The Prince. In Niccolo Machiavelli, *The Prince and the Discourses*, 1–98. New York 1940

—— 40a: The Discourses. In Niccolo Machiavelli, *The Prince and the Discourses*, 99–540. New York 1940

MAÇOUDI, PO: Maçoudi. *Les Prairies d'Or*, texte et traduction par C. Barbier de Meynard and Pavet de Courteille. 9 v. Paris 1861–1874

MAENCHEN-HELFEN 39: Otto Maenchen-Helfen. The Ting-ling. *HJAS* 4: 77–86, 1939

DE MAILLA, HGC: J. A. M. de Mailla. *Histoire Générale de la Chine.* 13 v. Paris 1777–1785

MANCHURIA 32/33: *The Manchurian Year Book, 1932–33.* Tokyo 1933

MARCO POLO 03: *The Book of Ser Marco Polo*, tr. and ed., with notes, by Sir Henry Yule. 3d edition, revised throughout in the light of recent discoveries by Henri Cordier. 2 v. London 1903

—— 38: *Marco Polo, The Description of the World*, ed. by A. C. Moule and Paul Pelliot, I. London 1938

MARQUART 98: Jos. Marquart. *Die Chronologie der Alt-türkischen Inschriften.* Leipzig 1898

—— 12: ——. Ǧuwainī's Bericht über die Bekehrung der Uiguren. *SAW* 27: 486–502, 1912

—— 14: ——. Über das Volkstum der Komanen. Chap. 2 of W. Bang and J. Marquart, Osttürkische Dialektstudien. *Abhandlungen der Königlichen Gesellschaft der Wissenschaften zu Göttingen, Phil.-Histor. Klasse*, n.s., 13 (1): 1–238, 1914

MARTINIUS 1654: Martin Martinius. *Bellum Tartaricum, or the Conquest of the Great and most renowned Empire of China.* London 1654

MARVAZĪ 42: *Sharaf Al-Zamān Tāhir al-Marvazī on China, the Turks and India* (Arabic text (ca. A.D. 1120) with an English translation and commentary by V. Minorsky). London, Royal Asiatic Soc. 1942

MASPERO 10: Communautés et Moines Bouddhistes Chinois au IIe et IIIe Siècles. *BEFEO* 10: 222–232, 1910

MAUNDEVILLE 1839: *The Voiage and Travaile of Sir John Maundeville*, reprinted from the edition of 1725 with an introduction etc. by J. O. Halliwell. London 1839

MAWERDI 15: Mawerdi (Abou'l Hasan 'Ali). *Les Statuts Gouvernementaux ou Règles de Droit Public et Administratif*, tr. and annotated by E. Fagnan. Algiers 1915

MAYERS 78: William Frederick Mayers. *The Chinese Government.* Shanghai 1878

MENGES 33: Karl Menges. Volkskundliche Texte aus Ost-Türkistan. Aus dem Nachlass von N. Th. Katanov. *SAW* 32: 1173–1293, 1933

——: See Potapov and Menges

MERRIAM 38: John Campbell Merriam. *Some Aspects of Cooperative Research in History.* Carnegie Institution of Washington Supp. Publ., no 45, 1938

MEYER 24: Eduard Meyer. *Kleine Schriften*, I. Halle 1924

—— 26: ——. *Geschichte des Altertums*, I (2). Stuttgart and Berlin 1926

MEYER 18: Robert Meyer. The History and Development of Government Statistics in Austria. In John Koren, *The History of Statistics*, 85–122. New York 1918

MICHAEL 42: Franz Michael. *The Origin of Manchu Rule in China.* Baltimore 1942

MINORSKY 37: M. V. Minorsky. Une Nouvelle Source Musulmane sur l'Asie Centrale au XIe Siècle. *Comptes Rendus de l'Académie des Inscriptions et Belles-Lettres*, 317–324, 1937

MIRZA HAIDAR 98: *A History of the Moghuls of Central Asia*, being The Tarikh-i-Rashidi of Mirza Muhammad Haidar, Dughlat, ed. by N. Elias. London 1898

MITCHELL 40: William A. Mitchell. *Outlines of the World's Military History.* Harrisburg 1940

MOMMSEN 23: Theodor Mommsen. *Römische Geschichte*, I. Berlin 1923

MOREL 22: H. Morel. Les Campagnes Mongoles au XIIIe Siècle. *Revue Militaire Française* 4: 348–368, 1922

MORSE 08: Hosea Ballou Morse. *The Trade and Administration of the Chinese Empire.* London 1908

MOULE 30: A. C. Moule. *Christians in China Before the Year 1550.* London, New York, Toronto 1930

—— 31: ——. The Use of the Cross among the Nestorians in China. *TP* **28**: 78–86, 1931

MOULE AND CHUNG 39: A. C. Moule and Chung Kei-won. The *Ta-Ming Shih-Lu*. *TP* **35**: 289–328, 1939

MOULE AND PELLIOT: See Marco Polo 38

MUFAḌḌALĪYĀT 18: *The Mufaḍḍalīyāt, an Anthology of Ancient Arabian Odes*, compiled by Al-Mufaḍḍal son of Muḥammad according to the recension and with the commentary of Abū Muḥammad Al-Qāsim Ibn Muḥammad Al-Anbārī, ed. by Charles James Lyall, II. Oxford 1918

MÜLLER 12: F. W. K. Müller. Der Hofstaat eines Uiguren-Königs. In *Festschrift Vilhelm Thomsen zur Vollendung seines siebzigsten Lebensjahres am 25. Januar 1912 dargebracht von Freunden und Schülern*, 207–213. Leipzig 1912

—— 12a: ——. Ein Doppelblatt aus einem manichäischen Hymnenbuch (Maḥrnâmag). *AAW* **5**: 1–40, 1912

—— 15: ——. Zwei Pfahlinschriften aus den Turfanfunden. *AAW* **3**: 1–38, 1915

MULLIE 22: Jos. Mullie. Les Anciennes Villes de l'Empire des Grands Leao 大遼 au Royaume Mongol de Bārin. *TP* **21**: 105–231, 1922

—— 33: ——. Les Sépultures de K'ing des Leao. *TP* **30**: 1–25, 1933

—— 33a: ——. La Rivière Jao-Lo. *TP* **30**: 183–223. 1933

MURDOCK 41: George Peter Murdock. Paper read before the American Ethnological Society. Andover, Mass. December 1941

—— 43: ——. *Our Primitive Contemporaries.* New York 1943

NACHOD, GJ: O. Nachod. *Gechichte von Japan*, II. Leipzig 1929–1930

NAPOLEON 40: Maxims of Napoleon. In William A. Mitchell, *Outlines of the World's Military History*, 730–739. Harrisburg 1940

NĀZIM 31: Muhammad Nāzim. *The Life and Times of Sultan Mahmūd of Ghazna.* Cambridge 1931

NED: *A New English Dictionary on Historical Principles*, V (1). Oxford 1901

EN-NESAWI 95: Mohammed en-Nesawi. *Histoire du Sultan Djelal ed-din Mankobirti*, tr. from the Arab by O. Houdas. Paris 1895

NEUMANN 55: Karl Neumann. *Die Hellenen im Skythenlande*, I. Berlin 1855

NICKERSON 37: Hoffmann Nickerson. Warfare in the Roman Empire, the Dark and Middle Ages. *Warfare*, 191–408. Washington 1937

NIDHĀMĪ-I-'ARŪDĪ 99: The Chahār Maqāla ("Four Discourses") of Nidhāmī-i-'Arūdī-i-Samarqandī, tr. into English by Edward G. Browne. *JRAS* n.s. 31, **51**: 613–663, 757–840, 1899

NIZAM OUL-MOULK 93: *Siasset Namēh, Traité de Gouvernement composé pour le Sultan Melik-Châh par le Vizir Nizām oul-Moulk*, tr. by Charles Schefer. Paris 1893

NORTH MANCHURIA 24: *North Manchuria and the Chinese Eastern Railway.* Harbin 1924

ODORIC 91: *Les Voyages en Asie au XIVe Siècle du Bienheureux Frère Odoric de Pordenone*, with an introduction and notes by Henri Cordier. Paris 1891

OGDEN AND RICHARDS 25: C. K. Ogden and I. A. Richards. *The Meaning of Meaning.* New York 1925

OHLMARKS 39: Åke Ohlmarks. *Studien zum Problem des Schamanismus.* Lund 1939

D'OHSSON 1834: C. d'Ohsson. *Histoire des Mongols depuis Tchinguiz-Khan jusqu'à Timour Bey ou Tamerlan.* 4 v. The Hague and Amsterdam 1834

O'LEARY 27: DeLacy O'Leary. *Arabia before Muhammad.* London 1927

OLSHAUSEN 90: O. Olshausen. Bemerkungen über Steigbügel. *Verhandlungen der Berliner Gesellschaft für Anthropologie, Ethnologie und Urgeschichte: Zeitschrift für Ethnologie* **22**: 207–209, 1890

OMAN 24: Charles Oman. *A History of the Art of War in the Middle Ages.* 2 v. London 1924

—— 39: ——. *On the Writing of History.* New York 1939

OPPERT 70: Gustav Oppert. On the Kitai and Kara-Kitai. *Jour. Ethnol. Soc. London* **2**: 97–106, 1870

OTTONIS FRISINGENSIS CHRONICON: Ottonis Frisingensis Chronicon. In *Monumenta Germaniae Historica* XX: 83–301. Hanover 1868

PARKER 92–95 TST: E. H. Parker. The Turco-Scythian Tribes. *China Review* **20**: 1–24, 109–125, 1892–1893; **21**: 100–118, 129–137, 253–267, 291–301, 1894–1895

—— 95: ——. *A Thousand Years of the Tartars.* London 1895

—— 00: ——. The Cathayans. *The Imperial and Asiatic Quarterly Review*, ser. 3, **10**: 342–364, 1900

PARSONS 37: Talcott Parsons. Society. *Enc. SS* XIV: 225–231

PEISKER 24: Johann Peisker. The Asiatic Background. In *Cambridge Mediaeval History* I: 323–359, 1924

PELLIOT 04: Paul Pelliot. Deux Itinéraires de Chine en Inde à la Fin du VIIIe Siècle. *BEFEO* **4**: 131–413, 1904

—— 10: ——. Rapport . . . sur sa Mission au Turkestan Chinois. *BEFEO* **10**: 655–660, 1910

—— 12: ——. Les Noms Tibétains des *T'ou-yu-houen* et des *Ouigours*. *JA*, ser. 10, **20**: 520–523, 1912

—— 12a: ——. L'Origine du Nom de "Chine." *TP* **13**: 727–742, 1912

—— 12b: ——. Kao-tch'ang, Qočo, Houo-tcheou et Qarâ-Khodja. *JA*, ser. 10, **19**: 579–603, 1912

—— 13: ——. Addenda to Berthold Laufer's *Arabic and Chinese Trade in Walrus and Narwhal Ivory*. *TP* **14**: 365–370, 1913

—— 14: ——. Chrétiens d'Asie Centrale et d'Extrême-Orient. *TP* **15**: 623–644, 1914

—— 15: ——. L'Origine de T'ou-kiue, Nom Chinois des Turcs. *TP* **16**: 688–689, 1915

—— 15a: ——. Quelques Transcriptions Chinoises des Noms Tibétains. *TP* **16**: 1–26, 1915

—— 20: ——. A Propos des Comans. *JA*, ser. 11, **15**: 125–185, 1920

—— 21: ——. Notes sur les T'ou-yu-houen et les Sou-p'i. *TP* **20**: 323–331, 1921

—— 26: ——. Review of Commandant Lefebvre des Noëttes, *La Force motrice animale à travers les âges*, Paris, 1924. *TP* **24**: 256–268, 1926

—— 29: ——. L'Edition Collective des Œuvres de Wang Kuo-wei. *TP* **26**: 113–182, 1929

—— 29a· ——. Neuf Notes sur des Questions d'Asie Centrale. *TP* **26**: 202–265, 1929

—— 30: ——. Notes sur le "Turkestan" de M. W. Barthold. *TP* **27**: 12–56, 1930

—— 30a: ——. Sur *yam* ou *jam* Relais Postal. *TP* **27**: 192–195, 1930

—— 31: ——. *Haute Asie*. Paris 1931

—— 31a: ——. Review of Arthur Waley, *The Travels of an Alchemist*, etc. *TP* **28**: 413–428, 1931

—— 31b: ——. Review of G. D. Sanžejev, *Mančžuro-mongol'skije jazykovyje paralleli*. *TP* **28**: 113–118, 1931

—— 34: ——. Tokharien et Koutchéen. *JA* **224**: 23–106, 1934

——: See Chavannes-Pelliot

PERI 17: N. Peri. Hāritī la Mère-de-démons. *BEFEO* **17** (3): 1–102, 1917

PETECH 39: Luciano Petech. *A Study on the Chronicles of Ladakh*. Calcutta 1939

POPE AND ACKERMAN 38: A. U. Pope and P. Ackerman. *A Survey of Persian Art*, IV. London and New York 1938

POSTGATE 22: J. P. Postgate. *Translation and Translations*. London 1922

POTAPOV AND MENGES 34: L. P. Potapov and K. Menges. Materialien zur Volkskunde der Türkvölker des Altaj. *Mitteilungen des Seminars für Orientalische Sprachen zu Berlin* **37**: 53–104, 1934

PREJEVALSKY 76: N. Prejevalsky. *Mongolia, the Tangut Country, and the Solitudes of Northern Tibet*. 2 v. London 1876

PROCOPIUS 14: Procopius. *History of the Wars*, Books I and II, with an English translation by H. B. Dewing. London 1914

PROGRESS IN MANCHURIA 32: *Third Report on Progress in Manchuria*. Dairen 1932

RADIN 37: Paul Radin. *Primitive Religion*. New York 1937

RADLOFF, WB: Wilhelm Radloff. *Versuch eines Wörterbuches der Türkdialecte*. 4 v. St. Petersburg 1893–1911

—— 93: ——. *Aus Sibirien*. 2 v. Leipzig 1893

—— 95: ——. *Die Alttürkischen Inschriften der Mongolei*. St. Petersburg 1895

—— 97: ——. *Die Alttürkischen Inschriften der Mongolei*. n.f. St. Petersburg 1897

—— 99: ——. *Die Alttürkischen Inschriften der Mongolei*. 2 f. St. Petersburg 1899

RAMSEY 92: Samuel Ramsey. *The English Language and English Grammar*. New York and London 1892

RANKE 24: Leopold Ranke. *Deutsche Geschichte im Zeitalter der Reformation*. 5 v. Munich and Leipzig 1924

RASHĪD AD-DĪN 1833: Description de la Chine sous le Règne de la Dynastie Mongole, tr. du persan et accompagnée de notes par M. Klaproth. *JA*, ser. 2, **11**: 335–358, 447–470, 1833

—— 1836: *Histoire des Mongols de la Perse écrite en Persan par Rashid-Eldin*, publiée, traduite en Français, accompagnée de notes et d'un mémoire sur la vie et les ouvrages de l'auteur par M. Quatremère, I. Paris 1836

—— 14: Contemporary Notices of Cathay under the Mongols Extracted from the Historical Cyclopaedia of Rashīduddīn. In Yule, *Cathay and the Way Thither* III: 113–133. London 1914

RATCHNEVSKY 37: P. Ratchnevsky. *Un code des Yuan*. Bibliothèque de l'Institut des Hautes Etudes Chinoises IV. Paris 1937

READ 32: Bernard E. Read. *Chinese Materia Medica. Avian Drugs*. Peiping 1932

—— 36: ——. *Chinese Medicinal Plants from the Pên Ts'ao Kang Mu*. Peiping 1936

—— 39: ——. *Chinese Materia Medica. Fish Drugs*. Peiping 1939

READ 39/40: Thomas T. Read. The Earliest Industrial Uses of Coal. *Trans. Newcomen Soc.* **22**: 119–133, 1939–1940

REDFIELD 34: Robert Redfield and Alfonso Villa. *Chan Kom, a Maya Village*. Carnegie Inst. Washington, Publ. no. 448, 1934

—— 41: ——. *The Folk Culture of Yucatan*. Chicago 1941

REDFIELD, LINTON, HERSKOVITS 36: Robert Redfield, Ralph Linton, and M. J. Herskovits. A Memorandum for the Study of Acculturation. *AA* **38**: 149–152, 1936

REICHELT 27: Karl Ludwig Reichelt. *Truth and Tradition in Chinese Buddhism. A Study of Chinese Mahayana Buddhism*, tr. from the Norwegian by Kathrina Van Wagenen Bugge. Shanghai 1927

RÉMUSAT 1820: Abel Rémusat. *Recherches sur les Langues Tartares*. Paris 1820

—— 1829: ——. *Nouveaux Mélanges Asiatiques*. 2 v. Paris 1829

—— 1836: ——. *Foĕ Kouĕ Ki*. Paris 1836

RIASANOVSKY 37: V. A. Riasanovsky. *Fundamental Principles of Mongol Law*. Tientsin 1937

RICHARDS: See Ogden and Richards

RICKERT 29: Heinrich Rickert. *Die Grenzen der naturwissenschaftlichen Begriffsbildung*. Tübingen 1919

RITTER 19: Moriz Ritter. *Die Entwicklung der Geschichtswissenschaft*. Munich and Berlin 1919

RIVERS 24: W. H. R. Rivers. *Social Organization*. London 1924

ROBINSON 08: James Harvey Robinson. *History*. New York 1908

ROCKHILL 84: W. W. Rockhill. *The Life of the Buddha and the Early History of his Order*. Derived from Tibetan Works in the BKAH-HGYUR and BSTAN-HGYUR. London 1884

——: See Hirth and Rockhill

ROSTOVTZEFF 41: M. Rostovtzeff. *The Social and Economic History of the Hellenistic World*. 3 v. Oxford 1941

RUBRUCK 00: *The Journey of William of Rubruck to the Eastern Parts of the World, 1253–55, as Narrated by Himself, with Two Accounts of the Earlier Journey of John of Pian de Carpine*, tr. from the Latin and edited with an introductory notice by William Woodville Rockhill. London, The Hakluyt Society 1900

SAHA 30: K. B. Saha. *Economics of Rural Bengal.* Calcutta 1930

SAINT-DENYS 76: *Ethnographie des Peuples Etrangers à la Chine. Ouvrage composé au XIIIᵉ Siècle de notre Ere par Ma-Touan-Lin*, traduit pour la première fois du chinois avec un commentaire perpétuel par le Marquis d'Hervey de Saint-Denys. Orientaux. Paris 1876

SALMONY 43: Alfred Salmony. The Find from Kopeny in the Yenisei Valley, a Siberian Gold Treasure of the Migration Period. *Gazette des Beaux-Arts* **23**: 71–82, 1943

SANŽEJEV 30: G. D. Sanžejev. *Darxaty.* Academy of Sciences of the USSR. Leningrad 1930

SAPIR 21: E. Sapir. *Language. An Introduction to the Study of Speech.* New York 1921

SAXE 41: Marshall Maurice de Saxe. My Reveries upon the Art of War, tr. by Major Thomas R. Phillips. In *Roots of Strategy*, ed. by Thomas R. Phillips, 177–300. New York 1941

SCHAEDER 27: Hans Heinrich Schaeder. Urform und Fortbildungen des Manichäischen Systems. *Vorträge der Bibliothek Warburg 1924–1925*, 65–157. Leipzig and Berlin 1927

SCHAKIR-ZADE 31: Tahir Schakir-zade. *Grundzüge der Nomadenwirtschaft. Betrachtung des Wirtschaftslebens der sibirisch-centralasiatischen Nomadenvölker.* Heidelberg 1931

SCHLEGEL 96: Gustave Schlegel. Review of Inscriptions de l'Orkhon déchiffrées par Vilh. Thomsen. *TP*, ser. 1, **7**: 176–191, 1896

SCHMIDT 23: P. P. Schmidt. The Language of the Olča. *Acta Universitatis Latviensis* **3**: 229–288, 1923

SCHOTT 74: Wilhelm Schott. Zur Uigurenfrage. *AAW*, Nr. 5: 102–121, 1874

—— 76: ——. Zur Uigurenfrage . . . Zweite Abteilung. *AAW*, Nr. 2: 27–57, 1876

—— 80: ——. Kitai und Karakitai, ein Beitrag zur Geschichte Ost- und Innerasiens. *AAW*, Nr. 1: 3–20, 1880

SCHRADER 29: O. Schrader. Steigbügel. *Reallexikon der Indogermanischen Altertumskunde* **2**: 470, 1929

SCHROEDER: See Ettinghausen and Schroeder

SCHULTE 00: Aloys Schulte. *Geschichte des mittelalterlichen Handels und Verkehrs zwischen Westdeutschland und mit Ausschluss von Venedig.* 2 v. Leipzig 1900

SCHUYLER 77: Eugene Schuyler. *Turkistan, Notes of a Journey in Khokand, Bukhara, and Kuldja.* 2 v. New York 1877

SCHWARZ 12: Paul Schwarz. *Iran im Mittelalter nach den arabischen Geographen*, III. Leipzig 1912

SEIGNOBOS 01: Ch. Seignobos. *La Méthode Historique appliquée aux Sciences Sociales.* Paris 1901

——: See Langlois and Seignobos

SHEPPARD 29: E. W. Sheppard. Military Methods of the Mongols. *Army Quart.* **18**: 305–315, 1929

SHIRASAKI: See Yano and Shirasaki

SHIRATORI 02: K. Shiratori. Sinologische Beiträge zur Geschichte der Türk-Völker: Über die Sprache der Hiungnu und der Tunghu-Stämme. *Bulletin de l'Académie Impériale des Sciences de St. Petersbourg* **17** (2): 01–033, 1902

—— 26: ——. A Study on the Titles Kaghan and Katun. *MRDTB* **1**: 1–39, 1926

SHIROKOGOROFF 24: S. M. Shirokogoroff. *Social Organization of the Manchus.* Shanghai 1924

—— 33: ——. *Social Organization of the Northern Tungus.* Shanghai 1933

SHOTWELL 39: James T. Shotwell. *The History of History*, I. New York 1939

SMITH 37: Adam Smith. *An Inquiry into the Nature and Causes of the Wealth of Nations.* New York, Modern Library 1937

SOED: *The Shorter Oxford English Dictionary on Historical Principles.* 2 v. Oxford 1936

SOMBART 19: Werner Sombart. *Der moderne Kapitalismus.* 2 v. Munich and Leipzig 1919

SOOTHILL AND HODOUS 37: William Edward Soothill and Lewis Hodous. *A Dictionary of Chinese Buddhist Terms with Sanskrit and English Equivalents and a Sanskrit-Pali Index.* London 1937

SPECK 35: Frank G. Speck. *Naskapi.* Norman, Oklahoma 1935

SSANANG SSETSEN 1829: *Geschichte der Ost-Mongolen und Ihres Fürstenhauses, Verfasst von Ssanang Ssetsen*, tr. by I. J. Schmidt. St. Petersburg 1829

STEIN 07: M. Aurel Stein. *Ancient Khotan, Detailed report on archaeological explorations in Chinese Turkestan.* 2 v. Oxford 1907

—— 21: ——. *Serindia.* 3 v. Oxford 1921

—— 28: ——. *Innermost Asia.* Oxford 1928

STEIN 39: Rolf Stein. Leao-Tche (遼志). *TP* **35**: 1–154, 1939

STEINGASS 30: F. Steingass. *Persian-English Dictionary.* London 1892; 2nd ed. 1930

STRAKOSCH-GRASSMANN 93: Gustav Strakosch-Grassmann. *Der Einfall der Mongolen in Mitteleuropa in den Jahren 1241 und 1242.* Innsbruck 1893.

STRONG 36: William Duncan Strong. Anthropological Theory and Archaeological Fact. *Essays in Anthropology*, 359–370. Berkeley 1936

SUN, TSCQ: Sun Yat Sen. *The True Solution of the Chinese Question.* In 孫中山全集，續集. Shanghai 1928

—— YS 27: ——. *San Min Chu I, The Three Principles of the People*, tr. by Frank W. Price. Shanghai 1927

SYKES 30: Sir Percy Sykes. *History of Persia.* 2 v. London 1930

TABAKAT-I-NASIRI 81: *Tabakat-i-Nasiri. A General History of the Muhammadan Dynasties of Asia . . .*, tr. by Major H. G. Raverty. 2 v. London 1881

TABARI 71: *Chronique de Abou-Djafar-Mo'hammed-Ben-Djarīr-Ben-Yezid Tabari traduite sur la version persane d'Abou-'Ali Mo'hammed Bel'Ami*, d'après les manuscrits de Paris, de Gotha, de Londres et de Canterbury par M. Hermann Zotenberg, III. Paris 1871

TAKEKOSHI 30: Takekoshi Yōsaburō. *The Economic Aspects of the History of the Civilization of Japan.* 3 v. London 1930

TAWNEY 12: R. H. Tawney. *The Agrarian Problem in the Sixteenth Century.* London 1912

—— 31: ——. *Equality.* London 1931

694   BIBLIOGRAPHY

TCHANG 05: Mathias Tchang. *Synchronismes Chinois, Chronologie Complète et Concordance avec l'Ere Chrétienne de toutes les dates concernant l'histoire de l'Extrême-Orient.* Variétés Sinologiques no. 24. Shanghai 1905

TEGGART 16: Frederick J. Teggart. Prolegomena to History. In *Univ. of Calif. Publ. in History* IV (3): 155–292. Berkeley 1916

TÊNG AND BIGGERSTAFF 36: Têng Ssǔ-yü and Knight Biggerstaff. *An Annotated Bibliography of Selected Chinese Reference Works.* Yenching Jour. Chinese Studies, Mon. no. 12. Peiping 1936

THOMSEN 96: *Inscriptions de l'Orkhon*, déchiffrées par Vilhelm Thomsen. Mémoires de la Société Finnoougrienne V. Helsingfors 1896

—— 24: ——. Alttürkische Inschriften aus der Mongolei in Übersetzung und mit Einleitung. *Zeitschrift der Deutschen Morgenländischen Gesellschaft* n.f. **3**: 121–175. Berlin 1924

THUCYDIDES 34: *The Complete Writings of Thucydides.* New York, Modern Library 1934

THURNWALD 32: R. Thurnwald. *Werden, Wandel und Gestaltung von Familie, Verwandtschaft und Bünden.* Leipzig and Berlin 1932

—— 35: ——. *Werden, Wandel und Gestaltung von Staat und Kultur.* Leipzig and Berlin 1935

TIMKOWSKI 1827: George Timkowski. *Travels of the Russian Mission through Mongolia to China, and Residence in Peking in the Years 1820–1821.* 2 v. London 1827

TITIEV 43: Mischa Titiev. The Influence of Common Residence on the Unilateral Classification of Kindred. *AA* **45**: 511–530, 1943

TORII 14: Ryūzō Torii and Kimiko Torii. Etudes Archéologiques et Ethnologiques. Populations Primitives de la Mongolie Orientale. *Jour. Coll. Sci., Imperial Univ. of Tokyo* **36** (4): 1–100, 1914

—— 36: Ryūzō Torii. *Illustrations of Archaeology.* 4 v. Tokyo 1936.

TOYNBEE, SH: Arnold J. Toynbee. *A Study of History.* 6 v. London 1934–1939

TRITTON 30: A. S. Tritton. *The Caliphs and their Non-Muslim Subjects.* London etc. 1930

TUFAIL 27: *The Poems of Ṭufail Ibn 'Auf Al-Ghanawī and At-Ṭirimmāḥ Ibn Ḥakim Aṭ-Ṭa'yī.* Arabic text edited and translated by F. Krenkow. E. J. W. Gibb Memorial XXV. London 1927

UNGER 27: Eckhard Unger. *Assyrische und Babylonische Kunst.* Breslau 1927.

—— 28: ——. Steigbügel. *Reallexikon der Vorgeschichte*, ed. by Max Ebert, **12**: 392, 1928

VÁMBÉRY 85: Hermann Vámbéry. *Das Türkenvolk in seinen Ethnologischen und Ethnographischen Beziehungen.* Leipzig 1885

VÁRI 06: R. Vári. Zur Überlieferung mittelgriechischer Taktiter. *Byzantinische Zeitschrift* **15**: 47–87, 1906

VASIL'JEV 59: V. P. Vasil'jev. Istorija i Drevnosti Vostočnoj Časti Srednej Azii, ot X do XIII veka, s priloženijem perevoda kitajskix izvestij o Kidanax, Džurdžitax i Mongolo-Tatarax. *Trudy Vostočnovo Otdel. Imperator. Arxeol. Obščestva* **4**: 1–235, 1859

—— 60: See Wassiljew.

VAUDESCAL 14: Le Commandant Vaudescal. Les Pierres Gravées du CHÊ KĪNG CHĀN et le YŪN KIŪ SSÉU. *JA*, ser. 11, **3**: 375–459, 1914

VEGETIUS 41: Flavius Vegetius Renatus. The Military Institutions of the Romans, tr. by St. John Clarke. In *Roots of Strategy*, ed. by Major Thomas R. Phillips, 65–176. New York 1941

VERNADSKY 38: George Vernadsky. The Scope and Contents of Chingis Khan's *Yasa*. *HJAS* **3**: 337–360, 1938

—— 39: ——. Juwaini's Version of Chingis Khan's *Yasa*. *Annales de l'Institut Kondakov (Seminarium Kondakovianum)* **11**: 33–45, 1939

VISDELOU 1779: C. Visdelou. Histoire Abrégée de la Tartarie. *Bibliothèque Orientale* **4**: 42–296, 1779

DE VISSER 35: M. W. de Visser. *Ancient Buddhism in Japan*, II. Leiden 1935

VLADIMIRTSOV 30: B. Vladimirtsov. *The Life of Chingis-Khan*, tr. from the Russian by Prince D. S. Mirsky. London 1930

—— 34: ——. *Obščestvennyj stroj mongolov.* Leningrad 1934

WADA 38: Wada Sei. The Natives of the Lower Reaches of the Amur River as Represented in Chinese Records. *MRDTB* **10**: 41–102, 1938

WADDELL 95: L. A. Waddell. *The Buddhism of Tibet.* London 1895

WALEY 31: *The Travels of an Alchemist, The Journey of the Taoist Ch'ang-ch'un from China to Hindukush at the Summons of Chingiz Khan, Recorded by his Disciple Li Chih-ch'ang*, tr. with an introduction by Arthur Waley. London 1931

WALKER 39: C. C. Walker. *Jenghiz Khan.* London 1939

WARE 33: James R. Ware. Wei Shou on Buddhism. *TP* **30**: 100–181, 1933

WASHINGTON 1834: *The Writings of George Washington being his Correspondence, Addresses, Messages and other Papers, Official and Private*, by Jared Sparks, II, III, IV. Boston 1834

WASSILJEW 60: W. Wassiljew. *Der Buddhismus, seine Dogmen, Geschichte und Literatur.* St. Petersburg 1860

WEBER 20: Max Weber. *Gesammelte Aufsätze zur Religionssoziologie*, I. Tübingen 1920

—— 22: ——. *Gesammelte Aufsätze zur Wissenschaftslehre.* Tübingen 1922

WESTERMANN 29: W. L. Westermann. *Upon Slavery in Ptolemaic Egypt.* New York 1929

WILLIAMSON, WAS: H. R. Williamson. *Wang-An-shih* 王安石, *a Chinese Statesman and Educationalist of the Sung Dynasty.* 2 v. London 1935–1937

WITTFOGEL, OS: Karl A. Wittfogel. *Oriental Society* (ms)

—— 27: ——. Probleme der chinesischen Wirtschaftsgeschichte. *Archiv für Sozialwissenschaft und Sozialpolitik* **57**: 289–335, 1927

—— 31: ——. *Wirtschaft und Gesellschaft Chinas, Erster Teil, Produktivkräfte, Produktions- und Zirkulationsprozess.* Leipzig 1931.

—— 32: ——. Die natürlichen Ursachen der Wirtschaftsgeschichte. *Archiv für Sozialwissenschaft und Sozialpolitik* **67**: 466–492, 579–609, 711–731, 1932

—— 35: ——. The Foundations and Stages of Chinese Economic History. *Zeitschrift für Sozialforschung* **4**: 26–60, 1935

—— 36: ——. Wirtschaftsgeschichtliche Grundlagen der Entwicklung der Familienautorität. In *Studien über Autorität und Familie, Schriften des Instituts für Sozialforschung* V. Paris 1936

—— 37: ——. Review of Alfred Forke, *Geschichte der mittelalterlichen chinesischen Philosophie. Pacific Affairs* **10**: 210–212, 1937

—— 38: ——. Die Theorie der orientalischen Gesellschaft. *Zeitschrift für Sozialforschung* **7**: 90–122, 1938

—— 38a: ——. *New Light on Chinese Society.* New York 1938

—— 39: ——. The Society of Prehistoric China. *Zeitschrift für Sozialforschung* **8**, 1939

—— 40: ——. Meteorological Records from the Divination Inscriptions of Shang. *Geographical Review* **30**: 110–133, 1940

WÜSTENFELD 54: F. Wüstenfeld. *Vergleichungstabellen der Muhammedanischen und Christlichen Zeitrechnung.* Leipzig 1854

WYLD 29: Henry Cecil Wyld. *A Short History of English.* New York 1929

XENOPHON 25: Xenophon Scripta Minora, with an English translation by E. C. Marchant. In *The Cavalry Commander,* 233–293. New York 1925

—— 42: The Anabasis of Cyrus, tr. by Henry G. Dakyns. In *The Greek Historians,* ed. by Francis R. B. Godolphin, II: 222–365. New York 1942

YAMASHITA 36/37: Yamashita Taizo. A Kitan Variety of Sung Pottery Discovered in Jehol. *Monumenta Serica* **2**: 421–422, 1936–1937.

YANO AND SHIRASAKI 36: Yano Tsuneta and Shirasaki Kyoichi. *Nippon.* Tokyo 1936

YAQOUT 61: *Dictionnaire Géographique, Historique et Littéraire de la Perse et des Contrées Adjacentes, extrait du Mo'djem el-Bouldan de Yaqout et complété à l'aide de documents Arabes et Persans pour la plupart inédits* par C. Barbier de Meynard. Paris 1861

YEH CS 43: Yeh Ch'i-sun. Work of Academia Sinica 1937–1942. *Quart. Bull. Chinese Bibliog.* [English ed.], n.s. **3**: 7–20, 1943

YULE, CWT: Sir Henry Yule. *Cathay and the Way Thither.* New edition revised throughout in the light of recent discovery by Henri Cordier. 4 v. London, The Hakluyt Society 1913–1916

—— 03: ——. Introduction to *The Book of Ser Marco Polo.* London 1903

YUSUF 43: S. M. Yusuf. Al-Muhallab-Bin-Abī-Sufra: His Strategy and Qualities of Generalship. *Islamic Culture* **17** (1): 1–14, 1943

ZAKHAROV 25: Alexis Zakharov. Antiquities of Katanda (Altai). *Jour. Royal Anthrop. Inst. of Great Britain and Ireland* **55**: 37–57, 1925

ZAKHAROV 75: Ivan Zakharov. *Polnyj Mańčžursko-Russkij Slovař* [Complete Manchu Russian Dictionary]. St. Petersburg 1875

ZARNCKE 79: Friedrich Zarncke. Der Priester Johannes. *Abhandlungen der Philologisch-Historischen Classe der Königlich Sächsischen Gesellschaft der Wissenschaften* **7**: 827–1028. Leipzig 1879

ZI 94: Etienne (Siu) Zi. *Pratique des Examens Littéraires.* Variétés Sinologiques no. 5. Shanghai 1894

REFERENCE INDEX

For the abbreviations used see Bibliography. The heavy-faced numbers refer to the year of publication. In addition to the *Liao Shih* five Chinese sources are quoted elaborately: four dynastic histories, CS, SS, TS, and WTS, and the CTKC. In these five cases the chapters [*chüan*] are indicated by italicized numbers.

Aboul-Ghāzi **74**: 635, 663
Aboulfeda **1848**: 2, 517, 656
AJCTC: 152, 161, 166
Annales Admuntenses: 639
Arendt **34**: 505
Aristotle **41**: 29
Arosenius **18**: 31
Arrian **42**: 539
Aṭ-Ṭirimmāh **27**: 506

Balázs **31–33** BWT: 122, 124, 161, 172, 328, 330, 378, 379
Bales **37**: 11
Bang and Gabain **31**: 432, 433, 434
Bar Hebraeus **32**: 2, 506, 508, 653, 671
Barthold, "Balāsāghūn": 645; BH: 626, 655; KK: 620, 621, 622, 634, 643, 651, 653, 662, 665, 669, 670, 671, 672, 674; **97**: 84, 85, 199, 450, 526, 529; **01**: 307, 671; **28**: 1, 6, 27, 51, 52, 85, 93, 100, 104, 170, 253, 292, 307, 309, 357, 431, 517, 619, 620, 621, 625, 635, 639, 640, 641, 643, 644, 645, 647, 649, 650, 651, 652, 653, 655, 657, 659, 660, 661, 662, 663, 664, 666, 667, 668, 669; **35**: 2, 6, 21, 23, 84, 85, 93, 95, 103, 105, 106, 107, 108, 141, 142, 170, 307, 308, 517, 625, 645, 670; **35a**: 6, 17, 21, 625
BCP: 308
Beard **34**: 29, 30, 32
Beck **16**: 269
Bell **31**: 291
Belloc **14**: 517
Benedict **38**: 214, 215, 216, 218
Benjamin **1840**: 661, 662, 667, 671
Bergman **39**: 157
Bernheim **14**: 29, 30, 32
Berr **11**: 29
Berr and Febvre **37**: 29
Bērūnī **79**: 308, 309
Blochet **10**: 517
Bloomfield **41**: 38
Boas **21**: 203; **35**: 203; **37**: 214, 215, 216, 218; **40**: 46, 47
Bodde **36**: 270
Bogholm **39**: 23
Boodberg **34**: 106; **36**: 22, 429; **39**: 85, 106, 223, 224
Bréal **00**: 36
Bretschneider **88**: 45, 93, 95, 98, 100, 107, 108, 243, 325, 517, 617, 619,

620, 622, 624, 625, 626, 627, 629, 631, 634, 635, 638, 639, 640, 642, 643, 645, 659, 660, 661, 663, 664, 666, 668
Britton **38**: 216
Brockelmann **28**: 42, 60, 95, 96, 109, 170, 429, 431, 432, 433, 434, 508, 517, 645; **37**: 506
Browne **28**: 1, 253, 635, 670
Browne **33**: 307
Brunnert and Hagelstrom **12**: 11
Buck **30**: 213; **37a**: 122, 123, 172, 328, 329; **37b**: 19, 172; **37c**: 213
Buck **33**: 406
Bunzel **38**: 203
Bury **31**: 505, 507
Bushell **80**: 103, 107: **95/96**: 60, 97
Bu-ston **32**: 291
Butler **84**: 506; **25**: 506

Carl **26**: 12
Carpini **00**: 17, 170, 316, 508, 517, 664; **28**: 2, 17, 170, 201, 214, 366, 517, 523, 524, 651
Carter **31**: 152, 257, 292
CC: 181, 182
CCC: 335
CCCW: 293
CCHT: 255
CCITC: 134, 157, 427
CCKCT: 268
CCSLCT: 1
CCSSC: 222, 269, 271
CCTCCS: 225, 398, 534
CCWC: 240
CCWHTK: 11, 14, 462, 463
CCYL: 204
CFC: 156, 157
Chach-náma **67**: 506
Chang HL **30**: 308
Chavannes, "Khitans": 4; "Kin": 95; MH: 27, 38, 254, 398, 414, 617; **97**: 104; **97–98** VC: 43, 93, 95, 103, 106, 155, 170, 175, 176, 181, 617; **03**: 85, 91, 93, 105, 106, 107, 108, 109, 110, 429, 509; **03a**: 103; **04**: 49, 101; **04–05** ICC: 9; **07**: 103; **13**: 103, 670; **14**: 505; **16**: 61
Chavannes-Pelliot **13**: 1, 307, 308, 309, 607, 635
CHC: 283, 306
CHCF: 376
Ch'ên MC **36**: 217

Ch'ên S **36**: 573; **39**: 65, 615; **39a**: 454
Ch'ên Y **23**: 294, 309; **23a**: 308
CHHC: 8, 414, 636
Ch'i SH **38**: 534
Chin: 2, 16, 105, 430, 457
Chou: 2, 85, 223, 224, 274, 450, 457, 470, 524, 526, 533, 536
CHTSL: 3
Chu H **36**: 79
CHWC: 237, 308, 654
CJCSWC: 157, 244, 624, 642, 657, 661, 665, 669
CKC: 60, 61, 325
CKCCC: 563
CKL: 59, 238, 611, 625
CKTLHC: 150, 151, 152, 153
CKTSNP: 458
CL: 664
Clausewitz **57**: 30, 527, 530, 537, 538, 539
CLCS: 256, 307
CLLS: 414
CLP: 155
CMYS: 156
Columbus **70**: 2
Coole **36**: 170, 172
Coomaraswamy **32**: 505
Couvreur **11**: 59, 534; **13**: 279
CP: 188
CPMHPK: 180
CPTC: 243
Creel **37**: 26, 216; **37a**: 26, 216; **38**: 224
Creighton **07**: 29
Croce **15**: 29
CS *1*: 94, 111, 399, 421, 422, 426, 569 594; *2*: 7, 87, 163, 253, 404, 596, 598, 629; *3*: 128, 193, 311, 312, 339, 632, 633, 637, 659, 664; *4*: 253, 610, 643; *5*: 269; *6*: 116, 302; *7*: 8, 314, 335, 646, 659; *8*: 7, 8, 116, 125, 224, 648; *9*: 8, 253; *11*: 269; *12*: 611; *24*: 58, 63, 77, 89; *35*: 256; *42*: 343, 426; *43*: 307; *44*: 8, 426; *46*: 173, 190, 333; *47*: 29, 193, 195, 286, 312, 363, 370; *51*: 8, 253, 454, 456; *52*: 253, 460, 462; *53*: 253; *55*: 8, 137, 162, 228, 253, 290, 311, 411, 450; *56*: 228, 257, 311, 343, 344, 486; *57*: 158, 228, 280, 311, 488; *58*: 345, 637; *64*: 8, 235; *66*: 253; *67*: 238, 427, 595; *70*: 422; *72*: 598, 629; *73*: 253, 632; *74*: 422, 629, 633; *76*: 253; *78*: 285, 287, 456, 461; *82*: 209, 253;

ANALYTICAL INDEX